Religion in Today's World

The importance of religion and religious issues in today's world is undeniable. Yet *sociology of religion* as it is conventionally taught in most undergraduate curricula does not reach a broad, lower division student population. Often, the sociology of religion course is taught more as an "ivory tower subject" than as a contemporary, "issues-oriented" subject. With the publication of this new, innovative text/reader, instructors are given a text that accomplishes two important goals:

- first, an analytically rigorous presentation;
- and second, thanks to the five unique foundational essays connected to 32 adapted readings, that allows instructors to involve their undergraduate students in the broad debates and issues that will equip them to analyze, discuss, and make their own judgments about religion/society long after they move on from the course.

Melissa M. Wilcox is Associate Professor and Chair of Religion, and Director of Gender Studies at Whitman College in Walla Walla, Washington. She has been teaching courses on the sociology of religion for over ten years, and is the author or co-editor of three other books focusing on religion, sexuality, and gender.

Contemporary Sociological Perspectives

Edited by **Doug Hartmann**, University of Minnesota, **Valerie Jenness**, University of California, Irvine and **Jodi O'Brien**, Seattle University

This innovative series is for all readers interested in books that provide frameworks for making sense of the complexities of contemporary social life. Each of the books in this series uses a sociological lens to provide current critical and analytical perspectives on significant social issues, patterns and trends. The series consists of books that integrate the best ideas in sociological thought with an aim toward public education and engagement. These books are designed for use in the classroom as well as for scholars and socially curious general readers.

Published:

Political Justice and Religious Values by Charles F. Andrain

GIS and Spatial Analysis for the Social Sciences by Robert Nash Parker and Emily K. Asencio

Hoop Dreams on Wheels: Disability and the Competitive Wheelchair Athlete by Ronald J. Berger

The Internet and Social Inequalities by James C. Witte and Susan E. Mannon

Media and Middle Class Mom: Images and Realities of Work and Family by Lara Descartes and Conrad Kottak

Watching T.V. Is Not Required: Thinking about Media and Thinking about Thinking by Bernard McGrane and John Gunderson

Violence Against Women: Vulnerable Populations by Douglas Brownridge

State of Sex: Tourism, Sex and Sin in the New American Heartland by Barbara G. Brents, Crystal A. Jackson & Kate Hausbeck

Social Statistics: The Basics and Beyond by Thomas J. Linneman

Sociologists Backstage: Answers to 10 Questions About What They Do by Sarah Fenstermaker and Nikki Jones

Gender Circuits by Eve Shapiro

Surviving the Holocaust: A Life Course Perspective by Ronald Berger

Transforming Scholarship: Why Women's and Gender Studies Students Are Changing Themselves and the World by Michelle Berger and Cheryl Radeloff

Stargazing: Celebrity, Fame, and Social Interaction by Kerry Ferris and Scott Harris

The Senses of Self, Culture and Society by James Tyner

Who Lives, Who Dies, Who Decides? by Sheldon Ekland-Olson

Surviving Dictatorship by Jacqueline Adams

The Womanist Idea by Layli Maparyan

Social Theory Re-Wired: New Connections to Classical and Contemporary Perspectives by Wesley Longhofer and Daniel Winchester

Also from Routledge:

Sex/Gender: Biology in a Social World by Anne Fausto-Sterling

Ethnography and the City: Readings on Doing Urban Fieldwork by Richard Ocejo

The World's Cities: Contrasting Regional, National, and Global Perspectives by A.J. Jacobs

The Connected City by Zachary Neal

Sacred Ecology, third edition by Fikret Berkes

China and Globalization, third edition by Doug Guthrie

Applied Statistics for the Social and Health Sciences by Rachel Gordon

Religion in Today's World

Global Issues, Sociological Perspectives

Melissa M. Wilcox

Routledge
Taylor & Francis Group

NEW YORK AND LONDON

First published 2013
by Routledge
711 Third Avenue, New York, NY 10017

Simultaneously published in the UK
by Routledge
2 Park Square, Milton Park, Abingdon, Oxon OX14 4RN

Routledge is an imprint of the Taylor & Francis Group, an informa business

Library of Congress Cataloging in Publication Data
Wilcox, Melissa M., 1972–
Religion in today's world : global issues, sociological perspectives / Melissa M. Wilcox.
        p. cm. — (Contemporary sociological perspectives)
Includes bibliographical references and index.
    ISBN 978–0–415–50387–7 (pbk.) — ISBN–978–0–415–50386–0 (hardback) 1. Religion and
    sociology. I. Title.
    BL60.W535 2012
    306.6—dc23
                                                                              2012016604

ISBN: 978–0–415–50386–0 (hbk)
ISBN: 978–0–415–50387–7 (pbk)

Typeset in StoneSerif
by Swales & Willis Ltd, Exeter, Devon

Printed and bound in the United States of America by Sheridan Books, Inc. (a Sheridan Group Company) on acid-free paper.

Contents

Section II Religion and Social Institutions   **111**

ESSAY: "RELIGION, STATE, AND NATION"

Readings:

Religion, State, and Law   **125**

Religion and the Nation   **165**

Section III Religion and Social Power   **213**

Readings:

Section IV Religion and Social Movements   **319**

ESSAY: "CHANGING RELIGIONS, CHANGING WORLDS"

Readings:

Religion in Social Movements   **333**

Series Foreword

THIS INNOVATIVE SERIES IS for all readers interested in books that provide frameworks for making sense of the complexities of contemporary social life. Each of the books in this series uses a sociological lens to provide current critical and analytical perspectives on the best ideas in sociological thought with an aim toward publication education and engagement. These books are designed for use in the classroom as well as for scholars and socially curious general readers.

This innovative text/reader focuses on the significance of religion in contemporary society: what it is, how it functions to unite and divide people, and how it serves as a major social and political force. The engaging readings and essays will introduce students to broad debates and issues and will equip them to analyze, discuss, and make their own judgments about religion and society long after they move on from the courses.

Douglas Hartmann
Valerie Jenness
Jodi O'Brien
Series editors

Preface

INVESTIGATING SOCIOLOGICAL PERSPECTIVES ON religion can require significant research. There are classic articles to read, authors whose inclusion is a must, and alternate perspectives that can be hard to dig up if you're not already aware of them. The books that have existed up until now offer either a summary of these perspectives or simply a collection of articles with little connecting information at all. *Religion in Today's World* addresses the need for a comprehensive book that both includes key works and also places those works in the broader context of the sociology of religion. Designed as a hybrid between a textbook and a course reader, this text contains everything that an instructor or an interested general reader might need to explore the social dimensions of religion.

Social Scientific Perspectives on Religion

The social sciences, and the interdisciplinary field of religious studies, approach religion as a social phenomenon to be studied. There is no question here of the veracity of any religion; rather, the fact that someone believes certain things to be true, or holds certain practices to be effective, is in itself of interest. I often teach students to approach the study of religion using the tools suggested by early phenomenologist (and ancestor of the social sciences) Gerardus van der Leeuw (1938): *epoché* and *verstehen*. The first term, *epoché*, refers to a suspension of judgment. Through this lens, one approaches the religion to be studied not with questions of truth or falsehood, good or evil, but with questions about what truth is for the practitioners of that particular religion. This is where *verstehen*, or empathetic understanding, comes in. The social scientist of religion endeavors to comprehend the religion under study as best she can, striving as much as possible to mentally get inside the world of the religious practitioners in order to better understand the religion itself.

This is a very different approach from those that study religion in order to identify which is correct, or in order to fulfill a spiritual quest, or in order to better understand the "enemy." Neither, however, are social scientific approaches to religion actively sympathetic to the religion under study. This is not to say that social scientists are firmly objective; I am persuaded that all of us enter our work with our own personal biases and perspectives that are impossible to eradicate. Thus, our efforts at *epoché* and *verstehen* are always only partially successful. We can, though, be aware of our biases and our differing perspectives, and through a clear analysis of them and a balancing with others' (equally but differently skewed) perspectives, we can come to an approximation of objectivity about a religious phenomenon.

This book represents largely the perspectives of the sociology of religion, with some voices from the anthropology of religion and from religious studies itself. Readers will also notice a focus on qualitative readings; I have chosen primarily qualitative and theoretical reading selections because I believe both to be more accessible to a range of readers than most quantitative work. The readings included here encompass the work of early scholars and contemporary ones; the work of well-known scholars and more obscure ones; and studies of both mainstream and marginal topics in the study of religion.

Using this Book

The goal of *Religion in Today's World* is to provide a comprehensive introduction to sociological perspectives, and social scientific perspectives more broadly, on the phenomenon we call religion. The book is divided into five sections, covering different areas in the study of religion and society. The first questions what religion actually is, what its past has been, and what its future will be. The second section examines interactions between religion, state, and nation. The third takes up a topic that threads through much of the social science of religion without being clearly articulated: religion and social power. The fourth section considers the intersections of religion and social movements, in terms of both religion's role in social movements and religion itself as a social movement—here, the study of new religious movements comes into play. Finally, the fifth section considers some of the results of globalization and the resulting localization movement: immigration, transnationalism, and violence. Each section contains an introductory essay that covers key sociological concepts and findings relevant to the section's topic; what follow are several reading selections that either demonstrate the concepts covered or push them further. Every essay also includes an "extended application" that demonstrates how the concepts covered in the chapter can be applied to recent or contemporary issues.

This text can be used in many ways. A general reader unfamiliar with the social scientific study of religion may want to begin simply by reading the introductory essays in order, and then return to the selected readings. An instructor may wish to have students read through the entire textbook in order, or to rearrange by theme or chronology of articles. Those instructors with extensive experience in the sociology of religion may wish to assign the introductory essays as reviews or complements to class lectures, while less experienced instructors may find the essays helpful for introducing the key topics in each new section. Finally, the course reader aspect of the book's design allows both instructors and general readers to select the readings they find most helpful, to rearrange the order of the readings, or to read the book from cover to cover.

Two aspects of this text will be especially useful in classroom settings, although again they may also be of interest to the general reader. The first is the glossary, found in the back of the book, which contains concise definitions of key terms from the introductory essays. Instructors may wish to draw from this for vocabulary tests, or to refer students to it as a study aid. Second, each introductory essay concludes with exercises that can be completed for fun by a general reader, or as homework or in-class assignments for students.

Sociological perspectives on religion can open new windows onto this complex, socially and politically critical phenomenon. Discovering new perspectives on religion can be both challenging and delightful, and I wish you much enjoyment as you work through this book.

Bold-faced terms are defined in the Glossary Index.

Acknowledgments

MANY FACTORS SHAPE THE LIVES and experiences of academics, and many people have contributed to my development as a teacher of the sociology of religion. First thanks go to those who trained me in the field, especially my doctoral adviser, Clark Roof. Other sociologists of religion have taken me under their wings over the years, including especially Steve Warner, Nancy Ammerman, Mary Jo Neitz, Meredith McGuire, and Jim Spickard. Second, I wish to thank all of my students in Religion and Society over more than a decade, both at U.C. Santa Barbara and at Whitman College. Their insights and probing questions have pushed me to think more deeply and thoroughly about the concepts I am presenting, and their interactions with me have been fundamental in shaping this book. Third and most recently, thanks go to Jodi O'Brien, series editor, and Steve Rutter, publisher in the social sciences at Routledge. They approached me initially with the idea for the book, and have been supportive and encouraging throughout the process. The very existence, but also the shape of this book, is in large part due to them. I would also like to thank the following reviewers for their invaluable feedback:

Joy Charlton, Swarthmore College
Laura Edles, California State University, Northridge
Riad Nasser, Fairleigh Dickinson University
Michael R. Ott, Grand Valley State University
Frank J. Page, University of Utah
Jim Preston, Sonoma State University
Bhavani Sitaraman, University of Alabama in Huntsville
David Yamane, Wake Forest University

What is Religion?

Essay:
Tilting at Windmills
Defining and Predicting Religion

> **Before you begin reading this chapter, take a moment to write down your own definition of religion.**

Defining Religion

How did you define religion? Does your definition require a deity, or not? Does it include practice? Belief? A centralized institution? Dogma? Perhaps more importantly, what religion or religions did you have in mind, consciously or unconsciously, as you wrote your definition? If your definition centers on belief, for example, you are like many people in predominantly Protestant Christian countries such as the United States and Canada (excepting Quebec)—even if you are not yourself a Protestant.

When Protestantism developed in the sixteenth and seventeenth centuries in northern Europe, its proponents focused the religion on belief. Tired of the ornateness of Roman Catholic ritual as well as the role the priest played as middleman between **laypeople**[1] (those not consecrated as priests, nuns, or monks) and God, Protestant reformers stripped Catholic churches of their icons and statuary, placing a simple cross and the Bible front and center. Martin Luther preached the "priesthood of all believers," meaning that every Protestant could access the divine directly. Notice here, too, the emphasis on belief. How did believers connect to God? Through the sacred text, the Protestant Bible. Thus, Protestants have come to see religion largely through the lenses of belief and sacred text. As they have influenced cultures in which they were the numerical majority or the socially dominant group, Protestants have shaped those cultures' understandings of religion such that even non-Protestants in those cultures may come to see religion as a function primarily of belief and text. This definition plays an important role in what people see when they look at religion.

My brother and his wife once got into a debate over whether Unitarian Universalists are Protestant, having recently attended a U.U. religious service. Both of them are former debate competitors, so it was quite a conversation! He argued that Unitarian Universalists are not Protestant, because they are by definition universalists: they believe in the validity of all religions as paths to the sacred. She countered that they are in fact Protestant, because their rituals involve an invocation, communal greeting, prayer, hymns, and a sermon. What I find most interesting here is not who was right (they both were), but *why* each was making her or his specific argument. My brother, though not a Protestant, was raised with some exposure to Protestantism and little exposure to any other religions, whereas his wife was raised Hindu. Protestantism centers on belief, which my brother used to argue convincingly that Unitarian Universalists are *not* Protestant. Hinduism focuses more on ritual, which my sister-in-law used to argue, equally convincingly, that Unitarian Universalists *are* Protestant. Again, how we define religion can make a big difference in what we see when we look at it.

Although scholars continue to argue over what constitutes religion and how we should define it, they generally group definitions into two categories: **substantive** definitions and **functional** definitions. In a nutshell, substantive definitions describe what religion *is*, and functional definitions describe what religion *does*. Most of my students write substantive definitions when I ask them to define religion on the first day of class; you may have also written a substantive definition when you began reading this chapter. A substantive definition might describe particular aspects of religion, like having a deity or a sacred text. It might define religion structurally, such as stating that it is an institution or a system of belief. A functional definition would describe the functions of religion, perhaps by stating that religion serves to answer people's existential questions or to provide access to a superhuman realm. There is no single, correct definition of religion, nor are substantive or functional definitions necessarily better. However, each may have greater usefulness for particular purposes.

Substantive definitions are particularly useful for **quantitative**, especially survey-based, research. Consider this: if you wanted to survey a large number of people to find out about their religiousness (or lack thereof), what questions would you ask and what options would you have for the answers? You might ask your participants whether they affiliate themselves with particular religions, and you might include major religions in your society as answer options: Judaism, for example, or Buddhism. What if you wanted to know how involved they were in religion? You might ask how often they attend religious services, or how often they read a sacred text such as the Bible or the Qur an. These are all perfectly valid questions; however, like any survey questions on religion, they rely on a particular definition. These questions implicitly assume that religion is part of an organized institution and that it centers on group ritual and sacred texts—all substantive definitions of religion.

As useful as substantive definitions are, especially for large-scale studies, they also have drawbacks. Do you know anyone who considers herself or himself "spiritual but not religious"? Often such people practice their spirituality on their own, or through meetings such as meditation classes that aren't formally considered religious services. They may read inspirational writings, but not necessarily sacred texts. Such people appear irreligious in survey questions such as the ones discussed above. How much does that tell us about religion in a particular society, and how much does it tell us about our own definitions of religion?

Functional definitions of religion address some of these problems, but raise others. What if we used a functional definition of religion to design those survey questions I mentioned above? We might then ask whether there's anything in a participant's life that helps her or him feel connected to an ultimate reality (if we said to "God," we'd automatically be ruling out some religions that have many or no deities). But how would you design the answer choices for such a question? Functional definitions lend themselves more easily to **qualitative**, often interview-based, research. Functional definitions also let us explore the boundaries of religion. Why, for instance, do some people say quite seriously that football is their religion, or that they follow a particular musician "religiously"? Some scholars think that tells us something interesting about religion itself, and how it's understood in cultures that use the word in that way. Maybe football is a person's religion because she or he is deeply devoted to it; does that mean that religion is that which evokes a feeling of deep devotion? If so, what else might be considered religious? Nationalism? Political ideologies? Science? Some scholars think we can find new perspectives on people's unswerving dedication to, and their sense of meaning in, such apparently non-religious phenomena by examining them using ideas from the study of religion.

But wait. Science as a religion? Herein lies the drawback, for some people, of functional definitions of religion: they can push the boundaries too far. Some scholars find this boundary-pushing to be fascinating and informative; others feel that there is, ultimately, a fundamental difference between science, nationalism, and religion that gets erased by overly-broad functional definitions of religion. And some people, as we'll see below, find a combination of substantive and functional definitions to be the solution that capitalizes on the strengths of each type of definition while lessening the impact of the weaknesses.

Though scholars continue to argue over the best definition of religion, sociologist Peter Berger offers what may be the most practical advice when he says that "definitions are matters of taste" (1967:178). Different definitions, and different types of definition, are more or less useful and appropriate depending on the nature of the questions we wish to ask about religion. Anthropologist Clifford Geertz adds that "it is notorious that definitions establish nothing," but continues that, nonetheless, definitions may serve the useful function of allowing one to develop "a novel line of inquiry." Thus, Geertz proposes a definition that is still widely used by scholars of religion today, one that includes both substantive and functional elements:

> A religion is: (1) a system of symbols [the substantive part of the definition] which acts [here are the functional parts] to: (2) establish powerful, pervasive, and long-lasting moods and motivations in men by (3) formulating conceptions of a general order of existence and (4) clothing these conceptions with such an order of factuality that (5) the moods and motivations seem uniquely realistic.
>
> (1973:90)

As Talal Asad points out, though, there is still a drawback here: even Berger and Geertz, with their fairly permissive approaches to the definition of religion, assume that there *is* a phenomenon that can be named as religion, that exists as a part of many people's experience, and that can be defined in the same way across many different cultures. But this assumption is a product of both Christianity and Western colonialism: in other words, a product especially of early modern, colonial, Western Christianity. Indeed, the field of comparative religions, which eventually branched into religious studies and the sociology and anthropology of religion, has its roots in the efforts of Western Christians to prove the superiority of their own religion over the religions of other cultures. In order to achieve this goal, Western scholars had to determine, or perhaps create, a category of social institutions called religion that represented a trans-historical and cross-cultural constant in human society. Basing their definitions of religion on the religion that most of them knew best—Christianity—these early comparative scholars defined religion through texts and beliefs, and then went to other cultures to see what aspects of those cultures fit in the pre-defined box.

A number of seemingly odd consequences resulted from this approach. For example, early scholars of comparative religion argued over whether Buddhism was indeed a religion, since many of its branches are atheist. They "discovered" ancient South Asian ritual texts and declared them to be the true heart of a religion they named "Hinduism," after the Indus River. Hinduism as a unified, world religion did not exist prior to the work of these Western scholars; instead, in addition to religions like Islam, Christianity, Judaism, and Jainism, India was home to a family of related, localized practices, many of which had little or no relation to the ritual texts followed by a small cadre of elite men. Some Western scholars condemned these local traditions as superstitious accretions that drew Indians away from their "true religion," "Hinduism," and they used this condemnation in part to justify the colonization of South Asia by the British, explaining that South Asians needed to be brought back to their "real" religion as a part of the process of "civilization" (that is, Europeanization). Indigenous traditions in other parts of the world suffered a similar fate, especially those that relied on oral rather than written tradition and thus had no "sacred texts."

So, if some "religions" focus on beliefs and texts, and some "religions" focus on practices, if some are atheist and others polytheist (that is, they have multiple deities), what, if anything, do they all have in common? This is the challenge that Asad implicitly raises. Can we speak about "religions" around the world and know what we're talking about? Scholars of religion continue to believe that there is some utility in examining that which theologian Paul Tillich defined simply as "ultimate concern," around the world. However, such scholars take the cautions raised above into account. They often are explicit about their own definitions of religion, and about how those definitions shape what they see when they look at different people's sources of "ultimate concern."

Another approach to defining religion is **inductive** rather than **deductive**. Deductive reasoning begins with a theory and a hypothesis, which it then proceeds to test. This is the model in which one defines religion and then sets out to find what fits the definition. Inductive reasoning, on the other hand, begins not with a theory or a definition but with observation. Inductively, we might ask: how do the participants in a particular research project define religion? What counts for them, and what can we learn about religion by studying those definitions rather than relying on our own? Of course, there is a complication to this simple distinction between inductive and deductive reasoning: many scholars would argue that, as thinking beings who operate within specific worldviews, humans always have a definition or a theory in the backs of our minds that shapes our observations of the world. Even if you're a Westerner, it's easy to see the problematic assumptions underlying such mistakes as the Western rejection of local South Asian traditions, because cultures have changed since that time and Westerners now have different perspectives. It's worthwhile to ask: what assumptions do we unconsciously make today, even in inductive research, that will stand out as glaring mistakes several generations from now?

Meredith McGuire helpfully delineates a number of these questions in her exploration of the social power dynamics underlying traditional social scientific definitions of religion. This reading selection is drawn from a larger work in which McGuire advocates the inductive approach to religion described above, beginning with the lives of individual laypeople and studying not which "religion" they subscribe to, but rather how they live their religion from day to day. This approach, and the title of McGuire's book, is *Lived Religion*. Using an inductive, **lived religion** approach, we can examine the practices and beliefs of the non-elite, including non-dominant and disempowered groups. As McGuire notes, such a perspective gives us a very different picture of religion than do the deductive and elite-focused perspectives discussed above.

Religion's Past: Evolutionary Perspectives

Many people wonder: where does religion come from? As you might now guess, this is a much more complicated question than it at first appears to be—in large part because in order to answer the question we have first to decide what we mean by religion, and whether it's a phenomenon that is the same or similar, and thus comparable, across cultures. Furthermore, although we have some ancient versions of sacred texts, the oral traditions of the past have been lost except as they exist today in unbroken lineages—something still possible, but increasingly rare in indigenous populations since Western colonization and the Christianization that often accompanied it. Archaeological evidence does offer a rich history of what many archaeologists have presumed to be religious beliefs and rituals, but again here we run into the problem of definitions determining what we find.

An excellent example of this problem comes from famous (or perhaps infamous) archaeologist Marija Gimbutas. A respected scholar who published throughout the middle and late twentieth century, Gimbutas rose to public fame in the 1980s when she developed a theory that the numerous prehistoric female figurines unearthed across Europe and the Mediterranean were evidence of the widespread worship of a Great Goddess. Many feminists of the time rejoiced to have scholarly support for an important feminist "sacred story": that the patriarchal societies and religions of the contemporary world had been preceded by cultures that revered women and were perhaps even matriarchal. Gimbutas's work raised an important point: up until that time, female figurines had often been interpreted as images of humans, not of deities, because mostly-male archaeologists from cultures with male deities had some implicit assumptions about how a deity would look. But did Gimbutas's own assumptions shape her reading of these figurines, too? Just as her predecessors had seen human figures because they expected prehistoric deities to be male, perhaps Gimbutas saw goddesses because she expected prehistoric deities to be female. When studying cultures that have left few other traces, we have little way of telling who is right.

Other problematic approaches also arise in the search for religion's origins. One of these was common among late nineteenth- and early twentieth-century scholars: the evolutionary perspective. In the mid-nineteenth century, Charles Darwin revolutionized Western outlooks on history and the living world with his theory of evolution. Though Darwin's ideas applied only to organisms, it took little time for other scholars to begin developing evolutionary theories about cultures and societies: a perspective called **social Darwinism**. Just as Darwin sketched out an evolutionary vision in which humans were the pinnacle, so social Darwinist scholars developed an evolutionary story about societies in which northern and western Europeans were the end point. Not surprisingly, this story fed into another story, one in which it was the responsibility of the "more advanced" cultures to colonize the less advanced (poet Rudyard Kipling famously called this "the white man's burden"). Since this perspective held that "survival of the fittest" applied to cultures as well as organisms, cultural genocide in the interest of Westernizing a colonized people was considered necessary and even inevitable. Some white anthropologists working with native North American cultures in this period went so far as to steal sacred objects in order to preserve the remnants of a culture they believed would soon become "extinct."

With social Darwinism at its height just as social scientific perspectives on religion were developing, it isn't surprising that evolutionary perspectives would dominate early scholars' approaches to the origins of religion, as well. And this approach was not limited to Christian scholars, either: two of the most important examples come from scholars of Jewish heritage.

Émile Durkheim is one of the best-known early commentators on religion, and is also considered one of the founders of the field of sociology. In *The Elementary Forms of the Religious Life* (published in French in 1912 and in English in 1915), Durkheim set out to determine the origins of religion. Relying on the biological theory that the least developed species was necessarily the oldest one, Durkheim began by seeking the "least developed" or, in his terms, the "most primitive" religion. For Durkheim, this meant the simplest religion, but in making his choice he also took into account Western assumptions about the evolutionary status of societies. Settling, as many Westerners did at the time, on aboriginal Australians as the least evolutionarily developed culture, Durkheim concluded that aboriginal religious practices were necessarily the oldest in the world, and therefore the closest to the origins of religion (notice the implicit assumption that aboriginal religious practices have remained unchanged throughout the centuries). By reading other Westerners' reports of aboriginal practices, Durkheim proceeded to develop his hypothesis about the origins of religion—which, he suggested, must be social.

As Durkheim tells the story, the source of religion is **collective effervescence**—the feeling of excitement and power that one gets from being in a crowd. Have you ever felt the energy of a crowd at a concert, a major football game, or a political protest? That's what Durkheim had in mind. Collective effervescence, for Durkheim, is a situation in which the whole becomes greater than the sum of its parts. Each individual in the crowd may add a certain level of excitement or energy, but the energy of the crowd is stronger than the energy of all of those individuals. Durkheim believed that ancient peoples felt the energy of the crowd when they gathered together for communal festivals. Misidentifying it as something external to themselves, they called it sacred and began to revere it. Since it happened only when they were together as a clan or tribe, they believed that the sacred was somehow linked to the clan itself. Their **collective representation**, the animal that represented the clan, thus became a representative of the sacred and a recipient of special reverence.

As Durkheim describes it, the social institution of religion developed from this initial perception of the clan and its collective representation as the source of the sacred. Since the experience of collective effervescence is fleeting, collective representations over time become detached from their experiential roots and become institutionalized as the beliefs and rituals we know as religion.

Another evolutionary perspective on religion, published just over a decade after Durkheim's work, offers a vastly different account of religion's origins. Sigmund Freud, the famed founder of psychoanalysis, saw religion as the product of an underdeveloped (male) social psyche. Freud's widely known theory of the Oedipal complex held that boys, through a primal and forbidden attraction to their mothers, came to fear their fathers' potential punishment. Because of this fear, they developed a distant relationship with their fathers and, unless this complex was resolved, forever lived in simultaneous need and fear of a father figure. When Freud turned his attention to religion (of which he mostly knew only Judaism and Christianity), he saw in God a punishing, fearsome father figure who also protected his children from the adverse events of life. Recognizing this figure as being similar to the Oedipal father, Freud suggested that religion itself was an illusion, a form of wish fulfillment (the male wish for the father figure) that provided an escape from the difficulties of life.

For Freud, religion also filled the role of the superego, an aspect of the fully developed psyche that, he believed, controlled the anti-social urges of the "primitive" id. Therefore, for Freud, religiousness in a society was a sign of an underdeveloped social psyche, one in which an externally-imposed superego was necessary because the internal superego had not developed sufficiently, and one in which the Oedipal conflict had not been resolved.

Like all of us, Durkheim and Freud were clearly influenced both by their times and by their particular perspectives on religion: the former anthropological, the latter psychological. Though the anthropology of religion and the psychology of religion still exist today, there is less of an impulse within them to figure out the origins of religion because of the problems with definition and evidence. While some neuroscientists are interested in determining which aspects of the brain are active during religious experiences, the social sciences of religion have largely moved away from the quest for religion's origins.

This is especially true for evolutionary theories of religion's development that smack of social Darwinism. On the other hand, the social sciences have remained fascinated with predictions about religion's future.

The Future of Religion

The book in which Freud developed his ideas on religion was entitled *The Future of an Illusion*. What did Freud see as the future of religion? Like many Western intellectuals in the late nineteenth and early twentieth centuries, Freud believed that the end of religion was in sight, both because people were beginning to lose their belief in religion and because for societies to mature their citizens needed to develop their own, internal superegos rather than relying on an external, prosthetic, and ultimately ineffective superego. Freud's take-home message? Grow up, society, and start following science rather than God!

Early sociologist Max Weber also foretold the inevitable end of religion based on what he saw around him, though for Weber this was a bleak image rather than one of progress as it was for Freud. Weber's understanding of religion, which I will discuss in more depth in the following chapter, centered on the idea that beliefs interact in important ways with other social institutions, especially the economy. Weber argued that Protestantism, and especially the Calvinist branch of Protestantism brought over by the Puritans, had a lot to do with the development and eventual success of capitalism in the United States. Calvinism lent ultimate meaning to work in one's profession, making such work not only enjoyable but eternally rewarding. But by his own time, Weber thought, religion was dying out; Western societies were experiencing the **disenchantment of the world**. Because so many formerly mysterious phenomena could now be explained scientifically, a sense of awe and mystery was leaving the world.

Have you ever made a papier-mâché balloon? You blow up a balloon, cover it with strips of paper soaked in a hardening agent, and once it dries you have a thick, stiff form of a balloon. Then you pop the balloon, leaving just the form. That's what the disenchantment of the world was like for Weber. Calvinism had given shape and form to capitalism, had filled it out and given it life, but then scientific advancements had popped the balloon, leaving just the empty shell of capitalism. People continued to work, often gruelingly hard in Weber's time, but without the fulfillment that Calvinism had provided. Weber called this structure the "iron cage," or (in a more recent translation) a "steel-hard casing" that locked each worker inside of the structures of capitalism itself. Weber and Freud, and many of their contemporaries, agreed that religion was dying in all "modern" societies, but they disagreed on how welcome such a change might be.

Especially for sociologists in the United States, the 1950s brought a hiatus in theories about the end of religion. Traditional religious affiliation soared in this period of global insecurity and mainstream cultural conformity. As men returned from fighting in World War II, women were strongly encouraged to give up the jobs they held during the war and become homemakers. Those women who could not follow this mandate, usually due to poverty, racism, and/or single marital status, were made to feel inferior as mothers and/or wives in addition to facing often-extreme sexism in the workplace. The Cold War had begun between the United States and the Soviet Union, and communism had come to be associated with atheism (as well as with other forms of social nonconformity such as Civil Rights activism, feminism, pacifism, and homosexuality). How to be a "true" American, in these times? Attend a mainstream religious organization—Protestant, Catholic, or Jewish—with your well-organized, heterosexual, dual-parent, nuclear family.

And then the 1960s came. Attendance at traditional, white religious organizations dropped dramatically as the 1960s counterculture emphasized nonconformity: "tune in, turn on, drop out" was the motto of the time. Sociological concern about the end of religion reached a new height in response to these changes, despite rapid growth in new, often countercultural, religious movements. Tracking solely traditional religious groups such as mainline Protestant churches (Lutherans, Presbyterians, Methodists, and so on) over time, sociologists saw only a steep decline in religion as the 1960s went on and gave way to the 1970s. For most sociologists of the time—and unlike for many late nineteenth- and early twentieth-century commentators—this change presented a fundamental problem. Peter Berger articulated it particularly clearly in *The Sacred Canopy* (1967), where he named the change **secularization**.

As Berger points out, the term "secularization" has had many meanings over the years, and indeed, it continues to have a variety of meanings among sociologists. As Berger defines it in the reading selection included here, secularization is "the process by which sectors of society and culture are removed from the domination of religious institutions and symbols." Notice that this does not necessarily mean the disappearance of religion altogether, but rather its **privatization**. Berger understood religion, in societies dominated by one major tradition, as the "sacred canopy" of that society. Like a rented canopy erected on a lawn for a party, the sacred canopy served two main purposes. First, it defined the boundaries of that society: those standing under the canopy are party guests, while those strolling around outside or standing under another canopy may not be, and likewise, those following the society's religion are members of that society, while those who do not follow the religion may not be. Second, the sacred canopy provided shelter by answering the existential questions of life, just as a party canopy protects guests from the weather. Secularization, then, as the privatization of religion, turns the party canopy into individual umbrellas. Mainly the result of industrial capitalism (here we see the influence of Weber on Berger's thought), secularization in Berger's eyes is potentially harmful to a society because it may cause a loss of identity, unity, and existential security.

Furthermore, Berger adds that there may also be a "secularization of consciousness," wherein an increasing number of people "look upon the world and their own lives without the benefit of religious interpretations." For Berger, the secularization of consciousness comes about in part because of religious pluralism, which undermines what Berger called **plausibility structures**. Not a literal structure like a building, plausibility structures are instead social structures that support particular worldviews. Imagine for a moment that you follow a minority religion with some beliefs not accepted by the general population around you. For the sake of argument, we'll say that this religion focuses on the idea that the founders of your country were aliens from another planet who must be worshipped as gods. As long as you are a part of your religious community, in touch with them either in person or virtually by telephone or Internet, you can sustain this belief. Your community of like-minded believers, your plausibility structure, supports your beliefs and reinforces your sense of their plausibility. But what happens when, say, you go to university? You tell your new friends about your beliefs; they respond incredulously. The more you are exposed to others' worldviews, and the more others question your worldview, the weaker your plausibility structure is. As a result, your sense that your beliefs are plausible weakens, too. For this reason, Berger thought that **religious pluralism**—the presence and interaction of multiple religions in a society—was another cause of secularization.

Secularization theory held sway in the sociology of religion for much of the twentieth century. Especially in the 1960s, 1970s, and 1980s, sociologists fretted about the decline of traditional religion, the irreligiousness of young people, and the rise of what Robert Bellah and his colleagues famously called **Sheilaism**. Named for the pseudonym, "Sheila Larson," of a participant in their study, "Sheilaism" referred to a form of **religious individualism** that Bellah and his colleagues found fairly widespread among the U.S. population they studied for their landmark book, *Habits of the Heart* (1985). Religious individualism represented the extreme of the structural aspect of secularization that Berger had described. "Sheila" didn't go to church, and didn't have a particular religion with which she was affiliated. She just followed her own beliefs, which she dubbed "Sheilaism."

Not until the early 1990s did many sociologists begin to ask whether Sheila's definition of religion might tell us something interesting, rather than simply dire, about contemporary religion in the United States and perhaps in other Western countries as well. One significant turning point in this thought process was a lengthy 1993 article by R. Stephen Warner, in which Warner identified what he called a "new paradigm" in the sociology of religion. Identifying the "old paradigm" with Berger and his followers, Warner suggested that those using the old paradigm were encountering increasing difficulties with fitting their research findings into their theories. Secularization, Warner argued, was simply not happening, despite sociologists' expectations to the contrary. Instead, he drew on a study conducted by two other sociologists (Roof and McKinney, 1987) to argue that the emerging pattern of religiousness in the United States is one of **religious voluntarism**. Sociologists had noticed many people leaving the religions in which they were raised, for instance, but had only recently begun asking where those people were going. As it turns out, many of them were not leaving all religion behind, or even abandoning the faith of their parents; rather, they were **switching** to another branch of that same religion. Certainly, the numbers of religious "nones" (those who answered "none" when asked what religion they were affiliated with) had risen, but they had not even surpassed 10 percent of the general U.S. population.[2] Furthermore, even "nones" may have a form of spiritual belief or practice. Far from dying, Warner argued, religion was changing instead, and sociologists needed to attend to the ways in which that was happening both across society and within individual lives.

Just a few years later, Peter Berger officially renounced his theory of secularization. Like Warner, Berger thought that the weight of the evidence against secularization was too strong for the theory to hold up any longer. Especially looking across the world,

Berger saw two major, global revivals of religion—that of Islam and that of evangelical Christianity—that defied explanation through the lenses of secularization. Both revivals were enormously diverse, not only in cultures but also in theologies and politics, and therefore neither could be passed off as some sort of residual trace or last gasp of an otherwise dying phenomenon. Furthermore, Berger offers two potential exceptions to the idea of religious resurgence, one of which he immediately disproves. Western Europe has long been the main model for secularization: with church attendance having dropped dramatically over the twentieth century and showing no signs of recovery, sociologists continue to point to countries such as the UK and France as proof that secularization is real. Yet Berger notes an important objection to this line of argument, and I would add another. As with Warner's ideas about religion in the United States, Berger points out that a drop in church attendance (and I choose the word "church" rather than "religious" advisedly) does not necessarily mean a drop in religiousness; it can also indicate a change in *how*, rather than *whether*, people express religion. Furthermore, I would add that by focusing on churches, such arguments implicitly define those who attend synagogues, mosques, and temples as non-European. If we say that religion is dying in Europe, what are we saying about European Muslims or Hindus, among which it appears to be alive and well?

Berger's second exception to the failure of secularization theory is his most ironic and most brilliant point: if secularization exists, he argues, it does so solely among Western-educated, elite intellectuals: the heirs to the Enlightenment tradition that provided the roots of secularization theory in the first place. Secularization thereby becomes a self-fulfilling prophecy carried out among members of an elite cadre who have failed to see beyond their own secular noses.

Yet secularization theory still has its proponents. One is University of Aberdeen (Scotland) professor Steve Bruce. Located in one of the most apparently secular regions of the world, Bruce continues to publish books and articles advocating the view that Western Europe secularized over the course of the nineteenth and twentieth centuries, that this process is irreversible, and that other industrial countries will follow this same course. In the article included here, Bruce challenges Berger's recantation of secularization theory on the basis of these arguments. First, he suggests, religious revival in the United States is not as evident as Berger and others think it is. Second, Bruce explains that the decline observed in liberal Christianity is a logical outcome of secularization. Third, he counters Berger's suggestion that religion in Europe has been changing more than it has been declining, and finally, he challenges the relevance of Berger's point about the tenacity of religion outside of Europe and North America. It's important to note here that Bruce's argument, like Berger's initial theory and his recantation, is based on a very specific definition of secularization that includes the fragmentation and privatization of religion. Though Bruce clearly sees such phenomena as leading to the eventual disappearance of religion as a whole, such a disappearance is not itself what most sociologists mean when they argue over the existence of secularization.

In distinct contrast to Bruce's argument, and as evidence that Europeans are just as conflicted as North American scholars over the question of the future of religion, Paul Heelas and Linda Woodhead suggest that the change taking place in Europe, at least, is from one type of religion to another rather than from religiousness to secularity. Heelas and Woodhead describe a larger cultural shift they term the **subjective turn**: a shift from what they call **life-as**, or living one's life through **ascribed** (socially given) roles, to what they call **subjective-life**, or life defined by one's own experiences and relationships to others. In the realm of practice and belief, they distinguish between religion (life-as) and spirituality (subjective-life), and argue that even as traditional religions do seem to be on the decline in Western societies, spirituality in both its individual and communal forms is on the rise.

In support of their argument, Heelas and Woodhead offer a study of what they call the "holistic milieu" in and around the largely-white town of Kendal in the northwest of England. Sometimes referred to as "New Age spirituality," the holistic milieu includes a wide range of beliefs and, especially, practices that focus on inner self-development. Some of these practices are interpersonal and others individual; for comparison with congregational life-as religious activities, Heelas and Woodhead focused on the interpersonal. These included everything from yoga to massage, meditation to aromatherapy. Examining both the congregational and the holistic milieux from quantitative and qualitative perspectives, Heelas and Woodhead demonstrate a marked decline in the congregational milieu and a marked increase in the holistic one. They explain this change through the subjective turn, or what they also term the **subjectivization thesis**.

As our reading selection demonstrates, Heelas and Woodhead also find significant gender and age factors in the subjective turn. In fact, we know that despite fairly common restrictions on their formal leadership roles, laywomen in Western countries have for centuries been more likely than laymen to be involved in Christianity. In Judaism the picture is somewhat more complicated; not surprisingly, this distinction comes about in large part because of differences in gender expectations between traditional Jewish and traditional Christian cultures. Heelas and Woodhead come to a similar conclusion regarding gender expectations; they argue that Western women's ascribed social roles as caregivers and nurturers make those who enact such roles more likely to be drawn to the caring and nurturing environment of the holistic milieu than are traditionally-gendered men. Surprisingly, Heelas and Woodhead share this interest in gender and the secularization thesis with only a few other scholars. Significantly, though, most of the scholars who pay close attention to gender in religion also argue against secularization theories.

In addition to drawing predominantly women, the holistic milieu in Kendal also draws mostly those in middle age. Heelas and Woodhead offer a number of speculations as to why this might be, largely having to do with typical life stages in Western societies that prevent or encourage involvement in holistic activities. Here, too, we have broader evidence of the effect of age on religious involvement, whether in life-as religion or in subjective-life spirituality. An additional factor, not mentioned by the authors, that may affect the age at which people become involved in the holistic milieu is economic. Many of the practices that Heelas and Woodhead identify within this milieu are quite expensive, inviting not only further age-based analysis but also a class-based analysis of involvement in subjective-life spirituality.

In the end, determining the future of religion is at least as difficult as defining this complex human phenomenon. This is especially true because predictions of the future of religion rely, in part, on how one defines religion to begin with. On the one hand, few would argue that in large-scale societies religion serves as a unifying force in the same way as in small-scale, traditional societies. On the other hand, plenty of debate still exists over whether the loss of the unifying force should be identified with secularization, and if so, what other changes in the societal life of religion might accompany secularization. Are post-industrial societies becoming less religious? Yes and no. They are at least becoming *differently* religious, which means they are less religious in the old ways than they used to be. Most scholars tend to agree, though, that religion is not simply dying out, any more than it is simply remaining the same. Religious change is likely not a new development, either, as both historians and historical sociologists like to remind us.

Despite the complexity of contemporary post-industrial societies, however, theories of secularization and even counter-theories to secularization have presented a surprisingly monolithic image of religious change. Scholars examining these "big-picture" questions rarely raise questions of socioeconomic status, ethnicity, national origin, gender, or sexual orientation in their work, with the result that their findings and therefore their theories often reflect the religious tendencies of socially dominant groups. We can conclude this section, then, with a question to ponder: just as Berger notes that elite intellectuals are the one group among which the secularization theory actually appears valid, might it also be the case that secularization is a white, Western-born, male, and perhaps even heterosexual phenomenon?

Conclusion

Take a moment to re-examine your definition of religion. Would you change it after having read this essay? If so, how? If not, why not? Given the extent to which our definitions shape what we find when we look for religion, being cognizant of your own definition will help you to examine the readings in the rest of this book, as well as your own ideas about religion and society, with a more critical eye.

At a certain level, the entire field of the sociology of religion (like all of sociology, really) is **socially constructed**; that is, the field itself was formed and defined through social processes. It bases its existence on a phenomenon that Western intellectuals came to consider a cross-cultural social institution, and that they consequently determined to study comparatively, but as Asad especially shows us, the concept of religion itself has a very specific, Western Christian history. On the other hand, to paraphrase gender theorist Judith Butler, the fact that something is socially constructed doesn't make its effects less real. "Hinduism" may be the invention of British colonists, but millions of people today, in South Asia and elsewhere, consider it their ancestral religion. Many others, especially in English-speaking, post-industrial societies like the United Kingdom, Canada, and the United States, consider "spirituality" and "religion" to be radically different. Both of these are the very real social results of what started out as Western intellectual constructs.

Since the effects of social constructs can be quite tricky to predict, it is perhaps no surprise that the scholars of the late nineteenth and early twentieth centuries erred in predicting the future death of religion. But since definitions of religion vary so widely, it also is no surprise that contemporary scholars can't seem to agree on whether religion is dying or thriving in contemporary societies. More is at issue here than simply what counts as religion, however. Both the definition and the future of religion provide excellent examples of intellectual disagreement—which many would say is a crucial part of the life of the mind.

Extended Application

Many of the concepts explained in this chapter pertain especially clearly to the question of religion among lesbian, gay, bisexual, transgender, and queer (LGBTQ) people. It's not uncommon, both within and outside of LGBTQ communities, for people to assume that LGBTQ people as a whole aren't religious. But this assumption is based, in turn, on several other assumptions about religion. Let's look at those through the lens of this chapter's concepts.

First, we need to consider the definition of religion. What do people mean when they say that LGBTQ people aren't religious? There is often an assumption that religiosity refers to adherence to a particular religious institution, an organized world religion like Conservative Judaism, Sunni Islam, or Roman Catholicism. Furthermore, some people assume that all organized religions are socially conservative and therefore unwelcoming to LGBTQ people. Both of these assumptions are problematic. As we've seen, religion extends beyond institutional and well-known world religions to encompass a wide variety of practices, beliefs, and even material objects and social relationships. In part because of the breadth of religion, it is highly unlikely—and, especially in lived religion, quite untrue—that all religion is socially conservative. But as we've seen, our definitions of religion shape what we see. Some people in the United States and other predominantly Christian countries even assume (sometimes unconsciously) that "religious" means "Christian." Some Christians and non-Christians alike also assume that "Christianity" means "conservative Christianity." Given all of these assumptions—that religion refers to institutionalized, world religions and perhaps specifically to Christianity; that all organized religion is socially conservative; and that Christianity is especially so—it's no wonder that some people assume that LGBTQ people aren't religious.

What happens if we start, instead, with an inductive approach to the definition of religion? Like many others in the United States, LGBTQ people are often reluctant to say they're religious. Quite a few of them, though, identify as spiritual.[3] So what do religion and spirituality mean to such people? Everything they mean to the broader population. LGBTQ-identified people are Christian, Jewish, Muslim, Buddhist, Hindu, Taoist, Wiccan, New Age, metaphysical, and many other religious identities. Some attend LGBTQ-focused religious events, mostly in the context of Judaism and Christianity; others attend religious events targeted at all people, or targeted specifically at heterosexual and cisgender (non-transgender) people. Some are closeted or stealth in their religious practices, others open. And while many are both socially and religiously liberal, LGBTQ populations include

Orthodox Jews, conservative evangelical Protestants, conservative Roman Catholics, Mormons, conservative Muslims, and Eastern Orthodox Christians, among others.

A lived religion perspective tells us not only about this religious diversity, but also about the diversity outside of traditional religions. For many years, researchers and religious leaders who worked with LGBTQ-focused Roman Catholic, Jewish, and Protestant congregations noticed that these groups tended to be largely male. Some wondered what the congregations were doing wrong, since they seemed unable to attract women. Some assumed that lesbian, bisexual, transgender, and queer women weren't religious. Once we began asking women about their experiences rather than making assumptions, however, we discovered something very interesting: they often did identify as spiritual, but they weren't necessarily focused on any single religious tradition, or even any religious tradition at all (Wilcox, 2009). A few were fairly focused on a single congregation, such as an LGBTQ-centered conservative church or a heterosexual/cisgender-centered synagogue. Many, though, attended religious or spiritual events at a variety of organizations, and added personal practice into the mix as well. One lesbian woman, for example, taught yoga, maintained a vegetarian diet, and attended services and classes at a very large Religious Science church (a non-Christian relative of Christian Science). Still others found their spiritual resources in activities not usually understood as religious at all, such as a transgender woman who found billiards tournaments spiritual, and a lesbian who practiced her spirituality by leading hikes for the local gay and lesbian chapter of the Sierra Club.

So, wait—is this religion at all? This question goes back to our definitions, and speaks directly to the debate over secularization theory. Some sociologists, relying on definitions of religion that emphasize traditional, socially conservative institutions have declared lesbian and bisexual women to be quite low in religiosity. But these are the same measures by which religion itself seems to be disappearing. Steve Bruce might agree that queer women are an excellent example of secularization. Yet, Paul Heelas and Linda Woodhead would say that they are practitioners of subjective-life spirituality. Whom do you think is right, and why?

Exercise

Check out the dynamics of religion and spirituality for yourself. In your class, or using an anonymous, online survey tool or even Facebook, ask your friends the following questions:

- On a scale of 1–10, with 1 being the lowest, how religious are you?
- On a scale of 1–10, with 1 being the lowest, how spiritual are you?
- What do you do to practice your religion and/or your spirituality?
- How often do you do at least one of the things you listed above?

Then take a look at your results. What's the average "religion" score? What's the average "spirituality" score? Which is higher (this will vary depending on the country you're in, the region within that country, and your group of friends)? What is the average frequency of religious and/or spiritual practice among your class or your group of friends?

Were you surprised by the answers to the question about practices? What about the averages? Discuss your findings with your friends or classmates. Based on what you've learned and read, what is your evaluation of secularization theory?

Notes

1. Bold-faced terms are defined in the Glossary.
2. In 2005, Warner noted that this trend in the U.S. Population of "nones" had shifted. He writes: "a distinct change from a claim I made in the 1993 article [is that] those raised with no religion are now as likely as those raised with a religion to maintain the religious, or irreligious, status of their upbringing" (Warner 2005: 279).
3. We don't know exactly how many this is, because no survey yet conducted in the United States has asked well-defined, detailed questions about *both* religion *and* gender and sexual identities. The failure to ask good survey questions can translate, as in this case, to a lack of knowledge that can have serious social consequences.

1

The Construction of Religion as an Anthropological Category

Talal Asad

IN MUCH NINETEENTH-CENTURY evolutionary thought, religion was considered to be an early human condition from which modern law, science, and politics emerged and became detached.[1] In this century most anthropologists have abandoned Victorian evolutionary ideas, and many have challenged the rationalist notion that religion is simply a primitive and therefore outmoded form of the institutions we now encounter in truer form (law, politics, science) in modern life. For these twentieth-century anthropologists, religion is not an archaic mode of scientific thinking, nor of any other secular endeavor we value today; it is, on the contrary, a distinctive space of human practice and belief which cannot be reduced to any other. From this it seems to follow that the essence of religion is not to be confused with, say, the essence of politics, although in many societies the two may overlap and be intertwined.

In a characteristically subtle passage, Louis Dumont has told us that medieval Christendom was one such composite society:

> I shall take it for granted that a change in relations entails a change in whatever is related. If throughout our history religion has developed (to a large extent, with some other influences at play) a revolution in social values and has given birth by scissiparity, as it were, to an autonomous world of political

institutions and speculations, then surely religion itself will have changed in the process. Of some important and visible changes we are all aware, but, I submit, we are not aware of the change in the very nature of religion as lived by any given individual, say a Catholic. Everyone knows that religion was formerly a matter of the group and has become a matter of the individual (in principle, and in practice at least in many environments and situations). But if we go on to assert that this change is correlated with the birth of the modern State, the proposition is not such a commonplace as the previous one. Let us go a little further: medieval religion was a great cloak—I am thinking of the Mantle of Our Lady of Mercy. Once it became an individual affair, it lost its all-embracing capacity and became one among other apparently equal considerations, of which the political was the first born. Each individual may, of course, and perhaps even will, recognise religion (or philosophy), as the same all-embracing consideration as it used to be *socially*. Yet on the level of social consensus or ideology, the same person will switch to a different configuration of values in which autonomous values (religious, political, etc.) are seemingly juxtaposed, much as individuals are juxtaposed in society. (1971, 32; emphasis in original)

According to this view, medieval religion, pervading or encompassing other categories, is nevertheless *analytically* identifiable. It is this fact that makes it possible to say that religion has the same essence today as it had in the Middle Ages, although its social extension and function were different in the two epochs. Yet the insistence that religion has an autonomous essence—not to be confused with the essence of science, or of politics, or of common sense—invites us to define religion (like any essence) as a transhistorical and transcultural phenomenon. It may be a happy accident that this effort of defining religion converges with the liberal demand in our time that it be kept quite separate from politics, law, and science—spaces in which varieties of power and reason articulate our distinctively modern life. This definition is at once part of a strategy (for secular liberals) of the confinement, and (for liberal Christians) of the defense of religion.

Yet this separation of religion from power is a modern Western norm, the product of a unique post-Reformation history. The attempt to understand Muslim traditions by insisting that in them religion and politics (two essences modern society tries to keep conceptually and practically apart) are coupled must, in my view, lead to failure. At its most dubious, such attempts encourage us to take up an a priori position in which religious discourse in the political arena is seen as a disguise for political power.

In what follows I want to examine the ways in which the theoretical search for an essence of religion invites us to separate it conceptually from the domain of power. I shall do this by exploring a universalist definition of religion offered by an eminent anthropologist: Clifford Geertz's "Religion as a Cultural System."[2] I stress that this is not primarily a critical review of Geertz's ideas on religion—if that had been my aim I would have addressed myself to the entire corpus of his writings on religion in Indonesia and Morocco. My intention in this chapter is to try to identify some of the historical shifts that have produced our concept of religion as the concept of a trans-historical essence—and Geertz's article is merely my starting point.

It is part of my basic argument that socially identifiable forms, preconditions, and effects of what was regarded as religion in the medieval Christian epoch were quite different from those so considered in modern society? I want to get at this well-known fact while trying to avoid a simple nominalism. What we call "religious power" was differently distributed and had a different thrust. There were different ways in which it created and worked through legal institutions, different selves that it shaped and responded to, and different categories of knowledge which it authorized and made available. Nevertheless, what the anthropologist is confronted with, as a consequence, is not merely an arbitrary collection of elements and processes that we happen to call "religion." For the entire phenomenon is to be seen in large measure in the context of Christian attempts to achieve a coherence in doctrines and practices, rules and regulations, even if that was a state never fully attained. My argument is that there cannot be a universal definition of religion, not only because its constituent elements and relationships are historically specific, but because that "definition is itself the historical product of discursive processes."

A universal (i.e., anthropological) definition is, however, precisely what Geertz aims at: A *religion*, he proposes, is "(1) a system of symbols which act to (2) establish powerful, pervasive, and long-lasting moods and motivations in men by (3) formulating conceptions of a general order of existence and (4) clothing these conceptions with such an aura of factuality that (5) the moods and motivations seem uniquely realistic" (90). In what follows I shall examine this definition, not only in order to test its interlinked assertions, but also to flesh out the counterclaim that a transhistorical definition of religion is not viable.

THE CONCEPT OF SYMBOL AS A CLUE TO THE ESSENCE OF RELIGION

Geertz sees his first task as the definition of symbol: "any object, act, event, quality, or relation which serves as a vehicle for a conception—the conception is the symbol's 'meaning' " (91). But this simple, clear statement—in which *symbol* (any object, etc.) is differentiated from but linked to *conception* (its meaning)—is later supplemented by others not entirely consistent with it, for it turns out that the symbol is not an object that serves as a vehicle for a conception, *it is itself the conception*. Thus, in the statement "The number 6, written, imagined, laid out as a row of stones, or even punched into the program tapes of a computer, is a symbol" (91), what constitutes all these diverse representations as versions of the same symbol ("the number 6") is of course *a conception*. Furthermore, Geertz sometimes seems to suggest that even as a conception a symbol has an intrinsic connection with empirical events from which it is merely "theoretically" separable: "the symbolic dimension of social events is, like the psychological, itself theoretically abstractable from these events as empirical totalities" (91). At other times, however, he stresses the importance of keeping symbols and empirical objects quite separate: "there is something to be said for not confusing our traffic with symbols with our traffic with objects or human beings, for these latter are not in themselves symbols, however often they may function as such" (92). Thus, "symbol" is sometimes an aspect of reality, sometimes of its representation.[3]

These divergencies are symptoms of the fact that cognitive questions are mixed up in this account with communicative ones, and this makes it difficult to inquire into the ways in which discourse and understanding are connected in social practice. To begin with we might say, as a number of writers have done, that a symbol is not an object or event that serves to carry a meaning but a set of relationships between objects or events uniquely brought together as complexes or as concepts,[4] having at once an intellectual, instrumental, and emotional significance.[5] If we define symbol along these lines,[6] a number of questions can be raised about the conditions that explain how such complexes and concepts come to be formed, and in particular how their formation is related to

varieties of practice. Half a century ago, Vygotsky was able to show how the development of children's intellect is dependent on the internalization of social speech.[7] This means that the formation of what we have here called "symbols" (complexes, concepts) is conditioned by the social relations in which the growing child is involved—by the social activities that he or she is permitted or encouraged or obliged to undertake—in which other symbols (speech and significant movements) are crucial. The conditions (discursive and nondiscursive) that explain how symbols come to be constructed, and how some of them are established as natural or authoritative as opposed to others, then become an important object of anthropological inquiry. It must be stressed that this is not a matter of urging the study of the origin and function of symbols in addition to their meaning—such a distinction is not relevant here. What is being argued is that the authoritative status of representations/discourses is dependent on the appropriate production of other representations/discourses; the two are intrinsically and not just temporally connected.

Systems of symbols, says Geertz, are also *culture patterns*, and they constitute "extrinsic sources of information" (92). Extrinsic, because "they lie outside the boundaries of the individual organism as such in that inter-subjective world of common understandings into which all human individuals are born" (92). And sources of information in the sense that "they provide a blueprint or template in terms of which processes external to themselves can be given a definite form" (92). Thus, culture patterns, we are told, may be thought of as "models *for* reality" as well as "models *of* reality."[8]

This part of the discussion does open up possibilities by speaking of modeling: that is, it allows for the possibility of conceptualizing discourses in the process of elaboration, modification, testing, and so forth. Unfortunately, Geertz quickly regresses to his earlier position: "culture patterns have an intrinsic double aspect," he writes; "they give meaning, that is objective conceptual form, to social and psychological reality both by shaping themselves to it and by shaping it to themselves" (1973, 93). This alleged dialectical tendency toward isomorphism, incidentally, makes it difficult to understand how social change can ever occur. The basic problem, however, is not with the idea of mirror images as such but with the assumption that there are two separate levels—the cultural, on the one side (consisting of symbols) and the social and psychological, on the other—which interact. This resort to Parsonian theory creates a logical space for defining the essence of religion. By adopting it, Geertz moves away from a notion of symbols that are intrinsic to signifying and organizing practices, and back to a notion of symbols as meaning-carrying objects external to social conditions and states of the self ("social and psychological reality").

This is not to say that Geertz doesn't think of symbols as "doing" something. In a way that recalls older anthropological approaches to ritual,[9] he states that religious symbols act "by inducing in the worshipper a certain distinctive set of dispositions (tendencies, capacities, propensities, skills, habits, liabilities, proneness) which lend a chronic character to the flow of his activity and the quality of his experience" (95). And here again, symbols are set apart from mental states. But how plausible are these propositions? Can we, for example, predict the "distinctive" set of dispositions for a Christian worshiper in modern, industrial society? Alternatively, can we say of someone with a "distinctive" set of dispositions that he is or is not a Christian?[10] The answer to both questions must surely be no. The reason, of course, is that it is not simply worship but social, political, and economic institutions in general,[11] within which individual biographies are lived out, that lend a stable character to the flow of a Christian's activity and to the quality of her experience.

Religious symbols, Geertz elaborates, produce two kinds of dispositions, *moods* and *motivations:* "motivations are 'made meaningful' with reference to the ends towards which they are conceived to conduce, whereas moods are 'made meaningful'

with reference to the conditions from which they are conceived to spring" (97). Now, a Christian might say that this is not their essence, because religious symbols, even when failing to produce moods and motivations, are still religious (i.e., true) symbols—that religious symbols possess a truth independent of their effectiveness. Yet surely even a committed Christian cannot be unconcerned at the existence of truthful symbols that appear to be largely powerless in modern society. He will rightly want to ask: What are the conditions in which religious symbols can actually produce religious dispositions? Or, as a nonbeliever would put it: How does (religious) power create (religious) truth?

The relation between power and truth is an ancient theme, and no one has dealt with it more impressively in Christian thought than St. Augustine. Augustine developed his views on the creative religious function of power after his experience with the Donatist heresy, insisting that coercion was a condition for the realization of truth, and discipline essential to its maintenance.

> For a Donatist, Augustine's attitude to coercion was a blatant denial of Christian teaching: God had made men free to choose good or evil; a policy which forced this choice was plainly irreligious. The Donatist writers quoted the same passages from the Bible in favour of free will, as Pelagius would later quote. In his reply, Augustine already gave them the same answer as he would give to the Pelagians: the final, individual act of choice must be spontaneous; but this act of choice could be prepared by a long process, which men did not necessarily choose for themselves, but which was often imposed on them, against their will, by God. This was a corrective process of "teaching," *eruditio*, and warning, *admonitio*, which might even include fear, constraint, and external inconveniences: "Let constraint be found outside; it is inside that the will is born."

Augustine had become convinced that men needed such firm handling. He summed up his attitude in one word: *disciplina*. He thought of this *disciplina*, not as many of his more traditional

Roman contemporaries did, as the static preservation of a "Roman way of life." For him it was an essentially active process of corrective punishment, "a softening-up process," a "teaching by inconveniences"—*a per molestias eruditio.* In the Old Testament, God had taught his wayward Chosen People through just such a process of *disciplina*, checking and punishing their evil tendencies by a whole series of divinely-ordained disasters. The persecution of the Donatists was another "controlled catastrophe" imposed by God, mediated, on this occasion, by the laws of the Christian Emperors. . . .

Augustine's view of the Fall of mankind determined his attitude to society. Fallen men had come to need restraint. Even man's greatest achievements had been made possible only by a "straightjacket" of unremitting harshness, Augustine was a great intellect, with a healthy respect for the achievements of human reason. Yet he was obsessed by the difficulties of thought, and by the long, coercive processes, reaching back into the horrors of his own schooldays, that had made this intellectual activity possible; so "ready to lie down" was the fallen human mind. He said he would rather die than become a child again. Nonetheless, the terrors of that time had been strictly necessary; for they were part of the awesome discipline of God, "from the schoolmasters' canes to the agonies of the martyrs," by which human beings were recalled, by suffering, from their own disastrous inclinations. (Brown 1967, 236–38)

Isn't Geertz's formula too simple to accommodate the force of this religious symbolism? Note that here it is not mere symbols that implant true Christian dispositions, but power—ranging all the way from laws (imperial and ecclesiastical) and other sanctions (hellfire, death, salvation, good repute, peace) to the disciplinary activities of social institutions (family, school, city, church) and of human bodies (fasting, prayer, obedience, penance). Augustine was quite clear that power, the effect of an entire network of motivated practices, assumes a religious form because of the end to which it is directed, for human events are the instruments of God. It was not the mind that moved spontaneously to religious truth, but power that created the conditions for experiencing that truth.[12] Particular discourses and practices were to be systematically excluded, forbidden, denounced—made as much as possible unthinkable; others were to be included, allowed, praised, and drawn into the narrative of sacred truth. The configurations of power in this sense have, of course, varied profoundly in Christendom from one epoch to another—from Augustine's time, through the Middle Ages, to the industrial capitalist West of today. The patterns of religious moods and motivations, the possibilities for religious knowledge and truth, have all varied with them and been conditioned by them. Even Augustine held that although religious truth was eternal, the means for securing human access to it were not.

FROM READING SYMBOLS TO ANALYZING PRACTICES

One consequence of assuming a symbolic system separate from practices is that important distinctions are sometimes obscured, or even explicitly denied. "That the symbols or symbol systems which induce and define dispositions we set off as religious and those which place these dispositions in a cosmic framework are the same symbols ought to occasion no surprise" (Geertz, 98). But it does surprise! Let us grant that religious dispositions are crucially dependent on certain religious symbols, that such symbols operate in a way integral to religious motivation and religious mood. Even so, the symbolic process by which the concepts of religious motivation and mood are placed within "a cosmic framework" is surely quite a different operation, and therefore the signs involved are quite different. Put another way, theological discourse is not identical with either moral attitudes or liturgical discourses—of which, among other things, theology speaks.[13] Thoughtful

Christians will concede that, although theology has an essential function, theological discourse does not necessarily induce religious dispositions, and that, conversely, having religious dispositions does not necessarily depend on a clear-cut conception of the cosmic framework on the part of a religious actor. Discourse involved in practice is not the same as that involved in speaking about practice. It is a modern idea that a practitioner cannot know how to live religiously without being able to articulate that knowledge.

Geertz's reason for merging the two kinds of discursive process seems to spring from a wish to distinguish in general between religious and secular dispositions The statement quoted above is elaborated as follows: "For what else do we mean by saying that a particular mood of awe is religious and not secular, except that it springs from entertaining a conception of all-pervading vitality like mana and not from a visit to the Grand Canyon? Or that a particular case of asceticism is an example of a religious motivation except that it is directed toward the achievement of an unconditioned end like nirvana and not a conditioned one like weight-reduction? If sacred symbols did not at one and the same time induce dispositions in human beings and formulate . . . general ideas of order, then the empirical differentia of religious activity or religious experience would not exist" (98). The argument that a particular disposition is religious partly because it occupies a conceptual place within a cosmic framework appears plausible, but only because it presupposes a question that must be made explicit: how do authorizing processes represent practices, utterances, or dispositions so that they can be discursively related to general (cosmic) ideas of order? In short, the question pertains to the authorizing process by which "religion" is created.

The ways in which authorizing discourses, presupposing and expounding a cosmology, systematically redefined religious spaces have been of profound importance in the history of Western society. In the Middle Ages, such discourses ranged over an enormous domain, defining and creating religion: rejecting "pagan" practices or accepting them;[14] authenticating particular miracles and relics (the two confirmed each other);[15] authorizing shrines;[16] compiling saints' lives, both as a model of and as a model for the Truth;[17] requiring the regular telling of sinful thoughts, words, and deeds to a priestly confessor and giving absolution to a penitent;[18] regularizing popular social movements into Rule-following Orders (for example, the Franciscans), or denouncing them for heresy or for verging on the heretical (for example, the Beguines).[19] The medieval Church did not attempt to establish absolute uniformity of practice; on the contrary, its authoritative discourse was always concerned to specify differences, gradations, exceptions. What it sought was the subjection of all practice to a unified authority, to a single authentic source that could tell truth from falsehood. It was the early Christian Fathers who established the principle that only a single Church could become the source of authenticating discourse.[20] They knew that the "symbols" embodied in the practice of self-confessed Christians are not always identical with the theory of the "one true Church," that religion requires authorized practice and authorizing doctrine, and that there is always a tension between them—sometimes breaking into heresy, the subversion of Truth—which underlines the creative role of institutional power.[21]

The medieval Church was always clear about why there was a continuous need to distinguish knowledge from falsehood (religion from what sought to subvert it), as well as the sacred from the profane (religion from what was outside it), distinctions for which the authoritative discourses, the teachings and practices of the Church, not the convictions of the practitioner, were the final test.[22] Several times before the Reformation, the boundary between the religious and the secular was redrawn, but always the formal authority of the Church remained preeminent. In later centuries, with the triumphant rise of modern science, modern production, and the modern state, the churches would also be clear about the need to distinguish the religious from the secular, shifting, as they did so, the weight of religion more and more onto the moods and motivations of the individual believer. Discipline (intellectual and social) would, in this period, gradually abandon religious space, letting "belief," "conscience," "sensibility" take its place.[23] *But theory would still be needed to define religion.*

THE CONSTRUCTION OF RELIGION IN EARLY MODERN EUROPE

It was in the seventeenth century, following the fragmentation of the unity and authority of the Roman church and the consequent wars of religion, which tore European principalities apart, that the earliest systematic attempts at producing a universal definition of religion were made. Herbert's *De veritate* was a significant step in this definitional history. "Lord Herbert," writes Willey,

> differs from such men as Baxter, Cromwell, or Jeremy Taylor mainly in that, not content with reducing the creed to the minimum number possible of fundamentals, he goes behind Christianity itself, and tries to formulate a belief which shall command the universal assent of all men as men. It must be remembered that the old simple situation, in which Christendom pictured itself as the world, with only the foul paynim outside and the semi-tolerated Jews within the gates, had passed away for ever. Exploration and commerce had widened the horizon, and in many writers of the century one can see that the religions of the East, however imperfectly known, were beginning to press upon the European consciousness. It was a pioneer-interest in these religions, together with the customary preoccupation of Renaissance scholars with the mythologies of classical antiquity, which led Lord Herbert to seek a common denominator for all religions, and thus to provide, as he hoped, the much-needed eirenicon for seventeenth-century disputes. (1934, 114)

Thus, Herbert produced a substantive definition of what later came to be formulated as Natural Religion—in terms of beliefs (about a supreme power), practices (its ordered worship), and ethics (a code of conduct based on rewards and punishments after this life)—said to exist in all societies.[24] This emphasis on belief meant that henceforth religion could be conceived as a set of propositions to which believers gave assent, and which could therefore be judged and compared as between different religions and as against natural science (Harrison 1990).

The idea of scripture (a divinely produced/ interpreted text) was not essential to this "common denominator" of religions partly because Christians had become more familiar, through trade and colonization, with societies that lacked writing. But a more important reason lies in the shift in attention that occurred in the seventeenth century from God's words to God's works. "Nature" became the real space of divine writing, and eventually the indisputable authority for the truth of all sacred texts written in merely human language (the Old Testament and the New). Thus:

> Locke's *The Reasonableness of Christianity* popularized a new version of Christianity by reducing its doctrine to the lowest common denominator of belief in Jesus as the Messiah, whose advent had been foretold in the prophecies of the Old Testament. Even this reduced creed was to be measured against the background of Natural Religion and of the Religion of Natural Science, so that Revelation in addition to being required to justify itself by Locke's standard, had to present itself as a republication of Natural Religion. For a time indeed the Word of God assumed a secondary position to his works as set forth in the created universe. For whereas the testimony of the latter was universal and ubiquitous, the evidence of Revelation was confined to sacred books written in dead languages, whose interpretation was not agreed even amongst professed Christians, and which related moreover to distant events which had occurred in remote times and in places far

removed from the centres of learning and civilization. (Sykes 1975, 195–96)

In this way, Natural Religion not only became a universal phenomenon but began to be demarcated from, and was also supportive of, a newly emerging domain of natural science. I want to emphasize that the idea of Natural Religion was a crucial step in the formation of the modern concept of religious belief, experience, and practice, and that it was an idea developed in response to problems specific to Christian theology at a particular historical juncture.

By 1795, Kant was able to produce a fully essentialized idea of religion which could be counterposed to its phenomenal forms: "There may certainly be different historical *confessions*;" he wrote,

> although these have nothing to do with religion itself but only with changes in the means used to further religion, and are thus the province of historical research. And there may be just as many religious *books* (the Zend-Avesta, the Vedas, the Koran, etc.). But there can only be *one religion* which is valid for all men and at all times. Thus the different confessions can scarcely be more than the vehicles of religion; these are fortuitous, and may vary with differences in time or place. (Kant 1991, 114)

From here, the classification of historical confessions into lower and higher religions became an increasingly popular option for philosophers, theologians, missionaries, and anthropologists in the nineteenth and twentieth centuries. As to whether any particular tribe has existed without any form of religion whatever was often raised as a question,[25] but this was recognized as an empirical matter not affecting the essence of religion itself.

Thus, what appears to anthropologists today to be self-evident, namely that religion is essentially a matter of symbolic meanings linked to ideas of general order (expressed through either or both rite and doctrine), that it has generic functions/features, and that it must not be confused with any of its particular historical or cultural forms, is in fact a view that has a specific Christian history. From being a concrete set of practical rules attached to specific processes of power and knowledge, religion has come to be abstracted and universalized.[26] In this movement we have not merely an increase in religious toleration, certainly not merely a new scientific discovery, but the mutation of a concept and a range of social practices which is itself part of a wider change in the modern landscape of power and knowledge. That change included a new kind of state, a new kind of science, a new kind of legal and moral subject. To understand this mutation it is essential to keep clearly distinct that which theology tends to obscure: the occurrence of events (utterances, practices, dispositions) and the authorizing processes that give those events meaning and embody that meaning in concrete institutions.

RELIGION AS MEANING AND RELIGIOUS MEANINGS

The equation between two levels of discourse (symbols that induce dispositions and those that place the idea of those dispositions discursively in a cosmic framework) is not the only problematic thing in this part of Geertz's discussion. He also appears, inadvertently, to be taking up the standpoint of theology. This happens when he insists on the primacy of meaning without regard to the processes by which meanings are constructed "What any particular religion affirms about the fundamental nature of reality may be obscure, shallow, or, all too often, perverse," he writes, "but it must, if it is not to consist of the mere collection of received practices and conventional sentiments we usually refer to as moralism, affirm something" (98–99).

The requirement of affirmation is apparently innocent and logical, but through it the entire field of evangelism was historically opened up, in particular the work of European missionaries in Asia, Africa, and Latin America. The demand that the received practices must *affirm something about the fundamental nature of reality*, that it should therefore always be possible to state meanings for them which are not plain nonsense, is the first condition for determining whether they belong to "religion." The unevangelized come to be seen typically either as those who have practices but affirm nothing, in which case meaning can be attributed to their practices (thus making them vulnerable), or as those who do affirm something (probably "obscure, shallow, or perverse"), an affirmation that can therefore be dismissed. In the one case, religious theory becomes necessary for a correct reading of the mute ritual hieroglyphics of others, for reducing their practices to texts; in the other, it is essential for judging the validity of their cosmological utterances. But always, there must be something that exists beyond the observed practices, the heard utterances, the written words, and it is the function of religious theory to reach into, and to bring out, that background by giving them meaning.[27]

Geertz is thus right to make a connection between religious theory and practice, but wrong to see it as essentially cognitive, as a means by which a disembodied mind can identify religion from an Archimedean point. The connection between religious theory and practice is fundamentally a matter of intervention—of constructing religion in the world (not in the mind) through definitional discourses, interpreting true meanings, excluding some utterances and practices and including others. Hence my repeated question: how does theoretical discourse actually define religion? What are the historical conditions in which it can act effectively as a demand for the imitation, or the prohibition, or the authentication of truthful utterances and practices? How does power create religion?

What kinds of affirmation, of meaning, must be identified with practice in order for it to qualify as religion? According to Geertz, it is because all human beings have a profound need for a general order of existence that religious symbols function to fulfill that need. It follows that human beings have a deep dread of disorder. "There are at least three points where chaos—a tumult of events which lack not just interpretations but *interpretability*— threatens to break in upon man: at the limits of his analytic capabilities, at the limits of his powers of endurance, and at the limits of his moral insight" (100). It is the function of religious symbols to meet perceived threats to order at each of these points (intellectual, physical, and moral): "The Problem of Meaning in each of its intergrading aspects . . . is a matter of affirming, or at least recognizing, the inescapability of ignorance, pain, and injustice on the human plane while simultaneously denying that these irrationalities are characteristic of the world as a whole. And it is in terms of religious symbolism, a symbolism relating man's sphere of existence to a wider sphere within which it is conceived to rest, that both the affirmation and the denial are made" (108).

Notice how the reasoning seems now to have shifted its ground from the claim that religion must affirm something specific about the nature of reality (however obscure, shallow, or perverse) to the bland suggestion that religion is ultimately a matter of having a positive attitude toward the problem of disorder, of affirming simply that in some sense or other the world as a whole is explicable, justifiable, bearable.[28] This modest view of religion (which would have horrified the early Christian Fathers or medieval churchmen)[29] is a product of the only legitimate space allowed to Christianity by post-Enlightenment society, the right to individual *belief*: the human condition is full of ignorance, pain, and injustice, and religious symbols are a means of coming positively to terms with that condition. One consequence is that this view would in principle render any philosophy that performs such a function into religion (to the annoyance of the nineteenth-century rationalist), or alternatively, make it possible to think of religion as a more primitive, a less adult mode of coming to terms with the human condition (to the annoyance of the modern

Christian). In either case, the suggestion that religion has a universal function in belief is one indication of how marginal religion has become in modern industrial society as the site for producing disciplined knowledge and personal discipline. As such it comes to resemble the conception Marx had of religion as ideology—that is, as a mode of consciousness which is other than consciousness of reality, external to the relations of production, producing no knowledge, but expressing at once the anguish of the oppressed and a spurious consolation.

Geertz has much more to say, however, on the elusive question of religious meaning: not only do religious symbols formulate conceptions of a general order of existence, they also clothe those conceptions with an aura of factuality. This, we are told, is "the problem of belief." *Religious belief* always involves "the prior acceptance of authority," which transforms experience: "The existence of bafflement, pain, and moral paradox—of the Problem of Meaning—is one of the things that drives men toward belief in gods, devils, spirits, totemic principles, or the spiritual efficacy of cannibalism, . . . but it is not the basis upon which those beliefs rest, but rather their most important field of application" (109). This seems to imply that religious belief stands independently of the worldly conditions that produce bafflement, pain, and moral paradox, although that belief is primarily a way of coming to terms with them. But surely this is mistaken, on logical grounds as well as historical, for changes in the object of belief change that belief; and as the world changes, so do the objects of belief and the specific forms of bafflement and moral paradox that are a part of that world. What the Christian believes today about God, life after death, the universe, is not what he believed a millennium ago—nor is the way he responds to ignorance, pain, and injustice the same now as it was then. The medieval valorization of pain as the mode of participating in Christ's suffering contrasts sharply with the modern Catholic perception of pain as an evil

to be fought against and overcome as Christ the Healer did. That difference is clearly related to the post-Enlightenment secularization of Western society and to the moral language which that society now authorizes.[30]

Geertz's treatment of religious belief, which lies at the core of his conception of religion, is a modern, privatized Christian one because and to the extent that it emphasizes the priority of belief as a state of mind rather than as constituting activity in the world: "The basic axiom underlying what we may perhaps call 'the religious perspective' is everywhere the same: he who would know must first believe" (110). In modern society, where knowledge is rooted either in an a-Christian everyday life or in an a-religious science, the Christian apologist tends not to regard belief as the conclusion to a knowledge process but as its precondition. However, the knowledge that he promises will not pass (nor, in fairness, does he claim, that it will pass) for knowledge of social life, still less for the systematic knowledge of objects that natural science provides. Her claim is to a particular state of mind, a sense of conviction, not to a corpus of practical knowledge. But the reversal of belief and knowledge she demands was not a basic axiom to, say, pious learned Christians of the twelfth century, for whom knowledge and belief were not so clearly at odds. On the contrary, Christian belief would then have been built on knowledge—knowledge of theological doctrine, of canon law and Church courts, of the details of clerical liberties, of the powers of ecclesiastical office (over souls, bodies, properties), of the preconditions and effects of confession, of the rules of religious orders, of the locations and virtues of shrines, of the lives of the saints, and so forth. Familiarity with all such (religious) knowledge was a precondition for normal social life, and belief (embodied in practice and discourse) an orientation for effective activity in it—whether on the part of the religious clergy, the secular clergy, or the laity. Because of this, the form and texture and function of their beliefs would have been different from the form and texture and function of contemporary belief—and so too of their doubts and their disbelief.

The assumption that belief is a distinctive mental state characteristic of all religions has been the subject of discussion by contemporary scholars. Thus, Needham (1972) has interestingly argued that belief is nowhere a distinct mode of consciousness, nor a necessary institution for the conduct of social life. Southwold (1979) takes an almost diametrically opposed view, asserting that questions of belief do relate to distinctive mental states and that they are relevant in any and every society, since "to believe" always designates a relation between a believer and a proposition and through it to reality. Harré (1981, 82), in a criticism of Needham, makes the more persuasive case that "belief is a mental state, a grounded disposition, but it is confined to people who have certain social institutions and practices."

At any rate, I think it is not too unreasonable to maintain that "the basic axiom" underlying what Geertz calls "the religious perspective" is *not* everywhere the same. It is preeminently the Christian church that has occupied itself with identifying, cultivating, and testing belief as a verbalizable inner condition of true religion.[31]

RELIGION AS A PERSPECTIVE

The phenomenological vocabulary that Geertz employs raises two interesting questions, one regarding its coherence and the other concerning its adequacy to a modern cognitivist notion of religion. I want to suggest that although this vocabulary is theoretically incoherent, it is socially quite compatible with the privatized idea of religion in modern society.

Thus, "the religious perspective," we are told, is one among several—common-sense, scientific, aesthetic—and it differs from these as follows. It differs from the *common-sense* perspective, because it "moves beyond the realities of everyday life to

wider ones which correct and complete them, and [because] its defining concern is not action upon those wider realities but acceptance of them, faith in them." It is unlike the *scientific* perspective, because "it questions the realities of everyday life not out of an institutionalized scepticism which dissolves the world's givenness into a swirl of probabilistic hypotheses, but in terms of what it takes to be wider, nonhypothetical truths." And it is distinguished from the *aesthetic* perspective, because "instead of effecting a disengagement from the whole question of factuality, deliberately manufacturing an air of semblance and illusion, it deepens the concern with fact and seeks to create an aura of utter actuality" (112). In other words, although the religious perspective is not exactly rational, it is not irrational either.

It would not be difficult to state one's disagreement with this summary of what common sense, science, and aesthetics are about.[32] But my point is that the optional flavor conveyed by the term *perspective* is surely misleading when it is applied equally to science and to religion in modern society: religion is indeed now optional in a way that science is not. Scientific practices, techniques, knowledges, permeate and create the very fibers of social life in ways that religion no longer does.[33] In that sense, religion today *is* a perspective (or an "attitude," as Geertz sometimes calls it), but science is not. In that sense, too, science is not to be found in every society, past and present. We shall see in a moment the difficulties that Geertz's perspectivism gets him into, but before that I need to examine his analysis of the mechanics of reality maintenance at work in religion.

Consistent with previous arguments about the functions of religious symbols is Geertz's remark that "it is in ritual—that is, consecrated behavior—that this conviction that religious conceptions are veridical and that religious directives are sound is somehow generated" (112). The long passage from which this is taken swings back and forth between arbitrary speculations about what goes on in the consciousness of officiants and unfounded asser-tions about ritual as imprinting. At first sight, this seems a curious combination of introspectionist psychology with a behaviorist one—but as Vygotsky (1978, 58–59) argued long ago, the two are by no means inconsistent, insofar as both assume that psychological phenomena consist essentially in the consequence of various stimulating environments.

Geertz postulates the function of rituals in generating religious conviction ("In these plastic dramas men attain their faith as they portray it" [114]), but how or why this happens is nowhere explained. Indeed, he concedes that such a religious state is not always achieved in religious ritual: "Of course, all cultural performances are not religious performances, and the line between those that are, and artistic, or even political, ones is often not so easy to draw in practice, for, like social forms, symbolic forms can serve multiple purposes" (113). But the question remains: What is it that ensures the participant's taking the symbolic forms in the way that leads to faith if the line between religious and nonreligious perspectives is not so easy to draw? Mustn't the ability and the will to adopt a religious standpoint be present prior to the ritual performance? That is precisely why a simple stim-ulus-response model of how ritual works will not do. And if that is the case, then ritual in the sense of a sacred performance cannot be the place where religious faith is attained, but the manner in which it is (literally) played out. If we are to understand how this happens, we must examine not only the sacred performance itself but also the entire range of available disciplinary activities, of institutional forms of knowledge and practice, within which dispositions are formed and sustained and through which the possibilities of attaining the truth are marked out—as Augustine clearly saw.

I have noted more than once Geertz's concern to define religious symbols according to universal, cognitive criteria, to distinguish the religious perspective clearly from nonreligious ones. The separation of religion from science, common sense,

aesthetics, politics, and so on, allows him to defend it against charges of irrationality. If religion has a distinctive perspective (its own truth, as Durkheim would have said) and performs an indispensable function, it does not in essence compete with others and cannot, therefore, be accused of generating false consciousness. Yet in a way this defense is equivocal. Religious symbols create dispositions, Geertz observes, which seem uniquely realistic. Is this the point of view of a reasonably confident agent (who must always operate within the dense-ness of historically given probabilities) or that of a skeptical observer (who can see through the repre-sentations of reality to the reality itself)? It is never clear. And it is never clear because this kind of phenomenological approach doesn't make it easy to examine whether, and if so to what extent and in what ways, religious experience relates to some-thing in the real world that believers inhabit. This is partly because religious symbols are treated, in circular fashion, as the precondition for religious experience (which, like any experience, must, by definition, be genuine), rather than as one condition for engaging with life.

Toward the end of his essay, Geertz attempts to connect, instead of separating, the religious perspec-tive and the common-sense one—and the result reveals an ambiguity basic to his entire approach. First, invoking Schutz, Geertz states that the everyday world of common-sense objects and prac-tical acts is common to all human beings because their survival depends on it: "A man, even large groups of men, may be aesthetically insensitive, religiously unconcerned, and unequipped to pursue formal scientific analysis, but he cannot be completely lacking in common sense and survive" (119). Next, he informs us that individuals move "back and forth between the religious perspective and the common-sense perspective" (119). These perspectives are so utterly different, he declares, that only "Kierkegaardian leaps" (120) can cover the cultural gaps that separate them. Then, the phenomenological conclusion: "Having ritually 'leapt' . . . into the framework of meaning which religious conceptions define, and the ritual ended, returned again to the common-sense world, a man is—unless, as sometimes happens, the experience fails to register—changed. *And as he is changed, so also is the common-sense world*, for it is now seen as but the partial form of a wider reality which corrects and completes it" (122; emphasis added).

This curious account of shifting perspectives and changing worlds is puzzling—as indeed it is in Schutz himself. It is not clear, for example, whether the religious framework and the common-sense world, between which the individual moves, are independent of him or not. Most of what Geertz has said at the beginning of his essay would imply that they are independent (cf. 92), and his remark about common sense being vital to every man's survival also enforces this reading. Yet it is also suggested that as the believer changes his perspective, so he himself changes; and that as he changes, so too is his common-sense world changed and corrected. So the latter, at any rate, is not independent of his moves. But it would appear from the account that the religious world *is* independent, since it is the source of distinctive experience for the believer, and through that experience, a source of change in the common-sense world: there is no suggestion anywhere that the religious world (or perspective) is ever affected by experience in the common-sense world.

This last point is consistent with the phenomenological approach in which religious symbols are sui generis, marking out an independent religious domain. But in the present context it presents the reader with a paradox: the world of common sense is always common to all human beings, and quite distinct from the religious world, which in turn differs from one group to another, as one culture differs from another; but experience of the religious world affects the common-sense world, and so the distinctiveness of the two kinds of world is modified, and the common-sense world comes to differ, from one group to another, as one culture differs from another. The paradox results from an ambiguous

phenomenology in which reality is at once the distance of an agent's social perspective from the truth, measurable only by the privileged observer, and also the substantive knowledge of a socially constructed world available to both agent and observer, but to the latter only through the former.[34]

CONCLUSION

Perhaps we can learn something from this paradox which will help us evaluate Geertz's confident conclusion: "The anthropological study of religion is therefore a two-stage operation: first, an analysis of the system of meanings embodied in the symbols which make up *the religion proper* and, second, the relating of these systems to social-structural and psychological processes" (125; emphasis added). How sensible this sounds, yet how mistaken, surely, it is. If religious symbols are understood, on the analogy with words, as vehicles for meaning, can such meanings be established independently of the form of life in which they are used? If religious symbols are to be taken as the signatures of a sacred text, can we know what they mean without regard to the social disciplines by which their correct reading is secured? If religious symbols are to be thought of as the concepts by which experiences are organized, can we say much about them without considering how they come to be authorized? Even if it be claimed that what is experienced through religious symbols is not, in essence, the social world but the spiritual,[35] is it possible to assert that conditions in the social world have nothing to do with making that kind of experience accessible? Is the concept of religious training entirely vacuous?

The two stages that Geertz proposes are, I would suggest, one. Religious symbols—whether one thinks of them in terms of communication or of cognition, of guiding action or of expressing emotion—cannot be understood independently of their historical relations with nonreligious symbols or of their articulations in and of social life, in which work and power are always crucial. My argument, I must stress, is not just that religious symbols are intimately linked to social life (and so change with it), or that they usually support dominant political power (and occasionally oppose it). It is that different kinds of practice and discourse are intrinsic to the field in which religious representations (like any representation) acquire their identity and their truthfulness. From this it does not follow that the meanings of religious practices and utterances are to be sought in social phenomena, but only that their possibility and their authoritative status are to be explained as products of historically distinctive disciplines and forces. The anthropological student of *particular* religions should therefore begin from this point, in a sense unpacking the comprehensive concept which he or she translates as "religion" into heterogeneous elements according to its historical character.

A final word of caution. Hasty readers might conclude that my discussion of the Christian religion is skewed towards an authoritarian, centralized, elite perspective, and that consequently it fails to take into account the religions of heterodox believers, of resistant peasantries, of all those who cannot be completely controlled by the orthodox church. Or, worse still, that my discussion has no bearing on nondisciplinarian, voluntaristic, localized cults of noncentralized religions such as Hinduism. But that conclusion would be a misunderstanding of this chapter, seeing in it an attempt to advocate a better anthropological definition of religion than Geertz has done. Nothing could be farther from my intention. If my effort reads in large part like a brief sketch of transmutations in Christianity from the Middle Ages until today, then that is not because I have arbitrarily confined my ethnographic examples to one religion. My aim has been to problematize the idea of an anthropological definition of religion by assigning that endeavor to a particular history of knowledge and power (including a particular understanding of our legitimate past and future) out of which the modern world has been constructed.[36]

NOTES

1. Thus, Fustel de Coulanges 1873. Originally published in French in 1864, this was an influential work in the history of several overlapping disciplines—anthropology, biblical studies, and classics.
2. Originally published in 1966, it was reprinted in his widely acclaimed *The Interpretation of Cultures* (1973).
3. Compare Peirce's more rigorous account of *representations*. "A representation is an object which stands for another so that an experience of the former affords us a knowledge of the latter. There must be three essential conditions to which every representation must conform. It must in the first place like any other object have qualities independent of its meaning. . . . In the 2nd place a representation must have a real causal connection with its object. . . . In the third place, every representation addresses itself to a mind. It is only in so far as it does this that it is a representation" (Peirce 1986, 62).
4. Vygotsky (1962) makes crucial analytical distinctions in the development of conceptual thought: heaps, complexes, pseudoconcepts, and true concepts. Although, according to Vygotsky, these represent stages in the development of children's use of language, the earlier stages persist into adult life.
5. Cf. Collingwood (1938, bk. 2) for a discussion of the integral connection between thought and emotion, where it is argued that there is no such thing as a universal emotional function accompanying all conceptualization/communication: every distinctive cognitive/communicative activity has its own specific emotional cast. If this view is valid, then the notion of a generalized religious emotion (or mood) may be questioned.
6. The argument that symbols *organize practice*, and consequently the structure of cognition, is central to Vygotsky's genetic psychology—see especially "Tool and Symbol in Child Development," in Vygotsky 1978. A cognitive conception of symbols has recently been revived by Sperber (1975). A similar view was taken much earlier by Lien-hardt (1961).
7. "The history of the process of *the internalization of social speech* is also the history of the socialization of children's practical intellect" (Vygotsky 1978, 27). See also Luria and Yudovich 1971.
8. Or, as Kroeber and Kluckhohn (1952, 181) put it much earlier, "Culture consists of patterns, explicit and implicit, of and for behaviour acquired and transmitted by symbols."

9. If we set aside Radcliffe-Brown's well-known preoccupation with social cohesion, we may recall that he too was concerned to specify certain kinds of psychological states said to be induced by religious symbols: "Rites can be seen to be the regulated symbolic expressions of certain sentiments (which control the behaviour of the individual in his relation to others). Rites can therefore be shown to have a specific social function when, and to the extent that, they have for their effect to regulate, maintain and transmit from one generation to another sentiments on which the constitution of society depends" (1952, 157).

10. Some ways in which symbolization (discourse) can *disguise lack of distinctiveness* are well brought out in MacIntyre's trenchant critique of contemporary Christian writers, where he argues that "Christians behave like everyone else but use a different vocabulary in characterising their behaviour, and also to conceal their lack of distinctiveness" (1971, 24).

11. The phenomenon of declining church attendance in modern industrial society and its progressive marginalization (in Europe, at least) to those sectors of the population not directly involved in the industrial work process illustrates the argument that if we must look for causal explanations in this area, then socioeconomic conditions in general will appear to be the independent variable and formal worship the dependent. See the interesting discussion in Luckman 1967, chap. 2.

12. This was why Augustine eventually came around to the view that insincere conversion was not a problem (Chadwick 1967, 222–24).

13. A modern theologian puts it: "The difference between the professing, proclaiming and orienting way of speaking on the one hand, and descriptive speech on the other, is sometimes formulated as the difference between 'speaking about' and 'speaking to.' As soon as these two ways of speaking are confused, the original and unique character of religious speech, so it is said, is corrupted so that reality-for-the-believer can no longer 'appear' to him as it appears in professing speech" (Luijpen 1973, 90–91).

14. The series of booklets known as Penitential manuals, with the aid of which Christian discipline was imposed on Western Europe from roughly the fifth to the tenth centuries, contains much material on pagan practices penalized as un-Christian. So, for example, "The taking of vows or releasing from them by springs or trees or lattices, anywhere except in a church, and partaking of food or drink in these places sacred to the folk-deities, are offenses condemned" (quoted in McNeill 1933, 456). (For further details, see McNeill and Gamer 1938.) At the same time, Pope Gregory the Great (A.D. 540–604) "urged that the Church should take over old pagan temples and festivals and give them a Christian meaning". (Chadwick 1967, 254). The apparent inconsistency of these two attitudes (rejection or incorporation of pagan practices) is less important than the systematic exercise of Church authority by which meaning was assigned.

15. "On the one hand, then, bishops complained of crude and too-avid beliefs in unauthorized and unexamined wonders and miracles, while on the other theologians (possibly also these same bishops) tried to come to terms with the matter. Although they attempted to define miracle by appeals to universal natural law, such definitions were not entirely successful, and in specific, individual cases, common sense was a better guide than medieval cosmology. When papal commissioners sat down to hear testimony about Thomas Cantilupe's miracles at London and Hereford in 1307 they had in front of them a schedule of things to ask about such wondrous events: they wanted to know, for example, how the witness came to learn of the miracle, what words were used by those who prayed for the miracle, whether any herbs, stones, other natural or medicinal preparations or incantations had accompanied the miracle; the witness was expected to say something about the age and social situation of the person experiencing the miracle, where he came from and of what family; whether the witness knew the subject before as well as after the miracle, what illness was involved, how many days he had seen the ill person before the cure; whether the cure was complete and how long it took for completion. Of course witnesses were also asked what year, month, day, place and in whose presence the wonderful event itself occurred" (Finucane 1977, 53).

16. By being authorized, shrines in turn served to confirm ecclesiastical authority: "The bishops of Western Europe came to orchestrate the cult of the saints in such a way as to base their power within the old Roman cities on these new 'towns outside the town.' Yet it was through a studiously articulated relationship with great shrines that lay at some distance from the city—St. Peter's, on the Vatican Hill outside Rome, Saint Martin's, a little beyond the walls of Tours—that the bishops of the former cities

of the Roman Empire rose to prominence in early medieval Europe" (Brown 1981, 8).

17. The life of St. Antony by Athanasius was the model for medieval hagiographies, and the Antonine sequence of early life, crisis and conversion, probation and temptation, privation and renunciation, miraculous power, together with knowledge and authority, was reproduced again and again in that literature (Baker 1972, 41).

18. The Lateran Council of 1215 declared that annual private confession should be mandatory for all Christians: "Every *fidelis* of either sex shall after the attainment of years of discretion separately confess his sins with all fidelity to his priest at least once in the year: and shall endeavour to fulfil the penance imposed upon him to the best of his ability, reverently receiving the sacrament of the Eucharist at least at Easter: unless it happens that by the counsel of his own priest for some reasonable cause, he hold that he should abstain for a time from the reception of the sacrament: otherwise let him during life be repelled from entering the church, and when dead let him lack Christian burial. Wherefore let this salutary statute be frequently published in churches, lest any assume a veil of excuse in the blindness of ignorance" (quoted in Watkins 1920, 748–49).

19. For a brief introduction to the varying reaction of ecclesiastical authority to the Franciscans and the Beguines, see Southern 1970, chaps. 6, 7. "Beguines" was the name given to groups of celibate women dedicated to the religious life but not owing obedience to ecclesiastical authority. They flourished in the towns of western Germany and the Low Countries but were criticized, denounced, and finally suppressed in the early fifteenth century.

20. Thus, Cyprian: "If a man does not hold this unity of the Church, does he believe himself to hold the faith? If a man withstands and resists the Church, is he confident that he is in the Church? For the blessed Apostle Paul has the same teaching, and sets forth the sacrament of unity, when he says, "There is one body, one Spirit, one hope of our calling, one Lord, one faith, one baptism, one God.' This unity we ought firmly to hold and defend, especially we who preside in the Church as bishops that we may prove the episcopate also to be itself one and undivided. Let no one deceive the brethren by falsehood; let no one corrupt the truth of our faith by faithless transgression" (quoted in Bettenson 1956, 264).

21. The Church always exercised the authority to read Christian *practice* for its religious truth. In this context, it is interesting that the word *heresy* at first designated all kinds of errors, including errors "unconsciously" involved in some activity *(simoniaca haersis)*, and it acquired its specific modern meaning (the verbal formulation of denial or doubt of any defined doctrine of the Catholic church) only in the course of the methodological controversies of the sixteenth century (Chenu 1968, 276).

22. In the early Middle Ages, monastic discipline was the principal basis of religiosity. Knowles (1963, 3) observes that from roughly the sixth to the twelfth centuries, "monastic life based on the Rule of St. Benedict was everywhere the norm and exercised from time to time a paramount influence on the spiritual, intellectual, liturgical and apostolic life of the Western Church. . . . the only type of religious life available in the countries concerned was monastic, and the only monastic code was the Rule of St. Benedict." During the period the very term *religious* was therefore reserved for those living in monastic communities; with the later emergence of nonmonastic orders, the term came to be used for all who had taken lifelong vows by which they were set apart from the ordinary members of the Church (Southern 1970, 214). The extension and simultaneous transformation of the religious disciplines to lay sections of society from the twelfth century onward (Chenu 1968) contributed to the Church's authority becoming more pervasive, more complex, and more contradictory than before—and so too the articulation of the concept and practice of lay religion.

23. Thus enabling the Victorian anthropologist and biblical scholar Robertson Smith to say that in the age of scientific historiography, "it will no longer be the results of theology that we are required to defend, but something prior to theology. What we shall have to defend is not our Christian knowledge, but our Christian belief" (1912, 110). Christian belief is no longer expected to fasten on the Bible as divine revelation but as "the record of divine revelation—the record of those historical facts in which God has revealed himself to man" (1912, 123). Therefore, the principles of historical interpretation were no longer strictly Christian, only the beliefs which that interpretation served.

24. When Christian missionaries found themselves in culturally unfamiliar territory, the problem of identifying "religion" became a matter of considerable

theoretical difficulty and practical importance. For example, "The Jesuits in China contended that the reverence for ancestors was a social, not a religious, act, or that if religious, it was hardly different from Catholic prayers for the dead. They wished the Chinese to regard Christianity, not as a replacement, not as a new religion, but as the highest fulfillment of their finest aspirations. But to their opponents the Jesuits appeared to be merely lax. In 1631 a Franciscan and a Dominican from the Spanish zone of Manila travelled (illegally, from the Portuguese viewpoint) to Peking and found that to translate the word *mass*, the Jesuit catechism used the character *tsi*, which was the Chinese description of the ceremonies of ancestor-worship. One night they went in disguise to such a ceremony, observed Chinese Christians participating and were scandalized at what they saw. So began the quarrel of 'the rites,' which plagued the eastern missions for a century and more" (Chadwick 1964, 338).

25. For example, by Tylor in the chapter "Animism" in part 2 of *Primitive Culture*.

26. Phases in the gradual evacuation of specificity from public religious discourse in the eighteenth century are described in some detail in Gay 1973.

27. The way in which representations of occurrences were transformed into meanings by Christian theology is analyzed by Auerbach in his classic study of representations of reality in Western literature and briefly summed up in this passage: "The total content of the sacred writings was placed in an exegetic context which often removed the thing told very far away from its sensory base, in that the reader or listener was forced to turn his attention away from the sensory occurrence and toward its meaning. This implied the danger that the visual element of the occurrences might succumb under the dense texture of meanings. Let one example stand for many: It is a visually dramatic occurrence that God made Eve, the first woman, from Adam's rib while Adam lay asleep; so too is it that a soldier pierced Jesus' side, as he hung dead on the cross, so that blood and water flowed out. But when these two occurrences are exegetically interrelated in the doctrine that Adam's sleep is a figure of Christ's death-sleep; that, as from the wound in Adam's side mankind's primordial mother after the flesh, Eve, was born, so from the wound in Christ's side was born the mother of all men after the spirit, the Church (blood and water are sacramental symbols)—then the sensory occurrence

pales before the power of the figural meaning. What is perceived by the hearer or reader . . . is weak as a sensory impression, and all one's interest is directed toward the context of meanings. In comparison, the Greco-Roman specimens of realistic presentation are, though less serious and fraught with problems and far more limited in their conception of historical movement, nevertheless perfectly integrated in their sensory substance. They do not know the antagonism between sensory appearance and meaning, an antagonism which permeates the early, and indeed the whole, Christian view of reality" (1953, 48–49). As Auerbach goes on to demonstrate, Christian theory in the later Middle Ages invested representations of everyday life with characteristic figural meanings, and so with the possibilities for distinctive kinds of religious experience. Figural interpretation, in Auerbach's usage, is not synonymous with symbolism. The latter is close to allegory, in which the symbol is substituted for the object symbolized. In figural interpretation the representation of an event (Adam's sleep) is made explicit by the representation of another event (Christ's death) that is its meaning. The latter representation fulfills the former (the technical term, Auerbach tells us, was *figuram implere*)—it is *implicit* in it.

28. Cf. Douglas (1975, 76): "The person without religion would be the person content to do without explanations of certain kinds, or content to behave in society without a single unifying principle validating the social order."

29. When the fifth-century bishop of Javols spread Christianity into the Auvergne, he found the peasants "celebrating a three-day festival with offerings on the edge of a marsh. . . . 'Nulla est religio in stagno,' he said: There can be no religion in a swamp" (Brown 1981, 125). For medieval Christians, religion was not a universal phenomenon: religion was a site on which universal truth was produced, and it was clear to them that truth was not produced universally.

30. As a contemporary Catholic theologian puts it: "The secularistic challenge, even though separating many aspects of life from the religious field, brings with it a more sound, interpretative equilibrium: the natural phenomena, even though sometimes difficult to understand, have their cause and roots in processes that can and must be recognized. It is man's job, therefore, to enter into this cognitive analysis of the meaning of suffering, in order to be able to affront

and conquer it. The contemporary condition of man, of the believer on the threshold of the third millennium, is undoubtedly more adult and more mature and allows a new approach to the problem of human suffering" (Autiero 1987, 124).

31. I have attempted a description of one aspect of this process in Asad 1986b.

32. Philosophical attempts to define science have not reached a firm consensus. In the Anglo-Saxon world, recent arguments have been formulated in and around the works of Popper, Kuhn, Lakatos, Feyerabend, Hacking, and others; in France, those of Bachelard and Canguilhem. One important tendency has been to abandon the attempt at solving what is known in the literature as the demarcation problem, which is based on the assumption that there must be a single, essential, scientific method. The idea that the scientist "dissolves the world's givenness into a swirl of probabilistic hypotheses" is as questionable as the complementary suggestion that in religion there is no scope for experimentation. On this latter point, there is massive evidence of experiment, even if we went no farther than the history of Christian asceticism. Equally, the suggestion that art is a matter of "effecting a disengagement from the whole question of factuality, deliberately manufacturing an air of semblance and illusion" would not be taken as self-evident by all writers and artists. For example, when the art critic John Berger argues, in his brilliant essay "The Moment of Cubism," that cubism "changed the nature of the relationship between the painted image and reality, and by so doing expressed a new relationship between man and reality" (1972, 145), we learn something about cubism's concern to redefine visual factuality.

33. In case some readers are tempted to think that what I am talking about is not science (theory) but technology (practical application), whereas Geertz is concerned only with the former, I would stress that any attempt to make a sharp distinction between the two is based on an oversimplified view of the historical practice of both (cf. Musson and Robinson 1969). My point is that science and technology *together* are basic to the structure of modern lives, individual and collective, and that religion, in any but the most vacuous sense, is not.

34. In the introduction to his 1983 collection of essays, Geertz seems to want to abandon this perspectival approach: "The debate over whether [art] is an applicable category in 'non-Western' or 'pre-Modern' contexts has, even when compared to similar debates concerning 'religion,' 'science,' 'ideology,' or 'law,' been peculiarly unrelenting. It has also been peculiarly unproductive. Whatever you want to call a cave wall crowded with overlapping images of transfixed animals, a temple tower shaped to a phallus, a feathered shield, a calligraphic scroll, or a tattooed face, you still have *the phenomenon* to deal with, as well as perhaps the sense that to add kula exchange or the Doomsday Book would be to spoil the series. The question is not whether art (or anything else) is universal; it is whether one can talk about West African carving, New Guinea palm-leaf painting, quattrocento picture making, and Moroccan versifying in such a way as to cause them to shed some sort of light on one another" (1983, 11; emphasis added). The answer to this question must surely be: yes, of course one should try to talk about disparate things in relation to one another, but what exactly is the purpose of constructing a series whose items can all easily be recognized by cultivated Westerners as instances of *the phenomenon* of art? Of course, any one thing may shed light on another. But is it not precisely when one abandons conventional perspectives, or preestablished series, for opportunistic comparison that illumination (as opposed to recognition) *may* be achieved? Think of Hofstadter's splendid *Gödel, Escher, Bach* (1979), for instance,

35. Cf. the final chapter in Evans-Pritchard 1956, and also the conclusion to Evans-Pritchard 1965.

36. Such endeavors are unceasing. As a recent, engaging study by Tambiah (1990, 6) puts it in the first chapter: "In our discussion hereafter I shall try to argue that from a general anthropological standpoint the distinctive feature of religion as a generic concept lies not in the domain of belief and its 'rational accounting' of the workings of the universe, but in a special awareness of the transcendent, and the acts of symbolic communication that attempt to realize that awareness and live by its promptings."

2

Contested Meanings and Definitional Boundaries: Historicizing the Sociology of Religion

Meredith B. McGuire

RESEARCHERS SOMETIMES discover that assumptions, embedded in their field's basic definitions; get in the way of understanding the phenomenon they are observing. The realization comes as a jolt, because it means that the way we have learned to think about a phenomenon is now hindering our ability to understand what we are observing.[1] Any mature ethnographer of religion has probably had this experience many times, because it is part of the process that makes ethnography such a difficult, albeit rewarding, way of studying religion.[2]

One such jarring research experience happened to me in early 1981, as I was beginning a study of nonmedical healing. I recorded these events in my field notes:

> The healing service took place in an attractive suburban Episcopalian church, the members of which were generally upper-middle class and well-educated. The Sunday evening Eucharistic service each week was designated as a healing service, with scripture readings, prayers, and other elements of the liturgy focused on health and healing. A regular and important part of these services (as I discovered later) occurred after the Eucharist, when the celebrant offered to bless salt and oil for home prayer for healing. With a rustling of brown paper

wrappers, the congregation hurriedly opened the spouts of salt boxes and lids of cooking oil bottles so the blessing could "get in."

I was only mildly surprised that these Episcopalians had revived a centuries-old tradition of promoting health and healing with blessed substances. What startled me, however, was the magical image of the blessing that these well-educated suburbanites obviously used: Their practice implied that they had to physically open the containers so that the blessing would reach the contents and thus its power would be effectively contained and transported home, in order for that power to heal at a distant location.

Doing good ethnography required me to examine my own reactions: Why was I startled? If I had observed Ecuadorian *campesinos* engaging in the same practice, I would not have been surprised. Were my reactions in this fieldwork perhaps biased by sociology's assumptions that religion should be "purified" of material concerns and magical thought? What had I assumed about the concepts of "magic" and "religion" that made it difficult for me to understand the ready mingling of magical practices and thinking in these contemporary Episcopalians' religious lives? In these people's lived experience, it was all part of practicing their religion.

At the time, I resolved my conceptual quandary by avoiding the concept of religion and focusing only on a concept that applied well to widely varying (religious and nonreligious) groups in my study: the notion of healing power (e.g., where it was located and how it was tapped, how it got to where it was needed, and what practices promoted its effectiveness). In the subsequent quarter century, however, I have experienced many such problems with the way sociology of religion defines religion and religiosity. Are magic and religion necessarily separate and mutually exclusive or are they integrated in many people's lived religions? Is the realm of the sacred always set apart from the profane, or do people sometimes experience the sacred as part of their work-a-day lives and mundane domestic existence? Is "folk" or "popular" or "non-official" religiosity any less religious than "official" or "church" religiosity? Does "religion" have to pertain to a deity or the supernatural, or could someone be equally religious without worshiping some suprahuman being?

Perhaps sociology, as a discipline, has uncritically adopted a post-Reformation "Protestant"[3] purism that excludes from our purview a large range of practices and beliefs that are, in fact, important parts of the lived religions of many individuals today. Perhaps too, sociology's disciplinary focus on what people believe, affirm, and think, as indicators of their religion and religiosity, is based on Reformation-era theological ideas that privilege belief over practice. If those assessments are correct, then sociology's conceptual apparatus is simply inadequate for understanding people's lived religion. It is thus necessary to examine and reconsider sociology's core definitions, then to refocus our research and methodological strategies accordingly.

I propose that we begin by trying to understand the nature of reiigion and religiosity in Europe before the Reformation era—before the foundation of a Christian denomination called Episcopalian, and long before anyone would have questioned the appropriateness of a congregation taking blessed substances home in order to carry divine healing power to where and when it was needed. The various "stories"[4] sociologists use to explain the place of religion in modern societies are all based on definitional assumptions. For example, many sociologists and anthropologists assume that in all religions there is a radical dichotomy between the sacred and the profane. Accordingly, religious behavior involves treating sacred places, time, and objects with a sense of profound respect and awe and protecting the sacred from contamination by the profane. If people's actual religious practices in other cultures or other times in history, involve melding the sacred and profane, should we conclude that they are not really religious? Or, rather, should we reconsider our assumptions about a sacred-profane dichotomy and what practices count as "religious"?

In this chapter, I will examine how the definitions of what is properly "religion" and "religious" changed during a long period of upheaval in which many people vied, sometimes violently, over precisely those borderlines. Which issues were so critical that people would exert enormous effort and power to control the resulting boundaries? Specifically, I examine four issues that, I believe, are particularly important for understanding that what scholars nowadays think of as definitive of "real" religion and religious action is itself a social construction[5], the result of human struggles over cultural resources and power:

The location of the sacred. Where is the sacred found and how do humans get in touch with it? Is the sacred an integral part of everyday space, time, and social relationships, or is it radically apart from the "profane" world of everyday life? What practices do people engage in to connect with the realm of the sacred?

The nature of divine power. How is divine power exercised in the world? Does it regularly break through in "miracles," changing individuals' situations and affecting the course of events in the world? Is divine power channeled through human actions, and is it responsive to magical rituals?

The focus of individual religious expression. What is really important for each individual to do or to believe in order to be religiously "in good standing"? How does (or should) the individual integrate religious belief and/or practice with other aspects of life?

The purity and authenticity of religious tradition and group identity. Who is authentically "one of us"? Who can authoritatively determine what beliefs and practices are true to a religion's tradition, as opposed to what is misled, alien, or downright heretical? When an individual modifies or selects religious practices to make them more relevant in everyday life, is that person still practicing the group's religion?

Recognizing that these definitional boundaries are social constructions does not mean we must discard the concepts, but does require us to realize that the resulting distinctions are not inherent properties of "religion" or "the sacred." And it requires that we notice how such factors as social class and political or military power shaped the resulting definitions to privilege some groups' religious practices and to marginalize others.'

Certain ways of being religious were once common or even the norm but after a long struggle came to be treated as unacceptable (even sinful or heretical). This chapter sketches the premodern notions that allowed those beliefs and practices to be understood as properly "religious."

HISTORICAL CONTESTS AND THE CREATION OF DEFINITIONAL BOUNDARIES

Sociology of religion needs a much deeper appreciation of the historical context of its core definitions. Drawing boundaries is a political and sociohistorical process. Definitional boundaries are the outcomes of *contested meanings*; that is, people have

actively exerted their power to affect the outcome and to resist others' efforts to gain control. The resulting boundaries must be understood in the sociohistorical context of that struggle. For Europe and the Americas, dramatic changes in the definitional boundaries of acceptable Christian belief and practice occurred between roughly 1400 and 1700 CE. The intense conflicts within and among religious groups during those centuries illustrate the uses of power in defining religion.

Some historians refer to this period as the Long Reformation because of the sociopolitical prominence of ongoing religious controversies.[6] While Protestant historians and apologists first applied the term "reformation" to their own foundational religiopolitical standpoint vis-à-vis the Catholic Church, most social historians now emphasize that both Catholic and Protestant churches experienced a series of change-promoting movements that aimed to reform Christianity. These reformations were about literally re-forming, re-shaping, and re-defining the core of Christian faith and practice.[7]

The extensive redrawing of religious boundaries during the Long Reformation took place in the context of other massive changes in wider sociopolitical and cultural boundaries. One of the main changes involved the development and elaboration of cultural distinctions between people. Thus, for example, social elites marked and exaggerated the differences between themselves and nonelite social groups, elaborating norms for etiquette, decorum, and demeanor. Some historians examining laypersons' religious practices during this transition period argue that the boundaries around what eventually came to be viewed as proper religious behavior were central to producing and reproducing social elites, as distinguished from common folks. As these boundaries became established norms, aspiring elites and middle classes gradually adopted them as definitive of proper behavior.[8]

Another set of boundaries that were redrawn pertained to people's sense of group identity. Whereas in late medieval times, people's group-identity was grounded in the cultural homogeneity of their local community, that homogeneity was disrupted by struggles over the redefinition of religious, social, and political units. People could no longer assume that others in the same community were like themselves in important areas such as religion, political allegiance, and social class. For example, one might have a stronger sense of identity with others of the same religious "confession" (e.g., Lutheran, Catholic) than with others who shared the same grazing lands or occupation but not "confession." Religious boundaries became especially important in this period of intense demarcation of *cultural identity* in new and complex constellations.

At the same time, religious and civil authorities created and emphasized greater distinction between the social center and the periphery, widening the exercise of their power over politico-religious units (e.g., canton, diocese) and bringing remote rural areas under tighter control.[9] Thus, cultural identity markers were frequently linked with political identity markers, such that decades-long religious wars and recurring violence toward religiopolitical Others eventually reshaped Europe.[10] The contested boundaries between "us" and "them" were, thus, also at stake in the historical processes of defining religion.

Why do sociologists need to pay attention to the historical struggles by which definitive boundaries were established? When we fail to recognize that our conceptual apparatus has been shaped by such battles over boundaries, we risk misapprehending our data and misusing our sociological interpretations. A prime example of such failing is sociologists Rod Stark and Roger Finke's misuses of historical accounts of medieval European religion. They depict medieval Christians as having a very low degree of religiosity, based on such indicators as the paucity and small capacity of parish churches, laypeople's sparse church attendance and infrequent reception of Communion, improper behavior in church, and widespread ignorance of church doctrines and church-prescribed religious practices

(such as how to recite the Apostles' Creed).[11] Their interpretations are limited by an overly institutional conception of religion that is utterly anachronistic.[12] All of those indicators are based on norms for religious behavior that became established, in most of western Europe, only in the modern era.

Our discipline's conceptual tools are, thus, limited by a Eurocentric bias. They do not adequately apply to non-Western religions, especially those religions that are not structured at all like Western religious organizations with "membership" of individuals. Anthropologist Talal Asad has argued that an anthropology (and, I would add, sociology) of religion was made possible by the development, in Western history, of a concept of religion as an objective reality—something that exists universally in the real world, and can be "discovered" and objectively studied.[13] Asad researched the genealogies of "religion" and several related core concepts (e.g., "ritual") to demonstrate how scholarly discourse itself has been shaped by important historical shifts in how power is exercised, how self and society are linked, and how human bodies and emotions are engaged in religion.[14] Unearthing the genealogies of our conceptual tools enables us to understand their limitations. It reminds us that both the social "reality" we study and our ways of thinking about that reality are products of a process of social construction in which human factors of power and privilege play a significant role.[15]

How can we interpret the changes in the social location of religion and the changed place of religion in individual lives if we fail to recognize that our field's core conceptual distinctions are themselves social products? For instance, how can we interpret comparative rates of church membership without acknowledging that the very definition and meaning of membership changed dramatically? How can we compare individual patterns of religiosity over time without admitting that what we researchers count as "religious" is completely different from what, for example, fourteenth-century persons in Languedoc, for example, considered "religious?"[16] Are there not serious biases affecting our interpretations if we privilege, by our fundamental definitions, those expressions of religion that served (intentionally or not) the political purposes of social elites, colonial powers, males, and victors?

To acknowledge that our concepts are the social products of historical contests does not mean we must discard them altogether or must despair of ever having useful conceptual tools. Rather, by historicizing the sociology of religion, we can begin to have a far more critical appreciation of our conceptual tools, as well as a much better understanding of the far-reaching societal changes we seek to interpret.

What were people's religious lives like before these definitional boundaries were drawn? Who were the contesting factions and how did they exert their interests and their meanings over the disputed boundaries? This transition period creates many problems if we are trying to understand ordinary laypeople's as well as elite individuals' religious expressions, because when these various reformation movements "dismantled medieval Christianity, they transformed the definition of religion itself."[17] In recent years, historians have published volumes of careful scholarship on ordinary people's religious practices and meanings in various parts of Europe and the Americas before, during, and after this critical redefining transition.[18] Their findings show that many sociologists' assumptions about religion, magic, the supernatural, and the sacred and the profane are based on faulty, biased readings of history.[19]

Let us examine some of the contested religious meanings around which political and cultural struggles centered in the transitional period of late medieval and early modem times.

CONTESTED MEANINGS: WHERE IS THE SACRED LOCATED?

Late medieval religion was not, of course, a unified, homogenous entity. Indeed, several historians have argued that one of the hotly contested projects of many Protestant and Catholic reformation movements was to consolidate authority over religious belief and practice in order to make it less heterogeneous.[20] Religious beliefs and practices tied to the location of the sacred help explain this considerable diversity in three ways: (1) localistic practices varied greatly because the sacred was rooted in local geography; (2) individuals could eclectically choose their own devotional options from a large repertoire of locally acceptable practices; and (3) in people's experience, sacred space and time were pervasive and not limited to the church or its rituals. The following sketches serve to give a sense of how the location of the sacred could produce such great diversity of belief, practice, and experience within the same religion.

Some sociologists have treated medieval Europe as monolithically Catholic-Christian. But they have failed to appreciate the enormous diversity that existed within that era's practice of Christianity. Stark and Finke argue that religion of that era epitomizes a religious market monopoly.[21] Their error is due, in large part, to a narrowly Protestant misreading of Catholicism generally, because Catholicism has long encouraged a considerable amount of internal diversity.[22] The market analogy, in particular, does not fit the patterns of medieval Christianity. Although virtually all persons were members of a single church, that membership was a minor part of their religion-as-lived. Individuals' actual lived religions were highly diverse, somewhat eclectic, and much more central to their everyday lives than was the church part alone. When there is only one food market in town, it cannot be said to hold a monopoly if the residents grow most of their own food.

Localism and Heterogeneity

There was enormous difference between one part of Europe and another. Indeed, religion, often varied considerably from a community in one valley to the next valley. For instance, the patron saint of one village—around whose patronage many communal religious rituals revolved—might go completely unnoticed in the everyday practices of persons living in nearby villages, which had their own patron saints. Because these practices pertained to a specific geographical place and historical community, they were immensely resistant to the efforts of outsiders to change them. Changes did occur, though, usually gradually and from within.[23] For instance, villagers might increase devotion to a saint whose help appeared to be especially effective in time of an epidemic, or they might lose interest in a practice, such as use of water from a holy well, when it failed to be particularly effective.

Such localism was one of the key characteristics of late medieval religious expression. The modern Westerner is often disturbed by the level of diversity and apparent inconsistency of such highly localistic religion: With that much variation, how can one consider it to be all the *same* religion? But that is precisely the point! So long as they observed a few highly important common translocal practices (*not* common beliefs), people's participation in their immediate community's religious practices made them confident that their religion was "Christian." These localistic ritual practices confirmed community social bonds and ties with the land, which may have been important sources of medieval Christianity's strength. But they also suggest why it simply did not matter to most participants that, in many respects, their regular religious practices differed from those of other Christian villages.

What were the important Christian practices most people held in common and would expect anywhere? Core practices included baptism (for oneself and one's family), attending Sunday Mass whenever practicable, making confession and receiving Communion at least once a year during Easter week, and using some basic prayers (usually the Ave Maria and Pater Noster).[24] We get a clue that ordinary people understood these practices as a

central core from the testimony of a character witness for an Inquisition suspect:

> "When he is not tending the herds and is at home in winter or when it rains, or during such times, he always goes to Mass; he always makes the sign of the cross when the Ave Maria tolls, he recites the Ave Maria, crossing himself first, he rests the oxen from their work at that time; blesses the bread and offers thanks to God after he has eaten; when he goes out to Mass he has a rosary in his hands; in church he is respectful and recites the rosary, and so he performs all the duties of a good Christian."[25]

This peasant from a remote valley in what is now Italy had good reason to expect that the inquisitor—an educated (and dangerous) stranger from a completely different social world—would recognize these religious practices as universally accepted definitive characteristics of a "good Christian." In his experience, lived entirely in the local village context, "good Christians" were, by definition, those who engaged in just such Christian practices.

Cultic Diversity and Devotional Options

Localism was not the only source of widespread heterogeneity. Another important source was individuals' relative freedom to choose (from a large, locally available repertoire), the specific religious practices and cultic devotions they used in their own lives, according to their specific needs. Furthermore, individuals could shape their own understandings of the saints and the meanings of their devotions toward them.[26] For example, one woman's everyday devotional practices might include seeking help from a saint known for protecting and healing children, devotions at a nearby holy well known for promoting fertility, involvement in rituals for the patron saint of her valley, and such routine women's religious responsibilities as the daily blessing of the hearth on rekindling the fire. An older neighbor would have very different everyday religious practices: She might say similar blessings on the hearth and the kitchen, seek a different holy well (perhaps one for the health and fertility of her barnyard animals), pay little or no attention to cults of saints protecting children, but seek the help of those saints who help persons with aches and pains, failing memories, and sore throats.

The men in their households would have different religious practices. One might seek help from the patron saint of farmers; another from the patron of fishermen or smithies. One might choose to tap divine power at an ancient cairn, another at a grotto, and another at a mountaintop shrine. Individual reverence (for example, toward Mary, the mother of Jesus) also varied (by locality, by gender, or by personal preference) as to what image of the holy person was the object of devotional prayers. For example, some people revered the Mary-of-Sorrows, others the Mary-Queen-of-Heaven, or any number of other manifestations of Mary as a holy or powerful religious figure.[27]

Such choice of personal and family religious practices, combined with localistic practices, resulted in a somewhat eclectic pattern of religiosity that differed in many important particulars from that of similar persons elsewhere in the same culture.[28] In order to understand the quality of their religion-as-lived, we need to appreciate how these diverse individual practices made sense in their everyday lives.

Sacred Space and Sacred Time

In premodern Europe, religious meanings pertained to everyday experiences of time and space, such that—without necessarily ever being conscious of it—ordinary people subjectively participated in these religious meanings regularly throughout each day. While people clearly recognized an important distinction between the sacred and the profane, in practice they observed no tidy boundaries between sacred and profane space and time.[29] There appears to have been a casual familiarity with what modern

people would consider to be sacred space. This familiarity is in marked contrast with the modern conception of sacred space that is set apart and not used for nonreligious purposes, that is treated with awe and reverence, such that "religious" people respect that space with "proper" behavior, such as attentiveness and decorum. Sociologists who treat such church-defined reverence toward the sacred as a core indicator of religiosity thus fail to notice the many other ways people have of being religious.

The medieval sense of sacred space was that it was nearly ubiquitous and highly accessible to everyone. In both rural and urban settings, the entire local landscape had something of a "sacred overlay."[30] All the people in the community knew numerous spaces where they could readily contact the divine—a votive shrine at a crossroads, a holy well, a home altar, a standing stone or cairn. Often, these places were more important in people's religiosity than the church building and grounds, because they were experienced as more awe-inspiring and imbued with sacred power than the church or its parts.

Most people in a community may have considered their church building itself to be more sacred than most other buildings because of the many ritual exorcisms and blessings on it. However, various parts of the church and churchyard were considered to have different degrees of holiness.[31] The demarcations between these spaces were thus ritually useful and meaningful, because the simple ritual act of moving one's body or an object from one space to a more sacred one would be experienced, by all those acculturated to that sense of space, as a highly meaningful act.[32]

Medieval people certainly considered some space more "sacred" than other space, but they had a very different notion (compared to, say, twentieth-century sensibilities) of what was proper behavior when present in that space. Because people thought of the church space as familiar and communal, they considered it no sacrilege to hold wakes and feast-day celebrations in the nave of the church.[33] They made no tidy boundaries between the religious and nonreligious activities these celebrations entailed. For instance, the wake had obvious religious significance as part of the larger communal ritual response to death, but wake festivities also included lots of eating, drinking, music, flirting and bawdy jokes, games, and jesting.[34]

People's casual familiarity with sacred space applied even during the Mass, the central church-oriented religious event of the routine week. One historian has summarized:

> on the face of it, medieval people would seem to have behaved informally, if not irreverently, at Mass. Apparently, scuffles broke out in parish churches, people sat on the altar steps or squatted on the floor, nipped out at intervals to the wine shop, talked, laughed, scratched, hawked, coughed and spat. They left the service as soon as they decently could, and used the premises for assignations, seductions, flirtations and sales.[35]

In church, some sacred time (like space) was more sacred than others. So, while Mass time generally might have been more holy than work time, within the Mass time, only the period surrounding the consecration of bread and wine was particularly sacred; within that period, the actual elevation of the consecrated host was the solemn moment for most congregants. It was not a breach of community norms to be inattentive in the early parts of the Mass or to leave the service after the elevation had occurred.[36]

The diffuseness of the sacred and its interpenetration with the profane in people's everyday lives were also due, in large part, to how thoroughly a complex series of calendrical rituals structured those lives. In addition to the major liturgical seasons (e.g., Advent, Christmastide, Lent, Easter, and Pentecost) established by the church, there were numerous special holy days to observe by abstention from work, attending Mass, or participating in processions, communal feasts, and private celebrations. Each locality also celebrated the special days

associated with its community's own shrines and local patron saints. One historian noted: "To fifteenth-and early sixteenth-century sensibilities the liturgical year was spread over twelve months, . . . and *none of it was secular.*"[37]

Calendrical rituals served to order the experience of time, establishing routines and schedules and creating a sense of *shared temporal regularity.*[38] Not only the liturgical year but also the days of the week and the hours of the day had ritual significance. Just as school bells, "rush hour," and the "six o'clock news" shape some of people's collective temporal regularity nowadays, pre-modern people experienced time through such, calendrical rituals as the daily ringing of Angelus bells, community celebrations of the Sabbath, and numerous seasonal rituals. These calendrical rituals produced a pervasive religiosity that was inherently communal, rather than individual.[39]

Especially solemn feast days were obligatory: Nonobservance (e.g., working a normal workday) was a serious sin. In a typical late medieval German town, for example, solemn feasts included Christmas, Easter, seven major feasts of the Virgin, the feasts of John the Baptist, feasts of the individual apostles, and the feast of the Discovery of the True Cross. Then, local patron saints merited another ten or twelve solemn feast days, and some nonobligatory celebrations as well.[40] Often the local patron saints' feasts were, in practice, more important than those of the officially recognized, higher saints.[41] Feasts were observed with liturgical (i.e., formal church ritual), paraliturgical, and nonliturgical celebrations. For instance, a village celebrating an important holy day might have a religious procession from the parish church's gate through the town and valley to a nearby shrine site, followed by an outdoor celebration of the Mass at the shrine, and later a special meal, with dancing and merriment around a bonfire. Of this day-long celebration, only the Mass was a formal church ritual, but the entire day's activities were part of observing the holy day.

The liturgical cycle shaped the Christian year with rituals for all the important seasons, needs, and emotions. The feast of the Purification of the Virgin (known as Candlemas), on February 2, exemplifies how people used liturgical, paraliturgical, and nonliturgical rituals together to channel divine power to affect their everyday material world. Because the central features of Candlemas itself were generally the same throughout most of Europe, we can draw on historical evidence from diverse countries. Local practices, however, varied in other meanings attached to the beginning of February and the entire ritual cycle of spring. For example, many German-speaking areas also celebrated a weather-predicting saint's day, such that there was religious significance to what Americans now know as "Groundhog Day." The feast of the Purification was also celebrated as St. Bridget's Day[42] in Ireland. In practice, Candlemas was clearly the celebration, simultaneously, of both these Christian saints' themes and the important Feast of Lights of various early European pagan religions. The pagan celebrations also evoked the themes of light, life, and renewal, so the Christian rituals reverberated with powerful cultural meanings.[43]

In church liturgy, the Candlemas feast symbolized the purity of the Virgin and coming of the light of the world (Christ). It was the main feast in a larger cycle of feasts of saints whose celebrations are linked with blessings for new spring life and mating, favorable weather for planting and vine-tending, blessings of animals against sickness, and so on.[44] In popular practice, Candlemas was both a large communal celebration with elaborate processions and, for individuals and families, the source of ritually blessed candles that each household used for protection, healing, and purification throughout the year.

For medieval people, time mattered. Dangerous periods of seasonal transition, such as planting or harvest time, required the ritual protection of the sacred. The ritual calendar also "structured the expression of the deep emotions of grief, love, and hope according to a seasonal and weekly, even hourly pattern."[45] If we consider also the extensive paraliturgical and nonliturgical ritual calendar, we can better appreciate how simply participating in ritual practices structured people's emotional and social experiences, giving them meaning by practice, rather than by ideas or verbal explanations.[46]

Our modern image of a sacred-profane dichotomy does not really apply to the sense of sacred time and space in medieval religion. On the contrary, more often the sacred was experienced as arising *from within* profane space and everyday, mundane activities. Indeed, sacred events/time "could enter the flow of merely human time," and certain religious practices promoted that sense of elision of time.[47]

Rather than diminishing the quality of experience of the sacred, such diffuseness in everyday life made the sacred more useful. Consider, for example, the quotidian usefulness of sacred power infused into blessed substances that one sixteenth-century commentator alluded to approvingly:

> People of old showed great zeal for all kinds of blessings by the Church, and everyone wanted to share in them. . . . Each Sunday, the old Christians went in crowds to the blessing of holy water and salt, and every week each person supplied his house with holy water and blessed salt . . . so that everyone had something blessed on his table the whole week through.[48]

Both the premodern persons described in this example and the suburban congregation I observed in the 1980s ritually used the blessed substances to carry divine power to where they needed it, for such uses as anointing sick family members or a protective blessing of all before they left the house each morning. Even though they may have viewed the priest's blessing as having greater effectiveness than a layperson's, the act of blessing people, places, or things was an important everyday religious practice. Ordinary laypersons, not ritual specialists, performed much—probably most—ritual practice.

Laypersons performed rituals, sometimes precisely, sometimes carelessly, throughout their daily lives, so that divine power might be brought to bear, even if in minute quantities, on their everyday needs and concerns.

This easy familiarity with the realm of the sacred was closely tied to how people used their religious practices as a means of tapping sacred power. People had a relationship with the saints. Veneration of saints was linked to getting concrete help from them to meet family or community needs, but saints who failed to fulfill their role were angrily chided or even abused. For instance, in Germany people called on St. Urban, the patron saint of vintners, to provide good weather for harvesting the grapes. When the weather on St. Urban's feast day was good, people honored him and appreciated his protection of the harvest, but if the weather was bad, his image was thrown in the mud.[49]

One of the effects (if not also one of the goals) of the Protestant and Catholic reformation movements was to limit the realm of the sacred, presumably making it more valuable, set apart, and awesome. A related end was to control the uses ordinary people could make of sacred power. This control was effected by drawing boundaries around the location of the sacred. It had to be differentiated from the everyday, mundane world of the common folk. The new delineations separated sacred space from people's profane space and sacred time from their everyday profane time. According to the logic of popular religion, the sacred pervaded the realm of the profane. Early modern reformation movements contested that sense; they proclaimed that the sacred and profane had to be ritually separated.

Rather than take the notion of a clear sacred-profane dichotomy for granted as a defining feature of religion, what would we understand about individuals' religious lives—now, as well as four centuries ago—if we considered the possibility that some, perhaps many, religious persons experience the sacred as arising *within* the profane world?[50] Many scholars of religion have used a similar dichotomy as definitive: the distinction between magic and religion.[51] Although religious leaders had tried for centuries to control the practice of important rituals, the Long Reformation was a period in which the boundary between religious and magical ritual was theologically and organizationally contested and fortified.[52] In rethinking our conceptual tools, it would be fruitful to examine some cultural understandings of religious, magical, and miraculous powers that were common in the late medieval era, before the definitive boundaries of religion and the religious were redrawn.

CONTESTED MEANINGS: MIRACLE, MAGIC, AND RELIGIOUS POWER

As part of their attack on popular uses of sacred power, various agents of reform tried to distinguish religion from magic and to eliminate magical elements from religious practice. For all practical purposes, the definitional boundary between magic and religion did not exist in the late medieval popular imagination. Most people had a magical image of the power of much religious and parareligious ritual. For example, people considered the candles blessed in church at Candlemas to be imbued with sacred power that could be transmitted to where it was needed for protection. Thus, during the dangerous time of childbirth, blessed candles were lit to keep evil spirits from mother and child. Each year, on the ritual calendar's New Year, the head of the household inscribed, in candle wax, a protective mark of blessing on the doors of the house and barn. People also used the blessed candles for healing, burning them at the bedside of the sick, and for purification, burning one to expel evil spirits or ghosts from an afflicted house.[53] Thus, religious uses of these candles seemed entirely consistent with a magical image of their efficacy.

One of the reasons we misinterpret medieval religious practice as merely "superstitious" or "irrational" is that we fail to grasp practitioners' conception of religious power. A mode of action is not irrational if a person perceives it to work. Given their conception of religious power, medieval persons were reasonable to consider ritual actions to be the appropriate and efficacious way to meet certain needs and to accomplish certain tasks. People experienced that power as real. These cultures socialized their members' very senses to perceive divine power.[54] Thus, not only did they *think* about this religious power differently than do most twenty-first-century Europeans but also they had regular experiences in which they *sensed* it.[55] Divine power was not just a matter of belief; it was an awesome and important reality in people's lives.

Historian Edward Muir has argued compellingly that the central contested issue of the Long Reformation was the meaning of ritual action. He observed that the "generalized concept of *ritual* as a distinct kind of activity came into being" during this critical period.[56] That concept was used to distinguish—to mark a boundary—between "true religion" (the religious practices of whoever was making the distinction) and "mere ritual" (the religious practices of the Other).

More important than these rhetorical distinctions, though, was that the Long Reformation resulted in a whole range of new interpretations of ritual *action*—hotly contested debates about the answer to the question "What do rites do?"[57] At one extreme was a dogmatic Catholic answer. Rites were real actions. As such, they had the power to bring something into being (e.g., a marriage), to literally enact something (e.g., the anointment of an emperor or bishop), and to make something present (e.g., Christ's presence in the Mass). At the other extreme was one Protestant (and humanist) position that rites were no more than representations, a form of communication by which meaning is represented symbolically. Accordingly, Communion rituals were reminders of the Last Supper; the rituals of anointment were symbols of an office-holder's change of status, and Christ's presence among

gathered believers was metaphorical, not physically real.[58] Other Protestant (and later Catholic) positions were somewhere between these two extremes. This historical process constructing a boundary between "real" religion and "mere" ritual is closely linked with the transition between premodern emphasis on practices by means of which people are religious and the modern emphasis on what and how religious persons believe.

Not only church rites but also everyday ritual practices were considered to have a real physical, as well as spiritual, efficacy. For example, the act of blessing someone, something, or someplace meant literally *doing* something that had the power to change the circumstances of that person, object, or place. People incorporated blessings on a household in their greeting on entering, and other blessings were part of such everyday acts as lighting the fire in the hearth. Parents blessed their children and other members of the household. Workers blessed their tools and often their products-in-process. Blessing was a literal, not merely metaphorical, act of using divine power. Because the power of blessing was considered to be an active power, people used many ritual blessings to channel divine power to where it was needed.[59]

People regularly sought the priest's blessings, especially when the liturgical calendar provided for them. For example, blessings on the feast of St. Blasius, February 3, were considered especially effective, for curing illness in humans and cattle. Laypersons, however, could also effectively do the blessing. For example, the head of the household was usually the one to perform the annual blessing of the house and barn on the feast of Epiphany— the religious new year.[60] Similarly, laypersons regularly performed blessings of people, animals, and inanimate objects, by using either a ritual prayer and action or a previously blessed object to pass the blessing on to another person or thing needful of it. Before the Long Reformation, church officials had little control over laypersons' access to or uses of such sacred power.

In late medieval times, many people experienced miracles as real. Medieval religiosity was based on the expectation of miracles, the breakthrough of divine power to affect people's everyday, material lives. "Of course," divine power could save the crops, heal sick people, and protect loved ones from harm! The only question was how to obtain that divine intervention for one's own life. Although sometimes it seemed capricious, this religious power was not utterly without order. People believed that it sometimes accomplished an immanent justice, for example punishing people's sins through plague or crop failure.[61] They thought of the power of the miraculous as reflecting the order of the cosmos; for example, the calendrical ritual order anticipated manifestations of divine power according to the order of nature's seasons.[62]

Divine power was susceptible to something of a contract with a community. In exchange for the community's devotions and faithful practice of necessary rituals, the powers would become that community's protectors and benefactors.[63] The saints personified this relationship.[64] People believed that they could channel divine power directly, without clerical mediation, to where it was needed. Saints' miracles could erupt anywhere.[65] And people could tap the saints' power themselves at home, at wayside shrines, in the fields, on the roads, wherever and whenever needed.[66] Rituals were thus the means by which cosmic order could be brought to bear on everyday life, giving ordinary people access to divine power and thereby a measure of control in the face of the chaos of life.[67] While God might be named as the ultimate source of all this power, in everyday life spiritual powers were treated as more widespread and less remote.

The religious power to help was simultaneously the power to harm.[68] Evil spirits were not the only source of dangerous power; in some instances, the saints were also considered malevolent for using their power to harm humans.[69] Thus, community rituals needed to propitiate these spiritual powers in order to escape their wrath.[70] This notion of religious power also suggests why people often did not care whether the power that accomplished their goal was "good" or "bad" in the eyes of religious authorities. To them, demonic power was merely an alternative means to tap efficacious power. Historians note, for example, instances in which weather bells were blessed in the name of the divinity and, when they did not bring favorable weather, were reblessed in the name of the devil.[71]

The pervasive influence of so many dangerous powers meant that people needed regular ritual practices for protection. There were numerous liturgical and extraliturgical prayers to drive away dangerous spirits and protective symbols one could wear or place on one's house and barn, as well as community works and prayers that might attract helpful spirits.[72] Each candle blessed at Candlemas, for example, was imbued with protective power, because its ritual blessing included the pronouncement that "wherever it shall be lit or set up, the devil may flee away in fear and trembling with all his ministers, out of those dwelling, and never presume again to disquiet your servants."[73] Furthermore, because there was no tidy boundary between the sacred and profane, these ritual actions were integrated in everyday life with other, more purely utilitarian actions, such as the planting of seed, the lighting of the hearth fire, and putting children to bed.

Thus, knowledge of effective ritual actions was valued knowledge. For example, a good mother would know that taking care of a sick child included use of blessed candles and oil, as well as prayers to exorcise the sick room of any bad spirits; she would know how to collect herbs for a healing tea and how to say the correct ritual words while brewing it; she would sponge the fevered child with cool compresses, while addressing prayers to a saint known to be especially effective in curing little ones. Such religious actions were not viewed as apart from purely instrumental ones; ritual prayers were an integral part of how one correctly performed the instrumental tasks. Thus, a mother who did not know these healing practices or who failed to do them properly would be deemed inadequate.[74]

Nevertheless, ritual effectiveness depended on performance, not intention or individual consciousness. Thus, a ritual action performed correctly was believed to be more effective than one performed incorrectly, even if the incorrect actions were done with greater earnestness and fervor. Likewise, actions done with sacrilegious intent or even by accident could effectively tap religious power if they happened to be performed correctly. The tale of the sorcerer's apprentice (even in its trivialized Disney cartoon version) illustrates this conception of performative power. Everyday ritual and magic were intertwined, making the distinction between religious practices and magical practices impossible.[75]

Knowledge of effective ritual actions was thus a potential source of individual power. Priests, as well as midwives, herbalists, bone-setters, healers, diviners, fire(burn)-drawers, and sorcerers, were respected and feared for knowing effective ritual actions the average person in the community did not know. Priest-craft and witch-craft were distinguished not by differences in effectiveness but by presumed benevolent or malevolent intent.[76]

Especially outside the cities, Christian priests were not, in their religious practices, much different from ordinary people. Priests did, however, have a few important ritual roles: They were the only ones who could legitimately perform the Mass, the central and most powerful ritual act. They were the ritual specialists the community sought out to lead processions and pilgrimages and other devotions in honor of local saints. And their ritual efficacy was sought to bless places and objects that were used for channeling divine power to where people needed it. Priests were asked to bless weapons, farm tools, ornaments, fields, and farm animals.[77] In particular, clerical blessings of sacramentals—the many nonliturgical religious objects, such as holy water and candles, that people could use at home in ritual practices and devotions—multiplied ritual opportunities for laypersons to channel divine power.[78]

Delimiting Sacred Power: Magic

The reformation movements—both Protestant and Catholic—attacked the popular idea of sacred power. Reformers tried to distinguish "true" religion from "mere" magic, and by the end of the Long Reformation, most religious organizations severely sanctioned unapproved persons' exercise of sacred power. The sociopolitical effect was the consolidation and control of power. For instance, if a "wise woman" healer successfully healed a sick person, the churches' interpretation was that she did so with the aid of the devil and must be punished severely.[79] Catholic reformation movements did not totally eliminate lay access to magical power. The Catholic Church still allowed some devotions and use of sacramentals to which many members attached magical meanings. Church authorities decried magic, however, and tried to centralize the mediation of divine power in church-approved rituals performed by priests who were under stricter control of the hierarchy.

Various Protestant reformation movements tried to eliminate magic from religion altogether, in part by stripping the churches and worship services of the material and ritual stuff with which magical action is accomplished.[80] Although Protestant religion-as-preached attempted to create a firm dichotomy between religion and magic, historians have shown that popular Protestant religion-as-practiced has not made such tidy distinctions. Because of the importance of the words of scripture in Protestantism, much Protestant magic was based on the magical use of the Bible or scripturally based charms.[81] For example, in the nineteenth and twentieth centuries (as well as today), many Protestants continued to use Bibles for divination or scraps of paper with verses of scripture for charms.[82] Ron (see chapter 1), who made a point of saying ". . . in Jesus' name" with, every prayer for protection or petition, was engaged in a similar practice.[83]

Delimiting Sacred Power: Miracle

The Catholic reformation movements kept more of the earlier notion of "miracle," but tried to limit "true" miracles to church-approved mediators of divine power. In particular, they emphasized the miraculous qualities of the Eucharist, in which Christ became fully present in the consecrated Communion host. Only priests were allowed to perform the church-approved rituals through which this miracle occurred, and the Catholic reformation movements increasingly emphasized priests as the proper mediators of divine power in the administration of all church-approved sacraments. The other ordinary channel to divine power was through the saints—persons who had been so holy while alive that they were believed to be closer to the "ear" of God after death. Before the Long Reformation, local convention and popular practice established and recognized the vast majority of saints.[84]

Between the thirteenth and seventeenth centuries, church authorities gradually centralized control of the process of canonization by which saints were officially recognized. The faithful were important in the process of canonization, because evidence of the saint's performance of miracles was a necessary criterion. Without ordinary people's believing in and seeking miracles, saints could not be acclaimed before the Congregation of Rites. By the end of the Long Reformation, however, the process was so formalized that laypeople's testimony was neither sought nor welcomed; thus the church of Rome seldom authorized or recognized popular saints.[85] Nevertheless, popular Catholicism, a vital part of many people's religious practice even today, continued the older notion of miracle and the intervention of the divine through the saints.[86]

Protestant churches, in a long series of reformation movements, tried to limit the possibility of "miracle" to acts of God alone. Many tried to reduce laypeople's use of intermediaries to God's miraculous power. The concept of "disenchantment of the world" developed by classical social theorist Max Weber aptly describes the Protestant churches' attempt to circumscribe the realm of sacred powers.[87] But by focusing on Protestant reformers' theology and Protestant leaders' teachings, Weber and other scholars of religion failed to understand the nature of popular Protestantism. Historian Robert Scribner, concludes: "I do not think that the thesis about the 'disenchantment of the world' will any longer pass muster as a historically accurate description."[88]

The issue for sociological understanding of religion is not how Protestant or Catholic reformation movements changed the church teachings on magic and miracle. The point is that magic and miracle were once completely interwoven with religion; they were integrally part of how people understood religious power. Powerful figures, such as ecclesiastical authorities, leaders of religious movements, and social elites, asserted dramatically different meanings, trying to limit people's access to and uses of religious power. After a long period of cultural and social structural change, certain official meanings delimiting what should be considered "real" religion prevailed, even though many people's religious practice did not fit those official limits. Scholars' definitional boundaries that distinguish magic from religion are themselves social products of that contest and thus culturally and historically bound.

CONTESTED MEANINGS: PRIVILEGING BELIEF VERSUS PRIVILEGING PRACTICE

Sociologists rely very heavily on the assumption that people's religion and religiosity can be identified, measured, and understood by finding out what they believe, but such operational definitions are socially constructed and the results of considerable wrangling (especially during the Long Reformation).

Rather than focus on what people believe, by contrast, late medieval religion privileged practice, not only in the ideals for religious virtuosi but also in the expectations for ordinary laypersons. Being a "good" Christian was defined in terms of a few prescribed occasional practices such as properly observing certain holy days, to which people added a myriad of everyday religious practices such as pronouncing blessings on entering a house or crossing themselves when passing a cemetery. A religious person was one who engaged in religious practices, of which only a few were done in church or under clergy auspices. The practice of many quotidian rituals involved people's bodies and emotions in religious experience and expression.

Historian Peter Burke points out that the medieval pattern of calendrical rituals created balance between addressing the needs of the upper body and the lower body—cognitive and spiritual aspects balanced against supposedly baser bodily needs and appetites—such as for food, sex, procreation, health. By contrast, the reform movements of the early modern period recognized only the upper body as proper to religiosity. The rest was treated as sacrilegious and dangerous.[89]

Burke likened the contested boundaries to the images in Brueghel's sixteenth-century painting "The Fight between Carnival and Lent." The painting depicts a busy town square full of people engaged in practices associated with paraliturgical celebrations of these two seasons. In the foreground is a mock jousting match between figures representing Carnival and Lent. Carnival is depicted as a fat man astride a wine barrel, bearing a cooking skewer with remains of a roast pig and propelled by jesters, musicians, and costumed merrymakers. The opposing figure represents Lent, gaunt and pale, with flatbread and fish, and armed with a baker's paddle. His entourage consists of a monk and a dour old lady, with some children eating flatbread. The painting contrasts Lenten somber dress, sobriety, penance, abstinence, and almsgiving with Carnival

games, contests, dancing, feasting, sexuality, and mockery. Burke argues that before the sixteenth century, these opposing figures were balanced, emotionally and ritually. The Long Reformation was something of a metaphorical battle between Carnival and Lent, and Lent won.[90]

Most reform movements—Protestant and Catholic alike—emphasized bodily control and propriety, especially regarding sexuality. This development had strong religious connotations, but it was also part of the larger "civilizing process" that was linked to the differentiation of social class elites.[91] Thus, the churches became places where the newly marked boundaries between sacred and profane were ritually observed with newly distinguished, class-based norms of propriety and gentility. Religious people were those who showed respect for the sacred in church by controlling their bodies and deporting themselves with proper postures, gestures, and other tightly controlled behaviors. Ordinary people's religious practices, regardless of official religious affiliation, were—by definition—not genteel enough. For example, both Protestant and Catholic clergy in rural Ireland struggled well into the nineteenth century to suppress the popular religious practices surrounding wakes, weddings, and "patterns" (patron saint festivals)—not because of theological concerns but because these practices were viewed as licentious, rowdy, and improper.[92]

At the same time, reform movements tried to eliminate or tightly control the richly sensual aspects of religious practice, opposing the popular emphasis' on spectacle and visual imagery. Muir argues that the Long Reformation represented, in essence, a revolution in ritual theory: The old ritual had privileged practice, while the new ritual privileged cognition—such as hearing preaching, assenting to creeds, reading and thinking about passages of the Bible. Protestant reformers generally went further than Catholic reformers by starkly' eradicating sensual elements, for example, drastically reducing the visual impact of church interiors, presumably to focus attention on the words being pronounced there.[93] The Catholic reformation movements also distrusted much of the sensual appeal of visual displays, mystery plays, religious dances, and paraliturgical processions. Their success in holding on to members in the face of vigorous early Protestant appeals, however, may be partly due to carefully controlled use of sensual elements, such as the lavish baroque decoration of Jesuit churches.[94] Much later—as late as the mid-twentieth century in some places—Catholic authorities, too, discouraged sensual religiosity.

In early modern times, nascent elites contested meanings that the religion of the common people promoted. After Lent won the ritual battle, religion came to be identified with the "higher" or more "spiritual" aspects of human existence. Human material concerns and pleasures, human bodies and extreme emotions came to be defined as not proper to religion or religiosity. There may have been only a relatively brief period (perhaps 100 to 150 years) in Europe and North America when religious organizations and elites were sufficiently influential to shape wider societal ideas about "proper" religious comportment and modes of religious expression. In most of northern Europe and North America, church-promoted norms of bodily and emotional constraint, together with emphasis on church-authorized religious belief and knowledge, appear to have influenced individual religion more widely between the 1850s and the 1950s than any time before or since. If that assessment is correct, it means that our sociological forefathers' vantage point for theorizing religion occurred in the middle of a brief historical blip during which religious institutions had unusual cultural influence. In light of these major historical shifts, we need to rethink the usefulness of sociological concepts that privilege religious belief, attitudes, opinions, and knowledge, while ignoring or marginalizing religious practice—especially its bodily and emotional components.

CONTESTED MEANINGS: PURITY AND AUTHENTICITY OF RELIGIOUS TRADITIONS AND IDENTITIES

The period of transition between the late medieval and early modern periods was also a time when boundaries between "us" and "them" were created or fortified. Anthropologist Mary Douglas suggests that societies with particular fear of pollution are those obsessed with a sense of danger from people crossing symbolic boundaries.[95] Late medieval society already had many such pollution fears, as exemplified by many myths of Jewish or Moorish desecration of Christian symbols, but the centuries of reformation movements multiplied the contested boundaries between peoples and increased the sense of fear of pollution. Inquisitions and witch hunts were among the more violent outcomes, justifying their violence as necessary to purify the community of dangerous elements. In Spain, for example, Jews who had converted to Christianity (often out of fear of persecution) were particularly suspect; thus the early stages of the Spanish Inquisition were devoted to delineating a boundary between true and fake converts.[96]

Although there had been efforts to denounce heretical teachings since the early centuries of Christianity, earlier disputes over boundaries had been generally confined to teachers and theologians. Along with the shift to emphasizing belief over practice, church authorities during this early modern period of transition turned the focus of heresy examinations to ordinary church members.[97] It was no longer sufficient that Christians simply engage in certain core religious practices; if they also held unorthodox beliefs, they must not communicate them to others.

Historian Carlo Ginzburg analyzed records of sixteenth- and seventeenth-century Inquisition trials of people involved in syncretic agrarian cults in remote parts of what is now northern Italy.[98] The Inquisition was not much concerned with these peasants' theological errors; rather, it was interested mainly in determining whether their practices constituted instances of witchcraft. Ginzburg's study shows clearly that the definitional boundaries of the idea of witchcraft were constructed and expanded specifically in this period of transition. The idea of witchcraft was a project of an intellectual elite of inquisitors. They justified their power to prosecute witchcraft trials by claiming knowledge that uniquely qualified them to identify who fit the very category—witchcraft—they were defining and decrying as a serious problem. The social construction of strong boundaries around true religion (or true religious power) was itself an exercise in power, exercised not only in the courts but also physically on the bodies of those branded as witches or heretics.

Purity concerns mixed with issues of authenticity. In practice, no religion is uninfluenced by its cultural and historical setting. All religions absorb cultural elements (including religious elements) from their surroundings as they develop over time.[99]

European Christian beliefs and practices historically were no less syncretic than those of colonized indigenous peoples of Mexico, but the Inquisition doubted the authenticity of many Mexicans' beliefs and practices.[100] Many Protestant movements were even more radical in their attempt to divest their religion of all impurities. Interestingly, most of Europe's witchcraft trials occurred in cultural borderlands or culturally diverse regions, such as the Franco-Spanish Basque area or the lower Rhine.[101] Defending symbolic borders of "authentic" religion was, at the same time, a way of defending permeable cultural borders.

THE PLACE OF POWER IN BOUNDARY CONTESTS

Anthropologist Eric Wolff asserts that structural power—the power to determine the terms of discourse—is a particularly effective and invisible

form of power.[102] In all of the aforementioned cultural and political contests of meaning, the winners were those who could set the terms of discourse for the others: the courtly mannered elites defining propriety; leaders of religious sects setting the terms for who would be accepted into their membership as religiously qualified; the inquisitors and religious judges defining orthodoxy (correct belief) and orthopraxy (correct practice); the bishops and higher clergy centralizing their control over practices in the hinterlands; regional religiopolitical powers centralizing their control over previously autonomous towns and city-states, and so on.

Those who eventually lost the definitional battles put up considerable resistance and struggle, but the net outcome was that many of their most valued religious practices no longer counted as religion. Powerful social and cultural groups changed the terms of discourse about religion. They had drawn new definitional boundaries.

CONCLUSION

If we fail to recognize the contested nature of definitional boundaries, we risk adopting an overly institutional—and historically inaccurate—view of religion. That is, we risk entertaining the mistaken notion that religion is a thing, an entity that exists in the real world with its distinguishing features objectively "given" and not subject to historical or cultural change. Sociology needs to historicize not only its debates about secularization[103] but also its use of core concepts defining religion and religiosity.

How can we understand the changing place of religion in society if our very definitional boundaries have resulted from some of the changes we hope to analyze? Such historically and culturally bound conceptual limits prevent us from adequately understanding *non*-European religious expressions—especially popular religion and other indigenous religious expression not made in the image of modern Euro-American religion. What does awareness of historical contests tell us about contemporary contests over the relevant boundaries of religion"? Are there important differences today, compared with early modern times, in the locus of structural power—especially the power to define the terms of discourse about religion? These are all questions scholars might fruitfully examine.

NOTES

1. This problem of basic conceptual assumptions not "fitting" the data is true in the natural sciences, too, as Thomas Kuhn noted in his analysis of how resistant scientists are to paradigm shifts. See Kuhn (1970).
2. For several essays on this reflexiveness in the ethnography of religion, see Spickard et al. (2002).
3. My usage of the term "Protestant" here refers not to specific Protestant beliefs and practices but to an image of "religion" as stripped of "magical" or "superstitious" elements. This concept was promoted especially by many Protestant groups during the Long Reformation, a historical development described further in this chapter.
4. According to James Spickard (2006), scholars' interpretations of the place of religion in modern societies are best understood as stories or narratives, rather than theories, because interpretations that follow a particular story use a common story line. The six main stories that sociological interpretations tell include: secularization, religious reorganization, individualization, supply-side of religious markets, resurgent conservative religion, and globalization.
5. On a social constructionist approach to the sociology of religion, see especially Beckford (2003). For an excellent critical essay about the scholarly quest to distinguish "real" religion from other religion, see Orsi (2005: 177–204).
6. See Muir (1997: 6).
7. Especially useful sources on the Protestant and Catholic Reformation movements include: Forster (1992); Ginzburg (1983); Luria (1989); Martin (1993); Muir (1997); Scribner (1984a; 1984b; 1990).
8. Elias (1978; 1982); Mellor and Shilling (1994).
9. Forster (1992).
10. On the political uses of constructed cultural distintions, see Anderson; (1991); Bauman (1992); Bourdieu (1984); Elias (1978).
11. Stark and Finke (2000: 63–72).
12. Applying such overly institutional criteria, derived from certain patterns of religious practice and characteristic of only a limited region of Europe, also results in some ethnocentric assumptions about religion and religious practices. Indeed, some of those indicators have never been appropriate for the equally old Christian traditions of eastern Europe (e.g., Romanian or Russian Orthodox) or Jewish traditions in both western and eastern Europe.
13. Asad (1993). Similarly, Peter Beyer's (1998) work shows that scholars have uncritically accepted the concept of "religions" (as in "world religions"), even though it was socially constructed as a political project. In an encyclopedic coverage of nonelite religious practice in both Western and non-Western religions, Steven Sharot (2001) shows clearly that Western definitions of religion simply do not fit Asian religions-as-practiced.
14. Asad (1988; 1993).
15. See Beckford (2003: 71).
16. I use this example because we have a highly readable historical account of peasants' everyday life, beliefs, and practices in such a village in the early 1300s. LeRoy Ladurie (1978).
17. Obelkevich (1979: 5).
18. Following the conventions used by the historians cited in this chapter, the late medieval period here refers roughly to 1300–1500 CE, with considerable regional variability in the timing and degree of various reformation movements' impact. The early modern period began in the 1500s in several parts of Europe but evolved sporadically and unevenly, lasting well into the 1800s (and even later, in some isolated cultural pockets).
19. These brief sketches cannot convey the complexity and nuances of the considerable historical literature on religion during this transitional period, but they suffice to raise important questions about sociology's definitional boundaries.
20. See Christian (1981); Forster (1992).
21. Stark and Finke (2000).
22. Carroll (1996).
23. Christian (1981: 178–80).
24. The Ave Maria was a short Latin prayer (often called "Hail Mary" in English) based on the gospel words of the angel to Mary at the annunciation. Saying this

prayer was recommended for all, especially twice a day (early morning and early evening) when they heard the Angelus bell tolling. It was later incorporated into the Rosary, a series of prayers with many Ave Marias and Pater Nosters; to keep track of where they were in the order of these prayers, most people used a string of different sized beads, which itself came to be called the "rosary." The Pater Noster was a longer, difficult Latin prayer (called the "Lord's Prayer" or the "Our Father" in English). Teaching the Pater Noster was a major catechetical effort for priests and parents, because teaching a long and difficult Latin prayer to someone partially literate (at best) required commitment (such that one English curate enjoyed telling a story of how he had tricked a plowman into learning his Pater Noster). Knowing and using the Pater Noster prayer regularly was also an expected part of the common Christian core religious practices (Duffy 1992).

25. Quoted in Ginzburg (1983: 120).
26. Luria (1991: 106–36).
27. Lionel Rothkrug (1979) documents the correlation between the late medieval Bavarian devotions toward Mary as "Queen of Heaven" and the promulgation, mainly by Franciscan friars, of an imperial image of God, Christendom, and Mary. By contrast, in the culturally similar region of Swabia, a different preaching order, the Dominicans, promoted devotions toward Mary that expressed a piety contrary to the imperial one of Bavaria. By devotions at shrines to Mary's image as the Suffering One and the Sorrowing Mother of the crucified Christ (as in a Pietà), people in the region of Swabia and the Rhineland emphasized Mary's (and, by extension, God's) identification with humanity and human (particularly mothers') tribulations.
28. Wilson (2000: 25–50).
29. Scribner (1984a),
30. Christian (1981: 176).
31. Hayes (2003: Ch.1); Mullett (1987: 46–47).
32. See, for example, Muir (1997: 21).
33. Burke (1978: 109).
34. Hayes (2003).
35. Mullett (1987: 46).
36. Mullett (1987: 46–47); see also Duffy (1992: 95–101, 117).
37. Duffy (1992: 47), emphasis added.
38. Muir (1997: 55–179); Wilson (2000).
39. Scribner (1984b).
40. Scribner (1984b: 51).

41. Muir (1997: 71).
42. St. Bridget, one of the most important popular saints of Ireland, was not canonized as a saint by the Roman church, but her feast day, February 1, has been celebrated as part of the Catholic liturgical calendar, even in modern times. Bridget is depicted with a flame over her head, and her feast day is part of the ritual calendar's celebration of the season of Candlemas (Scribner 1984a). Her connection with candle flame and "light" may be due to her resemblance to female "keepers of the flame," who were key figures in early spring religious rituals in pre-Christian Celtic religion ("Celtic Religion," 1996).
43. Muir (1997: 61–63).
44. Scribner (1984a: 19–22).
45. Muir (1997: 79).
46. See Bourdieu (1977: 114–24).
47. Scribner (1994).
48. Quoted in Scribner (1984b: 73).
49. Scribner (1984a: 25). See also Ashley and Sheingorn (1992).
50. In the early chapters of *The Sociology of Religion*, Weber (1963) clearly includes these premodern European religious conceptions of the location of the sacred as pertaining to "religion." His extensive use of historical and crosscultural examples to tease out conceptually the differentiation of institutionally specialized religious roles and organization is both exemplary and problematic.

     Weber's use of dichotomous conceptions may represent the imposition of modern, Western scholarly patterns of thought on religious worldviews with a different "logic," according to Cristián Parker (1994; 1996). Durkheim used the sacred/profane dichotomy as *definitive* of the religious sphere. His assumption that these are mutually exclusive categories may have blinded him to any "elementary forms" (his term) of religion that addressed the sacred within the profane. For instance, Durkheim does not consider women's religious roles, which European observers may have seen as "merely" profane actions (if, indeed, they were even noticeable to outsider males, on whose chronicles Durkheim relied for his anthropological empirical base).
51. Historically, it was primarily Christian theologians, religious leaders, and agents of social control who attempted to make the definitive boundaries between religion and magic utterly dichotomous and exclusive. Scholars of religion have often accepted the distinction, perhaps trying to translate it into terms that

might be more valid crossculturally. For example, historian Keith Thomas (1971) treated religion and magic as opposites in his detailed account of the impact of the Long Reformation in England. He depicted Christians before the reformation movements as heavily preoccupied with magic, including magical approaches to church rituals and celebrations. Accordingly, he saw religion prevailing and magic declining in the subsequent developments in England, Increasingly, however, anthropologists of religion and theorists of ritual have argued that it is more useful to see religious/magical orientations and modes of action as being so closely related that attempting tidy distinctions between them only serves to distract us from understanding the importance of what they have in common; see especially Bell (1997: 46–52). Tambiah (1990: 105–10) suggests some other ways of thinking about these orientations to the world; I find especially fruitful for understanding the complexities of individuals' lived religion his analytical distinction between "participation" and "causality" as orientations.

52. Scribner (1993); Wilson (2000); Kaelber (1998).
53. Scribner (1984a).
54. Bourdieu's (1977) concept of "habitus" suggests how senses are *social* and how practices (e.g., ritual) shape the body and emotions in prereflective meanings.
55. See McGuire (1996).
56. Muir (1997: 7). See also Asad (1993).
57. Muir (1997).
58. Muir (1997: 8, 186–212).
59. Muir (1997).
60. Scribner (1984b: 62–68).
61. Vauchez (1993: 88).
62. Scribner (1984a: 18).
63. Christian (1981); Muir (1997: 157); Mullett (1987: 48–49).
64. There was no necessary connection between the saints officially recognized by the church and those to whom local popular devotion was directed. Many popular saints had not lived historically, but that fact was not what mattered in people's veneration. What mattered was whether prayers addressed through that saint worked. If devotions to a saint were effective in meeting people's needs, regardless of whether the story of that saint's life was factual, then they were considered worth performing. Guinefort, a highly popular saint in what is now France, was a greyhound. According to her legend, she saved the life of her master's baby by killing a snake, but was subsequently killed because he had thought she had tried

to harm the child. When he discovered his mistake, he was so full of remorse that he honored his dog with a proper burial and grave marker. Popular sainthood came later, when people discovered that prayers to the faithful greyhound were effective in curing sick babies. Eventually, a substantial cult grew, involving ritual practices to tap the spiritual powers mediated through this saint (Schmitt 1983).
65. Luria (1989: 93–94).
66. During the Long Reformation, Catholic reformers attempted to eliminate devotions to local saints and substitute centralized devotions to church-wide saints, such as various cults of Mary. In place of local popular saints, church authorities promoted new saints and brought the definition of saints firmly under ecclesiastical control in the process of canonization. However, "many new saints had little popular appeal; their cults did not spread widely, and therefore, they had little impact on popular spirituality" (Luria 1991: 110). Mostly the new saints were those who inspired the elites (e.g., Francis de Sales, John of the Cross, Charles Borromeo). The new saints who became popular among nonelite people were those whose "miracles responded directly to the material needs of everyday peasant life" (111).

Many scholars of religion fail to realize that this historical shift away from the people's connection with popular spirituality was a project only of western European reformers, not of all Christian groups of that era. Thus, they cannot understand Eastern Christian (e.g., Eastern Orthodox) practices such as the popular selection of some persons who are eventually recognized as saints, popular practices in pilgrimage, and the importance of embodied practices (e.g., kissing ikons), which have continued, as central, to this day in many parts of the world where the Long Reformation did not occur to rule them out (Kokosalakis 1987; 1995); (Dubisch 1990).
67. Muir (1997: 16).
68. This perspective is still salient in many religions today, including among Christians. Many scholars, however, want to distance themselves from any notion of religion that encompasses such an image of sacred power; perhaps this attitude explains part of the vehemence of some scholars' objections to sociologist Michael Carroll's (1992) book *Madonnas That Maim*. Robert Orsi forthrightly addresses this scholarly ambivalence toward the very idea of a sacred power that can harm as well as help in *Between Heaven and Earth* (2005).

69. Ashley and Sheingorn (1992).
70. Luria (1989: 104).
71. Scribner (1984a: 25).
72. Liturgical prayers were those embedded in the Mass, for example in conjunction with celebration of a saint's day; extraliturgical prayers included popular devotional prayers that were typically transmitted by laypersons, whether or not they were also encouraged by local clergy.
73. Quoted in Duffy (1992: 16).
74. Note that similar valuable role-specific knowledge later got women into serious trouble with both Protestant and Catholic authorities because it made them suspect of witchcraft (Ehrenreich and English 1973).
75. See Wilson (2000: 421–68).
76. Muir (1997: 216–18).
77. Morris (1989: 502).
78. Scribner (1993).
79. The most notorious instance of this is the *Malleus Maleficarum*, a sixteenth-century manual for identifying witches and other humans whose "powers" were believed to come from evil rather than divine sources. Protestant persecutions of witches and others with unapproved powers were based on similar notions of divine power. Noting that learned men who engaged in occult sciences and licit magic were far less endangered by witch hunts than were women or indigenous peoples in the New World, Williams (1995) argues that accusations of witchcraft were, at root, about the exercise of power over a threatening Other. By defining witchcraft, powerful men were "defining dominion." See also Midelfort (1982); Monter (1983).
80. Duffy (1992).
81. Scribner (1993).
82. See Hall (1989); McDannell (1995).
83. This kind of ritual use of "words of power" blurs any distinction between religion and magic (Wilson 2000: 429–32). See also McGuire (1983a).
84. Because Eastern Orthodox churches (in what are now Greece and Russia, for instance) did not experience these historical transformations, they have retained many elements (such as the importance of ordinary laypeople's recognition of a holy personage as a saint) that pertained in Western Christianity before the Long Reformation (Kokosalakis 1987).
85. Luria (1991: 114–17).
86. Orsi (1997).
87. Weber (1958: 105).
88. Scribner (1993: 493).
89. Burke (1978).
90. Burke (1978).
91. Elias (1978).
92. Connolly (1982); Taylor (1995).
93. Muir (1997).
94. Stevens-Arroyo (1998).
95. Douglas (1966).
96. Longhurst (1962).
97. For example, they suspected such seemingly innocuous people as artisan apprentices, literate millers, and anomalous women (Ginzburg 1980; 1983; Martin 1987; Midelfort 1982; Tedeschi 1991).
98. Ginzburg (1983).
99. Shaw and Stewart (1994).
100. Interestingly, for example, some of the earliest ethnographies of New World indigenous peoples were produced to provide the guardians of the official religion (i.e., the Inquisition in Mexico) with a way to distinguish the people's Catholic faith from vestiges of indigenous religiosity (Martin 1994).
101. Monter (1983).
102. Wolff (1990).
103. As suggested in Carroll (1995); Gorski (2000).

3

Selections from The Sacred Canopy: Elements of a Sociological Theory of Religion

Peter L. Berger

THE TERM "SECULARIZATION" has had a somewhat adventurous history. It was originally employed in the wake of the Wars of Religion to denote the removal of territory or property from the control of ecclesiastical authorities. In Roman canon law the same term has come to denote the return to the "world" of a person in orders. In both these usages, whatever the disputes in particular instances, the term could be used in a purely descriptive and non-evaluative way. This, of course, has not been the case in the usage of more recent times. The term "secularization," and even more its derivative "secularism," has been employed as an ideological concept highly charged with evaluative connotations, sometimes positive and sometimes negative. In anti-clerical and "progressive" circles it has come to stand for the liberation of modern man from religious tutelage, while in circles connected with the traditional churches it has been attacked as "de-Christianization," "paganization," and the like. Both these ideologically charged perspectives, within which the same empirical phenomena appear with opposite value indices, can be rather entertainingly observed in the work of sociologists of religion inspired, respectively, by Marxist and Christian viewpoints. The situation has not been clarified by the fact that since World. War II a number of theologians, mainly Protestants taking up certain strands in the later thought of

Dietrich Bonhoeffer, have reversed the previous Christian evaluation of "secularization" and hailed it as a realization of crucial motifs of Christianity itself. Not surprisingly, the position has been advanced that, in view of this ideological furor, the term should be abandoned as confusing if not downright meaningless.

We would not agree with this position, despite the justification of the ideological analysis on which it is based. The term "secularization" refers to empirically available processes of great importance in modern Western history. Whether these processes are to be deplored or welcomed is, of course, irrelevant within the universe of discourse of the historian or the sociologist. It is possible, actually without too great an effort, to describe the empirical phenomenon without taking up an evaluative stance. It is also possible to inquire into its historical origins, *including* its historical connection with Christianity, without asserting that this represents either a fulfillment or a degeneration of the latter. This point should be particularly stressed in view of the current discussion among theologians. It is one thing to maintain that there is a relationship of historical causality between Christianity and certain features of the modern world. It is an altogether different matter to say that, "therefore," the modern world, including its secular character, must be seen as some sort of logical realization of Christianity. A salutary thing to remember in this connection is that most historical relationships are ironical in character, or, to put it differently, that the course of history has little to do with the intrinsic logic of ideas that served as causal factors in it.

It is not difficult to put forth a simple definition of secularization for the purpose at hand. By secularization we mean the process by which sectors of society and culture are removed from the domination of religious institutions and symbols. When we speak of society and institutions in modern Western history, of course, secularization manifests itself in the evacuation by the Christian churches of areas previously under their control or influence—as in the separation of church and state, or in the expropriation of church lands, or in the emancipation of education from ecclesiastical authority. When we speak of culture and symbols, however, we imply that secularization is more than a social-structural process. It affects the totality of cultural life and of ideation, and may be observed in the decline of religious contents in the arts, in philosophy, in literature and, most important of all, in the rise of science as an autonomous, thoroughly secular perspective on the world. Moreover, it is implied here that the process of secularization has a subjective side as well. As there is a secularization of society and culture, so is there a secularization of consciousness. Put simply, this means that the modern West has produced an increasing number of individuals who look upon the world and their own lives without the benefit of religious interpretations.

While secularization may be viewed as a global phenomenon of modern societies, it is not uniformly distributed within them. Different groups of the population have been affected by it differently. Thus it has been found that the impact of secularization has tended to be stronger on men than on women, on people in the middle age range than on the very young and the old, in the cities than in the country, on classes directly connected with modern industrial production (particularly the working class) than on those of more traditional occupations (such as artisans or small shopkeepers), on Protestants and

Jews than on Catholics, and the like. At least as far as Europe is concerned, it is possible to say with some confidence, on the basis of these data, that church-related religiosity is strongest (and thus, at any rate, social-structural secularization least) on the margins of modern industrial society, both in terms of marginal classes (such as the remnants of old petty bourgeoisies) and marginal individuals (such as those eliminated from the work process). The situation is different in America, where the churches still occupy a more central symbolic position, but it may be argued that they have succeeded in keeping this position only by becoming highly secularized themselves, so that the European and American cases represent two variations on the same underlying theme of global secularization. What is more, it appears that the same secularizing forces have now become worldwide in the course of westernization and modernization. Most of the available data, to be sure, pertain to the social-structural manifestations of secularization rather than to the secularization of consciousness, but we have enough data to indicate the massive presence of the latter in the contemporary West. We cannot here pursue the interesting question of the extent to which there may be, so to speak, asymmetry between these two dimensions of secularization, so that there may not only be secularization of consciousness within the traditional religious institutions but also a continuation of more or less traditional motifs of religious consciousness outside their previous institutional contexts.

If, for heuristic purposes, we were to take an epidemiological viewpoint with regard to secularization, it would be natural to ask what are its "carriers". In other words, what socio-cultural processes and groups serve as vehicles or mediators of secularization? Viewed from outside Western civilization (say, by a concerned Hindu traditionalist), the answer is obviously that it is that civilization as a whole in its spread around the world (and it need hardly be emphasized that, from that viewpoint, Communism and modern nationalism are just as much manifestations of Westernization as their "imperialist" predecessors). Viewed from inside Western civilization (say, by a worried Spanish country priest), the original "carrier" of secularization is the modern economic process, that is, the dynamic of industrial capitalism. To be sure, it may be "secondary" effects of this dynamic that constitute the immediate problem (for example, the secularizing contents of modern mass media or the influences of a heterogeneous mass of tourists brought in by modern means of transportation). But it does not take long to trace these "secondary" effects back to their original source in the expanding capitalist-industrial economy. In those parts of the Western world where industrialism has taken socialist forms of organization, closeness to the processes of industrial production and its concomitant styles of life continues to be the principal determinant of secularization. Today, it would seem, it is industrial society in itself that is secularizing, with its divergent ideological legitimations serving merely as modifications of the global secularization process. Thus the anti-religious propaganda and repressive measures of Marxist regimes naturally affect the secularization process (though, perhaps, not always in quite the way intended by their initiators), as do the pro-religious policies of various governments outside the Marxist sphere. It seems likely, however, that both these political-ideological attitudes must reckon with basic societal forces that antedate the particular policies in question and over which governments have only limited control. This state of affairs becomes amusingly evident when we see very similar sociological data for socialist and non-socialist countries (say, with regard to the secularity of the working class and the religiosity of the peasants) used by Marxist observers as an occasion to bemoan the limited effectiveness of "scientific atheist" agitation and by Christian observers to lament the failures of evangelism, to the point where one is tempted to suggest that the two groups might get together and comfort each other.

We would regard it as axiomatic that a historical phenomenon of such scope will not be amenable to any monocausal explanations. Thus we have no interest in denigrating any of the various factors that have been suggested as causes of secularization (such as, for example, the pervasive influence of modern science). Nor are we interested, in the present context, in the establishment of a hierarchy of causes. We are interested, however, in the question of the extent to which the Western religious tradition may have carried the seeds of secularization within itself. If this can be maintained, as we think it can, it should be clear from our systematic considerations that the religious factor must *not* be considered as operating in isolation from other factors, but rather as standing in an ongoing dialectical relationship with the "practical" infrastructure of social life. In other words, nothing could be farther from our minds than to propose an "idealist" explanation of secularization. It should also be clear that any demonstration of the secularizing consequences of the Western religious tradition tells us nothing about the intentions of those who shaped and carried on this tradition.

The suspicion that there may be an inherent connection between Christianity and the character of the modern Western world is by no means new. At least since Hegel the connection has been repeatedly asserted by historians, philosophers, theologians, though, of course, their evaluation of this has varied greatly. Thus the modern world could be interpreted as a higher realization of the Christian spirit (as Hegel interpreted it), or Christianity could be regarded as the principal pathogenic factor responsible for the supposedly sorry state of the modern world (as, for instance, by Schopenhauer and Nietzsche). The notion that a peculiar role in the establishment of the modern world was played by Protestantism has, of course, been a matter of widespread discussion among sociologists and historians for the last fifty years or so.

[. . .]

In terms of the general socio-religious processes discussed in the first part of this book, secularization has posited an altogether novel situation for modern man. Probably for the first time in history, the religious legitimations of the world have lost their plausibility not only for a few intellectuals and other marginal individuals but for broad masses of entire societies. This opened up an acute crisis not only for the nomization of the large social institutions but for that of individual biographies. In other words, there has arisen a problem of "meaningfulness" not only for such institutions as the state or of the economy but for the ordinary routines of everyday life. The problem has, of course, been intensely conscious to various theoreticians (philosophers, theologians, psychologists, and so forth), but there is good reason to think that it is also prominent in the minds of ordinary people not normally given to theoretical speculations and interested simply in solving the crises of their own lives. Most importantly, the peculiar Christian theodicy of suffering lost its plausibility and thereby the way was opened for a variety of secularized soteriologies, most of which, however, proved quite incapable of legitimating the sorrows of individual life even when they achieved some plausibility in the legitimation of history. And finally the collapse of the alienated structures of the Christian worldview released movements of critical thought that radically de-alienated and "humanized" social reality (the sociological perspective being one of these movements), an achievement that often enough was bought at the price of severe anomy and existential anxiety. What all of this means for contemporary society is the principal question for an empirical sociology of knowledge. Within our present considerations we cannot deal with all this except tangentially. The question, though, that we will turn to next is what the process of secularization has meant for the traditional religious contents and for the institutions that embody, them.

[. . .]

One of the most obvious ways in which secularization has affected the man in the street is as a "crisis of credibility" in religion. Put differently, secularization has resulted in a widespread collapse of the plausibility of traditional religious definitions of reality. This manifestation of secularization on the level of consciousness ("subjective secularization," if one wishes) has its correlate on the social-structural level (as "objective secularization"). Subjectively, the man in the street tends to be uncertain about religious matters. Objectively, the man in the street is confronted with a wide variey of religious and other reality-defining agencies that compete for his allegiance or at least attention, and none of which is in a position to coerce him into allegiance. In other words, the phenomenon called "pluralism" is a social-structural correlate of the secularization of consciousness. This relationship invites sociological analysis.

Such analysis affords a very nice opportunity to show *in concreto* the dialectical relationship between religion and its infrastructure that has previously been developed theoretically. It is possible to analyze secularization in such a way that it appears as a "reflection" of concrete infrastructural processes in modern society. This is all the more convincing because secularization appears to be a "negative" phenomenon, that is, it seems to be without causal efficacy of its own and continually dependent upon processes other than itself. Such an analysis, however, remains convincing only if the contemporary situation is viewed in isolation from its historical background. Religion under the impact of secularization can, indeed, be analyzed convincingly as a "dependent variable" *today*. As soon, though, as one asks about the historical origins of secularization the problem poses itself in quite different terms. As we have tried to indicate, one is then led to consider specific elements of the religious tradition of Western culture precisely as historical forces, that is, as "independent variables."

The dialectical relationship between religion and society thus precludes the doctrinaire approaches of either "idealism" or "materialism." It is possible to show in concrete instances how religious "ideas," even very abstruse ones, led to empirically available changes in the social structure.

In other instances, it is possible to show how empirically available structural changes had effects on the level of religious consciousness and ideation. Only a dialectical understanding of these relationships avoids the distortions of the one-sidedly "idealist" and "materialist" interpretations. Such a dialectical understanding will insist upon the rootage of all consciousness, religious or other, in the world of everyday *praxis*, but it will be very careful not to conceive of this rootage in terms of mechanistic causality.

A quite different matter is the potency of religion to "act back" upon its infrastructure in specific historical situations. On this it is possible to say that such potency varies greatly in different situations. Thus religion might appear as a formative force in one situation and as a dependent formation in the situation following historically. One may describe such change as a "reversal" in the "direction" of causal efficacy as between religion and its respective infrastructures. The phenomenon under consideration here is a case in point. Religious developments originating in the Biblical tradition may be seen as causal factors in the formation of the modern secularized world. Once formed, however, this world precisely precludes the continuing efficacy of religion as a formative force. We would contend that here lies the great historical irony in the relation between religion and secularization, an irony that can be graphically put by saying that, historically speaking, Christianity has been its own gravedigger. In looking at the collapse of plausibility suffered by religion in the contemporary situation, *hic et nunc*, it is logical to begin with social structure and to go on to consciousness and ideation, rather than the reverse. Quite apart from its theoretical justification, this procedure will avoid the pitfall (to which religiously inclined observers are particularly prone) of

ascribing secularization to some mysterious spiritual and intellectual fall from grace. Rather it will show the rootage of this fall from grace (the term is descriptively useful) in empirically available social-structural processes.

The original "locale" of secularization, as we have indicated, was in the economic area, specifically, in those sectors of the economy being formed by the capitalistic and industrial processes. Consequently, different strata of modern society has been affected by secularization differentially in terms of their closeness to or distance from these processes. Highly secularized strata emerged in the immediate proximity of these same processes. In other words, modern industrial society has produced a centrally "located" sector that is something like a "liberated territory" with respect to religion. Secularization has moved "outwards" from this sector into other areas of society. One interesting consequence of this has been a tendency for religion to be "polarized" between the most public and the most private sectors of the institutional order, specifically between the institutions of the state and the family. Even at a point of far-reaching secularization of everyday life as lived at work and in the relationships that surround work one may still find religious symbols attached to the institutions of state and family. For instance, at a point where everyone takes for granted that "religion stops at the factory gate," it may nevertheless be also taken for granted that one does not inaugurate either a war or a marriage without the traditional religious symbolizations.

A way of putting this in terms of common sociological parlance is to say that there has been a "cultural lag" between the secularization of the economy on the one hand and that of the state and the family on the other.

[. . .]

4

Selections from "Work in Progress Toward a New Paradigm for the Sociological Study of Religion in the United States"[1]

R. Stephen Warner

INTRODUCTION

The sociology of American religion is undergoing a period of ferment, interpreted herein as a paradigm shift in process. This article is at once a partial review of a vast, rapidly growing literature and an attempt at theoretical integration that draws tendentiously on certain strains within that literature. Thus the article is part of the very process it heralds.

The older paradigm—identified here with the early work of Peter Berger (1969, 1970)—is still cited by a great many researchers in the field and remains useful for understanding aspects of the phenomenology of religious life. However, those who use the older paradigm to interpret American religious organization—congregations, denominations, special purpose groups, and more—face increasing interpretive difficulties and decreasing rhetorical confidence. The newer paradigm—consciously under development by only a handful of independent investigators—stands a better chance of providing intellectual coherence to the field.

The newer paradigm stems not from the old one (Tschannen 1991), which was developed to account for the European experience, but from an entirely independent vision inspired by American history. [. . .]

The focus throughout is sociological, on religion as an institutional sector (Friedland and Alford 1991) rather than a primarily cultural or psychological phenomenon, and comparative in conception, focusing on the distinctive parameters of religion in American society, rather than on the evolution of "religion" as a generic phenomenon. Unless otherwise indicated, "America" refers to the United States and, for stylistic convenience, "American" to things pertaining to the society, government, or people of the United States. [. . .]

VI. THE "NEW" VOLUNTARISM

The preceding four sections have developed four distinctive and perennial aspects of American religion which, under different rubrics, have received the attention of contemporary researchers and which, considered theoretically, pose an alternative to the older paradigm. With appropriate complications and qualifications, religion in the United States is and has long been (*a*) disestablished, (*b*) culturally pluralistic, (*c*) structurally adaptable, and (*d*) empowering. My final topic is the recent (i.e., post-1960s) complex of individualized religious identification—including conversion to new religious identities and the assertive embrace of old ones, as well as apostasy on a wide scale—that I will follow Roof and McKinney (1987) in referring to as "the new voluntarism."[2] The contemporary scene seems sufficiently discontinuous with the patterns described more than a generation ago by Herberg (1960) to raise the question whether the American institutional complex portrayed in this article persists or whether, as the older paradigm would have it, we are witnessing the latest stage of "secularization."

Consider these figures: between one-third and one-half of those responding to polls have changed denominations in their lives, some of them only to switch back to the affiliation of their youth, more to an adjoining denomination, but many to religious disaffiliation (Hadaway and Marler 1991a; Roof and McKinney 1987, p. 165). One-fifth of those raised Catholic no longer identify with that faith, and they include an estimated one million Hispanics who have gone over to Protestantism within the past 15 years (Greeley 1990, p. 120). The proportion of Americans claiming no religious preference (the people sociologists of religion call "nones") has jumped from 2%–3% a generation ago to 7%–9% today. Moreover, with the exception of African-Americans, nones do not as a whole occupy alienated or marginal status in U.S. society (Glenn 1987; Roof and McKinney 1987, p. 99; Kosmin, Keysar, and Lerer 1991). Probably as radical as switching—and certainly as unsettling to loved ones—are such surprises as the Pentecostal spirit baptism of lifelong devoted Catholics (Neitz 1987), born-again evangelicalism among mainline Protestants (Warner 1988), and the "return" of nominal Jews to an orthodoxy they had never before embraced (Davidman 1991; Kaufman 1991).

The voluntarism is attitudinal as well. Gallup (1988, p. 3) reports that 80% of Americans agree that the individual "should arrive at his or her religious beliefs independent of any church or synagogue" (see also Roof and McKinney 1987, p. 57). Roof (1993) and his associates have tracked accounts of spiritual trajectories of "baby boomers" away from

and back toward conventional religion and many syncretic alternatives. Phillip Hammond (1988, p. 5) speaks of a growing shift from "collective-expressive" church membership in the past to "individual-expressive" religious involvement—voluntary and independent of other social ties—today (see also Hammond 1992). Samuel Heilman (1990, p. 195) writes that, "for the contemporary Jew, corporate identity diminishes and ascription gives way to achievement and autonomy as the most powerful determinants of identity." Elsewhere I have written that evangelical Protestantism upholds an ethic of achieved rather than ascribed recruitment (Warner 1988, pp. 52–53, 72, 292–93). It is true by definition that membership in a new denomination such as the Metropolitan Community Church is an achieved status; this is true as well as for the Vineyard, one of several conservative Christian protodenominations emerging out of the late 1960s Jesus movement and appealing primarily to baby boomers (Perrin and Mauss 1991). These are inherently churches of converts.

In other words, both religious disaffiliation and religious conservatism benefit from "achieved" religiosity; the United States has seen both religious revival and apostasy (Chaves 1989; Roozen, McKinney, and Thompson 1990). Taken-for-granted, traditional religion is passé. Born-again, return-to-the-fold neotraditional religion is all the rage.

The authors of *Habits of the Heart* (Bellah et al. 1985) have most eloquently lamented these individualistic trends. Although they recognize that Americans, no matter how individualistic, seek out like-minded others, they fear that the resulting associations are only "lifestyle enclaves," a term they intend to connote shallowness and mutual narcissism. "When we hear such phrases as 'the gay community' or 'the Japanese-American community,' we need to know a great deal before we can decide the degree to which they are genuine communities and the degree to which they are lifestyle enclaves" (Bellah et al. 1985, pp. 74–75). These authors worry about a culture that encourages Americans "to choose the groups with which [they] want to identify" (p. 154), and they propose instead, in the spirit of the older paradigm, that "there is a givenness about the community and the tradition. They are not normally a matter of individual choice" (p. 227).

I do not wish to dismiss the concerns of Bellah and his colleagues, but there is considerable evidence that religious switchers are morally serious. Kristin Luker reports that nearly 20% of the pro-life activists in her study of the abortion controversy were "converts to Catholicism, people who have actively chosen to follow a given religious faith, in striking contrast to the pro-choice people, who have actively chosen not to follow any" (Luker 1984, p. 196). Evidence that FitzGerald's social centrifuge contributes to moral coherence is presented in Roof and McKinney's analysis of 1972–84 General Social Survey data, which indicates that Protestants' inveterate switching of denominations is increasingly motivated by moral culture instead of socioeconomic status. Those shifting their allegiance to the liberal Protestant denominations like the Episcopal and the Presbyterian churches are more liberal on matters of women's rights and racial justice than those raised in these communities, while those gravitating to conservative bodies like the Southern Baptists and the Nazarenes are accentuating those bodies' conservatism on sexual morality (Roof and McKinney 1987, pp. 218, 220, 222).[3] Switching is decreasingly likely to mirror upward social mobility and to represent instead genuine religious change; "switchers are, in a very real sense, converts" (Hadaway and Marler 1991a, p. 22). Protestant switching is not entropic (Sullins 1992).

Switching includes the disaffiliation of dropouts, to be sure, but for those who shift from one faith community to another it also means greater religious involvement–contributing money to the church, frequent prayer and Bible reading, being "born again," being in agreement with the moral culture of their newfound reference group, searching

for more meaning in religious participation (Roof and McKinney 1987; Hadaway and Marler, 1991a; Mauss and Perrin 1991). Conservative churches that expect high levels of involvement are organizational beneficiaries of such switching patterns (Mauss and Perrin 1991; Roof and McKinney 1987, pp. 177–79), but liberal churches that take strong stands and make strong demands can attract newcomers as well (Matters 1992; Wiltfang and McAdam 1991).

We also know that irreligion in the United States replicates itself across generations less effectively than active religious preference. Though the proportion of "nones" has roughly tripled since the 1950s, nones tend to generate additional nones less efficiently than Protestants, Catholics, and Jews do their own kind (Roof and McKinney 1987, p. 169). This may be in part because, in a religious society such as ours, nones are surrounded more by religion than by irreligion. Men are more likely to lack religion than women, but religiously indifferent fathers are particularly poor in passing on their indifference to their offspring. Moreover, the *rate* of disaffiliation is declining. Disaffiliation was common in the young adulthood of baby boomers but is less so more recently (Hadaway and Marler 1991a). Religion is still a prime idiom by which Americans identify themselves.

Yet religion need not represent something in which people are primordially rooted. Religious affiliation in the United States is not tribal. The freedom of Americans to choose with whom they will congregate in service of their most basic values is a freedom not to "pass" as biological kin but to partake as full legatees of cultural traditions that add depth and richness to the association. Literate converts to a religion of the book have immediate access to its communal memory. The religious groups that seem to work best in cosmopolitan America are those that recognize the mobility of their members and bring them into contact with great cultural traditions by incessantly and elaborately recounting the founding narrative (Warner 1988, chap. 9).

It is helpful in this regard to think of religion in the United States as being subject to the decoupling of culture and social structure (Bell 1976). Religiously, relevant statuses are increasingly random with respect to the standard categories of social structure (Caplow 1985; Hammond 1992; Hadaway and Marler 1991a). Thus the new paradigm is not surprised by news of people with modern intellectual resources who reject secularity in favor of "Bible-based" Christianity and "observant" Judaism. Susan Rose (1987, p. 255) tells of women in an upstate New York religious commune who "knowingly and willingly stepped down and relinquished their authority and power" because they valued relationships with men. Nancy Ammerman (1987, pp. 26–31, 72–102) studied a fundamentalist church in New England whose members were demographically and educationally clustered slightly on the more privileged side of the surrounding middle-class suburb but who withdrew morally from what they felt to be an alien world. Lynn Davidman (1991, chap. 5) spent time with converts to orthodox Judaism in Manhattan— young, educated, well-employed women who found in traditional religion a legitimation for the families they hoped to create. In each of these studies, religious commitments helped people set and maintain priorities in a time of perceived bewildering choice.

Has American religion become rootless, evanescent, or arbitrary? No. The breakdown of ascription may be welcomed when, like members of the Metropolitan Community Church, its beneficiaries are convinced that they have been freed to acknowledge their true nature. What the new religious voluntarism amounts to is a centrifugal process, sorting elemental qualities on the basis of which identities are constructed. The evangelical Presbyterians I met in Mendocino, California, had in common not their denominational or educational backgrounds but their histories as migrants to an idealized small town. Their pastor's preaching united their ideological neoparochialism with the theology he had learned in seminary so as to give their

common narrative deep resonance (Warner 1988, pp. 86–87, 205–8). In this way, the breakdown of ascriptive ties to religion can enhance, rather than reduce, the elemental nature that believers attribute to their experiences. From this point of view, social ascription that denies one's true being is seen as arbitrary, while a new-found religion is self-affirming.

I do not wish to overestimate either the extent or the appeal of religious mobility, nor ignore the pain that often accompanies it. Once having chosen a religious home, one is supposed to be and likely to be loyal, and it is probably true that someone dissatisfied with her or his church is as likely to turn away from churches altogether as to seek a church more conformable to personal needs, at least in the short run. There is a norm to the effect that shopping for religion is wrong, and talk of a "religious market" is highly offensive to many people, particularly when it suggests an instrumental attitude toward religion, or ecclesiastical social climbing. Such a norm is no doubt functional for the stability of religious organizations.

What facilitates religious mobility despite such a norm and despite investments in religious capital (Iannaccone 1990) are several social facts, including aggressive proselytization; the emphasis on loyalty to God over institutions, that is part of the evangelical—and hence mainline Protestant—tradition; members' intermittent involvement, such that some who are formally church members may not feel committed and therefore not disloyal when they leave; life-cycle events such as marriage, particularly religious intermarriage; children, for whom one may want to choose an appropriate Sunday school; and geographic mobility. Geographic mobility requires people to choose a church. Since denominations are not homogeneous, the church of one's former denomination in the new location may not "feel right." Denominations themselves change, and the switcher may well perceive that it is not she or he who left the fold.

More research is needed on the question whether rates of religious mobility have recently increased over those prevalent in the 1950s, as has been argued by Roof and McKinney (1987) among others. Yet it should be borne in mind that religious individualism and denomination switching characterized earlier periods of U.S. history, particularly the "awakenings" that took place around 1800–30 and 1890–1920.[4] It was in the former period that the numerical dominance of what later came to be called the liberal Protestant denominations was eclipsed by the surge of the evangelical Methodists and Baptists. The latter period saw the rise of the Holiness, Pentecostal, and fundamentalist movements, the recent visibility of which has so greatly altered the profile of late 20th-century U.S. religion.

Like the present, these were times of massive geographical and social mobility, when individuals could not effectively follow in the footsteps of their parents but had to "start over" for themselves (FitzGerald 1986, pp. 383–414; see Ryan [1981] for the earlier period and Thomas [1989] for the later). Large numbers heeded the messages of religious innovators, and from these times of intense, revivalistic competition new institutions were born, institutions with the potential to solidify into powerful organizations and even rigid bureaucracies (Pritchard 1984; Barfoot and Sheppard 1980; Poloma 1989). Before entertaining the hypothesis that a new religious order prevails in the United States, it is worthwhile to mine the analogies between the present and the American past.

Such an analogy occurred to the anthropologist Riv-Ellen Prell as she looked back on her study of the early 1970s Egalitarian Minyan in Los Angeles. Prell (1989, p. 27) "came to understand the strong parallels between Minyan members and their parents' generation's constructions of Judaism." "I was struck," she writes, "by what these parallels revealed about American religion, namely that religion had been voluntaristic in America ever since immigrants arrived. What appeared, for example, as a counterculture rebellion had its roots deep in immigrants' attempts to maintain their Judaism within American society."

CONCLUSION: THE NEW PARADIGM AND THE AGENDA OF THE FIELD

It is conventional to conclude a paper with a call for more research, but this article—both a research review and a proposal—is such a call. I have highlighted recent work of many scholars, interpreting their findings as only loosely bound (if at all) to the older paradigm. My proposal claims that recent work is more compellingly framed in terms of the newer paradigm. The nascent paradigm itself is the self-conscious project of only a few scholars (without anyone's permission having been asked, it is reasonable in this connection to name Theodore Caplow, Roger Finke. Andrew Greeley, Nathan Hatch, Laurence Iannaccone, Mary Jo Neitz, Daniel Olson, and Rodney Stark), and they do not form a solidary group but a loose school of thought with a common focus on the distinctive institutional parameters of the U.S. religious system—particularly the combination of disestablishment and institutional vitality—as the analytic norm for the study of religion.

Some scholars who are aware of the theoretical ambitions of the new paradigm have spoken out in opposition to it (e.g., Lechner 1991; Breault 1989a), but most scholars in the field are uninvolved in the debate. Yet my claim here is that, because so much recent research focuses in fact on U.S. religious institutions, there is an immanent direction to the research programs even of those not involved in debates over paradigms. Progress in that direction could be facilitated if, in the work of such persons, the presuppositions of the new paradigm were substituted for the old. If that substitution were widespread, several consequences would ensue:

> Students of religious communities and subcultures would focus more on the building of religious institutions and the role of religion in social mobilization and relatively less on the erection and maintenance of plausibility structures.

Students of religious organization would focus as much on the rise of new religious organizations (e.g., Perrin and Mauss 1991) as the decline of old ones (e.g., Hoge and Roozen 1979), even though data would be intrinsically more difficult to find; those who focus on individuals and organizations would analyze entrepreneurial (Kwilecki 1987; Harrell 1985; Stout 1991) as well as bureaucratic (Chaves 1991a) and professional (Charlton 1978; Carroll et al. 1983) religious careers.

Students of social change would investigate the ways in which religion alternatively facilitates and inhibits collective action but would extend their time horizon for these processes to the span of a generation and complicate their models to include indirect effects of group solidarity.

Students of the intersection of biography and social history would assume that individual religious affiliation is not an ascriptive identity set for life but something that can be affirmed and later denied, or vice versa.

The paradigm debate does not crucially impinge on all areas of research in the field; in particular, studies of religious cultures and religious social psychology are less centrally implicated in a paradigm shift whose level of analysis is organizational. Nonetheless it is a radical decision to choose to focus on the European experience of religious monopoly or on the American case of religious cacophony as the analytic norm, or paradigmatic situation, of religion.

Researchers in the field agree that sociology of religion should not be sealed off from the rest of sociology. This article is based on the assumption that the field contributes most when it recognizes that its empirical field constitutes a central institutional sphere of U.S. society. The nonexclusive strategy taken here has been to codify a paradigm adequate to the best-documented case—the United States—both so that researchers on that case can better understand their findings and so that the parameters of the case itself can be identified. Thus there has just begun one critical line of research that

attempts to specify the determinants of the American religious system. Is the key to American religious vitality given in Tocqueville's analysis of the historically apolitical stance of most U.S. religious groups, the notion that American religion has largely stayed out of politics? (See, e.g., Caplow 1985.) Or is religious pluralism the key, as Finke and Stark (1988) would have it, the sheer variety of religious choices? Or is it deregulation, the lack of either subsidy or state oversight of religious organizations? (See Greeley 1989, pp. 126–27; Iannaccone 1991; Chaves and Cann 1992.) Comparative institutional research, unburdened of the secularization expectations of the older paradigm, will serve to demystify the concept of American exceptionalism (Tiryakian 1991). Until that has been accomplished, the exception may well be taken as the rule.

NOTES

1.   Research for this article began when I was a visiting member of the Institute for Advanced Study, Princeton, New Jersey. Earlier formulations were presented to audiences at the institute in October 1988, Princeton Theological Seminary in February 1989, a joint session of the American Sociological Association and the Association for the Sociology of Religion in San Francisco in August 1989, the Humanities Research Forum and the Office of Social Science Research of the University of Illinois at Chicago in January 1990, the Department of Sociology at Northwestern University in October 1991, and Swarthmore College in Novembers 1991. I am indebted to members of these audiences for their reactions, to numerous colleagues for advice and commentary, and to the Institute for Advanced Study, the Rockefeller Foundation, the National Endowment for the Humanities, the University of Illinois at Chicago, and Northwestern University for support. Rather than implicate by name any of the many individuals who have commented on previous drafts and assisted with this one, I wish to express my deep appreciation to all of them, as well as to four referees for the *American Journal of Sociology*. Correspondence may be directed to R. Stephen Warner, Department of Sociology (M/C 312),

University of Illinois at Chicago, Box 4348, Chicago, Illinois 60607–7140.

2. The concept of "voluntarism," as used here, stands in the tradition of American religious studies rather than sociological theory. Sometimes called "voluntaryism" (Ahlstrom 1972, pp. 382–83), the religious studies concept refers to the *concrete* institutional facts of separation of church and state and religious freedom in the postrevolutionary United States and the consequent need for churches to rely on persuasion rather than coercion for their support (Littel 1962; Mead 1963). Such "voluntarism," strange and remarkable to Europeans, "became a matter of course to Americans" (Rowe 1924, p. 53), and over time it evolved into the religious system portrayed here. The "voluntarism" of sociological theory, particularly associated with the early work of Talcott Parsons, concerns the *analytic* question of the categories needed for the analysis of individual action (Alexander 1982). Insofar as Parsons, himself raised a liberal Protestant, conceived modern social order to minimize coercion, the two concepts were no doubt related in his mind. Moreover, since the "new voluntarism" complex conceptualizes an additional, perhaps temporary, movement toward individualism in religion (referred to below as a disjunction of culture and social structure), the phenomena it delimits are closer still (albeit not identical) to the theorists' concerns. The new voluntarism has also been called the "third disestablishment" (Roof and McKinney 1987; Hammond 1992).

3. Roof and McKinney (1987) measure mobility of identifiers, not members, across "families" of denominations, not denominations per se. Thus, for their research purposes, Presbyterians are the same as Episcopalians since both are "liberal Protestants," Lutherans and Methodists are alike "moderate Protestants," and Southern Baptists and Pentecostals are "conservative Protestants." The cultural sorting they map, therefore, is ambiguous with respect to the hypothesis of the declining significance of denominational identities, strictly speaking.

4. The dates are from McLoughlin (1978).

5

The Desecularization of the World: A Global Overview

Peter L. Berger

A FEW YEARS AGO the first volume coming out of the so-called Fundamentalism Project landed on my desk. The Fundamentalism Project was very generously funded by the MacArthur Foundation and chaired by Martin Marty, the distinguished church historian at the University of Chicago. A number of very reputable scholars took part in it, and the published results are of generally excellent quality. But my contemplation of this first volume gave me what has been called an *"aha!* experience." The book was very big, sitting there on my desk—a "book-weapon," the kind that could do serious injury. So I asked myself, why would the MacArthur Foundation shell out several million dollars to support an international study of religious fundamentalists?

Two answers came to mind. The first was obvious and not very interesting. The MacArthur Foundation is a very progressive outfit; it understands fundamentalists to be anti-progressive; the Project, then, was a matter of knowing one's enemies. But there was also a more interesting answer. "Fundamentalism" is considered a strange, hard-to-understand phenomenon; the purpose of the Project was to delve into this alien world and make it more understandable. But to whom? *Who* finds this world strange? Well, the answer to *that* question was easy: people to whom the officials of the MacArthur Foundation normally talk, such as

professors at elite American universities. And with this came the aha! experience. The concern that must have led to this Project was based on an upside-down perception of the world, according to which "fundamentalism" (which, when all is said and done, usually refers to any sort of passionate religious movement) is a rare, hard-to-explain thing. But a look either at history or at the contemporary world reveals that what is rare is not the phenomenon itself but knowledge of it. The difficult-to-understand phenomenon is not Iranian mullahs but American university professors—it might be worth a multi-million-dollar project to try to explain that!

Mistakes of Secularization Theory

My point is that the assumption that we live in a secularized world is false. The world today, with some exceptions to which I will come presently, is as furiously religious as it ever was, and in some places more so than ever. This means that a whole body of literature by historians and social scientists loosely labeled "secularization theory" is essentially mistaken. In my early work I contributed to this literature. I was in good company—most sociologists of religion had similar views, and we had good reasons for holding them. Some of the writings we produced still stand up. (As I like to tell my students, one advantage of being a social scientist, as against being, say, a philosopher or a theologian, is that you can have as much fun when your theories are falsified as when they are verified!)

Although the term "secularization theory" refers to works from the 1950s and 1960s, the key idea of the theory can indeed be traced to the Enlightenment. That idea is simple: Modernization necessarily leads to a decline of religion, both in society and in the minds of individuals. And it is precisely this key idea that has turned out to be wrong. To be sure, modernization has had some secularizing effects, more in some places than in others. But it has also provoked powerful movements of counter-secularization. Also, secularization on the societal level is not necessarily linked to secularization on the level of individual consciousness. Certain religious institutions have lost power and influence in many societies, but both old and new religious beliefs and practices have nevertheless continued in the lives of individuals, sometimes taking new institutional forms and sometimes leading to great explosions of religious fervor. Conversely, religiously identified institutions can play social or political roles even when very few people believe or practice the religion that the institutions represent. To say the least, the relation between religion and modernity is rather complicated.

The proposition that modernity necessarily leads to a decline of religion is, in principle, "value free." That is, it can be affirmed both by people who think it is good news and by people who think it is very bad news. Most Enlightenment thinkers and most progressive-minded people ever since have tended toward the idea that secularization is a good thing, at least insofar as it does away with religious phenomena that are "backward," "superstitious," or "reactionary" (a religious residue purged of these negative characteristics may still be deemed acceptable). But religious people, including those with very traditional or orthodox beliefs, have also affirmed the modernity/secularity linkage, and have

greatly bemoaned it. Some have then defined modernity as the enemy, to be fought whenever possible. Others have, on the contrary, seen modernity as some kind of invincible world view to which religious beliefs and practices should adapt themselves. In other words, *rejection* and *adaptation* are two strategies open to religious communities in a world understood to be secularized. As is always the case when strategies are based on mistaken perceptions of the terrain, both strategies have had very doubtful results.

It is possible, of course, to reject any number of modern ideas and values theoretically, but making this rejection stick in the lives of people is much harder. To do that requires one of two strategies. The first is *religious revolution:* one tries to take over society as a whole and make one's counter-modern religion obligatory for everyone—a difficult enterprise in most countries in the contemporary world. (Franco tried in Spain and failed; the mullahs are still at it in Iran and a couple of other places.) And this *does* have to do with modernization, which brings about very heterogeneous societies and a quantum leap in intercultural communication, two factors favoring pluralism and *not* favoring the establishment (or reestablishment) of religious monopolies. The other possible way of getting people to reject modern ideas and values in their lives is to create *religious subcultures* designed to keep out the influences of the outside society. That is a somewhat more promising exercise than religious revolution, but it too is fraught with difficulty: Modern culture is a very powerful force, and an immense effort is required to maintain enclaves with an airtight defense system. Ask the Amish in eastern Pennsylvania. Or ask a Hasidic rabbi in the Williamsburg section of Brooklyn.

Interestingly, secularization theory has also been falsified by the results of adaptation strategies by religious institutions. If we really lived in a highly secularized world, then religious institutions could be expected to survive to the degree that they manage to adapt to secularity. That has been the empirical assumption of adaptation strategies. What has in fact occurred is that, by and large, religious communities have survived and even flourished to the degree that they have *not* tried to adapt themselves to the alleged requirements of a secularized world. To put it simply, experiments with secularized religion have generally failed; religious movements with beliefs and practices dripping with reactionary supernaturalism (the kind utterly beyond the pale at self-respecting faculty parties) have widely succeeded.

The Catholic Church vs. Modernity

The struggle with modernity in the Roman Catholic Church nicely illustrates the difficulties of various strategies. In the wake of the Enlightenment and its multiple revolutions, the initial response by the Church was militant and then defiant rejection. Perhaps the most magnificent moment of that defiance came in 1870, when the First Vatican Council solemnly proclaimed the infallibility of the Pope and the immaculate conception of Mary, literally in the face of the Enlightenment about to occupy Rome in the shape of the army of Victor Emmanuel I. (The disdain was mutual. If you have ever visited the Roman monument to the Bersaglieri, the elite army units that occupied the Eternal City in the name of the Italian *Risorgimento,* you may have noticed the placement of the heroic figure in his Bersaglieri uniform—he is positioned so that his behind points exactly toward the Vatican.)

The Second Vatican Council, almost a hundred years later, considerably modified this rejectionist stance, guided as it was by the notion of *aggiornamento,* bringing the Church up to date—that is, up to date with the modern world. (I remember asking a Protestant theologian what he thought would happen at the Council—this was before it had convened; he replied that he didn't know but he was sure they would not read the minutes of the last meeting!) The Second Vatican Council was supposed to open windows, specifically the windows of the Catholic subculture that had been constructed when it became clear that the overall society could not be reconquered. In the United States, this Catholic subculture has been quite impressive right up to the very recent past. The trouble with opening windows is that you can't control what comes in, and a lot has come in—indeed, the whole turbulent world of modern culture—that has been very troubling to the Church. Under the current pontificate the Church has been steering a nuanced course between rejection and adaptation, with mixed results in different countries.

This is as good a point as any to mention that all my observations here are intended to be "value free"; that is, I am trying to look at the current religious scene objectively. For the duration of this exercise I have put aside my own religious beliefs. As a sociologist of religion, I find it probable that Rome had to do some reining in on the level of both doctrine and practice, in the wake of the institutional disturbances that followed Vatican II. To say this, however, in no way implies my theological agreement with what has been happening in the Roman Catholic Church under the present pontificate. Indeed, if I were Roman Catholic, I would have considerable misgivings about these developments. But I am a liberal Protestant (the adjective refers to my religious position and not to my politics), and I have no immediate existential stake in what is happening within the Roman community. I am speaking here as a sociologist, in which capacity I can claim a certain competence; I have no theological credentials.

THE GLOBAL RELIGIOUS SCENE

On the international religious scene, it is conservative or orthodox or traditionalist movements that are on the rise almost everywhere. These movements are precisely the ones that rejected an *aggiornamento* with modernity as defined by progressive intellectuals. Conversely, religious movements and institutions that have made great efforts to conform to a perceived modernity are almost everywhere on the decline. In the United States this has been a much commented upon fact, exemplified by the decline of so-called mainline Protestantism and the concomitant rise of Evangelicalism; but the United States is by no means unusual in this.

Nor is Protestantism. The conservative thrust in the Roman Catholic Church under John Paul II has borne fruit in both number of converts and renewed enthusiasm among native Catholics, especially in non-Western countries. Following the collapse of the Soviet Union there occurred a remarkable revival of the Orthodox Church in Russia. The most rapidly growing Jewish groups, both in Israel and in the Diaspora, are Orthodox. There have been similarly vigorous upsurges of conservative religion in all the other major religious communities—Islam, Hinduism, Buddhism—as well as revival movements in smaller communities (such as Shintō in Japan and Sikhism in India). These developments differ greatly in their social and political implications. What they have in common is their unambiguously *religious* inspiration. Consequently, taken together they provide a massive falsification of the idea that modernization and secularization are cognate phenomena. At the very least they show that *counter*-secularization is at least as important a phenomenon in the contemporary world as secularization.

Both in the media and in scholarly publications, these movements are often subsumed under the category of "fundamentalism." This is not a felicitous term, not only because it carries a pejorative undertone but also because it derives from the history of American Protestantism, where it has a specific reference that is distortive if extended to other religious traditions. All the same, the term has some suggestive use if one wishes to explain the aforementioned developments. It suggests a combination of several features—great religious passion, a defiance of what others have defined as the *Zeitgeist,* and a return to traditional sources of religious

authority. These are indeed common features across cultural boundaries. And they do reflect the presence of secularizing forces, since they must be understood as a reaction *against* those forces. (In that sense, at least, something of the old secularization theory may be said to hold up, in a rather backhanded way.) This interplay of secularizing and counter-secularizing forces is, I would contend, one of the most important topics for a sociology of contemporary religion, but far too large to consider here. I can only drop a hint: Modernity, for fully understandable reasons, undermines all the old certainties; uncertainty is a condition that many people find very hard to bear; therefore, any movement (not only a religious one) that promises to provide or to renew certainty has a ready market.

Differences Among Thriving Movements

While the aforementioned common features are important, an analysis of the social and political impact of the various religious upsurges must also take full account of their differences. This becomes clear when one looks at what are arguably the two most dynamic religious upsurges in the world today, the Islamic and the Evangelical; the comparison also underlines the weakness of the category of "fundamentalism" as applied to both.

The Islamic upsurge, because of its more immediately obvious political ramifications, is better known. Yet it would be a serious error to see it only through a political lens. It is an impressive revival of emphatically *religious* commitments. And it is of vast geographical scope, affecting every single Muslim country from North Africa to South-east Asia. It continues to gain converts, especially in sub-Saharan Africa (where it is often in head-on competition with Christianity). It is becoming very visible in the burgeoning Muslim communities in Europe and, to a much lesser extent, in North America. Everywhere it is bringing about a restoration, not only of Islamic beliefs but of distinctively Islamic life-styles, which in many ways directly contradict modern ideas—such as ideas about the relation of religion and the state, the role of women, moral codes of everyday behavior, and the boundaries of religious and moral tolerance. The Islamic revival is by no means restricted to the less modernized or "backward" sectors of society, as progressive intellectuals still like to think. On the contrary, it is very strong in cities with a high degree of modernization, and in a number of countries it is particularly visible among people with Western-style higher education—in Egypt and Turkey, for example, many daughters of secularized professionals are putting on the veil and other accoutrements of Islamic modesty.

Yet there are also great differences within the movement. Even within the Middle East, the Islamic heartland, there are both religiously and politically important differences between Sunni and Shiite revivals—Islamic conservatism means very different things in, say, Saudi Arabia and Iran. Away from the Middle East, the differences become even greater. Thus in Indonesia, the most populous Muslim country in the world, a very powerful revival movement, the Nudhat'ul-Ulama, is avowedly pro-democracy and pro-pluralism, the very opposite of what is commonly viewed as Muslim "fundamentalism." Where the political circumstances allow this, there is in many places a lively discussion about the relation of Islam to various modern realities, and there are sharp disagreements among individuals who are equally committed to a revitalized Islam. Still, for reasons deeply grounded in the core of the tradition, it is probably fair to say that, on the whole, Islam has had a difficult time coming to terms with key modern institutions, such as pluralism, democracy, and the market economy.

The Evangelical upsurge is just as breathtaking in scope. Geographically that scope is even wider. It has gained huge numbers of converts in East Asia—in all the Chinese communities (including, despite severe persecution, mainland China) and in South Korea, the Philippines, across the South Pacific, throughout sub-Saharan Africa (where it is often

synthetized with elements of traditional African religion), apparently in parts of ex-Communist Europe. But the most remarkable success has occurred in Latin America; there are now thought to be between forty and fifty million Evangelical Protestants south of the U.S. border, the great majority of them first-generation Protestants. The most numerous component within the Evangelical upsurge is Pentecostalism, which combines biblical orthodoxy and a rigorous morality with an ecstatic form of worship and an emphasis on spiritual healing. Especially in Latin America, conversion to Protestantism brings about a cultural transformation—new attitudes toward work and consumption, a new educational ethos, and a violent rejection of traditional *machismo* (women play a key role in the Evangelical churches).

The origins of this worldwide Evangelical upsurge are in the United States, from which the missionaries first went out. But it is very important to understand that, virtually everywhere and emphatically in Latin America, this new Evangelicalism is thoroughly indigenous and no longer dependent on support from U.S. fellow believers—indeed, Latin American Evangelicals have been sending missionaries to the Hispanic community in this country, where there has been a comparable flurry of conversions.

Needless to say, the religious contents of the Islamic and Evangelical revivals are totally different. So are the social and political consequences (of which I will say more later). But the two developments also differ in another very important respect: The Islamic movement is occurring primarily in countries that are already Muslim or among Muslim emigrants (as in Europe), while the Evangelical movement is growing dramatically throughout the world in countries where this type of religion was previously unknown or very marginal.

Exceptions to the Desecularization Thesis

Let me, then, repeat what I said a while back: The world today is massively religious, is *anything but* the secularized world that had been predicted (whether joyfully or despondently) by so many analysts of modernity. There are, however, two exceptions to this proposition, one somewhat unclear, the other very clear.

The first apparent exception is Europe—more specifically, Europe west of what used to be called the Iron Curtain (the developments in the formerly Communist countries are as yet very under-researched and unclear). In Western Europe, if nowhere else, the old secularization theory would seem to hold. With increasing modernization there has been an increase in key indicators of secularization, both on the level of expressed beliefs (especially those that could be called orthodox in Protestant or Catholic terms) and, dramatically, on the level of church-related behavior—attendance at services of worship, adherence to church-dictated codes of personal behavior (especially with regard to sexuality, reproduction, and marriage), recruitment to the clergy. These phenomena, long observed in the northern countries of the continent, have since World War II rapidly engulfed the south. Thus Italy and Spain have experienced a rapid decline in church-related religion. So has Greece, thereby undercutting the claim of Catholic conservatives that Vatican II is to be blamed for the decline. There is now a massively secular Euro-culture, and what has happened in the south can be simply described (though not thereby explained) by that culture's invasion of these countries. It is not fanciful to predict that there will be similar developments in Eastern Europe, precisely to the degree that these countries too will be integrated into the new Europe.

While these facts are not in dispute, a number of recent works in the sociology of religion, notably in France, Britain, and Scandinavia, have questioned the term "secularization" as applied to these developments. A body of data indicates strong survivals of religion, most of it generally Christian in nature, despite the widespread alienation from the organized churches. A shift in the institutional location of religion, then, rather than secularization, would be a more accurate description of the European situation. All the same, Europe stands out as quite different from other parts of the world, and certainly from the United States. One of the most interesting puzzles in the sociology of religion is why Americans are so much more religious *as well as* more churchly than Europeans.

The other exception to the desecularization thesis is less ambiguous. There exists an international subculture composed of people with Western-type higher education, especially in the humanities and social sciences, that is indeed secularized. This subculture is the principal "carrier" of progressive, Enlightened beliefs and values. While its members are relatively thin on the ground, they are very influential, as they control the institutions that provide the "official" definitions of reality, notably the educational system, the media of mass communication, and the higher reaches of the legal system. They are remarkably similar all over the world today, as they have been for a long time (though, as we have seen, there are also defectors from this subculture, especially in the Muslim countries). Again, regrettably, I cannot speculate here as to why people with this type of education should be so prone to secularization. I can only point out that what we have here is a globalized *elite* culture.

In country after country, then, religious upsurges have a strongly populist character. Over and beyond the purely religious motives, these are movements of protest and resistance *against* a secular elite. The so-called culture war in the United States emphatically shares this feature. I may observe in passing that the plausibility of secularization theory owes much to this international subculture. When intellectuals travel, they usually touch down in intellectual circles—that is, among people much like themselves. They can easily fall into the misconception that these people reflect the overall visited society, which, of course, is a big mistake. Picture a secular intellectual from Western Europe socializing with colleagues at the faculty club of the University of Texas. He may think he is back home. But then picture him trying to drive through the traffic jam on Sunday morning in downtown Austin—or, heaven help him, turning on his car radio! What happens then is a severe jolt of what anthropologists call culture shock.

RESURGENT RELIGION: ORIGINS AND PROSPECTS

After this somewhat breathless *tour d'horizon* of the global religious scene, let me turn to some the questions posed for discussion in this set of essays. *First, what are the origins of the worldwide resurgence of religion?* Two possible answers have already been mentioned. One: Modernity tends to undermine the taken-for-granted certainties by which people lived through most of history. This is an uncomfortable state of affairs, for many an intolerable one, and religious movements that claim to give certainty have great appeal. Two: A purely secular view of reality has its principal social location in an elite culture that, not surprisingly, is resented by large numbers of people who are not part of it but who feel its influence (most troublingly, as their children are subjected to an education that ignores or even directly attacks their own beliefs and values). Religious movements with a strongly anti-secular bent can therefore appeal to people with resentments that sometimes have quite non-religious sources.

But I would refer once more to the little story with which I began, about American foundation officials worried about "fundamentalism." In one sense, there is nothing to explain here. Strongly felt religion has always been around; what needs explanation is its absence rather than its presence. Modern secularity is a much more puzzling phenomenon than all these religious explosions—if you will, the University of Chicago is a more interesting topic for the sociology of religion than the Islamic schools of Qom. In other words, the phenomena under consideration here on one level

simply serve to demonstrate continuity in the place of religion in human experience.

Second, what is the likely future course of this religious resurgence? Given the considerable variety of important religious movements in the contemporary world, it would make little, sense to venture a global prognosis. Predictions, if one dares to make them at all, will be more useful if applied to much narrower situations. One prediction, though, can be made with some assurance: There is no reason to think the world of the twenty-first century will be any less religious than the world is today. A minority of sociologists of religion have been trying to salvage the old secularization theory by what I would call the last-ditch thesis: Modernization *does* secularize, and movements like the Islamic and the Evangelical ones represent last-ditch defenses by religion that cannot last; eventually, secularity will triumph—or, to put it less respectfully, eventually Iranian mullahs, Pentecostal preachers, and Tibetan lamas will all think and act like professors of literature at American universities. I find this thesis singularly unpersuasive.

Having made this general prediction—that the world of the next century will not be less religious than the world of today—I will have to speculate very differently regarding different sectors of the religious scene. For example, I think that the most militant Islamic movements will find it hard to maintain their present stance *vis-à-vis* modernity once they succeed in taking over the governments of their countries (this, it seems, is already happening in Iran). I also think that Pentecostalism, as it exists today among mostly poor and uneducated people, is unlikely to retain its present religious and moral characteristics unchanged, as many of these people experience upward social mobility (this has already been observed extensively in the United States). Generally, many of these religious movements are linked to non-religious forces of one sort or another, and the future course of the former will be at least partially determined by the course of the latter. In the United States, for instance, militant Evangelicalism will have a different future course if some of its causes succeed in the political and legal arenas than if it continues to be frustrated in these arenas. Also, in religion as in every other area of human endeavor, individual personalities play a much larger role than most social scientists and historians are willing to concede. There might have been an Islamic revolution in Iran without the Ayatollah Khomeini, but it would probably have looked quite different. No one can predict the appearance of charismatic figures who will launch powerful religious movements in unexpected places. Who knows—perhaps the next religious upsurge in America will occur among disenchanted post-modernist academics!

Third, do the resurgent religions differ in their critique of the secular order? Yes, of course they do, depending on their particular belief systems. Cardinal Ratzinger and the Dalai Lama will be troubled by different aspects of contemporary secular culture. What both will agree upon, however, is the shallowness of a culture that tries to get along without any transcendent points of reference. And they will have good reasons to support this view. The religious impulse, the quest for meaning that transcends the restricted space of empirical existence in this world, has been a perennial feature of humanity. (This is not a theological statement but an anthropological one—an agnostic or even an atheist philosopher may well agree with it.) It would require something close to a mutation of the species to extinguish this impulse for good. The more radical thinkers of the Enlightenment and their more recent intellectual descendants hoped for something like this, of course. So far it has not happened, and as I have argued, it is unlikely to happen in the foreseeable future. The critique of secularity common to all the resurgent movements is that human existence bereft of transcendence is an impoverished and finally untenable condition.

To the extent that secularity today has a specifically modern form (there were earlier forms in, for example, versions of Confucianism and Hellenistic culture), the critique of secularity also entails a critique of at least these aspects of modernity. Beyond that, however, different religious movements differ in their relation to modernity. As I have said, an argument can be made that the Islamic resurgence strongly tends toward a negative view of modernity; in places it is downright anti-modern or counter-modernizing, as in its view of the role of women. By contrast, I think it can be shown that the Evangelical resurgence is positively modernizing in most places where it occurs, clearly so in Latin America. The new Evangelicals throw aside many of the traditions that have been obstacles to modernization—*machismo*, for one, and also the subservience to hierarchy that has been endemic to Iberian Catholicism. Their churches encourage values and behavior patterns that contribute to modernization. To take just one important case in point: In order to participate fully in the life of their congregations, Evangelicals will want to read the Bible; this desire to read the Bible encourages literacy and, beyond this, a positive attitude toward education and self-improvement. They also will want to be able to join in the discussion of congregational affairs, since those matters are largely in the hands of laypersons (indeed, largely in the hands of women); this lay operation of churches necessitates training in administrative skills, including the conduct of public meetings and the keeping of financial accounts. It is not fanciful to suggest that in this way Evangelical congregations serve—inadvertently, to be sure—as schools for democracy and for social mobility.

RELIGIOUS RESURGENCE AND WORLD AFFAIRS

Other questions posed for discussion in this volume concern the relation of the religious resurgence to a number of issues not linked to religion.

■ First, *international politics*. Here one comes up head-on against the thesis, eloquently proposed not long ago by Samuel Huntington, that, with the end of the Cold War, international affairs will be affected by a "clash of civilizations" rather than by ideological conflicts. There is something to be said for this thesis. The great ideological conflict that animated the Cold War is certainly dormant for the moment, but I, for one, would not bet on its final demise. Nor can we be sure that new ideological conflicts may not arise in the future. To the extent that nationalism is an ideology (more accurately, each nationalism has its *own* ideology), ideology is alive and well in a long list of countries.

It is also plausible that, in the absence of the overarching confrontation between Soviet Communism and the American-led West, cultural animosities suppressed during the Cold War period are surfacing. Some of these animosities have themselves taken on an ideological form, as in the assertion of a distinctive Asian identity by a number of governments and intellectual groups in East and South-east Asia. This ideology has become especially visible in debates over the allegedly ethnocentric/Eurocentric character of human rights as propagated by the United States and other Western governments and governmental organizations. But it would probably be an exaggeration to see these debates as signaling a clash of civilizations. The situation closest to a religiously defined clash of civilizations would come about if the world-view of the most radical branches of the Islamic resurgence came to be established within a wider spectrum of countries and became the basis of the foreign policies of these countries. As yet this has not happened.

To assess the role of religion in international politics, it would be useful to distinguish between political movements that are genuinely inspired by religion and those that use religion as a convenient legitimation for political agendas based on quite non-religious interests. Such a distinction is difficult but not impossible. Thus there is no reason to doubt that the suicide bombers of the Islamic Haws movement truly believe in the religious motives they avow. By contrast, there is good reason to

doubt that the three parties involved in the Bosnian conflict, commonly represented as a clash between religions, are really inspired by religious ideas. I think it was P. J. O'Rourke who observed that these three parties are of the same race, speak the same language, and are distinguished only by their religion, which none of them believe. The same skepticism about the religious nature of an allegedly religious conflict is expressed in the following joke from Northern Ireland: As a man walks down a dark street in Belfast, a gunman jumps out of a doorway, holds a gun to his head, and asks, "Are you Protestant or Catholic?" The man stutters, "Well, actually, I'm an atheist." "Ah yes," says the gunman, "but are you a Protestant or a Catholic atheist?"

■ Second, *war and peace*. It would be nice to be able to say that religion is everywhere a force for peace. Unfortunately, it is not. Very probably religion in the modern world more often fosters war, both between and within nations. Religious institutions and movements are fanning wars and civil wars on the Indian subcontinent, in the Balkans, in the Middle East, and in Africa, to mention only the most obvious cases. Occasionally, indeed, religious institutions try to resist warlike policies or to mediate between conflicting parties. The Vatican mediated successfully in some international disputes in Latin America. There have been religiously inspired peace movements in several countries (including the United States, during the Vietnam War). Both Protestant and Catholic clergy have tried to mediate the conflict in Northern Ireland, though with notable lack of success.

But it is probably a mistake to look here simply at the actions of formal religious institutions or groups. There may be a diffusion of religious values in a society that could have peace-prone consequences even in the absence of formal actions by church bodies. For example, some analysts have argued that the wide diffusion of Christian values played a mediating role in the process that ended the apartheid regime in South Africa, even though the churches were mostly polarized between the two sides of the conflict, at least until the last few years of the regime, when the Dutch Reformed Church reversed its position on apartheid.

■ Third, *economic development*. The basic text on the relation of religion and economic development is, of course, the German sociologist Max Weber's 1905 work *The Protestant Ethic and the Spirit of Capitalism*. Scholars have been arguing over the thesis of this book for over ninety years. However one comes out on this (I happen to be an unreconstructed Weberian), it is clear that some values foster modern economic development more than others. Something *like* Weber's "Protestant ethic" is probably functional in an early phase of capitalist growth—an ethic, whether religiously inspired or not, that values personal discipline, hard work, frugality, and a respect for learning. The new Evangelicalism in Latin America exhibits these values in virtually crystalline purity, so that my own mental subtitle for the research project on this topic conducted by the center I direct at Boston University has been, "Max Weber is alive and well and living in Guatemala." Conversely, Iberian Catholicism, as it was established in Latin America, clearly does *not* foster such values.

But religious traditions can change. Spain experienced a remarkably successful period of economic development beginning in the waning years of the Franco regime, and one of the important factors was the influence of Opus Dei, which combined rigorous theological orthodoxy with a market-friendly openness in economic matters. I have suggested that Islam, by and large, has difficulties with a modern market economy; yet Muslim emigrants have done remarkably well in a number of countries (for instance, in sub-Saharan Africa), and there is a powerful Islamic movement in Indonesia that might yet play a role analogous to that of Opus Dei in the Catholic world. I should add that for years now there has been an extended debate over the part played by Confucian-inspired values in the economic success stories of East Asia; if one is to credit the "post-Confucian thesis" and

also to allow that Confucianism is a religion, then here would be a very important religious contribution to economic development.

One morally troubling aspect of this matter is that values functional at one period of economic development may not be functional at another. The values of the "Protestant ethic" or a functional equivalent thereof are probably essential during the phase that Walt Rostow called "the take-off," but may not be so in a later phase. Much less austere values may be more functional in the so-called post-industrial economies of Europe, North America, and East Asia. For example, frugality, however admirable from a moral viewpoint, may actually be a vice economically speaking. Although undisciplined hedonists have a hard time climbing out of primitive poverty, they can do well in the high-tech, knowledge-driven economies of the advanced societies.

■ Finally, *human rights and social justice*. Religious institutions have, of course, made many statements on human rights and social justice. Some of these have had important political consequences, as in the civil-rights struggle in the United States and the collapse of Communist regimes in Europe. But, as mentioned previously, there are different religiously articulated views about the nature of human rights. The same goes for ideas about social justice: what is justice to some groups is gross injustice to others. Sometimes it is very clear that positions taken by religious groups on such matters are based on a religious rationale; the principled opposition to abortion and contraception by the Roman Catholic Church is such a clear case. At other times, though, positions on social justice, even if legitimated by religious rhetoric, reflect the location of the religious functionaries in this or that network of non-religious social classes and interests. To stay with the same example, I think that this is the case with most of the positions taken by American Catholic institutions on social-justice issues other than those relating to sexuality and reproduction.

I have dealt very briefly with immensely complex matters. I was asked to give a global overview, and that is what I have tried to do. There is no way that I can end this with some sort of uplifting sermon. Both those who have great hopes for the role of religion in the affairs of this world and those who *fear* this role must be disappointed by the factual evidence. In assessing this role, there is no alternative to a nuanced, case-by-case approach. But one statement can be made with great confidence: Those who neglect religion in their analyses of contemporary affairs do so at great peril.

6

The Curious Case of the Unnecessary Recantation: Berger and Secularization

Steve Bruce

INTRODUCTION

Until the 1980s, most social scientists supposed that the modern world was becoming increasingly Godless. Peter Berger was influential in developing the secularization thesis (though 'paradigm' might better describe what is a complex and at times only loosely articulated body of descriptions and explanations). He is also the most eminent of those who now challenge the thesis. In 1974 he began to question his own conclusions: 'In the last few years I have come to believe that many observers of the religious scene (I among them) have over-estimated both the degree and irreversibility of secularization' (1974b, p. 16). Two decades later his reservations had hardened into repudiation: 'The big mistake, which I shared with everyone who worked in this area in the 1950s and '60s, was to believe that modernity necessarily leads to a decline in religion' (1998, p. 782).

Whether trying to save an intellectual hero from himself is treacherous, I am not sure. But it is certainly arrogant. I wish to argue, despite what Berger now says, that his original contributions to the secularization approach remain valid, that he is confessing to sins he did not commit, and that his arguments against his own views are unpersuasive.

BERGER'S CONTRIBUTIONS TO SECULARIZATION

Berger's early work already contains two very different voices: the sociologist and the Lutheran. It could well be that his changing assessment of secularization is a product of the changing balance within his own character of the social scientist and the Christian. However, why someone believes something and whether it is true are two separate questions. I will confine myself to assessing the case he now makes against secularization and say no more about why he might now wish to find persuasive what did not convince him forty years ago.

Berger made two important contributions to the secularization approach. First, he strengthened Max Weber's stress on the increased rationalization of the world. Berger's early essay (1963c) on the Israelite prophets was important in locating the seeds of rationality in the monotheism of the Old Testament, thereby contributing to the argument of Weber, Ernst Troeltsch, Robert Merton, and David Martin that Judaism, Christianity, and Protestantism inadvertently and ironically incubated and nurtured the seeds of their own decline. By simplifying the supernatural, by permitting what pleased God to become codified, routinized and rationalized, and by making the operations of the divine predictable, this strand permitted the growth of science and technology and aided the rise of capitalism. The connections are complicated but we can find in Berger's early work the argument that one type of religion was centrally implicated in modernization and helped to create the conditions in which large numbers of people could come to live without much or any religion.

Berger's other contribution came as part of promoting the phenomenology of Alfred Schutz. In particular, he drew our attention to the impact of the 'pluralization of life-worlds' on the 'plausibility' of religious belief-systems:

> Our situation is characterized by a market of world views, simultaneously in competition with each other. In this situation the maintenance of certitudes that go much beyond the empirical necessities of the society and the individual to function is very difficult indeed. Inasmuch as religion essentially rests upon supernatural certitudes, the pluralistic situation is a secularizing one and, ipso facto, plunges religion into a crisis of credibility.
>
> (1979b, p. 213)

Although Berger spends most of his time on the social-psychological consequences of cultural diversity, he is fully aware of the political and social consequences. If it has to encompass diversity, the modernizing state – unless it is prepared to accept high levels of social conflict (and none were) – has to become increasingly religiously neutral. The public square is gradually evacuated. This not only removes formal state support for a particular religion. More importantly, and this is where Berger's focus on 'taken-for grantedness' is vital, it removes a whole range of opportunities for the religious tradition to be reinforced in day-to-day interaction. Where a community shares a common religion, big events such as births, deaths and marriages can be glossed by the church and thereby reinforce its beliefs. The passing of the seasons can be similarly treated. And everyday conversation can reinforce the shared beliefs as people gloss even mundane matters such as the weather in religious terms. The fragmentation of the religious culture into a range of competing alternatives drastically curtails the social reinforcement of belief.

RECANTATION

Since 1974 Berger has offered a number of reasons for doubting his initial confidence that modernity undermined religion. Before considering them, we might note that his recent writings on religion take the form of lectures or articles written for popular journals (a lot of them religious). Hence his comments are brief, popular in style, and lack the detailed qualifications that he would doubtless have added had he been writing a book-length treatment or an academic journal article. It may well be that his views have been revised less than would appear from one or two brief statements.

With varying degrees of commitment to them, Berger has offered the following as reasons to revise his confidence in the secularization thesis: (a) the growth of conservative and evangelical churches in the United States; (b) the decline of liberal churches; (c) the persistence of interest in religion (if not church-going) in other Western societies; and (d) the vitality of religion in other parts of the world.

Religious Revival in the United States

Berger has made far less of this than others and he rightly expresses some doubt about the extent of evangelical growth in the United States. But he none the less refers to it in the context of discussing liberal failure (of which more below). I am even less persuaded by the claims for revival in the heartland of modernity. Much church growth has been the result not of increased popularity but of population increase and increased longevity.

There is also a crucial issue of time-frames. I will return to this, but the crucial test for any theory of social change is not what happens in a range of societies in the same year but what happens when the changes that purportedly cause secularization occur. Thus if we believe that urbanization is a key consideration (either as an autonomous cause or as a surrogate for some more nebulous change with which it coincides), we should compare levels of religious vitality in societies A and B when they are equally urban. The United States did not reach until the 1920s the degree of urbanization of Britain in the 1850s. I do not want to pursue the point here, but there is a case to be made that because the onset of modernization was much later in the United States and in some European countries, its impact will be felt proportionately later. There is certainly considerable evidence that church membership and attendance is now declining in the United States (Hadaway, Marler and Chaves, 1993).

Equally importantly, as Wilson (1968) argued thirty years ago, much of American religion has become what, for the sake of brevity, we might call 'secular'. From the fundamentalist breakaway until the 1970s, American evangelicals prided themselves on having avoided the 'easy-believism', secularity, and self-interest of Norman Vincent Peale's 'power of positive thinking'. But many evangelicals now embrace the very liberal and permissive lifestyle their parents and grandparents so vehemently opposed. Asceticism is largely dead and as evangelicals have become more like everyone else in behaviour, so they have lost ideological distinctiveness. Sacrifice has gone. Heaven remains but hell is barely mentioned. Believers now feel free to select. Most significantly, there is a clear change in attitudes to the reach of religion. James Davidson Hunter's (1987) work on young evangelicals in the early 1980s shows that many accepted the requirements of the gospel for themselves but were no longer sure that they were binding on others. Unless this germ of relativism is killed off, it is hard to see what will prevent the conservative wing of American Protestantism following the mainstream churches. To his credit, Berger refers to Hunter's work and

thus uses the apparent strength of American religion in a much more nuanced way than does, for example, Jeffrey Hadden (1987).

Rather than cite a wide range of sources for the various elements of this description, I will offer a general observation of Wade Clark Roof's as support for the general assertion that the general direction of change in American religion is that predicted by Berger: 'the religious stance today is more internal than external, more individual than institutional, more experiential than cerebral, more private than public' (Roof, 1996, p. 153).

Liberal Failure

As well as offering conservative 'growth' as evidence of the general (and unexpected) vitality of religion, Berger has presented liberal decline as evidence that the secularization thesis is mistaken. 'If we really lived in a highly secularised world, then religious institutions could be expected to survive to the degree that they manage to adapt to secularism' (1997b, p. 33). This is a curious argument because it is not at all clear why adapting to secularism should mean imitating it and there is nothing about Berger's original arguments for secularization that requires such a link. Although committed to the same core ideas as Berger, I have been arguing since 1982 that liberal religion has been precarious because the tolerance and individualism at the heart of its ideology undermined the cohesion that is required for a large variety of organizational tasks that are vital to the survival of any shared belief system (Bruce, 1982, 1999). Some aspects of liberal religion (such as the unfortunate fondness for claiming aspects of secular culture as being more Christian than Christian ideas) are conscious attempts to regain relevance by aping the secular world and are doomed to failure. But the roots of its problems are not specific innovations; it is the diffuseness that permits such innovations and diffuseness is a result of secularization, not a deliberate attempt to 'adapt' to it.

Religion in 'Secular' Europe

Berger is much impressed by Grace Davie's (1994) thesis that the decline in participation in religious institutions should not be taken as a decline in religious interest *per se*. He summarizes her work thus:

> What she found is that, despite the dramatic decline in church participation and expressed orthodox beliefs, a lively religious scene exists. Much of it is very loosely organized (for instance, in private gatherings of people) and has odd do-it-yourself characteristics . . . the presence of these phenomena casts doubt on any flat assertion to the effect that Western Europe is secular territory.
>
> (1998, p. 796)

That depends. First, I am less impressed by the claims for 'private gatherings' than is Berger, Attitudinal survey data show a steady fall in orthodox Christian beliefs and even for such nebulous claims as a self-description as 'religious' (Gill, Hadaway and Marler, 1998). Second, the numbers involved in such organized religious innovations as there have been (the rise of the 'new churches', for example) are of a different order of magnitude than the losses to the mainstream churches: in thousands rather than in the millions that would be required to offset the losses. Third, for reasons I will pursue below, there are very good grounds for supposing that the 'odd do-it-yourself characteristics' will make it hard for such innovations to be sustained, reproduced or transmitted.

Religion in the Second and Third Worlds

Berger would probably not dissent much from the above; he makes relatively little of signs of religious resurgence in western Europe. What most causes him to doubt the inevitability of secularization is the evidence that 'Most of the world today is as religious as ever it was, and in a good many locales, more religious than ever' (1998, p. 782). Although I am a committed proponent of the secularization

thesis, I would have no trouble at all in endorsing the first half of that sentence. Indeed I have long argued that religion, when combined with ethnicity, remains a far more potent force than social class. One only has to consider the wars in the former Yugoslavia, Afghanistan or the Caucasus, or the rise of Islamic fundamentalism to recognize that religion is very important. Without considering the religious element, we cannot explain why some of the former Warsaw Pact countries better resisted Soviet communism than others (Bruce, 1999). However, I have some difficulty with the second half of Berger's proposition. We need to be very careful in how we describe religious change. In many parts of Latin America, a taken-for-granted Catholic culture, heavily informed by pre-Christian spirit cults, has been replaced by an increasingly secular society with very large numbers of highly committed Protestant Christians. It would seem a particularly Protestant view to describe the latter as more religious than the former. While we would describe the spread of Orthodoxy to former Russian Communist Party cadres as 'more religion', would we use the same description for an increase in frequency of church attendance by elderly peasants who had never given up their faith? I can think of many places where religious people are 'reforming', and I can think of places where the end of secularist repression has led to more and more open religious observance. But I cannot think of any major reversals in fairly thoroughly secular settings. There is no religious resurgence in Germany, Britain, the Netherlands or Denmark.

But, more importantly, I cannot understand why Berger thinks that religious vitality in the Third World has any bearing on his work on secularization. To return to the point introduced above, the secularization thesis is not a claim that the passage of time undermines religion. Rather, it is a number of related claims about the impact of certain social changes in certain circumstances. Obviously the claim that pluralism requires the state to become increasingly neutral on matters of faith refers only to democracies (or at least to polities informed by the general principle that all people are much-of-a-muchness) and to a very limited range of autocracies that have good reason to wish to avoid religious and ethnic conflict. Otherwise one gets the more common reaction to diversity, which is to murder or expel the deviants. Berger (1969c) knows this: he offers the post-Reformation wars of religion as an example of the extermination response and the 'territorial formula' of the Treaty of Westphalia that ended those wars as an example of the segregation response (pp. 48–9). Creating a climate in which alternatives can peacefully co-exist and compete on equal terms is just one of the possible responses, and it is typical only of modern liberal democracies. Berger has written about the circumstances under which he expects one aspect of modernization to weaken religion; it is hard to see why, thirty years later, he presents as evidence against his original arguments the fate of religion in quite different circumstances.

Similarly, the claim that pluralism undermines the certainty with which any group can hold its beliefs implies a number of things about the *source* of pluralism. Berger offers many observations about the differential plausibility of different sources of knowledge and information. Although I cannot recall one place where he spells this out, I have always assumed that the cognitive threat of pluralism varies in ways that can at least partly be explained by Bergeresque sociological observations about power, plausibility and authority. Berger and Luckmann (1966c) certainly provide the framework for elaborating the challenges of different sources of pluralism in their work on 'machineries of universe-maintenance' (pp. 122–46). While they are not talking specifically about religion, the following comment about the nihilation of deviant views is apposite: 'The threat to the social definitions of reality is neutralized by assigning an inferior onto-logical status, and thereby a not-to-be-taken seri-ously cognitive status, to all definitions existing outside the symbolic universe' (1966c, p. 133).

When Irish Catholics migrated to Scotland in large numbers in the late nineteenth century, Scots Presbyterians did not immediately lose confidence in their own world-view. Instead, they dismissed the religion of the Irish by creating invidious stereotypes of its carriers: they portrayed the Irish as drunken, illiterate, intemperate, compliant, slothful layabouts.

Berger and Luckmann (1966c) add that nihila-tion 'involves the more ambitious attempt to account for all deviant definitions of reality in terms of concepts belonging to one's own universe' (p. 133). Again Scottish Presbyterians can provide a fine illustration of people explaining the errors of others in a way that bolstered their own beliefs. They dealt with the fact that, taken globally, Presbyterians were a very small minority by arguing (a) that societies differed in their intellectual matu-rity and (b) that God in his kindness had revealed himself to various societies in a form which, with their limited intellects, they could comprehend. So child-like Hottentots were animists. God had shown himself to the Arabs, who were more advanced, as Allah. The southern Europeans, who were more advanced yet, had been gifted with Catholic Christianity. And God had shown himself in his full and complete revelation to the most advanced people: Scottish Presbyterians. Muslims perform a similar trick with their view that Islam is the final revelation that encompasses and supersedes the previously flawed versions of Judaism and Christianity.

The early historians who traced their own people back to Adam knew that other peoples claimed similar origins. They also knew that non-Christian civilizations had Adam-like Creation myths and Flood stories. Rather than seeing similar alternatives as casting doubt on the unique truth-fulness of their particular version, they took the popularity of such stories as proof that something like them must be true, and then asserted that their version was indeed the true undistorted one. Rather than see the Hindu trinity of Brahma, Vishnu and Shiva as evidence that trinity stories were a commonplace best explained by similarities of human imagination, Christians confronting Hinduism saw it as proof that man had a 'God-given faculty for reason [that] inclined him towards the core tenets of Christian belief [which were] . . . of course, buried in heathen culture cladding' (Kidd, 1999, p. 42).

While it is interesting to explore nihilation strategies, they do not explain their own success. It remains a sociological issue why they work at some times and not at others. It would be a mammoth task to pursue this question, and I will make only a few brief suggestions here. One point that is well elaborated in more abstract terms by Berger and Luckmann is that it is much easier to dismiss the culture of foreigners than to dismiss the religious diversity that results from fission within one's own religious tradition. The ignorance of the backward can be tolerated and forgiven. The defiance or deviancy of people 'like us' cannot as readily be neutralized.

A second point is that wealth (or other sources of high status) confers a degree of plausibility on any deviant minority. Some local magnates victimized George Fox, the Quaker founder, but many others took him into their homes and listened to him politely because he was a gentleman. As the Quakers and Methodists rose in social status, so the objections to them fell away. Partly this is a matter of power. The wealthy man has greater resources to sustain or promote his protest. Catholicism survived in parts of the north-east of Scotland because a number of powerful landed figures refused to join the Reformation and were able to protect their servants. But it is also a matter of persuasiveness; many of the invidious stereotypes used to blacken Irish labourers could not be deployed for the Quaker brewer and the Methodist manufacturer. But then wealth and high status are not always a protection; nor do they guarantee that the views of the carriers will be sympathetically heard.

But this sort of detail is secondary to the general point: Berger himself knows that the consequences of various elements of modernization differ according to circumstances. No one who understands the work of Berger (or Weber, Troeltsch, Wilson or Martin) would regard the explanation given there of what has happened in the past of some societies as being a template for the future of very different ones. In the same way that we must regard Weber's Protestant Ethic thesis as being historically specific, so we must regard the secularization thesis as being an account of the past of western Europe (and its settler society offshoots) that is only generalizable to other settings *to the extent that the specific elements are reproduced in those settings*. As Iran is unlike Essex in most regards, I see no reason why the secularization thesis should fall because the religious evolution of these places has differed.

That being said, there is one element of Berger's secularization work that is perhaps vulnerable to the criticisms of the mature Berger. And that is his exploration of the connections between technology and secularization. It has long been a staple of the secularization approach that technology undermines religion because it gives better solutions to specific problems and thus reduces the occasions for a recourse to religious explanations and offices. It also gives us an increased sense of mastery over our own affairs. To those observations about the effects of the *content* of technological advance, Berger, in association with Brigitte Berger and Hansfried Kellner (1974), added an interesting claim about the subtle psychological effects of the method of technology. Technological production assumes that every object can be reduced to a series of infinitely replaceable components: the switch for any 1996 Dimplex Model 3 radiator will fit any 1996 Dimplex Model 3 radiator. Similarly, all actions can be broken down to their essential components and endlessly repeated, each time with the same effect. Technology also supposes constant change and regular reflexive monitoring. If production processes can be improved, then they are improved. Nothing is sacred; nothing is unique. People who use modern technology cannot help but be influenced by the assumption of instrumental rationality.

This does seem to be a universal and predictive claim. If Berger, Berger and Kellner are right, as technological work spreads around the globe so it should create a more secular climate. If the nations of the Middle or Far East are able to adopt modern technology without there being some corresponding decline in religious vitality or change in the religious climate, then this specific element of the secularization approach fails, or, at the very least, requires substantial embellishment. Although the prediction may not have been met in every circumstance, it does seem to have been borne out in the general patterns identified by Ronald Inglehardt (1990; 1997). In almost every society for which data are available, economic growth and industrialization have been accompanied by a decline in commitment to the traditional religion.

If the expectation has not been met in every setting, this may mean not that the general expectation is false but that the effects of one social force are offset by another. It may well be that Berger is right about technological consciousness and hence that scientists and technicians and industrial workers in Iran, for example, were more likely to be subtly secular than village dwellers and agricultural workers. There is some evidence for such a conclusion. But such a difference may well have been overridden by the more powerful and immediate effects of the social unrest and cultural responses that the Shah's rule produced in Iran. The failure of the Shah's strategy to promote economic development by imitating the science and culture of the West combined with his repressive response to dissent to create a powerful resentment among members of the very class that was furthest from traditional Islam. Their faith might have been weakened by technological consciousness. But in their particular situation they were also alienated from what was taken to be the Western model of development by specific attacks on them as the potential carriers of democracy and by the failure of the economic

reforms to deliver results. Some at least of that class were then recruited to the radical movement and to the Islamic branch of that movement. All this tells us is that the real world is far more complicated than our models; that sociology cannot be conducted without economics, political science, geography and history.

In summary, the evidence cited by Berger does not lead me to join him in his recantation. First, I do not find the data which he offers as persuasive or compelling as he does. Second, I do not share his view of the status of the secularization approach. I have always thought that it was an historical explanation of specific changes in the religious climate of particular societies. It only has implications for other societies to the extent that the causes implicated in the original basis for the thesis are repeated elsewhere.

Theoretical Reservations

In addition to the above evidence-driven doubts, Berger also offers theoretical reasons for doubting his earlier writings, which were mostly of a functionalist nature. Talking of anomie, he wrote:

> Individuals can live in such a condition, unhappy though it is, for a long time. Societies probably cannot (though the phrase 'a long time' means something different for a society and an individual). . . . societies afflicted with widespread anomie have either perished or have regenerated themselves through a renascence of their fundamental values. For reasons that are probably rooted in the constitution of man, such renascences have usually had a powerful religious dimension.
>
> (1979b, p. 235)

He makes the same point in condemning alternative sources of meaning:

> I am impressed by the intrinsic inability of secularized world views to answer the deeper questions of the human condition, questions of

whence, whether, and why. These seem to be ineradicable and they are answered only in the most banal ways by the ersatz religions of secularism.

(1974b, p. 15)

We may accept that any major pulling together of very large numbers of people is likely to have a religious ideological base. We may accept that any grand cultural solution to the problem of anomie will be religious. However, I am not persuaded that 'needs' must always be met. People need food but die of starvation. We may need cultural consensus and fail to achieve it. Indeed Berger's own observations about the deleterious effects of pluralization would suggest that we can yearn all we like but still be unable to reverse the changes that undermine the plausibility of religious belief systems. When applied to abstractions such as social systems, the functionalist language of needs is even more unconvincing. Functionalist biology works because we know what counts as liver failure: the person turns yellow and dies. System failure allows us to work back to the 'needs' of the organism. It is difficult to reason in the same way from societies. Although Berger uses the term 'perish', this is metaphorical. Societies constantly change. Some changes are more dramatic than others but at what point do we pronounce one incarnation 'dead' and christen the new one? If we cannot translate the metaphor into a technically viable concept, then the functionalist claims become untestable.

Although it does not necessarily lead to the conclusion that severe social problems will inevitably call forth a religious revival, there is a more moderate form of the functionalist claim that is implied in the grander version. We could argue (and hope to demonstrate) that religious societies are 'healthier' than non-religious ones. There is a considerable empirical literature that tries to test such claims and the best that can be said at present is that the case is not proven. It would certainly be hard to assert that the United States, with its higher rates of church adherence, shows fewer marks of social disorganization or lower indices of deviance than the United Kingdom or the Netherlands or Sweden. But, even if there were bodies of convincing evidence that getting right with Jesus would make us as individuals happier and make our societies more pleasant, it does not follow that a religious revival will occur. The obstacles to such a response are obvious. Berger, like the rest of us, recognizes that one of the master features of modern societies is individual autonomy. This could be spelt out in more detail, but I am sure few will dissent from the view that modern societies are unusual not only in the degree of freedom of action they permit their citizens in private, but also in the extent to which they permit freedom of thought.

We long ago accepted that in matters of art and music appreciation, for example, authoritative judgements were impossible (and offensive because they are 'undemocratic'). 'I may not know much about art but I know what I like' used to be a sentiment imputed by the *cognoscenti* to the lower middle and working classes as an insult. Now it is a basic operating procedure. Even in fields of knowledge such as science and medicine, where most thoughtful people would insist that there is truth and there is falsehood, we are reluctant to insist that this or that view is just plain stupid. In matters of religion, personal preference has long dominated the mainstream churches and, as I have suggested above, is now becoming common even in churches that fifty years ago prided themselves on requiring subscription to an orthodoxy. And it is even more the case for those outside and on the fringes of the main religious traditions. A respondent in a study of New Age religion put it bluntly when he said: 'I have a problem with a lot of mainstream religion, because they're fucking with other people's business' (Bloch, 1998, p. 295). Although no wise man says 'never', it is remarkably difficult to see what circumstances will causes Westerners to give up their freedom to differ or agree to narrow the range of areas in which differences of taste are legitimate.

Or to put it more practically, politicians and lay people are keen to insist that social evils be eradicated by everyone else getting back to *their* basics; we hear very few voices willing to give up their preferences in order to support someone else's programme. To return to Berger, even if he is right to identify some social problems that could be resolved with a religious renascence, the pluralism which he did so much to bring to our attention prevents the mobilization of a common response to those problems.

THE FUTURE OF LIBERAL RELIGION

I have taken Berger's reservations about the secularization thesis and his revisions at their strongest. Yet it is clear that Berger remains committed to one of his original observations: the role that pluralism plays in undermining certainty. For example, in 1998, he wrote: 'whether we like it or not, if we are honest, religion for us cannot be based on knowledge, only on belief. The question is how we cope with this situation. Can we live with it?' (p. 782).

The crux of the matter can be put either in terms of belief systems or in terms of forms of association. This simplifies, but we can describe some belief systems as 'strong' and others as 'weak' or 'diffuse'. I should stress (because it is misunderstood) that this is a sociological consideration and involves no suggestion that strong beliefs are better than weak ones or that 'true religion' must be 'strong'. The strong-weak characterization was popularized by Dean Kelley in his explanation of *Why the Conservative Churches are Growing* (1972). In Hoge's (1979) summary:

> Strong churches are characterized by a demand for high commitment from their members. They exact discipline over both beliefs and lifestyle. They have missionary zeal with an eagerness to tell the good news to all persons. They are absolutistic about

beliefs. Their beliefs are a total closed system, sufficient for all purposes, needing no revision and permitting none. They require conformity in lifestyle, often involving certain avoidances of non-members or use of distinctive visible marks or uniforms.

(p. 179)

The behavioural characteristics in the first four sentences and the last sentence follow from the characteristics of the beliefs given in the fifth sentence. In order to be strict and maintain zeal, believers must view their beliefs as authoritative. If one permits that there are a variety of sources of truth and a variety of equally legitimate sources of interpretation, then one inevitably has diversity and a tolerant attitude to those who differ.

Allowing for some slippage, we can describe conservative Catholicism and evangelical or fundamentalist Protestantism as 'strong' and the liberal variants of Christianity as 'weak'. Elsewhere I have explored the problems of strong religion (Bruce, 1999), and will only say here that the sacrifices it requires (primarily of social isolation and the forgoing of individual liberty) seem willingly made by large numbers only in circumstances that are relatively rare in the West: for example, where the believers are geographically isolated or otherwise already excluded from the social mainstream. But we can let that pass because what is at issue in Berger's revision is the future of liberal religion. He believes that it is possible for people to sustain a loose and amorphous faith that accepts uncertainty. I disagree.

My empirical grounds for disagreeing are simply that secularization seems to have had the greatest impact, as Berger notes, on religions that are denominational rather than sectarian. In the United Kingdom, for example, the rare incidents of net growth or stability are to be found among the sects; the mainstream churches have been declining for fifty years and continue to do so. In 1979, about 12 per cent of the English attended church. In 1989 the figure was 10 per cent. In 1999, it was just under 8 per cent (Brierley, 1999).

My theoretical grounds are extensive (see Bruce, 1999). But the basic disagreements can be readily conveyed. First, I believe Berger exaggerates the stability of liberal Christianity because he fails to appreciate the extent to which its cohesion is an historical contingency. The essential diffuseness of liberal religion is a constant: as soon as one permits that the truth can take a variety of forms, the epistemological basis for discipline is removed and proliferation of permissible interpretations is possible. However, the degree of cohesion in liberal religion is variable, and currently mainstream churches retain some coherence from their more orthodox past. All the major denominations began life as churches or sects. This is often repeated in the biographies of individuals. Most of those responsible for the development of liberal Protestantism, either as an intellectual force or in its organizational form in the ecumenical movement, were raised in conservative homes. They found it possible to be undogmatic about their faith because they had been thoroughly socialized in the dogmas. The problem is that this cultural capital, like the invested financial capital that provides a very large part of the funds for the liberal denominations, is a wasting asset. With each generation that passes, commitment to the core beliefs (and even knowledge of them) becomes weaker and weaker.

A further sense in which denominational Christianity is precarious is that much of its appeal rested on a contrast with sectarian Christianity. Many liberals of Berger's generation were attracted to their present faith because it was a liberation from the stifling orthodoxies of their upbringing. So long as sectarian religion was popular the liberal alternative had a pool from which it could recruit. An open prison seems like a welcome release to someone who transfers from a high security prison. But for the ever-increasing number of people who have not been socialized in a sectarian version of the Christian faith, the liberal version has very little appeal.

Finally, I would like to mention reproduction. Crucial to the fate of liberal, diffuse, denominational religion is success in transmitting it to the next generation. Let us put the problem in a contrast of two imaginary couples. The liberal Protestant, because he does not have a hard line between the saved and the unregenerate, marries a non-practising Jew. He continues in his faith but what does that couple transmit to its children? How can they insist that the children go regularly to Sunday school, read their Bibles every night, and have family prayers before meals? If their children develop any interest in religion at all, it is likely to be the autonomous open seeking perspective of those who end up creating their own mixture from a wide variety of religious traditions. Now imagine an evangelical Baptist. He spends a lot of time in church-related activities and marries another evangelical Baptist. They send their children to an independent Christian school, have family prayers and Bible studies, and intensively socialize their children in their faith. Of three children one may fall away, but there is a good chance that at least one of the other two will continue in that faith.

This, then, is the core of my disagreement with Berger's view of liberal religion. He believes that its appeal will allow it to survive the organizational problems inherent in having a diffuse belief-system. I think not. If there is no reversal in membership trends that have been stable for fifty years, British Methodism will disappear entirely around 2030. If we wish to identify a model in our days of what religion beyond the sects will look like in fifty years' time, we should look not at the liberal Christian denominations, which are doomed, but at the world of New Age spirituality: a world in which individuals select from a global cafeteria ideas, rituals and therapies that appeal to them. Precisely because they are so thoroughly individualized, such beliefs will have very little impact even on those who carry them – let alone on their wider societies.

CONCLUSION

Had I thought that Berger was offering some universal template for social evolution, I would never have been attracted by his arguments. Had I thought that he was arguing that secularization was inevitable, I would not have become a disciple. I take the early Berger to be arguing the following: insofar as anything in this life is certain, it is that secularization of a certain type and extent is *irreversible* because the conditions required to construct, sustain, and reproduce across generations a shared supernatural world-view are destroyed by individualism and pluralism. I see nothing in the First World to make me believe that he needs to recant. Far from getting them wrong, the changes since 1960 have been those Berger predicted: increased individual autonomy; increased compartmentalization, decline of authority, and declining indices of involvement. Whether the societies of the Second and Third Worlds will evolve in the same direction is a fascinating question. Inglehart's massive cross-national surveys (1990; 1997) suggest a strong and almost universal connection between increasing prosperity and a decline in commitment to religious orthodoxies. But in any case what happens in Africa or Asia, though it is important for illuminating the conditions for secularization, does not bear critically on the value of the secularization thesis for explaining what happened in the rise of the first generation of modern industrial societies.

7

Selections from "Bringing the Sacred to Life: Explaining Sacralization and Secularization"

Paul Heelas and Linda Woodhead

Become what you are! (Friedrich Nietzsche, 1981, p. 252)

I am a part of all that I have met. (Alfred Lord Tennyson, 'Ulysses')

'Personal experience' constitutes 'personality'. (Max Weber, in Gerth and Mills, 1997, p. 137)

For many people today, to set aside their own path in order to conform to some external authority just doesn't seem comprehensible as a form of spiritual life. (Charles Taylor, 2002, p. 101)

Contemporary quests for spirituality are really yearnings for a reconstructed interior life. (Wade Clark Roof, 1999, p. 35)

W E HAVE SEEN THAT THERE is a connection between the associational activities of subjective-life spirituality and growth on the one hand, and the associational activities of life-as religion and overall decline on the other. But why should the numbers involved in the holistic milieu be growing whilst the total number involved in the congregational domain is declining? In this chapter we offer the 'subjectivization thesis' as an explanation of the co-existence of secularization and sacralization in the contemporary sacred landscape. After a brief introduction to the thesis, we use it first to explain the growth of the holistic milieu, then the decline of the congregational domain. Our aim is

not only to illuminate the evidence by way of the theory, but to test the theory by way of the evidence. As we do so we refine the thesis in order to take account of some of the most striking features of the contemporary sacred landscape, including the crucial role played by gender. Above all, we argue that by way of this single theory it is possible to make sense of apparently contradictory trends – towards growth in some forms of associational activity oriented towards the sacred, and decline in others.

THE SUBJECTIVIZATION THESIS

In a nutshell, the subjectivization thesis states that 'the massive subjective turn of modern culture' favours and reinforces those (subjective-life) forms of spirituality which resource unique subjectivities and treat them as a primary source of significance, and undermines those (life-as) forms of religion which do not. In other words, the thesis explains the varied fortunes of different forms of religion and spirituality today by reference to a single process – the widespread cultural shift in emphasis from the value ascribed to life-as to the value ascribed to subjective-life. This does not, however, imply that the subjective turn will necessarily encourage people to stay (or become) involved in associational forms of religion or spirituality – merely that *if* they are (or do), their involvement is more likely to be with those which cultivate subjective-life than those which prioritize life-as beliefs and values.

Underlying the subjectivization thesis is the Durkheimian principle that people are more likely to be involved with forms of the sacred which are 'consistent with their ongoing values and beliefs' – as Joseph Tamney (2002, p. 227) puts it – than with those which are not. In a society in which life-as roles are central, one can therefore expect to find forms of life-as religion which reinforce and legitimate those roles, and support and resource people in living life in terms of them, to be doing better than those forms of spirituality which undermine or ignore such roles. (For example, in highly stratified, hierarchical societies charismatic forms of spirituality with egalitarian tendencies are unlikely to become mainstream.) Conversely, when the cultivation of unique subjective-lives has greater cultural priority in society, then those forms of spirituality which cater for subjective-life tasks – offering individuals a sense of harmony and serenity, for example – are likely to fare much better. This is not to imply that religion is merely an epiphenomenon of culture, nor to deny that there can be 'prophetic' forms of religion and spirituality which challenge prevailing cultural values. It is merely to suggest that the latter will be marginal rather than dominant in the sacred landscape of their time.

When we apply the general Durkheimian principle to a society characterized by the subjective turn, we can see that it is reasonable to expect that the greater the number of those who prioritize subjective-life as their source of significance, the greater the likelihood that forms of the sacred which work for them will grow. Conversely, the smaller the pool of people who prioritize life-as as their primary source of significance, the greater the likelihood that forms of the sacred which work for them will decline.[1]

The evidence which undergirds the claim that there has been a massive turn to subjective-life in contemporary Western societies is weighty. Ronald Inglehart's analysis of successive rounds of value surveys shows that the number of 'post-materialists' has been growing steadily, both in absolute terms and relative to the number of 'materialists'. The latter are those whose prime concern is with obtaining the material necessities and securities of life, whilst the former are those who value self-expression and are intent on 'maximizing subjective well-being' (1997, p. 36). 'In 1970–71', writes Inglehart,

> Materialists held an overwhelming numerical preponderance over postmaterialists, outnumbering them by nearly four to one, By 1990, the balance had shifted dramatically, to a point where materialists outnumbered postmaterialists by only four to three. Projections . . . suggest that by the year 2000 materialists and postmaterialists will be about equally numerous in many Western countries' (1997, p. 35).

A growing body of literature exploring various aspects of the subjective turn supports Inglehart's findings. Charles Taylor's work has already been mentioned. Other influential studies include Robert Bellah et al's *Habits of the Heart* (1985), Anthony Giddens's *The Transformation of Intimacy* (1993), Martin Gross's *The Psychological Society* (1979), Philip Rieff's *The Triumph of the Therapeutic* (1987), Richard Sennett's *The Fall of Public Man* (1977), Joseph Veroff et al's *The Inner American* (1981), and Daniel Yankelovich's *New Rules* (1981). None of this literature suggests that the subjective turn has affected the whole of Western culture, nor that all Westerners now subscribe to subjective-life values. The suggestion is rather that the turn is becoming increasingly influential and thereby placing life-as values increasingly on the defensive.

As we have suggested previously in the volume, the subjective turn is bound up with the development of a wide array of provisions and activities. To give just a few examples, the 'disciplined' family of traditional values has increasingly been replaced by the expressive family of emotional bonds. The hierarchical command structure of the old-style business, where everyone has their place, now has to compete with flatter, more fluid and individual-worker-centred systems, and with business cultures which promise to 'bring life back to work' and encourage people to 'grow' in their 'learning environments' by way of a self-work ethic (work which enables one to 'work' on oneself). Similarly, educational provisions have shifted in emphasis from authoritative teaching of the facts of the matter to 'bringing out' the abilities of the child. Personal, relational life now has less to do with belonging to a specific, ordered community, and more to do with developing an array of interactions which serve to cater for different aspects of subjective-life concern. Voluntary associations, which have grown since the 1950s in Britain, show a distinct shift from those run along life-as lines (traditional women's organizations and trade unions are in decline) to those of a more 'quality of subjective-life' variety (support groups and preschool play groups are growing). Nursing and caring staff are encouraged to pay as much attention as possible to the quality of life of their patients (in rehabilitation wards for the elderly, for example). Complementary and alternative medicine, which includes emphasis on the importance of the healing of feelings, grows in significance annually, as do hospices in which the subjective lives of the terminally ill and their family become the focus of attention and care. Similarly, the number of counsellors, therapists and (most recently) 'life trainers' has expanded significantly since the 1960s.[2]

One can also cite the growing cultural prominence of provisions which enable people to reflect on private or subjective-life. For example, daytime TV shows probe life-issues; *Big Brother* and other reality TV shows display people's lives; biographies and autobiographies increasingly take the form of what Virginia Woolf called 'life-writing' or 'the writing of

the self'; books and articles devoted to matters of psychology and self-help proliferate; even the weather forecast ceases to be an authoritatively intoned summary of meteorological 'facts' and becomes the weather-with-feeling. In the realm of advertising, the trend is also towards the personalized: the presentation of variety to cater for individual tastes, and the appeal to the life-enhancing. And last, but by no means least, there is the role played by what might be called 'the ethic of subjectivity', which is evident in the value attached to self-expression and fulfilment; to doing 'what feels right', 'following your heart', 'being true to yourself, cultivating 'emotional intelligence' and respecting other people's feelings. Very telling in this regard is the value which has come to be attributed to 'feeling', and being 'comfortable' (as in 'how do you feel about that?' and 'are you comfortable with this decision?').

Though many more examples could be given of how cultural provisions and activities have become more person-centred and subjectivity-centred, this should suffice to give an indication of the cultural significance of the subjective turn. It is not our intention to evaluate this turn, nor to decide whether it is really as liberating as many feel it to be. No doubt many institutions that embrace the turn have developed sophisticated new methods of control and regulation, including accountability systems, inspections, mentoring, job descriptions and performance-related pay. No doubt the subjective turn flourishes, in part, because it proves compatible with the demands of late capitalism (for flexibility of labour, individual entrepreneurship, 'expressive' consumption and so on) (Rose, 1999). But important though they may be, none of these considerations alters the fact that very significant cultural value has come to be ascribed to being treated as a uniquely valuable person, finding out about oneself, expressing oneself, discovering one's own way of becoming all that one can (reasonably) be – themes, we shall shortly see, which are central to the most widespread cultural expression of the turn to date, namely subjective wellbeing culture.

Meanwhile, the idea of denying or sacrificing oneself for the sake of a supra-self order of things, or even of living by reference to such an order, becomes culturally marginal. Deference to 'higher authority' could hardly be said to be at the forefront of recent cultural change.

It can safely be concluded that the subjective turn, from life as 'expected', 'given' and 'laid down' to the interior experiences of subjective-life, is of considerable significance. Given the Durkheimian principle, we would expect the realm of associational activities focused on the sacred to be affected accordingly, with the subjective-life activities of the holistic milieu growing *because* they cater for the subjective turn of the culture, and the life-as activities of the congregational domain declining *because* they do not cater for the turn to subjective-life. As we have seen in previous chapters, this expectation seems to be fulfilled insofar as we have detected a pattern whereby those forms of the sacred which cater for the cultivation of unique subjective-life are faring better than those which do not. What we hope to demonstrate in this chapter is that this pattern is not a mere coincidence, but that it is their ability or inability to cater for the subjective turn which is a key *cause* of the growth or decline of those different forms of associational activity orientated towards the sacred.

It could, of course, be objected that the subjectivization pattern is a mere coincidence, and that secularization and sacralization in the contemporary sacred landscape should therefore be explained by other factors. For example, it might be argued that people are leaving the churches because they have lost their faith rather than because their subjective-lives are not being catered for. In order to strengthen the case for the subjectivization thesis we must therefore appeal to independent evidence that the subjective turn is indeed operative. We must show that an important reason for the growth of the holistic milieu is that it *in fact* caters for people who identify with the cultural turn, and that an important reason for the decline of the

congregational domain is that selves valuing subjective-life as a source of significance have *in fact* stopped attending.

Not that we wish to suggest that the subjectivization thesis could ever bear the burden of explaining sacralization and secularization *in toto*. It would be unrealistic to imagine that there could be any single cause of such massive and complex phenomena. We are proposing the subjectivization factor only as one explanation amongst others in relation to religious and spiritual decline or growth, and we would expect to bolt on other, complementary, factors as and when the evidence suggested that was appropriate. However, since we find a good deal of evidence to support the subjectivization thesis, and little that counts against it, we have considerable confidence in its value. If not the only key to explaining change, it certainly invokes a dynamic that should not be ignored.

REVISITING THE SUBJECTIVIZATION THESIS: THE GROWTH OF THE HOLISTIC MILIEU AND THE SIGNIFICANCE OF GENDER AND AGE

The Gender Puzzle

According to our questionnaire survey, 80 per cent of those active in the holistic milieu of Kendal and environs are female; 78 per cent of groups are led or facilitated by women; 80 per cent of one-to-one practitioners are women.[3] The conclusion is obvious: much of the growth of associational, holistic spiritualities of life is due to the fact that women have decided to participate. Why should this be the case?

We are immediately faced with a puzzle. We have been arguing that the subjective turn plays a key role in explaining the growth of the holistic milieu. Most generally, the subjective turn involves the turn to what Dick Houtman and Peter Mascini (2002) call 'moral individualism' – namely 'the granting of a moral primacy to individual liberty' (p. 459). The person serves as the locus of moral authority, with value being attached to staying true to oneself rather than succumbing to outside agency. However, as Houtman and Mascini also say, 'We know of no research demonstrating gender differences with respect to [moral] individualism' (p. 464).[4] Hence our puzzle – if indeed the gender ratio is 50:50 among subjectivized selves as gauged by moral autonomy, how are we to explain the fact that the ratio of the holistic milieu is 80:20 in favour of women?

Revisiting the Subjectivization Thesis

The answer must lie with the fact that the subjective turn involves not one but two modes of moral individualism or autonomous selfhood. One is more characteristic of men, which means they are not likely to be attracted to the associational activities of subjective wellbeing culture in general or the holistic milieu in particular. The other largely involves women, which means they are much more likely to be attracted to these spheres. Though the subjective turn is so often discussed as a single and undifferentiated process, we must therefore revisit and refine it in the light of our empirial findings.

Most comprehensively, and by definition, the subjective turn is the turn to the autonomous self. It is a turn away from being told what or how to be yourself to *having the freedom to be yourself*. To be, or become, oneself obviously entails that one assumes – by way of culture and/or experience – that one *has* a self to be and become; you cannot be autonomous without having what Lionel Trilling (1974) refers to as the 'internal space' from which to act (p. 24). Since the autonomous self cannot be a life-as self, it must be based not on external obligation but on what one 'is' – one's own unique subjective-life. So one acts on the basis of an intuition that all is not well with a situation, or on the inner promptings of one's conscience, or the realization that a relationship is having a negative effect on one's sense of

wellbeing, the sense one gets that another person is in distress, and so on.

But the direction that subjective-life may take as it extends out beyond its autonomous basis can vary. Our findings suggest that this variation can be thought of in terms of a spectrum between two poles. At one extreme lies what we will call *individuated subjectivism* and at the other *relational subjectivism*, with many intermediate positions in between. Every person who tries to live by the authority of subjective-life rather than, or together with, external guidance or dictation can be located somewhere along this spectrum.

The position of the individuated subjectivist is well described by Clifford Geertz (1984) when he writes of 'The Western conception of the person as a bounded, unique, more or less integrated motivational and cognitive universe, a dynamic center of awareness, emotion, judgement, and action organized into a distinctive whole and set contrastively both against other such wholes and against its social and natural background' (p. 126). At this end of the spectrum of the subjective turn, the 'voice of the unique' lies with the experience of the self operating as a (relatively) self-contained entity. Typically, subjective-life is catered for by going outside oneself to find external solutions, rather than by going deeper into one's inner life. The quality of subjective-life is enhanced by addressing the problem of not feeling successful enough, of not having enough pleasurable experiences, of not having achieved all one might achieve, and so on. Subjectivities are catered for by going out into the world to procure the commodities (a new house) or success (promotion) which serve desire, happiness or contentment. (Bellah et al. (1985), in the footsteps of Durkheim, refer to this position as 'utilitarian individualism'.) The emphasis is on subjective-life developed by way of atomized (self-reliant, self-sufficient) agency, on the self as unique and distinct. Competition is likely to be a more important theme than the connections of personal relationships, and there are obvious links between this mode of selfhood, possessive individualism, and entrepreneurial capitalism.

At the other end of the spectrum the subjective turn takes a relational mode. The commitment to autonomous subjective-life and the cultivation of the unique remains, but with an emphasis on the relational and going deeper. Steven Lukes (1973) writes that 'The very idea of *self*-development logically implies that the development is autonomously pursued – though clearly its course can be *substantially assisted* by providing the appropriate conditions and encouragements' (p. 136; our emphasis). Although the point is often neglected in the literature on the subjective turn, as is indicated by the fact that the term 'expressive *individualism*' is often used in this connection (see, for example, Bellah et al., 1985), Lukes reminds us that other people can have an important role to play. One can, of course, seek to cultivate one's subjective-life by oneself. Hermits aside, though, it is surely the case that the cultivation of subjective-life best takes place in the context of personal encounters: 'talking things through' with a friend; visiting a therapist, counsellor or human resource specialist; reading biographies or autobiographies; viewing close relationships on TV; reflecting on one's relationship with one's children or parents; discussing bad or good personality qualities with pupils at primary school, and so on. And unlike individuated (let alone life-as) modes of subjective-life, relational subjectivism is associated with the tendency to *go deeper*, one finds out more about oneself by discussing one's anger with a close friend or by dealing with jealousy with a lover, for example. Finally, it must be emphasized that the relational mode of subjective-life selfhood need *not* imply a diminution of the unique, autonomy or moral individualism. Since no one person has the same relationships as another, the more variegated the relational life the, more unique the 'me' becomes – with the 'voice of the unique' speaking accordingly. Recalling the words of Carson McCullers, cited at the end of the Introduction to this volume, relational subjectivity is all about 'the

we of me' – developing one's own subjective-life, be/coming oneself, relating to one's life, *through* one's relationships. In this context interdependence goes together with independence.[5]

Previously in this volume we have tended to refer to what Charles Taylor (1991) calls 'the massive subjective turn of modern culture' (p. 26) in its most general sense, as having to do with the turn to autonomy and the subjective-life which is thereby entailed. Prompted by our research findings and the gender puzzle, we must now nuance this usage more precisely. Taylor completes the sentence above by speaking of the subjective turn as being towards 'a new form of inwardness, in which we come to think of ourselves as beings with inner depths' (p. 26). Without disagreeing, we note that the subjective turn *can* go all the way to such 'depths' (typically involving, we would argue, relational subjectivism), *or* remain at the level of a more individuated and externally orientated form of subjectivism (often dismissive of the deeper subjective turn). By broadening out our understanding of the turn in this way, we have therefore distinguished between two modes or aspects of autonomous personhood: individuated subjectivism, where the strong tendency is to be externally orientated, seeking indirect solutions (material, etc.) to cater for subjective-life, and relational subjectivism, where the tendency is towards concentrating more directly on the exploration of the intricacies of the inner life. And as we shall now see, this distinction enables us to tackle tile gender puzzle.

Relationality

Given that both women and men are equally subjectivized in the general autonomous/moral individualism sense, we have to explain why women are more likely than men to be attracted to the holistic milieu and subjective wellbeing culture. So let us apply our distinction – between relational and individuated forms of subjective-life – to the puzzle of explaining why more women than men are attracted to subjective wellbeing culture and the holistic milieu. The key to solving the puzzle is that more women than men tend to emphasize relational subjective-life, and conversely that more men than women tend to emphasize the individuated or distinct variant. Accordingly, since subjective wellbeing culture and the holistic milieu is so relational, their provisions or activities attract subjectively orientated women (in particular) who seek to develop their subjective-lives through associational encounters. And since much of subjective wellbeing culture and the holistic milieu *in toto* emphasize 'inner' relationality, their provisions or activities are considerably less likely to appeal to those men (in particular) who seek to develop their subjective-lives by going out into the world to achieve and compete whilst retaining their own boundaries and sense of being in control. Hence the high percentage of women in the milieu.

In order to substantiate these points in greater detail, the first thing to re-emphasize is the strongly relational nature of the holistic milieu. In answer to the (single response) question 'Which of the following is the best description of your core beliefs about spirituality?', 21 per cent of respondents to the holistic milieu questionnaire used in the Kendal Project answered 'Spirituality is being a decent and caring person'; 20 per cent 'Spirituality is love'; and 10 per cent 'Spirituality is healing oneself and others'. In other words, over half associate spirituality with relationality. What is more, in response to another question ('Do you believe in any of the following?'), 82 per cent expressed belief in 'some sort of spirit or life force that pervades all that lives'. Recalling Chapter One, it is also clear that practitioners in the holistic milieu of Kendal and environs – and no doubt elsewhere – are very much concerned with developing close, *reciprocal*, egalitarian, trusting, holistic relationships with their participants. What matters is intimate disclosure, the encounters of what Giddens (1992) calls the 'pure relationship'. What matters is growing oneself through the experiences of associational activities.

Whether it be practitioners, one-to-one or group participants, the important thing is to share, express, care and to go beyond the 'the distinct' as that is marked out by life-as roles, rules and conventions. The spiritual dimension is (basically) understood as the dimension at which all life connects, and where the individual realizes her or his true nature in relationship with the 'whole'.[6]

Granted that the milieu is strongly relational, what is the evidence to support our argument that this is a key factor in explaining the predominance of women? More exactly, what is the evidence that more women than men seek to develop their subjective-lives through relationships – and so are more likely to turn to relational, holistic milieu activities? An important source of evidence is provided by subjective wellbeing culture. Many more women than men are active in this culture, with many encountering provisions, or participating in activities, of a relational kind. Of particular note, significantly more women than men are active in person-centred occupations where subjective wellbeing values are important – nursing, caring, primary school teaching and human resource development, for example. Research carried out by Thomas, Nicholl and Coleman (2001) on associational CAM activities shows that the female-male ratio is 60:40 in favour of women (with over 70 per cent of 'over the counter' sales being to women). (See also Wootton and Sparber, 2001.) Jackie Stacey (2000) reports that 67 per cent of those purchasing 'healing and self-improvement/awareness' literature are women (p. 117). Debra Gimlin, in her *Body Work. Beauty and Self-Image in American Culture* (2002) finds women to be preponderant, with (for instance) 90 per cent of both students and instructors of aerobics being female (p. 51). In their study of the beauty salon, Ursula Sharma and Paula Black (1999) find women – for there are virtually no men – to be adopting an increasingly 'therapeutic' dimension, encounters within the salon providing the opportunity for discussing personal issues, especially relationships. Our own relatively informal research indicates that women outnumber men in fitness and health centres, and that very few men indeed are to be found in holistic spas. Likewise, content analysis indicates that there are vastly more articles in magazines and newspapers dwelling on subjective wellbeing for women than on subjective wellbeing for men. More generally, Paul Ray and Sherry Anderson (2000) report that there are twice as many women as men amongst the 24 million 'core cultural creatives' (people greatly concerned with quality of life issues) in the USA, with 91 per cent of core cultural creatives affirming that 'helping other people' is 'very or extremely important' and 89 per cent believing that 'every person has a unique gift to offer' (p. 15).

Cutting a long story short, what we find is that whether we look at person-centred occupations, CAM, those health and fitness activities which involve self-expression (as provided by Fitness First, for example), or the literature which encourages self-development through 'relational' activities like gardening, cooking or interior design, those active in subjective well-being culture are by no means unfamiliar with 'the we of me'. And since those attaching importance to the relational path to experiential wellbeing are predominantly women, it makes perfect sense that those who turn to the associational activities of the holistic milieu are also predominantly women. Conversely, it makes equal sense to conclude that an important reason why significantly fewer men are active in the milieu is that fewer are accustomed to, or value, the intimate, expressive, relational path to subjective well-being – indeed, that many are threatened by what an interconnected 'we' might do to the 'me' as a (relatively) protected, guarded, bounded, private entity. In the words of Calvin Mercer and Thomas Durham (1999), 'people with a masculine orientation are too agentic, self-differentiating, and analytical to become engulfed in the mystical experience' (p. 180).[7]

Having established that more women than men are involved with subjective wellbeing culture,

and so are more likely to come across, and be attracted by, holistic milieu activities, we might leave it at that. But that still leaves open the fascinating question of *why* this should be: why women should be more likely to fall at the relational end of the spectrum of subjectivism than the individuated end, and hence be more attracted to subjective wellbeing culture, and the holistic milieu, in greater numbers than men (thus contributing substantially to the growth of the milieu). Without attempting to give anything like a full response to this question, we can identify some key considerations.

Most have to do with deeply entrenched cultural values and divisions of labour. On the basis of what must surely be the most comprehensive review of relevant large-scale surveys to date, Geert Hofstede (2001) concludes that 'almost universally women attach more importance to social goals such as relationships, helping others, and the physical environment, and men attach more importance to ego goals such as career and money' (p. 279). On the basis of their survey carried out in the USA, Joseph Veroff et al. (1981) find that 'women orient their behavior and self-definition toward other people more than men do' (p. 128), and note that 'more men than women give positive differentiations of the self from other people' (p. 125) and that women 'hold more internal aspirations for identity' (p. 127); and Francesca Cancian (1987) writes of the 'opposition of masculine freedom to develop oneself vs. feminine attachment to others' (p. 6), continuing, 'women are expected to be responsible for close relationships, and men to be independent and preoccupied with work' (pp. 10–11). Citing Carol Gilligan's (1982) research on the psychological development of men and women, she agrees that from the male cultural perspective, 'development itself comes to be identified with separation, and attachments appear to be developmental impediments', and that 'Women emphasize attachment in their personal development' (p. 5).[8]

Subjective wellbeing culture aside, women continue to have prime responsibility for the subjective wellbeing of others, whether close family and friends or those with whom they interact in voluntary or paid work. As noted above, they still outnumber men in the 'caring' professions. Even when care for subjective wellbeing is not part of the 'job description', women may still find themselves taking responsibility for this, as Rosemary Pringle (1989) finds in the case of secretaries, Lisa Adkins (1995) for women in the tourist industry, Arlie Hochschild (1983) for air hostesses, and Margaretha Järvinen (1993) for women in the sex industry, In the home women continue to have more responsibility for childcare than men, whether they are full-time mothers or working mothers. Julia Brannen and Peter Moss's (1991) study of 250 dual-earner households after the birth of a first child finds that it is women rather than men who become the 'managers' of the new lifestyle and take prime responsibility for childcare. Similarly, Hochschild's (1989) study of dual-earner parents in the USA found that domestic work was shared in only 18 per cent of households, and that 'most women still did most of the work' (p. 20). Women also take more responsibility for the subjective wellbeing of their spouse and other close kin. Husbands aside, Christine Delphy and Diana Leonard (1992) find that more than 1 in 10 adult women in Britain have someone other than a child who 'depends on them for some sort of care', and that the number rises for women over 40 (pp. 228–36). Micaela di Leonardo (1987) explores how women also take responsibility for maintaining kin relationships between households by way of 'the conception, maintenance and ritual celebration of ties, including visits, letters, telephone calls, presents and cards to kin; the organisation of holiday gatherings; the creation of quasi-kin relationships . . . the mental reflection on all these activities' (pp. 442–3). Robert Putnam (2000) supplies quantitative evidence to support these observations, adding that 'Although American boys and girls in the 1990s used computers almost equally, boys were more likely to use them to play games; girls more to email friends' (p. 95).

It is not simply that women find themselves with primary responsibility for the wellbeing of those close to them, but that they tend to take responsibility for care of the *whole* person — body, mind and sometimes spirit. In some workplaces, this is becoming more formalized and recognized, as in schools and hospitals (see Chapter Three pp. 71–2), but in general women's primary responsibility of care for mind and body is culturally expected, even though it is given little cultural validation (Hochschild, 2003). As Dorothy Smith (1974) puts it in her famous essay on why male academics are more able than women to cultivate 'disembodied reason', men characteristically spend far less time caring for 'the particularities of persons in their full organic immediacy' (p. 66). Women are more likely to spend time looking after the bodies of children and other dependents, cooking in order to nourish bodies, and cleaning, purchasing and sprucing in order to turn 'houses into homes' (Delphy and Leonard, 1992). Where mind and spirit are concerned, women also undertake a majority of what Hochschild (1983) calls the 'emotional labour' required to maintain subjective wellbeing, whether in comforting children, supporting and chatting with friends, or flattering men and making them feel (sexually) good about themselves. Sally Cline and Dale Spender (1988) find that even in conversation women spend more time 'feeding' the interchange, especially when they are talking to men.

Given that more women than men are concerned with the *personal* subjective wellbeing of others in their everyday lives, it is not surprising to find that they are more likely to enter subjective wellbeing culture and/or the holistic milieu. Quite simply, subjective wellbeing culture caters for those who already value being caring and expressive, being a person through reciprocal relationships, who appreciate the value of improving the quality of subjective-life – rather than concentrating on improving the quality of life by way of autonomous, individuated and competitive agency in the world.

Going Deeper

Thus far our exploration of the 'gender puzzle' has worked from the most specific (the holistic milieu), through subjective wellbeing culture, to the most general (the culture at large). It is time to reverse the order, to trace paths from the most general into the milieu.

Consider a young woman leaving school to start a career in a person-centred job like nursing. Even if she is no longer motivated by Christian teachings about women's 'calling' to care for others (as many nurses once were), she is likely to be already embedded in personal relationships as a key source of significance – at home (perhaps helping her mother care for other members of the family), at school (Collins, 1997) and during leisure time, with all that that entails with regard to the value of going 'deeper' into friendships. Being primed in this way to value the care of others, she may view nursing as an attractive option because of the opportunities it offers for 'whole person care'. But as the years roll by, disillusionment may set in. The mission statement of the ward might be about 'wellbeing', but the reality of the ward is that there is simply not enough time to talk with patients about their subjective wellbeing concerns. The 'iron cage' of bureaucracy and targets dominates life. So what can be done to 'go deeper and become more authentic'? Looking for more opportunity to improve quality of life, looking for greater recognition of what she has to contribute, looking for a more congenial space to care for her own subjective wellbeing as well as that of others, the nurse begins to engage with holistic milieu activities on a one-evening-a week basis. Her intention may be to explore ways of enhancing her contribution to the workplace and alleviate the more life-as, iron cage, aspects of her working environment. Our nurse might not go any further. Or she might join the ranks of those seeking to become a holistic milieu practitioner. (We estimate that about a sixth of those active in the holistic milieu of Kendal and environs aim to join the sixth who are already practitioners.) After some time as a 'learning' participant, she decides to go part-time in nursing, or perhaps give it up altogether, in order to escape from the restrictive life by setting up an outlet offering some form of body-mind-spirituality provision in the holistic milieu.

Evidence from the Kendal Project, particularly interviews which provided life-histories, suggest that our nurse is far from unusual. A related pathway into the holistic milieu may be from other forms of work, in other professions besides the caring professions, which have been found to ride roughshod over wellbeing issues (care of self and others). Alternatively, given the responsibility for holistic care that women often assume in the home setting, they may enter the holistic milieu by a domestic route. Whatever route they take, it is likely that those who enter subjective wellbeing culture and the holistic milieu will be seeking not only to continue or deepen a responsibility of care for others, but also to devote more attention to their own wellbeing. Women who have been devoted to 'giving out' for many years (caring for the family, caring for the home) may feel that their own subjective wellbeing is restricted, by duties or obligations, or neglected, perhaps by an individuated husband or by thoughtless teenagers. (Interestingly, the first usage recorded by the *Oxford English Dictionary* runs, 'Man did but from the well-being of this life from woman take', dated 1613.) They may feel that the time has come to balance care for others with care for self, and to seek greater 'harmony' in their lives. They have forgotten, or not been able, to care for their own wellbeing. The time comes when giving out needs to be complemented by 'taking in'. Women – most especially those who are not dominated by life-as roles and who thus appreciate what subjective-life relationality can offer – accordingly turn to where support can be found.

According to this account, many of the women who turn to holistic milieu activities are primarily concerned with caring for their own subjective wellbeing (of body, mind and spirit). The value of caring for others is by no means absent in the milieu, practitioners in particular attaching great importance to this. But a considerable amount of evidence from Kendal and elsewhere suggests that care for the self is at least as important. What matters, in this regard, is engaging with activities which enable one to address the problem of the 'drained-out' self – by being cared for, touched and listened to; by exploring ways of cultivating a sense of being recognized, valued, affirmed or esteemed; by cultivating a sense of being what one has to offer as a unique person.[9]

As for the evidence, the reader will recall from Chapter One that the characteristic language of the milieu of Kendal and environs makes frequent reference to the attention paid to 'your true nature', 'the essence of the person' and the 'deep inner self'. The theme of 'integration' and 'centring' is also encountered, the implication being that lives dispersed by way of looking after a diverse array of concerns can achieve a better 'balance' and 'harmony' of responsibilities and be re-integrated. Likewise, there is a strong emphasis on what is offered by way of easing stress, fatigue, low energy levels and 'blocked' energies. As we saw earlier in this chapter, 'health and fitness' is the single most important reason given for current participation in the activities of the holistic milieu, with 'stress relief' being third. The significance of bodily issues as a reason for being active in the holistic milieu should not be underestimated (see the 'Age' subsection, below, for further discussion), though it is also important to note that in a holistic context it is not apt to completely separate bodily concerns from other dimensions of health and wellbeing. In her research amongst those active in holistic wellbeing in Lancaster (20 miles to the south of Kendal), Eeva Sointu (2004) argues that what women experience above all in the holistic milieu is 'recognition', with body, mind and spirit concerns being. taken more seriously than in other spheres of their life. These are issues of personal concern that may not be taken seriously by a husband, that can perhaps not be voiced to colleagues, which might be dismissed as trivial or untreatable by a GP, but which can be heard and recognized by a (normally female) practitioner or fellow-participant. In the process one's sense of oneself grows, as does one's self-esteem and ability to face, deal with, understand and 'manage' one's subjectivities.

Whether the emphasis lies with relationships, as with patients in a hospital, one's spouse or one's friends, or issues more specifically focused on one's personal subjective wellbeing, as with feeling in tune with oneself, or both in tandem, the paths to the holistic milieu which we have been dwelling on have one thing in common: relationality. In answer to the (open-ended) question of the holistic milieu questionnaire, 'What would you say are the three most important problems facing you, personally, these days?', by far the most recurrent topic concerns relationships. It is not just that self issues are being dealt with in a relational context, they are also being placed in a framework that seeks to restore healthy relation between body, mind and spirit, and between self and others. Help is offered in dealing with relationships which are currently hindering the experiencing of oneself as complete and integrated – relationships that are too restrictive or demanding to allow one to creatively develop one's unique gifts and the full range of what one has to offer by way of oneself. Linda McGarvey speaks for many in the holistic milieu of Kendal and environs when she refers to people seeking 'the journey towards wholeness'; 'people are finding out who they really are, and not who they've been taught to be or what their life experiences have taught them'; participants are finding out 'fully who we can be'; people want 'to connect with who they are and the potential of who they are'. In short, the mode of *relational autonomous subjectivism* cultivated in the holistic milieu enable many participants to explore more deeply what they already know to be the case – that they have more to offer, both with regard to themselves and to others – than is allowed expression in everyday, relational and other, spheres of life.[10]

Drawing our exploration of the role played by gender to a close, there are two remaining topics to address. First, although the holistic milieu attracts women seeking greater depth in their lives and relationships, Kendal Project findings do not support the view that those attracted are especially unhappy with their everyday lives nor suffering from significant forms of 'deprivation'. Questionnaire results show that almost 80 per cent rate their satisfaction with their home life between 8 and 10, where 10 is most satisfied, the mean of 8.1 comparing with the national mean of 7.9 (Heald, 2000); that 71 per cent say their health is 'very good' or 'good' compared with the national figure of 70 per cent (Heald, 2000); that around 80 per cent of those in employment rate their level of work satisfaction at 6 to 10 on the scale of work satisfaction (10 being most satisfied); and that 51 per cent are married – very close to Heald's (2000) figure of 54 per cent for Britain. (See also note 9, p. 167.) The conclusion to be drawn is that the holistic milieu appeals to those who are sufficiently satisfied with their lives to believe that they are worth improving, but sufficiently dissatisfied to believe such improvement is desirable. It takes both humility ('my life is not as good as it could be') and confidence ('I have the potential to be a better person/I deserve a better life') to enter.

The second topic involves looking at the other side of the coin, namely why men only comprise some 20 per cent of the milieu in Kendal and environs, and around the same percentage elsewhere. As we have already suggested, men with a subjective-life bent are more likely to be individuated than women, and thus might well be dismissive of the intimate, self-disclosing relationality of the majority of holistic milieu activities. The ideals of masculinity to which many men aspire involve maintaining relatively clear boundaries between self and others, and going out in the world to exercise their autonomy and competitive spirit to achieve

subjective well-being. As one holistic practitioner told us with a smile, 'Men do like to be in charge, and this is something they can't be in charge of!' As one of our male postgraduates commented, 'Why should men enter the milieu when there's nothing tangible to achieve?'. It is not that men do not desire subjective wellbeing, but they may find it difficult to acknowledge their need and desire, and even more difficult to explicitly ask for or offer help in the cultivation of subjective wellbeing (just as men are somewhat more reluctant to visit the doctor than are women). As holistic milieu practitioner Tessa Logan put it, 'I'm sorry to say it, but women are more open than men. They talk about intimate things more. Men are more guarded and protective of their views. They tend to talk more about things like sport'. Furthermore, the masculine ideal of autonomy and self-sufficiency may explain why it is relatively common to hear men (and sometimes women) dismissing subjective wellbeing culture and the holistic milieu as 'narcissistic', 'pampering', and 'touchy-feely'. Equally, the attachment of many men to the ideal of 'rational' autonomy may be the cause of another common cluster of negative comments about the 'irrational', 'unscientific', 'unprofessional', 'not qualified', 'flaky', 'mumbo-jumbo', 'intangible' nature of the holistic milieu.

Age

Not only is the gender profile of the holistic milieu of Kendal and environs significantly different from the general population, so too is the age profile. Seventy three per cent of all those active in the holistic milieu of Kendal and environs are aged 45 and over, with 55 per cent of all participants aged between 40 and 59 – in Kendal as a whole, only 12 per cent fall into the latter age range. Forty five per cent of all those active in the milieu are women aged between 40 and 60, with the equivalent figure for males being just 10 per cent.[11] Furthermore, the majority of participants have not been involved prior to mid-life. This is indicated by the fact that under 15 per cent of respondents to the holistic milieu questionnaire are in their twenties and thirties; it is even more strongly indicated by the fact that around 40 per cent of practitioners (who are much more likely to have been involved in the milieu for longer periods than most participants) have only been practising for up to four years. In addition, given the growth of the milieu during the 1990s (when it tripled in size), and given the age profile, it stands to reason that many must have entered during mid-life. So how are we to explain the 'mid-life factor' – why the majority of participants only enter the holistic milieu in mid-life?

Although we do not have as much systematic evidence as we would like, it is clear that a considerable numbers of those active in the milieu – most obviously practitioners (around one sixth of participants) and those clients and group members who are most involved (around another sixth) in that many of them are intending to become practitioners in the future – have downsized or downshifted.[12] Accordingly, let us see if the literature on downshifting can shed light on the mid-life issue.

According to Clive Hamilton's (2003) research, '25 per cent of British adults aged 30–59 have downshifted over the last ten years', the average reduction in income being 40 per cent (pp, vii, viii). ('Downshifters' are defined as those who agree with the question, 'In the last ten years have you voluntarily made a long-term change in your lifestyle, other than planned retirement, which has resulted in you earning less money?' (p. vii)). Figures are much the same for the USA. What is significant with regard to our age puzzle is that the primary reason given for downshifting by people in their thirties and forties is that they want to spend 'more time with family' – 37.5 per cent of this age range give this answer, compared with just 19 per cent of those in their fifties (p. 20). What people in their fifties are much more likely to say (25 per cent, this making this the second most important reason for

downshifting overall) is that they are seeking a 'healthier lifestyle'. Only 9 per cent of those in their thirties and forties give this response (p. 20)

The picture which emerges is of younger adults prioritizing relationality and the fulfilment of family life (and perhaps friendship networks as well), and of older adults prioritizing health. This is not so surprising, given that the younger are much more likely to be raising families, whilst the children of older people have very probably left home (in Kendal and environs, for example, only 19 per cent of respondents to the holistic milieu questionnaire report they have children aged under 18 living in their household, compared with the national figure of 35 per cent (Heald, 2000)). And of course, the older one becomes, the more health concerns are likely to loom large.

Applying this to explain the 'mid-life factor', the likelihood is that younger parents (whether single or married) will be too involved with the relationalities of family life, and/or friendship networks that may have persisted from their student days, to feel that they would benefit from exploring their subjective-lives further by entering the holistic milieu. In addition, and bearing in mind the numbers of women in their twenties, thirties and forties who now also go out to work, it is also highly likely that few women feel that they have the time to add another sphere of activities to their constant round of work and home. (See Hochschild, 1997, on the 'time bind'; and Hochschild, 2003, p. 2 on the point that in the USA in 2000 close to 70 per cent of married women worked for pay, compared to 40 per cent in 1950 and less than a fifth in 1900.) However, as the family diminishes in size, with teenagers going off to college or university or leaving home to get a job elsewhere, relational life at home diminishes as a source of significance. And for many parents who, these days, are tending to have children later in life than in the past, this may coincide with entering their later forties and fifties. All of which conspires to make the motivation to look beyond the home to find ways of improving the quality of relational subjective-life much stronger. For women sympathetic to relational subjective-life values, the holistic milieu beckons. With more time and freedom to look beyond the home, and accumulated experiences on which to draw and reflect, they may enter into holistic activities in order to improve the quality of their lives and relationships. More specifically, some might well be seeking to reactivate the relationality which they nostalgically recall from the times at college or university, before they got swamped by family and work.

As we saw earlier in this chapter, Kendalians involved with the holistic milieu refer to 'health and fitness' concerns as their primary reason for originally embarking on the activities with which they are currently involved. A separate (open-ended) question enquiring about the main problems facing them also shows that health and fitness are important concerns. This very much matches Hamilton's (2003) finding that health is prioritized by those who downsize and who are aged between 50 and 60. Responses to our open question make it very clear that 'health' rather than 'illness' is the operative word in this context. (As noted above, most report 'very good' or 'good' health.) Given their age, it is not surprising that these 'later mid-lifers' should be more aware of 'ageing' than younger people, and more concerned to do something about it. Whilst specific ailments like fatigue, a bad back, headaches and so on may prompt people to enter the milieu, care for the 'whole person' is likely to become a more pressing concern – not least because the 'spirit' of the milieu encourages participants to think and act in a more holistic way. And the cultivation of the whole person, with the energy flowing through the self, should mean that they are in the best possible shape to stay 'young' longer – to weather the storms which inevitably lie ahead.

Further research is required in order to probe deeper into the 'mid-life factor'. Interviews carried out during the Kendal Project suggest further

hypotheses that could be tested. It could be argued, for example, that it takes time to accumulate the life-experiences which may take one to the holistic milieu (the divorce, the sense of fragmentation which can arise from running a home and going out to work, the 'unresolved' issues about relationships, the emerging sense of 'who I am') which come to the fore as one gets older and has more time (with the teenagers having left home, etc.) to reflect on how to 'work things out'. Or that it is largely in the second half of life that people become aware of the limits of life, of 'time running out', of the importance of making the most of what is left ('life is not a dress rehearsal'). As an informant from nearby Lancaster says, 'People who find themselves in holistic activities – they've probably had a journey to get to that point . . . and they've probably developed some self-awareness'. For women in particular, it may take until mid-life to rid themselves of the widespread cultural belief that their happiness comes from 'outside' (by way of the 'knight in shining armour', the romance, the perfect family, the beautiful house) and to realize that they need to take responsibility for their own happiness (Langford, 1999). It could also be argued that it takes time to become disillusioned by what various forms of 'life-as' have to offer, including mainstream professions (not least caring wellbeing professions), and to reach the point where one is no longer willing to put up with bureaucratic restrictions ('I finally realized that I couldn't influence the system'). Then again it could be argued that for many women who juggle the demands of work and family it is not until mid-life that they have the opportunity (the money, and the time, particularly if they have taken early retirement,[13] to explore aspects of their personal lives which have not been catered for by work and home life — perhaps self-esteem, perhaps a desire to reactivate the relationality of their youth, perhaps simply a desire to live a 'richer' life.[14]

Finally, what of people who have yet to reach 30 years of age? As Inglehart's (1997) survey findings indicate, younger people are more likely to value subjective-life than older people (and see Houtman and Mascini, 2002, p. 465). Research from a more ethnographic point of view supports the judgement that many younger people are deeply involved in relational subjective-life and value it highly (see, for example, Collins, 1997 on schools. Lynch, 2002 on clubbing). Given this orientation, one might expect young people to find the basic values of the holistic milieu congenial, and to be more involved with activities than we found to be the case in Kendal and environs (where only just over 1 per cent of participants are aged between 20 and 30). This is another issue which requires further research. What we can hypothesize is that a great many pre-30s (not just in Kendal, of course, but more generally) have ample relationaiity by way of the mobile phone, the love affairs, the extensive friendship networks, the clubs and bars, the personalized work groups. Subjective-life is rich and full in such regards, which means there is little if any need for the holistic milieu to serve as a source of relational significance. Health is likely to be as good as it is ever going to be. In addition, very long working hours (typical, for example, of work in finance, media or advertising, industries), and the desire to keep up with all the friends and forge intimate relationships, leaves very little time to become involved with holistic activities. And finally, the limits of 'life' have not yet made themselves felt. (See Heelas and Seel, 2003 for further discussion.)

Counter-Evidence and Argument

As well as amassing evidence that supports the subjectivization thesis, it is important to consider what might count against it. Most important in this regard is the body of literature that suggests that 'strict' and 'conservative' churches are growing rather than declining, and that it is their life-as strictness and conservatism that causes them to grow. This case is made most powerfully in Dean Kelley's *Why Conservative Churches are Growing* ([1972] 1995), and has been restated by Laurence Iannaccone (1994), Roger Finke and Rodney Stark (1992) and Stark and Finke (2000). Insofar as the category of what Kelley calls 'strict religion' might be thought to be close to what we are calling 'life-as religion', this seems to contradict the subjectivization thesis. The latter leads us to expect that life-as religion will decline as the subjective turn takes hold, whereas Kelley can be read to be claiming that life as religion has been doing well since the seventies.

The contradiction may not be as great as it seems. For one thing, we have never suggested that the subjective turn characterizes the whole of Western culture, nor that individuals are powerless to resist it. It is highly likely that pockets of life-as culture will persist, that certain varieties of Christianity will form such pockets, that Christianity can and will be effectively mobilized in Durtheimian fashion to support threatened forms of life-as (for example, traditional gender roles), and that under such circumstances Christianity may do well, becoming a 'haven' or Counter-culture for those who wish to resist the subjective turn of the wider culture. This outcome is particularly likely in a country as large as the United States, where congregations of difference are able to shelter from the subjective turn within a sub-culture of their own making (with home schooling, Christian universities, Christian television channels and so on). In all these respects we can agree with Kelley, Stark and others regarding the relative success of 'conservative' religion since the seventies, especially in the USA. The point at which we part company with them, however, is the point at which they suggest that conservative religion may come to occupy more than a minority position in the society and culture of subjectivized societies. As Christian Smith's (1998) recent study of American evangelicalism indicates, the 'protesting' counter-cultural status of such congregations is likely to energize and sustain them, whilst also ensuring that they will not expand greatly if at all beyond their current size nor shed their 'beleaguered' status.

We also believe that the Kelley thesis fails to differentiate sufficiently between what we have been calling religions of difference and religions of experiential difference. As we have seen in the previous chapter, the latter have demonstrated greater vitality than the former since the seventies. As we have also seen, the latter are significantly more subjectivized than the former, albeit not as subjectivized as holistic spirituality. As a growing number of studies suggest, the success of congregations of experiential difference appears to lie not so much in their strictness, as in their ability to combine normative strictness with attention to and reconstruction of inner lives (Tipton, 1982; Shibley, 1996; Miller, 1997; Griffith, 1997; Tamney, 2002). As Mark Shibley (1996) puts it in his study of Southern Baptist congregations, those that fare best do so 'precisely because they attend to the therapeutic needs of individuals' (p. 137); as one of our students puts it, such congregations are attractive to subjectivized selves because 'the self becomes important to God'; as a convert from Roman Catholicism to a charismatic congregation explained, 'I was looking for *life*. That life flow . . .' (Hoge et al., 1981, p. 121). Since we have been arguing that the relative success of 'strict' congregations is actually the success of congregations in which an overarching framework of theistic authority is combined with concern for the healing, cultivation and enrichment of subjective-life, the fortunes of this variety of congregation confirm rather than disconfirm the subjectivization claim and thesis (though not the spiritual revolution claim):[15]

The Subjectivization Thesis: Explaining the General and Varied Fortunes of the Congregational Domain

To sum up this discussion of congregational decline, our argument in general has been that the congregational domain's failure to retain or attract subjective-life orientated selves has been a significant cause of its decline. This stands in stark contrast to the success of holistic forms of spirituality, which have proliferated because they have been able to capitalize on the wider – and growing – cultural demand for subjective wellbeing.

Further support for the subjectivization thesis arises from the fact that it makes perfect sense of the varied fortunes within the congregational domain which were uncovered in the previous chapter. Given the increasing momentum of the subjective turn and the quest for personal wellbeing, the subjectivization thesis would predict that congregations of humanity will be faring worst, since they offer least by way of subjective wellbeing. It would predict that congregations of difference will be faring better insofar as they offer to enhance subjective wellbeing by reconstructing inner lives through conformity to God's laws. And it would predict that congregations of experiential difference and experiential humanity will be faring best, due to their ability to bring the sacred within the realm of personal experience, where it may have a direct impact on subjective-life and well-being.[16] As we have seen in Chapter Three (pp. 60–7) all these predictions are borne out by the facts.

CONCLUSION

Madeleine Bunting (1996) writes, 'People are turning inside themselves for answers rather than looking to external religions which people have to fit into rather than finding something which fits them. People are taking more control over all aspects of their life, spiritual and health, rather than letting other people tell them what to do or believe' (p. 3), Not many people these days would say 'yes' to Thomas Carlyle's question in his 1840 lectures *On Heroes, Hero-Worship and the Heroic in History*: '. . . does not every true man feel that he is himself made higher by doing reverence to what is really above him?'. For the pressing values of the culture in which we live are along the lines of 'Life is not made for you; you have to make it' or 'Take responsibility for finding your own ways of being and fulfilling yourself'. In the words of Zygmunt Bauman (2000), 'Needing to *become* what one *is* is the feature of modern living' (p. 32), And in the words of Gordon Allport (1962), what matters is 'the *right* of every individual to work out his own philosophy of life to find his personal niche in creation, as best he can. His freedom to do so will be greater if he sees clearly the forces of culture and conformity that invite him to be content with a merely *second-hand* and therefore for him, with an immature religion' (pp. vii–viii; our emphases).

The basic premise of the subjectivization thesis is perfectly simple. With ever-increasing numbers of people having come to value what subjective-life has to offer, the tendency is for forms of associational activity that locate the sacred within to be doing well. For when the sacred, or spirituality, is experienced as lying at the heart of who you are, as coming from 'You' (not least by way of relationships) it can hardly dictate or constrain who you are. How can spirituality impose a life on you when it is experienced to be your true life? By contrast, with ever-declining numbers of people having faith in life-as values, the trend is for forms of associational activity, where the sacred operates from without, to be in overall decline. For religion which tells you what to believe and how to behave is out of tune with a culture which believes that it is up to us to seek out appropriate answers for ourselves. How can any other source tell me how to live my life, when only I can know from inside who I really am and what I may become? In short, subjective-life spirituality serves and reflects contemporary core values, in particular those associated with going deeper into Trilling's 'internal space' in order to 'live *out*' of one's life. The thrust of life-as religion, on the other hand, is to rein in the potentially anarchic and 'selfish' possibilities of 'being yourself only better'.

This is not to deny that life-as religion can change and that some important changes in a subjectivized direction can be observed. Queen Victoria's first Prime Minister, Lord Melbourne, is reported to have complained, after hearing an evangelical sermon, that 'Things have come to a pretty pass when religion is allowed to invade the sphere of private life'. Times have certainly moved on. We have seen that those forms of congregational religion which have done most to cater for the enhancement of 'private life' are faring significantly better than others, thereby lending further support to the subjectivization thesis – but not going so far as to support the spiritual revolution claim.

Although we have been concentrating on the holistic milieu and the congregational domain in this chapter, the subjectivization thesis can also be used to help explain changes that are underway beyond these two associational heartlands. There is a clear link, for example, between the trend towards more subjectivized (child-centred) teaching in primary schools, and (patient-centred) caring in the NHS, and the growth of subjective-life spirituality in these spheres. (This is not to deny that other factors have a role to play, most obviously that inclusive spirituality works in multicultural settings, whereas more exclusivistic life-as religion runs into the difficulty of not being able to cater for a diverse spread of faith.) There are also pretty clear links between the increasing popularity of subjective-life values, the shift to mind-body-spirit provisions in the general culture, and the increasing popularity of beliefs of a non-theistic, inner variety among the population.

In this chapter we have concentrated on providing evidence to support the subjectivization thesis as it applies to Britain (and in some measure to the USA). Clearly, the thesis is only of explanatory value when and where the subjective turn is in evidence. We are not for one moment suggesting that it is relevant to the situation in sub-Saharan Africa, for example, where the subjective turn is scarcely in evidence, where life-as religion is flourishing, and where there are much more pressing needs than the cultivation of unique subjectivities – most especially sustaining life-itself.

One thing we have not concentrated on in this chapter is the fact that the subjective turn has gathered pace at a time – during and since the sixties – when overall associational involvement with the sacred has been in decline. At least in Britain, and almost certainly in the USA, the growth of the holistic milieu has not compensated for the decline of the congregational domain, The 'massive subjective turn of modern culture', it thus appears, has resulted in the secularization of the associationai territory as a whole. In a volume devoted to exploring the decline of life-as religion and the growth of subjective-life spirituality, we cannot enter into the complicated matter of establishing whether there is a causal link between the subjective turn and overall secularization – and thereby establishing the significance, or lack of significance, of other developments (such as increasing pressures on the time available to women who go out to work and run the home). (For ingenious and pioneering theoretical and empirical work on such matters, see Houtman and Mascini, 2002 – research which does much to confirm the subjectivization thesis, and which has the added advantage of testing a rival theory of change, namely rationalization; see also Yves Lambert, 1999 for a programmatic statement.)[17] Here we limit ourselves to just one point: that the main reason for overall secularization is probably that the holistic milieu has – to date – attracted a relatively small constituency. We have noted that the intimate and personally relational concerns of the milieu are likely to alienate those – especially many men — who seek to develop the quality of their subjective-lives by acting as individuated selves in the world; that during the last few decades the milieu does not seem to have attracted many younger people; and, we can add, that it has not appealed to elderly people who continue to support the life-as values in which they were raised. The simple fact that the holistic milieu has not

exercised a wider appeal can thus greatly help explain why its growth has not been able to compensate for congregational domain decline.[18]

We draw this chapter to a close with an argument which we think sets a research agenda for the future. Although the subjective turn is unquestionably a major feature of the cultural landscape in which we dwell, a great deal supports the contention that another major feature has emerged in the form of 'new' versions of life-as regulation and control with forceful life-as capacities. One can think of the technologies of surveillance (which force one to drive *as* a good motorist, for example) or the auditing, monitoring, inspecting, the performance-related pay and the public performance tables, which impose themselves within the modern workplace, and require one to work as the institution demands if one is to be successful. Without going into any more details, it is perfectly clear that we spend a great deal of time in a world of 'meet them or else . . .' targets, the process of targeting meaning that we have to channel our efforts in highly regulated ways – thereby serving to instil a very effective, because apparently self-chosen, life-as dimension to significant parts of many peoples' lives.

Our culture is experiencing a fundamental clash of values: on the one hand those associated with the cultivation of unique subjectivities, on the other those associated with the iron cage of having to live *the targeted-life*. In some spheres, like public-sector teaching or nursing, the clash may be acute. In others it may be better 'managed'. But given the prevalence of this clash, and given the preference on the part of increasing numbers of people for finding the freedom, the opportunity to be and become themselves, it is likely that many will use their 'free' time to seek liberation from their standard/ized, in effect *regimented*, work lives. If they engage with associational forms of the sacred, they are therefore much more likely to be involved with freedom-loving spiritualities of life than with role-enforcing life-as religion. Seeking to escape from externally imposed targets elsewhere in their lives, they will not want more of the same in the sphere of the sacred.

NOTES

1. Durkheim (1971) himself very much concentrated on explaining traditional life-as religion (defined as 'a unified system of beliefs and practices relative to sacred things, that is to say, things set apart and forbidden' (p. 47)) by reference to life-as socio-cultural formations. He did not apply his replication approach to explain another form of the sacred which, like so many others of his time, he was acutely aware was a growing force, namely one which consists 'entirely in internal and subjective states, and which would be constructed freely by each of us' (p. 47).

2. See Hall (1999) on voluntary associations; see also Putnam (2000, pp. 183–4) and Veroff et al (1981, p. 537). For an example of the subjectivization of politics, see Mulgan (1994) on how personal sources of significance can inform a 'new politics' of 'life values'; Chambers (1997), who defines wellbeing as 'the experience of good quality of life' rather than in terms of 'wealth' (p. 9), addresses the world of development agencies (see also Nussbaum and Glover, 1996).

3. Gender findings from Kendal are very much in line with those reported from elsewhere. See, for example, Brown (1997, p. 95); Frisk (2003, p. 243); Houtman and Mascini (2002, p. 468); Jones (2003); Lowendahl (2002); McGuire (1988, p. 12); Rose (1998, p. 6); Wootton and Sparber (2001) and Sharma (1995, e.g. p. 35) for CAM. The 'Yoga in America' questionnaire carried out by the Harris Interactive Service Bureau (2003) finds that 76.9 per cent of practitioners are women.

4. It is indicative that Inglehart, Basanez and Moreno (1998) find a very small difference between the percentages of males and females holding post-materialist values (V405). See also Mitchell (1983, p. 279).

5. Some excellent illustrations of what we mean by relational subjectivism, interfusing the relational with the autonomous, are provided by many of the great Romantics, Lukes (1973), writing that for Wilhelm von Humboldt, for example, the ' "true end of man" was "the highest and most harmonious

development of his powers to a consistent whole" [but] whose "highest ideal [was] the co-existence of human beings", constituted in "a union in which each strives to develop himself from his own inmost nature" ' (p. 68). More recently, consider Cancian's work (1987), whose general theme is that couples increasingly combine self-development with commitment, and whose conclusion is that 'There is plenty of evidence that the interest in personal growth during the seventies was linked to close relationships; intimacy, not isolation, was a sign of the developed self' (p. 9; see also p. 39). Another good example, now regarding the contemporary situation, is provided by Richard Sennett (1977), writing that 'The reigning aspiration today is to develop individual personality through experiences of closeness and warmth with others' (p. 259). See also Giddens (1993) and, from a social constructivist point of view, Gergen (1987). Or we might think of Brother David Steindl-Rast: 'When I talk about a shift to "personal experience", I don't mean "private". "Personal" is defined in terms of your relations . . . You become a person more deeply through your relations to other persons' (cited by Cimino and Latrin, 2002, p. 16).

6. Farias (forthcoming) provides a sophisticated social psychological analysis of what he calls 'New Age', showing that what he calls a 'hybrid form of individualism' emphasizes both the subjective-life of the 'holistic' and 'personal autonomy' (p. 12). This is characterized as 'holistic individualism' (p. 13). And see Hedges and Beckford on 'Holism, Healing and the New Age' (2000) and their exploration of the theme that 'The true self is not . . . an island or an atom: it is only one part of a much larger whole' (p. 172).

7. It could be objected at this point that some holistic milieu activities are not especially holistically interpersonal or intimate. Many yoga groups, for example, involve individual practice with little verbal self-disclosure. Our response is that bodily movement is highly expressive, communicative, self-disclosing, with relationships being established with the practitioner. Furthermore, the perception of many men is that yoga groups – predominantly involving women – are contexts which belong to women and where your body is going to be revealed: perhaps in ways which are going to make men feel clumsy and awkward. How many middle-aged men want their bodies to be taken seriously in public?

8. As to why there should be a gendered division of labour, debate currently rages between earlier feminist analyses which attributed differences to an early, somewhat passive, process of socialization (e.g. De Beauvoir, 1993; Gilligan, 1982) and more 'postmodern' feminist analyses which place more emphasis on the active and discursive negotiation of sex roles throughout a lifetime (e.g. Stanley and Wise, 1983; Davies, 1989; Butter, 1990).

9. Care for the body may be an obvious place to start, particularly since women's responsibilities often leave them with less time for themselves than men, more tired than men, and reporting lower levels of health (Brannen and Moss, 1991). Having someone else take care of their bodies may be full of significance for the authorization and enhancement of subjective-life, particularly if Adkins (1995) is right in her observation that women are more likely then men to feel 'limited ownership of their bodies' (p. 159). Adkin's point is echoed by Gilligan (2002) and by Young (1990) in her aptly titled discussion of 'Throwing it like a Girl'. Both authors investigate psychological and other causes of women's limited ownership of their bodies and (in Gilligan's case) of men's limited ownership of emotional vulnerability and relationality.

10. One way of conceptualizing the holistic milieu is as an experimental social space in which women are attempting to retain commitment to relationality, but to give this commitment – which has previously been validated by now threatened institutions of life-as like the church – a new, more subjectivized basis. In other words, many activities in the holistic milieu represent an attempt to reconcile the (often) culturally divergent imperatives to 'be all I can be' and retain commitment to care and relationality. If this characterization is correct, then the milieu is undertaking what Hochschild (2003) considers to be the most pressing need of our times, reconciliation between 'care' and 'the demands of our workplaces, the equality of the sexes, and the very structure of honour in modern life' (p. 3).

11. The age profile of Kendal is very much in line with England and Wales, the 2001 Census showing (for example) that 19.56 per cent of the population of Kendal are aged between 45 and 59, the equivalent figure for England and Wales being 18.93 per cent. The age profile of the holistic milieu is much the same elsewhere, including the USA: sec Heelas and Secl (2003); McGuire (1988, p. 13); Cimino and Lattin (2002, p. 27); Wootton and Sparber (2001) for CAM. See www.kendalproject.org.uk for an age profile graph for the holistic milieu of Kendal and environs.

12. Regarding practitioners, many have given up careers which leave little or no time for milieu activities, moving to jobs which enable them to practise for two or three days a week, earning (on average) around £20 an hour.

13. 21 per cent of participants in the holistic milieu of Kendal and environs are retired.

14. Although we do not have the space to explore the full implications of the fact here, it is significant that Hall (1999) reports that voluntary associations as a whole are 'For the most part . . . the preserve of those in middle age' (p. 455). Thinking back to points raised earlier in this chapter, it is also noteworthy that those involved in voluntary associations are increasingly drawn from the ranks of women (p. 437); that involvement correlates with level of education (p. 435); and that the large majority are middle-class (p. 438). It is clear that much the same socio-demographic factors are at work as with regard to holistic milieu participation. Hall himself draws particular attention to the role played by higher levels of education, especially of women (p. 437); see also Sharma (1995, chapters 1 and 3) on complementary medicine.

15. A number of studies which have tested Kelley's thesis by looking for factors that predict growth (or decline) failed to find a significant correlation with congregational strictness (see, for example, Hoge and Roozen, 1979 and Perry and Hoge, 1981). Studies of church leavers in both the UK and USA both find that dropouts are more likely to say they left because their congregation was 'too conservative' (around 33 per cent) than 'too liberal' (around 7 per cent) (Richter and Francis, 1998, p. 118; Hoge et al., 1981, p. 96 – both arrive at exactly the same figures). In a recent study, Thompson, Carroll and Hoge (1993) found that 'being theologically liberal was a plus for church growth' (p. 197).

16. Some congregations of experiential difference in Britain, and many more in the USA, go even further by offering material prosperity and/or healing of the body – perhaps by way of a 'miracle' (see, for example, McGuire, 1988; Percy, 1996; Poloma and Hoelter, 1998).

17. The research of Inglehart and associates is also highly relevant to the general argument of this chapter,

Ingelhart (1997) stating that 'Despite their, relative alienation from traditional religion . . . postmaterialists are *more* apt than the materialists to spend time thinking about the meaning and purpose of life. . . . Traditional beliefs and the established religious organizations may be losing their adherents, but spiritual concerns are becoming more widespread' (p. 285; see also p. 284; and Inglehart, 1990, pp. 187, 192).

18. The fact that the associational territory is in overall decline alone suffices to explain why we distance ourselves from those who adopt a homeostatic view with regard to the fortunes of different forms of the sacred – namely that as one form of the sacred declines another will grow to take its place (see, for example, Stark 1985). It can be added that *if* trends in Kendal and environs carry on as charted from the 1960s, the 2001 figure of 9.5 per cent for the congregational domain and the holistic milieu will not be matched until approaching the end of the century.

Religion and Social Institutions

Essay:
Religion, State, and Nation

Protestant Footprints

Let's go back to Weber's "iron cage." How, in Weber's estimation, did the United States get to that point? In the sociology of religion, Weber is best known for his lengthy essay, *The Protestant Ethic and the Spirit of Capitalism*—whose title pretty much sums up the work. Weber argued that there was a deep connection between the economy and the dominant religious perspective in any given society. In the case of capitalism, he began with the observation that this economic system was in his time particularly successful in the United States. He wanted to know, why was this the case? Why hadn't Europe, for instance, developed in the same way? Weber suggested that the answer lay in the close similarities between the ethos of Martin Luther's and John Calvin's Protestantism, which had been transmitted quite strongly into U.S. culture, and the ethos needed for the successful development of a capitalist economic system. Let's see how this worked.

For Weber, there are several important pieces to the **Protestant ethic**. One of these, drawn from the work of Martin Luther, is the value placed on hard work within a **calling**. Rather than teaching that only priests had a divine calling to their jobs, Luther taught that God called each person to a particular form of earthly labor. Therefore, to work within one's calling was to do honor to God. Work in the secular world, for Luther, became sacred.

The second important piece of the Protestant ethic, for Weber, was what he called **inner-worldly asceticism**. Rather than referring to some internal world, for Weber this term meant asceticism *in the world*. Before the Protestant reformation, asceticism in Western Europe generally referred to the practice of monks, priests, and nuns—people called **religious** (as a noun) who had dedicated their lives to the Church—though, of course, there are many religions around the world in which ascetic practices play a part. Asceticism involves a variety of modes of self-control or self-denial, ranging from restricting one's food intake, to engaging in various methods of physical pain, to relishing in one's illnesses as a form of self-chastisement, all with the aim of increasing one's religious focus, spiritual power, or connection to the divine. So what is inner-worldly asceticism? Like other forms of asceticism, it involves self-control and self-denial, but unlike most ascetic practices, it doesn't involve withdrawing from the world. Instead, inner-worldly asceticism appears as frugality and the avoidance of luxuries and self-indulgence.

The final important piece in Weber's understanding of the Protestant ethic is the Calvinist concept of **predestination**. Calvin believed that God determined, far in advance, whether any individual person would be saved and sent to heaven, or damned and sent to hell. Moreover, God's choices would be evident in people's lives: those whom God had determined to save would be materially successful, while the damned wouldn't receive the same reward. But God was tricky: God would also test people by giving them riches or poverty they didn't deserve.

You'd think that such a belief would lead to resignation and hopelessness; but consider it in classroom terms for a minute. If you walked in on the first day of class and your professor said, "I've already determined who's going to pass this class and who's going to fail, and you can't drop the class," what would your first question be? Probably, "OK, so am I going to pass or fail?" Your instructor might answer, "I can't tell you, but you'll know." So you'd probably do your best in the class in order to prove that you were one of the ones destined to pass, right? Weber argues that Calvin's doctrine of predestination had the same result. People tried very hard to live the most upstanding lives in their communities, and to get ahead financially, in order to prove (to themselves as well as to others) their blessed status in the eyes of God.

Now let's look at the link between this Protestant ethic and what Weber defined as the **spirit of capitalism**. What does one need in order to successfully develop a capitalist economy? One needs entrepreneurs, people who work tirelessly and re-invest most if not all of their earnings. One also needs workers who won't go on strike, who won't demand expensive pay raises or other benefits, and who will work long, hard hours and accept their place in life. Does this sound a little like the Protestant ethic? Weber thought so. He argued that the particular combination of Lutheranism and Calvinism that had established itself as the culturally dominant religion in the United States provided the country with exactly the factors needed to promote the rapid and successful development of capitalism. And, Weber thought, as long as this Protestant ethic was in place, even those who were being exploited by entrepreneurial employers at least were able to see a higher purpose—their divine calling—in their work. After the disenchantment of the world, however, which we considered in Chapter 1, the sense of divine impetus disappeared from the world of work, leaving especially the workers bereft of any greater meaning to their work—thus, as Weber put it, trapped in the "iron cage" of a disenchanted capitalism.

The Protestant ethic is one example of what I like to call **Protestant footprints** in U.S. culture. When you walk along a beach, you leave footprints that stay behind even when you aren't there anymore. Likewise, although there are relatively few strict Calvinists in the United States in the twenty-first century, Calvinists' important role in shaping U.S. culture in the colonial period left footprints in the culture that linger on. Historian Catherine Albanese (1992) suggests that these footprints cover more features of the culture than just the Protestant ethic; in fact, she argues for the presence of a widespread **public Protestantism** in the country. This includes both explicit and implicit Protestant elements. Explicit Protestant elements are those that are ostensibly religious but have come to be claimed as simply part of U.S. culture. For example, Christmas is a federal holiday in the United States but Eid al-Fitr (Muslim), Rosh Hashanah (Jewish), and Three Kings' Day (Roman Catholic) are not. Think about how the school year is structured—people in the United States generally refer to "winter break" and "spring break" now, but it's hardly a coincidence that winter break includes Christmas and spring break generally includes Easter (on the Western Christian calendar).

But what about people who celebrate Christmas with Santa and Easter with the Easter bunny, and who don't consider themselves Christian at all? Here again, Albanese would see a perfect example of public Protestantism: the infusion of Protestant practices into the broader U.S. culture. Though it isn't popular to use this term, people can be "culturally Protestant" just as some people identify as "culturally Jewish" or "culturally Muslim"— nonbelievers who still observe some of the practices of the religion.

For Albanese, the implicit elements of Protestantism in U.S. culture reflect patterns of Protestant belief and practice that come to shape the mainstream culture and even to influence the ways in which non-Protestants practice their religions in the United States. These include such elements as revivalism (the practice of large-scale religious or spiritual gatherings), individualism and voluntarism, and **millennialism** (a tendency to believe in events, secular or sacred, that will bring about radical change in the world). For many in the United States, for instance, the advent of the year 2000 was a millennial event. To some Christians, it heralded the second coming of Christ, since in Christian belief Jesus was born at the beginning of the Common Era (that is, the year 0). To others, the turn of the millennium threatened a technological end of the world, with computers programmed only up to 1999 shutting down and threatening global financial collapse. During December 1999, some people in the United States stocked up on food and other supplies, took extra money out of the bank, and prepared for the end, whether sacred or technological. This is an excellent example of the millennialism that Protestantism has left as one of its footprints in the culture.

We've been talking specifically about the United States here, but what about other cultures? In another of his works ("Sociology of Religion," in *Economy and Society*), Weber attempted to expand on his theory by examining several different cultures and subcultures around the world, tracing the relationship between the dominant religion in each culture and the dominant economic system. In part because Western scholars' knowledge of world religions was weak at the time, and in part because Weber appears to have attempted to fit each culture into his theory, this aspect of his work is weaker than his ideas on the Protestant ethic. However, it perhaps goes without saying that the culturally dominant religion in any society shapes that society significantly, regardless of the number of actual practitioners of the religion or the legal connection between the dominant religion and the state.

Religion, Law, and the State

But wait a minute—doesn't the United States have a "wall of separation" between "church" and state? Well, this is where it gets interesting. The "wall of separation" is actually

Thomas Jefferson's wording, and is not in the Constitution. Here's what the U.S. Constitution says about religion (aside from making use of the word "God" from time to time), as part of the First Amendment in the Bill of Rights:

> *Congress shall make no law respecting the establishment of religion, or prohibiting the free exercise thereof.*

People who study and apply the First Amendment generally divide this part of it into two **religion clauses**. The first part, before the comma, is the **establishment clause**, and the second part is called the **free exercise clause**. Let's look more closely at both of those.

It's easy to misread the establishment clause as being about a religious establishment: that is, an institution. Instead, the clause refers to a practice, common in the world at the time the Constitution was framed and still quite common today, of *establishing* a particular religion as the official religion of a country. The framers of the Constitution generally came from British backgrounds, and in the British Empire the Anglican Church was (and in today's England, still is) the established church. Anglican doctrine was taught in schools, and Anglican priests paid by the government. Some of the British colonies in North America had established religions, too, but after some argument the framers of the Constitution agreed that this was a bad idea for their new country. Interestingly enough, this was in part because of the influence of Protestantism. Most Protestants believed (and most still do) that true adherence to a religion could only come about because of individual choice. People forced into a religion, they thought, were not true converts because they hadn't considered and freely chosen the religion. For these reasons, the framers of the U.S. Constitution thought it made little sense for the state to force people into adhering to any particular religion: thus, they approved the establishment clause.

The free exercise clause has deep roots in U.S. colonial history, since many free men and women of European descent who came to the colonies, especially early on, did so because of religious oppression at home. Many were part of the Puritan movement, which faced severe repression especially in England but also in other northern European countries. With some of their ancestors having fled to the colonies to escape religious persecution, many of the Constitution's framers were eager to outlaw such persecution in their new country.

So far, the religion clauses seem pretty simple, right? But as time went on and challenges to the limits of these clauses arose, things got complicated. For one thing, until the passage of the Fourteenth Amendment in 1868, each state was allowed to make its own laws regarding religion; the First Amendment applied only in U.S. territories. For that reason there were few religion cases in the Supreme Court prior to the late nineteenth century. One well-known case, decided in 1879, offered an indication that legal interpretation of the religion clauses wasn't as clear-cut as it might seem. *Reynolds* v. *United States* involved a Mormon man who had two wives (the Church of Jesus Christ of Latter-day Saints allowed the practice of "plural marriage," or polygyny—a man having more than one wife—until 1890). Since polygamy (having more than one spouse) was against federal law and Reynolds was living in Utah, a U.S. territory at the time, Reynolds was prosecuted. He appealed the prosecution, claiming that the free exercise clause of the First Amendment protected his right to religiously-motivated polygamy. In deciding in the government's favor and upholding the ban on even religiously-motivated polygamy, the Supreme Court took its first step in establishing that religious belief is more clearly protected by the First Amendment than is religious practice. In a country with Protestant footprints, this isn't too surprising since, as we saw in Chapter 1, Protestantism itself focuses on belief and thus Protestant cultures tend to define religion in terms of belief.

Public Protestantism has also affected which religions were considered protected (that is, considered "religion" at all) in the United States. For instance, in the late nineteenth century and the first part of the twentieth century, many traditional Native American practices were banned or severely restricted. As central parts of Native American lifeways, these practices would easily be considered religious by most of the definitions we developed in Chapter 1; to Protestants, however, they looked nothing like religion. Arguing that the framers of the Constitution intended to protect the rights of people from different *Christian* sects, those implementing and enforcing the Native American ritual bans denied that they were violating the First Amendment. Today most people would argue differently, but in response many Native Americans and their allies would point to the 1990 case, *Employment Division* v. *Smith*.

Alfred Smith and his colleague Galen Black were both members of the Native American Church, a blending of Christian and indigenous traditions that includes the ritual use of a hallucinogen called **peyote**. They were also drug counselors with a private company. When a drug test showed peyote in their systems, both men were fired. Because they had been fired for misconduct, the State of Oregon refused them unemployment compensation. Although the First Amendment does not speak to whether a private firm can fire someone based on her or his religious practices, Smith and Black argued that it does address the question of whether the state can refuse unemployment benefits to those fired for religious reasons. Furthermore, in 1978 Congress had passed the American Indian Religious Freedom Act, or AIRFA, essentially affirming that the First Amendment applied to Native Americans too. But the Supreme Court, to the surprise of many, took Oregon's side. Such an uproar ensued that in 1993 Congress passed the Religious Freedom Restoration Act (RFRA), which in essence ordered the Supreme Court to allow the violation of the free exercise clause only when the government can prove a compelling interest in doing so. The language of the RFRA makes it clear that Congress believed that this "compelling interest test," part of the "Sherbert test" in use by the courts since the late 1960s, had been abandoned in *Smith*. The final blow in this fight landed in 1997, when in *City of Boerne, Texas* v. *Flores* the Supreme Court ruled the RFRA unconstitutional.

Though First Amendment jurisprudence is far too complex to review thoroughly in this book, it is worth saying that the major battles over the religion clauses have generally involved at least one of four issues: the definition of "religion," the definition of "exercise," the definition of "establishment," and the potential conflict between the two clauses. We've already seen that definitions can be tricky, and you can imagine how much trickier they become when a Supreme Court case is at stake. But conflict between two clauses that were written as a pair? Let's take a closer look.

Consider the case of the public display of the Ten Commandments on government property. Some Christians, especially those who arranged for the display, might consider it reflective of their free exercise rights: in displaying the Ten Commandments they are sharing their beliefs with others, as many believe Jesus commanded them to do. Yet others, often but not always non-Christians, view such displays as a violation of the establishment clause, because in allowing the display to be on public land the government is implicitly supporting one religion over others. Who's right? The Supreme Court decided two such cases simultaneously in 2005: *Van Orden* v. *Perry* and *McCreary County* v. *ACLU of Kentucky*. The first case, which originated in Texas, concerned a monument of the Ten Commandments, placed at the Texas State Capitol by the Fraternal Order of Eagles with the support of Cecil B. deMille, who had recently directed and produced his epic film, *The Ten Commandments*. The second case centered on two large, public displays of the Ten Commandments in two county courthouses in Kentucky. The cases sound alike, but the Supreme Court, in two 5-4 decisions, decided them differently. The Texas monument was allowed to stand, while the Kentucky ones were ordered to be removed. The key difference between the cases was the Court's opinion regarding the purpose of the monument. Was it secular and cultural, or explicitly religious? In the Texas case, the Court ruled that the display had been meant for secular purposes; in Kentucky, the Court decided, it had been for religious purposes. Thus, among two otherwise quite similar displays on public property, the one stood and the other did not.

We have examined in depth the relationship between religion and the state in the United States, but this relationship is one that every state must work out. Of particular interest here are states whose relationship to religion is changing, because of changes in the state, changes in the religion, or both. Yoshiko Ashiwa, for instance, demonstrates that there has been a great deal of complexity and variation in the modern Chinese state's attitude toward religion. Two movements of the early twentieth century (one nationalist, the other communist) that were designed to eradicate religious spaces in China led to the reorganization of Buddhism. The changes in Chinese Buddhist organizations, this author argues, made Buddhism into a religion that could fit within the modern state. Yet, despite the assurance of freedom of religious belief for non-Party members, during the Cultural Revolution the Chinese state mandated the destruction of all temples. In another reversal, by the early 1980s the Chinese government had opened up a narrow space for certain recognized religions. Though following Marx's belief that religion would fade away as communism came into full being in the country, China's government allowed the regulated existence of five major religions and at the same time continued its ban on all others, including those considered to be acting against the interests of the state.

As complex as the interaction between religion and the state has been in China, it has been even more so within the central Asian nations studied by Chris Hann and Mathijs Pelkmans. Here, we get another perspective on religion in China—this time, Islam in the western Chinese province of Xinjiang. Islam, on the one hand, is one of the five religions currently recognized by the Chinese state and, on the other hand, is sometimes considered by the state to be a carrier of Uighur separatism; thus, in addition to the various reversals of religious fortunes in all of China during the twentieth century, Islam has seen further complications in the Chinese government's determination of its level of threat to the state.

In addition to Chinese Islam, Hann and Pelkmans examine the interactions between religion, state, and nationalism in the former Soviet republics of Kyrgyzstan and Turkmenistan. Unlike China, which has wavered quite a bit in its stance on religion, the USSR had a firm and long-standing policy of religious repression. As a result, some aspects of Islamic practice underwent a process that Hann and Pelkmans term **folklorization**: that is, they became separated from the religion and became simply part of what it meant to be Kyrgyz or Turkmen. Upon the fall of the Soviet Union, some Western scholars predicted a ballooning of religious activity in the former Soviet republics, while others suggested that religion had been killed off by the Soviet regimes and would not be revived. As Hann and Pelkmans demonstrate, the picture is much more complicated than these all-or-nothing scenarios imagined, and involves both the **state**, or the official organizations of government, and the **nation**, or what historian Benedict Anderson (1983) called the "imagined community" of people. Recognizing the power of religion to unite people, in the aftermath of the dissolution of the Soviet Union both the Turkmen and Kyrgyz governments drew on Islam to identify what it meant to be a part of their nation. Though this process worked quite differently in the two countries, in both cases it involved combining Islamic teachings with local practices and national heroes' stories, such that being Muslim became inextricable from being a part of the nation. As Muslim traditionalists and Christian missionaries came into these countries such narratives weakened, perhaps proving that, contra Peter Berger's concept of the sacred canopy, religion by itself cannot hold an otherwise fragmented nation *or* state together.

Religion and the Nation

Even within the United States, sociologists and other scholars of religion have long argued about the role of religion in the nation. This question became especially pressing for some sociologists of religion in the 1960s when, as we saw in Chapter 1, traditional religions experienced a significant decline. Peter Berger bemoaned the loss of a "sacred canopy" in the United States, and his contemporary, Robert Bellah, likewise felt the nation was on the verge of an important loss. In 1966, drawing on the work of Jean-Jacques Rousseau, Bellah termed this loss a deterioration of the nation's **civil religion**.

Civil religion, for Bellah, seems to have meant several things. First and perhaps foremost, it meant *the nation in religion*: the idea that the nation itself was answerable to a higher power. In his famous article on civil religion, Bellah opened with a consideration of John F. Kennedy's inaugural address and its references to God, then moved to examine the role that the idea of God played in the speeches and writings of the founders of the country. He concluded that this civil religion presented the nation, and especially its president, as deeply connected to a monotheistic deity through both that deity's commitment to the country and the country's commitment to carrying out the work of the deity. The second piece of civil religion, for Bellah, linked closely to the first: it was *religion in the nation*, or the presence of religious themes in the national culture. Bellah noted, for example, the advent of themes of "death, sacrifice, and rebirth" in the North during the Civil War. These two pieces of Bellah's civil religion, taken together, encompass what Albanese would later term public Protestantism.

But it is the third aspect of civil religion that has been best remembered in association with the term: the role of the *nation as religion*. Using a functional definition of religion, we can discover significant similarities between devotion to the nation and devotion to another ultimate concern. If the ultimate concern in civil religion is the nation itself—let's say the United States for the sake of example—what might be the sacred texts? The Declaration of Independence, perhaps, or the Constitution. Saints? George Washington, Thomas Jefferson, and other founders. Martyrs? Abraham Lincoln and, some would say, Martin Luther King, Jr. What about religious holidays? We have the Fourth of July, Memorial Day, Presidents' Day, Martin Luther King Day, Thanksgiving. Hymns? The national anthem, "America the Beautiful," "My Country 'Tis of Thee" (which, not coincidentally, is sung to the tune of Great Britain's national anthem). Sacred stories? There are so many, from Paul Revere's ride to warn colonists of the advance of British troops to George Washington's act of cutting down a cherry tree. Rituals? Perhaps reciting the Pledge of Allegiance, or singing the national anthem.

One aspect of the U.S. nation that supports Bellah's ideas is the addition of the words "under God" to the Pledge of Allegiance and the words "In God We Trust" to the national currency. Both of these additions took place in the mid-1950s, when the country was embroiled in the Cold War. With the "red scare" in full swing, many in the United States were eager to define their country as the opposite of communism. Marx's adamant opposition to religion made religiosity one of the ways to prove one's opposition to communism. Thus, references to God became central to the country's spending practices and to declarations of fealty. First Amendment challenges have occasionally been raised against these references to the divine, but they have always met with severe opposition. In 2004, for instance, Michael Newdow took the issue all the way to the Supreme Court. In *Newdow v. Elk Grove Unified School District*, Newdow, an atheist, claimed that the daily recitation of the Pledge of Allegiance in his daughter's kindergarten class represented an imposition of religion. Though First Amendment case history has established that saying the Pledge must be optional for students with religious objections, Newdow argued that the regular recitation and the participation of the majority of students still constituted a form of religious establishment.

Though the district court in which Newdow first filed the case ruled that the Pledge did not violate the First Amendment, the Ninth Circuit Court of Appeals ruled that it did. The public outcry following this ruling was enormous. Congress passed two resolutions condemning the circuit court's ruling, and finally nearly unanimously passed a bill re-authorizing the Pledge of Allegiance (in its post-1950s form). George H.W. Bush signed the bill into law in 2002, and the Newdow case headed to the Supreme Court. Some believe that, given the heated political climate, the Supreme Court "ducked" the question. In a rather anticlimactic finish to this high-profile case, the Court ruled that Newdow, a divorced parent who did not hold primary custody of his daughter, had no standing to bring the case in the first place. Thus, it dismissed the case without considering the constitutional question. Still, the uproar caused by the case is evidence in support of Bellah's civil religion thesis: it is rare for Congress to react at all, let alone so swiftly, to a circuit court decision.

Since Bellah's article was published in 1967, scholars of religion have argued over the merits of his thesis. One of the most trenchant critiques, raised repeatedly, has been the question of who is included in this supposedly national religion. Most, if not all, of its prominent figures are men, and most, if not all, are white, Northern, elite, heterosexual, and fully abled. Some scholars, like historian Charles Reagan Wilson (1980), have argued for the existence of multiple civil religions in the United States, especially in the South and North during the Civil War. Others have dismissed the idea of civil religion outright as a myopic, elitist concept. Religious studies scholar Charles Long is one of the latter.

For Long, the concept of separate civil religions belies the fact that everyone living in the United States has shaped religion, and civil religion, in that country. But as their experiences have differed, especially by race, each of those people has also experienced different religions and different understandings of state and nation. So the differences are there, but they cannot be described as separate. Rather, they intertwine and interact constantly.

One example of this interaction is the relationship between religion and black nationalism. The black nationalist movements began in the late nineteenth century, when African Americans realized that the abolition of slavery did not mean the abolition of prejudicial treatment against them. Some black nationalists were Christian, some were atheist, and some followed new religious movements based in a blending of Islam, esoteric Christianity, and nationalism. Beginning with Noble Drew Ali's Moorish Science Temple in the 1910s and 1920s, these movements gave rise to a series of prophets over the course of the next decades. Though the Moorish Science Temple is still around, the most prominent of those prophets was Elijah Muhammad, the founder of the Nation of Islam. As a student of Wali or Wallace Fard, who later became regarded as a reincarnation of the divine on earth, Elijah came to be seen as the new Muhammad. He famously taught a creation story that neatly countered the racist stories, commonly told by white Christians at the time, of Africans descending from animals in the Garden of Eden, or being "cursed" with dark skin because of the misdeeds of Noah's son Ham. Elijah Muhammad taught instead that God had created humanity dark-skinned, but that an evil scientist (a common theme in literature of the day) had made a race of white-skinned devils. God had allowed these devils to rule over God's people, but had placed a time limit on their reign. Elijah Muhammad taught that the limit was to be reached imminently, at which point the white devils would be defeated and God's (dark-skinned) people allowed to rule again.

The Nation of Islam offered a potent combination of affirming beliefs and inspirational practices, with its proud men's militia and upstanding women's auxiliary. It inspired such leaders and public figures as Malcolm X and Muhammad Ali, and was one of the driving forces in the rise of the Black Power movement. And although Elijah Muhammad's son disbanded the movement in the mid-1980s, officially declaring all black Muslims to be a part of the Sunni branch of Islam, Minister Louis Farrakhan almost immediately revived it.

Despite its strengths, though, like all nationalisms the Nation of Islam has also had its problems. For instance, while it provided important roles for women, especially in its early years, the movement has always advocated very traditional gender roles that have drawn objections from feminists within and beyond African-American communities. Also like many nationalisms, and especially since the rise of Farrakhan, the Nation has alienated some of its former allies, including Jewish communities, through its exclusionary and often outright offensive comments and practices. In fact, at times representatives of Farrakhan's Nation have even met with white nationalists (who also tend to be anti-Semitic) to discuss their shared belief in the necessary separation of blacks and whites in the United States.

The combination of nationalism and religion, then, is both a potent and an unpredictable one. Mark Juergensmeyer, a sociologist who has devoted significant time to understanding religious violence, demonstrates the complex relationship between religious beliefs and both Christian nationalism and white nationalism in recent U.S. history. Christian nationalism, in the United States and elsewhere, has often been characterized by a belief that God has commanded Christians to institute Christian rule and Biblical law (or a very conservative interpretation thereof) throughout the world. When combined with the long-standing belief of some U.S. Christians that North America will be the site of the second coming of Christ, this form of Christian nationalism has led to the organization of groups dedicated to making the United States into an explicitly (conservative) Christian nation. Some, like former Religious Right leader Jerry Falwell, have followed the typical political channels of fundraising, lobbying, and electoral politics in their attempt to institute the Christian nation. Others, such as conservative Christian activist and convicted abortion clinic bomber Michael Bray, have taken more direct and violent routes. While not all nationalism ends in violence, extreme nationalism in combination with powerful religious convictions can prove quite dangerous.

The truth of this statement is nowhere so clear as in the conclusion to Walter Skya's book, *Japan's Holy War*. What Skya perhaps hyperbolically terms "radical Shintō ultranationalism" in the early twentieth century led directly to Japan's efforts to overtake East Asia, its ultimate goal to literally rule the world, and its general inability to believe in the possibility of failure. A religious nationalist force backed by a dedicated military that cannot conceive of its own failure is extremely dangerous both to its enemies (because of its determination and fearlessness) and to its own people (because of the hidden weaknesses brought about by a disbelief in the possibility of failure). And indeed, not only did Japan wreak havoc on its enemies, both in Asia and elsewhere in the world during World War II, it also ultimately lost the war in a spectacular and horrific way: the U.S. decision to visit nuclear devastation on Hiroshima and Nagasaki.

Lest Skya's discussion lead too easily to a condemnation of Japanese "fundamentalism" or even Islamic "fundamentalism" (both problematic terms, since "fundamentalism" refers to a specific theological movement within Christianity), we would do well to look again at the United States. Skya's description of "radical Shintō ultranationalism," in fact, looks suspiciously like Bellah's "civil religion in America," except that Skya disapproves of his subject while Bellah seems to endorse his. Skya describes Shintō nationalist beliefs that the nation has descended from the divine and is ultimately both approved by and responsible to that divine figure. Through these beliefs, nationalists were able to argue for the infallibility of their nation and to develop a powerful sense of national commitment among many of the Japanese people. Sound familiar?

So is religious nationalism the same thing as civil religion? Perhaps it is, and perhaps we call it religious nationalism when we disapprove and civil religion (or patriotism) when we approve. In closing our discussion, let's return to Bellah and consider whether this insight allows us to better understand both his work and that of his critics.

If civil religion in the United States is another term for religious (or, in some cases, quasi-religious) nationalism, then the repeated invocation of God in presidential addresses is not particularly surprising. We've seen that religion, in its interactions with both the state and the nation, can be used to bolster the legitimacy of the regime in power and to create a sense of national identity. In fact, strengthening the national identity may be another reason for the addition of God to the Pledge of Allegiance and the national motto in the 1950s. When a president invokes the divine, he is hinting or even stating outright that he has a divine mandate to rule. Such a mandate can become very dangerous when the president uses it to authorize attacks on or invasions of other countries, or to authorize the repression of groups within his own country. Likewise for the religion of the nation: with both a divine mandate and a position as itself divine, the nation at the center of any religious nationalism—whether a nation-state or an ethnic or religious community— becomes powerful and justified in its actions.

Viewing civil religion as a form of religious nationalism also clarifies some of the aspects of Bellah's theory that have been challenged over the years—especially the exclusions that Long and others have criticized. As Skya demonstrates, religious nationalism is generally in the hands of a particular, often dominant group (national elites in the case of religious nationalism in a nation-state, or men in the case of ethnic/racial nationalisms). Logically, then, the ethos of that nationalism would speak most forcefully to members of that dominant group, and would exclude or marginalize, either intentionally or unintentionally, those outside of the group. Bellah, himself a member of the dominant group as a white, male academic at a prestigious institution, failed to see the exclusionary nature of civil religion/U.S. religious nationalism because he was included. Power is always easier to see when you don't hold it than it is when you do.

Extended Application

It is often said that the best unifier is a common enemy, and indeed, nationalisms are particularly potent when the members of a nation feel threatened externally. The insights of the authors in this section can help us to understand the powerful and ultimately fateful reactions in the United States to the terrorist attacks of September 11, 2001.

When members of the international guerrilla network, al-Qaeda, hijacked four airplanes and flew them into New York City's World Trade Center towers and the Pentagon in Washington, D.C. (in the fourth plane, passengers overpowered the hijackers and crashed the plane in a field in Pennsylvania), many people around the world experienced shock and grief at the death and destruction that followed. People from the United States, unaccustomed to external attacks on their own territory, felt these emotions particularly acutely, along with a sense of violation and fear. Yet, by the following day, expressions of nationalism and civil religion had far outpaced those of grief. U.S. flags sprouted along freeway overpasses, from front yards, and from car windows. Members of Congress gathered on the steps of the Capitol building to sing an a cappella version of "God Bless America," and that phrase appeared on billboards, banners, even electronic reader boards that normally advertised daily specials. When the stores ran out of flags, the newspapers printed full-spread, full-color flags for their readers to clip out, and flag images for computer wallpaper spread rapidly over the Internet. Where "God Bless America" didn't appear, the words were, instead, "United We Stand."

To many, these responses may seem obvious and unsurprising. But we can learn a lot by asking some probing questions. Who was standing, for instance, and why were they united? Against whom? And why were God and the flag so important in the aftermath of the September 11 attacks? Why nationalism instead of grief?

Let's go back to Bellah to answer these questions, and think about what aspects of the mainstream U.S. civil religion were implicated in the September 11 attacks. How did the mainstream representations of the United States—in presidential speeches, major newspaper editorials, and the like—imagine the country before September of 2001? I have suggested in the past (see Wilcox, 2006) that there are six key elements to the U.S. self-image: omnipotence, omniscience, impregnability, divine election, supreme goodness, and a salvific mission to the world. Many of these are interconnected, and many are tied up with the country's self-image as the "leader of the free world."

Omnipotence refers to the state of being all-powerful. With a very large and well-trained military force and an immense stockpile of weapons, the United States sees itself as an extremely powerful country—perhaps the most powerful in the world. Economically, although the twenty-first century has seen a dwindling of U.S. dominance, the country still sees itself as a financial powerhouse. And diplomatically, the United States represents itself as a staunch and forceful ally with the ability to resolve disputes and enforce international agreements. The September 11 attacks brought this omnipotence into question: if the United States was all-powerful, how could two of its most iconic buildings, one of which represented its military, be attacked?

Omniscience means being all-knowing. With intelligence operatives active throughout the world and a network of technologically advanced spying devices in place, the United States often claims to both its citizens and its enemies that it can spot and stop any and all planned attacks on its soil or its interests around the world. While claiming to protect the privacy of its citizens, the country at the same time suggests that there is no privacy whatsoever for its enemies, implying that it knows less about its citizens only because it chooses to respect their privacy, not because it has no way of seeing into their personal affairs. The September 11 attacks undermined this part of the nation's self-image, as well: if the United States was omniscient, how could it have been ignorant of such a large-scale plan of attack? Some conspiracy theorists even went so far as to speculate that the United States remained omniscient: it had known about the attacks, they claimed, and President Bush either had allowed them or even had planned them himself. The story of omniscience can be extremely difficult to let go.

Belief in the country's omnipotence and omniscience led directly to belief in its impregnability. In 2001, the United States had not been attacked on its own soil by an external enemy for nearly 60 years: since Japan bombed Hawaii's Pearl Harbor in 1941. Even the Pearl Harbor bombing had not been an attack on the U.S. mainland. An attack not only on the mainland, but on highly symbolic buildings, including the nerve center of the nation's military and intelligence forces, was completely unprecedented. If the United States had seen itself as impregnable before the attacks, afterward it saw itself as penetrated. News reports of the attacks even used words evoking rape, such as "violation."

The concept of divine election links directly to Bellah's idea of civil religion: it means that the country sees itself as specially chosen by God. Some Christians in the United States believe that their country will be the site of the return of Christ and the location of the post-apocalyptic kingdom of God. Others, in a slightly more secularized version of this belief, believe that God has shown particular favor to the United States and has blessed it with prosperity and safety. Remember the Calvinists who worked so hard in order to gain the material benefits that would prove they had been predestined as the chosen of God? The United States has done much the same thing, making use of its economic and military successes to argue that it is God's chosen country. But how could God's chosen country be attacked in such a spectacular and devastating manner? The September 11 attacks brought the country's sense of divine election into question, too.

Along with divine election came a sense of the country as supremely good. Not only blessed by God, the United States saw itself as a representative of good around the globe, bringing food and shelter to the needy and freedom and democracy to those struggling under the leadership of dictators. As with the above aspects of the civil religion, this one required some psychological blinders to be believed, since poverty was on the rise in the early twenty-first century United States even as the wealthy grew wealthier, and since the United States had been involved throughout its history in numerous wars and colonial adventures of dubious value to the inhabitants of the regions where they had been waged. Yet, one of the most common questions in the press after the September 11 attacks was the incredulous, "Why do they hate us?" Many in the country were so convinced of the supreme goodness of the United States that they could not fathom why anyone would want to attack their country.

Supreme goodness and divine election combine to produce a sense of divine calling to a salvific mission in the world. As the self-styled "leader of the free world," the United States believed (and still believes) itself to have a mission to spread democracy, and often capitalism, to countries around the globe. To this end, the country has been involved in countless diplomatic efforts, United Nations peacekeeping forces, and self-initiated wars. Yet, according to the videos broadcast by the late al-Qaeda leader Osama bin Laden, al-Qaeda targeted the United States for attack because its efforts, at least in the Middle East, were unwanted. How can a supremely good nation, divinely chosen for a salvific mission to the world, be rebuffed by those it is attempting to "save"? The September 11 attacks raised a powerful challenge to the U.S. sense of salvific mission.

The al-Qaeda attacks challenged the nation's civil religion—the nation in religion, the religion in the nation, and the nation as religion—through undermining its sense of omnipotence, omniscience, impregnability, divine election, supreme goodness, and salvific mission in the world. With the civil religion powerfully challenged in this way, it seems less surprising that people across the United States would respond by displaying one of the most powerful collective representations of the nation: the U.S. flag. Furthermore, the appearance of God seems less remarkable in this light: if the nation's sense of divine election had been challenged, then of course its leaders and members would respond with "God Bless America." And the ubiquity of "United We Stand"? Unity reinforced the ongoing existence of the nation, and standing together reinforced its strength.

We can take this civil religion analysis further by returning to Skya's reflections on religious nationalism. Whereas Japan in the early twentieth century was a religiously nationalist country that could not conceive of defeat, the United States in the early twenty-first was one whose religious nationalism had been challenged and had returned with renewed vigor, and one threatened with defeat that had responded with even greater determination to succeed. If Japan was dangerous in the early twentieth century, the United States in the early twenty-first was even more so. It responded to the challenge to its religious nationalism globally by re-emphasizing its omnipotence, invading first Afghanistan and then Iraq. To underline its omniscience it restricted civil liberties for citizens but especially for non-citizens, visitors and residents alike. It reinforced impregnability by implementing draconian security measures at all ports and points of entry, reinforced divine election by stressing God's blessing of the country, and refocused attention on its supreme goodness and divine election by insisting that its invasions were bringing democracy to the citizens of Afghanistan and Iraq. While civil religion and religious nationalism can be dangerous when unchallenged, perhaps they are even more so when challenged.

Exercises:

1.   Spend some time watching national politicians' speeches and other representations of the nation. Do you think there is a mainstream civil religion in your country today? If so, of what does it consist? Make a list of what you think are the components of that civil religion, and compare it to your friends' and/or classmates' lists.

2.   Was the U.S. Ninth Circuit Court correct to declare the presence of "under God" in the Pledge of Allegiance to be unconstitutional? Organize a debate between yourself and your friends or classmates on this issue. Just for fun, randomly assign people to a side. Then partway through the debate, allow people to switch to the side they most support.

8

Positioning Religion in Modernity: State and Buddhism in China

Yoshiko Ashiwa

MODERNITY AND THE CREATION OF THE SPACE OF RELIGION

The late nineteenth and early twentieth centuries were a time in Asia of shaping modernity by, actively or passively, reshaping Western modernity. This dynamic transformation involved various projects that demanded the abandonment or reform of previous ideologies, systems, institutions, and consciousness. One of the projects of this modernity was religion. The term "religion" was translated from European languages into Asian ones, creating such neologisms as *shūkyō, zongjiao*, and *agama* that spread among intellectuals and political elites in Asia, who quickly adapted "religion" into their modern thinking as a necessary space for the making of a modern state. Therefore, in seeking a modern state, a space of religion newly emerged as part of this indispensable apparatus of modernity. The space of religion was constituted mainly by two actors. One was politicians and state officials, who promulgated modern constitutions, laws, and regulations regarding religion, often through conflicts and tensions linked to local politics and value systems. The other was reformist religious leaders and laypersons, who advocated the making of modern teachings, disciplines, and organizations within the established world religions, such as Buddhism and Christianity, in cooperation with or opposition, to state elites.

Hence, a space of religion emerges through modern state formation. This dynamic process involves the efforts to position religion undertaken by both religious reformers and state elites. In considering this process, this chapter explores several questions. How do the state and modern nation system relate to and mutually compose each other? How does the space of religion emerge through this process and what are its attributes? What influence does the process have on the beliefs of individuals? In the context of China the state elite has sustained a strong self-consciousness of modernizing from the late nineteenth century. Even today the state elite in the People's Republic, including officials of the Chinese Communist Party (Party) and the government, has a strong consciousness of China as being "in the process of developing toward socialist modernization" and forcefully imposes it on the people. An examination of the efforts to impose the modern concept of religion on Buddhism during the 1920s and 1930s and then in the 1980s and 1990s illuminates the historically ongoing process of the creation of a space of religion and the process of state formation.

According to Henri Lefebvre (1991), space is constituted by the integration of physical, institutional, and semiotic aspects. In the Chinese context of modernity, the physical space of religion refers to sites, including land, buildings, and monuments, that have been repeatedly destroyed and rebuilt throughout history, especially from the latter half of the nineteenth century, when China entered modernity during a period of extreme political turmoil. Repeated destruction and reconstruction reflects contestation over the modern concept of religion and attempts to impose it. Institutional space refers to religion in law and regulations controlled or defined by the state, and also religion as defined by associations, devotee societies, temple administration, and seminaries. Semiotic space refers to the meanings and discourses of religion through the practice of rituals and religious activities, which include beliefs. This chapter focuses on the institutional aspects linked to the physical and semiotic aspects, a focus expressed through the phrase "positioning of religion in space." A major attribute of modernity is that the space of religion emerges and is positioned on the platform of the modern state through projects to institutionalize certain principles that create, reshape, and allocate situations, peoples, and organizations. Thus, modernity is not a one-sided project of the state to discipline people's thoughts but is a reciprocal project of religions and states reshaping themselves and each other.

Projects of Modernity

Earlier modernization theorists such as Talcott Parsons, Daniel Lerner, and Clifford Geertz posited a paradigm of an abstracted single path of Western modernization as an ideal, universal process. However, this paradigm, which maintained that Asian countries are in earlier stages of this linear, universal modernization, has been acutely questioned and criticized. For example, Talal Asad (1993) has pointed out Clifford Geertz's confusion, or rather ambiguities, of linear Western history of modernization and indigenous histories and cultures. Contemporary social theories increasingly recognize "modernity" as, multiple projects or "a series of inter-linked projects" that, as Asad writes,

can be attained through various routes and processes in both Western and Asian societies.

> It is right to say that "modernity" is neither a totally coherent object nor a clearly bounded one, and that many of its elements originate in relations with the histories of peoples outside Europe. Modernity is a project—or rather, a series of interlinked projects—that certain people in power seek to achieve. The project aims at institutionalizing a number of (sometimes conflicting, often evolving) principles: constitutionalism, moral autonomy, democracy, human rights, civil equality, industry, consumerism, freedom of the market—and secularism. (Asad 2003: 13)

Asad's definition of modernity has two significant points. First, it is noteworthy that he defines the essential characteristics of modernity as something furthered by specific persons wielding subjective power. Modernity is not something that emerges spontaneously from the everyday lives of people who are embedded in enduring styles and values, but instead is an amalgamation of ongoing projects furthered by politicians, intellectuals, capitalists, state bureaucrats, and other power elites. Second, he stresses that these projects of modernity intentionally aim at institutionalizing such modern "new" principles as constitutionalism, industry, nationalism, civil rights and market economy human rights, civil society, and secularism. These projects are intertwined with modern state formation and the institutionalization of these principles.

Modernity is multiple projects or, rather a series of interlinked projects, of which religion is a part. Initiated by power holders, religion is directly linked to state formation through the institutionalization of such principles as secularism. Asad mostly emphasizes the institutionalization of principles of secularism as the foundation of the state. In this chapter I will argue that this institutionalization and counterinstitutionalization of religion are achieved through allocations and configurations of people, power, organizations, physical land, and property ownership through which the principles are represented.

Spread of Religious Space to Asia

Asia entered modernity through the collapse and reorganization of previous political regimes in the context of multiplying contacts with the West. These contacts consisted of new interstate relations, commodity exchanges, and popular flows (of immigrants, adventurers, ideologues, businesspeople) made possible by advances in transportation and domestic political turmoil. This period saw the beginnings of movements of large-scale globalization that connected the societies of the West and Asia through the expansion of colonialism, capitalism, and mass migration. This triggered the emergence of unprecedented spaces. It also led to the establishment in Asia of many spaces that were constituted by conflicts, contradictions, resistance, and amalgamation, such as the absolutizing and relativizing of Western values and their refusal and acceptance, and imitation and transformations, that were occurring under the coercive power of colonization, imperialism, capitalism, and efforts at modern state formation in Asia.

This process can be described as the fermentation of modernity, as Asian elites haphazardly formed myriad ideologies from pieces that incorporated a wide range of modern Western thought: Enlightenment history, scientism, rationalization, evolutionism, imperialism, anti-imperialism, socialism, pan-Asianism, Marxism, democracy, ethnicity, secularism, asceticism, spiritualism, and so on. These pieces of thought and ideologies, in other words sets of value systems, were combined and woven in integrated and contradictory fashions into numerous indigenous slogans, writings, and policies that composed the activities and disciplines of movements. Prasenjit Duara (1994) writes that some of these ideologies and movements triggered bifurcated histories that were then variously suppressed, absorbed, or ignored by the state as it

made a master narrative of modernization. It is through this process that religious space was formed.

An active space of religion constituted by these multiple ideologies and movements rapidly emerged in this period. However, it appeared not only in Asian countries that were struggling to form modern states but also through the expansion of such discursive spaces in the West as: Oriental studies, the study of Eastern religions, and the separation of religious studies from theology at Chicago, Oxford, and Heidelberg universities; the salons of politicians, intellectuals, and entrepreneurs; the 1893 World Parliament of Religion at the Chicago Exposition; the numerous ecumenical encounters of missionaries and scholars organized by Christians, which included meetings of entrepreneurs, bureaucrats, intellectuals, and revolutionaries from the West and Asia. On the one hand, in this space of religion in the West there can be seen emerging a powerfully resonant orientalism and relativization of the values of Christianity to encompass non-Christian religions. On the other hand, in Asia the activities of capitalists, bureaucrats, intellectuals, clergy, and revolutionaries constructed and institutionalized the space of religion alongside such other new spaces as a modern economy, politics, and science.

Over this period movements in Sri Lanka, Thailand, Burma, Japan, China, and other Asian countries created an indigenous conceptual term of "religion" that was equivalent to the English word "religion." This subsequently promoted the representation and acceptance of the concept and the classification and reform of extant beliefs to fit the category of "religion." In the case of Buddhism, its fit to the category of "religion" developed through imitating and adapting Christian missionary ethics and techniques, and through attempts to position and institutionalize Buddhism within the process of state building. This led Buddhism, as a modern religion, to accommodate ethnocentrism, modernist clergy and devotees, rationalism, and anti-imperialism, and then to internalize them. Furthermore, in this historical process the depth of the rationalism, pan-Asianism, and cosmopolitanism of the emerging space of religion was as remarkable as its novelty. Intersections among the Sri Lankan reformer of Buddhism Anagarika Dharmapala, the Chinese Buddhist devotee Yang Wenhui, who proposed the modern reform of Chinese Buddhism, the monk Taixu, who actively pursued the modernization of Chinese Buddhism, and the Japanese scholarly monk Nanjō Fumio, who assisted Max Muller and other Asianists, were constituted by ideas, networks, and encounters in Japan, Sri Lanka, North America, and Europe. The thoughts and understandings nourished in these interactions were mutually catalytic, and inspired the emergence and growth of new movements in these regions. These movements were a driving force of numerous projects that constituted modernity.

Spread of Religious Space to China

Religion in contemporary China has been involved in a continuous series of such projects of modernity. Religion was in decline during the troubled state-building of the Republican era and the first decade of the People's Republic of China. It was decisively suppressed during the decade-long Cultural Revolution (1966–76). Then, following the major shift toward a market economy from the late 1970s, religious activities were officially sanctioned and swiftly reemerged (Luo 1991; MacInnis 1989). According to a survey by university-based researchers, China has 300 million religious believers above the age of sixteen. Buddhists, Daoists, Catholics, Muslims, and Protestants account for 67.4 percent of these believers. About 200 million are Buddhists, Daoists, or worshippers of the Dragon King, God of Fortune, and other figures, while about 40 million are Protestants (*Wenweipo* 2007; Wu 2007).

There are various explanations for this rapid revival of religion. One is that the change in state policy toward religion from 1979 has released people's suppressed desire for religion, and enabled them to find in religion an alternative to communist ideology (Overmyer 2003). Another explanation, reflecting the role of the Catholic Church in the collapse of communist party-states in Eastern Europe, sees the revival as a shift to a more liberal state with an emerging civil society brought about by a newly tolerant religious policy (Madsen 1998). However, these interpretations are inadequate because they presuppose a sharp disjuncture of the circumstances surrounding religion before and after 1979. A close examination of the empirical details of the religious revival after 1979, such as the interaction between the state and religious organizations, and the conflicts and accommodations of religion and political ideologies, shows that the more long-term accumulation of cultural, historical, and social forms of capital before what appears as a conspicuous change around 1979 prepared a multilayered foundation and ideological basis for the emergence of the space of religion. Furthermore, these capital forms have emerged almost unnoticed in local fields of revival with significant political meanings.

An explanation of the contemporary revival of religion should go beyond a focus on the period since the new state religious policies that were introduced in 1979 or even from the founding of the People's Republic of China. The revival is imbricated in aspects of religious organization and teachings that predate not only the 1979 policy changes but also the 1949 establishment of the new state. Therefore, an explanation of the revival needs to be grounded in the seeds of the projects of modernity sown around the turn of the twentieth century from which the space of religion emerged.

As Asad points out, modernity is neither coherent nor totally bounded from other phenomena. If we assume that modernity is a continuum of interlinked multiple projects or if, as Duara (1995) says, bifurcated histories are hidden behind the linear history that constructs the master narrative, then the contemporary revival of religion, especially Buddhism, can be seen as the resulting integration of parts of all these multiple projects or bifurcated histories. Religion in China has to be viewed as a thread of the fabric of modernity, the design of which began to take distinctive and visible form around the end of the nineteenth century.

STIRRINGS TOWARD THE MODERN STATE AND THE SPACE OF RELIGION

By the late nineteenth century the Qing dynasty was collapsing from challenges both internal (such as from the Taiping Rebellion) and external (such as from the Opium War). There began at this time reform and institutionalization by the religions themselves to become modern and fit the space of religion, which the modern state was also struggling to create. From the state powerholders' point of view, which had been inconsistent in regard to the positioning of religion in the state system and ideology, the work of positioning religion in the system was, in fact, part of a very careful arranging that was directly linked to the building of the modern state itself. This generated various arguments and debates about religion that were linked to power struggles within the state but that also enabled the state to recognize the existence of religion, underscoring how the placement of religion within the state system is a crucial part of the process of modern state formation.

Among the modernist political and cultural elites were many who sought a subjective amalgamation of technology and the Chinese spirit. These persons included intellectuals and elite government bureaucrats, some of whom were also political activists and revolutionaries, and most of whom had the experience of living and traveling in Western countries as well as Japan. They used the knowledge they acquired abroad to achieve a breakthrough in China's confrontation with the chaotic situation. Many had a keen interest in Buddhism, because

they saw the possibility of reforming it to be a modern religion to express an essential core of Chineseness as an alternative to Christianity. However, Buddhism in the late Qing dynasty had reached a nadir as many temples were abandoned or inhabited by self-ordained monks and other self-styled practitioners. During this time Buddhist teachings were barely kept alive among scattered lay-intellectual devotees (*jushi*) who collected, studied, and edited Buddhist sutras.[1] Buddhism faced further challenges from Christian missionaries who were vigorously proselytizing among people from all walks of life—from the worldly and powerful to the parochial and poor.

In the early twentieth century, the Republican state launched the Convert Temples to Schools Movement (*miaochan xingxue yundong*) and the Smashing Superstition Movement (*mixin dapo yundong*). These movements deepened Buddhism's dire straits, accelerating modern reform efforts within Buddhism by active and enlightened monks and devotees.

The Smashing Superstition Movement: Demolishing Superstition and Dispositioning Local Power

When the Nationalist Party took power in the provinces around Shanghai in the 1920s, a movement to ban "superstition" and "sorcery" by destroying temples and idols was underway. Called the Smashing Superstition Movement, it was initiated by political reformists in local Nationalist Party branches at the county level and below. A study by Mitani Takashi (1978) shows how this movement reflected not only the antipathy of "science" toward "superstition" but also the complexity of politics at that time. The movement's key promoters were younger members of local party branches influenced by the May Fourth Movement of 1919 to uphold democracy and science, and who were also interested in communism. After receiving a modern education in urban centers after 1919 that promoted belief in democracy and science, they returned to their hometowns as schoolteachers and local intellectuals. They became the majority in local Nationalist Party branches and were the local leaders of the movement to smash the shrines and idols that the people worshipped. Their consciousness is evident in one of their publications.

> We must make the people thoroughly understand the exercise of the rights of the people and propel them toward the rational way so as to completely free them from the trap of old conventions. Divine authority is an obstacle to the development of the people's rights and the societal evolution. A society based on divine authority can never coexist with the new society based on the Three Principles of the People. (Chou 1927)

These young party members viewed the masses as obstinately believing in divine oracles and prophets, obeying traditional authority and conventions, failing to comprehend individual rights, and accepting subjugation by local landowners. Therefore, they viewed the destruction of temples and idols as necessary to enlighten, train, and guide the people, in order to direct them away from their false ideas and subjugation toward democracy and science.

Mitani points out that the political aspects of the Smashing Superstition Movement reflected the contemporary political split between the Nationalist and Communist parties. First, the movement was an explicit action by young Nationalist Party members to resist the conservatism among some central bureaucrats in the national capital of Nanjing. The central state, led by Chiang Kai-shek, desperately needed the support of capitalists and warlords. But the young members of local Nationalist Party branches were idealists who, influenced by communism, sought to awaken the masses for radical revolution. Their condemnation of what the conservatives stood for led them to launch the Smashing Superstition Movement.

Second, the Smashing Superstition Movement aimed to undermine the power and prestige of the landowners and gentry class who, as major local power holders, were in charge of the festivals, gods, and temples that the movement attacked. As a result, the new authority established in the center was expanding its control over the old power of local society. The state was attempting to reorganize the government administration but its weak local control made even tax collection difficult, while entrenched landowners and gentry still held power in county governments. Therefore, the destruction of the traditions controlled by these local power holders symbolically expressed the new power of the central government and the invasion of ideology, smashing and conquering the ideology and social structure of local entrenched authorities. The destruction of local beliefs, organizations, and sites controlled by these old entrenched authorities exposed symbolically and revealed practically the destruction of the old order and the power of the new regime.

In the early stage of the Smashing Superstition Movement all religious activities were considered premodern, unenlightened superstition. Buddhist and Daoist temples were included as targets of attack along with local deities. Buddhists complained to the Nanjing government about the attacks, and in response the central state issued *Standards for Preserving and Abandoning Gods and Shrines (Shenci cunfei biaojun)* that decreed what could and could be not be attacked and destroyed. The major criteria for determining whether a site should be destroyed or preserved were historical importance and scientific significance. The criteria had two categories defining sites to be preserved. One was the sage category (*xianzhelei*), which consisted of deities that had contributed to the nation, state, and society, possessed scholarly knowledge that had benefited the people, or had exhibited a loyalty, devotion, filial piety, and justice that inspired pride among the masses, such the agriculture god (Shennong), Confucius, and Guanweng. The second category to be preserved was the religious category (*zongjiaolei*): it consisted of "pure and true" teachings that ordinary people could believe in, such as Buddhism and parts of Daoism. The next two categories designated sites to be destroyed. The old gods category (*gushenlei*) referred to the gods that had been worshipped before the development of science but had since become meaningless, such as the gods of the sun, moon, and stars. The minor spirits category (*yincilei*) consisted of plant and animal spirits, such as the cow goblin and the snake god, that could also be destroyed (Mitani 1978: 10). However, these guidelines were not observed. They had been devised by upper class intellectuals on the basis of science and rationalism, but were interpreted locally as justifying the destruction of all religion. This was understandable because in the chaotic circumstances of Buddhism many temples were derelict and self-styled practitioners abounded, making it difficult to distinguish between Buddhist temples and those of the old gods and minor spirits. Furthermore, it is probable that the local people were not conscious of any clear-cut distinction between the categories. Therefore, the Smashing Superstition Movement launched in 1928 angered the masses of people and turned them against the central state being formed by the Nationalist Party and toward the Communist Party.

Two things are clear as a result of the Smashing Superstition Movement. One is that the actions and behavior toward religion created a space for it in which rationalism, scienticism, and enlightenment thinking—disciplines of modernity—clearly appeared in the space of religion. Second, the space of religion is highly vulnerable, and its manipulation and institutionalization had large influences on the process of reforming and organizing the political structure of the new regime and exhibiting its power.

The Convert Temples to Schools Movement: The Utility of Religious Facilities

A new movement was launched at the same time as the Smashing Superstition Movement to confiscate temple property for the construction of vocational schools and libraries to educate the masses. This use of temples for public education had first been advocated in a essay "Exhortation to Study" (*Quan xue bian*) written in 1901 by Zhang Zhidong, an enthusiastic proponent of adapting Western thought and technology to China. At that time it led to a movement to appropriate temples for schools that shook Buddhist indifference to the drastic changes occurring in society. The movement was revived in the late 1920s by Tai Shuangqiu, a modern rationalist with a doctorate in education from Columbia University who taught at Jiangsu University. In an article titled "The Converting Temples to Schools Movement" he called for the rapid dissemination of compulsory education. He saw the entry of children into temples to become clerics as a serious obstacle to modern education, and viewed temple property and wealth as a huge reservoir of capital for the construction of a modern education system as the foundation of the state. The Convert Temples to Schools Movement encouraged local education bureaus and universities to occupy temple lands and buildings, expel the clergy and confiscate their wealth, and reconstitute the temples as modern schools. This movement spread concurrently with the Smashing Superstition Movement.

However, the Convert Temples to Schools Movement contradicted the *Regulations for the Supervision of Monasteries and Temples* issued earlier, in 1915, by Yuan Shikai, then president of China, which stipulated that "Temples should not be abandoned and eliminated" and "Temple wealth and property should not be subject to occupation, confiscation, and fines based on pretexts" (Ohira 2002). The contradiction reflects two contesting themes of modern ideology. One is that the enlightened modern state guarantees freedom of religion while the second is that it promotes rational religion and the abandoning of premodern superstition. This contradiction led to several legal cases. Ohira summarizes one such case that was reported in the *Jiangsu Provincial Government Communiqué*

(*Jiangsu sheng zhengfu gongbao*). The abbot of Yuntaishan Faqi Temple, Guanyun county, in Zhejiang province, was sued and arrested for his "wrong behavior." The Nationalist Party county branch ordered the temple's property and wealth to be used for educational purposes. Central University (*Zhongyang daxue*) applied to the county government to do so, and the temple's property was duly confiscated. The county government allocated 40 percent of the temple's wealth for education and 60 percent for temple maintenance. However, the Jiangsu Buddhist Federation (*Jiangsu Fojiao lianhehui*), which took legal ownership of the temple after the abbot's arrest, refused to accept this and demanded the return of the property, upon which now stood a school and agriculture research center. This caught the county government between the Convert Temples to Schools Movement and the *Regulations*, the former decreeing the utilization of temple property for education, and the latter prohibiting the occupation and confiscation of temple property. The local government appealed to higher levels of the government for a resolution to this case. However, the provincial government only gave an ambiguous response, which restrained hasty confiscations but did not touch on the issue of the ownership of temple property. Nevertheless, in restraining confiscations, the provincial government determined that the Convert Temples to Schools Movement enlarged the interests of the government organizations, such as the university and Ministry of Education, whereas the Smashing Superstition Movement was based on the Nationalist Party's guidance (*zhidao*). The Nationalist Party criticized this decision with the counter argument that, "The Smashing Superstition Movement is not related to temple land and property. The provincial declaration to stop the movement and protect religion is contrary to the party's policy principles" (Ohira 2002). The Nationalist Party criticized the government for its inadequate study of the party's spirit. Despite a subsequent amendment to the *Regulations*, the contradiction still remained over

the legitimacy of smashing religions labeled as "premodern superstition" and the confiscation of temple property for the public good, while, as a modern state, guaranteeing freedom of religion.

With regard to modernity, the Convert Temples to Schools Movement generated three important consequences. First, Buddhists voluntarily started to make their own organizations. In 1912 the Chinese Buddhist Association (*Zhonghua Fojiao zonghui*) was established by the monk Jing'an, as the first nationwide organization in China for the purpose of protecting temple wealth and property. However, the state soon forced it to dissolve, leaving only local organizations, such as the aforementioned Jiangsu Buddhist Federation. During the Convert Temples to Schools Movement in the late 1920s, the first national meeting of the All-China Buddhist Representative Conference (*Quanguo Fojiao daibiao huiyi*) was convened to oppose the movement and reform Buddhism. The conference inaugurated a new national Chinese Buddhist Association that had the support of Chiang Kai-shek. The Convert Temples to Schools Movement compelled Buddhists to organize as a collective entity that could negotiate with other forces in society to oppose confiscation of temple property. This is the moment when Buddhism entered a new venue of political institutionalization during the process of modern state formation; Buddhism dressed up as "religion" that could cooperate and resist the power of the central authorities who were making a modern state.

Second, the Convert Temples to Schools Movement created a shared recognition among the new state, Buddhists, and the masses that the public interest was a significant criterion and discourse for evaluation and legitimacy. With regard to who and what constituted the "public interest," however, there were differences in the modern state system according to which subject was making the claim. Most intellectuals viewed temples as feudal remnants that harmed people's livelihood and urged that the labor of clergy and temple wealth be put to public use. The state declared that religion could not passively orient itself to the public interest through rituals and beliefs but had to commit temple resources to benefit society through social welfare and philanthropic projects. Thereupon, Buddhists began to use temple property to promote the public benefit and, furthermore, to undertake a reform of Buddhist teachings that emphasized the benefit for people in this world rather than in the other world after death. Putting aside differences in the interpretations of public benefit, the rise of the concept of public interest underscores the significance of temple property, facilities, and wealth as a public space. The modern state principle, "public, collective bodies that do not contribute to the public interest should not be recognized" became established as a norm with absolute legitimacy, even within the reformist ideas to modernize Buddhism.

Third, the Convert Temples to Schools Movement furthered a new recognition of religion and religious sites as a key arena of contestation over the institutionalization of property rights, ideology, and authority in the modern state system. The aforementioned examples illuminate the struggles over power and ideology between the center and local state, government and party, and enlightened young elites and conservative landowners. At issue were the interpretation and handling of religious issues that were created by juridical and administrative decision-making regarding property rights that reached from the local to national levels. Regarding religion, there were conflicts between, for example, the Ministry of Education and the Nationalist Party. Moreover, the conflicts involved not only a clash between premodern and modern ideologies but even disputes within the ideology of modernity. A tension between the modern principles of individual freedom of belief and upholding the public interest occurred in the context of the Convert Temples to Schools Movement and the *Regulations for the Control of Monasteries and Temples*. The Convert Temples to Schools Movement was a

modernizing project that sought a position for religion vis-à-vis the central state, which was in the process of modern state formation. In this moment of crises, there arose a group of Buddhists who subjectively participated in state formation.

The Reform Movement of Buddhism: Modernization from Within

Although Buddhism was in decline in the late nineteenth century, a modern reform movement was growing among a small number of Buddhists. Two of the movement's representative leaders were the lay devotee Yang Wenhui and the monk Taixu, both of whom were deeply aware of the changes in the world outside China. Yang Wenhui had lived in Europe as a member of the Chinese legation in the late Qing dynasty. There he met many people working on Buddhism, including Max Müller at Oxford University and Nanjio Bunyiu (Nanjō Bunyū), the scholar-monk of the Honganji sect who assisted Müller in editing and translating Buddhist sutras. In Europe Yang witnessed how Christianity was positioned within the system of the modern state and also how Buddhism, which had almost disappeared in China, was a newly established academic discipline in such prominent universities as Oxford. Upon his return to China, he resigned his government post to concentrate on collecting Buddhist texts. He met Anagarika Dharmapala, a prominent reformer of Buddhism in Sri Lanka, when Dharmapala visited China after attending the 1893 World Parliament of Religions in Chicago. He was impressed by Dharmapala's efforts to return Buddhism to India, spread Buddhism throughout the world, and promote the modern reform of Buddhism. Yang edited and printed the scattered Buddhist sutras he was collecting, and established the Jetavana Hermitage (*Zkihuan jingshe*) for the innovative, modern Buddhist education of monks and devotees. His emphasis on Buddhist education, the modernization of Buddhism, and Buddhism's contribution to society influenced enlightened devotees who became thinkers, political activists, and reformers. One of the first students of the Jetavana Hermitage was the young monk Taixu. A disciple of the monk Jing'an, who advocated the reform of Buddhism along traditional lines, Taixu dedicated himself to the modernization of Buddhist teachings, pedagogy, and the monastic system in the troubled years when Buddhism was under attack by the Smashing Superstition and Convert Temples to Schools movements during the turbulent emergence of the modern state (Ohira 2000; Pittman 2001).

Taixu made three major contributions.[2] First, the he advocated a Buddhist reform movement that would be guided by "three revolutions": a "revolution of teaching and doctrines" (*jiaoli*) a "revolution of institutions" (*jiaozhi*), and a "revolution of religious property" (*jiaochan*). Regarding the doctrinal revolution, Taixu believed that Buddhism should be concerned not with problems after death but with those of the living world. Thus he advocated social salvation, studying the truth of human life, and contributing to the progress of human beings. Regarding the institutional revolution, Taixu worked to reform the monastic system and established monastery schools that were organized along modern lines. Instruction was to be in classrooms with standardized grading and a curriculum that included not only Buddhist texts but also secular subjects, some of which were also just newly emerging in the West, such as "Western history, Asian history, the history of Theravada and other Buddhist traditions, literature, mathematics, psychology, and sociology. His essay "Reorganization of the Sangha System" (*Zhengli cengjia zhidu lun*), written between the two waves of the Convert Temples to Schools Movement, advocated the rationalization of temple management and the economic self-sufficiency of the clergy. By the revolution of religious property he meant that temple property should not be privately owned by abbots but rather collectively shared by all the monks residing in a temple. Through these three

revolutions Taixu envisioned the emergence of a new type of Buddhism that could be active in the real world: he called it "human Buddhism" (*renjian Fojiao*), contrasted it with the Buddhism that was focused on rituals and meditation, and he devoted his life to it.

Second, Taixu was oriented toward a "world Buddhism." Influenced by Yang Wenhui, he had a strong vision of Buddhism as a universal religion that was equivalent to Western Christianity. He saw China as the center of Buddhism for promoting its worldwide spread.[3] However, his orientation to world Buddhism was limited, because his apparent cosmopolitanism was contradicted by strong Chinese nationalism and he confined his appeal to Chinese audiences domestically and overseas (Ashiwa 2002).

Third, Taixu cultivated a large web of personal connections, among Buddhists as well as in secular fields. In his youth he had steeped himself in new intellectual streams by reading Tolstoy, Marx, Bakunin, and Kotoku Shusui (a socialist anarchist), and had been involved in socialist activities and discussions with anarchists. His acquaintances included Christian missionaries, Japanese Buddhists, politicians, scholars, lay devotees in business communities in China and abroad, and revolutionaries. At a later stage of his life he developed and maintained collaborative ties with central political leaders including a close relationship with Chiang Kaishek. Chiang dispatched him as special envoy to India and other South Asian countries during World War II to promote solidarity with Buddhist countries and gain allies against the Japanese and communists.

During the domestic political turbulence of modern state formation, the meaning and very existence of Buddhism was questioned and passed through the sieve of modernity. Some Buddhists worked for the survival of Buddhism by seeking to adapt it to the new conditions and ideologies of the modern state. Trained by intellectuals and enlightened lay devotees, they started to recognize the shape of religion that the modern state system requires. The modern state system itself, too, was taking shape through many projects, one of which was positioning religion within it. Buddhists' recognition of their situation was the starting point for a project to further the modern reform of the monastic system and Buddhist teachings by promoting a human Buddhism that sought to integrate Buddhist contributions to the lay world with Buddhist teachings.

However, the ongoing political turbulence from the Japanese invasion in the 1930s to the founding of the People's Republic of China hindered the reform of Buddhism. Taixu died in 1947, only two years before the creation of a communist country. After 1949 the Party issued new regulations that severely restricted all religions, including Buddhism, except when religion suited state purposes. The space for religion that had just started to emerge in China was cast aside.

I stress that in this early period of modern state formation, Buddhism had an opportunity to reform itself by modernizing and gain a legitimate space to expand inside the modern state. A space for Buddhism emerged through such multiple projects as the Convert Temples to Schools Movement and reform movements within Buddhism that comprised networks of practical activities among Buddhist clerics and devotees, expansion of social reform movements, the position of Buddhism in the laws and regulations enacted by the state, and the expansion of human Buddhism and imagination. The integration of this space with other newly emerging spaces of modernity, such as the economy, education, and diplomacy gradually took shape.

This space of religion, created by the critical condition of religion in China, was not limited to the domestic order. Clergy who were escaping the suppression and crackdown on Buddhism joined the flow of people and capital that had been moving abroad since the late nineteenth century and established temples in overseas Chinese communities. Many of these clerics were supporters of modern

reform Buddhism influenced by Taixu yet their interpretations and practices were diverse. After a half century this space of Buddhism abroad based on overseas Chinese networks came to play a significant role in the movement for the revival of Buddhism in China from the 1980s (Ashiwa and Wank 2005).

REVIVAL OF BUDDHISM SINCE THE OPEN ECONOMIC POLICY

The constitution of the newly established state of the People's Republic of China recognized freedom of religion, despite the Party's embrace of the atheistic ideology of Marxism-Leninism (Leung 1995). Article 99 of the 1954 constitution says, "Citizens of the People's Republic of China enjoy freedom of religious belief." This principle has remained unchanged in successive constitutions. However, during the Cultural Revolution (1966–76) the state eliminated the space of religion. Religion came under attack during the national campaign to eradicate the "four olds" (*sijiu*)—old habits, ideas, customs, and beliefs—that were considered cultural barriers to realizing socialism. Unlike the Smashing Superstition Movement, this time the destruction of temples was complete. There was no room for Buddhism to resist or negotiate with the state. The physical space of religion ceased to exist.

From the early 1980s and the open economic policy, religion started to revive. In the southeast coastal areas the revival has been especially remarkable (Birnbaum 2003; Duara 1994; Luo 1991; MacInnis 1989; Waldron 1998). Buddhism entered a new, vigorous stage. The 1982 constitution proclaims, "The state protects legitimate religious activities. No person is permitted to use religion to conduct counterrevolutionary activities or activities which disrupt social order, harm the people's health, or obstruct the educational system of the country." In this section I discuss the attributes of the new religious space that suddenly reopened due to the changes in state policy, and the continuity and discontinuity of the space of religion between the time of Yang Wenhui and now.

State Control of Religious Space

The state established an ideological and administrative space of religion in the early 1980s for the purpose of promoting religious activities within limits. At first the state needed to legitimate the logic of this radical change of direction. The Party issued a document in 1982, *The Basic Viewpoint and Policy on the Religious Question during Our Country's Socialist Period*, that, consistent with Marxist historical materialism, maintains that China is developing toward communism and that religion will naturally disappear once communism is attained: until that time religion must be acknowledged and tolerated to prevent the emergence of splits among the people that would hinder the development of a powerful socialist state.

A classification system was introduced that distinguished religion from superstition, popular belief (*minjian xinyang*), and feudal superstition. It defined religion as having such attributes as a logical system of thought oriented to the afterlife that is contained in scriptures, specially trained clergy, and fixed sites for religious activities (temples, churches, etc.) managed by clergy. Based on this modern concept, the state recognized five religions—Buddhism, Catholicism, Islam, Protestantism, and Daoism. The basic condition that the state imposes on religion is "love the state, love religion" (*aiguo aijiao*), which means loyalty to the Party and government above all else: it should never be "love religion, love the state" (*aijiao aiguo*). Religious observances should be performed within designated "religious activity sites" and be financially self-sufficient. In addition, Party members are prohibited from believing in religion. Superstition consists of oracles and shamans, which have none of the characteristics of religion and are banned. In between religion and superstition there are many

gods and deities that do not belong to the five recognized religions but are worshipped by people in locales: these are considered "popular belief" (*minjian xinyang*). They often have fixed sites, but lack a logical system of thought and scriptures, and usually a professional clergy. However, activities involving popular beliefs that are acknowledged as having "historical" and "cultural" value are permitted so long as they are defined as "cultural" rather than "religious."

The space of religion in the Chinese state proceeds through the dual Party/government structure: the Party provides ideological guidance while the government furnishes administrative guidance. Religious matters are handled by both the State Administration for Religious Affairs in the government and the United Front Work Department (*Tongyi zhanxian bu*) in the Party.[4] The State Administration for Religious Affairs has offices the center, provincial, and county/city levels to implement the state's religious policy. The United Front Work Department is the Party agency that handles relations with non-Party social groups and members and supervises the religious associations of the five recognized religions, whose members are prominent clergy, devotees, and scholars.

Religious associations were created by the state in the 1950s to be a bridge between the various religions and the state. The basic tasks of the Buddhist Association of China are to support the implementation of religious policy, heighten Buddhists' awareness of socialism and patriotism, represent the legal rights and interests of Buddhists, and organize "normal" religious activities. In practice the Buddhist Association of China functions to avoid direct confrontation between Buddhists and the state, and is the key channel for coordinating the coexistence of state and religion (Ashiwa and Wank 2006). During the first stage of the revival of Buddhism, local Buddhist associations worked with the local United Front Work Department offices to identify clerics who could represent Buddhists in dealings with the state and overseas Chinese, and coordinate efforts to reclaim temple land and rebuild temples that had been used by the state in the 1950s and 1960s as military posts, tourist sites, government offices, schools, factories, and community centers.

Buddhist temples have considerable autonomy when it comes to religious activities, such as rituals, teachings, and monastery regulations, although the space for religious activities is restricted to the temple site. While the clergy occasionally need advice from local Buddhist associations regarding formalities, they have the authority to control teaching and temple management. Rituals are the main performances at temples. Early morning and evening chanting is conducted daily, large rituals and festivals are performed according to the annual calendar, and numerous rituals for sending merit to ancestors are frequently conducted at the request of lay persons. Even the "relief of fiery mouths" (*fangyankou*)[5] ritual that, anthropologically speaking, contains many elements of exorcism and popular belief, is performed in temples without any questions being asked. The curriculum and management of Buddhist academies, which educate persons to be nuns and monks, are decided by the clergy. The curriculum for educating monks consists of Buddhist teachings as well as such secular subjects as mathematics, philosophy, foreign languages, sociology, psychology, and accounting. The daily routine of temples is controlled by the abbot or prior and based on the *baizhang qinggui*—the traditional regulations for monks drawn up by the monk Baizhang Huaihai (720–814) in the Tang dynasty.

Some temples have a large network overseas. The relationship of monks and donors abroad with specific temples in China has been reactivated since the late 1970s (Ashiwa and Wank 2005). There are now flows of donations to temples in China and exchanges of people. Young clerics in temples in China migrate to overseas temples as caretakers and many believers from abroad visit Buddhist sites in China as pilgrims and tourists. In this fashion the

interaction between believers in China and with those abroad is expanding the space for networks of Buddhism (Ashiwa and Wank 2005).

Religion is performed to the maximum extent possible within the limits set by the state. However, there is considerable flexibility in those limits depending upon the needs and power relations for implementing and improvising useful interpretations of regulations. By this collaboration and contestation, both the state and religion are actually making the space of "religion."

Revival of Nanputuo Temple

The mutual constitution of the space of "religion" can be viewed in the revival of Nanputuo Temple (*Nanputuosi*) in Xiamen city, Fujian province. The following account of the temple's revival is based on research conducted between 1989 and 2002.[6] It illuminates how religious space is institutionalized and acquires attributes through cooperation and contestation between religions and the state, and how this process has furthered China's economic development policies (see also Wank, this volume).

Nanputuo Temple is one of the first major Buddhist temples in China to have recovered after the Cultural Revolution. The temple compound has been restored and today there many more buildings than before the Cultural Revolution, many worshippers and tourists visit every day, and rituals are performed frequently. The temple's vitality can be traced to Fujian province's long history of Buddhism: as early as the Tang dynasty, one thousand years ago, the province was called "the land of Buddhism." Xiamen was one of the first treaty ports opened to foreign trade following China's defeat in the Opium War (1840–42) and its entrepot economy flourished. Emigration from Fujian increased and today the province is the ancestral homeland of many overseas Chinese. For emigrants embarking from Xiamen it was customary to visit Nanputuo Temple to pray for one's ancestors, a safe passage, and good fortune overseas. During the Cultural

Revolution the temple was sealed off and escaped major destruction, although a military observation post, factory, and school were established on the temple's land. By the late 1970s only a few monks remained, many fewer than the two hundred monks in the 1930s, at the temple's earlier peak. However, by the year 2002 there were about six hundred clergy in residence.

Several factors account for the temple's rapid revival. First, it has thick historical networks with overseas Chinese and clergy that have been reactivated since the late 1970s. Early in the twentieth century the temple's abbot, Huiquan, visited Chinese communities in Singapore, Hong Kong, and Malaya and established temples there (Ashiwa and Wank 2005). In 1980 a leading monk in Nanputuo Temple wrote letters to the clergy residing in these temples overseas. Clergy and devotees overseas, many with personal ties to Nanputuo Temple, were pleased to hear of the revival of Buddhism in the temple and donated funds for its restoration, as well as the rebuilding of other of Xiamen's temples.

Second, Nanputuo Temple was also a major site of Taixu's modern Buddhist reform movement in the early twentieth century. At that time Xiamen was a key locus of modernity in China with many foreign residents and numerous banks, universities, churches, and the marked presence of Western culture. The temple attracted patrons among new bourgeois youth who were interested in modernizing Buddhism and concerned about the spread of Christianity, which was especially visible in the treaty ports. By the 1920s the temple was a spearhead of modern Buddhist re-form. Originally of the Linji sect, it became ecumenical (*shifang conglin*) in 1924 and instituted a system for the democratic election of the abbot by the temple's clergy. The following year the Minnan Buddhist Academy (*Minnan Foxueyuan*) with Taixu as its head was established for the modern education of clergy. Reform was facilitated by the lack of a strong historical tradition of Buddhism in Xiamen. By the 1920s

the temple showed much vitality and was a center of modern reform.

The temple's historical link to Taixu has enhanced its legitimacy since the late 1970s. State religious policy has similarities to Taixu's human Buddhism with its emphasis on patriotism, societal contributions, and anti-superstition.[7] In his day, Taixu had sought to persuade the Nationalist Party elite that Buddhism could make a useful contribution to state building. Now the Nanputuo clergy invoke the image of Taixu to present the temple as having a thoroughly modern face to both the state and the people through such actions as reopening the Minnan Buddhist Academy, celebrating the hundredth anniversary of Taixu's birth, publishing special issues of the *Minnan Buddhist Academy Journal* on Taixu, and restoring the Taixu memorial stone and his meditation hut behind the temple. Clearly, Nanputuo Temple's historical links with Taixu have been effectively used by the temple to gain legitimacy to revive and expand in the context of the current state as a modern temple of "human Buddhism" for the public welfare. The modern reform Buddhism that Taixu promoted matches the need of the Party to make the state a modern one that acknowledges a space of religion.

The third reason for Nanputuo's rapid revival is that the temple started to reproduce its human capital early on. As soon as the restoration of the temple compound got underway in the early 1980s, the head monk revived the Minnan Buddhist Academy and the first class graduated in 1989. The same year Fujian province's first ordination ceremony since the Cultural Revolution was held at Guanghua Temple. Over five hundred monks and nuns were ordained, most of whom were elderly clerics from rural areas who had been forced to return to lay life during the Cultural Revolution and intended to return to their rural temples after ordination. But in the ordination ceremony, the fresh faces of the young nuns and monks from the Minnan Buddhist Academy stood out. Full of eagerness to be clerics, they had also studied such secular subjects as accounting and foreign languages and were assuming important roles in rituals and administration in Nanputuo Temple. This caused the power of actual management of the temple to shift from the Xiamen Religious Affairs Bureau to the young clerics. The rapidly growing number of young trained clerics also considerably raised the reputation of Nanputuo Temple by enabling it to conduct more rituals and send more young clergy to assume leading positions in overseas temples.

Redisposition of the System

The reemergence and growth of the market economy in China since 1979 has stimulated religion while the revival of Buddhism has also spurred the economy. This is especially apparent in Xiamen city, which was designated a Special Economic Zone by the central state in 1980 to attract business investment, particularly from Taiwan and overseas Chinese in Southeast Asia. The state also expected that the visible presence of religion would impress overseas Chinese with the openness of Chinese society, spurring them to invest. Expectations were especially high for Buddhism due to officials' assumption that many overseas Chinese businesspersons were Buddhists. Also, Nanputuo Temple itself was viewed by the Xiamen city government as an economic resource for the local tourist industry. However, the temple's success in addressing these various expectations soon strengthened it politically, which in turn led to conflicts between its clergy and the city government over the management of the temple. The ensuing confrontation redistributed power among the temple, city government, and other organizations.

At the start of the revival in the early 1980s when there were only a few monks in Xiamen, the monks and the Xiamen Religious Affairs Bureau worked closely with an elderly cleric named Miaozhan to revive the temple. The Xiamen Religious Affairs Bureau handled the temple's financial accounts and developed its commercial resources.[8]

However, as the number of administratively capable clerics increased during the 1980s tensions emerged between the clergy and the Xiamen Religious Affairs Bureau. The flashpoint was a highly profitable vegetarian restaurant in the temple that was managed by a layperson who had been appointed as temple accountant through his close tie with the chief of the Xiamen Religious Affairs Bureau. This lay manager had hired several hundred kin and friends of bureau officials to work in the restaurant, and distributed profits among them as bonuses while giving virtually nothing to the monks. In 1989 Miaozhan asserted the clergy's authority over the restaurant by appointing a recent graduate of the Minnan Buddhist Academy to manage the temple's commercial activities. But the Xiamen Religious Affairs Bureau, worried about losing control of the restaurant's rich income and employment, refused to acknowledge the appointment of this monk. In 1990, Miaozhan appealed to the Buddhist Association of China in Beijing. The association dispatched an investigative team to Xiamen to gather testimony for consideration back in Beijing by leading members of the Party and government. These officials affirmed the temple's ownership of the restaurant but recommended that it be leased to the lay manager, so as to avoid, in accordance with Buddhist precepts, the direct involvement of the clergy. This judgment supported the temple in principle while leaving the practical situation relatively unchanged. However, the appeal to the central authorities to resolve a local problem unexpectedly created a new direct link between the temple and the center that enhanced the latter's local control.

The implications of this new link became apparent when Miaozhan died in 1994. The issue of his successor as abbot created further conflict between the clergy and the officials of the Xiamen Religious Affairs Bureau, frightening other monks at Nanputuo Temple who were possible successors. The Buddhist Association of China in Beijing used this as an opening to nominate its own candidate, who had no connections to Xiamen or Nanputuo

Temple. Both the Xiamen Religious Affairs Bureau and Nanputuo Temple had no choice but to accept this candidate, despite the fact that the local election of the abbot was a major symbol of the temple's autonomy stemming from Taixu's time. This new abbot was in his forties and a member of the first graduating class of the China Buddhist Academy in Beijing since the Cultural Revolution as well as vice chair of the Buddhist Association of China. As a new-generation cleric he had an excellent grasp of temple management and the position of religion in China's socialist state; in fact, his graduating master's thesis was said to be on temple management. The replacement of the elderly Miaozhan, who had devoted much of his later life to reestablishing the vigor of Nanputuo Temple and rekindling ties with overseas Chinese, by the younger monk, Shenghui, who had a modern education in the center and fully accepted the position of religion in the communist state, symbolized the temple's realignment from a locally embedded temple to one closer to the central authorities. In this way, the involvement of the center in local politics reallocated local power relations and further implanted central control.

Nanputuo has developed itself subjectively, by utilizing its capital accumulated from the late nineteenth century, including its history as an enlightened temple and an important link in overseas networks, to coordinate interpretations of both the state and the temple, and to endeavor to duplicate the religious space defined by the state in the space of Buddhism, which the temple wants to expand. However, as a result Nanputuo is now being transformed into a temple that is closer to the state ideal of a model temple, and moving away from the local context and believers.

THE QUESTION OF BELIEF AND RELIGION

The policy of religious freedom in contemporary China is a part of the continuing process of state building and subjective modernization that stretches back to the beginning of the twentieth century. It is a new stage in the state's approach to religion that has been decided by the Party to complement its rejuvenation within the framework of the open economic policy. In this continuing project of modernity, which includes modern state building, the space of religion and its demarcation have been evolving, ever changing, and shifting according to the context of the times.

The Continuing Space of Modernity

The revival in Taixu and Yang Wenhui's time and the revival occurring since 1980 show both continuities and discontinuities. The most evident difference is that there now exists a stronger central state structure. The Party-state clearly intends to acknowledge religion as a necessary condition of a secular, modern state such as the People's Republic of China, and to include it in the state structure. The Chinese state has a clear and pragmatic purpose for linking the vital power of religion that has reemerged due to the open religious policy: to stimulate the economy. It expects that domestic and international tourism to temples will enrich local service industries and that overseas Chinese devotees will bring business opportunities. These contexts of reorienting the modern centralized state and the open economy through waves of globalization did not exist during the time of Taixu and Yang Wenhui.

However, the formation of the space of religion that has emerged since the early 1980s reveals certain continuities and similarities with the space of religion that began to take shape at the end of the nineteenth century. First, the late nineteenth century marked the beginning of a period of turmoil that stimulated flows of people abroad, including Buddhist clerics and devotees who had accumulated status and wealth overseas. These transnational flows went hand in hand with the expansion of the space of religion to overseas Chinese communities. This history constitutes capital for contemporary Buddhism. It has been reactivated through networks of people and money that have been flowing back to China (Ashiwa and Wank 2005). As noted above, this link between Buddhism and overseas Chinese is a major reason the state sees economic potential in Buddhism. A second continuity is that the institutionalizing of religion that involved the Chinese Buddhist Association in the 1920s and 1930s through its challenges to and negotiations with the state is proceeding now through the Buddhist Association of China. Both associations are significant linkages between the state and Buddhism. However, in the contemporary revival the Party and Buddhists are careful to avoid the kinds of earlier confrontations between Buddhism and the state by paying great attention to the formulation, interpretation, and implementation of laws regarding religion. Third, a century after Taixu's birth, his "human Buddhism" has been revived and is again being held up by both the Party and Buddhist clergy as an ideal modern Buddhism that contributes to the formation of a modern society and state (ruled by the Party). One of the intentions of the Party in reactivating the space of Buddhism is to provide support for the state's foreign diplomacy. This aim proceeds through cultural and academic exchanges with other Buddhist states, such as Japan and Myanmar, and with academic and religious institutions abroad. In this phase of efforts by the state and religion to rebuild the space which had once been devastated, the emphasis of contemporary Buddhism on continuity with the modern Buddhist reform advocated by Taixu is a collaboratively enacted heritage of intentional modernity agreed on by the state on the one hand, and Buddhist clergy and devotees on the other.

In addition, there are new dynamics in the contemporary revival. The reform of Buddhism toward a "religion under state guidance" is proceeding not by the exercise of the state's violent power as before, but rather by gradual transformations guided by the state and the Buddhist Association of China, as well as partly from within Buddhism. A centralized educational system based on the China Buddhist Academy in Beijing was established to train clerics who could fit the needs of the modern period. The academy is subject to strong political guidance by the Party and collaborates closely with it. The academy produces elite young clerics who are motivated to promote Buddhism in China's communist society. In the 1990s most of the elderly leaders of the religion who had survived the Cultural Revolution and contributed greatly to the revival of Buddhism in the 1980s were passing from the scene. These clergy had survived tumultuous times and contributed to the revival of Buddhism despite their old age. As living links with the past, they had enabled Buddhists to activate networks of overseas Chinese and to wield techniques for confronting the state that they had acquired through their earlier experiences. Among them was the aforementioned Miaozhan, leader of Nanputuo Temple's revival, who was eighty years old when he became abbot in 1990. The great respect and support he received from local believers and overseas Chinese enabled his temple to rapidly recover and expand. It also enabled him to appeal to the central authorities to help solve the temple's problems with the local government. However, his successor, Shenghui, represents a generation, in their twenties to forties, that was mostly educated in the aforementioned China Buddhist Academy and understands completely the position of "normal" religion in the state system and ideology. They are now becoming young abbots in local major temples and heads of Buddhist academies, and reproducing "modern" style Buddhism in China.

In contrast to the dynamics in the major temples described above, the efforts of lesser temples to gradually develop themselves by cultivating local as well as overseas devotees and believers through their own unique approaches cannot be overlooked. Xiamen's lesser temples pursue various strategies;

some play on the concern of the local government to promote tourism and local leisure spots by establishing vegetarian restaurants with a panoramic views, photo booths, and gift shops. Others are developing new sources of income by building large halls to perform masses for souls in hell or holding services to send merit to the spirits of the ancestors. One temple for lay-nuns (*zhaigu*) has become a weekend community center for female devotees who are factory workers. In Xiamen most of the secondary temples are maintained by clergy who come from southern Fujian province. They can communicate with the believers in the local Minnan dialect, which is highly effective in creating intimate relationships among clergy and local believers. At these other temples, the local believers can enjoy group activities such as pilgrimages and festivals organized together with the clerics, something that they cannot do at Nanputuo temple because most of the clergy are from rural areas in north and central China and speak Mandarin with a heavy accent that is difficult for local believers to understand. These lesser temples are under the control of the local Religious Affairs and Buddhist Association offices, and are inspected annually. The everyday lives of people are more closely woven into the "popular Buddhism" practiced in these lesser temples, such as funerals conducted with the help of the devotee associations, rituals for sending merit for ancestors, and praying for success in school exams and business deals. Even during the political turbulence of the first decades of the People's Republic of China this popular Buddhism that was tightly woven into the people's everyday life and customs continued to exist on a small scale and in underground activities, such as chanting accompanied by offerings of food and flowers (Welch 1968, 1972).

Problems with Falungong in 1999 caused the government to launch a "movement to suppress heterodoxy." Buddhist clergy, even in such major temples as Nanputuo, were very fearful that this movement would trigger the suppression of Buddhism because the label of heterodoxy that the state applied to Falungong was partly based on the fact that its teachings and practices were an amalgamation of Buddhist idioms and elements. Therefore, after the state campaign against Falungong began, Nanputuo promptly decided to issue booklets and put up wall posters in the temple claiming that Buddhism is not Falungong but rather a pure and legitimate religion recognized by the state that is firmly committed to the slogan "love the state, love religion." Small temples followed suit and started to pay more attention to keeping good relations with the local Religious Affairs and Buddhist Association offices in order to reinforce their status as practicing "pure" Buddhism.

The Place of Belief

According to Ann Anagnost (1987), in its drive for modernity the Chinese state continues to deploy the classifications of religion and superstition in order to legitimate the leading role of the Party. This echoes the movement initiated in the 1930s by the Nationalist Party to stamp out superstition. However, the contemporary situation under the Party is different. The Party is far less concerned with the "modernity/nonmodernity" of religion than was the state in the 1930s. In addition the Party's concern with "religion/superstition" merely follows the framework of the official definition and law regarding religion. With regard to Falungong, the Party's greatest fear is its power to mobilize and organize large numbers of people through its widespread and deep roots among the masses. The object of this fear is people's "belief," which is the source of Falungong's power and is stronger than the Party's ideology. This is evident in Falungong's power to drive its adherents to challenge the Party. When Falungong was still small and local and just starting to grow, its application to the Buddhist Association of China for official recognition as a Buddhist organization was rejected (Utiraruto, this volume). Yet the fact that Falungong could keep expanding its power to threaten state power despite the rejection as a legitimate religion shows that there is a space that "religion" as a system of legitimate institutions and organizations cannot control. This is the space of belief.

Although this chapter has not discussed the issue of belief, it is precisely belief that differentiates religion from all other projects of modernity that construct the state in terms of institutionalization and organization. In general, in the theory of modernity, belief is removed from the public space and sealed in an individual private space. In its aim to construct a modern state, the Chinese state is attempting to achieve precisely this sealing off of belief. The issue that the Chinese state is most concerned about and seeks to avoid is confrontation with "belief" because the state knows full well that "belief" can be a huge source of energy that can shake the state to its foundations as, for example, the Taiping Rebellion demonstrated. Therefore, any arguments about modernity and religion that focus only on institutions and state formation and avoid discussing belief are, perforce, deficient.

In the process of striving to be modern, both in the West and in the non-West, a crucial question is whether the state can successfully enclose belief within private space while expanding the institutionalization of the space of religion. At the same time, continuing waves of religious movements, such as religious fundamentalism, have emerged in modern contexts. In fact, religious fundamentalism is not a product of nonmodernity; religious fundamentalism and such modernized religions as reformed Buddhism, are both products of modernity. Valentine (2002) argues that both religious fundamentalism and modernized religion lead people to be cognizant of oneself and the world, and to consciously choose one "religion" and to become a "believer" of it with rational understanding and practice. He analytically distinguishes two types of consciousness of religion—epistemological and ontological. Epistemological religion is the aforementioned creation of modernity that

compels people to rationally and cognitively choose one religion rather than another. Ontological religion is the belief of "being" as a part of the culture and customs into which a person is born: people are "in" the religion by living their everyday lives. Valentine argues that the introduction of epistemological religion into ontological religion in Asia during the colonial period through numerous projects of modernity caused, by the late nineteenth century, a reaction among the "awakened" believers of the non-Christian traditions that took shape in the reform movements of Buddhism and Hinduism. Since then, ontological belief has diminished and has been left out of the public scene. It has been either forgotten or has only existed in the everyday customs of popular religions, such as the discursive space of "popular Buddhism," "superstition," and "culture and customs."

It is very illuminating to see how the Chinese state institutionally deals with beliefs that do not fit its definition of religion. Good examples are the Mazu belief, which has many enthusiastic adherents in southern China, Taiwan, and overseas, and the Three-in-One (*Sanyijiao*), which has a long history in Fujian province (Dean 1998). As Chau (2009) shows, negotiations among the local Religious Affairs Bureau offices and other state agencies and believers' groups enable these beliefs to legitimate their activities within state discursive institutions by positioning them as "popular belief" and "local customs" (*difang chuantong*), or in other words, as "cultural" phenomena that have tourist and historical value. In this formulation, the domestic and foreign pilgrims and participants who visit the sites revered by these beliefs are considered tourists contributing to the local economy or persons expressing patriotism.[9]

However, the populace continues to have an ontological consciousness of being Buddhist and they are familiar with Buddhism as social and domestic customs of everyday life (which institutionalizes popular belief as "culture"). This leads to confrontations between people's popular beliefs and the Buddhism practiced in temples. A telling example is the attempt to prevent people from burning paper money in Nanputuo Temple on Guanyin's Birthday because the clergy and state officials consider it a "superstition." The temple has banned burning paper money in the main compound, requiring it be burned outside the temple. Such confrontations of "belief" with modern "religion" may generate extreme mass behavior without any flexibility to negotiate. It could cause people to question and challenge the Party's inviolable principle of "love the state, love religion." This questioning could then confront people with the choice of choosing between "love religion" and "love the state," and place the former over the latter. To avoid a situation where this choice comes to be seen as absolutely inevitable, religions and the state will have to make ongoing efforts. While not yet visibly expressed, the question of the strength or pureness of belief will eventually emerge.

CONCLUSION

The creation of modernity is represented in the formation of the space of the modern state and the space of religion. In other words, the formation of each space mutually constrains and promotes the other through multiple projects of modernity. In this process, both religion and the state seek to define themselves. This process is constituted by an inclusion that defines oneself, an exclusion that defines the other, and occasionally the creation of new third parties. These projects are never coherent, the spaces are not stable, and boundaries are being continuously created and re-created by both subjects to demarcate the other. This mutual characterization of space is an ongoing process of conflict, negotiation, collaboration, accommodation, resistance, and compromise. Because religion, more than other spaces, has attributes of unstable fluidity due to its specific basis of belief, thought, and teachings, the space of religion requires

multiple interpretations as well as multiple legitimacies depending on contexts and circumstances. The two periods discussed in this chapter, from the end of the Qing dynasty until 1949, and from the late 1970s to today, are remarkable for the great efforts to legitimately include religion within the state system, both as organizations as well as ideologies of practice. In these moments both the state and religion have aggressively moved to create their systems and position themselves vis-à-vis the other through the establishment of "religion" as concepts, institutions, teachings, and organizations.

The apparatus of the modern state takes shape and is forming by processes of selection and evaluation that institutionalize religion. Through projects of modernity, religions have adjusted their shape many times and in various ways. Religions both demand and necessitate the rearrangement of the state apparatus. In China, where modernization was promoted as the powerful master narrative for building the state, the state and religion are creating modernity by relating themselves to the creation of the space of religion.

NOTES

1. The importance of lay devotees in keeping Buddhism alive is reflected in the term "lay devotee Buddhism" (*jushi Fojiao*) that is often used to describe the Buddhism of this period.
2. The study of Taixu's contribution has grown over the past decade (see Pittman 2001).
3. Complex domestic politics, fierce criticism from Buddhist traditionalists, and conflicts among Buddhist reformers in China further stoked Taixu's eagerness to spread Buddhism abroad.
4. The state bureaucracy of religious management was called the Religious Affairs Office from 1951 to 1954 and the Bureau of Religious Affairs from 1954 until 1998. The current name—State Administration for Religious Affairs—was adopted in 1998. For ease of reference this chapter uses the current name to refer to post-1949 bureaucracy at the national level.
5. Hungry ghosts have very small throats and cannot drink water. Whenever they open their mouths fire

comes out and burns the food in front of them so they are always hungry. Only magic can open up their throats, extinguish the flames, and relieve their suffering.

6. An account of the fieldwork can be found in Wank (this volume).

7. On the historical links between Taixu and the state in the first years of the People's Republic, see Welch (1972).

8. The official name of the bureau is the Bureau of Ethnic and Religious Affairs of Xiamen (*Xiamen shi minzu yu zongjiao shiwu ju*). In this chapter the name is shortened to Xiamen Religious Affairs Bureau. For a discussion of the use of the same bureau to manage ethnic and religious affairs see Ashiwa and Wank (2006: 344n12).

9. Ontological belief can be seen in the chapter by Utiraruto (this volume). Falungong contains elements of fundamentalism from Buddhism and is a production of modernity but is also linked to *qigong*, which is constituted by many folk beliefs that are outside the state's medical establishment but widely held by the common people.

9

Realigning Religion and Power in Central Asia: Islam, Nation-State and (Post)Socialism

Chris Hann and Mathijs Pelkmans

IN APPARENT CORRESPONDENCE with the increasing interconnectedness of the world we live in, evident in the popularity of terms such as globalisation, transnationalism and cosmopolitanism, the objects and methods of social scientific research have undergone major changes in recent decades. Thus in the study of religion scholars have tended to move away from the classic Durkheimian argument that approaches religion as a collective representation of society (Durkheim 1917) and instead addressed the establishment of global networks.[1] At the same time social scientists (particularly anthropologists) have continued to insist on the significance of place and local variation. The culinary experience of McDonalds in East Asia is not what it is in North America (Watson 1997). As with food, so with religion: conservative Protestantism has been successfully disseminated from 'the West', but it has taken on myriad local forms and meanings, in which collective as well as individual identities are at stake.

Where religion is concerned, the point about diversity goes deeper. Religion has been central to a great deal of modern social science theory. Secularisation, in the sense of a decline in religious belief and practices, is still held by some scholars to be the inexorable concomitant of 'modernisation' (Norris & Inglehart 2004). From this perspective increased 'individualism' and Western patterns of differentiation, in which religion is allegedly confined to the private sphere, are taken to chart the path which the rest of the world will necessarily follow. The collapse of the Soviet bloc in the early 1990s was a significant factor in promoting a general sense of accelerated convergence and even of 'the end of history' (Fukuyama 1992). Fukuyama had in mind the worldwide triumph of liberal capitalism, but in Central Asia nationalism and the resurgence of Islam have been more conspicuous.[2] Here as elsewhere in the former bloc, post-socialist countries have abandoned their old ideology. Many of the barriers that formerly separated them from the rest of the world have been dismantled. The post-socialist states have been put under international pressure to implement religious rights, understood to be a basic human right; the metaphor of the religious marketplace has been widely applied (Pelkmans 2006a).[3] The impact of global currents, including New Age (Lindquist 2005) and evangelical Christianity (Wanner 2007), is well documented in many regions of the former USSR.

Yet the demise of socialism has had other, sometimes contradictory consequences. The USSR was replaced by a loose Commonwealth of

Independent States, most of which had difficulties in consolidating democratic institutions and the economic welfare of their populations. By contrast, it was relatively easy for them to demonstrate their sovereignty by taking action to control religious activity. In other words the new religious market-places were framed by new states. In countries where one religion had dominated for many centuries, new powerholders were easily tempted to draw on this tradition in order to strengthen their precarious legitimacy. This tendency from within to promote the 'nationalisation' of religion conflicted with the prescription from outside to guarantee citizens religious freedom and to allow proselytising. While similar tensions can be found in many parts of the world, we argue in this article that the legacy of the socialist era has been doubly decisive in Central Asia. First, it is important to recognise the long-term consequences of a political regime ostensibly committed to a rational, atheist model of modernity, and in certain periods severely repressive of religious communities. Secondly, however, those communities were never eliminated and the institutions through which they were defined and controlled under socialism were closely tied to a territorial system that was grounded in a principle of nationality (Pelkmans 2006b; Saroyan 1997, pp. 95–100).

The new public significance of religion in post-Soviet Central Asia since the 1990s is therefore indicative of more than what sociologist José Casanova termed the 'deprivatisation' of religion (1994). Casanova identified a significant religious shift from the individual, private level of religion to that of the public sphere, but the ties between this public sphere and the state were left largely invisible in his analysis. We argue that the concept of deprivatisation must be extended by uncovering a second dimension of the 'public versus private' dichotomy. For the political economist, deprivatisation generally means a movement opposed to the decentralising principle of the market, characterised by competition between

property-owning individual agents, towards a centralising principle of public ownership and regulation. This principle is usually known as 'nationalisation'; indeed, as we shall see, the deprivatisation of religion in Central Asia is tightly connected to the construction of new nations. The term '*étatization*' is equally appropriate, for we are also dealing here with the construction of new states. Even where the state has not changed structurally, state policies towards religion have shifted from disregard and hostility towards intensified co-option.

Our comparative analysis is designed to address institutional variety within contemporary Muslim Central Asia. While the new ex-Soviet states have been appropriating religion for legitimation purposes, China continues to view religion in general, and Islam in Xinjiang in particular, with extreme suspicion. Among the former, different forms of appropriation have shaped not only religious institutions and practices but the nature of the new state itself. In Weberian terms, recent developments illustrate the inadequacy of secular bureaucratic ideals based in rational-legal domination. The successors to the mantle of Marxism–Leninism have attempted in varying ways to adopt the mantle of tradition and to generate new forms of charisma in order to legitimate their power. Although the nation has become the ultimate 'imagined community', an exclusively secular ideology of nationhood is inadequate. Instead, older forms of religion are being adapted to serve new purposes: nothing less than the sacralisation of the modern state. This gives a renewed pertinence to the theories of Durkheim, commonly taken to be obsolete or irrelevant at this scale of social organisation. There is no doubt that some inhabitants of ex-Soviet Central Asia have begun to explore new forms of spirituality in a post-Durkheimian sense, above and beyond reference to their socio-political community (Lindquist 2005). But the new states have been hostile to such trends and instead worked hard to promote a Durkheimian congruence of religion and polity. It is too early to assess the long-term impact of their policies but, for the time being at least, some of these new nation states seem to wield formidable power over their citizens.

The article is structured as follows. Although our main arguments concern the legacies of socialism, we contextualise these by beginning with a brief outline of the *longue durée*. Islam, the dominant religion for many centuries was universal in the sense that its authority was ultimately known to be lodged in texts and in the *umma*. This religion was not bound to tribal or national identity.[4] Muslims who fell into the Russian colonial sphere, like those further east who were drawn into the Qing Empire and eventually incorporated into the People's Republic of China, even in periods of greatest isolation from the centres of Islam, never lost this sense of belonging to a world religion. Under socialism, a considerable degree of homogeneity was accomplished in the management of religion through secular institutions. After demonstrating how this worked, we go on to investigate the diversity of recent decades. For the ex-Soviet countries, we focus on two extreme cases. Turkmenistan was, from independence until his death in 2006, ruled by an authoritarian leader who pursued repressive policies towards religion and almost everything else. Kyrgyzstan, by contrast, has been generally recognised to be the most liberal state in the region. The comparative analysis shows that even the latter is characterised by strong tendencies to promote perceptions of Islam which link it to the nation and to 'cultural heritage'.

We include the Uyghurs of Xinjiang in the comparisons as a foil to the post-Soviet cases. They share the same linguistic and religious traditions, but obviously their structural position is now entirely different. Since 1955 this region has officially been known as the Xinjiang Uyghur Autonomous Region, but power is located in Beijing; the First Secretary of the Communist Party in the region has always been a Han Chinese, not a Uyghur Muslim. After a relatively liberal phase in the 1980s, we shall see that religion has in recent decades again

become a source of intense concern to the authorities; but the emphasis is still placed on co-option rather than repression.

In conclusion, we return to the basic question of how religion is manipulated and appropriated by worldly powerholders. The unifying model of modernity implemented under Marxist–Leninist–Maoist socialism has dissolved. Political contingencies have pushed Xinjiang and the ex-Soviet republics in apparently different directions. Yet there is a degree of unity among the latter in the way in which religion is now being tied to the nation state, in both 'liberal' and 'authoritarian' cases. In spite of the structural differences, similar elements of 'folklorisation' can be found in all three countries. These patterns are antithetical to the model of the 'competitive religious marketplace' that is promoted by powerful outside forces. However, this nationalisation-cum-*étatization* of Islam is an alternative, we suggest finally, that social scientists should not rush to condemn.

BEFORE SOCIALISM

The spread of Islam in Central Asia was a chequered and drawn out process. It roughly coincided with Central Asia's decline as a region of commercial and geopolitical significance. One major reason for this decline was the opening up of maritime routes between Europe, India and China, which undermined the overland caravan trade (Wolf 1982; Christian 2000, p. 6; Ptak 2007). The consolidation of Safavid Shii power in Iran and the southward expansion of Muscovy in the sixteenth century established major barriers to the north and south of the Caspian Sea. With these developments the Sunni world was cut into two parts, and the Turkic peoples of Central Asia became separated from their Sunni brethren in the rest of the Muslim world (Bennigsen & Bryan 2002, p. 249). Sufi orders, especially the Naqshbandiiyya, were the prime agents in complex conversion processes. They combined observance of the *sharia* with mystical and charismatic elements, and the tombs of their saints remain inscribed in the Central Asian landscape to this day (Zarcone 1999). As a result, to distinguish Orthodoxy from the 'little tradition' of Islam is especially problematic in this region.[5]

From the middle of the eighteenth century the tsarist empire expanded into Central Asia. Initially invited by economically weak Kazakh hordes to offer protection against Kalmuk raiders and Oirat warriors, this protection gradually metamorphosed into possession. Russia resumed its southward expansion in the middle of the nineteenth century, strengthening its hold over the Kokand Khanate and annexing it in 1876, while allowing the principalities of Bukhara and Khiva to persist into the twentieth century as quasi-independent protectorates (Becker 1968). Russian rule everywhere undermined the local legal arrangements that were exercised by native rulers, but a significant degree of legal pluralism based primarily on religious distinctiveness persisted to the end of the Empire (V. Martin 2001; Burbank 2007).

Although Han Chinese presence in Central Asia dates back more than 2,000 years, a significant military and political consolidation was accomplished by the Qing authorities in the mid-eighteenth century (Millward 1998; Perdue 2005). The vast region was officially given the name Xinjiang (New Territories) in 1884, but even after this date the colonisers did little to interfere with the authority exercised by local *begs* and elaborate systems of customary law (Bellér-Hann 2008; Millward 2007).

The coeval imperial powers had similar images of themselves as civilising forces and each built new colonial towns as a demonstration of its modernity. The Russians in particular could point to infrastructure improvements and the establishment of bureaucratic administration (Brower 2003, pp. 108–09). But as Brower points out, in their conception of a transformed Central Asia the tsarist authorities virtually ignored the local population, which they perceived as 'entirely alien' (2003,

p. 106). Neither the tsarist nor the Qing empires interfered significantly with religious practices. Proselytising by the Russian Orthodox Church, important in the colonisation of other parts of the tsarist empire, was generally discouraged in Central Asia (Geraci 2001; Geraci & Khodarkovsky 2001). The Russian administration, in particular under Governor-General von Kaufman, adopted an approach of minimal interference in religious affairs, believing in true Enlightenment style that with progress and development the role of Islam would dwindle (Brower 1997, pp. 116–18; Khalid 2006, pp. 36–38). The Qing dynasty was similarly tolerant. One significant factor in the commercial penetration of the region was the expansion of the Hui (Muslim Chinese, often called Tungans in the older literature), who established their own mosques, separate from those of the indigenous groups. The sedentary oasis dwellers were usually in this era known to foreigners as Turki.

By the end of the nineteenth century reform movements were spreading in both empires. The Jadidist attempts to modernise Islam, especially traditional forms of education, were modelled on earlier initiatives among the Tatars and in the Ottoman Empire (Khalid 1998, pp. 90–93). Some Russian officials, fearful of the impact of these new ideas, including the emerging pan-Turkic currents, came to the conclusion that they preferred the 'rigid, predictable instruction of the traditional Muslim maktab' (Brower 2003, p. 113). This was the era of the 'Great Game', in which internal political instability was accentuated by rivalry between the European powers (Hopkirk 1992). The principal sources of rebellions had little to do with the dissemination of reformist ideas from the West but rather with local grievances and poverty; the confiscation of land in favour of European settlers or Han Chinese was an important factor. The role of religious leaders in these rebellions, in particular Naqshbandi shaykhs, contributed to a hardening of religious differences between Muslim Central Asians and foreign colonisers. The dramatic rise and fall of

Yakub Beg (1820–1877), whose Muslim fervour mingled with traces of pan-Turkism, exemplified the interweaving of religion and politics in the era before modern political boundaries had been definitively fixed (Millward 2007).

Religion was a force feared by both imperial regimes in their last decades because of its perceived potential to unite the divergent Central Asian groups, either under the flag of Islam or in the cause of a pan-Turkic nationalism or some combination of the two (Carrère d'Éncausse 1994, p. 174). With the exception of the northern parts of Kazakhstan, Russians formed a very small minority in Central Asia up to the early twentieth century.[6] The indigenous population was classified as *inorodtsy* or 'alien', a term which established their juridical difference from the incoming Russians (Slocum 1998). Ideas about nationality were largely absent among the indigenous peoples, who defined themselves rather in terms of language, tribal affiliation, locality, and life style, all of which showed considerable flux and overlap. Only among parts of the educated elite—such as the Jadids—did modern notions of nationality start to gain importance (Khalid 1998). The same was true in Xinjiang. During the turbulent decades which followed the collapse of the Qing Empire in 1911, central power was repeatedly usurped by local warlords, both Han and Hui. In the inter-war decades Dzungaria (the northern part of the region) was heavily influenced by the Soviet Union, which supported the short-lived Republic of Eastern Turkestan (Forbes 1986).

UNDER SOCIALISM

First in the Soviet Union from the early 1920s and then in China from the early 1950s, socialist rule combated religious expression directly (albeit inconsistently, as we describe below). These repressive regimes relied on techniques of mass mobilisation and social engineering that were firmly rooted in the Western project of modernity (Hoffmann 2003,

p. 7; Arnason 1993). Certainly the objectification of religion as a specific compartment of social life amenable to state regulation had its precedents in Europe and contradicted Islamic teaching. Yet the attitudes of the new powerholders towards their periphery in Central Asia did not differ greatly from those of their predecessors: the key elements of continuity were a patronising teleology of backwardness giving way to progress, sedentary lifestyles replacing 'inefficient' pastoral ways of life, and 'superstition' and 'fanaticism' vanishing in a secular society that was to be guided by scientific atheism (Brower 2003, p. 176). Whereas the Tsarist Empire had grand development plans which failed to incorporate the inhabitants into their visions, the Bolsheviks and later the Maoists were committed to moulding their subjects into 'modern' socialist citizens through direct interventions affecting every level of social life. Indirect, group-specific forms of governance gave way to a standardised 'socialist legality' which, however imperfect in its workings, broke radically with the hierarchies of 'feudalism'. Arguably, especially in the Soviet case, the new forms of citizenship were no longer imperialist at all, since the minority nationalities of the periphery now enjoyed the same rights and obligations as the dominant nationality, *de facto* as well as *de jure*; in some respects they were the privileged objects of 'affirmative action' (T. Martin 2001; cf. Khalid 2007).

The influence of the established religious authorities and the significance of Islam in public life diminished rapidly as a result of the persecution of religious leaders and the closure of most mosques and *madrasahs*. In both the Soviet Union and China, numerous famous buildings were divested of their religious significance and were transformed into museums; others were adapted for still more profane purposes, such as to serve as granaries (Zarcone 1999). The requirements and opportunities of the new system, especially in towns and cities, which grew rapidly, created material incentives for subjects to direct their energies in new directions. Nevertheless, despite this ideological onslaught

Islam retained much of its social relevance, even for the most secularised sections of society. With brief exceptions, notably during anti-religious campaigns under Stalin in the 1930s and under Khrushchev in the late 1950s and early 1960s, and in China during the Great Leap Forward and the early years of the Cultural Revolution, it was still possible to make pilgrimages to shrines such as saints' tombs. While the public maintenance of Sufi traditions became impossible, the orders did not dissolve entirely (Bennigsen & Wimbush 1985, 1986). Religion retained its significance as a social marker in everyday life, for example through the dietary rules that inhibited contacts with Russians and Han. Observance of the daily ritual prayers as well as the Ramadan fast, not especially strict in the past, declined further. Extravagant expenditure on rituals was condemned by the Party, as it was by religious leaders; but the most important life-cycle rituals retained their Islamic character and these continued to be observed by the vast majority of the population, including Party members (Ro'i 2000, pp. 509–49).

Soviet Central Asia

Scholars continue to debate the extent to which the Soviet Union succeeded in its promotion of an atheist society. Some commentators have stressed the decline of religious knowledge and the destruction of religious institutions (Greeley 1994; Bourdeaux 1995). Others have emphasised the tenacity of religion in the face of political repression (Bennigsen & Wimbush 1986; Husband 2000). Sociological surveys conducted in Soviet Central Asia in the 1970s revealed that religious identification and practice among the Muslim population were much higher than among former Christians elsewhere in the USSR.[7] The diverging interpretations can be partially reconciled when the broader cultural politics of socialist rule, and especially the close connections between religious and ethno-national categories, are taken into account.

Soviet Central Asia acquired a new cartographic complexion in 1924 and the codification of nationality according to territorially defined ethno-national categories was arguably the most enduring measure undertaken by the Soviet regime (Hirsch 2005). The policy was predicated on Lenin's paradoxical statement that the surest way to unity in content was diversity in form (Slezkine 1994, p. 419). The new entities thus created were the Turkmen, Uzbek, Tajik, Kyrgyz and Kazakh Soviet Socialist Republics. The foundations of modern Uyghur identity were laid in the same period and gradually consolidated as a result of Soviet influence in Xinjiang in the 1930s and 1940s. The very concept of nationality (*natsional'nost*) was ambiguous: nationalities were seen as rooted in primordial ethnic groups, and yet it was the responsibility of the state to intervene and shape them into modern political units.[8] Over time, these new nationality categories became fundamental markers of identity, embedded not just in the administrative structure of the USSR, but also in people's consciousness. As Hirsch has shown, by the 1930s even rural and nomadic populations that had previously identified themselves with a particular tribe or locality were now affiliating themselves to nationalities (2005). Though previous points of reference did not disappear, the promotion of ethno-national categories and their endowment with standardised literary languages as well as a long list of 'cultural' attributes (such as cuisine, costume, dance and music) was an overwhelming success.

Religious practices, too, were increasingly framed around ideas of cultural heritage (Shahrani 1984). Thus a Kazakh who was a member of the Communist Party and who by definition held an atheist worldview would still claim to be a Muslim when asked to indicate his cultural background. From a local perspective the notion of 'atheist Muslim' was not perceived as a contradiction. The 'folklorisation' of religion (Peyrouse 2004; Pelkmans 2007) detached it from doctrine and spirituality and made it available as an instrument to emerging national elites whose lifestyles were highly secularised. In short, the socialist encoding of religious identities through nationality politics led in the USSR ineluctably to a folklorised, 'cultural' Islam, in which ties to national traditions were deemed more important than scriptural knowledge. Religion was thus not eliminated, but it was emptied of sacrality and rendered amenable to secular bureaucratic management. The Muslim Spiritual Board of Central Asia was created in 1943 by the Soviet Union at a time when the government was desperate to boost its popularity. It functioned as the officially recognised central institution of Islam in Soviet Central Asia until 1991. The leaders of this 'supranational religious body' were then transformed overnight into 'non-national' clerics (Akbarzadeh 2001, p. 457; Ro'i 2000). Each of the newly independent republics proceeded to create its own 'national muftiyate' (Saroyan 1997).

Xinjiang

Nationalities policy was one of many fields in which Mao Zedong drew directly on Soviet experience (including the theoretical work of the young Stalin). Anthropologists were called upon to help in classifying peoples and documenting their cultures (Dreyer 1976; Mackerras 1994; Gladney 2004). Eventually it was determined that the People's Republic was populated by a family of 56 nationalities (*minzu*), consisting of the Han, making up over 90% of the total population, and 55 minorities. The Uyghurs were by far the largest non-Han nationality in Xinjiang, but nine further Muslim minorities were also present in this region. China diverged crucially from the Soviet Union in adopting the model of a unitary 'nation-state'. (The Chinese Communist Party had previously endorsed the Leninist principle which allowed a theoretical right of secession, but this was quickly dropped when the Party came to power.) This multiethnic nation-state (*duo minzu guojia*) allowed for greater continuity with pre-socialist imperialism than was the case in

the Soviet Union. Due to heavy migration from 'inner China', the Han component of Xinjiang's population expanded rapidly in the course of socialist modernisation. They were almost as numerous as the Uyghurs by the end of the twentieth century and formed a majority in many districts (Toops 2004). The main contours of this cultural encounter were little changed from pre-socialist days and most Han still had ingrained notions of their 'civilizational' superiority (Harrell 1995). What was new was that, as a result of the *minzu* policies, as in the Soviet Union, the minorities had acquired much greater collective self-consciousness. This was especially true of the Uyghurs, implicitly encouraged to view Xinjiang as their homeland through the very name bestowed on the region.[9]

Chinese communist policies towards religion too were strongly influenced by Soviet precedents (MacInnis 1989). Freedom of belief and the right to practice 'normal religious activities' were guaranteed in successive constitutions, but the implementation of these rights varied greatly. In theory, great care was taken to distinguish recognised religions from 'feudal superstitions', but in practice the former were frequently subject to repressive measures such as in the condemnation of all 'wasteful' expenditure on ritual. A China Islamic Association was founded in 1953, only to be repeatedly abolished and revived in succeeding decades. A hierarchy of religious affairs bureaux was created at every level down to that of the township (village government). Through this machinery the party-state sought to maintain a balance between fulfilling constitutional commitments to religious toleration and maintaining strict control (Potter 2003). Although there has been some regional variation, notably in Tibet, in principle religion was rigorously excluded from the public sphere. Not only Communist Party members but all state cadres, including teachers, were expected to set an example by espousing and practising the principles of scientific atheism. At the same time it was recognised that religion was deeply embedded in everyday social life, and that, especially in politically sensitive minority regions, it would be counter-productive to ban low-level cadres from partici-pating in religious activities.

In Xinjiang this meant that, from the begin-ning of socialist rule, the major religious holidays were treated as 'ethnic traditions', in which all were able to participate. The new powerholders initially pursued conciliatory policies. Local *mollas* and *imams* were wooed by the regime and integrated through the Islamic Association into a 'united front' (*siyasi kengäş*) at all levels of the new political hier-archy. Later these policies hardened. Many mosques and shrines (*mazar*) were closed and damaged during the campaign against the 'Four Olds' and in the Cultural Revolution which followed (1966–1976). In the countryside the nature of collective labour in the communes hindered mosque atten-dance, even among peasants. Yet popular rituals (among the Uyghur above all *näzir* to commemo-rate the deceased) were still observed domestically, even in the most difficult years when resources to sustain commensality were most scarce. The author-ities made no attempt to prevent the religious observances of weddings and funerals; they simply looked the other way.

In the general loosening of controls which began after the death of Chairman Mao in 1976, the expansion of the market was not accompanied by an opening up of the religious marketplace. There was, however, an efflorescence of Islam throughout China, and nowhere more so than in Xinjiang.[10] When villagers once again had material resources at their disposal, however modest, one of their first spending priorities was the refurbishment (often complete reconstruction) of shrines and mosques. Defunct local mosque communities (*jemaät*) were reformed and the *mäzin* was once again allowed to utter the public call for prayer. If their old *imam* had died, the villagers now chose a replacement from among themselves; there were still plenty of suit-able candidates among those who had received an education before the abolition of the religious schools. Their credentials were recognised by the authorities. In the cities permission was granted on the major religious occasions for large congrega-tions to gather at the most famous mosques and to spill over into public space. From the early 1980s increasing numbers of the faithful were selected by the Regional Islamic Association to make the pilgrimage to Mecca at subsidised rates; permission was also granted to those able to afford it to make the *haj* independently of the Association.

These processes of resurgence were overwhelm-ingly spontaneous, but they were of course moni-tored by the authorities, who went so far as to allow the establishment of an Islamic Academy in Urumchi in 1987. The regulations preventing reli-gious activity on the part of those employed in the public sector were not changed, but there was more flexibility in their interpretation. For example, a teacher could attend his local mosque regularly after his retirement without having to worry about losing his pension, though he was still denied this freedom if he was a member of the Party. As in the USSR, religion was increasingly presented as one more feature of minority traditional customs; this categorisation seemed all the more plausible in China, given the fact that few of the dominant Han profess any religious allegiance. It thus became possible to conduct academic research into Uygher popular religion (Häbibulla 1993). During the 1980s small groups of Protestant missionaries, generally funded from the USA or Hong Kong, were able to establish themselves at higher education institu-tions in the region; although unable to proselytise publicly, their 'private' campus activities were not hindered by the authorities.[11]

AFTER 1991

Throughout former Soviet Central Asia almost all domains of social life were transformed following the demise of socialism. Religion could now be actively embraced and appropriated. Former communist leaders were quick to adopt religious rhetoric and in all five newly independent republics 'Islamic heritage' became an important element in promoting viable national identities. These amalgamations of nationalist and religious ideologies have assumed different forms throughout the region, but the tendency of the new governments to cultivate specific national forms of Islam to underpin nation-building was found everywhere.

These nationalised versions of Islam were soon called into question on several fronts. Although the extension of the 'cultural Islam' of the socialist era provided a ready-made collective identity in the wake of the Soviet collapse, and was particularly convenient to those who considered themselves 'not very religious', the product was too anodyne to satisfy significant portions of the population. Three challenges can be distinguished. First, newly pious Muslims criticised the officially sanctioned model of Islam as an instrumentalised distortion of the true faith. Secondly, 'national Islam' can only be as strong as the nation state itself; in a weak or 'failed' state such a model could quickly lose its appeal. Thirdly, the ideal of a national religion clashes with international expectations that democratic countries should allow a free market of denominations as a central element of universal human rights. These factors interact in diverse ways in the countries of the region. We shall focus our discussion in this section on two 'most different' cases, Kyrgyzstan and Turkmenistan, which nonetheless exhibit common elements. After comparing recent trends in Xinjiang, we shall return to these common elements in the concluding discussion.

Kyrgyzstan

Kyrgyzstan was the first of the post-Soviet Central Asian republics to adopt the (neoliberal) market ideology preached by the international community.[12] The country's lack of natural resources and its land-locked position left its government little choice but to comply with the demands of international organisations such as the International Monetary Fund (IMF), the World Bank, and the United Nations (UN). A series of wide-ranging reforms addressed not only the political and economic spheres but also the position of religion. Unlike neighbouring republics, which introduced similar constitutional guarantees of freedom of religion, in Kyrgyzstan most political restraints on religious expression really were lifted. However, there were numerous unintended consequences. Economic liberalisation was chaotically implemented, brought benefits primarily to a small group of political entrepreneurs, and failed to generate sustainable economic growth. Religious liberalisation also had unexpected outcomes. While the Kyrgyz government had reckoned with a revival of locally rooted faiths—primarily Sunni Islam but also Orthodox Christianity—the liberal policies led within a few years to a proliferation of groups not previously active in the country. The most conspicuous success was enjoyed by religious groups employing dreamlike images of 'the West' or claiming to offer other answers to the dislocations produced by 'the transition'.[13]

These trends were not yet visible in the early 1990s. Both in official discourse and popular imagination, to be a Kyrgyz meant being a (moderate) Muslim. In everyday speech, Kyrgyz described their Uzbek neighbours as 'more Muslim' and attributed their own less dogmatic brand of faith to their nomadic past. When talking about religious expression they tended to stress life-cycle events such as funerals, weddings, and circumcision rituals, events that are seen as quintessentially Kyrgyz, but which do not necessarily conform to textually based interpretations of Islam. These themes were reflected in official state discourse about the relation between religion and nationality. President Akaev liked to stress that the Kyrgyz were liberal Muslims whose nomadic past ensured that they would always keep a 'healthy distance' from religious extremism.[14] Islam was valued as a part of Kyrgyz tradition and history, while the intrinsic qualities of Islam as a faith were rarely mentioned in official rhetoric. When addressing issues of spirituality, political leaders often invoked not Islam but rather the *Manas* epic, which revolves around the life of the mythical hero Manas, who united the 40 Kyrgyz tribes and defeated many enemies. Throughout the 1990s the Kyrgyz government presented this epic as a model for moral and spiritual guidance to the Kyrgyz nation (Marat 2008; van der Heide 2008). Schoolchildren were taught about the seven lessons or commandments of Manas: patriotism, unity of the nation, international cooperation, defence of the state, humanism, harmony with nature, and the aspiration to obtain knowledge and skills (Akaev 2003, pp. 420–24). Even if citizens did not necessarily embrace all seven commandments (Marat 2008; van der Heide 2008, pp. 274–75), the flood of popular publications and spectacular public events helped to elevate this already well known epic to the status of a national ideology. Celebrated narrators of the epic (*manaschis*) were given prominent places in the new pantheon of national heroes. During Pelkmans' first fieldwork in the country in 1995, he heard many Kyrgyz proudly proclaim the uniqueness of the Manas epic. Children enthusiastically memorised parts of it, sometimes hoping to become a *manaschi*. Manas qualified as the ultimate national symbol in part at least due to the hero's ambiguous religious credentials: he could be portrayed both as a devout Muslim and as a 'secular' national hero. During the celebrations of the epic's symbolic millennium in 1995, Islam was rarely mentioned. One observer argued that many Kyrgyz were unaware that Manas was a Muslim (Wasilewski 1997, p. 87). Whether or not this was the case, it is significant that religious identification was little stressed in these celebrations, or in other domains of public life in the mid-1990s.

This ideology and the accompanying symbols of national unity worked well enough so long as Kyrgyz independence was a source of common pride and government rhetoric of a transition to

affluence remained credible. However, they began to lose their appeal in the early 2000s as it became increasingly obvious that the living standards of most citizens were not rising at all.[15] Many Kyrgyzstani citizens nowadays date significant changes in the religious landscape from this phase. As examples they state that larger numbers of women started to wear the veil, while both men and women observed *Ramadan* more strictly; they also identify an intensified presence of Christian and Muslim missionaries (the latter known as *davatchi*) in this period. This religious renewal in the second decade of post-socialism challenged the hitherto accepted boundaries between what was religion and what was culture. As McBrien's research in a small town in southern Kyrgyzstan shows, forms of Islam which stressed more literal interpretations of the Quran became increasingly influential after the turn of the century. Highly self-conscious Muslims addressed false conceptions of Islam in their teachings and sought to transform life-cycle rituals into 'religiously pure' events. By abolishing the 'traditional' wedding party, prohibiting the serving of alcohol, enforcing gender segregation and inviting religious specialists as wedding speakers, these self-conscious Muslims challenged tacitly accepted notions of what was Islamic and what was not. They disconnected being Muslim from national affiliation, stressing the supranational character of Islam rather than its relation to tradition and history (McBrien 2006a). Evidence from other regions also shows growing support for more conservative or textually oriented forms of Islam, particularly among rural youth and the disadvantaged in the urban sector (Heyat 2004).

While new manifestations of Islam are sources of controversy because they erode the links between religion and culture, the tensions are even starker in relation to conversion to Christianity, an increasingly common phenomenon in Kyrgyzstan over the last ten years. A basic strategy of Protestant churches to overcome the 'ethnic barrier' has been to disconnect religious and ethnic categories, thereby rejecting the established fusion of 'Kyrgyzness' and 'Muslimness'. In particular, neo-Pentecostal churches have recruited strongly by advancing a kind of 'spiritual modernity' that, in addition to salvation, stresses that everyone can attain prosperity, health and success in this world through faithful prayer. This message has proven very attractive to the poorer layers of Kyrgyz society, especially to those who are in one way or the other way outsiders to their own community. The stories told by new Christians to explain their conversion highlighted personal crises caused by addiction, divorce, unemployment, or migration; joining neo-Pentecostal churches helped them to cope with these difficulties. In a survey of 120 members of a neo-Pentecostal church in southern Kyrgyzstan, the majority (71%) was found to consist of recent rural-urban migrants; 30% were divorced or widowed women. Many of the people in these partly overlapping categories evidently found themselves detached from their familial networks and thus more 'free' to pursue alternative worldviews, while the intense community life of the Pentecostal church was particularly attractive to those who had to struggle to find their niche in the post-Soviet urban setting.[16]

If membership of faith-oriented Muslim and Christian movements was potentially empowering for the individuals involved, it also created tensions within families and local communities (McBrien & Pelkmans 2008). The increasing popularity of these movements also caused much unease among the largely secularised political elite of Kyrgyzstan. In recent years the state Committee for Religious Affairs has expressed the view that religious liberalisation has gone too far and noted that 'developed European states' also have their methods for dealing with disruptive religious trends (Murzakhalilov 2004, pp. 86–87). These officials would prefer to hold on to the established synthesis according to which Islam is an indispensable, central element of Kyrgyz identity. In practice, however, Protestant proselytism continued unabated at least until 2008,

and it was the Islamic reform movements which had to pay the price of fading liberalism because of their perceived links to political extremism and even to terrorism (Pelkmans 2006a, p. 37; McBrien & Pelkmans 2008).[17]

In summary, we can say that the post-socialist trajectory of Kyrgyzstan has been shaped by a genuine attempt to conform to externally-determined international standards of modernity, but this effort was undermined by the destabilising effects of policies of deregulation and liberalisation. Subsequently the political authorities have been trying to reassert controls, not least in the sphere of religion. The Soviet doctrines of ethnicity and nationality discussed in the preceding section have continued to shape public debates and governmental attitudes towards religion. The present situation remains unstable and haphazard, as became clear in the revolution of 2005, which unseated President Akaev, and in the political unrest which has continued since. The state has been no more successful in charting a viable religious path than it has been in the political and economic spheres. Attempts to forge a distinctively Kyrgyz identity on the basis of a 'liberal' Islam appear to be failing and the country remains vulnerable both to internal factional divisions and to destabilising transnational forces.

Turkmenistan

Although one might expect the Turkmen case to bear some resemblance to that of the Kyrgyz, given the common significance of nomadic tribal organisation in their history, in fact political and religious developments since independence in Turkmenistan have been very different.[18] Whereas Kyrgyzstan liberalised, Turkmenistan remained under the rule of a single party (renamed the Democratic Party of Turkmenistan, *Türkmenistanyn Demokratik Partiýasy*) and a leader whose personality cult was more extreme than anything since the cult of Stalin. The *nomenklatura* system remained largely unchanged and acceptable political activity continued to be understood in terms of 'unreserved popular support for the leadership' (Akbarzadeh 1999, p. 272). State functionaries were expected to contribute to the glorification of President Niyazov, who in 1993, following the precedent of Mustafa Kemal 'Atatürk' in Turkey, assigned to himself the title 'Turkmenbashi' (leader or head of the Turkmens). As in Stalinist times, state functionaries devoted much time and energy to fawning over their great leader (Denison 2007). Turkmenbashi, like other statesmen of his sort, regularly appeared on television urging his subjects to be more restrained in their displays of glorification.

If Stalin's goal of 'Socialism in One Country' has been perversely renewed in a new form in contemporary Turkmenistan, this was due largely to the fact that vast oil and gas fields allowed the regime to go its own way and ignore international pressure. Yet the new forms of authoritarianism differed from the old. It was not just that Marxist notions of class and labour vanished: the Soviet ideal that its republics should be 'national in form and socialist in content' was radically reconfigured. As Edgar concluded, the Soviet project to construct 'a unified Turkmen nation and . . . modern, socialist society' enjoyed more success with the former goal than with the latter (2004, pp. 261, 265). After 1991 the Turkmen elite quickly abandoned atheist and socialist ideology and incorporated ideas about spirituality that were imagined to be in line with the 'national spirit'. Turkmenbashi had an early sense of the important role that Islam could play in his project, as his *hajj* in 1992 testified. Initially it seems that the political leadership looked to Islam to exert a civilising force, a policy attested in the promotion of educational and architectural ties with internationally recognised Islamic centres. At the same time though, the concept of a distinctively Turkmen Islam became very prominent. The Turkmen government promoted its vision of Islam as an intrinsic part of the country's national identity, as conducive to stability and progress, and above all as a means of sacralising the power of the president.

What emerged was a state-imposed version of Islam centred on the god-like figure of Niyazov-Turkmenbashi. The leader went so far as to cast himself as a new Prophet, and set his own sacred book, the *Ruhnama* ('book of the soul'), almost on a par with the Quran. The longest portions of the book are devoted to presenting Turkmen history from its most flattering (sometimes blatantly invented) side and to outlining the moral obligations of the citizens. Key historical sections deal with the Quran, God, and the Prophet Muhammad. Niyazov mentions differences between the *Ruhnama* and the Quran. At one point he writes: 'The Turkmens' *Ruhnama* is not a religious book. . . . God's book, the Quran, is sacred and cannot be replaced or compared to any other book' (Turkmenbashi 2005, p. 21). However, in the text the *Ruhnama* is in fact compared to the Quran repeatedly (Turkmenbashi 2005, pp. 9, 21, 22); its author is described as interpreting and translating the Quran (Turkmenbashi 2005, p. 13) and even as carrying out God's will (Turkmenbashi 2005, pp. 19, 29, 44, 45). Moreover, the public dissemination of the *Ruhnama* as a sacred book and the inscription of excerpts from it on minarets of newly built mosques underlined Turkmenbashi's attempts at sacralising 'secular' power.

The *Ruhnama* is not to be dismissed as a quirk of eccentric self-indulgence: it has been a powerful means of disseminating ideological messages. By tying spiritual heritage to Turkmen heroes, national monuments, and of course to the Muslim qualities of the country's president, the regime promoted a vision of 'Turkmen Islam' analogous in principle to that of 'Kyrgyz Islam' but yet very different in practice, above all because there was little or no scope to put forward other points of view. To disseminate this spiritual agenda among the population the *Ruhnama* was made obligatory teaching material in schools and universities, where it infiltrated the curriculum in virtually every subject (Mills 2005, p. 204). Knowledge of this text became a prerequisite for obtaining any official position; it was often considered more important than professional knowledge. While in Kyrgyzstan the promotion of the Manas epic ran parallel to religious structures, in Turkmenistan a concerted effort was made to fuse official ideology with religious teachings. Imams were obliged to display the *Ruhnama* inside mosques and to incorporate it into their religious teachings. Resistance to this defamation of Islam was suppressed through arrests and replacing key figures within Turkmenistan's Muslim Religious Board (the controlling organ for all official Muslim clerics).

The full effects of these extraordinary policies in everyday life are unclear, since it has not been possible until now to carry out extended fieldwork. Some parents have reportedly complained that their children have started to accept official ideology as reflecting reality (International Crisis Group 2003).[19] Open critique has been rare, but this does not mean that no alternative visions of Islam exist (Kehl-Bodrogi 2006). The official form of Islam is ubiquitous in public life and clerics are invited to most public ceremonies to lend a veneer of legitimacy. However, mosques (including new edifices such as the colossal Turkmenbashi Spirituality Mosque in the leader's home village) seem to have remained conspicuously empty (Lewis 2008, p. 107). Rather, religious renewal seems to revolve around two possibilities. On the one hand there is a continuing (perhaps growing) tendency for people to visit shrines and venerate saints. This type of religious expression is generally tolerated by the Turkmen regime as it conforms to the official vision of a distinctively Turkmen Islam. On the other hand Kehl-Bodrogi (2006) has also detected a hardening of religious enthusiasm, notably a shift towards 'Wahhabi' sentiments, and a revulsion against the ways in which their regime has 'corrupted' Islam among those who are the material losers of transformation processes. It remains to be seen if these trends will continue in the post-Turkmenbashi period. Political change has been very slow since the leader's death in December 2006. The new government has toned down the cult of personality surrounding its former leader, but religious expression continues to be closely monitored, manipulated and controlled heavy-handedly.[20]

The smooth incorporation of religion into national narratives suggests that it is unhelpful to see the year that the Soviet Union collapsed (1991) as a turning point in religious life. The increased importance and visibility of religion did not challenge the new regimes, but rather allowed them to capitalise on ideas of a synthesis of religion and nationality that many of their citizens shared. While the differences between Turkmenistan and Kyrgyzstan are certainly considerable, there is an important similarity. It is not hard to see why the new elites throughout the region should draw in this way on religion as part of their nation building. The post-socialist states emerged on the basis of boundaries, criteria and definitions worked out in the early socialist period. Some of the identities had much older roots, but the process of constructing imagined 'national' communities accelerated greatly in the socialist era. However, at the time of independence a secular notion of nationality alone was insufficient to fill the void left by the disappearance of the Soviet state and of Marxist–Leninist ideology. Islam was available to fill the gap, to provide an additional element of 'enchantment' for the new imagined community, which was based on the nation. It was able to do so, we suggest, in large part thanks to the considerable success of secularisation policies in the socialist era. This ensured that, while Islam remained very much alive at the level of everyday practices, in terms of both dogma and spirituality its appeal was limited. Few Central Asian Muslims found the imagined community of the universal *umma* more attractive than the imagined community of the new nation state. Thus post-socialist leaders throughout this region were able to co-opt Islam into their nation-state projects, and the continued caricaturing of a Wahhabi threat has been a central element of this strategy.[21] The extent to which such co-option of religion retains its attraction to broad layers of the population, especially in cases like that of Kyrgyzstan, where the state itself has shown increasing signs of disintegration, can only be assessed through further empirical investigation.

Xinjiang

While the newly independent republics of the former Soviet Union can be termed post-socialist, Xinjiang remains an integral unit of a nation state that still proclaims itself socialist. The appropriateness of this term is of course open to debate. As elsewhere in China, in the cities of Xinjiang a new consumerist understanding of modernity has emerged since the economic reforms launched in the early 1980s. The benefits of these policies have been augmented more recently by huge state investments to 'develop the western regions'. This urban prosperity has greatly widened social inequalities. Relatively little wealth has filtered down to the countryside, but here too the previous socialist models have been largely replaced. Since the early 1980s the household has been reinstated as the main unit of production and consumption.

As far as religion is concerned, the dramatic efflorescence of the 1980s has not been sustained. However, in both town and countryside mosque attendance seems to have held up well. The fact that the authorities have regularly found it necessary to speak out in condemnation of other forms of assembly, including informal women's prayer groups, and sometimes to punish participants with heavy fines, is a further indication that the material prosperity of the 'socialist commodity economy' has not so far led to a general decline in personal or collective religiosity. Repressive measures intensified in the course of the 1990s, as the Chinese government's 'strike hard' campaign associated Islam with 'Wahhabis' and Uyghur separatism ('splittism'). Tensions have been concentrated in southern regions, notably Kashgar, which have the highest proportion of Uyghurs and which have

largely missed out on the benefits of economic growth (Potter 2003, p. 14; Fuller & Lipman 2004).[22] But in other regions too, many Uyghurs are still unable to practise their faith as they would wish. Retired cadres are generally able to participate in the religious life of their community without sanctions, but Party membership still poses a formidable problem (and it has become virtually impossible to renounce this allegiance). It is bitterly frustrating to be denied the possibility of going on the *hajj* for this reason, especially if other family members and even one's own spouse can make the pilgrimage. The authorities have continued to increase the opportunities to do so through organised parties, but they have clamped down on individual travel. As in earlier decades, infringement of the regulations by an individual can lead to sanctions affecting the entire extended family.

It is rumoured among Xinjiang Uyghurs that many of the early graduates of Urumchi's Islamic Academy encountered political difficulties and that some ended up in gaol. In recent years admission has been even more tightly screened. Whereas Chinese Muslims (Hui) were previously educated separately from Turkic Muslims, in 2005 unified classes were introduced and the use of Mandarin intensified. With a reported 150 graduates annually, progress is being made towards introducing a system of salaried *imams* resembling that of Kemalist Turkey and other Central Asian states (notably Turkmenistan and Uzbekistan). As the old peasant *imams* die, they are increasingly replaced by government appointees from outside the *jemaät*. While some villagers are suspicious of these 'government sponsored' clerics, most are respectful of their educational qualifications; it has become common for larger communities to petition the state authorities to be allocated such a qualified *imam*. Meanwhile some of those who remain from the older generation of peasant *imams* have also been added to the state payroll and now receive a regular 'subsistence allowance'. At the local (township) level, all *imams* are regularly convened for political training sessions; some of those considered most influential, notably religious representatives at the United Front committees, are selected to participate in annual excursions. In these and other ways the authorities have intensified the long-term policy of 'winning over, uniting, and educating [politically] the religious professionals' (MacInnis 1989, p. 3). Some Uyghurs perceive this as a very welcome intertwining of religious and secular hierarchies, but at the same time the Chinese understanding of laicism insists on maintaining the strictest exclusion of religion from the public sphere; in stark contrast to the post-Soviet states, religion can have no place in the country's schools.[23]

Whereas the earlier socialist decades had witnessed an unlikely convergence of militant socialists and Islamic reformers, both of whom disapproved of 'popular' religious practices involving costly rituals, power-holders have in recent decades become more fearful of 'fundamentalist' influences seeping through much more porous frontiers, including those with the ex-Soviet states. As a result, like their counterparts in the ex-Soviet states they have made concessions to the heritage of the 'little tradition', notably the more famous tombs and shrines; although strictly controlled by the authorities, these can be visited by individuals and even by larger groups of pilgrims. In the eastern Tienshan mountains, community rainmaking rituals are classified not as superstition but as 'normal religious activity'. The authorities take no steps to prevent nocturnal Sufi chanting during Ramadan, nor do they intervene in the conduct of *näzir* commemorations of the dead, though in some circles these rituals have become a focus for costly status competition. The tendency to folklorisation has also been intensified. For example, the rituals of the Festival of Sacrifice (*Qurban Häyt*), such as traditional *sama* dancing in Kashgar, are nowadays presented to tourists as another example of 'national folkways' (Waite, 2010).

At the same time the folklorisation of Islam in Xinjiang necessarily differs from the adaptations found in the newly independent neighbouring states. Cultural policy-makers in China have sought to modify the implicit congruence of ethnic group and religion by highlighting the complex legacies of earlier religious traditions. Thus while the Ramadan and Sacrifice Festivals remain the major public holidays for Xinjiang Muslims, in recent years Nevruz (*Noruz*) celebrations at the Spring equinox have become the object of much symbolic investment, for example in schools and the wider cultural public sphere. It is proclaimed in the media that *Noruz* is the third major *häyt* of the Uyghur people, following *Rozä* and *Qurban*. Special emphasis is placed on the ancient, non-Islamic roots of this spring festival. Whereas in the post-Soviet cases attention is concentrated on one nation, in Xinjiang it is emphasised that *Noruz* is a national (*milli*) festival for all the Turkic peoples of Central Asia (links to the Iranian world are ignored or downplayed). This new ritual has replaced earlier spring customs, which virtually no one can now recall. The new mediatised *Noruz* has considerable appeal to urban and rural Uyghurs alike (Hann 2008).

In summary, whereas in ex-Soviet Central Asia religion has become a major presence in the public sphere, in Xinjiang, established mechanisms to confine religion to the private sphere have been intensified since the early 1990s. Primarily through the Religious Affairs Bureaux, the authorities control Islamic institutions, monitor every kind of religious assembly and pilgrimage site, encourage citizens to see the dominant faith in wider geographical and historical contexts so that it cannot be identified with any particular ethno-national identity, and prevent proselytising.[24] The need for state vigilance to monitor 'illegal religious activities' is attributed to the activities of small groups of Uyghur political activists. But given that Xinjiang has many Muslims who are not Uyghur, including a significant number who speak only Chinese and have virtually no interaction with Turkic speakers, it is hard to see how 'political Islam' could mobilise a unified opposition to Han powerholders. This diversity is greater than any internal diversity in the ex-Soviet cases.

CONCLUSION

That Soviet and Maoist socialist modernities differed from their Western counterparts is obvious. In this article we have explored various forms of religious appropriation and the shifting relations between secular power and religion in Islamic Central Asia, focusing on socialist legacies but integrating discussion of both the pre-socialist and the post-socialist eras in order to unravel the larger dynamics at work. Colonisation by the empires of Russia and China began in earnest in the eighteenth century, but pre-socialist rulers made little effort to engage with the native populations they encountered and did not meddle with their religion. The boundaries between Russian and Chinese spheres of influence were not definitively settled until the middle of the twentieth century, when the entire region became socialist. The new powerholders aimed to create socialist citizens and religion was banned from the public sphere. In practice it was often viewed identically with superstition. Secularisation proceeded rapidly, especially in the larger cities, though many forms of popular practice continued. Citizens were encouraged through the educational system and the media to perceive their *natsional'nost* or *minzu* as an entity to which they had been loyal since time immemorial. From this new secular perspective, Islam, although central to everyday manifestations of cultural identity, was a relatively recent historical accretion.

Both in Xinjiang and in the former Soviet republics evidence from recent fieldwork suggests that Islam has retained and may even be gaining strength in the private sphere, in the extent to which it structures and gives meaning to individual lives in an era in which the expansion of the market economy has confronted increasing numbers of citizens with new uncertainties and existential insecurity. In the public sphere, however, there is a marked contrast. Despite the common element of folklorisation and some regional variation, China has continued to implement an even stricter version

of laicism than that implemented in Western Eurasia by states such as France and Turkey. Suspicion of Islam has been exacerbated by the alleged connection to terrorism, though the presence in Xinjiang of numerous non-Turkic Muslim minorities militates against any possibility of a tight alliance between religion and nationality.[25] In the former Soviet republics, by contrast, religion did not simply revive after independence; it became a crucial element of nation-state legitimation. Here the universal community of Islam is increasingly divided according to national boundaries first drawn under socialism.

These complex entanglements of the religious and the secular have implications for sociological theorising about religion and modernity. In the early 1990s, José Casanova (1994) provided a valuable conceptual map to rethink secularisation theory, especially those strands in it which assume clear differentiation between the religious and the secular, as well as between the public and the private. His focus on 'modern forms of public religion that are not intrinsically incompatible with differentiated modern structures', allowed him to argue that the 'deprivatisation' of religion could contribute positively to 'the public sphere of modern civil societies' (Casanova 2006, p. 13). In his influential critique of Casanova, Talal Asad argued that this might be wishful thinking. From his point of view, 'no movement that aspires to more than mere belief or inconsequential talk in public can remain indifferent to state power in a secular world' (1999, p. 191). The secular state is bound to continue to police the limits of religious action, or alternatively to collapse the boundary between the religious and the secular.

The Xinjiang case represents the first of these alternatives, that is, the secular authorities continue to define and police legitimate religious expression. Here, militant secularism is regularly reasserted, despite the trend to folklorisation and a greater tolerance of the popular heritage of Sufism. But neither Asad's reflections on the boundaries of the secular nor Casanova's thesis of deprivatisation are very helpful in understanding the post-Soviet cases. Both authors focus on religious movements 'entering' public and political spheres, which in Casanova's depiction are inherently secular. This deprivatisation of religion is imagined as a one-way process, in the course of which religion inserts itself in the secular realm. The reverse process, that is, the insertion of the state into the religious realm, is not closely scrutinised. By interpreting deprivatisation in terms of nationalisation, we have tried to draw attention to this reverse process. The Kyrgyz and Turkmen cases show some of the ways in which the 'secular' can encroach into the religious. If the Kyrgyzstan government appropriated 'folkloristic' notions of Islam to boost its own status, the Turkmenistan regime has cloaked itself more fully in religious garments, presenting the nation, the state, and above all its leadership as the new *sacra*.

Given the very different circumstances in which their own religious communities operate, Western observers are unlikely to sympathise with the policies of these secular powerholders, whether they emphasise control, as in Xinjiang, or legitimation, as in the ex-Soviet republics. The tendency to appropriate Islam as national heritage appears especially anachronistic in today's increasingly transnational world. This is a variant of modernity that goes against the grain of liberal ideology. But, before judging by the standard of the cosmopolitan human rights activists, it is necessary to recognise the larger dilemmas. The promotion of religious human rights and the concomitant ideal of a 'religious marketplace' prioritise individual freedom of expression, but the unbridled religious market may lead in practice to social friction and new pathologies. Irrespective of how we assess the successes of Protestant missions and 'Wahhabi' activists in Kyrgyzstan, we should not rush to condemn a state which attempts to counteract these arguably disintegrating forces by reifying elements of local syncretism in order to package them as national heritage. Of course, the same nationalising tendencies may

also result in repugnant extremes. Turkmenba-shi's colonisation of Islam aimed to sacralise his authoritarian rule and led to the repression of religious forms that deviated from the straightjacket set by the state. These cases thus warn against eager adoption of either extreme on the continuum between religious market and monopoly. They draw attention to the multiple ways in which Islam, nationality, and state power are being recombined in the aftermath of the radical secularising impact of Marxist–Leninist–Maoist socialism.

NOTES

1. For example, for the case of evangelical Christianity see Coleman (2000) and Robbins (2004).
2. Definitions of Central Asia vary. Our case materials in this article are taken from the Muslim Turkic zone between Turkmenistan and Xinjiang. Not all of the indigenous Muslim populations are Turkic (the Tajiks are the most significant non-Turkic group). Afghanistan's encounter with Soviet socialism was far from insignificant but will not be considered here. Similarly, although Buddhist traditions in adjacent zones of Inner Asia raise some comparable issues, we cannot pursue them in this article.
3. The influential model of the 'marketplace' is driven primarily by the experiences of North America, in much the same way that traditional secularisation theory has been driven by the experiences of Western Europe. In North America, Islam may now be following the path trodden by Judaism and Catholicism. In other words, despite the furor of the present 'war against terrorism', it appears to be on the way to becoming fully accepted as one further denomination on the marketplace. But the United States is a country populated largely by increasingly diverse waves of immigrants and therefore quite unlike the Turkic-speaking Islamic populations of Central Asia that form the subject of this article. Islam has dominated this region for rather longer than Protestantism has been the dominant religion in the United States.
4. This is not to deny the importance of local structures, especially where kin groups played a central role in social organisation (Lemercier-Quelquejay 1984). The universal faith everywhere acquired a

local colour or context (Privratsky 2001). The point is that the religion as such transcended the local group (the neighbours were Muslim too) and even in the most remote tribal groups, at least some members were aware of the wider connections.

5. Even today, few Central Asian Muslims are aware of the Sunni–Shiite divide; nor are they aware of their common affiliation to the Hanafi school of law (*madhhab*).

6. It is estimated that in the Turkestan *guberniya* in 1913 only 6.3% of the population were Russians (Matley 1994, p. 105).

7. Researchers found that some 80% of the total non-Russian population were 'believers', whereas among the former Christians in the USSR about 80% were identified as atheists (Bennigsen & Bryan 2002, p. 252).

8. Slezkine provides a telling example of this paradoxical development in his description of the 1934 Congress of Soviet writers, which saw 'a curiously solemn parade of old-fashioned romantic nationalisms' (1994, p. 334). The new political entities were by no means fully congruent with the distribution of linguistic groups, and it was not possible to assign every nationality to a territorial 'homeland'.

9. Rudelson (1997) emphasises the continued significance of local identities in Xinjiang, but we follow Gladney (2004) in stressing the degree to which the policies of the socialist state have succeeded in overcoming both the oasis-based fragmentation of the sedentary Turkic-speaking population in the Tarim Basin and also the geographical and cultural boundary with Dzungaria in the north. Hoppe (1998) emphasises the 'cellular' diversity of inter-ethnic relations across the region; but he too notes that Han domination has led to an increased salience of ethnic allegiance among the minority nationalities.

10. See Dillon (1994); MacInnis (1989); Waite (2010); Zarcone 2001. Survey evidence from the 1980s confirmed the continuing 'profound social and ideological foundation' of religion in rural Xinjiang (MacInnis 1989, pp. 248–54).

11. Hann was able to observe them at close quarters in 1986 during his first fieldwork in Xinjiang, which was confined to the regional capital, Urumchi. Later field trips took him to urban Kashgar in 1996 and rural Qumul (Chinese: Hami) in 2006–2007. All fieldwork has been carried out together with Ildikó Bellér-Hann, in cooperation with local academic institutions; these projects had diverse priorities, but for obvious reasons religion was never one of them; the average duration of these field trips was a little over six months.

12. This section is based primarily on 14 months of field work by Pelkmans in 2003–2004, and a one-month follow-up trip in 2008. Another member of the 'Religion and Civil Society group' at the Max Planck Institute, Julie McBrien, also conducted fieldwork in a different location in Kyrgyzstan in 2003–2004 (McBrien 2006a; 2006b), during which period Hann made two short visits to the country; special thanks are due to Julie McBrien for her comments on this section.

13. These dreamlike images were explicitly used by a number of Pentecostal churches preaching a variant of the 'Gospel of Prosperity'. For a more elaborate analysis, see Pelkmans (2009).

14. See for example an interview with then President Akaev by R. Sagdeev, 24 June 1997, available at: www.eisenhowerinstitute.org, accessed 6 January 2008.

15. Van der Heide (2008, p. 279) similarly observed that Manas—as the symbol of national unity—quickly lost stature after the late 1990s.

16. For details on the survey, see Pelkmans (2009).

17. The government's latest attempt to reassert control includes a more restrictive religion law, signed by President Bakiev on 12 January 2009. This requires re-registration of all religious communities and bans unregistered religious activity, the involvement of children in religious activities, and 'persistent action aimed at converting followers from one faith to another'. The law has triggered a wave of protests from religious leaders and has not yet been implemented. As of May 2009, Government officials were claiming that they were still trying to resolve the major controversial issues. See http://www.forum18.org/Archive.php?article_id=1301, accessed on 9 June 2009.

18. Fieldwork in Turkmenistan was almost impossible during the first 15 years after independence. This section is based largely on a brief one-week visit by Pelkmans in 2006, when he attended an academic conference in the capital Ashkhabad, conducted interviews and visited several mosques. He was accompanied by our colleague Krisztina Kehl-Bodrogi, who has been able to make other short trips and kindly shared her impressions with us on numerous occasions. See in particular Kehl-Bodrogi (2006).

19. Attitudes towards Turkmenbashi's ideology have been difficult to ascertain. Several scholars have pointed out that, despite widespread scepticism among the general population, the level of 'belief appeared to be significantly higher among the youth (Denison 2007; Lewis 2008, p. 81, 92; Mills 2005, p. 196). During his visit in 2006, Pelkmans was struck by the comment of a cynical high school student who complained about her schoolmates talking about the *Ruhnama* as if it reflected reality.

20. See Forum 18 'Turkmenistan: Religious Freedom Survey, August 2008', available at: http://www.forum18.org/Archive.php?article_id=1167&pdf=Y, accessed 9 June 2009.

21. Uzbekistan, the largest state of the region, fits the pattern very well. Extreme pressure is applied to dissuade Uzbeks from conversion to Christianity, on the grounds that this religion is incompatible with their national identity (Hilgers 2006). Kazakhstan enjoys a more liberal reputation internationally (not unlike Kyrgyzstan); but here too, as in Uzbekistan, the president has regularly intervened in religious matters in a very personal way, for example in order to claim as a saint a celebrated Sufi scholar and mystic who embodies the best of the Kazakh people (Jessa 2006). The Tajik case is exceptional in numerous ways: it is the only post-Soviet state in the region where the dominant ethno-linguistic group is not Turkic, the only one to possess a substantial Islamic minority, and the only one which experienced civil war in the 1990s. Nonetheless Manja Stephan (2006) reports that here, too, the present powerholders are deploying notions of Tajik Islam and the Wahhabi threat in much the same way as their counterparts in the neighbouring ex-Soviet republics.

22. Some Uyghurs in other regions imagine that controls in the far south are overwhelmingly oppressive. This perception renders them grateful for the relative laxity, as they see it, shown by their own local authorities. Hann's personal observations (including a month spent touring the south in summer 2005) suggest, however, that the authorities maintain a high degree of uniformity in their policies towards religion. Regional variation is much greater in rural economic policy; constraints on the peasantry are much greater in the south.

23. Thus, while it is generally conceded that local religious leaders can play a valuable role in personal moral education (*tärbiyiläş*), they are not allowed to organise formal religious instruction for children. This therefore persists clandestinely; a young person wishing to proceed to higher education is taking a big risk if he or she attends such classes. Fieldwork by Hann in early 2007 was adversely affected by an incident which had taken place some 12 months earlier in a neighbouring community, when an *imam* was invited into a school to give classes in morality (*äxlaq*). This transgression of the line between the religious and the secular led to a series of corrective 'ideological instruction' campaigns at all levels of local society; the effect of these was to make many, especially junior officials, wary of all contacts with a foreign researcher, even to discuss topics unrelated to religion.

24. In 2006 Hann found that the missionary presence had declined substantially; it was now confined to a few families in Urumchi, the provincial capital.

25. During fieldwork in Xinjiang in August 2009, when this article was in press, Hann found that discontent over the government's religious policies remained strong among Uyghurs. However, no one considered religion to have been a major factor in causing the violence which on 5 July had left almost 200 dead in Urumchi.

10

Civil Religion in America

Robert N. Bellah

WHILE SOME HAVE ARGUED that Christianity is the national faith, and others that church and synagogue celebrate only the generalized religion of "the American Way of Life," few have realized that there actually exists alongside of and rather clearly differentiated from the churches an elaborate and well-institutionalized civil religion in America. This article argues not only that there is such a thing, but also that this religion-or perhaps better, this religious dimension-has its own seriousness and integrity and requires the same care in understanding that any other religion does.[1]

THE KENNEDY INAUGURAL

John F. Kennedy's inaugural address of January 20, 1961, serves as an example and a clue with which to introduce this complex subject. That address began:

> We observe today not a victory of party but a celebration of freedom-symbolizing an end as well as a beginning-signifying renewal as well as change. For I have sworn before you and Almighty God the same solemn oath our forebears prescribed nearly a century and three quarters ago.
>
> The world is very different now. For man holds in his mortal hands the power to abolish all forms of human poverty and to abolish all forms of human life. And yet the same revolutionary beliefs for which our forbears fought are still at issue around the globe-the belief that the rights of man

come not from the generosity of the state but from the hand of God.

And it concluded:

> Finally, whether you are citizens of America or of the world, ask of us the same high standards of strength and sacrifice that we shall ask of you. With a good conscience our only sure reward, with history the final judge of our deeds, let us go forth to lead the land we love, asking His blessing and His help, but knowing that here on earth God's work must truly be our own.

These are the three places in this brief address in which Kennedy mentioned the name of God. If we could understand why he mentioned God, the way in which he did, and what he meant to say in those three references, we would understand much about American civil religion. But this is not a simple or obvious task, and American students of religion would probably differ widely in their interpretation of these passages.

Let us consider first the placing of the three references. They occur in the two opening paragraphs and in the closing paragraph, thus providing a sort of frame for more concrete remarks that form the middle part of the speech. Looking beyond this particular speech, we would find that similar references to God are almost invariably to be found in the pronouncements of American presidents on solemn occasions, though usually not in the working messages that the President sends to Congress on various concrete issues. How, then, are we to interpret this placing of references to God?

It might be argued that the passages quoted reveal the essentially irrelevant role of religion in the very secular society that is America. The placing of the references in this speech as well as in public life generally indicates that religion "has only a ceremonial significance"; it gets only a sentimental nod that serves largely to placate the more unenlightened members of the community before a discussion of the really serious business with which religion has nothing whatever to do. A cynical observer might even say that an American President has to mention God or risk losing votes. A semblance of piety is merely one of the unwritten qualifications for the office, a bit more traditional than but not essentially different from the present-day requirement of a pleasing television personality.

But we know enough about the function of ceremonial and ritual in various societies to make us suspicious of dismissing something as unimportant because it is "only a ritual." What people say on solemn occasions need not be taken at face value, but it is often indicative of deep-seated values and commitments that are not made explicit in the course of everyday life. Following this line of argument, it is worth considering whether the very special placing of the references to God in Kennedy's address may not reveal something rather important and serious about religion in American life.

It might be countered that the very way in which Kennedy made his references reveals the essentially vestigial place of religion today. He did not refer to any religion in particular. He did not refer to Jesus Christ, or to Moses, or to the Christian church; certainly he did not refer to the Catholic church. In fact, his only reference was to the concept of God, a word that almost all Americans can accept but that means so many different things to so many different people that it is almost an empty sign. Is this not just another indication that in America religion is considered vaguely to be a good thing, but

that people care so little about it that it has lost any content whatever? Isn't Dwight Eisenhower reported to have said "Our government makes no sense unless it is founded in a deeply felt religious faith-and I don't care what it is,"[2] and isn't that a complete negation of any real religion?

These questions are worth pursuing because they raise the issue of how civil religion relates to the political society on the one hand and to private religious organization on the other. President Kennedy was a Christian, more specifically a Catholic Christian. Thus his general references to God do not mean that he lacked a specific religious commitment. But why, then, did he not include some remark to the effect that Christ is the Lord of the world or some indication of respect for the Catholic church? He did not because these are matters of his own private religious belief and of his own particular church; they are not matters relevant in any direct way to the conduct of his public office. Others with different religious views and commitments to different churches or denominations are equally qualified participants in the political process. The principle of separation of church and state guarantees the freedom of religious belief and association, but at the same time clearly segregates the religious sphere, which is considered to be essentially private, from the political one.

Considering the separation of church and state, how is a president justified in using the word "God" at all? The answer is that the separation of church and state has not denied the political realm a religious dimension. Although matters of personal religious belief, worship, and association are considered to be strictly private affairs, there are, at the same time, certain common elements of religious orientation that the great majority of Americans share. These have played a crucial role in the development of American institutions and still provide a religious dimension for the whole fabric of American life, including the political sphere. This public religious dimension is expressed in a set of beliefs, symbols, and rituals that I am calling American civil religion.

The inauguration of a president is an important ceremonial event in this religion. It reaffirms, among other things, the religious legitimation of the highest political authority.

Let us look more closely at what Kennedy actually said. First, he said, "I have sworn before you and Almighty God the same solemn oath our forbears prescribed nearly a century and three quarters ago." The oath is the oath of office, including the acceptance of the obligation to uphold the Constitution. He swears it before the people (you) and God. Beyond the Constitution, then, the president's obligation extends not only to the people but to God. In American political theory, sovereignty rests, of course, with the people, but implicitly, and often explicitly, the ultimate sovereignty has been attributed to God. This is the meaning of the motto, "In God we trust," as well as the inclusion of the phrase "under God" in the pledge to the flag. What difference does it make that sovereignty belongs to God? Though the will of the people as expressed in the majority vote is carefully institutionalized as the operative source of political authority, it is deprived of an ultimate significance. The will of the people is not itself the criterion of right and wrong. There is a higher criterion in terms of which this will can be judged; it is possible that the people may be wrong. The president's obligation extends to the higher criterion.

When Kennedy says that "the rights of man come not from the generosity of the state but from the hand of God," he is stressing this point again. It does not matter whether the state is the expression of the will of an autocratic monarch or of the "people"; the rights of man are more basic than any political structure and provide a point of revolutionary leverage from which any state structure may be radically altered. That is the basis for his reassertion of the revolutionary significance of America.

But the religious dimension of political life as recognized by Kennedy not only provides a grounding for the rights of man that makes any form of political absolutism illegitimate, it also provides a transcendent goal for the political process. This is implied in his final words that "here on earth God's work must truly be our own." What he means here is, I think, more clearly spelled out in a previous paragraph, the wording of which, incidentally, has a distinctly biblical ring:

> Now the trumpet summons us again-not as a call to bear arms, though arms we need-not as a call to battle, though embattled we are-but a call to bear the burden of a long twilight struggle, year in and year out, "rejoicing in hope, patient in tribulation"-a struggle against the common enemies of man: tyranny, poverty, disease and war itself.

The whole address can be understood as only the most recent statement of a theme that lies very deep in the American tradition, namely the obligation, both collective and individual, to carry out God's will on earth. This was the motivating spirit of those who founded America, and it has been present in every generation since. Just below the surface throughout Kennedy's inaugural address, it becomes explicit in the closing statement that God's work must be our own. That this very activist and noncontemplative conception of the fundamental religious obligation, which has been historically associated with the Protestant position, should be enunciated so clearly in the first major statement of the first Catholic president seems to underline how deeply established it is in the American outlook. Let us now consider the form and history of the civil religious tradition in which Kennedy was speaking.

THE IDEA OF A CIVIL RELIGION

The phrase "civil religion" is, of course, Rousseau's. In chapter 8, book 4 of *The Social Contract*, he outlines the simple dogmas of the civil religion: the existence of God, the life to come, the reward of virtue and the punishment of vice, and the exclusion of religious intolerance. All other religious opinions are outside the cognizance of the state and may be freely held by citizens. While the phrase "civil religion" was not used, to the best of my knowledge, by the founding fathers, and I am certainly not arguing for the particular influence of Rousseau, it is clear that similar ideas, as part of the cultural climate of the late eighteenth century, were to be found among the Americans. For example, Benjamin Franklin writes in his autobiography,

> I never was without some religious principles. I never doubted, for instance, the existence of the Deity; that he made the world and govern'd it by his Providence; that the most acceptable service of God was the doing of good to men; that our souls are immortal; and that all crime will be punished, and virtue rewarded either here or hereafter. These I esteemed the essentials of every religion; and, being to be found in all the religions we had in our country, I respected them all, tho' with different degrees of respect, as I found them more or less mix'd with other articles, which, without any tendency to inspire, promote or confirm morality, serv'd principally do divide us, and make us unfriendly to one another.

It is easy to dispose of this sort of position as essentially utilitarian in relation to religion. In Washington's Farewell Address (though the words may be Hamilton's) the utilitarian aspect is quite explicit:

> Of all the dispositions and habits which lead to political prosperity, Religion and Morality are indispensable supports. In vain would that man claim the tribute of Patriotism, who should labour to subvert these great Pillars of human happiness, these firmest props of the duties of men and citizens. The mere politician, equally with the pious man ought to cherish and respect them. A volume could not trace all their connections with private and public felicity. Let it simply be asked where is the security for property, for reputation, for life, if the sense of religious obligation *desert* the oaths, which are the instruments of investigation in Courts of Justice? And let us with caution indulge

the supposition, that morality can be maintained without religion. Whatever may be conceded to the influence of refined education on minds of peculiar structure, reason and experience both forbid us to expect that National morality can prevail in exclusion of religious principle.

But there is every reason to believe that religion, particularly the idea of God, played a constitutive role in the thought of the early American statesmen.

Kennedy's inaugural pointed to the religious aspect of the Declaration of Independence, and it might be well to look a that document a bit more closely. There are four references to God. The first speaks of the "Laws of Nature and of Nature's God" that entitle any people to be independent. The second is the famous statement that all men "are endowed by their Creator with certain inalienable Rights." Here Jefferson is locating the fundamental legitimacy of the new nation in a conception of "higher law" that is itself based on both classical natural law and biblical religion. The third is an appeal to "the Supreme Judge of the world for the rectitude of our intentions," and the last indicates "a firm reliance on the protection of divine Providence." In these last two references, a biblical God of history who stands in judgment over the world is indicated.

The intimate relation of these religious notions with the self-conception of the new republic is indicated by the frequency of their appearance in early official documents. For example, we find in Washington's first inaugural address of April 30, 1789:

> It would be peculiarly improper to omit in this first official act my fervent supplications to that Almighty Being who rules over the universe, who presides in the councils of nations, and whose providential aids can supply every defect, that His benediction may consecrate to the liberties and happiness of the people of the United States a Government instituted by themselves for these essential purposes, and may enable every instru-

ment employed in its administration to execute with success the functions allotted to his charge.

No people can be bound to acknowledge and adore the Invisible Hand which conducts the affairs of man more than those of the United States. Every step by which we have advanced to the character of an independent nation seems to have been distinguished by some token providential agency. .

The propitious smiles of Heaven can never be expected on a nation that disregards the eternal rules of order and right which Heaven itself has ordained. . The preservation of the sacred fire of liberty and the destiny of the republican model of government are justly considered, perhaps, as deeply, as finally, staked on the experiment intrusted to the hands of the American people.

Nor did these religious sentiments remain merely the personal expression of the President. At the request of both Houses of Congress, Washington proclaimed on October 3 of that same first year as President that November 26 should be "a day of public thanksgiving and prayer," the first Thanksgiving Day under the Constitution.

The words and acts of the founding fathers, especially the first few presidents, shaped the form and tone of the civil religion as it has been maintained ever since. Though much is selectively derived from Christianity, this religion is clearly not itself Christianity. For one thing, neither Washington nor Adams nor Jefferson mentions Christ in his inaugural address; nor do any of the subsequent presidents, although not one of them fails to mention God.[3] The God of the civil religion is not only rather "unitarian," he is also on the austere side, much more related to order, law, and right than to salvation and love. Even though he is somewhat deist in cast, he is by no means simply a watchmaker God. He is actively interested and involved in history, with a special concern for America. Here the analogy has much less to do with natural law than with ancient Israel; the equation of America with Israel in the idea of the "American Israel" is not infrequent.[4] What was implicit in the words of

Washington already quoted becomes explicit in Jefferson's second inaugural when he said: "I shall need, too, the favor of that Being in whose hands we are, who led our fathers, as Israel of old, from their native land and planted them in a country flowing with all the necessaries and comforts of life." Europe is Egypt; America, the promised land. God has led his people to establish a new sort of social order that shall be a light unto all the nations.[5] This theme, too, has been a continuous one in the civil religion. We have already alluded to it in the case of the Kennedy inaugural. We find it again in President Johnson's inaugural address:

> They came already here-the exile and the stranger, brave but frightened-to find a place where a man could be his own man. They made a covenant with this land. Conceived in justice, written in liberty, bound in union, it was meant one day to inspire the hopes of all mankind; and it binds us still. If we keep its terms, we shall flourish.

What we have, then, from the earliest years of the republic is a collection of beliefs, symbols, and rituals with respect to sacred things and institutionalized in a collectivity. This religion-there seems no other word for it-while not antithetical to and indeed sharing much in common with Christianity, was neither sectarian nor in any specific sense Christian. At a time when the society was overwhelmingly Christian, it seems unlikely that this lack of Christian reference was meant to spare the feelings of the tiny non-Christian minority. Rather, the civil religion expressed what those who set the precedents felt was appropriate under the circumstances. It reflected their private as well as public views. Nor was the civil religion simply "religion in general." While generality was undoubtedly seen as a virtue by some, as in the quotation from Franklin above, the civil religion was specific enough when it came to the topic of America. Precisely because of this specificity, the civil religion was saved from empty formalism and served as a genuine vehicle of national religious self-understanding.

But the civil religion was not, in the minds of Franklin, Washington, Jefferson, or other leaders, with the exception of a few radicals like Tom Paine, ever felt to be a substitute for Christianity. There was an implicit but quite clear division of function between the civil religion and Christianity. Under the doctrine of religious liberty, an exceptionally wide sphere of personal piety and voluntary social action was left to the churches. But the churches were neither to control the state nor to be controlled by it.

The national magistrate, whatever his private religious views, operates under the rubrics of the civil religion as long as he is in his official capacity, as we have already seen in the case of Kennedy. This accommodation was undoubtedly the product of a particular historical moment and of a cultural background dominated by Protestantism of several varieties and by the Enlightenment, but it has survived despite subsequent changes in the cultural and religious climate.

CIVIL WAR AND CIVIL RELIGION

Until the Civil War, the American civil religion focused above all on the event of the Revolution, which was seen as the final act of the Exodus from the old lands across the waters. The Declaration of Independence and the Constitution were the sacred scriptures and Washington the divinely appointed Moses who led his people out of the hands of tyranny. The Civil War, which Sidney Mead calls "the center of American history,"[6] was the second great event that involved the national self-understanding so deeply as to require expression in civil religion. In 1835, Alexis de Tocqueville wrote that the American republic has never really been tried and that victory in the Revolutionary War was more the result of British preoccupation elsewhere and the presence of a powerful ally than of any great military success of the Americans. But in 1861 the time of testing had indeed come. Not only did the

Civil War have the tragic intensity of fratricidal strife, but it was one of the bloodiest wars of the nineteenth century; the loss of life was far greater than any previously suffered by Americans.

The Civil War raised the deepest questions of national meaning. The man who not only formulated but in his own person embodied its meaning for Americans was Abraham Lincoln. For him the issue was not in the first instance slavery but "whether that nation, or any nation so conceived, and so dedicated, can long endure." He had said in Independence Hall in Philadelphia on February 22, 1861:

> All the political sentiments I entertain have been drawn, so far as I have been able to draw them, from the sentiments which originated in and were given to the world from this Hall. I have never had a feeling, politically, that did not spring from the sentiments embodied in the Declaration of Independence.[7]

The phrases of Jefferson constantly echo in Lincoln's speeches. His task was, first of all, to save the Union-not for America alone but for the meaning of America to the whole world so unforgettably etched in the last phrase of the Gettysburg Address.

But inevitably the issue of slavery as the deeper cause of the conflict had to be faced. In his second inaugural, Lincoln related slavery and the war in an ultimate perspective:

> If we shall suppose that American slavery is one of those offenses which, in the providence of God, must needs come, but which, having continued through His appointed time, He now wills to remove, and that He gives to both North and South this terrible war as the woe due to those by whom the offense came, shall we discern therein any departure from those divine attributes which the believers in a living God always ascribe to Him? Fondly do we hope, fervently do we pray, that this mighty scourge of war may speedily pass away. Yet, if God wills that it continue until all the wealth piled by the bondsman's two hundred and fifty years of unrequited toil shall be sunk, and until

every drop of blood drawn with the lash shall be paid by another drawn with the sword, as was said three thousand years ago, so still it must be said "the judgements of the Lord are true and righteous altogether."

But he closes on a note if not of redemption then of reconciliation: "With malice toward none, with charity for all."

With the Civil War, a new theme of death, sacrifice, and rebirth enters the new civil religion. It is symbolized in the life and death of Lincoln. Nowhere is it stated more vividly than in the Gettysburg Address, itself part of the Lincolnian "New Testament" among the civil scriptures. Robert Lowell has recently pointed out the "insistent use of birth images" in this speech explicitly devoted to "these honored dead": "brought forth," "conceived," "created," "a new birth of freedom." He goes on to say:

> The Gettysburg Address is a symbolic and sacramental act. Its verbal quality is resonance combined with a logical, matter of fact, prosaic brevity. . In his words, Lincoln symbolically died, just as the Union soldiers really died-and as he himself was soon really to die. By his words, he gave the field of battle a symbolic significance that it has lacked. For us and our country, he left Jefferson's ideals of freedom and equality joined to the Christian sacrificial act of death and rebirth. I believe this is the meaning that goes beyond sect or religion and beyond peace and war, and is now part of our lives as a challenge, obstacle and hope.[8]

Lowell is certainly right in pointing out the Christian quality of the symbolism here, but he is also right in quickly disavowing any sectarian implication. The earlier symbolism of the civil religion had been Hebraic without any specific sense of being Jewish. The Gettysburg symbolism (". those who here gave their lives, that that nation might live") is Christian without having anything to do with the Christian church.

The symbolic equation of Lincoln with Jesus was made relatively early. W. H. Herndon, who had been Lincoln's law partner, wrote:

> For fifty years God rolled Abraham Lincoln through his fiery furnace. He did it to try Abraham and to purify him for his purposes. This made Mr. Lincoln humble, tender, forbearing, sympathetic to suffering, kind, sensitive, tolerant; broadening, deepening and widening his whole nature; making him the noblest and loveliest character since Jesus Christ. I believe that Lincoln was God's chosen one.[9]

With the Christian archetype in the background, Lincoln, "our martyred president," was linked to the war dead, those who "gave the last full measure of devotion." The theme of sacrifice was indelibly written into the civil religion.

The new symbolism soon found both physical and ritualistic expression. The great number of the war dead required the establishment of a number of national cemeteries. Of these, Gettysburg National Cemetery, which Lincoln's famous address served to dedicate, has been overshadowed only by the Arlington National Cemetery. Begun somewhat vindictively on the Lee estate across the river from Washington, partly with the end that the Lee family could never reclaim it,[10] it has subsequently become the most hallowed monument of the civil religion. Not only was a section set aside for the confederate dead, but it has received the dead of each succeeding American war. It is the site of the one important new symbol to come out of World War I, the Tomb of the Unknown Soldier; more recently it has become the site of the tomb of another martyred President and its symbolic eternal flame.

Memorial Day, which grew out of the Civil War, gave ritual expression to the themes we have been discussing. As Lloyd Warner has so brilliantly analyzed it, the Memorial Day observance, especially in the towns and smaller cities of America, is a major event for the whole community involving a rededication to the martyred dead, to the spirit of sacrifice, and to the American vision.[11] Just as

Thanksgiving Day, which incidentally was securely institutionalized as an annual national holiday only under the presidency of Lincoln, serves to integrate the family into the civil religion, so Memorial Day has acted to integrate the local community into the national cult. Together with the less overtly religious Fourth of July and the more minor celebrations of Veterans Day and the birthdays of Washington and Lincoln, these two holidays provide an annual ritual calendar for the civil religion. The public school system serves as a particularly important context for the cultic celebration of the civil rituals.

THE CIVIL RELIGION TODAY

In reifying and giving a name to something that, though pervasive enough when you look at it, has gone on only semiconsciously, there is risk of severely distorting the data. But the reification and the naming have already begun. The religious critics of "religion in general," or of the "religion of the 'American Way of Life,' " or of "American Shintō" have really been talking about the civil religion. As usual in religious polemic, they take as criteria the best in their own religious tradition and as typical the worst in the tradition of the civil religion. Against these critics, I would argue that the civil religion at its best is a genuine apprehension of universal and transcendent religious reality as seen in or, one could almost say, as revealed through the experience of the American people. Like all religions, it has suffered various deformations and demonic distortions. At its best, it has neither been so general that it has lacked incisive relevance to the American scene nor so particular that it has placed American society above universal human values. I am not at all convinced that the leaders of the churches have consistently represented a higher level of religious insight than the spokesmen of the civil religion. Reinhold Niebuhr has this to say of Lincoln, who never joined a church and who certainly represents civil religion at its best:

An analysis of the religion of Abraham Lincoln in the context of the traditional religion of his time and place and of its polemical use on the slavery issue, which corrupted religious life in the days before and during the Civil War, must lead to the conclusion that Lincoln's religious convictions were superior in depth and purity to those, not only of the political leaders of his day, but of the religious leaders of the era.[12]

Perhaps the real animus of the religious critics has been not so much against the civil religion in itself but against its pervasive and dominating influence within the sphere of church religion. As S. M. Lipset has recently shown, American religion at least since the early nineteenth century has been predominantly activist, moralistic, and social rather than contemplative, theological, or innerly spiritual.[13] De Tocqueville spoke of American church religion as "a political institution which powerfully contributes to the maintenance of a democratic republic among the Americans"[14] by supplying a strong moral consensus amidst continuous political change. Henry Bargy in 1902 spoke of American church religion as "*la poésie du civisme.*"[15]

It is certainly true that the relation between religion and politics in America has been singularly smooth. This is in large part due to the dominant tradition. As de Tocqueville wrote:

> The greatest part of British America was peopled by men who, after having shaken off the authority of the Pope, acknowledged no other religious supremacy: they brought with them into the New World a form of Christianity which I cannot better describe than by styling it a democratic and republican religion.[16]

The churches opposed neither the Revolution nor the establishment of democratic institutions. Even when some of them opposed the full institutionalization of religious liberty, they accepted the final outcome with good grace and without nostalgia for the *ancien régime.*

The American civil religion was never anticlerical or militantly secular. On the contrary, it borrowed selectively from the religious tradition in such a way that the average American saw no conflict between the two. In this way, the civil religion was able to build up without any bitter struggle with the church powerful symbols of national solidarity and to mobilize deep levels of personal motivation for the attainment of national goals.

Such an achievement is by no means to be taken for granted. It would seem that the problem of a civil religion is quite general in modern societies and that the way it is solved or not solved will have repercussions in many spheres. One need only to think of France to see how differently things can go. The French Revolution was anticlerical to the core and attempted to set up an anti-Christian civil religion. Throughout modern French history, the chasm between traditional Catholic symbols and the symbolism of 1789 has been immense.

American civil religion is still very much alive. Just three years ago we participated in a vivid reenactment of the sacrifice theme in connection with the funeral of our assassinated President. The American Israel theme is clearly behind both Kennedy's New Frontier and Johnson's Great Society. Let me give just one recent illustration of how the civil religion serves to mobilize support for the attainment of national goals. On March 15, 1965, President Johnson went before Congress to ask for a strong voting-rights bill. Early in the speech he said:

> Rarely are we met with the challenge, not to our growth or abundance, or our welfare or our society-but rather to the values and the purposes and the meaning of our beloved nation.
>
> The issue of equal rights for American Negroes is such an issue. And should we double our wealth and conquer the stars and still be unequal to this issue, then we will have failed as a people and as a nation.
>
> For with a country as with a person, "What is a man profited, if he shall gain the whole world, and lose his own soul."

And in conclusion he said:

> Above the pyramid on the great seal of the United States it says in Latin, "God has favored our undertaking."
>
> God will not favor everything that we do. It is rather our duty to divine his will. I cannot help but believe that He truly understands and that He really favors the undertaking that we begin here tonight.[17]

The civil religion has not always been invoked in favor of worthy causes. On the domestic scene, an American-Legion type of ideology that fuses God, country, and flag has been used to attack nonconformist and liberal ideas and groups of all kinds. Still, it has been difficult to use the words of Jefferson and Lincoln to support special interests and undermine personal freedom. The defenders of slavery before the Civil War came to reject the thinking of the Declaration of Independence. Some of the most consistent of them turned against not only Jeffersonian democracy but Reformation religion; they dreamed of a South dominated by medieval chivalry and divine-right monarchy.[18] For all the overt religiosity of the radical right today, their relation to the civil religious consensus is tenuous, as when the John Birch Society attacks the central American symbol of Democracy itself.

With respect to America's role in the world, the dangers of distortion are greater and the built-in safeguards of the tradition weaker. The theme of the American Israel was used, almost from the beginning, as a justification for the shameful treatment of the Indians so characteristic of our history. It can be overtly or implicitly linked to the ideal of manifest destiny that has been used to legitimate several adventures in imperialism since the early nineteenth century. Never has the danger been greater than today. The issue is not so much one of imperial expansion, of which we are accused, as of the tendency to assimilate all governments or parties in the world that support our immediate policies or call upon our help by invoking the notion of free institutions and democratic values. Those nations that are for the moment "on our side" become "the free world." A repressive and unstable military dictatorship in South Vietnam becomes "the free people of South Vietnam and their government." It is then part of the role of America as the New Jerusalem and "the last best hope of earth" to defend such governments with treasure and eventually with blood. When our soldiers are actually dying, it becomes possible to consecrate the struggle further by invoking the great theme of sacrifice. For the majority of the American people who are unable to judge whether the people in South Vietnam (or wherever) are "free like us," such arguments are convincing. Fortunately President Johnson has been less ready to assert that "God has favored our undertaking" in the case of Vietnam than with respect to civil rights. But others are not so hesitant. The civil religion has exercised long-term pressure for the humane solution of our greatest domestic problem, the treatment of the Negro American. It remains to be seen how relevant it can become for our role in the world at large, and whether we can effectually stand for "the revolutionary beliefs for which our forbears fought," in John F. Kennedy's words.

The civil religion is obviously involved in the most pressing moral and political issues of the day. But it is also caught in another kind of crisis, theoretical and theological, of which it is at the moment largely unaware. "God" has clearly been a central symbol in the civil religion from the beginning and remains so today. This symbol is just as central to the civil religion as it is to Judaism or Christianity. In the late eighteenth century this posed no problem; even Tom Paine, contrary to his detractors, was not an atheist. From left to right and regardless of church or sect, all could accept the idea of God. But today, as even *Time* has recognized, the meaning of "God" is by no means so clear or so obvious. There is no formal creed in the civil religion. We have had a Catholic President; it is conceivable that we could have a Jewish one. But could we have an agnostic president? Could a man

with conscientious scruples about using the word "God" the way Kennedy and Johnson have used it be elected chief magistrate of our country? If the whole God symbolism requires reformulation, there will be obvious consequences for the civil religion, consequences perhaps of liberal alienation and of fundamentalist ossification that have not so far been prominent in this realm. The civil religion has been a point of articulation between the profoundest commitments of Western religious and philosophical tradition and the common beliefs of ordinary Americans. It is not too soon to consider how the deepening theological crisis may affect the future of this articulation.

THE THIRD TIME OF TRIAL

In conclusion it may be worthwhile to relate the civil religion to the most serious situation that we as Americans now face, what I call the third time of trial. The first time of trial had to do with the question of independence, whether we should or could run our own affairs in our own way. The second time of trial was over the issue of slavery, which in turn was only the most salient aspect of the more general problem of the full institutionalization of democracy within our country. This second problem we are still far from solving though we have some notable successes to our credit. But we have been overtaken by a third great problem that has led to a third great crisis, in the midst of which we stand. This is the problem of responsible action in a revolutionary world, a world seeking to attain many of the things, material and spiritual, that we have already attained. Americans have, from the beginning, been aware of the responsibility and the significance our republican experiment has for the whole world. The first internal political polarization in the new nation had to do with our attitude toward the French Revolution. But we were small and weak then, and "foreign entanglements" seemed to threaten our very survival. During the last century, our relevance for the world was not forgotten, but our role was seen as purely exemplary. Our democratic republic rebuked tyranny by merely existing. Just after World War I we were on the brink of taking a different role in the world, but once again we turned our backs.

Since World War II the old pattern has become impossible. Every president since Franklin Roosevelt has been groping toward a new pattern of action in the world, one that would be consonant with our power and our responsibilities. For Truman and for the period dominated by John Foster Dulles that pattern was seen to be the great Manichean confrontation of East and West, the confrontation of democracy and "the false philosophy of Communism" that provided the structure of Truman's inaugural address. But with the last years of Eisenhower and with the successive two presidents, the pattern began to shift. The great problems came to be seen as caused not solely by the evil intent of any one group of men. For Kennedy it was not so much a struggle against particular men as against "the common enemies of man: tyranny, poverty, disease and war itself."

But in the midst of this trend toward a less primitive conception of ourselves and our world, we have somehow, without anyone really intending it, stumbled into a military confrontation where we have come to feel that our honor is at stake. We have in a moment of uncertainty been tempted to rely on our overwhelming physical power rather than on our intelligence, and we have, in part, succumbed to this temptation. Bewildered and unnerved when our terrible power fails to bring immediate success, we are at the edge of a chasm the depth of which no man knows.

I cannot help but think of Robinson Jeffers, whose poetry seems more apt now than when it was written, when he said:

Unhappy country, what wings you have!
Weep (it is frequent in human affairs), weep for
the terrible magnificence of the means,

The ridiculous incompetence of the reasons, the
bloody and shabby
Pathos of the result.

But as so often before in similar times, we have a man of prophetic stature, without the bitterness or misanthropy of Jeffers, who, as Lincoln before him, calls this nation to its judgment:

When a nation is very powerful but lacking in self-confidence, it is likely to behave in a manner that is dangerous both to itself and to others.

Gradually but unmistakably, America is succumbing to that arrogance of power which has afflicted, weakened and in some cases destroyed great nations in the past.

If the war goes on and expands, if that fatal process continues to accelerate until America becomes what it is not now and never has been, a seeker after unlimited power and empire, then Vietnam will have had a mighty and tragic fallout indeed. I do not believe that will happen. I am very apprehensive but I still remain hopeful, and even confident, that America, with its humane and democratic traditions, will find the wisdom to match its power.[19]

Without an awareness that our nation stands under higher judgment, the tradition of the civil religion would be dangerous indeed. Fortunately, the prophetic voices have never been lacking. Our present situation brings to mind the Mexican-American war that Lincoln, among so many others, opposed. The spirit of civil disobedience that is alive today in the civil rights movement and the opposition to the Vietnam War was already clearly outlined by Henry David Thoreau when he wrote, "If the law is of such a nature that it requires you to be an agent of injustice to another, then I say, break the law. Thoreau's words, "I would remind my countrymen that they are men first, and Americans at a late and convenient hour,"[20] provide an essential standard for any adequate thought and action in our third time of trial. As Americans, we have been well favored in the world, but it is as men that we will be judged.

Out of the first and second times of trial have come, as we have seen, the major symbols of the American civil religion. There seems little doubt that a successful negotiation of this third time of trial-the attainment of some kind of viable and coherent world order-would precipitate a major new set of symbolic forms. So far the flickering flame of the United Nations burns too low to be the focus of a cult, but the emergence of a genuine transnational sovereignty would certainly change this. It would necessitate the incorporation of vital international symbolism into our civil religion, or, perhaps a better way of putting it, it would result in American civil religion becoming simply one part of a new civil religion of the world. It is useless to speculate on the form such a civil religion might take, though it obviously would draw on religious traditions beyond the sphere of biblical religion alone. Fortunately, since the American civil religion is not the worship of the American nation but an understanding of the American experience in the light of ultimate and universal reality, the reorganization entailed by such a new situation need not disrupt the American civil religion's continuity. A world civil religion could be accepted as a fulfillment and not as a denial of American civil religion. Indeed, such an outcome has been the eschatological hope of American civil religion from the beginning. To deny such an outcome would be to deny the meaning of America itself.

Behind the civil religion at every point lie biblical archetypes: Exodus, Chosen People, Promised Land, New Jerusalem, and Sacrificial Death and Rebirth. But it is also genuinely American and genuinely new. It has its own prophets and its own martyrs, its own sacred events and sacred places, its own solemn rituals and symbols. It is concerned that America be a society as perfectly in accord with the will of God as men can make it, and a light to all nations.

It has often been used and is being used today as a cloak for petty interests and ugly passions. It is

in need-as any living faith-of continual reformation, of being measured by universal standards. But it is not evident that it is incapable of growth and new insight.

It does not make any decisions for us. It does not remove us from moral ambiguity, from being, in Lincoln's fine phrase, an "almost chosen people." But it is a heritage of moral and religious experience from which we still have much to learn as we formulate the decisions that lie ahead.

NOTES

1. Why something so obvious should have escaped serious analytical attention is itself an interesting problem. Part of the reason is probably the controversial nature of the subject. From the earliest years of the nineteenth century, conservative religious and political groups have argued that Christianity is, in fact, the national religion. Some of them from time to time and as recently as the 1950s proposed constitutional amendments that would explicitly recognize the sovereignty of Christ. In defending the doctrine of separation of church and state, opponents of such groups have denied that the national polity has, intrinsically, anything to do with religion at all. The moderates on this issue have insisted that the American state has taken a permissive and indeed supportive attitude toward religious groups (tax exemptions, et cetera), thus favoring religion but still missing the positive institutionalization with which I am concerned. But part of the reason this issue has been left in obscurity is certainly due to the peculiarly Western concept of "religion" as denoting a single type of collectivity of which an individual can be a member of one and only one at a time. The Durkheimian notion that every group has a religious dimension, which would be seen as obvious in southern or eastern Asia, is foreign to us. This obscures the recognition of such dimensions in our society.
2. Eisenhower (1955), p. 97.
3. God is mentioned or referred to in all inaugural addresses but Washington's second, which is a very brief (two paragraphs) and perfunctory acknowledgement. It is not without interest that the actual word "God" does not appear until Monroe's second

inaugural, March 5, 1821. In his first inaugural, Washington refers to God as "that Almighty Being who rules the universe," "Great Author of every public and private good," "Invisible Hand," and "benign Parent of the Human Race." John Adams refers to God as "Providence," "Being who is supreme over all," "Patron of Order," "Fountain of Justice," and "Protector in all ages of the world of virtuous liberty." Jefferson speaks of "that Infinite Power which rules the destinies of the universe," and "that Being in whose hands we are." Madison speaks of "that Almighty Being whose power regulates the destiny of nations," and "Heaven." Monroe uses "Providence" and "the Almighty" in his first inaugural and finally "Almighty God" in his second. See *Inaugural Addresses of the Presidents of the United States from George Washington 1789 to Harry S. Truman 1949*, 82d Congress, 2d Session, House Document No. 540, 1952.

4. For example, Abiel Abbot, pastor of the First Church in Haverhill, Massachusetts, delivered a Thanksgiving sermon in 1799, *Traits of Resemblance in the People of the United States of America to Ancient Israel*, in which he said, "It has been often remarked that the people of the United States come nearer to a parallel with Ancient Israel, than any other nation upon the globe. Hence 'Our American Israel' is a term frequently used; and common consent allows it apt and proper." In Kohn (1961), p. 665.

5. That the Mosaic analogy was present in the minds of leaders at the very moment of the birth of the republic is indicated in the designs proposed by Franklin and Jefferson for the seal of the United States of America. Together with Adams, they formed a committee of three delegated by the Continental Congress on July 4, 1776, to draw up the new device. "Franklin proposed as the device Moses lifting up his wand and dividing the Red Sea while Pharaoh was overwhelmed by its waters, with the motto 'Rebellion to tyrants is obedience to God.' Jefferson proposed the children of Israel in the wilderness 'led by a cloud by day and a pillar of fire at night.' " Stokes (1950), pp. 467–68.

6. Mead (1963), p. 12.

7. Abraham Lincoln, in Nevins (1964), p. 39.

8. Robert Lowell, in Nevins (1964) pp. 88–89.

9. William Henry Herndon, in Eddy (1941), p. 162.

10. Decker and McSween (1892), pp. 60–67.

11. How extensive the activity associated with Memorial Day can be is indicated by Warner: "The sacred symbolic behavior of Memorial Day, in which scores of the town's organizations are involved, is ordinarily divided into four periods. During the year separate rituals are held by many of the associations for their dead, and many of these activities are connected with later Memorial Day events. In the second phase, preparations are made during the last three or four weeks for the ceremony itself, and some of the associations perform public rituals. The third phase consists of scores of rituals held in all the cemeteries, churches, and halls of the associations. These rituals consist of speeches and highly ritualized behavior. They last for two days and are climaxed by the fourth and last phase, in which all the separate celebrants gather in the center of the business district on the afternoon of Memorial Day. The separate organizations, with their members in uniform or with fitting insignia, march through the town, visit the shrines and monuments of the hero dead, and, finally, enter the cemetery. Here dozens of ceremonies are held, most of them highly symbolic and formalized." During these various ceremonies Lincoln is continually referred to and the Gettysburg Address recited many times. Warner (1962), pp. 8–9.

12. Reinhold Niebuhr, "The Religion of Abraham Lincoln," in Nevins (1964), p. 72. William J. Wolfe of the Episcopal Theological School in Cambridge, Massachusetts, has written: "Lincoln is one of the greatest theologians of America-not in the technical meaning of producing a system of doctrine, certainly not as a defender of some one denomination, but in the sense of seeing the hand of God intimately in the affairs of nations. Just so the prophets of Israel criticized the events of their day from the perspective of the God who is concerned for history, and who reveals His will within it. Lincoln now stands among God's latter day prophets." Niebuhr (1963), p. 24.

13. Lipset (1964), chap. 4.

14. Tocqueville (1954), p. 310.

15. Bargy (1902), p. 31.

16. de Tocqueville (1954), 311. Later he says, "In the United States even the religion of most of the citizens is republican, since it submits the truths of the other world to private judgment, as in politics the care of their temporal interests is abandoned to the good sense of the people. Thus every man is allowed freely to take that road which he thinks will lead him to heaven, just as the law permits

every citizen to have the right of choosing his own government" (p. 436).

17. Lyndon B. Johnson, in U.S., *Congressional Record*, House, March 15, 1965, pp. 4924, 4926.

18. See Hartz (1955).

19. Senator J. William Fullbright, speech of April 28, 1966, as reported in *The New York Times*, April 29, 1966.

20. Henry David Thoreau, In Arieli (1964), p. 274.

11

Civil Rights–Civil Religion: Visible People and Invisible People

Charles H. Long

AMERICAN RELIGION IS USUALLY understood as the religion of European immigrants transplanted into the American soil. Most general texts that deal with this topic begin with the coming of the Puritans, continue through to the breakdown of the Puritan theocratic ideal and on to the new light, old light debate of the Presbyterians. We are then treated to a description of the great awakenings and the religion of the pioneers as they moved across the American landscape.

Other texts pay equal attention to the different religious communities of the thirteen original colonies and their histories. More precise and detailed work in the area of American religious history has shown that certain themes tend to run through much of this history, becoming the threads with which American religious life weaves its fabric of meanings. Thus the notions of wilderness, new land, errands, and so on, form the symbolic threads of the American religious tradition.

In this vein some historians have more recently become interested in what is now called American civil religion. "Civil religion" is an exceedingly vague phrase, and attempts to define it have often led to more ambiguity. However, some basic notions are involved in the phrase. Greater clarity might be forthcoming if the phrase is placed in the context of the French sociological tradition from Denis Fustel Coulange's *The Ancient City* to Émile Durkheim's

The Elementary Forms of the Religious Life. Works in this tradition define and locate religion as either a projection of the image of society into objective and sacred symbols or as a correlate of the structure of society. If notions such as these are applied to American religion, the emphasis falls on the religious meanings implicit in the founding documents of the American Republic: the Declaration of Independence and the Constitution. As such, the religious vision stemming from this orientation differs from that of the revealed religion, Christianity; for the revealed religion offers salvation to all human beings regardless of circumstance whereas, in the civil religion, salvation is seen within the context of belonging to the American national community. But the American national community in its ideals and history also offers salvation to all, since it has defined itself as a community that includes peoples from all over the world who seek the forms of freedom and order enunciated in the founding documents.

Civil Religion emerges as a parallel structure alongside revealed religion and its institutions, or it may find expression through revealed religion, or again it may borrow symbols from the revealed religion. Issues of this kind are exhaustively discussed in H. Richard Niebuhr's *Christ and Culture*, where a typology of the possible range of relationships is described in detail.

If American religion is dealt with in either of these two ways or in a combination of these ways, we must note some glaring omissions. Let me raise the issue by asking a simple question, the answer to which will raise a serious issue of method and description. What is meant by "American" and by "religion" in the phrase "American religion"? If by "American" we mean European Christian immigrants and their progeny, then we have overlooked American Indians and Afro-Americans. And if religion is defined as revealed Christianity and its institutions, we have overlooked much of the religion of Afro-Americans, American aborigines, Asian Americans, the Jewish communities, and others. Even from the point of view of civil religion it is not clear, from the perspective of the various national and ethnic communities, there has ever been a consistent meaning of the national symbols and their meanings. In short, a great many of the writings and discussions on the topic of American religion have been consciously or unconsciously ideological, serving to enhance, justify, and render sacred the history of European immigrants in this land.

Indeed, this approach to American religion has rendered the religious reality of non-Europeans to a state of invisibility, and thus the invisibility of the non-European in America arises as a fundamental issue of American history at this juncture. How are we to understand this invisibility and how are we to deal with it as a creative methodological issue? It is no longer possible for us to add the "invisible ones" as addenda to a European-dominated historical method, for such a procedure fails to take into account the relationships of the ones omitted throughout the history of religion in America. Nor is it possible for us, simply in imitation of the historical method and historiography we are criticizing, to begin the project of writing history in which the ideological values of blacks or American Indians dominate. This procedure has no merit, for it could not make sense of that problem of invisibility which allowed us to raise the issue of our

discussion. The issue raised here is a subtle one, and questions must be asked concerning the nature of historical method. Reference has already been made to the issue of concealment as described by Sidney Mead in his *The Lively Experiment*. Allow me to add another statement in regard to this same matter. Ralph Ellison, in his prologue to his novel *Invisible Man*, writes:

> I am an invisible man. No, I am not a spook like those who haunted Edgar Allan Poe; nor am I one of your Hollywood-movie ectoplasms. I am a man of substance, of flesh and bone, fiber, and liquids —and I might even be said to possess a mind. I am invisible, understand, simply because people refuse to see me. Like the bodiless heads you sometimes see in circus side-shows, it is as though I have been surrounded by mirrors of hard distorting glass. When they approach me they see only my surroundings, themselves, or figments of their imagination—indeed, everything and anything except me.
>
> Nor is my invisibility exactly a matter of a biochemical accident of my epidermis. That inevitability to which I refer occurs because of a peculiar disposition of the eyes of those with whom I come in contact. A matter of construction of the inner eyes, those eyes with which they look through their physical eyes upon reality. . . . You wonder whether you aren't simply a phantom in other people's minds.

Mead's statement and this one by Ellison deal with the issues of concealment and invisibility. From the point of view of a religious historian, these statements carry great import, for they refer to definitive and fundamental modes of orientation of the American tradition of history and religious history. The statements have to do with the American cultural language, the American mode of perception, and the American religion. "The mighty saga of the outward acts" is a description of the origins not simply of an American language rooted in the physical conquest of space but equally of a language which is the expression of a hermeneutics of conquest and suppression. It is a cultural language that conceals the inner depths, the archaic dimensions of the dominant peoples in the country, while at the same time it renders invisible all those who fail to partake of this language and its underlying cultural experience. The religion of the American people centers around the telling and retelling of the mighty deeds of the white conquerors. This story hides the true experience of Americans from their very eyes. The invisibility of Indians and blacks is matched by a void or a deeper invisibility within the consciousness of white Americans. The inordinate fear they have of minorities is an expression of the fear they have when they contemplate the possibility of seeing themselves as they really are.

This American cultural language is not a recent creation. It is a cosmogonic language, a language of beginnings; it structures the American myth of the beginnings, and has continued to express the synchronic dimensions of American cultural life since that time. It is a language forged by the Puritans and the Jeffersonians and carried on by succeeding generations. The Puritan "errand in the wilderness" was undertaken in the name of religious freedom, a freedom that would allow the colonists from Europe to divine the Word of God in a manner appropriate to their dispositions and knowledge, and a freedom to show this light of the gospel to all human beings, both far and near. This wilderness was, in following the biblical paradigm, a place of retreat from the world for prayer and reflection upon divine meanings. And again, this wilderness was paradise, a space overflowing with the bounty of creation. These meanings of the wilderness are undercut when they confront the American aborigines. The aborigines do not partake of these Puritan understandings of their culture and lands. Even when the aborigines become the teachers of the Puritans, the Puritan cultural languages fail to take cognizance through an alteration of their own language; or even when they are treated benignly by the aborigines, the shift in

language and thus in cultural perception does not take place. The aborigine is a wilderness creature who, like the wilderness itself, must be conquered. The conquest of the aborigine began in the seventeenth century and continues into the present. The linking of the aboriginal cultures with the wilderness and the subsequent conquest of both raise issues of race and ecology. These are issues that point up an inherent hermeneutical structure in American historical and religious interpretation.

The Jeffersonian language is equally ambiguous, and this ambiguity is made more intense by the factor of self-consciousness. Unlike the Puritans who wished to be a light unto Europe, the Jeffersonians were thrilled by the possibilities of creating a free society in a new land. They were enlightened people who had thought about the meaning of freedom as an essential ingredient of human societies. Around the issue of slavery was to be played the poignant and commiserating drama of the Jeffersonian conscience; Jefferson is the archetype of the sophisticated liberal. But this issue is deeper than the biography of Jefferson; Jefferson is the hand behind the Declaration of Independence and one of the moving spirits of the Constitution; these are the founding documents, the structures of cosmogony. Through these documents the character of the Jeffersonians and the structure of American cultural language gain a definitive form.

The compromise over slavery at the beginning, in the formation and promulgation of the Constitution, is the archetype of that long series of compromises concerning the freedom of black Americans within the American national community. This first compromise sets the tone for what is almost a ritual of language concerning the nature of black freedom and, consequently, the meaning of freedom in the American Republic. Indeed, we are able to discern almost precisely the one-hundred-year periods in which the Jeffersonian cultural and linguistic compromises rise to an intense and violent level; where the antinomies of its inner structure are exposed. These are cycles of American history. From 1776 to the 1860s is almost a hundred years, and from the Civil War to the 1960s and 1970s is another hundred-year period. These cycles represent dramatic rituals of the archetypes of American history and religion.

At each of these mythical cycles the opportunity is presented for a change of the ritual, for a break in the repetition of this kind of eternal return. It was present in 1776, and then again in the bloody Civil War, and then again in the 1960s with the Kennedys and Martin Luther King, Jr., and Malcolm X; but at each of these junctures the American revolution is aborted and clever priests of our national language and apparatus, skillful in the ways of ritual purity and manipulation, come upon the scene to ensure the repetition of the American ritual.

It is from this perspective that we must understand the meaning of religion in America from the point of view of one who is not a part of the heritage of European immigrants. In this sense, the distinction between civil religion and church religion is not one that looms large for us. In the first place, it is the overwhelming reality of the white presence in any of its various forms that becomes the crucial issue. Whether this presence was legitimated by power executed illegally, or whether in institution or custom, its reality, as far as blacks were concerned through most of their history, carried the force of legal sanction enforced by power. The black response to this cultural reality is part of the civil rights struggle in the history of American blacks.

The fact that black churches have been the locus of the civil rights struggle is not incidental, for the civil rights struggle represented the black confrontation with an American myth that dehumanized the black persons being. The struggle was a mode of affirmation on the part of blacks and a protest in the name of human rights and freedom. The location of this struggle in the church enabled the civil rights movement to take on the resources of black cultural life in the form of organization,

music, and artistic expression, and in the gathering of limited economic resources. The civil rights movement has been one of protest and exposition — a protest in the name of freedom and an exposition of the hypocrisy of the American cultural language. But more than hypocrisy was being exposed in this movement, for at points the American system was seen as a gross irrationality or a rationalized demonism. This is religious language and the expression of religious experience. The vicissitudes of the black struggle against the American myth can be traced from recalcitrant slaves through persons symbolized by the names of Nat Turner, Denmark Vesey, David Walker, Marcus Garvey, W. E. B. DuBois, Martin Luther King, Jr., and others.

To the extent that the struggle for black freedom was carried on through the seeking of legal redress and petition, it participated in and made use of the American cultural language; for in this affirmation there is the tacit acceptance of the American language as adequate for the expression of human freedom for all the American people. But something more is at work here within the black communities. First of all, the very organization of black people meant that they were not invisible to each other; their humanity was affirmed within their communities. Second, they came to know the meaning of the American cultural language in all of its subtleties and antinomies, or, to use a colloquial expression, they came to know the Man. Third, and probably more important, they came to a knowledge and experienced *another reality*, a reality not created or given by the Man. This otherness is expressed in the spirituals as God, or as a mode of perception that is not under the judgment of the oppressors. It is equally expressed in the practical and concrete proposals that speak of *another space*, whether Africa or another geographical location, or heaven. This sense of otherness, or the sense of the other that has arisen out of the black experience, is present when the black communities contemplate the meaning of America as a free society; for if blacks are to be free in American society, this society will indeed have to become a radically different one, *an-other* place.

In the light of this perspective on American religion, let us ask our second question: How is it possible to do justice to the facts of American religious history and at the same time overcome the concealment of peoples? How might it be possible to make visible those who have been rendered invisible religiously and historically? The issue has to do with the network, the nexus, onto which and out of which the facts are generated and interpreted. I am raising a question that is close to the problem of myth.

If we take myth as defined by Mircea Eliade—namely, that myth is a *true* story—then it is the question of a rendering of American religion as a story that does justice to the inner-life meanings and vitalities of those who were made invisible in the old interpretive schema, and it should be a true story that can halt the repressive concealment that has characterized so much of American history.

As in all hermeneutical procedures, one must take account of the misunderstandings and misinterpretations; only by going through these can we arrive at meanings that are substantive. I have stated above that I wish to be faithful to the facts of American history and religion; my problem, or better, the problematical issue, centers around the matrix or pattern onto which these facts are spread. The issue is one of the relationship between authenticity and truth as involving both the facts and the interpretations of these facts. Myth emerges as a category at this point, because I am interested in telling a story of America that is both true and authentic—a story that can respond to an objective and felt meaning of all Americans, a *true story* of the American peoples that moves beyond concealment and invisibilities.

In the telling of the story of America and American cultural reality, we have been dominated by one tradition, the tradition of "the mighty saga of the outward acts," told and retold in such a manner, "until it overshadowed and suppressed the equally vital but more somber story of the *inner experience.*"

The telling and the retelling of the American experience in this mode have created a normative historical judgment and ideology of the American experience. The *historical* telling of this story has in the form of historiography relegated itself to a position of objectivity in terms of the canons of scholarship; it has become identified with truth and legitimacy. Those identified with this approach have not openly asked the question of why they wish the facts to conform to this conception of the truth of the American reality, or better, why certain facts were chosen as the sinew of this truth.

Most interpretations of American religion, whether from the point of view of the revealed tradition or the civil tradition, have been involved with an ideological concealment of the reality of the inner dynamics of their own religio-cultural psychic reality and a correlative repression and concealment of the reality of others. This procedure has been undertaken to give American reality a normative mode of interpretation centered in one tradition. This mode of interpretation has a hallowed position in Western intellectual thought. It constitutes the problematic and resolution of the issue of the episteme. The notion of the episteme constitutes a problem for any form of coherence, and as understood in this context it is the issue of the normative center of interpretation of American religion.

The invocation of the notion of the episteme is an indication of the seriousness of this problem at the level of method. While the notion of the episteme as a pre-methodological meaning allowed for an organizing principle of coherence and provided a normative structure for the organization of data, it simultaneously operated as a center, a presence, making possible the permutation or transformation of other data. "The mighty saga of the outward acts" represents the data produced from the unknown, suppressed, never revealed "inner depths." It is this ideological construct that forces all other traditions to remain in their places — places allocated to them by the centering of this "great tradition."

The concealment and correlative invisibility of various and sundry American peoples result from this methodological centeredness of the American episteme. But even when this tradition is the normative center, we observe that it cannot be known in itself. It is known only through the data that it generates about itself and others. Once this is revealed, we are able to see the contradiction; it constitutes a coherence encompassed by a contradiction, and from a hermeneutical point of view this issues into a problem of desire. It is precisely this desire to uncover, reveal, make visible, the truth of the American reality that explains the violent centennial outbreaks of the American antinomies.

On the practical level, a method must be found whereby we deal with the religious history of all the American peoples. I suggest that we might begin by defining this culture as an Aboriginal-Euro-African culture. The terms should not be seen as simply additive or descriptive. The terms are relational. This means that these meanings should always form the background for any discussion of American religion at any historical period. They are not simply additive, that is, I am not suggesting them because I wish to include all the peoples in America in this methodological paradigm. I am saying that once the singularity of a normative tradition is overcome, the problem of inclusion of all peoples will no longer be at issue. The notion of equality which is part and parcel of the American cultural language must express itself in theoretical terms also; we must work for a meaning of this notion that has relevance for historical method. The question of the meaning of American religion in its revealed or civil forms calls for new theoretical considerations.

In this short essay I have attempted to raise certain theoretical problems in relationship to historical method and historiography of American religion. New understandings of this history will be forthcoming with a change of consciousness; with this I agree, but my emphasis has been directed toward changes on the levels of the intellectual and theoretical expressions of human consciousness.

NOTE

One sees again the influence of Sidney Mead's work *The Lively Experiment: The Shaping of Christianity in America* (New York: Harper & Row, 1963).

I am indebted to works txiat have come from the history of religions methods and from what has come to be known as the "structural schools." In the former, Mircea Eliade's *The Myth of the Eternal Return*, trans. Millard R. Trask (New York, Pantheon Books, 1954), and in the latter Claude Lévi-Strauss's *The Savage Mind* (Chicago: University of Chicago Press, 1970), and Jacques Derrida's programmatic essay, "Structure, Sign, and Play in the Discourse of the Human Sciences," in *The Structuralist Controversy*, ed. Richard A. Macksey and Eugenio Donato (Baltimore: Johns Hopkins Press, 1970), have been of particular importance to me.

12

The Militant Christian Right in the United States

Mark Juergensmeyer

RECENT MOVEMENTS OF RELIGIOUS activism in the United States also respond to a perception of secular society's moral deficiencies. At times this religious dimension has taken a turn toward politics. Politicized religion in the United States is not, in itself, a new thing. American patriotism has often been fused with biblical images and Protestant Christian rhetoric, creating a "civil religion" that has been as nationalist in its own way as the Muslim Brotherhood in Egypt or the Rashtriya Swayamsevak Sangh in India. Periodically in American history, separatist movements have created their own ideal societies; native peoples have used symbols from their religious heritage to define an identity of their own that insulates them from absorption into the dominant society.[1]

What was new about American religious politics in the late twentieth century was the way that religion became infused into a radical critique of the secular political order. Though Christianity has always contained the idea of a kingdom of God that contrasts with the worldly human order, the notion of a catastrophic moment in history in which this godly kingdom intersects with the human order is peculiar to Evangelical Protestant Christianity. It began to take shape in the modern era with the theology of John Nelson Darby, a nineteenth-century British theologian, who believed that the time of the kingdom would be at hand when pious

Christians experienced the "rapture" of being united with heavenly existence. This vision reemerged with remarkable popularity in the United States after the end of the Cold War. It has provided the framework for the *Left Behind* novels of Tim LaHaye and Jerry Jenkins, which have sold tens of millions of copies. Many of the sixteen volumes in the series made the *New York Times* best-seller list.[2]

The evangelical Christian movement in the United States that is the audience for the *Left Behind* books has had a profound impact on American politics. It required American political society to take on a Christian character in order to fulfill society's role in the coming of Christ.[3] Even though there were two branches of millenarian thinking about the return of Christ's kingdom to earth—premillennarian and postmillenarian, the first envisioning Christ to come again to reign on earth for a thousand years and the other imagining the return of Christ at the end of a thousand-year period—both posited the need for a virtuous political order in order to make possible the expected messianic return. Thus Christian politics was not only desirable; it was a theological necessity.

At the end of the Cold War the talk of a "new world order" alarmed many evangelical Christians, who took this to mean the global domination of secular government. Some conservative Christians interpreted it as opening up American society to a variety of religions, races, and sexual orientations, all of which they regarded as contrary to their desire for a Christian nation that would fulfill the messianic expectations of the coming of Christ. As a result, many evangelical Christians turned to electoral politics to increase their power, and in the late twentieth century, their efforts bore fruit.[4]

One branch of postmillennial evangelical thought that had considerable political impact was Dominion Theology. This theological position maintained that Christianity had to assert the dominion of God over all creation, including secular politics and society, in order for messianic expectations to be fulfilled. This point of view—articulated by such right-wing Protestant evangelicals as Jerry Falwell and Pat Robertson—led to a burst of social and political activism in the Christian right in the 1980s and 1990s. It also corresponded with the thinking of many Christians who had become politically active in their efforts to prohibit abortion in the United States.

The Christian movement opposing abortions is permeated with ideas from Dominion Theology.[5] Randall Terry, founder of the militant Operation Rescue organization and a writer for the Dominion magazine *Crosswinds*, helped craft the magazine's "Manifesto for the Christian Church." The manifesto asserted that America should "function as a Christian nation" and opposed such "social moral evils" of secular society as "abortion on demand, fornication, homosexuality, sexual entertainment, state usurpation of parental rights and God-given liberties, statist-collectivist theft from citizens through devaluation of their money and redistribution of their wealth, and evolutionism taught as a monopoly viewpoint in the public schools."[6]

At the extreme right wing of Dominion Theology is a relatively obscure theological movement, Reconstruction Theology, whose exponents seek to create a Christian theocratic state. Leaders of the Reconstruction movement trace their ideas, which they sometimes called "theonomy," to Cornelius Van Til, a twentieth-century Presbyterian

professor of theology at Princeton Seminary who followed the teachings of the sixteenth-century Reformation theologian John Calvin regarding the necessity for presupposing the authority of God in all worldly matters. Followers of Van Til, including his former students Greg Bahnsen and Rousas John Rushdoony, and Rushdoony's son-in-law, Gary North, adopted this "presuppositionalism," with all its implications for the role of religion in political life, as a doctrine.

Reconstruction writers regard the history of Protestant politics since the early years of the Reformation as having taken a bad turn, and they are especially unhappy with the Enlightenment formulation of the separation of church and state. They feel it necessary to "reconstruct" Christian society by turning to the Bible as the basis for a nation's law and social order. To propagate these views, the Reconstructionists established the Institute for Christian Economics in Tyler, Texas, and the Chalcedon Foundation in Vallecito, California. They published a journal and a steady stream of books and booklets on the theological justification for interjecting Christian ideas into economic, legal, and political life.[7]

According to the most prolific Reconstruction writer, Gary North, it is "the moral obligation of Christians to recapture every institution for Jesus Christ."[8] He regarded this as especially so in the United States, where secular law as construed by the Supreme Court and defended by secular politicians has been moving in what Rushdoony and others regarded as a decidedly un-Christian direction, particularly in matters regarding abortion and homosexuality. What the Reconstructionists ultimately wanted, however, was more than the rejection of secularism. Like other theologians who invoked the biblical concept of "dominion," they reasoned that Christians, as the new chosen people of God, were destined to dominate the world.

One of the followers of Reconstruction thought was Michael Bray, a Lutheran pastor in Maryland who was convicted and served prison time for bombing clinics that performed abortions on the East Coast. Bray had studied the writings of Reconstruction Theology authors extensively and owned a shelf of their books. He and his friend Presbyterian pastor Paul Hill regarded their political actions as sanctioned by the Bible and Christian history as interpreted by Reconstruction theologians. Hill had once studied with a founder of the movement, Greg Bahnsen, at the Reformed Theological Seminary in Jackson, Mississippi.[9]

In my conversations with Michael Bray, he maintained that the idea of a society based on Christian morality was not a new one, and he emphasized the "re-" in "reconstruction."[10] Although Bray rejected the pope's authority, he valued much of the Roman Catholic Church's social teachings and greatly admired the tradition of canon law. Only recently in history, he observed, had political order in Europe and America not been based on biblical concepts. Opposed to the disestablishment of the political role of the church, Bray labeled himself an "antidisestablishmentarian."

Bray was serious about bringing Christian politics into power. He said that it is possible, under the right conditions, for a Christian revolution to sweep across the United States and bring in its wake constitutional changes that would make biblical law the basis of social legislation. Failing that, Bray envisaged a new federalism that would allow individual states to experiment with religious politics on their own. When I asked Bray what state might be ready for such an experiment, he hesitated and then suggested Louisiana and Mississippi, or, he added, "maybe one of the Dakotas."

Bray justified violence as an appropriate response to what he regarded as the secular captivity of American society. In an arresting book, *A Time to Kill*, Bray used biblical references and theological justifications for warfare—including those propounded (or so Bray believed) by liberal Protestant theologians Dietrich Bonhoeffer and Rein-hold Niebuhr—to justify his position.[11] His friend Paul Hill took this advice seriously. In 1994, Hill approached a medical doctor who was about to enter a clinic in Pensacola, Florida, that performed abortions and shot the doctor, John Britton, and his escort, killing them both. Hill said that in the days preceding the attack, he had opened his Bible and found verses that he thought were speaking to him and directing him to this action.[12] Hill was immediately apprehended, convicted of murder, and some ten years later was executed for the crime by the state of Florida.

Not all Reconstruction thinkers have endorsed the use of violence, especially the kind that Bray and Hill justified. As Reconstruction author Gary North admitted, "there is division in the theonomic camp" over violence, especially with regard to anti-abortion activities. Some months before killing Dr. Britton and his escort, Hill—apparently hoping for North's advance approval—sent North a letter, along with a draft of an essay justifying such killings in part on theonomic grounds. North ultimately responded, but only after the murders had been committed. North regretted that he was too late to deter Hill from his "terrible direction" and chastised Hill in an open letter, published as a booklet, denouncing Hill's views as "vigilante theology."[13] According to North, biblical law provides limited exceptions to the commandment "Thou shalt not kill" (Exodus 20:13), but in terms similar to just-war doctrine: when one is authorized to do so by "a covenantal agent" in wartime, to defend one's household, to execute a convicted criminal, to avenge the death of one's kin, to save an entire nation, or to stop moral transgressors from bringing bloodguilt on an entire community.[14]

Hill—joined by Bray—responded to North's letter. They argued that many of those conditions applied to the legal status of abortion in the United States. Writing from his prison cell in Starke, Florida, Paul Hill maintained that the biblical commandment against murder also "requires using the means necessary to defend against murder—including lethal force."[15] He went on to say that he regarded "the cutting edge of Satan's current attack" to be "the abortionist's knife" and that his actions therefore had ultimate theological significance.[16] Bray, in *A Time to Kill*, addressed North's concern about the authorization of violence by a legitimate authority or "a covenantal agent," as North put it. Bray raised the possibility of a "righteous rebellion."[17] Just as liberation theologians justified the use of unauthorized force for the sake of their vision of a moral order, Bray saw the legitimacy of using violence not only to resist what he regarded as murder—abortion—but also to help bring about the Christian political order envisioned by Reconstruction thinkers such as Gary North. In Bray's mind, a little violence was a small price to pay for the possibility of fulfilling God's law and establishing His kingdom on earth.

Another strand of radical religious thought—Christian Identity—had relatively few qualms about the use of violence. This strand of Protestant Christian thought is based on the notions of racial supremacy and biblical law and has had enormous influence on some of the most radical Christian movements in America.[18] It has been in the background of such extremist groups as the Posse Comitatus, the Order, the Aryan Nations, the supporters of Randy Weaver at Ruby Ridge, Herbert Armstrong's Worldwide Church of God, the Freeman Compound, and the World Church of the Creator. It is popular among many militia movements and motivated Buford Furrow in his 1999 assault on a Jewish center in Granada Hills, California. Christian Identity ideas were also in the background of the thinking of Timothy McVeigh, the convicted perpetrator of the 1595 Oklahoma City bombing, and Eric Robert Rudolph, who bombed the Olympic Park in Atlanta in 1996.

Timothy McVeigh was exposed to Identity thinking through the militia culture with which he was associated and through his contacts with the Christian Identity encampment, Elohim City, on the Oklahoma-Arkansas border. Although there is no evidence that McVeigh was ever affiliated with the commune, phone calls he made to Elohim City

in the months before the bombing are a matter of record, including one made two weeks before the bombing.[19] McVeigh likely visited the site, since he once received a citation for a minor traffic offense ten miles from the commune on the only access road leading to it. McVeigh also imbibed Identity ideas, or similar concepts, through such publications as *The Patriot Report*, an Arkansas-based Christian Identity newsletter that McVeigh received, and perhaps most of all from *The Turner Diaries*.[20] According to McVeigh's friends, this was "his favorite book"; it was "his bible," some said.[21] According to one gun collector who saw McVeigh frequently at gun shows, he hawked the book at bargain prices, and it was always at his side.[22] More to the point, McVeigh's telephone records indicate that despite his denials, he had talked directly with the author of the novel on several occasions, including a conversation shortly before the Oklahoma City bombing.[23]

The author of McVeigh's favorite novel was William Pierce, who received a Ph.D. from the University of Colorado, once taught physics at Oregon State University, and for a time served as a writer for the American Nazi Party. Although he denied any affiliation with the Christian Identity movement—and in fact attacked the clubbishness of most Identity groups—Pierce's ideas are virtually indistinguishable from Identity thinking. In 1984 Pierce proclaimed himself the founder of a religious compound very similar to those associated with the Christian Identity movement. He called it the Cosmotheist Community.[24]

Pierce's novel, written under the pseudonym Andrew Macdonald, was the main vehicle for his Identity/Cosmotheist ideas. Published in 1978, it describes an apocalyptic battle between freedom fighters and a dictatorial American government. The novel soon became an underground classic, selling 200,000 copies in gun shows and through mail-order catalogues. It served as the blueprint for such activists as Robert Matthews, who was implicated in the 1984 assassination of a Jewish talk-show host in Denver. Matthews, like Timothy McVeigh, seems to have taken seriously the novel's predictions of the encroachment of government control in America and the resistance by a guerrilla band known as "the Order." Matthews called his own movement "the Order," and the modus operandi McVeigh used in destroying the Oklahoma City federal building was almost exactly the same as the one used by patriotic guerrillas to attack government buildings in Pierce's novel.

Although written almost eighteen years before the r 995 Oklahoma City bombing, a section of *The Turner Diaries* reads almost like a news account of the event. It recounts in chilling detail its hero's bombing of the federal office building with a truckload of "a little under 5,000 pounds" of ammonium nitrate fertilizer and fuel oil. Timothy McVeigh's own truck carried 4,400 pounds of the same mixture, packaged and transported exactly as described in the novel. In Pierce's novel, the bombing was directed against the perceived evils of the government and sought to arouse the fighting spirit of all "free men."[25] Such efforts were necessary, according to Pierce, because of the dictatorial secularism that had been imposed on American society as the result of an elaborate conspiracy orchestrated by Jews and liberals desperately seeking to deprive Christian society of its freedom and its spiritual moorings.

Pierce and Christian Identity activists yearned for a revolution that would undo America's separation of church and state; in fact, disdaining organized religion, they sought to merge "religion and state" in a new society governed by religious law. That aspiration may explain why so many Identity groups lived in theocratic societies such as Elohim City, the Freeman Compound, the Aryan Nations compound, and Pierce's Cosmotheist Community. Although these religious communalists believed in capitalism, many held property in common. They also shared an apocalyptic view of history and an even more conspiratorial view of government than the Re-constructionists. They believed that the great

confrontation between freedom and a government-imposed slavery was close at hand and that their militant efforts might awaken the spirit of the freedom-loving masses. These ideas came to Timothy McVeigh from "William Pierce *and The Turner Diaries* and indirectly from the theories of Christian Identity.

Christian Identity thought originated in the movement of British Israelism in the nineteenth century. According to Michael Barkun, who has written extensively about the movement, one of the founding fathers was John Wilson, whose central work, *Lectures on Our Israelitish Origin*, brought the message to a large British and Irish middle-class audience.[26] Wilson claimed that Jesus had been an Aryan, not a Semite; that the migrating Israelite tribes from the northern kingdom of Israel were in fact blue-eyed Aryans who somehow ended up in the British Isles; and that the "Lost Sheep of the House of Israel" were none other than present-day Englishmen.[27] According to later versions of this theory, people who claim to be Jews are imposters. Some versions of Identity thinking regard them as descendants of an illicit sexual act between Eve and Satan; other versions identify them as aliens from outer space. In either case, Identity thinking claims that the people known as Jews pretend to be Jews in order to assert their superiority in a scheme to control the world. According to Wilson, the Jews' plot is allegedly supported by the secret Protestant order of Freemasons.

British Israelism came to the United States in the early twentieth century through the teachings of the evangelist Gerald L. K. Smith and the writings of William Cameron, a publicist for the automobile magnate Henry Ford.[28] Ford himself supported many of Cameron's views and published a book of anti-Semitic essays written by Cameron but attributed to Ford, *The International Jew: The World's Foremost Problem*. Cameron conveyed such Christian Identity tenets as the necessity for the Anglo-Saxon race to retain its purity and political dominance and the need for Western societies to establish a biblical basis for governance. The Christian Identity philosophy was promoted further by Bertram Comparet, a deputy district attorney in San Diego, and Wesley Swift, a Ku Klux Klan member who founded the Church of Jesus Christ-Christian in 1946. This church was the basis for the Christian Defense League, organized by Bill Gale at his ranch in Mariposa, California, in the 1960s, a movement that spawned both the Posse Comitatus and the Aryan Nations.[29]

British Israelism appealed to some members of the elite of nineteenth-century British society, but by the time these ideas came to the United States, the ideology had taken a more strident and political turn. Most of the followers of Christian Identity were relatively benign, and according to Jeffrey Kaplan, who has studied contemporary Christian Identity groups in the American Midwest and Northwest, their ideas tended to be simplified in the public mind and the groups reduced to the ranks of "monsters" in America's right-wing fringe.[30] Though that may be true, the fact remains that the ideology underlay a strain of violent religious activism in American society in the late twentieth century.

In recent decades the largest concentration of Christian Identity groups in the United States was in Idaho—centered on the Aryan Nations compound near Hayden Lake—and in the southern Midwest near the Oklahoma-Arkansas-Missouri borders. In that location a Christian Identity group called the Covenant, the Sword and the Arm of the Lord (CSA) established a 224-acre community and a paramilitary school, which it named the Endtime Overcomer Survival Training School.[31] Nearby, Christian Identity minister Robert Millar and former Nazi Party member Glenn Miller established Elohim City, whose members stockpiled weapons and prepared themselves for "a Branch Davidian-type raid" by the federal Bureau of Alcohol, Tobacco, and Firearms.[32] It was this Christian Identity encampment that Timothy McVeigh contacted shortly before the Oklahoma City bombing.

The American incarnation of Christian Identity incorporated many of the British movement's paranoid views, updated to reflect the social anxieties of many contemporary Americans. The United Nations and the Democratic Party were alleged to be accomplices in a joint Jewish-Masonic conspiracy to control the world and deprive individuals of their freedom. In a 1982 Identity pamphlet, Jews were described as "parasites and vultures" who controlled the world through international banking.[33] The establishment of the International Monetary Fund, the introduction of magnetized credit cards, and the establishment of paper money not backed by gold or silver were listed as the final steps in "Satan's Plan."[34]

Gun control is also an important issue to Christian Identity supporters, since they believe that this is how the "Jewish-UN-liberal conspirators," as they call them, intend to eliminate the last possibilities of rebellion against centralized power. These "conspirators" are thought to be intent on depriving individuals of the weapons they might use to defend themselves or free their countrymen from a tyrannical state. This obsession with gun control has made many Christian Identity followers natural allies with the National Rifle Association. The association's rhetoric has played a significant role in legitimizing Christian Identity members' fears of the evil intentions behind governmental gun control and has provided a public voice for their paranoid views.

By the last decade of the twentieth century, the Christian Identity movement had become publicly identified as one of the leading voices of America's radical right. At that time the dean of the movement was Richard Butler, a former Presbyterian minister sometimes described as "the elder statesman of American hate."[35] Butler's designated successor was Neumann Britton of Escondido, California. Although Butler's Aryan Nations compound in Idaho consisted of only a handful of supporters on a twenty-acre farm, its website received over five hundred hits a day. Moreover, the movement received an infusion of financial support from two Silicon Valley entrepreneurs, Carl E. Story and R. Vincent Bertollinni. Their organization, the Eleventh Hour Remnant Messenger, is said to have spent a million dollars promoting Christian Identity ideas as of 1999. It was also said to have had access to fifty million more. One of the projects they funded was the mass mailing of a videotape of Butler presenting his Christian Identity theory of "Adam's pure blood seed-line," and the alleged global conspiracy to destroy it.[36]

At the extreme fringes of the Christian Identity movement have been rogue terrorists. Some were closely linked to Identity organizations. Buford Furrow—the man who attacked the Jewish day-care center in Los Angeles—once lived in Butler's compound and had married Matthews' widow. Benjamin Smith, the 1999 Fourth of July sniper in Illinois and Indiana, belonged to an Identity-like church that eschewed other Identity groups and, for that matter, all of Christianity. Others were like Timothy McVeigh, whose group was virtually an anti-organization: a nameless, close-knit cadre that shared Identity beliefs but did not have formal ties to organized Identity groups.

One of the most elusive of the lone-wolf Christian Identity terrorists was Eric Robert Rudoph, who was captured in 2003 after having successfully dodged a massive and well-publicized seven-year manhunt. In 2005 Rudolph pleaded guilty to a long list of charges, including bombing abortion clinics in Birmingham, Alabama, and Atlanta, Georgia and a lesbian bar in Atlanta, and exploding a bomb at the 1996 Atlanta Olympics that killed three and injured 150. What these incidents had in common is their relationship to what many Christian activists regard as sexual immorality: abortion and homosexuality. According to another Christian activist, Michael Bray, Rudolph's anger at the Olympic organizers came in part because the carriers of the Olympic torch, which passed through the southern United States on its way to Atlanta, skirted one county in North Carolina that had approved an ordinance declaring that "sodomy is not consistent with the values of the community." Rudolph is said to have interpreted this detour in the torch's journey as a pro-gay stance on the part of the Olympic organizers.[37]

In a broad sense, Rudolph was concerned about the permissiveness of secular authorities in the United States and "the atheistic internationalism" controlling one side of what Bray called "the culture war" in modern society.[38] These concerns are shared by many Christian activists, but in Rudolph's case they were associated especially with the ideas of the Christian Identity movement with which Rudolph became familiar in childhood. At one time he and his mother stayed at the American Identity compound led by Dan Gayman, and there are press reports that Rudolph knew the late Identity preacher Nord Davis.

The world as envisioned by Eric Robert Rudolph, Timothy McVeigh, Buford Furrow, Benjamin Smith, "William Pierce, Richard Butler, and Michael Bray—by followers of both Christian Identity and Reconstruction thought—is a world at war. Identity preachers have cited the biblical accounts of Michael the Archangel destroying the offspring of evil to point to a hidden, albeit cosmic, war between the forces of darkness and the forces of light.[39] Reconstruction thinkers have also seen the world enmeshed in a great moral struggle. "There is murder going on," Mike Bray explained, "which we have to stop." In the Christian Identity view of the world, the struggle is a secret war between colossal evil forces allied with the United Nations, the United States, and other government powers, and a small band of the enlightened few who recognized these invisible enemies for what the Identity followers thought they were—satanic powers, in their view—and were sufficiently courageous to battle them. Although Bray rejected much of Christian Identity's conspiratorial view of the world and specifically decried its anti-Semitism, he valued its commitment to fight against secular forms of evil and its insistence on the need for a Christian social order.

As Mike Bray explained, his justification of violence against abortion clinics was not the result of a personal vendetta against agencies with which he and others had moral differences, but the consequence of a grand religious vision. His position was part of a great crusade conducted by a Christian subculture in America that considered itself at war with the larger society, and to some extent was victimized by it. Armed with the theological explanations of Reconstruction and Christian Identity writers, this subculture saw itself justified in its violent responses to a vast and violent repression waged by secular (and, in some versions of this vision, Jewish) agents of a satanic force.[40]

Mike Bray and his network of associates around the country saw themselves engaged in violence not for its own sake but as a response to the institutional violence of what they regarded as a repressive secular government. Those within his culture did not view his burning of abortion clinics as an assault on civil liberties or as a vengeful and hateful crime. Instead, Bray was seen as firing the opening salvos in a great defensive Christian struggle against the secular state, a contest between the forces of spiritual truth and heathen darkness, in which the moral character of America as a righteous nation hung in the balance.

NOTES

1. See, for instance, Weston LaBarre, *The Ghost Dance: The Origins of Religion* (New York: Dell, 1970).
2. The first in the series is Tim F. LaHaye and Jerry Jenkins, *Left Behind: A Novel of the Earth's Last Days* (Carol Stream, Ill.: Tyndale Publishing House, 2000). For an analysis of the series as a publishing phenomenon, see Glenn Shuck, *Marks of the Beast: The* Left Behind *Novels and the Struggle for Evangelical Identity* (New York: New York University Press, 2004); Michael Standaert, *Skipping Towards Armageddon: The Politics and Propaganda of the* Left Behind *Novels* (Brooklyn, N.Y.: Soft Skull Press, 2006); and the essays in Bruce David Forbes and Jeanne Halgren Kilde, eds., *Rapture, Revelation, and the End Times:*

Exploring the Left Behind *Series* (New York: Palgrave Macmillan, 2004).

3. For a discussion of the rise of Christian religious political movements at the turn of the twenty-first century, see Michelle Goldberg, *Kingdom Coming: The Rise of Christian Nationalism* (New York: W.W. Norton, 2007); Chris Hedges, *American Fascists: The Christian Right and the War on America* (New York: Free Press, 2007); and Kevin Phillips, *American Theocracy: The Peril and Politics of Radical Religion, Oil, and Borrowed Money in the 21st Century* (New York: Penguin, 2007).
4. See, for instance, Stephen Bruce, "The Moral Majority: The Politics of Fundamentalism in Secular Society," in Lionel Caplan, ed., *Studies in Religious Fundamentalism* (Albany: State University of New York Press, 1987); and Capps, *The New Religious Right.*
5. Bruce Barron, *Heaven on Earth? The Social and Political Agendas of Dominion Theology* (Minneapolis: Zondervan, 1992.).
6. "Manifesto for the Christian Church," *Crosswinds.* Quoted in Chip Berlet, John Salvi, *Abortion Clinic Violence, and Catholic Right Conspiracism* (Somerville, Mass.: Political Research Associates, 1996), 8.
7. The book that established Reconstruction Theology as a movement is Rousas John Rushdoony's two-volume *Institutes of Biblical Law* (Nutley, N.J.: Craig Press, 1973). Introductions to Cornelius Van Til's thought are found in R.J. Rushdoony, *By What Standard?* (Tyler, Tex.: Thoburn Press, 1978), and Richard Pratt, *Every Thought Captive* (Phillipsburg, N.J.: Presbyterian and Reformed Publishing Company, 1982.). The journal of Reconstruction thought, *Chalcedon Report,* is published in Vallecito, California.
8. Gary North, *Backward, Christian Soldiers? An Action Manual for Christian Reconstruction* (Tyler, Tex.: Institute for Christian Economics, 1984), 267. According to North, the four main tenets of Christian Reconstruction are biblical law, optimistic eschatology, predestination, and "presuppositional apologetics," which North defines as a "philosophical defense of the faith" *(Backward, Christian Soldiers?* 267). North has authored or edited over twenty books, including *An Introduction to Christian Economics* (Tyler, Tex.: Institute for Christian Economics, 1973), *Unconditional Surrender; God's Program for Victory* (Tyler, Tex.: Institute for Christian Economics, 1988), *and Millennialism and Social Theory* (Tyler, Tex.: Institute for Christian Economics, 1990).

9. Gary North, *Lone Gunners for Jesus: Letters to Paul J. Hill* (Tyler, Tex.: Institute for Christian Economics, 1994), 2.

10. Interview with Michael Bray, Reformation Lutheran Church, Bowie, Maryland, March 20, 1998.

11. Michael Bray, *A Time to Kill: A Study Considering the Use of Force and Abortion* (Portland, Oregon: Advocates for Life, 1994).

12. Paul Hill explains the reasons for the shooting in his autobiographical statement "I Shot an Abortionist," on the Army of God website (www.armyof-god.com/PHilL_ShortShot.html).

13. North, *Lone Gunners for Jesus*, 25.

14. Ibid.

15. Paul Hill, *Paul Hill Speaks* (pamphlet published by Reformation Press, Bowie, Maryland, June 1997), 1.

16. Ibid., 2.

17. Bray, *A Time to Kill*, 158.

18. Chester L. Quarles, *Christian Identity: The Aryan American Bloodline Religion* (Jefferson, N.C.: McFarland & Co., 2004). For a discussion of the significance of the radical Christian right on American politics and society, see Hedges, *American Fascists*; Goldberg, *Kingdom Coming*; Clyde Wilcox and Carin Larson, *Onward Christian Soldiers: The Religious Right in American Politics* (Boulder, Colo.: Westview Press, 2006); Robert Booth Fowler, Allen D. Hertzke, and Laura R. Olson, *Religion and Politics in America: Faith, Culture, and Strategic Choices* (Boulder, Colo.: Westview Press, 2004); and William Martin, *With God on Our Side: The Rise of the Religious Right in America* (New York: Broadway, 2005).

19. Morris Dees, *Gathering Storm: America's Militia Threat* (New York: HarperCollins, 1996), 165. Reports of McVeigh visiting Elohim City are made in David Hoffman, *The Oklahoma City Bombing and the Politics of Terror* (Venice, Calif.: Feral House, 1998), 83–84.

20. Andrew Macdonald [William Pierce], *The Turner Diaries* (New York: Barricade Books, 1996) (originally published by National Alliance Vanguard Books, Arlington, Va., in 1978).

21. Dees, *Gathering Storm*, 154.

22. Ibid., 158.

23. Although Pierce, the author of *The Turner Diaries*, denies knowing McVeigh or talking to him, two separate law enforcement sources claim to have telephone records proving that McVeigh placed a lengthy call to Pierce's unlisted number in West Virginia in the weeks before the bombing. This information was first reported by CNN and is mentioned in Dees, *Gathering Storm*, 165.

24. Amy C. Solnin, *William L. Pierce, Novelist of Hate: Research Report of the Anti-Defamation League* (New York: Anti-Defamation League, 1995), 8.

25. Macdonald [Pierce], *Turner Diaries*, 64.

26. Michael Barkun, *Religion and the Racist Right: The Origins of the Christian Identity Movement* (Chapel Hill: University of North Carolina Press, 1994).

27. Barkun, *Religion and the Racist Right*, 7.

28. Leonard Zeskind, *The "Christian Identity" Movement: Analyzing Its Theological Rationalization for Racist and Anti-Semitic Violence* (New York: Division of Church and Society of the National Council of Churches of Christ in the U.S.A., 1986), 12.

29. Zeskind, *"Christian Identity" Movement*, 14.

30. Jeffrey Kaplan, *Radical Religion in America: Millenarian Movements from the Far Right to the Children of Noah* (Syracuse, N.Y.: Syracuse University Press, 1997), 175.

31. Zeskind, *"Christian Identity" Movement*, 45.

32. Gerald Baumgarten, *Paranoia as Patriotism: Far-Right Influences on the Militia Movement* (New York: Anti-Defamation League, 1995), 17.

33. Gordon "Jack" Mohr (founder of the Christian Patriot Defense League), "Know Your Enemies," 1982 pamphlet, quoted in James Aho, *The Politics of Righteousness: Idaho Christian Patriotism* (Seattle: University of Washington Press, 1990), 96.

34. Aho, *Politics of Righteousness*, 91.

35. Kim Murphy, "Last Stand of an Aging Aryan," *Los Angeles Times*, January 10, 1999, A1.

36. Kim Murphy, "Hate's Affluent New Godfathers," *Los Angeles Times*, January 10, 1999, A14.

37. Michael Bray, "Running with Rudolph," *Capitol Area Christian News* 28 (Winter 1998–99): 2. Eric Rudolph's own explanation of why he exploded the bomb at Centennial Park emphasizes the attempt to punish and embarrass the United States government for its stand on abortion. See his autobiographical statement on the Army of God website (www.armyofgod. com/EricRudolphAtlantaCourtStatement.html).

38. Bray, "Running with Rudolph," 2.

39. Aho, *Politics of Righteousness*, 85.

40. I explore further this discussion of Christian activism in America in my book *Terror in the Mind of God*, where parts of this section were first published.

13

Selections from Japan's Holy War: the Ideology of Radical Shintō Ultranationalism

Walter A. Skya

In reading the history of nations, we find that, like individuals, they have their whims and their peculiarities; their seasons of excitement and recklessness, when they care not what they do. . . . We see one nation suddenly seized with a fierce desire of military glory; another as suddenly becoming crazed upon a religious scruple; and neither of them recovering its senses until it has shed rivers of blood and sowed a harvest of groans and tears, to be reaped by its posterity.

—CHARLES MACKAY, *Memoirs of Extraordinary Popular Delusions and the Madness of Crowds*, xix

[. . .]

IN WAR WITHOUT MERCY, John Dower exposed the racism in America toward the Japanese people as a whole during the Pacific War. Japanese were considered "subhuman and repulsive" by many Americans. In daily conversation, Americans tended to refer to their wartime enemies, Germany and Japan, as "Hitler and the Japs" or "the Nazis and the Japs." Dower pointed out that the implication of perceiving the enemy as "Nazis" and "Japs" was enormous, for "this left the space for the recognition of the 'good German,' but scant comparable place for 'good' Japanese."[1] Racism was certainly a major factor in the inability or the unwillingness of many Americans to distinguish between "good Japanese" and "bad Japanese," but another, important but overlooked factor may have significantly exacerbated the problem: the failure to identify our real enemy in Japan. What was the Japanese ideological equivalent of German Nazis or Italian Fascists? The average American on the street during World War Two simply did not know, but this was certainly not due to Americans' personal faults or prejudices. It was not clear even to the director Frank Capra. In his wartime propaganda film *Prelude to War*, the first in the series of seven *Why We Fight* films, Capra presented a picture of the development of the dictatorships in Germany, Italy, and Japan, When the time came to identify America's ideological enemies, Capra told viewers that the enemy in Germany was National Socialism, or simply "Nazism," and in Italy it was "Fascism." When he came to the case of Japan, he said, "They [the Japanese] have lots of names for them [the extremist nationalists]." Simply put, Capra and the U.S. War Department could not identify a specific ideological enemy in Japan. But one should not fault him, either, because even after more than six decades since the end of the Second World War, the average American still does not know. The blame must lie with the failure of American scholars to deal adequately with one of the most fundamental issues in modern Japanese history, as well as in the history of World War Two: the failure to identify the enemy. Clearly, we must recognize that this is a conceptual void that must be filled.

If we do not wish to continue to make villains of all Japanese when we speak about the Second World War and Japan's role in waging that war, we must make an effort to identify this ideological enemy. One can give easy reasons for this failure to identify the ideology of extreme nationalism in prewar Japan. For example, unlike in the cases of Germany and Italy, no one, easily identifiable radical nationalist group took power in Japan, This presents a major problem, but it is not the whole problem. Who were the Japanese theorists of the radical right? What did they write? This study was first undertaken at least in part to attempt to fill this ideological void. I hope it has succeeded in laying the ideological foundations for further studies of the interaction of ideology and political groups or individual actors in prewar Japan.

PURSUING THEOLOGICAL-IDEOLOGICAL PURITY, TERRORISM, AND DREAMS OF WORLD DOMINATION

In this study of the main developments and trends within State Shintō ideology from 1890 to 1937, I have argued that the ideological equivalent of Nazism and Fascism in Japan was radical Shintō ultranationalism. I have also argued that radical Shintō ultranationalism was a totalitarian ideology and a massed-based radical religion of völkisch nationalism, much like Nazism in Germany. It grew out of an extreme form of religious fundamentalism that had begun to emerge at the center of political and ideological discourse in Japan at the beginning of the twentieth century. The story of the rise and fall of radical Shintō ultranationalism is not just about ideological contestation in the past century. It may also offer a lesson about the extent of the immense challenges we face at the beginning of this new century between extremist political religions, particularly radical Islamic fundamentalism, and other radical religious movements that now confront Western-style secular nationalism.

[. . .] the aim of the pure Shintō fundamentalist revival movement of the late Tokugawa period was to fight a religious and ideological battle against all things foreign, particularly Chinese. The attack on Chinese and other Asian ideologies, religions, and systems of thought by Shintō fundamentalists such as Kamo Mabuchi and Motoori Norinaga in the eighteenth century did not cease, however, with the end of the Tokugawa regime and feudalism. The pure Shintō fundamentalist movements of the late nineteenth century and early twentieth century led by Hozumi Yatsuka, Uesugi Shinkichi, and Kakehi Katsuhiko represented a revival of the Kokugaku (National Learning) Movement of the Tokugawa period in a new form. They were religious purists who sought to purge the Japanese state of foreign ideologies. The Shintō ultranationalists' assault on Asian thought, as well as on the new ideological threat from the Western world, continued until the end of the Second World War.

A prime example of this search for religious purification and anti-foreignism can be found in the thought of the radical Shintō ultranationalist Yamada Yoshio (1875–1958), who was just briefly introduced in the previous chapter. Yamada was a well-respected scholar of Japanese language and literature who hailed from Toyama Prefecture in central Japan. Very much a self-made man, having achieved success and recognition by his own efforts, he earned a teaching certificate mostly through independent study. Upon obtaining his teaching credentials, he secured a job as a schoolteacher and taught at a number of elementary and middle schools. He eventually worked his way up to teach in higher education and finally became a professor at Tōhoku Imperial University in 1927. However, the pinnacle of his professional academic career came with his appointment as president of Kōgakkan University in 1940, one of the two large Shintō theological universities responsible for the training of Shintō priests. Kōgakkan had been established in 1882 under the name Jingū Kokugakuin near the Ise Shrine as part of a government effort to establish an institution of higher learning with the mission to develop a coherent Shintō doctrine following the so-called pantheon dispute of the 1870s.[2] The school was later moved to Uji Yamada, where it was reestablished as a Shintō training institute of the Ministry of Home Affairs. As a government-funded State Shintō religious institution, Kōgakkan would be forced to close down by General Douglas MacArthur's occupation authorities in 1945, but it reopened in 1952 at its original location as a private university. As mentioned in the previous chapter, Yamada also moved into the political limelight at the height of his academic career when he became a member of the House of Peers in 1944.

During the American occupation of Japan, MacArthur carried out purges that aimed to "eliminate for all time the authority and influence of those who [had] deceived and misled the people of Japan into embarking on world conquest." Purge Directive SCAP AG 091.1 (January 4, 1946) GS, "Removal and Exclusion of Undesirable Personnel from Public Office," guided the removal from public office of all persons who had been "active exponents of militaristic nationalism and aggression."[3] Yamada was among the people forbidden by the directive to hold public or educational office. It is noteworthy that although Yamada was one of the members of the official compilation committee that rewrote the original manuscript of *Fundamentals of Our National Polity*, he apparently was purged not on that basis but because of his numerous other ultranationalist activities and writings. In other words, Yamada is an excellent example of a radical Shintō ultranationalist who came to dominate the prewar Shintō religious establishment.

Taken as a whole, Yamada's writings during the wartime period reveal a fixed mental attitude that predetermined the responses to, and interpretations of, any given set of situations. A classic example of this was that he continued to spout the rhetoric of Japan's purity and divine nature and its invulnerability to defeat and failure while stubbornly clinging on to the erroneous notion that the Chinese people somehow lacked a genuine sense of national cohesiveness and nationalism many years after the tenacity with which the Chinese resistance to Japan's occupation had been clearly and courageously displayed to the world. One example of this can be seen in his essay "Shinkoku Nihon no Shimei to Kokumin no Kakugo (Divine Japan's Mission and the Nation's Resolve)," which appeared in the September 1943 issue of *Chūō Kōron*.

Yamada began the essay by telling readers that Japan's unique kokutai could be understood in all its magnificence and glory only by adopting a purely Japanese perspective on Japanese history. He charged that Japanese history, for the most part, had not been written from a purely Japanese consciousness, as was in the case of earlier works in Japanese history, such as the Great History of Japan and the Chronicle of Gods and Sovereigns. He lamented that he could find very few books on Japanese history that were written from the perspective of Japan's miraculous kokutai. Yamada provided concrete examples of what he meant by saying that Japanese history was not being presented from a consciousness of Japan's kokutai. For example, he attacked Japanese historians for structuring Japanese history from what he considered essentially a Chinese-inspired perspective of history: the rise and fall of dynasties. Employing the Chinese historical method in analyzing Japanese history, Japanese historians had formulated the period in Japanese history in which the Fujiwara regency was powerful as the Fujiwara Period; the period of the regency of the Kamakura government was likewise called the Kamakura Period. The years in power by the Ashikaga and Tokugawa feudal clans were called the Ashikaga Period and the Tokugawa Period, respectively. Yamada asserted that viewing Japanese history as the rise and fall of these powerful families and governments was to use a historical interpretation very close to that used by Chinese historians to analyze their own history. Thus, this type of periodization of Japanese history by Japanese historians amounted to nothing less than a Sinofication of Japanese history—a Sinofication that subverted the spirit of Japan's true history based on the kokutai, which was a history of the unbroken line of emperors, from the age of the gods:

> Conventional historians in our country . . . undoubtedly adopted this form of periodization as if to compare these periods in Japanese history with the rise and fall of dynasties in the history of China. Many modern scholars have mistaken this view of the repeated rise and fall of regimes in China and the Western world as the essence of history. They have based their theories on the fundamentally erroneous view of history which ignores the sacred essence of our country. The reason Rai San Yō (1780–1832) wrote a kind of national history called "The Unofficial History of Japan" centered on the rise and fall of regencies generation after generation was because he fell into the trap [of writing from such a viewpoint] that any scholar of Chinese history might do. However, since this is an "unofficial history," there is no need to pursue this matter further, but it does go to show that this method of compiling history is, for the most part, easily copied by scholars who have learned Chinese history.[4]

Yamada also charged that the factual information Japanese were required to learn in schools also did not focus on Japan's unique kokutai. As a simple illustration of this, he noted that if one were to ask a Japanese subject who had completed at least compulsory education the name of the third Tokugawa Shōgun, one would expect to hear a correct answer. Similarly, an educated Japanese subject could readily answer that the eleventh Shōgun was Ienari. But if one were to ask any Japanese who was the third emperor from Emperor Jimmu, could he or she answer correctly? Or if one were to ask who was the eighth emperor or the eleventh emperor, could he or she reply correctly? Most likely not, Yamada lamented. Yamada charged that the problem lay in education based on the memorization of facts and terminology without providing the slightest clue as to what the facts meant or how they came to have historical significance from the Shintō perspective. Citing another example, a Japanese young person

was likely to know the name Seiitaishōgun, Yamada said, but was very unlikely to know the name of the particular emperor who appointed the warriors Seiitaishōgun and the rationale for it.

In short, what all these examples added up to in Yamada's mind was that the Japanese people were learning Japanese history from a certain type of historiography that originated in China, that they were learning facts not centrally relevant to Japan's kokutai, and that they were memorizing facts without learning the ideas behind them.

Needless to say, this seeking of ideological and religious purity can be dangerous to an individual, a nation, and even an entire civilization, for ideological blinders distort reality, and that can lead to destruction. For example, Yamada claimed contemptuously that the history of China was not a history of a nation (kuni) that was born, matured, and continues to live and develop in the present. Rather, it was the history of a geographical region (chiiki) called China that had seen the rise and fall of some fifty-odd states in chronological order. These Chinese states had no common relationship or common connecting thread or logical link.[5] The history of each Chinese dynasty was no more than a history of a "victorious state (shōkoku)," which he defined as a state that had destroyed the imperial household of the previous dynasty and replaced it with its own rulers. Accordingly, the history of the Yuan Dynasty period was written by the Ming Dynasty; the history of the Ming Dynasty was written by the Qing Dynasty. If one read the history of China by Chinese scholars, according to Yamada, one could easily see that the people who wrote the history were neither tied by blood (ketsueki) nor were they sympathetic to the peoples concerned.[6] That is to say, such histories were written from the standpoint of conquerors who had revised the history of the previous dynastic period to cover their own crimes and present themselves in a favorable light among their contemporaries. Consequently, Chinese history lacked a continuous genuine national spirit. Crudely speaking, he said, it was the same as if a burglar or a thief had broken into somebody's house, killed the master of the house, occupied the house, and then had written a history of the house and the generations of its occupants from the viewpoint of a criminal. Anyone would be appalled by such events. Nevertheless, this was the kind of history that had been written in China by the Chinese for thousands of years.

For Yamada, the Chinese state represented a clear and obvious example of a typical non-ethnically based state. It therefore lacked a homogeneous historical culture. An alien group ruled over the Chinese masses. Accordingly, when one referred to "China," it meant merely a geographical or a territorial entity. He seems to have implied that China was a cluster of different races or ethnic groups in that no identifiable blood ties linked everyone to the nation:

> It can be said that the history of our country is like one person's life history from its birth to the present if one compares it to a human being. The history of other countries is different. Take, for example, the case of China. From the age of the Three Sovereigns and the Five Emperors to the present it is merely a compilation of records of the rise and fall of various states. Accordingly, if one speaks of the history of China in general, it is not a history in which the country called China continued to survive, but it only refers to the histories of more than 50 individual, disconnected, states compiled chronologically as they rose and fell in a region called China. Furthermore, the history of each state is a history of a so-called victorious state. What is a victorious state? It is a state which destroyed the loyal family of a previous dynasty, and declared it the winning state over the state they overthrew and conquered. . . . As to the history of China, the people who write it are tied neither by blood nor emotional bonds; neither do they have common interest. It is written from the same standpoint of a disinterested third party. While that may have its good points, one writes what is good and rewrites what is not good. However, there is no way for ideals to be handed

down and carried on, and absolutely no way for a coherent spirit to flow through its history. . . . To think that there is a coherent spirit . . . is to think that there is a spiritual connection between an assailant and a victim when the burglar breaks into a house and kills the master of the house and then settles down there. . . . This kind of history, even if it continues for 3,000 or 5,000 years, cannot be thought of as the history [of one nation].

For Yamada, this was not the case just for the history of China. It was the same for all countries in the Orient and the Occident.[7]

This idea that China was really not a nation was common among nearly all Japanese radical Shintō ultranationalist thinkers and was one argument they used to justify taking over territory in China. Herbert Bix also brought out this point and implied that Emperor Hirohito and Prime Minister Hirota (1936–37) also held such a view. "Also like the emperor," Bix wrote, "Hirota shared an assumption that many Japanese officers considered self-evident: China was neither a nation nor a people but merely a territorial designation, and Japan was entitled to rearrange that territory and take whatever parts it wished."[8] In another passage in which Yamada linked China and the West, he said, "Both the Chinese people and the Western peoples are similarly individualistic."[9] This is not to say that he felt the Chinese were similar to the Western peoples in all respects, but from the radical Shintō ultranationalist point of view, the Chinese were considered to be closer to Western peoples in a fundamental way than they were to the Japanese. Yamada also insisted that while the Japanese people had a nation-centered ideology, the Chinese, like the Westerners, had an individual-centered ideology.

This perception of China was commonplace among Japanese radical Shintō ultranationalists, as has been shown in the thought of Hozumi Yatsuka, which completely demolished the erroneous notion that all Asians have common underlying cultural traits. Western historiography tends to emphasize a link between Shintō ultranationalist thought and pan-Asianism in the sense of having "Asian" values, and the Second World War in Asia is sometimes characterized as a war between Asia and the Western world. But the logic of the ideology of Shintō ultranationalism in Japan clearly denies this. State Shintō and Shintō ultranationalism were inherently anti-Asian. They were also anti-Buddhist and anti-Confucian, the two leading systems of continental Asian thought derived from India and China.

Bombarding the Japanese masses with outdated perceptions of China and the Chinese people, Yamada and other radical Shintō ultranationalists kept the Japanese people from acquiring any realistic understanding of the realities of China in the 1930s and 1940s. They simply reinforced the prevalent attitude among the Japanese that, since the Chinese people had no true sense of nationhood, they should be easily conquered. But nothing could have been further from the truth, Chinese nationalist consciousness grew more intense as Japan continued to wage war. The historian Ienaga Saburō blamed Japan's disaster in the Second World War on its contemptuous attitude toward the Chinese. Ienaga began his analysis of Japan's defeat in the Second World War in Asia, which he referred to as the "fifteen-year war," with a chapter titled "Misconceptions about China and Korea,"[10] For Ienaga, the Second World War in Asia was all about Japan's attempt to conquer China. He emphasized that Japan's long-held misconception that the Chinese had no sense of nationhood blinded the Japanese leadership into thinking that China could be subdued with little effort. This was Japan's "colossal blunder" in the war, he stated.[11] He lamented the fact that "a domestic political force capable of preventing aggression against China just did not exist" in Japan.[12] But why? Ienaga's answer to this was that contempt toward the Chinese had been so ingrained in the minds of the Japanese, at least since Japan's victory in the Qing Dynasty–Japan War of 1894–95. But he did not mean to say that all intelligent Japanese were unaware of the rise

of Chinese mass nationalism in the first decades of the twentieth century. As an example, he quoted Yanaihara Tadao, a Tokyo Imperial University scholar and specialist on Japanese colonial policy, warning the Japanese of danger in China in a lecture in November 1936:

> Assertions that the Chinese have no sense of nationhood and so forth are outdated. The Chinese of today are not the Chinese of old. I have heard that there are Chinese who say, "If China goes to war with Japan, we will probably lose at first. But there are 400 million of us, so we can afford to lose 300 million and still have 100 million left. With three Chinese soldiers to every one Japanese, we must resist and defend our nation's sovereignty.[13]

Again, in February 1937, just a few months before the China Incident, or the outbreak of Japan's full-fledged invasion of China, Yanaihara stated the following in an article in *Chūō Kōron*:

> The key to our relations with China lies in understanding that China is a national state on its way to unification and reconstruction. Only a policy based on a perception of China which affirms and asserts that national unity will help China, help Japan, and contribute to the peace of Asia. Implementation by force or arbitrary policies contrary to this rational view will bring a disaster that will haunt us for generations, will inflict suffering on China, and will destroy the peace of Asia.[14]

This turned out to be a very prophetic statement.

What is remarkable is that Yamada and other radical Shintō ultranationalists were still preaching the same fallacies about the lack of nationalism in the Chinese collective consciousness six years after Japan's full invasion of China and after Japan had clearly become bogged down in its war with China and was fighting a world war, as well. By 1941, "nearly 300,000 Japanese soldiers had died in China, and over a million were deployed across the country, occupying most of its major cities, all of its ports, and most of the rail lines connecting them. Millions of Chinese had perished, and still no end was in sight."[15] Clearly, with such a high death toll, the Chinese were in no mood to surrender. What Yanaihara had heard from nationalistic Chinese in 1937 was turning out to be quite accurate. And the "rational views" regarding China that Yanaihara mentioned were apparently still not being heard in Japan, The rational views of secular thinkers had long been silenced by the Japanese state in the hands of radical Shintō ultranationists who promoted the rise and spread of militant Shintō fundamentalism. The thoughts of most Japanese had been formed by the writings of the true believers such as Yamada, who were motivated and driven by theology. Since, they genuinely believed that Japan had never been defeated in war in its 2,600 year history, to even entertain the idea that Japan could possibly be defeated in war was considered blasphemy toward the collective Japanese national entity, the kokutai. After all, was not Japan destined to lead the work prophesied under "Eight Corners of the World under One Roof"?

For Yamada, Japan was the nation of the gods: "When we say that our Japan is a divine country, it is of course based on the fact that the two gods Izanagi and Izanami created this country."[16] That is to say, Yamada was a committed creationist, a true believer in the Japanese Shintō story of creation. He further reasoned that since the imperial ancestors were gods and the Japanese people were descendants of those gods, all of the Japanese people, too, as children of the gods, must also be gods. Therefore, "Being a divine country is not just a metaphor, or a figure of speech but a fact and a reality in our country."[17]

Being a divine nation and a divine people also dictated that there must be a divine mission for the country:

The fact that our country is a divine country created by the gods also directly indicates the mission of the Empire. ... This country was not born by chance, but was born in order to fulfill the purposes prescribed by *Amaterasu ōmikami*. It may be that she

is a sacred country in order to realize this mission. Looking back on our real history, we find thit Japan has gradually become prosperous since the Age of the Gods, and it has never yet been invaded or suppressed as other foreign countries have. Upon deep reflection, this seems to be due to sacred and profound facts that are unfathomable to us.[18]

But what was that mission? Yamada was clear on that issue, too:

What should be the work of the divine nation of Japan? What should its mission be? As every Japanese person nowadays knows, it was clearly indicated in the Imperial Proclamation of Emperor Jimmu "Eight strings mike a house (*Hakkō o matte ic to nasu*)." What is a house? We can understand this when we look at our individual life. Even if we go out, engage in various activities, encounter difficulties, and feel uneasy, once, we go home, we can enjoy our own living there. Thus, a house is a base where people feel at ease and carry on their lives. The "eight strings (*hakkō*)" in the phrase "eight strings make a house" means "in all directions (*shihokappō*)." I believe that "eight strings mike a house" signifies Emperor Jimmu's desire to let everyone and everything, have peace of mind and enjoy living. . . . It is conceivable that the thought of "the whole world makes a house" is the purpose of the Greater East Asian War at the present time. However, we can clearly see that this desire of Emperor Jimmu did not start only with Emperor Jimmu when we read the Imperial Proclamation of Emperor Jimmu. This is the desire of *Amaterasu Ōmikami*.[19]

As indicated in this statement, the idea of "eight strings make a house" was taken from a passage in the chapter on Emperor Jimmu in the *Nihon Shoki*, which reads, "Thereafter the capital may be extended so as to embrace all the six cardinal points, and the eight cords may be converted so as to form a roof."[20] In prewar Japanese literature, this phrase became popularly known as *hakkō ichiu*, or "the whole world under one roof," and was used to justify carrying out the Greater East Asian War as the necessary first step in the establishment of a new world order by the Japanese nation.

Yamada made another comment on the ultimate purpose of the Greater East Asian War, which is worth quoting at length:

> What we have to seriously consider about the current Greater East Asian War is that our enemies England and America are also making a desperate effort in this war. At this time, even if there is the slightest inattention on our part, the enemy may seize the opportunity, and this could possibly lead to disaster. Therefore, our hundred million people must unite and become one in heart and show not one bit of carelessness. But by that alone we cannot achieve the purpose of this sacred war. . . . [S]ince the war naturally came about as a result of the destruction of the League of Nations, it must be said that the focus of the war should now be on whether or not England and America are still allowed to maintain a world order. When the war broke out, England and America were still in control of the world. We the Japanese people may end up by facing the same fate as our fellow countrymen encountered in Guadalcanal. We Japanese should first realize this point. . . . Our immediate mission is to . . . realize the Imperial ideal of "the whole world under one roof." For this purpose, we must engage in facing, solidifying, and stabilizing other countries in the world who are wandering aimlessly. This is the original mission of the divine country of Japan. This Greater East Asian War was started to force England and America to relinquish their position of world leadership, and ultimately to establish a new order to secure a just and lasting peace.[21]

Thus, from what we have found in the writings of Yamada Yoshio, Japanese expansionism was internally derived from its sense of mission to establish a new world order. Accordingly, anything short of achieving that objective would be tantamount to defeat.

[. . .] there were several forms of Shintō ultranationalism. Hozumi Yatsuka's Meiji Shintō ultranationalism was an ultraconservative form of Shintō

ultranationalism that sought to push back the clock, at least in a political sense, and re-create a Shintō theocracy. The most militant of the radical Shintō ultranationalist movements, which encouraged terrorism, can be loosely associated with the thought of Uesugi Shinkichi. This is by no means to imply that all terrorist groups or individual terrorists in the 1920s and 1930s who saw themselves as executioners carrying out the will of the emperor can be traced to a cohesive network that Uesugi had built. It does, however, suggest that autonomously operating radical Shintō ultranationalist groups and individuals shared his religious ideology. Uesugi provided the ideological leadership and the theological justification for terrorism, In prewar Japan, radical Shintō ultranationalist groups frequently disbanded and reemerged under new names. We find that the radical Shintō ultranationalist groups with no apparent connections to each other nevertheless advanced the same extremist agendas.

The ultimate purpose of the individual in Uesugi's radical Shintō ultranationalist ideology was to die for the emperor, the act through which one's own being would merge into the mystical body of the emperor, thus closing the gap between one's existential being and one's essential being. This meant in actual practice seeking death by eliminating individuals who refused to follow what they considered the true will of the emperor or by destroying corrupt institutions that stood in the way between the emperor and the masses. Accordingly, such terrorist activities were directed primarily not against foreigners but against Japanese in positions of power and influence who were considered apostate. As has been discussed, the Japanese state was gripped by a religious fundamentalism so powerful and pervasive that even the radical Shintō ultranationalist terrorists were praised by the masses for their purity and devotion and purely innocent victims were thought to have deserved death at the hands of the true believers. By contrast, the ultimate purpose of Kakehi's radical Shintō ultranationalism was to die for the emperor by carrying out the emperor's task of destroying the Western-controlled secular world order—beginning with the "liberation" of China from the clutches of Western ideology and Western civilization—and creating a Japanese emperor-centered world order in its place. This was very much the ideology of the Control Faction in the military and was more directed toward outsiders by waging war and dying on the battlefield to create the emperor-centered world order.

[. . .]

In the prewar period, Japan, together with its German and Italian allies, waged war against the rest of the world. How to win this war was an important topic of discussion in Japan in the early 1940s. For instance, in November 1943, on the eve of the second anniversary of the start of the Pacific War, a symposium was held in Tokyo to discuss the theme "The Greater East Asian War and National Politics." This was just one of a number of symposiums organized during the Pacific War years. A wide range of issues on war goals and the means necessary to achieve these goals were discussed at the symposium, which appeared in print in the December 1943 issue of the widely read and highly respected intellectual journal *Chūō Kōron*. The participants in this particular round-table discussion, conducted on November 6, 1943, were Hanami Tatsuji, editor-in-chief of the *Yamato Newspaper*; Mitsuda Iwao, a political and social critic; Nakano Tomio, a professor at Waseda University; and Tsuguno Kunitoshi of the General Affairs Department of the Imperial Rule Assistance Political Association.[22]

The moderator of the symposium opened the session by asking the panelists to restate the meaning of the Greater East Asian War and, in light of the current situation, to reflect on some of the problems facing Japan in China and elsewhere in East Asia. Hanami began by saying that the Greater East Asian War was a war that was being fought to create a "new world order."[23] He also stated that this was something that everyone in Japan should know. But he also said that many people still had to have a clearer understanding of the role that Japan was to play in

the East Asian community and the new world order. On this point, he emphasized that Japan would play a pivotal rote in this new world order because that order itself ultimately had to be based on the imperial way (*Kōdō*),[24] the spirit of the Japanese state since its founding in ancient times. He firmly believed that the imperial way was the original way of mankind and of the world and that humanity had no choice other than to return to this great way if global order and peace were to be maintained.

Nakano Tomio also placed much emphasis on the point that Japan's kokutai spirit was the only viable basis for a world order. He agreed with Hanami's remarks and added to them by pointing out that the spirit of Japan's kokutai was fundamentally opposed to constitutional forms of government. He further noted that Western theories of liberalism, democracy, and Marxism were not comprehensive worldviews. They were no more than partial views of the human condition. If one wished to take as a worldview a perspective that encompassed the entire universe, including all aspects of human life, then the political theories and political principles devised by the Western world thus far would not qualify. On the contrary, Nakano asserted; "It is Japan's world view that is a real worldview."[25] In other words, the Western world never really produced a true worldview; and it was the worldview founded on Japan's kokutai that was the only true worldview on which to establish a new world order. Nakano's reference to liberalism and Marxism implied that neither the American-inspired Wilsonian ideal of a world order bated on liberal-democratic internationalism nor the Soviet-led Marxist vision of a world order was a worldview that could guarantee world peace and order.

The participants in the symposium sought to drive home the point that the Greater East Asian War was not merely a "defensive war (*jiei no sen*)" to free the peoples in East Asia from Western imperialism by expelling the Europeans and the Americans, only to let each individual country in Asia go its own way.[26] Hanami stressed this point in his opening remarks. He said that it had to be embedded in the people's minds that the political aim of the Greater East Asian War was the consolidation of East Asia using the imperial way as the foundation of unity. This was to be a major stepping stone to the establishment of the Japan-centered world order. Hanami also added that it was a "holy war."[27] Mitsuda Iwao also viewed the war in East Asia as the first step in the establishment of a new world order. In fact, he referred to the war as a "war for world reform (*sekai ishhin sen*)."[28]

Having restated the fundamental goal of the Greater East Asian War to be the consolidation of East Asia as the first step toward a new world order, the participants then began to identify problems and discuss ways in which these problems might be solved if Japan were to be successful in establishing this new world order. As for unity in East Asia, the principal stumbling block was China. China, of course, is the largest country in East Asia in terms of both population and size. The Japanese could not possibly succeed in their initial goal of the Greater East Asian War without winning over the Chinese. As Hanami saw it, the crux of the "China problem (*Shina no mondai*) was that the Chinese stilt had their own vision for the construction of a modern state that was ultimately in conflict with Japan's vision of a new East Asian order under the emperor."[29] The Chinese ideals for the establishment of a new China were ultimately based on the ideals of the so-called *San Min Chui* (Three People's Principles)—nationalism, democracy and land nationalization—articulated at the turn of the century by the father of the Chinese revolution, Sun Yat-sen, The first principle of Chinese nationalism was originally aimed against rule by the Manchu people as well against imperialist incursions by the Western powers and Japan. The Chinese wanted to be ruled by the Chinese people. The second of the Three People's Principles was that China was eventually to evolve into a democracy. This, too was in opposition to the Japanese imperial way. With these visions of the state, Japan and China were bound to come into conflict.

Hanami did not frontally attack the Three People's Principles and insist that the Chinese abandon them. That would have been political suicide for furthering Japanese–Chinese relations. Instead, he called for a "correct interpretation of the Three People's Principles based on the imperial way."[30] That is, Hanami in effect suggested as a solution to the China problem that the Chinese be allowed to retain the ideals of the Three People's Principles but interpret them in such a way as to gut them of all real content. Recalling the discussion of *Fundamentals of Our National Polity* in chapter 9 about the sublimation of foreign ideologies, this was an inverse application of the same principle. The Japanese radical Shintō ultranationalists suggested that the only viable solution at the time was to bring about the complete sublimation of the ideals of the modern Chinese state into the Japanese kokutai.

The last topic brought up for discussion was the "Greater East Asian War as a War for World Reform (*sekai ishin sen to shite Dai Tōa Senso*)."[31] Mitsuda reiterated that the war ultimately was being fought to establish a new world order. The hegemonic kingly ways of European civilization and Chinese civilization in the past, as well as the present republican and democratic ways of America, could never serve as a solid basis of a world order for all people. The only viable way to achieve a lasting world order was the imperial way. It is instructive to note here that nobody suggested trying to find a way to unite the peoples of East Asia under a common spiritual heritage such as Buddhism, a universal religion that had spread throughout the major countries of the region. But the reason for this should be clear: that would have negated their justification for waging this war.

[. . .]

THE FAILURE OF RADICAL SHINTŌ ULTRANATIONALISM AS A UNIVERSAL IDEOLOGY

The ultimate goal of radical Shintō ultranationalism in the Second World War was to establish a new world order based on Japanese imperial rule to replace the Wilsonian-inspired world order of democratic internationalism, institutionalized through the League of Nations after the First World War. This goal was enunciated by virtually every radical Shintō ultranationalist thinker, politician, and military man in the 1930s and the 1940s. This study has introduced some of the principal theoreticians of radical Shintō ultranationalism who articulated this global vision, but there were many more. For instance, Daniel Holtom, who wrote on Shintō ultranationalism in the midst of the Pacific War in the 1940s, quoted Admiral Yonai Mitsumasa speaking as the newly appointed prime minister in January 1940: "The principle of the whole world under one roof embodies the spirit which the Empire was founded by jimmu Tennō. My understanding is that this is the spirit of making the boundless virtues of the Emperor prevail throughout the whole world."[32] Holtom also cited Konoe Fumimaro, who in July 1940 replaced Yonai as prime minister, proclaiming: "The basic aim of Japan's national policy lies in the firm establishment of world peace in accordance with the lofty spirit of *Hakko Ichi-u*, in which the country was founded."[33] Holtom also noted a very interesting piece of information in a footnote:

> In the spring of 1940 a monument to the spirit of "the whole world under one roof" was erected in the city of Miyazaki, Kyushu, at a cost of some six hundred thousand yen. It stands on Hakko Hill in the form of a great tower of ferroconcrete, overlooking the Hyuga Straits and rising to a height of more than a hundred feet. In outline it suggests the shape of a Shintō *gōhei* the zigzag purification device in common use at the shrines. On each of the four sides of the pillar is a representation of a human figure, symbolizing the four primary agencies wherewith Japan attains the realization of her mission in the world—commerce and industry, fishing, agriculture, and war.[34]

General Araki Sadao, who was serving as minister of education in 1938, wrote in an article titled "State and Education" in the journal *Contemporary Japan* in December 1938:

> The Japanese conception of political origin lies in the very law of nature in conformity with Divine Will. According to our belief, Japan was founded by the Sun Goddess, *Amaterasu-Omikami*, who is revered by the entire nation for her all-pervading virtues, and from whom our Imperial House is descended. We, therefore are proud to look upon our Emperor as the fountain-head of our national life. In this respect our Empire rests upon the foundation of blood relationship which far transcends mere morality, and our Ruler is viewed in the light of a super-moral being. . . .
>
> The *Tenno*, by which name our Sovereign is known, embodies in Himself the spirit of the deities of the primordial universe, as well as the guiding spirit of government, manifested by His divine ancestress, *Amaterasu-Omikami*. His august virtues thus pervade both time and space, and He reigns over His people with love and benevolence.[35]

One could go on and on citing such statements by Japanese leaders. Indeed, it would be no exaggeration to say that radical Shintō ultra-nationalist thought and the idea of global imperial rule deeply permeated the minds of the Japanese people as a whole as well as those of its its leaders. John Dower noted:

> Only a handful of academics emerged from the war with their reputations enhanced for not having been swept along by the tides of ultranationalism. . . . There was no counterpart to the principled resistance that a small but heroic number of intellectuals, leftists, church people, and military officers had mounted against National Socialism in Germany in the same period. There was very little indeed in which intellectuals could take pride where their behavior prior to August 15, 1945 was concerned.[36]

It must be noted that another explosion of radical Shintō ultranationalist writings occurred in the early 1940s, but covering this requires another study. For example, Satō Tsūji, a scholar of German literature and philosophy who in 1943 became a member of the Ministry of Education's National Spirit Cultural Research Institute and later was president of Kōgakkan University published his monumental *Kōdō no Tetsugaku* [The Philosophy of the Imperial Way] in 1942. Still another important work by a radical Shintō ultranationalist intellectual in the 1940s is Nakashiba Suezumi's *Kōdō Sekaí Kan* (World View of the Imperial Way; 1942).

This vision of a new world order ruled over and governed by the Japanese emperor-deity was prophesied in scripture. Indeed, it was the radical Shintō ultranationalists' purpose in life to contribute to the fulfillment of this prophesy. It was their belief that only the emperor could rule the world with total impartiality and benevolence. And, as we have seen in the state theories of Uesugi Shinkichi and Kakehi Katsuhiko, for the Japanese people themselves, radical Shintō ultranationalist ideology envisioned an egalitarian society in which every individual was equal in the eyes of the emperor. The Utopian objective for the individual in his or her relationship with the emperor was to lose the ego—that thinking, feeling, and acting self that is conscious of the self and aware of the distinction of the self from the selves of others—and merge the self totally into the mystical body of the emperor.

However, the problem of how to export this ideology to the non-Japanese people of the conquered lands became a more critical issue as the war progressed. Thinkers critical of Shintō ultranationalism such as Kita Ikki had raised this issue in the first decade of the twentieth century, during the early stages of Japanese expansionism. Radical Shintō ultra-nationalists, as well as other ideologues, were aware that one cannot create a world order based on sheer military power. This issue of how to rule over an empire composed of other ethnic peoples and races was also an issue of which Holtom was keenly aware. He wrote:

The rise of modern Japan to ascendancy in Far Eastern affairs has been accompanied by an impressive geographical expansion. This territorial growth—achieved mainly by the force of arms—has been safeguarded by the extension of elaborate political and military administration, and this in turn has been accompanied by economic and cultural penetrations that are only beginning to reveal their vast possibilities for the reordering of the new areas of control. . . . In manufacturing, agriculture, mining, engineering, business, education, and religion, Japan is projecting something like a migration onto the mainland, which, if carried through even to partial conclusion, will leave very little as it was either for continental eastern Asia or for Japan. And even though the actual movements of population may not be relatively large, the completeness of the controls which the Japanese genius for paternalistic organization is in process of establishing over conquered peoples threatens a momentous change to the story of mankind. . . . The part which the national religion has played in this great movement is not inconsiderable. The tenacity with which the Japanese government has pressed the Shintō issue in Korea and elsewhere points to its significance as the guarantee of the establishment of inner authority over subjected peoples.[37]

The goal, of course, was somehow to induce non-Japanese to embrace radical Shintō ultranationalist ideology. But this proved to be no easy task. The crux of the problem was that radical Shintō ultranationalism was in essence an ethnic or Volk-based ideology that lacked a universal message with which all peoples of the world could enthusiastically identify. [. . .] Further, the Japanese themselves, imbued with this ideology for decades, were unprepared mentally and psychologically for the task of converting the non-Japanese masses to radical Shintō ultranationalism. Holtom noted that Horie Hideo, an authority on Shintō, tried to deal with this vexing problem in an article titled "The Shintō Shrine Problem Overseas," in the 1939 issue of *Skūkyō Nenkan (Yearbook of Religion)*. In a summary of Horie's article, Holtom wrote:

The major problem, argues Horie, is that of adjustment of the exclusively nationalistic aspects of State Shintō to the universalism that ought to inhere in constructive international intercourse. The existence of the former elements is first recognized and strongly emphasized. The author calls attention to the consciousness of unique racial integrity that underlies the thinking of the Japanese people. He begins with the doctrine of the one-tribe origin of the nation. The true members of the Japanese race regard themselves [as offspring] of the gods. They believe that their state was brought into being by the *kami* and that the people are the descendants of these ancestral deities. They hold that, in spite of the infusion of the blood of other peoples in times past, the genuine Yamato stock predominates and that for the most part the breed is pure. Communal solidarity is guaranteed and preserved by this fact of direct divine descent and by the bonds of spiritual communion with the gods.[38]

What Horie said about the essence of State Shintō is exactly what the radical Shintō ultranationalists had been articulating for decades. However, after Horie admitted that ethnicity was at the core of State Shintō, according to Holtom, he went on to say:

The nationalistic character found in the shrines does not inevitably veto a universal character. In cases where members of our Japanese race [*sic*; ethnic nation]—so rich in the sentiment of reverence—are living together in a land with foreigners of like tendencies the practice of worshiping together at the shrines is not merely a matter to which there is no objection, rather it should be welcomed. Shintō, the Great Way of the Gods, is not a thing which the state or the people of the nation should regard selfishly. Shintō is broad. It includes humanitarianism and righteousness. The spirit of Shintō, which is the fundamental directive principle of our national life, must be utilized for the purpose of elevating the races of neighboring territories where the national relationships are complicated. Indeed, by means of this spirit of Shintō foreign peoples must also be evangelized. The self-interested internationalism, which has come into existence apart from the give and take of ordinary intercourse and which up to now fought with the weapons of craft and deception, must be brought to its senses by the saving presence of the pure and holy spirit of Shintō.[39]

There is no reason to doubt Horie's sincerity in wanting to lift up the neighboring Asian peoples by encouraging them to worship the Japanese gods in the shrines. But one should hardly be surprised to discover that such a message would fall on deaf ears. If Horie was addressing Asian peoples in Japanese conquered territories, this was the equivalent to a man throwing a few scraps of bones to hungry dogs running down the street. In terms of ideology, Japanese radical Shintō ultranationalists might as well have been from another planet; their State Shintō ideology was totally alien to Asian peoples. Besides, other Asians for the most part were already acting and operating within the ideological orbit of the Western world, whether republican or communist, which the Japanese utterly failed to understand. Even Douglas MacArthur alluded to this when he remarked, "Tucked away there in the North Pacific, the Japanese had little or no realization of how the rest of the world lived. They had evolved a feudalistic system of totalitarianism which had produced results which were almost like reading the pages of mythology."[40]

Holtom also had expressed strong reservations about this and noted that trying to spread State Shintō ideology was hampered by three factors: (1) the government-inspired doctrine that the essence of sincerity consisted of conformity to rule; (2) the conception of the national expansion process as involving the full assimilation of conquered peoples; and (3) the inseparable connection between Shintō and political administration. In regard to the first point, when asked what value Shintō had to offer applicable to all mankind, radical Shintō ultranationalists claimed that "sincerity" was the universal value of State Shintō that was the equivalent to Christian love and to Buddhist compassion. But this virtue of "sincerity"—the equivalent saying "one heart, one virtue"—meant becoming one with the emperor. When asked what this might mean to a Manchurian subject under Japanese rule, a non-Japanese resident candidly replied, "It means a heart of fear and a virtue of absolute obedience."[41] As anyone even remotely familiar with the history of modern Chinese history knows, nationalism had been spreading rapidly among the Chinese masses since the May 4, 1919, Movement, and the Chinese people were certainly in no mood to identify with a foreign emperor whose troop were occupying their land and when their people were being massacred in the name of that emperor. The original policy of "assimilation" in Korea and Taiwan, for all practical purposes, meant "cultural genocide"—the cultural extermination or destruction of an entire people or ethnic group. These Asians in essence were expected to become fictive Japanese. Needless to say, this was no way to establish an "inner authority over the subjected peoples." Finally, Holtom acknowledged that radical Shintō ultranationalism was a religion of national expansionism. Its ideal of egalitarianism of all people under the emperor did not apply to non-Japanese peoples. Therefore, the ideal could not be realistically exported and accepted beyond the Japanese völkisch or ethnic group.

To circumvent this ideological dilemma and come up with some kind of viable blueprint or set of ideological guidelines for Japanese officials involved in the practical planning and administration of Japan's conquered areas, radical Shintō ultranationalists finally resorted to a partial resurrecting of the Meiji conceptualization of a hierarchical order of rule articulated by theorists such as Hozumi Yatsuka. They also incorporated new ideas from abroad, especially German Nazism. This authoritarian model of "conservative Shintō ultranationalism" was

resurrected and rearticulated to apply to Japanese rule of non-Japanese peoples. Insofar as it served as an ideological basis of a world order, this development within radical Shintō ultranationalist ideology was a sure indication of the theoretical breakdown of the ideology when it came to justifying global rule. It simply did not contain egalitarian universal values. But the potential long-range outcome of a failure to articulate adequately an ideological justification for ruling over a vast empire would also result in certain disaster. For that reason, Japanese radical Shintō ultranationalists had to come up with alternative solutions to the dilemma. An excellent example of this can be seen in the 1943 document *An Investigation of Global Policy with the Yamato Race* [*sic; Ethnic Nation*] *as Nucleus* that Dower discussed in his powerful work *War without Mercy*.[42] More than anything, this document seems to indicate that Japan's global ideological policy was in shambles and that its fanatical militant Shintō ultranationalist leaders were desperate to try anything.

As shown in Dower's analysis of *An Investigation of Global Policy*, which was compiled by forty researchers working for the Population and Race (Ethnic Nation) Section of the Research Bureau of the Ministry of Health and Welfare, the Japanese were even seriously contemplating drastic measures such as a long-range plan to relocate on a massive scale Koreans and Taiwanese:

> Concerning the Koreans and Formosans, the report was exceedingly harsh. They were described as being especially suitable to carry out the heavy physical work of a protracted war. Given their high birth rates, resistance of Japanization, and strategic locations, special care had to be taken to prevent them from becoming "parasites" within the empire. Once the war was over, Koreans living within Japan proper should be sent home; those living near the Soviet border should be replaced by Japanese settlers; and, in general, Koreans should be encouraged to emigrate to harsh and thinly populated places such as New Guinea.[43]

It is instructive to keep in mind that the Taiwanese and Koreans were the first people to fall under Japanese rule. By the 1940s, the Koreans had been under direct Japanese rule for more than three decades and the Taiwanese more than four decades. Obviously, the Japanese policy of cultural genocide was not working, and the Japanese were by that time clearly fed up with having the Taiwanese and the Koreans living in the core area of the new world order they were trying to create. It seems that they had no real, "proper place" within that order. Advocating the physical removal of the Koreans was only one or two steps away from a final solution such as the one the Nazis developed for the Jews. This Japanese proposal to encourage the Koreans to emigrate to New Guinea recalls the Nazi proposal to have the European Jews emigrate to Madagascar.

But the radical Shintō ultranationalists were not having problems with just the Taiwanese and the Koreans. Contact with the peoples of Asia that was too close was also considered dangerous for the long-range survival of the empire and, eventually, global rule. Dower noted: "Concerning overseas Japanese, admonitions against racial [ethnic] intermarriage were a standard part of policy documents, and the 1943 report spelled out the rationale for this: intermarriage would destroy the 'national spirit' of the Yamato Race [ethnic nation],"[44] Not only would it destroy the national spirit of the Yamato ethnic nation; it would, in the long run, destroy the ethnic nation itself. This is what the radical Shintō ultranationalists feared most, and this mind-set goes back to what Hozumi Yatsuka was talking about in the late nineteenth century. With this attitude toward other races and ethnic groups, the only way to secure the stability of the empire and the conquered lands theoretically was to export Japanese overseas in numbers large enough to dominate them. The detailed plan for the "blood of the Yamato race [ethnic nation]" to be "planted in the soil" of the various countries is just one of the fascinating aspects of this incredible

document."[45] Everything according to radical Shintō ultranationalism was centered on Japan, and theoretically there was no room for anything else. They even went so far as to redraw the maps of the world. Since Japan was the first land created by the gods Izanagi and Izanami, Japan was considered the center of the world. Accordingly, one finds Komaki Tsuneki's proposal to place Japan at the center of a world map, going so far as to rename the continents and designate all the oceans of the world the "Great Sea of Japan."[46]

From our analysis of the ideology of radical Shintō ultanationalism, one should not be surprised by the fact that Japan had no reliable Asian ally in the Second World War. Radical Shintō ultranationalism was not the type of ideology that could give meaning for people outside the Japanese ethnic group. Only a universal ideology can unite peoples of different national origins and give them a shared sense of identity and a purpose to work together to make a better world for all. This study should make it very clear that the Japanese could never have won the ideological battle, for only the globalization of a universal religion or universal ideology ultimately could have succeeded. The United States, for example, attempts to promote democracy and human rights globally by supporting democratic elements in countries around the world. Democracy can also be induced from the outside by military forces as in the case of Germany and Japan after the Second World War, but it is not necessary. Various strategies can be utilized for that purpose. The critical point is that democratic institutions and values of human rights can be exported. Likewise, the other major ideology of the twentieth century, communism (and its various ideological derivatives), can also be exported. The communist nations had supported indigenous communist movements in countries around the world. This is not to suggest that exporting universal values is easy. One of the great lessons of the twentieth century and now the twenty-first century is that democracy is not easily exportable, as Americans are now finding out in

Iraq and other areas of the Middle East. It is extremely difficult even under the best circumstances, and in places where relative success stories are found, such as Taiwan and the Republic of Korea, it has taken decades of careful nurturing and massive assistance from the United States. Radical Shintō ultranationalism could not be spread by such means. In other words, the globalization of an ethnic religion could not possibly have succeeded.

Shintō ideology and theology utterly failed to break out of the narrow confines of ethnicity within which it had been imprisoned since ancient times. It had not advanced beyond the late Tokugawa period, when Hirata Atsutane had first articulated his cosmology. In *Tama no Miha-shira* (Pillar of the Soul), Hirata claimed that Japan and the Japanese were superior to all other lands and peoples because in the Shintō story of genesis Japan was born as the result of the union of the gods Izanagi and Izanami and its people were the descendants of the gods, while foreign peoples and foreign countries were formed out of the foam of the sea. The Shintō story contained no monogenetic theory of the origins of man, and no serious attempt was ever made to evolve Shintō into a genuinely universal religion.

Japanese Shintō ultranationalists were victims of their own delusions of grandeur and power. All of them were highly religious people—Shintō fundamentalists[47]—and as such they believed in the core doctrines of Shintō ultranationalism: the divine descent and divinity of the living emperor; the divine origins of the Japanese ethnic group as against the divine origins or natural evolutionary origins of man; and the divine source of political authority stemming from the ancestral deity Amaterasu Ōmikami. These doctrines were common to all Shintō ultra-nationalists as much as the crucifixion or resurrection of Jesus Christ is to Christians. Accordingly, for all these radical Shintō ultranationalist theorists, sovereignty resided in the emperor, and no human law was capable of restraining the sovereign emperor. Nevertheless, within this common framework, major differences

did exist among Shintō ultranationalists in their articulations of emperor ideology. Hozumi Yatsuka started with the principle of the family, and on the basis of the family he built the structure of the state. Uesugi Shinkichi, on the contrary, virtually ignored the family and took the state, which, to him was composed of individuals who were all equal in the mystical body of the emperor interacting in a spatial-temporal matrix, as his starting point. For Kakehi, the state was really religion. He focused on the divine nature of the emperor and the mystical relationship between the emperor and the masses. Shintō ultranationalism, in short, contained a multiplicity of distinct articulations.

Hozumi's conservative Shintō ultranationalism inherited the task of defending the authoritarian political order in the late Meiji period against liberalism and democratic institutions by demonstrating its ability to defend the sovereignty of the emperor and thereby the interests of the elite ruling oligarchy. Based on the traditional patriarchal construction of state and society, Hozumi's formulation of emperor ideology allowed for no participation of the masses in politics. Hozumi had linked the emperor system to the state much in the same way Europeans had connected the monarchy to the state in the sixteenth century and seventeenth century. But such a theory of state was effective as an ideology only in a premodern society. Consequently, by the second decade of the twentieth century it came to represent a reactionary force and was in danger of losing its appeal to the people, who were, using the words of Hegel, rapidly becoming "a law unto themselves." By then, no longer could it be correct to say that the state consisted of the emperor and his subjects, if by "subjects" one meant nonpolitical, scattered, and unorganized individuals.

Ideological challenges coming from liberalism and socialism articulated in the form of German state-sovereignty theories in the Meiji period and *minponshugi* in the Taishō period were, for the most part, responses to Hozumi Yatsuka's formulation of emperor ideology. If it were not to become ossified and corroded and thereby lose its ideological hegemony. Shintō ultranationalism had to be rearticulated. Correctly perceiving the inherent weakness of Hozumi's formulation of emperor ideology, Uesugi Shinkichi and Kakehi Katsuhiko reformulated it to accommodate the new political and social realities brought on by the politicization of the masses. It had to be redefined and its relevance reproduced without losing the validity of its central tenets.

To construct an ideology welding absolute monarchy to the politicized masses was a formidable task, indeed, that could be accomplished only by means of a fiction. Uesugi's emperor ideology had sought to convince the masses that what they desired was really what the emperor desired. He had to convince them that their wishes were identical to those of the emperor—that indeed, they were really a part of the emperor rather than independent beings who had consciousness of their own individuality. Kakehi's emperor ideology sought to create this identity between the emperor and the masses by indoctrinating the latter through devotion, prayer, adoration, and sacrifice to the emperor. In both Uesugi's metaphysics and Kakehi's mystical religious doctrines, this identity between the emperor and the masses was theoretically worked out. The findings of the study suggest that it was in this way that radical Shintō ultra-nationalist ideology, Japan's "myth of the twentieth century," succeeded in organizing and mobilizing the masses and in remaining the dominant ideology throughout the first half of the twentieth century. This transformation of emperor ideology from a traditional form of absolutism to a modern, mass-based egalitarian state structure under the emperor represented one of the most important political developments in modern Japanese history—more important than the turn from constitutional monarchy to absolute monarchy—for it required the transformation of the consciousness of men on a massive scale. The dynamics involved in the process of the mass transformation of the consciousness of the Japanese people from a traditional form of absolutism to a consciousness of totally identifying one's own being with the emperor is best illustrated by the story "A Sailor's Mother" that elementary-school children were required to recite throughout the Taishō and Shōwa periods:[48]

It was the time of the War of 1894–1895. One day on our ship the Takachiho, a sailor was weeping as he read a letter written in a women's handwriting. A passing lieutenant saw him and, thinking his behavior unmanly, said, "Hey, what have we here? Has life become so valuable? Are you afraid to die? Are you lonely for your wife and children? Don't you think it's an honor to become a soldier and go to war—What kind of attitude is that?"

"Sir, don't think that of me . . ."

[The officer reads the letter:]

"You said you did not fight In the battle of Feng-tao, and you did not accomplish much in the August 10th attack at Weihaiwei either. I am very disappointed in you. Why did you go into battle? Wasn't it to sacrifice your life to repay the emperor? The people in the village are good to me and offer help all the time, saying kindly: 'It must be hard for you having your only son off fighting for the country. Please don't hesitate to tell us if there is anything we can do.' Whenever I see their faces, I am reminded of your cowardice and I feel as if my heart will break. So every day I go to the shrine of Hachiman and pray that you will distinguish yourself in battle. Of course I am human, too, and cannot at all bring myself to hate my own child. Please try to understand my feelings as I write this letter. . . ."

[The officer apologized.]

"I'm sorry. I can only admire your mother's spirit."

The sailor, who had been listening with lowered head, saluted and, smiling, left.[49]

Irokawa Daikichi noted that "A Sailor's Mother" illustrated "the close relation between filial piety and loyalty on the part of the ordinary people and the common soldier."[50] Quite frankly, I am at a loss to explain what Irokawa meant by this statement. If the story was supposed to illustrate filial piety, it was a filial piety so twisted and mangled that it is unrecognizable. It is inconceivable that this story has anything to do with illustrating the close association between loyalty to the emperor and filial piety. Just the opposite: the story signified, if anything, the demise of the value of filial piety in Japanese society. Filial piety—and, definitely, filial piety in the Confucian ideal—required that a son should protect his own life to care for his parents. In the traditional patriarchal construction of state and society, loyalty to the king or the emperor was construed as an *extension* of filial piety. In other words, devotion one has to one's parents is extended to the emperor. Loyalty to the emperor is thus promoted alongside filial piety.

In the story, morality is used to destroy any emotional attachment that a person may have even to one's own family or spouse or children. It was designed to destroy the sphere of the individual's inner life of freedom from radical Shintō ultranationalist ideology. It recognized no limits on its penetration into the thoughts and daily life of the individual. The moral of the story is to induce total devotion to the emperor. To die for the emperor, the individual must obliterate any real affection between the individual and his loved ones. In the story, the lieutenant mistakenly chides the young sailor for weeping for what at first he imagines as his longing for his wife and children. "Are you afraid to die?" asked the lieutenant. The implication here, of course, is that any feeling that the sailor may have had for his wife and children would weaken his resolve to die for the emperor. The lieutenant is delighted when he reads the letter and finds out that the sailor's mother has scolded her son for not seeking death in battle for the emperor. In the mother's thinking, too, the son is not supposed to be concerned about her or the family. She feels that her "heart will break" if her son does not die in battle.

From the viewpoint of radical Shintō ultranationalist ideology, the mother and the lieutenant were the exemplary personalities. They were the ones responsible for sending millions of Japanese to their deaths in the name of the emperor. But to do this, the most fundamental of human emotions had to be destroyed. Even the slightest of feelings or emotions for loved ones indicated weakness and less than total commitment and devotion to the emperor. "A Sailor's Mother" portends the type of thinking that was to dominate the Japanese state in the 1930s and the 1940s. Anyone who had been in the way of this form of religious ultranationalism was driven from power and influence in Japanese society. What happened to Minobe Tastukichi and his organ theory of the state is a good example of this.

Of course, it is possible that not everyone in Japan in the 1930s and the 1940s came to believe in the divinity of the emperor, despite the decades of mass indoctrination of radical Shintō ultranationalist ideology. Perhaps groups and individuals resisted to the bitter end, as Ienaga Saburo tried to show in the chapter "Dissent and Resistance: Change from Within" of his book *The Pacific War, 1931–1945*. But one thing is unquestionable: the massive impact of this radical form of Shintō nationalism on the life of the Japanese people in the first half of the twentieth century.

NOTES

1   Dower, *War without Mercy*, 78–79.
2   This dispute arose from a proposal by Takatomi Senge (1845–1918), chief priest of the Grand Shrine of Izumo, who maintained that O-kuni-nushi-no-mikoto should be added to the official pantheon consisting of Amaterasu Ōmikami and the three creation deities Ame-no-minaka-nushi-no-kami, Takami-musubi-kami, and Kami-musubi-no-kami, who were the center of worship of the Great Promulgation Campaign, a movement by the Meiji government from 1870 to 1884 to articulate a national religion. This was challenged by priests of the Grand Shrine of Ise. The dispute spread throughout Japan.

3 Quoted in Hall, *Kokutai no Hongi*, 6.
4 Yamada, "Shinkoku Nihon no Shimei to Kokumin no Kakugo," 3.
5 Ibid., 2.
6 Ibid.
7 Ibid.
8 Bix, *Hirohito and the Making of Modern Japan*, 306–7.
9 Yamada, "Shinkoku Nihon no Shimei to Kokumin no Kakugo," 8.
10 Ienaga, *The Pacific War, 1931–1945*, 3–12.
11 Ibid., 85.
12 Ibid., 3.
13 Ibid., 86–87.
14 Ibid., 87.
15 Cook and Cook, *Japan at War*, 23.
16 Yamada, "Shinkoku Nihon no Shimei to Kokumin no Kakugo," 5.
17 Ibid.
18 Ibid., 12.
19 Ibid., 9.
20 Aston, *Nihongi*, 131.
21 Yamada, "Shinkoku Nihon no Shimei to Kokumin no Kakugo," 16.
22 The Imperial Rule Assistant Political Association (Yokusan Seiji Kai) was formed in 1942 in conjunction with the Imperial Rule Association as the sole legal political party. The Imperial Rule Assistant Political Association itself was formally organized in 1940 following the dissolution of all political parties in the Japanese parliament. Its purpose was guarantee that the parliament was totally cooperative with the political leadership and promoted national unity.
23 *Chūō Kōron*, December 1943, 30.
24 An excellent work on the philosophy of the Imperial Way is Satō, *Philosophy of the Imperial Way*, which was written in 1941, at the beginning of the Pacific War. Although his philosophy is not covered in this study, he was a leading ultranationalist scholar of the 1940s. He taught at Kōgakkan University.
25 *Chūō Korōn*, 33.
26 Ibid., 31.
27 Ibid., 32.
28 Ibid.
29 Ibid., 31.
30 Ibid.
31 Ibid.
32 Holtom, *Modern Japan and Shintō Nationalism*, 22.
33 Ibid., 22.
34 Ibid., 27.
35 Ibid., 11.
36 Dower, *Embracing Defeat*, 233–34.
37 Holtom, *Modern Japan and Shintō Nationalism*, 153–54.
38 Ibid. 157.
39 Ibid., 158–59.
40 Dower, *Empire and Aftermath*, 278.
41 Holtom, *Modern Japan and Shintō Nationalism*, 162.
42 Dower, *War without Mercy*.
43 Ibid., 289.
44 Ibid., 277.
45 Ibid., 267.
46 Ibid., 273.
47 I should point out that the word "fundamentalism" in this study has two meanings. First, it refers to the historical meaning of the word, which dates back to the early part of the twentieth century when American Protestant evangelists sought to clarify the "fundamentals" of the Christian faith in the face of what they perceived to have been the onslaught of secularism and to reassert the truths and doctrines of the inerrant Bible. In a comparable way, the Shintō fundamentalists labored to reassert the Shintō truths and doctrines, integrating them into their interpretations of the Constitution of the Empire of Japan and using them to develop elaborate theories of state. Hozumi Yatsuka, Uesugi Shinkichi, Kakehi Katsuhiko, and other Shintō ultranationalist theorists did all this in the face of what they perceived to be the weakening of the traditional conception of the Japanese state by rational, Western-oriented emperor-as-organ theorists in particular, and by the secularization spreading in Japanese politics and society in general. Second, fundamentalism refers to the fanatical commitment to act in radical ways because of religious conviction.
48 This story is quoted in full from Irokawa, "The Emperor System as a Spiritual Structure," 305–6.
49 Ibid.
50 Ibid., 305.

Religion and Social Power

Essay:
Religion, Oppression, and Resistance

Ask many people today to define "religion," and they will respond by describing dogmatic dedication to a massive, bureaucratic institution. Sometimes in the United States we hear the expression, "don't drink the Kool-Aid," meaning: don't get taken in by an ideology, a personage, or a fad to the extent that you give your life to it. The saying is a reference (albeit a slightly mistaken one) to the 1978 deaths of Peoples Temple members from poisoned Flavor-Aid. Though many people today no longer know why Kool-Aid stands in for a kind of fatal gullibility in common idiom, it's clear that popular opinions of religion expect it to be a source of oppression rather than an opportunity for resistance. As we've seen since the beginning of this book, however, religion is a complicated phenomenon, and thus, we might expect that its relationship to social power would be complicated as well. In fact, were we to sum it up, we might describe religion as a whole, in its relationship to social power, as both strikingly *powerful* and immeasurably *malleable*. These two factors, taken together, help to explain why religion can be at times so dangerous to oppressed groups, and at other times such a powerful force for social justice.

The readings included in this section, and those not included but covered below, reflect scholars' attempts to grapple with the complexity of the relationship between religion and social power from the mid-nineteenth century up through the early twenty-first century. Each scholar's approach is significantly shaped by social and historical location, both her own and those of the communities with which she or he worked. Taken together, these readings provide a picture of scholarly debate over the role of religion—a debate that is driven, in part, by the very complexity we've been considering.

Karl Marx: "The opium of the people"

Karl Marx is perhaps best known for his co-authorship (with Friedrich Engels) of the *Communist Manifesto*. But his ideas also continue to shape the ways in which many cultures and states regard religion today. In philosophical circles, Marx is known for developing a **materialist** (material-based) understanding of the world that was opposed to the **idealist** (idea-based) understanding common in his day. For idealists, it was people's ideas that shaped the world around them; for instance, an idealist might argue that because European Christianity envisioned a hierarchical order to the world, European states were historically hierarchical as well. Marx argued the opposite: "Life is not determined by consciousness, but consciousness by life" (1974: 67). For Marx, the material conditions in which people lived fundamentally shaped their understanding of the world around them. Thus, he argued that the forms that Christian belief took among the working classes of his day were the result of living in an unequal and exploitive economic system, rather than the other way around.

Though not from a working-class background himself, Marx was centrally concerned with improving the lives of the working classes, or the **proletariat**, in Europe. Born and raised in Germany, Marx also lived in England for some time. In the mid-nineteenth century both countries were in the throes of the Industrial Revolution. Where once a great deal of the population had been rural, now people were moving to the cities as their crops failed, their landlords turned them out or proved too harsh, or their families outgrew their ancestral land holdings. Factories were springing up throughout urban areas and were often staffed in large part by those from the countryside, but there weren't yet any regulations regarding the length of the work day or the work week, safety in the workplace, minimum wages, or the minimum age of a worker. Factories were often crowded, dangerous places where children and adults worked side by side for 12- or 16-hour shifts, six and sometimes seven days a week, for very little pay. The owners of the factories, meanwhile, benefited enormously from this unregulated, inexpensive labor, and a new wealthy class developed that Marx called the **bourgeoisie**. Marx wondered why the proletariat, so much larger in numbers than the bourgeoisie, did not revolt against the conditions in which they lived, and he developed a theory that relied on the concepts of **ideology** and **superstructure**. It was ideology, or a system of politically and economically charged beliefs, that kept the proletariat in line; the superstructure, or the social institutions that promoted that ideology, held the system in place.

This is where religion comes in. Remember that, with his main experience being in Germany and England, Marx was exposed largely to Christianity. More importantly, he was exposed to state churches—institutions supported and controlled by the government. For Marx, then, religion was central to the continued oppression of the proletariat, both as ideology (in the beliefs it taught) and as part of the superstructure (in its institutional aspect).

So what of Marx's materialist theory—doesn't that suggest that the proletariat had some control over their religious beliefs? Yes, in that Marx thought they were drawn to particular beliefs because of their economic status. But Marx also thought that those beliefs were in the interest of the bourgeoisie because they kept the proletariat obedient. In a nutshell, Marx believed that *religion kept the working classes from revolting*. How did it have this power?

Marx's most famous statement on religion is that "it is the opium of the people [the proletariat]." This comment is often misunderstood because today we know opium primarily as a recreational drug; indeed, it was used as such in Europe during Marx's time as well. Opium derivatives, though, are widely used today to relive severe pain, and opium also had such a use in nineteenth-century Europe. For Marx, then, religion was not the recreational drug of the people so much as it was the morphine of the people: it soothed the severe pain the proletariat felt as a result of their oppression. Such a property was a double-edged sword, because Marx also believed that it was this pain that would drive the eventual revolution of the proletariat. With their pain assuaged, Marx thought, the down-trodden would not demand a better life. The solution was to wean them off the painkiller, to stop treating the symptoms and attack the illness—economic disparity—instead.

Antonio Gramsci: Hegemony and Counter-hegemony

Italian Marxist Antonio Gramsci offers a slightly more complex take on religion than Marx's; Gramsci's work demonstrates some of the ways in which Marxist thought can form the basis for a nuanced theory of religion and social power. An activist and author from a poor background, Gramsci was jailed by Mussolini's government in 1926 for his political activities. Although he had published a handful of articles prior to his imprisonment, while behind bars he began writing notes for a major work. Unfortunately, he suffered from ill health while in prison, and he died a few years after being released. The major work was never written, but the notebooks remain, containing thousands of pages of Gramsci's thought in fragmented and scattered form, sometimes expressed in euphemisms so as to escape censorship. Selections from the notebooks were translated into English in the early 1970s (Gramsci, 1972; see also Gramsci, 1992, 1995), and Gramsci's work quickly became influential both within and beyond English-speaking Marxist circles. Interestingly, though, Gramsci's take on religion is far less well known than his theories of social power.

Gramsci was centrally concerned with a single question: why had the proletariat revolution not come to pass in Italy? Marx's writings made it clear that revolution was nearly inevitable, a product of a sort of economic evolution, and yet the working classes in Italy had not revolted. What was going on? Gramsci's answer to this question was the concept of **hegemony**. Gramsci believed that there were two main ways in which a dominant group could hold onto social power: first, through force, and second (and more sustainably), through hegemony. We might define hegemony here as a situation in which an unequal social power relationship is made to appear natural, legitimate, and inevitable. In the face of such apparent givenness, oppressed groups essentially consent to and even embrace their own oppression. This strategy works, according to Gramsci, as long as the oppressed group does not develop a revolutionary consciousness, and as long as their mistreatment is not extremely severe; in these two cases, force becomes necessary to maintain the social power system.

The concept of hegemony can seem fairly daunting—how does one break out of it? Gramsci suggested that it was possible to develop **counter-hegemony** as well. A counter-hegemonic worldview would see the non-dominant group's oppression as neither inevitable nor natural, and as clearly illegitimate. It might hold to a vision of equality as the hegemonic reality, or hold that the true order of the world was the superiority of the currently-oppressed group. Either way, Gramsci believed that counter-hegemony could release oppressed groups from the hold of a hegemonic worldview, and thus spark the long-awaited revolution.

Living as he did in Italy in the early twentieth century, Gramsci conceptualized religion largely through the role of the Roman Catholic Church in Italian society. Often working hand-in-hand with the fascist government, the Church appeared to Gramsci as an important source of hegemony. Here, Gramsci seems to agree with Marx on religion, but perhaps even more so: religion is not so much an opiate as it is a dirty trick orchestrated by dominant groups to keep other people down. Yet, Gramsci was willing to go further, in that he suggested that the religious beliefs of the proletariat contained the seeds of counter-hegemony. While he believed that these seeds would never by themselves bear fruit, he nonetheless saw a role for religion other than that of supporting the status quo.

W.E.B. Du Bois—Black Religion as Complex Phenomenon

W.E.B. Du Bois, the first African American to graduate from Harvard and one of the earliest black sociologists, devoted his career to the study of black communities and especially to analyzing and seeking to remedy the racism faced by African Americans. Some of his most well-known ideas can be found in his third book, a collection of essays entitled *The Souls of Black Folk* (1903). Du Bois was the first to describe the experience of living as a member of an oppressed group in a larger society as a "double consciousness" in which one lived as both a member of the whole (for Du Bois, an American) and a member of a group of "Others" (a black man), and in which one learned to see oneself always through the eyes of the dominant group. It was Du Bois who pioneered the concept (now often considered elitist) of the "talented tenth," the 10 percent of African Americans who, he believed, would through their abilities bring all black people to equality with whites.

Du Bois was also one of the earliest truly insightful observers of the roles played by religion in African-American communities. Though a product of his time and culture, and therefore dismissive of the African indigenous practices that influenced early slaves in the Americas, Du Bois looked closely at the role of Christianity in two of its forms during slavery: the Christianity of slaves and that of free blacks. Here we begin to see the complexity of religion in Du Bois's estimation, for on the one hand Du Bois notes that the slaveholders seized on Christian teachings of peace and obedience in order to keep slaves in their control, and on the other hand he stresses the importance for free blacks of believing that judgment day was imminent. Thus, though he sounds like Marx when discussing slave religion, Du Bois simultaneously allows for religion to play a role in the abolitionist movement.

Du Bois was also a keen observer and critic of religion in the communities around him. He noticed, for instance, that black churches had a wide variety of functions in the lives of their members—functions that often were fulfilled for whites by other social institutions from which blacks were barred by racism. The importance of the church in African American communities has often been noted by other scholars since Du Bois first pointed it out. Furthermore, Du Bois warned his readers against the complacency or hopelessness he saw in contemporary Southern black religion and the radicalism he saw in the contemporary North. Yet, at the point where he wrote *The Souls of Black Folk*, Du Bois continued to believe in the transformative potential of "the deep religious feeling of the real Negro heart," a power that he believed would eventually bring about the end of racism. By the end of his life, however, Du Bois had given up on this vision and had renounced his U.S. citizenship, moving to Ghana, where he died in 1963.

Bruce Lincoln: The Power of Discourse

Contemporary historian of religion Bruce Lincoln (1989) offers a **discursive**, or discourse-based, analysis of religion and social power. Though clearly influenced by Gramsci, Lincoln develops his ideas about the religion–power relationship from his study of a wide range of historic religious beliefs and practices. Reiterating Gramsci's point that social power can be maintained either through force or through socio-cultural influence, Lincoln points to the power of **discourse**—cultural communication, whether verbal or symbolic—to maintain or overturn a system. In effect, Lincoln redefines both hegemony and counter-hegemony as the effects of discourse.

For Lincoln, discourse can take a number of different forms; as a scholar of religion, he is especially interested in the religious forms it may take, which he identifies as ritual, classification, and myth. In ritual and classification he sees discourse in its symbolic form, whereas in myth it is more often verbal. For instance, when in some liberal Protestant churches a same-sex couple is allowed to take communion together (a ritual that remembers and honors the life of Jesus), the literal words of the ritual are the same as when a different-sex couple receives communion together. The symbolism, however, of a same-sex couple standing or kneeling where many Christians would expect to see a different-sex couple is a powerful political and theological statement. Likewise for classification: to consider women and men to be equally valuable but to contribute to Orthodox Jewish life in fundamentally different ways (including the vastly different number of *mitzvoth*, or commandments, required of each: 613 for men and three for women) is to say something very different about the distribution of social power along gender lines than to consider women and men to make similar contributions to Jewish life, as in more liberal branches of Judaism. This is not to make the simplistic argument that Orthodox women are oppressed as women and liberal Jewish women are not, but rather to say that which sex holds social power, when, and where is different in Orthodox worlds than in more liberal ones. How people are classified religiously can make a difference in social power dynamics.

Lincoln makes the intriguing observation that much myth (meaning sacred story) is very similar to history, except that it carries greater import, a world-making power that Lincoln terms "authority." Lincoln therefore suggests that we should view stories of the past as being of one of four types: fable, which does not have "authority" and also neither claims nor is believed to be true; legend, which has no "authority" and is not believed to be true but does claim to be true; history, which both claims and is believed to be true but does not have "authority," and myth, which has truth claims, credibility, and authority. This taxonomy is interesting because Lincoln claims that it has practical application: if a particular myth serves to keep the social power system intact, then revolutionaries need only remove its authority, or better yet, its credibility as well, demoting it to a legend, in order to release its hold. The reverse is also true, of course. For example, in convincing Native Americans to convert to Christianity (and therefore also to accept European colonization), missionaries often demoted Native sacred stories to the status of legends. Still today, most non-Natives as well as some Native Americans use this term to refer to these stories, whereas others have reclaimed them as sacred or have discovered new stories (sometimes in combination with Christianity, sometimes not) that support Native resistance movements.

Lara Medina: Living in the Middle

Historian Lara Medina picks up on the religious realities of colonization in her consideration of the meanings of the Nahuatl word *nepantla*. Meaning "in the middle," the term has been taken in a negative light as a sort of indecisiveness, a cultural and religious form of sitting on the fence. Medina argues, however, that *nepantla* indicates a strategy for living with two cultures—perhaps a practical response to Du Bois's "double consciousness."

In making this argument, Medina builds upon the classic work of Chicana lesbian feminist theorist Gloria Anzaldúa. In 1987, Anzaldúa published a book of essays that developed, among other ideas, the concept she called *mestizaje*. Meaning "mixedness," the term literally refers to people who are multiracial, especially Mexicans of combined indigenous and Spanish descent (as Anzaldúa points out, this is the majority of Mexicans). As Anzaldúa uses the term, however, *mestizaje* can refer to a number of different experiences of mixedness that affect Mexicans and Chicana/os, especially women (she refers to women of multiracial heritage as *mestizas*). Anzaldúa stresses what she calls "a consciousness of the Borderlands," a consciousness shaped by the common Chicana/o experience of belonging to two nations (Mexico and the United States), yet being seen as belonging to neither. Scorned in Mexico for their U.S. ways and their inability with Spanish, Anzaldúa says, at the same time Chicana/os face racism in the United States and the accusation that they don't belong.

Yet, for Anzaldúa as for Medina, the consciousness of the borderlands is a positive aspect of living in two cultures simultaneously. Anzaldúa sees in this consciousness a contrast and potential alternative to what she considers the problematically linear, rigid tendencies of Western thought. *Mestiza* consciousness (a term Anzaldúa uses interchangeably with "consciousness of the Borderlands") is supple enough to live in two cultures at once and to tolerate and oppose rejection from both. As Medina explains, all too often this ability to live in the middle is viewed by others as indecisiveness, lack of commitment to indigenous identity, or an inability to assimilate into the colonizing culture. While she accepts that confusion is one aspect of middle spaces, she also argues that such spaces have a second aspect of **agency**: the ability to act in ways that shape the world around one. Religiously, this might mean locating one's beliefs and practices in between indigenous and colonizing religions, integrating the two into what Medina calls *"nepantla* spirituality." This also is exactly the process by which religions such as Vodou emerged.

Karen McCarthy Brown: "The realm of the possible and practical"

Anthropologist Karen McCarthy Brown spent nearly a decade during the 1980s coming to know Mama Lola (also called Alourdes), a Haitian Vodou priestess (*manbo*) in New York City. Though her biography of Mama Lola ranges over a wide variety of topics, Brown's commentary on the role of Vodou in politics and in the everyday lives of its practitioners adds further complexity to the oppression-or-resistance dichotomy we see in Du Bois's work. With its focus on "the realm of the possible and practical," Vodou is neither a source of outright resistance nor an "opium of the people." Instead, it provides its practitioners with tools to address, quietly and subtly, the injustices of their everyday lives.

Vodou is one member of a family of **African diasporic religions** that came into being during the slave trade in the Americas, specifically where white Roman Catholics controlled practitioners of West African indigenous religions. Overseers often forced the slaves to cease practicing their ancestral religion and to practice Roman Catholicism instead. Faced with the potentially serious consequences of disregarding the traditional spirits, the slaves seem to have concluded that the Roman Catholic vision of the non-human world was in fact quite close to their own: it included a deity who ran everything but often paid little direct attention to individual humans, and a wide range of sacred beings who did interact quite closely with humankind. There were even Roman Catholic saints who had similar areas of specialization to those found among the traditional African spirits. Over time the slaves came to see the saints and the spirits as representing the same beings, and they blended Catholicism with their ancestral religion to produce the African diasporic religions. In the global North the best-known members of this large family of religions are perhaps Haitian Vodou and Cuban/Puerto Rican Santería, but many other, related religions are now practiced around the world.

Practice of an African diasporic religion involves maintaining a close relationship with the spirits, who like some Catholic saints are both generous and demanding. A participant will generally have a particularly close relationship with one or more spirits and will be said to be the "spouse" or "child" of that spirit, depending on the tradition. Spirits interact directly with the human community through a form of spirit possession in which the spirit "mounts" a human "horse" (often that spirit's spouse or child), taking over the person's consciousness and body for a period of time in order to greet people, chastise some, and advise others. Practitioners keep altars to the spirits and honor them by wearing a spirit's colors, by making offerings of food or drink, and by tending to the altar. Divination is also a common practice.

Given Vodou's roots in a slave culture surreptitiously practicing an ancestral religion in the context of forced conversion, it is logical that the religion would offer subtle forms of resistance rather than open encouragement of revolution. This is not to say that Vodou practitioners did not play important roles in Haiti's independence struggles, for clearly they did. However, the bulk of the religion's history relates most closely to what Brown calls "the realm of the possible and practical." As immigrants of African descent in New York City, Mama Lola and her family face racism, classism, nationalism, sexism, and religious prejudice—not as separate entities but as "intersecting" ones. Developed by legal scholar Kimberlé Crenshaw (1991), the concept of **intersectionality** demonstrates that different forms of social power interact with and shape each other. Thus, when Brown notes in passing the role that she played when she attended the courthouse with Alourdes and Maggie, she stresses both race and class as factors: "my white face, my polite requests, and the right clothes." As Haitian immigrants, Alourdes and Maggie have few of the markers of social power that are recognized in the United States, but they do have the spirits, to whom they turn to ensure William's freedom. Though some might argue that their efforts with the spirits distract Alourdes and Maggie from directly confronting a racist and classist system, such an argument implicitly defines the spirits as fictional or at least ineffectual, suggesting that Vodou practitioners suffer from what Marx would have called "false consciousness." This is too simple an approach to such a complex human phenomenon.

Cheryl Townsend Gilkes: "Dual-sex politics"

Sociologist Cheryl Townsend Gilkes (2001) offers another complex view of the dynamics of religion and social power in her study of women's roles in the "Sanctified" (Holiness and Pentecostal) black churches. Writing in the mid-1980s, Gilkes offers a nuanced response to the often starkly-defined debates over women's roles in religion that took place as part of the largely white-controlled feminist movement in academia at the time. On one side of the debate were feminists such as Mary Daly, who argued that traditional religions were all irretrievably patriarchal and that women should be creating their own religious beliefs and practices that reflected feminist values. On the other side were feminists like Daly's rival Rosemary Radford Ruether, a Christian theologian who saw hope for reforming traditional religions from within and could often be scornful toward new feminist religions. Interestingly, neither of these sides allowed room for women to live in a *nepantla* space between feminism and male-focused religions, yet as Gilkes shows us, many women did so.

Gilkes also wrote within the context of feminism's growing crisis over intersectionality. Though the term would not be coined until 1991, the idea that women's experience of gender was fundamentally shaped by other social factors such as race and class drove passionate feminist debates in the 1980s, as white feminists increasingly began to listen to the voices of feminists of color. Dominant both in publication and as the public face of feminism, many white, middle-class feminists in the 1970s and early 1980s attempted to rally women based on an assumption of shared oppression as women. Because they believed that all women experienced the same oppression on the basis of sex even if they also experienced other forms of oppression, such feminists designed the platform of this generation of feminism to focus on what they assumed were a set of shared goals. As they were to learn from women of color, third-world women and working-class white women, these assumptions were false. Likewise, the analyses offered by feminists such as Daly and Ruether in the 1970s and 1980s addressed women's roles in religion with little or no attention to the dynamics of race and class. Their debate had little relevance to the experiences of many women of color, a fact Gilkes pointedly refers to in her essays from this period.

Moving beyond the traditional-versus-newly-created debates in feminist religion, Gilkes offers a nuanced reading of women's roles in the Pentecostal-Holiness traditions, churches that have often been assumed to be misogynist and patriarchal. Their history itself, however, is far more complex. Churches in the Holiness traditions hold that the Holy Spirit can not only release humans from culpability for past sins but, through what is called a "second blessing," "sanctification," or "holiness," can also remove the human tendency to sin. Since sanctification does not vary by gender, both women and men (these churches do not recognize genders outside of this binary) equally become "Saints." As Gilkes points out, for African Americans suffering under grinding racism in the late nineteenth and early twentieth centuries, to be told that one has been perfected by God is a powerful experience —one even more powerful for African American women than for African American men because of the intersections of sexism and racism with which these women lived.

The Pentecostal movement that developed in part out of the late nineteenth-century Holiness movement also saw a great deal of gender and racial diversity. This movement focused on a belief that people today can experience the same "gifts of the Spirit," or charismatic gifts, that Jesus's apostles experienced after his death. These included *glossolalia* or the ability to "speak in tongues" (originally believed to be foreign languages, but now more commonly interpreted as the language of the angels or a private prayer language), the ability to prophesy, the ability to interpret prophecy, and the experience of being "slain in the Spirit," a trancelike state in which participants often report a sense of immense closeness to God. The first person in contemporary times to speak in tongues was a woman: Agnes Ozman, a student at Bethel Bible College in Topeka, Kansas, experienced glossolalia on January 1, 1901. When her teacher founded a college in Houston, Texas, an African American man named William Seymour began attending. Forced at first to sit outside and listen through the window because he was black, Seymour nonetheless took his lessons to heart. In 1906, an African American woman who had been a classmate of his invited Seymour to preach at her multiracial church in Los Angeles. The resulting eruption of charismatic gifts lasted for several years, and came to be known as the Azusa Street revival, after the location of the church where Seymour preached. Out of these revivals arose the Pentecostal movement, which interwove with the Holiness movement to such an extent that they are now often referred to as the Pentecostal-Holiness movement.

Like many new religions, the Pentecostal-Holiness movement was initially both gender- and racially-inclusive. Also like many new religions, as it grew and became more organized it lost some of that inclusiveness. Denominations formed in part around racial identity, such that Pentecostal-Holiness churches quickly became mostly white or mostly black (now, of course, there are other racial/ethnic groups involved in these traditions as well—most notably Latina/os). Despite the important roles played by women in the founding of the movement, many Pentecostal-Holiness churches also began to teach that women should not preach in the pulpit. On the surface, then, it would appear that this branch of Christianity falls outside of the feminist debate in which Gilkes intervened: neither an all-new, feminist religion nor a reformed, feminist version of old tradition, the Pentecostal-Holiness traditions would be rejected if not ignored by many feminists as simply oppressive to women.

Gilkes disagrees with this easy dismissal. Looking more deeply into the Pentecostal-Holiness churches, she finds not only denominations that allow and encourage women's pastoral leadership, but also myriad other ways in which women hold authority in this movement. As W.E.B. Du Bois noted that the black church offers services to the black community that racism prevents them from accessing elsewhere, so Gilkes notes the importance of Pentecostal-Holiness churches for black women specifically. Strict dress codes, for example, presented black women as upstanding and modest, contrary to white racist assumptions that black women were morally depraved and sexually ravenous. Women's leadership roles in the churches provided professional experience that was difficult to obtain elsewhere. And the churches placed a strong emphasis on education for both men and women. In all, Gilkes argues, to condemn this tradition within the black church as patriarchal and misogynist simply because women cannot preach in some denominations and are required to dress in certain ways is to miss completely the ways in which such churches combated both internalized and externalized forms of racism and sexism in black women's lives.

R. Marie Griffith: Submission as Liberation

Can we make the same argument for white women in contemporary evangelical churches? This is the question that religion scholar Marie Griffith asks (Griffith, 1997). During the mid-twentieth century, the "spirit-filled" churches became quite socially marginal, especially in white society. But one of the consequences of the focus on emotion and the rise of new religious movements in the 1960s counterculture was the re-popularization of the Christian gifts of the Spirit. Now spreading beyond the Pentecostal and Holiness churches, the charismatic gifts started what has come to be known as the evangelical or charismatic movement within Christianity. Evangelical churches now exist in many denominations and, although they tend strongly toward social conservatism, even include socially liberal churches and churches with a predominantly lesbian, gay, bisexual, and transgender congregation. Griffith, though, is interested in women's roles in the more socially conservative evangelical churches. When these churches were beginning to grow in the 1970s and 1980s, they did not allow women to preach from the pulpit or to teach men in any way. Even the women's organization Griffith studied, a Christian **parachurch organization** or non-affiliated group called Women's Aglow Fellowship, had male oversight. Conservative evangelical churches in the 1970s taught that a wife should submit to her husband in all things, even enduring emotional and physical abuse in order to stay true to God's commands. Though Griffith notes that the doctrine of female submission changed through the 1980s to become "mutual submission" of husband and wife to each other, the question of women's power and agency in this movement remains.

Griffith leaves the answer to this question somewhat ambiguous, but offers her readers the perspectives of Aglow members to consider. Importantly, the women Griffith studied repeatedly speak of submission—both to husbands and to God—as an experience of liberation and empowerment. This presents a similar dilemma for interpreters as the questions raised by Brown's study of social power in Vodou. To interpret people's experiences of empowerment as self-delusion or a kind of Marxist false consciousness is clearly too simple an explanation, and yet it is also difficult for non-evangelicals to accept that submission to another's power can be a form of liberation. How can we simultaneously take people's own experiences seriously and think about what those experiences mean for our understanding of religion and human agency? Anthropologist Saba Mahmood offers one way out of this dilemma.

Saba Mahmood

Mahmood's timely book, *Politics of Piety* (2005), was published when both Muslims and non-Muslims in Western countries had been barraged for four years with images of the "oppressed Muslim woman"—three words that seem to have been stuck together with Superglue in the twenty-first century West. Many non-Muslims exposed to these images came to wrongly identify the Muslim veil with the full cover of the *burqa* and to confuse governments that enforced dress codes with women who freely chose to cover themselves. Even Muslim women who wore the far more common *hijab* (headscarf) were often treated by non-Muslims in the United States and elsewhere in the West as downtrodden and controlled by their husbands and their religion. Indeed, many non-Muslim feminists have over the years condemned the entire religion of Islam as patriarchal and misogynist —conveniently ignoring the long tradition of women's rights activism within Muslim countries such as Egypt and Morocco.

A secular feminist who grew up within leftist activist circles in Pakistan, Mahmood began to ask why the powerful nationalist movements of the early and mid-twentieth century that had freed many predominantly Muslim societies from European colonization had developed into conservative Islamic states or at least had seen a rise in the popularity of conservative Islam. As she recounts in the preface to *Politics of Piety*, Mahmood and her fellow activists initially turned to Marxist and political explanations for the popularity of religion in these recently decolonized societies. Over time, though, Mahmood came to believe that these explanations were inadequate, and as a result she traveled to Egypt to study women's involvement in the Islamic Piety movement. Her work focused on the women's mosque movement, a loose grouping of women teachers (*dā'iyāt*) and their adult women students who met regularly in mosques to discuss Islamic doctrine.

Though the mosque movement is part of the larger, socially conservative Islamic revival movement in Egypt, and though the women in the mosque movement often espoused values that Western feminists would see as patriarchal and oppressive to women, Mahmood suggests a much more careful approach to the movement and its participants. Critically, rather than ask what Western feminist theory can bring to an understanding of the mosque movement, Mahmood asks what an understanding of the mosque movement can bring to Western feminist theory. She begins by dismantling the concept of *agency*, or the ability to act in one's own interest, reconstructing it as a multifaceted phenomenon evidenced in the lives of the women in the mosque movement. Next up for retooling is the by-now famous theory of gender performativity articulated by feminist theorist Judith Butler; Mahmood argues that although women's "virtuous actions" in the mosque movement appear to fit nicely within Butler's theory of performativity, such actions also add nuance to the theory and bring critical questions to bear on it. Finally, she turns to the dilemma that Griffith raises: how can we understand women's ability to survive and even happily thrive under restrictive and patriarchal conditions? By taking women's experiences seriously and conceptualizing agency as always constrained and shaped by social forces, Mahmood offers her readers an understanding of the lives of conservative Muslim women that not only complicates questions of oppression and resistance but also pushes secular feminist theories and politics to broaden their scope in order to be applicable to women's lives outside of the secular West.

Andrew K.T. Yip: Bringing the Self into the Sacred Text

One particularly striking finding that has emerged in the development of research on religion among lesbian, gay, and bisexual (LGB) people is the importance of individual interpretations of religion. Many who are not themselves both LGB and religious assume that these two identities cannot go together because, supposedly, traditional religions condemn same-sex eroticism. However, many LGB Jews, Christians, Muslims, Buddhists, Hindus, and members of other religions would beg to differ, and in fact prominent branches of Judaism, Christianity, and Buddhism are openly welcoming of LGB people. In the case of religious groups that do make clear their opposition to same-sex eroticism, then, the question becomes not whether LGB people can be involved in such a religion (they can, and are), but how they manage what would seem to be a significant case of **cognitive dissonance**—a clash between two central aspects of one's self-concept.

One answer to this question is that sometimes the cognitive dissonance fails to emerge at all, or emerges only briefly. My favorite example in this case is a participant in a study I conducted in the late 1990s. Raised by missionaries with the Fundamentalist Churches of America, this man would seem to be the perfect candidate for strong homophobia and biphobia. However, one day when he was in his early twenties, he prayed to God to help him to know himself better. God answered his prayer with the revelation that this young man was gay. In response, he went through his concordance (a kind of index to the Bible) seeking texts on homosexuality. Upon reading all of the passages (seven of them, by most people's count), he concluded that they weren't a big deal, and went on with his life as a gay, conservative Christian.

In other cases, a sense of cognitive dissonance does develop, and religious LGB people often initially address it in one of two ways: by rejecting the LGB identity or by rejecting the religious identity. Over time, though, some people come to reconcile these two identities—so how do they do it? This is where individual interpretations of religion come in. Although it is nothing new for people to have their own, unique relationships to their religious traditions, it would appear that there has been a rise in this phenomenon in Western countries beginning in the 1960s. As a result, people are more willing to do what sociologist Lynn Resnick Dufour (2000) has called "sifting through tradition": filtering their religious traditions through their own values and beliefs. Thus, some LGB people in traditional religions come to the conclusion that their sexual orientation is no barrier to their participation in the religion.

While people may resolve the tension between their sexual and religious identities by themselves, what remains for many is the problem of how to explain this resolution through the lens of the tradition—especially when the tradition interprets certain sacred stories or texts as condemning same-sex eroticism. By using in-depth interviews with research participants, sociologist Andrew K.T. Yip explored how LGB Christians and Muslims in the United Kingdom solve this problem. His findings, which relate closely to studies of LGB Christians, Jews, and Muslims in the United States, France, and Canada as well as to the work of LGB theologians, indicate three strategies that can be utilized individually or in tandem with regard to religious texts that may condemn same-sex eroticism. Participants challenged the authority of the text itself by questioning its authenticity, its transmission, or its origin. They challenged the authority of interpreters who claim that the text opposes same-sex eroticism, and they interpreted the text through their own experience. By thus creating a sacred text that not only does not condemn but actually welcomes or even includes LGB people, the participants in Yip's study created space for themselves in a religion in which they strongly felt they belonged.

Noach Dzmura: Reading Transgender People in Jewish Tradition

Despite the growth of research on sexual orientation and religion, gender history and gender identity have received short shrift in the social scientific study of religion. The final selection in this chapter, then, provides a transgender-focused example of the strategies Yip and others have seen among lesbian, gay, and bisexual members of traditional religions. The term "transgender," as it is used here, refers to a wide range of people (see Valentine, 2007): those who cross-dress for pleasure but do not identify solely with a different gender from the one they were assigned at birth; those who do disidentify with their socially assigned gender, whether through considering themselves "genderqueer" (gendered outside of the binary) or a member of the gender "opposite" to their birth sex; and those who, through some combination of hormone treatment or surgery, have altered their primary and secondary sexual characteristics and often consider themselves transsexual or formerly transgender.

Noach Dzmura, an essayist and transgender activist who holds an advanced degree in Jewish Studies, focuses his re-reading on a text drawn from the body of Jewish writing known as the Talmud. This vast collection of writings by early rabbis contains both legal and Biblical commentary, and is the source to which many Jews turn (either directly or through their rabbis) for clarification of the Biblical text. Though there is little mention in either the Hebrew Bible or the Talmud of people we might today consider transgender, one brief Biblical passage (Deuteronomy 22:5) forbids a woman to wear a man's garment and vice versa. Jewish tradition also forbids bodily alterations, and the rabbis raise questions about the status of a man with damaged testicles (but they neither state nor deny that such a being might be another sex or gender). Thus, within Jewish tradition there is little for transgender people to work with, and what is there is mostly either ambiguous or unsupportive. Transgender people within the more liberal branches of Judaism draw on their denominations' modernizing approach to tradition, challenging the text (as Yip notes for LGB Christians and Muslims) by questioning its contemporary relevance. Dzmura, however, takes Yip's third approach: he reads himself and other transgender and intersex people into the text through his translation of and commentary on a Talmudic passage on the "hermaphrodite"—people who today would term themselves "intersex."

Conclusions: Powerful and Malleable

Is religion an opiate? It can be, but it is also many, many other things. As I mentioned at the beginning of this essay, we can think of religion as being both very malleable and a very powerful source of human inspiration and action. At times religion soothes the pain of oppression, and that function can at times serve to prevent revolution. But Marx, working as we all do within a limited historical and geographic context, had a very limited view of religion based primarily on the state churches of Germany and England. Gramsci's vision of the weak potential of proletarian religion also reflected his limited exposure to religion, but his acknowledgment of something other than the Vatican's Roman Catholicism demonstrates the nuance that enters the study of religion and social power when one begins to take a lived religion approach to one's studies. Indeed, Du Bois demonstrates exactly this nuance as he considers the roles of black religion in the United States—both oppressor and liberator, depending on what group held control over the interpretation of the religion. Among these four authors, however, it is Lincoln's widely comparative approach that, perhaps appropriately, demonstrates in detail the force and malleability of religion in its relationship to social power.

The readings that follow add detail to these theories, as well as providing an increasingly complex picture. Even for Du Bois and Lincoln, there is still a clear, binary opposition between religion supporting the status quo and religion promoting revolution. Medina, Brown, and Mahmood all question that binary. Beginning with Medina's invocation of *nepantla* and *mestizaje*, continuing on through Brown's description of the powers of Vodou, and culminating in Mahmood's challenge to Western feminist concepts of agency, this middle group of readings stresses the ways in which religion, too, is part of intersectionality, an aspect of people's lives that interacts with social power in complex and sometimes surprising ways. The final two readings by Yip and Dzmura demonstrate in detail a few of the ways in which the relationship between religion and social power can work. Though these last articles return us, to a certain extent, to the individualist concept of agency that Mahmood criticizes, it is important not to forget that even here we see those individuals interacting with, and thus centrally shaped by, a religious tradition. What would it mean to approach the study of religion in LGBT communities with Mahmood's critical attitude toward individualist agency? It would mean, I think, an even greater attention to the roles played by societies and traditions as well as a careful approach to the roles of individualism in creating, maintaining, and negotiating LGBT and religious identities themselves. As you peruse the readings in this section, consider what your own understanding is of the relationship between religion and social power. How does your exposure to religion, along with your geographic, historical, and social context, shape your theories?

Extended Application

Marx and Gramsci both saw in institutionalized Christianity a potent source of oppression of the poor. Even though Gramsci believed that religion held seeds of liberatory potential, it was specifically the religion of laypeople and not that of religious institutions that he had in mind. Yet a young Roman Catholic priest from South America offered a different perspective and started a groundswell among Christian intellectuals, and eventually those of other religions as well, with his development of the school of thought known as **liberation theology**.

A Peruvian of both Spanish and indigenous descent, Father Gustavo Gutiérrez was extensively educated in South America and in Europe in the mid-twentieth century. He was involved with Catholic social action in his youth in the 1930s and 1940s, and brought that perspective as well as his own background into his theological studies. Gutiérrez argued that the Roman Catholic Church had its priorities wrong, and that God maintains what Gutiérrez called "a preferential option for the poor": that is to say, God's representatives on earth to pay special attention to the poor rather than lavishing attention on the wealthy, as Gutiérrez had seen many representatives of the Roman Catholic Church do. If God has a preferential option for the poor, Gutiérrez argued, then priests should be flocking to poverty-stricken areas and working to fill the needs they encounter there. They should be helping to organize the poor and striving for economic justice, even if that meant resisting those in power who contribute generously to the Church. Gutiérrez, and those who followed in his footsteps, began to work in poor areas of South and Central America to create *comunidades de base*, or "base communities." Using their understanding of Christianity, they began to politically mobilize the poor.

While Marx would hardly have predicted the success of Gutiérrez's ideas, he would indeed have expected that liberation theology would not sit well with the upper echelons of the Roman Catholic Church. While enthusiasts, including many vowed religious (priests, monks, and nuns) as well as lay theologians, began to hold conferences on liberation theology in South America, the Church hierarchy responded with suspicion and often outright hostility. The movement remains influential, however, and in addition Gutiérrez's work has sparked several other important theological developments both within and beyond Christianity.

One particularly important theologian influenced by liberation theology is James Cone. The author in 1969 of *Black Theology and Black Power*, Cone was the first to link liberation theology to struggles for racial justice. Responding to Malcolm X's challenge that blacks in the United States were worshipping a white Jesus and a white God, Cone set out to think about how the radical ideals[1] of the Black Power movement might be applied to Christianity. In so doing, he was challenging accepted activist ideas (as well as established Christian ones) as much as Gutiérrez had done. Where Gutiérrez challenged traditional Marxist thought by bringing Christianity to bear on economic justice, Cone challenged the Black Power movement by bringing Christianity to bear on racial justice. Because they were convinced that Christianity had become the religion of whites in general and white racists in particular, many in the Black Power movement advocated the complete departure of blacks from that religion. Though the Civil Rights movement, under the leadership of Martin Luther King, was deeply linked to Christianity, the Black Power movement had stronger allegiances to the Nation of Islam, when it had religious allegiances at all. In bringing together the radicalism of Black Power with the social justice focus of liberation theology, Cone pioneered a new theological approach—black theology, or black liberation theology—that is still widely influential today.

Like the split between the Black Power and Civil Rights movements, the second-wave feminist movement of the 1960s, 1970s, and 1980s was also split between liberal and radical branches. Both developed theological approaches; as in the split between the Black Civil Rights and Black Power movements, Christianity was best represented in the liberal branch of feminism. Yet, the perspectives of liberation theology wove both through feminist Christian and feminist Jewish theology, as well as through what many radical feminists came to call "thealogy." In this case, God had a preferential option not specifically for the poor, but for women, who were not represented in the traditional divine imaginings of Christianity and Judaism.

Liberal and radical feminists, reformers and revolutionaries alike, had no quarrel over the status of women in traditional Christianity or Judaism. To paraphrase Marx (who, indeed, was quite influential in much of feminism), feminists saw traditional religion as the opiate of women, promising them future rewards for accepting their oppression and soothing the pain of sexism so that they refrained from revolting. And some feminists left the analysis there: religion was a carrier of women's oppression, and feminists should have nothing more to do with it. Others, though, saw revolutionary as well as repressive potential in religion. Some chose to reclaim feminine imagery of the traditional deity in Judaism and Christianity, representing God as multi-gendered, non-gendered, or distinctly feminine. Others, seeing in traditional religions a pattern of sexism that they thought was too engrained to break, explored the feminine divine—goddesses, mostly—in religions outside the **Abrahamic** traditions of Judaism, Christianity, and Islam. Some of these "thealogians" ("thea" means "goddess" in Greek) explored contemporary religions such as Hinduism, the neopagan movement, or indigenous North American or African traditions, while others delved into European and Middle Eastern history for their visions of the feminine divine. As feminism moved into its third wave in the 1990s and into the twenty-first century, feminist theology has developed and changed like all schools of thought, remaining a vibrant approach to the question of religion, oppression, and resistance.

Out of the early feminist explorations, and influenced as well by the work of Cone and other black theologians, came the rise of womanist theology. This approach to thinking about the divine also has both Christian and non-Christian advocates, as well as those who blend the two approaches. It was shaped most fundamentally by the work of novelist and essayist Alice Walker, who in 1984 published a definition of the term "womanist." Though it is too long to reproduce here, Walker's definition crystallized what many women of color had been feeling about the feminist movement: it was on the right track, but something was missing. The feminism that was being published and generally represented in the public sphere at the time had little to no analysis of racial or economic justice. It didn't take into account the fact that some women also experienced oppression in these other ways, and that oppression was fundamentally tied to their experiences of sexism. Womanist theology undertook to add that analysis, present since the early days of feminism but absent from the movement's public face, back into the picture. Both it and *mujerista* theology, which developed from a combination of womanist, feminist, and liberation theologies, took their theological explorations back to the people in much the way that Gutiérrez did. Asking what women of color already thought about the sacred, asking what they needed from a theologian, brought theology again out of the intellectual clouds in which it can travel, and grounded it in the lives of laypeople.

A final branch of theological inquiry and production that was influenced by these movements is gay and lesbian theology, which later came to encompass bisexual and transgender theology and eventually developed a new branch, blended with the school of thought known as queer theory, called queer theology. Gay and lesbian theologians of the 1960s and 1970s were impressed by the work of liberation theology, black theology, and feminist theology; in fact, lesbians were some of the most prominent feminist theologians and thealogians. As with other theologians whose work developed from liberation theology, lesbian, gay, bisexual, and transgender (LGBT) theologians and thealogians argue that the divine has a special concern for oppression: in this case, oppression on the basis of sexual and gender identity. Working within and outside of Christianity and Judaism, and eventually branching along with feminist theology into other religions as well, LGBT and queer theologies explore the experiences of LGBT and queer-identified people with the sacred as well as the religious implications of what we might call the divine "preferential option for the queer."

More than any other descendant of liberation theology, at least when taken as a group, LGBT thea/ologians tell of their own struggles to see their worth through the eyes of the divine. So, for all of these groups—the poor, people of color, women, LGBTQ people, and all of those who occupy more than one of these subject positions—religion remains a potent source of oppression. It has been amply proven, however, also to be a potent source of resistance. Opiate and liberator both, religion continues to demonstrate complexity far beyond what is encompassed by any single theory of its function.

Exercises

1. Explore a religion you're familiar with, either through your own experience or that of family or friends. What resources does it have for resistance? What potential does it have for oppression? Does it have a history of use for oppression and/or resistance?
2. Design a hypothetical religion from the ground up. Can you make one with no potential for oppression, or no potential for resistance? What do your findings tell you about religion?

Note

1. I use the term "radical" here to refer to movements desiring wholesale social change, as opposed to "liberal" movements that work within the existing system to create change. "Radical" as I use it does not mean "extremist."

14

Introduction to the Contribution to the Critique of Hegel's Philosophy of Law

Karl Marx

The following passage is the opening statement of this early (1844) work, which concludes with the identification of the proletariat as the only agent that can carry out the revolutionary transformation of society Marx is calling for.

FOR GERMANY THE *criticism of religion* is in the main complete, and criticism of religion is the premise of all criticism.

The *profane* existence of error is discredited after its *heavenly oratio pro aris et focis* has been disproved. Man, who looked for a superhuman being in the fantastic reality of heaven and found nothing there but the *reflection* of himself, will no longer be disposed to find but the *semblance* of himself, only an inhuman being, where he seeks and must seek his true reality.

The basis of irreligious criticism is: *Man makes religion*, religion does not make man. Religion is the self-consciousness and self-esteem of man who has either not yet found himself or has already lost himself again. But *man* is no abstract being encamped outside the world. Man is *the world of man*, the state, society. This state, this society, produce religion, an *inverted world-consciousness*, because they are an *inverted world*. Religion is the general theory of that world, its encyclopaedic compendium, its logic in a popular form, its spiritualistic *point d'honneur*, its enthusiasm, its moral sanction, its solemn complement, its universal source of consolation and justification. It is the

fantastic realisation of the human essence because the *human essence* has no true reality. The struggle against religion is therefore indirectly a fight against *the world* of which religion is the spiritual *aroma*.

Religious distress is at the same time the *expression* of real distress and also the *protest* against real distress. Religion is the sigh of the oppressed creature, the heart of a heartless world, just as it is the spirit of spiritless conditions. It is the *opium* of the people.

To abolish religion as the *illusory* happiness of the people is to demand their *real* happiness. The demand to give up illusions about the existing state of affairs is the *demand to give up a state of affairs which needs illusions*. The criticism of religion is therefore *in embryo the criticism of the vale of tears*, the *halo* of which is religion.

Criticism has torn up the imaginary flowers from the chain not so that man shall wear the unadorned, bleak chain but so that he will shake off the chain and pluck the living flower. The criticism of religion disillusions man to make him think and act and shape his reality like a man who has been disillusioned and has come to reason, so that he will revolve round himself and therefore round his true sun. Religion is only the illusory sun which revolves round man as long as he does not revolve round himself.

The *task of history*, therefore, once the *world beyond the truth* has disappeared, is to establish the *truth of this world*. The immediate *task of philosophy*, which is at the service of history, once the *holy form* of human self-estrangement has been unmasked, is to unmask self-estrangement in its *unholy forms*. Thus the criticism of heaven turns into the criticism of the earth, the *criticism of religion* into the *criticism of law* and the *criticism of theology* into the *criticism of politics*.

15

"Of Our Spiritual Strivings" and "Of the Faith of the Fathers"

W.E.B. Du Bois

OF OUR SPIRITUAL STRIVINGS

O water, voice of my heart, crying in the sand,
All night long crying with a mournful cry,
As I lie and listen, and cannot understand
The voice of my heart in my side or the voice of
   the sea,
O water, crying for rest, Is it I, is it I?
All night long the water is crying to me.

Unresting water, there shall never be rest
Till the last moon droop, and the last tide fail,
And the fire of the end begin to burn in the
   west;
And the heart shall be weary and wonder and cry
   like the sea,
All life long crying without avail.
As the water all night long Is crying to me.

ARTHUR SYMONS.

Between me and the other world there is ever an unasked question: unasked by some through feelings of delicacy; by others through the difficulty of rightly framing it. All, nevertheless, flutter round it. They approach me in a half-hesitant sort of way, eye me curiously or compassionately, and then, instead of saying directly. How does it feel to be a problem? they say, I know an excellent colored man in my town; or, I fought at Mechaniecsville; or, Do not these Southern outrages make your blood boil? At these I smile, or am interested, or reduce the boiling to a simmer, as the occasion may require. To the real question, How does it feel to be a problem? I answer seldom a word.

And yet, being a problem is a strange experience,—peculiar even for one who has never been anything else, save perhaps in babyhood and in Europe. It is in the early days of rollicking boyhood that the revelation first bursts upon one, all in a day, as it were. I remember well when the shadow swept across me. I was a little thing, away up in the hills of New England, where the dark Housatonic winds between Hoosac and Taghkanic to the sea. In a wee wooden schoolhouse, something put it into the boys' and girls' heads to buy gorgeous visiting-cards—ten cents a package—and exchange. The exchange was merry, till one-girl, a tall newcomer, refused my card,—refused it peremptorily, with a glance. Then it dawned upon me with a certain suddenness that I was different from the others; or like, mayhap, in heart and life and longing, but shut out from their world by a vast veil. I had thereafter no desire to tear down that veil, to creep through, I held all beyond it in common contempt, and lived above it in a region of blue sky and great wandering shadows. That sky was bluest when I could beat my mates at examination-time, or beat them at a foot-race, or even beat their stringy heads. Alas, with the years all this fine contempt began to fade; for the words I longed for, and all their dazzling opportunities, were theirs, not mine. But they should not keep these prizes, I said; some, all, I would wrest from them. Just how I would do it I could never decide: by reading law, by healing the sick, by telling the wonderful tales that swam in my head,—some way. With other black boys the strife was not so fiercely sunny: their youth shrunk into tasteless sycophancy, or into silent hatred of the pale world about them and mocking distrust of everything white; or wasted itself in a bitter cry, Why did God make me an outcast and a stranger in mine own house? The shades of the prison-house closed round about us all: walls strait and stubborn to the whitest, but relentlessly narrow, tall, and unscalable to sons of night who must plod darkly on in resignation, or beat unavailing palms against the stone, or steadily, half hopelessly, watch the streak of blue above.

After the Egyptian and Indian, the Greek and Roman, the Teuton and Mongolian, the Negro is a sort of seventh son, born with a veil, and gifted with second-sight in this American world,—a world which yields him no true self-consciousness, but only lets him see himself through the revelation of the other world. It is a peculiar sensation, this double-consciousness, this sense of always looking at one's self through the eyes of others, of measuring one's soul by the tape of a world that looks on in amused contempt and pity. One ever feels his twoness,—an American, a Negro; two souls, two thoughts, two unreconciled strivings; two warring ideals in one dark body, whose dogged strength alone keeps it from being torn asunder.

The history of the American Negro is the history of this strife,—this longing to attain self-conscious manhood, to merge his double self into a better and truer self. In this merging he wishes neither of the older selves to be lost He would not Africanize America, for America has too much to teach the world and Africa. He would not bleach his Negro soul in a flood of white Americanism, for he knows that Negro blood has a message for the world. He simply wishes to make it possible for a man to be both a Negro and an American, without being cursed and spit upon by his fellows, without having the doors of Opportunity closed roughly in his face.

This, then, is the end of his striving: to be a co-worker in the kingdom of culture, to escape both death and isolation, to husband and use his best powers and his latent genius. These powers of body and mind have in the past been strangely wasted, dispersed, or forgotten. The shadow of a mighty Negro past flits through the tale of Ethiopia the Shadowy and of Egypt the Sphinx. Through history, the powers of single black men flash here and there like falling stars, and die sometimes before the world has rightly gauged their brightness. Here in America, in the few days since Emancipation, the black man's turning hither and thither in hesitant and doubtful striving has often made his very strength to lose effectiveness, to seem like absence of power, like weakness. And yet it is not weakness,—it is the contradiction of double aims. The double-aimed struggle of the blade artisan—on the one hand to escape white contempt for a nation of mere hewers of wood and drawers of water, and on the other hand to plough and nail and dig for a poverty-stricken horde—could only result in making him a poor craftsman, for he had but half a heart in either cause. By the poverty and ignorance of his people, the Negro minister or doctor was tempted toward quackery and demagogy; and by the criticism of the other world, toward ideals that made him ashamed of his lowly tasks. The would-be black *savant* was confronted by the paradox that the knowledge his people needed was a twice-told tale to his white neighbors, while the knowledge which would teach the white world was Greek to his own flesh and blood. The innate love of harmony and beauty that set the ruder souls of his people a-dancing and a-singing raised but confusion and doubt in the soul of the black artist; for the beauty revealed to him was the soul-beauty of a race which his larger audience despised, and he could not articulate the message of another people. This waste of double aims, this seeking to satisfy two unreconciled ideals, has wrought sad havoc with the courage and faith and deeds of ten thousand thousand people,—has sent them often wooing false gods and invoking false means of salvation, and at times has even seemed about to make them ashamed of themselves.

Away back in the days of bondage they thought to see in one divine event the end of all doubt and disappointment; few men ever worshipped Freedom with half such unquestioning faith as did the American Negro for two centuries. To him, so far as he thought and dreamed, slavery was indeed the sum of all villainies, the cause of all sorrow, the root of all prejudice; Emancipation was the key to a promised land of sweeter beauty than ever stretched before the eyes of wearied Israelites. In song and exhortation swelled one refrain—Liberty; in his tears and curses the God he implored had Freedom in his right hand. At last it came,—suddenly, fearfully, like a dream. With one wild carnival of blood and passion came the message in his own plaintive cadences:—

"Shout, O children!
Shout, you're free!
For God has bought your liberty!"

Years have passed away since then,—ten, twenty, forty; forty years of national life, forty years of renewal and development, and yet the swarthy spectre sits in its accustomed seat at the Nation's feast. In vain do we cry to this our vastest social problem:—

"Take any shape but that, and my firm nerves
Shall never tremble!"

The Nation has not yet found peace from its sins; the freedman has not yet found in freedom his promised land. Whatever of good may have come

in these years of change, the shadow of a deep disappointment rests upon the Negro people,—a disappointment all the more bitter because the unattained ideal was unbounded save by the simple ignorance of a lowly people.

The first decade was merely a prolongation of the vain search for freedom, the boon that seemed ever barely to elude their grasp,—like a tantalizing will-o'-the-wisp, maddening and misleading the headless host. The holocaust of war, the terrors of the Ku-Klux Klan, the lies of carpet-baggers, the disorganization of industry, and the contradictory advice of friends and foes, left the bewildered serf with no new watchword beyond the old cry for freedom. As the time flew, however, he began to grasp a new idea. The ideal of liberty demanded for its attainment powerful means, and these the Fifteenth Amendment gave him. The ballot, which before he had looked upon as a visible sign of freedom, he now regarded as the chief means of gaining and perfecting the liberty with which war had partially endowed him. And why not? Had not votes made war and emancipated millions? Had not votes enfranchised the freedmen? Was anything impossible to a power that had done all this? A million black men started with renewed zeal to vote themselves into the kingdom. So the decade flew away, the revolution of 1876 came, and left the half-free serf weary, wondering, but still inspired. Slowly but steadily, in the following years, a new vision began gradually to replace the dream of political power,—a powerful movement, the rise of another ideal to guide the unguided, another pillar of fire by night after a clouded day. It was the ideal of "book-learning"; the curiosity, born of compulsory ignorance, to know and test the power of the cabalistic letters of the white man, the longing to know. Here at last seemed to have been discovered the mountain path to Canaan; longer than the highway of Emancipation and law, steep and rugged, but straight, leading to heights high enough to overlook life.

Up the new path the advance guard toiled, slowly, heavily, doggedly; only those who have watched and guided the faltering feet, the misty minds, the dull understandings, of the dark pupils of these schools know how faithfully, how piteously, this people strove to learn. It was weary work. The cold statistician wrote down the inches of progress here and there, noted also where here and there a foot had slipped or some one had fallen. To the tired climbers, the horizon was ever dark, the mists were often cold, the Canaan was always dim and far away. If, however, the vistas disclosed as yet no goal, no resting-place, little but flattery and criticism, the journey at least gave leisure for reflection and self-examination; it changed the child of Emancipation to the youth with dawning self-consciousness, self-realization, self-respect. In those sombre forests of his striving his own soul rose before him, and he saw himself,—darkly as through a veil; and yet he saw in himself some faint revelation of his power, of his mission. He began to have a dim feeling that, to attain his place in the world, he must be himself, and not another. For the first time he sought to analyze the burden he bore upon his back, that dead-weight of social degradation partially masked behind a half-named Negro problem. He felt his poverty; without a cent, without a home, without land, tools, or savings, he had entered into competition with rich, landed, skilled neighbors. To be a poor man is hard, but to be a poor race in a land of dollars is the very bottom of hardships. He felt the weight of his ignorance,—not simply of letters, but of life, of business, of the humanities; the accumulated sloth and shirking and awkwardness of decades and centuries shackled his hands and feet. Nor was his burden all poverty and ignorance. The red stain of bastardy, which two centuries of systematic legal defilement of Negro women had stamped upon his race, meant not only the loss of ancient African chastity, but also the hereditary weight of a mass of corruption from white adulterers, threatening almost the obliteration of the Negro home.

A people thus handicapped ought not to be asked to race with the world, but rather allowed to give all its time and thought to its own social problems. But alas! while sociologists gleefully count his bastards and his prostitutes, the very soul of the toiling, sweating black man is darkened by the shadow of a vast despair. Men call the shadow prejudice, and learnedly explain it as the natural defence of culture against barbarism, learning against ignorance, purity against crime, the "higher" against the "lower" races. To which the Negro cries Amen! and swears that to so much of this strange prejudice as is founded on just homage to civilization, culture, righteousness, and progress, he humbly bows and meekly does obeisance. But before that nameless prejudice, that leaps beyond, all this he stands helpless, dismayed, and well-nigh speechless; before that personal disrespect and mockery, the ridicule and systematic humiliation, the distortion of fact and wanton license of fancy, the cynical ignoring of the better and the boisterous welcoming of the worse, the all-pervading desire to inculcate disdain for everything black, from Toussaint to the devil,—before this there rises a sickening despair that would disarm and discourage any nation, save that black host to whom "discouragement" is an unwritten word.

But the facing of so vast a prejudice could not but bring the inevitable self-questioning, self-disparagement, and lowering of ideals which ever accompany repression and breed in an atmosphere of contempt and hate. Whisperings and portents came borne upon the four winds: Lo! we are diseased and dying, cried the dark hosts; we cannot write, our voting is vain; what need of education, since we must always cook and serve? And the Nation echoed and enforced this self-criticism, saying: Be content to be servants, and nothing more; what need of higher culture for half-men? Away with the black man's ballot, by force or fraud,—and behold the suicide of a race! Nevertheless, out of the evil came something of good,—the more careful adjustment of education to real life, the clearer perception of the Negroes' social responsibilities, and the sobering realization of the meaning of progress.

So dawned the time of *Sturm und Drang*: storm and stress to-day rocks our little boat on the mad waters of the world-sea; there is within and without the sound of conflict, the burning of body and rending of soul; inspiration strives with doubt, and faith with vain questionings. The bright ideals of the past,—physical freedom, political power, the training of brains and the training of hands,—all these in turn have waxed and waned, until even the last grows dim and overcast. Are they all wrong,—all false? No, not that, but each alone was over-simple and incomplete,—the dreams of a credulous race-childhood, or the fond imaginings of the other world which does not know and does not want to know our power. To be really true, all these ideals must be melted and welded into one. The training of the schools we need to-day more than ever,—the training of deft hands, quick eyes and ears, and above all the broader, deeper, higher culture of gifted minds and pure hearts. The power of the ballot we need in sheer self-defence,—else what shall save us from a second slavery? Freedom, too, the long sought, we still seek,—the freedom of life and limb, the freedom to work and think, the freedom to love and aspire. Work, culture, liberty,—all these we need, not singly but together, not successively but together, each growing and aiding each, and all striving toward that vaster ideal that swims before the Negro people, the ideal of human brotherhood, gained through the unifying ideal of Race; the ideal of fostering and developing the traits and talents of the Negro, not in opposition to or contempt for other races, but rather in large conformity to the greater ideals of the American Republic, in order that some day on American soil two world-races may give each to each those characteristics both so sadly lack. We the darker ones come even now not altogether empty-handed: there are to-day no truer exponents of the pure human spirit of the Declaration of Independence than the American Negroes; there is no .true American music but the wild sweet melodies of the Negro slave; the American fairy tales and folklore are Indian and African; and, all in all, we black men seem the sole oasis of simple faith and reverence in a dusty desert of dollars, and smartness. Will America be poorer if she replace her brutal dyspeptic blundering with light-hearted but determined Negro humility? or her coarse and cruel wit with loving jovial good-humor? or her vulgar music with the soul of the Sorrow Songs?

Merely a concrete test of the underlying principles of the great republic is the Negro Problem, and the spiritual striving of the freedmen's sons is the travail of souls whose burden is almost beyond the measure of their strength, but who bear it in the name of an historic race, in the name of this the land of their fathers' fathers, and in the name of human opportunity.

And now what I have briefly sketched in large outline let me on coming pages tell again in many ways, with loving emphasis and deeper detail, that men may listen to the striving in the souls of black folk.

OF THE FAITH OF THE FATHERS

Dim face of Beauty haunting all the world,
Fair face of Beauty all too fair to see,
Where the lost stars adown the heavens are
    hurled,—
There, there alone for thee
May white peace be.

Beauty, sad face of Beauty, Mystery, Wonder,
What are these dreams to foolish babbling men
Who cry with little noises 'neath the thunder
Of Ages ground to sand,
To a little sand.

FIONA MACLEOD

It was out in the country, far from home, far from my foster home, on a dark Sunday night. The road wandered from our rambling log-house up the stony bed of a creek, past wheat and corn, until we could hear dimly across the fields a rhythmic cadence of song,—soft, thrilling, powerful, that swelled and died sorrowfully in our ears. I was a country school-teacher then, fresh from the East, and had never seen a Southern Negro revival. To be sure, we in Berkshire were not perhaps as stiff and formal as they in Suffolk of olden time; yet we were very quiet and subdued, and I know not what would have happened those clear Sabbath mornings had some one punctuated the sermon with a wild scream, or interrupted the long prayer with a loud Amen! And so most striking to me, as I approached the village and the little plain church perched aloft, was the air of intense excitement that possessed that mass of black folk. A sort of suppressed terror hung in the air and seemed to seize us, —a pythian madness, a demoniac possession, that lent terrible reality to song and word. The black and massive form of the preacher swayed and quivered as the words crowded to his lips and flew at us in singular eloquence. The people moaned and fluttered, and then the gaunt-cheeked brown woman beside me suddenly leaped straight into the air and shrieked like a lost soul, while round about came wail and groan and outcry, and a scene of human passion such as I had never conceived before.

Those who have not thus witnessed the frenzy of a Negro revival in the untouched backwoods of the South can but dimly realize the religious feeling of the slave; as described, such scenes appear grotesque: and funny, but as seen they are awful. Three things characterized this religion of the slave,—the Preacher, the Music, and the Frenzy. The Preacher is the most unique personality developed by the Negro on American soil. A leader, a politician, an orator, a "boss," an intriguer, an idealist,— all these he is, and ever, too, the centre of a group of men, now twenty, now a thousand in number. The combination of a certain adroitness with deep-seated earnestness, of tact with consummate ability,

gave him his preëminence, and helps maintain it. The type, of course, varies according to time and place, from the West Indies in the sixteenth century to New England in the nine-teenth, and from the Mississippi bottoms to cities like New Orleans or New York.

The Music of Negro religion is that plaintive rhythmic melody, with its touching minor cadences, which, despite caricature and defilement, still remains the most original and beautiful expression of human life and longing yet born on American soil. Sprung from the African forests, where its counterpart can still be heard, it was adapted, changed, and intensified by the tragic soul-life of the slave, until, under the stress of law and whip, it became the one true expression of a people's sorrow, despair, and hope.

Finally the Frenzy of "Shouting," when the Spirit of the Lord passed by, and, seizing the devotee, made him mad with supernatural joy, was the last essential of Negro religion and the one more devoutly believed in than all the rest. It varied in expression from the silent rapt countenance or the low murmur and moan to the mad abandon of physical fervor,—the stamping, shrieking, and shouting, the rushing to and fro and wild waving of arms, the weeping and laughing, the vision and the trance. All this is nothing new in the world, but old as religion, as Delphi and Endor. And so firm a hold did it have on the Negro, that many generations firmly believed that without this visible manifestation of the God there could be no true communion with the Invisible.

These were the characteristics of Negro religious life as developed up to the time of Emancipation. Since under the peculiar circumstances of the black man's environment they were the one expression of his higher life, they are of deep interest to the student of his development, both socially and psychologically. Numerous are the attractive lines of inquiry that here group themselves. What did slavery mean to the African savage? What was his attitude toward the World and Life?

What seemed to him good and evil,—God and Devil? Whither went his longings and strivings, and wherefore were his heart-burnings and disappointments? Answers to such questions can come only from a study of Negro religion as a development, through its gradual changes from the heathenism of the Gold Coast to the institutional Negro church of Chicago.

Moreover, the religious growth of millions of men, even though they be slaves, cannot be without potent influence upon their contemporaries. The Methodists and Baptists of America owe much of their condition to the silent but potent influence of their millions of Negro converts. Especially is this noticeable in the South, where theology and religious philosophy are on this account a long way behind the North, and where the religion of the poor whites is a plain copy of Negro thought and methods. The mass of "gospel" hymns which has swept through American churches and well-nigh ruined our sense of song consists largely of debased imitations of Negro melodies made by ears that caught the jingle but not the music, the body but not the soul, of the Jubilee songs. It is thus clear that the study of Negro religion is not only a vital part of the history of the Negro in America, but an interesting part of American history.

The Negro church of to-day is the social centre of Negro life in the United States, and the most characteristic expression of African character. Take a typical church in a small Virginia town: it is the "First Baptist"—a roomy brick edifice seating five hundred or more persons, tastefully finished in Georgia pine, with a carpet, a small organ, and stained-glass windows. Underneath is a large assembly room with benches. This building is the central club-house of a community of a thousand or more Negroes. Various organizations meet here,— the church proper, the Sunday-school, two or three insurance societies, women's societies, secret societies, and mass meetings of various kinds. Entertainments, suppers, and lectures are held beside the five or six regular weekly religious services; Considerable sums of money are collected and expended here, employment is found for the idle, strangers are introduced, news is disseminated and charity distributed. At the same time this social, intellectual, and economic centre is a religious centre of great power. Depravity, Sin, Redemption, Heaven, Hell, and Damnation are preached twice a Sunday after the crops are laid by; and few indeed of the community have the hardihood to withstand conversion. Back of this more formal religion, the Church often stands as a real conserver of morals, a strengthener of family life, and the final authority on what is Good and Right.

Thus one can see in the Negro church to-day, reproduced in microcosm, all the great world from, which the Negro is cut off by color-prejudice and social condition. In the great city churches the same tendency is noticeable and in many respects emphasized. A great church like the Bethel of Philadelphia, has over eleven hundred members, an edifice seating fifteen hundred persons and valued at one hundred thousand dollars, an annual budget of five thousand dollars, and a government consisting of a pastor with several assisting local preachers, an executive and legislative board, financial boards and tax collectors; general church meetings for making laws; sub-divided groups led by class leaders, a company of militia, and twenty-four auxiliary societies. The activity of a church like this is immense and far-reaching, and the bishops who preside over these organizations throughout the land are among the most powerful Negro rulers in the world.

Such churches are really governments of men, and consequently a little investigation reveals the curious fact that, in the South, at least, practically every American Negro is a church member. Some, to be sure, are not regularly enrolled, and a few do not habitually attend services; but, practically, a proscribed people must have a social centre, and that centre for this people is the Negro church. The census of 1890 showed nearly twenty-four thousand Negro churches in the country, with a total enrolled membership of over two and a half millions, or ten actual church members to every twenty-eight persons, and in some Southern States one in every two persons. Besides these there is the large number who, while not enrolled as members, attend and take part in many of the activities of the church. There is an organized Negro church for every sixty black families in the nation, and in some States for every forty families, owning, on an average, a thousand dollars worth of property each, or nearly twenty-six million dollars in all.

Such, then, is the large development of the Negro church since Emancipation. The question now is, What have been the successive steps of this social history, and what are the present tendencies? First, we must realize that no such institution as the Negro church could rear itself without definite historical foundations. These foundations we can find if we remember that the social history of the Negro did not start in America. He was brought from a definite social environment,—the polygamous clan life under the headship of the chief and the potent influence of the priest. His religion was nature-worship, with profound belief in invisible surrounding influences, good and bad, and his worship was through incantation and sacrifice. The first rude change in this life was the slave ship and the West Indian sugar-fields. The plantation organization replaced the clan and tribe, and the white master replaced the chief with far greater and more despotic powers. Forced and long-continued toil became the rule of life, the old ties of blood relationship and kinship disappeared, and instead of the family appeared a new polygamy and polyandry, which, in some cases, almost reached promiscuity. It was a terrific social revolution, and yet some traces were retained of the former group life, and the chief remaining institution was the Priest or Medicine-man. He early appeared on the plantation and found his function as the healer of the sick, the interpreter of the Unknown, the comforter of the sorrowing, the supernatural avenger of wrong, and the one who rudely but picturesquely expressed the longing, disappointment, and resentment of a stolen and oppressed people. Thus, as bard, physician, judge, and priest, within the narrow limits allowed by the slave system, rose the Negro preacher, and under him the first church was not at first by any means Christian nor definitely organized; rather it was an adaptation and mingling of heathen rites among the members of each plantation, and roughly designated as Voodooism. Association with the masters, missionary, effort and motives of expediency gave these rites an early venee of Christianity, and after the lapse of many generations the Negro church became Christian.

Two characteristic things must be noticed in regard to the church. First, it became almost entirely Baptist and Methodist in faith; secondly, as a social institution it antedated by many decades the monogamic Negro home. From the very circumstances of its beginning, the church was confined to the plantation, and consisted primarily of a series of disconnected units; although, later on, some freedom of movement was allowed, still this geographical limitation was always important and was one cause of the spread of the decentralized and democratic Baptist faith among the slaves. At the same time, the visible rite of baptism appealed strongly to their mystic temperament. To-day the Baptist Church is still largest in membership among Negroes, and has a million and a half communicants. Next in popularity came the churches organized in connection with the white neighboring churches, chiefly Baptist and Methodist, with a few Episcopalian and others. The Methodists still form the second greatest denomination, with nearly a million members. The faith of these two leading denominations was more suited to the slave church from the prominence they gave to religious feeling and fervor. The Negro membership in other denominations has always been small and relatively unimportant, although the Episcopalians and Presbyterians are gaining among the more intelligent classes to-day, and the Catholic Church is making headway in certain sections. After Emancipation, and still earlier in the North, the Negro churches largely severed such affiliations as they had had with the white churches, either by choice or by compulsion. The Baptist churches became independent, but the Methodists were compelled early to unite for purposes of episcopal government. This gave rise to the great African Methodist Church, (the greatest Negro organization in the world, to the Zion Church and the Colored Methodist, and to the black conferences and churches in this and other denominations.

The second fact noted, namely, that the Negro church antedates the Negro home, leads to an explanation of much that is paradoxical in this communistic institution and in the morals of its members. But especially it leads us to regard this institution as peculiarly the expression of the inner ethical life of a people in a sense seldom true elsewhere. Let us turn, then, from the outer physical development of the church to the more important inner ethical life of the people who compose it. The Negro has already been pointed out many times as a religious animal,— a being of that deep emotional nature which turns instinctively toward the supernatural. Endowed with a rich tropical imagination and a keen, delicate appreciation of Nature, the transplanted African lived in a world animate with gods and devils, elves and witches; full of strange influences,—of Good to be implored, of Evil to be propitiated. Slavery, then, was to him the dark triumph of Evil over him. All the hateful powers of the Under-world were striving against him, and a spirit of revolt and revenge filled his heart. He called up all the resources of heathenism to aid,—exorcism and witch-craft, the mysterious Obi worship with its barbarious rites, spells, and blood-sacrifice even, now and then, of human victims. Weird midnight orgies and mystic conjurations were invoked, the witch-woman and the voodoo-priest became the centre of Negro group life, and that vein of vague superstition which characterizes the unlettered Negro even to-day was deepened and strengthened.

In spite, however, of such success as that of the fierce Maroons, the Danish blacks, and others, the spirit of revolt gradually died away under the untiring energy and superior strength of the slave masters. By the middle of the eighteenth century the black slave had sunk, with hushed murmurs, to his place at the bottom of a new economic system, and was unconsciously ripe for a new philosophy of life. Nothing suited his condition then better than the doctrines of passive submission embodied in the newly learned Christinity. Slave masters early realized this, and cheerfully aided religious propaganda within certain bounds. The long system of repression and degradation of the Negro tended to emphasize the elements of his character which made him a valuable chattel: courtesy became humility, moral strength degenerated into submission, and the exquisite native appreciation of the beautiful became an infinite capacity for dumb suffering. The Negro, losing the joy of this world, eagerly seized upon the offered conceptions of the next, the avenging Spirit of the Lord enjoining patience in this world, under sorrow and tribulation until the Great Day when He should lead His dark (children home,—this became his comforting dream. His preacher repeated the prophecy, and his bards sang,—

> "Children, we all shall be free
> When the Lord shall appeal!"

This deep religious fatalism, painted so beautifully in "Uncle Tom," came soon to breed, as all fatalistic faiths will, the sensualist side by side with the martyr. Under the lax moral life of the plantation, where marriage was a farce, laziness a virtue, and property a theft, a religion of resignation and submission degenerated easily, in less strenuous minds, into a philosophy of indulgence and crime. Many of the worst characteristics of the Negro masses of to-day had their seed in this period of the slave's ethical growth. Here it was that the Home was ruined under the very shadow of the Church, white and black; here habits of shiftlessness took root, and sullen hopelessness replaced hopeful strife.

With the beginning of the abolition movement and the gradual growth of a class of free Negroes came a change. We often neglect the influence of the freedman before the war, because of the paucity of his numbers and the small weight he had in the history of the nation. But we must not forget that his chief influence was internal,—was exerted on the black world; and that there he was the ethical and social leader. Huddled as he was in a few centres like Philadelphia, New York, and New Orleans, the masses of the freedmen sank into poverty and listlessness; but not all of them. The free Negro leader early arose and his chief characteristic was intense earnestness and deep feeling on the slavery question. Freedom became to him a real thing and not a dream. His religion became darker and more intense, and into his ethics crept a note of revenge, into his songs a day of reckoning close at hand. The "Coming of the Lord" swept this side of Death, and came to be a thing to be hoped for in this day. Through fugitive slaves and irrepressible discussion this desire for freedom seized the black millions still in bondage, and became their one ideal of life. The black bards caught new notes, and sometimes even dared to sing,—

> "O Freedom, O Freedom, O Freedom over me!
> Before I'll be a slave
> I'll be buried in my grave,
> And go home to my Lord,
> And be free."

For fifty years Negro religion thus transformed itself and identified itself with the dream of Abolition, until that which was a radical fad in the white North and an anarchistic plot in the white South had become a religion to the black world. Thus, when Emancipation finally came, it seemed to the freedman a literal Coming of the Lord. His fervid imagination was stirred as never before, by the tramp of armies, the blood and dust of battle, and the wail and whirl of social upheaval. He stood dumb and motionless before the whirlwind: what had he to do with it? Was it not the Lord's doing, and marvellous in his eyes? Joyed and bewildered with what came, he stood awaiting new wonders till

the inevitable Age of Reaction swept over the nation and brought the crisis of today.

It is difficult to explain clearly the present critical stage of Negro religion. First, we must remember that living as the blacks do in close contact with a great modern nation, and sharing, although imperfectly, the soul-life of that nation, they must necessarily be affected more or less directly by all the religious and ethical forces that are to-day moving the United States. These questions and movements are, however, overshadowed and dwarfed by the (to them) all-important question of their civil, political, and economic status. They must perpetually discuss the "Negro Problem,"—must live, move, and have their being in it, and interpret all else in its light or darkness. With this come, too, peculiar problems of their inner life,— of the status of women, the maintenance of Home, the training of children, the accumulation of wealth, and the prevention of crime. All this must mean a time of intense ethical ferment, of religious heart-searching and intellectual unrest. From the double life every American Negro must live, as a Negro and as an American, as swept on by the current of the nineteenth while yet struggling in the eddies of the fifteenth century,—from this must arise a painful self-consciousness, an almost morbid sense of personality and a moral hesitancy which is fatal to self-confidence. The worlds within and without the Veil of Color are changing, and changing rapidly, but not at the same rate, not in the same way; and this must produce a peculiar wrenching of the soul, a peculiar sense of doubt and bewilderment. Such a double life, with double thoughts, double duties, and double social classes, must give rise to double words and double ideals, and tempt the mind to pretence or revolt, to hypocrisy or radicalism.

In some such doubtful words and phrases can one perhaps most clearly picture the peculiar ethical paradox that faces the Negro of to-day and is tingeing and changing his religious life. Feeling that his rights and his dearest ideals are being trampled upon, that the public conscience is ever more deaf to his righteous appeal, and that all the reactionary forces of prejudice, greed, and revenge are daily gaining new strength and fresh allies, the Negro faces no enviable dilemma. Conscious of his impotence, and pessimistic, he often becomes bitter and vindictive; and his religion, instead of a worship, is a complaint and a curse, a wail rather than a hope, a sneer rather than a faith. On the other hand, another type of mind, shrewder and keener and more tortuous too, sees in the very strength of the anti-Negro movement its patent weaknesses, and with Jesuitic casuistry is deterred by no ethical considerations in the endeavor to turn this weakness to the black man's strength. Thus we have two great and hardly reconcilable streams of thought and ethical strivings; the danger of the one lies in anarchy, that of the other in hypocrisy. The one type of Negro stands almost ready to curse God and die, and the other is too often found a traitor to right and a coward before force; the one is wedded to ideals remote, whimsical, perhaps impossible of realization; the other forgets that life is more than meat and the body more than raiment. But, after all, is not this simply the writhing of the age translated into black,—the triumph of the Lie which today, with its false culture, faces the hideousness of the anarchist assassin?

To-day the two groups of Negroes, the one in the North, the other in the South, represent these divergent ethical tendencies, the first tending toward radicalism, the other toward hypocritical compromise. It is no idle regret with which the white South mourns the loss of the old-time Negro,—the frank, honest, simple old servant who stood for the earlier religious age of submission and humility. With all his laziness and lack of many elements of true manhood, he was at least open-hearted, faithful, and sincere. To-day he is gone, but who is to blame for his going? Is it not those very persons who mourn for him? Is it not the tendency, born of Reconstruction and Reaction, to found a society on lawlessness and deception, to tamper with the moral fibre of a naturally honest and straightforward people until the whites threaten to become ungovernable tyrants and the blacks criminals and hypocrites? Deception is the natural defence of the weak against the strong, and the South used it for many years against its conquerors; to-day it must be prepared to see its black proletariat turn that same two-edged weapon against itself. And how natural this is! The death of Denmark Vesey and Nat Turner proved long since to the Negro the present hopelessness of physical defence. Political defence is becoming less and less available, and economic defence is still only partially effective. But there is a patent defence at hand,—the defence of deception and flattery, of cajoling and lying. It is the same defence which peasants of the Middle Age used and which left its stamp on their character for centuries. To-day the young Negro of the South who would succeed cannot be frank and outspoken, honest and self-assertive, but rather he is daily tempted to be silent and wary, politic and sly; he must flatter and be pleasant, endure petty insults with a smile, shut his eyes to wrong; in too many cases he sees positive personal advantage in deception and lying. His real thoughts, his real aspirations, must be guarded in whispers; he must not criticise, he must not complain. Patience, humility, and adroitness must, in these growing black youth, replace impulse, manliness, and courage. With this sacrifice there is an economic opening, and perhaps peace and some prosperity. Without this there is riot, migration, or crime. Nor is this situation peculiar, to the Southern United States, is it not rather the only method by which undeveloped races have gained the right to share modern culture? The price of culture is a Lie.

On the other hand, in the North the tendency is to emphasize the radicalism of the Negro. Driven from his birthright in the South by a situation at which every fibre of his more outspoken and assertive nature revolts, he finds himself in a land where he can scarcely earn a decent living amid the harsh competition and the color discrimination. At the same time, through schools and periodicals, discussions and lectures, he is intellectually quickened and awakened. The soul, long pent up and dwarfed, suddenly expands in new-found freedom. What wonder that every tendency is to excess,—radical complaint, radical remedies, bitter denunciation or angry silence. Some sink, some rise. The criminal and the sensualist leave the church for the gambling-hell and the brothel, and fill the slums of Chicago and Baltimore; the better classes segregate themselves from the group-life of both white and black, and form an aristocracy, cultured but pessimistic, whose bitter criticism stings while it points out no way of escape. They despise the submission and subserviency of the Southern Negroes, but offer no other means by which a poor and oppressed minority can exist side by side with its masters. Feeling deeply and keenly the tendencies and opportunities of the age in which they live, their souls are bitter at the fate which drops the Veil between; and the very fact that this bitterness is natural and justifiable only serves to intensify it and make it more maddening.

Between the two extreme types of ethical attitude which I have thus sought to make clear wavers the mass of the millions of Negroes, North and South; and their religious life and activity partake of this social conflict within their ranks. Their churches are differentiating,—now into groups of cold, fashionable devotees, in no way distinguishable from similar white groups save in color of skin; now into large social and business institutions catering to the desire for information and amusement of their members, warily avoiding unpleasant questions both within and without the black world, and preaching in effect if not in word: *Dum vivimus, vivamus.*

But back of this still broods silently the deep religious feeling of the real Negro heart, the stirring, un-guided might of powerful human souls who have lost the guiding star of the past and seek in the great night a new religious ideal. Some day the Awakening will come, when the pent-up vigor of ten million souls shall sweep irresistibly toward the Goal, out of the Valley of the Shadow of Death, where all that makes life worth living—Liberty, Justice, and Right—is marked "For White People Only."

16

Nepantla *Spirituality: Negotiating Multiple Religious Identities among U.S. Latinas*

Lara Medina

I was born and live in that in-between space, *nepantla*, the borderlands. (Anzaldúa, 1993:114)[1]

IN 1987, GLORIA ANZALDÚA PUBLISHED *Borderlands/La Frontera: The New Mestiza*, a foundational book for the further development of Chicana feminist thought and praxis. At the time, I was completing a masters' in theology at the Graduate Theological Union in Berkeley. I considered the book to be a "new Chicana bible." Her articulation of the pain yet creativity of living on physical, psychological, sexual, and spiritual borders resonated profoundly with my own experiences of growing up Chicana. Straddling borders or the spaces "wherever two or more cultures edge each other" had become a way of life for me and other brown women constantly learning how to survive in a white-dominated society. All people of color in the United States share this challenge, but Anzaldúa addressed this space of discomfort and contradiction from a specific cultural and gendered perspective. Anzaldúa has gifted Chicanas with a theory with which to articulate our personal and communal pain leading to a "new mestiza consciousness," one that moves toward "a more whole perspective, one that includes rather than excludes" (1987:79). For Anzaldúa, a central aspect of this new consciousness is the healing of the dark-skinned Indian woman within Chicanas/os who has been "silenced, gagged,

caged, bound into servitude . . ." (Ibid.:23). La India's voice, wisdom, and spirit could redeem the fragmentation of our spiritual, psychological, and physical selves that had conformed to the dualistic paradigm of Western thought and culture.

One year later, the publication of *Hispanic Women: Prophetic Voice in the Church* by Ada María Isasi-Díaz and Yolanda Tarango offered another foundational text for the articulation of Latina feminist thought and praxis. The authors wrote candidly of the alienation and hurt that Latinas have experienced in the Catholic Church and within Latino cultures due to sexism and internalized racism. Their starting point was the daily experiences of Latinas in a white dominant society and church. By intertwining cultural theology, feminist theology, and liberation theology they offered an accessible methodology to enable Latinas to articulate their "understandings of the divine" and to effect social change. Through sharing our stories, analyzing the systemic causes of our shared pain, liturgizing from a feminist perspective, and strategizing to bring forth change, Latinas could give birth "to new elements, to a new reality" (1988:xiii). Validating the fusion of Amerindian, African, and Christian beliefs and practices "as the most operative system of symbols used by Hispanic women . . . [that] could well offer needed correctives to some of the religious understandings of official Christianity"

(Ibid.: 67) sanctioned my own growing awareness of the critical need to recognize Indigenous epistemologies within a Chicana/o theology. My master's thesis would argue that the reinterpretation and reclamation of Indigenous epistemology is a vital task for a Chicano/a liberation theology as Indigenous ways of knowing are foundational to Chicano/a ways of being in the world. It is the deepest source for our valuing communal responsibility, interdependency, reciprocity, sacrifice, truth through artistic expression, intuitive knowledge, respect for elders, humility, sacredness within nature, and the interconnectedness of all living things. As Anzaldúa prophesied, the Indigenous mother was truly emerging from the darkness "to fight for her own skin and a piece of ground to stand on, a ground from which to view the world — a perspective, a home ground where she can plumb the rich ancestral roots into her own ample mestiza heart" (1987:23). The question for Anzaldúa and myself became, "How could I reconcile the two, the, pagan and the Christian?" (Ibid.: 38).

Reconciling the pagan and the Christian for colonized and Christianized people can be an arduous process. The reconciling must take place in the depth of one's being rather than as a mere acceptance of a syncretic symbol system or a mestiza identity formed from the best of two or more cultures. The concept of *mestizaje*, although useful to emphasize the racial/ethnic mixture of Chicanos and other Latinos, and the blending of cultures that create a mestizo/a identity, can also easily diminish the significance of the Indigenous worldview within the *mestizaje* and the conditions under which it has struggled to survive. As Anzaldúa later stated, "Beware of *el romance del mestizaje. . . . Puede set una ficción*" (1993:111).[2] True reconciliation between the Indigenous and the Christian requires the privileging of the mother culture, the Indigenous, until the Indigenous can be fully respected.

According to Webster's New World Dictionary, to reconcile means: (1) "to make friendly again or win over to a friendly attitude; (2) to settle (a quarrel or dispute) or compose (a difference); (3) to . . . bring, into harmony; and (4) to make content, submissive, or acquiescent (to) [to become reconciled to one's lot]." For mixed race peoples, existing in harmony is often an oxymoron and submitting or acquiescing is no longer a viable option. How then can "the pagan and the Christian" truly reconcile?

The ancestral experience of violent contact, colonization, miscegenation, and transculturation beginning in the sixteenth century between Indigenous, European, and African peoples that created the mestiza, the mulatto, and the Afromestizo, also created the potential for their descendants to hold diverse worldviews and religions in balance (Aguirre Beltrán, 1946; Bennett, 2003). But colonizing powers had a different agenda and the African and Indigenous epistemology would be supplanted or forced underground. Not being willing to give up their ancestral deities and being forced to accept a new way left many Indigenous people in between worlds, discerning how best to survive. The well-known phrase "idols behind altars" offered an attempt to understand one strategy of survival, but as David Carrasco so brilliantly elucidates, "There were idols behind altars but it is imperative to look at the entire scene, the idol and the altar as the relationship to be understood" (1995:74). Indigenous peoples did not merely resist the imposition of Christianity but they responded to the foreign tradition by crafting their religiosity, developing unsanctioned traditions, reinforcing their community networks, and ultimately asserting their religious autonomy.[3] They became Christian on their own terms and in the process Christianity was changed.

The first victims of colonization found themselves in *nepantla*, a Nahuatl term meaning in the middle, or the middle place.[4] According to Nahautl scholar Fermin Herrera, the word *nepantla* means a middle place and is usually attached to nouns.[5] For example, *tlalli* means land and *tlalnepantla* means middle of the earth. To be "in *nepantla*" could then imply to be at the center.

The use of *nepantla* was recorded by the Dominican friar Diego Durán, in the sixteenth century in *Historia de las Indias de Nueva España y Islas de Tierra Firme*. I quote the passage at length:

> Once I questioned an Indian regarding certain things, particularly why he had gone dragging himself about, gathering monies, with bad nights and worse days, and having gathered so much money through so much trouble he put on a wedding and invited the entire town and spent everything. Thus reprimanding him for the evil thing he had done, he answered me: Father, do not be frightened because we are still *nepantla*, and since I understood what he meant to say by that phrase and metaphor,: which means to be in the middle, I insisted that he tell me in what middle it was in which they found themselves. He told me that since they were still not well rooted in the faith, I should not be surprised that they were still neutral, that they neither answered to one faith or the other or, better said, that they believed in God and at the same time keep their ancient customs and demonic rites. And this is what he meant by his abominable excuse that they still remained in the middle and were neutral. (1867–80:268)

The friar's apparent lack of regard or understanding of Indigenous communal responsibility, communal obligations, and communal celebrations marking rites of passage clearly blurred his interaction with the native elder. Within indigenous epistemology, community participation symbolizes the strength of a community and is proof of one's belonging in a community.[6] Instead, the friar found this behavior to be an "evil thing" and condemned the actions. In addition to his lack of understanding of the traditions of the Nahuas, the possibility of their believing in the Christian God *and* maintaining their ancient customs repulsed the missionary.

According to the renowned scholar of Mesoamerican studies Miguel León-Portilla, this response of the "elder Indian" exemplified "the trauma of nepantlism." He elaborates:

> The ancient institutions had been condemned and mortally wounded, while the ones the friars imposed were still strange and at times incomprehensible. Consequently, the Indians found themselves *nepantla*, "in between." The commitment to forcing change had wounded the very values and foundations of the indigenous world. (1990:10)

León-Portilla further adds:

> The violent attacks against the indigenous religion and traditions, the death of the gods, and the difficulty in accepting the new teachings as true had already affected the people deeply and had brought about, as a consequence, the appearance of nepantlism. The concept of nepantlism, "to remain in the middle," one of *the greatest dangers* of culture contact ruled by the desire to impose change, retains its full significance, applicable to any meaningful understanding of similar situations. (Ibid.:11)

León-Portilla's often quoted interpretation of the exchange of words between the friar and the "wise old native" presumes indecisiveness on the elder's part. His use of the term *nepantla* is assumed to mean confusion and conflict, the result of imposed change. Clearly, the native peoples experienced psychological, physical, and spiritual violation, and subsequently found themselves caught or bound between worlds leading to inner and outer turmoil. But the elder himself stated that they were neutral, implying their unwillingness to take sides in the religious conquest. As a matter of survival, they would choose both religions. And as he told the friar, "Do not be frightened."

I would like to elaborate on the elder's response and suggest a different interpretation for his decision, an interpretation that broadens the concept of *nepantla* and illuminates the multifacetedness of "being in the middle." So I raise the following questions: Is it not possible that the elder was referring to his survival strategy of remaining in the middle, the neutral space, by describing how his people must and could incorporate Christianity into their native worldview, but also must and could hold on to their traditional beliefs and practices? Could the elder have been maneuvering the fissures, boundaries, and borders of his changed world by claiming the middle space, the center space, the space of meaning-making where his people's religious and cultural agency could construct new ways or simply provide space for both religions to coexist side by side? In other words, for the elder, the pagan and the Christian could coexist in harmony, in a middle space, a neutral space where one does not have power over the over. Perhaps what appeared to the friar and to León-Portilla to be a state of confusion and ambiguity was the manner in which the elder attempted to hold on to his dignity and to the ways of his ancestors. The elder wisely and consciously chose the middle space, the center, for his worldview was large enough to encompass multiple manifestations of the divine. From this perspective, *nepantla*, the middle place, presumes agency, not confusion.

My interpretation of *nepantla* in this manner suggests that there is duality within *nepantla*, a transparent side where there is clarity and; self-determination, and a shadow side, where diversity confuses and creates disorientation. As such, I argue that *nepantla* is a multifaceted psychic and spiritual space composed of complementary opposites: obscurity and clarity.

Bipolar duality consisting of complementary opposites is a constant within Indigenous Mesoamerican understandings of the universe (Marcos, 1995) and illuminates the duality I propose within *nepantla*. As duality or complementary opposites exist in all things, neplanta itself is comprised of the shadow side or the bewildering state of uncertainty, and the transparent side or the state of clarity and meaning making.

According to Mexican anthropologist Sylvia Marcos, "the duality implicit in Mesoamerican cosmology was constantly in flux and never fixed or

static . . . movement gave its impulse to everything . . . everything flowed between opposite poles" (1995:30). For border people, people who live in the physical and psychological terrain where diverse cultures clash, at times converge, and ultimately coexist (not without tension) there is constant movement, constant fluidity.

Whereas fluidity remains constant, the cosmos naturally reestablishes equilibrium as "the critical point of balance had to be found in continual movement" (Ibid.:30). Maintaining balance/equilibrium in all things, including oneself, is the moral responsibility of all individuals. Without balanced individuals, the community cannot exist in harmony. Balance was achieved not by "negating the opposite but rather by advancing toward it and embracing it, in an attempt to find the ever-shifting center of balance" (Ibid.:31). The confusion of *nepantla* must be embraced and worked through in order to reach the balanced state of clarity on the opposite pole within *nepantla*. The elder and his people had to move toward Christianity and embrace it as the opposite in order to survive and regain balance in their changing world. But the opposite, the native worldview, was/is held on to in order to sustain balance.

My use of *nepantla* differs from the concept of syncretism that refers to the blending of diverse beliefs and practices into new and distinct forms. The term "syncretism" is often used to describe Latin American religions resulting from the European imposition of Christianity upon native religions. Scholars are realizing the limitations of this term as it can easily silence complex historical contexts, power relations, and the "phenomenological distress" in which syncretic traditions evolved. According to David Carrasco, syncretism "can be useful when viewed as a 'tool for interpretation' rather than as a description of social patterns" (1995:71). As such, he suggests redesigning the tool to better understand the dynamics of Latino cultures and religions. Refining syncretism as shared culture, Carrasco illuminates what took place throughout colonial Latin America, in the "contact zone of incomplete and developing forms where the social and symbolic relations were permeated by conflict and loss, coercion and indigenous urging more than adherence" (Ibid.:78). Syncretism when understood as shared culture reveals the agency and ingenuity of the Indigenous to transform Christianity for their benefit. For example, a crucifix made of cornhusks conjoins the sacrifice of Christ with the sacredness of maize and "the cosmo-magical powers stemming from the earth" (Ibid.:76).

Syncretism as shared culture also exemplifies a middle space, and as such holds a place within *nepantla*, but as Klor de Alva points out, "*Nepantlaism* should never be confused with syncretism, which is, in both a historical and a psychological sense, the consequence of nepantlaism." *Nepantla* as a multifaceted psychological and spiritual space provides for pre-Christian Indigenous traditions and syncretic Christianity to coexist, side by side, in mutual harmony and respect. In *nepantla*, there is room for all. *Nepantla* provides a place where the Indigenous elders and their descendants can survive, rest, and prosper. In the transparency of *nepantla*, there are no power struggles regarding who holds "the truth." While *nepantla* as a harmonious space might seem to contradict the mystico-militarism that existed within the Mexica culture, it is important to remember that the poets and philosophers, the *tlamatinime*, advocated a peaceful coexistence with all of humanity. Mexica culture, like all cultures, was/is not homogeneous.

León-Portilla's interpretation of *nepantla* as a place of conflict and confusion has influenced the writing and artistic productions of many Chicana scholars and artists, but they too have broadened its meaning. Anzaldúa refers to "mental and emotional states of perplexity ... psychic restlessness ... mental nepantlism, an Aztec word meaning torn between ways" (1987:78). In later work, she refers to *nepantla* as the site of transformation. *Nepantla* is referred: to as "the dark cave of creativity ... one that brings a new state of understanding"

(1993:113). Cultural theorist Laura Pérez (in chapter 11) refers to the "*susto* of *nepantla*" (the frightening of *nepantla*), But she also sees "that 'in between' space *al revés*, in reverse, not only as something powerful, but indeed as emblematic of the nature of being and meaning." Yreina Cervantez's lithograph triptych titled *Nepantla* images the severity of colonizing forces to obliterate and reconfigure the native, and the artist's response to move "beyond *nepantla*," into a place of power and self-determination. These insightful and groundbreaking works candidly describe the turmoil and self-doubt that exist within the shadow side of *nepantla* as well as calling the reader/viewer to transformation beyond the disorientation and obscurity of *nepantla*. *Nepantla* is the liminal space that can confuse its occupants but also has the ability to transform them.

NEPANTLA SPIRITUALITY IN PEDAGOGY

In my teaching about Chicanos/as and religion, I encounter many students who are spiritually searching. They are searching for more knowledge about themselves and their God. Many express interest in learning about their Indigenous roots, knowledge that has been denied them in the Western educational system. Most have only studied religion in catechism classes and have never openly challenged Christian doctrine. The class intends to provide the opportunity to question religious "truths" constructed within historical and gendered contexts so they may think critically about their own traditions and their own cultures. It is through the process of critical thinking about religion that healing from the psychic wounds of spiritual colonization can occur. My emphasis on Indigenous epistemology challenges the majority to confront their internalized biases toward non-Christian and non-Western worldviews. For Chicanos/as who are products of cultural *mestizaje* within a legacy of colonization, reconciling the differences and discovering the similarities between Christian and Indigenous traditions offers healing. Healing in this context is about bringing forth self-knowledge and historical consciousness so that one may claim religious agency, or the ability to determine for oneself what is morally and ethically just, and what enables communication with spiritual sources. For the young women in the class, discussions about moral authority over one's body constitute a central part of the healing process. The personal nature of the student's interest in religion definitely influences the course design.

Many students reveal their parents' concern that in college they will leave their Christian upbringing behind and turn to Indigenous ways or forget about spirituality altogether. To help the students bridge their worlds, I introduce the concept of *nepantla* spirituality,[7] spirituality at the biological and cultural crossroads where diverse elements converge, at times in tension and at other times in cohesion. It is a spirituality that allows the Christian and the Indigenous to coexist in harmony. The use of the Nahuatl term to distinguish this spirituality privileges and reinforces the Indigenous epistemoiogy active within *nepantla*.

As in any relationship coexistence is not always easy, but once the tensions of *nepantla* are understood and confronted, and the native-Self is recovered and continuously healed, *nepantla*, or the middle space, becomes a psychological, spiritual, and political space that Latinos/as transform as a site of meaning making and healing. Rather than being limited by confusion or ambiguity, Latinos/as act as subjects in deciding how diverse religious and cultural forces can or cannot work together. Like the native elder of the sixteenth century, they creatively maneuver the fissures, boundaries, and borders and consciously make choices about what aspects of diverse worldviews nurture the complexity of their spiritual and biological *mestizaje*, and what for them enables communication with spiritual

forces. Within *nepantla*, Chicanas/os and other Latinos can have the wisdom of both the Indigenous and the Christian.

A significant amount of class time is spent on understanding the Mexican Indigenous/Chicano tradition of honoring and communing with the dead through *Días de los muertos*. As in many Indigenous cultures around the world, with exceptions of course, the dead or the ancestors play a key part in cultural continuity. The ancestors guide the living, offer protection, and renew the living. Constructing sacred space in their honor, leaving them gifts of food and drink, spending time with their spirits, and sharing in oral tradition ensures family stability and most importantly reminds the living of their historical lineage. For marginalized peoples in the United States, the simple act of remembering their family history holds spiritual and political significance. Whether celebrating the dead takes place in public processions, cemeteries, gatherings in cultural centers, or in the privacy of a family altar, the tradition rejects mainstream attempts to ignore the histories and traditions of non-white and mixed race peoples. Through public ritual, marginalized "others" claim public space and reject any efforts to dismiss their presence in an increasingly segregated society. The tradition challenges a society that privileges youth and silences the dead. Teaching about this tradition underscores the distinctiveness of non-Western epistemologies where the living and the dead depend on each other.

Students are required to construct *ofrendas* (offerings) to a deceased member of their family or community. The *ofrenda* can be designed in a box that can be easily carried to class. They must design the container with symbols and photos that represent the life of the deceased. In their oral presentations they offer a brief biographical sketch followed by an explanation of the symbols they chose to represent the deceased. For many of the students, building the *ofrenda*, explaining it to the class, and writing a summary facilitates a healing process by enabling them to confront the pain of loss. Many students express how meaningful the assignment is not only for themselves, but also for their families. Oftentimes they will have to ask a parent to tell them more about a deceased family member and the exchange facilitates the sharing of family history previously untold.[8]

The symbols chosen by the students to represent family members oftentimes reflect *nepantla* spirituality as the *ofrendas* contain elements of Indigenous spirituality alongside elements found meaningful in Catholic Christianity. Catholic icons share physical space with Indigenous elements such as soil, water, fire, herbs, and images of Mesoamerican deities. The dual symbol system represents not confusion, but rather choice about what objects and natural resources reflect the fullness of their identity and spirituality.

To further the experience of *nepantla* spirituality, I respectfully offer those students seeking connection to their Indigenous ancestral ways the opportunity to participate in a *temazcal* or purification/sweat ceremony, an ancient ceremony indigenous to the Americas. Many Chicanas/os have learned the purification ceremony from Lakota people who have been willing to share their tradition, the *inipi*, as a way to bring balance to the world and strength to those in solidarity with native peoples.[9] Many Chicanas/os who are seeking their way home to the Indigenous mother have rediscovered the sweat ceremony. As Chief Lame Deer of the Lakota states, "it gives them their identity back" (1972:5). Some Chicanas/os also have learned the tradition from their Mexican Indigenous elders or peers who have maintained the purification ceremony. While the actual sweathouse will look different depending on the tradition being followed, the sweat ceremony is a sacred ceremony for many native peoples of the Americas and must not be taken lightly. It is centered on prayer, sacrifice, and both physical and spiritual renewal.

Native American (Abenaki) Joseph Bruchac, in his very useful book *The Native American Sweat Lodge:*

History and Legends, describes some of the distinctive features of the Lakota *inipi* and the *temazcalli* of the Native peoples of Mexico.[10] The *inipi* is a semipermanent dome structure made from willow branches:

> [The] Vapor-bath sweat involves heating stones in a fire outside the lodge. The stones are carried inside, the lodge is sealed [traditionally with animal skins but now with heavy blankets], and after cedar and sweet grass are placed on the stones, water is poured to create steam. When the sweat is concluded, the participants leave the sweat lodge. (1993:11)

In contrast, the *temazcalli*:

> is a permanent structure . . . made out of stone or adobe bricks. The fire for the *temescal* [*sic*] is built in an oven which is adjacent to the sweating chamber, sharing a wall with it and sometimes with a heating duct to conduct the fire's heat into the chamber. The fire heats the stones so thoroughly and intensely that the heat is conducted through them into the room where the sweating takes place . . . more often than not, water is poured onto the stones of that heated wall. Often, the water has special medicinal herbs mixed in with it. (Ibid.:11–13)

What Bruchac does not describe for both traditions is the lengthy, process of building the sweathouse, gathering the lava rocks, building the sacred fire, and the many prayers/songs and teachings that compose crucial parts of the ceremonies.

Temazcalli in Nahuatl means bathhouse or sweathouse. *Tema* is to bathe and *calli* is house. The custom of purifying and healing oneself through ritual sweating is an ancient tradition common to many northern and southern native peoples of this hemisphere. At the time of the European invasions of the Americas the sweat bath was an integral part of the daily practice of native peoples. The Spanish missionaries wrote extensively on the tradition they encountered in Mexico. Diego Durán, the same missionary who encountered the elder previously discussed, described succinctly what he saw: "These bath houses can hold ten persons in a squatting position. The entrance is very low and narrow. People enter one-by-one and on all fours" (Ibid.:17). And Friar Bernardino de Sahagún observed that ritual participants prayed and chanted as the *temazcalli* "restored their bodies, their nerves. Those who are as if faint with sickness are there calmed, strengthened" (Ibid.). According to Bruchac, "For the Aztecs, the vapor bath was the favorite remedy for almost every ill" (Ibid.).[11]

Despite the presence of the sweat bath in parts of ancient Europe, for Spaniards and other Europeans from the fifteenth to the eighteenth century, bathing and sinfulness went hand in hand. The emphasis on bathing that the native people valued appeared appalling to the colonizers throughout the Americas. This helps to explain their efforts to eradicate ritual sweating, which was a form of cleansing and praying (Ibid.:17–18; see also Giedion, 1948).

The banning of the sweat bath for native peoples beginning in the sixteenth century proved devastating to their spiritual and physical well-being. Bruchac cites a poignant example based on an interview with a Mayan elder named Tata Julian from the pueblo Todos Santos:

> In the college we had to bathe in cold water. I went to the chief and said, "Señor, it is the custom in my pueblo for the *naturales* to take sweat baths. Here there is no sweat bath. Will you give me permission to heat a little water for a bath?" He would not give me permission. After I had been there a year and six months, we all became sick with much *chor* [dysentery]. All of us were sick, sick every day. They gave us just tea; no coffee. Many *naturales* died. We became so weak that we could not walk. More and more of the *naturales* died. Then my thoughts went back to *Todos Santos*. I knew that if I did not escape I would never see my pueblo again. Señorita, as weak as I was I escaped one night and I returned to my pueblo. (Ibid.:20)

Spanish missionaries denounced sweat baths, and by 1873 the U.S. government prohibited the tradition for Native Americans. Many native peoples in the United States lost the tradition over time. The Lakota, however, managed to withstand colonizing powers waged against the *inipi*. The Indigenous of the south also preserved this most important spiritual and cultural practice.

The *temazcal* has been referred to as "the mother of all medicines." As one Chicana says about her first experience in the purification ceremony:

> I felt like I was home. I felt like I went back five hundred years. I could feel the spiritual connection to those original ceremonies and to my ancestors, and I never felt like that before. I really felt a deep spiritual inner connection.[12]

When one enters the *temazcal* or the *inipi* on all fours and kisses mother earth to ask her permission to enter, one is beginning the return to the Indigenous mother. Entering the *temazcal* or the *inipi* is like (re)entering the womb of the creator mother. Being enveloped by her warmth and immersed in the darkness of her womb enables the participants to purge themselves of their burdens. Sitting in a circle in the darkness reminds us all of our inherent equality. It is a visceral returning to the unconditional love of the divine mother. Offering songs and prayers of thanksgiving to the four sacred cardinal directions of the universe, to the creator and to one's ancestors opens the communication between the living, the divine, and the dead. Prayers for one's personal needs and the needs of others are shared.

The lava rocks brought into the *inipi* embody the spirits of the ancestors. When the water is poured over them, they emit ancestral spirit and ancestral knowledge. The steam that is created offers the breath of the creator. Lakota Chief Lame Deer states, "The steam in essence is the Grandfather's breath combining together our prayers, the air, the water, the fire which is in the rocks, and our mother the earth" (1972:2).

The process of sweating in the ceremony requires physical and emotional sacrifice. It is a process of letting go of one's fears, of letting go of material and temporal concerns. It is a process that requires trust, trust in one's creator and trust in the ceremonial leader. Leading, a *temazcal* requires specialized training, ceremonial knowledge, and intuitive skills. The water pourer or ceremonial leader ministers to the participants. He or she invites participation, shares teachings, leads in prayer and song, and paces the process of the ceremony. The *inipi* ritual is divided into four parts coinciding with the four cardinal directions and the four stages in life. The Lakota ceremony often includes the sharing of the sacred pipe during the four resting periods when the "door" of the sweathouse is opened.[13] The *temazcal* is often in two parts. Both ceremonies may be compared to the sacrament of the Eucharist in the Catholic tradition or *La Santa Cena* in the Pentecostal tradition in that the participants are led into communion with their creator and the participants are spiritually transformed.

When the ceremony is over, the participants crawl out of the sweathouse, the womb, feeling reborn, renewed, and purified. "We rinse off and the sweat from our bodies is an offering of ourselves back to Mother Earth, who gave us life" (Ibid.:4). Sacrifice, reciprocity, and renewal underscore the dynamics of the purification ceremony.

For students to reconcile with Christianity and the often-rigid paradigm they were taught, I draw from the theory of transformation proposed a decade ago by Chicano sociologist David Abalos. Essential to this theory is the awareness of one's true self or the sacred source within each individual that enables one to shape one's life based on justice, love, and solidarity with humankind. Fragmentation or alienation occurs when one has been conditioned to image the sacred source, or God, as solely outside of oneself, beyond one's personal and social reality. "A disconnection from one's sacred sources and from one's self leaves others to play god" (1986:5).

According to Abalos, it is the quality of the relationship between the person and the sacred that is important. He distinguishes between "three gods who correspond to three fundamentally different ways of living."

> Two of these gods are false gods or idols, and only the god of transformation allows us to fully participate. Thus the god of emanation is a divinity that embraces us and protects us. But we cannot struggle or talk back. We must be perpetual children to be protected by this mother-god-Church. Others link us to the god of incoherence that will help us triumph over others if we are good. This is a capitalistic god that urges us to . . . seek power. It is only the transforming god who asks/needs our participation in completing the creation of divinity, community, world, and our own selfhood. (Ibid.:8)

The god of transformation requires humans to critique unhealthy relationships and systems of oppression, reconstruct new ones, and critique them again. This never-ending process will offer liberation, or the inherent right and ability to shape one's life and environment based on justice and solidarity. Liberation does not mean an irresponsible autonomy that allows one to do what is most advantageous for personal gain. Rather, liberation offers the freedom to create conditions that provide all persons with equal respect and opportunity.

All three gods can be found within Christianity, but individuals must choose which god they are to follow. Jesus' work offered hope to the marginalized as he challenged the oppressive religious and political structures of his time. His message required the "transformation of all reality — personal, social, and even cosmic" (Sobrino, 1978:356). Jesus did not believe in a God who was totally other, totally beyond the human situation. According to liberation theologian Jon Sobrino, "Jesus unmasked people's domination of others in the name of religion, people's manipulation of the mystery of God . . . to avoid the obligations of justice" (Ibid.:366). Jesus challenged an access to God limited to worship, prayer, or academic knowledge. For Jesus access to God was in challenging injustice for the liberation of the oppressed. Jesus chose the god of transformation, yet the ecclesial institutions of power that came after in his name promoted the gods of emanation and incoherence.

Christian doctrine has presented Jesus primarily as the necessary sacrifice for individual salvation. He is considered to have paid the price for human redemption through his death, a once and for all act of penance demanded by an angry but forgiving God. Such a Christology does not concern itself with the social sin that brought Jesus to the cross or the manner in which the horror of the crucifixion affected Godself, the sacred source of life.

But when the death of Jesus is understood as the result of his bold criticism of unjust religious and political systems, then the god of transformation is revealed. This transforming love is revealed through the resurrection. When the followers of Jesus heard of his rising from the dead, they heard of a power that overcame the darkness of the cross, the darkness of the social sin that had killed him. They experienced a response from God that transformed the evil and they experienced hope against injustice. Understanding the resurrection requires hope in transformation. The resurrection then calls the hopeful to responsible action in the challenging and reconstruction of oppressive structures and relationships. Thus, resurrection occurs every time marginalized people attempt to challenge oppression. Christian faith cannot rest on the notion of personal salvation but ultimately must be a functional, just, and liberating way of acting in history.

CONCLUSION

Many Chicanos and Chicanas find empowering the possibility of being able to participate in both Indigenous and Christian spirituality. As one student states,

I feel more at peace with myself now, there is nothing wrong with me trying to practice indigenismo. . . . I don't see myself as only Catholic. . . . I don't want to leave Catholicism, but I have always felt a strong connection to the earth, to herbs, and especially to the ocean. I now feel at peace being in the middle, being in *nepantla*.[14]

Or as another student wrote,

Nepantla spirituality is a useful concept because many people feel that Catholicism alone will not satisfy their spiritual needs. *Nepantla* is the common ground, where both Indigenous and Christian religions can meet.

To be *en nepantla* is to exist on the border, on the boundaries of cultures and social structures, where life is in constant motion, in constant fluidity. To be *en nepantla* also means to be in the center of things, to exist in the middle places where all things come together. *Nepantla*, the center place, is a place of balance, a place of equilibrium, or, as discussed earlier, a place of chaos and confusion. Border people, *las mestizas y los mestizos*, constantly live *en nepantla*. We can never leave the middle space as that is where we were created, in "the contact zone" (Carrasco, 1995:78). As Anzaldúa stated, "As you make your way through life, *nepantla* itself becomes the place you live in most of the time — home" (2002:548). How we choose to occupy our home is crucial. *Nepantla* spirituality offers a choice, a choice to exclude or to include.

NOTES

1. While I was completing this essay the great Chicana cultural theorist Gloria Anzaldúa unexpectedly died on May 16, 2004, of complications related to diabetes. I most respectfully dedicate this essay to her.
2. "Beware of romanticizing *mestizaje* . . . it could be fictional."
3. Roberto R. Treviño named these aspects of religious agency in his study on turn-of-the-century Tejano

Catholics. See "The Handbook of Texas Online," *www.tsha.utexas.edu/handbook/online/articles/print/ MM/pqmcf.html.*

4. Nahuatl is the language of the Nahuas, the largest Indigenous ethnic/cultural group in the central valley of Mexico in the 1500s. Nahuatl is widely spoken today in this region of Mexico.

5. Fermin Herrera is a professor of Chicano/a studies at California State University, North-ridge and author of *Nahuatl-English, English-Nahuatl*, Hippocrene Books Concise Dictionary, 2004.

6. Examples of communal responsibility in helping to make celebrations a success can still be found in contemporary indigenous communities today. The communal participation is proof of one's belonging to the community. One example occurs in the video *Blossoms of Fire.*

7. I define spirituality as the multiple ways in which persons maintain and nurture balanced relationships with themselves, others, the world, and their creator or creation.

8. See Matovina and Riebe-Estrella, 2002, for a lengthy discussion of the Mexicano/Chicano tradition of honoring the dead.

9. I have been trained according to the Lakota *inipi* tradition, but I have also experienced the Mexican *temazcal*. The traditions differ in the structure of the sweat house, the use of herbs, the prayers and songs. I belong to a woman's spiritual circle that practices the *inipi* tradition.

10. There are many other kinds of sweathouses in the Americas depending on the region, traditions, and natural resources available. The Lakota *inipi* and the Mexican *temazcalli* are the most widely used today in North America.

11. The practice of sweating also thrived in ancient Europe, specifically among the Greeks, Romans, Scythians (present-day Russia), Slavs, Scandinavians, and Celts, and also in the Arab world, ancient Japan, and parts of Africa. The Russian, Scandinavian, and African sweat traditions in particular, had physical and spiritual therapeutic properties as does the northern and southern Indigenous American sweat bath. See Bruchac, 1993:14–16; and also Aaland, 1978.

12. Interview conducted by author with Virginia Espino, March 1994.

13. The sacred pipe is shared only if a pipe carrier is present in the ceremony. The pipe is an extremely sacred object; the pipe and the tobacco are used to help send prayers to the Creator.

14. Interview conducted by author with Celia Ramos, May 2004.

Selections from Mama Lola: A Vodou Priestess in Brooklyn

Karen McCarthy Brown

VODOU AND POLITICS

People often ask if I think Vodou keeps the people of Haiti poor and oppressed. I respond that although Vodou, like every other religion, has sometimes been misused by tyrants and scoundrels alike, guns and money have far more to do with perpetuating the suffering of Haitians than religion does. Vodou comments on and shapes life, but it hardly creates it ex nihilo. If the Haitian army were not thoroughly corrupt, if little Haiti were not in the backyard of one of the world superpowers, if Haitians in New York were not regularly losing jobs because someone fears that they have AIDS or practice "black magic," then perhaps a question could be raised as to whether Vodou is a positive force in Haiti. But if those things were different, Vodou would also be different. Vodou works within the realm of the possible and practical.

At times in the distant past, and once in the recent past, revolutionary change seemed possible. In the war that eventually liberated the Haitian slaves, traditional religion played a key organizational role. It also played a role, although it is not yet clear how large a one, in the freedom movements surrounding Jean Claude Duvalier's ouster in 1986. Yet, for the great majority of Haitians, their experiences of repression at home and racism abroad have been far too tangible, persistent, and

effective to nurture revolutionary ideas. When the use of force seems suicidal, Vodou introduces Ogou Badagri to teach the lessons of pride and endurance. And there is also Agèou, the liar, who teaches people how to duck, how to bob and feint. These are the practical survival skills Haitians use every day of their lives.

Bobbing and feinting come naturally to adults who have lived under the severe political repression of Duvalierist Haiti. For example, even legal immigrants in New York use a variety of names for themselves—one for family, another for co-workers, yet another for the telephone company. Secretiveness is a lesson taught by example and one that children learn early. Although the young children in Alourdes's household were born in the United States and have no firsthand experience of Haiti's repressive political climate, they too have come to recognize the usefulness of Ogou's skillful deception. No one has to remind them that the drama of Vodou that goes on regularly within their home is not to be discussed outside.

Alourdes and Maggie are convinced that their well-being, even their survival, depends on service to the spirits. The depth of their commitment explains the fierce pride with which they hold on to their controversial religious practice. Maggie once told this story: "When we just moved in the neighborhood, my brother William told his friends that my mother does Vodou and stuff like that. And then all these people have in their mind that she is a Vodou lady, she is bad. Most of the neighborhood people don't bother talking to us . . . which I don't care about anyway! We just keep ourself to ourself."

Sometimes even the people Alourdes successfully treats remain ambivalent about Vodou. They come alone and at night; they ask her not to tell anyone they have been to see her. Alourdes accepts the attitudes of her clients and neighbors without agreeing with them. And, to some extent, she adjusts her behavior to take account of such prejudice. She does her healing work in a small basement room that can be locked against the prying eyes of strangers. When I first met her, the altars in that room were on tables, in the open. Over the years, the tables have gradually been exchanged for cabinets with doors that can be closed. Reactions to prejudice have also shaped Vodou rituals in New York. "Here, you just invite couple people. They come in, sit down, clap the hand," Alourdes said. "But in Haiti, they have big yard. You can invite a lot'a people. They beat the drum. Here, you cannot do that because of the neighbor."

American popular culture dwells on images of Vodou's malevolence, an attitude as nonsensical as equating Catholicism with Satanism. The understanding most North Americans have of Vodou is derived mainly from its portrayal in novels, films, and television, where images of sorcerers, *zonbi*, snakes, blood, and violence abound. In the United States, the word *voodoo* is used in a casual and derogatory way to indicate anything on a spectrum from the deceptive to the downright evil. If it were not so clear that racism underlies these distortions, it would be hard to understand why this kind of stereotyping is tolerated for an African-based religion when it would not be tolerated for other religions.

The negative portrayal of Vodou in the press, in novels, and in travelers' accounts began in earnest shortly after the Haitian slaves won their freedom, a period in which slavery was still practiced in the United States and in many European colonies. The argument was often explicitly made that the barbarism of their religion clearly demonstrated that Haitians were incapable of governing themselves—an argument used by the United States and several countries in Europe to justify their refusal to recognize the fledgling black republic. Racism is more covert and convoluted these days, but the same stereotypes of Vodou still serve its purposes. One of the central ways such propaganda works is by characterizing Vodou as in every way the opposite of "true" religion, that is, of Christianity. This description is ironic, for people who serve the Vodou spirits consider themselves good Christians.

Haitians see no conflict between practicing Catholicism and serving the spirits, whom they never refer to as deities. "They have only one God for everybody, and I think everybody love God," Alourdes said. "I love God plenty. I got confidence in God. But I love my spirit, too, because they help me. If God don't give that help, that strength—spirit can do that for you."

Bondye (God) is singular and supreme in Haitian Vodou. He is a deity with roots in the Christian god as well as in the so-called high gods of West Africa. Yet in the Haitian view of things, Bondye, like his African models, rarely gets involved with individual human lives. Attention to the everyday drama of life is the work of his "angels," the Vodou spirits. Of course, equating Bondye and the Christian god and calling the Vodou spirits his angels are also political strategies that have roots going back to the time of slavery.

"OGOU BADAGRI, WHAT ARE YOU DOING THERE?"

Vodou is different for each person who deeply engages with it, because each person concentrates on his or her own particular spirits. Although Alourdes routinely honors all the major spirits, she has half a dozen on whom she focuses most of her ritual activity. It is understood within Vodou that the spirits select their special devotees, not the reverse. The spirits Alourdes concentrates on are those who have "chosen" her, who "love" her, and whose "protection" she has inherited from earlier generations within her family. They are the ones featured on her altars and routinely called on for assistance in her healing practice. Singly and in relation, these spirits, who give their names to the chapters in this book, shape and guide her professional and personal life.

Alourdes makes no major decision without consulting one or more of these spirits. All significant events are filtered through the sieve of their personalities, and their character traits and patterns of behavior frame her choices. But the spirits are not moral exemplars. Nor do they dictate exactly what she is to do, although from time to time some of the spirits give advice. More commonly, through possession-performance, the spirits explore all the potentialities, constructive and destructive, in a given life situation. In this way they provide the images that allow Alourdes to reflect on problems and to make her own choices about the most appropriate and effective ways of dealing with them.

Within Alourdes's group of special spirits, one stands out. He is her *mèt tèt* (the master of her head), Ogou Badagri. But the dominance of Ogou Badagri in her life and in her character does not go unchecked. The other spirits with whom she has a close relationship counterbalance Ogou Badagri's weight. For example, even if a situation has called out the aggression of the Ogou in Alourdes, Gede can possess her and put the matter in an entirely different light through his iconoclastic humor. Thus her view of the world and the moral choices she makes within it emerge from the chemistry of the interaction among her spirits.

The personality of the *mèt tèt* and that of the devotee tend to coincide, an intimate tie hinted at in the occasional identification of the "big guardian angel" (*gwo bònanj*), one dimension of what might

be called a person's soul, with the Vodou spirit who is his or her *mèt tèt*. Diagnosing which spirit is a person's *mèt tèt*, something that is not determined by inheritance alone, amounts to a kind of personality typing. Thus, someone with Ogou as a *mèt tèt* is expected to be brave, assertive, loyal, and so forth. The specific Ogou identified as the master of the head adds nuance to this general portrait. For example, all the Ogou are quick to anger, and some mete out stiff punishment to offenders. Alourdes once said that Ogou Feray has been known to bang his sword on his own head—that is, on the head of his horse—when that horse had made him mad. But Badagri, Alourdes's Ogou, handles his anger in another way: he withdraws and withholds. "When he angry, you just don't see him. You feel it, but you call him . . . he don't come," Alourdes said. The way she herself deals with anger reflects the Badagri "in her head." Tempered by life, she is never frivolous with this potent emotion. I have seen her sulk and withdraw many times, but I have never seen her rant and rave.

Ogou Badagri possesses Alourdes more frequently than any other spirit, with the possible exception of Gede. He is almost always involved in treating the problems her clients bring to her. Because Alourdes has gone through the Vodou marriage to Ogou Badagri, she calls him her "husband."[1] She sets aside one night a week for him. On this night, she receives the handsome soldier in dreams, and no human lover shares her bed. On Wednesday, Ogou's day, Alourdes always wears his color, red.

In describing Ogou Badagri, Alourdes could well be describing herself. Badagri will not tolerate injustice. To illustrate this trait, Alourdes gives a homely example: "If you nagging people—you know, teasing—when they don't do nothing, he can get mad about that." Disloyalty is equally intolerable: "If you do something, like, you make money for him and you spend it for no reason—that make him very angry."

Badagri is also known for his good looks, his generosity ("he love to give—even he angry, he give; he like to spoil people"), his expertise in treating people's problems ("he just father for everybody; he love to make treatment"), and his penchant for hard work ("he *love* hard work"). But the most striking part of Ogou Badagri's character is his ability to endure in the face of trials that would break many others. This quality is portrayed in Alourdes's favorite song for him, depicting a conversation between Ogou Feray, head of the army, and Badagri, the loyal soldier who stands guard:

> *Ogou Badagri, sa ou ap fè la?*
> *Ou sèviye; m'ap reveye.*
> *M'ta dòmi, Feray; m'envi dòmi, o.*
> *M'ta dòmi, Feray; m'pase dòmi, o.*
> *Se nan lagè mwen ye! Ou mèt m'reveye!*
> *O Feray, o.*
> *Gason lagè mwen ye! Yo mèt m'reveye!*

> Ogou Badagri, what are you doing there?
> You are on watch; I am going to wake you.
> I would sleep, Feray; I need to sleep, oh.
> I would sleep, Feray; I am beyond sleep, oh.
> There is a war going on! You must wake me!
> O Feray, oh.
> I am a soldier! They must wake me!

Forsaking attack, Alourdes, like Badagri, chooses watchfulness. She draws her power around her like a cloak, holding it close to her body. She does not dream of extending herself outward and conquering the world. Rather, she controls what experience has taught her she is able to control—herself. As it does in Ogou Badagri, Alourdes's fighting spirit comes to a keen focus in her pride and self-respect. Her current life strategy is to follow the rules, conserve her energy, and practice constant vigilance. This strategy has gotten her through both short-term crises and long-term hardship. Like Badagri, Alourdes endures.

"THE POLICE WILL ARREST ME"

In March of 1981, Alourdes's strategy was challenged. Her son William was arrested for purse snatching. Her first response was disbelief that anyone in her family could do such a thing. Then came anger, which quickly gave way to fear, as she was forced to deal with the police and the courts, institutions she deeply distrusted.

Alourdes has four children, three of whom were born in Haiti; William is the youngest of these three. William suffered brain damage from a bout of meningitis in infancy. Years later, testing by the New York City public school system indicated that his IQ was between 55 and 57. In the tradition of Haitian families, there has never been any thought of putting William in an institution. His place in Alourdes's household is guaranteed; and in the event of Alourdes's death, Maggie would assume the same commitment. Underlying this stance is an unarticulated belief that ignoring family responsibilities endangers the care and protection of the spirits. In providing the considerable care William requires, Alourdes and Maggie do not consider themselves martyrs. Neither do they infantilize William. He can be difficult, and Maggie and Alourdes do not spare him when they are annoyed.

William was twenty-one when he was arrested. He had the tall, strong body of a man, although his mind and heart were still those of a child. He vacillated between cloying eagerness to please and stubborn resistance to rules. Entrusted with two subway tokens and money for lunch, William made his own way each day to the trade school he attended in Greenwich Village. If he got in trouble, it was usually because he gave his lunch money away or got sidetracked on his way home. William could not say no. He would do anything for anyone if it would earn him a thank-you or a moment to bask in the glow of friendship. Although the full story was not known at first, this need to please had led to his involvement in the purse snatching. Another young man from the trade school had actually taken the purse. He had given it to William to hold, and William had complied. Because the other boy was too young to face criminal charges, William went through the frightening experience of jail and court appearances alone.

The police advised Maggie and Alourdes to be at the court-house at ten o'clock on the morning after William's arrest. I arranged to pick them up in Brooklyn at nine-thirty. Snow was coming down fast and thick that day. The roads were slippery and the driving difficult. Maggie answered the door, looking dreadful. She wore no makeup and had done nothing with her hair but comb it to a stand-off. She paced the hallway in her overcoat, shaking. Maggie had not slept. "I am too nervous," she said. "You got to get those name for me. I cannot do it. We got to know the police officer' name . . . the judge' name . . . the name of that woman with the pocketbook. If we got those name, my mother can fix it."

I found Alourdes sitting on her bed watching television. Although we were running late, she said we could not leave until her friend Soeurette arrived. Insecurity had generalized itself, and Soeurette had been called to watch the empty house while we were gone. With her back to me, Alourdes kept a dispassionate eye on the television. After a time, she began to talk in a small, tired voice.

"I hope," she said (meaning "I wish"), "my mother is here and I just a little girl, and I don't have no responsibility. I just eat . . . I sleep . . . I play. When I was little girl, I say, 'Oh, boy, when I am going to grow up?' Now I am sorry. You give them everything they want, a bed to sleep in, food to eat. If they need shoes, you give them shoes, clothes, everything they want. . . . Oh, boy, I hope my mother is here. When I little girl, she give me everything . . . well, maybe if I could not get shoes right now, I get them next year! Same thing."

Then, in a more desperate tone, Alourdes continued: "Why they not call me and tell me William is dead? Just tell me come down to that place where they keep dead people and get him. Then I call you, Karen. You help me. We sad. Then it's finish. Why he not just dead?" I stood staring at Alourdes's back, unsure whether these words had offended my sense of compassion or my sense of propriety.

Soeurette bustled in the door shortly after ten. Alourdes greeted her with a sullen stare, followed by accusations. Like a nervous, clucking hen, Soeurette responded, "It not my fault, *cheri*. The car had no heat, and we had to drive slow." Excuses are mandatory; it is not mandatory that they have any logic.

The snow continued to fall in huge feathery flakes. The wind on the Brooklyn Bridge blew the snow up, down, and sideways all at once. The tension inside the car mounted. Alourdes withdrew into herself. Sitting in the front passenger seat, she hunched her shoulders and hung her head, staring at her fingers as she braided and unbraided the fringe on her wool scarf. Maggie was more anxious than depressed, talking nonstop. She made occasional brave attempts at light conversation, but more often she fell into blaming either William or herself for the crisis. Throughout the short trip, she scrambled around the back of my station wagon using her mittens to wipe off the windows.

We soon confronted the imperial architecture of the criminal courts building in lower Manhattan, at 100 Centre Street. The heavy revolving door could have accommodated a person ten feet tall. Inside, the marble was cold and endless. Feet wet with snow made us feel even more precarious. This was purgatory, the ultimate in liminal places. The hallways seemed wider than the offices that clung along their edges, yet these huge hollow spaces were not waiting rooms. There were no chairs or benches, no ashtrays. People smoked furtively, getting away with something each time they put out a cigarette on the floor. Purgatory did not provide public restrooms. We had to get directions, negotiate a maze, and then ask permission to use a toilet that seemed to be there for someone else. The building overwhelmed Alourdes. "Oh, boy, this building solid . . . yes!" she said, craning her neck at a massive marble pillar. "Look at that staircase—iron!" "Tel-e-phone," she read, tracing her finger over brass letters set in marble. "Telephone in there? Oh, boy, this building . . . everywhere gold . . . beautiful . . . yes."

A few basic rules, quickly learned, helped us sort out the social parade moving through the halls of the building. The accused were black or Hispanic and wore scruffy clothes. Lawyers were white and wore suits. Anyone dressed like the Marlboro man in jeans, a flannel shirt, and a down vest was a police officer waiting to testify. Although we had been told that in 90 percent of the cases no family members showed up, dozens of them were roaming the halls. A slender Puerto Rican woman with tight jeans and red, brimming eyes yanked her daughter's arm and screamed: "You better behave or—!"

Officer Reese flinched and instinctively backed off when Alourdes greeted him with the question: "You the man who arrest my son?" Reese was short and kind, paunchy and puffy-eyed. As the day wore on, the smell of alcohol came on his breath, yet he never seemed drunk, only tired. He told us what to do to move things along, and he waited patiently outside the doors of the crime bureaucracy. "It doesn't bother me," he said, "I get paid for it." Later, he offered an indirect apology: "I've seen too many things. I'm suspicious. I didn't know if William— that's his name? —is retarded or just putting me on. I thought maybe he was making fun of me. That happens, you know." Reese's partner was a tall black man named Matthews, who took the time to talk with William and uncover his innocence of spirit. He described William as "hurt by a night in the slammer" and a long day in the "holding pens."

Hours passed as we moved from office to office checking on the progress of William's case. We made the rounds from the room on the second floor where papers are compiled, to the docket room where each case is assigned a number, to the little window with bars on the first floor where a list of the next cases to be heard is available. My white face, my polite requests, and the right clothes (I was wearing my grandmother's old rabbit coat, which, if not inspected too closely, could pass for something finer) got me quicker and more courteous

responses than others seemed to be receiving. The face behind the barred window asked: "Are you the attorney?"

When there was nothing more to do but wait, I looked at Alourdes and said, "Aren't you warm? Don't you want to untie your scarf . . . open your coat?" "Yes," she replied but made no move, so I untied her scarf and unfastened the top button of her coat. She suffered my attentions in an unprotesting, even grateful, way, as a child might. Alourdes gave herself over to me much as she surrendered to the legal system, trusting that she would be told the right way to do things.

Maggie, however, was filled with venom from the moment we first found ourselves dwarfed by the pillars of justice. "You know what I am going to do? I am going to beat him with a *resiyòl. Resiyòl* is a thing like . . . a . . . a . . . whip. In Haiti they use that on animals. They use that on people, too!" And moments later: "You know what I am going to do? I'm going to kick him in the knockers," she said, jerking her knee up sharply. "You see how I am going to do it?"

When Alourdes talked, which was not often, she also blamed William. "Why he got to do that? He know he can't bring no pocketbook back to my house." But she also questioned: "William not like that. You know me, Karen. All the time, I just leave my pocketbook. Also I got two big jar full of dime and quarter. He never take nothing." In her mind, William's major offense was disloyalty. "When he do something like this, he not just do it hisself. He got family behind him. We got to come down here. We got to talk to policeman. When I little girl, sometime I bad—but not like this. I never do nothing serious. I know I got my mother . . . my father to think about."

It had already been a long day, and I was finding it difficult to think of anything to say to Alourdes. I searched lamely for an encouraging word: "You know, someday we will laugh about all of this. It will be funny." Alourdes, who had been dry-eyed all day, began to cry. Her crying was more movement than sound; she bent over and covered her face, and her body quaked like a mountain about to erupt.

Eventually we learned that William would be arraigned in night court, which did not convene for several hours. Alourdes would have stood in purgatory and waited patiently for her turn. Maggie, however, wanted to go back home, "pick up the children, do the laundry." Given the chill inside and the weather outside, neither idea seemed practical to me, so I talked them into going out to eat. Snow and wind were driving in our faces as we walked toward Baxter Street and Forlini's northern Italian cuisine. Alourdes, like an oversized elf in her brown coat and peaked hood, bent into the wind and cried: "*Wot! Woy!* I can't walk! Help me!"

It was early, and Forlini's was virtually empty. White cloths were spread on all the tables except one, the booth in the back of the restaurant, closest to the kitchen. Stifling her initial impulse to seat us there, the hostess directed us to the booth in front of it. Alourdes tucked her napkin under her chin, "so I don't get no food fall on my clothes," and told me to order for her. We each had a glass of red wine. Maggie had soup, and Alourdes and I split an order of stuffed shells with a green salad.

Alourdes commented on her inability to drink: "One little glass of wine and my head begin to spin." Picking up her wine glass and swaying from side to side, she demonstrated how alcohol affects her. (I had a brief but alarming fantasy of having to move Alourdes's unconscious body the length of a restaurant in which waiters carried folded linen napkins over their arms.)

"But what I don't understand," Alourdes said, sitting up straight and looking chipper for the first time all day, "is how the spirit can drink. Papa Ogou come, he drink a lot of rum. He drink but . . . when he gone, I don't feel nothing." "You don't smell no alcohol on your breath, nothing!" Maggie added in an animated voice. The waiter checking accounts at the booth behind us turned to look at

us over the banquette. Switching from English to Creole, we continued the conversation in our private language.

Maggie and Alourdes seemed grateful for a moment in which to act as if tragedy were not lurking around the corner. But before long William was once again the topic of conversation. So far, there had been no opportunity to talk with him, and no one had been able to give us any answers about what had happened. (Later, we would all be surprised that we assumed William took the purse.)

"Why he got to do that?" Alourdes fumed. "Dummy," Maggie interjected. Hesitantly, I entered the fray. "I don't want to interfere in your family life . . .," I began. Simultaneous protests came from Maggie and Alourdes: "Don't say that! You are family." And so I talked about my fear that William would close down if they were too hard on him. I suggested that maybe that night they should simply tell him they loved him; tomorrow they could tell him that what he had done was wrong. "He has already had enough of a lesson for today," I concluded. The wine had made us earnest, and I was vaguely aware that the rhythms of our speech (often shifting into English mid-sentence and then back to Creole before the thought was complete) were careening around the restaurant.

Maggie became painfully self-reflective. "You know, you are right. Just now I am thinking about some things. I call William 'dummy,' and all the time he wanting to kiss me, and I am busy and I say to him, 'Don't do that.' I should not be like that." More quietly and using English, as she usually does when talking about her life in New York, Maggie continued: "You know I am sitting here with my college degree [an associate's degree in early childhood education from Brooklyn College], and I take all these classes, and I don't know nothing. Maybe if I could just go back and get my books. . . . If I could read, maybe, Piaget—and there was another book, I cannot remember that name—if I could read, maybe I could understand. I could set up a program to help William. I am his sister!"

Alourdes reflected, too. "I am always saying to William, 'Why don't you just get out and leave me alone?' And I mean that." We finally settled on a comparison between William and the children, Kumar and Michael. William was like a child who needed both punishment and love. The conversation seemed important, and things seemed clearer. The wine helped to sustain both impressions.

While we were in the restaurant, darkness fell and the snow stopped. Alourdes was more relaxed on the walk back to the courthouse, and, after two glasses of wine apiece, Maggie and I were even looser. Impulsively, I leaned over backward on the trunk of a car, into a virgin crust of snow with two inches of powder beneath. Flapping my arms up and down several times, I made a snow angel for Alourdes and Maggie. They had never seen one.

The arraignment happened quickly. The Legal Aid Society had appointed an attorney who was soothing but not very interested in giving or receiving information. He rushed into the courtroom only minutes before William's case was called. After shaking hands all around, the attorney drew us outside for a hasty consultation. When Maggie launched into a stream of explanations and questions, he hushed her with a question of his own: "Did any of you know the woman whose purse was stolen?"

"What was her name again?" I asked, catching Maggie's eye and winking. "Pointer," he said, "Laura Pointer." Back in the courtroom, I took out the envelope from a telephone bill received that morning. I wrote "Laura Pointer" beneath the names of the judge and the arresting officers, folded the envelope, and handed it to Maggie. Accessory to magic!

William came through the door beside the judge's bench, a uniformed officer holding his left arm. The official procedure passed in largely inaudible tones at the front of the courtroom. The only comment from the lawyer that drifted our way was about the other boy taking the bag and handing it

to William. A court date was set, March 26, and William was released without bail.

Outside the courtroom, the attorney explained that there had been an offer of a misdemeanor charge, but he had advised William not to plead guilty to anything. "Stay in touch," he said, handing me his card, and then he ran off toward another courtroom and another case. We stood in the now-familiar hall-way for several minutes more: William, Alourdes, Maggie, myself, and the two arresting officers. The relief we felt at William's release was palpable. Everyone was thanking everyone else profusely—everyone except William, who looked dazed.

In the midst of the hubbub, Maggie grabbed the lawyer's card from my hand and said to Officer Reese: "See! See, I will show you if I was lying. I was not lying, you will see. Here, William. Read this! Read this line!" The line on the card read "Associate Attorney." William made a good guess. "Lawyer," he said. Officer Matthews shoved aside the awkward moment with a comment as unrealistic as it was caring: "I used to have trouble with reading, too. I understand. You can do it, William. Don't you ever believe that you can't. You just have to work at it."

Maggie had not cried all day, not until the moment it was clear that William would be released without bail. Then she had turned to me with a hoarse whisper: "Get me out of here!" Her muffled sobs had accompanied us out of the courtroom. In the hallway, Maggie's emotional spin began again. The talk came faster and faster; things were said too many times and too loudly. Whatever restraint Maggie intended to exercise with William was gone by the time we cleared the door and felt the cold air in our faces.

"Did you take that pocketbook?" Maggie snapped. William started to protest, but no one listened. Then Maggie linked her arm with William's and struck up another tune. "Anything you ever want, you just come to me. I will give it to you. You know you always got your sister." William said nothing.

"THE JUDGE WILL NOT CONDEMN ME"

Maggie took charge after that first day in court. She kept track of the details of William's case, making regular telephone calls to the Legal Aid office. Her calls were not always returned. In fact, as the hearing date of March 26 approached, it became more and more difficult to get anyone there to speak with her. The evening before William was to appear in court, the lawyer finally called. He did not know how the district attorney intended to proceed with the case; the prognosis was "anybody's guess." The family was nevertheless to show up at ten o'clock the next morning. And, oh, yes, he would not be able to be there, but the new attorney assigned to the case would have a complete set of his notes.

When I went to pick up Alourdes and Maggie this time, the mood was different. They were both dressed up and looking good, both wearing new wigs. Alourdes met me at the door, all sugar: "Karen, *ba'm nouvèl ou* [give me news of yourself]. Did you dream about me last night?" Her question caught me off guard: "Well . . . er . . . uh . . . I really don't know. I dreamed a lot last night, but I can't remember." I tend to take Alourdes too literally. In fact, her question was simply the prelude to telling me about her own dream. She launched into the account before I was in the door.

"I dream my mother last night . . . like I just forget she dead. In that dream, it like my mother sleeping, and she just wake up and hear me talking. My mother say to me, 'What that you say?' I say 'I don't say nothing. I just sitting here.' She say, 'Who that you talking with? I don't believe you!' She take a flashlight and shine it all around, and she say, 'I see you talking to somebody . . . I see that!' "

Alourdes's dream made me smile. If only in sleep, she had succeeded in becoming a young girl again, with no responsibility. I had heard many stories about her clandestine courtships as a young woman, and I also knew that, with little or no electricity in the poor sections of Port-au-Prince, using a flashlight would be one sure way for anxious mothers to ascertain what was going on in the yards that serve as living rooms in these areas. "Whenever I dream my mother," Alourdes concluded, "I know everything going to be okay. She come to me like that and I know." Although good luck was clearly in the air, Alourdes hedged her bets by stopping in her altar room to splash herself with specially prepared perfumes.

This time, we waited in the wide marble halls of 100 Centre Street for only two hours. Just after noon, we learned that William's case had been postponed until April 20 and that the judge had excused William from appearing then. The new lawyer told us that he hoped to have the matter resolved before the hearing date. He explained that we might not know anything definite until the last minute.

"Is anybody listening to me?" he hollered with good humor. "You are going to get a letter. It will look very official. It will say: 'If you do not show up in court on April 20, a warrant will be issued for your arrest.' You can ignore that letter because the judge has excused William. The computer will go ahead and send out the letter anyway. But you do not have to come. Do you understand?" Without a moment's hesitation, Alourdes responded, "I get a letter like that, say they going to come arrest me, put me in jail, I going to come!"

Maggie's attitude was different. "I am tired of all this trouble!" she shouted as we pushed through the revolving door of the courthouse into a clear sunny day. "This stuff going to be finish! It better be, or I am going to kill them. Papa Danbala! He is number one on my list. Then come Papa Ogou. I am tired of trouble. All the time, trouble! But, Karen," she said, moving her speech rapidly from high notes to low, "I really think everything going to be okay. Last night, for the first time, I sleep. You know I don't sleep. I don't eat. And now I just want to sit down and relaaaaaaax! So now I know my guardian angel is quiet, and everything going to be okay. You know, before, when we was here, *tèt mwen boulvèse* [my head was turned around], and my angel got no peace. Then I don't sleep. No dream. I could not even think. Now I am coming along. If I sleep enough, I will conquer the world! But I don't got to tell you that. You know that, right?"

Maggie suddenly shouted: "You know too much, Karen!" Seeing my startled response, she laughed and continued in an ordinary conversational tone, "You my friend and you around a lot, and sometimes I just tell you things. You see thing, you hear thing. I think those spirit say, 'Karen know too much.' It is like the Mafia—once you know too much, then they got to Christian [baptize] you. I think you going to have to go to Haiti like me, get your head washed . . . you know." She grinned mischievously.

In another lightning change of mood, Maggie turned to William: "When we get home, I got to call the police. They say we got to keep them informed, what you are doing. 'Cause if you don't behave, they going to put you in jail." She gave me an exaggerated wink and whispered: "I am just trying to scare him lately."

Sometime in mid-April, the telephone call came. No one seemed surprised, and no one made much of it. With the help of school records and test scores procured by Maggie, the district attorney had finally been convinced that William was retarded. All charges against him were dropped.

DIFFERENT KINDS OF OGOU POWER

Alourdes and Maggie have each carved out a place in the New World, in New York. Their roles and attitudes differ, in part because they have lived different lives. One way to capture this difference would be to say that Alourdes is a Haitian who lives in the United States, whereas her daughter is an American who spent the first twelve years of her life in Haiti.

One afternoon in 1983, Alourdes was dreaming aloud about going back to Haiti. "Nobody don't like New York! If I got money, I be gone right back to my country. I take the front room of my mother' house, open a little boutique. Nothing big . . . just a little place. I sell hat . . . dress."

"You do that! Not me," was Maggie's quick retort. "I don't care what anybody say about New York. It is better here. I am staying. You can have your Baby Doc, your Duvalier, your Tonton Makout. Not me!" "Tonton Makout don't bother me," Alourdes said simply. "I just mind my business. I don't have nothing to do with them."

Alourdes avoids all public authority structures in the United States, as she did in Haiti. When William got in trouble with the police, there was no question that Maggie would be the family's front-line representative. Once Maggie was clear about William's actual role in the incident, she took on this task in a fighting spirit rooted in the assumption that a mistake had been made and that, furthermore, she was not powerless to do something about it. It would not have occurred to Alourdes that she could call the police and the courts to account on a matter of principle or law. In her mind, they represent a force as irrational as nature itself. She challenged them instead through the intervention of the spirits, just as Philo had when the courts took away her home. It was Alourdes who would not leave for the courthouse until she visited her altar room, and it was she who first asked for the names of the people involved in the case. She did not want to harm them, but she did want to ensure that they could not harm her.

Alourdes's attitude toward those who have authority is based in experiences that go far back in her life. One early lesson concerned her older brother Jean, who had to leave Haiti when he was nineteen. A colonel in the Haitian army had his eye on Jean's girlfriend. Philo heard through her network of loyal clients that soldiers were plotting to kill her son to get him out of the colonel's way. By calling in favors wherever and however she could, Philo managed to short-circuit the lengthy emigration process, and she had Jean out of the country in days. "That's the way it is," Jean said to me on one of his rare visits to Alourdes's home in Brooklyn. "Any government official. Get a mistress, build her a house, give her a BMW. Whatever they have to do to get what they want, they do it."

Since the days of Dessalines, the Haitian army has functioned with few checks on its power. Around soldiers, violence erupts in arbitrary and shocking ways, sparked as often by their own greed or fragile pride as by crime or political dissent. Anyone who has spent much time walking the streets of Port-au-Prince has seen examples. These streets were Alourdes's world until she was in her late twenties. Experience has led her to conclude that survival depends on slipping through the cracks in the system. Specifically, it is necessary to cultivate invisibility around anyone who may be threatening. Alourdes credits her Vodou spirits with granting her this invisibility: "All my life, I'm walking in the street . . . I'm walking very proud and healthy and protected. Even . . . I . . . I a woman—that don't make no difference! They cannot talk to me. I pass near those people, they don't see me. Because I got protection, I got a *gad* [guard, a protective charm]. Spirit put that *gad* in me for protection. I got protection from awful people, *ennviyou* [envious] people, violent people."

Yet Alourdes acknowledges that this spiritual gift has limitations. "Let me tell you something, protection don't mean you can go fight. No, no, no, no, no. That not protection. Protection mean people can't harm you for no reason, just because you don't do nothing. But you got to protect yourself, too. You got two eye to look. If a car coming, I not going stand up in front of that car just so I see if I got protection. No. If I stand up in front of that car, that car going hit me."

Now middle-aged, Alourdes has begun to exhibit a conservatism that would not have been possible for her as a young woman, when she was still struggling to make a place for herself in the

world. Her work as a *manbo* enables her to confine herself largely to her house, a place where she is in control. Alourdes seldom leaves home. When she does go out, careful planning ensures that her transit will be smooth and that the reception at her destination will be consonant with her well-developed self-esteem. The sources of Alourdes's conservatism, her current tendency to make a fortress of her home, could be examined in terms of a lesson Ogou teaches. One of his songs seems to describe the wounds to the heart and to the will that can result from too much life experience, too much pain and struggle. This song, addressed to the battle-seasoned chief of the Ogou, Sen Jak Majè, consists of the name of the spirit and one other line: "*M'blese, m'pa wè san mwen* [I'm wounded, but I don't see my blood]."

The early part of Alourdes's life was a constant struggle. She is still bruised and has reason to be wary of the larger world. For a brief period when she was a teenager, beautiful and high-spirited, Alourdes thought she had escaped forever from the hunger and demeaning poverty of her childhood. She talked her mother into letting her audition for a place in Haiti's Troupe Folklorique, and, to the surprise of everyone but the self-confident fifteen-year-old, she was successful. In no time, she became the lead singer with this group, which performed both popular and traditional religious music and dance.

But the excitement and glamour of her career soon ended, as did the brief marriage that followed it. Before long, Alourdes found herself on her own and responsible for three children. It was impossible to find steady work, and there was never enough money. At times, she fed her children salt water, as her own mother had done with her, so they would feel they had something in their bellies. "That time was awful for me. My mother have to pay my rent. When my mother don't have nothing . . . if she don't have money, she don't cook—nobody eat that day."

These hard times eventually made Alourdes decide to leave Haiti. And yet, during her first years in New York, things were not much easier. It was difficult to find a good job, her health failed, and it took a long time to save enough money to bring her children from Haiti. Then, not long after the family was reunited, another crisis hit, in 1965.

Alourdes was getting ready to make the trip home to undergo initiation into the Vodou priesthood. It was winter, and the tiny apartment she was renting had no central heat. Her landlord provided an electric space heater, but its defective wiring started a fire in the middle of the night. The fire took everything—her refrigerator, a new television, even the hundred dollars in cash a friend had given her to take to his family in Port-au-Prince. Half asleep and scrambling to get his pants on, Jean-Pierre, then fifteen, sustained burns on his back and neck from a flaming curtain. He was sent to the hospital, while Alourdes, Maggie, and little William were taken in by friends. The Red Cross gave them new shoes, warm clothing, and coupons for food.

These days, Alourdes can say proudly that she owns her own home and requires no outside help to feed and clothe her family. In the row house in Fort Greene, she and Maggie support a lively, three-generation household. Alourdes credits her chief protector, Ogou Badagri, with the security she now enjoys, and she can detect his presence throughout her early life as well. "Let me give you a story about me," Alourdes once offered. "Wednesday is Papa Ogou' day, right? I born on Wednesday. I married on Wednesday. Maggie born on Wednesday. Jean-Pierre born on Wednesday. I come to New York on Wednesday. If I got an appointment with somebody, I have to do any business, I have to go out for any reason—I go on Wednesday. I don't have no luck on Monday."

Maggie's story is different. She knew hunger and poverty as a child, but she simply accepted them as children are wont to do. For Maggie, the real struggles began when she came to the United States. It was in New York that she learned to fight. When Maggie tells stories about her first few months in school in New York City, she reveals a

twelve-year-old self more frightened and more aggressive than the worldly wise and resilient mother of two who is now my friend.

"I had just come to that school, and they look at me, they think, 'That black girl!' They think I'm ugly. And I don't speak no English. We got all kind'a people in that school: white, black, Puerto Rican. Each one have some kind'a gang. These white girls jump on me and beat me up. I did not even start it, and they expel me for that! But you should of seen me, Karen; I was big then." Maggie's solemn face broke into a huge grin. "I was soooooooooo big." She planted her feet wide apart and took big thumping steps across the room. "I just walk like this. My stomach stick out to here, and my rear end just stick out like this."

In a matter-of-fact tone, she completed the story. "They took that girl to the hospital. I cut her here and here," Maggie said, vaguely gesturing toward her face and upper arm. "When I first come, I always carry a little knife, like a penknife—right here." She snapped the waistband on her skirt. "When all them white girls jump on me, I just cut one. So they put me out for three weeks. But when I come back, everybody like me! I was the leader, the leader of everybody—black, white, Puerto Rican. I was soooooo big!"

One day, when Alourdes was singing Ogou songs for my tape recorder, we came to one for Ogou Achade:

> *Baton pase nan men mwen, Achade,*
> *Pou chyen raje mòde mwen.*

> The club passes into my hand, Achade,
> For the mad dog bites me.

When she finished singing, Alourdes exclaimed: "That's me! That's my protection. Nobody can't touch me." Maggie could have made the same point and meant it more literally, although the adult Maggie would never wear a knife in her waistband.

As an adult, Maggie, like Alourdes, has learned the value of knowing how to slip by unnoticed. Like

Alourdes, she cites the spirits as the source of this talent: "When I'm on the street, it's like people don't see me. Or if I'm talking, they don't hear me. I'm like the wind . . . just passing by!" But Maggie is not Alourdes, and she will still take on a good verbal fight with bill collectors and Vodou spirits alike. Fighting with the spirits was Maggie's first response to the arrival of serious trouble in January of 1981.

For several months before this, Maggie had been preoccupied with financial problems. She and Alourdes were nearly ten thousand dollars in debt, and Maggie's annual salary was not much more than five thousand dollars. She was constantly scheming and juggling scarce resources. Lying awake one night in mid-January, she conceived a plan. Early the following morning, she and Alourdes made a trip to the bank. Maggie intended to borrow a thousand dollars on her Visa card to pay their overdue fuel bill, but the bank teller informed her that there were new credit rules. She could have only three hundred fifty dollars. "Why is that?" Maggie demanded. "I got a two-thousand credit line, and once before I got seven hundred on that Visa card."

With indignation rising in her voice, Maggie later described her reaction: "I got so mad, 'cause I don't know anything about no new rules! When I hear that—only three hundred fifty dollars!—I get so upset. I'm so mad. I just go. My mother and I walk and walk. We left the house, it was nine o'clock in the morning, and by the time we get back, it was one-thirty. We just walk and walk. We nearly freeze to death! And then when I get home, I come in, put another sweater and my hat, and go out again and walk. We don't know what we doing to do! I was gone all day. My head ache, my body ache. I take two Sinutab and go to bed."

While Maggie was lying down late that afternoon, Alourdes went to the basement. She found the entire lower floor filled with steam. Maggie said later, "I'm upstairs, and I hear that scream. . . . If Mommie was the kind'a person who have heart attack, she would be dead!" The fuel tank for their

furnace had been nearly empty that morning, and the suppliers had refused to deliver more oil until the bill was paid—prompting Maggie's rush to borrow money. During the long, troubled walk, the fuel tank had gone dry, and the heat went off. The pipes froze and burst, and Maggie and Alourdes were now faced with expensive furnace repairs.

Late the same day, Maggie recounted the story for me over the phone. When she finished, there was a long silence. Then she said defiantly: "You know what I did, Karen? I talk to my people. I talk to Papa Ogou. I tell him, 'I'm going to give you one month! I need one thousand dollar. By two month from now, I'm going to need two thousand. I want it now! I'm tired of waiting! We always borrowing money from this one . . . Visa or something . . . to pay someone else. I'm tired of that! I've had enough! I want my own money!' I tell Papa Ogou I'm going to give him one month, and then I'm going to go downstairs to the altar and break everything up. I tell him, 'You better shape it or ship it! That's right! You better shape it or ship it, 'cause I am tired of waiting.' "

Sounding more depressed than angry, Maggie continued: "I don't know, Karen. Mommie say to me, 'Look, you know everything going to be all right.' But I don't know, sometime I just don't think there is any God up there." I had never heard Maggie say anything like that, and I could think of nothing to say in response. Through the long silence on the telephone, I could feel her groping for her customary strength and ironic humor. At last, she laughed.

"You know, all this time, I'm just buying thing, buying thing. All the time buying." She giggled conspiratorially and asked if I knew what she had done just the day before. "Some man come to the house, and I bought an encyclopedia for the kids. Just a little encyclopedia, but two hundred and fifty dollars! I give him a check for fifty dollars, and now I'm going to have to call him and tell him to hold that check until next Tuesday. I want my own money, Karen. I'm tired of just having other people's money. Those spirit got to help me! But all the time they just giving me trouble. I am tired of it, Karen. I am tired!"

The broken furnace was only the first in a long list of things that went wrong in Maggie's life throughout the opening months of 1981. She contracted chicken pox; she lost her job; William was arrested; and, just a few days after that, Maggie's floor of their home in Brooklyn was robbed. "Now that robber! All my jewelry! My camera—I just buy that camera! I don't even make one payment to Mastercard yet."

Maggie decided the spirits were harassing her, as they had done before, because they wanted her to become a *manbo* like her mother. By the time William's problem with the court was resolved, the other crises had receded into the past, and Maggie had become philosophical: "This bad luck, it begin with me when I get chicken pox, and it end with me, with that robber. That's it! Now those spirit know I know what they want." Ogou provides the weapon to fight mad dogs. But at times the source of trouble is Ogou himself.

> *Sen Jak pa la.*
> *Se chyen ki la.*
>
> Saint James's not there.
> It's a dog who's there.

When I first met her, in 1978, Maggie said, "Work with the spirit run in my family—my grandmother, my mother. People coming in here to see my mother all hour of the day and night. She never too tired to see people. She just like my grandmother, always helping people." Maggie hesitated before she continued with this train of thought. "My mother, my grandmother—they don't ever have no money. They just giving . . . always giving. I don't want to be like them!" But then, with resignation in her voice, Maggie added, "Seem to be each time I say I don't want to be like them, something pulling me back . . . saying, 'You can't do that!' "

In the summer of 1981, Maggie finally gave in to the will of the spirits, much as her mother had done a quarter of a century earlier. She went to Haiti to take the *ason*. She did not do so with dreams of wealth and success. She went out of the conviction that initiation would reinforce her bonds with her family and that bonding with family, living and dead, represented her best hope for peace and security.

Vodou does reinforce family ties. In the presence of Ogou, however, this statement must be qualified. Alourdes and Maggie discuss family with great warmth and feeling; there is no question of their deep commitment to each other and to their children. And they both speak lovingly of the extended family, a good part of it still in Haiti. Nevertheless, although they expend considerable energy nurturing family roots, both acknowledge that these links no longer sustain them the way they should.

Their fears are often apparent in discussions of what they would do in the case of a real crisis—a serious illness or a death in the household. With characteristic exaggeration, Maggie once said to me, "I don't have no friend. Even if my mother die . . . I could call Madame François. I could call her, and after that the very next person I call would be you. I don't got nobody to ask." Alourdes's complaint is not very different: "I use to got so many friend in Haiti. Now . . . nobody! I go to Haiti, everybody happy, happy, happy. I see my daddy. I see my sister. Then what I going do? You know, me and my father never get along together. After one week, they tired with you. Where my friend? They in Miami. They in Chicago. They in New York. And I even don't see them."

When this mood sets in, Maggie and Alourdes seem more willing to lay their bets on new friends and new ways of handling the challenges of life than to count on family. Such judgments do not mean that they have rejected their family any more than that they have rejected their Vodou roots. But both family and religion have been redefined. Relative newcomers in their lives, people such as myself, carry fictive kinship titles—Alourdes calls me her daughter, and Maggie calls me her sister. And the family of spirits has been rearranged as well. Azaka, the rural country cousin, is faithfully honored once a year, but he is seldom called at other times. Papa Ogou is the most frequent spirit guest in their home. He is the one who clears a path through the social forest and generally assists in taking on the challenges of the new.

NOTE

1. The *mèt tèt* is not the only appropriate candidate for marriage. Alourdes, for example, has also married Kouzen and Danbala.

18

Agency, Gender, and Embodiment

Saba Mahmood

WHILE IN THE EARLIER chapters of this book I explored how the ethical practices of the mosque movement have been shaped by, and in turn transformed, the social field of Egyptian secularity in unexpected ways, here I want to focus on how we might think about these ethical practices in the context of relations of gender inequality. Given the overwhelming tendency of mosque movement participants to accept the patriarchal assumptions at the core of the orthodox Islamic tradition, this chapter is animated by the following questions: What were the terms the mosque participants used to negotiate the demands of the orthodox Islamic tradition in order to master this tradition? What were the different modalities of agency that were operative in these negotiations? What difference does it make analytically if we attend to the terms internal to this discourse of negotiation and struggle? And what challenges do these terms pose to notions of agency, performativity, and resistance presupposed within liberal and poststructuralist feminist scholarship?

In chapter 1, I argued for uncoupling the analytical notion of agency from the politically prescriptive project of feminism, with its propensity to valorize those operations of power that subvert and resignify the hegemonic discourses of gender and sexuality. I have argued that to the extent that feminist scholarship emphasizes this politically subversive form of agency, it has ignored other modalities of agency whose meaning and effect are not captured within the logic of subversion and resignification of hegemonic terms of discourse. In this chapter, I want to attend not only to the different meanings of agency as they emerge within the practices of the mosque movement, but also to the kinds of analytical questions that are opened up when agency is analyzed in some of its other modalities—questions that remain submerged, I would contend, if agency is analyzed in terms of resistance to the subordinating function of power.

I should make clear that my exploration of the multiple forms agency takes is not simply a hermeneutical exercise, one that is indifferent to feminism's interest in theorizing about the possibility of transforming relations of gender subordination. Rather, I would argue that any discussion of the issue of transformation must begin with an analysis of the specific practices of subjectivation that make the subjects of a particular social imaginary possible.[1] In the context of the mosque movement, this means closely analyzing the scaffolding of practices—both argumentative and embodied—that secured the mosque participants' attachment to patriarchal forms of life that, in turn, provided the necessary conditions for both their subordination and their agency. One of the questions I hope to address is: how does the particularity of this attachment challenge familiar ways of conceptualizing "subordination" and "change" within liberal and poststructuralist feminist debates?

Finally, since much of the analytical labor of this book is directed at the specificity of terms internal to the practices of the mosque movement, I would like to remind the reader that the force of these terms derives not from the motivations and intentions of the actors but from their inextricable entanglement within conflicting and overlapping historical formations. My project is therefore based on a double disavowal of the humanist subject. The first disavowal is evident in my exploration of certain notions of agency that cannot be reconciled with the project of recuperating the lost voices of those who are written out of "hegemonic feminist narratives," to bring their humanism and strivings to light—precisely because to do so would be to underwrite all over again the narrative of the sovereign subject as the author of "her voice" and "her-story."

My project's second disavowal of the humanist subject is manifest in my refusal to recuperate the members of the mosque movement either as "subaltern feminists" or as the "fundamentalist Others" of feminism's progressive agenda. To do so, in my opinion, would be to reinscribe a familiar way of being human that a particular narrative of personhood and politics has made available to us, forcing the aporetic multiplicity of commitments and projects to fit into this exhausted narrative mold. Instead, my ruminations on the practices of the women's mosque movement are aimed at unsettling key assumptions at the center of liberal thought through which movements of this kind are often judged. Such judgments do not always simply entail the ipso facto rejection of these movements as antithetical to feminist agendas (e.g., Moghissi 1999); they also at times seek to embrace such movements as forms of feminism, thus enfolding them into a liberal imaginary (e.g., Fernea 1998). By tracing in this chapter the multiple modalities of agency that informed the practices of the mosque participants, I hope to redress the profound inability within current feminist political thought to envision valuable forms of human flourishing outside the bounds of a liberal progressive imaginary.

ETHICAL FORMATION

In order to begin tugging at the multiple twines that hold this object called agency in its stable locution, let me begin with an ethnographic vignette that focuses on one of the most feminine of Islamic virtues, *al-ḥayāʾ* (shyness, diffidence, modesty), a virtue that was considered necessary to the achievement of piety by the mosque participants I worked with. In what follows, I want to examine the kind of agency that was involved when a novice tried to perfect this virtue, and how its performance problematizes certain aspects of current theorizations within feminist theory about the role embodied behavior plays in the constitution of the subject.

In the course of my fieldwork, I had come to spend time with a group of four working women, in their mid- to late thirties, who were employed in the public and private sectors of the Egyptian economy. In addition to attending the mosque lessons, the four also met as a group to read and discuss issues of Islamic ethical practice and Quranic exegesis. Given the stringent demands their desire to abide by high standards of piety placed on them, these women often had to struggle against the secular ethos that permeated their lives and made their realization of piety somewhat difficult. They often talked about the pressures they faced as working women, which included negotiating close interactions with unrelated male colleagues, riding public transportation in mixed-sex compartments, overhearing conversations (given the close proximity of their coworkers) that were impious in character and tone, and so on. Often this situation was further compounded by the resistance these women encountered in their attempts to live a pious life from their family members—particularly from male members—who were opposed to stringent forms of religious devotion.

When these women met as a group, their discussions often focused on two challenges they constantly had to face in their attempts to maintain a pious lifestyle. One was learning to live amicably with people—both colleagues and immediate kin—who constantly placed them in situations that were far from optimal for the realization of piety in day-to-day life. The second challenge was in the internal struggle they had to engage in within themselves in a world that constantly beckoned them to behave in unpious ways.

On this particular day, the group had been reading passages from the Quran and discussing its practical significance for their daily conduct. The Quranic chapter under discussion was "The Story" (Surat al-Qaṣaṣ), which discusses the virtue of shyness or modesty (al-ḥayā'), a coveted virtue for pious Muslims in general and women in particular. To practice al-ḥayā means to be diffident, modest, and able to feel and enact shyness. While all of the Islamic virtues are gendered (in that their measure and standards vary when applied to men versus women), this is particularly true of shyness and modesty (al-ḥayā'). The struggle involved in cultivating the virtue of shyness was brought home to me when, in the course of a discussion about the exegesis of "The Story," one of the women, Amal, drew our attention to verse 25. This verse is about a woman walking shyly—with al-ḥayā'—toward Moses to ask him to approach her father for her hand in marriage. Unlike the other women in the group, Amal was particularly outspoken and confident, and would seldom hesitate to assert herself in social situations with men or women. Normally I would not have described her as shy, because I considered shyness to be antithetical to qualities of candidness and self-confidence in a person. Yet, as I was to learn, Amal had learned to be outspoken in a way that was in keeping with Islamic standards of reserve, restraint, and modesty required of pious Muslim women. The conversation proceeded as follows.

Contemplating the word istiḥayā', which is form ten of the substantive ḥayā',[2] Amal said, "I used to think that even though shyness [al-ḥayā'] was required of us by God, if I acted shyly it would be hypocritical [nifāq] because I didn't actually feel it inside of me. Then one day, in reading verse 25 in Surat al-Qaṣaṣ ["The Story"] I realized that al-ḥayā' was among the good deeds [huwwa min al-aʿmāl a-ṣaliḥa], and given my natural lack of shyness [al-ḥayā'], I had to make or create it first. I realized that making [ṣanaʿ] it in yourself is not hypocrisy, and that eventually your inside learns to have ḥayā' too." Here she looked at me and explained the meaning of the word istiḥyā': "It means making oneself shy, even if it means creating it [Yaʿni ya Saba, yiʿmil nafsu yit-kisif ḥatta lau ṣanaʿti]." She continued with her point, "And finally I understood that once you do this, the sense of shyness [al-ḥayā'] eventually imprints itself on your inside [as-shuʿūr yiṭbaʿ ʿala guwwaki]."

Another friend, Nama, a single woman in her early thirties, who had been sitting and listening, added: "It's just like the veil [ḥijāb]. In the beginning when you wear it, you're embarrassed [maksūfa] and don't want to wear it because people say that you look older and unattractive, that you won't get married, and will never find a husband. But you *must* wear the veil, first because it is God's command [ḥukm allah], and then, with time, because your inside learns to feel shy without the veil, and if you take it off, your entire being feels uncomfortable [mish rāḍī] about it."

To many readers this conversation may exemplify an obsequious deference to social norms that both reflects and reproduces women's subordination. Indeed, Amal's struggle with herself to become shy may appear to be no more than an instance of the internalization of standards of effeminate behavior, one that contributes little to our understanding of agency. Yet if we think of "agency" not simply as a synonym for resistance to social norms but as a modality of action, then this conversation raises some interesting questions about the kind of relationship established between the subject and the norm, between performative behavior and inward disposition. To begin with, what is striking here is that instead of innate human desires eliciting outward forms of conduct, it is the sequence of practices and actions one is engaged in that determines one's desires and emotions. In other words, action does not issue forth from natural feelings but *creates* them. Furthermore, pursuant to the behaviorist tradition of Aristotelian moral philosophy discussed in chapter 4, it is through repeated *bodily acts* that one trains one's memory, desire, and intellect to behave according to established standards of conduct.[3] Notably, Amal *does not* regard simulating shyness in the initial stages of her self-cultivation to be hypocritical, as it would be in certain liberal conceptions of the self where a dissonance between internal feelings and external expressions would be considered a form of dishonesty or self-betrayal (as captured in the phrase: "How can I do something sincerely when my heart is not in it?"). Instead, taking the absence of shyness as a marker of an incomplete learning process, Amal further develops the quality of shyness by synchronizing her outward behavior with her inward motives until the discrepancy between the two is dissolved. This is an example of a mutually constitutive relationship between body learning and body sense—as Nama says, your body literally comes to feel uncomfortable if you do *not* veil.

Secondly, what is also significant in this program of self-cultivation is that bodily acts—like wearing the veil or conducting oneself modestly in interactions with people (especially men)—do not serve as manipulable masks in a game of public presentation, detachable from an essential interiorized self. Rather they are the *critical markers* of piety as well as the *ineluctable means* by which one trains oneself to be pious. While wearing the veil serves at first as a means to tutor oneself in the attribute of shyness, it is also simultaneously integral to the practice of shyness: one cannot simply discard the veil once a modest deportment has been acquired, because the veil itself is part of what defines that deportment.[4] This is a crucial aspect of the disciplinary program pursued by the participants of the mosque movement, the significance of which is elided when the veil is understood solely in terms of its symbolic value as a marker of women's subordination or Islamic identity.

A substantial body of literature in feminist theory argues that patriarchal ideologies—whether nationalist, religious, medical, or aesthetic in character—work by objectifying women's bodies and subjecting them to masculinist systems of representation, thereby negating and distorting women's own experience of their corporeality and subjectivity (Bordo 1993; Göle 1996; Mani 1998; E. Martin 1987). In this view, the virtue of al-ḥayāʾ (shyness or modesty) can be understood as yet another example of the subjection of women's bodies to masculinist or patriarchal valuations, images, and representational logic. A feminist strategy aimed at unsettling such a circumscription would try to expose al-ḥayāʾ for its negative valuation of women, simultaneously bringing to the fore alternative representations and experiences of the feminine body that are denied, submerged, or repressed by its masculinist logic.

A different perspective within feminist theory regards the recuperation of "women's experience" to be an impossible task, since the condition for the possibility of any discourse, or for that matter "thought itself" (Colebrook 2000b, 35), is the rendering of certain materialities and subjectivities as the constitutive outside of the discourse. In this view, there is no recuperable ontological "thereness" to this abjected materiality (such as "a feminine experience"), because the abject can only be conceived in relation to hegemonic terms of the discourse, "at and as its most tenuous borders" (Butler 1993, 8). A well-known political intervention arising out of this analytic aims to demonstrate the impossibility of "giving voice" to the subalterity of any abject being—thereby exposing the violence endemic to thought itself. This intervention is famously captured in Gayatri Spivak's rhetorical question, "Can the Subaltern Speak?" (Spivak 1988).

The analysis I have presented of the practice of al-ḥayāʾ (and the practice of veiling) departs from both these perspectives: I do not regard female subjectivity as that which belies masculinist representations; nor do I see this subjectivity as a sign of the abject materiality that discourse cannot articulate. Rather, I believe that the body's relationship to discourse is variable and that it seldom simply follows either of the paths laid out by these two perspectives within feminist theory. In regard to the feminist argument that privileges the role representations play in securing male domination, it is important to note that even though the concept of al-ḥayāʾ embeds a masculinist understanding of gendered bodies, far more is at stake in the practice of al-ḥayāʾ than this framework allows, as is evident from the conversation between Amal and her friend Nama. Crucial to their understanding of al-ḥayāʾ as an embodied practice is an entire conceptualization of the role the body plays in the making of the self, one in which the outward behavior of the body constitutes both the potentiality and the means through which inferiority is realized (see chapter 4). A feminist strategy that seeks to unsettle such a conceptualization cannot simply intervene in the system of representation that devalues the feminine body, but must also engage the very armature of attachments between outward behavioral forms and the sedimented subjectivity that al-ḥayāʾ enacts. Representation is only one issue among many in the ethical relationship of the body to the self and others, and it does not by any means determine the form this relationship takes.

Similarly, I remain skeptical of the second feminist framing, in which the corporeal is analyzed on the model of language, as the constitutive outside of discourse itself. In this framework, it would be possible to read al-ḥayāʾ as an instantiation of the control a masculinist imaginary must assert over the dangerous supplement femininity signifies in Islamic thought. Such a reading is dissatisfying to me because the relationship it assumes between the body and discourse, one modeled on a linguistic theory of signification, is inadequate to the imaginary of the mosque movement. Various aspects of

this argument will become clear in the next section when I address the notion of performativity underlying the Aristotelian model of ethical formation the mosque participants followed. Suffice it to say here that the mosque women's practices of modesty and femininity do not signify the abjectness of the feminine within Islamic discourse, but articulate a positive and immanent discourse of being in the world. This discourse requires that we carefully examine the *work that bodily practices perform* in creating a subject that is pious in its formation.

To elucidate these points, it might be instructive to juxtapose the mosque participants' understanding of al-ḥayāʾ with a view that takes the pietists to task for making modesty dependent upon the particularity of attire (such as the veil). The contrastive understanding of modesty or al-ḥayāʾ (also known as *iḥtishām*) that results from such a juxtaposition was articulated forcefully by a prominent Egyptian public figure, Muhammad Said Ashmawi, who has been a leading voice for "liberal Islam" in the Arab world.[5] He is a frequent contributor to the liberal-nationalist magazine *Rūz al-Yūsuf*, which I quoted from earlier. In a series of exchanges in this magazine, Ashmawi challenged the then-mufti of Egypt, Sayyid Tantawi, for upholding the position that the adoption of the veil is obligatory upon all Muslim women (farḍ) (Ashmawi 1994a, 1994b; Tantawi 1994). Ashmawi's general argument is that the practice of veiling was a regional custom in pre-Islamic Arabia that has mistakenly been assigned a divine status. His writings represent one of the more eloquent arguments for separating the virtue of modesty from the injunction to veil in Egypt today:

> The real meaning of the veil [ḥijāb] lies in thwarting the self from straying toward lust or illicit sexual desires, and keeping away from sinful behavior, without having to conjoin this [understanding] with particular forms of clothing and attire. As for modesty [iḥtishām] and lack of exhibitionism ['adam ah-tabarruj] in clothing and outward

appearance [*maẓhar*], this is something that is imperative, and any wise person would agree with it and any decent person would abide by it. (Ashmawi 1994b, 25)

Note that for Ashmawi, unlike for the women I worked with, modesty is less a divinely ordained virtue than it is an attribute of a "decent and wise person," and in this sense is similar to any other human attribute that marks a person as respectable. Furthermore, for Ashmawi the proper locus of the attribute of modesty is the interiority of the individual, which then has an effect on outward behavior. In other words, for Ashmawi modesty is not so much an attribute of the body as it is a characteristic of the individual's interiority, which is then expressed in bodily form. In contrast, for the women I worked with, this relationship between interiority and exteriority was almost reversed: a modest bodily form (the veiled body) did not simply express the self's interiority but was the means by which it was acquired. Since the mosque participants regarded outward bodily markers as an ineluctable means to the virtue of modesty, the body's precise movements, behaviors, and gestures were all made the object of their efforts to live by the code of modesty.

Performativity and the Subject

It might seem to the reader that the differences between these two perspectives are minor and inconsequential since, ultimately, both understandings of modesty have the same effect on the social field: they both proscribe what Ashmawi calls "illicit sexual desires and sinful behavior." Disagreement about whether or not one should veil may appear to be minor to those who believe it is the moral principle of the regulation of sexuality, shared by Ashmawi and the mosque participants, that matters. The idea that such differences are minor accords with various aspects of the Kantian model of ethics discussed in chapters 1 and 4; however, from an Aristotelian point of view, the difference between Ashmawi's understanding of modesty and that of the mosque participants is immense. In the Aristotelian worldview, ethical conduct is not simply a matter of the effect one's behavior produces in the world but depends crucially upon the precise form that behavior takes: both the acquisition and the consummation of ethical virtues devolve upon the proper enactment of prescribed bodily behaviors, gestures, and markers (MacIntyre 1966). Thus, an act is judged to be ethical in this tradition not simply because it accomplishes the social objective it is meant to achieve but also because it enacts this objective in the manner and form it is supposed to an ethical act is, to borrow J. L. Austin's term, "felicitous" only if it achieves its goals in a prescribed behavioral form (Austin 1994).

Certain aspects of this Aristotelian model of ethical formation resonate with J. L. Austin's concept of the performative, especially as this concept has been conjoined with an analysis of subject formation in Judith Butler's work (1993, 1997a), which I touched upon briefly in chapter 1. It is instructive to examine this resonance closely for at least two reasons: one, because such an examination reveals the kinds of questions about bodily performance and subjectivity that are important to foreground in order to understand the force this Aristotelian tradition of ethical formation commands among the mosque participants; and two, because such an examination reveals the kind of analytical labor one needs to perform in order to make the ethnographic particularity of a social formation speak generatively to philosophical concepts—concepts whose anthropological assumptions are often taken for granted.

A performative, which for Austin is primarily a speech act, for Butler includes both bodily and speech acts through which subjects are formed. Butler, in her adoption of Derrida's interpretation of performativity as an "iterable practice" (Derrida 1988), formulates a theory of subject formation in which performativity becomes "one of the influential rituals by which subjects are formed and reformulated" (1997a, 160). Butler is careful to point out the difference between performance as a "bounded act," and performativity, which "consists in a reiteration of norms which precede, constrain, and exceed the performer and in that sense cannot be taken as the fabrication of the performer's 'will' or 'choice'" (Butler 1993, 234).[6] In *Excitable Speech*, Butler spells out the role bodily performatives play in the constitution of the subject. She argues that "bodily habitus constitutes a tacit form of performativity, a citational chain lived and believed at the level of the body" (1997a, 155) such that the materiality of the subject comes to be enacted through a series of embodied performatives.[7]

As I discussed earlier, Butler's conception of performativity is also at the core of her theory of agency: she claims that the iterable and repetitive character of the performatives makes the structure of norms vulnerable and unstable because the reiteration may fail, be resignified, or be reappropriated for purposes other than the consolidation of norms. This leads Butler to argue: "That no social formation can endure without becoming reinstated, and that every reinstatement puts the 'structure' in question at risk suggests the possibility of its undoing is at once the condition of possibility of the structure itself" (1997b, 14). In other words, what makes the structure of norms stable—the reiterative character of bodily and speech performatives—is also that which makes the structure susceptible to change and resignification.[8]

Butler's notion of performativity and the labor it enacts in the constitution of the subject may at first glance seem to be a useful way of analyzing the mosque participants' emphasis on embodied virtues in the formation of a pious self. Both views (the mosque participants' and Butler's) suggest that it is through the repeated performance of virtuous practices (norms in Butler's terms) that the subject's will, desire, intellect, and body come to acquire a particular form. The mosque participants' understanding of virtues may be rendered in Butlerian terms in that they regard virtuous performances not so much as manifestations of their will but more as actions that produce the will in its particularity. In this conception, one might say that the pious subject does not precede the performance of normative virtues but is enacted through the performance. Virtuous actions may well be understood as performatives; they enact that which they name: a virtuous self.

Despite these resonances between Butler's notion of performativity and the mosque participants' understanding of virtuous action, it would be a mistake to assume that the logic of piety practices can be so easily accommodated within Butler's theoretical language. Butler herself cautions against such a "technological approach" to theory wherein "the theory is articulated on its self-sufficiency, and then shifts register only for the pedagogical purpose of illustrating an already accomplished truth" (Butler, Laclau, and Žižek 2000, 26). Such a perfunctory approach to theory is inadequate, Butler argues, because theoretical formulations often ensue from particular examples and are therefore constitutively stained by that particularity. In order to make a particular theoretical formulation travel across cultural and historical specificities, one needs to rethink the structure of assumptions that underlies a theoretical formulation and perform the difficult task of translation and reformulation.[9] If we take this insight seriously, then the question we need to ask of Butler's theorization of performativity is: how does a consideration of the mosque participants' understanding of virtuous action make us rethink the labor performativity enacts in the constitution of the pious subject?

To address this question, I believe that it is necessary to think through three important dimensions of the articulation of performativity in regard to subject formation: (a) the sequencing of the performatives and their interrelationship; (b) the place of language in the analysis of performativity; and (c) different articulations of the notions of "subversion," "change," or "destabilization" across different models of performativity. One of the crucial differences between Butler's model of the performative and the one implicitly informing the practices of the mosque movement lies in how each performative is related to the ones that follow and precede it. The model of ethical formation followed by the mosque participants emphasizes the sedimented and cumulative character of reiterated performatives, where each performative builds on prior ones, and a carefully calibrated system exists by which differences between reiterations are judged in terms of how successfully (or not) the performance has taken root in the body and mind. Thus the mosque participants—no matter how pious they were—exercised great vigilance in scrutinizing themselves to gauge how well (or poorly) their performances had actually taken root in their dispositions (as Amal and Nama do in the conversation described earlier in this chapter).

Significantly, the question of the disruption of norms is posed differently in the model governing the mosque movement from how it is posed in the model derived from the examples that Butler provides. Not only are the standards by which an action is perceived to have failed or succeeded different, but the practices that *follow* the identification of an act (as successful or failed) are also distinct. Consider for example Butler's discussion of drag queens (in "Gender Is Burning") who parody dominant heterosexual norms and in so doing expose "the imitative structure by which hegemonic gender is itself produced and disputes heterosexuality's claim on naturalness and originality" (Butler 1993, 125). What is significant here is that as the drag queen becomes more successful in her approximation of heterosexual norms of femininity, the challenge her performance poses to the stability of these norms also increases. The excellence of her performance, in other words, exposes the vulnerability of heterosexual norms and puts their naturalized stability at risk. For the mosque participants, on the other hand, excellence at piety does not put the structure that governs its normativity at risk but rather consolidates it.

Furthermore, when, in Butler's example, a drag queen's performance fails to approximate the ideal of femininity, Butler reads this failure as a sign of the intrinsic inability of the performative structure of heteronormativity to realize its own ideals. In contrast, in the model operative among the mosque participants, a person's failure to enact a virtue successfully is perceived to be the marker of an inadequately formed self, one in which the interiority and exteriority of the person are improperly aligned. The recognition of this disjuncture in turn requires one to undertake a specific series of steps to rectify the situation—steps that build upon the rooted and sedimented character of prior performances of normative virtues. Amal, in the conversation cited above, describes how she followed her initial inability to simulate shyness successfully with repeated acts of shyness that in turn produced the cumulative effect of a shy interiority and disposition. Drag queens may also expend a similar kind of effort in order to better approximate dominant feminine norms, but what is different is that they take the disjuncture between what is socially performed and what is biologically attributed as necessary to the very structure of their performance. For the mosque participants, in contrast, the relevant disjuncture is that between a religious norm (or ideal) and its actual performance: their actions are aimed at precisely *overcoming* this disjuncture.

One reason these two understandings of performative behavior differ from each other is based in the contrastive conceptions of embodied materiality that underlie them. Butler understands the materiality of the body on the model of language, and analyzes the power of bodily performatives in terms of processes of signification whose disruptive potential lies in the indeterminate character of signs. In response to those who charge her with practicing a kind of linguistic reductionism, Butler insists that the body is not reducible to discourse or speech, since "the relationship between speech and the body is that of a chiasmus. Speech is bodily, but the body exceeds the speech it occasions; and speech remains irreducible to the bodily means of its enunciation" (Butler 1997a, 155–56). So how are we to understand this chiasmus? For Butler, the answer lies in formulating a theory of signification that is always operative—whether acknowledged or not—when one tries to speak about this chiasmus, because in speaking one renders discursive what is extra- or nondiscursive (Butler 1993, 11). The discursive terms, in turn, become constitutive of the extra-discursive realms of the body because of the formative power of language to constitute that which it represents.[10] Butler remains skeptical of approaches that leave the relationship between discursive and extra-discursive forms of materiality open and untheorized, and seeks to demonstrate the power of an analysis that foregrounds the significatory aspects of the body.[11]

It is important to point out here that there are a range of theorists who may agree with Butler about the chiasmic relationship between the body and discourse, but for whom a theory of signification does not quite address a basic problem: how do we develop a vocabulary for thinking conceptually about forms of corporeality that, while efficacious in behavior, do not lend themselves easily to representation, elucidation, and a logic of signs and symbols (see, for example, T. Asad 1993; Connolly 1999; Grosz 1994; Massumi 2002). For these scholars, a theory of linguistic signification does not quite apprehend the power that corporeality commands in the making of subjects and objects. These scholars, of course, speak from within a long philosophical tradition that extends from Spinoza to Bergson to Merleau-Ponty and, more recently, to Deleuze.

In light of this ongoing debate, a consideration of the mosque participants' understanding of virtuous action raises yet another set of interesting questions regarding Butler's emphasis on the significatory aspects of bodily performatives. As I mentioned earlier, the mosque participants do not understand the body as a sign of the self's inferiority but as a means of developing the self's potentiality. (Potentiality here refers not to a generic human faculty but to the abilities one acquires through specific kinds of embodied training and knowledge, see p. 147.) As described in chapter 4, the mosque participants are in fact strongly critical of the nationalist-identitarian interpretations of religiosity because these views treat the body primarily as a sign of the self rather than as a means to its formation. One might say that for the mosque participants, therefore, the body is not apprehensible through its ability to function as a sign but encompasses an entire manner of being and acting in which the body serves as the developable means for its consummation. In light of this, it is important to ask whether a theory of embodied performativity that assumes a theory of linguistic signification (as necessary to its articulation) is adequate for analyzing formulations of the body that insist on the inadequacy of the body to function as a sign?

The fact that the mosque participants treat the body as a medium for, rather than a sign of, the self also has consequences for how subversion or destabilization of norms might operate within such an imaginary. Note that the mosque participants regard both *compliance to* and *rebellion against* norms as dependent upon the teachability of the body—what I called the "docility of the body" in chapter 1—such that both virtuous and unvirtuous dispositions are neccesarily learned. This means that the possibility for disrupting the structural stability of norms depends upon *literally* retutoring the body rather than on destabilizing the referential structure of the sign, or, for that matter, positing an alternative representational logic that challenges masculinist readings of feminine corporeality. Thus, anyone interested in reforming this tradition cannot simply assume that resignifying Islamic practices and virtues (like modesty or donning the veil) would change the meaning of these practices for the mosque participants; rather, what is required is a much deeper engagement with the architecture of the self that undergirds a particular mode of living and attachment, of which modesty/veiling are a part.

The recalcitrant character of the structure of orthodox Islamic norms contrasts dramatically with the politics of resignification that Butler's formulation of performativity presupposes. Butler argues that the body is knowable through language (even if it is not reducible to language); corporeal politics for her often ensue from those features of signification and reference that destabilize the referential structure. In Butler's conception, insofar as the force of the body is knowable through the system of signification, challenges to the system come from interventions in the significatory features of that system. For example, Butler analyzes the reappropriation of the term "queer," which was historically used as a form of hate speech against lesbians and gays, but which has now come to serve as a positive term of self-identification. For Butler the appropriation of the term "queer" works by redirecting the force of the reiterative structure of homophobic norms and tethering the term to a different context of valences, meanings, and histories. What is notable for the purpose of my argument here is that it is a change in the referential structure of the sign that destabilizes the normative meaning and force of the term "queer." In the case of the mosque movement, as I have argued above, a change in the referential structure of the system of signs cannot produce the same effect of destabilization. Any attempt to destabilize the normative structure must also take into account the specificity of embodied practices and virtues, and the kind of work they perform on the self, recognizing that any transformation of their meaning requires an engagement with the technical and embodied armature through which these practices are attached to the self.

My somewhat long foray into Butler's theory of embodied performativity elucidates, I hope, the range of productive questions that are generated through an encounter between philosophical "generality" and ethnographic "particularity"—an encounter that makes clear the constitutive role "examples" play in the formulation of theoretical concepts. Moreover, an analysis of the historical and cultural particularity of the process of subjectivation reveals not only distinct understandings of the performative subject but also the perspectival shifts one needs to take into account when talking about politics of resistance and subversion.

TO ENDURE IS TO ENACT?

In this section I would like to return to the exploration of different modalities of agency whose operations escape the logic of resistance and subversion of norms. In what follows I will investigate how suffering and survival—two modalities of existence that are often considered to be the antithesis of agency—came to be articulated within the lives of women who live under the pressures of a patriarchal system that requires them to conform to the rigid demands of heterosexual monogamy. Given that these conditions of gender inequality uniformly affect Egyptian women, regardless of their religious persuasion, I am particularly interested in understanding how a life lived in accordance with Islamic virtues affects a woman's ability to inhabit the structure of patriarchal norms. What resources and capacities does a pious lifestyle make available to women of the mosque movement, and how do their modes of inhabiting these structures differ from women for whom the resources of survival lie elsewhere? In particular I want to understand the practical and conceptual implications of a religious imaginary in which humans are considered to be only partially responsible for their own actions, versus an imaginary in which humans are regarded as the sole authors of their actions. It is not so much the epistemological repercussions of these different accounts of human action that interest me (cf. Chakrabarty 2000; Hollywood 2004), but how these two accounts affect women's ability to survive within a system of in-equality and to flourish despite its constraints.

In what follows, I will juxtapose an example drawn from the life of a woman who was part of the mosque movement with another taken from the life of a woman who considered herself a "secular Muslim," and who was often critical of the virtues that the mosque participants regard as necessary to the realization of their ability to live as Muslims. I want to highlight the strikingly different ways in which these two women dealt with the pressures of being single in a society where heterosexual marriage is regarded as a compulsory norm. Even though it would be customary to consider one of these strategies "more agentival" than the other, I wish to show that such a reading is in fact reductive of the efforts entailed in the learning and practicing of virtues—virtues that might not be palatable to humanist sensibilities but are nonetheless constitutive of agency in important ways.

The full extent to which single women in Egypt are subjected to the pressure to get married was revealed to me in a conversation with Nadia, a woman I had come to know through her work in the mosques. Nadia was in her mid-thirties and had been married for a couple of years, but did not have any children; she and her husband lived in a small apartment in a lower-middle-income neighborhood of Cairo. She taught in a primary school close to her home, and twice a week after work she taught Quranic recitation to young children in the Nafisa mosque as part of what she considered her contribution to the ongoing work of daʿwa. Afterward, she would often stay to attend the lesson at the mosque delivered by one of the better-known dāʿiyat. Sometimes, after the lesson, I would catch a bus back with her and her friends. The ride was long and we would often have a chance to chat.

During one of these rides, I observed a conversation between Nadia and her longtime friend Iman, who was in her late twenties and who also volunteered at the mosque. Iman seemed agitated that day and, upon getting on the bus, immediately spoke to Nadia about her dilemma. A male colleague who was married to another woman had apparently approached her to ask her hand in marriage.[12] By Egyptian standards Iman was well over the

marriageable age. Iman was agitated because although the man was very well respected at her place of work and she had always held him in high regard, he already had a first wife. She was confused about what she should do, and was asking Nadia for advice. Much to my surprise, Nadia advised Iman to tell this man to approach her parents formally to ask for her hand in marriage, and to allow her parents to investigate the man's background in order to ascertain whether he was a suitable match for her.

I was taken aback by this response because I had expected Nadia to tell Iman not to think about this issue any further, since not only had the man broken the rules for proper conduct by approaching Iman directly instead of her parents, but he was also already married. I had come to respect Nadia's ability to uphold rigorous standards of pious behavior: on numerous occasions I had seen her give up opportunities that would have accrued her material and social advantages for the sake of her principles. So a week later, when I was alone with Nadia, I asked her the question that had been bothering me: why did she not tell Iman to cut off any connection with this man?

Nadia seemed a little puzzled and asked me why I thought this was proper advice. When I explained, she said, "But there is nothing wrong in a man approaching a woman for her hand in marriage directly as long as his intent is serious and he is not playing with her. This occurred many times even at the time of the Prophet."

I interrupted her and said, "But what about the fact that he is already married?" Nadia looked at me and asked, "You think that she shouldn't consider marriage to an already married man?" I nodded yes. Nadia gave me a long and contemplative look, and said, "I don't know how it is in the United States, but this issue is not that simple here in Egypt [il-masʾila di mish sahla fi maṣr]. Marriage is a very big problem here. A woman who is not married is rejected by the entire society as if she has some disease [il-maraḍ], as if she is a thief [ḥarāmi]. It is an issue that is very painful indeed [*hadhahi mas'ila muẓlima jiddan, jiddan ḥaqīqi*]."

I asked Nadia what she meant by this. She replied: "If you are unmarried after the age of say late teens or early twenties—as is the case with Iman— everyone around you treats you like you have a defect [*al-naqṣ*]. Wherever you go, you are asked, 'Why didn't you get married [*matgawwaztīsh ley*]?' Everyone knows that you can't offer to marry a man, that you have to wait until a man approaches you. Yet they act as if the decision is in your hands! You know I did not get married until I was thirty-four years old: I stopped visiting my relatives, which is socially improper, because every time I would go I would encounter the same questions. What is even worse is that your [immediate] family starts to think that you have some failing [*il-'ēb*] in you because no man has approached you for marriage. They treat you as if you have a disease."

Nadia paused reflectively for a moment and then continued: "It's not as if those who are married necessarily have a happy life. For marriage is a blessing [*na'ma*], but it can also be a trial/problem [*fitna*]. For there are husbands who are cruel [*qāṣi*]; they beat their wives, bring other wives into the same house, and don't give each an equal share. But these people who make fun of you for not being married don't think about this aspect of marriage, and only stress marriage as a blessing [*na'ma*]. Even if a woman has a horrible husband, and has a hard married life, she will still make an effort to make you feel bad for not being married."

I was surprised at Nadia's clarity about the injustice of this situation toward women and the perils of marriage. I asked Nadia if single men were treated in the same way. Nadia replied resoundingly, "Of course not! For the assumption is that a man, if he wanted to, could have proposed to any woman: if he is not married it's because he *didn't want* to, or there was no woman who deserved him. But for the woman it is assumed that no one wanted *her* because it's not up to her to make the first move." Nadia shook her head again, and went on,

"No, this situation is very hard and a killer [*il-mauḍū' ṣa'b wi qātil*], O Saba. You have to have a very strong personality [*shakhṣiyya qawiyya*] for all of this not to affect you because eventually you also start thinking that there is something deeply wrong with you that explains why you are not married."

I asked her what she meant by being strong. Nadia said in response, "You must be patient in the face of difficulty [*lāzim tikūni ṣābira*], trust in God [*tawwakali 'ala allah*], and accept the fact that this is what He has willed as your fate [*qaḍā'*]; if you complain about it all the time, then you are denying that it is only God who has the wisdom to know why we live in the conditions we do and not humans." I asked Nadia if she had been able to achieve such a state of mind, given that she was married quite late. Nadia answered in an unexpected manner. She said, "O Saba, you don't learn to become patient [*ṣābira*] or trust in God [*mutawakkila*] only when you face difficulties. There are many people who face difficulties, and may not even complain, but they are not *ṣābirīn* [patient, enduring]. You practice the virtue of patience [*ṣabr*] because it is a good deed [*al-'amal al-ṣāliḥ*], regardless of your situation: whether your life is difficult or happy. In fact, practicing patience in the face of happiness is even more difficult."

Noting my look of surprise, Nadia said: "Yes, because think of how often people turn to God only when they have difficult times, and often forget Him in times of comfort. To practice patience in moments of your life when you are happy is to be mindful of His rights [*ḥaqqahu*] upon you at all times." I asked Nadia, "But I thought you said that one needs to have patience so as to be able to deal with one's difficulties?" Nadia responded by saying, "It is a secondary consequence [*al-natīja al-thānawiyya*] of your doing good deeds, among them the virtue of patience. God is merciful and He rewards you by giving you the capacity to be courageous in moments of difficulty. But you should practice ṣabr [patience] because this is the right thing to do in the path of God [*fi sabīl lillah*]."

I came back from my conversation with Nadia quite struck by the clarity with which she outlined the predicament of women in Egyptian society: a situation created and regulated by social norms for which women were in turn blamed. Nadia was also clear that women did not deserve the treatment they received, and that many of those she loved (including her kin) were equally responsible for the pain that had been inflicted on her when she was single. While polygamy is allowed in Islam, Nadia and other participants of the mosque movement would often point out that, according to the Quran, marriage to more than one woman is conditional upon the ability of a man to treat all his wives equally (emotionally and materially), a condition almost impossible to fulfill.[13] For this reason, polygamous marriages are understood to create difficult situations for women, and the mosque participants generally advise against it.[14] Nadia's advice to Iman that she consider marriage to a married man, however, was based on a recognition of the extreme difficulty entailed in living as a single woman in Egypt.

While Nadia's response about having to make such choices resonated with other, secular, Egyptian friends of mine, her advocacy of the cultivation of the virtue of ṣabr (roughly meaning "to persevere in the face of difficulty without complaint") was problematic for them.[15] Ṣabr invokes in the minds of many the passivity women are often encouraged to cultivate in the face of injustice. My friend Sana, for example, concurred with Nadia's description of how difficult life could be for a single woman in Egypt, but strongly disagreed with her advice regarding ṣabr.

Sana was a single professional woman in her mid-thirties who came from an upper-middle-class family—a self-professed "secular Muslim" whom I had come to know through a group of friends at the American University in Cairo. In response to my recounting of the conversation with Nadia, Sana said, "Ṣabr is an important Islamic principle, but these religious types [mutadayyinīn] think it's a solution to everything. It's such a passive way of dealing with this situation." While Sana, too, believed that a woman needed to have a "strong personality" (shakhṣiyya qawiyya) in order to be able to deal with such a circumstance, for her this meant acquiring self-esteem or self-confidence (thiqa fil-nafs wal-dhāt). As she explained, "Self-esteem makes you independent of what other people think of you. You begin to think of your worth not in terms of marriage and men, but in terms of who you really are, and in my case, I draw pride from my work and that I am good at it. Where does ṣabr get you? Instead of helping you to improve your situation, it just leads you to accept it as fate—passively."

While Nadia and Sana shared their recognition of the painful situation single women face, they differed markedly in their respective engagements with this suffering, each enacting a different modality of agency in the face of it. For Sana the ability to survive the situation she faced lay in seeking self-empowerment through the cultivation of self-esteem, a psychological capacity that, in her view, enabled one to pursue self-directed choices and actions unhindered by other people's opinions. In this view, self-esteem is useful precisely because it is a means to achieving self-directed goals.[16] For Sana one of the important arenas for acquiring this self-esteem was her professional career and achievements. Nadia also worked, but clearly did not regard her professional work in the same manner.

Importantly, in Nadia's view, the practice of ṣabr does not necessarily make one immune to being hurt by others' opinions: one undertakes the practice of ṣabr first and foremost because it is an essential attribute of a pious character, an attribute to be cultivated regardless of the situation one faces. Rather than alleviating suffering, ṣabr allows one to bear and live hardship *correctly* as prescribed by one tradition of Islamic self-cultivation.[17] As Nadia says, if the practice of ṣabr fortifies one's ability to deal with social suffering, this is a secondary, not essential, consequence. Justification for the exercise of ṣabr, in other words, resides neither in its ability to reduce suffering nor in its ability to help one realize one's self-directed choices and/or goals. When I pressed Nadia for further explanation, she gave me the example of Ayyub, who is known in Islam for his exemplary patience in the face of extreme physical and social hardship (Ayyub is the equivalent of Job in the Judeo-Christian tradition). Nadia noted that Ayyub is famous *not* for his ability to rise above the pain, but precisely for the manner in which he *lived* his pain. Ayyub's perseverance did not decrease his suffering: it ended only when God had deemed it time for it to end. In this view, it is not only the lack of complaint in the face of hardship, but the way in which ṣabr infuses one's life and mode of being that makes one a *ṣābira* (one who exercises ṣabr). As Nadia notes in the conversation reported earlier, while ṣabr is realized through practical tasks, its consummation does not lie in practice alone.

Importantly, Nadia's conception of ṣabr is linked to the idea of divine causality, the wisdom of which cannot be deciphered by mere human intelligence. Many secular-oriented Muslims,[18] like Sana above, regard such an approach to life as defeatist and fatalist—as an acceptance of social injustice whose real origins lie in structures of patriarchy and social arrangements, rather than in God's will manifest as fate (qaḍāʾ). According to this logic, holding humans responsible for unjust social arrangements allows for the possibility of change, which a divine causality forecloses. Note, however, that the weight Nadia accords to fate does not absolve humans from responsibility for the unjust circumstances single women face. Rather, as she pointed out to me later, predestination is one thing and choice another (al-qadr shaiʾ wal-ikhtiyār shaiʾ ākhir): while God determines one's fate (for example, whether someone is poor or wealthy), human beings still choose how to deal with their situations (for example, one can either steal or use lawful means to ameliorate one's situation of poverty). What we have here is a notion of human agency, defined in terms of individual responsibility, that is bounded by both an eschatological structure *and* a social one.

Importantly, this account privileges neither the relational nor the autonomous self so familiar to anthropologists (Joseph 1999), but a conception of individual ethics whereby each person is responsible for her own actions.[19]

Just as the practice of self-esteem structured the possibilities of action that were open to Sana, so did the realization of ṣabr for Nadia, enabling certain ways of being and foreclosing others. It is clear that certain virtues (such as humility, modesty, and shyness) have lost their value in the liberal imagination and are considered emblematic of passivity and inaction, especially if they don't uphold the autonomy of the individual: ṣabr may, in this view, mark an inadequacy of action, a failure to act under the inertia of tradition. But ṣabr in the sense described by Nadia and others does not mark a reluctance to act. Rather, it is integral to a constructive project: it is a site of considerable investment, struggle, and achievement. What Nadia's and Sana's discussions reveal are two different modes of engaging with social injustice, one grounded in a tradition that we have come to value, and another in a nonliberal tradition that is being resuscitated by the movement I worked with.

Note that even though Nadia regarded herself as only partially responsible for the actions she undertook (the divine being at least equally responsible for her situation), this should not lead us to think that she was therefore less likely to work at changing the social conditions under which she lived. Neither she nor Sana, for a variety of reasons, could pursue the project of reforming the oppressive situation they were forced to inhabit. The exercise of ṣabr did not hinder Nadia from embarking on a project of social reform any more than the practice of self-esteem enabled Sana to do so. One should not, therefore, draw unwarranted correlations between a secular orientation and the ability to transform conditions of social injustice. Further, it is important to point out that to analyze people's actions in terms of realized or frustrated attempts at social transformation is necessarily to reduce the heterogeneity of life to the rather flat narrative of succumbing to or resisting relations of domination. Just as our own lives don't fit neatly into such a paradigm, neither should we apply such a reduction to the lives of women like Nadia and Sana, or to movements of moral reform such as the one discussed here.

THE PARADOXES OF PIETY

As I suggested in chapter 1, it is possible to read many of the practices of the mosque participants as having the effect of undermining the authority of a variety of dominant norms, institutions, and structures. Indeed, my analysis of the overall aims of the mosque movement shows that challenging secular-liberal norms—whether of sociability or governance—remains central to the movement's self-understanding. Moreover, regardless of the movement's self-understanding, the objective effects that the movement has produced within the Egyptian social field de facto pose stiff impediments to the process of secularization. Despite this acknowledgment, as I suggested before, it would be a mistake to analyze the complexity of this movement through the lens of resistance insomuch as such a reading flattens out an entire dimension of the force this movement commands and the transformations it has spawned within the social and political fields.

This caution against reading the agency of this movement primarily in terms of resistance holds even more weight when we turn our attention to the analysis of gender relations. In what follows, I want to show why this is the case through ethnographic examples in which women may be seen as resisting aspects of male kin authority. While conceding that one of the effects of the mosque participants' pursuit of piety is the destabilization of certain norms of male kin authority, I want to argue that attention to the terms and concepts deployed by women in these struggles directs us to

analytical questions that are closed off by an undue emphasis on resistance. The discourse of the mosque movement is shot through; of course, with assumptions that secure male domination: an analysis that focuses on terms internal to the discourse of piety must also engage the entire edifice of male superiority upon which this discourse is built. Indeed, my analysis of the mosque participants' practices of pedagogy and ritual observance (in chapters 3 and 4) is in part an exposition of this point. But the fact that discourses of piety and male superiority are ineluctably intertwined does not mean that we can assume that the women who inhabit this conjoined matrix are motivated by the desire to subvert or resist terms that secure male domination; neither can we assume that an analysis that focuses on the subversive effects their practices produce adequately captures the meanings[20] of these practices, that is, what these practices "do" within the discursive context of their enactment. Let me elaborate.

The pursuit of piety often subjected the mosque participants to a contradictory set of demands, the negotiation of which often required maintaining a delicate balance between the moral codes that could be transgressed and those that were mandatory. One common dilemma the mosque participants faced was the opposition they encountered to their involvement in da'wa activities from their immediate male kin, who, according to the Islamic juristic tradition, are supposed to be the guardians of women's moral and physical well-being. In order to remain active in the field of da'wa, and sometimes even to abide by rigorous standards of piety, these women often had to go against their male kin, who exercised tremendous authority in their lives, authority that was sanctioned not only by divine injunctions but also by Egyptian custom.

Consider for example the struggles a woman called Abir had with her husband regarding her involvement in da'wa activities. 1 had met Abir during one of the lessons delivered in the low-income Ayesha mosque and, over a period of a year and a half, came to know her and her family quite well. Abir was thirty years old and had three children at the time. Her husband was a lawyer and worked two jobs in order to make ends meet. Abir would sew clothes for her neighbors to supplement their income, and also received financial help from her family, who lived only a few doors down from her. Like many young women of her class and background, Abir was not raised to be religiously observant, and showed me pictures from her youth when she, like other neighborhood girls, wore short skirts and makeup, flaunting the conventions of modest comportment. Abir recounted how, as a young woman, she had seldom performed any of the obligatory acts of worship and, on the occasions when she did, she did so more out of custom (*'āda*) than out of an awareness of all that was involved in such acts. Only in the last several years had Abir become interested in issues of piety, an interest she pursued actively by attending mosque lessons, reading the Quran, and listening to taped religious sermons that she would borrow from a neighborhood kiosk. Over time, Abir became increasingly more diligent in the performance of religious duties (including praying five times a day and fasting during Ramadan). She donned the headscarf, and then, after a few months, switched to the full body and face veil (niqāb). In addition, she stopped socializing with Jamal's male friends and colleagues, refusing to help him entertain them at home.

Abir's transformation was astonishing to her entire family, but it was most disturbing to her husband, Jamal. Jamal was not particularly religious, even though he considered himself a Muslim—if an errant one. He seldom performed any of his religious obligations and, much to Abir's consternation, sometimes drank alcohol and indulged his taste for X-rated films. Given his desire for upward mobility—which required him to appear (what Abir called) "civilized and urbane" (*mutahaḍḍir*) in front of his friends and colleagues—Jamal was increasingly uncomfortable with the orthodox Islamic sociability his wife seemed to be cultivating at an alarming rate, the full face and body veil (niqāb)

being its most "backward" (*mutakhallif*) sign. He was worried, and let Abir know in no uncertain terms that he wanted a more worldly and stylish wife who could facilitate his entry and acceptance into a class higher than his own.

Things became far more tense between them when Abir enrolled in a two-year program at a nongovernmental institute of da'wa so she could train to become a dā'iya. She had been attending the local mosque lessons, and felt that she would make a more effective teacher than the local dā'iyāt if she had the proper training. Jamal did not take her seriously at first, thinking that she would soon grow tired of the study this program required, coupled with the long commute and daily child care and housework. But Abir proved to be resolute and tenacious: she knew that if she was lax in her duties toward the house, her children, or Jamal, she did not stand a chance. So she was especially diligent in taking care of all household responsibilities on the days she attended the da'wa institute, and even took her son with her so that Jamal would not have to watch him when he returned from work.

Jamal tried several tactics to dissuade Abir. He learned quickly that his sarcastic remarks about her social "backwardness" did not get him very far: Abir would retort by pointing out how shortsighted he was to privilege his desire for worldly rewards over those in the Hereafter. She would also ridicule his desire to appear "civilized and urbane," calling it a blind emulation of Western values. Consequently, Jamal changed his tactic and started to use religious arguments to criticize Abir, pointing out that she was disobeying Islamic standards of proper wifely conduct when she disobeyed the wishes and commands of her husband. He would also occasionally threaten to take a second wife, as part of his rights as a Muslim man, if she did not change her ways. On one occasion, when he had just finished making this threat in front of her family and myself, Abir responded by saying, "You keep insisting on this right God has given you [to marry another woman]. Why don't you first take care of *His* rights over *you* [*ḥaqq allāh ʿēlaik?*]" It was clear to everyone that she was talking about Jamal's laxity in the performance of prayers, particularly since just an hour before, Abir had asked him, as the man of the household, to lead the evening prayer (*ṣalāt al-maghrib*)—a call he had ignored while continuing to watch television. Abir had eventually led the prayers herself for the women present in the house. Jamal was silenced by Abir's retort, but he did not refrain from continuing to harass her. At one point, after a particularly harsh argument between the two of them, I asked Abir, when we were alone, if she would consider giving up her daʿwa studies due to Jamal's opposition. She answered resolutely, "No! Even if he took an absolute stand on the issue [*hatta lau kān itmassik li-mauqif*], I would not give up daʿwa."

In response to Jamal's increasing pressure, Abir adjusted her own behavior. Much to her family's surprise, she became uncharacteristically gentle with Jamal, while using other means of persuasion with him. In particularly tense moments, she would at times cajole or humor him, and at times embarrass him by taking the higher moral ground (as in the scene just described). She also started to pray regularly for Jamal to his face, pointedly asking for God's pardon (*maghfira*) and blessings (*baraka*), not only in this life but in the Hereafter. The phrase "*rabbinna yihdīk, ya rabb!*" ("May our Lord show you the straight path, O Lord!") became a refrain in her interactions with Jamal. Sometimes she would play tape-recorded sermons at full volume in the house, especially on Fridays when he was home, that focused on scenes of death, tortures in hell, and the day of final reckoning with God. Thus, in order to make Jamal feel vulnerable, Abir invoked destiny and death (reminding him of the Hereafter when he would face God), urging him to accord these their due by being more religiously observant.

All of these strategies eventually had a cumulative effect on Jamal and, even though he never stopped pressuring Abir to abandon her studies at the daʿwa institute, the intensity with which he did

so declined. He even started to pray more regularly, and to visit the mosque occasionally with her. More importantly for Abir, he stopped indulging his taste for alcohol and X-rated films at home.

What is important to note in this account is that none of Abir's arguments would have had an effect on Jamal had he not shared with her some sort of a commitment to their underlying assumptions—such as belief in the Hereafter, the inevitability that God's wrath will be unleashed on those who habitually disobey His commands, and so on. Abir's persuasion worked with Jamal in part because he considered himself to be a Muslim, albeit one who was negligent in his practice and prone to sinful acts. As an example of this, even when he did not pray in response to her repeated enjoinders, he did not offer a reasoned argument for his refusal in the way an unbeliever might have when faced with a similar situation. Certain shared moral orientations structured the possibilities of the argument, and thus the shape of the conflict, between them. When confronted with the moral force of Abir's arguments, Jamal could not simply deny their truth. As Abir once explained to me, for Jamal to reject her moral arguments would be tantamount "to denying God's truth, something even he is not willing to risk." The force of Abir's persuasion lay partly in her perseverance, and partly in the tradition of authority she invoked to reform her husband, who was equally—if errantly—bound to the sensibilities of this tradition. In other words, Abir's effectiveness was not an individual but a collaborative achievement, a product of the shared matrix of background practices, sensibilities, and orientations that structured Jamal and Abir's exchanges.

Secondly, it is also important to note that Abir's enrollment in the daʿwa institute against the wishes of her husband would not be condoned by majority of the *dāʿiyāt* and Muslim jurists. This is because, as I explained in chapter 2, while daʿwa is regarded a voluntary act for women, obedience to one's husband is considered an obligation to which every Muslim woman is bound.[21] Abir was aware of the risks she was taking in pursuing her commitment to da'wa: Jamal's threats to divorce her, or to find a second wife, were not entirely empty since he was within his rights as a Muslim man to do so in the eyes of the sharīʿa. Abir was able to hold her position in part because she could claim a higher moral ground than her husband. Her training in da'wa had given her substantial authority from which to speak and challenge her husband on issues of proper Islamic conduct. For example, as she learned more about the modern interpretation of da'wa from the institute where she attended classes, she started to justify her participation in da'wa using the argument, now popular among many Islamist thinkers (see chapter 2), that da'wa was no longer considered a collective duty but an individual duty that was incumbent upon each and every Muslim to undertake—a change that had come about precisely because people like Jamal had lost the ability to know what it meant to live as Muslims.[22] Paradoxically, Abir's ability to break from the norms of what it meant to be a dutiful wife were predicated upon her learning to perfect a tradition that accorded her a subordinate status to her husband. Abir's divergence from approved standards of wifely conduct, therefore, did not represent a break with the significatory system of Islamic norms, but was saturated with them, and enabled by the capacities that the practice of these norms endowed her with.

It is tempting to read Abir's actions through the lens of subordination and resistance: her ability to pursue da'wa work against her husband's wishes may well be seen as an expression of her desire to resist the control her husband was trying to exert over her actions. Or, from a perspective that does not privilege the sovereign agent, Abir's use of religious arguments may be understood as a simultaneous reiteration and resignification of religious norms, whereby patriarchal religious practices and arguments are assigned new meanings and valences. While both analyses are plausible, they remain inadequately attentive to the forms of reasoning, network of relations, concepts, and practices that

were internal to Abir's actions. For example, what troubled Abir was not the authority Jamal commanded over her (upheld by divine injunctions), but his impious behavior and his attempts to dissuade her from what she considered to be her obligations toward God. For Abir, the demand to live piously required the practice of a range of Islamic virtues and the creation of optimal conditions under which they could be realized. Thus Abir's complicated evaluations and decisions were aimed toward goals whose sense is not captured by terms such as *obedience* versus *rebellion, compliance* versus *resistance*, or submission versus *subversion*. These terms belong more to a feminist discourse than to the discourse of piety precisely because these terms have relevance for certain actions but not others. Abir's defiance of social and patriarchal norms is, therefore, best explored through an analysis of the ends toward which it was aimed, and the terms of being, affectivity, and responsibility that constituted the grammar of her actions.[23]

Daʿwa and Kinship Demands

The significance of an analysis that attends to the grammar of concepts within which a set of actions are located may be further elaborated through another example, one that is well known and often cited among those who are familiar with the figure of Zaynab al-Ghazali. As I mentioned in chapter 2, Zaynab al-Ghazali is regarded as a pioneering figure in the field of women's da'wa in Egypt; she is also well known for having served as a leader of the Islamist political group the Muslim Brotherhood in the 1950s and 1960s. Given her public profile and political activism, al-Ghazali has been seen as a paradoxical figure who urged other women to abide by their duties as mothers, wives, and daughters, but lived her own life in a manner that challenged these traditional roles (Ahmed 1992; Hoffman 1985). An often-cited example of this seeming contradiction is al-Ghazali's account of how she divorced her first husband whom she claimed interfered with her "struggle in the path of God" (*jihād fi sabīl lillāh*), and then married her second husband on the condition that he not intervene in her work of daʿwa (Z. al-Ghazali 1995; Hoffman 1985, 236–37).

In her well-known autobiographical account, *Days from My Life* (*Ayyām min ḥayātī*), al-Ghazali reports an exchange with her second husband, who, upon seeing the frequency of her meetings with male members of the Muslim Brotherhood increase, had inquired about the nature of her work. According to al-Ghazali, since the Brotherhood was under strict government surveillance, with many of its leaders in Egyptian jails, her work with the Brotherhood had to be performed clandestinely, and she refused to share the exact nature of this work with her husband. When he probed, she conceded that her work with the Brotherhood could endanger her life, but reminded him of the agreement they had come to before their marriage:

> I cannot ask you today to join me in this struggle [jihād] but it is within my rights to stipulate [*ashtaraṭ ʿalayka*] that you not prevent me from my struggle in the path of God [jihādi fi sabīl lillāh), and that the day this [task] places upon me the responsibility of joining the ranks of the strugglers [*mujāhidīn*] you do not ask me what I am doing. But let the trust be complete between us, between a man who wanted to marry a woman who has offered herself to the struggle in the name of God and the establishment of the Islamic state since she was eighteen years old. If the interests of marriage conflict with the call to God [*al-daʿwa ʾila allāh*], then marriage will come to an end and the call [to God] [daʿwa] will prevail in my whole being/existence. . . . I know it is within your rights to order me, and it is incumbent upon me to grant you [your wishes], but God is greater in us than ourselves and His cail is dearer to us than our existence. (Z. al-Ghazali 1995, 34–35)

In commenting on this passage, feminist historian Leila Ahmed points out that al-Ghazali's own choices in life "flagrantly undercut her statements on the role of women in Islamic society" (Ahmed 1992, 199-200). This contradiction is most apparent, in Ahmed's view, when al-Ghazalt gives herself permission to place her work above her "obligations to raise a family," but does not extend the same right to other Muslim women (Ahmed 1992, 200).[24] While I do not deny that al-Ghazali's life has entailed many contradictions,[25] I think it is possible to understand her prescriptions for Muslim women as consistent with the conditions she stipulated in her own marriage. Notably, al-Ghazali does not argue that the pursuit of *any* kind of work in a woman's life permits her to excuse herself from familial duties (as Ahmed suggests): only her work "in the path of God" (fi sabīl lillāh) allows her to do so, and only in those situations where her kinship responsibilities interfere with her commitment to serving God. According to al-Ghazali, had she been able to bear children, her choices would have been more complicated because, as she expressed to me in one of my interviews with her, this would not have left her "free to devote herself to the path of God" (Cairo, 22 July 1996). She also talks about this in an interview that was published in a Saudi women's magazine called *Sayyidati* (Hindawi 1997). In this interview, al-Ghazali explains her decision to seek divorce from her first husband by saying, "It was God's wisdom that He did not divert me from my [religious] activities by endowing me with a son, or blessing me with children. I was, however, and still am, a mother to all Muslims. Thus, confronted with the treasure and ardor of this call [to daʿwa], I was not able to keep myself from responding to it. When my [first] husband refused to let me continue my daʿwa activities, I asked him for a divorce and this was how it happened" (Hindawi 1997, 72).

Two doctrinal presuppositions are at the core of Zaynab al-Ghazali's argument. One is the position within Islamic jurisprudence, and commonly espoused by contemporary daʿiyāt and the ʿulamāʾ, that a woman's foremost duty is to her parents before marriage, and to her husband and offspring after marriage, and that this responsibility is second only to her responsibility toward God. Only in situations where a woman's loyalty to God is compromised by her obligations toward her husband and family is there space for debate on this issue, and it is within this space that al-Ghazali formulates her dissent against her husband.

Zaynab al-Ghazali's argument also turns upon another important distinction made by Muslim jurists between one's *material* and *spiritual* responsibilities toward one's kin—both of which are organized along lines of age, gender, and kinship hierarchy. In this moral universe, while women are responsible for the *physical well-being* of both their husbands and children in the eyes of God, they are accountable only for their own and their children's *moral conduct*—not that of their husbands. Husbands, on the other hand, by virtue of the authority they command over their wives and children, are accountable for their *moral conduct* as well as their *social and physical well-being*. Thus, while inferiors and superiors have mutual *material* responsibilities toward each other (in the sense that wives, husbands, and children are obligated to care for one another's material comforts, albeit in different ways), it is husbands who are accountable for their wives' virtue, while wives are accountable only for the moral conduct of their children. This distinction allowed al-Ghazali to argue that her inability to bear children had "freed her" to pursue da'wa activities, something she would have been unable to do if she were encumbered by the responsibility for her children's moral and physical well-being.

Al-Ghazali's ability to break successfully from traditional norms of familial duty should be understood, as I suggested in chapter 2, within the context of her considerable exposure to a well-developed discourse of women's rights at the turn of the twentieth century, a discourse that had been crucial to her formation as an activist. Indeed, it is quite possible to read al-Ghazaii's ability to stipulate conditions in both her marriages as a function of the opportunities that were opened up for women

of her socioeconomic background in the 1930s and 1940s in Egypt and the new consciousness this had facilitated regarding the role women had come to play in the public domain.

While this social and historical context is undoubtedly important for explicating al-Ghazali's actions in her personal and public life, it would be a mistake to ignore the specificity of doctrinal reasoning and its governing logic that accorded her actions a particular force—a force whose valence would be quite different if her arguments had relied upon the claim that women should be granted rights equal to those enjoyed by men within Islam in regard to marriage, divorce, and other kinship responsibilities. Al-Ghazali's actions and her justifications for her actions did not, in fact, depend on such an argument for equal rights. Instead her argument pivoted upon the concept of "moral and physical responsibility" that she as a Muslim woman owed to her immediate kin. In al-Ghazali's reasoning, her ability to break from these responsibilities was a function of her childless status. Whether we agree with the politics this reasoning advances or not, the discursive effects that follow from her invocation of this concept of moral responsibility explain both the power she commands as an "Islamic" (rather than a "feminist") activist in the Muslim world today and the immense legitimacy her life story has accorded juristic Islamic discourse on kinship—particularly for those who want to pursue a lifestyle that breaks from the traditional demands of this discourse while at the same time abiding by its central tenets and principles.

Here I do not mean to suggest that the effect of al'Ghazali's abidance by the terms of juristic discourse is best understood in terms of the lifestyles it has legitimized; rather, my point is that her narrative account should be analyzed in terms of the particular field of arguments it has made available to Muslim women and the possibilities for action these arguments have opened and foreclosed for them. It is this dimension of al-Ghazali's reasoning that I have wanted to emphasize, particularly because it is often ignored and elided in accounts that explain her actions in terms of the universal logic of "structural changes" that modernity has heralded in non-Western societies like Egypt. While these "structural changes" provide an important backdrop for understanding al-Ghazali's speech and actions, they have little power when it comes to explicating the force her life story commands in the field of Islamist activism.

Doctrinal (ir)resolutions

While many of the problems that al-Ghazali and Abir faced in their pursuit of piety were related to their goal of becoming trained dāʿiyāt, women who did not have such ambitions also encountered structurally similar problems. Given that Islamic jurisprudence regards men to be the moral and physical guardians of women,[26] participants in the mosque movement often complained that living with male kin who were not as religiously devout compromised their own standards of piety. The problem seemed to be particularly acute for a woman who was married to what the mosque participants called "al-zauj al-ʿāṣi" (a disobedient husband)—this concern was widely discussed not only in the mosque circles but also in religious advice columns in newspapers. In the eyes of the sharīʿa, even though a woman is not responsible for her husband's moral conduct but only her own and her children's, her husband's behavior nonetheless profoundly affects her own pursuit of a virtuous life, given the moral authority he commands over her and his offspring as their custodian. Faced with such a situation, it is not easy for a woman to challenge her husband's conduct or to seek divorce, given the stigma of being a divorcée in Egyptian society and the restrictions Islamic law places on a woman's right to divorce. It was, therefore, very common during the mosque lessons to hear the audiences ask the dāʿiyāt what a woman should do if she was married to a husband who lived a sinful

existence by the standards of virtuous Muslim conduct.

There is no simple doctrinal resolution to this problem. The responses of the dāʿiyāt varied and the women were urged to pursue a variety of means to come to terms with the contradictions posed by the conflicting demands of loyalty to God versus fidelity to one's (sinful) husband. Most dāʿiyāt, whether at the upper-middle-, middle-, or lower-income mosques, argued that since men are the custodians (auliyāʾ; singular: wali) of female kin in Islam, and not the other way around, women are not accountable in the eyes of God for the actions of their adult male kin. They advised women to try persuading their "disobedient husbands" to reform their behavior, and in the event they failed, to continue living with them with the understanding that they would have to be extra vigilant in monitoring their own conduct.

I questioned some of the dāʿiyāt and the mosque participants about the contradictions this advice generated in a woman's life, since living with an impious husband would force her into situations that compromised her ability to live by acceptable standards of virtuous conduct. Most of them acknowledged that their recommendations did not constitute the best solution to the problem at hand, but insisted that most women had no choice. Some of the dāʿiyāt said, "If we advised women to seek divorce from disobedient husbands, we would de facto be asking half the population of married Egyptian women to be divorcées!"—implying that they thought a large number of Egyptian men were impious. Some argued that the fact that women are not held accountable for their husband's conduct is a blessing God has bestowed upon women—one that frees them to pursue piety without having to worry about the conduct of male kin—while men are burdened with having to account for their wives' actions as well as their own.

Other dāʿiyāt, such as Hajja Asma, who had been Zaynab al-Ghazali's student and now served as a dāʿiya in a local mosque, answered the question very differently.[27] During an afternoon lesson, when Hajja Asma was presented with this question by a woman in her mid-thirties from among a group of twelve middle-class housewives, she started by inquiring about the nature of the husband's sins. Once it was established that they were "grave sins" (al-kabā'ir)—such as refusing to pray regularly (qaṣr al-ṣalāt qāṣiran), engaging in illicit sexual activity (zinā'), and drinking alcohol—she advised the woman to employ a variety of strategies to convince her husband to change his conduct. She said:

> The first step is to cry in front of your husband, and make him realize that you are worried for him because of what God will do to him given his conduct. Don't think that this crying is in vain [mafish fā'ida bi] because crying is known to have melted the hearts of many. One of my neighbors convinced her husband to start praying regularly this way. She also brought other pressures to bear on him by having me talk to him, because she knows that he respects me and would be embarrassed [maksūf] if I were to question him about prayers. But if you find that crying does not seem to have results, then the next step you can take is to stop sharing meals with him [baṭṭali it-taʿm maʿa]. Eventually this is bound to have an effect, especially because men usually have stronger willpower than women and when a man sees a woman stronger than him he is moved by her persistence and strength [istimrāriha wi quwwatiha].

At this point one of the women listening to Hajja Asma asked, "What if none of this has an effect on him [matitʿashirīshi bi]?" Hajja Asma replied, "The final and last thing you can try is to refuse to sleep with him [baṭṭali al-ishrʿa maʿa]." There was a palpable silence among the women at this point, and then a woman in her early thirties said in a low voice, "What if that doesn't work?" An older woman in her late sixties added loudly in response, "Yes, this happens a lot! [ʿaiwa, da ḥaṣal kitīr]." Hajja Asma nodded in agreement and said,

"If none of this works, and you are certain that you have tried everything—and *only you can judge how hard you have tried*—and he still does not change his ways, then you have the right to demand a divorce from him [ʿaleyki ḥaqq tuṭlubi it-ṭalāq minnu]."

Some of the women gasped in surprise: "Yā!" ("Yā!" is an expression of surprise women often use in Egyptian colloquial Arabic). Noting this reaction, Hajja Asma responded, "Of course—what else can you do [hatiʿmli 'ēh]? Live with a sinning husband, raise your children in a sinful atmosphere—who will then grow up to be like him? How can you be obedient to God if you are living with a man like this [tikūni fi-ṭ-ṭāsʿat allāh izāy lamma tikūni maʿa rāgil zayyu]?" She continued, "If it was only a matter of him being harsh with you [lau kān, qāṣi maʿaki], or having a rough temperament [tabīʿatu kān khishn], then you could have endured it [titṣabbiri ʿaley]. But this is something you cannot be patient about or forebear: it is an issue between you and your God."

Hajja Asma's words were received with somber silence, since divorce is not something that is easy for Egyptian women to contemplate given the social taboos associated with it, the bias against women in Egyptian law regarding child custody, and the economic hardship a divorcée must face in raising her children. Moreover, as I mentioned earlier, Islamic law does not make it easy for a woman to seek divorce, even in such a situation. In talking to Hajja Asma later, it was obvious to me that divorce was not something she took lightly either. Notably, Hajja Asma emphasized (as she does above) that if a woman was faced with a husband who had a harsh temperament, it was her obligation to be patient, given that patience (ṣabr) is an Islamic virtue that she should cultivate as a pious Muslim. But to practice forbearance in a situation where God's *claims over her* were being compromised, was to place her own interests (in terms of the security and safety marriage provides) above her commitment to God. When I asked the other dāʿiyāt and their audiences what they thought of Hajja Asma's response, they argued that not all women would have the courage and strength to risk the scorn and hardship a divorcée would be subjected to in Egyptian society in order to uphold high standards of virtuous conduct. Among the dāʿiyāt who took such a position, some of them said that women like Hajja Asma "were true slaves of God [*humma ʿibād ʿibād allāh ḥaqīqiyyan*]!"

As is clear from these disparate answers, the choice between submission to God's will and being obedient to one's husband did not follow a straightforward rule, and at times placed contradictory demands on the mosque participants. As a result, women were called upon to make complex judgments that entailed an interpretation of the Islamic corpus as well as their own sense of responsibility in the situation.[28] The questions the audience members posed, and the answers the dāʿiyāt provided, assumed that a woman is responsible for herself and her moral actions; the anguish underlying these queries was a product of both the sense of moral responsibility these women felt and the limited scope of choices available to them within orthodox Islamic tradition.

Within the moral-ethical framework articulated by Hajja Asma, a woman must, prior to asking for divorce, have a clear understanding of the order of priorities entailed in God's commands so that she challenges her husband only on those issues that compromise her ability to live as a dutiful Muslim. According to Hajja Asma's framework, if husbands interfere with matters pertaining to voluntary, rather than obligatory, acts (such as praying in a mosque instead of at home, practicing supererogatory fasts, undertaking daʿwa, or wearing the full face and body veil), then women are advised to give up these practices and to not disobey their husbands' wishes and commands. Similarly, a husband's harsh treatment of his wife is not regarded as sufficient reason to seek a divorce (although Egyptian women have been known to do so). Only when the nature of a husband's conduct is such that it violates key Islamic injunctions and moral codes, making it

impossible for a woman to realize the basic tenets of virtuous conduct in her own and her children's lives, is she allowed to resort to divorce.

When viewed from a feminist perspective, the choices open to the mosque participants appear quite limited. The constraining nature of these alternatives notwithstanding, I would argue that they nonetheless represent forms of reasoning that must be explored on their own terms if one is to understand the structuring conditions of this form of ethical life and the forms of agency they entail. Note that the various paths followed by the women do not suggest the application of a universal moral rule (in the Kantian sense), but are closer to what Foucault calls ethics: the careful scrutiny one applies to one's daily actions in order to shape oneself to live in accordance with a particular model of behavior. Thus, Hajja Asma's advice entails a variety of techniques of introspection and argument, including: examining oneself to determine whether one has exhausted all possible means of persuading one's husband prior to asking for a divorce; being honest with oneself in such an examination, since no one else can make such a judgment; and employing a variety of techniques of persuasion, both oral and embodied, to change the immoral ways of the husband. This stands in contrast to the kind of self-scrutiny applied by a woman who chooses to stay with an impious husband: such a woman must constantly watch that she does not use her husband's behavior as an excuse for her own religious laxity, assess her intentions and motivations for the actions she pursues, make sure she does everything in her capacity to raise her children in accord with standards of pious conduct, and so on. In both situations, moral injunctions are not juridically enforced but are self-monitored and entail an entire set of ascetic practices in which the individual engages in an interpretive activity, in accord with sharīʿa guidelines, to determine how best to live by Islamic moral codes and regulations.

Only through attention to these kinds of specificities can we begin to grasp the different modalities of agency involved in enacting, transgressing, or inhabiting ethical norms and moral principles. The analysis I have presented here should not be confused with a hermeneutical approach, one that focuses on the meanings that particular utterances, discourses, and practices convey. Rather, the framework I have suggested analyzes the *work* that discursive practices perform in making possible particular kinds of subjects. From this perspective, when assessing the violence that particular systems of gender inequality enact on women, it is not enough to simply point out, for example, that a tradition of female piety or modesty serves to give legitimacy to women's subordination. Rather it is only by exploring these traditions in relation to the practical engagements and forms of life in which they are embedded that we can come to understand the significance of that subordination to the women who embody it.

Finally, in respect to agency, my arguments in this chapter show that the analytical payback in detaching the concept of agency from the trope of resistance lies in the series of questions such a move opens up in regard to issues of performativity, transgression, suffering, survival, and the articulation of the body within different conceptions of the subject. I have insisted that it is best not to propose *a* theory of agency but to analyze agency in terms of the different modalities it takes and the grammar of concepts in which its particular affect, meaning, and form resides. Insomuch as this kind of analysis suggests that different modalities of agency require different kinds of bodily capacities, it forces us to ask whether acts of resistance (to systems of gender hierarchy) also devolve upon the ability of the body to behave in particular ways. From this perspective, transgressing gender norms may not be a matter of transforming "consciousness" or effecting change in the significatory system of gender, but might well require the retraining of sensibilities, affect, desire, and sentiments—those registers of corporeality that often escape the logic of representation and symbolic articulation.

NOTES

1. I am in agreement with anthropologists such as Jane Collier, Marilyn Strathern, and Sylvia Yanagisako who have argued that all cultures and societies are predicated upon relations of gender inequality, and that the task of the anthropologist is to show how a culturally specific system of inequality (and its twin, equality) is constructed, practiced, and maintained (Collier 1988, 1997; Collier and Yanagisako 1989; Strathern 1988). My only caveat is that I do not believe that there is a single arrangement of gender inequality that characterizes a particular culture; rather, I believe that different arrangements of gender inequality often coexist within a given culture, the specific forms of which are a product of the particular discursive formation chat each arrangement is a part of.

2. Most Arabic verbs are based on a triconsonantal root from which ten verbal forms (and sometimes fifteen) are derived.

3. It is interesting to note that the women I worked with did not actually employ the body-mind distinction I use in my analysis. In referring to shyness, for example, they talked about it as a way of being and acting such that any separation between mind and body was difficult to discern. I have retained the mind-body distinction for analytical purposes, the goal being to understand the specific relation articulated between the two in this tradition of self-formation.

4. This concept can perhaps be illuminated by analogy to two different models of dieting: an older model in which the practice of dieting is understood to be a temporary and instrumental solution to the problem of weight gain; and a more contemporary model in which dieting is understood to be synonymous with a healthy and nutritious lifestyle. The second model presupposes an ethical relationship between oneself and the rest of the world and in this sense is similar to what Foucault called "practices of the care of the self." The differences between the two models point to the fact that it does not mean much to simply note that systems of power mark their truth on human bodies through disciplines of self-formation. In order to understand the force these disciplines command, one needs to explicate the conceptual relationship articulated between different aspects of the body and the particular notion of the self that animates distinct disciplinary regimes.

5. Ashmawi served as the chief justice of the Criminal Court of Egypt and as a professor of Islamic and Comparative Law at Cairo University. For an overview of his work on Islamic legal theory, see Hallaq 1997, 231–54.

6. An important aspect of Butler's formulation of performativity is its relationship to concepts in psychoanalytic theory. On this relationship, see the chapter "Critically Queer" in Butler 1993.

7. See Amy Hollywood's excellent discussion of Butler's analysis of embodied performativity and its relationship to the concept of ritual (2002).

8. While Butler remains indebted to Derrida in this formulation, she also departs from him by placing a stronger emphasis on the historically sedimented quality of performatives. See Butler 1997a, 147–50.

9. Butler argues this point eloquently in her recent work: "no assertion of universality takes place apart from a cultural norm, and, given the array of contesting norms that constitute the international field, no assertion can be made without at once requiring a cultural translation. Without translation, the very concept of universality cannot cross the linguistic borders it claims, in principle, to be able to cross. Or we might put it another way: without translation, the only way the assertion of universality can cross a border is through colonial and expansionist logic" (Butler, Laclau, and Žižek 2000, 35).

10. Note that Butler's focus on the formative power of discourse posits a strong critique of a representational model of language. Her objections are twofold: one, that this model incorrectly presupposes chat language is anterior to the object it represents, when it in fact constitutes the object as well; two, that this model presumes a relationship of exteriority between language and power, when, in essence, language is not simply a tool for power but is itself a form of power. On these points, see Butler's critique of Bourdieu's representational theory of language in Butler 1997c; also see Butler and Connolly 2000.

11. In response to a question posed by William Connolly about the nondiscursive character of bodily practices, Butler argues: "To focus on linguistic practice here and non-linguistic practice there, and to claim that both are important is still not to focus on the relation between them, It is that relation that I think we still do not know how to think. . . . It will not be easy to say that power backs language when one form that power takes is language. Similarly, it will not be possible to look at non-discursive practices

when it turns out that our very way of delimiting and conceptualizing the practice depends on the formative power of a certain conceptual discourse. We are in each of these cases caught in a chiasmus relation, one in which the terms to be related also partake of one another, but do not collapse into one another" (Butler and Connolly 2000).

12. Islamic jurisprudence permits men to have up to four wives.

13. Both the Hanbali and Maliki schools of Islamic jurisprudence permit a woman to stipulate in her marriage contract that if the husband takes a second wife, she has the right to seek divorce. What is quite clear is that none of the schools give the woman the legal right to prevent her husband from taking a second wife. For recent debates on polygamy among contemporary religious scholars in Egypt, see Skovgaard-Petersen 1997, 169–70, 232–33.

14. This is further augmented by the liberal ideal of nuclear family and companionate marriage, which, as Lila Abu-Lughod points out (1998), has increasingly become the norm among Islamists as well as secular-liberal Egyptians.

15. I have retained the use of ṣabr in this discussion rather than its common English translation, "patience," because ṣabr communicates a sense not quite captured by the latter: one of perseverance, endurance of hardship without complaint, and steadfastness.

16. In the language of positive freedom, Sana may be understood to be a "free agent" because she appears to formulate her projects in accord with her own desires, values, and goals, and not those of others.

17. For contemporary discussions of ṣabr among leaders of the Islamic Revival, see M. al-Ghazali 1990; al-Qaradawi 1989.

18. As I indicated in chapter 1, I am using "secular-oriented Muslims" as shorthand to refer to those for whom religious practice has limited relevance outside of personal devotion. See chapter 2 for my discussion of how the term "secularism" is used by the mosque participants in Egypt today.

19. Notably, Sunni Islam shares with Protestantism two central ideas. First, they both share the assumption that each follower of the tradition is potentially capable of inculcating the highest virtues internal to the tradition and is responsible for the self-discipline necessary to achieve this goal (even though divine grace plays a central role in both traditions), Second, they both share the assumption that the highest

virtues of the tradition must be pursued while one is immersed in the practicalities of daily life, rather than through seclusion in an enclosed community (of nuns, priests, or monks), or a predefined religious order (as is the case in certain strains of Christianity, Hinduism, and Buddhism). Consequently all of life is regarded as the stage on which these values and attitudes are enacted, making any separation between the secular and the sacred difficult to maintain.

20. Obviously, my use of the term "meaning" here goes well beyond mere sense and reference.

21. Even among those writers who argue that da'wa in the modern period has acquired the status of an individual duty (farḍ al-'ain) rather than a collective duty (farḍ al-kifāya), da'wa is still considered, for women, an obligation secondary to their duties as wives, mothers, and daughters. This position is upheld not only by men but also by women, like Zaynab al-Ghazali, who have advocated for women's increased participation in the field of da'wa (see Z. al-Ghazali 1996a, 39; al-Hashimi 1990, 237).

22. Jamal could have countered this argument by pointing out that most proponents of da'wa consider it to be a woman's duty only if da'wa does not interfere with her service to her husband and children (see note above). But since Jamal was unfamiliar with these debates about da'wa, he was unable to make this argument.

23. My insistence throughout this book that we attend to the terms and concepts informing the actions of the mosque participants does not aim to simply reproduce "folk categories." Rather, my argument is that attention to these terms and concepts is necessary to rethinking analytical questions about regnant notions of agency in the social sciences and feminist theory. In this sense, my approach to the analysis of concepts is informed by the philosopher Ian Hacking who notes, "a concept is nothing other than a word in its sites. That means attending to a variety of types of sites: the sentences in which the word is actually (not potentially) used, those who speak those sentences, with what authority, in what institutional settings, in order to influence whom, with what consequences for the speakers" (Hacking 2002, 17).

24. Hoffman (1985) offers a similar reading of these passages.

25. In her two-volume book addressed to Muslim women in Egypt, al-Ghazali calls on women to enter the field of da'wa (Z. al-Ghazali 1994a, 1996a). However, she advises a woman dā'iya to concentrate her efforts on other women because "she can understand their temperaments, circumstances and characteristics, and therefore will succeed in reaching their hearts and solving their problems, and [be able] to follow their issues" (1994a, 2). While al-Ghazali conducted da'wa among women for a period of thirteen years, she also worked with men when she joined the Muslim Brotherhood as part of what she considered her work in da'wa. She rose to a position of leadership among the Muslim Brothers during a period when the majority of its top leaders were in jail and played a key role in coordinating the activities of the Brothers, a role for which she was later imprisoned. Clearly, her advice to women dā'iyāt—to primarily focus on other women—was not something she followed in her own life.

26. The Quranic verse often cited to support this position states, "Men shall take full care of women with the bounties which God has bestowed more abundantly on the former than on the latter" (al-rijāl qawwamūn 'ala al-nisā', verse 34 from Sūrat al-Nisā ["The-Woman"]).

27. Hajja Asma was the only dā'iya I worked with who talked openly about her sympathies with the Muslim Brotherhood. As a result, she often had to move from mosque to mosque under government pressure and was only able to offer lessons sporadically.

28. To make informed decisions about such an issue, Muslims often turn to a mufti (juriconsult) who, after consulting various established opinions and evaluating the individual situation, issues a fatwa that is legally nonbinding. In the context of the mosque lessons, the dā'iyāt, though not trained to be muftis, in practice enact this role by helping women interpret the shari'a in light of their personal situations. For more complex issues, the dā'iyāt often refer their audiences to a qualified mufti.

Queering Religious Texts: An Exploration of British Non-heterosexual Christians' and Muslims' Strategy of Constructing Sexuality-affirming Hermeneutics

Andrew K.T. Yip

INTRODUCTION

In spite of increasing social and legal normalization of non-heterosexuality (specifically homosexuality) in western society, non-heterosexuals[1] with religious faith continue to grapple with censure of their sexuality within religious communities. Notwithstanding the gradual ascendancy of their own voices and their supporters', their progressive efforts for change continue to experience resistance from conservative quarters of the religious communities. Within the Christian community, this resistance has been demonstrated since May 2003 by the controversy surrounding the appointment of the publicly gay Jeffrey John as the Bishop of Reading, and his subsequent withdrawal as a result of the threat of disintegration of the international Anglican Communion (e.g. Yip and Keenan, 2004). Such resistance is also clearly manifested in the Vatican's latest document on human sexuality, issued in June 2003, that continues to pathologize homosexuality and same-sex relationships (Congregation for the Doctrine of the Faith, 2003); and in the protestations against the election of Gene Robinson as Bishop of New Hampshire, the

first openly gay Bishop in the worldwide Anglican Communion (e.g. *USA Today*, 2003).

Similar discourse is evident in the Muslim community in the West, though not as common and widely reported. In 2001 in the Netherlands, for instance, imam Khalil El Moumni declared on national television that homosexuality was a disease, a sin, and a threat to social fabric, sending far-reaching ripples throughout Dutch society (for more details see Hekma, 2002).

Empirical research shows that non-heterosexual Christians and Muslims develop diverse strategies to manage the lack of acceptance experienced by them in religious communities.[2] While some conceal their sexuality in religious communities for fear of stigmatization (e.g. Yip, 1997), some discard religion altogether in order to reduce or resolve the psychological dissonance generated by the seemingly unbridgeable chasm between their sexuality and religious faith (e.g. Mahaffy, 1996; Safra Project, 2002). Some also refrain from 'practising' their sexuality through, among others, spiritual assistance from the so-called 'ex-gay movement'[3] (e.g. Naz Project, 2000; Ponticelli, 1996). Others attempt to minimize stigmatization by distancing themselves from religious communities but still keeping their religious faith through privatized practices such as prayer (e.g. Yip, 2000).[4] In addition, some search for accepting religious enclaves and thrive in such an environment (e.g. Lukenbill, 1998; Rodriguez and Ouellette, 2000). Finally, some remain in religious communities despite potential stigmatization, with the hope of effecting positive change from inside (e.g. Dillon, 1999; Yip, 2003a, 2003b). On the whole, these diverse strategies reflect how individuals with dissident and counter-normative identities manage social exclusion. The dynamics of such exclusion is complex; these strategies are inter-related, and their employment is context specific. In general, they are employed not only to defend, but also to construct space for the reinforcement of their dissident identity.

This article provides an in-depth analysis of a specific strategy that relates to and informs some of the strategies outlined above. Specifically, it presents narratives that demonstrate non-heterosexual Christians and Muslims constructing sexuality-affirming hermeneutics of religious texts to legitimize their sexuality theologically and also uncover 'queer' meanings in such texts for their own consumption and spiritual nourishment. This process is part and parcel of identity construction and management, aided by printed theological resources, the internet (e.g. on-line discussions or self-study of material) and support networks (e.g. support groups). It is important to state at the outset that individual non-heterosexual Christians and Muslims demonstrate varying degrees of competence in the employment of this strategy, depending significantly on their theological knowledge.

RELIGIOUS TEXTS AS THE PRIMARY BASIS OF CENSURE OF HOMOSEXUALITY

Christianity and Islam are scriptural religions with written texts as the lynchpin of their teachings on,

inter alia, sexual morality (e.g. Parrinder, 1996; Ridgeon, 2003). Thus, religious texts constitute the primary, though not exclusive, basis for the censure of homosexuality. The significance of the Bible was incontrovertibly highlighted in the recent controversies mentioned earlier. In the debates about the appointment of Jeffrey John, both his supporters and opponents resorted to the Bible to buttress their arguments. In their open letter expressing their concern about the appointment, nine bishops base their opposition primarily 'in the light of Scripture' (*The Guardian*, 2003). In defending Jeffrey John, Richard Harries, the Bishop of Oxford who appointed him, asserts that he 'could see nothing in the Bible' against John's celibate same-sex relationship (*The Sunday Times*, 2003). In both cases, the Bible as a divine text – and therefore of higher authority to humans – underlines the discourse and reverse discourse. Indeed, the significance of religious texts is undeniable. Even opponents with scarce theological knowledge often use clichés such as 'The Bible says so' or 'The *Qur'an* says it is wrong', to justify their stance against homosexuality. Though lacking in theological sophistication, such popular discourse reflects its significant textual underpinnings.

Against this backdrop, it is not surprising that non-heterosexual Christians and Muslims engage with religious texts to construct space not only to contest for acceptance, but also to generate theological capital for their own spiritual nourishment. Within Christianity, it is widely perceived that the Bible explicitly or implicitly censures homosexuality. The traditional – and still dominant – discourse of binary sexuality hegemonizes heterosexuality (particularly within marriage), and problematizes homosexuality. Biblical passages that are used to support this discourse are: Genesis 19 (e.g. most famously the story of Sodom and Gomorra), Leviticus 18:22 and 20:13, Deuteronomy 23:18, Romans 1:26–27, I Corinthians 6:9 and I Timothy 1:10, 18–32. In the past two decades, however, the emergence of lesbian and gay-affirming theology has rattled religious orthodoxy and offered significant resources to non-heterosexual Christians for the individual and collective construction of a reverse discourse (e.g. Jordan, 2000; Stuart, 1995), as I demonstrate later.

Islam, on the other hand, has a greater repertoire of religious texts in this respect. In addition to the *Qur'an*, which most Muslims consider the literal and unabridged words of *Allah*, the *Shari'ah* ('Whole duty of Mankind' [An-Na'im, 1990: 11], a text on moral and pastoral theology; laws for public and private life), and the *Hadith* (Sayings of the Prophet Muhammad) are also significant. Similar to the Christian discourse on sexuality, the Islamic discourse also hegemonizes heterosexuality within marriage, and renders homosexuality a revolt against *Allah* and violation of nature (Bouhdiba, 1998; Green and Numrich, 2001). Jamal (2001), for instance, argues that the story of Lot, which is mentioned in 14 of the 114 *suras* (chapters) in the *Qur'an* (e.g. 6: 85–87; 38: 11–14; 54: 33–40), is commonly used as the basis for censuring homosexuality (Jamal, 2001). Unlike Christian theology of sexuality, however, there are at present limited efforts in Islamic theology which offer non-heterosexual Muslims resources to construct a reverse discourse. The works of Jamal (2001), Malik (2003) and Nahas (1998, 2001; cf. Hekma, 2002) are distinct exceptions.

It is important to acknowledge that, despite the sharing of sexual identification and similarity in certain experiences (e.g. being stigmatized), non-heterosexual Christians and Muslims in Britain – and the West in general – differ in some significant ways. As mentioned, the former have witnessed significant growth in theological resources that affirm their sexuality. Such theological capital, however, is scarce for non-heterosexual Muslims. There is also a higher degree of internal pluralism within Christianity (some argue that this is evidence of secularization), compared to Islam, which opens up more space for dissident identities and alternative religious practices. Indeed, Islam in

the West, being a minority religion, also heightens expectation of adherence and conformity, as a form of cultural defence (Bruce, 2002; Roald, 2001). Further, Islam plays a significant role in ethnic identification among British Muslims, who are primarily of South Asian origin. Within the Muslim community, homosexuality is widely perceived as a 'western disease', a natural outcome of the West's secularity and cultural degeneracy (Naz Project, 1999; Yip, 2004). Non-heterosexual Christians are generally spared of such cultural complexities that significantly inform identity construction. In addition, Muslims face much prejudice in western societies, evidenced, for instance, in debates around state aid to Islamic schools and the wearing of *hijab* in school. Some argue that such prejudice has proliferated since the unfortunate event of September 11 (e.g. Fetzer and Soper, 2003). Finally, non-heterosexual Christians also have substantially more established support networks than non-heterosexual Muslims.[5] This has a significant impact on the availability of religious and social capital for identity construction and management. In short, it is important to be aware of the differences in the social positions of these two groups. Nevertheless, they all face varying degrees of religious exclusion on the ground of their sexuality.

In this specific strategy of queering religious texts, Goss (2002), with specific reference to Christian texts, argues that to 'queer' is 'to spoil or interfere with' (p. xiv). Queering religious texts, therefore, has a de-stabilizing effect, through the transgression and de-construction of naturalized and normalized hermeneutics, which reinforces heteronormativity. As I demonstrate, queering exposes the socio-cultural embeddedness and temporal specificity of the texts, as well as the ideological framework of the authority that constructs such hermeneutics. This strategy, closely informed by and intertwined with theological resources, can be divided into three approaches:

1   critique of traditional interpretation of specific passages in the texts;
2   critique of interpretative authority of religious authority structures and figures; and
3   re-casting religious texts.

Before discussing these approaches, I first provide a brief account of the research.

THE RESEARCH

The qualitative data presented in this article are drawn from two separate but conceptually related projects. The first project, conducted in 1997–8, involves in-depth interviews with 25 women and 36 men who are self-identified Christian and lesbian/gay/bisexual. The second project, on non-heterosexual Muslims, involves in-depth interviews with 20 women and 22 men, and two focus groups, conducted in 2001–2. Both projects aim to examine three levels of the participants' life circumstances and lived experiences. These levels are:

1   individual (e.g. how they reconcile the seemingly contradictory sexual and religious dimensions of their identity);
2   interpersonal (e.g. how they organize social relations with potentially stigmatizing social audiences such as the religious community and family); and
3   intergroup (e.g. how they access and manage involvement in support networks).

This article, however, focuses only on the individual level.

In view of the 'hidden population' status of the participants (particularly in the case of non-heterosexual Muslims), a variety of sampling methods were employed to construct non-probability convenience samples. These methods are: support group networks, non-heterosexual press, personal networks, snowballing, and publicity in non-heterosexual events/meetings.

There are similarities between the two samples, for instance, the majority of them live in Greater London and the southeast of England (71% non-heterosexual Muslims and 80% of non-heterosexual Christians). They are highly educated (52% of non-heterosexual Muslims and 89% of non-heterosexual Christians have at least a first degree), and the majority are in full-time employment (76% of non-heterosexual Muslims and 72% of non-heterosexual Christians). Almost all of the non-heterosexual Christian sample are white (97%), but none of non-heterosexual Muslims are, with 88 percent being of South Asian origin. Further, 64 percent of the non-heterosexual Muslims are under the age of 30, but only 48 percent of the non-heterosexual Christian sample are in this category.

CRITIQUE OF TRADITIONAL INTERPRETATION OF SPECIFIC TEXTUAL PASSAGES: A DEFENSIVE APPROACH

The majority of the participants acknowledge that homosexuality is presented in a negative light in some parts of religious texts. Thus, this approach focuses on *alternative* textual interpretations with the primary objective being to defend the acceptability of their sexuality, drawing upon theological resources, of which the participants demonstrate varying degrees of knowledge. In general, there are two dimensions to this defensive approach.

1 Engagement *within* the Framework of this Specific Corpus of Textual Material, by Constructing an Alternative and Sexuality-affirming Interpretation

Through this, the participants expose the inaccuracy of traditional interpretation, attempting to undermine its theological credibility and moral authority, and in return, enhance their own. One of the most commonly used passages in the censure of homosexuality in both Christianity and Islam is the story of Sodom and Gomorra in relation to Lot, Abraham's cousin (Genesis 19 of the Bible and *suras* 6 and 38 of the *Qur'an*). In both theological and popular discourses, the destruction of Sodom and Gomorra is often used as evidence of God's punishment for the 'sinful' same-sex sexual acts that occurred. Therefore, it is unsurprising that participants take issue with such interpretation, as demonstrated by the following narratives:

> The traditional interpretation of those passages that appear to speak against homosexuality is not accurate. I have read enough in this area to be convinced that the Church has got it wrong. They misunderstood male prostitution as homosexuality, for example [referring to Deuteronomy 23:18]. You get people who argue that 'Oh, Sodom and Gomorra is the story about God's punishment for gay people.' That's bullshit. There are tons of good books out there now to show that actually it is about inhospitality. (Sandra, a lesbian Christian in her 30s)

> I had assumed, like most Muslims, that Islam was very homophobic and the penalty for being gay was death. But I have since done some reading and discussed it a lot with people who know more about Islam than I do. I now know that there are various interpretations of what the *Qur'an* says. . . . I turned to the passage most Muslims would turn to – the story of the Prophet of Lot. I read and re-read it in English and Arabic, because it didn't occur to me that it was referring to sexuality at all. . . . So, as I discussed it more [on-line and in a support group] and read more, I became convinced by the argument that the passage didn't refer specifically to homosexuality, but to various things like inhospitality and the [negative] treatment of guests. That was a huge sense of relief! (Jamila, a self-identified queer Muslim in her 20s)

These narratives are clearly informed by lesbian and gay-affirming theology. This body of theology – which often examines original languages of the texts – has argued that the destruction of the cities was actually due to inhospitality to strangers and sexual violence (e.g. Goss, 2002; Jamal, 2001; Nahas, 1998). In the same vein, Nahas (1998, 2001) argues that although the *Shar'iah* is generally negative towards homosexuality, it also mentions that same-sex sexual acts are only punishable if they are observed by four witnesses. This problematizes the Islamic position on homosexual acts in private, particularly within the context of a loving and committed relationship.

Evidently, the participants engage with such alternative theological material to undermine the basis of the traditional interpretation that stigmatizes homosexuality. Significantly, they do not challenge the content of the religious texts, thus respecting their sanctity. However, they contest the accuracy and therefore the hegemony of the traditional interpretation of such texts. Through this, they construct themselves as victims (and indeed survivors) of religious ignorance and prejudice.

2 Contextualizing the Textual Material by Highlighting its Historic and Cultural Specificity, thus its Inapplicability to Contemporary Sociocultural Context

Here, the participants highlight the cultural and historical specificity of the traditional interpretation of homosexuality, which might appear negative, but is nevertheless inapplicable to contemporary society with its modern understanding of the diversity of human sexuality. In other words, they challenge the inerrancy and the literal usage of such texts on the basis that texts are discursively produced, therefore historical, temporal, and cultural specificity must be emphasized. Ian, a gay priest in his 50s, asserts the importance of such contextualization.

> So what if the Bible says some negative things about homosexuality? It was written ages ago,

when people did not have the scientific knowledge we now have about human sexuality. The culture was so rigid then when it comes to sex. How could you apply the standards and norms then to our life now? We have moved on. We should move on from that . . . I think that's the problem. The Church thinks that our understanding of sexuality doesn't change, or shouldn't change. But we do change, as individuals and a society.

Ian's argument is consistent with that of Shazia, a lesbian Muslim in her 30s:

I always question the *Hadith*, because the earliest *Hadith* was written 300 to 400 years after the death of the prophet Muhammad. So how true can that be? And at that time there was a lot of political people in Islam and Islamic tribes, so a lot of *Hadith* were written in a time of political upheaval, [with the] pressures to contain [a] society that needs order, rules, regulations. . . . The *Shari'ah* has come from the *Hadith* and also the *Qur'an*. But the *Shari'ah* has a lot to do with men specifically, and people controlling the masses. The *Shari'ah* has gone a long way to continue the bigotry and prejudice that lies in our Islamic cultures today, on homosexuality and many other subjects such as women.

These narratives resonate with the postmodernist approach that 'queer' theologians favour, that knowledge is discursively produced, and should not be universalized and generalized across time and space. For instance, lesbian and gay-affirming Christian theologians (e.g. Stuart, 2003) have argued that Leviticus 18:22 and 20:13 do not condemn sex between men. Rather, they censure 'a man lying with a man as a woman' (taking on the female role), which reflects socio-cultural significance and rigid symbolism of gender-specific sex roles within a particular historical context. Similarly, they assert that homosexual acts that the Apostle Paul censures (e.g. Romans 1:26–27; I Corinthians 6:9) actually refer to cult prostitution, which should have no bearing on contemporary same-sex relationships.

Within Islam, An-Na'im (1990) – with specific reference to civil liberties, human rights and international laws – asserts that the *Shari'ah* was developed based on Muslims' experience and understanding in Medina in the 7th century. Far from being divine and immutable, the *Shari'ah* is constructed, based on human interpretation of other Islamic sources within a specific cultural and historical context. Therefore, the interpretation and practice of it needs to be contextualized, as long as it is consistent with fundamental sources of Islam. Although An-Na'im makes no reference to sexuality in his arguments, works such as his contribute indirectly to non-heterosexual Muslims' consideration of Islamic written sources.

In sum, this defensive approach aims to defend the participants' sexuality by engaging with the same textual material, but offering an alternative de-stigmatizing light. Further, temporal and socio-cultural relevance is greatly emphasized. On the whole, it is a form of defensive apologetics. This is complemented by an offensive approach, to which I now turn.

CRITIQUE OF INTERPRETIVE AUTHORITY OF RELIGIOUS AUTHORITY STRUCTURES: AN OFFENSIVE APPROACH

Given the perceived divine authority of religious texts, it is unsurprising that religious authority structures employ them to buttress the absolutism of their own moral authority. Against this backdrop, the participants launch an offensive against religious authority structures and figures, so as to discredit their credibility and moral authority, and in turn weaken their discourse. Underpinning this approach is the argument that the engagement with texts cannot be separated from the power behind the interpretation and propagation. Participants raised two dimensions to this approach, which again appear to be informed by lesbian and gay-affirming theology.

1 Deconstructing and Challenging the Hegemonic Discourse of Religious Authority Structures

This dimension emphasizes the heterosexist bias embedded in the interpretation of religious texts and institutional pronouncements that censure homosexuality, as illustrated in the following narrative:

> I feel sometimes, all these people who issue these hard-line statements against homosexuality are repressed homosexuals themselves. To them homophobia is the biggest shield for their own [homo]sexuality. I mean, if you go to any little town in any Muslim country, the religious leaders are always involved with homosexuality. *Imams* have bad reputation in Pakistan in certain districts . . . for having sex with men. (Omar, a gay Muslim in his late 20s)

Omar might have exaggerated his observation. However, the thrust of his argument discredits the assumed intellectual and moral objectivity of religious authority figures. Empirical research has shown that younger Muslims in the West do challenge imams from their countries of origin (who are often not fluent in western languages) who attempt to re-enact the traditional version of Islam, which in their view, may not be totally appropriate for their western social environment (e.g. Smith, 2002). The employment of this offensive is also evident among non-heterosexual Christians, such as Margaret, a bisexual Christian in her 40s:

> I think the Church generally does not know how to deal with issues about sexuality, or anything to do with the body really. I think the Church is doing more damage than good, both to itself and the people it's supposed to be caring for. I often ask myself why I don't just walk away.

Besides undermining the moral credibility and intellectual objectivity of religious authority structures, the participants are also highly critical of their 'selective fundamentalism', namely their focus on homosexuality, and neglect of other 'abominations' mentioned in religious texts (e.g. wearing a mixed fibre jacket and eating shellfish).

This method is consistent with that widely used by feminist Christians and Muslims to challenge androcentric and patriarchal hermeneutics of religious texts and the construction of sexist theology (e.g. Jobling, 2002; Mernissi, 1991). By expressing doubt over religious authority structures and their discourse, the participants argue for the reliance on their own reasoning as the definitive interpretive authority of religious texts, to which I now turn.

2 Relocating Interpretive Authority from Institution to the Self

Having discredited the interpretive authority of religious authority structures, the participants relocate this authority to their self, using their personal experience as non-heterosexual believers as the interpretive lens. In this case, queering texts means personalizing and individualizing the interpretation of texts, by adopting a hermeneutic lens based on the authority of self. The following narratives demonstrate this:

> Anyone who goes to the *Qur'an* as a text is reading it . . . through their understanding of that reading. It's how you perceive the text. So between ten people who read the same sentence, we can perceive it in ten different ways. . . . So [the *Shari'ah*] are man made laws and they have come through male reasoning and interpretation. Do I wish to live my life according to that? Certainly not. . . . For me it's much more a personal thing. (Hasima, a lesbian Muslim in her early 20s)

> I think at the end of the day, my experience as a lesbian Christian will determine how I live. Okay, I listen to what the Church or Christian traditions have to say about sexuality and other things. I also

read the Bible. But at the end of the day, it's our conscience that counts, isn't it? Who is the Church to tell me that my life is a mistake? Yes, I did screw things up. But now I am happy as I am. The relationship with [her partner] has a lot to do with it. . . . So yes, my reference point is my own experience. (Sally, in her 40s)

These narratives illustrate clearly the participants' attempts to bring their self into the reading of texts. Such religious individualism, for non-heterosexuals with religious faith, is often a dissident identity management strategy (Wilcox, 2002, 2003; Yip, 2002, 2003a). Reading religious texts, therefore, becomes an exercise to seek guidance rather than approval, as they learn to trust their personal experiences as the 'spirit of truth' (Stuart, 1997a: 20; see also Stuart, 2003). It is important to acknowledge that the participants – in line with lesbian and gay theology – generally do not discount the value, relevance and indeed sanctity of the texts. However, they wrestle the authentic interpretive authority from religious authority structures and relocate it to their self – their own reflection, evaluation and experience. This is consistent with Koch's (2001) encouragement to non-heterosexual Christians to 'cruise' the texts, with their personal experience in the driving seat in the journey of textual exploration. The practice of this is elaborated in the next approach.

RE-CASTING RELIGIOUS TEXTS: A CREATIVE APPROACH

Compared to the first two, this approach is the least commonly used and sophisticated, primarily because the theological capital that underpins it is the most recently developed. Significantly, this approach moves beyond the framework of the moral debate about homosexuality, in which the first two approaches are embedded. Here, the participants focus on using the texts for spiritual growth. This approach, however, is significantly

uncommon among non-heterosexual Muslims at present. This, as mentioned, is a reflection of the significant discrepancy in theological and cultural resources between them and their Christian counterparts. There are two dimensions to this approach.

1 'Outing' the Texts

Goss (2002) defines 'outing' religious texts as the attempt to discover queer voices in them and to use them to inform non-heterosexual Christian living. In other words, accounts of same-sex intimacy and love are embedded within religious texts, but have been silenced. Such 'subjugated knowledge' ought to be used not only to justify same-sex intimacy and love, but also offer insights into dynamics of same-sex intimacy. Biblical accounts of the relationships of Naomi and Ruth (the book of Ruth), Jonathan and David (I and II Samuel), and Jesus and his disciples (the Gospel of John) are commonly used (e.g. Stuart, 2003). John, a gay Christian in his 50s, demonstrates his employment of such 'subjugated knowledge':

I draw so much comfort and confidence from the intimacy between David and Jonathan, or Ruth and Naomi. Their stories show us that same-sex love is possible [and] there is no need to be ashamed of it . . . Jesus himself was so close to his disciples. I have read that there are probably homosexual feelings between them. I think he opened the door for us. No need to be ashamed, really. I think we should focus on learning from these examples and enrich our own relationships.

2 'Befriending' the Texts

In this related dimension, the participants attempt to uncover implicit non-heterosexual subjectivity within the texts. A good example of this is their attempt to 'queer' Christ by focusing on his humanity, emphasizing his role as a champion of victims of social injustice and a radical political activist who transgressed traditional social order and power structure. Through this, the solidarity between Christ and non-heterosexual as the oppressed is established. Thus, Christ's suffering, as Goss (2002) argues, encompasses non-heterosexuals' suffering; and gay bashing becomes Christ bashing. The following narrative illustrates this central point:

> I see Jesus as a champion for marginalized people, like poor people, black people, and gay people. I really believe in it. He wasn't afraid of authority and really spoke his mind to defend social justice. I know deep inside that he understands me and knows the pains I go through [she is not open about her sexuality in the church for fear of rejection]. Hopefully, one day I feel strong enough to stand up and be counted in the church. I really hope so. (Maria, a lesbian Christian in her late 30s)

This view of Christ is prevalent among non-heterosexual Christians (e.g. Yip, 2003b). Another less common identification with Christ centres on his sexuality, as James, a gay Christian in his early 60s, asserts:

> Yes, Jesus is the Son of God. But he was also human. He felt pain when he was crucified. He had desires and urges like you and me. I think he must have had sexual feelings too. Otherwise, how could he be totally human like you and me? You see? I think he must have felt sexually attracted to people around him, maybe his own disciples too.

James' argument is consistent with theological efforts to construct Christ as a sexual being, which challenges the traditional conception of him as asexual or celibate (e.g. in emphasizing Christ's supposedly homoerotic relationship with Mark and Lazarus. See, for example, Bohache, 2003; Goss, 2002). This explicit allusion to Christ's sexuality accentuates his humanity, since being sexual is part and parcel of being human.

Another central Biblical figure who has been subjected to such 'queering', albeit to a much lesser extent, is the Apostle Paul. This is not surprising as some of his epistles are commonly used to justify the censure of homosexuality. Joy, a lesbian Christian who is clearly informed by Spong's (1991) controversial claim that Paul was 'gay', argues:

> I have read books which claim that Paul was gay himself. But he couldn't express it, you know, at the time. [It] must be tough for gay people then. . . . So we can understand why he is so negative about homosexuality in the Bible. I think he hated himself for being gay.

By constructing the texts as 'gay-friendly' through the reading of them from a queer social location, the texts are transformed into not only narratives of resistance (against censure), but also narratives of spiritual nourishment. This process promotes truth-claims that affirm their identity as well as nourishing their spirituality. Koch (2001), for instance, argues that non-heterosexual Christians should move away from the hermeneutical paradigm to defend themselves against the traditional interpretation of religious texts. Instead, they should use a 'homoerotic approach' that stems from internal knowledge – the self – which ' "cruises" the Bible for pleasure and moments of delightful encounter with those characters and stories which offer moments of identification, point of connection and the possibility of transformation' (p. 10).

Injecting 'queer' meanings to texts, therefore, becomes an important component of this process. For instance, there are efforts to inject homoeroticism into *Song of Songs*, the treatise to love in the Old Testament (e.g. King, 2000; Moore, 2001). The keyword in this effort is 'reclaiming', which signifies their intention to reclaim space that has been eradicated through traditional heterosexist hermeneutics.

Such 'befriending' of religious texts is relatively absent in Islamic theology and among non-heterosexual Muslims. The social position of homosexuality within the Muslim community and

Islamic theological discourses means that non-heterosexual Muslims have only recently begun the defensive – and to a much lesser extent, the offensive – approaches discussed above.

Beyond central religious texts, lesbian and gay-affirming Christian theology has also developed texts to affirm same-sex rituals, drawing upon the Bible and other sources (e.g. Kittredge and Sherwood, 1995; Stuart, 1992). A small minority of participants report that they have used such texts to celebrate their relationships.

CONCLUSIONS

Christian and Islamic religious texts have played a primary role in the censure of homosexuality. Not surprisingly, radical lesbian and gay theologians have called them 'texts of terror' that commit 'textual violence' to non-heterosexual believers, making them victims of 'biblical terrorism' (e.g. Goss, 1993, 2002). While participants of these research projects were less radical and forceful in their articulation of this issue, they nevertheless engage with such texts to construct sexuality-affirming hermeneutics, involving not just the texts, but also the interpretative authority of such texts. By no means do I claim that such endeavour is peculiar to contemporary society. What is significant is that, in contemporary society, social processes such as de-traditionalization and individualization *increasingly* empower the self over the institution as the basis of such self-directed hermeneutics that constitutes identity construction.

In this respect, this article has highlighted three multi-dimensional approaches – defensive, offensive and creative. Significantly, the engagement with such texts highlights the participants' view about their continued relevance to contemporary society. Nevertheless, such texts are no longer treated as an infallible prescriptive moral template, but as a set of moral guidelines with, at best, an advisory role. The reflection and evaluation of such texts, and the practice of principles gained from them, is no longer the preserve of religious authority structures, but their own. This process humanizes the texts, emphasizing the believer's moral right to choose and select from a repertoire, rather than being constrained by it (Dufour, 2000; Wilcox, 2002, 2003). Thus, the empirical 'what is' (based on personal experience) is prioritized over the theological 'what ought to be' (i.e. institutional perspective) (McFadyen, 2000).

In doing so, the participants bring the texts in line with their lived experiences by bringing the self into the reading (Stone, 2001a; Stuart, 1997b). This is reflective of recent developments in biblical hermeneutics (less so in *Qur'anic* hermeneutics) in which 'readers also bring a particular "self" to the text which is shaped by a variety of factors such as race, ethnicity, gender, class, religious affiliations, socioeconomic standing, education, and we would add, sexual orientation' (Goss and West, 2000: 4). In the same vein, Lozada (2000) has argued that biblical interpretation is not independent of one's identity, and the identity of the interpreter is interconnected with the production of meaning.

On the whole, this strategy highlights the discursiveness, situatedness and fluidity of religious texts – their meanings and teachings. By transgressing traditional discourse, such attempts are rebellious and liberative, as well as personally and socially transformative. In many ways, the fundamental operational principle of this strategy is not new. Feminist, black, post-colonial and liberation theologies, to name a few, have all attempted to contest boundaries legitimized by patriarchal, sexist, Eurocentric, and middle-class hermeneutics (e.g. Althaus-Reid, 2003; Beaman, 1999; Gutierrez, 2001; Roald, 1997). Indeed, as Bardella (2001: 117) argues, this is a kind of liberation theology that aims to 'theologically recontexualize the metaphysical dimension of homosexuality, to construct a spiritual discourse that includes lesbians and gays'. In this, we can see the intersection of the secular, the political, the theological, and the personal. Like other socially disadvantaged social groups whose voices are marginalized in religious communities, non-heterosexual Christians and Muslims, in the words of Johnson (2003: 166), attempt to insert their pictures into their 'faith family photo album, not as apologia, but a gift to the tradition'.

This strategy is not without its critics. For instance, the third – creative – approach to 'out' and 'befriend' texts has been criticized for imposing the contemporary template of sexuality and identity on the Apostle Paul and Christ, thus making the same mistake of cultural blindness which they critique. Stone (2001b) also argues that there is not, and should not be, a single 'queer method', which assumes uniformity among people who share the same label or social location. Religious, material and cultural diversity within the non-heterosexual community makes such a strategy rather limited. Further, the current 'queering the text' strategy has been criticized for being excessively individualistic and personalistic – even narcissistic – and devoid of political and historical context and meaning.

Nevertheless, Bowler's (1991; cf. Ford, 1999: 136) powerful words succinctly underline the participants' need to undermine the presumed infallibility of religious authority structures and their interpretative objectivity:

> The consequences of treating the scripture as though history and personality made no difference to the words and content of scripture have been, in Christian history, horrendous. By lifting a text from its content and treating it as a timeless truth, Christians claimed scriptural warrant for their murder of Jews (Matthew 27:25); by lifting a text, Christians found warrant for burning women whom they regarded as witches (Exodus 22:18); by lifting a text, Christians justified slavery and apartheid (Genesis 9:25); by lifting a text, Christians found justification for executing homosexuals (Leviticus 20:13); by lifting a text (Genesis 3:16), Christians found warrant for the subordination of

women to men, so that they came to be regarded as 'a sort of infant', incapable of taking charge of their own bodies, finances or lives.

The data presented in this article lend credence to the neosecularization thesis which argues that secularization does not mean the decline or even disappearance of religion. Rather, it signifies the declining significance and influence of religious authority structures in contemporary western society. This occurs in tandem with the ascendancy of self in the fashioning and construction of individual and social life (Yamane, 1997; Yip, 2002). Internal and external pluralism within the religious landscape in contemporary western society has led to increasing diversity in religious expressions, practices and identities. Indeed, religious orientation, identity and practices have become increasingly internally referential and reflexively organized, prioritizing human subjectivity. There is a perceptible relocation of interpretive authority to the self, buttressed by broad humanistic – often anti-authoritarian – values such as social justice, human rights, personal responsibility, liberty and diversity (e.g. Repstad, 2003). This is particularly true among religious people with dissident identities (Wilcox, 2002, 2003; Yip 2002, 2003c).

This development in the religious landscape is of course reflective of the contemporary western society as a whole. Processes such as de-traditionalization and individualization have significantly undermined the basis of traditional authority, leading to the empowerment of the self. Life, therefore, has become increasingly a strategic trajectory in the construction of social biography (e.g. Bauman, 2001b; Giddens and Pierson, 1998).

Indeed, in the case of non-heterosexual Christians and Muslims, queering religious texts becomes one of the strategies to construct 'do-it-yourself' social biographies to achieve identity coherence and continuity. Nevertheless, I must reiterate the importance of appreciating the different levels of efforts between these two religious groups due to the discrepancy in theological and social capital. I envisage that younger generations of non-heterosexual Muslims would lead the way for such progress. This is because empirical research on younger generations of British Muslims has shown that their identities, compared to those of the older generations, are more contested and reflexive, as a result of a broader cultural repertoire that selectively incorporates their cultures of origin and western values of personal freedom and liberty (e.g. Husain and O'Brien, 2001; Manji, 2003; Samad, 1998).

ACKNOWLEDGMENTS

Data on non-heterosexual Christians are drawn from a project funded by Nottingham Trent University. I gratefully acknowledge the support from the University, all user groups and participants. Data on non-heterosexual Muslims are drawn from an ESRC-funded project entitled *A Minority within a Minority: British Non-heterosexual Muslims* (Award No. R000223530). I gratefully acknowledge the support from the ESRC, all user groups and participants. I also wish to thank the three anonymous referees and Michael Keenan for their helpful comments.

NOTES

1. 'Non-heterosexual' is a contentious term. Some consider it pejorative because it labels people against the perceived norm of heterosexuality, thus reinforcing heteronormativity. They prefer 'lesbian, gay, and bisexual'. This phrase itself is unsatisfactory, as others insist on prolonging it, in the name of inclusivity, by adding 'transgendered', 'queer', and more

recently, 'intersex'. I decided to use 'non-heterosexual' throughout the text (except where there is a need to specify) primarily because it embraces all the labels used by participants – 'gay', 'lesbian', 'bisexual', 'homosexual' and 'queer' – to represent their dissident identity, in contrast to 'heterosexual'.

2. In the past decade, there has been a burgeoning corpus of sociological and psychological research on non-heterosexual Christians. However, this is not the case for non-heterosexual Muslims. The data on non-heterosexual Muslims presented in this article are drawn from the very first piece of sociological research on this sexual minority, although there have been several publications by support groups, based on anecdotal evidence and personal testimonies (all cited in this article).

3. There is diversity in the ideological framework of the 'ex-gay movement'. Some are tolerant of 'homosexual orientation' but not 'homosexual practice', thus abstinence is imposed. Others adopt a more stringent approach and attempt to 'heal' with their 'stepping out of homosexuality' programme. In general, all groups emphasize the importance of spiritual intervention and discipline. Examples of such groups are: *True Freedom Trust* (in the UK), *Exodus International* and *Living Water* (both in the USA).

4. Hower (2003) reports that while 60 percent of the lesbian and gay population in the USA are affiliated to a religion, only 38 percent practise their faith publicly (e.g. participating in church activities).

5. For instance, the *Lesbian and Gay Christian Movement* has a membership of more than 3000, with local groups across the UK. There are also many other non-heterosexual Christian groups organized by profession, gender and denomination. In comparison, support groups for non-heterosexual Muslims are a recent occurrence, the *Al-Fatiha Foundation* (in the USA) and *Al-Fatiha UK* were established in 1998 and 1999 respectively (*Al-Fatiha UK* changed its name to *Imaan* in April 2004). Other groups include Safra Project (UK) and the Yoesuf Foundation (The Netherlands; see Nahas, 2004).

20

"Intersexed Bodies in Mishnah: A Translation and an Activist's Reading of Mishnah Androgynos" and "An Ancient Strategy for Managing Gender Ambiguity"

Noach Dzmura

INTERSEXED BODIES IN MISHNAH

[Concerning the hermaphrodite]: There are in him manners[1] equivalent[2] to men, there are in her manners equivalent to women, there are in hir manners equivalent to men and women, and there are in zir[3] manners equivalent to neither men nor women.[4]

This first paragraph acts as a table of contents for a set of communal obligations, organizing the material that follows in the next four paragraphs by topic sentence. The hermaphrodite may exhibit behaviors that signal maleness, femaleness, "both sexes," and "neither sex" to the community.

Manners equivalent in them to men: he conveys Levitical impurity in semen like men; he may marry but may not be married to a man, like men; like men he may not be alone with women; he may not be sustained with the daughters in matters of inheritance like men; he is obligated to all the mitzvot proclaimed in the Torah, like men; he may not put on female clothing or cut [his hair as women do] like men; he may not make himself impure by corpses like men; he may not transgress "you shall not round off" "you shall not mar" like men.

His external appearance is male. His public behavior is male. He behaves toward women as a heterosexual man. However, his male exterior conceals female genitalia. He is not a man, but his community may see a man when they look at him.

Manners equivalent in them to women: she may become Levitically impure with menstrual blood like women; she may not be alone with men like women; she may not contract a levirate marriage like women; like women she does not receive a portion [of the inheritance] with the sons; she may not share in the holiest things like women; she is unfit to give any testimony mandated in the Torah like women; if she had prohibited intercourse her sons are prohibited from qualifying for priesthood like women.

She may be capable of pregnancy, so her behavior toward men is female (avoiding one-on-one social contact). Because she appears male, observers of her female-coded behavior toward men might not know how to interpret her behavior; perhaps it would seem a gender-variant masculinity. Since this is the way she is obligated to behave, her gender-variant form of masculinity might eventually be viewed as "another acceptable type of man"—that is, unless she is mistakenly perceived as (simply) male. To, prevent such mistakes, some form of perception management is required.

Manners equivalent in them to (both) men and women: s/he is obligated for damages incurred as though s/he were a man or a woman; the one who kills hir intentionally is put to death; if unintentionally the murderer receives asylum in the cities of refuge; hir mother will observe, on account of hir birth, the period of blood purification as if she had borne both a female and a male child, and brings an offering on account of the child as though both a male and female child had been born; s/he inherits all (if s/he is an only child) the inheritance like men and women; s/he eats holy things eaten outside of Jerusalem like men and women; if one said, "I am a Nazirite if this is both a man and a woman," then he is a Nazirite.

This paragraph insures that s/he receives basic human rights, just as both men and women do. "Both" in this paragraph indicates equivalence to men and women, "sameness." "Neither" (in the next paragraph) indicates "otherness" or dissimilarity to other humans.

*The last two paragraphs of Androgynos are peculiar in that they spell out obligations **for others** in the community rather than for the hermaphrodite: "hir murderer" is mentioned, as is "hir mother," and an anonymous "they" who incur no obligation because of hir action or inaction, and finally the "one" who takes a Nazirite vow on the condition of hir "bothness" or hir "neitherness."*

Manners equivalent in them to neither men nor women: they are not obligated on account of hir uncleanness; they do not burn (an offering) on account of hir uncleanness; zie cannot be subject to valuation like neither men nor women; zie cannot be sold as a Hebrew slave like neither men nor women; and if a person said, "I am a Nazirite if this is neither a man nor a woman" then he is a Nazirite. Rabbi Yosi says, "*Androgynos* is a being created in zir own image and the sages could not decide whether he was a man or she was a woman, but *tumtum* is judged either a doubtful man or a doubtful woman."

The writers of this text involve others in the process of ritually calling attention to the hermaphrodite as a human who exhibits "bothness" and "neitherness"— characteristics which would otherwise be hidden under hir slightly feminized (as described on the previous page) masculine behavior and appearance. The hermaphrodite is a special case—no other set of religious obligations crosses gender boundaries or requires the assistance of other community members to help realize the truth about a person's communal behavior.

To this activist (who often engages in managing communal perceptions about transgender "bothness" and "neitherness" that is hidden under a single-sex appearance), the writers of this text appear to have performed the postmodern task of managing perceptions about this dual-sex being, so that the community might recognize the truth of a complicated sex, rather than make a mistake and misinterpret a being who looks and behaves in public like a man.

AN ANCIENT STRATEGY FOR MANAGING GENDER AMBIGUITY

Western cultures deal with gender in terms of binary norms, instantaneous categorization, and certainty. Transgender people force us to confront gender in a more complicated way, tacitly or overtly positing a hard to define "third space" that exists outside the gender binary. It can be hard to categorize a person in a gender category, and harder still to remain certain about gender as a person transitions. Transgender ideologies ask us to recognize and grow comfortable with ambiguity and uncertainty. Transgender ideologies ask us to support transpeople in both their binary and their nonbinary self-identifications—even when such identifications occur simultaneously. How do we develop the tools to see the world in this unfamiliar way? These challenging postmodern propositions are not entirely without precedent in the ancient world. Mishnah Androgynos introduces and reifies three postmodern ideas about the management of gender ambiguity:

1) Ambiguity or indeterminacy can serve as a valid category of recognition, a "third space" in the context of a binary norm. In the same way, an electron in particle physics is said to be located within a cloud of possibilities rather than in a specific, predeterminable position. All possible positions within a common set are equally likely, equally true. Rather than certainty, this category of recognition is characterized by doubt. In other words, like Schrödinger's cat, which is both dead and alive until such time as an observation is made, the Mishnaic hermaphrodite is single-sexed and double-sexed and neither-sexed all at the same time—at least until the law requires a movement toward one state or another.

2) The category of third space embraces each pole of the normative binary and recognizes a space beyond it. A common set of options co-exist within this third space, from which situational or relative truths may be extracted. These situationally applied truths do not invalidate the third space's overarching ambiguity. Rather, the situation-specific truths (certainties like "male," "female," "both," or "neither") exist for a brief time in a longer-term container of indeterminacy (an uncertainty that contains "male," "female," "both," and "neither"). Interestingly, third space introduces the idea of *time* to the consideration of gender.

3) In order to collectively recognize an ambiguous or indeterminate third space alongside a recognized binary requires training (in the form of a statement of identity followed by reinforcement by another member of the community and renegotiation of terms between community members) about two simultaneous realities: a situational truth plus the recognition of third space as an overarching category. When such reinforcement occurs in Mishnah Androgynos, the rabbis seem uncharacteristically to be showing us that social role is not the sole determinant of gender; rather, the community participates in constructing the hermaphrodite's nonbinary gender identity.

The essay below shows how, against academic convention, I imagined these postmodern ideas in an ancient text. The subheading "It Takes a Village" takes readers past the surface to the underlying tensions in Androgynos, and shows how time and communal assistance are implicated in gendering the hermaphrodite. The subheading "Doubt and Difference: Translation Notes" shows how ambiguity-over-time acquires the stability required to comprise a category of recognition.

It Takes a Village

Since God commanded two genders ("male and female created he them," Gen. 1:27), the rabbis were limited in how they could approach the obligations of another human type. The strategy they arrive at is almost unique in rabbinic literature. S/he is to perform some behaviors in the way a man does, some behaviors in the way a woman does, some behaviors in the way both men and women perform them, and some behaviors as they are performed uniquely by a person who is neither man nor woman.[5]

On the surface, Androgynos appears to describe a separate human category that is strikingly balanced, covering each of the gender possibilities equally (equivalent to men, equivalent to women), and also seeming to see past the binary sex/gender system to encompass a being who embodies both genders, or neither (that is, equivalent to both men and women, equivalent to neither men nor women). Once one looks carefully at the way Androgynos is structured, this apparent democratic instinct seems much more complicated, and tells us that the rabbis maintained masculine dominance even within a dual-sex individual.[6]

Jewish religious obligations in antiquity circumscribed a wide range of personal behaviors, including such things as hair and clothing styles, the type of offerings one brought to the temple, laws of inheritance, and avoidance of the opposite sex before marriage.

These obligations were markedly different for members of each sex. If an observer did not know a person's gender in this ancient society from the clothing they wore (hard to imagine this situation, since clothing was gender-coded, but play along with me in this thought experiment), the observer would soon be able to identify a man or a woman via their daily duties. Mishnah Androgynos (translated above) organizes a set of religious obligations for a person with two sexes—two sets of genitals, one male and one female. Historically, such a person was referred to as a *hermaphrodite*. True hermaphroditism is mythical, but a condition called *pseudohermaphroditism* does occur (rarely), and other intersex conditions (genitalia that exhibit some aspects of both sexes) are quite common. If these ancient words might be said to apply to any modern persons Androgynos applies to intersexed people.[7] I think it is also helpful to classify some transpeople (including myself) in the same category as the intersexed, because our hormonally and surgically altered bodies retain characteristics of both sexes.

The authors of Androgynos didn't think of gender as a set of rules that could be modified according to a personal truth of an incongruent relationship between the physical sex of a body and the gender identity one expresses, but there's nothing to prevent readers of that ancient text today from thinking that way. This text, studied in synagogues today, can be useful in sharing with one's community those complicated personal truths about gender, which might then be incorporated into communal perceptions. In this essay, I want to put forth the idea that the ancient authors of Androgynos seem to have understood that it takes a village to communicate a complicated truth, in surprising agreement with the postmodern idea that perceptions of reality are socially constructed—and communally altered.

The Mishnah did not outline a distinct "third gender space" for the hermaphrodite that was easy to identify. Instead, the authors borrowed some behaviors from men and some from women, and cobbled together an ambiguous dual gender characterized by doubt.[8] The intersexed person the Mishnah is concerned with has a set of prescribed obligations that intentionally cross gender boundaries. Nevertheless, Mishnah Androgynos sets out a consistent prescription of behaviors such that, if an observer watched such a person long enough in the performance of hir daily duties, that observer would be able to correctly identify the person as a hermaphrodite, having distinguished both male-and female-coded behaviors. An observer's *certain* classification of the person as a hermaphrodite could only be made when other community members were observed together with the presumptive hermaphrodite. Those behaviors in Mishnah Androgynos that label a hermaphrodite as belonging to a category that is "both male and female" or "neither male nor female" are performed by other community members on behalf of the presumptive hermaphrodite (see paragraphs four and five of the translation, above).

How does such confused gender-coding play out socially? There was no real community governed by Mishnaic law; rather, in the Mishnah the rabbis constructed a legal fiction to flesh out and test the law. Engaging the imagination to construct a hypothetical social life for this fictitious ancient community can be a useful activity for thinking about gender in present-day society. Rather than being simple to decode and mutually exclusive, like the obligations for men and women, the gender identity for the intersexed person is ambiguous and challenging to decode. It takes time and observation in context to understand the hermaphrodite's behavior. Because this being's obligations required hir to cross genders, s/he might have been difficult to "read" and thus hard for a hypothetical observer to correctly and infallibly identify. If one did not observe the presumptive hermaphrodite for a long period of time together with other community members, one could make a mistake in identifying the sex and gender of the hermaphrodite.

An example: Hir dress and public behavior are patterned after male behavior. Hir external appearance follows a male pattern. Hir public behavior is male. S/he avoids one-on-one contact with women like any other unmarried man. However, hir male exterior conceals female genitalia. S/he is not a man, but hir community may see a man when they look at hir, because most of the public behavior s/he is required to perform marks hir as a man. However, since the hermaphrodite may be capable of pregnancy, s/he is required to avoid one-on-one social contact with men, too. Hir avoidance of both male and female companionship might appear strange and uncategorizable. If the hypothetical observer saw only a few public behaviors, such an observer might mistakenly identify the hermaphrodite as a man, since, according to the rabbinic prescription in Androgynos, s/he dresses like a man and only performs a few, relatively private female-coded behaviors.

To prevent such mistakes (and such mistakes were directly linked to divine displeasure in the hypothetical construct of Mishnaic "society"), it seems to me that the authors of the Mishnah obligated other people to reinforce the gender of the intersexual—by publicly identifying the hermaphrodite's dual-sex status. One example: Hir mother is required to bring an offering to the temple when s/he is born. Rather than bringing the offering for a male child or a female child, she brings both sorts of offerings. Her community, who knows she did not give birth to twins, will get the message that her child is intersex. The mother's offering is a gender code. Another example: On certain unspecified occasions, a person is required to stand up and make a claim (supported by a vow of increased piety if the statement is true—called a Nazirite vow) that a hermaphrodite has male and female genitals, and therefore is neither male nor female. Nazirite vows were often made to support the truth of a statement that might otherwise be contested. In a culture where gender is a rigid binary, gender variance is invisible. Gender-variant bodies have no specific language, no categories of recognition. If what we talk about shapes and defines our reality, gender

variance is wraith-like, visible only as deviation or *averah* (transgression). So it seems that even the ancients who wrote the Mishnah recognized as we do today that it takes a village to construct, reinforce, and police collective understanding of a nonbinary gender identity.

Today in Western cultures, many people mix or cross the binary lines of culturally specific gender-identifying behaviors. While we still attempt to classify people in gender boxes based on their behavior choices, transgender reality tells us that's no longer possible. Sight alone cannot tell us the entire truth about a person's gender. When I walk down the street, for example, people see a large bearded man. The reality of my female history is not apparent to the casual observer. To really understand my gender identity (if I didn't tell you outright), you would have to observe me and my community for a longer period of time, and allow the community to tell the story. Just like the hermaphrodite, whose story of dual sex must be told to the community by hir mother (when she makes the offerings at temple for both a boy child and a girl child) and by the Nazirites (who make the claim that s/he is both male and female and therefore not simply male or female), my story is told by my mother (who remembers her long-ago daughter with longing but speaks of her present-day son with love) and by my community (who know me as FTM and as an openly transgender activist). It takes a storyteller's eye to put together the full tale of a complicated gender identity.

Doubt and Difference: Translation Notes

Gender is what we do rather than what we are. Gender is a complex set of negotiated performances that indicate or divert attention from our hidden sexual organs and broadcast our sexual roles and preferences, rather than a simple binary code for what is between our legs. What gender is occupied by a person who has two sets of genitals? Since gender can also be described as one's sociosexual role, I think Mishnah Androgynos is an attempt to find a solution to that problem.

As an activist, I embrace this small corner of the Jewish canon as the core text for transgender inclusion.[9] While some academics and many present-day rabbis hold that the rabbinic hermaphrodite is a mythical creature not unlike the *koi* (an imaginary animal that is half domestic and half wild), I'd like to push this text put front and into our communities to discuss how gender variance can be accommodated within the existing binary, but also may push our capacity to recognize more than two genders in a sustained and systematic way.[10] More than any generic biblical text proclaiming the need for treating all people fairly "even to the stranger in your midst," the text of Mishnah Bikkurim chapter 4 says *of what fairness might consist*, and assures basic human rights are granted while "what is fair" is negotiated between members of a compassionate community. Mishnah Androgynos introduces the postmodern idea that—for all genders—one's social role is not the sole determinant of gender, and that certain negotiated alliances can foster recognition of a variant gender identity.

My version of Androgynos (appearing on pages 163–66) contains several key differences from typical academic and religious translations. The Hebrew word *derachim* (ways, manners, things) and the word *shaveh* (like, equivalent to) open interpretive possibilities in the text. Take for example the translations by classical commentators Pinchas Kehati and Herbert Danby. Pinchas Kehati translates *derachim* as "ways": "The *androgynos* is in some ways (*derachim*) like to men, in some ways like to women, and in some ways like to both men and women, and in some ways like to neither men nor women."[11] Herbert Danby translates *derachim* as "things": "The *androgynos* is in some things (*derachim*) like men, in some things like women, and in some things like both men and women, and in some things like neither men nor women."[12]

A reader of the Kehati or the Danby translations may be confused. A question remains as to whether "ways" refers to the physiology of the hermaphrodite, or hir behavior. One might ask the same question of Danby's "things"—must a body perform a certain way because one is equipped with certain things (a penis, perhaps, or both a penis and a vagina), or do the "things" refer to the behaviors one performs? A reader may also question the meaning of the word "like." Does it convey the meaning of identity (that is, "the same as"), parody or charade (almost, not quite), similarity (resemblance or approximation), or identity of behavior across differences of physiology? In reference to the text of Androgynos, if a hermaphrodite performs behavior assigned to women, does s/he *become* a woman, for that moment, under the law? Is she a half woman, whose male half remains unobligated during that momentary span of time? Or, is zie obligated like a woman and like a man at the same time, with halves of hir body compelled by different obligations? Or, is s/he truly "a creature in hir own image" only able to perform a parody of the behavior a (complete/whole/real) woman (or man) would perform?[13] Is the hermaphrodite who inherits from hir father's estate "acting like a man" or "really a man?" How much of that assessment depends on who is looking? I ask these questions to explore how an activist only peripherally influenced by scholarship (or halacha) might conceive of one kind of Jewish gender, the relationship between bodies and behaviors, and the communal implications of the hermaphrodite's carefully constructed gender performance.

In my translation, I chose to translate *derachim* as "manner" over "ways" or "things" to emphasize that the text is speaking primarily of behavior, although behavior almost always links to a particular anatomy. For the word *shaveh*, I chose "equivalent" over "like" to emphasize what I believe is the text's focus, which is not at all a matter of resemblance or parody, but rather, a matter of an authorized approximation. The hermaphrodite "does masculine" with the masculine half of hir body while the female half remains null. The result, rather than absolute ambiguity, is a limited (ephemeral?) typology: for the duration of the performance of the masculine act, there are two kinds of masculinity, one hermaphroditic, one male. The same applies to feminine acts.

As long as these categories are equivalent (*shaveh*) rather than hierarchical, the idea that there might be recognized, authorized, or negotiated "kinds" or "types" of masculinity and femininity is liberating for gender-variant persons in the present day.

The cumulative result of these word choices is to recognize in this text not simply a body of legal precedents (as some academics and some rabbis might view it), but to see the establishment of normative behavior and appearance of a hermaphrodite. Norms of behavior and appearance are actions that we perform—or performatives—for gender expression. Rather than an abstract legal document, the text describes norms of behavior and elucidates the ways the community may respond to enforce or police those norms.

In my translation, I substituted gender-variant pronouns (s/he and hir) because they help a reader of present-day American English (with its strict binary gender system) to keep the hermaphrodite's dual gender in mind. This option is not available in Hebrew, which defaults to a normative masculine gender (and therefore genders the hermaphrodite masculine). When reading the Hebrew I found it easy to let the hermaphrodite's male gender pronouns enable him to "pass for male." I think the loss of visibility of hir female aspects and dual nature were rabbinic concerns as well (see my translation of Androgynos for a discussion).

Perception is crucial to Jewish notions of gender. In fact, one minority Orthodox ruling on the "true gender" of a postoperative transsexual is based on the idea that perception carries halacha.[14] According to this *possuk* (rabbinic legal decision maker), a transsexual woman is a woman.

Safek (in the final paragraph of the translation) can mean both "divided" and "doubtful." The word

safek is used in Androgynos to describe the sex *tumtum* (*safek zachar v safek n'kevah*—a "doubtful man or a doubtful woman").[15] What the phrase means is that the *tumtum* might be a man or a woman, but there is no way to be sure until/unless surgery to remove the skin flap over the genitals is performed. *Safek* is later used in the Talmud to describe the sexual status of the hermaphrodite when considering whether s/he should be circumcised on the Sabbath. In this instance, the hermaphrodite is referred to as *safek zachar* (a "divided man," or the male half of a dual-sex person). Reading the modern world onto an ancient text in the way only an activist can, both senses of the word *safek* (as "doubtful" and as "divided") could be used in the case of the hermaphrodite, as a descriptor for gender that is uncertain. The hermaphrodite is a divided man/woman whose obligations to society variously express any of the following: sexual doubling, common asexualized humanity, maleness, or femaleness. Any of hir prescribed behaviors may result in the perceiver's doubt. If she is obligated according to hir "bothness" her masculinity and her femininity are covered over. If she is obligated according to her masculinity, her femininity and her "bothness" are covered over. There are additional permutations, but I won't spell them all out.

For academics, the modern concept of gender should not be brought into discussion of ancient texts; it's a modern construct and therefore irrelevant. As an activist outside of the academy, I am free to offer the word *safek*, inclusive of the connotations of both division and doubt, as a word that might describe the gender of a hermaphrodite.

The idea of official sanction of "true gender" that may be perceived as multiple, and "stable gender" that may be perceived as ambiguous (*safek*) offers potentially transformative options to the present day. In addition, it is liberating to recognize the hermaphrodite's gender as an expression of productive ambiguity rather than as a place of binary fixity, oppression, and/or repression.[16]

I'd like to put forward the idea that the perception of doubt or ambiguity about a person's gender is as valid a perception as is certainty. I'd like to hold up the irresolvability of the *androgynos's* gender identity as a desired condition. The irresolvable discomfort of the perceiver and the perceived that is inspired by doubt when one is confronted by a gender outside the ordinary is exactly the state that should be nurtured in Jews seeking to include transgender lives in their midst. It is a state wherein the participants are awake and aware to truth and human compassion, and the ability to relate as human companions is opened.

NOTES

1. Alternative translations for the Hebrew word *derachim:* "manners," "ways," "things."
2. Alternative translations for the Hebrew word *shaveh:* "equivalent to," "similar to," "like."
3. *Zie* and *hir* are gender-neutral pronouns. Hebrew is a binary-gendered language, and the hermaphrodite is referred to in the masculine. I use this and other gender-neutral pronouns in my translation. I got the idea to use male, female, binary gender inclusive *(s/he)*, and binary gender exclusive *(zie, hir)* pronouns from Reuben Zellman.
4. Charlotte Elisheva Fonrobert translates this passage: "[As far as the] androginos [is concerned]: there are *with* regard to him [grammatical gender] *ways* in which he is *similar* to men, and there are ways with regard to him in which he is similar to women, and there are ways with regard to him in which he is similar to both men and women, and there are ways in which he is dissimilar from both men and women" (emphasis mine). Fonrobert, "Regulating the Human Body," 273. I include this substantially similar translation here to emphasize differences (*with* vs. *in; ways* vs. *manner; similar* vs. *equivalent*). See my essay "An Ancient Strategy for Managing Gender Ambiguity" later in this volume for more about these choices.
5. *S/he* is a pronoun that combines both male and female pronouns.
6. Fonrobert, "Regulating the Human Body."

7. Elliot Kukla and Reuben Zellman assert that intersexed people are a present-day analog of the Mishnaic hermaphrodite in the essay "Created by the Hand of Heaven" later in this anthology.
8. The last line of Mishnah Androgynos bears repetition here: "Rabbi Yosi says, '*Androgynos* is a being created in zir own image and the sages *could not decide* whether he was a man or she was a woman" .'
9. The Mishnah is the core text upon which is built the three hundred years of Rabbinic discussion that forms the Gemara, and together the Mishnah and Gemara are commonly known as the Talmud, a collection of halacha (law) and aggadah (story). The Mishnah was collected earlier than the Talmud (circa 200 CE), and not everything in the Mishnah became a subject of the Gemara. The Mishnah was studied in its own right, too, as training material for aspiring rabbis. For these and other reasons it is still studied today. Mishnah Androgynos is a five-paragraph text tacked (in a late redaction) onto the tail end of the tractate concerning agricultural matters, called Zeraim, or Seeds. Mishnah Androgynos deals in a sustained way with the ritual obligations of a hermaphrodite, conceived by the rabbis as a human in possession of a set of male genitals and a set of female genitals. While Androgynos appears only in some versions of the Mishnah, it always (and perhaps more properly) appears in an earlier collection of legal writings called the Tosefta. I refer to it as Mishnah here simply because it was this context in which I first found Androgynos. The texts are substantially the same from both sources; the only changes are to the number and order of listed obligations. The overall structure of the hermaphrodite's social role (and masculine gender presentation) is the same in all the texts. Mishnah Androgynos does not have a corresponding Gemara, but its subject (the hermaphrodite) is referenced close to three hundred times in the Talmud as a "special case" whose obligations vary from those of normative men and women.
10. The rabbis specify that the *koi* (Tosefta Bikkurim 1) is to be treated in some things like a wild animal, in some things like a domestic animal, in some things like both a wild and a domestic animal, and in some things like neither a wild nor a domestic animal. The *koi* is a mythical creature (sometimes described as half goat and half cow) employed by the rabbis to test the limits of the law.
11. Kehati, (1996), 52.

12. Danby,(1933), 97–98.

13. Tosefta Bikkurim 2:7, "*androgynos biria bifnei atzmo hu.*"

14. Tzitz Eliezer; see Beth Orens's essay "Judaism and Gender Issues" in this volume for more information.

15. A *tumtum* is a second human of variable gender in rabbinic texts. The *tumtum* is either a man or a woman whose sex cannot be known until/unless a flap of skin covering the genitals is removed.

16. I owe the idea of productive ambiguity to Ann Burlein's article "The Productive Power of Ambiguity: Rethinking Homosexuality through the Virtual and Developmental Systems Theory" *Hypatia* 20, no. 1 (Winter 2005); 21–53.

Religion and Social Movements

Essay:
Changing Religions, Changing Worlds

The Metropolitan Community Church (MCC) began in 1968 with the explicit goal of serving lesbian, gay, bisexual, transgender, and queer (LGBTQ) Christians. Its founder, the Reverend Troy Perry, has been an activist in LGBTQ communities since the church first opened its doors—or rather, since he opened the doors of his home to the first worshippers in his church. Perry has fasted, marched, spoken out, and married people in the interest of LGBTQ rights; in fact, despite a common assumption on the part of both LGBTQ people and straight, cisgender (non-transgender) people that LGBTQ people aren't religious, Perry not only has attracted an international following of over 40,000, but has also been a fixture in mainstream gay and lesbian activism. Furthermore, since Perry attracted like-minded clergy and theologians, the MCC has become central to the development of LGBTQ-positive Christian theology and even played an important role in the founding of the first LGBTQ synagogue, Los Angeles's Beth Chayim Chadashim. Thus, the MCC has two relationships to social movements: first, as a religious institution it is itself a social movement, and second, it has served as an important resource for broader LGBTQ social movements.

The purpose of this chapter is to examine the relationship between religion and social movements, first in terms of the resources religion can bring to social movements and second in terms of how religious organizations themselves function as social movements. Although sociologists have written a great deal about how religious beliefs affect political opinions, there is relatively little sociological literature that examines in a theoretical way the connections between social activism and religion. Sociologist Otto Maduro's early book, *Religion and Social Conflicts* (1982), is an exception to this rule. Maduro takes up several aspects of the relationship between religion and social conflict, including society's role in shaping religion and the effects of social conflict on religion. Of greatest interest for our purposes here, however, is the section of the book in which Maduro considers the direct relationships between religion and social movements, including religion's ability to hinder such movements and its ability to help them.

Religion in Social Movements

Taking his cue from Marx and Gramsci but going much further than either of those earlier thinkers, Maduro examines the relationship between religion and class-based oppression in Latin America. Working primarily on a theoretical level, Maduro performs an intellectual act that would surprise most Marxist theorists: he makes use of Marxist concepts to argue that religion not only suppresses revolution but also can encourage it.

Religion, Maduro suggests, shapes society through shaping the worldview of a people. When religion supports a hegemonic system (see Chapter 3), it does so through that system's co-optation of the clergy, the religious leaders. Hegemonic systems also repress insurgent religions, co-opt or annihilate indigenous religions, and remove the "means of religious production" from the oppressed group. That is to say, hegemonic systems take over the functions of producing religious thought, certifying religious leaders, and conducting religious ritual. Not only does such a takeover demoralize the oppressed group by removing control over their traditions, Maduro argues, but it also removes that group's ability to utilize religion as a mode of resistance.

Maduro adds that churches (despite the Christocentric term, he means organized, monotheistic religion in general) can play a socially conservative role—that is, they can conserve the status quo—by "produc[ing] a unitive and ambiguous religious discourse." In addition, smaller religious movements can fragment or, as Marx argued, pacify non-dominant social groups.

But this is not the end of the story, and here Maduro parts ways with most Marxist thinkers. Since Maduro holds that religion shapes society through its control over the social worldview (in a society dominated by a single religion, at least), he follows Gramsci in arguing that religion can produce a revolutionary worldview as well as an oppressive one. In addition, Maduro suggests that religion can address "class consciousness," "class organization," and "class mobilization." Religion, in other words, can be a potent source of revolution. It is important to note here that central to Maduro's argument is the idea that a non-dominant group should have its own religion; in this way, the group can control the religious worldview and leadership for itself. However, Maduro also believes that there is potential for revolution from within traditional religions. In this case, he says, the priests of that religion (here he is thinking predominantly of Roman Catholicism) serve as Gramscian **organic intellectuals**.

Like Maduro, Gramsci was concerned about the creation of worldviews (though he didn't use that term). He worried that even revolutionary ideas were too often created by intellectuals, like Marx, who had no roots in the communities they were trying to help, and that this lack of connection weakened the potential their ideas had to create change. Gramsci, who himself was from a working-class background, advocated the education of people from within oppressed communities who could learn the intellectual traditions of the dominant group but could also think differently about those traditions so as to adapt them for use by oppressed groups. The organic intellectual would then return to her or his community and make use of her or his education to create social change.

An excellent example of an organic intellectual within religion, and surely someone Maduro had in mind, is Gustavo Gutiérrez, the founder of liberation theology (see the Extended Application in Chapter 3). Another is Metropolitan Community Church founder Troy Perry, a trained pastor of a highly conservative church who came out as gay and lost his congregation, his ordination, and his family. Furthermore, MCC is an important example of Maduro's claim that oppressed groups need their own religion. Though MCC is a branch of Christianity, it is an autonomous denomination. It serves primarily people who experience oppression on the basis of their sexual orientation and/ or gender identity, and it has served as an important resource for social change.

Sociologist Christian Smith (1996) offers some perspectives on exactly how organized religious groups like MCC can offer support to social movements of all kinds. Focused less specifically on social justice than Maduro is, Smith considers a variety of social movements in their relationship to religion, and offers a systematic evaluation of the resources religion can bring to social movements. He begins with the importance of transcendent motivation, or the power of the belief that one is working for a higher purpose beyond the human realm. Sociologists have long noted that such religious **legitimations** are particularly powerful ways of justifying social relations, but generally such observations have focused on maintaining the social status quo: using religion to justify a deep division between rich and poor, for example. While this is certainly one legitimating function of religion, Smith points out that religious legitimations can serve to support revolutionary struggle, as well. Other aspects of a religious worldview, such as an emphasis on values that support a protest movement or what Smith terms the ideological "flexibility" of religion, can also be important motivators for social action.

A second set of religious resources that Smith identifies centers on the religious organization itself, and the ways in which it can support social movements. These include, for Smith, trained leaders, money, an already-gathered group of potential participants, established modes of communication with participants and with other organizations, established social structures, and the basic office tools (and workers, though Smith mentions them only in his list of office tools) of any social movement. As Smith puts it, because religious organizations are already organized, they can serve as "movement midwives" (1996:16), providing the support and knowledge needed to birth a new social movement.

A third aspect of religion's contribution to social movements, Smith believes, is social-psychological: the importance of a shared identity. People who otherwise do not know each other can bond quickly around a shared identity, and religion is one aspect of identity that can function in this way. Likewise, the religions that concern Smith are large, organized ones that often have a multi-national and trans-cultural presence, allowing religion-based social movements to spread widely and rapidly. Organized religion also has a complex relationship to the state that can help in religion's support of social movements. First, especially in contexts where the religion is dominant in a particular society, some repressive regimes allow privileges to religious personnel that they would not allow to other organizers. With greater freedom of movement and perhaps of speech, such religious leaders can support the development of social resistance. Second, organized religions often are defensive of the boundaries between themselves and the state. When a state begins to threaten an organized religion, that religion, Smith argues, becomes a site of resistance to the state.

The first three articles in this section provide examples that allow us to explore and apply Maduro's and Smith's ideas on religion and social movements. In "Faith-Based, Multiethnic Tenant Organizing," Jeung offers evidence that strongly supports Smith's argument that religion provides organizational resources to social movements. Jeung tells the story of Oak Park, a grossly substandard housing development in Oakland, California, that housed primarily poor immigrants, many of them undocumented Latinos or Cambodian refugees. Fearing the state because of their former lives under a repressive regime or because of their undocumented status, the tenants at Oak Park were divided by language and nationality, and reticent to approach authorities about the severe problems affecting their residence. Jeung's group, a Christian ministry with a special calling to live and work with people in poverty, served as what Jeung calls a "bridge organization," providing the other Oak Park tenants with resources and social capital to which they otherwise might not have had access. In the end, the tenants formed an association and successfully brought suit against their landlord, forcing the landlord to sell the property and pay damages to the tenants.

Though Jeung focuses primarily on the organizational resources that religion brought to Oak Park, and only briefly discusses the importance of religious belief and practice in the housing struggle, our next article offers a clear and particularly intriguing examination of the role of religious belief in social activism. Contrary to popular belief, the same religion can take many different sides in a social movement, and such is the case with Christianity, Judaism, and the U.S. movements around the issue of same-sex marriage. Campbell and Robinson frame their article as a discussion of the validity of the idea that the United States is engaged in a "culture war" over same-sex marriage. While, as Campbell and Robinson acknowledge, the term "culture war" has been misused and has come to mean something different in popular usage than it meant when the term was coined (see Hunter, 1991), they continue to believe that the term is useful when defined as a shift in the focus of religious loyalties: from loyalty to a denomination or religion, to loyalty to certain political and/or ethical beliefs. This shift has resulted in the formation of numerous parachurch organizations.

In the context of same-sex marriage, Campbell and Robinson point out, the best-known parachurch organizations are the ones that oppose legalizing such marriages. In part, the authors argue, this is because conservative parachurch organizations are larger, more national, and better networked than liberal ones. In other words, they have greater **social capital** and better resources to offer the anti-marriage movement. However, Campbell and Robinson also note the important fact that there *are* parachurch organizations working in support of legalizing same-sex marriage. Supported by liberal Protestant denominations such as the United Church of Christ, interfaith denominations like the Unitarian Universalists, and non-Orthodox Jewish denominations,[1] these parachurch organizations lobby, educate, and fundraise in support of same-sex marriage, and provide a religious counterpoint to their conservative opponents. As Maduro argues, religion can be a powerful force both for maintaining the status quo and for revolutionizing it.

In light of Maduro's interest in revolutionizing the status quo, the next article is particularly relevant. Smith and Beaman focus on an international organization known as Trident Ploughshares that, although not explicitly religious, attracts activists whose religious beliefs support social action in the interest of peace. In the case of the "Trident Three," who partially destroyed a nuclear weapons control station in Scotland, one activist was a Quaker and the other two were not explicitly religious but cited a sense of moral obligation in defending their actions in court. The pacifist beliefs of Quakers (among other religions), as well as a non-religious but powerful moral conviction against violence, function as legitimations and motivations for political protest—motivations so powerful that people like the Trident Three are willing to face arrest and prosecution in the interest of bringing nuclear weapons issues into the judicial sphere. Moral conviction, both explicitly religious and apparently secular, can thus legitimate actions otherwise seen as morally reprehensible, such as the destruction of state property.

As Smith and Beaman demonstrate, though, the British High Court replaced the defendants' narrative of transcendent moral convictions with its own narrative of transcendent reason; in so doing, it reduced the actions of the Trident Three to "subversion by three eccentric women." Eccentricity is not only a term often used to dismiss the beliefs or actions of women; it is also a term used to de-legitimate religious beliefs and practices. By removing the women's actions from the realm of the transcendent and global, and reading them instead as irrational, individual acts, the court challenged the activists' moral authority and their rationality. In this case, then, we can see the action of religion on social movements from two perspectives: the importance of religious (including ethical) legitimations for social action, and the power of removing or discounting the religious aspect in order to de-legitimate a social movement.

Religions as Social Movements

But religions not only *affect* social movements; in themselves, they *are* social movements. And they come in a variety of forms, from small-scale movements to social institutions. Many sociologists distinguish these movements using the terms **church, denomination, sect,** and **cult**. The differences between these types of religious movement lie in the movements' **sense of legitimacy** and their *tension with society* (see McGuire, 2008). Especially because of the question of tension with society, the same religion can be classified differently depending on its social and historical location. Let's take a look at these categories.

According to this schema, a church or a churchly group is any religion (despite the Christocentric term) that has a unique sense of legitimacy—that is, believes that it has the only route to the ultimate truth—and is in low tension with society—it is widely accepted and it, in turn, accepts the mainstream society as it is. If a religion is widely accepted and holds that no other religion has access to the truth, it is likely a legally or socially established religion. In other words, it is likely to be the officially or unofficially dominant religion of the society. For example, in medieval Europe the Roman Catholic Church held a churchly position, but in many European countries it no longer does so. In some majority-Muslim countries today, such as Iran or Pakistan, Islam holds a churchly posi-tion; in others, such as Indonesia, other religions are given more of a place at the social table, and Islam is more a denominational religion.

A denominational group, like a churchly one, is in low tension with society. However, unlike a churchly group, it has a pluralistic sense of legitimacy: it sees other religions as having at least some validity. Denominational groups are widely socially accepted and are generally accepting of the society around them, but while they may attract large numbers of people their presence in that society is not exclusive. The Roman Catholic Church in the United States today is denominational; Buddhism is denominational not only in the United States but also in some Asian countries.

Some Christian groups in the United States and elsewhere today are denominational, but others are sectarian. A sectarian group has a unique sense of legitimacy and high tension with society. As a result, sectarian groups are often in social, political, or legal conflict with the society around them. The Amish in the United States address their tension with society by living apart; their separateness has been the source of some impor-tant court cases on the First Amendment. But in some cases, such as the Branch Davidians in Waco, Texas, the tension with society has exploded into violence.

The Branch Davidians broke off from the Seventh-day Adventist Church in the early twentieth century. In the early 1990s they were living communally outside of Waco, supporting themselves by working in the community and by selling weapons at gun shows. Though Christian, they were in high tension with society because they believed that the return of Jesus to earth was imminent, and that all governments but that of God would be destroyed. Furthermore, they had a strongly unique sense of legitimacy: they believed that their current leader, David Koresh, was a figure referred to in the Christian Biblical book *Revelation to John* (or *Revelations*), and they believed that when the end of the world came, they would be on the front lines of the army of God.

The combination of high social tension with weapons dealing was too much for the federal government, and in 1993 the Bureau of Alcohol, Tobacco, and Firearms (ATF) raided the Branch Davidians' home. The Davidians, expecting the army of Satan to chal-lenge them but expecting the challenge to come in Jerusalem rather than in Texas, fought back and began to re-think their beliefs about the end times. Both sides suffered casualties and the ATF was forced to retreat; soon thereafter the Federal Bureau of Investigation (FBI) sent in a Hostage Rescue Team and a team of negotiators. Besieged by the forces of a government they already considered suspicious, the Branch Davidians began to come to the conclusion that the first battle between the armies of God and Satan was taking place. Meanwhile, the FBI had decided that it was dealing with a dangerous "cult." With this level of tension and misunderstanding, a violent outcome was nearly inevitable. Indeed, on April 19, 1993 the FBI invaded the Branch Davidians' home. A disastrous fire of uncer-tain cause erupted, and most of the members of the sect were killed.

The stereotype of the "cult" was part of the impetus for the FBI's approach to the Branch Davidians. Yet, for sociologists the term is simply a descriptor for a group in high tension with society and having a pluralistic sense of legitimacy. Cultic groups, in socio-logical terms, may not be well regarded by the mainstream society and may not approve of that society, but they also believe that they are not the sole group with access to the truth. High tension with society can still lead to confrontation, but such groups' pluralism sometimes softens those confrontations to a certain extent. Wicca, an earth-focused new religious movement that is fairly prominent in many English-speaking Western countries, is one example of a cultic group. Wiccans have faced significant confrontations with neighbors and with law enforcement because of their social tension, and especially because many Christians incorrectly believe Wiccans to be worshippers of Satan. Yet, they are also often participants in more liberal interfaith organizations, and have worked together with liberal parachurch groups on political issues, especially those involving the environment.

So, if cultic groups are pluralistic and in high tension with society, what about the word "cult"? In much of the English-speaking world, this term evokes the image of a group of brainwashed followers in the thrall of a charismatic but mentally disturbed, manipulative, and egocentric leader. While it's true that there are and have been religious leaders who are more centered on their own interests than those of their congregants, such leaders are relatively rare and appear in mainstream religions as well as marginalized ones. Furthermore, as both psychological and sociological research have shown, the possibility of "brainwashing"—erasing someone's personality, beliefs, and values and replacing them with those of the brainwasher—is non-existent (see Richardson, 2004). Certainly, some religious movements (like some other social movements) are manipulative and even coercive; again, this can happen in both marginalized and more mainstream religions. But the brainwashing thesis itself has been disproven, and the "cult" stereotype causes more problems than it solves. In fact, it is often applied to any religious movement in high tension with society. "Cult" designates social opprobrium more than it describes anything realistic about the group in question.

Because of the baggage carried by the term "cult," many sociologists today avoid using the word. Instead, we term groups *new religious movements* to emphasize that they're similar to other new social movements. There's a great deal to be learned about religion through the study of new and established religious movements, especially once we escape the assumptions imposed by the use of pejorative terms such as "cult."

You may be wondering at this point: "So if brainwashing doesn't exist, why and how do people join new religious movements?" Many sociologists have asked exactly that question; in fact, they have broadened it to ask how and why, in general, people convert into and out of religions. Sociologists Rodney Stark and Roger Finke have long taken an interest in the development of new religious movements, and are leading proponents of a concept termed **rational choice theory** (for an overview, see Stark and Finke, 2000). This theory, developed from economic principles, suggests that people weigh costs and benefits, not just belief systems, when deciding to join or disaffiliate from a religion. These costs and benefits are not strictly financial, but have to do with maximizing less tangible assets such as eternal rewards, social capital, and religious capital. *Social capital* refers to the tangible and intangible sources of power one holds within a particular society, such as respect, education, unearned privilege, or the power to make decisions that affect others' lives. **Religious capital** is a special kind of social capital that functions within a religious group; it includes such assets as religious education, knowledge of rituals, and status and respect within the tradition. Stark and Finke suggest that decisions to join a particular religious group are affected significantly by the need to conserve social and religious capital. They link this to another conclusion drawn by sociologists of religion: that conversion is also heavily reliant on **social networks**. People rarely join religions in which they know no one, and they rarely leave religions in which they have a large number of social ties. The religious movements, then, which grow most rapidly are often those that rely heavily on social networks for their recruitment: friend networks, family networks, and employment networks, to name a few. The rapidly-growing yet relatively young Church of Jesus Christ of Latter-Day Saints (the LDS Church, or Mormons), provides a clear example of this pattern, as Stark and Finke demonstrate. While rational choice theory is still under much debate among sociologists, the importance of social networks in conversion has been repeatedly proven.

The study of new religious movements also provides sociologists with the opportunity to consider how religions change over time, especially as they grow. New religions often rely on the **charisma** of a founder or prophet; indeed, world religions such as Christianity, Islam, and Buddhism had such a figure (Jesus, Muhammad, and the Buddha, respectively). Joseph Smith played this role for the LDS Church, and in more recent movements other figures such as Sun Myung Moon of the Unification Church or A.C. Bhaktivedanta Swami Prabhupada of the International Society for Krishna Consciousness have served as the charismatic founders of religious movements. Eventually, though, religious movements that are successful in drawing followers grow to the point where the founder's charisma cannot reach everyone, and where some organizational structure becomes necessary. The religion must go through a process that Max Weber called the **routinization of charisma**: it must find a way to communicate the charisma of the founder to all members, and it must develop forms of organization that allow the religion to function while not obscuring the critical element of charisma. Routinization is an especially important process as the founder ages, because the death of the founder presents new religions with their most powerful challenge, and those religions that have already routinized are often better prepared to survive this traumatic period.

A second significant challenge to any religion comes about when, as social psychologist Leon Festinger and his co-authors put it, "prophecy fails" (1956). William Shaffir's article shows us that the challenge is especially pressing when a leader's death represents a failure of prophecy. The Lubavitchers are a relatively new movement within Judaism, having been founded in seventeenth-century Eastern Europe. A strongly pietist movement, focused on reverence of the divine, Lubavitchers also treat their leaders, or Rebbes, with great reverence. In the late twentieth century the current Rebbe began to teach that the coming of the Messiah, the savior who would bring about the restoration of the Jews to their holy land and the rebuilding of the Temple in Jerusalem, was imminent. Some of his followers soon came to believe that the Rebbe himself was the Messiah, and that when Jews had sufficiently prepared themselves, he would reveal his true nature. As Messiah, of course, the Rebbe was expected to be immortal; thus, when he fell gravely ill in 1992 the prophesied arrival of the Messiah came into question. And, although the Rebbe was not the founder of the Lubavitch movement, as the sole leader who had been specially chosen by his predecessor he played an important and charismatic role in this pietist movement. He also had not named a successor. Thus, the movement faced several key issues: its leader, though not a founder, was nonetheless its central charismatic figure; routinization of charisma had partially taken place over the centuries, but without a designated successor it was incomplete; and, should the Rebbe die, the "prophecy" that he was the Messiah would fail.

In 1994, the Rebbe did pass away, and his movement was left with questions of succession and a failed prophecy. Yet, Shaffir demonstrates that, as in the case of many other "failed" prophecies, the Rebbe's death led not to the dissolution of the movement but to the reinterpretation of the prophecy. Many Lubavitchers continued to believe that the Rebbe had been the Messiah; however, they came to understand his death as meaning that they had not done enough to bring about the expected messianic redemption. Rather than leave the movement, as one might expect those disillusioned by a failed prophecy to do, they not only stayed but recruited new members through their focus on redoubling efforts to be deserving of the arrival of the Messiah. Some believed the Rebbe to have been resurrected; in fact, Shaffir tells us that many Lubavitchers kept vigil outside of the mausoleum in which he was buried in the hope of witnessing his resurrection. Others believed him to have died bodily but to have lived on in spiritual form. In the end, while some left the movement, Lubavitcher Judaism was strengthened by its reinterpretation of the death of its leader and the apparent "failure" of the prophecy surrounding him.

A more recent new religious movement that has survived the death of its founder is the Church of Satan, included here both because it demonstrates the ways in which new religious movements reflect the culture around them and because it is perhaps the clearest example of a new religious movement that has been misunderstood through the rubric of the "cult." Founded in 1966 by Anton Szandor LaVey, the Church of Satan was influenced by a long tradition of Western (especially British and U.S.) occultism and interest in sex magic, but also by the counterculture of the 1960s and that culture's sexual and religious experimentation. LaVey designed his religion quite explicitly along the lines of violating social norms while simultaneously, as Urban shows, reinforcing some of those same norms.

For LaVey, the figure of Satan represented all that was opposed to Christianity. The latter religion, he believed, focused on suppressing all of the natural instincts of humanity; LaVey, on the contrary, felt that such instincts should be freely expressed. In advocating the rejection of Christianity, LaVey came to frame his religion around the worship of Satan, where Satan represented the earthly, the physical, the human instincts for food and indulgence and sex. Furthermore, there is little doubt that LaVey delighted in his role as provocateur and social transgressor. Drawing on centuries-old Christian legends of the Satanic Black Mass, as well as the more recent occult traditions developed by figures such as Aleister Crowley, LaVey developed a ritual that parodied and inverted Christian imagery and liturgy while simultaneously taking a tongue-in-cheek approach to contemporary cultural fears of the "Satanist." Performed on a woman's naked body and including the invocation of Christian demons as well as the desecration of various Christian symbols, LaVey's Black Mass in the early years of the Church of Satan is very evidently, in Urban's words, an "explicit, exaggerated, even ridiculous form of transgression." Like most parody, it was poorly received by the target religion.

More to the point, though, and much to LaVey's amusement, non-Satanists took the religion very, very seriously. In fact, because of a number of cultural factors including perhaps LaVey's influence, the United States in the 1980s saw a widespread Satanism scare, with Satanists being blamed for everything from ritual child abuse to killing pets to recording secret messages in heavy metal music. Still today, the term "Satanist" can automatically evoke the classic image of the "cult," along with all of the suspicions often leveled at new religious movements: mistreatment of women and children, undermining the dominant religion, and undermining the government. The last charge has little truth to it, although the undermining of Christianity was clearly one of LaVey's goals. Children are not a part of the Church of Satan, but as Urban points out, the role of women may be open to greater criticism.

The late 1960s was the height of the "sexual revolution," which some women found liberating but others, especially those who were unmarried, found simply increased the demands of men for sex and increased the difficulty of refusing to have sex. In such an environment, it is not surprising that some women would find the Satanic emphasis on sex to be liberating; yet, one could also argue that turning one's passive, naked body into an altar is the height of objectification. We are left with the fact that some women did, and still do, find the movement liberating, and must therefore ask whether it is most accurate to accept a "cult" stereotype, to accept the testimony of movement members, or to try to reach a more complicated understanding of the gender dynamics of this new religious movement. It is probably clear that I favor the latter, and toward that end it is worth adding that people often find liberation in the inversion of repressive stereotypes. While inverting the stereotypes re-values them—in this case, changing the valuation of women as passive sexual objects by elevating the "Whore of Babylon" to sacred status—it also leaves the stereotypes in place. Other new religious movements of the time performed similar though less transgressive acts of gender re-valuation; only a few groups have been willing to challenge gender stereotypes head-on.

Conclusions

Religions can be fruitfully approached both as influences on social movements and as social movements in their own right. As influences on social movements, religions can offer a wide variety of resources, from the concrete (such as offices and staff) to the cultural (such as legitimations and sacred histories). Marx and Gramsci may have been on the right track in their approaches to religion as opiate and as resistance-in-infancy, but both men focused primarily on the dominant religion in their societies. As sociologists have come increasingly to attend to non-dominant religions, our picture of the influence religion has on social movements has become increasingly complex. Religion is powerful but malleable, and thus has a great deal to offer both socially conservative and socially resistant causes.

Religion has increasingly come to be understood through the broader lens of social movement theory. In viewing religions as social movements, we can attain a greater understanding of members' involvement, of growth and change in religions, of the roles of leaders and other authority figures, and of the interactions of belief and practice with social structure both within and beyond each religion. Approaching religion as a social movement helps us to move beyond the image of the "antisocial cult" to question popular representations of new religious movements, and it helps us to see how such movements arise from and exist in conversation with their broader social surroundings. Finally, approaching religions as social movements gives us a foothold from which to consider the topics of this book's final section: the local and global impact of religions on the societies in which their adherents live, and the impact of globalization on religion.

Extended Application

In 1954, shortly after England's anti-witchcraft laws had been repealed, Gerald B. Gardner published a book entitled *Witchcraft Today*. An avid occultist with a long-standing connection to well-known students of ritual magic, Gardner claimed to be the first modern, non-hereditary initiate into the pre-Christian religion of ancient England. That religion, Gardner told his readers, had been the real target of the medieval European witch-hunts. As Gardner's story went, to protect themselves the practitioners went underground with their religion. Practicing only at home behind shuttered windows, they turned "witchcraft" into a family affair rather than the communal religion it had been previously. Each person kept a diary of successful rituals, called a "book of shadows," and upon her or his death that book passed to a descendant, who would memorize the book and then burn it. In this way, Gardner claimed, the ancient religions of Europe had been preserved all the way to the twentieth century. Then, a group, or coven, of hereditary witches had agreed to initiate him, and with the repeal of the English anti-witchcraft laws had allowed him to publish their secrets.

The religion Gardner described was one focused on nature and on the agricultural cycles of the year. It had two central deities, referred to by various names but often simply known as "the Goddess" and "the God." Lovers and creators, the Goddess and the God were also represented ritually by the high priest and high priestess of a coven. The religion had no evil figure or deity and did not imagine the world through a dichotomy of good and evil, but rather considered life to be intrinsically good and the world to be composed through balance rather than duality. The covens that Gardner described were small groups of 13, roughly balanced between men and women, who met to revere the Goddess and the God, to observe agricultural and astrological holidays and to conduct ritual magic. To Gardner, "magic" meant the use of incantations and rituals to create desired change in the world.

Gardner's book soon began to gather a following among others interested in the occult. By the early 1960s it had made its way across the Atlantic to North America, where it encountered that continent's growing counterculture. As in England, in North America Gardner's influence was mediated not only by his books but, after his death in 1964, by the work of his student, Doreen Valiente. Valiente expanded upon Gardner's writings, providing the religion with its basic ethical statement, a growing set of sacred stories, and its alternate name: Wicca. Wiccans make ethical decisions based on two main guidelines: the Wiccan Rede (pronounced "reed") introduced by Valiente, and the Rule of Three. The Rede states, "An [if] it harm none, do as ye will," and the Rule of Three prescribes that all actions, for good or ill, will return to their originator three times over. In a nutshell: harm none, and be careful what you do because it will come back to you.

Historians interested in Wicca generally disagree with Gardner's version of the religion's origins, deeming it part of the Wiccan "sacred story." In Lincoln's systematization of narrative (see Chapter 3), this story would be considered "myth"—it claims to be true, is believed to be true, and carries sacred authority. Many historians, whose version of the story carries little sacred authority with Wiccans, point to the connections between Gardner and famous occultist Aleister Crowley (also, incidentally, an inspiration for the Church of Satan), as well as Gardner's long-standing interest in the occult, and argue that Wicca's origins lie with Gardner himself. Since some connection to a historical narrative seems to be important for the attraction of a new religion and the longevity of an established one, it comes as little surprise that Gardner might have fabricated his story about the coven of hereditary witches. Regardless of what Gardner's experiences may have been, many Wiccans continue to hold that their religion at least echoes that of ancient, pre-Christian Europeans. And this controversy over Wiccan history in no way invalidates the religion itself for sociologists, whose concern is, after all, not with the verity of any given religion. Rather, the controversy is one more fascinating example of the ways in which religions and their followers seek a sense of authenticity.

Gardner died less than ten years after revealing his religion in print. However, Wicca provides an interesting case of the routinization of charisma. Gardner's charisma was contained in his writing, for it was through his books even more than his personal teaching that the religion spread. In addition, Gardner had students whose own writings —especially those of Doreen Valiente—helped to spread the religion further. And because Wicca did not develop a hierarchy beyond that of the high priest and the high priestess in their individual covens, there was less need for a formal routinization. Wicca spread organically, "virally" we would say now, through publications and classes, in the fertile environment of the 1960s counterculture. With Gardner's books—and those of his students, and of later Wiccans who also claimed hereditary initiation—as the religion's central recruitment factor, Wicca had multiple, relatively permanent sources of charisma. Today those sources of charisma are well-represented online, giving the religion an even more widespread locus of recruitment and contributing to its continued thriving.

With its lack of organized hierarchy and its tendency to spread through publications and local classes rather than through officially-sanctioned educational initiatives, Wicca would seem to be a religion poorly suited to offer the kinds of resources for social movements that Maduro and Smith describe. Two branches of the religion, however, prove otherwise. One began with an explicitly political intent; the other was influenced early on by anarchism and over time developed resources for political activism.

In 1971, as feminism was developing a separatist branch that held that women needed to work separately from men for their own liberation, feminist activist Zsuzsanna "Z"

Budapest decided that feminism needed a spiritual base. Together with several other women, she founded the Susan B. Anthony Coven #1 (named after an early feminist activist) in a suburb of Los Angeles. In a 1979 book Budapest would claim to be a hereditary witch herself, and to have learned everything she knew from her Hungarian mother, who in turn had learned from her own mother in a long line of purely matrilineal descent. The religion as Budapest describes it, though, bears many similarities to that of Gardner, Valiente, and other Wiccans who came after them. It incorporates more ancient and contemporary goddesses, and demotes the God to secondary importance. It also contains a number of rituals that are in keeping with cultural feminists' focus on celebrating the milestones of women's lives and healing from patriarchy and violence. Most importantly, Budapest's religion is only for "women-born-women"—that is, those people assigned female at birth and continuing to identify as female. The cycle of the year in this version of witchcraft is much the same as Gardner's, as are the descriptions of basic ritual practices. Like Gardner, Budapest drew on texts about witchcraft and the occult that preceded her, while solidifying the historical credentials of her religion by attributing it to her heritage.

Budapest's religion was termed Dianic witchcraft or Dianic Wicca after the Roman goddess Diana, who spent much of her time in the company of women. Not only was it an explicitly feminist religion, it also had explicit political aims. Budapest's 1979 book, for instance, contains a spell that has proved quite controversial in Wiccan circles: a hex, or curse. Because of the Rule of Three and the Rede, most Wiccans consider cursing people to be extremely unwise as well as unethical. Budapest, though, explains her hex as calling a person's "karma" back on him immediately, and warns that the witch's own "karma" will be called back on her immediately as well. Significantly, Budapest's hex was intended to be used against a rapist, at a time when it was even more difficult than it is now in the United States for a woman to successfully bring rape charges against anyone. In the absence of an effective judicial system, Budapest's followers took justice into their own hands.

A student of Budapest's, Miriam Simos, liked the activism of Budapest's branch of Wicca but was uncomfortable with the separatism. After moving to San Francisco from Los Angeles, she studied with a high priest from another Wiccan tradition. Living and spending time with anarchists and other political activists, she drew all of these influences together into a movement that eventually became yet another branch of Wicca. During this time she took on the name of Starhawk in recognition of a sacred vision. In 1978, Starhawk and others founded the Reclaiming Collective, a group of Wiccan and more generally neo-pagan practitioners who worked together to explore the ways in which the practice of Wiccan rituals and magic could create real, tangible change in themselves and in the world. Starhawk and Z. Budapest published their first books at the same time in 1979, introducing people in many English-speaking countries to these two feminist branches of Wicca. Both would later publish more books for their established and new followers to read; as Budapest's became more focused on women's intimate and personal lives in keeping with her cultural feminist focus, Starhawk's came to focus ever more intently on an analysis of the connections between sacred practice and social power. Over the past decades, Starhawk has come to be known as an international activist dedicated to anti-war and environmental causes.

In the late 1990s, the Reclaiming Collective faced an unusual challenge in the routinization of charisma: Starhawk's teachings had spread so widely through her books, through workshops organized by the collective, and through members of the collective moving away from San Francisco, that new covens had formed across the world whose members wished to affiliate with Reclaiming. Starhawk has maintained that she never intended to start a new religious movement—but sometimes religions start without the permission of their founders. In response to the wishes of other, Reclaiming-inspired covens, the Reclaiming Collective framed a series of principles by which all affiliated covens would agree to abide. These explicitly include activism for social justice, and Reclaiming covens tend to draw members who are interested in creating social change, whether through magic, protest, or magical protest. As the Collective was always run on anarchist principles of consensus and rotating leadership, Starhawk has steadfastly refused any formal leadership position in Reclaiming, beyond that inevitably attributed to her through her writing and teaching career. Thus, using very different models for the combination of religion and activism, Z. Budapest and Starhawk have created, from the very personal, secretive religion Gardner described, one that plays a vibrant, if small, role in contemporary politics.

Exercises

1. Explore a new religious movement in your area—one that started after 1900. Here are some possible questions to ask participants or leaders:
    a. When and how did the group begin?
    b. Is the founder still alive? If not, did the group change after the founder's death, and how or why not? How does the group maintain the founder's teachings?
    c. Is the group connected to any social movements? If so, in what ways? If not, why not?
    d. How did your interviewee become interested in the group? What does she or he value most highly about the group?
2. Explore a social movement that has ties to religion. Compare religion's role in this group with Maduro's and Smith's ideas about religion and social movements. Do aspects of this movement match Maduro's and Smith's theories? Does religion interact with this movement in ways that Maduro and Smith don't mention?

Note

1. Since the publication of Campbell and Robinson's article, Conservative Judaism has approved same-sex marriages and the ordination of lesbian and gay clergy.

21

Faith-Based, Multiethnic Tenant Organizing: The Oak Park Story

Russell Jeung

ON A BRIGHT SAN FRANCISCO morning in the fall of 2000, an unlikely group emerged laughing from an ornate skyscraper.[1] Among the three dozen assembled were undocumented residents from Mexico, a European American minister, Cambodian refugees, and a Taiwanese American city planner. They had just won almost one million dollars from their landlord in one of the largest legal settlements of its kind (DeFao 2000). In addition to winning monetary damages for forty-four households, the group's victory transformed the complex into brand new apartments that are held permanently at affordable rents. Overcoming obstacles of race and class, the Oak Park Tenants Association is a model of faith-based, multiethnic community organizing.

This housing victory was unlikely because it involved primarily Latinos, some of whom avoid the government for documentation reasons, and Cambodians, who had been tortured by their government (Counts 1999a; Ochs and Payes 2003). Linguistic isolation prevented them from understanding the American legal system or fully integrating into this society (Bolivar et al. 2002). And because the tenants were on public assistance or worked as day laborers, they could not afford other housing if they were to be forced out. Despite these fears and structural barriers, the tenants organized against substandard living conditions

that threatened their health and safety. Remarkably, these two ethnic groups joined together as a tenants association and remained united throughout the three-year struggle. The anomalous success of their efforts demonstrates the need for communities to build upon both the ethnic and religious social capital of low-income communities. Similarly, this case study demonstrates how faith-based organizers required both kinds of capital to bond the tenants and bridge them to outside resources.

THEORIES OF SOCIAL CAPITAL AND COMMUNITY ORGANIZING

Both social movement research and community organizing literature assert the social capital is a necessary factor for group mobilization. Robert Putnam's *Bowling Alone: The Collapse and Revival of American Community* distinguishes two dimensions of social capital. According to Putnam, "social capital refers to connections among individuals—social networks and the norms of reciprocity and trustworthiness that arise from them" (Putnam 2000, 19). This capital may be "bridging" and encompass people across social cleavages, or it may be "bonding" and reinforce exclusive identities. For example, religious institutions may bridge Latinos and Asians as they attend a Catholic church and connect them to job opportunities offered by other parishioners. On the other hand, a Buddhist temple may merely bond those who are Thai because of the language and rituals employed. For those in low-income communities, social capital is especially important because they have less access to human capital (education) and physical capital compared to other communities.

Richard Wood (2002) applies these concepts about social capital in his comparison of race-based and faith-based community organizing. He argues that multiracial groups have restricted access to social capital in that racial groups usually have little trust and interaction with one another. Consequently, organizers of multiracial organizations expend considerable efforts building trust among racial groups. Faith-based organizers, on the other hand, can draw upon networks established within congregations. More significantly, religion offers both a rich symbolic culture (songs, scriptures) and structural information channels to mobilize members (Greeley 1997; Wood 1997). As a result, faith-based community organizing groups serve as better bridging institutions than race-based ones.

FAITH-BASED ORGANIZING OF IMMIGRANTS

Similarly, Mark Warren observes the difficulty in organizing these largely immigrant communities. He explains, "We simply do not have very many institutions in which Americans from different racial groups cooperate with each other" (Warren 2001, 27). He suggests that networks of faith-based organizations offer space where multiethnic groups can cooperate and participate in politics. Organizers in these faith-based, immigrant networks have utilized four key principles that they have found to be successful. First, they apply the "Iron Rule" that organizers should not do for others what they can do for themselves. Instead, they aim to develop

local leadership and organizational capacity so that groups themselves can voice and lobby for their concerns.

Second, immigrants organize around issues of self-interest that tend to be broad based. Mary Ochs and Mayron Payes observe that recent newcomers "will not find their new living conditions in the U.S something to organize about," but will address issues when they "experience extreme discrimination or victimization" (Ochs and Payes 2003, 20). Both community organizations and unions now acknowledge that immigrant organizing should be done in and out of the workplace and should be holistic in concerns (Louie 1992; Wong 1994).

Third, faith-based organizers recognize that ethnic faith-based institutions offer great networking opportunities. Unfortunately, community activists have ignored these temples and congregations for a variety of reasons (Yoo 1999). However, the faith communities offer immigrants safe places to voice their fears and issues. These indigenous organizations often operate like large, extended families and can turn out numbers at direct action events (Bolivar et al. 2002).[2]

Lastly, organizing immigrants requires an understanding of the group's history and traditions, as well as their community strengths (Gutierrez et al. 1996). Besides building upon family and religious networks, organizations can mobilize through ethnic markets and media. To agitate groups to action, organizers have learned they must earn the right to meddle by building personal relationship and valuing the group's traditions (Noden 2002).

These understandings of social capital and the principles of faith-based organizing have arisen from case studies of successful organizing networks. Organizers work with multiple organizations that usually share the same general faith. In contrast, this case study of Oak Park involves immigrants coming from Buddhist, Catholic, and evangelical Protestant backgrounds. Furthermore, the tenants did not belong to preexisting formal organizations. In fact, the Cambodians and Latinos living in this apartment complex had occasional conflicts with one another as a result of language barriers and mistrust. The organizers at Oak Park, therefore, needed to establish both trusting relationships and a new organization in order to mobilize successfully.

PARTICIPATORY ACTION RESEARCH METHODS

This study is the result of participatory action research over twelve years. As a Chinese American sociologist, I moved into Oak Park in 1992 to learn about the adjustment of Southeast Asian families to low-income, urban settings. I entered this field site through introductions by staff of Harbor House, a Christian ministry in the neighborhood. As my roommate and I developed relationships with our neighbors, youth and parents asked for assistance in their education and in dealing with government agencies. I quickly realized that I could not study these families as an objective outsider. Instead, they became like extended family members to me as they welcomed me to their homes, fed me, and protected me in various situations. As a fellow Asian American, I did not want only to document the lives of Cambodian Americans, but also to empower my community. Subsequently, other Christians volunteering with Harbor House and I became actively engaged with our neighbors around issues affecting immigrants.

Our organizing efforts around the housing conditions at Oak Park came after six years of building relationships and trust. Four years after winning this legal settlement in 2000, I have interviewed 25 percent of the households who participated in the case with the help of Spanish and Khmer translators. To do so, we did utilize social capital within the local ethnic groups as well as the resources of our faith-based group.

OAK PARK APARTMENTS: HISTORY AND DEMOGRAPHICS

Oak Park Apartments originally was a fifty-six-unit apartment complex in the San Antonio/Fruitvale district of Oakland, California. The one-bedroom apartments all faced a central courtyard, which filled with scores of children after school. With an average family size of more than six persons, Oak Park children had to sleep in the living rooms. In fact, the complex was well known for being an overcrowded tenement for recently arrived refugees.[3]

Oak Park's neighborhood is an exemplar of an impoverished, underclass barrio. According to the 2000 U.S. Census, the community was 52 percent Hispanic, 25 percent Asian, 16 percent African American, 3 percent white, and 1 percent Native American or Pacific Islander. Children and youth dominate the streets, with 36 percent of the population under eighteen. Locked out of job markets because of language and immigration status, 51 percent of those over sixteen were not employed, and 54 percent received some type of public assistance. One-third of the families in the neighborhood were below the poverty level and 62 percent had not completed high school.

Those living at Oak Park were even worse off than their neighbors. The Cambodians, who arrived in the mid-1980s, had gone through the genocidal killing fields of the Pol Pot regime and still suffer greatly from posttraumatic stress syndrome. One forty-four-year-old woman, Sarah Prum, shared her experiences about this time: "I was about fifteen years old when the Khmer Rouge came into Cambodia, and they took both my mom and dad and killed them. My oldest sister had a nephew who was about a year old. They tossed him up and had him fall onto a rifle bayonet. Later, life at the work camp was very hard. We had no food. A half-cup of rice had to be shared between about thirty people. I dug up for potatoes in the fields for food to eat. We worked at early sunrise . . . from five in the morning to midnight."[4] The ravages of war and the refugee experience created such dislocation that few could concentrate to learn English and gain meaningful employment.

The Latino families also moved to Oak Park for the low rents. By the mid-1990s, 45 percent of Oak Park households were Cambodian, 45 percent were Latino, and the rest included Chinese Americans, African Americans, European Americans, and Native Americans. The Latinos, many of them undocumented, had to survive on day labor work. Francisco Martinez described the hardships of moving to Oakland in order to support his family:

We brought [our oldest daughter] here at three months, when she was very small. And we crossed [the border] . . . My God, how one dares to do things! We crossed hugging her and running. I tried to bring her by getting her a passport, but I couldn't because, well, it was not possible. And I did not have enough money to do that. So, I tried to cross the border.

That first year was stressful because when you arrive in a new place, it's difficult. You have to learn how to get a job—someone has to teach you the streets, how to go on the major streets to look for your jobs.

Because of their undocumented status, families could only find temporary work without benefits. Latinos and Cambodians banded with co-ethnics at Oak Park for mutual support in adjustment, job information, and local resources offered by the government and nonprofits. Sitha Le, a mother of five, whose husband had left, explained why she moved to Oak Park: "At Oak Park I saw a lot of Cambodian people, and I liked living near to other Cambodian people. If I have a problem, I can go to talk to them, get some advice or suggestions for what I can do to solve a problem. If we're sick, we can help to take care of each other. I didn't really know anyone here before I moved here, but it was easy to get to know them, and I became friends with

the people here." Similarly, Mexican families encouraged other family members to rent at Oak Park so that they could look out for one another, and to have close access to bilingual educational and health resources.

While these two ethnic groups lived side-by-side at Oak Park, they rarely interacted with one another because of language differences. Even the children remain segregated as the local school tracked them into different bilingual programs. The older youth maintained friendships along racial lines and gang affiliations. Periodically, contentious interactions would escalate into racialized conflicts. Because individuals could not distinguish the members of another group, they tended to blame an entire group for problems rather than seeking to hold an individual responsible. Mrs. Le complained about the ethnic conflict and perception of out-group homogeneity: "We've had some problems with other members living in Oak Park from different ethnic groups. Some people have accused my kids of stealing their things, a computer laptop, and they called the police. I was very afraid."

Another group came to Oak Park in the 1990s, but religious faith connected them rather than ethnic bonds. In the late 1980s, a nonprofit organization, Harbor House, began offering English as a Second Language (ESL) tutoring at Oak Park as part of its Christian ministry to refugees. When Daniel Schmitz arrived in 1989 to start a cleaning business that employed refugees, Harbor House had already developed trust with the tenants. As another Harbor House volunteer, I moved to Oak Park in 1992 to do participant observation research with Southeast Asian youth (Jeung 2002). As we got to know our neighbors, they began to ask for assistance, so Schmitz and I began a tutoring program, ESL classes, and a mentorship group for boys. Other college graduates interested in doing urban ministry came to volunteer, and by 1997 evangelical Christians rented five Oak Park units. Soon independent from Harbor House and loosely organized as Oak Park Ministries (OPM), this collection of whites, Latinos, and Chinese Americans brought in other volunteers to run the programs.

Carlos Flores, a second-generation Latino who was raised in the Assemblies of God church, learned about doing urban ministry from John Perkins, a founder of the Christian Community Development Association. Perkins teaches that urban ministry requires three R's: the relocation of Christians to low-income areas, reconciliation between racial groups, and redistribution of wealth and resources. Flores explained that he wanted to join a group doing such a ministry. Furthermore, he found the spiritual community of believers pivotal to his activism:

> My main reason I moved into Oak Park was that I saw what God was already doing there and wanted to become a part of it. The community drew me— seeing how people shared their life together. It wasn't just people moving in to do cool things, but I had a sense that it was driven by God.

> By deciding to live here, I am making this neighborhood now my community. This is the place where I'm going to work out my salvation, the context where I want to live out my daily faith walk with God and to love others. We're working out what it means for my neighbors to follow God, and for myself to follow God.

OAK PARK'S HOUSING CONDITIONS

During the 1990s, two individuals owned this complex and held it under as a corporate entity, Oak Park Apartments. The first Cambodians who moved there in 1984 could not recall the landlords ever making any capital improvements or repairs to the building. Mr. Schmitz attempted to make some needed repairs when he worked as the on-site manager in 1997, but he eventually quit because of the lack of maintenance funds. He observed: "Our building takes in $25,000 per month, and I was only given $150 a month for repairs. What I saw in this building, and in other buildings they

own, was active, calculated neglect—not just passive neglect. They would find out about dangerous situations and make it seem like they were repaired" (Counts 1999).

In the winter of 1997–98, El Nino rains flooded the Oak Park courtyard, backed up the sewers, and leaked through the roof. Gabrielle Alvarez, wife of Francisco Martinez, remembers how sewage ruined their entire apartment: "Around 1998 all the filth started coming out of the bathroom. We went to do the wash and when we returned, the whole hallway, everything was full of water! At that time I didn't have the money to just go somewhere else to sleep with my kids. And it was worse when it dried. A smell lingered that no one could stomach. It took two days to clean up, but the smell lasted more than a week." As those on the bottom floor were flooded, those on the second floor had to put out thirty-gallon garbage cans to collect the rainwater leaking through the ceiling. Dara Pheng, a sixty-nine-year-old grandmother receiving a Section 8 housing waiver, suffered the worst: "I lived on the second floor and the roof leaked a lot. It leaked so much, all over the place! Parts of the roof fell into the house. My bedroom wasn't leaking with rain, but the walls were kind of moldy. I had maggots in my home—it was like rice everywhere."

The landlords also failed to manage and maintain the property properly. Trash littered the building, the complex lacked fire extinguishers, and extermination service was a rarity. Mice and roaches overran the complex. Gabrielle Alvarez joked about the situation: "We couldn't stand the cockroaches. Honestly, one went into Mario's ear! He got sick twice, and he came out of the hospital. The second time he came out, a cockroach went into his ear. We were almost going to take him right back to the hospital! In the hospital they asked us where we lived and how the situation was in our apartment. They said we should move." Although the tenants complained about the lack of security at Oak Park and about the housing conditions, the management did not respond. Dara Pheng expressed her anger over the negligence: "I called the manager and asked him about fixing the leaking, but he never fixed it. I wasn't well during all the raining and leaking. I got rashes and things all over my back and body. I made complaints, but he looked at it and said the problems were minor and didn't fix anything."

Inside apartments, mold blackened entire walls as the rains brought about damp conditions. The environmental conditions created by the mold and roaches led to extremely high asthma rates at Oak Park. That year, at least eight households had to make emergency room visits because of asthma attacks. Later, when we tested six children from three different households, all had mold spores found in their bloodstream. Unfortunately, because of their lack of income, the families had to endure these conditions as their children became sick.

OPM members living at Oak Park suffered through the same conditions. A three-by-five-foot piece of the ceiling, under the weight of gallons of rainwater, fell onto one woman's bed. During a shower, another tenant's hand went through the rotted bathroom wall when he tried to brace himself against it. By the end of 1997, OPM members began to take more decisive actions.

BONDS OF TENANT SOLIDARITY: BUILDING UPON ETHNIC SOCIAL CAPITAL

To organize their fellow tenants at Oak Park, OPM members drew upon the respective ethnic bonds of the Cambodians and Latinos. Along with calling upon the trust and respect that they had earned from their neighbors, they were able to form the Oak Park Tenants Association to take a collective stand. By helping tenants recognize their common concerns, they helped establish the group identity of the tenants association.

As stated earlier, both the ethnic communities possessed extended familial networks within Oak

Park. Francisco Martinez and Gabrielle Alvarez vocally supported the lawsuit and facilitated organizing through their relationships with others at Oak Park. Gabrielle Alvarez was close to her next-door neighbors, who would cook and sell tamales together. Francisco Martinez developed friendships with men of other Spanish-speaking households and assisted them in getting work.[5] These personal ties later would provide the trust necessary to work together in suing the landlord.

In addition, the ESL classes encouraged further face-to-face interaction and group activity, especially among the Cambodian tenants. At the twice-a-week ESL classes, mothers would share stories of their past and their daily concerns. The year following the stabbing of the Mexican tenant, these Cambodians decided to continue their New Year festivities but invited Latino participation in a community potluck. Over three hundred persons celebrated together that year. Salsa music followed tunes of traditional Khmer folkdances, with the Macarena being played every third song. Sarah Prum brightened when she recalled, "I liked the feasts and potlucks we had. Everyone would gather together and everyone would cook food to eat together. We had special cultural dances."

The ESL classes also facilitated collective action among the Cambodians. When the U.S. Congress introduced welfare reform along with the Republican "Contract with America," the Cambodians became alarmed that their sole means of subsistence would be cut because they were noncitizens. During the ESL classes, tenants learned of legislative updates and wrote letters to legislators. OPM members, who considered this scapegoating of immigrants as unjust, actively lobbied against the reform and supported their neighbors' struggle. OPM member Alice Wu, a second-generation Taiwanese American, explained her concern for immigrants:

> Immigrants have a special vulnerability, not knowing the laws of the land, and being seen as foreigners. I think I have compassion for this

vulnerability partly because my own parents were immigrants, and I know there were times that they were taken advantage of in this new land.

I think God also has a special affinity for immigrants, especially for refugees from war, and understands the longing they feel for a home that is comfortable. We should be "groaning inwardly as we wait eagerly" (Rom 8:23) for the hope of our redemption. I believe God has more in store for us, for our immigrant neighbors, for our imperfect world, and I do groan inwardly along with my neighbors as we believe God is not yet done.

When the legislation passed, the ESL classes became citizenship classes so that the students could continue to receive needed benefits. This early organizing effort helped the Cambodians recognize their common plight as ethnic minorities in the United States.

Because the tenants were accustomed to meeting in the apartments of OPM members for party planning, ESL classes, or potlucks, they did not hesitate to attend meetings regarding Oak Park's living conditions. In the first tenants' meeting with Oak Park management in December 1997, representatives identified their most serious issues: leaking roofs, sewage problems, security, and infestation. The management claimed that plans were under way to renovate the buildings, but the meeting devolved into a shouting match, and even greater mistrust of the landlord resulted. With the failure of mediation, OPM members then investigated the possibility of a lawsuit to bring the building up to code. Through church contacts at the Alameda County Legal Assistance Center, we met with a private housing attorney who agreed to take the case on retainer.

While the five OPM households could have sued their landlord on their own, the attorney recommended that securing other plaintiffs with egregious complaints would bolster the case. OPM then met with each household individually, asking them about the damages caused by rain and mold and informing them of their housing rights. The

families were clearly hesitant to resist the landlord. Like her fellow tenants, Sitha Le was uninformed of her rights and fearful of government or landlord retaliation: "I didn't know my rights or the process of suing. I was living in Oak Park and thought it was wrong to complain and make reports on the bad conditions the landlord made us to live in. I was afraid to join the lawsuit because I didn't really know what would happen, and I was afraid of getting into any controversy because I was on welfare." Alvarez expressed similar concerns: "I was scared at first, thinking they might throw us out on the street. I first thought we shouldn't get involved because they'll kick us out and we'd have to look for another apartment. Other places say you can't have kids, or this and that, a lot of requirements. They also ask for large deposits, and we couldn't afford such changes."

When the prospects of organizing a large number of tenants seemed unlikely, the landlords paradoxically assisted us by raising the rents. This final straw outraged the tenants, who could not afford higher rents given their fixed incomes. The Cambodian grandmothers, especially, felt free to vent their wrath toward the landlord. Touch Chen, another senior citizen on Section 8, summarized the tenants' feelings: "I joined the lawsuit because the landlord wouldn't fix anything and the conditions were so bad in the apartments. We have rodents everywhere, there was mold in the walls, and the ceiling was leaking. And so we all got together to join this lawsuit because we were angry that the landlord didn't care and nothing was being fixed."

Once a few other tenants agreed to sue, OPM called larger group meetings. These group meetings especially capitalized on the close ties of the ethnic groups. For Khmer translation, we obtained the free services of Suon In, a leader at the Cambodian Buddhist Temple and staff person for Asian Community Mental Health Services. His involvement at the temple made a recognized and trusted partner in the organizing effort. Carlos Flores, one of the OPM members, worked as a community organizer for another nonprofit and used his language skills to facilitate the Spanish-speaking meeting. He explained his approach toward organizing: "People have a desire to make things better for themselves, to make things that are unjust just. But a lot of times, people don't know how to do so even though they see something is really wrong. Organizing brings a broader perspective of the wider, systemic injustices. God really wants justice to happen, so organizing people for justice on earth brings hope to people and a wider perspective. And that's related to my faith in the gospel."

Each person interviewed answered that they participated in the lawsuit because they saw their co-ethnics also suing. Believing that the situation could not get much worse, Juan Avila threw his lot in with the group: "I saw that everyone was joining. Daniel had told me that there was an option. If we win, good. And if we don't, we don't. So that's why we joined in the suit—we weren't sure if we were going to win or not. But then I told him, well, just put us down, we're with you, whatever happens, happens." Likewise, Sophal Chan, a grandfather with two children who each had their own apartments at Oak Park, decided to join once he saw the group unity: "I heard people talking about the lawsuit and that's how I knew about it. I heard everybody talking about it. After talking with a lot of people and my wife, and seeing everyone joining the lawsuit, I decided to join too." The family networks, the face-to-face communication, and the easy access to one another served as ethnic social capital that facilitated a group identity and collective action. Using bilingual leaders to lead meetings and garnering the support of the elders were two culturally sensitive methods to mobilize this ethnic social capital.

The personal relationships that OPM organizers had formed with their fellow tenants were another form of bonding social capital. Having attended their marriages and funerals, tutored their children,

and acted as their English teachers, OPM members built particularly strong ties with the Cambodians. We traded on this earned respect to gather the tenants to group meetings and secure a hearing. The younger tenants decided to sue based on rational choices and their confidence in the organizers. Ra Chhom explained: "When Russell and everyone talked with us, told us the process, and gave us all the information, we decided to join the lawsuit. Yes, I thought it was a good idea. Since Russell and everyone were helping with it, we felt they knew what they were doing and felt confident about joining the lawsuit. We weren't afraid." On the other hand, the older tenants made their decisions mostly on the basis of their loyalty to the OPM members. Sam Kong joked: "I trusted Russell and everyone so I signed the papers. If we lost and I got evicted I would go live with Russell! He loves the Cambodians, kids and all. We can all go live in a big house together. I joined to support Russell, Dan, and the others." For him, joining the lawsuit was an act of reciprocity to repay OPM members for their work in the community. While we thought we acted to empower him, we later learned that Kong was doing us a favor.

The family ties and close interactions promoted ethnic social capital, but they also led to ethnic divisions. To overcome mistrust and segregation, OPM attempted to forge a group identity as tenants. Large trilingual group meetings, held in our cramped living room, brought the ethnic groups together. In these sessions, Martinez recognized that the tenants shared the same issues: "For my part, when we joined the lawsuit nobody knew if we were going to win or not. What helped us was when we all got together. You know the saying; 'There is strength in numbers'? In these apartments there are many tenants. If we all have the same problems, like with the electricity coming and going, and we come together, we can do anything."

Moreover, Kong commented on the similar material conditions that the ethnic groups faced:

"We are all people in the same situation going through the same things, and we just need to help each other and work together. It doesn't matter to me what race someone is, as long as we are together and working together." Meanwhile, OPM organizers recognized that the Cambodians and Latinos were being exploited precisely because they were low-income tenants who were unlikely to complain. Given this exploitation, "their outcries for social justice overcame their ethnic boundaries," commented OPM member Alice Wu. "I think the Tenants Association overcame ethnic barriers because the residents saw we were all having the same problems and were in this together, and they knew that we [the organizers] were there to help. They also trusted us because we played with and tutored their kids, both Cambodian and Mexican kids. So I think the kids were a big part of bridging the trust gaps, even as they helped to bridge the language gaps by translating for their parents."

With high amounts of trust and reciprocity, forty-four of the fifty-six households at Oak Park joined the lawsuit by February 1998, much to the surprise of the attorney. In total, we had 197 plaintiffs in our case, almost all of whom were noncitizen, limited English-speaking, and low-income immigrants.

SUSTAINING THE LAWSUIT: BRIDGING SOCIAL CAPITAL

Once we initiated the lawsuit, our landlords did not bring the building up to code as expected but allowed the building to fall into even greater disrepair. They apparently tried to delay court hearings and outlast the tenants, who began to move away over time for various reasons. To bring more pressure to bear on our landlords, OPM members and our attorney strategized to gain city government support and garner media attention. The active involvement of these two

institutions bolstered the tenants' morale. As symbolic cues, their actions became important for the cognitive liberation of the tenants, who saw that their efforts could be successful (McAdam 1982).

The lawsuit required the documentation of the housing violations at Oak Park by city code inspectors. Because previous inspectors had not been thorough, I contacted district council member Ignacio De La Fuente. I had worked as an assistant to another city council member, and my relationships with the city officials proved quite helpful. De La Fuente's new assistant, Libby Schaaf, took on the Oak Park case as one of her top assignments. With their influence, a comprehensive team of health, building, fire, and police inspectors visited Oak Park in April 1999 and cited the landlords with forty-three code violations. In addition to levying fines, they placed a $50,000 lien on the property. Avila observed the effect of official city involvement: "When the government came, we thought this was for real, and that maybe we were going to win. When the person came from the city and told us that all of this was wrong, he said we would win the case. And when a person like that comes here it's not just to visit. He said there were many irregularities here: there are dead rats; there are lots of things that are not right. This gave me encouragement because I saw him when he was saying all of this." Unfortunately, the inspectors also declared Oak Park Apartments as substandard, which threatened the community's survival, as we feared being relocated.

OPM members believe that their faith practices and beliefs sustained them during this difficult period. The group met weekly to study the Bible, as well as to share and pray about their different ministries. Carlos Flores recalls that "there were times during the lawsuit that were very distressing, that we let down all the people. It was really scary, the possibility that people would be displaced and the community would break up. OPM meetings helped challenge my faith and grow. Most encouraging was listening to people sharing about the different ministries—how different kids changed or made decisions to follow God—and being able to pray about those things. If one person was feeling down, others would pick them up. Sticking together through everything was really positive."

In June 1999 the landlords claimed corporate bankruptcy and the building went into federal receivership (Counts 1999). The tenants association discussed mass relocation to other sites as a likely event. More vacant units became boarded so that Oak Park looked increasingly like an abandoned slum. In October 1999, Section 8 officials gave thirty-day notices to the grandmothers Pheng and Chen because Oak Park failed to pass their inspections.

These events would have broken the tenants association if not for continued media attention. In October 1999, reporters gathered again at Oak Park to hear that De La Fuente's Decent Housing Task Force had named it as one of the city's seven worst slums (DeFao 1999).[6] The press, both mainstream and ethnic, helped the tenants feel that they were not alone in their cause. Sarah Prum stated: "News about the lawsuit with Oak Park was even on the news in Long Beach. People I know there called and asked me what was going on and asked me what I was doing on the news." This attention further strengthened the tenants' ethnic social capital in that they felt they became celebrities in their own communities. Gabrielle Alvarez exclaimed: "I went to Mexico, and a cousin of mine said, 'I know that woman!' She saw me here in Oakland on TV. The same with my mom, she said she saw me on the news. We became famous because of our situation, to try to better it."

Fortunately, in July 2000 the City Attorney's Office developed a creditors' plan in which the City of Oakland, Fannie Mae, and the tenants would jointly take over Oak Park through bankruptcy proceedings. This concerted strategy brought the landlord back to the negotiating table. The tenants agreed to settle their case only on the condition that Oak Park be sold, be brought up to code, and made permanent, affordable housing.

Finally, almost four years after the initial organizing efforts, the Oak Park Tenants Association achieved their housing victory. We received $950,000 in damages and gained permanent, affordable housing. The tenants learned invaluable lessons about their rights and their abilities to effect change. Juan Avila encouraged others to organize in similar ways: "I learned that united, there is strength and you can do more things. If we hadn't joined together, nothing would have happened. My brother-in-law lives in apartments that are all messed up. I would tell him to unite. And they've even seen us on TV there. But they lack a lawyer and a person that helps them organize. The conditions are bad but they don't organize. They need some sort of union."

The bridging social capital that the OPM members brought to the Oak Park Tenants Association was invaluable. Because of their own religious faith, they remained committed to loving their neighbors and to seeking social justice. Their networks with attorneys, government officials, media, and nonprofit organizations proved significant in each step of the organizing process. Not only did they bridge the Oak Park Tenants Association to outside resources, but they also facilitated communication between Cambodian and Latino families. Since the lawsuit, Oak Park families continue to join together to do youth organizing, intergenerational family events, and, of course, for parties.

CONCLUSION

The victory of the Oak Park Tenants Association illustrates key lessons for organizing immigrant communities. In contrast to Putnam's thesis that Americans demonstrate declining social capital, newcomers to the United States possess much ethnic social capital that becomes intensified through the immigration process. The strong familial ties and close, face-to-face interaction of these communities facilitates mass mobilization. While faith-based organizers stress utilizing preexisting ethnic organizations, the Oak Park experience indicates that new multiethnic organizations can be established when groups are in close proximity and share common agendas.

Religious groups, such as OPM, may bring bridging social capital to these marginalized communities. OPM members developed long-term relationships over a period of years with their neighbors so that they could bridge the Cambodian tenants with the Latinos. While secular tenant organizers might build trusting relationships in order to secure winnable victories, OPM organizers established relationships in order to follow God, to build community, and to love their neighbors. The group's corporate faith practices encouraged them to persevere as tenants at Oak Park. Even when the building was condemned and no legal settlement seemed foreseeable, these evangelical Christians stood by their neighbors. As Pastor Dan Schmitz has written, "Contextualizing the gospel, I think, means taking care of people's physical needs, seeing the love of Jesus in very practical terms. That's really the focus of our ministry—it's being obedient, expecting God to work in our midst without presupposing what that looks like" (Schmitz 2001). Importantly, OPM itself was a multiethnic group, and other tenants could identify with them along ethnic and racial lines. They then called on the trust and friendships that had been established to invite households to attend tenant association meetings and to participate in the lawsuit.

The bridging capital of OPM members also connected the community with outside resources. By working with a leader from the Cambodian Buddhist temple, OPM secured even further credibility with the refugees. Visits by government officials and the media encouraged the tenants and reinforced their sense of efficacy. Contacts with and assistance from these entities were instrumental in forcing the landlord to settle.

This bridging capital helped our neighbors forge identities as not only Cambodian or Mexican but also as immigrant tenants with rights. Along with winning the lawsuit and helping Oakland establish a Decent Housing Month, the Oak Park tenants gained a new sense of power. Ra Chhom reflected, "The main thing I've learned, that I can hold on to, is that I have rights. If I am in a living situation where I'm renting a place with bad conditions, I have rights. And I can take action and not just allow what is happening to continue. If our lives or our families' health are at risk or something, then we can do something about that." In the same way, even the faith-based organizers learned something about faith and hope. Alice Wu Cardona concludes: "I learned that God really is above all other powers, and that He truly is a God of justice! I hadn't expected much from our lawsuit, but it seemed the faithful thing to do at the time, having exhausted all other reasonable avenues to make Oak Park decently habitable. I think before the lawsuit, I had some vague idea of God's justice coming into play in the last days. But the Oak Park lawsuit showed me that God can and will bring about justice in the here and now, for the poor and the voiceless, for people that He loves."

NOTES

1. The author wishes to acknowledge Carlos Flores and Rebecca Chhom for their interviewing and translating assistance, as well as Joan Jeung, Matthew Jeung, Daniel Schmitz, Shauna Olson Hong, and Alice Wu Cardona for their support on this project.
2. Organizers have learned that Southeast Asians have not been responsive to door-knocking recruitment techniques. On the other hand, they have been able to tap into preexisting organizations to help Cambodians engage politically (Hoyt 2002; Noden 2002).
3. To highlight the negative environmental impacts of these new populations, the *San Francisco Chronicle*

published photographs of Oak Park that showed idle Mien women with babies on their backs and toddlers at their feet (Gilliam 1989).

4. Pseudonyms of some tenants are used to protect my respondents' anonymity and confidentiality.

5. Similarly, many Cambodian tenants brought their relatives to live there, and at least four marriages were arranged among Oak Park families.

6. I was one of the tenant representatives on the task force that included property owners and city officials.

22

Religious Coalitions for and against Gay Marriage: The Culture War Rages On

David C. Campbell and Carin Robinson

"WE COME HERE TODAY for the audience of One," proclaimed the president of the Family Research Council, Tony Perkins. He stood before a cheering crowd gathered for the Mayday for Marriage rally on the National Mall in Washington, DC. "While our troops battle terrorists and tyrants abroad, a parallel battle rages here on our soil for the family and ultimately the future of our nation."[1] On October 15, 2004, more than two hundred thousand people gathered in Washington to defend what they see to be the traditional definition of marriage as being between one man and one woman. The Mayday for Marriage movement was organized in response to the rise of same-sex marriage on the national political agenda—on the West Coast the mayor of San Francisco had authorized the marriage of same-sex couples, on the East Coast the Supreme Judicial Court of Massachusetts had issued a ruling mandating gay marriages in the Bay State, and in between gay marriages were being performed in a handful of jurisdictions. A number of conservative pro-family groups such as the Family Research Council have since mobilized to host rallies across the country, attracting defenders of traditional marriage from a variety of denominations and faiths. To foreshadow the argument of this chapter—namely, that opposition to gay marriage unites religious traditionalists across the denominational spectrum—it is interesting to note that though the Family Research Council's constituency is predominantly white evangelicals, Mayday for Marriage was begun by an African American pastor.[2]

At the rally in Washington, the speakers included Rabbi Daniel Lapin, who encouraged attendees to "remember marriage at the voting booth." A Catholic group, the American Society for the Defense of Tradition, Family, and Property, waved banners and cheered following the rabbi's speech. An English-speaking Chinese pastor translated the message for members of his congregation, who stood holding a sign that read "Marriage = 1 Man + 1 Woman" in English and their native language. An Assemblies of God group joined hands to pray for the speakers. Members of a local African American church served as volunteers helping pass out programs, humming to the worship band playing "Great Is Thy Faithfulness" in the background. Gary Bauer, a prominent spokesperson for the Christian Right, proclaimed to the attendees, "You are not some small special interest group. You are America. You are the heart of America."

The religious and racial diversity present at the Mayday for Marriage rally is significant. Had there been any mention of welfare policy, the death penalty, or the Iraq War, the coalition would have dissolved. Their theological disagreements are even deeper; these groups are divided over such fundamentals as the divinity of Jesus Christ, speaking in tongues, and the afterlife. Groups with sharp disagreements about theology and in some cases a history of deep antagonism nonetheless stood side by side in opposition to same-sex marriage. Or, more accurately, people within these groups who hold traditional beliefs have found that they have more in common with other traditionalists, even those of other faiths, than members of their own religion who hold what are often called progressive beliefs.[3] For example, although many traditional Catholics attended the rally, their progressive counterparts stayed home. A similar divide is apparent within Judaism. The Union of Orthodox Jewish Congregations of America has joined white evangelical groups in calling for an amendment to the U.S. Constitution defining marriage as a union between a man and a woman. In contrast, the Union of Reform Judaism and the Central Conference of American Rabbis view gay marriage as a civil right and therefore support gay unions.

THE AMERICAN RELIGIOUS LANDSCAPE

The religious coalitions that have formed around the issue of gay marriage reflect a significant development in American religion and the way it shapes our politics. Only a few decades ago, the salient religious divide in American politics was defined by the boundaries between religious traditions, as famously summarized in the title of a well-known book by sociologist Will Herberg in 1955: *Protestant—Catholic—Jew*. Times have changed. Today, the salient divide is not *between* religious traditions but *within* them—in virtually every major religion in America, a split has developed between traditionalist and progressive factions. Although in each tradition the proximate sources of disagreement center on indigenous doctrinal disputes, at their roots these disputes all hinge on the source of

ultimate authority. In the words of the sociologist James Davison Hunter, traditionalists believe in an "external, definable, and transcendent authority," whereas progressives are more willing to adapt their moral beliefs to "the prevailing assumptions of contemporary life" (1991, 44, 45). This fundamental division in the way moral questions are answered is not contained to arcane theological questions but spills over into opinions about politically relevant issues such as gay marriage. Thus, traditionalists from within various branches of Protestantism have joined forces with like-minded Catholics, Mormons, Jews, and Muslims to oppose gay marriage because they all share a belief in a transcendent authority, namely God, that holds the institution of marriage as limited to relationships between men and women. Although they have had a lower profile, some religious progressives have similarly allied with secularists in favor of same-sex marriages. Like the traditionalists, they, too, may appeal to God to justify their position, but in doing so they are more likely to speak of justice, equality, and inclusiveness than moral absolutes, having refracted their understanding of scripture through the prism of contemporary American society.

A common but often misused way to describe the intradenominational fissure we observe concerning gay marriage is as an example of the culture war in American politics. We use this term advisedly, aware that it borders on the hyperbolic. Nonetheless, its original usage aptly describes the coalitions that have formed regarding gay marriage. The term was popularized by James Davison Hunter, who used it to describe coalitions among traditionalists and progressives across denominational lines, especially with regard to issues of public policy such as abortion and pornography. The same development had also been carefully chronicled by Robert Wuthnow in *The Restructuring of American Religion* (1998), but *restructuring* does not have the same ring as *culture war*, and so it is the latter term that has gained wide usage. In 1992, when failed presidential candidate Pat Buchanan reached for a phrase to rally the moral conservatives who were increasingly congregating in the Republican Party, he declared that America was embroiled in a culture war. Interestingly, Buchanan himself exemplified what Wuthnow meant by the restructuring of American religion and what Hunter described as the culture war. Buchanan is a devout Catholic, but he found the most enthusiastic audience for his brand of red-meat conservatism among evangelical Protestants.

Since entering the public lexicon, the term *culture war* has morphed from the meaning Hunter assigned to it. Although it originally described the historically unusual development of religious coalitions that supersede denominational borders, it has come to be used as a short-hand description for the prominence of hot-button social issues such as abortion, gender roles, and homosexual rights. More recently, it has also been increasingly invoked as half-description, half-explanation of the perceived polarization within the American electorate. This latter usage has become so common among political pundits, in fact, that the political scientist Morris Fiorina (2005) has recently published a book in which he repudiates it. His book, however, only questions the term *culture war* as it is used to describe a highly polarized electorate, not Hunter's original definition. Indeed, Fiorina's thesis is quite consistent with Hunter's original formulation. Fiorina argues, convincingly, that Americans appear closely divided politically because when they go to the polls their choices are increasingly limited to political extremists. The general public is not as polarized as are political elites. Similarly, Hunter explicitly argues that the culture war he describes is most pronounced among social and political elites, in particular those within religious organizations.

In explaining how the culture war (or restructuring) framework illuminates the religious coalitions that have formed with regard to gay marriage, we begin with the attitudes in the general public. Because we would expect the lines between traditionalists and progressives to be blurrier among the mass public than among elites, public opinion data constitute a "hard case" for the culture war thesis. Nonetheless, we find patterns that reflect a divide between religious traditionalists and progressives regarding the subject of gay marriage that transcends denominational affiliation. We then turn to detailing the ways in which leaders of religious groups with a political dimension and political groups with a religious dimension have formed such coalitions, primarily in opposition. As we explain in greater depth, the anti–gay marriage movement reflects previous coalitions formed to deal with other cultural issues, such as abortion and opposition to the Equal Rights Amendment. Not only did those previous campaigns establish the institutional infrastructure for a campaign against gay marriage by forging a sense of shared purpose among religious traditionalists across denominational lines, but they also introduced culturally conservative groups to the strategies and technologies of modern political campaigns. The campaign against gay marriage thus represents the second generation of cultural conservatism, and it is far more politically sophisticated than the early stages of similar campaigns. In addition, this second generation is far more diverse than the first, both religiously and racially. Although the early leaders of the religious Right spoke of a big tent under which Protestants, Catholics, Jews, Mormons, and others would unite, in reality the movement was predominantly composed of white evangelicals.[4] The coalition against gay marriage, in contrast, is much more ecumenical and, consequently, more ethnically diverse.

THE CULTURE WAR IN THE TRENCHES

Although we would expect to see the greatest evidence of the culture war among the generals, the attitudes of the infantry are relevant also. Leaders must have someone to lead, and so political and religious elites cannot fall out of step with their constituencies. Is there evidence that the interfaith coalitions that characterize "culture war" politics describe attitudes about gay marriage? The strongest statement of the culture war hypothesis is that it predicts that divisions concerning gay marriage should be greater *within* than *between* religious traditions. Within religious traditions, we should see that adherents with divergent degrees of traditionalism differ in their attitudes regarding gay marriage to a greater extent than do people of different religious traditions. For example, a traditionalist Catholic should have more in common with a traditionalist evangelical Protestant than with a progressive Catholic.

To test whether this is the case, we turned to the 2004 National Election Study (NES), whose respondents were asked, "Should same-sex couples be allowed to marry, or do you think they should not be allowed to marry?" They were given the explicit option of indicating that gay marriage should or should not be allowed, and they could volunteer other responses, for example, expressing support for civil unions. For simplicity of presentation, we report the percentage of respondents who explicitly opposed any form of legal recognition for homosexual relationships. We divided NES respondents into four religious traditions based on a standard denominational classification system: White Evangelical Protestants, Mainline Protestants, Catholics, and Black Protestants (Steensland 2000; Kellstedt et al. 1996). Note that the category "Black Protestants" consists of all Protestants, either evangelical or mainline, who are African American, while Catholics can be of any race. Obviously, this is not an exhaustive list of religious traditions in America, but other groups such as Jews, Mormons, and Muslims, are too small to be adequately represented in a survey the size of the 2004 NES (roughly twelve hundred people).

To distinguish between progressives and traditionalists within each religious tradition we relied on an index of four questions, each of which taps into moral traditionalism. Respondents were asked

the extent to which they agree with each of the following four statements:

1. The world is always changing and we should adjust our view of moral behavior to those changes.
2. The newer lifestyles are contributing to the breakdown of our society.
3. We should be more tolerant of people who choose to live according to their own moral standards, even if they are very different from our own.
4. This country would have many fewer problems if there were more emphasis on traditional family ties.

We used factor analysis, a statistical technique that compresses the four questions into a single index, and then divided the resulting scores into four quartiles.

Figure 6.1 displays the percentage of those within each religious tradition who oppose gay marriage,[5] dividing people within each tradition between those in the lowest and the highest quartiles of the moral traditionalism index. If the strongest version of the culture war hypothesis were to hold, we should see no difference in attitudes regarding gay marriage across religious

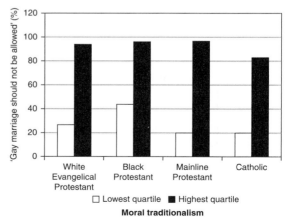

Figure 6.1 Opposition to gay marriage by religious tradition.

traditions—people with the same score on the traditionalism index should share the same level of opposition to gay marriage, regardless of their religious tradition.

The strong version of the culture war hypothesis finds considerable support in figure 6.1. Among people in the lowest quartile of the moral traditionalism index, opposition to gay marriage is very similar regardless of religious tradition. Only 21 percent of Catholics and mainline Protestants, for example, oppose gay marriage. The figure for evangelicals is only slightly higher at 27 percent. The one group with noticeably stronger opposition to gay marriage is black Protestants, at 44 percent. At the high end of the traditionalism index, the similarities are even more apparent. The levels of opposition to gay marriage among evangelicals, mainline Protestants, and black Protestants are 94, 97, and 97 percent, respectively. In this case, Catholics are slightly less likely to oppose gay marriage, because "only" 82 percent are against it. A quick glance at figure 6.1 makes clear that, consistent with the culture war hypothesis, moral traditionalism is a far better way to predict opposition to gay marriage than religious tradition.

These data about general public opinion are suggestive, but they can only reveal the *potential* for interfaith coalitions to form to address the subject of gay marriage. The coalitions themselves are actually forged or not, as the case may be, among political and religious leaders. It is thus among the generals that culture war politics should be most evident, and so that is where we turn our attention.

WHO WORKS WITH WHOM, AND WHY DO THEY WORK TOGETHER?

As we trace the coalitions that have formed concerning the subject of gay marriage, the key test of the culture war hypothesis is whether they fulfill two conditions. First, as with the public opinion data, we should see divisions defined more by

tensions within religious traditions than between them. Second, we should observe leaders of different religious traditions actually working together in the common cause of opposing gay marriage.

The story of the coalitions working against gay marriage begins long before this particular issue rose on the public agenda. The groups that are now mobilized against gay marriage have their roots in the New Christian Right movement, which began in the mid-1970s as white conservative Christians entered the political scene to speak out against feminism, the legalization of abortion, and the general decay of what they considered to be "family values." Originally the movement was ostensibly ecumenical, as evidenced by the names of two early members: the Religious Roundtable and the Moral Majority. These were groups with aspirations of assembling a broad, ecumenical membership as their leaders sought to attract religious conservatives from Protestantism, Catholicism, and Judaism alike. Notwithstanding a few notable Jewish and Catholic members, however, the awakening of religious conservatives in the 1970s and 1980s was largely an evangelical Protestant affair. In the early 1990s the Christian Coalition arose from the ashes of Pat Robertson's run for the presidency and inherited the institutional legacy of the Christian Right movement. Like its predecessors, it, too, sought to broaden its appeal to groups other than white evangelical Christians. And, also like its predecessors, the Christian Coalition was largely unsuccessful in trying to enlarge its tent (Robinson 2006).

Today, the religious coalitions that have formed to oppose gay marriage are far more ecumenical in their composition. Though having a narrow political focus, the range of participants has greater breadth than the original Christian Right, which was concerned with multiple issues. As was showcased at the Mayday for Marriage rally, participants come from a wider array of religions and races than was the case for the Christian Right movement in the 1980s and 1990s. Indeed, the presence of rabbis at the rally underscored that concern about gay marriage is not confined to Christianity. The old Christian Right laid the foundation, but the structure has taken a different shape.

Given the way the story is covered in the news media, it is easy to miss the interracial, trans-denominational nature of the coalition against gay marriage. Because much of it is built on the preceding movement, it is tempting to assume that this is the Christian Coalition all over again. As a case in point, consider how coverage of the Mayday for Marriage rally fed that impression. Speakers at the rally included James Dobson, Gary Bauer, and Chuck Colson, all seminal figures in Christian Right circles. These are well-known, media-savvy figures, and so the news media gravitated toward them in their coverage. Consequently, the media portrayed the rally, and thus opposition to gay marriage generally, as dominated by white evangelicals. Scratch the surface of the movement, however, and you will find evangelical and mainline Protestants, conservative Catholics, orthodox Jews, and even Muslims. Because many of the spokespeople for these groups are relatively new to the political stage, they do not get the airtime afforded the familiar faces. Notwithstanding the way the movement is portrayed in the news, however, the denominational diversity that characterizes it is evidence favoring one criterion for culture war politics—a coalition that transcends denominational boundaries.

We have thus far focused on the rally as an exemplar of the anti-gay marriage coalition. But is it truly representative of the groups working against marriage for homosexuals? Far from being an isolated example, the rally fully reflects the cooperation across multiple denominations and religious traditions among gay marriage opponents. Other examples abound. Consider one of the earliest ballot initiatives against gay marriage, Proposition 22 in California, which was on the ballot in 2000. The campaign in favor of Proposition 22 featured cooperation among Catholics, evangelical Protestants, and Mormons, groups that had worked together previously, notably in opposition to pornography. Given the sharp theological disputes between these groups, especially the tensions between evangelicals and Mormons, this ecumenical partnership is remarkable (Campbell and Monson 2002).

Another case in point is the Arlington Group, a coalition of socially conservative supporters of the Marriage Amendment Project (MAP), an organization that serves as the nexus for groups working to pass an amendment to the federal Constitution that would define marriage as the union of one man and one woman. The Arlington Group is committed to defending traditional marriage in addition to addressing other issues of moral concern such as abortion and judicial activism. During the 2004 election cycle, the Arlington Group created another entity, MAP, to spearhead the work on the marriage issue specifically.[6] Although the Arlington Group is housed in the Family Research Council's facility in Washington, DC, and is associated with Christian Right groups such as Focus on the Family and the American Family Association, more than fifty religious or political organizations are members, and the list is anything but homogeneous. From denominational groups such as the Southern Baptist Convention and the Missouri Synod of the Lutheran Church to interest groups such as the Catholic Citizenship, Family, and Human Rights Institute and the Coalition of African American Pastors to state organizations such as Family First of Nebraska and the Center for Arizona Policy, the Arlington Group represents the breadth of the movement.

The number of groups that are under the Arlington Group's umbrella is actually a conservative estimate of the number of religious groups that oppose gay marriage because some gay marriage opponents do not favor a constitutional amendment and thus choose not to affiliate with the Arlington Group. Moreover, the Islam Society for North America, once part of the MAP, voluntarily left the project because of concern that any direct association with Muslims might tarnish the group's public image, owing to anti-Muslim sentiment following the terrorist attacks of September 11, 2001. Also, according to the coalition's staff, the Union of Orthodox Jewish Congregations of America has worked with MAP to pass the amendment but was never listed as a participating organization (Slatter 2004). Therefore, although the Arlington Group's supporters do not make up an exhaustive list of the organizations opposed to gay marriage, they are nonetheless evidence of the cooperation taking place across denominations, and the Arlington Group is on the front line of the culture war.

A similarly broad coalition characterizes the Alliance for Marriage, another group that opposes gay marriage but also seeks to defend traditional marriage more broadly by addressing issues such as divorce and social welfare policies that discourage marriage. Although it calls for an amendment to the Constitution to ban gay marriage, the Alliance for Marriage has worked less with interest groups associated with the Christian Right than with individual leaders within denominations. For example, the alliance's board of directors includes a rabbi, a Muslim, a minister from the African Methodist Episcopal church, a Hispanic pastor, and a Chinese minister, as well as a number of professors from Catholic universities.

Both the Arlington Group and the Alliance for Marriage provide evidence that opposition to gay marriage has brought together religious conservatives of varied backgrounds, fulfilling one criterion for culture war politics. The second criterion is evidence of tension within a given religious tradition between opponents and supporters of gay marriage. Nowhere has such tension been more apparent than within the black church. Most scholars of religion believe that predominantly African American denominations constitute a separate religious tradition within America because of their unique evolutionary path through the slavery, Jim Crow, and civil rights eras (Harris 1999; Lincoln and Mamiya 1990; Steensland 2000). And within

this tradition, there has been a pitched battle about gay marriage. Many African American clergy are theologically conservative and therefore oppose the practice. A number of conservative black ministers have aligned with white evangelicals to fight it. For example, the Traditional Values Coalition, a nondenominational grassroots church lobby that represents more than forty-three thousand congregations, has hosted a number of events specifically targeting the black churches within their constituency. "We're looking for African-American clergy members who have local authority, and we're getting them to hold a summit on marriage, just one issue," the chairman of the Traditional Values Coalition, Reverend Louis Sheldon, said in one media report (quoted in Banerjee 2005). A number of black leaders spoke at the Mayday for Marriage rally, including Bishop Harry R. Jackson Jr., the pastor of the Hope Christian Church in College Park, Maryland, who said the opening prayer. Jackson has said that blacks are especially attuned to the hardship of broken marriages, single parenting, and babies being born out of wedlock. Jackson said, "The bottom line is not about being anti-homosexual—it is about family reconstruction" (quoted in Chang 2005). Jackson and other African American clergy have joined with the Arlington Group, the Alliance for Marriage, or the Traditional Values Coalition to work against gay marriage.

Not all black clergy oppose gay marriage, however. Within the black church we observe the now-familiar split between traditionalists and progressives. In contrast to clergy members such as Harry Jackson, a number of the most prominent African American religious leaders have defined gay marriage as a civil rights issue and thus support the notion of granting marriage benefits to homosexuals. A common line of reasoning among this group is to draw a parallel with the bans on interracial marriage, which the civil rights movement worked successfully to end (Williams 2004). Former Democratic presidential candidate Al Sharpton shares these sentiments and has publicly endorsed same-sex marriage, going to great lengths to criticize the Republican Party for using the issue to target the religious black community (Finnegan 2004). After giving a sermon to Atlanta's Butler Street African Methodist Episcopal Church, Sharpton said, "George Bush manipulated a lot of religious feelings about marriage" and used gay marriage to draw attention away from Iraq and other policy positions that might not be as popular with the African American community (quoted in Plummer 2005). Perhaps the divide within the black church over gay marriage is best exemplified by the public split within the family of Martin Luther King Jr. King's widow, Coretta Scott King, favored same-sex marriage, and King's daughter, Bernice King, opposes it. Coretta Scott King repeatedly compared homophobia with racism and was convinced that her husband would support granting rights to homosexuals if he were alive today. In contrast, King's daughter, who says homosexuality is a sin, is an elder at an Atlanta church that organized a march in opposition to gay marriage in December 2004. She led the march, which began at her father's grave (Barry 2004).

The divide between traditionalists and progressives is also apparent within Judaism. In 1996, when gay marriage had only begun to emerge on the nation's political agenda, the Reform movement within Judaism took a liberal position with respect to this issue. The Central Conference of American Rabbis (CCAR) within the movement passed a resolution opposing any government action that would prohibit same-sex couples from marrying. The congregational arm of Reform Judaism echoed this resolution a year later, saying that they would support legislation allowing same-sex marriage. Within the Conservative Rabbinical Assembly there is an endorsement of gay rights coupled with an intentional silence on the issue of gay marriage. In fact, a small number of Conservative rabbis have performed same-sex Jewish weddings. These groups stand in contrast to the Orthodox Jews who

participated in the Mayday for Marriage rally and support the Arlington Group's agenda.

Many Catholic groups—but, pointedly, not all—have also joined with Jews and evangelical Protestants to oppose gay marriage. As a telling example of the fracture within Catholicism over the issue, we point to the divide between the two dioceses in the state of Virginia:[7] the Diocese of Arlington and the Diocese of Richmond. In 2004 the two dioceses jointly adopted a legislative agenda but then individually chose to give priority to various aspects of that agenda. The Arlington Diocese tends to focus on abortion and the traditional family structure, whereas the Richmond group focuses on issues relating to poverty and social justice. The Richmond Diocese has not come out in favor of same-sex marriage, but to our knowledge, it has not taken great strides in speaking out against the issue, either. Moreover, the diocese has taken more liberal positions when the issue of homosexuality has been addressed by the Virginia State Legislature. For instance, it supported amending the state's hate crimes law to include homosexuals. In contrast, the Arlington Diocese opposed the measure. The bishop of Arlington has been vocal about his opposition to same-sex marriage, addressing the subject in a homily to his congregants prior to the 2004 election. The differing orientation of the two dioceses is reflected in the religious coalitions in which they participate at the state level. The Richmond Diocese tends to cooperate with more progressive groups such as the Virginia Interfaith Center for Public Policy. The Arlington Diocese has worked closely with Focus on the Family and the Family Research Council's state affiliates to defend traditional marriage and other social conservative policies.

The tension over homosexuality within a number of mainline Protestant denominations echoes and amplifies the debate within Catholicism, the black church, and Judaism. For example, the United Methodist Church has been driven by an internal debate about gay marriage—as a matter not only of public policy but also church policy. In 1999, sixty-eight Methodist ministers presided over a lesbian couple's wedding as an act of protest of church law, which prohibits such ceremonies. The case brought against them was eventually dismissed, suggesting that there is substantial support for same-sex marriage within the church body. This support, though, was not enough to rescind the policy prohibiting same-sex marriage at the 2004 General Conference, where a spirited debate about the subject was conducted. The intensity of the debate is unsurprising; in a case that drew national attention, in March 2004 a jury of Methodist clergy members in Washington State acquitted a fellow minister of violating church law by being in a lesbian relationship. But then a few months later, a similar trial in Pennsylvania resulted in a guilty verdict issued against another lesbian minister, and as a result she was defrocked but was allowed to serve as a layperson in the church (Banerjee 2004). The lesbian minister appealed the ruling, and in May 2005 a committee reversed the decision made by the lower clergy court, citing technical grounds. (The church had never defined the term *practicing homosexual,* which was the basis of the charges brought against the minister.) In October 2005, however, the Judicial Council, the highest court in the Methodist Church, agreed with the original jury's verdict opposing "self-avowed practicing" homosexuals in ordained ministry (Cooperman 2005). The council also said that homosexuals have no immediate right to church membership and reinstated a Virginia minister who had been suspended by a bishop for not allowing a gay man to become a member of his congregation.

The Episcopal Church has been similarly divided about homosexuality, with the ordination of an openly gay bishop leading some Episcopal conservatives to threaten a schism within the church. Although there is obvious sympathy for gay marriage among some of the Episcopal hierarchy (Newman 2005), the Episcopal Church does not officially perform same-sex marriage ceremonies.

Although there are numerous examples of organizations that have united traditionalist denominations in opposition to gay marriage, examples of religious progressives who have banded together to support homosexual unions are few. The religious progressives who are in favor of allowing same-sex marriage are not mobilized to the degree that religious traditionalists are. They are smaller in number than the traditionalists, and either as a cause or as a consequence, they do not have an infrastructure, comparable to the Christian Right's to bring their convictions into the political realm.

The group Clergy for Fairness is the exception that proves the rule. The interfaith group of religious leaders came together in 2006 to oppose a federal amendment to the Constitution that would ban same-sex marriage. In the summer of that year, the group maintained a regular presence in Washington, DC, as both houses of Congress debated the amendment. Representatives of Clergy for Fairness from numerous states visited congressional offices and hosted press conferences. The organization's Web site is perhaps the most sophisticated of its kind, providing links to sample sermons from various religious traditions and talking points about religious liberty and discrimination. Although united in their opposition to a federal amendment, the clergy do not necessarily agree on all issues related to homosexuality and same-sex marriage. Nor does the group take a position with respect to state constitutional amendments regarding same-sex marriage or civil unions.

Other religious groups that support civil marriage rights for same-sex couples are regionally based. The Religious Coalition for the Freedom to Marry, a small interfaith group of clergy, is limited to the New England states and thus a bit player at best in the national drama that is playing out. Similarly, the Colorado Clergy for Equality in Marriage (CCEM) is a group of 104 clergy members from across denominations, working in support of gay unions in the state. Again, there appears to be little coordination between CCEM and any groups on the national stage. The mobilization among religious progressives in support of same-sex marriage rights is hardly an analog to the interfaith organizations which oppose gay marriage.

It seems that the liberal mainline denominations, such as the Episcopal Church and the Methodist Church, are too consumed with the issue of homosexuality within the church to expend much energy on the issue beyond the church. And though there are individual denominations that support same-sex marriages, they represent a minuscule portion of the overall religious landscape. The Unitarian Universalist Association (UUA), a representative body of UU churches, has showed support for same-sex marriage since 1970. Similarly, the United Church of Christ (UCC) officially came out in favor of gay marriage in a 1975 resolution and reasserted its commitment in 2005.[8] In an attempt to show its inclusiveness, in 2004 the UCC ran a television ad showing a same-sex couple being turned away by an unidentified church, only to be welcomed by a UCC church.[9]

Yet the UCC, one of America's most liberal denominations, is not immune from the traditionalist-progressive divide. Because the UCC is composed of autonomous local churches, the General Synod has little authority over individual church practices. So, for example, when the Western North Carolina Association of local UCC churches banned the ordination of openly gay clergy members in 2003, the General Synod had no authority to overrule the act. Other UCC churches have been critical of the governing body's support of same-sex marriage. The First Church of Christ in Wethersfield, Connecticut, the largest UCC church in New England, voted to become independent of the UCC denomination in 2004, explaining that its decision was largely due to the denomination's position regarding gay marriage and other social issues ("Largest UCC church in New England votes to become independent" 2004).

In reviewing the evidence given above, can we say that the religious coalitions surrounding gay marriage support the culture war thesis? Recall the two criteria for observing a culture war among elites: (1) cooperation among leaders of different religious traditions and (2) greater divisions within than between religious traditions. We have seen that both criteria are met, although perhaps the first to a greater extent than the second. Among gay marriage opponents we find a historically remarkable degree of ecumenism, exceeding the breadth of coalitions formed concerning other cultural issues such as abortion and the Equal Rights Amendment. Traditionalist Protestants, Catholics, and Jews alike have united in their opposition to gay marriage. On the other hand, although religious progressives are more naturally inclined toward interfaith cooperation, there are few examples of ecumenical action among gay marriage proponents. In this conflict, one side significantly outnumbers the other.

We also see some evidence for the other criterion, namely, divisions within religious traditions. Within Catholicism and various strains of Protestantism, religious leaders are split with regard to the question of gay marriage. One should not exaggerate the transdenominational nature of opinions about the issue, however. Certainly, the traditionalist-progressive split is salient, but this does not mean that denominations have ceased to matter. A Southern Baptist, regardless of her traditionalism, is more likely to oppose gay marriage than an Episcopalian, notwithstanding the Episcopalian's degree of orthodoxy. It would appear that when we look within denominations, the biggest fights over gay marriage occur inside liberal churches—whose congregants appear less unified in their progressivism than conservative church members are cohesively committed to traditionalism.

WHAT STRATEGIES HAVE THEY EMPLOYED?

The breadth of the coalition against gay marriage is interesting as an example of the fault lines that have formed with regard to cultural issues in American politics. Its significance is more than merely academic, however, because the transdenominational nature of the movement is an important element in its political success. The efforts to build a diverse coalition—in terms of race and religion—underscore the political sophistication of the religious activists who oppose gay marriage. They understand the fundamental rule in a participatory political system: numbers matter. Elected officials are more likely to listen to a large group representing more voters than a smaller group representing fewer voters; all else being equal, a broad coalition beats a narrow one every time. And for the battle over gay marriage, the coalition of opponents has been broad indeed.

Why is there such a broad coalition opposing gay marriage? Given the widespread opposition to the practice, as illustrated in figure 6.1, it may seem inevitable that the opposition to it would have a wide base. But there is nothing inevitable about the institutions that have been developed to lead the charge against gay marriage.

Although the widespread opposition to gay marriage is a necessary condition for a broad coalition, it is not sufficient. The breadth of the coalition is also the result of political experience gained over the previous generation of cultural battles and the political infrastructure that has been built to fight those battles. The coalition is in large part the result of a deliberate strategy employed by evangelical conservatives since the issue first gained national prominence in the mid-1990s, when the Defense of Marriage Act was passed in Congress and signed by Bill Clinton. The specific strategy in play consists of diversifying the coalition opposed to gay marriage, amending state constitutions to ban gay marriage, and, finally, creating the "perfect storm" so that the conditions will be right to pass an amendment to the U.S. Constitution defining marriage as the union of a man and a woman.

A good example of a Christian Right activist who has recognized the political advantage of a diverse coalition working against gay marriage is Matt Daniels of the Alliance for Marriage. Recognizing the limits of the prolife movement, which largely consists of white evangelicals and Catholics,[10] Daniels sought to create a multiracial movement in defense of heterosexual marriage. A Chinese pastor serving on the advisory board of the alliance notes that Daniels selected advisors and board members with the idea of bringing together people of diverse faiths and races (Wong 2004). As noted above, the Arlington Group is another example of Christian Right leaders' organizing an infrastructure composed of diverse religions and denominations to respond to gay marriage. After the groups were linked at the national level, the local and state affiliates came to coordinate with one another, an important development because the battle over traditional marriage has primarily been waged at the state and local levels.[11]

Examining one state in particular illustrates the political strategy of gay marriage opponents. On November 2, 2004, Ohioans voted to ban the recognition of same-sex marriage by amending the state constitution. The success of this ballot initiative was largely a result of coordination between Ohio affiliates of socially conservative advocacy groups and their national parent organizations. The leading figure in Ohio, Phil Burress, was a familiar face in local Christian Right circles, having run an antipornography group since the early 1990s.[12] When Hawaii's state supreme court issued a ruling in favor of allowing same-sex marriage in 1993, Burress began committing most of his time to fighting gay marriage in his own state. He started the Ohio Campaign to Protect Marriage, now a state affiliate of Focus on the Family and the Family Research Council. To assist Burress and his supporters, these and other national groups contacted their members in Ohio to mobilize them in response to the issue. The American Family Association, for example, sent out mass emails to sixty thousand supporters who live in Ohio to encourage them to sign the petition needed to get the issue on the ballot and then turn out to vote in November. Representatives from the Ohio group met with national leaders regularly. Part of the strategy involved discussing how to conduct outreach to leaders within other religious traditions in the state. As a result, staffers from the Ohio Campaign to Protect Marriage visited a large mosque in the greater Cincinnati area to encourage its members to support the state's ban on gay marriage (Miller 2005). The Ohio group also worked closely with African American churches to gather signatures for the petition. Further broadening the coalition, all twelve Catholic bishops in Ohio made a public statement in support of the state's marriage amendment. With these interfaith relationships in place, the Ohio Campaign to Protect Marriage was able to gather 575,000 signatures in fewer than ninety days to put a measure on the Ohio ballot. Sixty-two percent voted in favor, and thus a ban on same-sex marriage was written into the state constitution.[13]

The example of Ohio, like that of California, mentioned earlier, demonstrates that the religious diversity among groups opposed to gay marriage is not restricted to the national level. Although evangelical groups appear to be spearheading the cause, they depend on a larger community of religious believers to achieve political success. And we expect to see further interreligious cooperation because the success of the Ohio campaign now serves as a template for anti–gay marriage campaigns in other states. Soon after the 2004 election season, which resulted in bans on same-sex marriage added to the constitutions of twelve states,[14] Burress and other religious leaders met in Washington, DC, to discuss the following year's constitutional amendment battles in other states. By igniting support for traditional marriage at the grass roots, leaders at the national level hope to spur constituents to pressure their representatives and senators to support the amendment to the U.S. Constitution. To that end, they remain focused on the states.

As evidenced by the decision to build support for a gay marriage ban state by state, leaders in the

movement against the practice have displayed a considerable degree of political sophistication (not to mention patience). This is nowhere more apparent than in their negotiations concerning the federal marriage amendment. Although it is certain to fail in the short term, it will be repeatedly introduced in the years to come. Conservative religious leaders do not expect success immediately. Years ago, prior to the first introduction of the amendment, leaders of the Christian Right met with members of Congress to determine a realistic strategy for enacting a constitutional amendment. They realized the limitations they faced in a contentious Congress and chose to work within those constraints, as illustrated by the wording selected for the amendment. A ban on civil unions, they were told, would never happen. And so instead of an amendment that would explicitly ban civil unions and gay marriage, they opted for one that would prohibit homosexual marriages only. The majority of groups represented by the movement to defend traditional marriage also oppose civil unions, but many of them were willing to focus their efforts on marriage as a political compromise. According to Allison Slatter of the Arlington Group's Marriage Amendment Project, trying to outlaw civil unions would have been political suicide. Using a metaphor that resonates with our discussion of the culture war, she said, "Civil unions require a nuke and nuking is not popular. Restricting marriage to man and woman would require circular strikes, and those are acceptable. We pinpoint the area most troublesome and we stop that" (Slatter 2004). Focus on the Family, equally opposed to civil unions, agreed that pushing for an amendment to address civil unions would not be politically expedient. Instead, Focus on the Family believes that it must defend traditional marriage before attempting to outlaw civil unions as well. "Being an incrementalist is not an unprincipled approach," said Peter Brandt, the group's vice president of public policy (Brandt 2004). Brandt thinks it wiser to turn to the states to adopt the language necessary to ban civil unions.[15]

Contrast this flexibility with earlier incarnations of the Christian Right movement, which was characterized by absolutism with regard to moral issues. As it has become a more politically sophisticated movement, it has recognized the value of getting half a loaf when the whole loaf is out of reach. The evolving strategy of abortion opponents illustrates this change. When the Christian Right first appeared on the national political landscape, its leaders and organizations took a hard-line stand against abortion, supporting nothing less than an absolute ban on all abortions. In more recent years, however abortion opponents have adopted an incremental strategy by working to enact a prohibition on "partial-birth abortion" (known to abortion rights advocates as "intact dilation and extraction"), supporting parental notification laws, and the like (Saletan 2003). As applied to abortion, the incremental strategy appears to be working. Not only have numerous limitations and restrictions on abortion been successfully enacted, but recent years have seen a small shift toward prolife attitudes among the general public—two developments that are clearly related, although the direction of causality is unclear (Wilcox and Norrander 2002). Incrementalism with respect to abortion has served as a template for the strategy to oppose gay marriage. The half loaf of a gay marriage ban that permits civil unions is better than trying and failing to obtain the whole loaf of banning both.

CONCLUSION

We have seen that the religious coalitions that have formed around the issue of gay marriage—especially in opposition to it—are evidence of what James Davison Hunter memorably labeled "culture war politics." The term is incendiary and perhaps misleading, but the interfaith cooperation it is meant to describe nonetheless includes the groups

working to thwart gay marriage in the United States. In its current configuration, the debate about the practice pits opponents comprised largely of traditionalists spanning the religious spectrum against advocates who are predominantly secular but are joined by a small number of religious progressives. We stress that we are not saying that religious traditions are irrelevant in shaping opinions regarding gay marriage. To the contrary, members of different religious traditions vary systematically in their opposition to gay marriage. But the differences among religious traditions are surpassed by the differences within them. Your level of traditionalism within your church matters more than which church you go to.

At the moment, the opponents of gay marriage have the upper hand. Supporters of marriage among homosexuals are in the minority, as evidenced by public opinion polls and the overwhelming margins of victory for ballot initiatives to ban marriage between homosexual couples. As we look toward the future, however, should we expect to see the "culture war" continue? There are two ways to read the tea leaves. On one hand, attitudes toward homosexuality are becoming increasingly liberal, largely because young people are more accepting of homosexuals and gay marriage than their elders. Young people are also less likely than their elders to endorse morally traditionalist opinions. For example, 36 percent of Americans over the age of fifty-five are in the bottom half of the moral traditionalism index introduced above, compared to 72 percent of people under the age of thirty. As time marches on, those young people will come to occupy an ever-larger share of the population. It is thus tempting to say that we should expect to see a cessation of hostilities in the culture war—at least along the front line of gay marriage—in much the same way that racial attitudes changed dramatically over the course of a generation. It is also portentous, however, that the gap in attitudes toward gay marriage between young people at the bottom and at the top of the moral traditionalism index mirrors what we see among their elders. The former gap in is 28 percentage points. Among people over fifty-five, the gap is 32 points. In other words, we see that young people, taken as a whole, have more liberal attitudes about gay marriage than do their elders. Yet among young people, there remains a clear distinction between traditionalists and progressives. This sharp divide suggests that the most apt analogy for attitudes about gay marriage may be not public opinion regarding civil rights. Rather, perhaps a better comparison is with attitudes about abortion, which have remained sharply polarized for decades. If so, we can expect the battle over gay marriage to be with us for a long time.

NOTES

1. Tony Perkins, president of the Family Research Council, in remarks made to attendees at the Mayday for Marriage rally in Washington, DC, on October 15, 2004, and printed in the event's program.
2. Ken Hutcherson, senior pastor at Antioch Bible Church in Kirkland, Washington, organized the first Mayday for Marriage Rally, in Seattle. It drew approximately twenty thousand people.
3. Terms such as *traditional* and *progressive* are contested. Since these are the terms Hunter uses in *Culture Wars*, we have adopted them. We prefer them to *conservative* and *liberal,* since these terms confuse theology with political ideology.
4. For an overview of the composition of the Christian Right, see Wilcox and Larson (2006), chap. 2.
5. This includes any other type of legal recognition for homosexual relationships. To keep things simple, we simply refer to "opposing gay marriage," which should be understood as including opposition to civil unions.
6. After 2005, MAP no longer existed as a separate entity, though the goal of barring same-sex marriage remains a prominent interest of the Arlington Group.
7. For a discussion of religious lobbying activity in Virginia, including a summary of its two Catholic dioceses, see Larson, Madland, and Wilcox (2006).
8. On July 4, 2005, at the Twenty-fifth General Synod of the United Church of Christ, delegates voted to adopt the resolution "In Support of Equal Rights for

All." http://www.ucc.org/synod/resolutions/gsrev 25–7.pdf (accessed October 17, 2006).
9. Both NBC and CBS refused to air the advertisement, deeming it too controversial.
10. For an overview of the composition of the prolife movement, see Luker (1985) and Maxwell (2002).
11. To understand the strategy one must have some understanding of the structural organization of Christian Right groups. Many national-level groups, such as the Family Research Council, Focus on the Family, and the Christian Coalition, have state affiliates that share the policy platform of the national body. When cooperation is taking place on the national scale, cooperation between state affiliates is likely to follow.
12. For a profile of Phil Burress and his work in defense of traditional marriage, see Dao (2004).
13. In 2004 the wording of state amendments went largely uncontested among the religious groups opposed to gay marriage. Burress, a staunch social conservative, was the original architect of the Ohio amendment, and he put forth a conservative text that banned same-sex contracts in addition to same-sex marriage. Activists from other states chose to pursue a ban on same-sex marriage that did not include a ban on civil unions, possibly thinking that this additional stipulation might decrease the chances of the amendment's passage. In Oregon, for example, an amendment banning same-sex civil unions would have been asking too much from a liberal-leaning state. Oregon voters did pass an amendment banning gay marriage but by only 58 percent, the smallest margin of any marriage amendment proposed in 2004. To date, the text of state amendments has been left up to the discretion or conviction of local evangelical activists and evangelical groups.
14. Two states voted to amend their constitutions prior to Election Day. Missouri citizens voted to amend the state constitution in August 2004 to define marriage as a union of a man and woman. Louisiana voted in September to amend its constitution, outlawing gay marriage as well as civil unions. In November, however, a Louisiana lower court judge overturned the state amendment, saying it was flawed because it included two purposes, banning gay marriage and civil unions, within one amendment. At this point, it seems likely that the ban will eventually be reinstated, however, if only because Louisiana's supreme court is an elected body, and

Louisianans voted overwhelmingly in favor of the ban (78 percent).

15. Not all socially conservative advocacy groups have been happy with this compromise. Concerned Women for America, for example, was so displeased with the failure of the amendment to address civil unions that it decided not to directly partner with the coalitions opposing gay marriage in April 2005.

23

Displacing Religion, Disarming Law: Situating Quaker Spirituality in the 'Trident Three' Case

Lisa Ann Smith and Lori G. Beaman

INTRODUCTION

In June of 1999, three middle-aged women—Angie Zelter, Ulla Roder and Ellen Moxley (the Trident Three)—boarded a Trident[1] control station stationed on a Scottish loch; with the use of their hands and small hammers they disabled much of the computer equipment aboard the station and threw all computer equipment that was not attached overboard. In total, they caused over £80,000 of damage and temporarily disarmed one third of Britain's nuclear weapons system. They subsequently sat atop the barge awaiting arrest, a pivotal part of their plan. Their nonviolent actions were strategically designed to provoke a legal reaction which would lead to a court case. In their defense, they argued that their actions were justified on the basis of the illegality of the use or threat to use nuclear weapons proclaimed by the International Court of Justice (ICOJ) in its advisory opinion on the Legality of the Threat or Use of Nuclear Weapons. In this opinion the International Court found that "the threat or use of nuclear weapons would generally be contrary to the rules of international law applicable in armed conflict, and in particular the principles and rules of humanitarian law" (ICOJ, *Legality of the Threat or Use of Nuclear Weapons (General List No. 95)*, section 1). The Trident Three hoped that the court would find in their favor and declare the govern-

ment's continued possession of nuclear weapons illegal.

The three women were members of Trident Ploughshares, a coalition of faith-based and radical political activists dedicated to stopping the proliferation of nuclear weapons on the basis of the Old Testament assertion to "beat swords into ploughshares." Its members, called Trident pledgers, were not strangers to the court as throughout the years many had openly sought prosecution in order to push for the abolition of nuclear weapons under law. The Trident Three came to be regarded among Trident pledgers, as well as nuclear disarmament activists more generally, as symbolic of the possibilities of nonviolent direct action. Their fame derived as much from the extent of the damage they caused as it did from the controversy provoked by the initial decision to acquit the three in the Lower Court.

In the court, the three women claimed that they were acting out of a sincere belief in their obligation as moral citizens to promote the values of nonviolence and peace. Ellen was clear that she drew from her spiritual beliefs as a Quaker; while Angie and Ulla made no mention of spiritual motivations and cited their deeply held moral convictions. These claims were reshaped by the court based on an alternative set of claims to authority—the rule of law. The court's claim to authority derived from law's status as an institution which embodies rationality, objectivity, and reason. The court's claim to transcendence derived from the fact that it was neutral and not affected by individual belief, opinion, or emotion. The appeal to a global position in the context of the case for both parties makes perfect sense as the destructive capacity of nuclear weapons makes them an inherently global issue. However, what is interesting is that religion, or any wider moral viewpoint, completely disappears in the court's judgment of the three women; yet it maintains and upholds its own position of transcendence.

The aim of this paper is to read the Trident Three case as a social text that reveals a confrontation between two worldviews, that of the court and that of the Trident Three. Beyond making a contribution to socio-legal scholarship, this paper seeks to contribute to two key areas: first, to the broader debate around the division between the sacred and the secular; second, to an understanding of the complexities of religiously informed political action and the influence of religion in social movements. The individual nature of religious practice and the diffuse nature of belief mean that Quakers, in particular, tend towards outward engagement with other secular and religious organizations (Smith, 2006). As Kent and Spickard (1994) argue, beyond being related to positions on particular issues, Quaker beliefs reflect a particular view of the value of political institutions, which has infiltrated and influenced "radical" political positions more generally. In the background of the Trident Three case, rather than being obvious and readily apparent, religion is a subtle presence within the group that both directly and indirectly informs their shared worldview. Quaker spirituality helps us to make sense of both how the women arrived in the courtroom and why they presented their legal argument in the way that they did. Further, in the legal decision, religion remains an undercurrent against which the court juxtaposes it own position.

Drawing on literature in critical legal studies (Mossman, 1987; Smart, 1989), sociology of religion and social movements (Smith, 1996; Williams and Kubal, 1999) we argue that there is a profound disjuncture between the ways in which the law and religious discourse frame the actions of the Trident Three. This paper contrasts these two discursive frameworks in order to explore the ways in which religious claims are reshaped by legal discourse as isolated actions rather than as actions set in a broader moral context with transcendental implications. In challenging the law on its own terrain, the Trident Three were subjected to its power to define and delimit the meaning of events. Our analysis contains two major components: tracing the background of the Trident Three and a critical discourse analysis (Fairclough, 1995) of the High Court judgment. We are not claiming to situate our analysis in a social movements framework; rather our project is to conduct a socio-legal analysis of competing discourses, paying particular attention to the ways in which power relations are worked out. However, we do acknowledge the contribution of social movements literature to an understanding of the ways in which groups deploy notions of "the good society" or "the public good" in order to ground their justification of choice of action (see especially Williams, 1995).

In carrying out this analysis we have paid particular attention to the subtleties of the court decision, which would be obscured by relying on a surface reading, or a reading that focused on the outcome only. We have deconstructed the court's version of events, focusing not only on what is within the narrative of the decision, but also on that which was constructed as being outside of the court's purview, or as being irrelevant. Our analysis recognizes both the broader context that influenced and preceded the specific action of the Trident Three and the specific space of the court room. Both are understood as having broader implications even though they may be seemingly confined by time and location. It is the interplay between religion, law, and action that emerges from a consideration of these multiple sources.

1. RELIGIOUS ACTIVISM IN CONTEXT

We conceptualize religion in a dynamic manner. As Robert Orsi (2003) puts it, "Religion is always religion-in-action, religion-in-relationships between people, between the way the world is and the way people imagine or want it to be" (Orsi, 2003: 172). Orsi's orientation is particularly useful for considering the manner in which religion plays a role in the case of the Trident Three, because it captures the idea that it is essential to move beyond the specificity of an individual's political action to how it fits into a broader set of social relationships and networks. Following the work of Orsi (2003) and Beckford (2003), we adopt a moderate constructionist approach to the study of religion. Religion is part of both complex social formations at the macro level and mundane practices in everyday life at the micro level. The case of the Trident Three highlights a unique intersection between personal belief and global systems of connection. Religious ideas and beliefs are active in challenging and resisting in ways that are not always obvious, in spite of the belief that we live in a secular society where religion is relegated to the private sphere.

While it is rare for theorists to completely discount the continued importance of religion as a political motivator, it is very common both in popular and scholarly discourse for the role of religion in the public sphere to be oversimplified in either a positive or a negative light (ter Haar, 2005). A large part of this mischaracterization originates in how religion and religious believers are conceptualized as practicing their religious beliefs only in private quarters. Central to this misconception is the belief that religion and religious belief are "private" matters, while politics is a "public" matter, and the two should not intersect.

Yet, issues of religious practice which supposedly occur in the private sphere continue to seep into public debates, and the nature of religious practice continues to affect and inform individuals' outward actions in the world. Further, even a cursory exploration into a variety of modern social movements reveals connections with religious individuals and groups. In fact, certain groups like the Quakers engender this type of integration because of their belief systems. However, there is nothing new in saying that religious groups have influenced nonviolence or peace activism or, even more generally, modern social movements. Elements of this confluence have been explored in depth by Smith (1996) and Williams and Kubal (1999). The Trident Three case offers an opportunity to explore the intersection of religion and social activism as a process involving a subtle weaving together. In this sense, the links between influence, individual practice, and belief need to be carefully attended to.

The actions of the Trident Three can only partially be understood through the conceptual frameworks of contemporary social movements. Christian Smith (1996) identifies numerous characteristics of such social movements, including shared identity and organizational resources. Against this backdrop social movements more generally should not be understood as strictly secular or religious, but rather spaces in which individuals bring a potentially diverse set of viewpoints together. As Pagnucco (1996) notes, "The American peace movement has always included a strong core of religious activists. Throughout American history, the historic peace churches, primarily the Quakers, have played key roles in the emergence of anti-war activism during wartime and have been carriers of the movement in less active times" (1996: 205). Ceadel (2002) notes that, in the British context, Quakers have similarly influenced the popularization of the peace movement. In this sense, religion can be understood as a potentially diffuse social entity that refers back to and interacts with secular society. The minimalist doctrine of the Quakers, their emphasis on social justice as an active and individual practice, and their loose organizational structure mean that they do not fit neat typologies. Further, their collaboration with those outside of the Quaker faith adds a unique dimension to the analysis. Especially intriguing is the shared liturgical act, whereby individual spirituality is tempered by and more fully realized in the context of a group.

2. THE QUAKER COMMITMENT TO PEACE AND SOCIAL JUSTICE

The Quaker movement emerged as an alternative Christianity in England in the 1600s under the guidance of George Fox. What sets Quakers apart as a religious group, and in particular as a Christian group, is the decentralized character of both their religious beliefs and their practice. The emphasis placed on the individual and the experiential nature of God means that Quaker expressions of spirituality are not manifested in strictly religious spaces. Because of this, Quakers are often found in organizations not directly linked to the organizational structure of Friends.[2] This helps us to make sense of their ongoing engagement in issues of peace and social justice from a nonviolent and pacifist standpoint in a diverse set of political spaces, both religious and secular.

The diffuse nature of Quaker spirituality also presents a unique challenge to social movements literature. For example, Williams argues that "Religion shapes the identity, the sense of solidarity, and the moral outrage that are integral to social-movements cultures. Motivated believers are at the core of any collective action[;] at the same time, religious doctrine and theology can offer coherent and elaborated cognitive rationales that diagnose social problems, prescribe possible solutions and justify the movement's action—often in the cause of universal verities" (1996: 377). The challenge presented by Quakers, and more specifically by the Trident Three case, is the complex way

in which religion is woven into the fabric of the actions of the Trident Three and the organizations in which they are involved. As we have already stated, the core of our focus in this paper is the discursive working-out of the actual court case, but clearly we cannot consider this without at least briefly acknowledging the cultural context of the case.

Dandelion (2004), Collins (2002), and Coleman and Collins (2000) emphasize that unity, and therefore the uniqueness of Quakers, is engendered through religious practice, rather than through a particular set of religious beliefs or texts. Interestingly, not all Quakers define God as the unifying force, because unity is derived from practice rather than from a religious belief system. As Bourke (2003) highlights, this helps us to understand why Quakers demonstrate diverse religious orientations, such as Christian, Buddhist, or Jewish, and yet share the same spiritual practice. In this sense, outward manifestations such as political activism and engagement in social justice derive from a shared worldview, rather than from a shared theology. This makes Quakers unique in both the secular and the religiously-based activist contexts. In the former, this is because their involvement in peace and social justice can be understood as an expression of their spiritual experience; in the latter, it is because the basis for their action is experience rather than religious doctrine.

Quakers view their society as a community of individuals participating in a religious movement, rather than a religious movement encompassing and dictating to a group (Byrd, 1960: 12). This belief is reflected in the decentralized character of Quaker meetings, which subscribe to no organizational hierarchy and have no set format. Worship meetings are held in silence; members may break the silence with prayer or song if they feel led to do so.

Quakers do not follow a religious leader or refer to a particular text in the formation of their ideas or beliefs. However, the fact that there is no overarching ideology associated with Quakers stands in contrast to the reality of their particular history of interactions with the law. Robert Byrd (1960) said of Quakers:

> There has never been a generation of Friends, including the present one, which has not seen an important segment of its membership in prison on grounds of conscience for one reason or another, beginning with the early Friends and their opposition to proving truthfulness in court by swearing oaths and extending to the present period when Friends have refused to establish their "non-disloyalty" by swearing to their innocence of traitorous activity. (Byrd, 1960: 36)

This inability to avoid imprisonment is not due to the propensity of Quakers to be criminals in the traditional sense, but rather relates to their particular religious views, which lead to an obligation to confront the law. The form of these actions—emphasizing nonviolence and pacifism—demonstrates congruence among Quakers about the value and importance of the individual and the experiential nature of religious beliefs, which can help us to understand how and why they challenge the law in the way that they do (Byrd, 1960: 6).

Quakers believe in the Inner Light or inherent integrity of every individual. "Every person, regardless of differences in ability, appearance, training or political or religious allegiance, possesses a creative, unifying quality—the dignity, worth or preciousness of the individual personality" (Byrd, 1960: 2). Quaker spiritual practice is meant to uphold this belief and foster the sacred character of the individual. The belief in the worth of each individual is also reflected in the way Quakers interact with other members of society, which is best expressed in the history of the Quaker Peace Testimony.[3] The Inner Light or "That of God in every man" refers to a belief that God is inherent in each individual and that spiritual practice involves developing this spirit of interconnectedness with other individuals (Byrd, 1960: 2). Quakers also emphasize the experiential nature of religious beliefs. The process of knowing God does not occur through reading or communication of doctrine and scripture, but rather through direct personal experience (Hoare: 2). Moreover, knowledge of God is demonstrated through and enhanced by action. Actions must therefore reflect one's spiritual beliefs, and in particular one's belief in the inherent integrity of the individual as an expression of God.

Quakers refuse to participate in violent processes despite legal mandates, e.g. mandatory military conscription, because doing so violates their integrity as individuals, as well as the integrity of others. Furthermore, they actively oppose laws which leave open the possibility of violence because doing nothing also violates one's integrity as an individual. "Doing good is not the fundamental reason . . . but the fact that he suffers a corrosion of spirit who stands by unconcerned in the presence of the burdened spirits of others" (Byrd, 1960: 17). Kent and Spickard (1994) highlight this ethic in the history of radical activism amongst American Quakers: ". . . all people are called to work for peace and justice. When political institutions do not further these ends, then those institutions must be opposed" (Kent and Spickard, 1994: 373).

The Quakers are in a unique position in that they are obligated, as a conscientious exercise, to disobey laws that support, allow or promote violence. Furthermore, because they perceive a unity amongst the worth of all individuals and believe that this unity transcends and is inherent to social interactions, there is no separation between the religious and the private. The government and the law have no ultimate value; they are seen as negotiable tools in enhancing the individual's capacity to know God. Kent and Spickard (1994) note that the ethic underpinning the tradition of radical Quaker politics is distinct from the mainstream civil religious tradition, which sees government and its institutions as manifested by the hand of God. Conversely, the Quaker sectarian tradition ". . . seeks to replace the social order by a new, purer, more just one. It sees in its own band of faithful the hope of a new society" (Kent and Spickard, 1994: 374). As Byrd has observed, throughout Quaker history, spending time in prison has been a central form of political protest. Like that of many other marginal religious groups, Quaker spirituality poses a challenge to attempts by the law to define religion and religious practice. The unique character of Quaker spiritual practice has meant that Quakers have influenced organizations in ways that fall outside of the realm of traditional understandings of religious expression.

Quakers have been extremely vocal and active in attempting to influence domestic and international policy and issues. This is often done through the auspices of Quaker-based organizations. Committees are developed by Quakers with a particular mandate in mind, and work towards policy development, public education, and direct action. Individual Quakers have also been extremely active in attempting to influence domestic and international policy and issues.[4] Quakers will often involve themselves in the political or legal realm as a personal expression of their spirituality, and band with likeminded organizations, both secular and religious. Maureen Waugh (2001) explores the tensions for Quakers inherent in working in mainstream politics because they hold a set of beliefs that do not correspond to the dominant majority in international peace work. She notes: "Quakers must reconcile their pacifist convictions with their perceived responsibilities as a 'Quaker citizen', and at the same time engage with the emergent realities of political power and the use of force at the inter-state level" (Waugh, 2001: 1). Despite these tensions, many Quakers continue to involve themselves in attempting to influence international politics and policy through mainstream institutions. However, because of these tensions, many Quakers instead seek to participate in organizations which align themselves with Quaker beliefs and ideas. Ellen Moxley, a Quaker and one of the Trident Three, became a pledger with Trident Ploughshares to campaign for nuclear disarmament. Her affiliation

with this organization can be understood by the fact that it facilitates legal disobedience with an underlying religiously based belief in non-violence.

The actions of Ellen Moxley, as well as those of other Quakers (Smith, 2006), demonstrates that the intensely individual expression of Quaker spirituality both leads to and to some extent requires integration with others, who are often non-Quakers. The integration of Quakers with non-Quaker organizations occurs both directly and indirectly. As mentioned above, Quakers often participate in like-minded organizations, such as Trident Ploughshares. Quaker beliefs and values often shape the strategies used by organizations. There are many non-Quakers who use Quaker values and beliefs in formulating their actions and strategies. Martin Ceadel (2002) notes the important role played by Quakers in the British peace movement because of their emphasis on pacifism. Quakers ". . . did much to achieve general acceptance of pacifism as more than a sectarian peculiarity or an excuse for avoiding dangerous citizenly duties" (Ceadel, 2002: 29). In this sense Quaker spirituality is mobilized through the secular peace movement.

Trident Ploughshares provides a platform for interested activists, like Ellen Moxley, who align on grounds, whether religious or political, that have a particular congruence with Quaker beliefs and ideas. Angie, Ulla and Ellen brought a diverse set of motivations and influences with them, some religious, some secular. While Angie and Ulla did not identify themselves as religious, they drew on Quaker strategies and other religious traditions in the interests of advancing their goals as secular political activists. Taking action that is nonviolent, open, and fully accountable resonates with Quaker beliefs in the inherent worth of the individual—both personally and collectively—and the experiential nature of spirituality. In her defense at trial, Ellen Moxley stated this feeling in the following way: "Doubtless you members of the jury would agree that sabotaging the ovens of Auschwitz would have been a moral duty. The moveable incinerator that is Trident is many times more lethal" (Ellen Moxley, cited in McIntosh, 2001: 3). Working towards disarmament is expressed as an obligation of the moral citizen to promote the values of nonviolence and peace, rooted in a belief of the universality of human worth.

3. TRIDENT PLOUGHSHARES AND THE BRITISH CONTEXT

The manner in which individuals engage with political issues is subject to the wider social and cultural context in which they live. As Byrne highlights, beginning in the 1970s and continuing into the 1980s in Britain, protest became firmly established as a "part of the array of actions citizens and groups might consider using to make themselves heard" (1997: 5). Further he notes the centrality played by the peace movement more generally, and nuclear disarmament in particular. The Trident Three and their action can thus be situated within a wider set of movements in Britain that sought to oppose nuclear weapons by influencing the government. Their organization, Trident Ploughshares, is similar to the Campaign for Nuclear Disarmament (CND). Both CND and Trident Ploughshares employ a number of strategies, from policy consultation to education and direct action employing nonviolence. Though they have sometimes trespassed (on private property), CND activists have tended to stay within the realm of "acceptable" protest, while it would seem (Byrne, 1988) that Trident pledgers have a greater tendency to trespass and destroy property.

In both CND and Trident Ploughshares, we see the influence of religious individuals and groups that espouse peace and a nonviolent philosophy. Similarly, the influence of religious groups is seen in many political organizations around the world, both within and across state boundaries. As we noted previously, churches rooted in a peace-centered ideology have played an important role in generating anti-war activism. Further, on an individual level many activists working within "secular" organizations continue to cite spiritual beliefs as one of the core reasons for their involvement (Byrne, 1997).

If we employ a more nuanced definition of religion, we must provide a more subtle consideration of the role of religion in the particular organization at issue in this case—Trident Ploughshares—and the subsequent action of the Trident Three. With this in mind it is imperative to pay attention to both the obvious and the more obscure elements of religious influence. The action taken by the Trident Three has a symbolic meaning that sought to transcend individual action in order to make a broader statement about nuclear arms, violence, and the world in which we live. Similarly, their actions have a broader sociological meaning that reveals the way in which religion motivates and informs individual and collective action, even when it is integrated with seemingly "secular" value systems and organizations.

Trident Ploughshares is founded on the biblical dictum to "beat swords into ploughshares." The name comes from Hebrew scripture; however Trident Ploughshares does not identify itself as a specifically Christian or Jewish movement. It brings together a wide range of people from many different faiths and philosophies—and is an excellent demonstration of the integration of the faith-based peace movement and the radical political secular movement (Zelter, 2001: 6). "Some people have seen their action arising out of the Biblical prophecy of Isaiah and as witnessing to the kingdom of God. Others, coming from a secular perspective, have viewed their action as being primarily motivated by a humanist or deeply held conscience commitment to nonviolence and solidarity with the poor" (Trident Ploughshares, 2001b: section 1.6, para. 3). The Trident Three demonstrate the diversity among Trident pledgers. Ellen Moxley is a Quaker, while Angie Zelter and Ulla Roder identify themselves as secular activists.

Despite differing orientations, Trident pledgers aim to disarm the United Kingdom's Trident nuclear weapons system. Pledgers to Trident Ploughshares have a common desire to abolish war "through an engagement in constructive conversion of arms and military related [sic] industry into life affirming [sic] production, and the development of nonviolent methods for resolving conflicts" (Trident Ploughshares, 2001b: section 1.6, para. 3). The strategies employed by Trident Ploughshares pledgers are guided by the following key ideas:

Nonviolence—the means used must reflect the ultimate vision for social change;

Openness—Trident is always informed of actions that will take place. There are no attempts to hide information or plans.

Accountability—Ploughshares activists always peacefully await arrest following each act in order to participate in a public conversation about the particular issues that the action raises (Trident Ploughshares, 2001b).

The goal of Trident Ploughshares is to work towards a democratic decision about nuclear disarmament through actively engaging and promoting dialogue. This often involves Trident pledgers spending extensive amounts of time in prison[5] and putting their lives at risk for a cause they believe in. Art Laffin, a Catholic Worker house member and a Trident Ploughshares pledger, expressed the ethic adopted in the following way: "In my view, the basic hope of Ploughshares actions is to communicate from the moment of entry into a plant or base—and throughout the court and prison witness—an underlying faith that the power of nonviolent love can overcome the forces of violence . . . We try to disarm ourselves by disarming weapons" (Trident Ploughshares, 2001b: section 1.6, para. 10). Given its advocacy of nonviolence, it is not surprising that Trident Ploughshares has attracted Quaker members like Ellen Moxley. While the original movement drew much of its

membership from the Catholic Worker houses and other communities such as Jonah House in Baltimore, the membership has evolved to embrace the peace traditions in many faith groups.

The development of the organization through collaboration, and in particular its stance on nonviolence, reveals that through the involvement of individual Quakers like Ellen, Quaker spirituality has had an influence on the group. Trident Ploughshares adopts a religious understanding of nonviolence that is informed by Quaker-based programs of active nonviolence, such as the Quaker Peace Action Caravan (Q-PAC) (1987) and Turning the Tide. Q-PAC was a project of Quaker Peace and Service, part of the Religious Society of Friends in Britain. "Q-PAC was to work with members of the Society of Friends, through established Quaker structures, to reach the general public" (Quaker Peace and Social Service, 1987: 1). Turning the Tide is a Quaker-based program for nonviolence and social change. It was commissioned by Trident Ploughshares to train pledgers in their affinity groups in the principles and practice of nonviolence as espoused by Trident Ploughshares. Workshops cover the principles of nonviolence, responses to violence, group processes, and personal empowerment. More in-depth workshops cover tactics and strategies, sustaining a campaign, and building strong action groups (Trident Ploughshares, 2001a). These Quaker programs, as well as Trident Ploughshares, define a religious understanding of nonviolence as "the ultimate goal of social change and the spirit in which it is carried out" (Turning the Tide: para. 2).

4. CONFRONTING LAW, CONSTRUCTING RELIGION

Richard Fenn (1982) offers a framework for understanding the legal diminishing of an act such as that carried out by the Trident Three. He argues that there is a profound disjuncture between legal and religious discourses, and focuses on the liturgical act to illustrate this point.

> Like all formal language, liturgical acts depend for their effectiveness on their ability to isolate purely personal or idiosyncratic factors. Liturgists do not permit the private, religious, or moral heresies of the faithful to interfere with the elegance and serenity of the ritual as a whole. But in the court-room the judge made frequent references to the personal and idiosyncratic on a number of occasions. The effect of those references was to discredit the moral persuasiveness of the defendants' arguments. (Fenn, 1982: 191)

The liturgical action of the Trident Three is reduced by the courts to an act of subversion by three eccentric women. This stands in contrast to an understanding of their actions as being global and timeless, as a "prophetic denunciation" (Fenn, 1982: 191). The law reduces actions to time, place, and act, whereas the Trident Three understand their actions in much broader terms.

We might describe the actions of the Trident Three as "parabolic deeds," defined by Pagnucco (1996) as "'unruly' or 'unconventional' direct action tactics such as war-tax resistance and civil disobedience that constitute moral acts of noncooperation with evil and forms of public witness that challenge the consciences of the American people" (Pagnucco, 1996: 206). Of course, the Trident Three are not American, but we argue that the notion of "parabolic deed" can apply in other contexts. Indeed, we would argue that the nuclear arms issue is conceptualized much more broadly than a local issue. Clearly, local resistance is necessary, but the Trident Three situate their parabolic deed in a global context.

Critical accounts of law tend to highlight the tendency for law to exercise power so as to maintain the status quo rather than to make space for alternative understandings of social reality. "The power of law is its ability to set the boundaries of normal while maintaining that its fact-finding abilities

produce a truth that is arrived at objectively and in a value-neutral way" (Beaman, 2002: 415). The seemingly technical and administrative position of the court can thus be reframed as conflicting with the ideological confluence represented by the Trident Three's legal argument; the court acts to uphold the bounded and secular nature of morality by rejecting the notion of the "global citizen" and the existence of any form of transcendent morality.

In the following section we seek to juxtapose these two discursive frameworks in order to explore the ways in which religious claims are reshaped by legal discourse as isolated actions rather than as actions set in a broader moral context with transcendent implications. We argue that this allowed the court to disengage with the broader moral questions raised by the women. The mechanisms of legal method allowed the discursive subversion of the central arguments of the women. In "Feminism and Legal Method: The Difference it Makes," Mary Jane Mossman identifies three principles of legal method: (1) the characterization of the issues; (2) the choice of legal precedent; and (3) the process of statutory interpretation (1987: 157). In analyzing the judgment we do not necessarily seek to justify a different outcome, but rather we seek to consider the manner in which the court arrived at its judgment and what this reveals about the power of law to define religion and religious viewpoints.

4.1. Characterizing the Issue

Mossman highlights how courts "consistently characterize legal issues as narrowly as possible, eschewing their "political" or "social" significance", by explaining "that the court is interested only in the law" (Mossman, 1987: 157). In the Trident Three case the process of characterization served to both narrow the issues before the court and delegitimize and individualize the action of the Trident Three.

The court began by narrowing the issue before them as one of local concern by asserting its authority to frame the relevant issues (and "non-issues") in the case and stated that it would be dealing only with issues which were questions of law. The court chastised the women for their attempts to present how *they* saw the issues and reasserted its ultimate authority to do so. "We think the respondents see the first argument, depending not on necessity but upon customary international law, as the more 'important' (perhaps because of a somewhat extraneous wish to have the Government's actions condemned as illegal or criminal, rather than for reasons directly connected with the issue of their own possible guilt)" (Trident v. Angela Zelter, Bodil Ulla Roder, Ellen Moxley, 2001: 10, para. 32). The court's tone juxtaposed its own authority and objective stance with the Trident Three's subjective position.

The court further individualized the objectives of the women and Trident Ploughshares by downplaying the extent to which they were part of a wider movement or organization of activists.

> . . . some emphasis was placed upon the respondent's membership of an organization which *apparently* takes an interest in questions of nuclear weapons and disarmament. That organization *apparently* has a number of principles or rules, by which members such as the respondents abide when taking action in furtherance of the organization's aims. . . . In many ways their action *appears* to have been a carefully chosen element in a widely-based political campaign. [emphasis added] (Trident, 2001: 7, para. 20)

In so doing, the court diminished the credibility of the Trident Three, characterizing them as dangerously subversive and anarchistic in contrast to the court, which adopted a reasoned approach. The court warned against the potential for anarchy inherent in supporting protesters of this kind. "The reason for such circumspection is clear—necessity can very easily become simply a mask for anarchy" (Trident, 2001: 16, para. 2). The court reinforced the law's authority by rendering it the only reasonable voice in a sea of dangerous action. Simultaneously, the court imposed its own moral standard, which draws authority from the rule of law and law's objectivity.

The court denied the possibility of expanding the legal framework to include the ruling of the International Court of Justice (ICOJ) by characterizing the issue before the court as one of domestic interpretation. "The only substantial issue relates to the contention that they were justified in inflicting that damage" (Trident, 2001: p. 10, para. 31) as outlined in Scottish law. By characterizing the case as an issue of domestic interpretation, the court denied the applicability of a global or unified vision, which the women claimed to represent. This put the Trident Three's individual culpability at the centre of the trial.

The court's political position is evident in its somewhat lengthy discussion on appropriate political behavior for a citizen (despite the fact that this had originally been characterized as a "non-issue"). The court distanced itself and the women's action from the broader ideological question—effectively minimizing any connection to broader social justice issues and to either a secular or a religious worldview. The way the court characterized both citizen interveners and global citizens had the effect of individualizing the actions of the women and denying their affiliation to a collective movement, and the claim that it was legitimately grounded in either shared secular or religious convictions. By situating the Trident Three's actions as individual it was easier for the court to discredit the inclusion of any type of worldview not associated with the rule of law. The Trident Three's sincerely held and unshakeable views were used to discredit their position. Attachment to a broader moral viewpoint through personal religious experience was further proof of the individual nature of their action. As Mossman points out, though, the ways in which issues are characterized involves choices by those participating in the legal process, including lawyers and judges. Thus the recognition of certain positions or arguments as worthy is largely a flexible matter, despite law's frequent claim to the contrary.

4.2. Using Precedents in the Common Law Tradition

In refusing to justify the action taken by the Trident Three, the court cited in particular a lack of precedent in incorporating international rulings in interpreting Scottish law. This approach allowed the court to situate the defense as falling outside of the boundaries of domestic law. The doctrine of precedent relies on past judgments to justify current decisions. Mossman points to "the negative effects of the doctrine of precedent on newly emerging claims to legal rights. If a precedent is required in order to uphold a claim, only existing claims will receive legal recognition. The doctrine of precedent thus becomes a powerful tool for maintaining the status quo and for rationalizing the denial of new claims" (Mossman, 1987: 159). Precedent can be used to justify a failure by law to address shifting social conditions by allowing courts to say "this is the way it has always been, therefore this is the way it shall be". In the Trident Three case, the court relied on the lack of precedent to assert that the actions of the Trident Three had no justification under Scottish law.

In its interpretation of the ICOJ advisory opinion, the court asserted that there was no precedent for applying international legal standards in the domestic court of Scotland. Furthermore, the court emphasized that the opinion was not an official judicial determination of customary international law (Trident, 2001: 21, para. 66). "And correspondingly, it is this court's function to reach its own conclusions as to the rules of customary international law, taking full account of, but not being bound by, the conclusions reached by the International Court of Justice" (Trident, 2001: 21, para. 66). This description of the role of the ICOJ placed the court in the convenient position of being

able to pick and choose from the ruling; the ICOJ exists to uphold international standards of human rights and justice and to prevent further atrocities. The court later stated that *even if* the ruling was relevant, the standards did not apply to the respondents.

> In any event, and even on the hypothesis of armed conflict and actual threat, customary international law does not entitle persons such as the respondents to intervene as self-appointed substitute law-enforcers with a right to commit what would otherwise be criminal offences in order to stop, or inhibit, the criminal acts of others. (Trident, 2001: 32: para. 99)
>
> . . . whatever drove them or compelled them to do as they did bears no resemblance to necessity in Scots [sic] law. (Trident, 2001: 33, para. 100)

The argument put forth by the court is all too familiar, and is always difficult to deal with at a pragmatic level, as the lack of precedent would seem to put the law in a straightjacket. It should also mean that the law is incapable of responding to social change and cultural context. We know that this is not so. The position taken by the Lower Court demonstrates the availability of choice in interpreting precedent. The Lower Court took the opinion that the issues raised were relevant and that international law did apply in Scottish law. The ruling of Sheriff Margaret Gimblett upheld the lack of criminal intent in the actions of the Trident Three: "The three took the view that if Trident is illegal, given the horrendous nature of nuclear weapons, they had the obligation in terms of international law to do whatever little they could to stop the deployment and use of nuclear weapons in situations which could be construed as a threat" (Trident, 2001: para. 15). However, recognizing her limited jurisdiction, Gimblett left the legal aspects of the case open for the Crown to appeal in the High Court. The Crown appealed to resolve questions of law arising from the case.

The High Court's interpretation of international legal standards is further puzzling and inconsistent in that it recognized that they exist to protect human rights abuses, but then suggested that it was up to each country to determine when to apply these standards. Nuclear weapons by their very nature are not confined to the boundaries of the nation state; they are inherently a global concern in their potential for a global impact. The ICOJ ruling relating to the proliferation of nuclear weapons was a response to historical atrocities. It was developed at the behest of the member states. It is therefore difficult to understand where the court did see it applying or how. This question, however, was left unanswered.

4.3. Interpreting Statutes

As Mossman notes, the way in which courts interpret statutes serves as a powerful tool for maintaining the status quo by preserving the power of the law to define the parameters of any issue in terms of standards that portray the law's intentions as neutral and objective. However, as she also points out—and the Trident Three case is no exception to her argument—more often than not, judges interpret statutes with reference to their own time and experiences while presenting decisions as being based on neutral and objective standards. Two issues relating to this process come to light upon analysis of the High Court judgment. The first relates to how the court interpreted the defense of "necessity" in relation to the Trident Three case, and the second to how the court interpreted its role in matters of "national" defense.

At the trial, the Trident Three relied on the common law defense of necessity, which is used to mitigate the element of criminal intent when an individual commits a criminal act in order to prevent death or injury being caused by an accident or another criminal act. The court noted that it can be used in relation to malicious damage, which was one of the charges against the Trident Three, "where

it prevents immediate danger to the life or health of an individual or that individual's companion" (Trident, 2001: 11, para. 34). The court also noted that the manner in which the Trident Three advanced the defense of necessity required not only that they prove the immediacy of the likelihood of injury or death, but also that the injury or death that would be caused was a result of illegal actions. In order to accept the defense, the court had to find that the actions of the government were illegal under customary international law, and further that these legal standards applied in the Scottish courts. The court further noted that their defense placed the Trident Three outside the bounds of "normal" peace protesters in that they sought not only to demonstrate in a public space, but also to have the court affirm their position by declaring the behavior of the government criminal. The court recognized that this was the Trident Three's intent; however, in placing the actions of the Trident Three outside the bounds of "normal" behavior for citizens engaged in political protest, the court condemned their position and dismissed the questions raised by the use of the defense in this context.

The court described the defense of necessity in extremely narrow terms: it referred only to a "personal" response by an "ordinary" person in circumstances where the danger prevented was imminent and the action taken direct. This interpretation of necessity meant that it applied only in circumstances where the action carried out had no broader moral vision, because necessity cannot be a planned process. The court refused to recognize the possibility that the government could engage in "criminal" behavior, which could be justifiably prevented by citizens. The court further expressed disbelief that the Trident Three did not wish to portray themselves as *just* political protesters. However, the appeal to necessity shocked the court, not only in its peculiarity but also in the idea it represented of the capacity of individuals to enact a vision beyond individual political beliefs.

In the court's view, the appeal to this broader context was not only undesirable but also reprehensible in distorting the function of the defense of necessity.

The court further drew on its interpretive capacity to distance the actions of the Trident Three as matters that were inappropriate for the court or the legal process. The court stated that nuclear weapons are an issue for parliament to resolve and that parliament had expressed no intention to include the ICOJ advisory opinion in Scottish law. The court expressed annoyance at being asked to adjudicate on an issue that it perceived not to be within its realm: "The defense of the realm against enemies is the responsibility of the executive, and not the courts of justice. It is par excellence a non-justiciable question" (Trident, 2001: 18, para. 57). The court depicted itself as powerless in this case. Interestingly, however, the court did suggest that there were circumstances under which the threat or use of nuclear weapons could be construed as criminal, yet it did not articulate what these circumstances might be. Ultimately, the court defined the questions raised by the Trident Three case as non-justiciable, meaning they were beyond the court's jurisdiction.

How the court framed the defense of necessity and its own role in relation to parliament provided a powerful framework through which to dismiss the claims put forth by the Trident Three. In its final statement, the court not only reasserted the invalidity of the defense under international law but also rejected the very issues raised by the women, specifically the use of violence in any instance: "And we feel obliged to add that even ignoring the issue of justiciability, we are not persuaded that the facts of what the respondents did, or anything in the nature of the deployment of Trident, indicate any foundation at all, in Scots or in international law, for a defense of justification" (Trident, 2001: 35, para. 113). This final paragraph of its decision reveals the extent to which the court sought to discredit the action taken by the Trident Three, and provided a powerful precedent for the rejection of similar claims from those who would dare to propose an alternative worldview to that of the supreme rule of law.

5. CONCLUSION

The case of the Trident Three suggests the need to rethink our understanding of the delineation of sacred and secular motivations in the context of political activism. The fact that the court in this case did not want to engage in a consideration of these motivations is concerning given the increasing attention paid to the connection between religious fundamentalism and international terrorism. This expresses only one view of the role of religion in informing modern political movements. The case of the Trident Three demonstrates that religion is, and has been, playing an equal role in informing the peace movement in political activism. But furthermore, that religion and spiritual beliefs are not always obvious in political activism and are often intertwined with secular motivations.

The rejection by the Scottish High Court of the broader vision presented by the Trident Three constitutes a rejection of any unified religious *or* secular movement to which the political actor can appeal. It is this closing of boundaries that portrays politics as a matter for government officials, with no connection to the *average* citizen. Beyond voting, the court makes no reference to the citizen's political role. This belief is tied to a specific set of assumptions that place the government and the courts—or the bounded state—as the highest authority in interpreting ethics and morality. However, this view is not shared by all citizens and excludes the possibility of advocating change from an alternative set of beliefs. In this paper, we have placed a particular focus on the diffuse nature of Quaker involvement in peace and social justice movements. Quakers hold a belief that dedicated individuals, both Quaker and non-Quaker, have a role and an obligation to challenge existing socio-political institutions like the law. They express the view that the worth of any law, whether domestic or international, lies in its capacity to allow us to relate with one another in a meaningful and constructive way. While the Trident Three case illustrates the ways in which so-called sacred and secular motivations overlap and are woven together, it also shows that the law ignores the complex weave of the fabric—in particular, in this case, by ignoring what Fenn describes as the shared liturgical aspect of the Trident Three's action.

Despite the overturning of the Trident Three's defense by the Scottish High Court, the impact of their action extends beyond this ruling. Trident pledgers continue to push the court to recognize that the Trident Three are not just a "few radical protesters", but that there are many more just like them; they share the same unshakeable vision as the Trident Three, of a world free of nuclear weapons. How the religious will continue to inform and build this movement is a story yet to be told.

NOTES

1. Trident is the United Kingdom's main nuclear weapons system and consists of four submarines, each of which can carry between 12 and 16 missiles, each capable of delivering up to ten 100-kiloton warheads to separate targets.

2. The terms Quaker and Friend can be used interchangeably.

3. For more information on the Quaker Peace Testimony see Ceadel (2002) or Brock (1990).

4. In many cases, their perceived interference in international policy has resulted directly in legislation, e.g. in 1801, when the American Congress opposed the peace efforts of a self-appointed Quaker diplomat and passed the Logan Act, which prevented private citizens from negotiating with foreign governments. Of course, Quakers continued to disobey this law (Kent and Spickard, 1994: 379).

5. Those convicted as a result of participating in Trident Ploughshares actions have received penalties ranging from suspended sentences to 18 years in prison. The average prison sentence has been between one and two years (Trident Ploughshares, 2001, section 1.6, para. 10). To date pledgers have suffered 2,200 arrests, 503 trials, 2,184 days spent in prison, and £72,819.50 in fines (Trident Ploughshares website, http://www.tridentploughshares.org).

24

When Prophecy is Not Validated: Explaining the Unexpected in a Messianic Campaign

William Shaffir

IN EARLIER ISSUES [. . .] I wrote about the campaign of the Lubavitch (Habad)[1] movement to popularize their conviction that the arrival of the Jewish Messiah was imminent.[2] Faithful believers asserted that it was their present Rebbe, the charismatic Rabbi Menachem Mendel Schneerson, who was the long-awaited Messiah and some of them begged him to 'reveal' himself. Advertisements appeared in *The New York Times* as well as in other newspapers, listing the events which were seen as harbingers of the Redemption, and announcing: 'The Era of Moshiach is upon us'.[3] That campaign had been given a dramatic momentum in April 1991, when the Lubavitch Rebbe delivered a memorable speech—later to be much quoted and analysed—in the course of which he had declared that he had done all that he could to spur Jews to work actively for the Messianic Redemption and that his followers must do the rest; he urged them: 'Now do everything you can to bring Moshiach, here and now, immediately'. Such a forceful command from their revered leader caused the Lubavitcher to begin at once an extensive and intensive campaign.

As that campaign was gaining in momentum, nearly a year later, in March 1992, the Rebbe suffered a stroke while he was visiting the grave of his predecessor and father-in-law; that was to be the first of a series of ailments which eventually deprived

the Rebbe of his power of speech and caused him at the end to lapse into total loss of consciousness. The faithful had to endure 'cognitive dissonance': the simultaneous presence of two inconsistent happenings, which can be expected to cause great stress. When events challenge belief, the response can be a reinterpretation of the basis of belief; the Rebbe was devoutly believed to be the Messiah, but he was very seriously incapacitated by his stroke and could communicate with any degree of certainty only by vague gestures of one hand, difficult to interpret with any assurance. That situation continued for two years. In my last article on the subject, published in the June 1994 issue of this journal, I commented that if the Rebbe failed to regain his health and to reveal himself as the Jewish Messiah, and died, his followers would be shaken as if by an earthquake and added:[4]

> . . . if all attempts to prolong the Rebbe's life fail and he is given a traditional Jewish burial, those followers who have resolutely maintained that their leader was undoubtedly the Messiah-in-waiting will then try to explain that the blame for the failure of the Rebbe to reveal himself as the true Messiah was precisely the result of those doubting Jews, who by being creatures of little faith, did not show enough commitment to provide the final impetus for the advent of the Redemption—so that the Rebbe had to die in despair.

(While the article was in press, the news came that he had in fact died and been buried and that was added in bold type at the end of that page.)

The Rebbe died in a New York hospital in the early hours of 12 June 1994, which was the third day (Gimmel in Hebrew) of the month of Tammuz in the Hebrew calendar and was buried before the end of that day. The prophecy that he had indeed been the Messiah had clearly not been confirmed, so far.

Ever since the Lubavitch Moshiach campaign had gained in momentum, when the Rebbe was already in his nineties, there was much speculation about what would happen to the movement when he died. He was childless, there was therefore no prospective dynastic successor, and no one seemed to know whether he had decided upon the man who would replace him as leader. The Lubavitcher's answer was that there would be no need for a successor, since the Rebbe would initiate the Redemption. However, he did die, there was obviously no Redemption, and he had been buried according to traditional Orthodox Jewish rites. In New York, in the expectation of the hysteria which might well follow the announcement of his death, there had been a special plan devised during the last period of his illness. It was code-named Operation Demise, and police, social workers, and psychiatrists were ready to go to the Crown Heights neighbourhood; the Lubavitch epicentre was at no. 770 Eastern Parkway. Everything was in place to provide counselling akin to that offered in a disaster zone.[5] Two days after his death, the opinion of a psychologist of religion was quoted in *The New York Times*: 'It's clear that the rebbe's death has created a crisis, but it's not an insurmountable one. Some people will expect a resurrection, but most will develop all kinds of rationalizations. . . . the majority of people are capable of accepting the explanations'.[6] Another psychologist commented: 'It does seem to make some sense psychologically, if what one is doing is drowning the dissonance with increased emphasis on one of the cognitions'.

Leon Festinger *et al.* published a study in 1956 entitled *When Prophecy Fails*.[7] A small apocalyptic group, in the American Midwest, with a science fiction eschatology, who claimed to be in communication with beings from Outer Space, had believed a prediction that on a specific day, a flood would inundate much of the Western Hemisphere and some members had gathered in a vigil, waiting for a flying saucer which they were confident would raise them and carry them to safety before the flood. But there was no flying saucer and no flood. The members of the group then concluded that they had been saved by God and went on to spread their particular gospel. Festinger and his co-authors concluded that the strong ties uniting the members of that group had helped them to overcome their shock at the failure of their predicted events to materialize. Those who were not very closely linked to their fellow-members, however, lost their faith —in contrast to those who proceeded to renew their efforts at proselytisation with great enthusiasm while enjoying a considerable amount of social support from the other believers. A. D. Shupe, referring to that study and to other research into religious movements, concluded: 'It is not unfulfilled prophecy *per se* that irrevocably disillusions believers, but rather it is the social conditions in which such disconfirmations are received that determine their ultimate impact on faith'.[8] J. G. Melton, in a later analysis of the reactions to a failure of prophecy, argued that it was a common error to suppose that millennial movements would be expected to disintegrate after a prediction had failed to materialize, since predictions are typically made within the context of a wider belief system. As a result, if a prediction fails, the members of the group do not abandon the movement but aim to resolve the dissonance while relying on the 'unfalsifiable beliefs out of which religious thought worlds are constructed [and] within that context believers can engage in a reaffirmation of basic faith and make a reappraisal of their predicament'.[9] In that way, the members are reassured that the prophecy had not failed but had merely been misunderstood.

In the present paper, I focus on the attempt by Lubavitcher to reconstruct and reinterpret the events surrounding the Rebbe's illness and death in order to deal with the reality of that death and of the failure of the prediction of imminent Redemption. I have gathered data from a number of sources: about 50 interviews, all in the English language, with Lubavitcher hassidim, including officials of the movement at various levels of the organizational hierarchy; the publications of the Lubavitcher literature about the Moshiach and the Moshiach campaign; and video and audio cassette tapes. Most of the interviews were carried out in Canada—in Toronto and Montreal—and in Israel; and I also spent brief but intensive periods at Lubavitch headquarters at 770 Eastern Parkway, in the Brooklyn district of Crown Heights, observing proceedings and chatting informally with the members whom I met there.

THE REBBE DIES

One despairing hassid told me soon after the Rebbe's death was announced: 'What happened was not only unexpected, it's much worse. This thing that we didn't believe would happen, happened. We really didn't believe it. I can tell you that I'm a broken man and Lubavitch is broken'. Other followers expressed the same sorrow and shock; they had known that the Rebbe was very seriously ill and that his condition had been deteriorating rapidly—but they devoutly believed that as a result of divine intercession, a miracle would restore him to health and vigour and he would continue to lead them in their messianic campaign. Some of them even convinced themselves that he would soon be resurrected. His death had received front-page coverage in *The New York Times*[10] and the article, framing a photograph of the Lubavitcher surrounding the coffin, stated:

Within hours of his death at 1:50 a.m., thousands of his followers began gathering on the streets around Lubavitch World Headquarters ... to mourn a teacher and scholar that most of them had hoped would reveal himself to be the Messiah before he died.

But when his plain pine coffin was borne out of the headquarters building into a light rain yesterday afternoon, a huge cry of grief shook the crowd of mourners jammed into Eastern Parkway which the Emergency Medical Service estimated at 12,000. The coffin, draped with the black coat of the Grand Rabbi, or Rebbe, as he was universally known, was supported by about 20 men, and it seemed in danger of toppling to the ground as Hasidim desperate with grief reached to touch it with their fingers or umbrellas. . . .

From the rooftops it appeared that a huge wave of black was cascading down the parkway, following the Rebbe's motorcade. Thousands of people ran until they could run no further, some collapsing into sobs.

The Jerusalem Post reported that in Israel many hundreds clamoured for plane tickets at Ben Gurion airport, some of them standing on counter-tops trying to get tickets, while others rushed in all directions when rumours spread that tickets were available in a particular area of the airport.[11] In Toronto, a charter flight left within hours of the announcement of the Rebbe's death, on 12 June, carrying a planeload of mourners.

Many believed the Rebbe to be immortal and could not be reconciled to the fact that he had indeed died: *The Forward*, an English weekly newspaper published in New York, reported a few days after the burial that a group asserted that their leader's resurrection was imminent and they were sleeping close to the Rebbe's grave, hoping to be the first to see their Messiah rise from the tomb.[12] The resurrection theme was to become within days the subject of public sermons within the movement. On the day of the funeral, moreover, a small group were dancing and singing outside the

Lubavitch headquarters, which unnerved the vast majority of the mourners. Allan Nadler described the scene immediately before the funeral cortege set out of the building:[13]

> Still, many of his faithful refuse to be deterred by so small a matter as Schneerson's mortality. When I arrived in Crown Heights that Sunday morning . . . I was amazed to see young Lubavitcher singing, dancing and drinking vodka directly across the street from 770 Eastern Parkway, the Lubavitch World Headquarters where the body of their beloved rebbe was lying . . . in shrouds on a wooden floor. Even more stunning was a small group of women encouraging the men with tambourines.

These individuals were convinced at the time that the Rebbe's death signalled the onset of the Redemption and one person was quoted as saying, '. . . any minute now the rebbe will rise up to take us all to Israel'.[14] The same was true of another group of adherents in Kfar Habad, the movement's stronghold in Israel: some hassidim refused to believe that their Rebbe had died, while others asserted that if he had died, it would be only to cause him to rise to redeem the Jews. A driver employed by Habad was quoted in the *Jerusalem Post* issue of 13 June, the day after the death and burial, as stating: 'This is a happy day, because this is the last day of exile', and with the chant of 'Moshiach, Moshiach, Moshiach' blaring from his van's loudspeakers, he added: 'We came here to cheer people up, to tell them this is the last day of exile'.[15]

The tragic news of the Rebbe's final deterioration in health spread quickly, only to be followed at first with the announcement that his heartbeat had stabilized; but soon after came a message on the beepers that it was urgently requested that *Tehillim* (Psalms) be recited, and a few minutes later there came the shattering words '*Borukh Dayan Ha'emes*' ('blessed is the true judge')[16]—the formula which broadcast the fact that the unthinkable had occurred, that the Rebbe had ceased to live. Then sirens were heard, arousing the Crown Heights

residents and informing them of the calamity. At 3:25 a.m., a police helicopter hovered over no. 770 and to the blaring sound of sirens, an ambulance arrived, a stretcher was carried out and taken into the building surrounded by members of the *ḥevra kadisha* (the burial society whose duty it is to prepare the body for interment), and the door of the building was quickly closed. Half an hour later, the followers were told that they would be permitted to enter the Rebbe's room and file through while reciting psalms. The funeral was to take place at 4 p.m. that afternoon.

At the cemetery, the Rebbe's grave had been dug to the immediate left of his predecessor's tomb, in the mausoleum, and the male mourners filed past one entrance and the females through another gate, and the *kriya* ceremony proceeded, the tearing of a garment worn by the mourner.[17] Meanwhile, at no. 770 the synagogue was filled with mourners sitting on the floor or on low stools, in the prescribed manner for *shiva*, the seven days of intense mourning. A hassid described the scene in his diary; it was printed in one of the publications of the movement:[18]

> The sound of weeping and lamentation has replaced yesterday's shock and stupor. Wherever you look in Crown Heights you see chasidim, alone and in small groups, standing and crying to themselves. . . . The front lawn of 770 is covered with people. . . . The benches along the parkway are packed with mourners, some of whom are nodding off after having been awake for almost two full days.
>
> Seven-seventy is packed with people. A steady stream of mourners continues to flow, coming and going. Men, women and children all try to come to terms with what has happened, but they cannot make peace with the new situation.
>
> They cannot understand what has happened. . . .

The majority of those with whom I had conversations in Toronto and in Montreal said that they had learnt the news of the Rebbe's death by a telephone call from a friend or relative, in the early hours of the morning. They already knew that the life of their Rebbe was despaired of by the physicians. One follower commented: 'I knew what that phone call meant. No one calls for social reasons at three o'clock in the morning'. Many of the women could tell that the Rebbe had died when they saw the faces of their husbands, when they had returned from the synagogue. One woman told me: 'As soon as I saw him, I knew. The look on his face said everything'. Another commented that no words were necessary when her husband came home: she just went to rouse their children to prepare them for the journey to Crown Heights: 'We were on the road in twenty minutes', she added.

The Rebbe had been well known as a Biblical scholar in both Jewish and non-Jewish informed circles and the activities of the Lubavitch were often reported in the press of various countries. Condolences were received from the President and the Vice-President of the United States, from the Chief Rabbi of the United Hebrew Congregations in London, from the Canadian Prime Minister, from a United States senator, the governor and the mayor of New York, and many other prominent persons.[19] He was hailed as 'a great leader', as one of the world's 'great moral and religious leaders', as a 'towering religious figure', while Jewish eulogies contained tributes to the Rebbe's efforts to combat assimilation and out-marriage. Such praise not only provided solace to the Lubavitcher in their grief but also confirmed the eminence of their revered leader and reflected the respect with which his scholarship and dedication were viewed by eminent individuals in many countries.

Since the Lubavitch had pursued with vigour their Moshiach campaign for several years, especially in the early 1990s, it was inevitable that comparisons would be drawn with other Messianic groups in Jewish history. The most widely-known, of course, was the case of Sabbatai Zvi who in the seventeenth century had attracted a wide following in Turkey, Italy, and Poland after he had proclaimed

himself to be the Jewish Messiah. He proved to be a false messiah, he was eventually converted to Islam, and his followers were engulfed in despair and bitterness, causing a proportion of them to abandon Judaism. In 1994, there was great concern lest the fact that the Rebbe had died, been buried, and not risen from the grave and showed himself to be the Messiah, lest that tragedy of unfulfilled promises of Redemption would result in very large defections from the Lubavitch movement.

There had been fierce condemnations of the Messianic campaign in the Rebbe's lifetime and his death only served to reinforce the case of the movement's critics. *The Forward* was still on the attack several months after the Rebbe's death; it stated that those who believed that '. . . the rebbe had misled his people during his lifetime, are now perturbed by the fact that a cluster of his most fanatic entourage is perpetuating what the critics see as the false and dangerous notion of Rabbi Schneerson as a super-mortal being'[20]—referring to those who supported the prediction that the Rebbe would without much delay rise from the grave. The paper went on to state that an eminent rabbi who was also a scholar had come to the conclusion that the Rebbe's followers were still deluded, that they failed 'to realize they have been duped by a charlatan who masqueraded as a saint'.[21]

Two weeks later, in December 1994, *The Forward* printed a front-page story with the headline: 'Rabbis Blast Lubavitcher Messianism' and the opening paragraph stated:[22]

> The Lubavitcher Chasidim of Crown Heights are alarming Jewish theologians with their growing fervor of their belief in the imminent "resurrection" of Menachem Mendel Schneerson as the "Messiah," and some critics are warning that eerie parallels to Christianity are flickering inside the Lubavitch movement.

The article was set around a photograph of Sabbatai Zvi, with the caption 'False Messiah', and referred to the continuing belief by followers of the Rebbe that he was indeed the real Jewish Messiah and that he would return to earth. Paradoxically, such attacks only seem to reinforce the commitment of the faithful to that belief.

The Forward also claimed that, several months after the Rebbe's death, '. . . some of his followers are in the throes of despair, and others are deeply disillusioned' and that his leadership might 'be to blame for the angst of the Jews of Crown Heights'.[23] In fact, the movement has experienced neither mass suicide nor even a minimal exodus from the Crown Heights area. While Lubavitcher with whom I had frequent conversations admitted freely that they were still shaken by the Rebbe's death, they insisted that they were still committed to their movement's style of Judaism. One of them told me:

> Generally speaking, if I tell you it didn't affect anyone, I'd be lying to you. But I don't know anybody who lost their faith or converted out of Yiddishkayt. No one shaved their beard, stopped putting *tefillin* [phylacteries], or took off their *shytl* [wig]. . . . To say that there aren't problems that people have to deal with, *bin eech kein mentsh nit* [I am not human]. We're not pure *neshomo* [soul].

There has been much soul-searching about the unfulfilled Messianic prophecy, with the death of the Rebbe. The adherents had been aware for months and years that the Rebbe's health was failing, since they were kept informed by daily reports of his condition, but they had still expected nothing less than a miraculous recovery and the realization of the Messianic prophecy. They had found reassurance in the fact (according to them) that the Rebbe had never been proved wrong in any of his advice or predictions and only a few days before his death, a Lubavitch publication stated:[24]

> As this newsletter goes to press, our beloved guide and mentor, . . . the Lubavitcher Rebbe . . . lies grievously ill. . . . It is now many weeks that the Rebbe lies unconscious. . . . Medically the situation seems hopeless. Naturally, rationally—it would seem appropriate to prepare for the "inevitable."

. . . the reaction of this Jew at a time when everything seems so hopeless, is one of unbridled hope in totally supernatural salvation. Even at this time, and perhaps precisely because of it, we remember that the same Rebbe who accurately predicted the safety of Israel during the Gulf War, in spite of countless indications to the contrary, has prophesied that the "time of your Redemption has arrived" —a prophecy in which we must continue to have absolute faith.

TECHNIQUES OF NEUTRALIZATION

We must now consider the techniques, the vocabulary of motives,[25] which the Lubavitcher commonly employed in order to neutralize any dissonant feelings and to reinforce their faith in the imminent Redemption by their King Messiah, their Rebbe. In order to minimize the disjuncture between their expectations and the obvious reality, they drew upon a series of explanations which would not only preserve but enhance their commitment to the messianic prophecy.

No single explanation is uniformly advanced by all the followers, but they all do adhere to the belief in Divine Providence, *hashgocheh protees*, a belief which provides them with the underlying foundation on which they rest their interpretations of the events preceding and following the Rebbe's death. For them, the hand of Divine Providence must be seen in all that occurs but God's intentions may be difficult to grasp with our finite intelligence. An article in a Lubavitch publication[26] stated three months after his death: 'Even with all the explanations which have been advanced, the bottom line is that we don't understand the ways of Hashem' (the Name: that is, God) and: 'Hashem has taken the Rebbe from our physical presence for reasons only He understands'.[27] Variations on this basic theme were consistently advanced during my conversations with the faithful. For example, a woman did not deny that the Rebbe's death had come as an enormous shock, but she remained firmly dedicated to the cause: 'If you believe that Hashem guides us in everything, then you accept what happens as for the good. Who knows why the Rebbe died? Only one thing is clear: it's part of Hashem's master plan'.

For an observant and pious believer, it is inconceivable that God could have erred in his judgment —while the Rebbe's statements on Redemption had the seal of prophetic utterance and must therefore not be considered as false assertions. If the prophecy must remain unchallenged, the Rebbe's statements had to be reinterpreted to conform to the present reality. One follower explained to me:

> We haven't been wrong [in identifying the Rebbe as the messiah]. We have only been wrong in assuming that this is going to happen in the rebbe's lifetime. . . . So we were wrong in the calculation of the timing . . . but not in terms of theology. To me nothing has changed except the Rebbe's presence.

I had a conversation with two Lubavitch women, in the course of which they stressed that the movement in general, and they in particular, had failed to comprehend adequately the Rebbe's views on Redemption; the fault for the misinterpretation was theirs alone, and one said:

> By now we have learned to realize that the only sure things are things we heard straight from the Rebbe. . . . The things the Rebbe said clearly in the last four years are things that always always happened. So the way we understood there would not be a period of no life [that is, the Rebbe would not die], on these things we were wrong. But those were our own views. As long as we are going on the words of the Rebbe, those things can't go wrong.

She concluded by saying that the followers were re-examining the statements of the Rebbe: 'Now, there are many things that people are finding in the words of the Rebbe'. The Rebbe's behaviour immediately before his first stroke in 1992 was carefully being reconsidered as it now seemed that there was evidence to show that he was fully aware that he was on the verge of death: 'Truthfully, on his own, for a half a year the Rebbe was preparing his staff, and the Rebbe was preparing all of us [for his death]', asserted a Lubavitcher. The Rebbe was able therefore to decide on the path to be taken after he had ceased to live. He could have ushered in the Redemption, if he had chosen to do so, but he had taken another course. A Lubavitch publication claimed: 'Our Rebbe . . . was just about ready to cross the finish line when he decided at the last second to give the baton . . . to us, and said, "It is now in your hands to bring Moshiach" '.[28]

The accusation that Lubavitcher failed to foresee (and therefore to be prepared for) the Rebbe's death was countered by the argument that the disappointment about the hopes for Redemption had occurred precisely because the present generation had failed to deserve Divine Redemption. A woman told me: 'Moshiach would have come, but we didn't merit it. . . . if we merited it, things would have worked out differently' and another follower had come to the same conclusion: 'If it didn't happen, this means we were not worthy of it'. There was some discussion of the various natural and supernatural sequences leading to the coming of the Jewish Messiah; I was told: 'We blew it. Obviously, whatever we have done is not enough' and by another follower: 'Obviously we didn't do everything right, or not enough. . . . Otherwise we wouldn't be discussing it now. We'd be sitting in the *Bays Hamikdosh* [the Holy Temple] and enjoying Moshiach and the Rebbe'.

Immediately after the Rebbe's death, there circulated a printed statement[29] on a single page from the Chairman of the International Campaign to Bring Moshiach; it included the following words:

> The rebbe's instructions are clear. It is up to us to respond. The campaign . . . urges all Jews to continue to carry out, with renewed vigor, the Rebbe's directive to study the sections of the Torah which discuss the Redemption and the coming of

Moshiach and to do more acts of goodness and kindness. . . .

The Rebbe, as we noted above, died and was buried on Sunday, 12 June 1994; and on the Sunday following the week-long traditional *Shiva*, a Moshiach Day was convened in Crown Heights. An afternoon teach-in lasted into early evening and was attended by several hundred members who were assured by a panel of rabbis that the Rebbe's prophecy remained as relevant after his death as it had been in his lifetime. All the speakers stressed that the Rebbe's guidance remained valid, reiterating what the chairman had stated in his opening statement to the gathering: 'As far as what we are supposed to do, we have to listen to what the Rebbe tells us. . . . There's no doubt that we will find in the Rebbe's words all that we need for every step of the way'. Indeed, on that day, that was the core theme of the various speakers. One declared:

And . . . he clearly gave us a program which is so meticulous. . . . He took us from step to step. Our work has been defined very very clearly. . . . And even though we may not be able to see him [the Rebbe] with our eyes . . . he's here with us today telling us what he told us for forty-four years. Nothing is missing in his instruction.

The Lubavitcher were told that in spite of suffering overwhelming grief in mourning for their revered leader, they had to take immediate action to obey the Rebbe's directives and the Rebbe's emissaries, the *shluchim*, who had gathered in Crown Heights for the funeral, were urged to pursue their activities as zealously as before. The report of a meeting of these emissaries contains the following passage:[30]

"We will continue!" was the sentiment of all the shluchim assembled in the room. Rabbi Shmuel Kaplan . . . chaired the event and said: ". . . we all know what the Rebbe wants of us, and each one of us knows his responsibility."

Rabbi Moshe Kotlarsky spoke in the same vein. "None of us knows what should be *said* at such a

bitter time. No one knows what to say, but we all know what to *do*.

. . . All participants spoke about the special mission and obligation of shluchim at this critical hour. . . .

A Lubavitch woman affirmed this decision when she told me in the course of an interview: 'The Rebbe told us what to do. The job the Rebbe gave us to do we must continue'. The followers also recalled the advice and comfort which Rabbi Schneerson had given when his predecessor had died and they read and re-read a letter he had written at the time of their bereavement. He had stated that 'salvation lies not in mourning, and that despair and sorrow do not lead towards light'[31] and he had then asserted as a second principal guideline that a true bonding with the Rebbe is derived from the study of his discourses and by fulfilling his requests. A Lubavitch publication commented on the first point, and an excerpt reads (*Gimmel Tammuz* refers to the day and the month on which the Rebbe had died):[32]

We have lost a limb. If we look at the events of Gimmel Tammuz with *fleishige oigen*—physical eyes—we lost our head . . . and our heart. Now we could walk around feeling totally handicapped, with little ability to overcome this shock to our lives. . . . The Rebbe never allowed us to look at anything in life negatively—how much more so in a situation like this.

One of the Rebbe's secretaries urged the members of the movement to remember that the Rebbe's presence must continue to dominate every aspect of their life (thus reiterating the Rebbe's own recommendation when his predecessor had died):[33]

The Alter Rebbe [the first Lubavitcher Rebbe] in Tanya [the first Lubavitcher Rebbe's work outlining the philosophy of Ḥabad] . . . quotes the Zohar, "A Tzaddik who departs from this world, is present in all the worlds more than he was during his lifetime." And the Alter Rebbe explains, that the Zohar also means to say, that the Tzaddik is present in this physical world more than during his life on this world. He also tells us that after the departure of the Neshomo [the soul] from this world, the Neshomo of the Tzaddik generates more strength and more Koach (power) to his devoted disciples.

In that context, a Lubavitcher commented: 'The leader remains a leader even now and even though not seen physically still remains a leader', then he cited sacred texts in support of that statement: 'It's also a principle in the Torah, the Zohar, and the Talmud that a *tsaddik* (righteous person) even after his death, his presence can be felt more than even before, not being limited by the physical body'. Another said: 'The Rebbe is here. We feel and sense this' and then gave several examples of the Rebbe's miraculous powers which were being manifested now, after his death. A third follower was convinced of the Rebbe's continued presence and support:

> I'd venture to say that I'm stronger now than before. Now I can't slow down because he [the Rebbe] sees me 24 hours a day. And I know that he sees me. If I can function today, it's only because he sees me. It is only because he gives me strength. . . .

The Rebbe had given a talk several months after his predecessor's death in 1950 and some of his advice contained in the record of that talk was repeatedly cited by the Lubavitcher to derive comfort in their mourning and grief several decades later:[34]

> . . . Even when we find ourselves in a low, fallen state, we should not feel removed from the Rebbe after his passing. We should know, that now too, the Rebbe answers and responds to questions . . . as before. . . . The Rebbe is here with us as before.

An editorial in a Lubavitch publication declared: 'The Rebbe remains our Rebbe, and we remain his chassidim',[35] adding that his death had been 'the most forceful event that has so dramatically changed our world. . . . We know that the "faithful shepherd does not abandon his flock" and he

continues to watch over us and guide us'.[36] The Rebbe's secretary asserted in another article: 'And just as the Rebbe served his flock before his departure, so is he continuing to serve them now, but with an increase both qualitatively and quantitatively'.[37]

Lubavitcher had to accept the fact that the Rebbe was no longer alive and they now came to believe that the unexpected tragedy of his demise might have been expected. Sources were being identified and interpreted to show that the Jewish Messiah would in fact die: this meant that the Rebbe's death was *not* a proof that he had been only a false Messiah. However, some followers did not immediately grasp that vindication; a woman commented: 'Everyone's confused and everyone doesn't know how to interpret this and how to understand it. . . . it forced a lot of people to go to the sources . . . and to find some consolation from this'. That reliance upon sources, or that use of the sources, was expressed again and again during the conversations I had. When I asked a Lubavitcher, whom I had known before the Rebbe's death, how he reconciled the fact that he had previously asserted that the Rebbe would not die with the reality that he had indeed died and been buried, he invoked the sources:

> There's also things which are written, which are predicted and which talk about this possibility. The Talmud talks about it, the Zohar says it in no uncertain terms, the Kabbalists speak about it. Moshiach will go through that period. There will be a period of moshiach dying and reviving.

Some Lubavitcher with whom I had conversations after the Rebbe's death were clearly not familiar with the texts of the sources, but they did not doubt their validity: 'There are several sources but I'm not exactly sure where'; but others demonstrated a measure of expert knowledge:

> We can talk about specific sources in the Talmud, in the Zohar specifically . . . that speak about

moshiach's passing away. There are contradictory statements in the Talmud about moshiach's arrival and they all boil down to two things: miraculous and natural . . . and within this miraculous and natural there are many stages. There can be sickness, natural recovery, severe sickness, miraculous recovery. . . . Different sources point to different possibilities. . . .

According to that follower, the scenario in the most extreme case was that the advent of the Messiah would be miraculous and would therefore involve the Rebbe's complete recovery. Sadly, he had to admit that clearly the miracle had not taken place, the Rebbe had not recovered, he had died: there had been several possibilities, according to the sources, for the Rebbe to have been restored to health and to have revealed himself as the Messiah but, he admitted, 'It didn't go that way'.

Although familiarity with the relevant sources had become more widespread after the Rebbe's death, their contents had been known also during his lifetime but had not been publicized. There were two reasons: first, no one dared to entertain the thought that the Rebbe might indeed die, especially as there were what they believed to be many signals to the contrary—he had successfully recovered from severe illnesses following his first stroke, to the amazement of qualified medical specialists; they were familiar with a particular religious tenet that the Messiah might manifest himself from either the living or the dead, but the indications at the time were that a living man would declare himself as the Messiah. The second reason was that the various sources dealing with the advent of the Messiah, in Biblical commentaries on the subject, were not derived from the actual texts of the Halakha, of Orthodox Jewish law; the important point to bear in mind was that predictions of that kind should not be expected inevitably to occur, to be realized literally. One of the speakers at the teach-in previously mentioned, stressed that all that is stated in the Midrash (the exposition and commentaries on the Old Testament) does not constitute a legal

ruling, is not embodied in the Halakha. 'It doesn't have to be fulfilled . . .' argued the speaker, adding that you cannot base Jewish law on the commentaries, which do not have the same legitimacy; but one must still heed the words of the Midrash, a competent religious exposition, although 'it doesn't mean that it's the way it's going to happen, but it's definitely a possibility', when it comes to predictions in the Midrash.

Such techniques of rationalization were not used by all the Lubavitcher, or not generally known to all, but they were a spur for the active members to encourage them in their Messianic proselytization and even in some cases to enhance their enthusiasm. The Lubavitcher retained their belief in the Rebbe's assurance that the redemptive process had begun: it was now their task to see that the necessary further steps were taken to fulfil the Messianic prophecy. A Lubavitch woman declared: 'The Rebbe said that the process has begun and everything that needs to be done to bring Moshiach has been done. The reservoir is filled, so it's filled. The Rebbe promised in the words of prophecy'. Another follower concurred: 'To me, nothing has changed except the Rebbe's presence. So I still look forward to the Rebbe's prediction. I believe it'll happen in our generation simply going by the Rebbe's track record'. It was that deep-seated confidence in the Rebbe's wisdom and in his knowledge of the Divine purpose that strengthened their devotion to him and to his teachings even after he had died and not risen from his grave. One woman supported her steadfast commitment with the use of the following analogy:

> So they stood there in front of the sea and Moishe [Moses] said 'Go'. Did anyone of them, in their wildest imagination, know they were going to cross the sea? Did anyone of them imagine the sea would split? A moment before it happened, nobody knew how they were going to cross the sea. So, in a way, we're standing in front of the sea and we know we are going to cross it. How it's going to happen, we'll see.

CONCLUSION

A Lubavitcher elaborated on the subject of the profound conviction of his fellow-members that the Messiah's advent would assuredly take place. He illustrated their adherence to that belief with the following tale:

> I'm not sure at which airport it was . . . A plane . . . full of hassidic Jews and they're waiting at the conveyer belt for their suitcases. There this Lubavitch man found himself standing between two Gerer hassidim. About one hundred suitcases passed and it just so happened that they happened to be standing right at the beginning where the valises start coming out. And they're standing for 15 minutes watching suitcases falling out and being sure that the next one is his. . . . So he [the Lubavitcher] turns around to them and says, 'You know, it's an amazing thing. The three of us are focused here on this opening and although hundreds of suitcases have passed, we're convinced that the next suitcase will be ours. And if another hundred suitcases are going to pass by, until the last suitcase, we are still going to be convinced that our suitcase is coming at any minute. And although a long time has passed, it doesn't diminish my ultimate belief that my suitcase is coming'. It's the same story with Moshiach. We've had two thousand years of suitcases travelling and flowing. . . . Nevertheless, I'm convinced that the next suitcase, the next moment, Moshiach is coming. . . . There's no question in my mind and I can talk for every hassid.

There is great variation in the manner in which different religious groups deal with their disillusionment or shock that the predictions of their leaders, which they had whole-heartedly believed, failed to materialise. In some cases, the reaction has been to persist in the commitment to their particular religious tenets, to find or manufacture explanations for the failure of the promised events, and to continue with their efforts to recruit more adherents; the overwhelming majority in the Lubavitch

movement reacted in that way. An article, marking the conclusion of the 30-day mourning period after the death and burial, stated in an English-language Lubavitch magazine:[38]

> Some antagonists had initially predicted a diminishing of Chabad activity after the Rebbe's passing, or even a complete breakdown and collapse of Lubavitch. Thank G-d, the doomsayers were proven false, and their bad predictions did not materialize. On the contrary, we are witnessing a worldwide spur of new activities, projects and institutions established in the Rebbe's honor.

That statement was indeed true: the December 1994 issue of *World of Lubavitch* listed 93 institutions which have been established since the Rebbe's death.[39] A journalist commented: 'If Chabad has managed to outwit despair, that is partly because hasidim believe the rebbe continues to guide and protect them; he has simply exchanged a physical for a spiritual body'.[40] That was also my own experience when hearing again and again the Lubavitcher say to me as if intoning a refrain: 'The Rebbe remains the Rebbe'. The most common theme in the prolific Lubavitch literature which was published after the Rebbe's death was that of the enduring value of his teachings and the validity of the belief that a Messianic Redemption would come to pass while the arguments to refute critics and doubters were advanced with force.

But such faithfulness and determination does not characterize all the members of the movement. In the matter of interpreting the last will and testament of the Rebbe, which was dated 14 February 1988 and filed for probate immediately after his burial, there was concern that he had left his entire estate—valued at about $50,000—to the Lubavitch movement but had left no instructions about the procedure for appointing his successor. Much significance was attached to the fact that he had named as his sole executor one of his senior secretaries—a man who had long opposed the rising tide of Messianism in the movement, a man who was reportedly the most pragmatic and conservative of his principal assistants. The role of an executor of a modest estate is theoretically a minor one; but in this particular case, his selection gave him a status superior to that of other members of the Rebbe's secretariat, and seemed to mark him as a man appointed by the revered Rebbe to exert considerable influence and authority to chart the movement's future along a conservative course.

It must be noted here that even in the Rebbe's lifetime, after his stroke had rendered him speechless and as his condition steadily deteriorated, there had been disagreements about the manner in which the Rebbe's teachings and advice were to be implemented. These disagreements had chiefly been voiced about the intensity of the Messianic proselytising campaign as well as about the confident tone used to identify the Rebbe as the Jewish Messiah who was about to manifest himself. Since his death, there have been disputes about what the Rebbe would have sanctioned if he had been still alive: for example, a Rabbi in Oxford who has been generally considered to be a follower of the Lubavitch movement was compelled to resign by the Lubavitch Foundation in Britain because it objected to the invitation he had extended to the prime minister of Israel to give a public lecture at Oxford University after he had been awarded the Nobel Prize for Peace. Since that prime minister had committed himself to surrendering some Holy Land territory during his peace negotiations with Palestinian leaders, it was argued that such an invitation was disrespectful to the Rebbe's memory:[41] the Rebbe had been firmly opposed to the surrender of Biblical Jewish land. The resulting conflict was publicized in the Jewish press in England and elsewhere, but the Lubavitcher have gone to some pains in cases such as these to describe such public disagreements as events of little significance.

The Rebbe's published works and the audio and video cassettes of his *farbrengens* (gatherings of his Hassidic followers) are readily available and enable the members of the movement to recall his extraordinary presence and the contents of his teachings. The vast organizational infrastructure which has shaped the movement provides it with a measure of momentum for the maintenance and the intensification of its activities. In this way, the Rebbe's death has failed to alter dramatically the movement's educational and religious endeavours.

Nevertheless, the faithful are now bereft of the living presence of their spiritual leader and there will have to be a decision eventually to designate a successor. A rising star in the Lubavitch intellectual firmament has stated boldly in print: 'Either our family gets closer, and the loss brings us together, or G-d forbid, the opposite'.[42] Clearly, the Lubavitch movement is not immune from the bitter dissensions and factionalism which occur in other religious groups when a momentous event causes shock, reappraisal of policies, and rivalries between potential new leaders. There is evidence now that there is some turmoil among the Lubavitch senior officials, with various segments which are each considering mobilizing support for the claim to best represent the Rebbe's legacy. It will not be easy for a successor to follow into the late Rebbe's footsteps and to provide the guidance and care which so endeared him to his followers. He had earned their affection and respect, their reverence, for decades and he was the central figure which provided the focus and unity of the movement.

ACKNOWLEDGEMENT

The research for this study has been supported by a grant from the Social Sciences and Humanities Research Council of Canada.

NOTES

1. The terms LHubavitch and Ḥabad are synonymous and refer to followers of the same hassidic sect. Ḥabad is an acronym for the Hebrew *hokhmah*, *binah*, and *da'at*—intelligence or wisdom, understanding, and

knowledge. In Israel the term Ḥabad is commonly used, while in North America the term Lubavitch or Lubavitcher is more popular.

2. See in *The Jewish Journal of Sociology* 'Jewish Messianism Lubavitch-Style: An Interim Report', vol. 35, no. 2, December 1993, and 'Interpreting Adversity: Dynamics of Commitment in a Messianic Redemption Campaign', vol. 36, no. 1, June 1994.
3. *The New York Times*, 22 August 1991.
4. W. Shaffir, op. cit. in Note 2 above, p. 52.
5. A New York congressman, who represents the Crown Heights district in the state assembly in Albany, remarked: 'It's a community in some ways in denial. . . . People are going to feel immensely let down when something they believed in for so long, the expectation that he would return after death, doesn't happen': see *Toronto Star*, 13 June 1994, p. A4.
6. *The New York Times*, 14 June 1994, p. A11.
7. See Leon Festinger, Henry W. Riecken, and Stanley Schachter, *When Prophecy Fails*, New York, 1956.
8. See Anson D. Shupe, Jr., *Six Perspectives on New Religions: A Case Study Approach*, New York, 1981, p. 141.
9. J. G. Melton, 'Spiritualization and Reaffirmation: What Really Happens When Prophecy Fails', *American Studies*, vol. 26, no. 2, 1987, p. 82.
10. *The New York Times*, op. cit. in Note 3 above, p. 1.
11. *The Jerusalem Post*, 14 June 1994, p. 1.
12. See *The Forward*, 17 June 1994, p. 1.
13. Allans Nadler, 'King Of Kings County', *The New Republic*, 11 July 1994, pp. 16–17.
14. Ibid., p. 17.
15. *The Jerusalem Post*, 13 June 1994, p. 1.
16. The blessing which mourners recite after death.
17. *Kriya* is the rending of the garment of the mourner. The rent, at least four inches long, is made in the lapel of an outer garment before the funeral. For parents, the *kriya* is made on the left side; for other relatives, on the right.
18. See *Chabad Magazine*, June 1994, p. 17.
19. Ibid.
20. See *The Forward*, 18 November 1994, p. 13.
21. Ibid.
22. *The Forward*, 2 December 1994, p. 1.
23. *The Forward*, 18 November 1994, p. 13.
24. See *N'shei Chabad Newsletter*, June 1994, p. 21.
25. C. Wright Mills, 'Situated Actions and Vocabularies of Motive' in *American Sociological Review*, vol. 5, no. 5, 1940, pp. 904–13.
26. See *N'shei Chabad Newsletter*, September 1994, p. 32.
27. Ibid.
28. *N'shei Chabad Newsletter*, September 1994, p. 34.
29. 'Moshiach And The Test of Faith', n.d.
30. *Chabad Magazine*, 18 June 1994, p. 22.
31. Ibid., p. 6.
32. *N'shei Chabad Newsletter*, September 1994, p. 33.
33. Ibid., p. 47.
34. *Chabad Magazine*, June 1994, p. 6.
35. Ibid., September 1994, p. 5.
36. Ibid.
37. *N'shei Chabad Newsletter*, September 1994, p. 47.
38. *Chabad Magazine*, August 1994, p. 47.
39. *World of Lubavitch*, December 1994, p. 4.
40. See *The Jerusalem Report*, 28 July 1994, p. 22.
41. See *The Forward*, 21 October 1994 and *The Canadian Jewish News*, 20 October 1994.
42. *Chabad Magazine*, August 1994, p. 78.

25

The Age of Satan: Satanic Sex and the Black Mass, from Fantasy to Reality

Hugh B. Urban

Our religion . . . is the only one, I think, in complete accordance with human nature. It is based on indulgence. Instead of commanding our members to repress their natural urges, we teach that they should follow them. This includes physical lusts, the desire for revenge, the drive for material possessions.

    ANTON SZANDOR LAVEY, interview with John Godwin, *Occult America*

In Anton's church all the Satanic fantasies became realities.

    BLANCHE BARTON, *The Secret Life of a Satanist*

IF THE 1950S WITNESSED A NEW flowering of sensual spirituality with the rise of neo-paganism, witchcraft; and Goddess worship, the late 1960s would give birth to even more radical and transgressive forms of sexual magic. As its founder, Anton Szandor LaVey (1930–97), observed, it is no accident that the modern Church of Satan was created in 1966—at the height of the countercultural revolution, amid a generation eager to transgress the boundaries of American society through drugs, music, and sexual experience.[1] And if the neo-pagans and Wiccans had "rediscovered" ancient traditions by creatively reimagining and reinventing them, so too LaVey and his followers would reimagine Satan and the Black Mass for a new generation.

As we saw in the first chapter, one of the darkest undercurrents running through the Western religious imagination, from pre-Christian times down to Aleister Crowley, was the nightmare of sexual license and the perversion of sacred ritual. This was a nightmare that had been foreshadowed in the attacks on the Gnostics, the heresies of the Cathars and Free Spirits, and the Templars, but it achieved perhaps its final form in the early modern period in the fantasy of the Black Mass—a complete inversion of the Holy Eucharist, usually involving some form of sexual perversion. While the Black Mass was primarily a matter of fantasy throughout the last five hundred years, LaVey's Church of Satan was among the first groups to make this fantasy a reality. Just as Crowley took the old narrative of perverse Gnostic rituals and created a "Gnostic Mass," and just as Gardner took the old narrative of witches' orgies and created a "Great Rite," so too, the modern Church of Satan would take the old narrative of orgiastic Black Masses and create a new ritual that at once enacts and ridicules these persistent fantasies of sex and magic.

Dressed in his absurd devil costume, complete with pointy horns and cape, LaVey represents a kind of parodic turn within the history of sexual magic, which recognizes the contrived nature of its own ritual performance: "We step on modern sacred cows. A modern-day form of the Black Mass might consist of such things as urinating on marijuana, crushing an LSD sugar cube underfoot, hanging a picture of Timothy Leary or a famous Indian guru upside down."[2] At the same time, however, LaVey would also be accused by many critics of selling out, commercializing the Church of Satan and transforming transgression itself into a kind of marketable commodity. Other disillusioned followers would also be deeply troubled by the powerful elements of misogyny, sexism, racism, and fascist tendencies within the church. But again, LaVey seemed at once aware and yet unbothered by this, and in fact he seemed quite happy to fleece any poor dupes who were stupid enough to take things too seriously: "P. T. Barnum said, 'A sucker is born every minute.' With the population explosion, by now there must be five."[3]

In this chapter, I will argue that the Church of Satan needs to be understood in the context of 1960s American culture amid the social trends variously called the countercultural revolution, the sexual revolution, and so forth. LaVey and his church, I will suggest, reflect many of the central tensions in American society in the late 1960s and 1970s. As Jeffrey Weeks observes, sexuality became a central source of tension, anxiety, and debate throughout the 1960s and 1970s, reflecting larger social fears about rapid social change and the increasing freedom of a new generation: "What was clearly taking place was a displacement of the anxieties aroused by the nature of the social changes, especially expressed in the growing autonomous styles of the various youth cultures, onto the terrain of sexuality, where hidden fears and social anxieties could most easily be stirred."[4] LaVey at once reflected and exploited these larger fears about sexuality, yet he did so in complex and contradictory ways. At the same time that he declared the dawn of a new Satanic age of sexual and personal freedom, LaVey also held some extremely conservative social and political views; at the same time that he proclaimed the autonomy of the individual ego

and its desires, he was also by his own admission a misogynist with attitudes toward women that many would find quite offensive. Like most of the figures we have examined so far, LaVey identified sexual liberation with an ideal of liberation on a much larger scale; however, in his case, this liberation was not a social and political revolution, but instead the liberation of the individual ego from all inhibition, guilt, or shame. As such, LaVey reflects much of the darker and less admirable side of the sexual revolution—a revolution that was still, in many ways, primarily "for men"[5] and less concerned with social justice than with individual gratification.

After a brief historical overview of the Black Mass in the Western imagination, I will examine LaVey's early life and his own version of the rite. I will then place LaVey's movement in the context of American culture of the late 1960s and 1970s, where it embodied some of the most intense anxieties and contradictions surrounding sexuality during these decades. Finally, I will discuss some of the criticisms brought against LaVey for his apparent sexism and reactionary politics, which would in turn give birth to a whole new series of Satanic offshoots. Although LaVey was often criticized for his offensive sexual and political views, he clearly helped revive the old nightmare of the Black Mass for a new generation of sexual magicians.

THE BLACK MASS: FROM MEDIEVAL FANTASY TO MODERN REALITY

[T]he practitioners of the Black Art in modern times [are] almost exclusively people of great wealth.

DENNIS WHEATLEY, *The Devil Rides Out*

Any ceremony considered a black mass must effectively shock and outrage, as this seems to be the measure of its success.

ANTON SZANDOR LAVEY, *The Satanic Bible*

The highly theatrical Black Mass performed by Anton LaVey and his followers drew upon a long, rich history of Christian nightmares of ritual inversion and demonic perversion. Indeed, it is in many ways the culmination of the long history or "recurring nightmare" of religious heresy and sexual subversion that we briefly retraced in chapter 1. As Jeffrey Burton Russell observes, however, the actual performance of the Black Mass does not in fact have a very ancient history; on the contrary, it is "for the most part a literary invention of the nineteenth-century occultists."[6] Despite its powerful role in the modern popular imagination, there is only scant evidence of any actual Black Mass being celebrated prior to the seventeenth century, and it achieves its now-famous form only in nineteenth-century novels.

Nonetheless, the modern Black Mass does draw on many older tropes in the Western religious imagination and is closely tied to the same fears of secret ritual, child sacrifice, and sexual perversion that surrounded both the early Christians and the early Christian heresies. Thus, one of the more infamous heresies of Middle Ages, the Brethren of the Free Spirit, was charged with performing such sacrilege as sexual intercourse on top of an altar during the act of consecration: "They . . . maintained that if a man and a woman had sexual intercourse on an altar at the same time as the consecration of the host, both acts would have the same worth."[7] Likewise, we saw that the Knights Templar were accused of both desecrating the Mass and various sexual transgressions, and finally the classic prototype of the Black Mass were the fantasies of the witches' Sabbath, with its invocation of the devil and free copulation with demons. As Stuart Clark observes, the witches' Sabbath was often described by the church demonologists and inquisitors as a complete inversion of the Mass, now dedicated to Satan as the "ape of God": "the devil [is] enthroned like God . . . together with altars, demons, 'saints,' music, hand-bells, crucifixes (with the arms lopped off), prelates, bishops, and priests . . . candles, aspersions (with the devil's urine). . . . After elevating the black host . . . the priest threw it down and ground it into pieces. One of the most important witches

confided . . . that she believe witchcraft to be a better religion than the one it simulated because its masses were more splendid."[8]

There is also evidence that the Eucharist itself had long been used for "magical" (and black magical) purposes, such as "to cause disease or to obtain love, or even to procure abortion or death."[9] The Council of Toledo in 1694, for example, condemned priests who celebrated a Mass for the dead naming not a dead man but a living victim whom it was intended to kill.[10] Even Catherine de' Medici (1519–1589), Queen of France, was alleged to have performed a Black Mass involving human sacrifice on behalf of her sick son, Philip.[11] Eventually, we find written texts with instructions for black magical uses of the Mass; probably the most notorious of these is the sixteenth-or seventeenth-century *Grimoire of Honorius*, attributed to Pope Honorius III, which contains various instructions for uses of the Mass (together with the sacrifice of a cock and other offerings), in order to summon spirits and make them do his bidding.[12]

The association of Satanism, the Mass, and sexual perversion was solidified in the popular imagination by several infamous figures of the late medieval and early modern period. The first was the French baron Gilles de Rais (1404–1440), a great military chief who fought at the side of Joan of Arc and became one of the wealthiest men in Europe. In 1440, however, de Rais was arrested and executed for a long series of horrifying crimes and would be remembered as one of the worst serial killers in history and a medieval predecessor of modern Satanic abuse narratives. Not only had he sexually abused and murdered dozens—perhaps hundreds—of children, but the baron was also alleged to have employed sorcerers and alchemists in the hopes of generating new wealth when his extravagant lifestyle threatened to bankrupt him.[13] According to some accounts, however, de Rais only once made use of the remains of a victim in a magical rite, and even then he was so seized by guilt that he gave the corpse a Christian burial.

The second, no less infamous story of sexual magic and the black arts is said to have occurred in the late seventeenth century at the court of Louis XIV. In a scandal of epic proportions, which involved allegations of abortions, child sacrifice, and poisoning among members of Louis' court, black magic and political intrigue became deeply entangled. Louis' mistress, Madame de Montespan, was apparently worried that the king's interest in her was waning and therefore turned to supernatural means. According to the charges leveled against her, she had first used various "powders" given to her by a fortune-teller called La Voison in order to inspire the king's affections. When this failed, she was said to have turned to still more extreme measures; in 1673, she was alleged to have participated in a Black Mass performed with the naked body of a woman as the altar, upon which communion was celebrated from a chalice containing wine mixed with the blood of an infant (three or four babies had been sacrificed, according to her accuser). During the ceremony, de Montespan recited the following incantation:

> Astaroth, Asmody, Prince of Friendship, I conjure you to accept the sacrifice of this infant I present to you for the things which I ask, which are that the friendship of the King . . . should continue towards me, that I should be honored by the princes and princesses of the court, that nothing I demand from the King should be denied me.[14]

The priest believed to be most deeply involved in the celebration of these Masses was Abbé Guiborg, who was described in particularly sinister terms by his interrogator, Nicolas de la Reynie: "He has cut the throats and sacrificed uncounted numbers of children on his infernal altar. . . . It is no ordinary man who thinks it a natural thing to sacrifice infants by slitting their throats and to say the Mass upon the bodies of naked women."[15]

Finally, de Montespan would also be implicated in an alleged attempt to poison the king himself, undertaken by one of her maid's, Mlle des Oeillets (the courier of the love powders). Des Oeillets had briefly received the sexual attention of the king and had borne a child by him, but she was soon cast aside and forgotten. Out of brokenhearted revenge, she was said to have enlisted the services of Guiborg in order to create a poison. According to Guiborg's confession,

> Clad in alb and stole I officiated at a conjuration . . . in the presence of La des Oeillets who wanted to put a death charm upon the king and was accompanied by a man who supplied the rubric of the conjuration. For the rite it was required to have the sperm of both sexes, but since des Oeillets was having her monthly period menstrual blood was used instead; the man with her went to the space between bed rail and the wall . . . and masturbated himself. I directed this semen into the Chalice.[16]

The combined wine, semen, and menstrual blood was then mixed with powdered bat blood and flour and taken away to be used as a deadly poison on the king. Although de Montespan was never proved guilty of involvement in this affair, these scandalous events did serve to destroy any remains of the king's love for her and permanently damaged her reputation.

Perhaps the most explicit connection between the Mass and sexual perversion, however, appears in the writings of the infamous pornographic novelist Marquis de Sade (1740–1814). Although he did not associate them with magic or Satanism, de Sade wrote several accounts of the Catholic Mass performed in explicit sexual settings. The most elaborate descriptions appear in his novels *Justine* and *Juliette*. The latter describes a Mass celebrated by Pope Pius himself in St. Peter's Cathedral, during which the sacred Host is defiled in all manner of sexual and scatological ways by His Holiness and Juliette: "The Host once consecrated, the acolyte brought it up to the stage and respectfully deposited it upon the tip of the papal prick, the very next moment the bugger claps it into my bum. . . . Sodomized by the Pope, the body of Jesus Christ nested in one's ass . . . what a rare delight."[17] As the

Marquis wrote in his *Lusts of the Libertines*, the Mass provides one of the best occasions for a variety of deliciously shocking transgressions:

[The libertine] fucks a whore throughout a Mass being held in his private chapel, and ejaculates furiously at the moment the host is raised aloft. . . .

He fucks whores on the holy altar while Mass is proclaimed, their naked arses spread apart on the sacred stone. . . .

He farts and has a whore fart into the holy chalice, they both piss into it, they both shit in it, and finally he splurts his spunk into the mess.

He makes a small boy shit onto the plate of the Eucharist, then devours the turd while the boy sucks his cock. . . .

He takes holy communion then, while the wafer is still in his mouth, has four whores shit upon it. . . .

He rubs the whore's clitoris with the Host until she drenches it with cunt-cream, then shoves it up her cunt and fucks her, ejaculating over it in turn.[18]

By the nineteenth century, these narratives of Black Masses and sexual perversion had entered fully into the European popular imagination. Arguably the most famous literary rendition of the Black Mass is J. K. Huysmans's classic decadent novel *Là bas* ("Down There"). Increasingly interested in the occult arts, witchcraft, and Satanism, Huysmans allegedly sought out a series of guides to lead him to the Black Mass. There is a great deal of controversy as to whether Huysmans ever did in fact witness a Black Mass or whether he simply fabricated the event and embellished the already long history of Western fantasies of satanic ritual. There are some firsthand reports that he was taken in person to performances of the Black Mass, but there are others, such as French occultist Joséphin Péladan, who charged that the book revealed an "absolute and definitive ignorance of the laws of satanism," and Papus (Gérard Encausse), who suggested that the author pilfered the whole thing from Larousse's *Encyclopedia*.[19]

According to Huysmans's account, however, he had in fact witnessed a Black Mass, at which he had seen a man later identified as Abbé Van Haecke. In Van Haecke, Huysmans believed he had discovered the "greatest satanist of all time, the Gilles de Rais of the nineteenth century."[20] In 1889, Huysmans encountered yet another controversial figure associated with illicit sex and black magic: the defrocked priest Abbé Boullan. Together with his companion, Sister Adèle Chevalier, Boullan had founded a religious community at Bellevue near Paris called the Society of the Reparation of Souls. Many have suspected that this may have been less a genuine religious order than a cloak for darker sexual and violent activities, ranging from fornication to ritual murder and sacrilege: "whenever a nun fell sick or complained of being tormented by the devil, Boullan would apply remedies compounded of consecrated hosts and faecal matter; and on 8 December 1860, at the end of his Mass, he sacrificed upon the altar a child which Adèle Chevalier had born him at the moment of Consecration."[21] In any case, Boullan was considered by many to be a truly evil character. As Stanislas de Guaita described him in his *Temple de Satan*, Boullan was a "pontiff of infamy, a base idol of the mystical Sodom, a magician of the worst type, a wretched criminal, an evil sorcerer, and the founder of an infamous sect."[22] Huysmans heard about Boullan in 1889 and sought him out in order to learn more of the occult. While Boullan denied being a Satanist, he did claim to be an authority on incubi and succubi and gave Huysmans more than enough information to write his novel.[23]

Boullan and van Haecke both appear as fictionalized characters in *Là bas*. The former appears in the character of the intelligent and learned priest, Dr. Johannes, while the latter appears as the sinister, fallen priest, Canon Docre, who officiates over the Black Mass that is at the center of the novel. The hero of the story and Huysmans's alter ego is Durtal, who happens to be researching the life of Gilles de Rais, and as part of his probing into the darkest side of human nature, seeks out a real performance of the Black Mass. Huysmans's account of the Mass is truly fantastic, weaving together all the old fantasies of blasphemy, sexual license, and transgression that run throughout the Western religious imagination. The Mass takes place in the remains of an old Ursuline convent, where the crucifix has been replaced with a grotesque image of Christ, whose grieving face has been transformed into "a bestial one twisted into a mean laugh. He was naked, and where the loincloth should have been, there was virile member projecting from a bush of horsehair."[24] Instead of a pure young child, the choir boy assisting in the Mass is a "fairy," while the priest, Canon Docre, wears a scarlet bonnet with two buffalo horns. In the course of his Mass, Docre derides Jesus as the "Artisan of Hoaxes, Bandit of Homage," who has caused the "Chicanery of thy . . . commercial representatives, thy Popes, to answer by dilatory excuses and evasive promises." Meanwhile, he praises Satan as the "King of the Disinherited, Son who art to overthrow the inexorable father," and celebrates his various sins:

> Master of slanders, Dispenser of the benefits of crime, Administrator of sumptuous sins and great vices, Satan, thee we adore, reasonable God, just God! Superadmirable legate of false trances . . . thou savest the honour of families by aborting wombs impregnated in the forgetfulness of the good orgasm . . . and thine obstetric spares the stillborn children the anguish of maturity, the contamination of original sin. . . .
>
> Hope of Virility, Anguish of the Empty Womb, thou dost not demand the bootless offering of chaste loins . . . thou alone receivest the carnal supplications and petitions of poor and avaricious families. Thou determinist the mother to sell her daughter, to give her son; thou aidest sterile and reprobate loves; Guardian of strident Neuroses, Leaden Tower of Hysteria, bloody Vase of Rape![25]

The whole scene culminates in a bizarre chaos of blasphemy and disgust, as the congregation—mostly prostitutes and degenerate old women—writhe madly on the floor while Docre chews up and spits out the host to be further desecrated:

> In a solemn but jerky voice he said "Hoc est enim corpus meum," then instead of kneeling . . . before the precious Body, he faced the congregation and appeared tumified, haggard, dripping with sweat. He staggered between the two choir boys who, raising the chausible, displayed his naked belly. Docre made a few passes and the host sailed, tainted and soiled, over the steps. . . . A whirlwind of hysteria shook the room. . . . Women rushed upon the Eucharist and, groveling in front of the altar, clawed from the bread humid particles and divine ordure. . . . Docre . . . frothing with rage, was chewing up sacramental wafers, taking them out of his mouth, wiping himself with them and distributing them to the women, who ground them underfoot, howling, or fell over each other struggling to get hold of them and violate them.
>
> The place was simply a madhouse, a monstrous pandemonium of prostitutes and maniacs.[26]

Although this account is probably the product of Huysmans's own vivid imagination and the long history of dark fantasies of the Christian world turned upside down, it would become one of the most widely read accounts of the Black Mass and a major influence on most later attempts to recreate it. Moreover, Huysmans was apparently so disturbed by his own research into the dark world of the occult that he became convinced of the existence of supernatural evil and eventually returned to the church; as he put it, "the devil drew me toward God."[27]

In the twentieth century, these fantasies of the inverted Mass would be still further elaborated in the wake of the Great Beast, Aleister Crowley. As we saw above, Crowley seemed to delight in his own reputation as the wickedest man in the world, notorious for his sexual transgressions and ritual performances. But his image became all the more infamous through various popular accounts of his activities in the media and in fiction, such as the works of the popular British author Dennis Wheatley (1897–1977). A caricature of Crowley appears in several of his novels, where circles of wealthy, intelligent, devil worshippers permeate British society (often in league with Nazis or Communists) and meet to hold occult rituals. His 1953 novel, *To the Devil—a Daughter*, uses Crowley as the model for its main villain, Ipsissimus Mocata, the head of a group of British Satanists. And his 1934 novel, *The Devil Rides Out*, provides a detailed account of a "sabbat" held in the English countryside by a group of wealthy, upper-class Satanists who arrive in a fleet of expensive automobiles; for, as Wheatley observes, "the practitioners of the Black Art in modern times were almost exclusively people of great wealth."[28] The ceremony is conducted by the devil himself, appearing as goat-headed creature who leads his worshippers in a ritual that enacts many of the old tropes: desecration of the crucifix, cannibalism, and so forth.

Just a few decades later, Anton Szandor LaVey would borrow from and exaggerate this trope of the Black Mass. His Satanic rites would be at once the culmination of this long history of fantasy surrounding the Black Mass and a kind of satirical play upon their frightening power in the modern imagination.

THE DAWN OF THE SATANIC AGE: ANTON SZANDOR LAVEY AND THE CHURCH OF SATAN

The devil does not exist. It is a false name invented by the Black Brothers to imply a unity in their ignorant muddle of dispersions. A devil who had unity would be a God.

ALEISTER CROWLEY, *Magic in Theory and Practice*

The Satanic Age started in 1966. That's when God was proclaimed dead, the Sexual Freedom League came into prominence and the hippies developed the free sex culture.

ANTON SZANDOR LAVEY, quoted in Arthur Lyons, *The Second Coming*

Portrayed as a former circus performer, lion trainer, police photographer, and the man who starred as the devil in Roman Polanski's film *Rosemary's Baby*, Anton Szandor LaVey would seem to be a character almost as colorful as the Great Beast, Aleister Crowley himself. Indeed, he seems in many ways a kind of American version of Crowley for a new age of sex and violence. As Blanche Barton described him, he was a figure of truly "Luciferian" pride and contradictions: "As a reflection of the three-dimensional villain [Satan], Anton LaVey is a complex and in many ways frighteningly deceptive man. Supremely ego-driven, he integrates characteristics most of us would think irreconcilable. Upon first meeting LaVey, many are disarmed by his wit, talent and an almost self-deprecating manner. Those who have the opportunity to be around him for any length of time eventually see a seething, brutal side to LaVey."[29] Barton's biography of LaVey, *The Secret Life of a Satanist*, is today the best-known account of LaVey's enigmatic life. It has, however, been seriously challenged by Lawrence Wright[30] and other critics who have found little evidence for many of the claims made in Barton's lively account (which was denounced as "a catalogue of lies" and "self-serving bullshit" by LaVey's own daughter Zeena).[31]

The now legendary narrative of LaVey's life as told by Barton goes briefly as follows: LaVey was born in Chicago in 1930, of French, Alsatian Russian, and Romanian descent, though he also claimed to possess gypsy blood and to have learned about vampires from his grandmother Luba Kolton. Brought up in San Francisco, LaVey was the proverbial boy who ran off to join the circus, leaving his family and school at age sixteen to play calliope at an amusement park; later he would join the Clyde Beatty Circus as a cage boy and later as an assistant lion tamer. LaVey also worked for some time as a calliope player and organist, performing for both the carnival dancers and for the Christian tent revivals—an experience which, he claims, proved to him the hypocrisy of Christianity and the deeper reality of carnal desire:

> On Saturday night I would see men lusting after half-naked girls dancing at the carnival and on Sunday morning when I was playing the organ for tent-show evangelists at the other end of the carnival lot I would see these same men sitting in the pews with their wives and children, asking God to forgive them and purge them of their carnal desires. . . . I knew then that the Christian Church thrives on hypocrisy and that man's carnal nature will out![32]

Another formative experience for LaVey was his time working as a criminal photographer for the San Francisco Police Department, where he regularly saw examples of horrible cruelty and bloodshed. If his organist days proved to him the reality of carnal desire and the hypocrisy of religion, his time as a police photographer proved to him the violence of human nature and the nonexistence of God: "There is nobody up there who gives a shit. Man is the only god. Man must be taught to answer to himself and other men for his actions."[33]

During the 1950s, LaVey also developed an interest in the occult and parapsychology. After studying the works of Crowley (which he ordered from Jack Parsons himself), he began to investigate reports of ghosts, UFOs, and other bizarre phenomena for the police department. Eventually, he would begin holding classes on esoteric subjects at his notorious Black House, a sprawling old Victorian manor which he had painted entirely black. In addition to his popular Friday night lectures on the occult, he began to hold "witches' workshops," where he would impart formulas to women willing to use them for their own self-glorification and power.[34] This gradually evolved into a more ritual sort of gathering, involving a parodic performance of the Black Mass, complete with desecrated hosts, inverted crosses, prayers recited backwards, and the like. Finally, choosing the dramatic occasion of *Walpurgisnacht*, 1966, LaVey shaved his head and proclaimed the formation of the Church of Satan. Thus 1966 was declared Year One, Anno Satanus: the first year of age of Satan.[35] LaVey's newly crafted image as the high priest of Satan was also clearly a parodic one, almost absurdly so. In addition to his Halloween-costume outfit with horns and cape, LaVey sported a pointed goatee that, as many have observed, made him look strikingly like the villain Ming the Merciless from the old Flash Gordon comic books.

Regardless of the truth of Barton's biography, LaVey's reputation as the high priest of Satan and the black pope for a new age of sensual religion spread rapidly. In 1967, a year after the founding of the church, Ira Levin published his popular Satanic horror novel, *Rosemary's Baby;* when Roman Polanski decided to turn it into a film, LaVey seemed a natural choice to serve as a technical advisor and even to appear as the Devil in the surreal impregnation scene. Here we find the ultimate act of sexual magic, and one that Crowley and Parsons had also hoped to realize: the incarnation of Satan himself, who enters this world through sexual union. In any case, Satan had now burst into the American popular imagination in full force and would soon appear throughout a whole new flood of popular literature on black magic and the occult.

Like Crowley before him, LaVey proudly declared all existing religious and moral systems deceased, bankrupt, hypocritical, and irrelevant. His own new creed is based on the fundamental acceptance that all religions are human creations, that all moral codes are relative and arbitrary, and that we may as well create a religion and morality that we can enjoy:

> I question all things. As I stand before the festering and varnished faces of your haughtiest moral dogmas, I write thereon in letters of blazing scorn: Lo and behold! All this fraud. . . .

No creed must be accepted upon authority of a "divine" nature. . . . No moral dogma must be taken for granted—no standard of measure deified. There is nothing inherently sacred about moral codes. Like the wooden idols of long ago, they are the work of human hands, and what man has made, man can destroy.[36]

The basic philosophy behind LaVey's new church is neither particularly original nor particularly complicated. It is perhaps best described as a kind of radical materialism and hedonistic individualism, which celebrates the human body, ego, and sensual pleasure—or in Barton's world, "a system based on rational self-interest, sensual indulgence, and the constructive use of alienation."[37] Much of LaVey's writing—such as *The Satanic Bible* and *The Satanic Witch*—bear strong resemblance to the works of Crowley, Friedrich Nietzsche's ideal of the will to power, and existentialism, with a dash of Ayn Rand thrown in for good measure. But LaVey also marketed his philosophy for a new generation of sexual freedom and individualism in the America of the 1960s and 1970s. The main point for LaVey is that Satanism does *not* mean worship of some actual anti-deity named Satan who is the opposite of some imagined God; rather, it is the rejection of all gods altogether and the warship of one's own individual self. Here Satan—meaning literally "the adversary"—is merely the symbol of the individual human ego. For "Religions and ideologies will come and go . . . but man's basic nature will remain the same. Yet only through understanding himself will he be able to embrace and cherish the demon within him."[38] What he created was, in effect, a response to the "turn on, tune in, drop out" idealism of the 1960s counterculture, a religion in which a person can "turn on" to the pleasures around him without "dropping out" of society.[39]

Like Crowley and Nietzsche, LaVey felt a particular disgust for Christianity, which he saw as a religion of weakness, repression, guilt, and hatred of the body: "The contemptible Judaeo-Christian religion is the root of our present misery, for it has taught us to repress our true, selfish feelings."[40] Yet LaVey was no less harsh in his criticism of the various forms of neo-paganism and witchcraft that had become so popular in the wake of Gardner's Wiccan revival; all of that nature worship and dancing around in naked circles is merely so much "namby-pamby ethicalism" mingled with "sanctimonious fraud" and "esoteric gibberish."[41]

LaVey's new religion was intended—much like Crowley's Abbey of Thelema—to shock conservative mainstream society out of its complacency and moral double standards.[42] What mankind needs now, he suggests, is a religion that worships the individual human being as a carnal beast with desires that need to be fulfilled.

1. Satan represents indulgence instead of abstinence!
2. Satan represents vital existence instead of spiritual pipe dreams! . . .
5. Satan represents vengeance instead of turning the other cheek! . . .
7. Satan represents man as just another animal, sometimes better, more often worse than those that walk on all-fours, who, because of his "divine spiritual and intellectual development," has become the most vicious animal of all!
8. Satan represents all of the so-called sins, as they all lead to physical, mental, or emotional gratification!
9. Satan has been the best friend the Church has ever had, as He has kept it in business all these years![43]

As such, LaVey claims, Satanism is the most honest and the most powerful religion in the world, for it is simply "a religion of the self," the reverence and worship of the individual ego, which openly acknowledges that it is, like all religions, not a divine revelation but a human invention: "Satanism is the only religion which serves to encourage and enhance one's individual preferences, so long as there is admission of those needs. . . . It's a celebration of individuality without hypocrisy."[44] Here LaVey seems to have created the ideal religion for the "Me-Generation," which follows shortly after the founding of his church in the 1970s.

At the same time, LaVey was also clearly marketing his church to a much larger, much less elite or esoteric audience than his occult predecessors like Crowley or Theodor Reuss. Thus his popular paperbacks are all sold widely in major bookstores, while the Church of Satan Web site advertises the movement with slogans like "Satan Wants You." As filmmaker Kenneth Anger observed, LaVey's Satanic philosophy was far less disciplined than even Crowley's sexual magic and was instead meant to be accessible to a wider public:

> Crowley would have been too much hard work for Anton. Anton may have been a little jealous of Crowley, he may have been a lot jealous. . . . There are aspects of Crowley that require a great deal of self-discipline. Anton's take on Satanism was to make it accessible for everyone—it's not a difficult esoteric philosophy.[45]

We might even say that LaVey represents the far more liberal American and Californian laid-back attitude toward magic and sexuality, which rejects once and for all even the lingering remnants of Victorian prudery still left in Crowley's magic.

The New Black Mass: Satanism and Sexual Liberation in the 1960s

> The reason there has always been such a fascination for witchcraft and sorcery is because it has been consistently considered taboo . . . nothing is so fascinating as that which is not meant to be seen.
> ANTON SZANDOR LAVEY, quoted in Barton, *The Secret Life of a Satanist*

O Infernal Majesty, condemn him to the Pit, evermore to suffer in perpetual anguish. Bring Thy wrath upon him, O Prince of Darkness, and rend

him that may know the extent of Thy anger, Call forth Thy legions that they may witness what we do in Thy name. Send forth thy messengers to proclaim this deed, and send the Christian minions staggering to their doom.
ANTON SZANDOR LAVEY, "Le Messe Noir," in *The Satanic Rituals*

Despite his rejection of most forms of neo-paganism, LaVey would also incorporate elaborate ritual and ceremony into his church. For LaVey, however, the power of ritual lies in its combination of "psychodrama and psychic direction." On the one hand, ritual creates a profound aesthetic or psychological effect. After all, "man needs ceremony, and ritual, fantasy and enchantment [the] wonder and fantasy which religion, in the past, has provided."[46] Or, as Gavin Baddeley nicely puts it, "Drama and melodrama are very meaningful. Bombast has its place in Satanism—in some ways, Satanism takes up where Catholicism leaves off."[47] Yet LaVey also acknowledges that this aesthetic and psychological drama generates a powerful energy that can be shaped and directed for magical ends.[48] And the most notorious of LaVey's ritual performances was his parodic re-creation of the Black Mass.

Although he would later downplay the performance of the Black Mass as outdated and ineffective, LaVey did celebrate several Masses in the early church, which helped in no small part to spread his reputation as the new Black Pope. "The rituals for the first year were largely intended as cathartic blasphemes against Christianity. The elements were consistent with the reports of Satanic worship from the famous writings of diabolists, such as the description in . . . *Là Bas*."[49] One of these Masses was recorded in 1968 and soon became the standard format for performances of the Black Mass throughout America and Europe. Performed upon the body of a naked woman as the altar, and involving the use of urine and explicit desecrations of the sacred Host, LaVey's Black Mass (*Le Messe Noir*) was at once an extreme performance and a ridiculous parody of the long nightmare of sexo-Eucharistic perversions that have so long haunted the Christian imagination. It is not entirely clear what LaVey's precise sources for *Le Messe Noir* were; he alludes to a nineteenth-century group in France called *Societé des Luciferiens*, along with the works of other nineteenth-century French authors like Huysmans and Baudelaire and a certain Legué (probably Gabriel Legué, rather than Georges as he cites him):[50]

> The *Black Mass* which follows is the version performed by the *Societé des Luciferiens* in late nineteenth and early twentieth century France. Obviously taken from prior *Messes Noir*, it also derives from the texts of the *Holy Bible*, the *Missale Romanum*, the work of Charles Baudelaire and Charles Marie-George Huysmans, and the records of Georges Legué. It is the most consistently Satanic version this author has encountered.[51]

In the early days of the Church of Satan, LaVey held performances of the Black Mass and other rites each Friday night at his Black House, which attracted not just the lunatic fringe of the Bay Area but a number of affluent individuals and celebrities (including, as we'll see below, Jayne Mansfield). The ritual was performed with almost absurdly demonic drama. Opening with booming chords from an organ, LaVey appeared wearing a horned cap and a long cape surrounded by black-robed worshippers; on the wall was the Sigil of Baphomet allegedly used by the Knights Templar in their perverse rites, and beneath it was the naked female body draped across the stone mantle over the fireplace. Extending a sword to the four directions, LaVey invoked Satan, Lucifer, Belial, and Leviathan and then passed around a chalice filled not with wine or blood but with some other beverage of choice (e.g., bourbon).

The text of LaVey's *Le Messe Noir* is a mixture of a Latin parody of the Catholic Mass and French and English prayers to Satan. Several paragraphs of the text are lifted word for word from Huysmans's Black Mass in *Là bas*, including the following Satanic rants:

> Thou, thou whom, in my quality of Priest, I force, whether thou wilt or no, to descend into this host, to incarnate thyself into this bread, Jesus, artisan of hoaxes, bandit of homages, robber of affection, hear! Since the day when thou didst issue from the complaisant bowels of a virgin, thou hast failed all thy engagements, belied all thy promises. Centuries have wept, awaiting thee, fugitive god, mute god! Thou wast to redeem man, and thou has not. Thou wast to appear in thy glory, and thou sleepest. Go, lie, say to the wretch who appeals to thee,
>
> "Hope, be patient, suffer; the hospital of souls will receive thee; the angels will assist thee; Heaven opens to thee." Imposter! Thou knowest well that the angels, disgusted at thy inertia, abandon thee![52]

LaVey's ritual also contains various instructions for the desecration of the ritual and the sacred Host by means of bodily fluids and sacrilegious acts involving urine, genitalia, and desecration. For example, the nun "lifts her habit and urinates into the font," after which an aspergeant is dipped into the urine and shaken in four directions. The wafer, which is to be made of turnip or coarse black bread, is placed "between the exposed breasts of the altar," then touched to the "vaginal area," and finally trampled by the priest, deacon, and subdeacon.[53]

Clearly, much of this ritual is aimed at a kind of explicit, exaggerated, even ridiculous form of transgression that goes even further in the direction of parodic inversion than Crowley's own extreme ritual transgressions. LaVey himself would more or less acknowledge as much, suggesting that the early Church of Satan had in a sense to use such extreme displays of Christian inversion in order to awaken the American public and make itself known to the world: "Any ceremony considered a black mass must effectively shock and outrage, as this seems to be the measure of its success."[54] Once the original shock had been made, however, these theatrical performances of the Black Mass were no longer really necessary:

> After that original blast, there was no need for the ongoing public spectacle and outrage of an inverted Catholic Mass anymore. Christianity was becoming weaker every day. That was just beating a dead horse. There were plenty of other sacred cows to attack, and that's what keeps Satanism vital and thriving.[55]

Nonetheless, despite the church's statements to the contrary, the La-Veyian style Black Mass, with the naked female altar has continued to be a thriving and theatrical aspect of Satanic worship throughout the world to this day. It seems to have been taken in some interesting new directions as well. Thus, one Satanic witch describes a New Year celebration in which she served not just as the altar but the dinner table for an elaborate Satanic smorgasbord:

> In the last Satanic New Year we had a huge party and it was really great. I was there at the private party in the evening on the table. We had dinner on me! . . . They put me on the table naked, they put all sorts of salads all over my body, and they ate off me with a spoon. It was absolutely fantastic.[56]

Yet to what degree such rituals are "fantastically" liberating and to what degree they only continue a deeper form of exploitation and misogyny remains open to question.

While LaVey's Black Mass involves primarily symbolic references to sexuality (the naked altar, touching the breasts and genitals, etc.), he does also recommend various other rites of a more explicitly sexual nature. *The Satanic Rituals* outlines three main types of ritual: sex rituals for the conjuration of lust, destructive rituals for the expression of anger or hatred, and compassionate rituals for helping oneself or others. The first of these might be considered the Satanic version of sex magic. Here the practitioner is to pray to the "great spawn of the abyss" to "send forth that messenger of voluptuous delights and let these obscene vistas of my dark desires take form in future deeds and doings." Then, in the case of a male, he should recite a prayer in rather Crowleyian prose that exalts his throbbing "rod" and its "venom" in the name of Pan:

> My rod is athrust! The penetrating force of my venom shall shatter the sanctity of that mind which is barren of lust; and as the seed falleth, so shall its vapours spread within that reeling brain benumbing it to helplessness according to my will! In the name of the great god Pan, may my secret thoughts be marshaled into the movements of the flesh of that which I desire!

The female, conversely, is to pray in the name of the whore of Babylon, celebrating her nectar-dripping loins and their "pollen":

> My loins are aflame! The dripping of the nectar from my eager cleft shall act as pollen to the slumbering brain, and the mind that feels not lust shall on a sudden reel with crazed impulse. . . . In the names of the great harlot of Babylon, and of Lilith and of Hecate, may my lust be fulfilled![57]

Here the sexuality and gender of both male and female are exaggerated in ways that go even further than the "woman is from the moon, man is from the sun" of the Wiccans. Now both male and female become hypereroticized lust-dripping creatures, the thrusting rod and the flaming loins aching for sexual satisfaction.

THE DARK SIDE OF THE SEXUAL REVOLUTION: SEXUAL LIBERATION, SATAN-STYLE

> Freud's "pleasure principle" should be known to be the highest motivator for any religion. . . .
>
> Never underestimate the sexual corollaries to fetishism/religion.
>
> ANTON SZANDOR LAVEY, "The World's Most Powerful Religion"

Unless we free ourselves from the ridiculous sexual standards of our present society, including the so-called sexual revolution, the neuroses caused by those stifling regulations will still persist.

ANTON SZANDOR LAVEY, *The Satanic Bible*

LaVey's new church was in many ways a simultaneous expression of and reaction against many of the changing attitudes toward sex and gender in the 1960s. Many of his works, such as *The Satanic Witch*, are at once classic expressions of the rhetoric of sexual liberation and also quite blatant statements of male chauvinism. Above all, his performance of the Black Mass—performed upon the living altar of a naked female body—is a kind of weird parodic experiment in both sexual revolution and ritual misogyny. In fact, LaVey himself acknowledges that the very symbolism and magical power of the Black Mass rests upon a fundamental male-female/dominant-receptive gender polarity that is directly opposed to modern forms of feminism:

Feminism negates and inverts the natural male/female interchange. There's a magnetic interaction between men and women that can be exploited for magical results. . . . It's been described as yin/yang, active/passive. . . . In Satanic ceremonies, it's the interplay between the dominant Priest and the receptive female altar. But feminists in their supposed quest for equality have tossed the baby out with the bathwater.[58]

As Steven Seidman suggests, the years between 1960 and 1980 in the United States witnessed a profound new "legitimation of the erotic aspects of sex" and a new valuation of sexual pleasure as a good in and of itself, even apart from love and marriage: "by the 1960s the pleasurable and expressive qualities of sex were appealed to as a sufficient justification of sex. Discourses . . . appeared that constructed sex as a domain of pleasure and self-expression requiring no higher purpose. . . . Eros was released from the culture of romance that gave birth to it."[59] Yet this new drive toward liberation was not limited to sexual freedom; rather, it was part of a larger countercultural phenomenon that also involved freedom in music, dress, hairstyle, drug use, and political resistance: "the 1960s saw the birth of a counter-culture, less apolitical than the working class culture, more challenging . . . of bourgeois hegemony. Music, clothes, style became the hallmark, the crack in the painwork of the traditional society that seemed to be vanishing forever. . . . [V]iolence, drugs and sex, three major preoccupations of the 1960s and 70s blended symbolically in the image of youth in revolt."[60] At the same time, this period witnessed a new expansion of sexuality into popular culture as a whole, particularly through advertising, the media, and the increasing commodification of sex through pornography:

By the 1960s there was undoubtedly an increasing eroticization of many aspects of social life, from the increasing sexual explicitness of advertising, where sex became an obvious inducement to ever-extending and often useless consumption, to the growing squalor and exploitativeness of pornography in major cities.[61]

Yet, as other, more critical authors have observed, this revolutionary call for the unleashing of eros was often largely in the service of male interests. As Sheila Jeffreys argues, it was typically men rather than women who benefited from this new sexual freedom, which allowed them to enjoy a wide array of libidinal pleasures often without accountability, all in the name of "sexual liberation." "The sexual revolution completed the sexualisation of women. Both married and unmarried women were expected to become experts in sexually servicing men, and to get over their own tastes and interests."[62] In sum, "the sex-rev failed because, Freudian or not, it failed to ask what women want."[63] Instead of genuine liberation or equality, what we find today is a remarkable proliferation of commodified forms of sexuality, pornography, and prostitution, which, as Dennis Altman observes, are largely "means of satisfying male 'desire' through the services, in both the corporeal and fantasy realms, of women."[64]

The Law of the Forbidden: Sexual Fetishism and Fantasy

[P]sychiatry had no room for the encouragement of fantasy or personal fetish. If anything it was about negating or subverting them. That's where I found my grey area—keeping and treasuring your fetishes, dreams and fantasies rather than subverting or expelling them.

ANTON SZANDOR LAVEY, interview with
Gavin Baddeley, *Lucifer Rising*

LaVey's new church was in many ways the epitome of this contradictory fusion of sexual liberation and male domination that ran throughout the "sexual revolution" as a whole. His writings repeatedly emphasize the need for full indulgence of one's sexual appetites, as well as a proud recognition of all one's most peculiar sexual proclivities. "Satanism *does* advocate free love, but only in the true sense of the word. Free love, in the Satanic concept, means exactly that— . . . freedom to indulge your sexual desires with as many others as you feel is necessary to satisfy your particular needs."[65] Thus, for example, pornography is by no means rejected but openly embraced as a celebration of our carnal nature: "Porn is inherently Satanic as an art form: it has no other role beside self-indulgence in its most basic form; it glorifies man's carnal nature, blending the most beautiful aspects of the human animal with the most debased."[66] Like Crowley before him, LaVey warned that sexual desires that are *not* indulged will simply turn into dangerous obsessions, neuroses, or worse: "If a person has no proper release for his desires, they rapidly build up and become compulsions."[67] And like Crowley, P. B. Randolph, Reuss, and others, LaVey taught methods of sex magic, or the release and channeling of sexual energy for magical aims; but his was, as he put it, "Sex magic without sanctimony."[68]

In certain respects, LaVey's concern with the liberation of sexuality went much further than most of the countercultural discourse of the 1960s. LaVey was not simply interested in liberating healthy, happy, pleasurable sex for a more open society; rather, he was particularly interested in exploring sexual areas that were considered most taboo: sexual fetishes and deviant desires of all varieties. We are all, in his opinion, "fetishists," with some form of deep, dark, deviant desire or other: "EVERY MAN IS A FETISHIST, YOU SIMPLY HAVE TO *DISCOVER* HIS FETISH."[69] Indeed, LaVey suggests that the sexual liberations of the 1960s had very quickly become boring and routine, simply because of the endless, easy access to free love. Exploring one's most idiosyncratic fetishes, conversely, makes sex dangerous, defiant, exciting again:

> Fetishism is . . . an effort to make sex exciting again. The experiments in "free love" of the 1960s and 1970s may have made promiscuity fashionable, . . . but they also demonstrated that . . . anything in endless, monotonous supply could become dull. . . . Christianity preaches that sex is merely a procreative act, devoid of pleasure. . . . Sexual activity wherein procreation is avoided . . . is therefore one of the most pleasurable blasphemies. Truly Satanic sex is where the individual indulges their own true personal proclivities.[70]

Like Crowley and Georges Bataille, LaVey was fascinated by the principle of transgression, the explicit violation of social and sexual taboos, or what he liked to call "the law of the forbidden." As De Sade and Bataille had also observed, the prohibition only tends to make the forbidden act all the more tantalizing, the act of violating the taboo all the more exhilarating. When asked by interviewer Gavin Baddeley "How much of the appeal of the occult, and Satanism in particular, derives from its secret, hidden character?" he replied:

> There's a big link with the "law of the forbidden," a concept pioneered by the photographer William Mortensen concerning the primal appeal of sex, sentiment and wonder. These are the basic human interests from which our compulsions and fetishes are derived. Like the fairground where people will pay to go into the freak tent to avert their eyes.[71]

Thus the law of the forbidden applies equally to our fascination with Satanism and the occult as well as to our fascination with sexual transgression and deviant desires. Just as "The reason there has always been a fascination for witchcraft and sorcery is because it has consistently been considered taboo," so too "sheer nudity in itself is usually not nearly as stimulating as a glimpse of the forbidden," for in both cases "NOTHING IS SO FASCINATING AS THAT WHICH IS NOT MEANT TO BE SEEN!"[72] In LaVey's opinion, we are all deviant and "nasty" at heart; indeed, our sexual fetishes and our fascination with the forbidden are what make us mature human animals: "all men are nasty little boys at heart. When the first sexual feelings and subsequent experimentation occurred in a man's life, he was acting in the capacity of a nasty little boy in ninety-nine percent of all cases … when a boy becomes a man, it is accompanied by lewd thoughts!"[73] In sum, whereas Randolph, Reuss, and other sexual magicians had identified sex as the innermost essence of the human being and the greatest source of magic, LaVey identifies *sexual fetishism and deviance* as the innermost core of human animality.

Thus, when performing sexual rituals, LaVey advises that the Satanist be constantly mindful of the transgressive, deviant, subversive nature of the act: "While performing your ritual, remain as aware as possible that you are doing something naughty, forbidden, possibly even nasty. … This is the time to turn unfounded guilts and inhibitions into an *advantage*!"[74] For it is in large part this sense of the forbidden or transgressive that gives the act its magical power.

The Satanic Witch: An Anti-Feminist Religion?

I'm a confirmed misogynist, but only because I'm such a pushover for feminine women.

ANTON SZANDOR LAVEY, quoted in Barton, *The Secret Life of a Satanist*

Women can exploit their differences to gain more power. … Advanced, Satanically-oriented women can choose their own lifestyle rather than have it thrust upon them. They can participate in all kinds of exercises, rituals if you will, to break down the brainwashing feminism has done on contemporary young women. Sadomasochistic revelries, shape-changing deviltry, discipline games—women are looking for more of that sort of thing in their private lives because it's the ideal therapy.

ANTON SZANDOR LAVEY, *The Satanic Witch*

Perhaps the most complex—and, to many, disturbing—aspect of LaVey's Satanic philosophy is his attitude toward women. As in most other aspects of his views, LaVey is proudly offensive and politically incorrect in his views on women. He does in fact argue for a certain kind of sexual liberation and empowerment of women, a recognition of the real power that women wield over men and can use to their advantage. As he puts it, "The witch has always been a rebel," who, with her subtle violations of taboos, "defies sacred cows the other women kneel before."[75] LaVey himself had a powerful attraction to and respect for particular kinds of women—most often the curvaceous, voluptuous, "truly female" types, such as Marilyn Monroe and Jayne Mansfield, both of whom had brief relationships with the Black Pope. After Mansfield's death in a car crash, LaVey praised her for her "hedonism and pure, selfish pursuits" in her "dedication to the ideals of Satan."[76] In Satanism, Mansfield "had found a philosophy through which she could be a businesswoman, an intellectual, a mother and a sexpot all at once."[77]

But at the same time, LaVey was also a staunch opponent of feminism, women's rights movements, and anything that weakened the distinctions between the sexes. As his daughter Zeena, observes, LaVey released his *Satanic Witch* in the same time period—and in many ways in response to—the Equal Rights Amendment and feminist activists like Gloria Steinem. Satanism was, in effect, a rejection of this "emasculation" of men and "de-feminizing" of women:

It was in this period of gender confusion and bra-burning bravado that the *Satanic Witch* was first published . . .. A diabolical textbook reinforcing traditional sex roles and "sexist" attitudes was viciously attacked in that shrilly militant, androgynous atmosphere.[78]

In LaVey's opinion, this whole period of time was "completely ass-backwards. Men were becoming emasculated, women were getting uglier, and adults in general were turning into one indeterminate sex in the name of liberation," which blurred the fundamental distinction between man and woman, creating a synthetic composite that represented the worst of both genders.[79]

In contrast to the "defeminizing" and "androgynizing" trends in modern women's movements, LaVey advocates what he calls a "true liberation for women brave enough to risk jealous ridicule from their 'sisters.' " Rather than an androgynous, desexualized being, the "truly liberated female" is the one who knows how to accentuate and make full use of her femininity, with all its curves and caprices; she "knows both how to use and enjoy men" and can "profit by her womanliness by manipulating the men she holds in contempt, while enjoying them." This would, LaVey suggests, herald a new and more authentic kind of feminism based on the recognition of the true nature of the female body as an object of carnal desire: "The woman who grasps and fully understands the mastery of the world inherent in this book's Satanic teachings will usher in a true feminism: the liberation of the demonic in every woman."[80] In contrast to the "flaccid, lackluster attitude" of the Wiccan and neo-pagan witches, the Satanic witches embody true "pride, identity and power" by accepting and affirming their distinctly feminine sexuality.[81]

Probably the best known artist for the Church of Satan was "Coop," much of whose work featured extremely voluptuous demon vixens sporting little apart from horns and pitchforks to adorn their large bottoms and bursting bosoms. As Coop argued in an interview with Gavin Baddeley, this is really what men want, and have always wanted from the dawn of time, in keeping with our own uniquely "male" and "female" animal natures:

> Women should look like women, and men should look like men. There's a reason that we have evolved into this state, and I can't see why we should throw that out of the window after it's worked for so many thousands of years. I think the image of the voluptuous woman is firmly planted in the darkest, least evolved parts of our brains. If you look at stone-age fetish figurines—like the famous Venus of Willendorf—they were just basically little statues of fat chicks that cavemen jerked off to.[82]

The ability to manipulate feminine sexuality in order to dominate men is the heart of sexual magic for the true Satanic witch. The wise witch can arouse and then draw upon the sexual energy in the men whom she captivates in order to use that energy for her own devices:

> Because their sexual energy is potential magical energy and nature intended that they be attracted to you, *men* are your best source of witch power . . . by your own sexual self-consciousness, you can draw this power from the men who need only to be placed within your magnetic field—produce an accelerated charge of sexual self-consciousness.[83]

Thus LaVey gives detailed instructions to the Satanic witch for her sexual-magical rituals designed to allure and seduce men. She might, for example, go out in public, highly made-up and wearing nothing but a coat over her naked body; she should then flaunt herself before every man she meets, imagining that she is totally naked. She should then go home, remove the coat, and stare at herself naked in the mirror, imagining herself from a man's perspective, feeling "completely exposed" as she "shamelessly flaunted" herself, imagine handsome men grabbing her, aroused and excited at the outrageous display of the sensual naked body:

Allow yourself to build as high a peak of sexual excitement as possible, masturbating yourself to a climax, attempting to feel as the man would as he watched the girl (you) perform such an act in public. As you are overcome by your sensual responses, close your eyes, fall to the floor, thrash about in wild abandon—or do whatever will contribute to the most intense orgasm. . . . As you are coming down from your climax, say to yourself, "I am a witch; I have power over men! I am a witch; I have power over men!"[84]

In short, the witch is not only to *become* a sexual object and focus of the male gaze; she is even to *internalize* that male gaze, subject herself to it in her imagination, and thereby use it to her own magical advantage.

Although LaVey claims that rituals like these are liberating and empowering for his female followers, there is little doubt that most feminists and anyone sympathetic to women's rights today would find his teachings deeply disturbing. He had no qualms about saying things that would make anyone with politically correct conscience cringe, such as: "all women are exhibitionists to a certain extent. The thrill that any healthy woman obtains when she knows she is exciting a desirable man is the most natural thing in the world."[85] But LaVey himself would most likely admit as much. He was an avowed "misogynist" who loathed the defeminization of women that he saw occurring during the 1960s, and he wanted nothing more than to "smash the current androgyny," to return to a world where "men look like men" (hard, cold, intellectual) and "women look like women" (soft, warm, emotional). As he put it in his usual uncompromising way,

I'm a confirmed misogynist, but only because I'm such a pushover for feminine women. A misogynist's disdain is based on jealousy. Seeing the power that aggressively passive women wield through their feminine wiles, he wishes he had a bit of it himself, secretly admires it, and seeks to capture it before it captures him. . . . We misogynists need

wanton, sleazy, yielding, soft women to augment our masculinity. I consider a well-adjusted heterosexual misogynist a bulwark against the most devastating form of defeminization.[86]

Not surprisingly, the publication of LaVey's *Satanic Witch* was met with mixed results. While some praised it as a visionary "breakthrough in understanding human motivation," many feminists responded with livid outrage, "public book burnings, pickets at stores."[87] LaVey, however, rather seemed to enjoy the controversy he'd created.

HEDONISM, INDIVIDUALISM, AND GREED: THE ULTIMATE "MODERN" RELIGION?

[T]his is a very selfish religion. We believe in greed, we believe in selfishness. We believe in all of the lustful thoughts that motivate men because that is man's natural feeling.

ANTON SZANDOR LAVEY, interview in the film, "Satanis: The Devil's Mass"

The philosophy of Satanism I follow is a modern invention, relevant to the modern age. We look at it from a fairly scientific, balanced point of view.

DAVID AUSTEN, High Priest of the Temple of Set, quoted in Baddeley, *Lucifer Rising*

As a religion that affirms the basic principles of egotism, sexual pleasure, and greed, a religion that values the principles of elitism and hierarchy, LaVey's church could be said to be in many ways an ideal religion for American capitalist society in the late twentieth century. If Crowley represents, in a sense, the "exhaustion of modernity" in Europe and England in the mid-twentieth century, then LaVey might be said to represent the *celebration of a new form of modernity* in America at the close of the twentieth century. After all, the basic ideals of modernism may have led to war, holocaust, and disaster in Europe, but the United States emerged from the war as the most powerful, arrogant, and rapidly growing force in global politics. LaVey's philosophy would seem in many ways to reflect a new confidence in the Crowleyian principles of individualism, radical freedom, amorality, and hedonism, which fit rather well with the basic principles of American capitalism. And LaVey's church would itself become quite successful commercially, rapidly growing into one of the most successful new religions on the American occult scene of the 1960s and 1970s.

Not all of LaVey's followers would agree with the direction his church was taking, however. Increasingly in the 1970s and 1980s, LaVey would face not just outrage from mainstream Christians and irate feminists, but also dissent from various church members who were increasingly disturbed by the seemingly fascistic and capitalistic tendencies within the movement.

Blessed Are the Strong

Smash the crumbling cross, for Might is right.
ANTON SZANDOR LAVEY, "Battle Hymn of the
Apocalypse," from *The Satanic Bible*

As with his outspoken misogyny and sexism, LaVey had no qualms about voicing an explicitly politically incorrect social vision based on hierarchy and the dominance of the strong over the weak. A highly elitist philosophy, taking a kind of Nietzschean will to power, the cult of the individual, and Darwinian survival of the fittest ideal to their furthest extremes, Satanism is based first and foremost on the power of the strong, willful individual over the dull conformity of the cowardly masses: "LaVey's world is self-indulgent, hedonistic, elitist . . . yet also brutal, opinionated, extreme. He needs no other humans to populate it, so any who come into his immediate circle enter understanding LaVey's emotional/psychological inaccessibility and distance."[88] Thus LaVey has his own Satanic inversion of the Sermon on the Mount, which celebrates not the weak and poor but the strong and greedy:

Blessed are the strong, for they shall possess the earth—Cursed are the weak, for they shall inherit the yoke!

Blessed are the powerful, for they shall be reverenced among men—Cursed are the feeble, for they shall be blotted out! . . .

Blessed are the iron-handed, for the unfit shall flee before them—Cursed are the poor in spirit, for they shall be spat upon.[89]

As LaVey's daughter Zeena comments, Satanic sexual practices can also be used as a form of eugenics: by learning to select the strong and dominant, while avoiding the weak and feeble, the Satanist can help to create a new breed of powerful individuals who rise above the dull herd: "*The Satanic Witch* . . . is a guide to selective breeding, a manual for eugenics—the lost science of preserving the able-bodied and able-minded while controlling the surplus population of the weak and incompetent."[90]

These elements of elitism, intolerance, and even eugenics did not always sit well with LaVey's followers. One of the most outspoken critics of the church has been Isaac Bonewits, who was a regular at LaVey's rituals as a teenager. He would later become shocked and horrified by the apparent racism, chauvinism, and elitism within the movement, describing Satanists as largely a bunch of "fascists, jerks and psychopaths."[91] He was particularly disturbed when he began to see elements of white supremacy and Nazism creep into the church:

Some were bringing authentic Ku Klux Klan robes and Nazi uniforms for the ceremonies. I was assured that the clothes were merely for "Satanic shock value" to jar people from their usual pattern of thinking. Then I would talk to the men wearing these clothes and realize they were not pretending anything. I noticed that there were no black members of the Church . . . and began to ask why.[92]

LaVey himself espoused no particular political views. Yet his highly elitist and hierarchical Satanic philosophy is clearly in many ways compatible with certain aspects of fascism, racism, and, as I would suggest, consumer capitalism.

Churchofsatan.com: Marketing Satan, Sex, and Liberation

Satanism as mass culture is great. . . . There's a great advantage in mainstreaming, and I'd be a hypocrite to dislike it.

ANTON SZANDOR LAVEY, interview with Gavin Baddeley, quoted in *Lucifer Rising*

LaVey's emphasis on the central values of egotism, hedonism, and personal satisfaction does seem to fit well with the larger economics patterns of consumer capitalism in late-twentieth-century America. Greed and acquisitiveness are, like all other vices, basic aspects of the human being and should therefore be affirmed and celebrated. Just as he rejects the idea of abstention in sexual matters, so too he rejects any pretence of poverty in the name of religion: "LaVey had no illusions about vows of poverty as a means of gaining spiritual redemption. For him magic was essentially about power—and wealth was a type of power. LaVey reserved the right to channel funds accruing to the church of Satan in any way, for any purpose he saw fit."[93] Eventually, in 1975, LaVey even began marketing the degrees of initiation within the church. Higher degrees could now be obtained by contributions in cash, real estate, or valuable objects of art: "priesthoods in the Church of Satan were available to those who demonstrated their success in the wider world—such demonstrations to include gifts of cash or valuable objects."[94]

Aagain, however, not all of LaVey's followers were happy with what they saw as blatant commercialism creeping into the church. One of the most notable critics of the church was Michael Aquino, a former high-ranking officer in the U.S. military intelligence, with service in Vietnam and a doctorate in political science to his name, who joined the church in 1969. Like Bonewits, Aquino began to feel that the church was beginning to attract the wrong sort of crowd—"a carnival of freaks," "sexually inadequate, social misfits, intellectual poseurs." The leadership had meanwhile fragmented into "petty squabbles over title, ranks and privileges" amid an ironic fraternity of individualists.[95] However, Aquino was even more disturbed by LaVey's policy of selling degrees, which he saw as the same sort of hypocrisy that Satanists had attacked in the mainstream Christian church: "If there had been a single unifying factor that had brought us to Satanism, it was the church's stand against hypocrisy. So when we learned of this policy, our reaction to it was that LaVey was betraying his office, betraying everything that he had worked for for so many years."[96] In 1975, Aquino broke from the church and founded his own new order, the Temple of. Set. Indeed, he claimed that Satan had revealed himself in his true and original form, the ancient Egyptian god Set, and had named Aquino as LaVey's replacement (as well as the successor to Aleister Crowley). In sum, "Just like the Pope in the sixteenth century, the Black Pope faced the challenge of attempted reform."[97]

The Church of Satan, I would suggest, is thus a striking illustration of the larger "cultural contradictions" surrounding sexuality, transgression, and liberation in the America of the 1960s and 1970s. Indeed, it shows very clearly the ways in which the very promise of sexual transgression and sociopolitical liberation themselves can become co-opted, commodified, and transformed into yet another profitable supermarket of American culture. As Altman suggests, this is a recurring theme throughout American society during these decades, as the "attempt to link sexuality with the political" gave way to a culture "where sexuality is more commonly linked with contemporary capitalism, and we increasingly think of ourselves as consumers rather than citizens."[98] As we will see in the following chapter, both the hope for liberation and the tendency toward commodification would become even more obvious in the closing decades of the twentieth century amid the strange new logic of late capitalism.

CONCLUSION: THE DEVIL IS WINNING

> Satan has been the best friend the Church has ever had, as He has kept it in business all these years!
>
> ANTON SZANDOR LAVEY, *The Satanic Bible*

> From a Satanic perspective, there's room for optimism. The Devil is winning.
>
> GAVIN BADDELEY, *Lucifer Rising*

If Crowley represented the darker side of the late Victorian era, with his love of transgression and violation of sexual taboos, then LaVey and his church show us the dark side of the 1960s and the sexual revolution. At the same time that he embodied many of the counterculture's ideals of sexual freedom and revolt against mainstream values, he also represented a striking reaction against the cultural revolution, a rejection of many "liberatory" phenomena such as feminism, equal rights, and anything smacking of socialism. As Bonewits and others observed, LaVey's church would often appear more politically conservative, even fascistic, than liberating. As LaVey himself argued, Satanism and the Black Mass have always been about the inversion or transgression of mainstream cultural values; thus, a modern Black Mass would have to reject or invert popular values such as the 1960s counterculture and liberalism itself:

> A black mass today would consist of blaspheming of such "sacred" topics as Eastern mysticism, psychiatry, the psychedelic movement, ultra-liberalism, etc. Patriotism-would be championed, drugs and their gurus defiled, acultural militants would be deified.[99]

In spite of, or perhaps *because of*, his politically incorrect philosophy, LaVey's church has continued

to flourish even after his death, attracting a variety of high-profile members, such as shock-rock artist Marilyn Manson among others. As Gavin Baddeley suggests, the devil has not gone out of favor with the end of the sexual revolution, but in many ways he seems stronger than ever in a new era of individualism, sexual freedom, and the relentless search for sensual pleasure:

> Satanists will continue to play with "spiritual nitroglycerine." . . . In embracing perennial Christian taboos . . . we intend to prevent present-day idiocies from dragging the next millennium into another miserable Dark Age. If a New Satanic Age is born, it will be born from the ideas of curiosity, independence and pleasure. From a Satanic perspective, there's room for optimism. The Devil is winning.[100]

At least in contemporary American consumer and corporate culture, it would seem that the principles of elitism, egotism, and greed and the logic of consumer capitalism are winning as well.

NOTES

1. Arthur Lyons, *The Second Coming: Satanism in America* (New York: Dodd, Mead, 1970), p. 1.
2. Anton Szandor LaVey, quoted in Lyons, *Second Coming*, p. 185.
3. Anton Szandor LaVey, conversation, 1986, quoted in Arthur Lyons, *Satan Wants You: The Cult of Devil Worship in America* (New York; Mysterious Press, 1988), p. 104.
4. Jeffrey Weeks, *Sex, Politics, and Society: The Regulation of Sexuality since 1800* (London: Longman, 1981), p. 254.
5. Sheila Jeffreys, "The Sexual Revolution Was for Men," in *Sexuality*, edited by Robert A. Nye (New York: Oxford University Press, 1999), pp. 132–33.
6. Jeffrey Burton Russell, *Witchcraft in the Middle Ages* (Ithaca, NY: Cornell University Press, 1972), p. 253.
7. Robert Lerner, *The Heresy of the Free Spirit in the Later Middle Ages* (Berkeley: University of California Press, 1972), pp. 10–11.
8. Stuart Clark, *Thinking with Demons: The Idea of Witchcraft in Early Modern Europe* (Oxford: Clarendon,

1997), p. 85, summarizing Pierre de Lancre, *Tableau de l'inconstance des mauvais anges et demons* (1612).

9. Russell, *Witchcraft*, p. 296 n. 12.

10. Richard Cavendish, *The Black Arts: An Absorbing Account of Witchcraft, Demonology, Astrology, and Other Mystical Practices throughout the Ages* (New York: Perigree Books, 1967), p. 327.

11. Aubrey Melech, *Missa Niger: La Messe Noire* (Northampton, U.K.: Sut Anubis, 1986), pp. 1–5. See H. T. F. Rhodes, *The Satanic Mass* (London: Rider, 1954).

12. Cavendish, *Black Arts*, pp. 328–29; cf. A.E. Waite, *The Book of Ceremonial Magic* (New York: University Books, 1961), p. 265. The *Grimoire* was first published in Rome in 1678.

13. Frances Winwar, *The Saint and the Devil; Joan of Arc and Gilles de Rais* (New York: Harper & Brothers, 1948), pp. 256–62.

14. Lisa Hilton, *Athénaïs: The Life of Louis XIV's Mistress, the Real Queen of France* (Boston: Little, Brown, 2002), p. 207.

15. Francis King, *Sexuality, Magic, and Perversion* (Secaucus, NJ: Citadel, 1971), pp. 69–70.

16. Ibid., pp. 72–73. See Hilton, *Athénaïs*, p. 217.

17. Marquis de Sade, *Juliette* (1797; reprint, New York: Grove Press, 1968), p. 802. For a discussion of de Sade and the "libertine body," see Marcel Hénaff, *Sade: The Invention of the Libertine Body* (Minneapolis: University of Minnesota Press, 1999).

18. Marquis de Sade, *Philosophy in the Boudoir*, translated by Meredith X. (New York: Creation Books, 2000), pp. 163–65.

19. Robert Baldick, introduction to J. K. Huysmans, *Down There (Là bas): A Study in Satanism*, translated by Keene Wallis (New Hyde Park, NY: University Books, 1958), pp. xv, xxiii.

20. Robert Baldick, *The Life of J.-K. Huysmans* (Oxford: Clarendon Press, 1955), pp. 149–50. "It was said of the Abbé that he had crosses tattooed in the soles of his feet, to be able to walk continually upon the symbol of Christ; . . . he obtained a hold over young people by means of lovely women and lavish meals, corrupting their morals and then forcing them into the darkest devilries" (Baldick, introduction to Huysmans, *Down There*, pp. xx–xxi).

21. Baldick, *Life of J.-K. Huysmans*, p. 155.

22. Baldick, introduction to Huysmans, *Down There*, p. vii.

23. Ibid., pp. xxii–xiii.

24. Huysmans, *Down There*, pp. 264–65.

25. Ibid., pp. 268–69.

26. Ibid., p. 272.

27. Baldick, introduction to Huysmans, *Down There*, pp. xxvi–vii.

28. Dennis Wheatley, *The Devil Rides Out* (London: Hutchinson, 1954), p. 84; Wheatley, *To the Devil a Daughter* (London: Hutchinson, 1953).

29. Blanche Barton, "About the Author," in Anton Szandor LaVey, *The Satanic Witch* (Los Angeles: Feral House, 1989), n.p.

30. Lawrence Wright, "It's Not Easy Being Evil in a World That's Gone to Hell," *Rolling Stone*, September 5, 1991, 63–68, 105–6. Wright claims there is no evidence that LaVey ever worked for Clyde Beatty Circus or the San Francisco Police Department, among other things.

31. Zeena Schreck (originally LaVey), letter to Michael Aquino, December 30,1990, quoted by Joe Abrams, "The Church of Satan," University of Virginia Religious Movements Homepage Project, http://religiousmovements.lib.virginia.edu/nrms/satanism/churchof.html (2000).

32. Blanche Barton, *The Secret Life of a Satanist: The Authorized Biography of Anton LaVey* (Los Angeles: Feral House, 1990), pp. 39–40.

33. LaVey, quoted in Burton H. Wolfe, *The Devil's Avenger* (New York: Pyramid Books, 1974), p. 52.

34. Barton, "About the Author," and *Secret Life*, pp. 61–68.

35. Bill Ellis, *Raising the Devil: Satanism, New Religions, and the Media* (Lexington: University Press of Kentucky, 2000), p. 169.

36. Anton Szandor LaVey, *The Satanic Bible* (New York: Avon, 1969), p. 31.

37. Barton, "About the Author."

38. LaVey, *Satanic Witch*, p. 266.

39. Nevill Drury, *The History of Magic in the Modern Age* (New York: Carroll & Graf, 1991), p. 192.

40. Russell, *History of Witchcraft*, p. 146.

41. LaVey, *Satanic Bible*, p. 21.

42. Drury, *History of Magic*, p. 190.

43. LaVey, *Satanic Bible*, p. 25.

44. Anton Szandor LaVey, "The World's Most Powerful Religion," The Church of Satan, www.churchofsatan.com/home.html.

45. "A Witness at Birth: Kenneth Anger on the Early Days of the Church of Satan," in Gavin Baddeley, *Lucifer Rising: Sin, Devil Worship, and Rock'n'Roll* (London: Plexus, 1999), p. 78.

46. LaVey, *Satanic Bible*, p. 53.

47. Baddeley, *Lucifer Rising*, p. 76.

48. LaVey, *Satanic Bible*, p. 110–13; Barton, *Secret Life*, p. 89.

49. Barton, *Secret Life*, p. 88.
50. Gabriel Legué, *La Messe Noire* (Paris: E. Fasquelle, 1903).
51. Anton Szandor LaVey, *The Satanic Rituals* (New York: Avon, 1972), p. 34.
52. Ibid., p. 49.
53. Ibid., pp. 43–51.
54. LaVey, *Satanic Bible*, p. 101.
55. LaVey, quoted in Barton, *Secret Life*, p. 125.
56. Baddeley, *Lucifer Rising*, p. 110.
57. LaVey, *Satanic Bible*, pp. 147–48.
58. LaVey, quoted in Barton, *Secret Life*, p. 172.
58. Steven Seidman, *Romantic Longings: Love in America, 1803–1989* (London: Routledge, 1991), p. 8.
60. Weeks, *Sex, Politics, and Society*, p. 255.
61. Ibid., p. 251.
62. Sheila Jeffreys, *Anticlimax: A Feminist Perspective on the Sexual Revolution* (Washington Square, NY: New York University Press, 1990), pp. 110–11. See also Linda Grant, *Sexing the Millennium: A Political History of the Sexual Revolution* (London: HarperCollins, 1993).
63. Julie Burchill, "Pleasure Principle," *Age* (Melbourne), June 6,1998.
64. Dennis Altman, *Global Sex* (Chicago: University of Chicago Press, 2001), p. 5.
65. LaVey, *Satanic Bible*, p. 66.
66. Baddeley, *Lucifer Rising*, p. 236.
67. LaVey, quoted in Lyons, *Satan Wants You*, p. 111.
68. LaVey, *Satanic Witch*, p. 235.
69. Ibid., p. 73.
70. Baddeley, *Lucifer Rising*, p. 236.
71. LaVey, quoted in Baddeley, *Lucifer Rising*, p. 76.
72. LaVey, *Satanic Witch*, pp. 140, 235.
73. Ibid., p. 144;
74. Ibid., p. 238.
75. Ibid., p. 125.
76. Barton, *Secret Life*, p. 114.
77. Blanche Barton, "Satanic Feminism," The Church of Satan, www.churchofsatan.com/home.html (1997).
78. Zeena LaVey, introduction to LaVey, *Satanic Witch*, n.p. "LaVey released *The Satanic Witch* at the height of feminist fervor. It was meant as an antidote to what LaVey has called the most aesthetically barren period in history" (Barton, *Secret Life*, p. 172).
79. Barton, *Secret Life*, p. 172.
80. Ibid.
81. Barton, "Satanic Feminism."
82. "Just a Horny L'il Devil: Coop's Reflections on the World," in Baddeley, *Lucifer Rising*, p. 245.
83. LaVey, *Satanic Witch*, p. 238.
84. Ibid., pp. 240–41.
85. Ibid., p. 237.
86. LaVey, quoted in Barton, *Secret Life*, p. 173.
87. Ibid., p. 172.
88. Barton, *Secret Life*, p. 225.
89. LaVey, *Satanic Bible*, p. 34.
90. Zeena LaVey, introduction to LaVey, *Satanic Witch*, n.p,
91. Isaac Bonewits, interviewed in the documentary "Witchcraft in America," Hex Productions and A&E Networks, Hearst/ABC/NBC (New York: A&E Home Video, 1993).
92. Bonewits, quoted in Ellis, *Raising the Devil*, p. 172.
93. Drury, *History of Magic*, p. 195.
94. Baddeley, *Lucifer Rising*, p. 102; cf. Drury, *History of Magic*, p. 196.
95. Ibid., p. 100.
96. Aquino, personal communication, quoted in Drury, *History of Magic*, p. 196.
97. Baddeley, *Lucifer Rising*, p. 102. Aquino's revelation resulted in *The Book of Coming Forth by Night*. See the Temple of Set Web site: www.xeper.org/pub/gil/xp_FS_gil. htm.
98. Altman, *Global Sex*, p. 105.
99. LaVey, *Satanic Bible*, p. 101.
100. Baddeley, *Lucifer Rising*, p. 238.

Religion, Local and Global

Essay:
Local and Global
Blurring the Boundaries

Some people say that our world has grown smaller; others say it has grown more complex. Whatever your interpretation, it's true that *something* has happened as travel has become easier for those who can afford it, as production and consumption have "gone global," and as staying in touch with someone across the world no longer means writing a letter that may arrive by ship and horseback six months later, but rather (again, for those who can afford such technology) turning on one's computer and opening up a video chat program. These changes and their consequences are often referred to as **globalization**. The process of globalization has affected everything from agriculture to economies to warfare, and from politics to art. Though many people regard religions as timeless and unchanging, globalization has also affected religion.

Some religions have had global goals from their inception. For instance, Jesus, the central figure of Christianity, commands his followers to go out and spread his teachings. Some branches of Islam and Buddhism are similarly inclined to share their wisdom with others. Other religions, such as some branches of Judaism, most of the family of traditions grouped under the term "Hinduism," and most indigenous religions, understand their practices and beliefs to be tied closely to their practitioners' ethnic identities. Such religions may actively oppose conversion. Still others, such as different branches of Judaism and Buddhism as well as some new religious movements, welcome converts but do not seek them out. But regardless of their attitudes toward conversion, all religions have been affected in one way or another by globalization.

Not all of these changes have been positive. After all, the beginnings of the globalization of capitalism lie in the European colonization of much of the rest of the globe. Battling each other for the natural resources, human resources, and supposedly "open" land in Asia, Africa, the Middle East, the Americas, and the Pacific, European forces over the course of several centuries committed both physical and cultural genocide around the world. In dividing the "newfound" territories among themselves, they redrew lines of ethnicity and nationality in ways that continue to disrupt political relations in many of these regions.

Culturally, one of the hallmarks of colonization was the effort to Europeanize and Christianize colonized peoples—to the extent that Europeans believed that was possible, which varied from continent to continent. Often these efforts were forcible, and sometimes they resulted in the partial or wholesale destruction of indigenous lifeways. More often, however, colonized people practiced what sociologists have come to term **brico-lage**: they drew from both European and indigenous traditions to create something entirely new. As discussed in Section 3, Vodou is one example of this pattern. African indigenous churches are another.

And the blending of religions went in more than one direction, though there are significant differences between being forced to convert to an invader's religion and choosing to adopt aspects of the indigenous religion of a region you've colonized. Again, where and when such borrowing took place was highly dependent on Europeans' attitude toward the particular peoples from whom they borrowed. Most people of European descent, for instance, viewed the indigenous religions of the Americas, Africa, and the Pacific as "primitive"; they believed the future of these religions was dim. On the other hand, in line with their view of Asians as the keepers of ancient wisdom, Europeans—and especially European scholars—were fascinated with Asian religions. As a result, in addition to *exporting* Christianity to Asian cultures, Europeans *imported* Asian religions, especially aspects of Hinduism and Buddhism, to their home countries. So unfamiliar were they with these religions that many of European descent initially had difficulty telling Hinduism and Buddhism apart. As a result, in the nineteenth century, most whites interested in Asian religions taught and practiced a rather garbled amalgam of Hinduism and Buddhism.

In the United States, a new global religious dynamic became especially apparent with the first World's Parliament of Religions at the 1893 World's Fair in Chicago, Illinois. While the indigenous traditions of Africa, the Pacific, and the Americas were relegated to zoo-like "villages" that purported to exhibit indigenous ways of life, leaders in several Asian religions were invited to share the stage with representatives of the **Abrahamic religions**. Some of these teachers stayed on in North America after the World's Fair, and developed a mostly wealthy, liberal, white following. Thus, Asian religions came to be exported as well, though in a very different context of power than that in which Christianity had been exported to Asia. Today, there is a thriving trade in religion, as teachers and practitioners migrate across the globe, although unequal economic and political relationships between countries still mean that such trade is not—perhaps never can be—neutral.

Globalization has brought with it both advantages and significant disadvantages for indigenous peoples. On the one hand, it has allowed for connections between leaders in various indigenous rights movements around the globe. The 2007 United Nations Declaration on the Rights of Indigenous Peoples is a prime example of the power such organizing can carry. On the other hand, globalization has often meant displacement from traditional lands. Such displacement, for many indigenous people, means more than simply the loss of a land base. Because their traditional lifeways (many argue that "religion" is an inappropriate term because tradition is woven into all aspects of life) center on particular geological structures and other physical aspects of one specific ecosystem, indigenous people find it extremely difficult to practice their traditions away from their ancestral lands. Thus, some have become part of a **localization** movement that has spread to encompass a wide variety of ethnic and religious groups. Localization focuses on connecting to one's immediate surroundings, and resisting globalization. Perhaps emblemized by the slogan, "Think globally, act locally," localization movements address a wide range of issues, from land rights and indigeneity to buying locally-produced foods. However, although religious leaders ranging from Christian to neo-pagan to indigenous are vocal supporters of localization movements, we have not yet seen a strong localization of religion outside of indigenous traditions. Many religions, it seems, are happy being global.

An interesting blurring of the lines between local and global is increasingly taking place; it's referred to as **transnationalism**. Marked by ongoing connections between sending and receiving countries, transnationalism complicates the older narrative of immigration as a final and complete break with one's home country. Under transnationalism, people, ideas, and objects flow back and forth across national borders. So do religions, in such forms as religious leaders who travel from the home country to teach their far-flung followers; religious pilgrims who travel to the home country to visit sacred sites; and religious paraphernalia imported from the home country. There is even virtual transnationalism now, as sociologist Peggy Levitt demonstrates in her discussion of the "new religious architecture" formed by religious transnationalism: in Brazil one can watch a Portuguese-language Mass taking place in Massachusetts, and eagerly seek out familiar faces among the Brazilian-American worshippers.

Like globalization, transnationalism is changing the face of religion around the world. In order to capitalize on the potential of globalization, some religions are following the lead of transnational corporations in their organization and activities. Levitt describes three such models. In the Catholic model, the presence of a clearly-defined and tightly run global hierarchy combines with national interests to create situations where Catholic funds follow Catholic people in their migrations. In the Protestant model, a less tightly organized but nonetheless somewhat centralized religion (the Southern Baptist Convention) has migrated to Brazil through missionary work, has taken on a distinctly Brazilian stamp, and has been re-exported back to the United States in forms that some non-Brazilian leaders in the United States find unusual—for good or for ill. And in Levitt's national model, some groups retain their national character but work transnationally as their followers relocate around the globe. Finally, Levitt proposes that we recognize a different model of transnational religion as well: that of "flexible specialization." Like some transnational corporations (Levitt gives the example of the clothing company Benetton), some religions are decentralized, allowing them to take different shapes according to the cultures, and subcultures, in which they find themselves. This strategy allows for significant innovation in the transnational "religious market," though it also sometimes produces misunderstandings or even competition among different members of the same religious organization as they work together to respond to different religious "niche markets."

Levitt's models focus especially on the flow of religions across borders, but of course people travel back and forth across those borders as well. One question that has intrigued students of immigration is how and why immigrants' religious practices change when they move to a new and often religiously different country. We know, for instance, that in the strongly Protestant context of the United States, many people from other religions have had to "Protestantize" their practices in order to fit in. In the nineteenth century, large numbers of Jews immigrated from Germany (earlier in the century) and from Eastern Europe (later in the century). Whereas in their home communities the synagogue had been a male-dominated space in which men stood to intone their prayers, in the U.S. context the more liberal branches of Judaism soon developed benches akin to church pews in which both men and women sat, songs akin to hymns, and even a weekly sermon and Sunday school for the children. Likewise, whereas in many majority-Muslim countries the mosque is a place for occasional visitation, especially for women, in the U.S. context the mosque has become a place to attend at least weekly, if not more often.

Furthermore, for many immigrants, communal religious spaces become a form of community center, offering classes for the first generation (those who were adults when they came to the receiving country) in the dominant language of their new country, in culture, in job-seeking, and the like. As immigrant communities stay on and grow in the receiving country, these religious community centers come to offer classes for the second generation (the first one born in the United States) and their third-generation children, as well. Whereas their parents and grandparents take classes in the new language, culture, and politics, the second and third generations might take classes in their ancestral language and religion, or classes on cooking in the traditional style. In this way, while religious communities help first-generation immigrants to assimilate, they offer the more assimilated second and third generations the opportunity to return, in part, to the culture of their ancestors.

As sociologist Ilana Akresh explains, this function as community center is one explanation for the increase in religious attendance among recent immigrants to the United States. Another explanation is the Protestantization described above: in a country where attendance at religious services is generally equated to "practicing" religion (thus the emphasis on religious attendance in survey research, for instance), one might shift from home practice toward greater involvement in a religious institution. Moving from a context where your religion is in the majority to one where it is a minority also has an effect. When your religion is no longer all around you, it becomes important to seek it out more often and more formally, in order to get the same level of exposure. All the same, it's worth noting the potential problems with the Protestant assumptions of much survey research on immigration and religion. Not all religions center on communal practice, for instance, or on weekly attendance. Therefore, attendance at "religious services" is a problematic measure of a person's religiosity outside of Protestantism and the more Protestantized religions in the United States. For instance, someone who tends a home altar daily but only goes to the local temple every few months will appear as relatively irreligious on such a measure, whereas someone who has shifted her religious practice to the temple-as-community-center will appear much more religious.

The underlying question here is one of **assimilation**: the process whereby immigrants become part of the varied cultures of their new home. Although this word has overtones of the loss of one's ancestral culture and wholesale adoption of the new culture, as sociologists use it "assimilation" has greater nuance. We can think, for example, of at least two processes of assimilation: **adhesive assimilation** and **segmented assimilation**. The former is the common image of assimilation: one *adheres* one's traditional culture to the new culture, becoming over the course of a few generations a part of that new culture (and transforming it in return). In segmented assimilation, however, because of greater ties or similarities to a particular *segment*, or subculture, of the receiving country, an immigrant group joins that subculture rather than assimilating into the larger culture. Sometimes religious similarities drive this form of assimilation, but in many countries it is due to other factors, which lead that society to see the immigrant group as more similar to a subculture than they are assimilable into the mainstream. Often in Western countries this apparent similarity is based on perceived race and on experiences of racism in the receiving country. Thus, for instance, many Caribbean immigrants to the United States who "read" (are socially perceived) as black assimilate within African American communities rather than within the heavily white mainstream culture.

Of course, this distinction between segmented and adhesive assimilation also relies on some problematic assumptions, the first of which is that there is a clearly distinguished mainstream into which one might assimilate. In the United States, for example, as in much of Europe, the so-called mainstream is really middle-class, white culture—a culture that remains fairly exclusive for a number of reasons. Yet this fact doesn't simply mean that all immigrants of color, poor immigrants, or non-Protestant immigrants will assimilate into a subculture that is completely separate from the mainstream, because as social theorists have taught us, it is nearly impossible for subcultures to shield their members from influence by the mainstream culture. We might instead say, then, that there are numerous sites and strategies for adjustment to a new culture. The young German Muslim women whom Synnøve Bendixsen studied are a case in point. Seeking what they term a "pure" form of Islam—that is, one that is (impossibly) separated from all cultural influence, these young women are grappling in creative ways with what it means to be both German and Muslim, bridging two cultures that often both see themselves as incompatible. As Bendixsen points out, it is in part the individualism pervading Western cultures —including Western religions—that allows these women to develop their own versions of Islam that are suited to their own cultural and subcultural locations.

Religion and Violence, Local and Global

So far, this chapter's discussion of globalization, localization, and transnationalism has focused primarily on peaceful interactions. But most religions have developed violent movements at some point during their history—and in most cases, they have developed violent movements recently, sometimes in direct response to globalization. This section explores the links between religion and violence on both local and global levels.

Western stereotypes of religion, or at least of what many Westerners term "spirituality," are generally peaceful. Many Westerners believe that "true" religion promotes understanding, generosity, and wisdom; from this perspective, the involvement of religion in violence is an aberration, a corruption of the essence of religion. Yet, religion and violence have been intertwined for millennia, especially though not only in the context of universalizing religions, which claim sole access to ultimate truth and reality. From a historical perspective, the contemporary violence we see associated with many religions is simply the most recent manifestation of a well-known propensity. On the other hand, some of this violence takes new forms, and some, old forms. Nancy Nason-Clark's ground-breaking research and activism in the area of religion and domestic violence tracks contemporary forms of a well-established, local form of religious violence and religious healing.

In the article included in this collection, Nason-Clark draws on her extensive research to present Christian faith-based approaches to domestic violence from the perspective of the survivor, the perpetrator, the counselor, and the community. Christianity here appears as a double-edged sword: on the one hand, Nason-Clark makes clear that abusive partners who are Christian use certain interpretations of Christian teachings as support for their violence—such as the belief, held by some Christians, that wives should be submissive to their husbands. On the other hand, for devoutly Christian survivors of domestic violence, Christianity can also be an important resource in healing. Here again we see the character of religion as both powerful and malleable.

The theme of religious responses to violence continues on both the local and the global levels in Janet Jacobs's study of ritual responses to the Holocaust. It is often said that genocide is a modern crime, that although mass murder has been committed throughout much of human history, the extermination of an entire people was not feasible until the development of modern weapons, transportation, and large-scale, global warfare. If this claim is true, then the Holocaust itself is a form of religious (and ethnic) violence that is beholden to globalization. And the global diaspora of Holocaust survivors also speaks to global politics and networks. Yet, the experience of surviving the Holocaust is very much a local one, both in terms of the differences in survivors' experiences depending on the region in which they lived and in terms of the very personal and familial impact of genocide. In Jacobs's study of the ritual transmission of trauma, and the ritual innovations of adult children of Holocaust survivors in an attempt to counter that trauma, we see the local and the global intertwining in ways not often articulated in the literature on globalization.

These first two examples of the connections between religion and violence, local and global, offer a fairly fluid and nuanced picture: Christianity is involved in both the perpetration of and the healing from domestic violence; Jewishness made one a target of the Holocaust but also served to express and eventually to resist that trauma. In other cases, though, the connections between religion and violence are more unambiguous. It is easy to come up with examples of religiously-motivated violence, from inter-religious wars to large-scale terrorist attacks to the individual terrorism of the religiously-motivated assassin. Some religious groups have been involved wholesale in violence, whether directed at them, by them, or a combination of both. In some cases the violence has been suicidal, as with Peoples Temple in Jonestown, Guyana and with the Heaven's Gate movement; in other cases it has been homicidal, as with the sarin gas attacks perpetrated by Aum Shinrikyo in the Tokyo subway; and in some cases it has been of more complex causes, such as with the Branch Davidians in Waco, Texas. Especially after the long siege of the Branch Davidians' home by federal forces in 1993, and the resulting firestorm that killed most of those in the building, scholars and others have been asking, "How do we predict when a religious group will become violent?" Contrary to popular belief, the fact that a group is reclusive, anti-social, or simply new and unfamiliar is insufficient to predict violence. In fact, most scholars of religion and violence believe that we *can't* predict religious violence. However, we can identify risk factors that, when properly understood, can help to diffuse a potentially violent situation.

Catherine Wessinger suggests that millennialism is a key factor in predicting religious violence. Not all millennial religions are violent; in fact, most aren't. However, as Wessinger points out, certain forms of millennialism are likely risk factors in religious violence, given the right situations. She distinguishes between *progressive* and *catastrophic* millennialism, the former being a belief in a gradual, peaceful change in the world and the latter a belief that the change will come suddenly and often violently. Even here, though we might assume from these definitions that catastrophic millennialism is inherently violent, it is important to be aware of context. For example, many people in the United States believe in catastrophic millennialism without becoming violent. Wessinger adds an important element here: both history and theory have shown that violence becomes more likely with catastrophic millennial groups that are internally *fragile* or externally *assaulted*. With this knowledge, we can't always prevent violence, but we can at least hope to lessen its likelihood through taking action to avoid assaulting (or appearing to assault) some millennial groups and through reacting cautiously to the fragility of others.

Yet, violence has become a global issue, and despite Wessinger's analysis of Aum Shinrikyo most of her examples are Western; indeed, most are from the U.S. context. Richard King's article, in challenging the Western bias of religion and violence scholars, closes this volume by bringing us back full-circle to the problem of defining religion. King notes that other prominent scholars of religion and violence, such as sociologist Mark Juergensmeyer and historian of religions Bruce Lincoln, approach their studies from the modern, Western perspective that religion is a separate institution that can be clearly distinguished from the secular, and that religion centers on morality and ethics. These assumptions, especially the second one, owe a great deal to the European Enlightenment. In their focus on reason as the height of human activity, Enlightenment thinkers decried much of religious practice as irrational "superstition." But they were willing to see one redeeming aspect in some religions: their focus on morality and ethics, both (to Enlightenment thinkers) products of reason. It was this perspective that led some European cultures, in the wake of the Enlightenment, to lessen the extent of their anti-Semitism and allow Jews to assimilate (provided they relinquished those ritual practices that Enlightenment thinkers believed were not related to reason).

Yet, as Section 1 discussed, not all religions stress ethics, morality, or even belief. Furthermore, many religions intertwine with the lives of their practitioners in such a way that those practitioners' lives cannot be easily separated into "secular" and "religious" dimensions. What becomes, then, of the association between "religion" and violence when, with Talal Asad and Richard King, we let go of the idea that there is the same, central essence to all religions? First, such a move challenges the automatic association between religion and violence (as King notes, whether this association refers to all religion as "bad," or to religion when it "goes bad," is irrelevant). Second, and perhaps most importantly, deconstructing the narrative of the "world religions" and of "religion and violence" forces us to take a closer look at all of the factors that play into different uses of violence.

The fire and deaths at the Branch Davidians' home in Waco were not due simply to the Branch Davidians' religion, nor simply to the aspects of FBI culture that viewed the Branch Davidians as a "cult," a perversion of Christianity, and an enemy of the state. Instead, the deaths—as best we can tell with evidence missing—were the result of a fatal combination of conflicting worldviews, suspicion, miscommunication, and, to some extent, subterfuge. Religion was part of the story, but only part of it. Likewise, and as King points out, the terrorist attacks in the United States on September 11, 2001 were only partly—perhaps even minimally—about religion. They had much more to do with the international economic and political policies of the United States, and the disastrous results of those policies for many Arab people, Muslim or not. Moving away from theories about the universality of religion forces us to examine less comfortable truths about the world around us. At its best, this is what sociology can bring to the study of religion.

Conclusions: Future Directions in the Sociology of Religion

In this volume, I've presented a picture of the past and present states of the sociological study of religion. In concluding, it seems only fitting to speculate about possible future directions in this field. These include an increased empirical focus on globalization and transnationalism, more work outside of Europe and the United States, more work on religions beyond Christianity and Western NRMs, moving away from Christocentrism and Eurocentrism, and paying increased attention to the social and religious margins in addition to the mainstream.

As this essay has made clear, globalization and transnationalism are prominent and important phenomena today. They affect many aspects of our lives, including religion. However, outside of studies on the religious lives of immigrants and on religion and violence, sociologists have produced relatively little in-depth work on these phenomena despite repeated statements of their importance. Peggy Levitt leads us in the right direction by pointing to the transnational connections of religious paraphernalia as well as religious people, but we stand to learn a great deal by studying the wider patterns of consumption of such religious objects and patronage of religious leaders, rather than focusing solely on their (also important) impact in communities of recent immigrants. We need to think more intensively about the impacts of globalization and transnationalism on the shape of religion today around the world, and on the recent history of religions.

Such a change in thinking would mean, in part, more work outside of Europe and the United States. While some might argue that an international focus is the realm of anthropology, it's important to remember that the division of labor between anthropology and sociology originated in attempts to study what we might call the "other within" and the "other without." Anthropology took responsibility for the "other without"—largely, those colonized by European countries—while sociology focused on the "other within"—recent immigrants, the poor, and the like. As the two fields have developed they have increasingly come to overlap in both topics and methods. Furthermore, both anthropology and sociology have been forced to change by those "others" who have themselves been trained in these fields and begun doing research. What do terms like "other within" and "other without" mean when the scholar is not from European, global North cultures? From such a perspective, study of the global North should be the subject of anthropology, and study of the global South the subject of sociology. Thus, the topical dividing line between these two fields has significantly eroded. Important differences remain in both theory and methods, but it is no longer considered inappropriate for sociologists to work outside of the global North.

Despite this shift in sociological areas of study, among sociologists of religion neither theory nor research practice has caught up with the change. Many of our survey instruments are still Christocentric—measuring religiosity by frequency of attendance and prayer, belief in God, and other questions that inadequately reflect many practitioners' experiences beyond Christianity. And some of our most important theoretical debates also betray this narrowness of definition. Take secularization, for example. The main source of debate in this area today is over whether "religion" has died out or shifted under the economic and cultural conditions of (post-)modernity. The arguments on both sides of the debate rely heavily on large-scale surveys of entire (white-dominated, culturally Christian) countries, as well as small-scale, in-depth studies of (white, culturally Christian) populations. In part because of a belief that immigrant communities aren't from "modern" countries and haven't been in the receiving countries long enough to be affected by modernity, such communities are neglected in these studies. Yet, to claim that, for instance, Europe has become secular is to erase the presence of devoutly religious Christians, Jews, Muslims, Hindus, Buddhists, and practitioners of other religions who are present but often invisible and segregated in European populations, thus implicitly defining Europe as being still the domain of whites.

Socially marginalized populations need to be as much a part of the sociology of religion as are the dominant groups; otherwise, we produce an incomplete picture of social reality. In fact, as a number of fields have learned, we stand to learn a great deal by studying from the margins—in this case, the margins of religion. In order to continue growing as a field, and in order to produce a fuller picture of what exactly religion is and how it interacts with society, sociologists need to study from the margins of religion. This means studying phenomena that are considered marginally religious in the social mainstream, such as new religious movements or "quasi-religious" cultural phenomena; studying those people considered marginally religious (such as those who call themselves "spiritual but not religious"); and studying people who are socially marginalized (the poor, people of color, immigrants, lesbian/gay/bisexual/transgender/queer people, and the like). In an interconnected yet still unjust world, sociologists of religion have the opportunity to shift relations of power by producing new systems of knowledge.

Extended Application

Downtown in the small town where I live, there used to be a Christian supply store. It sold everything from Bibles, to Christian-themed films and music, to t-shirts. Although we don't have supply stores for any other religions, I have no doubt that people here buy religiously-themed items online on a pretty regular basis. In a large, religiously diverse city one might find many different stores that carry what scholars call religious *material culture*: that is, material items used in religious practice. Many cities have a range from occult supply stores to *botánicas* (stores that carry herbs and other supplies for spiritualists and practitioners of the African blended religions) to South Asian markets that carry images of Hindu deities. Cities with such a diversity of religious commodities available for sale are evidence of a lengthy history of globalization and transnationalism, offering as they do supplies that come from around the world, for religious practitioners who come from around the world.

There's another aspect of religious transnationalism and commodification, though, beyond the use of religious material culture by practitioners of a religion, and that's the use of such material culture by those who don't identify with the religion. People who don't consider themselves Buddhist, for example, but believe that the Buddha was a wise being to be honored, may have statues of the Buddha in their homes or offices. There are even Buddhas for your car, and starter kits called "Buddha-in-a-Box"! In recent years, the image of the elephantine Hindu god Ganesh has been a popular decoration for everything from tote bags to dorm room walls—used most often by people who don't consider themselves Hindu. In fact, there is a history of the citizens of colonizing countries collecting the (often stolen) sacred objects of a people they had colonized, and certainly Europe and European-derived cultures such as white North Americans and Australians, have been among those guilty of such appropriation. In many cases, those sacred objects ended up in museums as "cultural artifacts." Some have been repatriated—that is, returned to the peoples from which they were taken—whereas others remain the subject of controversy.

In some ways, such controversy is a part of the tension described in this chapter between globalization and localization; and, in part, it derives from the inevitable dynamics of power that attend that tension. Part of the power-laden rhetoric of globalization is that of cultural sharing: we are all global citizens now, the logic goes, so it is appropriate for museums around the world to honor, recognize, and teach about cultures beyond their own, in part by displaying objects those cultures hold sacred. The logic of localization, on the other hand, argues that such objects belong with the culture they came from, in the place they came from. Significantly, it is often the cultures with which the objects originated that argue for the localization perspective. So should the situation be "finders, keepers"? Some would say yes, especially on the basis that museums have often paid great sums of money to acquire sacred objects, and have often bought them completely legitimately from art dealers, other museums, or private owners. Others would say no, because the context in which the sacred objects were taken, or even given, to their initial owners outside the originating culture was one of unequal power. Can a "gift" given under duress, or an object sold to buy food for the starving, really be considered to be traded fairly?

One way of addressing these challenges is through legislation. At the international level, the United Nations can encourage countries to return objects of value to other countries; at the national level, the process can have greater persuasiveness. For example, in 1990 the U.S. Congress passed NAGPRA, the North American Graves Protection and Repatriation Act. This act required all museums and federal agencies to investigate the cultural origins of their Native American artifacts and skeletal remains. In the case of artifacts of sacred or cultural significance, excluding human remains and "funerary objects," the museums were required to determine whether a particular tribe could be identified to whom the artifacts belonged, and to make that information publicly available. If a tribe requested the artifacts, they were to be returned. In the case of human remains or other objects associated with death, the museums were to seek out the tribe to which these materials belonged, if possible, and return them immediately.

Some readers may wonder, why was NAGPRA necessary? Why is religious material culture so important that the U.S. Congress passed a law requiring its repatriation? Certainly, some have argued, there are ornate altarpieces from Roman Catholic churches in many museums around the world, and Roman Catholics don't seem to be bothered. So what's the difference? It's two-fold. First, the altarpieces generally were not acquired by theft or threat. Second, they generally are not held in the museums of countries that have invaded and colonized Roman Catholic countries. Third, many of the most controversial museum holdings are of great cultural significance to some or all of the affected people. Imagine someone digging up your great-grandmother and displaying her skeleton in a museum, or stealing a Torah scroll or a rosary that's been in your congregation or your family for generations, and then putting it on display.

But there are examples of such controversies over material culture even among European countries. Perhaps the most well-known when I wrote this book was the struggle over the ownership of the Parthenon marbles on display in the British Museum in London. These marbles, including pieces of columns from the Greek Parthenon as well as statues and friezes, have been in the British museum since the early nineteenth century, when they were removed from the Parthenon by the British Ambassador to Constantinople (now Istanbul) and sold to the British government. The British Museum, having acquired the marbles fairly itself, argues that it does not need to repatriate the marbles; furthermore, for many years it argued that Greece did not have the proper facilities in which to store and exhibit them. In 2007, Greece completed a museum designed in part to house the marbles, yet the British government continues to argue for its own rightful ownership. As a more politically and economically powerful country than Greece, Britain is able to retain the marbles, at least for now, against the protests of its politically weaker neighbor to the south.

Just as we can't prevent globalization, which has been in process for several centuries, but must instead grapple with it as a fact of our current reality, so too we can't easily resolve the debates over religious material culture in the context of the mutually opposing movements of globalization and localization. What we can do, as sociologists and global citizens, is observe religious material culture around us. Where do you see religious material culture in your daily life? Do you make use of it? Do you see others—your family members or friends, for example—making use of it? Where do you see evidence of globalization in religious material culture? If you think about it, in the United States even religions such as the various branches of Protestantism that people tend to think of as uniquely American are evidence of globalization, because they developed from the earlier forms of Protestantism brought over by the early British invaders of North America. Do you see uses of religious material culture that are separated from the practitioners of religion? Even tea containers, as one of my students has pointed out, use images and words that evoke a diffuse sense of "Asian spirituality" to market their product.[1] What are the ethics of using such products, or of encouraging their use? Is religion something to be shared with everyone, or is there some aspect of cultural ownership to religious objects and images? These are the knotty questions that the globalization of religion has brought to many areas of the world. Your answer to them may depend not only on your religion—whether it's one that advocates sharing one's practices and beliefs with others, or one that argues your religion should stay within your culture—but also on your social location. In other words, do you belong to a religion or culture that has experienced repeated appropriation by others against your will, or do you belong to a religion or culture that is more likely to have engaged in such appropriation?

Regardless of your answers to the questions above, you can observe that religion and globalization are central aspects of the world around us. What impact this will have on religions and cultures in the future remains to be seen, but there is no doubt that it will be significant.

Exercises

1. Discuss the following with a classmate, friend, or family member: if King is correct that the most significant motivations for the September 11, 2001 attacks in the United States were economic and political, why have so many people, especially but not only in the United States, seen them as primarily religious?
2. Now that you've learned a lot about religion from reading this book, design a religion of your own. Imagine that a billionaire has offered a large start-up grant to the person with the most potentially successful proposal for a new religion, and write a grant application. Don't forget to name your religion!

Note

1. Thanks to Evan Randall for this insight.

26

A New Religious Architecture

Peggy Levitt

JAGDISH CHANDRA MAHARAJ, the leader of the Bhagat community, is visiting his followers. He left Elizabeth, New Jersey, at the crack of dawn to drive to his cousin's home in Chelmsford, Massachusetts. There he will meet for lunch and prayers with a small group of his closest associates before he leads a Janmashtami celebration for the entire Bhagat community in honor of Lord Krishna's birthday.

The past few years have not been easy for the Maharaj. I first visited him at his home in Punyiad, a small town about thirty kilometers from Baroda, in 1998. The condition of the road leading there was my first clue that all was not well. Once we turned off the highway, it took nearly half an hour to travel the less-than-two-mile stretch because the track was in such bad condition. When we got there, we were ushered into a spacious entrance hall, almost empty, except for a large, flat swing where the Maharaj receives visitors, and a few wooden sofas and chairs arranged near it. The building's dark coolness was a welcome respite from the midday sun.

The Maharaj is a slight, soft-spoken man with thinning gray hair. He appears more diminutive than he is because of his modest, unassuming manner and impish smile. After his wife served us lunch, we went into a back room, where he and I talked with help from a translator, while his son and advisers listened. No, he said, the Bhagats who go to America do not change. They continue to

live according to Indian values. They come back to visit him each time they return to India. Still, he clearly realized that changes were happening and that he needed to stay in better touch with his followers. He showed me a copy of a mimeographed, four-page magazine he had put together that he mailed to Bhagats around the world. The last page even included a message to the children of immigrants, written in broken English by his son and heir apparent, telling them how much the community needed them and urging them to stay within its fold.

During my second visit, it was clear that the Maharaj's troubles had only gotten worse. I met more and more Bhagats who spent much more time being Swadhyayees or Swaminarayan than they did in their own community. They complained that the Maharaj was weak. He refused to put on the stole of the guru, the ceremony that makes him the official head of their group, preferring instead to think of himself as doing social service. The community was in flux, they said, and his *kirtens* or lectures did not offer them much helpful advice.

Yet people continued to support the Bhagat samaj because "they were disappointed in Jagdish, not in their community." In Bodeli, we visited a new marriage hall covered with plaques honoring donors in the United States and the United Kingdom. During my next trip in 2001, we visited a school construction site that included a special English-language classroom to prepare kids to emigrate. The Maharaj knew about these efforts and gave his blessing, but he did not supervise them directly. Chapters of the Udah Bhagat Society, which includes Bhagats living in other districts near Baroda as well as Bodeli, had each formed their own trusts or charitable foundations, so they could collect and administer their own funds.

Loyalty was at a low point. When I asked the Maharaj if this "walkout" bothered him, he responded confidently that it did not as long as his followers came back to him. when they died. Even Bhagats who have been Swadhyayees during their lives, he said, will come back to be buried according to Bhagat traditions. He felt no need to proselytize. He was interested in quality not quantity. When you have the best product, he asserted, the customers come to you.

Many of his followers apparently felt otherwise. In addition to their dissatisfaction with his leadership, they also had concerns about money management. They disagreed with his refusal to officiate at intermarriages between Bhagats and people from outside the community, or at the thread ceremonies of their children. Times were changing, they said. They needed a visionary who could go with the flow and teach them what their tradition had to say about living in today's world. They still wanted to participate in Bhagat rituals, but more and more they wanted to do so without this Maharaj at the helm.

Leadership in the Bhagat Samaj is a family affair. The top decision makers in India and the United States are all related. It's a matter of trust. The leader of the community in the United States, who officiates at all formal celebrations, is the Maharaj's first cousin. Another first cousin, who lives in Baroda, also travels between India and the United States. More distant relatives also direct local chapters up and down the eastern seaboard. On his way back to New Jersey, the Maharaj would stop in Danbury and Stamford, where there were other Bhagat communities. He also planned to visit followers in Chicago, Florida, and Washington.

The house where the Maharaj lunched was very much like Pratik and Dipa's new home. Outside, young children and teenagers dressed in their best Indian clothing played in the driveway. As I entered, a group of women scurried to finish the meal they were preparing for the thirty-odd guests. The Maharaj was sitting in the living room with his wife. We ate lunch sitting on the floor and then, as in Punyiad, a small group of men accompanied the Maharaj into another room where we could talk.

He decided to visit America, he said, because he needed to be in closer contact with his followers. He was losing his grip and had to do something about it. He showed me a four-color booklet he brought with him explaining the teachings of Ram Kabir, written in Gujarati and translated into difficult-to-understand English. He hoped that by giving these out and meeting his followers, they would return to him.

The Janmashtami celebration was supposed to begin at 3:30 p.m. at an elementary school in Lowell. At 3:15, we were still in Chelmsford discussing the Bhagat community's future. The school was located about half an hour away. I left to go over and was greeted by what had become a familiar scene at many Gujarati celebrations. A small group rushed around frantically, trying to set up the audiovisual equipment before the guest of honor arrived. Others stood outside chatting in the parking lot. The children entertained themselves by running back and forth in the auditorium. Two sections of chairs, where men and women sit separately, had been arranged in rows facing the stage. The women not busy preparing the communal meal sat on their side, talking quietly together and admiring each other's children. Since some families came from far away and many are distantly related to each other, religious and cultural celebrations double as family reunions.

The word that comes to mind to describe how the Bhagats greeted their leader is "lukewarm." When his caravan finally arrived, everyone went out to the parking lot. He and his wife walked between two lines of chanting followers who showered flower petals on them. But the Maharaj's shyness and his followers' ambivalence were painfully apparent. The procession moved on to the auditorium stage, where a green carpet, strewn with flowers, had been laid out. The men gathered, sitting cross-legged, around the Maharaj. Some of the women also joined them on the stage and sat behind them. Various percussion instruments were distributed. The next hour was spent singing *Bhajans* or devotional hymns. The Maharaj was supposed to lead these, but again he was more than happy to pass the microphone to anyone who offered. When he did lead, his mumbling was barely audible.

Still, the group's prayers were spirited. People closed their eyes and swayed to the music. By the end of the day, the Maharaj had accomplished what he came for. By sharing prayers and a meal with his followers, he helped reaffirm their ties to the Bhagat community. The next day, he would be off doing similar damage control in Connecticut, in the hope that by the time he returned, the Bhagat Samaj would remain intact despite the widespread dispersion of its members.

The Maharaj's problem is not unique. Lots of religious communities have members around the world who are struggling to figure out how to belong to several places at once. Sending and receiving country political and cultural groups compete for their loyalties. The Maharaj is doing what many communities do: constructing a new religious architecture and way of working that responds better to the reality of members' everyday lives. Religion already comes equipped with messages and rituals that help followers negotiate the many layers of the global experience. Religious organizations are also changing to reflect that reality, creating dense, intricate webs linking local, regional, and national players. In the process, they invent new structures, job descriptions, and membership requirements, and reorder the organizational chart.

When you go to your local candy store to buy a Nestlé Crunch bar, you know that even if you just walked across the street to make your purchase, what you bought was probably manufactured hundreds of miles away. Not only that, global production and distribution networks make the same candy bar available in Mexico, Milan, or Manila. The McDonaldization of the world is old news.

Similarly, if you walk down the street in any immigrant neighborhood, you're likely to find homeland political party offices. The Dominican Revolutionary Party and the Party of Dominican Liberation, for example, organize their immigrant supporters into local chapters, citywide zones, regional sections, and national organizations that take orders from the national headquarters in Santo Domingo. Each party also belongs to an international network of like-minded groups. In the Dominican Revolutionary Party's case, the Socialist International—an umbrella for 161 social democratic, socialist, and labor political parties and organizations—supports its efforts and is supported by them. The Indian Bharatiya Janata Party and the Brazilian Worker's Party function in a similar way. Domestic politics, then, is not just produced inside the nation. It is also produced outside it by members of the diaspora who vote, lobby, and finance election campaigns as well as by international political organizations.

Increasingly, religious organizations are taking their place alongside these global corporate and political actors. Worldwide production and distribution networks also manufacture religious goods. The local mosque or church is just one brick in this extensive global religious architecture. Some structures simply connect immigrants with people in their homelands. Others link them to fellow believers around the world. As a result, like politics and economics, domestic religion is both transnationally and nationally produced.

THE TRANSNATIONAL RELIGIOUS CORPORATION: THE CATHOLIC VARIETY

Every Sunday morning, groups of families in Governador Valadares gather in their living rooms to watch the Catholic Mass broadcast on their local television. But this Mass is not taking place in Valadares or any other Brazilian city. It is a recording of the Portuguese Mass held at Saint Joseph's Church in Somerville, Massachusetts, where many Brazilian immigrants worship. People in Brazil watch, hoping to see their relatives.

These worshippers belong to one kind of transnational religious organization: a transnational religious corporation. Transnational religious corporations are eminently familiar. The Catholic Church is the "jewel in their crown." Workers around the world, at all levels of the organization, take orders from the same chief executive officer in Rome. The organizational chart and lines of authority are clear.[1] Workers fulfill similar functions and abide by the same employee manual. Worshippers in Valadares and Massachusetts use the same weekly prayer supplements. When parishes in Brazil earmark their collections for the homeless, parishioners in Boston mount a better neighborhood campaign so that congregations everywhere work on similar problems.

When migrants circulate in and out of parishes in the United States, Ireland, or Brazil, they are extending and customizing this powerful, well-established corporate structure. In each case, migration makes some aspects of organizational life transnational while others remain inside national borders. How the national and the transnational combine varies by organizational level. Local sending and receiving, country parishes in Brazil and Boston may work together, but the Brazilian and U.S. National Catholic Conferences may not. Likewise, migrants from Valadares sometimes participate in homeland activities, not because

they feel loyal to their sending parishes, but because they still want to be part of the Brazilian national church.

This was the case of Inishowen. The big church in Carndonough sits high above the town on a big, flat, open hilltop. Father Charles has served in the parish for over twenty years. Yes, he says, he knew many people had migrated to Boston. It was true there was a long tradition of that. But it didn't make much difference for the everyday life of the parish. "A couple of years ago, some fellows in Boston raised money to help replace the cupola, but that was about it." Instead, unlike many Latin American migrants who become the principal patrons of their sending community churches, the Irish church engaged in cross-border activities designed to reinforce migrants' ties to the national church as a whole.[2]

The New York City archdiocese, knew it needed help when the "new Irish" arrived en masse in the early 1980s. It turned to the Irish Episcopal Commission on Emigrants in Dublin, charged with caring for Irish emigrants around the world. The commission responded by loaning priests to New York. As more immigrants fanned out along the East Coast and to the Midwest, more priests followed.

That is how Father Patrick and Father Mike came to Boston. There were just too many Irish singles and newly married couples with young children who needed care. It was too much for Sister Lynn and Father Matthew, the team already working for the Boston archdiocese. Oddly enough, Patrick and Mike landed at Saint Brendan's because there were extra rooms at the rectory, not because migrants from Inishowen have been worshipping there for decades.

Father Mike said he decided to come to Boston because the Catholic Church is "a global organization and we are supposed to take care of Catholics everywhere." Father Patrick came because those abroad "still belong to the Irish family." Just as families do not abandon their relatives who move away, neither should churches or governments.

I don't know if you are a mother or not, but a mother doesn't say she is no longer responsible if her children go away. You want to know that if something happens, someone will be there who is attuned to their needs and can help them. You want to know that if something goes wrong, you can phone up and someone will watch out for them. A mother doesn't act like that, and neither should churches or the government. Irish emigrants show they still want to remain part of Ireland by the investments they make, the new homes they build, and the skills and ideas they import. It would be foolish of us to abandon our sons and daughters just because they no longer live among us. They still contribute so much to our lives.

The two priests set about getting to know the community by going to Gaelic football games and visiting the bars along Dorchester Avenue. Pretty soon, they set up a support group for new mothers, Irish-language classes, and a social club for singles, all under the umbrella of the new Irish Pastoral Center. They also filled in at christenings and funerals because the parish was short staffed.

It became clear to them early on that some people "had one foot in Ireland," so their programs should as well. "We talked about it and we decided that we needed to be where the people were," said Father Patrick. "If they wanted to be part of the parishes where they lived, we needed to help them. If they wanted to stay part of Ireland, we needed to help them do that too." At the premarital classes he offered, which you have to take if you want to be married in the church, he discussed how to get a mortgage or open a bank account in Boston and Ireland. He talked about getting a job and paying for college in both places. And because so many people actually go back to Ireland to tie the knot, the Pastoral Center assigned someone to help them complete the paperwork before they leave.

The Boston archdiocese and the Irish Catholic Church split the cost of the priests' living expenses.

The priests report to superiors in both countries. The Pastoral Center is also part of the Irish Apostolate/USA, a national umbrella group of programs for immigrants. Father Chris, an Irish priest working in Washington, DC, had to get permission to create it from the Irish Episcopal Commission on Emigrants and the National Council of Catholic Bishops. In the early 1990s, he went to Ireland to talk to people in the government about his concerns. "The people in America are not American citizens," he told the officials he met with. "They still need help. Without citizenship or a green card, they are very vulnerable. If the church does not help them, they will be in bad shape." From his point of view, the priests over in America don't work for the U.S. government or the church but for their Irish equivalents.

By 2001, the Irish Apostolate/USA was running programs up and down the East Coast as well as in Chicago, Milwaukee, and San Diego. During the summer, it sent chaplains to places like Ocean City, Maryland, where Irish students found seasonal work. Since Father Chris worked for the National Council's Office of Migrant and Refugee Services, if someone had a problem in a place where there was no specific official working with immigrants, he picked up the phone, called the local priest, and asked for help. In 1999, the Irish government supported these activities with a yearly grant of $300,000. In 2002, the amount grew to $453,000.[3] The National Council, private foundations, and "Irish Americans who have made good" also make occasional contributions. Each year, Father Chris sends reports to the Irish government about what he has accomplished.

The Catholic Church is a transnational corporation with discrete national units that function independently and as part of the larger operation at the same time. In the Inishowen case, the corporate structure broadened and deepened in response to migrants' cross-border lives. The Irish Pastoral Center's funding, leadership, and in part its services all operate across borders. Migrants express broad national and religious identities through their church membership. Belonging to a particular community or congregation mattered less to them than belonging to the Irish Catholic nation as a whole. As such, membership reaffirms Irishness and Irish ethnicity in America while also integrating migrants into the Catholic community worldwide.

THE TRANSNATIONAL CORPORATE MODEL: THE PROTESTANT EXPERIENCE

Transnational religious corporations also come in a Protestant variety. Pastor Carlos is the leader of the Church of the Good Shepherd, a large Baptist congregation in Valadares affiliated with the Southern Baptist Convention. He said that more than eighty of his members had joined "sister" congregations in Newark, New Jersey. When they leave Brazil, he gives them a *carta de transferência*, or a letter of introduction, to the Baptist Church where they are moving; if they don't come back to Valadares within three months, he tells them to switch their membership to their new congregation. While some colleagues allow people to be members of two churches at once, he thinks people need to decide which community they live in.

His church belongs to a national network that also links it to churches of the same denomination around the world. The Valadares statewide association includes congregations from over forty cities. The state group belongs to the national Convención Bautista Brasilera, started by the Southern Baptist Convention over a hundred years ago. The Southern Baptists maintain three offices in Rio, and until recently built, funded, and staffed many of its own churches. New congregations are now independent, though affiliated with the convention; they receive support for special missions. If Pastor Carlos needs help on a project, for example, he requests it from the Rio office, which then finds him a partner church in the United States. The national churches

also send representatives to the World Baptist Alliance, a transnational governing body.[4]

Scattered on the end tables in the waiting room at the Convención Bautista Brasilera office in Rio are copies of the monthly Portuguese-language magazine *O Jornal Batista*, filled with articles about the activities of congregations in Brazil, Florida, New Jersey, and Massachusetts. Churches advertise to attract new members. Convención staff encourage congregations in Brazil and overseas to coordinate more closely with each other. You can't force congregations to work together, they explained, but you can strongly suggest that they do their homework so they don't end up duplicating efforts by working in the same place. Back in Valadares, Pastor Carlos admitted he is building relationships beyond his denomination because so many of his members now belong to other Baptist denominations in the Northeast. "What's the difference between the Southern and the Northern?" he asked. "The doctrine is the same, it's just how we do things that is different."

NATIONAL GROUPS THAT WORK TRANSNATIONALLY

Groups like the ISSO and Swadhyaya are national religious corporations whose financing, leadership, and structures operate transnationally. They are globally managed with clear chains of command. As Gujaratis moved to the United Kingdom, South Africa, and the United States, they expanded their operations to serve their migrant clientele. The organizations they established reinforce members' ties to Indians around the world and the homeland in general.

Groups in the United States and the United Kingdom operate like chapters or franchises of their Indian headquarters. Franchises are firmly controlled and partially directed by homeland leaders who make most of the important decisions, to preserve the brand. Religious chapters, on the other hand, enjoy greater flexibility. While they are part of the corporate structure, they have more control over decision making and leadership. Everyday religious life grows out of an interactive conversation between leaders in India and the United States rather than a series of nonnegotiable directives.

Compared to their counterparts in the United Kingdom, the U.S. branches of these groups are relatively new.[5] Devesh was a founder of the ISSO in Lowell. When he first moved to the area, he traveled to New Jersey to go to temple. He remembers the day he realized enough people lived in Massachusetts that they could form their own group. At first, they met at someone's house and rented halls on holidays. When their leader visited in the mid-1980s, he gave them permission to build their own temple. Satsangees or Swaminarayan followers in Houston and Chicago were also building temples at that time. To help each other out they created a revolving loan fund. Each group contributed funds toward the temple in Houston. When it was completed, they set their sights on Chicago. "We helped each other," Devesh recalls, "not just with money, but with expertise. When we were buying land, the guys in Houston understood the real estate market and all that stuff." In fact, similar resource sharing enabled the Boston ISSO to build a new, much-larger headquarters, in a former Goodwill Industries warehouse that they converted into a temple complex in August 2006.

The ISSO leader, Acharya Shri Koshalendraprasadji, a direct descendant of Lord Swaminarayan, is considered God's incarnation on earth. According to Sandeep Dave, who supervises the group's overseas activities from Ahmedabad, "There is just one type of worship, one way of living, and one type of social action." But as people spread out more, "we felt the need for a structure that would protect Lord Swaminarayan's moral teachings." Each local group has a president, a vice president, and a secretary. Sadhus or sages are sent to areas where there are large communities. They offer guidance, enforce discipline, and set broad policy. In places where there is no sadhu in residence, local leaders move ahead on small things, but consult leaders back in Ahmedabad about big decisions. People in the United States are in constant contact with India and each other. They travel regularly to participate in temple inaugurations, celebrations, and national meetings. They often meet informally because they have become each other's closest friends and advisers.

The devotees of Bochasanwasi Shree Akshar Purushottam Swaminarayan Sanstha (BAPS), the other Swaminarayan denomination in the Northeast, reject the idea that Lord Swaminarayan has a representative on earth. They believe he lives through his saints. Pramukh Swami is their current leader. Maintaining their message as Satsangees moved around the world also concerned BAPS leaders, who created a worldwide organization in response.[6] Temples in the United States and the United Kingdom are integral pieces in their organizational chart. Initially, laypeople ran the BAPS temple in Massachusetts, but they answered to the sadhu in Flushing, New York. Now, the community has grown large enough to support its own *Pujari* or priest.

The ISSO and BAPS also organize their members into special-interest groups. People belong to the national and international organization through their membership in their local temple as well as their membership in smaller age- and gender-specific groups, which have national and international networks of their own.[7] The women's wing of BAPS, established in 1954, has chapters at each local temple, which in turn belong to the National and International Women's Wing. The idea, according to one of its directors, is to reinforce members' relationship to the organization in a variety of ways and reach out to them at specific stages of their lives. The same person who belonged to the youth group as a teenager participates in the Women's Wing as a young mother.[8]

FLEXIBLE SPECIALIZATION

The clothing manufacturer Benetton was the company célèbre in the late 1980s. It abandoned its central warehouse and one-size-fits-all product and distributed its operations among several locations to be able to respond quickly and with agility to slight changes in the market. If the most popular color in the new spring line turned out to be yellow, Benetton could switch its production to yellow in a matter of days. Economists hailed this flexible specialization as a way to remain competitive in a global market no longer driven by local tastes.

Flexible specialization represents a radical departure from assembly lines and their strict division of labor.[9] Multiskilled, adaptable workers use flexible manufacturing techniques to produce goods for relatively small, segmented markets. Loose, fluid partnerships between different parts of the supply chain arise organically rather than being imposed from above. Such groups function like Manuel Castells's network society.[10] Just, as decentralized, adaptive modes of production are better suited to the challenges of the global economy, so the flexible production and dissemination of religious goods may be better suited to meeting the needs of people of faith living in a global world.[11]

A second set of transnational religious organizations resembles this model. They are horizontally managed, loosely coupled changing sets of partnerships. Their organization is impermanent and unsystematic, arising in response to a particular moment's opportunities and needs. Decision making and power is decentralized, allowing actors to customize, downsize, or otherwise alter the way they do things to meet members' demands. Like their corporate counterparts, there are both transnational and national aspects to what they do.

One example of religious flexible specialization is the International Church of the Four Square Gospel (ICFSG). Aimee Semple McPherson founded the church in Los Angeles in 1924. It sent its first missionaries to Minas Gerais and São Paulo in 1951. Though a relatively small denomination in the United States, the ICFSG spread rapidly in Brazil. By 2001, there were an estimated ten thousand churches throughout the country, located primarily in Minas Gerais, Parana, Guarana, and São Paulo. Brazilian migration to the Northeast, and the American ICFSG's decision to focus on evangelization in the region, produced a reverse missionary movement to New England.

When I spoke to Pastor Gabriel, an ICFSG leader in Valadares, he estimated there were twenty-one churches in the city, each with at least a third of their members in the United States. These local groups formed part of an extensive national architecture. A six-member director's council runs his 3,500-member church. Ten local churches make a regional church, and regional churches are organized into state federations, belonging to the National Council in São Paulo. The Secretario Nacional de Missionario, operating in more than twenty countries, oversees the ICFSG's missionary activities.

Several types and layers of relationships produced the web of transnational ties connecting Boston and Brazil. For one thing, a number of migrants still belonged to their congregations in Valadares and continued to tithe there. Even people who transferred their membership to the United States still sent money back now and then in response to what Pastor Gabriel called their "diplomatic linkages." They sent him letters about what they were doing in America. He got calls all the time asking him to pray for people who had emigrated. And, he said, migrants continued to be present because their relatives still attended church every Sunday.

Relations between leaders in the United States and Brazil produced another layer of connection. Pastor Luis, who was responsible for much of the ICFSG's work with Brazilians in New England, keeps in close touch with his colleagues at home, including Pastor Gabriel in Valadares, leaders from his former church in São Paulo, and members of the ICFSG national board, on which he served before emigrating. He has two sets of pastoral credentials: one from the United States and one from the Brazilian national church.

Pastor Luis's networks and activities speak to the informal, flexible character of these arrangements. He had to get permission from the Brazilian national governing board to work in the United States. He got start-up funds from the U.S. ICFSG and a onetime $500 grant from his church in São Paulo to support his efforts. In 2000, he got additional funds from the Secretario Nacional de Missionario in Brazil, in part because the director is a personal friend. Mostly, he supports himself with income he earns from investments in Brazil.

Although Pastor Luis is no longer officially a leader in Brazil, he recognizes the importance of maintaining good relations with his homeland colleagues. He visits at least once a year and often invites pastors to preach in Massachusetts. He makes sure they know about his church-planting activities. He knows he will probably go back to Brazil someday, and in the meantime he can always count on his fellow pastors if he needs to.

Brazil-to-U.S.-oriented and U.S.-to-Brazil-oriented missions form another layer of connection. In 1994, the American ICFSG president began actively encouraging cooperation between national churches to heighten members' sense of belonging to a worldwide community. What started out as flexible specialization may turn into a transnational corporation. According to an American-born former missionary, who now has his own congregation in Massachusetts,

> Last year, the American president invited all the missions departments around the world to meet with him. I think he is trying to encourage us all to feel, whether we are Brazilian, Panamanian, or American, that we are all part of an international church with various national parts that work together. He is trying to bring about greater coordination in the mission activities, so that we don't duplicate our efforts. All of the countries are independent, equal members of the worldwide assembly that meets once a year, but this is an effort to strengthen our international church community.

THE TRANSNATIONAL SUPPLY CHAIN

Many religious groups operate primarily in the United States. They are only transnational in that they depend on inputs from abroad. Some are informal communities that meet every so often for prayers and religious education. Their members want to be connected to their culture and faith in some way, but they are not strongly attached to a particular version. They want to improvise, cobbling together a mix of religious practices that still have some roots in their homeland.

Growing up, Hetal Patel, a seventeen-year-old high school student, attended such a Satsang school, where he learned about Indian holidays as well as how to read and write in Gujarati.[12] Most of the other families did not consider themselves very religious. They didn't pray at home and were satisfied with the monthly meetings and holiday get-togethers the Satsang had to offer. There was no official leader—someone always took charge when something needed to get done.

They depended, though, on a steady supply of goods from India. The pictures and statues they put up when they prayed were all imported. So were the oils they used to care for the Gods, the CDs of prayers and chants they listened to, and the educational materials they used with the children. They often invited teachers from India to spend a week with them. These events were open to the public and were frequently well attended by native-born Americans interested in meditation and spirituality.

The Islamic Center of Hopkinton, which is loosely affiliated with the Ithna Ashari tradition within Shia Islam, is a second example of a group that relies on a transnational supply chain. The Shia are a minority in Pakistan as well as in Boston. While Sunni Muslims have no central organization or leader, and each mosque operates on its own, the Shia community has a federated administrative structure and imam.[13] While the Islamic Center functions autonomously, it is tied to other Shia groups in several ways. Its members look to imams from overseas when questions arise over ritual and practice. It regularly hosts preachers from around the world because the community cannot afford a full-time imam of its own. The community members import circular clay disks, made from soil from Karabala, Iraq, on which they rest their heads while praying, because the Prophet prayed with his head on the earth.[14]

THE INTERIOR DESIGN OF NEW RELIGIOUS ARCHITECTURES

When Nike manufactures sneakers with parts made in Asia and Latin America, it's not just the production process that is worldwide. The entire corporate operation goes global. The company's strategic planning, financing, and human resources manual must change to reflect its new circumstances. Managers have to be schooled in cross-cultural management. Those who oversee corporate giving have to rethink their approach to reflect the changing boundaries of the communities they serve.

The same is true for global religious groups. The religious organizational architecture changes and so does what goes on inside it. Many members live aspects of their religious lives via long distance. To keep them satisfied and supervised, religious groups have to invent new ways of operating. Global religiosity requires different kinds of leaders. It demands new production processes. It requires different ways of communicating with followers, and new technologies for doing so. It means revising the membership requirements so people can still fulfill them in their new homes. It means figuring out how to educate the next generation. All of this adds up to major changes in business as usual.

When members emigrate, religious communities can't depend on face-to-face contact between leaders and followers anymore. Groups develop long-distance leadership techniques, rescripting authority and who can assume it. Members who were unable to be leaders before can now step up to the plate.

Since many groups aren't large enough to support full-time clerics, those who are most knowledgeable generally take charge. Women, in particular, play more central roles. And because many mosques double as social centers and schools, women lead prayers, serve on boards of directors, and also run educational programs. Leila, a thirty-eight-year-old Pakistani migrant, is clear that

> women are the obvious answer. And they are ready and willing to step in. We pray separately, and there is still a tendency during social occasions for men and women to mingle among themselves. But I've been on the board several times in the past ten, eleven years in different positions and never felt sort of kept at the back, oh, she's a woman. I've become more vocal about my rights than I ever was. We are not going to let men tell us what to do. And, you know, they wouldn't try because they need us too much.

Female members of the ISSO and BAPS were particularly pleased by the enhanced opportunities emigration brought them. They are not allowed to speak directly to a sadhu; a "brother" or male member of the community must intervene on their behalf. While critics claim this is proof that the Swaminarayan faith treats women like second-class citizens, and that Hindu values are being used to justify keeping patriarchy intact, both immigrants and members in India adamantly rejected this view. They run the Women's Wing without men interfering, they said, so they have all the freedom they need. They have even more power now that their activities have expanded to serve members in England and the United States.

The relationship between leaders and their flocks also changes in transnational religious organizations. Like international aid workers and corporate executives, a cadre of religious leaders circulates around the world. The boundaries of the communities they serve and how familiar they are with their daily life contrasts markedly with religious leaders in the past who often served the same community for decades.

Ulf Hannerz makes the same argument about how globalization changed journalism. He jettisons the idea that the media is a single tribe, or that classic categories like staff correspondent, freelancer/stringer, or parachutist still hold. He reclassifies reporters as "spiralers" or "long-timers," depending on how they move through the globalized news landscape. The global networks and institutions these correspondents relate to may influence their work just as strongly as the foreign locality that is their beat. As such, foreign correspondents are crucial catalysts for the globalization of consciousness, or for driving the very same shared package of values of individualism, consumerism, self-actualization, and democracy that some of the people in chapter 4 subscribed to.[15]

Globalization also changes the way religious leaders relate to their territories. Their knowledge about and involvement in members' daily lives varies considerably. Some are firmly integrated into the local scene while others are themselves tourists. Some work for the same organization for many years while others change jobs and denominations frequently. What leaders experience in their last position strongly influences what they do in their next one. They are like pied pipers, accumulating opinions and strategies with each new encounter, which they then add to an ever-expanding repertoire. As such, like reporters, they drive the globalization of religious consciousness by carrying ideas and values from post to post.

Father Patrick, one of the Irish priests working with Inishoweners in Boston, is intimately acquainted with the people in his community and quite skilled at relating to people outside it. He interacts with parishioners in much the same way as the old-time parish priest who guided generations through the sacraments. The only difference is that Father Patrick's parish extends to Ireland. By joining the church's expatriate priest corps, he became part of a professional religious class, which also includes missionaries and other types of leaders, who circulate from one congregation to another.[16] They bring the lessons learned in their last post to the challenges of their new position, thereby spreading global religious consciousness.

Pastor Martin carries ideas and skills from, one religious organization to another. He came to Boston to work with a Baptist colleague who wanted to start a Portuguese-speaking congregation. When things didn't work out, Martin found work in a Presbyterian church. Being in the United States changed his views. He now believes you can "rewrite the book, within reason," rather than taking it literally. "Sometimes," he notes, "you just have to look around you and see that what you have always done doesn't work anymore." He recently returned to Valadares, where he started a nondenominational church mixing various denominational styles. He feels that it's OK to combine anything as long as it brings people closer to God. He does not rule out "migrating again" to the United States or another denomination. Like Father Patrick, each time he does, he integrates new tools into his kit.

These religious leaders come in contact with people outside the communities, they directly serve, albeit superficially. They know enough about what happens on the other side of their church's walls that they can help their members deal with it. In contrast, the sadhu at the ISSO temple relates to his followers completely differently. He knows little English. He cannot speak to women. He doesn't go out of the temple unless someone accompanies him. While he can advise them about life in India, he doesn't have a lot to say about life in the United States. His devotees are his guide, rather than the other way around. He is like an English-speaking business consultant working in a country where he doesn't know the language. By day he is the expert, but by night he becomes totally dependent on his hosts.

Pastor Elton also exemplifies this second type of leader, although not for lack of trying. He came from Brazil to lead a new Pentecostal congregation. He speaks little English and also relies heavily on his congregants to tell him what to do. His limits frustrate him deeply. "I have no time to learn English or to learn about the United States. The needs of my community are so great. But what kind of a leader can I be if I know so little about the world outside my church's doors?"

A third group of leaders parachutes in and out of the immigrant community before returning to their home base. They are like the business professionals who organize a one-day seminar yet aren't involved with the participants on an ongoing basis, nor are they expected to. Jagdish Chandra Maharaj and Didiji are parachuters. They make quick, symbolic visits to their followers and then move on. While members generally have little, if any, direct contact with them, they still feel as if they have a personal relationship with their leader. The leaders' short visits, whether they involve close physical proximity or a brief sighting from the other side of a packed football stadium, reinforce these bonds.

Religious organizations have to renegotiate the membership requirements when members change their address. They have to modify what they expect from their faithful, and what they are willing and able to give in return. They have to invent new ways to communicate and revise the messages they transmit. To ensure quality control, or that the message remains intact, and to make sure they are systematically disseminated to potential members, they have to tightly script their recruitment activities so that anyone, with little supervision, can perform them.

For example, Swadhyaya, BAPS, and the ISSO each have specific ways they spread "the word." An interchangeable, global cadre of religious workers efficiently follows this recipe. In India, Swadhyayees do Bhakti Pheri—visiting the same village every two weeks and talking to people about Dadaji's teachings. After months of repeated visits and getting to know people over time, some residents join the group. But members can't be expected to devote the same time and energy to Bhakti Pheri in the United States, where they barely have time to visit their own families. The new religious architecture's interior design has to be modified to reflect their changing circumstances.

Bhakti Pheri has been reinvented in America. People make monthly visits to communities where Indian families are living. They look in the phone book for addresses of Patels and knock on their doors. Since hospitality is a deeply held value, most people invite them in. Four weeks later, they drive up again, revisit the same families, and visit a few new ones. Eventually they create a new *parivar*, thus beginning the systematic replication of Swadhyaya throughout the region. Recently, members in Massachusetts have been visiting families in suburban New York, and Fiji and Trinidad, where they are reaching out to Gujaratis who have been living there for generations.

Swadhyayees also do Yogeshwar Krishi—devoting time to money-making activities and then giving away the profits to the poor. In Gujarat, commercial fishermen spend one or two days a month working on a fishing collective, or farmers dedicate time to a communal farm. In the United States, the function, if not the form, of Yogeshwar Krishi has been replicated. In Boston, Swadhyayees earned money assembling circuit boards for local computer companies. In Chicago, they made ink refills for pens.

Another example of changing religious production comes from the encounter between a Brazilian church and its American hosts, although in this case, what was imported was combined with established practice to produce something new. When he first came to Boston, Pastor Luis of the ICFSG said that planting churches was a high priority. The only problem was that his ideas about how that should be done differed markedly from his American superiors. The native-born pastors "took months," surveying the population, doing needs assessments, and checking out the competition. They were, in his words, "slower than molasses," and let far too many opportunities go by. "I understand that you have to be smart about these things. That you can't go around wasting resources. But I also know that there are people just waiting to accept God's word, and that someone will get to them if we don't get there first."

His strategy was to bring people together, convince them of God's truth, and, presto, a church is planted. And you do that any way you can. One time he rented a bus and invited a group of Brazilians to go with him to Connecticut to watch a soccer game. On the way down and back, he talked, evangelized, told stories about the Bible, and, by the time they got home, five new churches were created. When he told his American supervisors about it, they stared in amazement. But when he had started five churches for every one of theirs, they began to see the light. Now he does what he pleases and is considered a role model for others in the region. They, too, have become much more bold and creative in their outreach approach.

Technological innovations also enable people to continue to be full-fledged, long-distance members of their faith traditions. Religious communities have become quite skilled at using technology to further their cause. They change how people "attend" religious services and what happens once they are there. The Valadarenses described earlier in this chapter, who went to Mass in Boston by watching it on television in Brazil, are a case in point. The women seated at the back of Pramukh Swami's birthday celebration, who participate by watching the proceedings projected onto large video screens flanking the stage, get a much more

"up close and personal view" of him than they would if they simply sat in the back of the ten-thousand-plus crowd. Swadhyayees spend most of their time together watching videotapes of the *pravachans* or lectures Dadaji delivered each week in Bombay before he passed away.[17] Some videos now even come with English subtitles so that the second generation in America and the United Kingdom can understand them. Technology makes it possible for Dadaji to replicate himself and reach millions. It also makes it possible to control his message and make sure it doesn't get watered down.

Finally, not just the practice of religion changes when it is enacted transnationally but also how it is passed down to children. To stay viable among expatriates, groups have to figure out how to reproduce themselves and be meaningful to a second generation raised where different rules apply. In places like India or Pakistan, religion pervades every institution and interaction. Children generally receive some sort of religious education at school; their homes and neighborhoods are also living classrooms.

But in the United States, religious communities have to be much more purposeful. In response, Hindus and Muslims create their own versions of the ubiquitous Sunday schools and vacation Bible schools we are all familiar with. On any given Sunday, the mosque is filled with students of all ages, from kindergarten to high school, taught by parent volunteers. While adult Swadhyayees watch videos of Dadaji's lectures, their children are down the hall also discussing his message. Each summer, kids go away to Swadhyaya or Swaminarayan camp—an especially formative experience for youngsters growing up with few Indian neighbors.

What's particularly interesting is that many groups have created special homeland schools where children are sent for cultural immersion. Swadhyayees can enroll their children in a one-year post-high school "cultural education" course in Bombay. BAPS brings twenty-plus girls of high school age to live at the temple complex in

Ahmedabad each summer. It also opened a high school for nonresident Indians. The idea came from a Satsangee living in London who, the story goes, visited Pramukh Swami and placed a bag of money at his feet. He was fed up, he said, with how his children were growing up in England. Because Swaminarayans are such a minuscule minority, it's impossible to maintain their culture. "The kids can answer multiple choice questions," he complained, "but they can't write an essay about who they are." He donated money to build a school for girls that now has 350 students. Fifteen percent of the students are nonresident Indians; most come from the United States, but there are also students from the United Kingdom, Dubai, and Africa. Indian residents pay about $1,150; nonresident Indian families $1,800. You don't have to be Swaminarayan to attend.

It's not just Nike, Coca-Cola, or Benetton, for that matter, who are producing and distributing their products globally. Religious communities are also structured and operating across borders. They channel flows of ideas, rituals, and values. They bring people and practices from different places together under the same umbrella. The resulting encounters alter the fabric of everyday religious life. Moreover, they provide members with strong, intricate, multilayered webs of connections that are perfect platforms from which to live globally. They offer a haven in every port, be it London, Boston, or Bombay. They speak to the challenges of life in the neighborhood, the nation, and the universal human experience. They offer solutions to ideational and cultural clashes that reflect the transnational reality of migrants' lives. And because faith traditions respond so powerfully to globalization and have adopted so well to it, their architectures are likely to broaden and thicken.

"That's terrifying," Alice and Florence say. Al-Qaeda and Hezbollah are transnational religious organizations, and look where they have gotten us. Luis would agree, if he would just wake up to what is going on around him. And there is no doubt some

truth to what they say. There are too many religious groups that want to make the world over as they see fit and use violence to do so. But again, they represent religion at the margins. We don't yet know what the people in the religious middle say about putting their religious beliefs into practice.

NOTES

1. National and local churches enjoy varying degrees of autonomy. Vatican II, for example, reversed a century-long trend toward centralization by acknowledging the plurality of national Catholicisms at the same time that it instituted a set of liturgical changes that homogenized Catholicism around the world (Hervieu-Léger 2000). Catholic authorities' open acceptance of local popular religious forms or *inculturation* was also taken as an indicator of a heightened tolerance for more diverse practices.

2. See Menjívar 1999; Cook 2002; Peterson, Vásquez, and Williams 2001.

3. That same year, a task force composed of religious and organizational leaders and academics recommended an increase of up to €1 million ($1.2 million) for the Irish Episcopal Commission's work with emigrants in the United States (Task Force 2002). Although they did not receive the entire amount, Foreign Minister Brian Cowen did establish the "Irish Abroad Unit" within the Ministry of Foreign Affairs in 2004, and as of July 2006 the amount earmarked for U.S. groups topped $1 million (Department of Foreign Affairs, press release, July 26, 2006, available at http://www.foreignaffairs.gov.ie/Press_Releases/20060726/2122.htm).

4. Southern and Brazilian Baptists used to meet each other at the annual congresses of the Baptist World Alliance. The Southern Baptist Convention withdrew from the alliance in June 2004.

5. Groups of devotees (Satsangees) have been getting together informally to hold Satsang Sabhas in each other's homes throughout England since the 1960s (see http://www.swaminarayan.info/events/leicesterutsav/history.asp). According to its Web site, in 1976, the ISSO, headquartered in Leicester, was created "to further the Maharajashri's divine vision of creating a global Satsang network of young and old Satsangees across the continents." Presently, ISSO Europe has temples in Mariestad, Sweden, and

in Leicester, Streatham (London), and Portslade (Brighton), all in the United Kingdom. Additionally, there are Swaminarayan temples in Bolton, London (Willesden, Harrow, Forest Gate, and Woolwich), Cardiff, and Oldham. The Maharajashri's dream was carried to the United States in 1978 to "meet the religious needs of the present generations, rather than the future ones," with the help of a single devotee who offered to travel all over the United States with him. The result was the creation of numerous chapters (branches) across the North American continent, including Swaminarayan temples in Weehawken (New Jersey), Boston, Chicago, Houston, and Los Angeles (http://www.swaminarayan.info/isso/isso.asp). This follows a pattern in many immigrant religions that assume a congregational form when they are transplanted to the United States. This "de facto congregationalism" (see Warner 1993, 1066–67) follows and re-creates the Protestant model of voluntary church organization with lay leadership, rather than a universal or parish structure dictated from above (Yang and Ebaugh 2001; Bankston and Zhou 2000).

6. They divided India into four regions. Ahmedabad alone has forty-two temples, organized into three areas. Leaders attend a yearly religious retreat, where they choose projects to work on together. People who want to become leaders must pass a test demonstrating their mastery of the material. The most important leaders have passed nine levels of exams. For more on BAPS, see Williams 1988, 2001. See also Barot 2002 on the Swaminarayans, and Srivastava 1998 on Swadhyaya.

7. Swadhyaya also has the Bal Sanskar Kendra for young children, the Yuva Kendra and Divine Brain Trust for older children and young adults, and the Mehila Kendra for women.

8. Transnational political parties employ a similar strategy. Young people first participate in youth groups and then in groups for young adults. Ultimately, they graduate into groups of male and female supporters, often after a political education similar to the ISSO's nine exam levels.

9. The term "flexible specialization" was first introduced by Piore and Sabel (1984).

10. Castells's depiction of the current "information age" and his multivolume work about the emergence of a network society (1996, 1997, 1998) transformed the way many scholars conceptualized identity and social relationships in a global world. Network societies do not arise in response to globalization but the other way around—globalization is the consequence of a global network society (Rantanen 2005). A network society is one where decentralized, flexible, yet connected networks provide customized services and goods. Its "social structure is made of networks powered by microelectronics-based information and communication technologies" (Castells 2004, 1). In Castells's formulation, a network has no center, just interconnected multiple "nodes" that play multiple roles. Some nodes may be more important than others, based on what they contribute to the network's goals, but all are necessary for its performance. Networks continuously evolve and adapt, adding and deleting nodes as necessary and/or useful. Exchanges of flows or streams of information circulate through and between the nodes; there is no line in the sand between receivers and senders as traditionally conceived in communication research. Nor can there be any one model for network societies, Castells adamantly asserts (cited in Rantanen 2005)—they are inherently flexible, and may exhibit more or less connectivity according to the other social structures in a given society.

11. Peterson, Vásquez, and Williams (2001) make this same argument in their study of the Charismatic Catholic Renewal Movement. While parish life is characterized by a Fordist mode of production that results in a one-size-fits-all product, the renewal movement is post-Fordist, flexibly creating a customized product that is successful because it does not challenge established hierarchies.

12. Satsang means "the company of the truth." It is a gathering of seekers who chant, meditate, and listen to scriptural teachings or readings together.

13. Although they accept the rightful inheritance of the family of the Prophet Muhammad as leader of the Muslims, Shia groups are divided over who that leader is. Disputes over time have led to the establishment of distinct branches or denominations such as Dawoodi Ismaeli or Khoja. The Masumeen Center, or the Islamic Center of Hopkinton, is a Jaafari mosque, or one that follows the Ithna Ashari tradition within Shia Islam. The Jaafari community is the largest Shia community globally, and is predominant in southern Lebanon, southern Iraq, Bahrain, and Iran. The imam of a Shia mosque is someone who is learned in that tradition but does not necessarily come from the family of the Prophet Muhammad himself.

14. Karabala is believed to be the site where Imam Ali, the nephew and son-in-law of Prophet Muhammad, was martyred.
15. Hannerz 2004.
16. This is similar to Sklair's (2000) "transnational capitalist class" that promotes the globalization of capitalism and an associated consumer culture. This emerging class includes four main factions: the corporate (business executives and local affiliates), the state (globalizing bureaucrats and politicians), the technical (globalizing professionals), and the consumerist (merchants and media). Their (primarily economic) interests are globally linked and outwardly reaching, rather than locally situated, and they share similar tastes, lifestyles, educational levels, and consumption styles. Projecting themselves as citizens of the world as well as their nations, they include individuals such as Akio Morita (the founder of Sony) and Australian-born media mogul Rupert Murdoch.
17. According to Sheth (1994), the video baghan, or the act of receiving discourse through a video, has become a ritual in itself.

27

Immigrants' Religious Participation in the United States

Ilana Redstone Akresh

A N IMPORTANT QUESTION that has persisted in the literature on immigrants' religious participation in the US is what happens to their religious behaviour the longer they remain in the US. Immigrants come from a wide variety of religious backgrounds and practices, diversity that further highlights the importance of understanding these patterns. Much of the existing literature examining immigrants and religion has consisted of ethnographic studies focusing on small groups. While these studies have expanded our understanding of the links between religion and assimilation (Hurh and Kim 1990; Ebaugh and Chafetz 2000; Guest, 2003; Min and Kim 2003; Cavalcanti and Schleef 2005), between religion and the formation of ethnic identities (Bankston and Zhou 1996; Warner and Wittner 1998; Kurien 1998, 2001; Yang 2000; Cha 2001), between religion and transnationalism (Menjivar 1999) and between religion and positive acculturation and upward mobility (Bankston and Zhou 1995; Cao 2005), one important aspect of the role of religion on which they have remained largely silent is the link between immigrants' religious habits before and after coming to the US. Largely due to previous data limitations, this is the first large study able to consider this relationship and examine participation patterns across origin groups (Cadge and Ecklund 2007).

The shift in immigrant origins in the last four decades from being primarily European in nature to Asian and Latin American has also brought new diversity in religious backgrounds. In the early twentieth century, the foreign-born population was dominated by Catholics and Protestants (Herberg 1950). Although Catholics in particular continue to dominate numerically, there are now substantial Buddhist, Hindu and Muslim populations as well (Yang and Ebaugh 2001; Hirschman 2004). Data from the 2002 and 2004 General Social Survey on all foreign-born indicate that 39.4 per cent identify as Catholic, 24.1 per cent as Protestant, 2.1 as general Christian, 3.4 as Jewish, 4.6 as Muslim, 3.7 per cent as Orthodox Christian and 14.9 per cent report no religion.[1] The religious involvement of immigrants both shapes and is shaped by existing communities, making these patterns crucial for understanding immigrants' integration into the US. The primary contribution of the current study is to the understanding of immigrants' religious behaviour in the US after factoring in home-country practices. Without this, it has been impossible to distinguish between cohort differences in religiosity and real changes in individual behaviour. A secondary contribution is to inform the still contentious secularization paradigm that suggests that individuals will become more secular with modernization.

This work takes advantage of data from the 2003 cohort of the New Immigrant Survey (NIS) to examine religious participation among US immigrants systematically. The survey instrument includes questions concerning religious preference and participation in the US, in addition to soliciting information on the frequency of attendance prior to coming to the US. We know that migration disrupts religious participation (Wuthnow and Christiano 1979) and, in most cases, it will take time to make this transition complete. The current study shows evidence of an increase in participation, for some a rebound pattern, by immigrants the longer they remain in the US. Although this paper treats religious affiliation as a static state, clearly the potential for switching exists (see, for instance, work on Korean immigrants in Alba, Raboteau and Dewind 2009; Suh 2009). That said, the data indicate that 99 per cent of the NIS sample report that their current religious tradition is the same as that in which they themselves were raised, minimizing this confounding effect.

PRIOR STUDIES ON RELIGION WITH NEW IMMIGRANT SURVEY (2003 AND PILOT DATA)

In this section, I describe two studies that have used data from the New Immigrant Survey-Pilot (NIS-P) study, the pilot project for the data used in the current work. The first uses data from the NIS-P to examine religious service attendance. In that study, the authors find evidence supporting a negative relationship between time in the US and religious involvement (Cadge and Ecklund 2006). In other words, their work indicates that less assimilated immigrants are more likely to attend services regularly, suggesting decreased religious participation over time. The authors also find evidence supporting the fact that Christians are more likely to attend services regularly than are non-Christians. They attribute this both to the greater availability of Christian churches in the US and to the stronger requirement of weekly attendance for Christian than for Buddhist or Hindu practices (Cadge and Ecklund 2006). However, their study is subject to data limitations stemming from the use of the smaller pilot survey. They are restricted to a substantially smaller sample size that does not allow for an examination of region of origin differences, they have only two religion-based questions available and they have no information on the respondent's religious involvement prior to coming to the US. The full survey allows the current study to address each of these limitations directly.

The second work using NIS-P data takes a descriptive look at religious preference patterns (Jasso *et al.* 2003). This study, co-authored by the four principal investigators of the New Immigrant Survey, finds a substantially different distribution of religious preferences among the foreign born than among the native born.[2] For instance, the authors find that only two-thirds of the immigrant population is Christian compared with 82 per cent of the native born and that the proportion Catholic among immigrants is 42 per cent contrasted with 22 per cent among the native born (Jasso *et al.* 2003). Overall, their study points to several salient patterns of religious preference among immigrants that await further examination with the full survey (Jasso *et al.* 2003).

PERSPECTIVES ON IMMIGRANTS AND RELIGION

One of the reasons the current study is needed is that there are solid theoretical reasons one might expect religious participation to increase and to decrease with time in the US. In what follows, I outline each perspective.

Why Immigrants' Religious Participation might be Expected to Decline

As noted early on by Wuthnow and Christiano (1979), migration disrupts religious participation.

In their work looking at internal migration in the United States, they find that religious participation decreases with each subsequent migratory event. With international migrants, there are at least three reasons why one might expect to see a similar decline.

1. One might expect an initial decline after arrival if there is a delay in finding an appropriate and comfortable congregation to join. This might be particularly relevant for minority religions for which there are fewer places of worship. This pattern would suggest that the decline would be temporary and be followed by a subsequent restoration of previous levels.
2. Given that many immigrants come seeking job opportunities, one might expect a decline simply due to the amount of time committed to employment.
3. If religious attendance is used to buffer the adaptation process, participation might decline as time and comfort level in the US increase.
4. A fourth rationale for a decrease is linked to the secularization paradigm. In its simplest form, proponents of the traditional secularization paradigm argue that modernization is associated with a decrease in religious participation. This is thought to be linked to the increase in scientific explanations and technological advances providing explanations for previously unexplained or poorly explained phenomena. Although the validity of the 'traditional' secularization paradigm has been fiercely debated by sociologists, it has also displayed remarkable persistence as a framework for thinking about modern religious trends (Hadden 1987; Finke 1992; Stark 2000; Berger 2001; Bruce 2001; Hervieu-Léger 2001a; Woodhead, Heelas and Martin 2001). For immigrants, the theoretical association might be one that unfolds over space rather than over time. For US migrants who originate in countries that are less developed (or less 'modern') than the United States, a pattern consistent with the 'traditional' paradigm would predict a negative relationship between religious attendance and time in the US. Perhaps the most important flaw in this logic is the assumption that immigrants are, in fact, arriving from less 'developed' or less 'modern' countries. In reality, some come from the middle or upper middle echelons of the income distribution (Massey 1990; Massey, Durand and Malone 2002), further raising the questions as to the empirical nature of this relationship.

Why Immigrants' Religious Participation might be Expected to Increase

In contrast to the arguments developed above, there are also several reasons for predicting that immigrants' religious participation will *increase* after moving to the US. Other work has made it clear that these expectations are arguable only when the US is the destination because of its unique history, policies towards immigration and the interest in promoting religious and other types of diversity (Williams 1998). Recent work by Connor (2009) and Mooney (2009) also suggests that the effect of migration on religious participation depends heavily on the destination country. To this end, the US is uniquely open to almost all types of religious public expression.

1. If newcomers view belonging to a congregation as a pathway to a social network, this might suggest a rapid transition to a high level of religious participation. The benefits of belonging to this network have been explored in the theoretical work of Handlin (1951) and Herberg (1950) and include its ability to soothe the trauma of migration and provide continuity in newcomers' lives. Hirschman adds to these benefits religion's role in providing information

and opportunities, including the essential trading of information on employment, enrolling children in school and improving language skills through organized classes for new arrivals (Hirschman 2004). Along this line, religious participation has at least two potential roles in immigrants' lives (Foner and Alba 2008). In the first, it functions as a bridge connecting new arrivals to the community; churches, synagogues and temples serve an important role in providing information about jobs, housing and general information on survival in a new place (Barton 1975; Smith 1978; Foner and Alba 2008). In the second, it serves as a buffer against further integration into US mainstream society by limiting immigrants' exposure primarily to co-ethnics and reducing other incentives to adapt (Greeley 1972; Foner and Alba 2008). Clearly the two perspectives are not necessarily mutually exclusive. Religious participation could simultaneously offer information leading to jobs and mobility and buffer against the acquisition of host-country language and customs, particularly if the place of worship is highly concentrated with co-ethnics.

2. Other work (Portes, Escobar and Radford 2007) has shown that immigrants' links to transnational organizations strengthen as they remain in the US. If religious participation facilitates the formation and maintenance of transnational ties, one might expect a corresponding increase in attendance.

3. In contrast to the traditional secularization paradigm, advocates of a 'new' paradigm cite increasing religious participation in the United States as evidence that religion is not in decline (Lechner 1991; Warner 1993; Yamane 1997; Yang and Ebaugh 2001; Levitt 2007). In the Yang and Ebaugh (2001) study of immigrants conducted in Texas, the authors find that the religious pluralism associated with recent immigrants has led to a 'revitalization' of religion rather than a decline.

DATA

The data used in this study come from the New Immigrant Survey (NIS) 2003 cohort. The survey was originally pilot tested with a sample drawn in 1996 (refer to http://nis.princeton.edu for full information). The sampling frame for the NIS 2003 was immigrants granted legal permanent residency (LPR) between May and November of 2003 and the response rate was 69 per cent (Jasso *et al.* forthcoming). Although there are no known biases associated with the response rate, the sampling design dictates that undocumented migrants and others without LPR status are not eligible for inclusion. Compared to US migrants who do not have LPR status, those who do might have better networks or greater facility navigating the immigration system. Although those with LPR status may differ from those without it, the direction of the resulting bias with respect to the current analysis is not immediately clear. However, one could imagine that undocumented migrants might be more likely to draw from the unofficial support offered in a religious community. Further, undocumented migrants are largely comprised of Mexicans, a group that has a high level of religiosity both in their home country and in the US. They are also overwhelmingly Catholic and the church has been a strong advocate of their rights. This suggests that the overall finding in the current study of higher religious participation in the US is understated by the data.

Interviews were conducted in the language of the respondent's choice as soon as possible after legal permanent residency was granted and individuals who were new arrivals to the US as well as those who had adjusted their visa status were included in the sample (Jasso *et al.* forthcoming). This latter point means that there is substantial variation with respect to how long the respondents have been in the US. The survey methodology for the adult sample involved four strata: spouses of US citizens, employment principals, diversity principals and other immigrants (Jasso *et al.* forthcoming).[3] This analysis uses the adult sample, which was restricted to individuals who were at least 18 years old at the time of admission. Important for the current work, rather than asking an ambiguous question about year of arrival or year of immigration, which can lead to overestimates in the case of circular migration or underestimates in the presence of a migration history prior to the event of 'immigrating', the NIS allows for a cumulative measure of all time spent in the US (Redstone and Massey 2004).

The analysis uses individuals with valid responses on all variables of interest, yielding 6,381 observations. Of the 2,192 (8,573–6,381) cases that are dropped, 40 per cent are lost due to missing information on religious attendance in the US, 22 per cent are lost due to missing labour-force information and the remainder is lost due to various other covariates. With respect to age, sex, years of education and

English ability, differences between individuals with religious attendance information and those without are minimal in magnitude. The one dimension on which they differ substantially is US duration; the former have approximately 1.2 years more US experience than the latter. If newer arrivals are simply uncertain how to answer the religion questions posed in the survey, the results presented here are likely to understate the transition of increased participation as we are not accounting for a number of infrequent attendees who are also recent arrivals.

Religion questions in the NIS

The survey instrument for the NIS-2003 includes multiple questions on religion and participation which are described, along with possible responses, in Table 27.1. There are several important factors to

TABLE 27.1 NIS survey questions	SURVEY QUESTION	REPONSES AND CODING	VARIABLE MEASURING
	What religious tradition, if any, describes your current religion (You may mention more than one if you wish)?	Catholic, Orthodox Christian, Protestant, Muslim, Jewish, Buddhist, Hindu, No Religion, Some other religion, or can name an unlisted religion	Religious preference (independent variable)
	Since becoming a permanent resident, how many times have you attended religious services?	Using the frequency reported and dividing by the elapsed time between the date of admission to permanent residency and the interview data yields estimate of frequency of US attendance (religious participation in the US)	Religious attendance since legal permanent residency (dependent variable)
	Before coming to the United States to live, how often did you attend religious services in your country of last residence?	Categories ranging from never to more than once per day (religious participation in home country)	Religious attendance in home country (independent variable)
	Do you have a shrine, altar, or religious icons, paintings, or statues in your home?	1 if yes	Religious items in home (independent variable)

note in the survey questions. First, as the reader will note in the table, the questions used to elicit information on religious participation prior to migration and since being in the US are not the same. Ideally, the wording on the two points would be identical, thus minimizing error resulting from this discrepancy. This may introduce bias if the variation in the questions results in systematically different recall error or systematic differences in how individuals respond to the two types of wording, concerns I am unable to address. Second, the wording of the questions is biased toward religions that support regular communal worship. This is not a practice among Hindus or Buddhists, many of whom may have come to the United States without ever having formally belonged to a religious community. In addition, for members of some religions, in situations when they do worship communally, they do so at whatever temple or mosque is closest in proximity.

VARIABLES

Although the current study takes into account several factors that are expected to be associated with religious participation in the US, there are four covariates of primary importance. First is the ability to account for respondents' frequency of religious participation prior to coming to the US. This facilitates a more precise examination of whether immigrants change their religious behaviour after migration. Second is the identification of an individual's degree of US integration. The proxy measure, years of US experience, is not without controversy as assimilation occurs at different rates and can have different meanings across individuals. However, as one of the primary reasons for the inclusion of this variable is to provide a direct empirical test of whether immigrants increase or decrease their religious participation the longer they remain in the US, it remains the most appropriate measure in this case. Third are region of

origin indicators capturing differences across traditions and home-country habits respectively. As there are clearly important differences across religious traditions, indicators for Catholic, Orthodox Christian, Muslim, Jewish, Buddhist, Hindu and no religion (Protestant is omitted) are included throughout the analysis, but a discussion of these characteristics in the multivariate setting is beyond the scope of this analysis.

RESULTS

Table 27.2 presents selected characteristics for the pooled sample and by region of origin. The results in Table 27.2 also point to several interesting patterns with respect to religious attendance. More than half of the Western European group report never attending religious services in the US, while only 29 per cent of respondents from Mexico place themselves in this category. The same two groups constitute the highest (Mexico at 23 per cent) and lowest (Western European group at 9 per cent) concentrations of respondents indicating that they attend religious services at least once per week. With the exception of Mexico, the modal category for the remaining groups is 'never attends religious services'. In addition to immigrants from Mexico and South/Central America, Africans also have high levels of religious participation such that more than half report attending several times a year or more. Looking now to patterns prior to coming to the US, Asia demonstrates the highest percentage that reports never attending while Mexico has the lowest. This pattern for Asians is largely driven by Chinese immigrants, 85 per cent of whom never attended abroad. Here again the origin groups with the greatest frequencies attending once per week or more are Africa and Latin America. These patterns are broadly consistent with those found in Van Tubergen (2006), such that immigrants from more religious countries are more religious themselves. From these tabulations, it appears that substantial

TABLE 27.2

Selected sample characteristics

	POOLED SAMPLE (n = 6381)	SOUTH/ CENTRAL AMERICA, CARIBBEAN (n = 1429)	MEXICO (n = 911)	WESTERN EUROPE, AUSTRALIA, CANADA, NEW ZEALAND (n = 287)	EASTERN EUROPE, FORMER USSR (n = 803)	ASIA (1348)	INDIAN SUBCONTINENT, MIDDLE EAST (n = 924)	AFRICA (n = 679)
Years of US experience	4.39 (5.97)	6.93 (7.09)	7.46 (7.89)	4.69 (5.03)	2.43 (3.91)	2.87 (4.42)	3.36 (4.01)	1.51 (3.39)
Religious attendance in the US								
Never	39.32	35.55	28.98	54.01	45.83	47.26	38.74	32.25
Less than several times per year	15.89	17.14	15.48	17.42	16.06	9.42	22.73	16.49
Between several times per year and less than once per week	25.47	26.80	33.04	19.16	23.41	22.63	21.10	29.16
Once per week or more	19.32	20.50	22.50	9.41	14.69	20.70	17.42	22.09
Religious attendance while in home country								
Never	18.52	11.76	7.46	27.87	20.25	36.42	16.02	9.72
Less than several times per year	17.76	14.98	11.64	36.59	28.64	14.17	24.68	8.69
Between several times per year and less than once per week	16.93	19.03	20.97	15.33	21.42	9.50	19.26	13.99
Once per week or more	46.80	54.23	59.93	20.21	29.89	39.91	40.04	67.60
Has religious items at home	0.385	0.307	0.553	0.244	0.402	0.353	0.501	0.268

Note: Standard deviations are shown in parentheses below means.

transitioning occurs in the middle categories. For instance, 9.5 per cent of Asians report attendance between several times per year and less than once per week while in their home countries and 23 per cent place themselves in this category in the US.

Finally, a comparison of aggregate pre- and post-migration patterns indicates a decrease in attendance, confirming earlier work on the disruption of migration (e.g., Wuthnow and Christiano 1979) and highlighting the need to examine this question in a multivariate analysis setting. It is precisely because migration is a disruptive life event that the current study asks what happens after that disruption has passed and newcomers settle into their life in the US. These patterns are further explored in Tables 27.3 and 27.4 and in the discussion section.

Table 27.3 presents results from a multinomial logistic regression predicting religious attendance in the US, where the omitted category is 'never attends'.[4] The first specification (the first three columns) mimics previous work in that it does not account for the individual's religious participation prior to coming to the US. The positive and statistically significant coefficients on the indicator for years of US experience suggest that more time in the US is linked with increased religious participation, relative to never attending. Specifically, each additional year in the US increases the likelihood of attending in each frequency category by between 2 and 5 per cent (relative risk ratios available upon request). This is consistent with the 'new paradigm' discussed earlier and with the role of religion in the maintenance of transnational ties. This differs from the Cadge and Ecklund (2006) findings using the NIS-P, a distinction that merits future exploration.[5] Differences also emerge across region of origin and religious preferences. After accounting for other characteristics, immigrants from South/Central America and the Western European group are less likely than Mexicans to attend more than several times per year.

The final three columns of Table 27.3 contain a multinomial logit specification similar to the first, yet, in this case, religious attendance prior to coming to the US is included as an explanatory variable. Not surprisingly, this important factor has a strong, positive correlation with US religious attendance. The strong, positive relationship between years of US experience and religious frequency suggests that immigrants increase their religious participation the longer they remain in the US. In this specification, as in the previous, although the magnitude of the coefficients across the three equations is similar, they do differ from one another at the one percentage level. This suggests that there is a slightly stronger link between years in the US and the highest level of religious participation.

With respect to region of origin differences, the majority of categories maintain coefficients with magnitudes and significance levels similar to the first specification in Table 27.3. However, a notable difference is for immigrants from Africa. After accounting for religious practice prior to coming to the US, Africans are indistinguishable from Mexicans in their likelihood of attending with any level of frequency.

Table 27.4 displays only the coefficients on the years of US experience variable from MNL specifications separated by region of origin. Each individual regression includes the same covariates as in Table 27.3. Apparent from the disaggregated specifications is that the positive link between time in the US and religious frequency is not consistent across groups. Evidence of increased religious participation is observed among immigrants from South/Central America and the Caribbean (approximately a 2 to 5 per cent increase for each additional year in the US) and among those from Eastern Europe and the former USSR (an 8 to 19 per cent increase for each additional year in the US, relative risk ratios available upon request). Among African and Indian origin immigrants additional time in the US increases the likelihood of weekly or higher

TABLE 27.3 *Multinomial logistic regressions predicting religious attendance in the US*

OMITTED CATEGORY IS NEVER ATTENDS	WITHOUT CONTROL FOR RELIGIOUS INVOLVEMENT PRIOR TO MIGRATION			WITH CONTROL FOR RELIGIOUS INVOLVEMENT PRIOR TO MIGRATION		
	LESS THAN SEVERAL TIMES PER YEAR	BETWEEN SEVERAL TIMES PER YEAR AND LESS THAN ONCE PER WEEK	ONCE PER WEEK OR MORE	LESS THAN SEVERAL TIMES PER YEAR	BETWEEN SEVERAL TIMES PER YEAR AND LESS THAN ONCE PER WEEK	ONCE PER WEEK OR MORE
Years of US experience	0.023***(0.008)	0.025***(0.007)	0.039***(0.007)	0.026***(0.008)	0.029***(0.007)	0.044***(0.008)
Region of origin (omitted is Mexico)						
South/Central America, Caribbean	0.105(0.139)	−0.140(0.119)	−0.111(0.131)	0.063(0.141)	−0.186(0.123)	−0.184(0.136)
Western Europe, Australia, Canada, New Zealand	−0.235(0.228)	−0.631***(0.214)	−1.299***(0.263)	−0.086(0.232)	−0.358(0.222)	−0.953***(0.272)
Eastern Europe, former USSR	−0.010(0.180)	−0.211(0.157)	−0.478***(0.178)	0.032(0.185)	−0.113(0.163)	−0.292(0.185)
Asia	0.023(0.184)	0.596***(0.153)	0.784***(0.165)	0.190(0.189)	0.635***(0.162)	0.736***(0.174)
Indian subcontinent, Middle East	0.628***(0.226)	0.659***(0.209)	0.744***(0.220)	0.521**(0.231)	0.468**(0.216)	0.495**(0.229)
Africa	0.617***(0.204)	0.738***(0.178)	0.495***(0.192)	0.317(0.209)	0.274(0.184)	−0.064(0.201)
Attendance in home country (omitted is never)						
Less than several times per year	—	—	—	1.459***(0.172)	0.877***(0.167)	0.345*(0.180)
Between several times per year and less than once per week	—	—	—	1.893***(0.180)	1.803***(0.166)	1.124***(0.178)
Once per week or more	—	—	—	2.092***(0.172)	2.317***(0.157)	2.302***(0.160)
Constant	−1.941***(0.303)	−0.705***(0.259)	−1.097***(0.278)	−3.772***(0.350)	−2.597***(0.306)	−2.824***(0.325)
Observations	6381	6381	6381	6381	6381	6381
Pseudo R^2	0.122			0.161		

Notes: Regressions also control for age, female, years of education, number in the household under 18, employment status, hours worked per week, marital status, English proficiency and the presence of religious objects in the home. Standard errors in parentheses.

* significant at 10%; **significant at 5%; ***significant at 1%.

TABLE 27.4

Coefficients on years in the US: variables by region of origin resulting from multinomial logistic (MNL) regressions predicting US attendance (each column is a separate MNL specification while the outcomes are labeled as rows)

ATTENDANCE IN THE US (OMITTED CATEGORY IS NEVER ATTENDS)	SOUTH/CENTRAL AMERICA, CARIBBEAN	MEXICO	WESTERN EUROPE, AUSTRALIA, CANADA, NEW ZEALAND	EASTERN EUROPE, FORMER USSR	ASIA	INDIAN SUBCONTINENT, MIDDLE EAST	AFRICA
Less than several times per year	0.017 (0.013)	0.022 (0.014)	0.020 (0.040)	0.075** (0.038)	0.013 (0.030)	0.037 (0.029)	0.088* (0.046)
Between several times per year and less than once per week	0.032*** (0.011)	0.009 (0.012)	0.012 (0.040)	0.106*** (0.036)	0.034 (0.027)	0.042 (0.031)	0.052 (0.048)
Once per week or more	0.047*** (0.012)	−0.017 (0.014)	0.048 (0.054)	0.170*** (0.039)	0.106*** (0.026)	0.075** (0.033)	0.105** (0.045)
Observations	1429	911	287	803	1348	924	679
Pseudo R^2	0.103	0.091	0.287	0.236	0.324	0.185	0.181

Notes: Regressions include the same covariates shown in Table 27.2.

Standard errors in parentheses.

* significant at 10%; **significant at 5%; ***significant at 1%.

attendance, but has no relationship with lower frequencies of attendance.[6]

DISCUSSION

In this work, I have considered the religious lives of immigrants, informing the literature theoretically in our understanding of changes in religious participation after immigration. I have examined whether the evidence indicates a trend towards increasing or decreasing religious participation the longer immigrants remain in the US. Although these questions have been considered previously, this is the first analysis using a large data set allowing for comparison across groups.

Contrary to prior evidence, the results presented here suggest that there is a tendency towards greater religious attendance with increased time in the US and no evidence of a decline, consistent with the role of religion in the maintenance of social capital and with the 'new' paradigm of increased religious participation and religious pluralism (Warner 1993; Ebaugh and Chafetz 2000). I also find that taking into account past religious practice also explains some of the variation across origin groups, particular for African immigrants. Another possibility that has been offered is that religious participation increases with time in the US due to the loss of social status often associated with migration (Min 1992). This pattern is most pronounced for immigrants from South/Central America and from Eastern Europe.

Although the results shown here are also consistent with the possibility that it simply takes newcomers time to find a suitable place of worship in their new home, there are two reasons why this is not the most likely explanation. First, the empirical findings hold in statistical significant and in magnitude when the sample is restricted to family preference migrants (immigrants who achieve legal permanent residency through a family member who is either a permanent resident or a citizen).

This is important because these individuals probably arrive with a support network already in place and would not require the same adjustment period as an individual arriving with no social contacts. Second, although an adjustment period might explain the need for time in the US to find an appropriate place of worship in the new setting (in other words, attending at all versus not attending), it does not explain changes in the intensity of attendance.

An additional interpretation of this pattern is that is it a 'contextual effect'. In other words, if the US is more religious than immigrants' origin societies, as measured by religious participation, increased participation with time in the US would also be consistent with part of a broader process of adjustment to life in the US, again reinforcing religion's role in assimilation. Evidence on this is mixed: ancillary analysis of data from the World Values Survey for 1999–2004 for five of the largest immigrant-sending countries indicates that 58.4 per cent of Filipinos, 56 per cent of Mexicans, 2.2 of Chinese, 32 per cent of Indians and 3.8 per cent of Vietnamese, compared to 45.1 per cent from the United States, report attending religious services once per week or more.

Although this study has gone further than previous work in examining, on a large scale, the religious behaviour of immigrants, several questions remain unanswered and caveats must be mentioned. Concerning the former, the current work has focused on region of origin variation with respect to the relationship between time in the US and the outcome studied. A natural next step would be to study how other covariates vary along this dimension. Regarding the latter, in order better to untangle the question of the role of religion in immigrants' lives, one would like to have detailed information on both the church-related activities in which the individual participates and on the array of activities offered by the establishment. An additional omitted factor is residential context. Residence in an ethnically concentrated neighbourhood is likely to be associated with both an individual's religious participation and the ethnic composition of their gathering place. Unfortunately, the NIS at present does not release information on residential context, restricting this avenue of analysis. Additionally, little is known about an individual's ability to estimate the ethnic composition of his gathering place accurately. Without more detailed information, one might surmise that the potential for overestimation exists if the church or place of worship holds separate services in different languages and the respondent attends only the service in his native language. Finally, as with any cross-sectional dataset, results must be interpreted with caution and causal inferences should be avoided. Fortunately, the NIS-2003 will eventually be longitudinal so that researchers may observe how individuals fare over time.

NOTES

1. The General Social Survey is administered only in English, leading to a likely underrepresentation of immigrants. Other categories include 0.9 per cent identifying as Other, 2.9 per cent as Buddhist, 2.8 per cent as Hindu, 0.8 per cent as Other Eastern and 0.6 per cent as Inter-Denominational.

2. The four co-PIs for the NIS have an additional book chapter relating to religion, yet the results are similar to those described above (Jasso *et al.* 2000).

3. 'Principal' refers to 'the alien who applies for immigrant status and from whom another alien may derive lawful status under migration law or regulations (usually spouses or minor unmarried children)' (US Citizenship and Immigration Services definition).

4. A multinomial logit is preferred as the specification violates the proportional odds assumption necessary for an ordered logit specification.

5. One possibility for this difference is that immigrants arriving after September 11, 2001 feel greater urgency to connect with a social network and alleviate feelings of isolation and alienation. Additionally, the sample size for the NIS-pilot study is substantially smaller than for the full 2003 cohort, resulting in less statistical power in identifying significant relationships. Finally, religious participation is measured differently in the two studies, perhaps accounting for the variation in results.

6. As important differences emerged in Table 27.2 regarding subgroups of Asians, I re-specified the fifth column in Table 27.4, for Chinese, Filipino, Korean and Vietnamese immigrants separately. With one exception, none of the four major groups exhibited a significant relationship between time in the US and religious participation. The sole exception was that Vietnamese immigrants in the US for longer are more likely to attend once per week or more.

28

Islam as a New Urban Identity? Young Female Muslims Creating a Religious Youth Culture in Berlin

Synnøve Bendixsen

THE LANDSCAPE OF EUROPEAN cities has, since the 1960s, been influenced by immigration from former colonies or through working-contracts between European and non-European countries. In the last decade, Islam has become increasingly present in European societies through the global (negative) media focus, increased use of the veil (*hijab*) among young Muslims, and by replacement of the earlier provisory backyard mosques of the 1970s with purpose-built mosques of the late 1990s. Although the urban context is usually associated as a place where people turn away from religion and where religious communities fulfill few social roles,[1] the last decade has seen a return of religion within the urban space. Today, several youths from the second and third generation of migrants[2] in European cities are turning to Islam in a quest for authenticity, an individual identity, and as part of their group orientation. In Germany, the increased visual religious identification of youth with migrant backgrounds has caused surprise, stupefaction and excitement in a society largely believing that being German and Muslim is an oxymoron.

This chapter discusses the "turn to Islam" as a factor of identification among female youths born in Germany and addresses the following questions: How are youths embracing a religious lifestyle in the Western urban spaces compared to their parents? Can a Muslim identity be a way of situating oneself in western modernity, rather than a sign of enclosure or disavowal of the "modern" German?

First, I discuss the kind of identification with Islam among the young generation in Berlin and second, I examine their reasons for turning to Islam as a main reference point of identity. This chapter suggests that there is an increasing individualization of religious belonging at the same time that the German sociopolitical sphere is increasingly shaping the Muslim social field. I propose that a Muslim lifestyle does not necessarily involve segregation from the German society, but can, on the contrary, provide modes of situating oneself in the German social space. The data for this chapter is from an earlier fieldwork that included approximately fifty young female Muslims in Berlin (2004 to 2007).[3] The youths, from thirteen to thirty years old, have parents from Egypt, Turkey, and Palestine and participate in the organization called "Muslim Youth Germany" (*Muslimische Jugend in Deutschland e. V.*, MJD). This religious youth organization arranges weekly meetings in which I participated during my fieldwork.[4]

MUSLIM YOUTHS IN GERMANY

Islam in Germany is generally represented by the immigrant workers arriving largely from Turkey in the mid 1960s, and their children and grandchildren who were born and educated in Germany. Whereas the German public was less concerned with the religious orientation of their immigrant population up until the 1980s, this situation changed rapidly from the early 1990s onwards (Soysal 2003; Spielhaus 2006).[5] The discursive change in the German media and public discussion in defining its migrant population as *guestarbeiter* (guest worker) to "Turks" and today "Muslims" must be understood as a combination of the end of the "dream of return" both among the migrants and the German population, an increase of visualization of religious markers (i.e., building of mosques and donning the veil), and global events like the terrorist attacks in the United States on September 11, 2001, after which the world turned its focus on "Islam" and "Muslims."

Today, the German Muslim population is around 3.4 million with 213,000 living in Berlin, the capital. These numbers, however, need to be taken with care since statistics on religious belonging is not well designed and do not reflect whether or not the individual actually identifies with Islam (Spielhaus and Färber 2006). When talking about religious belonging among young females in Berlin, the large intra-generational differences must first be noted. While some youths can be called "chic" Muslims as they combine headscarf, strong make-up and sexy clothes; others veil with more modest dress comportment; and again, others are not *visually* practicing Islam, although some might try to lead a religious lifestyle in the sense that they pray and fast. In addition, among the secular youths, some continue to recognize a cultural affinity with Islam. In this paper, I discuss young Sunni Muslims[6] for whom Islam is their main point of identity.

"Identity" is not considered as static or fixed, but continuously (re)created or formed in social interaction—identity is about ascription, both by individuals themselves and of individuals by others (Jenkins 1996). Groups identify themselves and are categorized by others. In modern society, identity is continuously constructed and in flux (Hall 1996). I follow Richard Jenkins (1996) in that others' perception of one's person will affect the perception one has of oneself and one's categorized group. This is particularly true when a person belongs to a minority group which is educationally and socially situated in a position of minor influence in public discourse. Identity formation and influence from peer groups or lifestyle groups are particularly strong among young people, when many seek a "self," and a purpose in life and are dealing with questions on "who to identify with" (Widdicombe and Wooffitt 1995). A *religious identity* tends to be an identity which one was born into and socialized through the family and community. However, one of the characteristics of modern society is the increased leeway to choose and frame political and religious identities (Lipset and Rokkan 1967). A religious identity is not only the adherence to a particular religious or spiritual frame of reference, but also in relation to whether that religious belief becomes a resource which impacts one's daily life, feelings of belonging and representation.

Generational Changes in Religious Practices

Several researchers have pointed out the generational differences in religious identification among Muslim youths in West European societies compared to that of their parents (Nökel 2002; Tietze 2006). Transmission of religion from one generation to the other always implies some change in continuity (Hervieu-Leger 1998). Socialization of youths to religious norms and values takes place as a continuous cultural change, even if a society is tradition oriented (Hervieu-Leger 1998). Movement or migration adds another dimension to religious change as immigration always changes how religion is transmitted. Stephen Warner (1998: 3) asserts that "religious identities, often (but not always) mean more to [individuals] away from home, in their diaspora, than they did before, and those identities undergo more or less modification as the years pass." One main reason for this, is that "[t]he religious institutions they build, adapt, remodel and adopt become worlds unto themselves, "congregations," where new relations among members of the community—among men and women, parents and children, recent arrivals and those settled—are forged" (Warner 1998: 3). Furthermore, social alienation and frustration because of displacement impact ethnic and religious identification, and connected with the very move is the fact that religion and culture no longer are "prearranged identities" (Göle 2003: 813). By changing context, Islam is no longer automatically transmitted from one generation to another or considered as a norm taken for granted. Instead, the former conceptions of social practices are questioned and tested. Migration to societies that are highly modern adds to the escalation of generational change.

The religious identity among the youths in this study is characterized by three partly interrelated aspects which concurrently mark a distinction from their parents' religiosity, namely: an effort to draw a division between "pure" and "traditional" Islam, focus on improving one's knowledge of Islam, and effort to live out Islam in the German language and space. These aspects, as it will be suggested, make it possible for the youths to argue that being a Muslim and a German is not a contradiction.

First, the youth deem their parents as not observing Islam "correctly," but as performing a mixture of religious forms and traditions brought with them from their (Turkish) villages. The youths instead seek a "pure" or "true" Islam (Roy 2004), detached from culture, ethnicity and nation by going back to the sources, particularly the Koran, *Tafsir* (commentary of the Koran), and the *Sunna* (the exemplary practice of the Prophet Mohammed). For example, during one weekly religious youth meeting, Fatwa (twenty-five years old, Egyptian

parents) emphasized that some, in particular older women, exaggerate their tears during their prayer in Ramadan or funerals, constituting more of a "performance" or "a competition" of who is feeling the most religiously, or who was the closest to the dead. "This is tradition," she argues, and not "correct religious behavior." Here, the division between "correct" and "wrong" is reflected upon within the framework of distinguishing between "culture" and "religion."[7] Such reflections illustrate that a correct religious performance within this religious group is recognized by certain normative standards, against which flawed performances are distinguished and assessed (Hirschkind 2001). An act "must be described in terms of the conventions which make it meaningful *as a particular kind of activity*, one performs for certain reason and in accord with certain standards of excellence and understood as such by those who perform and respond to it" (Hirschkind 2001: 633).

The emphasis on distinguishing between "pure" and "traditional" Islam is part of religious reform movements as well as among more fundamental religious movements in several European countries (Roy 2004).[8] The youths are part of similar processes taking place in different European societies, and also globally, in what have been called a "revival of Islam." Since the beginning of the 1990s, researchers interviewing young South Asian Muslim women in England find that these females establish a clear division between "religion" and "culture," a distinction which for their parents are largely interchangeable areas (Knott and Khokher 1993).[9] This orientation toward Islam resembles that of the "objectification" processes of the religious imagination in the Muslim Middle East in the 1990s (Eickelman 1992: 643). With the objectification of the religious imagination, Dale Eickelman (1992) points to the consciousness process by which Muslims become aware of their identity as Muslims. In this process the subjects explicitly ask themselves "What is my religion? Why is it important to my life? and, How do my beliefs guide my conduct?"

(Eickelman 1992: 643). In the course of this objecti-fication, religion is not becoming uniform or mono-lithic, even if some religious actors promote this perception. The so-called "objectified conscious-ness" is realized through *a process of modernization,* where the expansion of literacy, access to education and modern technology, like the internet, contribute to diminish the dependence on more traditional established authorities to make sense of their religion (Ismail 2004: 624–625).

Second, one consequence of seeking a "pure" Islam is an attentiveness to continuously improving ones knowledge of Islam and performing "correct" religious obligations, both internally and exter-nally. The youths consider it insufficient to perform a religious act externally, meaning that one's body movements and comportment of the performance are correct. The internal, one's mind and thoughts, has to be included in the act in order for it to be judged as *a religiously moral act* (cf. Mahmood 2005).[10] I often hear youths point to the idea that if someone performs a good deed "just in order to tell others" and to demonstrate "how good one is," this deed fails to provide "good points" (as a "good deed" for Allah) since such an act must be performed with the "correct" intentions.[11] The following discussion illustrate this further: During one of the weekly religious meetings organized by the Muslim Youths Germany, Fatwa says: "I was thinking that from next Monday on we should fast, but I don't know if people are motivated?"[12] One of the girls exclaims: "If we know that twenty of us are fasting, should that not be motivating enough?" Fatwa agrees, and another young girl enthusiastically suggests that "fasting is also weight reducing" as an incentive to fast. In response, Somaya (eighteen years old, Sudanese parents) wrinkles her nose, stressing that "diet should not be the reason to perform the fast."

Community feelings foster individual incen-tives to perform a religiously motivated act, like fasting. Moreover, Somaya's comment here reflects the idea that the act of fasting is only religiously "valid" in so far as the person conducts the act with correct motivations and virtues. Cultivating these dispositions, the young participants in the study learn to differentiate between performing practices which are motivated by religious experiences, or coming from religious moods, vis-à-vis those coming from secular, materialistic, traditional or fashion moods. Fasting in itself is not sufficient to count as a compelling religious act. Rather, fasting is only religiously valid in so far as the person conducts the act with truthful motivations.[13] The quest for "correct" bodily and sensory practices is part of what recent Islamist movements are seeking to reinstate or protect (Mahmood 2005; Asad in Mahmood 1996).

Third, in their struggle to live a religiously oriented life, Muslim adolescents emphasize that this religious lifestyle is actually sought *in* German society. Most are particularly preoccupied with how to construct and negotiate a modern life in Germany without compromising what they feel are their reli-gious duties and obligations in their daily life. One of the youth comments: "Living in this society, there are distractions everywhere. It's more difficult to be motivated to keep all the obeisance and reli-gious needs." Consequently, many participate in religious groups and organizations as it aids disci-plining themselves, and to be with "similar people." In the religious weekly Muslim Youth Germany meetings, questions concerning how to live as a "good" Muslim in a society that is not only non-Muslim but also largely considered as secular, is a topic of constant concern. For example, during a question round among the youth, some of the females asked, "Is one allowed to show one's hair to a lesbian?" and "How can one avoid being influ-enced by fashion, or be diverted from their prayers by non-practicing friends or TV shows?"

One consequence of the youths' emphasis on practicing a "pure" Islam is that they seek answers and knowledge in books and through the internet, and are easily rejecting the religious authority of their parents who they believe are following a traditional Islam. This approach to Islam makes it possible for young females to de-legitimize their parents' "religious" positions as based on "culture." To some extent, this situation leads to a "crisis" of their parents' authority (Roy 2004; Khosrokhavar 1997: 144); the youths are not discussing religious issues with their parents and feeling that they know more about Islam than their parents call upon "a higher moral authority and greater Islamic knowledge" (Mahmood 2005: 116; Cesari 2003; Salih 2003; Jacobsen 2006). Sometimes the young women even attempt to influence their own mothers' practices, such as educing them to veil, and assess their parents critically for their lax religious lifestyle. In consequence, the age hierarchy under which textual authority is in voked and, to some extent, the youth can become religious educators of their parents.

However, even if I agree that the youths' individual orientation to Islam leads to some extent to emancipation or more freedom of movement, my fieldwork indicates that this aspect needs to be adjusted or modified. During my fieldwork I realized that the parent's authority is often *re-emphasized* through Islamic discourses. Presentations frequently stress the youths' obligations and duties as daughters (or sons), and the significant role and position of parents within Islam. Breaking with the family is considered as a great sin, and should be avoided as far as possible.

The changed role of religious authority of their parents indicates not only a generational shift, but also an increasing individuaiization of Muslim identity. How Islam is played out and how the youths are "being Muslims" are negotiated in relation to new religious authorities, including internet blogs, television preachers, books, religious groups and personal judgment. Furthermore, as the youths are not active in ethnic oriented mosques and organizations, they emphasize a universal Islam where the world wide *ummah* (community) is the reference, the youths' religious activities and identification are de-ethnicized. Turning to Islam is not making the youths feel more "Turkish" or "Egyptian." Rather, it detaches their ethnic identity from their religious identity. At the same time, many youths feel that it is difficult *feel* like a "German" due to continuous framing of Islam as incompatible with German values.

Representing Islam

Typically, the female youths are treated as non-German and/or as "others" by strangers they encounter in daily life and by their school teachers. This representation is related to stereotyping and prefabricated ways of looking at the headscarf by the media (Schiffer 2005). The habits of categorization are often related to second-hand experience, the media. Media is our most important source of information, in particular to themes which we otherwise have little access to, of which consequently media structures our perception (Schiffer 2005). Being German and Muslim is a problematic identification due to the current media framing of "Islamism" (*lslamismus*) and "terror," and the construction of "Islam as strangeness" (*Fremdheit*) (Schiffer 2005) and as representing values incompatible with German values. Islamism and the suppression of Muslim women are symbolized through the continued use of references to or images of the headscarf in the media. A chain of associations, by now unconsciously, has been constructed in that television or newspapers make use of women with headscarves in particular reports. This collective stereotyping or profiling of what "Muslims are" or how they are supposed to behave in which Islam apparently dictates how Muslims behave and think, is not only affecting how the non-Muslim population think about Muslims and Islam, but also how Muslims identify and behave in the European public spheres. This process is gendered in which the image of the veil is constructing an idea of Muslim women as submissive, subverted, traditional and/or passive.

A politician with migrant background is quoted in the tabloid newspaper, *Bild am Sonntag*, as appealing to Muslim women saying, "Arrive today, arrive in Germany. You live here, thus take off the headscarf!"[14] The statement suggests that wearing a headscarf is considered as incompatible with being German, or with having "arrived"—not only physically, but mentally or affectively—in German society. The relation between veiling and being perceived as a non-German becomes particularly clear when talking to German Muslim female converts. Both Muslim and non-Muslim population consider these women as no longer German once they don the veil. Also "born" Muslims feel a difference in the public perception of them after starting to veil. For example, Ines, a seventeen year old of Palestinian background believes that when she started to wear the headscarf, it changed the way her urban surroundings consider her. She narrates:

> Sometimes at the metro, there are like three people sitting across you, and they stare, look at you like this' [she looks at me from head to toe" 'as if they were in the Zoo . . . and I, like, think, come on hey, stop looking at me like that, as if I am a monkey in a cage! And sometimes you are also imagining it, like, that (you think) they are looking, and then there is maybe no one who is really looking at you, it drives you crazy . . . And then they ask why foreigners become criminals? Like, imagine, I feel it like that, and I am not even a foreigner, I am German. And they are still not treating me as a German. Imagine how it must feel for a real foreigner, someone who is not a German! . . . I have been German since I was able to think, and now, since when I started to wear a headscarf, I am not German anymore. They treat you differently, you can just feel it.

Ines feels that there is a clear change in how her immediate surroundings react and behave toward her after she started to veil (Bendixsen 2005). She personally does not see any contradiction in being German and veiled, but experiences that she is treated as a "foreigner" due to this practice. Growing up in a place where she seldom socialized with

people of migrant background, Ines had mostly "ethnic" German friends before the age of fourteen. After a turbulent youth, she turned more religious when she moved to Berlin and decided to veil at the age of seventeen. Until then, she says, she had no problems considering herself as a German, a feeling that changed after she visually expressed that she is a Muslim and the subsequent external reactions toward her. In the above conversation, she particularly emphasizes the experiences of being "othered" by gazes from strangers.

"German & Muslim = Good Like That"[15]

Several Muslim youths are trying to combine "being German" with "being Muslim." They employ several tactics[16] in pursuing this endeavor, including learning Islam in the German language, emphasizing certain common values and moralities, and trying to change the negative stereotyping of Islam in Germany. Without the intention of returning to their parents' homeland, many youths of the so-called second generation consciously learn about Islam in the German language in which they are more fluent (Nökel 2002). Consequently, youths can explain Islam to their non-Muslim surroundings in a more straightforward way. Furthermore, the majority focuses on how to best practice Islam, their religious behavior and belief, *in Germany*, which is considered a secular society.

Perhaps paradoxically, the females' religious identification can assist in embracing a German and "modern" identity. The youths encounter daily expectations which they feel are contradictory from those of their parents on the one hand, who fear that their daughters are becoming "too German," and from their teachers and peers, on the other, who they think will consider them as "too Turkish." The clear distinction that the youth make between ethnicity and religion makes it possible for them not to feel "betwixt and between" their parent's home country and Germany. Certain values, such as punctuality, honesty and hard work are appreciated both in Islam and in German culture. By framing these as "Islamic," the youths can negotiate a "third space" (Bhabha 1994).[17] For example, Fatima (thirty years old, Turkish parents) remarks that "religion can be a bridge," because it combines both; "one can say 'I am a Muslim' and it does not matter whether one is German, Turkish or Arabic." When young women look for a marriage partner, it is increasingly important that their future husband is a religiously observant Muslim, without regard for his ethnic background. The majority still marry within their ethnic groups—most likely due to language, social network and expectations from their parents. Nevertheless, a marriage choice is more complex, as Naila (seventeen years old, Egyptian parents) comments: "For sure, I will never marry an Egyptian from Egypt, you know," and explains that it is important that her future husband should not only be a Muslim, but also know the "European lifestyle."

The effort of living out a "correct" Islam by the youths is localized and situated in Germany as a non-Muslim society and as a place where many adolescents feel that "Islam is misunderstood and misrepresented." For example, at one Friday presentation in a German-speaking mosque which the youths often visit, the presenter says "Islam is being criticized because we are doing wrong things. We are mirroring Islam for these people, and when we mirror the wrong things then we are guilty in that they are not coming to Islam because we are mirroring wrong." Such utterance situates the religious practice of youths directly in their physical locality and suggests their larger duty to perform Islam "correctly" in a specific socio-historical context. The representative role the youth's sense as a consequence of "othering" processes cannot be underestimated.[18] Many youths, females in particular, experience being "walking representatives of Islam" in their daily life vis-à-vis both non-Muslims and the Muslim population. With this follows a feeling of obligation to improve the stained (Goffman 1963) image of Islam in the German public where they are depicted as suppressed or victims of patriarchal forces—thus at the same time, portraying "the Muslim man" as a suppressor.

What I call "daily micro-politics" are tactics (de Certeau 1984) the youth make use of in an effort to improve the negative representation of Muslims. Such tactics include a continuous attentiveness to how they behave in the street, such as smiling to strangers, being helpful, or to enhance their Islamic knowledge to improve their answers to questions about Islam. The self-awareness of representing Islam increases social pressure, from themselves, other Muslims and non-Muslims on the young females: as the females try to promote an authentic or ideological image of Islam and Muslims, it involves high demands on their daily behavior in the street. The price for "being in a community" (Bauman 2001a: 4) includes self-control and living up to constructed expectations on what it means to be a "good, correct Muslim."

The youths' identification with Islam is not only affected by their status as members of a post-migration religious minority (Cesari 2003), but also by global events, the introduction of technology and opportunities provided in the urban space. The transnational element of the youth's orientation to Islam as a consequence of modern technology cannot be underestimated; figures like Tariq Ramadan,[19] the Egyptian religious scholar al-Qaradawi[20] and the popular Egyptian television preacher Amr Khaled are references and authorities for youths all over the worldwide *ummah* (Mandaville 2005). Through the online discussion groups and cable TV shows, ideas and concepts are spread and discussed between different local spaces. The recent popular Baba Ali figuring in "ummah films" on YouTube is one example of a young, American-Iranian Muslim who creatively contributes to a transnational Muslim youth culture with his funny, satiric clips with titles such as "Culture vs. Islam," "Muslim while Flying," "Looking for a Spouse Online" and "The Parent Negotiations."[21]

Social class and educational level of youths affect how a religious identity is lived out (Ismail 2004; Salih 2003) and where they participate religiously (Bendixsen 2007). Emphasizing knowledge as the only way to live Islam "correctly" seems to attract youths who already are, or in the future will belong to an upward mobile part of the migrant population because of their parents' or own educational success. It can be suggested that educational level has a stronger effect on the youths' relation to Islam (cf. Salih 2003) than merely their economically defined class and migration background.

A MODERN MUSLIM IDENTITY?

The "turn to Islam" is an urban phenomenon in Germany, which can also be found in Cairo (Ismail 2006) and Istanbul (Sanktanber 2002). A city offers a variety of religious spaces representing different religious orientations and congregations providing particular "infrastructures of action" (Ismail 2006: 12). Salwa Ismail suggests that the "turn to Islam" within the urban space is not only a consequence of people moving from rural to urban, thus facing alienation in the urban anonymity and weakening of community structures. More important is mobilizing urban opportunities for a religious organization to situate its message in the social antagonism and positions that have historically always been a part of the urban landscape (Ismail 2006: 112–113). Religion can be practiced alone, by use of the many online groups on the internet, in new religious study groups, or in the more traditional, ethnically oriented mosques. The variety of religious spaces in urban Berlin makes it possible for the youth to pursue a more individual and privatized orientation toward Islam, and consequently, to develop a religious youth culture.

"Turning to Islam" as a focal orientation of identity involves not only a religious moral orientation, but certain aesthetic, search for "pious fun" and religious consumption. Religious businesses or religious consumption are part of the youths' identification with Islam; in "religious shops," particularly in Kreuzberg, Wedding and Neukölln,[22] the youths can purchase CD readings of the Koran, candies without gelatin,[23] Mecca Cola, a counseling book for food purchase for Muslims in Germany, and *hijab*-Barbie (Barbie with a veil) while listening to religious songs by Yusuf Islam or Ammer 114[24]—a German "Islamic" hip-hop artist. Information on which of the "Turkish" or "Arab" *Imbiss* are religiously "correct" is passed via word-of-mouth.[25] Islamic graffiti on the Berliner urban landscape such as "Muslims are the best. Live Allah!" or "Muslims love best" (Kaschuba 2007)[26] both challenge urban spaces and present spaces of belonging (Bendixsen 2007).

Turning to Islam also includes a consciousness on how Muslims dress in public, an effort to behave in a religiously correct manner in terms of gender relation in the public sphere, and refusal to visit places with high alcohol consumption. In this religious identity formation, several seek to improve themselves religiously by increasing their knowledge and enhancing their moral behavior, for example to pray more or to wear the headscarf. There are diverse reasons why young females decide to veil; some of the young women are forced by their parents, for others the headscarf is a fashion or a political statement, and some veil because of religious conviction. In the latter case, veiling is part of a continuous personal effort to improve themselves as "pious subjects" (Mahmood 2005), to please God and to reach Paradise in the afterlife. Seeing other veiled women in the street becomes part of their feeling of belonging in Berlin; "We are always so happy to see someone with a headscarf, particularly here [Reinickendorf] where there are not that many," exclaims one youth during a picnic. It improves their self-consciousness as Muslims and group identification with Islam in Berlin. The veil is not only a religious obligation, but in the socio-historical climate, it has turned into a symbol of solidarity among female Muslims and by wearing it, creates spaces of belonging in a non-Muslim society.

Salwa Ismail (2006) argues that "[t]he view of Islamism as anti-modern rests on the assumption that modernization is associated with secularization and the retreat of religion from the public sphere. Islamism thus appears as an expression of an anti-modern strand that, for some, is inherent in the religion" (Ismail 2006: 3).[27] Instead of considering Islamism as an anti-modern movement, Ismail refocuses our attention to its rejection of the Western perceived hegemonic ownership or mega-narrative of the modern.

In contrast to this perception, wearing headscarf with jeans and fashionable colors is not about bricolage, but an act through which the youths situate the religious practice in the society in which they live. Further, at a picnic with a group of veiled youths, Rüya says jokingly to her sisters, "We have to be modern, after all we are Muslims!" This narrative of modernity, uttered half playful and half serious, should be understood within a context where Islam and Muslims are considered as "traditional," backward and resisting the modern (secular) society. Even if Rüya recognizes that the non-Muslim German majority consider religious adherence to Islam as traditional, Rüya promotes modernity through her devotion to Islam as a spiritual and social self-fulfillment in Germany.

Living a religious life and seeking modernity is not contradictory for these youths. Scholars point out that even if the traditional systems of believing are rejected by modernity, belief is not abandoned (Casanova 2001; Berger 1999). Individual, self-reflection and search for knowledge are part of the youth's religious identity, an identity which is felt and lived out as a "free" and conscious choice. They continuously distinguish their religious practices from their parents, which they consider traditional. The females, for example, often joke and make fun of their mothers' "unfashionable headscarf," distinguishing their parent's practice from their own. Simultaneously, even if this religious identity is more individualized than their parents, it does not mean the end of orthodoxy or that they are creating

a random "pick and choose." The need for legitimacy and validation of the religious practice continues to be largely part of their religiosity. As Danièle Hervieu-Leger stresses "there is no religion without the authority of a tradition being invoked (whether explicitly, half-explicitly or implicitly) in support of the act of believing" (2000: 76).

Push and Pull Factors Illuminating "the Islamic Turn"

The question of why women embrace religious norms and religious communities has been central in studies on Muslim women since the 1990s and has been addressed in different ways. The fact that women embrace Islam and religious organizations regarded as subjecting female bodies to patriarchal gender structures have been considered as a paradox, or representing a "perplexing question" by feminist scholars (Moghadam 1994; Saghal and Yuval-Davis 1992). Some scholars have a tendency to consider women who actively participate in religious organizations as victims of "false consciousness"—disciplined by fundamentalist formations (Grewal and Kaplan 1994).[28] Related to the debate on multiculturalism, Susan Okin (1997), a liberal feminist philosopher, claims that there is an inescapable tension between gender equality ideals and cultural recognition of groups. Continuing in this vein of understanding, other scholars argue in a universalistic feminist matter, that though Muslim girls seem to choose wearing the veil, this does not mean that they are autonomous, as the veil is a (*the*) symbol of subordination (Badinter 1989). In this view, as the content of women's "cultural norms"—such as modesty, self-discipline, and seclusion—is in opposition to personal autonomy, the women risk to be subordinated by adhering to their cultural communities.

Since the 1990s several scholars argue that Muslim youth's "turn to Islam" is part of "identity politics" (Cesari 2003; Khosrokhavar 1997)—a modern phenomenon—with similarities to social movements. Just like other youth subcultures which have developed in the urban spaces throughout the years (Widdicombe and Wooffitt 1995) identification with Islam seems to be a response to socio-economic conditions. It is one possible way to create a space and place within a life-world which does not offer many positive prospects for a socially and economically secure future. As such, "being or becoming a Muslim" is seen as a possible solution toward discrimination (Cesari 2003), and a way out for youths who are more or less excluded or feel rejected from society and search for a purpose in life (Khosrokhavar 1997). Implied in this perception of young Muslims' activities is the idea that Muslims are searching to publicly articulate an "authenticity" (Göle 2003), often through symbols that represent their religious identity as a way to claim *recognition* from the larger society (cf. Fraser 2000).

Identifying with Islam is a way to gain more emancipation from their families. By referring to religious argumentations, youths easily legitimate certain aspirations such as education and working in public. Veiling provides girls more freedom in that their parents will trust their behavior more in public (cf. Jacobsen 2006; Salih 2003; Nökel 2002). Distinguishing Islam from tradition and customs also facilitates their refusal of certain stigmatizing practices, such as forced marriages and "honor killings." By positioning both as the result of tradition and not Islam, the youths argue that "it has nothing to do with me, as it has nothing to do with Islam" both to other Muslims and to non-Muslims.

At the same time, understanding the turn to a religious identification simply as a reaction to external social structures as push factors becomes a too functional analysis and neglects both the specific individual and the global processes of which their religious identification constitutes a part. During my fieldwork with the young females, I realized that one needs to take these youths' religiousness seriously. This includes a stronger focus on the females' religious agency as well as the pull factors from religious organizations. Religious agency, following Laura Leming (2007) is "a personal and collective claiming and enacting of dynamic religious identity. As *religious* identity, it may include, but is not limited to, a received or an acquired identity, whether passed on by family, religious group, or other social entity such as an educational community, or actively sought. To constitute religious *agency*, this identity is claimed and lived as one's own, with an insistence on active ownership" (Leming 2007: 74). This religious agency is, like all agencies, not situated in a vacuum, but is performed within particular socio-historical contexts.

The decision to participate in a Muslim organization or to identify with Islam is shaped by religious and spiritual desires and experiences.[29] Several young women start practicing Islam actively due to a dream related to their—until then—lax religious praxis or because they are feeling confused. "Being a Muslim" and struggling to become a "better" Muslim is also about seeking to identify oneself as a religious person where motivation to becoming a pious or virtuous subject is a vehicle for daily activities, including efforts to perform their five obligatory prayers, struggle to merge internal motivation with external motions, but also forming characteristics which they consider important in Islam, such as modesty and being helpful.

This religious agency is often neglected, perhaps because the "turn to Islam" is considered as an (unfortunate) return to tradition and parental home country's culture. What should be clear by now is that the youths are not (re)turning to a static, unchanging religious tradition. Rather, they are actively pursuing religious morals and values which are situated in their own material and socio-cultural living condition. This does not mean that the youths are creating an individual religion where they pick and choose from Islam as "religion a la carte" or a religious bricolage, which some scholars tend to suggest (cf. Kara-kasoglu 2003; Khosrokhavar 1997: 128). On the contrary, the youth's quest for a "pure" Islam where validation of the "correct performance" is situated within a search for authenticity makes it necessary to legitimate their practices, for themselves and their peers, by positioning these practices vis-à-vis the religious sources. Most religious actors need a religious community in order to be with "others like them" and to create a universe of meaning where "what makes sense to you also makes sense to me" (Hervieu-Leger 2001b: 167). An individual requires confirmation from outsiders for the meanings she/he makes use of in making sense and significance of their daily life (Hervieu-Leger 2001b).

One *pull* factor which is often ignored is the effort from religious organizations to attract the youths as these organizations may represent spaces where the youths are not "othered" or considered as abnormal. In continuation, Hans Joas (2004) points to the need for religious people to articulate their faith or their experience of self-transcendence—a practice which is difficult. Religious experiences happen to individuals and are felt or apprehended rather than cognitively recognized. Although these elements contribute to make the experiences real, they make them only real, as the phenomenologist William James ([1902] 1994) suggests, for those who experience them. Consequently, Joas (2004) emphasizes that people need spaces in where they can share these feelings and experiences with others who also experiences them, although in a different way. These *pull* factors from religiousness and religious organization must be included in a deeper understanding of the "turn to Islam."

expected to represent Islam in any situation. The conditions of community formation are upheld (Baumann 2001a), although the form of religious communities has changed. In this process, a new religious lifestyle among the young Muslims is developing in urban spaces.

Without undermining the authentic religious experience of the identification with Islam or Muslim identity, I suggest that this process has similarities to "lifestyle subcultures." The youths' focus on moral values and universality as a reaction both toward the secular, materialistic, and Eurocentric majority in society on the one hand, and a traditional, cultural, local and nostalgic orientation of the "migrant community" on the other. In this space, specialized religious knowledge becomes a kind of "subcultural capital" (cf. Thornton 1995). Noticeably, the youths most attracted to this religious identification are not uneducated youth, but those who in many ways, are the most equipped among the "migrant" youth, in the sense that they master the German language, focus on higher education and have ambitions of a future working career. At the same time as localizing themselves through the urgency of improving the image of Islam in Germany, they also transcend the physically bounded site by drawing on globalized networks and influences, (re)capitalizing on the Islamic notion of community, the *ummah*.

CONCLUSION

Is the combination of youth, religion and an urban lifestyle a contradiction? Or, is the urban space opening up for a variety of religious orientation in the twenty-first century, a period depicted as uncertain, ever changing and disintegrating communities? It is my perception that the modern process of individualization takes place (Bauman 2001a) at the same time as there is a continued process of ascription, categorization, and "othering" processes. Any individual outwardly resembling a Muslim is

NOTES

1. Some sociologists of religion have pointed to the perception that there is a necessary incompatibility between religion and modern, urban life was too quickly taken. Stark argues that in Japan folk religion "flourishes among the young, successful, educated urbanites." It is worth noting that Stark has been critiqued, justifiably so, on his particular selection of statistic and data in order to completely reject the thesis of secularization. See Stark (1999): 268.

2. The concept of second generation of migrants has been rightly problematized for constructing the idea

that people who are born in the country are still "migrant" just because their parents come from a different country. I still use the concept here for lack of a better concept that recognizes the particular sociaiization in a transnational space, meaning that they, through a *Biografiebildung* (biography formation) in their parent's home country—as well as in the migration "community," are embedded in familial and other relevant social relationships and networks. See Apitzsch (2003).

3. The participant observation (eighteen months) was conducted as part of my PhD thesis entitled "It's like doing SMS to Allah": Young Female Muslims Crafting a Religious Self in Berlin" in Social Anthropology at the Humboldt University (Berlin) and École des Hautes Études en Sciences Sociales (Paris), 2009.

4. The youth is the main focus of MJD as the stated goal is "to integrate Muslim youths by providing an opportunity to develop their creativity and talents *as young German Muslims* in the German language." See MJD, www.mjd-net.de (accessed February 1, 2008). Similar Muslim youth organisations exist in Austria, Italy, France, Sweden and Norway and MJD is represented at the European level by FEMYSO (Forum European Muslim Youth and Student Organisation) established in Leicester (UK) in 1996.

5. Like most European scholars, German scholars were mostly concerned with how ethnic and national identity and culture continued to have an impact on migrants' life choices up until the late 1980s. Particularly when large parts of the migrant population protested publicly in Britain during the Rushdie affair in 1989 scholars refocused their attention to the (changed) role of religion of migrants and their children born in Europe. See Steven Vertovec, "Religion and Diaspora" (paper presented at the conference on New Landscapes of Religion in the West, University of Oxford, September 27–29, 2000).

6. In Germany, the largest groups are the Sunni (approximately 2.2 million), followed by the Shiite (approximately 400,000), and the Alevite (approximately 340,000). See Below and Karakoyun (2007), 33.

7. Hirschkind, performing fieldwork in Egypt, similarly found that many were distressed by people crying during religious sermons for the "wrong" reasons. See Hirsckind (2001): 623–631.

8. Hermansen argues that "[i]nternationalist Muslim revivalist movements such as *Jama 'at Islami* [Islamic Party] and the Muslim Brotherhood (*Ikhwan al-Muslimin*) have encouraged this concept of a 'cultureless' Islam around the world." They are, she further holds, incorporating the identity element into the organization by insisting on "Muslim and proud of it." See Hermansen (2003), 309.

9. They reject their parents' conformity to ethnic traditions that the parents consider as emblematic of religiosity (e.g., manner of dress), while embracing a Muslim identity in and of itself. Among these young women, Knott and Khokher explain, there is a. "self-conscious exploration of the religion which was not relevant to the first generation." See Knot and Khoker (1993): 596.

10. Similarities can be found in Christianity.

11. It is the belief that doing "good deeds" *(al-amal al-saliha)* secures God's blessing and aids in the formation of virtuous dispositions. The good deeds must be performed with the right sincerity of intent (*al ikhlas*) in order to perceive "good points" believed to improve a Muslim's chance to enter paradise. See Mahmood (1998), 102–104.

12. Note that this was not during Ramadan. The youths are sometimes fasting throughout the year as an act that gives "good points," but also in order to complete their past Ramadan as women have to break the fasting month during their period of menstruation.

13. Note here the notion of *niyya* (Arab, "intention"). This notion emphasizes the importance of pronouncing the intention in the heart before performing the outer act in order for it to be a valid religious act in Islam. For example, the prayer, pilgrimage and fast are not valid if the proper intent is absent. One hadith (#1 in *al-Nawawi's* Forty Hadith) states that "actions are according to intent" or "actions are what they are by virtue of intent."

14. Ekin Deligöz, member of the Bundestag of the Green party, is quoted in Spiegel online as saying that prominent German-Turkish have appealed to Muslims in German to take off their headscarf as a sign of their willingness to integrate: "the person who veils is consciously bounding herself off from the German society" (my translation from German). Spiegel, *Deutsch-Türken gegen Kopftuch*, Spiegel, http://www.spiegel.de/politik/deutschland/0,I518,442656,00.html (accessed October 20, 2006).

15. My translation from the German: "Deutsch & Muslim = Gut so," written in a power point slide presented in the Berlin weekly meeting on the topic

"Muslim and German" by one of the national representatives of Muslim Youth Germany (MJD).

16. De Certeau makes a distinction between strategies and tactics: "A strategy assumes a place that can be circumscribed as proper and thus serve as the basis for generating relations with an exterior distinct from it . . . I call a 'tactic,' on the other hand, a calculus which cannot count on a 'proper' (a spatial or institutional location), nor thus on a borderline distinguishing the other as a visible totality. The place of a tactic belongs to the other . . . A tactic insinuates itself to the other's place, fragmentarily, without taking it over in its entirety, without being able to keep it at a distance." See Certeau (1984), xix.

17. Third spaces, according to Bhabha, are "discursive sites or conditions that ensure that the meaning and symbols of culture have no primordial unity or fixity; that even the same signs can be appropriated, translated, and rehistoricized anew." See Bhabha (1994), 37.

18. In postcolonial theory, which is my approach here, the notion of the "Other" refers to "the discursive production of another"—a process typified by the way in which Europe produces an Orient-as-other, also described as "othering." See Spivak ([1992] 1996). There is a general tendency to consider "others" as categorically and essentially different. In this idea of difference, are potentials for hierarchical and stereotypical thinking, which it is why the effect of "othering" bears resemblance to racism. See Zizek (1990): 50–62.

19. Ramadan in particular encourages young Muslims to regard their position in non-Muslim homelands not as one of weakness, but rather as a source of strength. See Mandaville (2005).

20. Al-Qaradawi produces a discourse, which is modern and moderate at the same time. Its more formal dimensions (using more traditional *fatwa* methodology or ruling on a question of Islamic law) preserve the authenticity of Islamic traditionalism. Religious programs on *al-Jazeera* and translations of his books have made him a representative of the most popular contemporary transnational Islamic discourses with devotees from the *banlieus* (suburbs) of Paris to the *pesantren* (Islamic boarding schools) of Southern Asia. See Mandaville (2005).

21. See Ummah Films, http://youtube.com/ummahfilms (accessed November 20, 2008).

22. These are neighborhoods in Berlin with a large representation of working class and population with immigrant background.

23. Many groceries contain the additive E441 (used in ice cream, chocolate, candies and different food products) which is produced through swine skin and the E47-E474 contains swine products, considered as *haram* (forbidden) to eat in Islam. There is a difference among Muslims in the degree to how careful one is concerning eating these products.

24. The number 114 refers to the number *of Surahs* (chapters) in the Koran.

25. Mandel has described how shopkeepers in Kreuzberg use the fear of *haram* (forbidden) meat and what is considered obligatory or *halal* (permitted) to their advantage. The result is an increase of shops that cater exclusively to Turks, creating a Muslim space in Germany, subdivided by Sunni or Alevi. She rightly points that this commercial orientation is also creating a place for migrants, on their own terms. See Mandel (1996), 147–166.

26. My own translation from the German language. Original: "Muslime sind die Besten. Es lebe Allah" and "Muslime lieben am besten." See Kaschuba (2007): 83.

27. Islamism is a contested term, and rightly so. Ismail refers to "Islamism" as both Islamist politics and re-Islamisation, the latter of which relates to my usage here. Islamisation is "the process whereby various domains of social life are invested with signs and symbols associated with Islamic cultural traditions, Examples of this process include the wearing of the *hijab* (veil), the consumption of religious literature and other religious commodities, the publicizing of symbols of religious identity, the reframing of economic activity in Islamic terms." See Ismail (2006), 2.

28. Bracke suggests how this idea of "false consciousness" is based on a gendered and ethnicized way of thinking. See Bracke (2003): 337.

29. As Rambo correctly intervenes: "[r]eligion and spirituality, like aesthetics, should be considered a domain of life and experience that has its own validity." There are, he continues, "experiences, both cognitive and affective, that are distinctive to religion and spirituality." See Rambo (1999): 264.

Christianity and the Experience of Domestic Violence: What Does Faith Have to Do with It?

Nancy Nason-Clark

DOMESTIC VIOLENCE is a pervasive reality that knows no boundaries of class, color, country, or faith perspective (Stirling, Cameron, Nason-Clark, & Miedema 2004; Timmins, 1995). Its prevalence around the world has been documented through statistics collected by government agencies, the World Health Organization, and the United Nations Secretariat (Kroeger & Nason-Clark, 2001/2010). Yet, religious voices are often silenced, or sidelined, and a holy hush still operates in many congregational or denominational circles (Nason-Clark, 2004; Fortune, 1991; Potter, 2007).

From the earliest days of the battered women's movement, there was a reluctance to see any perspective informed by religious language or passion as part of the *solution* to abuse (Brown & Bohn, 1989). Yet, it was undeniable that a woman's religious faith might shape her experience and disclosure of battery and the road she would choose to travel in her quest for wholeness in its aftermath (Boehm, Golec, Krahn and Smyth, 1999; Clarke, 1986; Fiorenza & Copeland, 1994; Halsey 1984). There was mounting evidence that some abused women were turning to their religious leaders for assistance (Rotunda, Williamson and Penfold, 2004;

Giesbrecht & Sevcik, 2000; Horton & Williamson, 1988; Weaver, 1993). But the story of what happened when men, women, and children looked to their faith community after terror occurred at home was yet to be told.

For almost twenty years, my research program has been attempting to fill this void through a series of studies—both quantitative and qualitative—aimed at understanding the interface between religion and domestic violence. Some religious survivors claim their faith sustains them through the protracted, ugly reality of domestic abuse. It empowers them, through spiritual and practical resources, to flee the abuse and seek safety and solace in a context free from the violence of the past. Others are consumed by the sacred silence, fighting demons both within and without. They are ultimately prevented from leaving behind the fear or reality of abuse.

There are many angles to the story of abuse in families of faith, some connected to survivors, or to perpetrators, or to those professionals who seek to offer them support or accountability in its aftermath. In this article, I propose to begin to unravel some of the complexities in the relationship between faith and domestic violence, and the struggle to build bridges between secular and sacred community response networks.

This article draws on results that emerge from the following studies:

- Tensions, Contradictions and Collaborations between clergy and transition house workers in Canada (Beaman-Hall & Nason-Clark, 1997; Nason-Clark, 1996).

- Pastoral Knowledge and Experience of Abuse in Congregational Life (Nason-Clark, 1997, 1998b).

- Pastoral Counseling and Abused Religious Women (Nason-Clark, 1999; Nason-Clark & Kroeger, 2004).

- Religious Women-Helping-Women Who are Abused (Beaman-Hall & Nason-Clark, 1997; Beaman-Hall & Nason-Clark, 1997b; Nason-Clark, 1995).

- Clergy in Mainline Denominations and Experience Responding to Abuse (Nason-Clark, 2000a, 2000d).

- Faith-Based Batterer Intervention Programs: a 10 Year File Study (Fisher-Townsend, Nason-Clark, Ruff, & Murphy, 2008; Nason-Clark, Murphy, Fisher-Townsend, & Ruff, 2003).

- Professionals Working with Male Batterers (Fisher-Townsend, 2008; Nason-Clark & Fisher-Townsend, 2005).

- Understanding the Stories of Men Who Act Abusively Over Time (Nason-Clark & Fisher-Townsend, 2008).

- Global Strategies to Understand and Respond to Abuse in Families of Faith (Nason-Clark, 2004).

I have attempted to harness some of the results from these selected studies to highlight four different perspectives, or experiences, which collectively help us to understand the web of connections surrounding Christianity and violence in the family context. Ultimately, we are challenged to ask: what does faith have to do with it?

FOUR PERSPECTIVES ON THE EXPERIENCE OF RELIGIOUS WOMEN WHO HAVE BEEN VIOLATED

Spiritual Dimensions of the Journey for a Survivor of Abuse

When religious women seek assistance from their pastor in the aftermath of domestic violence, they are looking for help with practical, emotional and spiritual needs (Nason-Clark and Kroeger, 2004). For women of faith, even some of the practical and emotional issues that surface have spiritual undertones. *Is it okay for a Christian to seek refuge at the local shelter? Should an abused woman enter the workforce, or continue to be a full-time mom? Does God expect a victim of her husband's abuse to forgive her husband seventy times seven?*

As a result, abused Christian women report that sometimes they feel pulled between what they perceive as the teachings of their church, including the behavior or advice of its leaders, and their personal safety and emotional health (Nason-Clark, 1999). Moreover, since many pastors do not refer abused women who seek their help to secular community-based agencies, women who look for help in a variety of contexts (both within and beyond the household of faith) may feel that they have let their faith community down. Religious women suffering abuse are often disappointed to find that there is limited awareness and understanding of domestic violence by their leaders, modest knowledge of the resources available, and a lack of ability (or discomfort) to offer them help of an explicitly religious nature (i.e., prayer, Bible readings, spiritual counsel) (Nason-Clark, 1998).

When religious leaders speak out about violence during the weekly routine of church life, its impact on those who have been violated is profound (Kroeger, Nason-Clark and Fisher-Townsend, 2008). However, one of the best-kept secrets of congregational life is the support that women of faith offer to each other in and beyond the local church setting

(Beaman-Hall and Nason-Clark, 1997b; Nason-Clark, 1995, 1997). One of the implications of this finding for those who practice social work is to gently encourage a woman of faith (who may feel cut off from her congregation or its leadership) to seek out other women in her church or religious network at her point of need. Like any disclosure of a personal nature, she will need to choose her confidantes wisely.

For over twenty years, through my research and speaking engagements, I have been hearing the stories of abused Christian women, told by survivors and those who have walked alongside them. Often their spiritual needs are primary on the road to personal well-being. Like a shattered window, an abused woman reports that her life as she knew it has been blown apart. Yet, the pastor and other community-based professionals, such as her lawyer, social worker, or advocates at a shelter, can help her to pick up the pieces of her broken life and reclaim strength and safety.

Many religious women want to maintain the illusion of an intact family (Nason-Clark, 1997; 2000a). She may be very reluctant to leave her husband and seek alternative solutions for personal safety and emotional health. She may cling unrelentingly to the promise she made, many years before, to love and honor her husband until death. She may feel it is her responsibility to keep on forgiving, to keep on trying to salvage the marriage, and to never give up hope that her husband might change. In point of fact, through our research we have found that most religious women who are abused do not consider themselves to be battered wives (Nason-Clark, 1996; 2004). On the contrary, they feel simply like their lives—and their families—are falling apart.

The resources that religious women seek in the aftermath of domestic violence in part differentiate them from other abused women. They are often very reluctant to seek secular, community-based sources of support, preferring to look to others of like-minded faith for assistance—pastors and lay alike. Since many faith communities place the intact family on a pedestal, religious women are especially prone to blame themselves for the abuse, believe they have promised God to stay married until death, and experience both the fear and reality of rejection at church when attempts to repair the relationship fail.

It is imperative that those in the helping professions—like social workers—understand some of the unique and specific needs of clients who are very religious. As a bridge builder, a social worker can help to build an alliance between a community-based agency and communities of faith. Sometimes these bridges will be one person at a time: an abused woman on her caseload and her pastor. Sometimes these bridges will be agency or congregation specific: the mental health clinic and a downtown historic church. Other times, as a case manager, the social worker may be encouraging other professionals with whom she or he works to include a faith perspective around the collaborative community table.

In the aftermath of violence in the life of an abused woman, there are so many questions to be answered, questions that can only be addressed by someone with spiritual credentials, like a religious leader, or in-depth religious knowledge, like a faith-enriched therapist. Whether an abused religious woman first seeks help in a community-based agency or a church, she should be able to expect that her story of abuse is taken seriously, that she is given accurate, practical advice, that her safety and security is the top priority, and that her faith perspective is understood and respected. For many Christian women of deep personal faith, the experience of domestic violence in the family context is intricately intertwined with her spiritual life in such a way that it would be impossible to understand one separate from the other.

Perspectives of Men Who Participate in Faith-Based Batterer Intervention Programs

Justice, accountability, and change are all imperative features of intervention services offered to men who abuse their wives or intimate partners. While some come voluntarily, most men who attend batterer intervention classes do so because they have little or no choice in the matter—they have been mandated by the courts as a result of a conviction for domestic violence, or referred by wives, therapists and/or clergy as a final gasp before the relationship is considered dead.

Religious women, in particular, are very hopeful that intervention programs can change violent men. Since many abused *religious* women do not wish to terminate their relationship with the abuser—either temporarily or forever—they hold out great faith that if only their partner were to attend such a program, the violence would cease and peace would be restored to the marriage. But is there any evidence upon which to base such hope?

In the first ever attempt to document empirically the characteristics of men who sought assistance from a faith-based batterers' intervention program in the United States, we analyzed over 1000 closed case files. Comparing this data to men in secular programs revealed that the faith-based program had a higher proportion of men who had witnessed or experienced abuse in their childhood homes, while rates of alcohol abuse and criminal histories were similar (Nason-Clark et al., 2003). Another finding to emerge from this data is the role of clergy in encouraging or "mandating" men who seek their spiritual help to attend a faith-based intervention program. In fact, men who were clergy-referred were more likely to complete (and graduate from) the 26 week program (followed by the six month monitoring phase, making a total of 52 weeks) than those whose attendance was mandated by a judge (Fisher-Townsend et al., 2008). Since the faith-based program participants have more life stability factors (currently married, employed, higher education, etc.) this may reinforce their willingness to complete the program and to alter their abusive ways (Nason-Clark et al., 2003). Sharing a religious worldview with the other

men in the program may actually provide a *safe place* for these abusive men to challenge themselves and each other, and look toward a day when their abusive past will no longer control their present reality (Nason-Clark, 2004).

Some men in the program do not complete the entire 52-week program and "graduate." Rather, they drop out, or attend only periodically—when a crisis occurs or an ultimatum is given. Those who are court-mandated must complete 52 classes or face the implications of their non-compliance. In this state-certified program, there are several groups a week, each with at least 15 men and two facilitators.

The curriculum is not dissimilar to that of a secular program, but the agency's staff includes only men and women committed to their Christian faith. When the men raise issues of spirituality, religion, or the Bible, the facilitators respond using the language of their various faith traditions. They are knowledgeable about the Bible and well prepared to counter any claims made by program participants that Scripture justifies abuse or violent acts. They hold men accountable using both secular and religious language. For men of faith, this is very powerful. Here a man's religious ideology is harnessed in ways that have the potential to nurture, monitor, and reinforce a violent-free future.

While we might be tempted to conclude that these results relate only to faith-based programs, there are some very important lessons here for those who work with the violated or those who act abusively. It is extremely useful to harness any spiritual resources that might add weight to either the criminal justice or therapeutic response to violence in the family context. For men of faith, the word of a pastor carries weight (Fisher-Townsend, Nason-Clark, Murphy and Ruff, 2008). Since many faith traditions offer a *language of hope* and a theology that includes *new beginnings*, building bridges between a religious man who acts abusively and his pastor increases the possibility of the man doing the work needed to change his behavior, while at the same time providing enhanced accountability as that work progresses.

Yet, there is great reluctance amongst batterers to assume responsibility for their actions (Ptacek, 1988b; Scott & Wolfe, 2000). When they begin the program, most of the men are unwilling—and some are unable—to interpret their acts as abusive. *I am not violent* is a common phrase used by the men in their early days of program attendance (Fisher-Townsend et al., 2008). Some interweave spiritual overtones. They talk about submission, or authority, or hierarchy in the family. But most talk only indirectly about these issues, choosing instead references to how she *pushed their buttons*. Men both justify what they have meted out to their partner and blame her for the abuse. Essentially, most of the men believe, at least in the early days of coming to the agency, that they are entitled to certain things in a relationship and angry when their expectations are not met.

When religious leaders are able to walk alongside abusive men who are committed to their religious tradition, everyone in the family has the potential of direct benefit. It is very powerful for a man who has acted abusively to see his faith community as supportive of his decision to change and pursue wholeness. In this way, pastors and other religious leaders are uniquely positioned to augment the process of recovery.

For social workers and others involved in the helping professions, it is critical to see the centrality of the religious belief system for many men who have acted abusively. It is a key component of their social context (DeKeseredy & MacLeod, 1998; Ptacek, 1988a), used to justify or defend their proclivity to power and control (Bancroft, 2002; Gondolf, 2002). Concepts such as submission reinforce these notions of religious entitlement (Shupe, Stacey, & Hazlewood, 1987). In this way, religious leaders and faith-enriched therapeutic staff are unique resources in any community-based efforts to create safe and peaceful homes. Faith is a core construct, central to any understanding of male entitlement, power and control.

Clergy Responding to Domestic Violence

From our studies of religious leaders, we have learned how difficult it is for pastors to see their intervention as successful if the marriage ended in divorce. Many clergy feel pressure to keep families together and marriages intact. In this way, pastoral counselors frequently find themselves in a very difficult double-bind: they are stalwart supporters of family values, including a reluctance to see any couples divorce, yet many of the families who seek their counsel need to separate in order to ensure the safety of all. Often with limited training, and a lack of resources at their disposal, they have not yet learned to identify that it is the relationship that has failed, not their advice.

Based upon data from over 300 conservative Protestant ministers, we learned that 98 percent have counseled a woman who has suffered from her husband's verbal aggression, 53 percent have helped a woman where the physical aggression of her partner involved activities like shoving or pushing, and 29 percent of pastors have been called upon to respond to a woman who has been repeatedly battered by her intimate partner.

While pastors differ greatly in their counseling experience and the advice that they offer, we found no evidence in our studies with pastors that they deliberately or directly dismiss an abused woman's call for help (Nason-Clark, 1997). Translating the rhetoric of "happy family living" into practical help for women, men, and couples in crisis is no easy task. It is time consuming and emotionally draining for the pastor, it is often discouraging, there are few simple answers, and the rewards can seem to be in short supply. As a result, pastoral counselors sometimes feel like they are caught in the cross-fire between the ideology of the family that their denominations and churches hold dear and the nature, severity, and persistence of male aggression and abuse. In reality, clergy are far more likely to offer practical advice and support than they are to provide direct spiritual counsel, or explicit religious activities like prayer.

However, pastors are often slow to suggest dissolution of even a violent marriage and quite optimistic about the possibility of change in the life of a man who has acted abusively. But clerical optimism is frequently tempered by the unwillingness of such men to engage in the therapeutic process or to change their violent ways. When abuse is obvious and unrelenting, clergy appear to be motivated to bring safety and security to all. However, when the severity and the impact of abuse are obscured by other factors like alcohol abuse, clergy appear to have greater difficulty both identifying the battery and understanding the need for safety or healing for the victims.

Referral networks can help to ensure that the experts are identified and that inadequate pastoral training does not translate into poor or life-threatening counsel for abused women and their children. For many religious leaders, faith is integral to any response to abuse. Through referrals, faith-enriched counselors in secular agencies, or personnel in faith-based counseling agencies have the opportunity to bridge the gap between religious and non-religious resources. By inviting religious leaders to participate in any coordinated community responses to combat domestic violence, secular workers in therapeutic or criminal justice environments become acquainted with the unique needs of highly religious men and women. As an added impact, religious leaders who may be reluctant to make the first step are educated about domestic violence and also benefit from their interface with counselors. As a result, clergy become better equipped to offer best practices to people of faith who suffer the impact of domestic violence, victim and victimizer alike.

The Coordinated Community Response

Building bridges of collaborative action between community agencies and religious congregations is an enormous challenge. While recent years have witnessed many innovative projects that involve selected features of a coordinated community response, such as specialized domestic violence courts, or law enforcement officers who are uniquely trained to respond to cases of domestic violence and work in a multi-disciplinary context, most community-enhanced efforts to combat domestic violence or respond to its victims do not include a role for spiritual leaders. However, pastors and other religious professionals play a critical role in calling religious men to accountability and offering spiritual and practical support to women and children who have been victimized by male aggression in the family context.

Over the years, our data has revealed several reasons why it is central to include religious leaders as part of any collaborative community response to domestic violence (Nason-Clark, 2006). These include the fact that religious leaders are chosen by many victims, chosen by some abusers, invested with moral authority, regarded as experts on marriage and the family, able to offer spiritual comfort and guidance, in regular contact with many who are marginalized by society, able to provide ongoing support after the crisis period is over, and skilled in talking about hope. Moreover, religious leaders provide educational and other resources to all age groups and many clergy have access to men, women and children at the point of individual crisis.

Religious women can be especially vulnerable when abused, for they are very likely to hold the intact family in high esteem and to consider separation and divorce as unsatisfactory options. Thus a community response needs to include input from various faith traditions if it wishes to meet the needs of all people who live in any given jurisdiction. When a pastor or other religious leader explains to a follower that "abuse is wrong" and a violation of how their faith tradition understands marriage before God, it has a powerful impact, much more powerful than the same words spoken by a social worker to an abused religious woman. Of course, not all members of faith communities will want assistance from their religious leader when domestic violence impacts the family home. However, for those who do, it is critical that such help be made available; it is critical, too, that the religious leader be informed and comfortable with referring parishioners to community agencies that work with victims or abusers. Referrals between resource providers are essential, yet our data has revealed that among those clergy who are poorly trained to respond to domestic violence, there is a great reluctance to refer those who do come for their help.

Since many faith traditions celebrate "family values," it is imperative that the leaders speak out when abuse becomes the reality of family life. A coordinated community response needs to include these voices—especially since they are invested with credibility by substantial numbers of people. As a result, they can offer comfort and guidance that is distinct from that offered in community-based agencies. As religious leaders, they speak the language of the spirit—using the sacred texts, prayers, and other rituals inherent in their faith tradition. Breaking the cycle of violence often requires both the input of secular culture and support from the religious community and its leadership. There are specific religious contours both to the abuse that is suffered by people of deep faith and to the healing journey. As a result, many in the secular therapeutic community do not like to work with clients who are particularly religious (Nason-Clark, McMullin, Fahlberg and Schaefer, 2009; Whipple 1987). Without spiritual credentials, these workers find it difficult to challenge the religious ideation that is believed by the victim or perpetrator to give license to abuse.

For collaborative ventures between churches and community agencies to be successful in the fight to end to domestic violence—what I like to call paving the pathway between the steeple and the shelter—personnel from both paradigms must recognize the need to work together (Nason-Clark,

1997). A cultural language that is devoid of religious symbols, meanings, and legitimacy is relatively powerless to alter a religious victim's resolve to stay in the marriage no matter what the cost. Moreover, curbing violent behavior amongst religious men who believe they are entitled by their tradition to behave in this way must include spiritual language condemning the violence and religious resources to empower hope and change. Correspondingly, the language of the spirit must also include references to practical resources and secular knowledge. Otherwise, spiritual language alone may compromise a *victim's* need for safety, security, and financial resources to care for herself and her children or a *perpetrator's* need for justice and restraint.

Building bridges takes time. It is hard work. It involves negotiating the delicate terrain of egos, values, disciplinary boundaries, and divergent strategies for a common goal. Yet, there is evidence that when you choose carefully with whom you will build bridges—looking for those with skills, training, and commitment—it is amazing what a coordinated community response can achieve (Nason-Clark, Mitchell, & Beaman, 2004).

WHAT DOES FAITH HAVE TO DO WITH DOMESTIC VIOLENCE?

Based on twenty years of social science research, there is ample evidence that religious faith and domestic violence are co-mingled. The story of why a religious woman, man, teen, or child looks to his or her faith community for help in the aftermath of domestic violence is replete with spiritual overtones, as it is with practical issues. The story of what happens when help is sought is more diverse. Looking at the interface between religion and domestic violence from different vantage points reveals several unique features of the journey towards justice, safety, healing, and wholeness for a religious victim or perpetrator of abuse. Whether an abused religious woman, or a religious man who acts abusively, is offered help first by their church, or through a community-based agency, it is critical that those who respond understand *both* the issue of domestic violence and the nature of religious faith. While safety and security must always be the first priority, accurate, practical advice is also imperative, offered in a way that respects one's faith traditions and professional best practices. Assisting men and women of deep faith in the aftermath of abuse in the family context often requires an in-depth knowledge of that community of faith. Many of the religious issues that surface require dialogue with someone possessing spiritual credentials—like a pastor—or spiritual sensitivity—like a faith-enriched therapist. In this way, religious leaders and agencies that offer either a faith-perspective or faith-sensitive staff are unique resources in any community-based effort to create safe and peaceful homes.

Perspectives informed by faith must be *part* of the solution to a community-based response to domestic violence. Perspectives informed by secular training, experience and credentials must be *part* of the solution to a faith-based response to domestic violence. For this to happen—for bridges to be built between churches and their communities and for the movement between them to be bi-directional—there must be mutual respect and mutual understanding, built on a foundational belief that ending domestic violence involves the entire community.

The Cross-Generational Transmission of Trauma: Ritual and Emotion among Survivors of the Holocaust

Janet Jacobs

OVER THE PAST TWO DECADES, the cross-generational transmission of trauma has become an increasingly important area of study. To a large extent this research has focused on second-generation Holocaust survivors who, according to the literature in the field, have "inherited" the post-traumatic symptoms of their traumatized parents. Beginning in 1966, psychiatric and psychological studies of the second generation of Holocaust survivors described the children of survivors as suffering from nightmares, guilt, depression, fear of death, sadness, and the presence of intrusive images (Baranowsky et al. 1998; Bergman and Jucovy 1982; Binder-Byrnes et al. 1998; Hass 1990; Holmes 1999; Prince 1985). Although research has found these symptoms to vary among second-generation survivors, the overall findings suggest that the Holocaust is "a dominant psychic reality" (Bergman and Jucovy 1982, 312) that is informed both the psychological and social development of the children of survivors. In particular, the research stresses the difficulty with which the second generation struggled to separate emotionally from their traumatized parents (Fonagy 1999; Kellerman 2001a; Sorscher and Cohen 1997).

In addition to posttraumatic stress disorder in the children of survivors, researchers investigate how older generations convey trauma to younger generations. The research focuses primarily on two modes of parental (first-generational) communication, which are obsessive storytelling and deep emotional silences (Baranowsky et al. 1998). In the first mode of communication, obsessive storytelling, parents were likely to speak continually and graphically about their experiences of Nazi persecution. Parents shared, even with young children, the horrors to which they and their relatives had been subjected. In the second mode of communication, deep emotional silences that are more difficult to articulate and assess, parental trauma was conveyed through what Bar-On (1995, 20) has termed "the untold story," feelings and emotions that permeated the survivor household. According to Bar-On (1995), it was these unspoken feelings that were most influential in the generational transmission of Holocaust trauma.

Although traumatic inheritance research is extensive and ongoing, little work exists on the social contexts in which survivors communicated told and untold stories to the children of survivors. More specifically, intergenerational transmission of trauma research tends to overlook the role that religion and family tradition have played in traumatic transference. This omission is especially glaring given the emotional quality of ritual behaviors. The goal of this study therefore is to explore the relationship between the cross-generational transmission of trauma and the observance of religious ritual in the post-Holocaust family. Based on a qualitative study of thirty-five second-generation survivors, I examine how families maintained Jewish rituals in the postwar home and how the ritual life of survivors conveyed the traumas of the past through the emotional dynamics of ritual observance. As an investigation into ritual and emotion in the post-Holocaust family, these research findings inform the study of the intergenerational transmission of trauma in three significant ways. First, I examine ritual as a site of traumatic transference. Second, I apply self-in-relation theory to the cross-generational transmission of trauma. Finally, I analyze ritual as a path to autonomy among second-generation Holocaust survivors.

METHOD AND PARTICIPANT CHARACTERISTICS

I conducted the research under the auspices of the University of Colorado in accordance with the guidelines for research on human subjects. I obtained participants for this study through contacts with Children of Holocaust Survivor organizations and using a snowball sampling methodology. I first approached two Children of Survivor organizations in the Rocky Mountain region that met regularly. I explained that I was interested in studying the effects of mass trauma on the second generation and would be interested in attending their meetings, if that was permissible, and in interviewing the members individually. Both groups were open to my research and invited me to their events and social gatherings. Consisting of between ten and fifteen members, the groups met to share their experiences of growing up in survivor households and to create friendships and social support systems with other second-generation survivors

with similar experiences and backgrounds. In addition to participant observation at these gatherings, I also conducted in-depth interviews with group members, as well as other second-generation survivors through snowball sampling. In extending the research beyond the Children of Survivor Organizations, I expanded the study to include second-generation survivors who were living in New York, Los Angeles, and Boston.

Altogether, I interviewed thirty-five second-generation survivors: seventeen women and eighteen men between the ages of forty-six and fifty-eight. The in-depth tape-recorded interviews ranged between two and four hours, and they were transcribed for the purposes of analysis. Using a life history approach, I followed an open-ended interview schedule focused on family history, the transmission of knowledge about the Holocaust, religious upbringing, and current spiritual beliefs and practices. The majority of the interviews took place in the homes of the participants, and I conducted all of the interviews ensuring confidentiality. Because of the familial location of the interview sites (e.g., family homes), respondents frequently shared photographs, family documents, and precious family artifacts that had survived the war. In some instances the process of sharing led to tours through the participant's home, as she or he pointed out framed photographs of their parents before and after the war and of other family members who did not survive. Other times, respondents produced carefully assembled scrapbooks that chronicled their parent's ordeal and survival in newspaper accounts published in local newspapers during the 1960s and 1970s. Thus, the interview settings were, in many cases, field sites in and of themselves— they were spaces of memory and family culture where participants framed recollections of the past and narratives of childhood by the familial surroundings that enriched and recalled the respondents' ties to loss, survival, and catastrophe.

My connection to the participants was intensified by the surroundings where the research took place, homes where families preserved the traumas of the past both in the material and emotional culture of the second generation. The in-depth interviews helped to strengthen my empathic bonds to the respondents to whom I already felt connected because of my own postwar Jewish childhood. In the East Coast suburb where my family lived, there was a small survivor community whose presence was acknowledged in whispers and lowered voices, quietly revering those who had "been in the camps." Decades later, when I approached the children of survivors for this research project, I carried with me my own memory of their imagined parents, shopkeepers, and teachers who had survived Auschwitz, Buchenwald, and Treblinka—sites of Nazi terror that, at an early age, had been indelibly inscribed into my own Jewish consciousness. As a result, the interviews were often deeply emotional both for the respondents and for me as each of us negotiated the feelings engendered by the persistence of traumatic memories and the recounting of a life personally informed by the Jewish genocide of World War II.

Although all of the study respondents were born to Jewish parents, importantly, the religious upbringing of the survivors was varied and diverse. Nearly half of the respondents grew up in conservative Jewish homes. Among the other half, five of the respondents were raised as Orthodox Jews, six as reform Jews, three without any denominational affiliation, three as atheists, and two as non-Jews— one Unitarian and one Catholic. At the time of the interviews, four respondents identified as Orthodox Jews, seven as Conservative Jews, six as Reform Jews, three as followers of Jewish Renewal (a modern-day egalitarian movements that has its roots in Hasidism), and ten as Jewish spiritual seekers who had not yet found a synagogue or movement with which to affiliate. One respondent identified as atheist, two as Unitarian, and two as Buddhist. Regardless of current religious affiliation, however, all of the respondents identified ethnically as Jewish. All participants were college educated and close to half held graduate degrees.

Participants were working in fields such as teaching, health care, accounting, domestic work, art, and filmmaking.

Finally, although this research, like previous studies, tends to group all second-generation survivors together for the purposes of research, the parental backgrounds of the participants were characterized by numerous differences. In this study alone, the parents of respondents came from diverse backgrounds, including Poland, Russia, Germany, Lithuania, the Czech Republic, Slovakia, France, and Italy. These differences informed both the survivors' refugee experiences and how they forged their Jewish identity through a cultural framework. Additionally, the conditions of survivorship were not the same for all first-generation parents. While some of the parents of the participants survived through hiding, other parents suffered in labor and death camps. These differences contextualized the transmission of trauma to the second generation and created an important backdrop for their connection to their parents' suffering. Beginning with a discussion of Jewish ritual in the survivor family, I explore the significance of ritual as a mode of traumatic transference and ritual innovation as a means of separation among adult children of survivors.

RITUAL AS A SITE OF POSTTRAUMATIC EMOTION

In the study of ritual and emotion, the work of Durkheim (1995) and Geertz (1973) elaborate how group rituals are the site of shared emotions that connect group members to an ancestral past. As a source of cohesion and memory, rituals provide a means to form and sustain group identity among individuals with a common history and shared culture. Scheff (1979) and Turner (1969) further examine the emotional character of ritual performance that allows participants to express and externalize repressed feeling states, creating conditions under which the cathartic release of emotion is made possible. Following these theorists, Bird (1995) explores how religious ritual functions particularly in the family, outlining four dimensions of family-based ritual practice. Among these dimensions are the expression of feelings that ordinarily are silenced in the family and the affirmation of cultural identity through the maintenance of religious traditions. These interrelated functions of family ritual, as articulated by Bird, were found to be especially significant in post-Holocaust families. Accordingly, familial ritual practice became an important site for the cross-generational transmission of trauma.

Turning to the study of posttraumatic stress disorder among survivor populations, Herman (1992) describes a cycle of emotional repression and expression where survivors vacillate between remembering and forgetting, a contradictory set of responses that result in a "dialectic of trauma." In this dialectic, states of rage, hatred, and grief alternate with periods of numbness and emotional disconnection. According to the accounts of the second generation, the cycle of expression became embedded in the ritual performances of the first generation who, through religious practice and traditions, relived the emotions of their traumatic past. In particular, the participants reported that the observance of Yom Kippur (the Day of Atonement), the holiest day of the Jewish year, was especially significant for the evocation of traumatic memory and the attending expression of traumatic feelings in the survivor household. As described in the narratives of the second generation, the observance of this religious holiday produced great emotional strain within families, as feelings of anger, guilt, and inconsolable sadness permeated the emotional dynamics of fasting and prayer. Aaron Hass (1990, 68–9), a scholar of Holocaust trauma and a second-generation survivor, describes the Yom Kippur ritualization of his father's Holocaust narrative in this way:

The ritual began when I was eight or nine years old and lasted for about ten years. It took place on the night of Yom Kippur. In observance of Jewish legal restrictions, our apartment in Brooklyn was dark except for a shaft of light coming from under the closed door of the bathroom. This streak would be our lantern in the blackness. One was not permitted to switch on electricity for twenty-four hours during this holy period.

The story was brief and always the same. The somber environment and the mystical day on which it was told lent an eeriness to the account. We lay on my parents' bed, my father laying on his side, I on my right side facing him. I could barely make out the outlines of his face. My father spoke in Yiddish. "We [the partisans] found out that a German officer would be at the farmhouse of a Pole who had betrayed Jews to him. The German was probably delivering two bottles of Vodka as payment for the two Jews the Pole handed over. We came in and they were drinking together. We tied them up and cut a small hole in each one's arm. For hours we put salt in the open wounds. Then we shot them both." My father's voice reflected an increasing bitterness as the story progressed. I absorbed my father's determination as he spoke, and I felt my anger swell. I was fascinated. I was also frightened.

In this autobiographical account, Hass (1990) captures the feelings his father's ritual storytelling aroused in the "eerie" atmosphere of Yom Kippur. In a complex ritual of religious observance, atrocity storytelling, and emotional exchange, Hass internalized both the anger of the perpetrator/father as well the fear of a young child who became witness to the scene of his father's rage and violence. As this case powerfully illustrates, the observance of the High Holy Days was framed by emotion-laden memories that were relived each year on Yom Kippur. Further, in Hass's recollection, the father symbolizes the rage and violence of the perpetrators while the German officer and the Polish informants represent the victims of torture and terror.

In comparison with Hass's (1990) experience, a number of respondents in this study reported that the anger and bitterness communicated during the observance of the High Holy days, and especially Yom Kippur, emanated from their parents' anger and rage, not at their German tormentors, but at a God who abandoned the Jews during their time of greatest need. Torn between moral outrage at a God who had let so many innocent Jews die and a deep moral commitment to keep Judaism alive, the first generation conveyed a complicated set of emotions that were brought on especially by the period of reflection and repentance that the holiday demanded. In the following account, a fifty-two-year-old participant raised in an orthodox home describes how his father's rage toward God became intertwined with the family's adherence to religious tradition:

> My Dad spoke of the Holocaust incessantly. From as early as I can remember, he spoke of his experiences before and during the war. . . . My Dad was raised by a very, the word he uses, is "pious" man. His father was extremely religious. He came from a large family. It was a very rigid reality. This is what life is about, studying Talmud and the Torah. It was really jammed down his throat. Then his dad, my grandfather, was taken away and murdered and the rest of the family was killed. My father and his brother were the only survivors. When he started to raise his own family, he was still coming from this place of guilt and anger. It was weird mixed messages. He was so non-religious and pissed off at God and he couldn't believe any of it, but yet he felt we had to observe all the laws and rituals. So it was kind of schizophrenic. I had to be Bar Mitzvahed—there was no choice—we had to keep kosher, keep the Sabbath, fast, light candles, and if my mother showed up at things without her wig, that was like heresy. But Yom Kippur? That was always the hardest, when the anger and bitterness was the strongest—it was just a kind of jammed down your throat—this is the way it is kind of thing without any depth—the only feelings were that of rage and bitterness.

As these two narratives illustrate, second-generation survivors associated the observance of Yom Kippur

with the remembrance of violence and rage in one case and the transmission of embittered feelings toward God in the other case. Although these accounts each offer a different perspective on the effects of anger in the intergenerational transference of trauma, both reveal the important role that the Yom Kippur ritual played in engendering memories of a specifically Jewish trauma and the posttraumatic feeling states that such memories invoke.

A second and equally powerful set of emotions triggered by the observance of Yom Kippur, the Day of Atonement, were those feelings associated with survivor guilt. The liturgy for this religious holiday involves the recitation of sins for which the supplicant asks God for forgiveness and mercy. As research on first-generation survivors has poignantly shown, the memory of survivorship was often accompanied by feelings of self-blame and guilt that, in the aftermath of catastrophe, contributed to the posttraumatic symptoms of the surviving generations (Herman 1992; Langer 1991). It is thus not surprising that Yom Kippur, with its emphasis on sin and self-recrimination, was often a difficult and angst-ridden holiday in the survivor family.

The narrative of a woman respondent illustrates this dimension of the High Holiday observance. Piecing together her mother's wartime experiences from stories she told her as a young child, the respondent, now in her fifties, recounted how her mother was deported to Auschwitz at age seventeen where she survived by working in a munitions factory. This participant described her mother as very beautiful and smart, a woman who lived by her wits and was able to sustain a privileged life as a prisoner. At the same time, the respondent said that although her mother spoke with pride of her survival, there was an unspoken subtext to her stories, an undercurrent of silence, regret, and guilt that surfaced especially during her observance of Yom Kippur:

> Surviving such a horrendous event, you can't begrudge anybody for doing what they had to do to

get by at Auschwitz. My mother suffers from survivor guilt, because there is another side of the story. Remember I told you there were nine siblings, including my own mother? I believe it was 1941; her mother and father went to some little town near Krakow where they were hiding. It was a tiny little village. My mother was in Krakow at that time and she heard that they were going to the village to kill all the Jews. She was able to get to a telephone and she called but there was no answer. She knew right then and there that that was it for her parents. Then her uncles, their children, her little nieces with whom she was very close—all killed.

My mother did not want to raise us Jewish. We were Unitarians. I think that being Jewish was too painful. Having said that she observed all the holidays. We had Passover, and Yom Kippur was very sad for her. She would gorge herself the day before so that she could spend the whole day fasting. . . . She would just lay in bed all day. My sister and I were scared because it was the one time a year when her feelings of guilt and grief overwhelmed her and she couldn't eat or move or even talk to us. There was just this silence and her pain.

As this account reveals, even in nonreligiously Jewish households, survivors observed the Yom Kippur ritual, maintaining a yearly tradition when people were able to give expression and make visible painful emotions in the postcatastrophe culture of the survivor family.

Along with fasting and the recalling of sins and wrongdoing, family members traditionally remember the dead on Yom Kippur. At the onset of the holiday, the lighting of memorial (Yahrzeit) candles in the home signals the beginning of a memorial period. Accordingly, study participants gave vivid and emotional accounts of kitchen countertops and dining room tables lined with ritual candles, small glass containers with Hebrew lettering that, for the child of survivors, came to symbolize the Jewish nature of traumatic loss. A woman in her sixties, whose father died when she was twelve, recounted an early childhood memory.

She framed her father's only connection to Judaism through this act of memorialization:

My father escaped from Bratislava, jumped the train and came to Italy. It is unclear whether his parents died in Theresienstadt or Auschwitz. My father grew up Jewish. My grandmother, my father's mother was orthodox and when he married my mother everyone said she was a foreign woman, even though she was a Jew, because she came from Italy. My mother did not keep a kosher home and she was not brought up in a religious home. After the war, my father was not religious but he kept Yom Kippur and Rosh Hashanah and he always lit a Yahrzeit candle for his father. That was very important to me—the only time I would see his grief, when his feelings were not hidden. I remember I talked to him about it and how important it was. And I light a Yahrzeit candle for him every day. I feel I owe it to him.

While Yom Kippur was clearly the most emotion-laden ritual in the survivor household, the participants also reported other forms of observance that left a deep impression on the second generation. Surrounded by sadness, loss, and anger, participants describe the ritual life of the family as joyless, rigid, and obligatory. A number of respondents remarked on the rigidity with which their families kept kosher, observed the Sabbath, or strictly maintained the dietary rules of Passover. Often their parents became angry or upset if someone violated a rule or law. Others remarked on the compulsive and often depressing observance of holidays such as Sukkoth (the Feast of the Tabernacles) that, while for other Jews were celebratory and festive, for their families were unhappy and despairing occasions:

My parents didn't take particular joy in practicing ritual. They felt that this was the way they were brought up and they didn't want us to lose the identity. I remember hating Sukkoth because we never did anything joyful or exciting. My father didn't go to work. We didn't go to school but there was no warmth, no bringing us together, just the persistent memory of who was not there, who would not be celebrating with us.

The findings on Yom Kippur and the persistence of other Jewish rituals among observant as well as nonobservant survivors suggest that in the aftermath of the Holocaust, ritual practice was one means by which older generations conveyed the emotional trauma of the catastrophe to the next generation. Along with the telling of atrocity narratives and/or the feeling-laden silences that were pervasive in the postwar family culture, the practice of ritual established a separate but compelling emotional space where children were witness to their parents' suffering and rage and where the emotional boundaries between the first and second generation became blurred within a ritualized context of Jewish observance. Thus, as an important site of emotional exchange, the significance of ritual for the intergenerational transmission of trauma can in part be explained through the paradigm of self-in-relation theory.

RITUAL AS A SITE OF EMOTIONAL EXCHANGE: SELF-IN-RELATION THEORY AND THE CROSS-GENERATIONAL TRANSMISSION OF TRAUMA

In the past decade, scholars put forward various theoretical models to explain the relationship between the intergenerational transmission of trauma and personality development in second-generation survivors. Within this field of study, Kellerman (2001b) notes the four prominent models of transmission that dominate the second-generation literature: psychoanalytic, social learning, communication, and relational theory. The psychoanalytic view suggests that the child "unconsciously absorbs the repressed and insufficiently worked-through Holocaust experiences of

survivor parents" (Kellerman 2001b, 260). The social learning and family system theories focus on the more overt ways in which survivor parents engaged in inadequate or destructive parenting behaviors while establishing closed family systems in which the interdependency between the child and the parent created an obstacle to the child's independence. And lastly, the relational model, based on object relations theory, emphasizes a psychodynamic in which the child internalizes the traumatized parent who then becomes a reflection of the child self (Holmes 1999).

Expanding on Kellerman's (2001b) discussion, a fifth model of transmission, the self-in-relation perspective (Chodorow 1978; Jordan et al. 1991), can add further insight on the child's identification with a traumatized parent. Originating out of the relational school of development, the self-in-relation paradigm takes as its starting point the exchange of feelings that, beginning in infancy, takes place between the child and caregiver. As such, this theory shifts the emphasis in development from the internalization of a parent-object to the emotional relationship that characterizes the parent-child dynamic. Feminist in orientation, self-in-relation theory highlights the value of empathy (the emotional identification with the feelings of others) in personality development and illuminates the way in which identity evolves out of the strong emotional connection that takes place between a parent and child:

> The earliest representation of the self, then, is of a self whose core—which is emotional—is attended by other(s) and in turn, begins to attend to the emotions of other(s). Part of the internal image of oneself includes feeling the other's emotions and *acting on* them as they are in interplay with one's own emotions. (Miller 1991, 14)

In applying the self-in-relation model to the findings on ritual and the transference of trauma, respondents' narratives suggest that the practice of ritual provided a familial space where an intense exchange of emotion took place between the first and second generations. This ritualized form of emotional exchange created a socio-emotional context for traumatic sharing where the emotional boundaries between parent and child were especially permeable. As a site of emotional transference, ritual played a significant role in establishing a relational environment that fostered, through empathy and connectivity, the child's emotional identification with a traumatized parent. Second-generation survivors thus describe themselves as "having absorbed" the trauma of their parents as if it were their own. Here a woman respondent, now in her fifties, describes this internalization of her parents' suffering:

> As a young child, what I lived was the emotional pain in my body that I was receiving from them. Children pick up everything. My parents lived in so much grief. How can you even imagine them emotionally surviving all that suffering? I intuited the pain that they lived in and that was in their bodies. I didn't know how to separate myself from it. Whatever my unconscious experience was, my life was about their pain and how to make it better, how not to feel it, whatever it was about.

Another respondent, whose mother survived Auschwitz, described the sense of shared terror that pervaded her dreams and nightmares:

> I used to have very bad dreams, totally about being captured. I have to tell you that I still have Holocaust dreams from time to time, about being raped, being rounded up, about being imprisoned.

While accounts like these were common among participants, others described the process of absorption as a kind of supernatural phenomenon in which the trauma of the first generation had somehow inexplicably become lodged in the collective unconscious of their children. One participant, whose mother's life had been fraught with emotion, offered this perspective on what she has come to understand as the second generation's propensity for "psychic" experiences:

> My mother was from Poland. She wound up in a forced labor camp and then there was something about Auschwitz and only her father survived. I had recurring dreams as a very small child, probably prior to age four that I remember to this day because they were recurring dreams. The dream always started with a panoramic view of the city. And understand that at three or four, I had never seen cobblestone streets. I had never seen such structures. Every time I had the dream, I remembered that I had had it before, but when I woke up I didn't remember it. And in the dream there was a panoramic view of the city. It was like I had a camera and I was panning slowly. I could draw it for you, to this day. Eventually it makes its way to the train station. It's a wooden train station. There is nothing metal. The station house, I see some poles, the ties are wood. And I see a train track and after a few minutes I see a man running down the train track, screaming. I had that dream I can't tell you how many times. And one time I woke up afterwards crying and my mother came into my room, and I remembered the dream and she said, "What's wrong?" And I told her the dream and my mother turned white as a sheet and she started to cry. She told me that she found out after the war, the Gestapo had come to take her family away while her father was out bartering food. When he came home, the family was gone. He heard they had been put on the transport and he ran down to the train tracks, crying, running after the train. She swore she never told me that. Obviously I was too little. How would I know that at three years old unless—and I believe there is kind of a higher mentality. There's a collective consciousness and every child of a Holocaust survivor I talked to believes the same thing. Every person in our group said they agreed. We remember things and recognize people in our life we have never met. I don't know how that is possible.

As these diverse narratives illustrate, second-generation survivors express shared knowledge of and feeling for their parent's trauma that, in part, can be explained by the transfer of emotion that took place during the ritual observances in the survivor household. Within the framework of self-in-relation theory, religious practice became a site of emotional exchange, contributing to the confusion between self and other in the second generation's remembrance and "re-experiencing" of Holocaust trauma. Consequently, study respondents, like other children of survivors, struggle to establish a separate and nontraumatized sense of self. Much of the second-generation research addresses the problem of enmeshment among children of survivors, emphasizing their need to find paths to autonomy that facilitate a healthy separation from the first generation (Kellerman 2001a). As the second set of findings of this study reveals, among the most important strategies for establishing a separate sense of self has been the reinvention of ritual among the second generation, a trend that reflects the adult child's desire to remain connected to his or her Jewish heritage while at the same time create a separate and distinct identity.

FORGING SEPARATE IDENTITIES: CULTURE BEARING AND THE REINVENTION OF JEWISH RITUAL AMONG SECOND-GENERATION SURVIVORS

The data from this study support strongly the finding that while ritual was a site of emotional exchange in the formative years of the second generation, in adulthood the practice of ritual facilitated a process of separation and individuation. Sociology of religion research points to a number of significant trends in religion and spirituality among the Baby Boomer generation. Among these trends, Roof (1999) and Wuthnow (1998) indicate a decisive turn toward religious creativity, individualism, and ritual invention. Like others of their generation who came of age in the cultural dislocations of the 1960s, children of Holocaust survivors embraced the values of religious experimentation and innova-

tion as they sought to negotiate the difficult emotional terrain of their survivor upbringing. Although the innovative strategies of the respondents look similar to their nonsurvivor counter parts, the social psychological lens through which the children of survivors sought out ritual innovation was distinctly different. As one respondent remarked:

> As a child of survivors, you feel this obligation to make sure Hitler doesn't succeed. At the same time, you don't want to do it the way your parents did—you want holidays to be fun, to bring joy. So I think you have to do more than just observe the rituals—you have to do it differently.

Faced with a moral obligation to preserve Judaism and a competing psychological need to separate from their traumatized Jewish parents, the second generation created new ritual forms that maintained Jewish tradition without reproducing the traumatizing ritual experiences of their childhood. Rejecting the sadness, grief, and rage of the first generation, the adult children of survivors intentionally and self-consciously reinvented Jewish customs in a manner that strongly differentiated their observance from that of their parents. Not surprisingly, among the rituals that were of particular importance to the project of creative innovation were those that focused on Yom Kippur. Given the significance of the Day of Atonement for the first generation, the majority of respondents sought ways to bring new meaning to a holy day that had deep associations with parental despair. A nonpracticing participant in his forties described the alternative ritual he created for the observance of this holiday:

> We don't do the High Holidays. I just can't resonate with them. I guess I am somewhat rebellious around Yom Kippur in particular, about fasting on that day. Yet, being the son of somebody who is a Holocaust survivor, it is hard for me to just ignore the traditions. There are times when I go off on my own for two or three days on a kind of vision quest.

I'll sit with myself and not eat and I try to think about what Yom Kippur is designed to do—what it is all about—what does it mean to repent when you have this terrible history.

This innovative approach to Yom Kippur is also found among other Jews in the United States, including those affiliated with the Jewish Renewal movement, who are seeking to create new ritual practices that incorporate meditation and prayer in natural and noninstitutionalized settings (Eisen 1998). For the second generation such alternatives had great appeal in part because they offered nontraditional modes of spiritual reflection that were far removed from the overwhelming emotional experiences that their parents had conveyed during High Holiday observance.

While new approaches to Yom Kippur were among the most solemn and serious of the ritual innovations, the reinvention of ritual among the respondents also included other customs, most notably those associated with the traditions of Sabbath and Passover. Recent surveys of Jews in the United States suggest that a little over a quarter of the Jewish population regularly prepare a traditional Friday night dinner to usher in the beginning of the Sabbath (Cohen 2006). Among study respondents, nearly one third of the participants routinely maintained Friday night dinners to foster a family culture of connection and relatedness. Here an unaffiliated respondent offers this view of the weekly Sabbath customs that she practices in her home:

I don't consider myself religiously Jewish at all. But I definitely practice the Jewish rituals. I made a chalice that I use for Friday night when we light the candles and say the blessings over the wine. We always have Friday night dinner. Our daughter thinks challah is the best food substance in the land. But Friday night candles are the most important ones for me. It keeps my relationship with my parents and yet because we do it so differently—with our own prayers and blessings and family time—it is our own.

Similarly, another respondent, also a mother, recast the melancholy Sabbath observance of her childhood through a lens of connection to family and friends:

The kids wouldn't give up Friday night for anything. It's the only time that we sit down together. It's a very special night for them. When we were kids, it was so different. It was just us with our parents. They were so busy trying to get life together there was no time for us really—not even on the Sabbath. Now we have our kids and our friends and we all get together and share the week with one another.

In both of these accounts, the respondents maintained the Sabbath, especially Friday night dinner, as a ritual of connectedness to reshape and sustain Jewish identity. The traditional concepts that mark the Sabbath as a liminal space separating the sacred from the profane are replaced with meaning systems emphasizing familial continuity and cultural connection. This phenomenon, documented in other research on Jewish women and tradition (Davidman and Tenenbaum 1994), was especially pronounced among daughters of survivors who tended to focus on the relational value of ritual rather than the importance of Jewish law for Sabbath observance.

The celebration of Passover offered yet another ritual context for innovation and creativity. Here, more than in any other ritual observance, the participants linked the remembrance of Jewish catastrophe with a moral imperative to move beyond an explicitly Jewish worldview, as one respondent, now a member of Jewish Renewal, explained:

The holiday that we do in our hearts is Passover. We try to be inclusive in those. We try to go beyond the concept of the slavery of Jews. When I was growing up, my family was always about us and them. That's what my family has always been about, us and them. So I try to be inclusive and open the idea up to the concept of slavery that we have in our world, in our hearts, ourselves, the prisons that we create for ourselves. In that way we don't hide that it comes from a Jewish thing, we talk about it. In that way we bring in some Jewish holidays but with a more universal understanding.

Significantly, Passover provided a ritual context for the second generation's shift from the "us and them" mentality that fueled the fears and anxieties of the first generation. Because the story of the Jews' enslavement in Egypt can be read as a timeless parable of resistance and empowerment, Passover became a valuable form of ritual observance for many of the respondents who, in seeking to resolve the tensions between a longing to remain connected to Jewish heritage and the need to distances themselves from the trauma of their parents, chose the story of the liberation of the Jews from Egypt as a tradition that could be adapted and made relevant for a contemporary perspective on enslavement and oppression. In expanding the notion of human suffering beyond the boundaries of Jewish experience, the children of survivors found ways to incorporate values of social justice into their ritual lives, an innovation that, in making a break from the past, helped to define an individual and separate identity.

Finally, for those participants who do not consider themselves to be religiously Jewish, the rituals that were most important were those that bestowed upon their children the "right" of Jewish identity. One respondent, currently a Unitarian, expressed great concern that her adopted child would not be considered Jewish unless she underwent a traditional conversion ceremony that included emergence in a mikveh (ritual bath). She sought out a rabbi who would perform this rite with her daughter:

> We were determined to have my daughter be Jewish and to take her to the mikveh. We tried. At the very last moment my daughter broke her leg and she had a stress fracture, so she had a brace on. The Rabbi in all of her wonderfulness said she couldn't go into the mikveh because the *mikveh*

had to touch all of her body parts. I thought she was joking initially, and she wasn't. She was very fundamentalist around this process. So at the very last moment, we went to a friend's swimming pool and we gave her Mogen David wine and we had challah and we sang. The swimming pool was the mikveh. She had been practicing how to jump in before the day and so she just jumped in. So she is Jewish and "they" can deal with it later.

This account highlights two significant qualities of the second generation. First, they desire to ensure the Jewishness of their children, regardless of their religious orientation. Second, this generation is willing to create new rituals when the traditional approach fails. In this narrative, the alternative mikveh rite, while a departure from traditional Jewish law, nevertheless met the individual criteria of the respondent whose openness and flexibility were characteristic of other children of survivors who prided themselves both on their creativity and their ability to distance themselves from the more painful aspects of their parents' ritual lives.

CONCLUSION

In bringing the varied findings of this research together, there are a number of important insights on the intergenerational transmission of trauma. Among the most significant insights are those that illuminate the ways in which ritual functioned as a site of emotional exchange in the post-Holocaust family, revealing an aspect of traumatic transference thus far overlooked in the psychological literature. In exploring the effects of ritual observance on the second generation, the research gives further support to the relational approach to the cross-generational transmission of trauma as this approach is viewed through the lens of self-in-relation theory. Additionally, the findings on ritual further an understanding of how children of survivors work to resolve their identification with a traumatized parent through the creation of new cultural forms that offer a path to autonomy and separation. Although ritual innovation is only one way the second generation seeks to unravel the deep and often troubling emotional connections to the first generation, this trend reveals the kinds of creative resolutions that succeeding generations have developed in response to the sometimes conflicting emotional needs that have framed the life experiences of children of survivors.

Future research on trauma and ritual might also consider the importance of ritual for collective memory in the survivor family. As this research has illustrated, in the aftermath of catastrophe and familial destruction, ritual appears to grow in importance as a source for the intergenerational transmission of trauma-based memories among survivors and their descendents. This finding has important implications for the study of mass trauma, family tradition, and collective memory, an area of research that can shed further light on religion and the formation of social memory. Future work in ritual and mass trauma might return to Halbwachs's (1992) work on religious tradition and collective memory, providing a contemporary consideration of the importance of family ritual as a vehicle for the construction of social memory and the transfer of traumatic emotion.

31

How the Millennium Comes Violently

Catherine L. Wessinger

Those who do not remember the past are condemned to repeat it.

—Sign at the Jonestown pavillion
(George Santayana)

RECENT EVENTS

The year 2000 is stimulating religious imaginations to spin millennial dreams. The new millennium is stimulating hopes that the limitations of the human condition will be transcended finally and completely. Scholars have termed this *hope for collective earthly or heavenly salvation* "millennialism" or "millenarianism," because, so often, the terrestrial perfection has been expected to last one thousand years. Many millennialists believe the transition will take place catastrophically, and sometimes this conflict expectation and its accompanying radical dualistic perspective have contributed to episodes of violence.

In the last decade of the twentieth century, a number of millennial groups involved in violence burst into the news. In 1992, the family of Randy and Vicki Weaver, who had strong millennial beliefs and had taken refuge in the mountains at Ruby Ridge, Idaho, was caught up in a conflict with law enforcement agents that killed Sam Weaver (age 14), Vicki Weaver, and U.S. Marshal William Degan.[1] In 1993, the Branch Davidians were subjected to not one, but two assaults by federal

officers, resulting in the deaths of four ATF agents and eighty Davidians. In October 1994, fifty-three members and former members of the Order of the Solar Temple (Ordre du Temple Solaire) were discovered dead in Quebec and Switzerland. Some were murdered and some committed suicide. At the winter solstice just before Christmas 1995, sixteen more members of the Solar Temple died in a group murder/suicide near Grenoble, France. On March 20, 1995, members of Aum Shinrikyo released sarin gas on Tokyo subway trains, injuring over 5,000 people and killing twelve. Aum members previously had committed a variety of murders, and they attempted to commit more murders after the Tokyo subway attack. The 1996 eighty-one-day standoff between FBI agents and the Montana Freemen contained an armed group that was part of a revolutionary movement in the United States that aimed to overthrow the federal government. On March 22, 1997, when the Hale-Bopp comet was closest to the earth, five more members of the Solar Temple committed suicide in Quebec, and thirty-nine members of Heaven's Gate began their group suicide near San Diego. On May 6, 1997, two more Heaven's Gate believers attempted suicide, and one succeeded. The Heaven's Gate believer who was revived at that time, Chuck Humphrey, committed suicide in February 1998.

Members of all of these groups were millennialists, as were members of the Peoples Temple, who, in 1978, committed murder and "revolutionary suicide" in and near Jonestown, Guyana. Millennial hopes are perennial and are not necessarily tied to unusual dates on the calendar. On November 18, 1978, Peoples Temple members opened fire on the party of U.S. Congressman Leo Ryan, who had just completed an unwelcome visit to Jonestown and was leaving with some defectors. Five people were killed, including Congressman Ryan, and ten were wounded. Back in Jonestown, the community gathered to commit suicide by drinking Fla-Vor-Aid laced with tranquilizers and cyanide. Some people, including children, were injected with the deadly potion. Nine hundred and nine people died in Jonestown, including 294 children under age nineteen. A loyal member of Peoples Temple stationed in Georgetown, Guyana, slit the throats of her three children and then killed herself. Four months later, Mike Prokes, the church's public relations man, called a news conference in a Modesto, California, motel. Prokes said, "I can't disassociate myself from the people who died, nor do I want to. The people weren't brainwashed fanatics or cultists; the Temple was not a cult." Then he went to the bathroom and shot himself.[2]

Each one of these cases teaches us that well-meaning and ordinary people (lower class, middle class, and upper class, young and old, people of all races, nationalities, and educational levels) can become caught up in religious systems and social dynamics that can culminate in violence and death. Jim Jones's sign at the Jonestown pavillion, quoting Santayana, is pertinent. If we neglect to study these millennial movements, and do not understand the dynamics that produce tragic violence, then these scenarios will continue to occur.

When we learn of an episode of violence involving a religious group, we distance those people from us by considering them to be brainwashed cultists who have nothing in common with ordinary people like ourselves. We make them completely "other" from ourselves. But in fact, members of these religious groups *are* ordinary people, who are sincerely committed to their religious beliefs. We need to recall that millennial beliefs are at the core of a number of mainstream scriptures, especially the Bible, and that these scriptures, therefore, serve as resources upon which religious people can draw.

After the deaths at Jonestown, the members of Peoples Temple were dehumanized, because we saw them in the news only as corpses.[3] The news media did not characterize the residents of Jonestown as good people who were committed to an ideal of interracial harmony and human equality. Peoples Temple members were building a community based on "apostolic socialism," in which financial resources were held in common to serve the needs of all community members. The members of the community worked for each others' well-being.

The Branch Davidians also were dehumanized in the news media. Because the FBI controlled the flow of information about the Davidians, the Davidians were not permitted to tell their side of the story. They were obstructed from explaining their religious beliefs to the American public. All we saw in the media were depictions of a deranged-looking David Koresh. The invisibility of the other Davidians made them into nonentities and created a cultural situation in which it became acceptable to exterminate them. By this I mean that, because the news did not depict the Davidians as human beings, the media coverage produced a cultural consensus that their deaths did not warrant public outcry against the excessive force used against them.[4] Seventy-four Davidians died in the fire on April 19, 1993. Of these, twenty-three were children, including two infants who were born after the death of their mothers.[5]

It is my hope that my comparative study of Jonestown, the Branch Davidians, Aum Shinrikyo, the Montana Freemen, the Solar Temple, Heaven's Gate, and Chen Tao[6] will enable ordinary people—religious believers, potential converts, news reporters, law enforcement agents, and scholars—to deal constructively with the dynamics of millennial groups and to avoid violence.

KEY TERMS

In understanding violent millennial groups, I have found Robert D. Baird's definition of religion to be useful. Utilizing the phrase coined by theologian Paul Tillich, Baird defines religion as "ultimate concern," and he defines ultimate concern as "a concern which *is more important than anything else in the universe for the person [or the group] involved.*"[7] Many of us are pragmatic and will change our ultimate concerns if placed in life-threatening situations. However, groups such as Jonestown, the Branch Davidians, Aum Shinrikyo, the Montana Freemen, the Solar Temple, and Heaven's Gate show us that people can be willing to kill or die for their ultimate concerns.

The ultimate concern of the Jonestown residents was to preserve their communal solidarity, and, thus, be an example that would help establish a future society free of racism, sexism, classism, and ageism. Jim Jones taught that a period of turmoil, race war, and nuclear destruction would precede the establishment of the perfect society, which he believed would be communist. The ultimate concern of the Branch Davidians was to be obedient to God's will as revealed in the Bible in order to be included in God's salvation kingdom. The Davidians believed that Koresh would be killed in armageddon[8] and then he would return to establish God's kingdom. The ultimate concern for Aum Shinrikyo devotees was the creation of communities of enlightened individuals, who would survive armageddon and establish the Buddhist millennial kingdom called Shambhala. The ultimate concern of the Montana Freemen was to overthrow the illegitimate American government to establish true American republics obedient to Yahweh's laws revealed in the Bible. These are all millennial goals involving the expectation that salvation will be terrestrial.

In millennial religions, however, the expectation of an earthly salvation also involves belief in heaven or an otherworld. This permits shifting to an expectation of a heavenly salvation if historical conditions disprove the earthly salvation. When the Solar Temple adepts decided that the world's population was stubbornly refusing to transform to create the Age of Aquarius, they shifted their expectation of terrestrial salvation to an otherworldly realm, to which they made several group "transits" by murder and group suicide.

Heaven's Gate serves as a reminder to scholars that millennial groups are not always concerned with terrestrial salvation. The Heaven's Gate class members saw the terrestrial world, which they designated the Human Kingdom, as sorely lacking in perfection. In order to achieve the Kingdom of Heaven, or what they termed The Level Above Human (T.E.L.A.H.), each believer had to learn how to overcome human desires. Ultimately, they abandoned their human bodies, their terrestrial "vehicles," confident that their souls were transferring into divinized extraterrestrial bodies in T.E.L.A.H. They believed that as inhabitants of T.E.L.A.H., they would travel the universe with their teachers, Ti and Do, in a "mothership." As T.E.L.A.H. inhabitants, they would spend eternity in service by guiding the evolution of life on various planets regarded as "gardens" for the growth of souls. They exited Earth in 1997 (they did not regard this as suicide), because catastrophic destruction was imminent due to an overgrowth of evil here in this "garden."

We need to note that increasingly in new religions, extraterrestrials and space aliens are the superhuman agents that act in the roles previously filled by God, gods, angels, and devils. The religious outlook remains the same; there is continued belief that there are normally unseen superhuman agents that affect us in our earthly existence for good or ill.

There are two primary types of millennialism, which I call catastrophic millennialism and progressive millennialism.[9]

Catastrophic millennialism involves a pessimistic view of humanity and society. We are so corrupt and sinful that the world as we know it must be destroyed and then created anew. This will be accomplished by God (or by superhuman agents such as extraterrestrials), perhaps with the assistance of human beings. The millennial kingdom will be created only after the violent destruction of the old world.

Progressive millennialism involves an optimistic view of human nature that became prevalent in the nineteenth century. Humans engaging in social work in harmony with the divine will can effect changes that non-catastrophically and progressively create the millennial kingdom.[10]

Believers in both catastrophic millennialism and progressive millennialism are certain that there is a divine (or superhuman) plan to establish the millennial kingdom. Both types of millennialism possess an urgent sense of the imminence of the millennial kingdom. Catastrophic millennialism and progressive millennialism differ on whether humanity contains enough positive potential to make the transition noncatastrophically or is so depraved that violent destruction of the old world is necessary before the millennial kingdom can be established.

Both catastrophic millennialism and progressive millennialism may or may not involve messianism.[11] I use the Hebrew word *messiah* to refer to an individual believed to be empowered by God (or a superhuman agent) to create the millennial kingdom. A messiah is always a prophet, but a prophet is not necessarily a messiah.[12] A *prophet* is someone who is believed to receive revelation from a normally unseen source, such as God, angels, ascended masters, or extraterrestrials. Both messiahs and prophets have charismatic authority (see the discussion of charisma in chapter 1), but the messiah is the individual believed to be empowered to bring about the millennial kingdom. The prophet may announce the imminent arrival of the millennial kingdom, and perhaps even the imminent arrival of the messiah, but the prophet who is not a messiah is not regarded as having the power to create the millennial kingdom.

THE DYNAMICS OF VIOLENCE

Catastrophic millennialism inherently possesses a dualistic worldview.[13] The world is seen as a battleground between good and evil, God and Satan, us and them. This radical dualism expects, and often produces, conflict. It identifies particular groups and individuals as enemies. It is the embattled worldview of people engaging in warfare. Many religious people hold this dualistic worldview and wage their warfare spiritually with prayers, faith, and worship as their weapons. But if the warfare becomes physical, people are killed, they kill others, people are martyred and die for a cause. Jonestown, the Branch Davidians, Aum Shinrikyo, and the Montana Freemen were catastrophic millennial groups willing to fight the battle on the physical level.

Catastrophic millennialism and progressive millennialism are not mutually exclusive. If a group experiences some prosperity, some success at building its millennial kingdom, the expectations of catastrophe may wane and progressive expectations will come to the fore. But if the group experiences conflict with "cultural opponents,"[14] if it experiences persecution, then the group may be pushed to exaggerated expectations of catastrophe and a radical dualism that tends toward paranoia.

I suggest that if members of a catastrophic millennial group perceive themselves as being persecuted by outside cultural opponents, and furthermore perceive that they are failing to achieve their ultimate concern, this will be a group that is likely to commit violent acts in order to preserve its ultimate concern.[15] In attempting to deal with such a catastrophic millennial group, it is counterproductive to undertake actions that make the members feel persecuted, and the worst thing to do is to apply increased pressure that causes the members to despair about achieving their ultimate goal. Persecution just confirms the millennial group's dualism and perception of being locked in a conflict with powerful and demonic enemies. If the group members are pushed to the point of despair about the success of their goal, they will not abandon their ultimate concern, but instead they will be motivated to take desperate actions to preserve it.

If, due to internal weaknesses and the experience of cultural opposition, a catastrophic millennial community gives up on the possibility of including individuals in the outside world in salvation and turns inward to ensure the salvation of its members alone, then violent actions are more likely to be committed. This was the point reached by the Jonestown residents and Aum Shinrikyo devotees as well as by the Solar Temple adepts and Heaven's Gate students. The violence may be directed outwardly against enemies, or it may be directed inwardly to control dissidents or perhaps to commit suicide and remove the group from the hopelessly corrupt world. Jonestown, Aum Shinrikyo, and the Solar Temple indicate that it is likely that *both* inwardly-directed and outwardly-directed violent acts will be committed.

In studying catastrophic millennial groups involved in violence, we need to distinguish between fragile groups that initiate violence to preserve their ultimate concern, and groups that are assaulted because law enforcement agents regard them as dangerous. There are also revolutionary millennial movements that possess theologies or ideologies that prompt believers to commit violent acts against enemies perceived as demonic or subhuman.

Fragile Millennial Groups that Initiate Violence due to Internal Weaknesses and Cultural Opposition

Jonestown and Aum Shinrikyo are examples of catastrophic millennial groups experiencing internal and external pressures that can produce violence.[16] Jonestown and Aum Shinrikyo are examples of fragile catastrophic millennial groups whose members commit violent acts because they feel persecuted and perceive their millennial goal (their ultimate concern) as failing.

Both Jim Jones and Shoko Asahara created stresses internal to the group that endangered the ultimate concern. Both leaders set goals for their groups that were impossible to achieve. Both Jones and Asahara were, by virtue of their own actions, in danger of failing to be the messiahs they claimed to be. Jones's descent into debilitating drug addiction after he moved to Jonestown intensified the pressure felt by the other leaders to keep Jonestown economically viable. Jonestown was in danger of failing as a communal experiment, and was suffering from Jones's erratic behavior when the unwanted visit by Congressman Leo Ryan, reporters, and concerned relatives—all perceived as enemies—pushed the community over the edge. Shoko Asahara styled himself as a perfect Buddha, a fully enlightened person with infallible powers of prophecy. He created stresses internal to Aum Shinrikyo by stipulating that an impossible number of individuals had to become renunciants (monastics). Once Asahara, as an infallible Buddha, predicted armageddon, then armageddon had to occur. Asahara's insistence that devotees perform violent acts of asceticism led to a devotee's death and subsequently the murder of an individual who wanted to defect. Aum Shinrikyo, therefore, possessed criminal secrets, and any investigation of the group endangered its ultimate concern of establishing the Buddhist millennial kingdom.[17]

The stresses internal to Jonestown and Aum Shinrikyo were exacerbated by the activities of outside opponents—concerned relatives, anticult activists, reporters, law enforcement agents, and government representatives—that caused members of both groups to feel persecuted. The response within both Jonestown and Aum Shinrikyo was to turn inward and give up on the outside society as being hopelessly corrupt and sinful. Jonestown residents opted to take revenge against their enemies by killing Congressman Ryan and attacking news reporters and defectors in Ryan's party, and then to preserve their communal solidarity by murdering their children and committing group suicide. Their revolutionary suicide in protest of corrupt capitalism was meant to prevent the further disruption of their community by defectors and outside opponents.[18] Aum Shinrikyo devotees committed a variety of murders to prevent defections and to silence outside opponents. They developed weapons of mass destruction for revolutionary purposes, but they utilized these weapons to wage war against their immediate enemies. The Tokyo subway gas attack had the short-term aim of preventing a massive police raid from being carried out against Aum communes. Fortunately, Japanese police were able to take the Aum leaders into custody before they became a full-fledged revolutionary millennial movement and initiated armageddon.

Both Jonestown residents and Aum Shinrikyo devotees possessed a radically dualistic worldview. The Jonestown leaders saw reality in terms of a conflict between communism and capitalism. Jim Jones used the biblical metaphor of "Babylon" to refer to evil capitalistic society.[19] The Aum guru and leaders saw reality in terms of a conflict between spirituality and materialism. Because Aum Shinrikyo concealed criminal secrets, its leaders saw every possibility of investigation as part of a conspiracy to destroy Aum. Residents of Jonestown and residents of the Aum communes felt persecuted and besieged by outside enemies. The integrity of their communes was threatened from within by potential and actual defectors.

Because of their fragility due to internal weaknesses, many of which were caused by their respective leaders and their experience of cultural opposition, Jonestown residents and Aum Shinrikyo devotees initiated violence to preserve their ultimate concerns. In both cases, violence was directed both inwardly against members and dissidents and outwardly against enemies.

The Solar Temple and Heaven's Gate, both treated in chapter 7, were also fragile millennial groups whose members committed violent acts to preserve their ultimate concerns. In the case of the Solar Temple, internal weaknesses, plus the experience of cultural opposition, caused the adepts to despair that the Age of Aquarius would be created on earth, so they opted to make a "transit" to a "heavenly" salvation on the star Sirius. Before leaving, they executed their enemies, and they murdered some less resolute Solar Temple members to assist them in making the transit. In the Heaven's Gate group, the two leaders, Ti and Do, had set impossible goals for their "class," and their dualistic catastrophic millennial worldview made the group's members extremely sensitive to any negative response to their message, which they interpreted as persecution. The Heaven's Gate class members committed suicide, which they regarded as an "exit" from Earth to enter the Kingdom of Heaven, to preserve their ultimate concern.

Assaulted Millennial Groups that are Attacked by Law Enforcement Agents because they are Perceived as Dangerous

Although the Branch Davidians also saw themselves in conflict with sinful "Babylon," they differ from Jonestown and Aum Shinrikyo because they never doubted the achievement of their ultimate concern.[20] All of the actions taken by the ATF and FBI agents[21] against the Davidians had the effect of confirming David Koresh's prophecies about the violent events of the endtime and thereby enhanced his authority as the messiah. The Branch Davidians were catastrophic millennialists and they felt persecuted, but their persecution strengthened their faith in David Koresh and his prophecies. They had no reason to doubt that God would accomplish the millennial kingdom. The events of the ATF assault and the fifty-one-day siege conducted by FBI agents confirmed that everything was going according to God's plan, and that David Koresh had the divinely-inspired ability to interpret the Bible. I believe that this explains why the Davidians were able to withstand such an incredible amount of persecution by law enforcement agents. The Davidians never gave up their efforts to convert individuals in the outside world because their persecution made it appear more likely that the ultimate concern would be achieved. David Koresh attempted to get his message out during the siege, and when that was prevented, he and other Davidians attempted to convert the FBI negotiators.

The problem was that the FBI agents were unequipped to understand the Bible-based language spoken by Koresh and the Davidians. The transcripts of the negotiation tapes[22] show that the Davidians tried valiantly throughout the siege to communicate and negotiate with the FBI agents, and that clearly indicates that the Davidians did not want to die. They believed that God might will them to die at the hands of agents of Babylon to initiate the catastrophic endtime, and they were willing to die for their ultimate concern, but *the Branch Davidians did not want to die*. The Davidians attempted to communicate with FBI agents up until the very end.

During the siege, at least one Davidian (Livingstone Fagan) came out of Mount Carmel for the purpose of explaining the Davidians' faith. Other Davidians came out for personal reasons or they sent their children out. The persecution confirmed Koresh's prophecies, so the community was not endangered when people chose to come out. But many Davidians stayed inside Mount Carmel because they were waiting for a revelation of God's will, and because each time Davidians came out, FBI agents punished them by escalating the psychological warfare.[23]

The Branch Davidian tragedy illustrates how law enforcement agents *should not* deal with armed catastrophic millennial groups.[24] To avoid violence, law enforcement agents have to take seriously the group's religious views and avoid acting in ways that make them appear to be the agents of Satan. In the event of a siege, group members should be offered terms that permit them to remain true to their ultimate concern even while surrendering. This was not done with the Branch Davidians, to a great extent because of the advice being given to

law enforcement agents by anticult activists.[25] Anticult activists possess their own radical dualistic worldview that perpetuates the prejudiced stereotype of the so-called cult.

After being ignored by the FBI when they offered their services, two Bible scholars, Dr. J. Phillip Arnold and Dr. James Tabor, pursued a plan to persuade the Davidians to surrender. Arnold and Tabor were concerned because the Davidians believed they were in the "Fifth Seal" of Revelation (Rev. 6: 9–11). The Davidians interpreted this Bible passage as a prediction that some of the members of the godly community would be killed by Babylon, and after a waiting period the rest of the community would be martyred.[26] Arnold and Tabor directed a radio broadcast to the Davidians in which they discussed the biblical prophecies. The Davidians were elated that *finally* someone was communicating with them who understood their Bible-based language.[27] Arnold and Tabor suggested that other prophecies in Revelation indicated that David Koresh should come out in order to present his interpretation of the Seven Seals to the world, even after being imprisoned. They argued that the waiting period described in the Fifth Seal would be longer than a few months. The Davidians should exit Mount Carmel because God did not intend them to be martyred there. Once out of Mount Carmel David Koresh would be able to spread his message of God's salvation to the rest of the world.

On April 14, 1993, Koresh sent out a letter in which he reported that he had received permission from God to write a "little book"[28] containing his interpretation of the Seven Seals. Koresh's letter said that once the manuscript was in safekeeping with Tabor and Arnold, he and the Davidians would come out.[29] The negotiation tapes reveal that the Davidians were heard cheering at the prospect of coming out.[30] On April 16, Koresh reported to the FBI that he had completed writing his interpretation of the First Seal.[31] When Attorney General Janet Reno asked if there were reasons to continue waiting and negotiating with the Davidians, FBI agents did not tell her about Koresh's promise to surrender. A woman who escaped the fire on April 19 carried out a disk that contained David Koresh's interpretation of the First Seal of Revelation, indicating that Koresh was sincere in his promise.[32]

J. Phillip Arnold and James Tabor succeeded in offering the Davidians a way they could remain true to their ultimate concern and still come out, but their successful efforts were nullified by the FBI gas and tank assault on April 19. During the assault, the Davidians probably concluded that the prophecies of Revelation were being fulfilled in their martyrdom at the hands of Babylon. Only nine Davidians escaped the fire.

Revolutionary Millennial Movements Possessing Theologies of Violence[33]

The eighty-one-day soft siege of the Montana Freemen in 1996 was handled correctly by the FBI. The standoff involved a group of armed people who aimed to spark "the second American revolution" to overthrow the federal government they identified as "Babylon" and to establish true American republics obedient to Yahweh and his laws. Revolutionary millennial movements have an inherent potential for violence because they aim to overthrow what they view as a persecuting government. The believers are convinced that they are participating in the divine plan to violently destroy the illicit government and then establish the millennial kingdom. They believe that violent revolution is necessary and divinely ordained in order to establish the millennial kingdom.

The Freemen indicate for us that there is no need to have a messiah or a guru in order to have a potentially violent religious movement. In 1996, the Freemen living in Justus Township were the most visible portion of an ongoing revolution against the American federal government. This revolutionary movement is a Euro-American nativist movement (see chapter 6). Extremist individuals associated with militias, white supremacist

groups, and the religion known as Christian Identity are committing acts of domestic terrorism, and federal and local law enforcement agents are working to contain this revolution.

Unlike Jonestown, the Branch Davidians, Aum Shinrikyo, and the Solar Temple, anticult activists were not opposing the Montana Freemen. The national news coverage of the Freemen was mediocre, but they were not demonized. Instead we saw the Freemen and their children on television, and we saw that they were human beings. The news coverage in the *Billings Gazette* was exceptionally good. Relatives of the Freemen were interviewed, and the Freemen were depicted as being farmers, ranchers, and working people with concerns that other Americans had.

During the Freemen standoff, FBI agents consulted scholars knowledgeable about millennial and new religious movements, including Dr. Michael Barkun, Dr. J. Phillip Arnold, Dr. Jean Rosenfeld, and myself. The scholars advising the FBI agents urged them to keep the siege low-key and to avoid making the Freemen feel persecuted. We urged the FBI agents to utilize third-party intermediaries (worldview translators),[34] who could understand the Freemen's worldview and speak the Freemen's language, but also who had the cognitive distance from the Freemen worldview to analyze it. We urged the FBI agents not to pressure the Freemen or cause them to despair of achieving their religious goal. Finally, we urged the FBI agents to offer terms to the Freemen that permitted them to simultaneously remain true to their ultimate concern and come out of Justus Township.

Toward the end of the Freemen standoff, J. Phillip Arnold spent four days with the FBI negotiators in Montana, which contributed to the breakthrough involving the exit of a couple along with the woman's two young daughters (ages eight and ten). FBI agents offered final terms to the remaining Freemen that reassured the Freemen they could continue striving to achieve their ultimate concern while in federal custody.[35] According to the Freemen perspective, they did not surrender, but took their fight against Babylon into the federal courts.[36] The Freemen were not put into a position in which they felt their only options were either to kill or die for their ultimate concern.[37]

CONCLUSION

The categories highlighted here—fragile millennial groups, assaulted millennial groups, and revolutionary millennial movements—can be seen as distinct moments on a continuum involving millennial beliefs and the potential for violence. A particular millennial group may possess several of these features simultaneously—fragility, revolutionary ideology and activity, and being subjected to assault. A group may move from one of these categories to another as it develops.[38] I have assigned one of these categories to each millennial group treated in this book according to whether the members or outside opponents initiated the violence, and whether a revolutionary ideology, fragility, or self-defense was the primary motivation for violent acts committed by believers.

Aum Shinrikyo possessed a revolutionary ideology and was actively acquiring weapons of mass destruction in preparation for initiating armageddon, but in fact, the violent acts committed by devotees were related to the fragility of Aum Shinrikyo and its endangered ultimate concern. Hence, I conclude that at the times of the sarin gas attack on the Tokyo subway and earlier acts of violence, Aum Shinrikyo was a fragile millennial group.

The Branch Davidians had revolutionary potential in that David Koresh taught that they would go to Israel and fight on the side of the Israelis against the United States and the United Nations in armageddon in 1995. Initially, the Davidians were not expecting armageddon to take place in Texas. David Koresh and one of his followers supported the group financially by buying and selling arms at gun shows.

No conclusive evidence has been produced that the Davidians' weapons were illegal, and in 1993 the Davidians were not preparing to fight armageddon against their Texas neighbors. ATF agents and FBI agents assaulted the Branch Davidians twice because they misunderstood their religious commitment and intention.

Jonestown, the Solar Temple, and Heaven's Gate were unambiguously fragile millennial groups, whose members committed violent acts to preserve their ultimate concerns. Each suffered from internal stresses that endangered their respective goals as well as from varying degrees of cultural opposition that members viewed as persecution.

The Montana Freemen were part of a diffuse revolutionary millennial movement in contemporary America, and the Freemen were prepared to commit violent acts, but if the Freemen, like similar Christian Identity communities in the United States, had experienced some success at building their millennial kingdom set apart from corrupt mainstream society, then the potential for violent acts committed by believers could have diminished over time.

It needs to be noted that catastrophic millennial beliefs do not necessarily cause violent episodes.[39] Numerous catastrophic millennial groups exist and have existed without getting caught up in violence.

On the other hand, every millennial movement is revolutionary in its hope for a radical transformation to a collective salvation.[40] A key issue in determining the potential for volatility is whether the believers expect that the transformation will be accomplished by divine intervention or by the active participation of the faithful in overthrowing the current sinful order. Under specific social conditions, otherwise peaceful catastrophic millennial groups may become assaulted or fragile.

The comparative study of Jonestown, the Branch Davidians, Aum Shinrikyo, the Montana Freemen, the Solar Temple, Heaven's Gate, and also of Chen Tao, reveals the persistent folly of a radical dualistic worldview, and shows that such "dichotomous thinking"[41] is found not only in members of catastrophic millennial groups, but also among defectors from new religious movements, anticult activists, law enforcement agents, and news reporters. It is all too human to see things in conflictual terms—us vs. the enemy, the good guys vs. the bad guys. The persistence of a radical dualistic view is seen in defectors from catastrophic millennial groups, who simply reverse those they define as the enemy. The religious group they have left and its leader are redefined as evil, and they work as passionately to destroy that group as they previously worked to promote it.[42] Law enforcement agents and members of the military are trained to see situations in terms of the good guys in conflict with the bad guys. Numerous retired police officers and former military personnel populate the continuing Euro-American nativist movement that includes the Freemen, constitution and Common Law study groups, and militias. They have merely redefined the federal government and its agents as evil, and they work passionately to destroy the government's dominance. Police officers and former military personnel were active in helping Aum Shinrikyo prepare to wage deadly armageddon against the population of Japan. In the cases of Jonestown, the Branch Davidians, and the Solar Temple, news reporters in search of sensationalized stories of conflict contributed to the tragic conclusions. The Heaven's Gate leader, Do, felt persecuted by the news media in the mid-1970s, and this contributed to his decision to lead his class to commit a group suicide more than twenty years later.

In order to deal constructively with members of unconventional religious groups, law enforcement agents, reporters, and scholars have to learn to regard the members as human beings possessing a sincere commitment to their ultimate concern. If people can regard each other as human beings, as persons like "us," and not as demonic and inhuman enemies, conflictual dualism on all sides will

diminish. For law enforcement agents, this means it is necessary to meet with members of new religious groups, listen to them, and, whenever possible, enlist their cooperation in the investigation of their activities. News reporters can contribute to peaceful dialogue rather than violent conflict by respectfully permitting members of unconventional religions to articulate their views and to be seen as human beings. Scholars need to promote increased public understanding of religion by making their expertise available to reporters, law enforcement agents, and the wider community. However, as scholars attempt to humanize the members of new religious movements for the general public, they should not be in the business of giving "clean bills of health" to particular groups. Aum Shinrikyo stands as a warning that sometimes NRMs contain nasty surprises. Scholars also should be leary of labeling a group as potentially dangerous given the propensity of law enforcement agents, reporters, relatives, and anticult activists to step up cultural opposition to unconventional groups. How to utilize skillfully the lessons learned from this comparative study remains at issue.

NOTES

1. Tom Morganthau, Michael Isikoff, and Bob Cohn, "The Echoes of Ruby Ridge," *Newsweek*, August 28, 1995, 25–28; Jess Walter, " 'Every Knee Shall Bow': Exclusive Book Excerpt," *Newsweek*, August 28, 1995, 29–33; Jess Walter, *Every Knee Shall Bow: The Truth and Tragedy of Ruby Ridge and the Randy Weaver Family* (New York: Harper Paperbacks, 1995).

2. John R. Hall, *Gone From the Promised Land: Jonestown in American Cultural History* (New Brunswick, N.J.: Transaction Books, 1987), 291.

3. I thank Rebecca Moore for sharing this observation with me.

4. James T. Richardson, "Manufacturing Consent about Koresh: A Structural Analysis of the Role of Media in the Waco Tragedy," in *Armageddon in Waco: Critical Perspectives on the Branch Davidian Conflict*, ed. Stuart A. Wright (Chicago: University of Chicago Press, 1995), 153–76. Richardson does not use the word

exterminate in his article, but he does point out that the news coverage of the Davidians made them into victims "unworthy" of the compassion of the general public.

5. James D. Tabor and Eugene V. Gallagher, *Why Waco? Cults and the Battle for Religious Freedom in America* (Berkeley: University of California Press, 1995), 3; Carol Moore, *The Davidian Massacre: Disturbing Questions about Waco Which Must Be Answered* (Franklin, Tenn., and Springfield, Va.: Legacy Communications and Gun Owners Foundation, 1995), xiii–xiv; Dick J. Reavis, *The Ashes of Waco: An Investigation* (New York: Simon & Schuster, 1995), 277.

    The two pregnant women were Aisha Gyarfas (17), who died of a gunshot wound, and Nicole Gent (23), who was killed by falling cement as she huddled with other women and the children in a room made of concrete blocks.

    In the ATF raid on Mount Carmel on Sunday, February 28, 1993, four ATF agents were killed, twenty ATF agents were wounded, five Davidians were killed, and four Davidians (including David Koresh) were wounded. That afternoon about 4:55 P.M., Michael Schroeder was shot and killed by ATF agents as he attempted to walk to Mount Carmel to rejoin his family.

6. The episode involving the Randy Weaver family is discussed in chapter 6.

7. Robert D. Baird, *Category Formation and the History of Religions* (The Hague: Mouton, 1971), 18. Baird's emphasis, my addition in brackets.

8. Armageddon in the book of Revelation refers to a place where the final battle between good and evil will occur. Throughout this book I use *armageddon* in its popular sense of the final battle that will destroy the world as we know it.

9. I offer these readily comprehensible terms as alternatives to the obscure and misleading terms used by historians, *pre-millennialism* and *post-millennialism*. See Catherine Wessinger, "Millennialism With and Without the Mayhem: Catastrophic and Progressive Expectations," in *Millennium, Messiahs, and Mayhem: Contemporary Apocalyptic Movements*, ed. Thomas Robbins and Susan J. Palmer (New York: Routledge, 1997), 47–59.

10. This is the type of millennialism I studied in *Annie Besant and Progressive Messianism* (Lewiston, N.Y.: Edwin Mellen Press, 1988).

    In *Millennialism, Persecution, and Violence: Historical Cases*, ed. Catherine Wessinger (Syracuse: Syracuse

University Press, 2000), the chapters by Robert Ellwood on German Nazis, Scott Lowe on Mao Zedong's Great Leap Forward in the People's Republic of China, and Richard Salter on the Khmer Rouge in Cambodia indicate that progressive millennialism can motivate revolutionary violence. Revolutionary progressive millennial beliefs promote violence, but it appears that *noncatastrophic* progressive millennialism as defined in this chapter is unlikely to promote violence. See the discussion in my introduction to *Millennialism, Persecution, and Violence*, "The Interacting Dynamics of Millennial Beliefs, Persecution, and Violence," 3–39. None of the groups studied here are noncatastrophic progressive millennialists or revolutionary progressive millennialists.

11. This assertion is contrary to most scholarly assumptions about "post-millennialism." See the discussion in Wessinger, "Millennialism With and Without the Mayhem."

12. See my discussion in "Interacting Dynamics of Millennial Beliefs, Persecution, and Violence."

13. Revolutionary progressive millennialism possesses the dualistic view found in catastrophic millennialism.

14. John R. Hall, "Public Narratives and the Apocalyptic Sect: From Jonestown to Mt. Carmel" in Wright, *Armageddon in Waco* 207.

15. I derived this thesis from reading simultaneously works of two scholars: Mary McCormick Maaga, "Triple Erasure: Women and Power in Peoples Temple," Ph.D. diss. Drew University, 1996; Ian Reader, *A Poisonous Cocktail? Aum Shinrikyo's Path to Violence* (Copenhagen: Nordic Institute of Asian Studies Books, 1996). I rely to a great extent on these works by Maaga and Reader in my description and analysis of events involving Jonestown and Aum Shinrikyo.

16. Millennial groups becoming involved in violence due to simultaneous endogenous and exogenous factors are also discussed in Thomas Robbins and Dick Anthony, "Sects and Violence: Factors Enhancing the Volatility of Marginal Religious Movements," in Wright, *Armageddon in Waco*, 236–59. In Wessinger, *Millennialism, Persecution, and Violence*, the fragile millennial groups discussed are Jonestown by Rebecca Moore, Solar Temple and Heaven's Gate by Massimo Introvigne, and Aum Shinrikyo by Ian Reader.

17. Ian Reader, "Imagined Persecution: Aum Shinrikyo, Millennialism, and the Legitimation of Violence," in

Wessinger, *Millennialism, Persecution, and Violence*, 158–82.

18. The Jonestown residents felt they had no other place to go. They did not view returning to American society with its capitalism and inequality as an option. They had explored relocating to Cuba or the U.S.S.R. with no result.

19. Hall, *Gone from the Promised Land*, 31, 145.

20. In Wessinger, *Millennialism, Persecution, and Violence*, other assaulted groups studied are the Mormons by Grant Underwood, the massacre of a Lakota Sioux band in 1890 at Wounded Knee by Michelene E. Pesantubbee, the Dreads in Dominica by Richard C. Salter, and the massacre of black Israelites at Bulhoek, South Africa, by Christine Steyn. Assaulted millennial groups are not rare.

21. These agencies are the Bureau of Alcohol, Tobacco, and Firearms, and the Federal Bureau of Investigation.

22. For studies of the Waco negotiations, see Eugene V. Gallagher, " 'Theology Is Life and Death': David Koresh on Violence, Persecution, and the Millennium," in Wessinger, *Millennialism, Persecution, and Violence*, 82–100; Jayne Seminare Docherty, "When the Parties Bring Their Gods to the Table: Learning Lessons from Waco," Ph.D. diss., 1998, George Mason University; and the forthcoming dissertation by Cary R.W. Voss, Communications, University of Kansas.

23. James Tabor, "The Events at Waco: An Interpretive Log," at <http://home.maine.rr.com/waco/ww.html>.

24. See Catherine Wessinger, "Review Essay: Understanding the Branch Davidian Tragedy," *Nova Religio: The Journal of Alternative and Emergent Religions* 1 (October 1997): 122–38. Information on *Nova Religio* can be found at <http://www.novareligio.com>.

25. See John R. Hall, "Public Narratives and the Apocalyptic Sect," 205–35; Nancy T. Ammerman, "Waco, Federal Law Enforcement, and Scholars of Religion," 282–96; Stuart A. Wright, "Construction and Escalation of a Cult Threat," 75–94; all in Wright, *Armageddon in Waco*; see also Tabor and Gallagher, *Why Waco?*

26. The Fifth Seal described in Revelation 6:9–11 is given below. The following is quoted in J. Phillip Arnold, "The Davidian Dilemma—To Obey God or Man?" in *From the Ashes: Making Sense of Waco*, ed. James R. Lewis (Lanham, Md.: Rowman & Littlefield, 1994), 25.

> And when he had opened the fifth seal, I saw under the altar the souls of *them that were slain* for the word of God, and for the testimony which they held: And they cried with a loud voice, saying, *How long*, Lord, holy and true, dost thou not judge and avenge our blood on them that dwell on the earth? And white robes were given unto every one of them; and it was said unto them, that they should *rest* yet for a little season, until their fellow servants also and their brethren, that should be *killed* as they were, should be fulfilled.

27. Negotiation tape no. 129, March 15, 1993, of Steve Schneider reporting the enthusiastic responses of Davidians to hearing on the radio Dr. J. Phillip Arnold discussing the Bible. Schneider asked that Dr. Arnold be permitted to discuss the biblical prophecies with David Koresh to see if Arnold could offer alternative interpretations. Schneider stated that if Arnold could prove by the biblical texts that the Davidians should come out, they would exit Mount Carmel regardless of whether or not David Koresh agreed with Arnold's interpretations.

    Audiotape of discussion of James Tabor and J. Phillip Arnold on the Ron Engleman radio talk show station KGBS on April 1, 1993; audiotape of "The Last Recorded Words of David Koresh April 16–18, 1993," narrated by James Tabor.

    On April 16, 1993, David Koresh enthusiastically discussed with a negotiator that when he had written his commentary on the Seven Seals, he and the Davidians would come out. Koresh explained that he would give the manuscript to James Tabor and Phillip Arnold for safekeeping, because they had expressed a sincere interest in his biblical interpretations. Koresh wanted his teachings preserved and disseminated in writing because he believed that once he was taken into custody, he would be presented to the public as a monstrosity.

    For the full story, see chapter 4.

28. This is a reference to a messenger with a "little book" in Revelation 10. See Tabor and Gallagher, *Why Waco?* 16.

29. Tabor and Gallagher, *Why Waco?* 15.

30. House of Representatives, *Investigation into the Activities of Federal Law Enforcement Agencies toward the Branch Davidians: Thirteenth Report by the Committee on Government Reform and Oversight Prepared in Conjunction with the Committee on the Judiciary together with Additional and Dissenting Views*, Report 104–749 (Washington, DC: U. S. Government Printing Office, 1996), 65.

31. "Last Recorded Words of David Koresh" audiotape.

32. For these events, see Tabor and Gallagher, *Why Waco?* James; D. Tabor, "Religious Discourse and Failed Negotiations: The Dynamics of Biblical Apocalypticism in Waco," in Wright, *Armageddon in Waco*, 263–81; James D. Tabor, "The Waco Tragedy: An Autobiographical Account of One Attempt to Prevent Disaster," in Lewis, *From the Ashes*, 13–21; Arnold, "Davidian Dilemma," 23–31.

33. In Wessinger, *Millennialism, Persecution, and Violence* the, revolutionary millennial groups studied are the Russian Old Believers by Thomas Robbins, the Taiping Revolution and Mao Zedong's Great Leap Forward by Scott Lowe, German Nazism by Robert Ellwood, the appropriation of *Lotus Sutra* millennialism by militant Japanese nationalists by Jacqueline Stone, the Khmer Rouge by Richard C. Salter, American Neo-Nazis by Jeffrey Kaplan, and the Montana Freemen by Jean E. Rosenfeld. Revolutionary millennial movements are very common and can cause massive suffering.

34. I thank Jayne Seminare Docherty for this term, *worldview translator*, which she uses in her dissertation. Docherty, "When the Parties Bring Their Gods to the Table." Docherty derived this phrase from Phillip Lucas, "How Future Wacos Might Be Avoided: Two Proposals," in Lewis, *From the Ashes*, 209–12.

35. The terms were reported in Clair Johnson, "Freemen deal includes 5: Negotiator spells out points in agreement," *Billings Gazette Online*, June 19, 1996.

36. Neill H. Payne, "Shades of Waco: CAUSE Negotiates Peaceful End to Siege of Justus Township Standoff," *The Balance: A Newsletter of Civil Rights and Current Events 7*, no. 2 (Summer 1996): 1–3.

37. The standoff was concluded peacefully because the Freemen were offered terms that permitted them to remain true to their ultimate concern. The peaceful resolution did *not* occur because their electricity was cut off although that may have been a contributing factor. Unlike their dealings with the Branch Davidians, FBI agents increased the pressure on the Freemen cautiously.

38. I thank Eugene V. Gallagher for stressing these points to me in personal communications.

39. I thank Lonnie Kliever and Grant Underwood for emphasizing this point to me in personal communications. See Grant Underwood, "Millennialism, Persecution, and Violence: The Mormons," in Wessinger, *Millennialism, Persecution, and Violence*, 43–61.

40. I thank Eugene V. Gallagher for emphasizing this to me in personal communications.

41. Linda E. Olds discusses the problematic features of dichotomous thinking in promoting patriarchy and sexism in *Fully Human: How Everyone Can Integrate the Benefits of Masculine and Feminine Sex Roles* (Englewood Cliffs, N.J.: Prentice-Hall, 1981).

42. For example, while a member of Peoples Temple, Tim Stoen idolized Jim Jones.

32

The Association of 'Religion' with Violence: Reflections on a Modern Trope

Richard King

Our conceptions of the world face the predicament of turning into ideologies the moment that they forget their own historicities.

(Dirlik 2000: 84).

Understanding the system of ideology that operates in one's own society is made difficult by two factors: (i) one's own consciousness is itself a product of that system, and (ii) the system's very success renders its operations invisible, since one is so consistently immersed in and bombarded by its products that one comes to mistake them (and the apparatus through which they are produced and disseminated) for nothing other than 'nature'.

(Lincoln 1996: Thesis 10).

The point is rather that the Enlightenment must examine itself.

(Adorno and Horkheimer 1972: xv).

IT IS A COMMONLY HELD view that 'religion' has a particular association with violence. Consider, however, a few salient facts and statistics about the contemporary world in which we live. In 2005 between 62 to 65 per cent of the world's total military budget was spent by five ostensibly 'secular' nation-states (the USA, the UK, France, Japan and China).[1] Of these five states, one in particular – the United States of America – has a military budget that accounts for almost half of the total global spending on the military (47 per cent in 2004). This

is almost *10 times* the amount spent by the next biggest spenders (the United Kingdom and France, both on 5 per cent). According to proposed spending plans for 2007, the US government will spend $1.2 billion a day, that is almost $14,000 per second, on its military budget.

Consider a different, but, in my view, equally pertinent set of statistics relating to another sphere of modern 'secular' activity – the rapidly expanding global economy. In the year 2000 while the sales of the top 200 multinational corporations constituted over a quarter of the world's total economic activity, these companies employed less than 1 per cent of the world's total workforce. The combined sales of these top 200 companies are *18 times* the size of the combined annual income of the 1.2 billion people living in 'severe' poverty.[2] In an interview with the British newspaper *The Independent* on 20 June 2005, Jeffrey Sachs, the Columbia University professor, economist and special advisor to the UN Secretary General Kofi Annan, made the following sobering remark to the interviewer:

Every day, your newspaper could put on its front page, 'More than 20,000 people died yesterday because of extreme poverty'. Every day. And every single one of those deaths is preventable. It's not just something that just happens, like rain. It is something that we can change in a short period of time.

(*Independent* 20 June 2005)

In a world characterized by an increasing concentration of wealth in the hands of a small percentage of the world's population and mass consumption levels in the 'developed world' reaching an unprecedented scale, the continued death of thousands of people in conditions of extreme poverty *every single day*, while others live in conditions of unparalled affluence, is surely the most scandalous example of ongoing systemic violence in human history. Yet we hardly ever hear about it. Place this gruesome statistic alongside the untold suffering and deaths caused by a century of world wars and genocides, few of which have an easily identifiable 'religious' dimension, and one wonders why the recurring issue of mass-mobilized forms of violence is so often seen to be a problem specifically associated with 'religion'. My suggestion in this paper is that the mainstream discourse on 'religion and violence' and the emphasis that has been placed upon this as a recurring problem of human history is the secularist equivalent of a 'lone gunman theory'. By focusing one's attention upon the apparently intolerant, dogmatic and socially disharmonious aspects of purportedly identifiable entities known as 'the religions', our attention is distracted from asking deeper, structural questions about violence as a condition of modern, 'everyday' life and about the involvement of human beings in the performance of such violence – whether grounded in (so-called) 'secular' or 'religious' forms of life. Whether intended or not (and I would concede that in many cases this is unreflective and unintentional) the way that the debate about violence has been framed effectively insulates the institutional forms, organizations and ideologies that govern modern ('secular') life from critical interrogation.

'RELIGION' AS *DOXA*

This volume of papers has been particularly concerned with South Asian traditions in both their ancient and contemporary forms and their complex relationship to the performance, justification and condemnation of acts of violence. In a broader cultural and intellectual context, these discussions have systematically been framed within a broader discursive context concerned with the global question of 'religion and violence', of which there is now a growing literature, both popular and academic. It is important, given this wider hermeneutic context, to examine the debate over 'religion and violence' and locate it within its own historical and cultural context. Only then will we be in a position to appreciate some of the specificities and issues involved in understanding 'the South Asian experience'.

This paper will take a step back from this discussion and ask some critical questions about the theoretical framework that underlies the 'religion and violence' debate in general. This analysis will be carried out through an examination of the work of two prominent scholars of religion who have published on this topic, namely, Mark Juergensmeyer (UC Santa Barbara) and Bruce Lincoln (University of Chicago). Both are highly respected academics and have not only produced scholarly work of extremely high quality but also made significant contributions to their respective fields of expertise. Both however, in slightly different ways, deploy a universalized category of 'religion' that ends up dulling rather than sharpening our attention to the particularities under discussion in the 'religion and violence' debate. This paper should not be read in any sense as an attempt to diminish the substantial contribution that both scholars have made to the academic body of knowledge, but is rather an attempt to tease out some of the cultural tropes at work in the field of study as a whole through an examination of two key contributors to the debate.

Like virtually all of the authors who have written on this theme, the work of Lincoln and Juergensmeyer carries forward certain cultural assumptions and tropes about the relationship between something called 'religion' – which both scholars see as a clearly identifiable phenomenon in the world – and a propensity for intolerance and acts of violence. I will attempt to demonstrate in this paper that both authors base their work upon prevailing Euro-American assumptions about the nature of religion and its association with conflict. These assumptions can broadly be classified as 'secularist' in tenor since they reflect the way that the debate about 'religion' has unfolded in a post-Enlightenment context (though this does not preclude the occurrence of such tropes in the work of more 'theologically' inclined defences of 'the religious' that have been precipitated by such critiques.)

The prevailing assumption that runs throughout the literature on this subject, whether addressed from a theological or 'insider' perspective or from a social scientific or historical point of view, reflects a wider 'common-sense' view of history in the Western world, which assumes that 'religion' and violence have had a long and murky history of association with one another. Consider for instance the following opening remarks by Stephen J. Stein in his 2002 review of recent literature on this theme:

> Religion and violence have never been strangers, nor are they in the contemporary world. Popular and scholarly attention to the troubling relationship between the two is fostered almost daily by media accounts of religiously influenced violence in seemingly every quarter of the globe. Muslims and Jews in the Middle East, Protestants and Catholics in Northern Ireland, antiabortionists in the United States, and anticultists in a variety of nations – these are the familiar examples of such conflict. . . . None of this is terribly mysterious. Religion has often (maybe always) operated in close proximity with violence, either as the object of, or the motivator of violence.
>
> (Stein 2002: 103)

What has made these assumptions so prevalent and uncontested is the fact that they remain deeply entrenched as key components of the myths of origin of modern 'secular' nation-states such as the United States of America and France. In so far as this is the case, such assumptions remain powerful and convincing tropes within dominant Euro-American constructions of 'modernity' and remain not only largely beyond question for those influenced by such myths, but also barely conscious in their operation. In this sense the underlying discourse of religion at work here represents a good example of what Pierre Bourdieu called a *doxa*, that is:

> the coincidence of the objective structures and the internalized structures which provides the illusion of immediate understanding, characteristic of practical experience of the familiar universe, and which at the same time excludes from that experience any inquiry as to its own conditions of possibility.
>
> (1990: 25–26)

For Bourdieu, a *doxa* occurs when a particular taxonomic system presents itself as corresponding to 'nature' – the way things really are, rather than as a culturally constructed artifice. It is constituted by that which is taken for granted in a specific social setting, that which remains literally unquestionable because its arbitrary and socially constructed origins have been occluded. *Doxa* forms the unquestioned truth or authority that frames the very possibilities of thought itself – the stage upon which orthodoxies and heterodoxies can be played out according to a set of rules and assumptions that none of the participants question (Bourdieu 1977: 164–71). According to Bourdieu, challenges to *doxa* require not only a crisis of some sort but also that those who have been dominated and interpellated by such assumptions develop the 'material and symbolic means' to challenge this construction of the real. The view that all of the major macro-traditions of the world (with the exception of the European Enlightenment tradition) are examples of a single genus 'religion', and that they therefore share certain characteristics with Christianity (the archetypal religion in all of these debates) is, I would suggest, a fundamental *doxa* of modernity. As Daniel Dubuisson has argued:

Created by the West, enshrined in Western episte-mology, and central to its identity, the concept of religion eventually came to be the core of the Western worldview. Since this notion is intrinsi-cally linked to all the philosophies, complementary or competing, that have been invented in the West, the West cannot, at the risk of its own disintegra-tion, do without it, because these global concep-tions would then decompose into scattered or juxtaposed fragments. . . . Would not abandoning the idea of religion be the equivalent for Western thought of abdicating part of its intellectual hege-mony over the world?

(2003: 94)

The denaturalization of the concept of 'religion' is a fairly recent consequence of the intellectual and cultural crisis that has occurred in the West in the late twentieth century as a result of the end of European colonialism. The rising challenge to the hegemony of Occidental theory has been slowly making an impression on all disciplines in the modern academy in a series of waves (post-modernism, post-structuralism, post-colonialism). It should come as no surprise then to discover that some of the most significant early contributions to unmasking the doxic status of the category of reli-gion in the modern world have been from scholars of non-European origin (see Asad 1993 and Balagangadhara 1994).

Once one considers the discourse of 'religion' to be a fundamental *doxa* of Euro-American modernity one begins to see how different ideological posi-tions involved in this debate engage in a struggle for supremacy based upon an underlying complicity about their object of study. For the secularists reli-gion tends towards zealotry, intolerance, dogma-tism and conflict. For apologists of religion, this is only the case when religious ideals have been misap-propriated for other ends or when 'religion goes bad'. There are various intermediary positions that one can take on this debate, but what they all have in common is first, the assumption that the complex macro-traditions that are classified by the universal category of 'religion' (however differently this term may be defined by each author) can all be denoted by implication when this term is employed in debates, and second, that 'religion' does not (and cannot) denote its opposite – those dimensions of life and ideologies that are to be classified as 'secular'. These assumptions, rendered invisible by the framing of debate in terms of a series of 'competing possibles', establish a censorship, which, as Bourdieu argued, is far more radical than one that is based upon a simple orthodoxy. Indeed, the construction of an orthodoxy and various competing hetero-doxies only serve to crowd our intellectual space with oppositional views that create the illusion that all options are being explored. In this way, such debates actually *delimit the universe of possible discourse* (Bourdieu 1977: 169).

Thus, before one is able to consider the ques-tion of violence and, say, South Asian traditions (the theme of this volume), one must confront a prior epistemological issue, namely what traces and assumptions are being carried forward when we use terms such as 'religion' and 'violence' in these contexts. Generally speaking, debates about 'reli-gion and violence' assume, often uncritically, that these categories are unproblematic and 'straightfor-ward' and can be universally applied in quite distinct cultural and historical situations. However, the history of the usages of both of these terms and their specific association with each other in the modern (by which I mean here, post-Enlightenment) world should be as much the subject of critical analysis as the case studies that we are so routinely offered of this apparently universal phenomenon.

THE ASSOCIATION OF RELIGION WITH CONFLICT IN EURO-AMERICAN MODERNITY

Contemporary debates about religion and violence in the West often focus upon the question of the possibility of a just or holy war, particularly after the attacks upon the World Trade Center in New York in September 2001. Western commentators have struggled to understand the motivations of the hijackers, particularly their willingness to die in the pursuit of their goals. It is not clear, however, that there is a specific and necessary correlation between suicide missions and 'religious traditions'. Robert Pape (2005) notes for instance that the pioneer and world leader in suicide attacks is an overtly secularist movement – the Marxist Tamil Tigers of Sri Lanka. Similarly, Diego Gambetta notes that:

> Contrary to a widespread belief, the majority of [suicide missions] have been carried out by secular rather than religious organizations. This suggests that if special and exalted motivations to self-sacrifice are involved, religious beliefs and preaching are not the only way to induce or to exploit them.
>
> (2005: viii–ix)

The attacks of 11 September 2001 on the United States of America by a small but well-organized group of radical Islamists however has breathed new life into the now well-established association of religion and violence and brought this issue into the forefront of public discussion. In a contemporary Western context this is usually framed according to the following clash of tropes about 'the religious': Do religions justify and cause violence or are they more appropriately seen as forces for peace and tolerance? In the context of secular forms of modernity, religion has been represented by some as a primary cause of social division, conflict and war, whilst others have argued that this is a distortion of the 'true' significance of religion, which, when properly adhered to, promotes peace, harmony, goodwill and social cohesion. On the one hand some writers suggest that religion is a primary producer of conflict and violence. For others this is only the case when 'religion becomes evil' (Kimball 2002).

A good example of the tension between these two tropes can be found in the work of Mark Juergensmeyer, perhaps the leading scholar in the study of religion and violence in the modern world. In a series of books (most notably, *The New Cold War? Religious Nationalism Confronts the Secular State* (1993) and *Terror in the Mind of God. The Global Rise of Religious Violence* (2000)) Juergensmeyer, examines what he perceives to be an alarming global rise in religious violence in recent years. His 2000 book (re-issued with a new preface after the events of 11 September 2001), is full of detailed analysis and important empirical data. It is based upon extensive interviews and, in some cases, unprecedented access to individuals involved in various forms of ideologically motivated violence. His analysis of this data, however, is severely skewed by his recourse to an uncritical notion of 'the religious'. The author expresses puzzlement that 'bad things are done by people who otherwise appear to be good – in cases of religious terrorism, by pious people dedicated to a moral vision of the world' (2000: 7). This perplexity reflects a popular understanding of 'religion' that relates it to the development of moral values within society and harmonious influences upon the behaviour of its individual adherents. The intrinsic moral goodness of religion is a constant theme throughout Juergensmeyer's work and is reiterated (for instance) in his concluding remarks in *Terror in the Mind of God*, where the author expresses the hope that religion can act as a 'moral beacon' to provide a 'cure' for contemporary religious violence:

> Religion gives spirit to public life and provides a beacon for moral order. At the same time it needs the temper of rationality and fair play that Enlightenment values give to civil society. Thus, religious violence cannot end until some accommodation can be forged between the two – some assertion of moderation in religion's passion, and some acknowledgement of religion in elevating the spiritual and moral values of public life. In a curious way, then, the cure for religious violence may ultimately lie in a renewed appreciation for religion itself.
>
> (2000: 243)

Juergensmeyer's response to 'the rise of religious violence' is to propose an accommodationist secularism, deriving from the values of the European Enlightenment, as the basis for mediating the problems of 'religious violence' in the contemporary world. This, of course, immediately raises the question of whether the liberal values of the Euro-American Enlightenment are really capable of mediating the competing claims of cultural traditions and ideologies on a worldwide scale. Global social and economic inequalities, many of them a direct historical consequence of the colonial reconfiguration of the globe by those same 'enlightened' Europeans (and now Americans), remain in place despite the rhetoric of the Western liberal tradition. Whilst secular forms of liberalism have significantly reconfigured the terrain and opened up opportunities for resisting oppressive regimes with the emphasis that they have placed upon individual human rights and freedoms, they have also sat rather too easily with colonialist agendas. It has proved far too easy to justify colonial aggression and domination under the cover of the spread of 'Western liberal values' and the claim to be exporting civilization and 'democracy' abroad.

Failure to acknowledge the murky history of complicity between Western secular liberalism and the colonial project however, continues for as long as one specifically associates violence and aggression with 'religious' worldviews rather than as a recurring feature of human ideologies in general (including Western secular liberalism). It may be argued that this has been an unfortunate feature of Western liberal regimes in the past, but that the colonial era has now ended. Unfortunately, the claim that Western liberalism, once purged of unpleasant associations is really a force for good, utilizes the same strategy of exclusion that is deployed by defenders of 'the religious'. On this view liberalism in itself is good, and should not be confused with 'liberalism gone bad'. Sadly, even attempts to consign the complicity of Western liberal discourse with colonial oppression to the dustbin of history does not sit easily with the current geopolitical situation in which we find ourselves at the beginning of the twenty-first century with the rise of a neo-liberal world order that seems intent on spreading its empire far and wide and the ongoing expression of military might by powerful Western nations in places such as Afghanistan and Iraq.

In the contemporary post-Cold War context there remains a widely perceived sense of social, economic and cultural injustice in relations between the West and the rest, a situation exacerbated in recent decades by the rise of neo-liberal forms of capitalism and a growing, rather than decreasing, gulf between rich and poor which is only likely to foster further examples of insurgency and violence.[3] Scholars discussing what they see as a resurgence of 'religious violence' have generally ignored such factors, partly because of an insufficiently critical engagement with dominant constructions of 'globalization' and its apparently wholesome and redemptive trajectory. They are also oriented away from such analysis by the assumption that, as a secular and economic phenomenon, contemporary global capitalism is beyond the remit of their discussion. The attack on the World Trade Center in New York in September 2001 was horrific and unjustifiable but it is surely of great significance that the choice of target was an iconic emblem of American/global capitalism. Clearly those who carried out and planned the attack saw this as an opportunity to speak to the sense of social and economic injustice felt by many in 'the Muslim world' in its relations with major Western powers such as the USA. European (and more recendy American-driven) colonialism has also been a significant historical factor in the contemporary rise of 'religious violence' across the globe. This colonial history, however, remains largely invisible to scholars such as Juergensmeyer, for whom an Enlightenment-centred (and largely American) view of history appears to be the only way forward,[4] since from such a perspective it becomes difficult to interrogate the darker side of Western secular modernity, which as Anibal Quijano (2000) has pointed out, is experienced as 'coloniality' by those outside the privileged domain of 'the First World'.

Crucial to the generic nature of the debate about 'religion' and violence is an uninterrogated and ahistorical construction of 'the religious'. A significant body of scholarly literature has now emerged since the 1990s that has called into question the universalization of this category from a variety of different perspectives.[5] As I have argued in *Orientalism and Religion* (1999), modern uses of the term 'religion' carry with them the cultural and historical traces of European Christian theological debates and, at least since the Enlightenment, the framing of 'the religious' as a universal category of world history to be firmly distinguished from more recent 'secular' ideologies. Indeed, it is important to appreciate that modern notions of 'the religions' were forged in an ideological context framed by the rise of secular humanism. The concept of religion carries forward cultural tropes that reflect its largely Christian history, but as a feature of Western constructions of modernity it remains essentially the product of a secularist conception of history.

Broadly speaking, 'secularization' – that complex series of processes related to the disestablishment of the Christian Church as a hegemonic force in European and American polities, is not, as is so often claimed, the death of religion but rather the very moment of its birth. It is during the Enlightenment that 'religion' became objectified as systems of belief and practices. This was only possible because the 'sacred canopy' of medieval Christendom had fragmented after the Protestant Reformation leading to a 'denaturalization' of a 'divinely ordained' social and political ordering of reality. The theocentric conception of the cosmos that had dominated in the medieval period also became increasingly displaced by an anthropocentric or humanistic vision of history. The invention of 'the religions' in the modern sense of the term is a consequence of these social processes and reflects

the conceptual distillation of a clearly distinguishable human phenomenon – the 'historical religions' – from a wider cultural dynamic. As John Bossy (1982) has suggested, the abstraction of something called 'the religions' (as well as their deployment as a category of universal history) would have been impossible before the social and political transformations of late sixteenth-/early seventeenth-century Europe. I will not dwell any further upon the debate about the historical construction of the religious as a category at this juncture because of limitations of space but instead refer the interested reader to the relevant literature on this topic. What emerges, however, from a serious consideration of these works is that one cannot apply the term 'religion' and its close correlates in a cross-cultural context without at least engaging reflexively with the history of the term and the multiple traces and resonances it carries in the contemporary Euro-American *imaginaire*. Failure to engage with the historical and culturally specific tropes of the 'religion and violence' debate constitutes not only a failure to recognize the Euro-American mindset which frames such discussions, but is also an abdication of the responsibility to apply the same degree of historicization (that is so often applied to the non-Western traditions under examination), to one's own primary categories of analysis.

How exactly then does the use of a 'catch all' category such as 'religion' aid us in understanding ideologically rooted acts of violence in the contemporary and ancient worlds? Clearly as a site of comparative analysis the *modern* concept of religion (which is nothing if it is not a *comparative* category – that is a conceptual site through which an imaginative act of comparison takes place) allows one to bring together apparently disparate cultural and historical phenomena into a single overarching framework. This has enabled those deploying this term to generate cross-cultural and transhistorical statements about otherwise widely divergent traditions and epochs. However, we should remain highly suspicious of the easy deployment of this category, particularly as it has been used in the 'religion and violence' debate, precisely *because* of its largely taken-for-granted status. The belief that there are 'religions' out there in the world is so culturally embedded in the modern imagination that it has become a 'common-sense' category or *doxa* to use Pierre Bourdieu's term. However, as Clifford Geertz (1983: ch. 4) has suggested, 'common-sense' is that which in its very taken-for-granted status requires the most rigorous interrogation.

The modern concept of 'religion' carries with it certain key assumptions about the world that are, as we shall see, ultimately grounded in a hegemonic Euro-American myth about the origins of 'modernity' and the birth of the secular nation-state. These assumptions are not ideologically neutral but rather are encoded according to a specifically European history of the world. This history reflects an extended series of conversations or 'cultural wars' in medieval and early modern Europe between various competing forms of Christianity as well as between Christianity and other traditions (usually classified at the time as Jewish, 'Mohammedan' and 'pagan' or 'heathen'). More recendy these controversies also incorporated the clash between 'secular' or humanistic movements and the fragmentation of the socio-political world of Christendom. These conflicts played a significant role, for instance, in the colonization of 'the New World' and have become enshrined in the foundational myths of origin for those nations that emerged from the revolutionary movements of the Enlightenment such as the United States of America and France. This has left a strong cultural imprint and suspicion of 'the religious' based upon a particular reading of European history that focuses upon 'the Wars of Religion' as the primary cause of social strife and factionalism. Important though these events have been, in planetary and macro-historical terms, such clashes have been decidedly local disputes, which only appear universal in import because of the way in which they have spilt over onto a global canvas

as a consequence of the European colonial reconfiguration of much of the planet in the last few centuries. Failure to appreciate the provincial origins (and traces) of the concept of religion in general and of the 'religion and violence' debate in particular, constitutes one of the most significant *theoretical* obstacles to any attempt to examine not only human propensities towards violence (regardless of whether this is framed as 'religious' or not) but also a broader, non-Eurocentric account of human history that takes account of its diversity and complexity.

How then is the term 'religion' operationalized within the 'religion and violence' debate? Juergensmeyer (2000: 10) characterizes the religious in terms of three features:

1. a transcendentally grounded moralism
2. the ritual intensity with which such acts are committed
3. images of struggle and transformation and concepts of a cosmic war between good and evil.

These features are fairly standard generalizations about 'the religious' in academic and journalistic literature on the subject. Another contributor to this debate, Bruce Lincoln, suggests a similar model of the religious involving the following four characteristics:

(a) a discourse that claims its concerns transcend the realm of the human, temporal, and contingent, while claiming for itself a similarly transcendent status; (b) a set of practices (ethical, ritual, and sometimes also aesthetic) informed and structured by that discourse; (c) a community organized around the discourse and its attendant practices, whose members regulate their identity with reference to them; and (d) an institutional system that regulates discourse, practices, and community, reproducing and modifying them over time, while still asserting their eternal validity and transcendent value. Whenever any of these components plays a role of some seriousness within a given conflict, one ought to acknowledge that the conflict has a religious dimension.

(1998: 65)

In his book *Holy Terrors* (2003), Lincoln reiterates the centrality of his 'four domains' of the religious. Moreover, he suggests, 'discourse becomes religious not simply by virtue of its content, but also from its claims to authority and truth' (2003: 5) and again 'religion begins with a discourse that constructs itself as divine and unfailing, through which deeds – any deeds – can be defined as moral' (2003: 16). The contrast between the human and the divine here make it absolutely clear that for Lincoln religion implies not only the postulation of these two categories but their explicit polarization. This characterization of the religious of course fits theistic (especially monotheistic) traditions, but it is not clear that it maps at all well in a broader global context.

The various features of 'the religious' highlighted by Juergensmeyer and Lincoln are in fact both too broad *and* too narrow to pick out the global phenomena that they wish to discuss. On the one hand such characterizations can equally apply to a whole host of apparently secular ideologies or movements in the modern world. The struggle for democracy, human rights, free-market capitalism, 'the American way of life', Communism, etc., all involve reference to some kind of transcendental signifier or value. These transcendental referents (whether identified as capital, nation, liberty, etc.) correspond to a set of ideals or values that remain as intangible, out of reach and 'incontestable' as the claims made on behalf of so-called 'religious' values and ideals. They are also similarly anchored in institutions, rituals and social practices that normalize and legitimate their own existence and authority. Contemporary proponents of capitalist neoliberalism – the current orthodoxy of the 'new world order' of globalization – continually imbue their own ideological claims with a magical air of incontestability. A regular mantra of the dominant

'transnational capitalist class' (Sklair 2001) – from corporate leaders to major politicians – is that 'there is no alternative' to globalization (which they read as both an ineluctable force of history and as an economically driven process). This feature of capitalist ideology in the post-Cold War context is increasingly being recognized by some scholars as exhibiting precisely the kinds of features that scholars such as Lincoln and Juergensmeyer associate exclusively with 'the religious' (see Cox 1999; Hopkins 2001; Loy 2002; Carrette and King 2005; Deutschmann 2001). This aspect of capitalism was perhaps first noticed by Walter Benjamin in 1921 in his originally unpublished fragment 'Capitalism as Religion':

> A Religion may be discerned in capitalism – that is to say, capitalism serves essentially to allay the same anxieties, torments, and disturbances to which the so-called religions offered answers. . . . Capitalism is a religion of pure cult, without dogma.

(Benjamin 1996 [1921]: 288–89)

Juergensmeyer's second point – that religious acts are carried out with 'ritual intensity', hardly picks out any clearly identifiable phenomena that we can describe as religious. This characterization builds upon older medieval uses of 'religious' which imply a firm adherence to one's faith (as in taking up a monastic life of 'holy orders'). Even today, when someone undertakes an activity with great resolve and determination we say that they are doing it 'religiously'. This 'cultic sense' of the term (as Jonathan Z. Smith (1998b: 270) describes it), connotes the idea of wilful and unwavering commitment and predisposes one to associate 'religiosity' with ritual repetition, zealotry and extremism. However, since one can 'be religious' in this general sense about anything (from mowing the lawn to looking both ways before crossing the road), in analytic terms it provides no help at all in pinpointing a specifically 'religious' dimension to certain practices. In fact, if anything, everyday usage suggests quite the opposite – namely that one can 'be religious' about a whole host of activities that have nothing to do with 'the religions'.

In a similar fashion, organized acts of violence and aggression carried out by apparently secular nation-states can be just as intense in their ritualized commitments as 'religious' ones, and can similarly polarize the world in terms of a primordial battle between good and evil (in George W. Bush's infamous words about the 'global war on terrorism' – 'you are either with us or you are against us'). This is a point well noted by Lincoln in his analysis of the common Manichean structure to Bush and Bin Laden's rhetoric, but in the case of the American President this is linked by the author to George W. Bush's well-publicized Christian allegiance. This is an easy target and allows Lincoln to continue pressing his case about the dangers of 'the religious' for civic society. It also ignores the continuity of Bush's stance with a broader civic tradition of American exceptionalism, which frequently utilizes a Manichean rhetoric and identifies the USA as the primary driving force of modernity and freedom in the world.[6] Moreover, as William Cavanaugh (2004: 31) notes in his own critique of the discourse of 'religion and violence', the question 'What you would be prepared to kill for?' offers stark empirical evidence that nationalism is a far greater incitement to violence in contemporary America than Christianity.

> What percentage would be willing to kill for their country? Whether we attempt to answer these questions by survey or by observing American Christians' behavior in wartime, it seems clear that, at least among American Christians, the nation-state – Hobbes' 'mortal god' – is subject to far more absolutist fervor than 'religion'. For most American Christians, even public evangelization is considered to be in poor taste, and yet many consider it their duty to go to war against whomever the president deems necessary.
>
> (Cavanaugh 2004: 31)

On the other hand, Lincoln and Juergensmeyer's accounts of the religious are also too narrow. Virtually all of the examples that Juergensmeyer uses to illustrate his points in *Terror in the Mind of God*, come from the Jewish, Christian and Islamic traditions and his explanation of the rationale behind such acts invariably appeals to a Manichean cosmic war between good and evil, notions of a struggle between martyrs and demons and a 'satanization' of the other (e.g. 2000: 163). These tropes are not so easily mapped onto the traditional categories of many of the South Asian traditions that Juergensmeyer refers to by implication. Indeed, the main example deployed in the book as an example of contemporary Buddhist violence is the Japanese sect Aum Shinrikyo. This movement is a small-scale and highly eclectic mixture of Buddhist, Śaivite, millenarianist Christian and New Age elements and is hardly representative of the Buddhist tradition as a whole. In making this point I should stress that I am not seeking to romanticize Asian traditions as somehow exempt from the charge that they have been involved in the legitimation and incitement of appalling acts of violence throughout their histories. My point is rather that it does not aid us in understanding these processes to label such traditions as 'religious'. There are a number of obvious examples, for instance, of Buddhist involvement in, and justification of, violent acts, both historical and contemporary (a point noted by Juergensmeyer in his 1993 work; see also Victoria 1997, 2003, Bartholomeusz 2002, and articles by Gethin and Schalk in this volume), but these are rarely dwelt upon by Juergensmeyer in his sweeping account of global terrorism in *Terror in the Mind of God*. Similarly, if one is seeking images of a battle for righteousness against evildoers one need look no further than Indian epics such as the *Mahābhārata* (again something that Juergensmeyer at least discusses in his 1993 work, but is missing from *Terror in the Mind of God* which focuses exclusively upon the contemporary context). However, despite these clear instances of the complicity between

South Asian traditions and the justification and incitement of violence, we should reject very clearly any suggestion that such examples express something 'essential' or even 'essentially religious' about 'Hindu culture' or South Asia, for this is to ignore the heterogeneity of South Asian history. As Lincoln notes:

> Every macro-entity that gets called a 'religion' – Buddhism, Islam or Christianity, for example – has countless internal varieties and subdivisions, each of which undergoes its own historic process of development and change.
>
> (2003: 8)

Indeed, we discover from Lincoln that 'no practices are inherently religious and any may acquire a religious character when connected to a religious discourse that constitutes them as such' (Lincoln 2003: 6). Despite this, Lincoln fails to dwell upon the possibility that the converse might also be the case – namely that the ideologies that are conventionally labelled 'secular' (including his own Enlightenment-grounded tradition of critique) might also exhibit qualities (such as intolerance and intellectual hubris) that the author otherwise associates with 'the religious'.[7] Again, developing one line of argument from Lincoln's analysis, one might ask if it is more appropriate in some instances to classify 'macro-traditions' such as Buddhism, Islam and Christianity – traditions that in their very heterogeneity also include a great deal that is pluralistic and 'tolerant' – as inclusive of trends within them that are more 'secular' than 'religious' (in the sense defined by Lincoln's 'four domains'). The reason that these theoretical possibilities are not explored in any depth by the author, I would suggest, is that to do so would disrupt the stability of the 'secular/religious' dichotomy in a way that would challenge Lincoln's own project, which is, as I read him, to offer a critique of 'the religions' (as he conceives them) based upon their transcendental claims to absolute authority.

The irony of the accounts offered by Juergensmeyer and Lincoln, which in this regard

are generally representative of the 'secularist' strand in the 'religion and violence' debate, is that they replicate a Manichean-style dualism of their own in the form of an uncritical and universalized dichotomy between the secular and the religious, and the explicit privileging of ideologies associated with the former not only as adequate and appropriate explanatory accounts of 'the real world' on the one hand but also as a framework for mediating cultural and ideological differences on a global scale on the other. Thus, a key element in both authors' characterization of the religious is their assumption that religions provide secondary interpretations of reality that build upon the more solid (more 'real'?) foundations of social, economic and political events. Juergensmeyer argues, for instance that:

> religious ideas have given a profundity and ideological clarity to what in many cases have been real experiences of economic destitution, social oppression, political corruption and a desperate need for the hope of rising above the limitations of modern life.
>
> (Juergensmeyer 2000: 242)

Here 'real experiences' are equated with the social, economic and political dimensions of life to which religious ideologies 'add' clarity and meaning. Again, elsewhere in the study (Juergensmeyer 2000: 161), the author sets up a dichotomy between 'religious images' on the one hand and 'real life situations' on the other. Similarly, for Lincoln, religious discourse is a worldly (*read*: social/economic/political) discourse that attempts to portray itself as 'otherworldly'. For Lincoln, dissent from this position, as in the claim that such analysis is reductionist, 'is meant to silence critique' (Thesis 12 of Lincoln's *Theses on Method*). This rebuttal of all criticism from traditions that do not accept Western social scientific categories as given, means effectively that Lincoln himself silences any criticism that does not conform to the canons of his own historicism. This reflects a tension in Lincoln's method between an acceptance of human fallibility on the one hand and a rejection of traditions of criticism that are not grounded in the secularist traditions of the European Enlightenment. This is encapsulated in Lincoln's 'Theses on Method' (1996) in the tension between his tenth and twelfth theses:

> Understanding the system of ideology that operates in one's own society is made difficult by two factors: (i) one's own consciousness is itself a product of that system, and (ii) the system's very success renders its operations invisible, since one is so consistently immersed in and bombarded by its products that one comes to mistake them (and the apparatus through which they are produced and disseminated) for nothing other than 'nature'.
>
> (Thesis 10)

> Although critical inquiry has become commonplace in other disciplines, it still offends many students of religion, who denounce it as 'reductionism'. This charge is meant to silence critique. The failure to treat religion 'as religion' – that is, the refusal to ratify its claim of transcendent nature and sacrosanct status – may be regarded as heresy and sacrilege by those who construct themselves as religious, but it is the starting point for those who construct themselves as historians.
>
> (Thesis 12)

Thesis ten is a classic statement of reflexivity. It is a recognition that there is no position from nowhere. Everyone, including the author, has blind spots deriving from their own cultural background and conditioning and this prevents us from seeing the world in an unmediated fashion. Thesis twelve, however, classifies any challenge to Lincoln's own Enlightenment-rooted historicism from a rival intellectual tradition as 'the silencing of critique'. In this context Lincoln seems to fall foul here of what I would call 'Bourdieu's paradox' (so named because it has become one of the classic criticisms of Bourdieu's conception of 'reflexive sociology'). In Bourdieu's case this involved the claim on the one hand that we are all caught in culturally specific webs of signification from which we cannot extricate ourselves (hence the need for reflexivity) and the contrary claim that only the sociologist is in a position to see these conditions and work to overturn them. This paradox is not insurmountable as long as one is prepared to accept that the sociologist's reflexivity is a relative rather than an absolute achievement, and on these terms I think it could be argued that Bourdieu manages to side-step such a critique. In the case of Lincoln, however, it is not clear that he would be prepared to give up his exclusivist claim that materialist/social scientific accounts of reality (deriving from the humanistic philosophies of the European Enlightenment) are both *more true* than any other (the 'religious' ones) and also *more capable of embodying tolerance* of differences. As a result virtually every other intellectual tradition in human history is framed as inferior to the humanistic traditions of Western modernity. The underlying burden of this ideology (and let us be clear that it *is* an ideology like all of the others) is to ensure that 'secular' and 'religious' discourses are not analysed on a level playing field – as different, and sometimes competing, ideologies or explanations of the world.

The consequence of this stance is that for Lincoln well-established social-scientific categories, deriving as they do from the specific cultural experiences of Northern Europeans and their American brethren, are naturalized and privileged over the categories of all other worldviews (which have already been interpellated and subalternized according to Lincoln's normative construction of 'the religious'). From this perspective all philosophies that do not express themselves according to the styles, traditions and categories of critical reflection that have been established by the secularist ideologies and disciplines of the European Enlightenment are assigned a subordinate or derivative status as explanations of the world. Indeed, for both Lincoln and Juergensmeyer 'religious' worldviews appear to operate at a secondary level as culturally specific and 'imagined' responses to the real world (of social, economic and political processes).

Thus, a similar sociologism[8] can be found in Juergensmeyer's work when he discusses attitudes towards death within the various 'religions':

> the Jewish notion of raising the dead, the Christian and Muslim notions of heaven and hell, the Roman Catholic notion of purgatory, the Buddhist idea of levels of consciousness (and in the Mahayana tradition, heavenly mansions), and the Hindu theory of karmic cycles of reincarnations – all of these offer ways of avoiding what humans know to be a fact: eventually they will die.
>
> (Juergensmeyer 2000: 158)

In this sweeping list, no account is taken, for instance, of the importance within Buddhist traditions of a contemplative recognition of the inevitability of one's own death or the traditional Hindu, Buddhist and Jain understanding of transmigration as a cycle of re-deaths (*punarmṛtyu*). Rather the impression is given that all religious traditions turn us away from a realization of the reality of death. This of course is precisely the rhetorical function of universalized terms like 'religion' in these contexts – to classify *by implication*. Again, one might ask why modern capitalism is not included in this list, since it also encourages individuals as consumers to avoid an awareness of the inevitability of their own death by promoting the pursuit of a bewildering array of consumable and 'life-enhancing' products that will provide you with *nirvana* in the here and now. Juergensmeyer, following the theories of Ernest Becker, implies that religion denies mortality and that he, as the secular social scientist, is in a privileged position to understand the reality of death.

Frequently one finds scholars relying on what one might call a 'base-line' definition of religion as belief in some kind of transcendental reality or being, beyond the material world. This for instance, is clearly the stance taken by Lincoln (1996: 225) who argues that religion is 'that discourse whose defining characteristic is to desire to speak of things eternal and transcendent with an authority equally transcendent and eternal'. The spirit of Edward B. Tylor (1832–1917) of course, hovers behind such definitions of the religious, with the emphasis placed upon *belief* in some form of supernatural, spiritual or transcendental being or reality beyond the material world of the here and now. Such definitions of the religious, however, privilege 'secular' or materialist presuppositions in at least two regards. First, such a construction of the religious is clearly 'theory-loaded' (Braun 2000: 11), since it presupposes that it already knows what constitutes the (materialist and historical) 'here and now' from which the transcendental pretensions of the religions are subsequendy projected. What precisely counts as the world 'out there' and what counts as 'the supernatural', however, constitutes one of the fundamental points at issue when different ideological constructions of reality confront each other. To define the 'religious' as that which claims to be more than it is (that is as postulating a *transcendent* authority that goes beyond its actual and *immanent* historical instantiation) is to presume the falsity of the systems being discussed and privileges materialist accounts of reality as 'given'.[9] One is entitled to ask what makes so-called 'secularist' accounts of the world any less involved in webs of cultural signification than so-called 'religious' accounts of reality. How exactly do secular social scientists learn to wrench themselves out of their own cultural conditioning – by fifting themselves up by their own bootstraps perhaps? The point of my rhetorical question, of course, is to highlight the *transcendentalist* nature of the historicist claim to have left behind (i.e. transcended) religious claims of transcendence. In such an account the cards have already been stacked in favour of a secularist worldview before the game even begins.

The supreme irony of such a position is that it is a materialist, 'secular', and historicist account of the world that is thereby granted transcendental authority – in that only from this perspective is one authorized to speak about cultural and historical contexts beyond their own milieu. The secularist claim to be able to speak about and mediate all rival claims is thus exposed as one of the very same 'bootstrap theories' or ontotheologies that are being criticized for being 'religious' – that is for claiming a totalizing, universal and transcendental authority. This is not easily seen because it is occluded by the use of the discourse of 'religion' to insulate certain ideologies (humanist/materialist ones) from critical engagement alongside the rest. The (post-Feuerbachian) projectionist claims being made here by scholars such as Lincoln also predispose us to read 'the religious' as being somehow character-ized by absolutist appeals to an unquestionable authority. This is clearly not the case for many of the traditions and movements that one might label 'religions' in conventional and popular parlance and is more a feature of self-contained, totalitarian or closed ideological systems in general. Such systems may or may not postulate ontologically transcendent or 'supernatural' realms in the narrow sense implied by Lincoln's Tylorian definition of the religious, but an exclusive focus upon these (through the deployment of the category of 'reli-gion') only succeeds in insulating secularist ideolo-gies from the same level of critical analysis. Such a move (and its investment in a particular construc-tion of 'the religious' as a foil to the secular) remains crucial to Lincoln's approach. However, once one challenges the necessary association of 'religion' with absolutist claims to authority, two possibilities emerge. First, that so-called 'secular' ideologies can also lead to totalitarian impulses (something that would be easy to demonstrate from even a cursory glance at twentieth-century history) and second, that tolerance of diversity (and the rejection of absolutism) can be expressed from 'within' a 'reli-gious' tradition (see Asad 1993: Chapter 6 for an interesting discussion of this). This is crucial in demonstrating that modern materialist ideologies do not monopolize the values of tolerance, humility and fallibilism.

Furthermore, it is not even clear that the Tylorian claim that religion is associated with the postulation of an *ontologically* transcendent reality or supernatural being will suffice as a definition of the subject-matter. First, it does not fit all of the cases that are popularly taken to be examples of 'religions' (consider for instance the Buddhist posi-tion that, as Nāgārjuna puts it, 'there is not the slightest difference between *saṃsāra* (this world) and *nirvāna* – the goal of liberation', *Madhyamaka-Kārikā* 25.19–20). Second, such constructions of the religious ignore the possibility that in a contempo-rary 'secularized' and scientific context, the tran-scendental has not disappeared, it has simply gone underground. After the apparent 'death of God', the so-called 'religious impulse' (which as we have seen for Lincoln seems to imply some kind of absolutist claim to authority) is likely to manifest itself in new and surprising ways, reflecting not only con-siderable local variations but also the cultural dominance of natural scientific explanations of the cosmos. This indeed may be a consequence of secularization when viewed as a process of differentiation (Casanova 1994). Conceding much of the traditional cosmological and metaphysical ground of explanation to the sciences, post-Enlightenment forms of 'religiosity' may well express themselves in a way that conforms to a scientific explanation of the world. This may make them appear decidedly 'secular' when in fact this is merely a reflection of the reconfiguration of the 'field of the religious' (if one insists on using this concept) or the 'metaphysical' in a post-scientific context. We should not be surprised therefore to find behavioural patterns, practices, beliefs and authority claims that might traditionally have been associated with 'the religions' (in Lincoln's terms), manifesting themselves in new apparentiy 'secular' and 'post-metaphysical' forms (as David Martin (1998: 40–41) has suggested). The modern authority of the natural sciences in a 'secularized' context has fundamentally transformed the ideological field in which fundamental worldviews, 'religions' (or 'cosmographic formations' as Dubuisson (2003) calls them) are now able to express themselves. One way of putting this would be to say that in certain contexts modern (and 'postmodern') secular ideologies, may themselves turn out to be 'religions' (again in Lincoln's sense of the term).

Given that humans inspired by avowedly secularist ideologies have been responsible for some of the most terrible atrocities and genocides of the twentieth century, one is entitled to ask why violence and intolerance continue to be associated with 'the religions' in particular and at the expense of seeing a similar complicity between violence and so-called 'secular' ideologies. Indeed, such are the problems involved in attempting to maintain a hard and fast distinction between the religious and the secular that I would suggest that we avoid this particular dichotomy as much as possible, since it simply does not aid us in understanding societies that do not easily conform to the social pattern that emerged in European and American societies influenced by Christian and Enlightenment-derived philosophies of the world. Moreover, in the context of the 'religion and violence' debate, the dichotomy between the secular and the religious has served to bolster the interests of two key constituencies involved in the controversy – the secularists and the religionists. Both have something to gain by maintaining and reproducing the language of 'religion' in this debate.

Much of the contemporary impetus behind the very idea that there is a sharp difference in type between 'the secular' and 'the religious' itself originates from within the interpretive framework of one particular ideological perspective – which, for want of a better word, we might label 'secularism'. The historical relationship between constructions of 'the religious' and 'the secular' is far too complex to allow such a simple dichotomy to be deployed usefully, for as Talal Asad has noted:

> The secular . . . is neither continuous with the religious that supposedly preceded it (that is, it is not the latest phase of a sacred origin) nor a simple break from it (that is, it is not the opposite, an essence that excludes the sacred). I take the secular to be a concept that brings together certain behaviours, knowledges, and sensibilities in modern life. To appreciate this it is not enough to show that what appears to be necessary is really contingent – that in certain respects, 'the secular' obviously overlaps with 'the religious'. It is a matter of showing how contingencies relate to changes in the grammar of concepts – that is, how the changes in concepts articulate changes in practices . . . the secular is neither singular in origin nor stable in its historical identity, although it works through a series of particular oppositions.
>
> (Asad 2003: 25)

Rather than focusing upon 'the problem of religion and violence', as if this reflected some sort of intrinsic or essential 'religious' quality that some ideologies possess and others do not, I suggest that one would do better to examine apparently 'secular' and 'religious' worldviews side by side. Only then are we likely to gain a greater comparative understanding of the human propensity to carry out ideologically rooted and 'communal' acts of violence upon each other.

One of the features that Juergensmeyer identifies as a characteristic of 'religious' acts of violence is the 'symbolic' and dramatic aspect of acts of 'religious terrorism', reflecting the sense in which they refer to something 'beyond their immediate target' (2000: 123). This is used by the author to suggest that such acts relate to 'other-worldly' or 'transcendental' goals. However, there is perhaps a more prosaic reason why groups like Aum Shinrikyo and al-Qaida engage in highly symbolic acts of violence and this has little to do with the purported 'religious' or transcendental nature of their goals. If the act is not an example of state-sponsored 'terrorism' (such as an attack on a sovereign nation or a bombing campaign on a civilian population) but is rather carried out by a relatively small-scale and disempowered group then there is little choice but to carry out highly *symbolic* acts of violence, since this is the most effective way of drawing widespread public attention to one's cause when faced with a radical asymmetry of power.[10] Juergensmeyer's point presumably is that the message or goal motivating the act transcends the particular focus of that attack, but this hardly makes such goals 'otherworldly' in nature (2000: 217). The implication drawn by Juergensmeyer about the 'otherworldly' nature of such acts is misleading. That this dichotomy between 'religious' and secular' uses of 'performance violence' cannot be maintained becomes clear, even on Juergensmeyer's own terms, when he acknowledges that the 'religions' (as he understands them) do not have a monopoly on such symbolic acts (2000: 216–17). As one frequently finds in literature on this theme, Juergensmeyer assumes before his analysis begins that religion and war have a long history of association (2000: 156) but this is hardly surprising given that the phenomena that he pinpoints as 'religious' relate to civilizations and traditions with long-standing and complex histories. The twentieth century has been scarred by the violent oppression of people by a number of totalitarian regimes (most notably Nazism and Stalinism) and two bloody world wars. The twenty-first century has begun in a similarly belligerent fashion. Are these wars religious in nature? To frame this point in a different way, is the problem of violence in human history one that is best laid at the door of *homo religiosus* or of *homo sapiens* in general? How does referring to this history in terms of 'religions' do anything other than insulate certain societies, institutions and ideologies (usually labelled 'secular') from a comparable degree of critical interrogation? As Talal Asad has suggested:

> The point that matters in the end, surely, is not the justification that is used (whether it be supernatural or worldly) but the behaviour that is justified. On this point, it must be said that the ruthlessness of secular practice yields nothing to the ferocity of (the) religious.
>
> (1993: 236)

Although Lincoln engages with Asad's critique of the universalization of 'religion' in *Holy Terrors*, he sidesteps the more radical implications of Asad's thesis by suggesting that all language (not just the construction of 'religion') 'is the historical product of discursive processes' (Lincoln 2003: 2) and by focusing on that aspect of Asad's critique that targets an extreme and privatized conception of 'the religious'. This, however, domesticates Asad's general critique of the concept of religion and also ignores the colonial issues that arise when one applies an Occidental concept that has played a crucial role in the identity-construction of the modern 'West' as a fundamental category in the study of non-Western civilizations and traditions. What we have in the deployment of the category of religion in these contexts is the projection of an 'insider category' from Lincoln's own cultural tradition, a notion that has a long and complicated history in the West and its application in cultural domains where, until comparatively recentiy, it had no role to play. This would not necessarily be a problem if it were not for the ideological baggage that the term 'religion' carries with it and the work it continues to do in fostering a sense of the distinctiveness and 'modernity' of Western civilization. This is all the more surprising since Lincoln asserts at this point in his discussion that 'the end result of our definitional labors ought to problematize and not normalize, the model that prompted their inception' (2003: 2).

Even more strikingly, at no point in *Terror in the Mind of God* does Juergensmeyer interrogate the concept of religion that is, of course, so crucial to his analysis. This is unfortunate because one of the issues here is precisely that of determining how – that is through what processes – certain institutions, traditions and civilizations have become characterized as 'religions' during the period of European colonial rule. To give an example, consider David Scott's work on Sri Lanka. Scott highlights the role of the British Colebrooke-Cameron reforms of the 1830s in re-structuring indigenous subjectivities and institutions, thereby creating an Anglicized middle-class elite in Śri Lanka and providing the conditions for the emergence of new reform-oriented trends such as Dharmapāla's modernist-oriented Buddhism. As Scott notes:

> Concepts like 'religion', 'state', and 'identity', are treated ahistorically insofar as they are made to refer to a set of timeless social-ideological formations as defining (or as *defining in the same way*) for say third-century inhabitants of the island as for contemporary Sinhalas. This conceptual/ideological projection of the present into the past (as a hermeneutic of the present) is possible only because these categories – religion, state, and so on – are the authoritative and normalized categories through which Universal History has been written, and through which the local histories of the colonial and postcolonial worlds have been constituted as so many variations on a common theme about the progressive making of modernity.
>
> (2000: 288–9)

The transformation of Sinhalese 'Buddhism' into a 'religion' in the modern sense of a total belief-system with clear (and largely closed) boundaries that differentiate it from other religions is a complex process. It was bound up with the activities of Christian missionaries (and their insistence that the native 'confess their faith' as a means of contestation and conversion to Christianity). It was also propelled by the colonial re-structuring of civil society and education, the impact of European scholarship on 'Buddhism' upon indigenous subjectivity and the activities of groups like the Theosophists in defending what they saw as 'the Buddhist faith' of the Śri Lankan people (Lopez 1998). Through all of these factors (which cannot be explored here in any detail), not only was something called 'Buddhism' born (translating indigenous notions of *baud-dhāgama* and *bauddha-śāsana* in the process) but this 'Buddhism' entered the colonial regime of knowledge as a 'religion' and a 'faith' amenable to a universalized discourse of 'world reli-

gions' that, as Tomoko Masuzawa (2005) has shown, only really emerged in the early twentieth century. This context severely complicates our attempts to analyse 'communal' and 'religious' violence in Śri Lanka. Similarly, as Arvind Mandair and Balbinder Bhogal have argued in this volume, European colonialism has played a crucial role in the construction of modern Sikh subjectivities. The issue here is not just that Western power has influenced the historical formation of the modern 'religions' of South Asia, but that the very characterization of the history of South Asian civilization (and by extension the rest of the 'non-Western' world) in terms of Euro-American notions of 'the religious' is itself problematic (King 1999; Peterson and Walhof 2002), see also Peter Gottschalk's contribution to this volume, pp. 195–210).

Moreover, once one begins to question the usefulness of the concept of 'religion' as a way of understanding ideologically rooted acts of violence, one might also ask why conflicts in South and West Asia are so often conceptualized differently from those involving Western nations. Why, as Peter Gottschalk has asked, is the American–Vietnamese war *never* represented as a clash between Christian and Buddhist civilizations, or the Quebeçois secessionist movement in Canada not seen as a Catholic struggle against a Protestant dominated nation, whilst South Asian cultures are so often represented in terms of a clash between *Hindu* and *Muslim*, or *Sinhalese Buddhist* versus *Hindu Tamil* (Gottschalk 2000: 12)? Is it that 'the religious' is supposed to have a greater significance in South Asian constructions of identity and community or is it rather that the supposedly 'religious dimension' of such phenomena has been over-determined in such accounts? To what extent is the *description* of violence in South Asia as 'religious' itself a product of the discursive transformations of these traditions in the modern world under the influence of European colonialism and orientalism?

To begin to answer some of these questions one must first understand the historical roots of the contemporary association of 'religion' with violence in Euro-American cultural contexts.

'THE WARS OF RELIGION' AS PART OF THE MYTH OF ORIGIN OF THE NATION-STATE

The modern association of violence with 'the religions' became firmly embedded in European (and early American) societies during the Enlightenment, where the underlying principles of modern liberalism were born. According to the secular myth surrounding the birth of the nation-state that most of us have inherited, the conflictual and violent nature of medieval Christian factions (often called 'The Wars of Religion') could only be resolved by some form of disestablishment of the Church and the State. By challenging the traditional social moral and philosophical authority of the Church, European and North American intellectuals sought to establish a framework for society and politics that avoided the religious conflicts of previous centuries. The most popular solution was to relegate the religious to the private sphere of life – to clearly demarcate it from the public realms of politics, science, philosophy and economics. This modern myth about the triumphant birth of the secular nation-state is deeply embedded in the consciousness of most Europeans and Americans. Thus, Bruce Lincoln (1998: 66) can declare, without any need for justification that 'The modern nation-state was created, in large measure, as a check against the violence and destruction unleashed in religious conflicts of this sort'.[11]

The taken-for-grantedness of this account of history obscures a considerably more complex understanding of the historical conditions under which the modern nation-state emerged. While it may have been the Protestant Reformation that broke the sacred canopy of medieval Christendom, thereby opening up the space for the emergence of proto-nation states (Philpott 2001), social turbulence during this period (called retrospectively the 'Wars of Religion') can just as easily be read as the product of the conflict between old and new regimes of regional power in early modern Europe. It is these regional power struggles, brought about by the fracturing of medieval Christendom that culminated in the sanctification of the sovereignty of the nation-state at the Peace of Westphalia in 1648. This coincides with the emergence of the modern concept of 'religion' as an identifiable phenomenon (Bossy 1982; Harrison 1990). The reification of this concept, I would argue, has played a crucial role in normalizing the sacred mythology of the modern 'secular' nation-state.

According to William Cavanaugh (1995), the modern (one might even say 'secular') concept of religion and its association with discord and violence emerged in this period primarily as a means of displacing the violence associated with the end of feudalism and the birth of the modern nation-state. Cavanaugh argues, therefore, that the story conveyed in conventional historical accounts 'puts the matter backwards':

> The 'Wars of Religion' were not the events, which necessitated the birth of the modern State; they were in fact themselves the birthpangs of the State. These wars were not simply a matter of conflict between 'Protestantism' and 'Catholicism', but were fought largely for the aggrandizement of the emerging State over the decaying remnants of the medieval ecclesial order. I do not wish merely to contend that political and economic factors played a central role in these wars, nor to make a facile reduction of religion to more mundane concerns. I will rather argue that to call these conflicts 'Wars of Religion' is an anachronism, for what was at issue in these wars was the very creation of religion as a set of privately held beliefs without direct political relevance. The creation of religion was necessitated by the new State's need to secure absolute sovereignty over its subjects.
>
> (Cavanaugh 1995: 398)

The Westphalian solution initiated the birth of the modern nation-state, with its clear territorial boundaries and the notion of national sovereignty. In Northern Europe the divergent Christian allegiances of citizens in the newly emerging nation-states were to be protected by 're-locating' them to the private sphere. The Enlightenment secularist model of course has also led to a prevailing belief in Northern Europe and its former colonies (including the USA) that politics and religion should not be mixed. I would like to highlight two consequences that have followed from this particular configuration of the religious. First, the Western liberal assumption that religion and politics represent two separate realms of human life has become a major stumbling block in Western attempts to understand the phenomenon of 'religious nationalism'. Once modern Western renderings of the secular/religious divide are accepted as the normative paradigm, examples of politically active and religious authority become easily predisposed to the image of the manipulative and opportunistic ideologue.[12] Groups that accept the secular authority of such a figure thus become represented as subject to some form of mass religious indoctrination. One does not have to look far to find contemporary examples of such a paradigm at work in Western representations of religions in the various mass media. In contrast to such reductionist approaches, we should, as Peter van der Veer argues, 'take religious discourse and practice as constitutive of changing social identities, rather than treating them as ideological smoke screens that hide the real clash of material interests and social classes' (van der Veer 1994: ix).

A second consequence of the secularist assumption that politics and religion are separate realms has been to perform a cognitive separation of acts of violence carried out by nation-states from acts of violence carried out in the name of 'religion'. The continued exclusion of acts of war and other state-sponsored acts of violence carried out by modern 'secular' nation-states in debates about violence and 'terrorism' is a reflection of the conceptual

difficulties that secular nationalist discourse has in looking beyond its own Euro-American cultural horizons. The modern secular nation-state was formed in a Euro-American context, where its very legitimacy was bound up with a denial of the violence associated with its own birth. In this context, forged in the crucible of Enlightenment anti-clericalism, the category of 'the religious' has becomes the primary foil, the point of conceptual displacement and the epistemological 'dumping ground' for secular modernity's own dark side. Similarly, the assumption that violence only occurs when 'religion becomes evil' (Kimball 2002), trades upon a conception of 'the religious' which divests the traditions so classified of their complexity and historical complicity in acts of oppression and violence.

What 'secularist' critics and 'religionist' defenders share in common in this debate is an investment in the production of a discourse of religion that can be easily deployed to justify not only their own institutional location as 'experts of religion' (of varying points of view) but also to bolster their particular ideological stake in the debate (whether 'pro-religious', 'anti-religious' or somewhere in-between). Lincoln, for instance, raises the stakes to the highest level when considering those who might dare to question that the secularism that emerged from the European Enlightenment is the only model possible for successfully mediating pluralities in society: 'When one rejects the Enlightenment's values en masse and dispenses with its model of culture, one risks not just a return of the repressed, but novel Wars of Religion' (Lincoln 2003: 61). In the face of such a challenge and in anticipation of such a charge, it is important that I reiterate that there is no sense at all in which the arguments in this paper constitute a rejection of 'Enlightenment values en masse' (many of which I share and hold dear), as if such a thing were even possible for a Western scholar like myself working in the academy and committed to its traditions of critical and disciplined inquiry. However, I think it behoves us as human beings to acknowledge that open-ended, tolerant and critical thinking of the kind valued by Lincoln and others (including myself), is *not* solely the provenance of the secular humanists of the European Enlightenment, and that a critique of absolutist claims to truth can be grounded in intellectual traditions other than the secularist hermeneutic of suspicion initiated by Marx, Freud and Nietzsche. To suggest otherwise is to do no less than assert the inherent superiority of modern Western civilization.

In this regard, in the post-9/11 world we have seen an unholy alliance between left- and right-wing thinkers. Moreover, the Enlightenment tradition of critical thought (which is itself heterogeneous) can also be applied reflexively to itself. Such moves undermine the exclusivist claim that 'only we have the answers'. It is important therefore to acknowledge the historicity of Enlightenment values and concepts (including ironically the historicity of historicism itself!)[13] as well as maintain a sense of humility when tempted to make totalizing and universalist claims about reality. Failure to perform this act of reflexivity in such contexts is to assert the privileged status of a secularized Enlightenment account of human history, or, in other words, to turn it, as Adorno and Horkheimer cautioned, into a new kind of totalizing myth. None of this precludes an acknowledgement of the tangible social achievements and practical advantages of adopting Western-style secularism, or what we might call (to use Lincoln's terms) a pluralistic and 'minimalist' approach to macro-traditions, but it is not clear to me why non-Western (and so-called 'religious') traditions cannot also serve as the basis for developing pluralistic, tolerant and inclusivist models of society. One might still wish to appeal to the ways in which models of society emerging from the European Enlightenment have promoted a democratically oriented culture of tolerance and some measure of protection for minorities, but again, one does not need to be a secular humanist to uphold such values. It is also important that we confront the darker side of Euro-American constructions of 'modernity/coloniality' (Quijano 2000) rather than shield these aspects from critical engagement by the normalization of an unexamined and secularist construction of 'religion'. Indeed, I would argue that those who wish to defend the merits of an Enlightenment-inspired 'secularist' position are better served on a global scale if they take seriously the fact that this is only one of a number of potential responses to the issue of mediating conflicts and divergent truth-claims in contemporary societies. One size may not fit all. The alternative in our new age of 'Empire', unfortunately, would seem to be to endorse a kind of *Pax Americana* by default.

The tragic irony of a secularist position that privileges its own standpoint as *uniquely* positioned to promote tolerance, pluralism and protection of the minorities in modern society is that, in the attempt to exclude 'religious' discourse from the public arena, the pluralistic ground upon which the secularist position stands becomes itself undermined. As William Connolly (1999) has argued, the sheer intensity of secularist resistance to traditional (so-called 'religious') dogmatisms can often lead to an unacknowledged immodesty of its own and a failure to acknowledge the possibility of what he calls 'asecular, non-theistic perspectives' that promote reverence, ethics and a civil society. The blind-spot of secularism occurs when it sets itself up as the authoritative centre of public discourse. Without decentering itself, secularism serves only to breed further opposition – thereby reproducing the very threat that it is designed to exclude. Thus, the secularist prophecy about 'religion' becomes self-fulfilling! The reproduction of authoritarian and fundamentalist discourses is of course the real danger of the binary logic at work in attempts to clearly differentiate 'religious' from 'secular' worldviews. If the options are so drastically reduced that 'you are either with us or against us' (to echo the words of George W. Bush) then the pluralistic vision that supposedly grounds a secularist vision of public life becomes undermined by an inability to take seriously the possibility of Christian, Buddhist, Hindu and Islamic correlates to the 'Western secular model'. As framed by Connolly, the key question (and response) becomes:

> Is it, again, possible to refashion secularism as a model of thinking, discourse and public life without lapsing into the 'opposite' view that 'Christianity' or 'the Judaeo-Christian tradition' must set the authoritative matrix of public life? Not if you think that the world comes predesigned with these two options alone.... *If* the objective [however] is to project your own perspective into the fray while also decentering the political imagination of the ensconced contestants so that each becomes an honored participant in a pluralistic culture rather than the authoritative embodiment of it, *then* the positive possibilities expand.
>
> (1999: 6)

To conclude, we would do well to try playing a different language game from the one that has characterized the 'religion and violence' debate. Such approaches must take seriously the fact that not all civilizations and traditions are mere correlates or carbon copies of European Christianity and that they are therefore not condemned (by virtue of belonging to the same genus – 'religion') to replicate the historical patterns of violence that have been laid at the feet of 'religion' in modern Euro-American accounts of history. To change the debate however, requires an acknowledgement that we have all been framed. The major 'macro-traditions' of the world, by virtue of their status as 'great civilizations', extend over a vast cultural, geographical and temporal range. Since they represent such a vast heterogeneity of movements, trends, beliefs and practices they can be characterized both as vehicles of violence on the one hand and of social harmony and moral selflessness on the other. It all depends upon the evidence that one chooses to highlight and the lenses one is wearing.

Despite, the enormous conceptual problems involved in attempting to maintain a strict dichotomy between 'religious' and 'secular' world-views, the discourse of 'religion and violence' has proved so popular precisely because it serves such powerful and deeply embedded interests. The overall effect of accounts of world history that rely on an uncritical deployment of the category of 'religion' is to reinforce an Orientalist vision of the world that posits 'the West' (however that putative entity may be denned) as a beacon of hope, tolerance, democracy and rationality in a world otherwise beset by the dark forces of superstition, intolerance and irrationality. The self-congratulatory rhetoric of such Euro-American tropes of course is exactly mirrored in the anti-Western rhetoric that has emerged, for instance, in Islamist portrayals of a decadent and irreligious West. This is a dangerous rhetorical game that we should be seeking to displace rather than escalate. Both stances, however, are challenged once one challenges the universalization of the discourse of religion upon which both positions rest. As Daniel Dubuisson (2003) has argued, such a critique goes to the heart of Western imperial power, since the universalized category of religion has played such a crucial role in the West's assertion of its own distinctiveness and superiority. Finally, failure to challenge this Euro/Americo-centric account of the world not only sets a paradigmatic limit on our attempts to understand ideologically rooted acts of violence in their complexity and diversity, but also does a violence to the cultures and civilizations of the non-Western world that it so actively frames.

NOTES

1. This statement requires some qualification. The USA, France and Japan have a constitutional separation of church and state. China remains, ostensibly at least, a socialist country, ruled by the Communist Party of China. Although there are a small number of state-regulated churches and temples, meaning that in practice there is no formal separation of church and state, the secularist ideology of the ruling party

severely restricts the role of 'religion' in public affairs. The United Kingdom has as its formal head of state a monarch, who is also the head of the Anglican Church. There is therefore an established church. However, the United Kingdom is in many respects a highly 'secularized' and multicultural society, with the Anglican Church having little more than a formalistic and ritual function with regard to the affairs of state. In their differently inflected fashions all exhibit a broadly 'secularist' approach to governance.

2. See Anderson and Cavanaugh (2000).

3. For an insightful but biting critique of contemporary neoliberalism and the violence it reaps upon societies, see Giroux (2004) and Brennan (2003).

4. Indeed, Juergensmeyer's work assumes a Western, (mostly North American audience) and at times appears to express the view that Enlightenment tolerance can only go so far, before lapsing back into some kind of *Pax Americana*:

> If we were to compile a list of those characteristics of religious nationalism *we* cannot live with and those *we* can live with, the first list must be quite lengthy. It would surely include the potential for demagoguery and dictatorship, the tendency to satanize the United States and to loathe western civilization, and the potential to become violent and intolerant. Most Americans, including myself, would agree that these are indeed *unacceptable* characteristics in any nation that wants to be part of the global community, and *we should not have to live with them*.
>
> (1993: 195, my italics for emphasis).

5. These works include: Cantwell Smith (1962); J.Z. Smith (1978, 1982, 1998); Despland (1979, 1999); Asad (1993); McCutcheon (1997); Dubuisson (2003); Fitzgerald (2000); Bossy (1982); Biller (1985); Harrison (1990); Despland and Vallee (eds) (1992); Cavanaugh (1995); Feil (1986, 1997); David Chidester (1996); Balagangadhara (1994); King (1999); Peterson and Walhof (eds) (2002); Masuzawa (2005).

6. Thus Eric Foner, a professor of history at Columbia University argues that Americans sometimes have the tendency to see enemies not just as opponents but as evil. Linked to that is the belief that America is the world's last best hope of liberty, so that those who oppose America become the enemies of freedom. Foner suggests that this is

> an unfortunate recurring pattern in American history. . . . We have a tendency in times of war

to adopt a Manichean vision of the world. It's a state of mind that makes us demonize the enemy and leads to a failure to see dissent as anything but treason.

> (Cited in Robert F. Worth, 'Truth, Right and the American Way; A Nation Defines Itself By Its Evil Enemies', *New York Times*, 22 February 2002)

7. That this position can be derived from Lincoln's work can be seen for instance in *Myth, Cosmos and Society* (1986: 164) where he suggests that 'an ideology – any ideology – is not just an ideal against which social reality is measured or an end toward the fulfillment of which groups and individuals aspire' but in fact also acts to persuade members of that group 'of the rightness of their lot in life, whatever that may be, and of the total social order'. Here all ideologies – whether secular or religious – it appears can function as religions in the later sense of Lincoln's 'four domains'.

8. I am using the term 'sociologism' here in the sense in which it is used by Talal Asad, that is as referring to the widespread scholarly belief that 'religious ideologies are said to get their real meaning from the political or economic structure, and the self-confirming methodology according to which this reductive semantic principle is evident to the (authoritative) anthropologist and not to the people being written about' (Asad 1993: 198–199). It should be clear from my arguments throughout this paper and elsewhere (e.g. King 1999) that the 'religionist' position (by which I mean the counter-claim, most often associated with the phenomenology or 'history of religions' school, that there is an autonomous realm known as religious') is equally problematic. Both positions are products of a Euro-Occidentalist view of the world.

9. One might argue that the underlying cosmologies of these worldviews do not necessarily presuppose a 'spiritual' or transcendental realm in the classical (that is 'pre-Enlightenment') sense of some kind of ethereal existence beyond the material 'here and now'. However, to construct 'religion' in this fashion is to use the term to denote *all* metaphysical systems that pre-existed or have yet to be reformulated by the rise of modern science and the various humanistic philosophies of the European Enlightenment. In other words, 'religion' comes to denote any worldview that does not conform to the metaphysics of contemporary materialism in positing the sole reality

of the material world. This approach privileges secularist philosophies (with 'religion' being defined in a circular manner as that which is not secularist). Such constructions not only privilege metaphysics and discourse as the ground for defining what is and is not religious but also obscure the fact that materialism is itself only one of a number of metaphysical interpretations of reality.

10. It is clear for instance from Jason Burke's work on al-Qaida (2003, 2004) that bin Laden's movement has always been a small-scale network of radical Islamists. Initially involved in fighting a guerrilla war to 'liberate' Afghanistan from Soviet rule (with the aid of the USA), they have been concerned more recendy with challenging what they saw as decadent rulers in the Middle East (such as the Saudi Arabian monarchy and the secular dictatorship of Saddam Hussein in Iraq) and also seeking to overthrow Western imperialist interests in that same region. The loose cadre of radicals surrounding Osama bin Laden (apparently first portrayed as a tight and coherent organization known as 'al-Qaida' by the FBI in 1998) have become emboldened and swelled in their ranks by the high-profile attacks of 9/11 and subsequent US military reactions to those attacks, such as the invasions of Afghanistan and Iraq. 'Al-Qaida' as a global label has now become an 'Islamic franchise' for a variety of radical Islamist groups responding to what they see as American-led imperial intervention in the Middle East on the part of certain Western nations.

11. See Lincoln, *Holy Terrors* (2003: 56–57) for a classic example of the Enlightenment seciuarist account of the 'Wars of religion' that underlies Lincoln's approach.

12. One consequence of this distinction has been to foster a suspicion amongst Westerners that any linkage of the two realms reflects a 'merely rhetorical' use of religious discourse to mask some underlying political, ideological or 'worldly' intention. This is a form of simplistic reductionism. This approach presupposes that religion and politics can, and indeed should, be distinguished and that the political dimension is the more fundamental of the two. The political meta-discourse is thus given ultimate explanatory status, explaining what has been hidden from view by religious discourse.

13. In making this point I am reminded of Bourdieu's declaration (2004) that to fulfill its own condition a reflexive sociology must also be a 'sociology of sociology' – that is, reflect upon its own socially constructed nature.

Works Cited

Aaland, Mikkel. 1978. *Sweat: The Illustrated History and Description of the Finnish Sauna, Russian Bania, Islamic Hammam, Japanese Mushi-Buro, Mexican Temescal, and American Indian and Eskimo Sweat Lodge*. Santa Barbara: Capra Press.

Abalos, David T. 1986. *Latinos in the United States: The Sacred and the Political*. South Bend: University of Notre Dame Press.

Abu-Lughod, Lila. 1998. "The Marriage of Feminism and Islamism in Egypt: Selective Repudiation as a Dynamic of Postcolonial Cultural Politics." In *Remaking Women: Feminism and Modernity in the Middle East*, ed. L. Abu-Lughod, 243–269. Princeton: Princeton University Press.

Adkins, Lisa. 1995. *Gendered Work: Sexuality, Family and the Labour Market*. Buckingham: Open University Press.

Adorno, Theodor and Max Horkheimer. 1972. *Dialectic of Enlightenment*. New York: Herder and Herder.

Aguirre Beltrán, Gonzalo. 1946. *La población negra de México, 1519–1810*. Mexico City: Ediciones Fuente Cultural.

Ahlstrom, Sydney. 1972. *A Religious History of the American People*. New Haven: Yale University Press.

Ahmed, Leila. 1992. *Women and Gender in Islam: Historical Roots of a Modern Debate*. New Haven: Yale University Press.

Aho, James. 1990. *The Politics of Righteousness: Idaho Christian Patriotism*. Seattle: University of Washington Press.

Akaev, A. 2003. *Kyrgyzskaya gosudarstvennost' i narodnyi epos "Manas"* Bishkek: Uchkun.

Akbarzadeh, S. 1999. "National Identity and Political Legitimacy in Turkmenistan." *Nationalities Papers* 27(2): 271–290.

Akbarzadeh, S. 2001. "Political Islam in Kyrgyzstan and Turkmenistan." *Central Asian Survey* 20(4): 451–465.

Alba, R., A.J. Raboteau and J. Dewind. 2009. *Immigration and Religion in America: Comparative and Historical Perspective*. New York: New York University Press

Albanese, Catherine L. 1992. *America: Religions and Religion*. 2nd edn. Belmont: Wadsworth.

Alexander, Jeffrey C. 1982. *Positivism, Presuppositions, and Current Controversies*. Vol. 1 of *Theoretical Logic in Sociology*. Berkeley and Los Angeles: University of California Press.

al-Ghazali, Muhammed. 1990. *al-Jānib al-'āṭifi min al-Islām*. Alexandria: Dār al-da'wa.

al-Ghazali, Zaynab. 1994a. *'ila ibnati: al-juz' al-awwal*. Cairo: Dār al-tauzī' wal-nashr al-islāmi.

al-Ghazali, Zaynab. 1995. *Ayyām min ḥayāti*. Cairo: Dār al-shurūq.

al-Ghazali, Zaynab. 1996. *'ila ibnati: al-juz' al-thāni*. Cairo: Dār al-tauzī' wal-nashr al-islāmiyya.

al-Hashimi, Ibn, ed. 1990. *Humūm al-mar'a al-muslima wal-dā'iya Zaynab al-Ghazali*. Cairo: Dār al-i'tiṣām.

Allport, Gordon. 1962. *The Individual and His Religion*. New York: Macmillan.

al-Qaradawi, Yusuf. 1989. *al-Ṣabr fi al-Qur'ān*. Cairo: Maktabat wahba.

Althaus-Reid, M. 2003. *The Queer God*. London: Routledge.

Altman, Dennis. *Global Sex*. Chicago: University of Chicago Press, 2001.

Ammerman, Nancy Tatom. 1987. *Bible Believers: Fundamentalists in the Modern World*. New Brunswick: Rutgers University Press.

Anagnost, Ann. 1987. "Politics and Magic in Contemporary China." *Modern China* 13(1): 40–61.

Anderson, Benedict. 1983. *Imagined Communities: Reflections on the Origin and Spread of Nationalism*. London: Verso.

Anderson, Benedict. 1991. *Imagined Communities: Reflections on the Origin and Spread of Nationalism*. Rev. and extended edn. London: Verso.

Anderson, Sarah and John Cavanaugh. 2000. *Top 200: The Rise of Global Corporate Power*. New York: The Institute for Policy Studies.

An-Na'im, A. 1990. *Towards an Islamic Reformation*. New York: Syracuse University Press.

Anzaldúa, Gloria. 1987. *Borderlands/La Frontera: The New Mestiza*. San Francisco: Aunt Lute Books.

Anzaldúa, Gloria. 1993, "Border Arte: Nepantla, El Lugar de la Frontera." In *La Frontera/La Border; Art About the Mexico/U.S. Border Experience*. San Diego: Centro Cultural de La Raza and Museum of Contemporary Art San Diego.

Anzaldúa, Gloria. 2002. "Now let us shift . . . the path of conocimiento . . . inner work, public acts." In *This Bridge We Call Home*, ed. Gloria Anzaldúa and AnaLouise Keating. New York: Routledge.

Apitzsch, Ursula. 2003. "Migrationsbiographien als Orte Transnationaler Räume." In *Migration, Biographie und Geschlechterverhältnisse*, ed. Ursula Apitzsch and Mechthild Jansen, 65–80. Münster: Verlag Westfälisches Dampfboot.

Arieli, Yehoshua. 1964. *Individualism and Nationalism in American Ideology*. Cambridge, MA: Harvard University Press.

Arnason, J.P. 1993. *The Future that Failed: Origins and Destinies of the Soviet Model*. New York: Routledge.

Arnold, J. Phillip. 1994. "The Davidian Dilemma – To Obey God or Man?" In *From the Ashes: Making Sense of Waco*, ed. James R. Lewis, 25. Lanham: Rowman & Littlefield.

Asad, Talal. 1986. "Medieval Heresy: An Anthropological View." *Social History* 11(3).

Asad, Talal. 1988. "Towards a Genealogy of the Concept of Ritual." In *Vernacular Christianity*, edited by W. James and D. H. Johnson, 73–87. New York: Lilian Barber Press.

Asad, Talal. 1993. *Genealogies of Religion: Discipline and Reasons of Power in Christianity and Islam*. Baltimore: Johns Hopkins University Press.

Asad, Talal. 1999. "Religion, Nation-State, Secularlism." In *Nation and Religion: Perspectives on Europe and Asia*, ed. P. van der Veer and H. Lehmann. Princeton: Princeton University Press.

Asad, Talal. 2003. *Formations of the Secular. Christianity, Islam, Modernity*. Stanford: Stanford University Press.

Ashiwa, Yoshiko. 2000. "Chūgoku ni okeru Bukkyō Bukkō no dōtai: kokka shakai to toranzunashonarizumu" (The Dynamics of the Buddhism Revival Movement in Southern China: State, Society and Transnationalism). In *Kokka-shakai tono kyōsei kankei: gendai Chūgoku no shakai kōzō no henyō* (The Symbiotic Relationship of State and Society: Transformation of Social Structure in Contemporary China), ed. Hishida Masaharu *et al.* Tokyo: Tōkyō daigauku shuppankai.

Ashiwa, Yoshiko. 2002. "Shūkyō no seiritsu to minzoku: Suriranka to Chūgoku no kindai Bukkyōkaikakusha nimiru kosumoporitanizumu no yukue" (The Formation of Religion and Nation: On Cosmopolitanism seen in Modern Reformists of Buddhism in Sri Lanka and China). In *Minzoku no undō to shidōshatachi* (Ethno-movements and their Leaders), ed. Etsuko Kuroda. Tokyo: Yamakawa shuppansha.

Ashiwa, Yoshiko. 2006. "State, Association, and Religion in Southeast China: The Politics of a Reviving Buddhist Temple." *Journal of Asian Studies* 65(2): 337–359.

Ashiwa, Yoshiko and David L. Wank. 2005. "The Globalization of Chinese Buddhism: Clergy and Devotee Networks in the Twentieth Century." *International Journal of Asian Studies* 2(2): 217–237.

Ashley, Kathleen and Pamela Sheingorn. 1992. "An Unsentimental View of Ritual in the Middle Ages or, Sainte Foy Was No Snow White." *Journal of Ritual Studies* 6(1): 63–85.

Ashmawi, Said Muhammed. 1994a. "Fatwa al-ḥijāb ghair shr'iyya." *Rūz al-Yūsuf*, August 8, 28.

Ashmawi, Said Muhammed. 1994b. "al-Ḥijāb laisa farīḍa." *Rūz al-Yūsuf*, June 13, 22.

Auerbach, E. 1953. *Mimesis*. Princeton: Princeton University Press.

Austin, J.L. 1994. *How to do Things with Words*. Ed. J.O. Urmson and M. Sbisà. Cambridge, MA: Harvard University Press.

Autiero, A. 1987. "The Interpretation of Pain: The Point of View of Catholic Theology." In *Pain: A Medical and Anthropological Challenge*, edited by J. Brihaye *et al.* New York: Springer-Verlag.

Baddeley, Gavin. 1999. *Lucifer Rising: Sin, Devil Worship, and Rock'n'Roll*. London: Plexus.

Badinter, Elisabeth. 1989. "Interview with L. Joffin." *Le Nouvel Observateur*, November 9–15, 7–11.

Baird, Robert D. 1971. *Category Formation and the History of Religions*. The Hague: Mouton.

Baker, D. 1972. "*Vir Dei*: A Secular Sanctity in The Early Tenth Century." In *Popular Belief and Practice*, edited by C.J. Cuming and D. Baker. Cambridge: Cambridge University Press.

Balagangadhara, S.N. 1994. "*The Heathen in His Blindness*": *Asia, the West and the Dynamic of Religion*. Leiden: E.J. Brill.

Baldick, Robert. 1955. *The Life of J.-K. Huysmans*. Oxford: Clarendon Press.

Bancroft, L. 2002. *Why does he do that? Inside the Minds of Angry and Controlling Men*. New York: G.P. Putnam's Sons.

Banerjee, Neela. 2004. "United Methodists Move to Defrock Lesbian." *New York Times*, December 3, A18.

Banerjee, Neela. 2005. "Black churches Struggle over their Role in Politics." *New York Times*, March 6, 23.

Bankston, C. and Zhou, M. 1995. "Religious Participation, Ethnic Identification, and Adaptation of Vietnamese Adolescents in an Immigrant Community." *The Sociological Quarterly* 36(3): 523–534.

Bankston, C. and Zhou, M. 1996 "The Ethnic Church, Ethnic Identification, and the Social Adjustment of Vietnamese Adolescents." *Review of Religious Research* 38: 18–37.

Bankston, Carl L.I. and Min Zhou. 2000. "De Facto Congregationalism and Socioeconomic Mobility in Laotian and Vietnamese Immigrant Communities: A Study of Religious Institutions and Economic Change." *Review of Religious Research* 41: 453–470.

Baranowsky, Anna B., Marta Young, Sue Johnson-Douglas, Lyn Williams-Keeler and Michael Mccarrey. 1998. "PTSD Transmission: A Review of Secondary Traumatization in Holocaust Survivor Families." *Canadian Psychology* 39: 247–256.

Bardella, C. 2001. "Queer Spirituality." *Social Compass* 48(1): 117–138.

Barfoot, Charles H. and Gerald T. Sheppard. 1980. "Prophetic vs. Priestly Religion: The Changing Role of Women Clergy in Classical Pentecostal Churches." *Review of Religious Research* 22(September): 2–10.

Bargy, Henry. 1902. *La Religion dans la Société aux États-Unis*. Paris: A. Colin.

Barkun, Michael. 1994. *Religion and the Racist Right: The Origins of the Christian Identity Movement*. Chapel Hill: University of North Carolina Press.

Bar-On, Dan. 1995. *Fear and Hope: Three Generations of the Holocaust*. Cambridge, MA: Harvard University Press.

Barot, Rohit. 2002. "Religion, Migration and Wealth Creation in the Swaminarayan Movement." In *The Transnational Family: New European Frontiers and Global Networks, Cross-cultural Perspectives on Women*, ed. Deborah Fahy Bryceson and Ulla Vuorela, 197–216. Oxford: Berg.

Barron, Bruce. 1992. *Heaven on Earth? The Social and Political Agendas of Dominion Theology*. Minneapolis: Zondervan.

Barry, Ellen. 2004. "March Clouded by Stand on Gay Unions." *Los Angeles Times*, December 11, A18.

Bartholomeusz, Tessa J. 2002. *In Defense of Dharma: Just-War Ideology in Buddhist Sri Lanka*. London and New York: RoutledgeCurzon.

Barton, Blanche. 1990. *The Secret Life of a Satanist: The Authorized Biography of Anton LaVey*. Los Angeles: Feral House.

Barton, J. J. 1975. *Peasants and Strangers*. Cambridge, MA: Harvard University Press.

Bauman, Zygmunt. 2000. *Liquid Modernity*. Cambridge: Polity.

Bauman, Zygmunt. 1992. "Soil, Blood and Identity." *Sociological Review* 40: 675–701.

Bauman, Zygmunt. 2001a. *Community: Seeking Safety in an Insecure World*. Malden: Blackwell.

Bauman, Zygmunt. 2001b. *The Individualized Society*. Cambridge: Polity Press.

Baumgarten, Gerald. 1995. *Paranoia as Patriotism: Far-Right Influences on the Militia Movement*. New York: Anti-Defamation League.

Beaman, L. 1999. *Shared Beliefs, Different Lives*. St Louis: Chalice Press.

Beaman, L. 2002. "Justice on the Margins: Wiccans and Freedom of Religion in North America." In *Knowledge Power Gender: Philosophy and the Future of the "Condition Féminine"*, ed. B. Christensen, A. Baum, S. Blattler, A. Kusser, I.M. Marti and B. Weisshaupt, 415–424. Zurich: Chronos Verlag.

Beaman-Hall, L. and N. Nason-Clark. 1997. "Partners or Protagonists? The Transition House Movement and Conservative Churches." *Affilia: Journal of Women and Social Work* 12(2): 176–196.

Beaman-Hall, L. and N. Nason-Clark. 1997b. "Translating Spiritual Commitment into Service: The Response of Evangelical Women to Wife Abuse." *Canadian Women Studies* 17(1): 58–61.

Becker, S. 1968. *Russia's Protectorates in Central Asia: Bukhara and Khiva, 1865–1924*. Cambridge, MA: Harvard University Press.

Beckford, J. 2003. *Social Theory and Religion*. Cambridge: Cambridge University Press.

Bell, Catherine. 1997. *Ritual: Perspectives and Dimensions*. New York: Oxford University Press.

Bell, Daniel. 1976. *The Cultural Contradictions of Capitalism*. New York: Basic.

Bellah, Robert N., Richard Madsen, William M. Sullivan, Ann Swidler and Steven M. Tipton. 1985. *Habits of the Heart: Individualism and Commitment in American Life*. Berkeley and Los Angeles: University of California Press.

Bellér-Hann, I. 2008. *Community Matters in Xinjiang 1880–1949: Towards a Historical Anthropology of the Uyghur*. Leiden: Brill.

Bendixsen, Synnøve. 2005. "Being Young, Muslim and Female. Creating Space of Belonging in Berlin." In *Hotel Berlin*, 88–99. Berliner Blätter, Berlin: Gesellschaft für Ethnographie (GfE) und dem Institut für Europäische Ethnologie der Humboldt-Universität zu Berlin.

Bendixsen, Synnøve. 2007. "Making Sense of the City: Religious Spaces of Young Muslim Females in Berlin." *Informationen zur Modernen Stadtgeschicht* 2: 51–65.

Bendixsen, Synnøve. 2009. " 'It's like doing SMS to Allah': Young Female Muslims Crafting a Religious Self in Berlin." Unpublished Ph.D. dissertation, Humboldt University (Berlin) and École des Hautes Études en Sciences Sociales (Paris).

Benjamin, Walter. 1921. "Capitalism as Religion." In *Selected Writings: Volume 1913–1926*, ed. Marcus Bullock and Michael W. Jennings, 288–289. London: Belnap Press, 1996.

Bennett, Hermann. 2003. *Africans in Colonial Mexico: Absolutism, Christianity and Afro-Creole Consciousness, 1570–1640*. Bloomington: Indiana University Press.

Bennigsen, A. and F. Bryan. 2002. "Islam in Central Asia." In *The Religious Traditions of Asia*, ed. J. Kitagawa. London: Routledge Curzon.

Bennigsen, A. and S.E. Wimbush. 1985. *Mystics and Commissars: Sufism in the Soviet Union*. London: Hurst.

Bennigsen, A. and S.E. Wimbush. 1986. *Muslims of the Soviet Empire: A Guide*. London: Hurst.

Berger, J. 1972. *Selected Essays and Articles*. Harmondsworth: Penguin.

Berger, Peter L. 1963. "Charisma and Ideological Innovation: The Social Location of Israelite Prophecy." *American Sociological Review* 28(6): 940–950.

Berger, Peter L. 1967. *The Sacred Canopy: Elements of a Sociological Theory of Religion*. Garden City: Doubleday.

Berger, Peter L. 1969. *The Social Reality of Religion*. London: Faber & Faber.

Berger, Peter L. 1970. *A Rumor of Angels: Modern Society and the Rediscovery of the Supernatural*. Garden City: Anchor.

Berger, Peter L. 1974b. *Religion in a Revolutionary Society*. Washington, DC: American Enterprise Institute for Public Policy Research.

Berger, Peter L. 1979b. *Facing up to Modernity*. Harmondsworth: Penguin Books.

Berger, Peter L. 1997b. "Against the Current." *Prospect*, March, 32–36.

Berger, Peter L. 1998. "Protestantism and the Quest of Certainty." *The Christian Century*, August 26 – September 2, 782–796.

Berger, Peter L. 1999. "The Desecularization of the World: A Global Overview." In *The Desecularization of the World: Resurgent Religion and World Politics*, ed. Peter Berger, 1–19. Cambridge: Wm.B. Eerdmans Publishing Co.

Berger, Peter L. 2001. "Reflections on the Sociology of Religion Today." *Sociology of Religion* 62(4): 443–454.

Berger, Peter L. and Thomas Luckmann. 1966c. *The Social Construction of Reality*. London: Allen Lane.

Berger, Peter L., Brigitte Berger and Hansfried Kellner. 1973. *The Homeless Mind: Modernization and Consciousness*. New York: Random House.

Bergman, Martin S. and Milton E. Jucovy. 1982. *Generations of the Holocaust*. New York: Basic Books.

Bettenson, H., ed. 1956. *The Early Christian Fathers*. London: Oxford University Press.

Beyer, Peter F. 1998. "The Modern Emergence of Religions and a Global System for Religion." *International Sociology* 13(2): 151–172.

Bhabha, Homi. 1994. *The Location of Culture*. New York: Routledge.

Biller, Peter. 1985. "Words and the Medieval Notion of 'Religion'." *Journal of Ecclesiastical History* 36(3): 351–369.

Binder-Brynes, Karen, Tamar Duvdevani, James Schmeilder, Milton Wainberg and Rachel Yehuda. 1998. "Vulnerability to Posttraumatic Stress Disorder in Adult Off-spring of Holocaust Survivors." *The American Journal of Psychiatry* 155: 1163–1171.

Bird, Frederick. 1995. "Family Rituals and Religion: A Functional Analysis of Jewish and Christian Family Ritual Practices." In *Ritual and Ethnic Identity: A Comparative Study of the Social Meaning of Liturgical Ritual in Synagogues*, ed. J.N. Lightstone and F.B. Bird, 185–195. Ontario: Wilfrid Laurier University Press.

Birnbaum, Raoul. 2003. "Buddhist China at the Century's Turn." *China Quarterly* 174(June): 428–450.

Bloch, John. 1998. "Individualism and Community in Alternative Spiritual 'Magic'." *Journal for the Scientific Study of Religion* 37: 286–302.

Boehm, R., J. Golec, R. Kahn and D. Smyth. 1999. *Lifelines: Culture, Spirituality and Family Violence: Understanding the Cultural and Spiritual Needs of Women who have Experienced Abuse.* Edmonton: The University of Alberta Press.

Bohache, T. 2003. "Embodiment as Incarnation: An Incipient Queer Christology." *Theology & Sexuality* 10(1): 9–29.

Bolivar, Wilfredo, Aaron Dorfman, Cristina Fundroa and Gerard Pean. 2002. "Unleash the Power of Immigrants . . . Organize!" *Social Policy* 2: 30–36.

Booth Fowler, Robert, Allen D. Hertzke and Laura R. Olson. 2004. *Religion and Politics in America: Faith, Culture, and Strategic Choices.* Boulder: Westview Press.

Bordo, Susan. 1993. *Unbearable Weight: Feminism, Western Culture, and the Body.* Berkeley and Los Angeles: University of California Press.

Bossy, John. 1982. "Some Elementary Forms of Durkheim." *Past and Present* 95(May): 3–18.

Bouhdiba, A. 1998. *Sexuality in Islam.* London: Saqi Books.

Bourdeaux, M. 1995. "Introduction." In *The Politics of Religion in Russia and the New States of Eurasia*, ed. M. Bourdeaux. Armonk: Sharpe.

Bourdieu, Pierre. 1977. *Outline of a Theory of Practice.* Cambridge: Cambridge University Press.

Bourdieu, Pierre. 1984. *Distinction: A Social Critique of the Judgement of Taste.* Cambridge, MA: Harvard University Press.

Bourdieu, Pierre. 1990. *Logic of Practice.* Stanford: Stanford University Press.

Bourdieu, Pierre. 2004 [2001]. *Science de la science et la réflexivité*, Edition Raisons d'Agir; English trans. Richard Nice, *Science of Science and Reflexivity.* Chicago: Chicago University Press.

Bourke, R. 2003. "Quaker Beliefs: Diverse yet Distinctive." *Quaker Studies* 7(2): 227–239.

Bowler, J. 1991. *A Year to Live.* London: SPCK.

Bracke, Sarah. 2003. "Author(iz)ing Agency: Feminist Scholars Making Sense of Women's Involvement in Religious 'Fundamentalist' Movements." *European Journal of Women's Studies* 10(3): 335–346.

Brandt, Peter. 2004. Interview by Carin Robinson, December 30.

Brannen, Julia and Peter Moss. 1991. *Managing Mothers: Dual Earner Households after Maternity Leave.* London: Unwin Hyman.

Braun, Willi. 2000. "Religion." In *Guide to the Study of Religion*, ed. Willi Braun and Russell T. McCutcheon, 3–20. London and New York: Cassell.

Bray, Michael. 1994. *A Time to Kill: A Study Considering the Use of Force and Abortion.* Portland: Advocates for Life.

Bray, Michael. 1998–1999. "Running with Rudolph." *Capitol Area Christian News* 28.

Breault, Kevin D. 1989a. "New Evidence on Religious Pluralism, Urbanism, and Religious Participation." *American Sociological Review* 54 (December): 1048–1053.

Brennan, Teresa. 2003. *Globalization and its Terrors: Daily Life in the West.* London: Routledge.

Brierley, Peter. 1999. *Religious Trends 2000/01*, No. 2. London: Christian Research.

Brierley, Peter. 2000. *The Tide is Running Out.* London: Christian Research.

Brock, P. 1990. *The Quaker Peace Testimony 1660–1914.* York: Sessions Book Trust.

Brower, D. 1997. "Islam and Ethnicity: Russian Colonial Policy in Turkestan." In *Russia's Orient: Imperial Borderlands and Peoples, 1700–1917*, ed. D. Brower and E. Lazzerini. Bloomington: Indiana University Press.

Brower, D. 2003. *Turkestan and the Fate of the Russian Empire.* London: Routledge.

Brown, J. and C. Bohn, eds. 1989. *Christianity, Patriarchy and Abuse: A Feminist Critique.* Cleveland: The Pilgrim Press.

Brown, Michael F. 1997. *The Channeling Zone: American Spirituality in an Anxious Age.* Cambridge, MA: Harvard University Press.

Brown, P. 1967. *Augustine of Hippo.* London: Faber & Faber.

Brown, P. 1981. *The Cult of the Saints: Its Rise and Function in Latin Christianity.* London: SCM.

Bruce, S. 1982. "The Student Christian Movement: A Nineteenth Century New Religious Movement and its Vicissitudes." *International Journal of Sociology and Social Policy* 2: 67–82.

Bruce, S. 1987. "The Moral Majority: The Politics of Fundamentalism in Secular Society." In *Studies in Religious Fundamentalism*, ed. Lionel Caplan. Albany: State University of New York Press.

Bruce, S. 1999. *Choice and Religion: A Critique of Rational Choice Theory.* Oxford: Oxford University Press.

Bruce, S. 2001. "The Curious Case of the Unnecessary Recantation: Berger and Secularization." In *Peter Berger and the Study of Religion*, ed. L. Woodhead, P. Heelas and D. Martin. New York: Routledge.

Bruce, S. 2002. *God is Dead*. Oxford: Oxford University Press.

Bruchac, Joseph. 1993. *The Native American Sweat Lodge: History and Legends*. Freedom, CA: Crossing Press.

Budapest, Zsuzsanna. 1979. *The Holy Book of Women's Mysteries*. Los Angeles: Susan B. Anthony Coven #1.

Bunting, Madeleine. 1996. "Shopping for God." *Guardian*, December 16, 2–3.

Burbank, J. 2007. "The Rights of Difference: Law and Citizenship in the Russian Empire." In *Imperial Formations*, ed. A. Stoler, C. McGranahan and P. Pedue. Santa Fe: School for Advanced Research Press.

Burchill, Julie. 1998. "Pleasure Principle." *Age* (Melbourne), June 6.

Burke, Jason. 2003. *Al-Qaida, Casting a Shadow of Terror*. London: I.B. Tauris.

Burke, Jason. 2004. *Al-Qaida: The True Story of Radical Islam*. London: I.B. Tauris.

Burke, Peter. 1978. *Popular Culture in Early Modern Europe*. London: Temple Smith.

Burlein, Ann. 2005. "The Productive Power of Ambiguity: Rethinking Homosexuality through the Virtual and Developmental Systems Theory." *Hypatia* 20(1): 21–53.

Butler, Judith. 1990: *Gender Trouble: Feminism and the Subversion of Identity*. New York: Routledge.

Butler, Judith. 1993. *Bodies that Matter: On the Discursive Limits of "Sex."* New York: Routledge.

Butler, Judith. 1997a. *Excitable Speech: A Politics of the Performative*. New York: Routledge.

Butler, Judith. 1997b. "Further Reflections on Conversations of Our Time." *Diacritics* 27(1): 13–15.

Butler, Judith. 1997c. *The Psychic Life of Power: Theories in Subjection*. Stanford: Stanford University Press.

Butler, Judith and William Connolly. 2000. "Politics, Power and Ethics: A Discussion between Judith Butler and William Connolly." *Theory and Event* 24(2), http:// muse.jhu.edu/journals/theory_and_event/v004/4.2butler.html.

Butler, Judith, Ernesto Laclau and Slavoj Žižek. 2000. *Contingency, Hegemony, Universality: Contemporary Dialogues on the Left*. London: Verso Press.

Byrd, R. 1960. *Quaker Ways in Foreign Policy*. Toronto: University of Toronto Press.

Byrne, P. 1988. *The Campaign for Nuclear Disarmament*. London: Croom Helm.

Byrne, P. 1997. *Social Movements in Britain*. London: Routledge.

Cadge, W. and E.H. Ecklund. 2006. "Religious Service Attendance among Immigrants: Evidence from the New Immigrant Survey-Pilot." *American Behavioral Scientist* 49(11): 1574–1596.

Cadge, W. and E.H. Ecklund. 2007. "Immigration and Religion." *Annual Review of Sociology* 33: 359–379

Campbell, David E. and J. Quin Monson. 2002. "Dry Kindling: A Political Profile of American Mormons." Paper presented at the Conference on Religion and American Political Behavior, Southern Methodist University, October 4.

Cancian, Francesca M. 1987. *Love in America: Gender and Self-Development*. Cambridge: Cambridge University Press.

Cao, N.L. 2005. "The Church as a Surrogate Family for Working Class Immigrant Chinese Youth: An Ethnography of Segmented Assimilation." *Sociology of Religion* 66(2): 183–200.

Caplow, Theodore. 1985. "Contrasting Trends in European and American Religion." *Sociological Analysis* 46(Summer): 101–108.

Capps, Walter H. 1990. *The New Religious Right*. Columbia: University of South Carolina Press.

Carrasco, David. 1995. "Jaguar Christians in the Contact Zone." In *Enigmatic Powers: Syncretism with African and Indigenous Peoples' Religions among Latinos*, ed. Anthony M. Stevens-Arroyo and Andres I. Pérez y Mena. New York: Bildner Center for Western Hemisphere Studies.

Carrère d'Encausse, H. 1994. "The Stirring of National Feeling." In *Central Asia: 130 Years of Russian Dominance, A Historical Overview*, 3rd edn, ed. E. Allworth. Durham, NC: Duke University Press.

Carrette, Jeremy and Richard King. 2005. *Selling Spirituality: The Silent Takeover of Religion*. London and New York: Routledge.

Carroll, Jackson W., Barbara Hargrove and Adair T. Lummis. 1983. *Women of the Cloth: A New Opportunity for the Churches*. San Francisco: Harper & Row.

Carroll, Michael P. 1992. *Madonnas That Maim: Popular Catholicism in Italy since the Fifteenth Century*. Baltimore: Johns Hopkins University Press.

Carroll, Michael P. 1995. "Rethinking Popular Catholicism in Pre-famine Ireland." *Journal for the Scientific Study of Religion* 34(3): 354–365.

Carroll, Michael P. 1996. "Stark Realities and Androcentric/Eurocentric Bias in the Sociology of Religion." *Sociology of Religion* 57(3): 225–240.

Casanova, J. 1994. *Public Religions in the Modern World*. Chicago: University of Chicago Press.

Casanova, J. 2001. "Secularization." In *International Encyclopedia of the Social and Behavioral Sciences*, ed. Neil J. Smelse and Paul B. Baltes, 13789–13791. Amsterdam: Elsevier.

Casanova, J. 2006. "Secularization Revisited: A Reply to Talal Asad." In *Powers of the Secular Modern: Talal Asad and His Interlocutors*, ed. D. Scott and C. Hirschkind. Stanford: Stanford University Press.

Castells, Manuel. 1996. *The Rise of the Network Society*. Cambridge, MA: Blackwell.

Castells, Manuel. 1997. *The Power of Identity*. Cambridge, MA: Blackwell.

Castells, Manuel. 2004. *The Network Society: A Cross-cultural Perspective*. Cheltenham: Edward Elgar.

Cavalcanti, H.B. and D. Schleef. 2005. "The Case for Secular Assimilation? The Latino Experience in Richmond, Virginia." *Journal for the Scientific Study of Religion* 44(4): 473–483.

Cavanaugh, William T. 1995. "A Fire Strong Enough To Consume the House: 'The Wars of Religion' and the Rise of the State." *Modern Theology* 11(4): 397–420.

Cavanaugh, William T. 2004. "Killing in the Name of God." *New Blackfriars* 85: 510–526.

Cavendish, Richard. 1967. *The Black Arts: An Absorbing Account of Witchcraft, Demonology, Astrology, and Other Mystical Practices throughout the Ages*. New York: Perigree Books.

Ceadel, M. 2002. "The Quaker Peace Testimony and its Contribution to the British Peace Movement: An Overview," *Quaker Studies* 7(1): 9–29.

"Celtic Religion." 1996. In *Encyclopedia of Religion on CD ROM*, 154–156. New York: Macmillan Library Reference.

Cesari, Joceline. 2003. "Muslim Minorities in Europe: The Silent Revolution." In *Modernizing Islam: Religion in the Public Sphere in the Middle East and in Europe*, edited by John Esposito and François Burgat, 251–269. New Jersey: Rutgers University Press.

Cha, P.T. 2001. "Ethnic Identity Formation and Participation in Immigrant Churches: Second Generation Korean American Experiences." In *Korean Americans and Their Religions: Pilgrim and Missionaries from a Different Shore*, ed. H.-Y. Kwon, K.C. Kim and R.S. Warner. University Park: Pennsylvania State University Press.

Chadwick, H. 1967. *The Early Church*. Harmondsworth: Penguin.

Chadwick, O. 1964. *The Reformation*. Harmondsworth: Penguin.

Chakrabarty, Dipesh. 2000. *Provincializing Europe: Postcolonial Thought and Historical Difference*. Princeton: Princeton University Press.

Chambers, Robert. 1997. *Whose Reality Counts? Putting the First Last*. London: Intermediate Technology.

Chang, Pauline. 2005. Interview posted January 17. The *Christian Post* online, www.christianpost.com/article/church/1841/section/interview.bishop.harry.s.jackson/1.htm (accessed March 30, 2005).

Charlton, Joy C. 1978. "Women Entering the Ordained Ministry: Contradictions and Dilemmas of Status." Paper presented at annual meeting of the Society for the Scientific Study of Religion, Hartford, CT.

Chau, A.Y. 2009. Expanding the Space of Popular Religion: Local Temple Activism and the Politics of Legitimation in Contemporary Rural China. In *Making Religion, Making the State: The Politics of Religion in Modern China*, ed. Yoshiko Ashiwa and David L. Wank, 211–240. Stanford: Stanford University Press.

Chaves, Mark. 1989. "Secularization *and* Religious Revival: Evidence from U.S. Church Attendance Rates, 1972–1986." *Journal for the Scientific Study of Religion* 28(December): 464–477.

Chaves, Mark. 1991a. "Segmentation in a Religious Labor Market." *Sociological Analysis* 52(Summer): 143–158.

Chaves, Mark and David E. Cann. 1992. "Regulation, Pluralism, and Religious Market Structure: Explaining Religious Vitality." *Rationality and Society* 4(July): 272–290.

Chenu, M.-D. 1968. *Nature, Man, and Society in the Twelfth Century: Essays on Theological Perspectives in the Latin West*. Chicago: University of Chicago Press.

Chidester, David. 1996. *Savage Systems: Colonialism and Comparative Religion in Southern Africa*. Charlottesville: University Press of Virginia.

Chinese Communist Party Central Committee (Zhonggong zhongyang). 1987 (1982). "Guanyu woguo shehuizhuyi shiqi zongjiao wentide jiben guandian he jiben zhengce" (Regarding the Basic Viewpoint and Policy on the Religious Question During Our Country's Socialist Period). In *Shiyijie sanzhong quanhui yilai zhongyao wenxian xuandu* (Collection of Important Documents Since the Third Plenum of the Eleventh Party Congress), vol. 1. Beijing: Renmin chubanshe.

Chodorow, Nancy. 1978. *The Reproduction of Mothering*. Berkeley: University of California Press.

Chou Wei. 1927. "Geming de Jiangsu nongmin" (Revolutionary Farmers of Jiangsu). *Buersaiweike* 1 (October).

Christian, D. 2000. "Silk Roads or Steppe Roads? The Silk Roads in World History." *Journal of World History* 11(1): 1–25.

Christian, William A., Jr. 1981. *Local Religion in Sixteenth-Century Spain*. Princeton: Princeton University Press.

Cimino, Richard and Don Lattin. 2002. *Shopping for Faith: American Religion in the New Millennium*. San Francisco: Jossey-Bass.

Clark, Stuart. 1997. *Thinking with Demons: The Idea of Witchcraft in Early Modern Europe*. Oxford: Clarendon.

Clarke, R.L. 1986. *Pastoral Care of Battered Women*. Philadelphia: Westminster Press.

Cline, Sally and Dale Spender. 1988. *Reflecting Men: At Twice their Natural Size*. London: Fontana.

Cohen, Steven. 2006. *The 2005 Boston Community Survey: Preliminary Findings*. Brandeis, MA: Steinhardt Social Research Institute.

Colebrook, Claire. 2000. "Incorporeality: The Ghostly Body of Metaphysics." *Body and Society* 6(2): 25–44.

Coleman, S. 2000. *The Globalisation of Charismatic Christianity: Spreading the Gospel of Prosperity*. Cambridge: Cambridge University Press.

Coleman, S. and P. Collins. 2000. "The 'Plain' and the 'Positive': Ritual, Experience and Aesthetics in Quakerism and Charismatic Christianity." *Journal of Contemporary Religion* 15(3): 317–329.

Collier, Jane. 1988. *Marriage and Inequality in Classless Societies*. Stanford: Stanford University Press.

Collier, Jane. 1997. *From Duty to Desire: Remaking Families in a Spanish Village*. Princeton: Princeton University Press.

Collier, Jane and Sylvia Yanagisako. 1989. "Theory in Anthropology since Feminist Practice." *Critique of Anthropology* IX(2): 27–37.

Collingwood, R.G. 1938. *The Principles of Art*. London: Oxford University Press.

Collins, P. 2002. "Discipline: The Codification of Quakerism as Orthopraxy, 1650–1738." *History and Anthropology* 13(2): 79–94.

Collins, Sylvia. 1997. *Young People's Faith in Later Modernity*. Guildford: University of Surrey Libary.

Cone, James H. 1969. *Black Theology and Black Power*. New York: Seabury Press.

Congregation for the Doctrine of the Faith. 2003. *Considerations Regarding Proposals to Give Legal Recognition to Unions between Homosexual Persons*. Rome: Offices of the Congregation for the Doctrine of the Faith.

Connolly, Sean J. 1982. *Priests and People in Pre-famine Ireland, 1780–1845*. Dublin: Gill and Macmillan.

Connolly, William E. 1999. *Why I am Not a Secularist*. Minneapolis: University of Minnesota Press.

Connor, P. 2009. "International Migration and Religious Participation: The Mediating Impact of Individual and Contextual Effects." *Sociological Forum* 24(4): 779–803.

Cook, David A. 2002. "Forty Years of Religion across Borders: Twilight of a Transnational Field?" In *Transnational Immigrant Networks*, ed. Ebaugh, H.R. and Chafetz, J.S. Lanham: Rowman & Littlefield.

Cooperman, Alan. 2005. "Lesbian Minister Defrocked by United Methodist Church." *Washington Post*, November 1, A3.

Coulanges, Fustel de. 1873. *The Ancient City: A Study on the Religion, Laws, and Institutions of Greece and Rome*. Boston: Lothrop, Lee and Shepherd.

Counts, Laura. 1999a. "A Clean Fight: Shabby Building Spurs Formation of Unlikely Tenants Coalition." *Oakland Tribune*, April 19, Local.

Counts, Laura. 1999b. "Oak Park Complex Stuck in Legal Battle: Owner Declares Bankruptcy." *Oakland Tribune*, June 25, Local.

Cox, Harvey. 1999. "The Market as God." *The Atlantic* (March): 18–23.

Crenshaw, Kimberlé. 1991. "Mapping the Margins: Intersectionality, Identity Politics, and Violence against Women of Color." *Stanford Law Review* 43(6): 1241–1299.

Crowley, Aleister. 1929. *Magick in Theory and Practice*. Paris: Lecram.

Danby, Herbert. 1933. *The Mishnah*. New York: Oxford University Press.

Dandelion, P. 2004. "Research Note: Implicit Conservatism in Liberal Religion: British Quakers as an 'Uncertain Sect'." *Journal of Contemporary Religion* 19(2): 219–229.

Dao, James. 2004. "Flush with Victory, Grass-roots Crusader against Same-sex Marriage Thinks Big." *New York Times*, November 23, A28.

Davidman, Lynn. 1991. *Tradition in a Rootless World: Women Turn to Orthodox Judaism*. Berkeley and Los Angeles: University of California Press.

Davidman, Lynn and Shelly Tenenbaum. 1994. "Toward a Feminist Sociology of American Jews." In *Feminist Perspectives on Jewish Studies*, ed. L. Davidman and S. Tenenbaum, 140–168. New Haven: Yale University Press.

Davie, Grace. 1994. *Religion in Britain since 1945: Believing without Belonging*. Oxford: Blackwell.

Davies, Bronwyn. 1989. *Frogs and Snails and Feminist Tales*. Sydney: Allen and Unwin.

De Beauvoir, Simone. 1993. *The Second Sex*. London: D. Campbell.

de Certeau, Michel. 1984. *The Practice of Everyday Life*. Berkeley: University of California Press.

de Tocqueville, Alexis. 1954. *Democracy in America*, vol. 1. Garden City: Doubleday & Co., Anchor Books.

Dean, Kenneth. 1995. *Taoist Ritual and Popular Cults of Southeast China*. Princeton: Princeton University Press.

Dean, Kenneth. 1998. *Lord of the Three in One: The Spread of a Cult in Southeast China*. Princeton: Princeton University Press.

Decker, Karl and Angus McSween. 1892. *Historic Arlington*. Washington, DC..

Dees, Morris. 1996. *Gathering Storm: America's Militia Threat*. New York: HarperCollins.

DeFao, Janine. 1999. "New Attack on Oakland Slumlords: City Levies Fins, Disgruntled Renters Sue." *San Francisco Chronicle*, October 29.

DeFao, Janine. 2000. "Oakland Tenants Get Big Settlement: Decrepit Apartments to Be Fixed Up." *San Francisco Chronicle*, October 17.

DeKeseredy, W. and L. MacLeod. 1998. *Woman Abuse: A Sociological Story*. Toronto: Harcourt Brace.

Delphy, Christine and Diana Leonard. 1992. *Familiar Exploitation: A New Analysis of Marriage in Contemporary American Societies*. Cambridge: Polity.

Denison, M. 2007. "Führerkult in Turkmenistan: Überwachsen und Überzeugen." *OstEuropa* 8–9: 209–233.

Derrida, Jacques. 1970. "Structure, Sign, and Play in the Discourse of the Human Sciences." In *The Structuralist Controversy*, ed. Richard A. Macksey and Eugenio Donato. Baltimore: Johns Hopkins Press.

Derrida, Jacques. 1988. "Signature Event Context." In *Limited Inc*, 1–23. Evanston: Northwestern University Press.

Derrida, Jacques. 1998. *In Search of Islamic Feminism: One Woman's Global Journey*. New York: Doubleday Press.

Despland, Michel. 1979. *La Religion en Occident: Evolution des idées et du vécu*, Héritage et projet, 23. Montreal: Fides.

Despland, Michel. 1999. *L'émergence des sciences de la religion. La monarchie de Juillet: un moment fondateur*. Paris: L'Harmattan.

Despland, Michel and Gérard Vallee, eds. 1992. *Religion in History: The Word, the Idea, the Reality*. Waterloo: Wilfred Laurier University Press.

Deutschmann, Christoph. 2001. "'The Promise of Absolute Wealth': Capitalism as a Religion?" *Thesis Eleven* 66(August): 32–56.

Dillon, M. 1994. "Muslim Communities in Contemporary China: The Resurgence of Islam After the Cultural Revolution." *Journal of Islamic Studies* 5(1): 70–101.

Dillon, M. 1999. *Catholic Identity*. Cambridge: Cambridge University Press.

Dirlik, Arif. 2000. *Postmodernity's Histories: The Past as Legacy and Project*. Lanham: Rowman & Littlefield.

Dobash, R.P. and R.E. Dobash. 1979. *Violence against Wives: A Case against the Patriarchy*. New York: Free Press.

Douglas, Mary. 1975. *Implicit Meanings*. London: Routledge and Kegan Paul.

Douglas, Mary. 1966. *Purity and Danger: An Analysis of Concepts of Pollution and Taboo*. New York: Praeger.

Dreyer, J.T. 1976. *China's Forty Millions: Minority Nationalities and National Integration in the People's Republic of China*. Cambridge, MA: Harvard University Press.

Drury, Nevill. 2000. *The History of Magic in the Modern Age*. New York: Carroll & Graf.

Duara, Prasenjit. 1995. "Campaigns against Religion and the Return of the Repressed." In *Rescuing History from the Nation: Questioning Narratives of Modern China*, 85–113. Chicago: University of Chicago Press.

Dubisch, Jill. 1990. "Pilgrimage and Popular Religion at a Greek Holy Shrine." In *Religious Orthodoxy and Popular Faith in European Society*, ed. Badone, E., 113–139. Princeton: Princeton University Press.

Dubuisson, Daniel. 2003 [1998]. *L'Occident et la religion: Mythes, science et idéologie*, Editions Complexe; English trans. William Sayers, *The Western Construction of Religion: Myths, Knowledge and Ideology*. Baltimore: Johns Hopkins University Press.

Duffy, Eamon. 1992. *The Stripping of the Altars: Traditional Religion in England, c.1400–c.1580*. New Haven: Yale University Press.

Dufour, L. 2000. "Sifting through the Tradition: The Creation of a Jewish Feminist Identity." *Journal for the Scientific Study of Religion* 39(1): 90–106.

Dumont, L. 1971. "Religion, Politics, and Society in the Individualistic Universe." *Proceedings of the Royal Anthropological Institute for 1970*.

Durán, Diego. 1867–1880. *Historia de las Indias de Nueva España y Islas de Tierra Firme*. Vol. 2. Mexico City: n.p.

Durkheim, Émile. [1915] 1965. *The Elementary Forms of the Religious Life*. Translated by J. W. Swain. New York: Free Press.

Durkheim, Émile [1915]1971: *The Elementary Forms of the Religious Life*. London: George Allen & Unwin.

Durkheim, Émile. 1995. *The Elementary Forms of Religious Life*. New York: Free Press.

Ebaugh, H.R. and Chafetz, J.S. 2000 *Religion and the New Immigrants: Continuities and Adaptations in Immigrant Congregations*. Walnut Creek: AltaMira Press

Edgar, A.L. 2004. *Tribal Nation: The Making of Soviet Turkmenistan*. Princeton: Princeton University Press.

Ehrenreich, Barbara and Deirdre English. 1973. *Witches, Midwives, and Nurses: A History of Women Healers*. New York: Feminist Press.

Eickelman, Dale F. 1992. "Mass Higher Education and the Religious Imagination in Contemporary Arab Society." *American Ethnologist* 19(4): 643–655.

Eisen, Arnold. 1998. *Rethinking Modern Judaism*. Chicago: University of Chicago Press.

Eisenhower, Dwight D. 1955. In Will Herberg, *Protestant-Catholic-Jew*, 97. Garden City: Doubleday & Co.

Eliade, Mircea. 1954. *The Myth of the Eternal Return*. Tr. Millard R. Trask. New York: Pantheon Books.

Elias, Norbert. 1978. *The Civilizing Process*, vol. 1: *The History of Manners*. Tr. E. Jephcott. New York: Pantheon Books.

Elias, Norbert. 1982. *Power and Civility*. Tr. E. Jephcott. *The Civilizing Process*, vol. 2. New York: Pantheon Books.

Ellis, Bill. 2000. *Raising the Devil: Satanism, New Religions, and the Media*. Lexington: University Press of Kentucky.

Evans-Pritchard, E.E. 1956. *Nuer Religion*. Oxford: Clarendon.

Evans-Pritchard, E.E. 1965. *Theories of Primitive Religion*. Oxford: Clarendon.

Fairclough, N. 1995. *Critical Discourse Analysis: The Critical Study of Language*. Boston: Addison Wesley.

Farias, Miguel. Forthcoming. *A Social-Psychological Study on the Adherence to the New Age Movement*. Oxford: Department of Experimental Psychology, University of Oxford.

Feil, Ernst. 1986. *Religio: die Geschichte eines neuzeitlichen Grundbegriffs vom Frühchristentum bis zur Reformation*, Forschung zur Kirchen- und Dogmengeschichte, 36. Göttingen: Vandenhoeck and Ruprecht.

Feil, Ernst 1997. *Religio II: die Geschichte eines neuzeitlichen Grundbegriffs zwischen Reformation und Rationalismus (ca. 1540–1620)*, Forschung zur Kirchen- und Dogmengeschichte, 70. Göttingen: Vandenhoeck and Ruprecht.

Fenn, R. 1982. *Liturgies and Trials: The Secularization of Religious Language*. New York: Pilgrim Press.

Festinger, Leon, Henry W. Riecken and Stanley Schachter. 1956. *When Prophecy Fails*. Minneapolis: University of Minnesota Press.

Fetzer, J. and J.C. Soper. 2003. "The Roots of Public Attitudes toward State Accommodation of European Muslims' Religious Practices Before and After September 11." *Journal for the Scientific Study of Religion* 42(2): 247–258.

Finke, Roger. 1992. "An Unsecular America." In *Religion and Modernization*, ed. S. Bruce. New York: Oxford University Press

Finke, Roger and Rodney Stark. 1988. "Religious Economies and Sacred Canopies: Religious Mobilization in American Cities." *American Sociological Review* 53(February): 41–49.

Finke, Roger and Rodney Stark. 1992. *The Churching of America, 1776–1990*. New Brunswick: Rutgers University Press.

Finnegan, Michael. 2004. "The Race for the White House; Jackson and Sharpton join Kerry on Trail; Black Voters are Urged to Focus on Quality of Life and not be Diverted by GOP 'Hot Button' Issues." *Los Angeles Times*, October 11, A13.

Finucane, R.C. 1977. *Miracles and Pilgrims: Popular Beliefs in Medieval England*. London: Dent.

Fiorenza, E.S. and M.S. Copeland, eds. 1994. *Violence against Women*. London: SCM Press.

Fiorina, Morris P., with Samuel J. Abrams and Jeremy C. Pope. 2005. *Culture War? The Myth of a Polarized America*. New York: Pearson Longman.

Fisher-Townsend, B. 2008. "Searching for the Missing Puzzle Piece: The Potential of Faith in Changing

Violent Behavior." In *Beyond Abuse in the Christian Home: Raising Voices for Change*, ed. C.C. Kroeger, N. Nason-Clark and B. Fisher-Townsend, 100–120. Eugene: Wipf and Stock.

Fisher-Townsend, B., N. Nason-Clark, L. Ruff and N. Murphy. 2008. "I am not Violent: Men's Experience in Group." In *Beyond Abuse in the Christian Home: Raising Voices for Change*, ed. C.C. Kroeger, N. Nason-Clark and B. Fisher-Townsend, 78–99. Eugene: Wipf and Stock.

FitzGerald, Frances. 1986. *Cities on a Hill: A Journey through Contemporary American Cultures*. New York: Simon & Schuster.

Fitzgerald, Timothy. 2000. *The Ideology of Religious Studies*. Oxford: Oxford University Press.

Fonagy, Peter. 1999. "The Transgenerational Transmission of Holocaust Trauma." *Attachment and Human Development* 1: 92–114.

Foner, N. and R. Alba. 2008. "Immigrant Religion in the U.S. and Western Europe: Bridge or Barrier to Inclusion?" *International Migration Review* 42(2): 360–393.

Forbes, A.D.W. 1986. *Warlords and Muslims in Chinese Central Asia: A Political History of Republican Sinkiang, 1911–1949*. New York: Cambridge University Press.

Forbes, Bruce David and Jeanne Halgren Kilde, eds. 2004. *Rapture, Revelation, and the End Times: Exploring the* Left Behind *Series*. New York: Palgrave Macmillan.

Ford, D. 1999. *Theology*. Oxford: Oxford University Press.

Forster, Mark R. 1992. *The Counter-Reformation in the Villages: Religion and Reform in the Bishopric of Speyer, 1560–1720*. Ithaca: Cornell University Press.

Fortune, M. 1991. *Violence in the Family: A Workshop Curriculum for Clergy and other Helpers*. Cleveland: The Pilgrim Press.

Fraser, Nancy. 2000. "Rethinking Recognition." *New Left Review* 3 (May/June): 107–120.

Friedland, Roger and Robert R. Alford. 1991. "Bringing Society Back In: Symbols, Practices, and Institutional Contradictions." In *The New Institutionalism in Organizational Analysis*, ed. Walter Powell and Paul J. DiMaggio, 232–263. Chicago: University of Chicago Press.

Frisk, Liselotte. 2003. "New Age Participants in Sweden. Background, Beliefs, Engagement and 'Conversion'." In *New Religions in a Postmodern World*, ed. Mikael Rothstein and Reender Kranenborg, 241–255. Aarhus: Aarhus University Press.

Fukuyama, F. 1992. *The End of History and the Last Man*. New York: Free Press.

Fuller, G.E. and J.N. Lipman. 2004. "Islam in Xinjiang." In *Xinjiang. China's Muslim Borderland*, ed. S.F. Starr. Armonk: M.E. Sharpe.

Gallup. 1988. *The Unchurched American—Ten Years Later*. Princeton: Princeton Religious Research Center.

Gambetta, Diego, ed. 2005. *Making Sense of Suicide Missions*. Oxford: Oxford University Press.

Gardner, Gerald. 1954. *Witchcraft Today*. London: Rider and Co.

Gay, P. 1973. *The Enlightenment: An Interpretation*. 2 vols. London: Wildwood House.

Geertz, Clifford. 1973. *The Interpretation of Cultures: Selected Essays*. New York: Basic Books.

Geertz, Clifford. 1983. *Local Knowledge: Further Essays in Interpretive Anthropology*. New York: Basic Books.

Geertz, Clifford. 1984. " 'From the Native's Point of View': On the Nature of Anthropological Understanding." In *Culture Theory. Essays on Mind, Self, and Emotion*, ed. Richard A. Shweder and Robert A. LeVine, 123–136. Cambridge: Cambridge University Press.

Geraci, R.P. 2001. "Going Abroad or Going to Russia? Orthodox Missionaries in the Kazakh Steppe, 1881–1917." In *Of Religion and Empire: Missions, Conversion, and Tolerance in Tsarist Russia*, ed. R.P. Geraci and M. Khodarkovsky. Ithaca: Cornell University Press.

Geraci, R.P. and M. Khodarkovsky, M. 2001. "Introduction." In *Of Religion and Empire: Missions, Conversion, and Tolerance in Tsarist Russia*, ed. R.P. Geraci and M. Khodarkovsky. Ithaca: Cornell University Press.

Gergen, Kenneth J. 1987. "Toward Self as Relationship." In *Self and Identity*, ed. Krysia Yardley and Terry Honess, 53–63. London: John Wiley & Sons.

Gerth, H.H. and C. Wright Mills. 1977. *From Max Weber. Essays in Sociology*. London: Routledge.

Giddens, Anthony. 1993. *The Transformation of Intimacy*. Stanford: Stanford University Press.

Giddens, Anthony. and C. Pierson. 1998. *Conversations with Anthony Giddens*. Cambridge: Polity Press.

Giedion, Siegfried. 1948. *Mechanization Takes Control*. New York: Oxford University Press.

Giesbrecht, N. and I. Sevcik. 2000. "The Process of Recovery and Rebuilding among Abused Women in Conservative Evangelical Subculture." *Journal of Family Violence* 15(3): 229–248.

Gilkes, Cheryl Townsend. 2001. *If It Wasn't for the Women: Black Women's Experience and Womanist Culture in Church and Community*. Maryknoll: Orbis Books.

Gill, Robin, C. Kirk Hadaway and Penny Long Marler. 1998. "Is Religious Belief Declining in Britain?" *Journal for the Scientific Study of Religion* 37: 507–516.

Gilliam, Harold. 1993. "Bursting at the Seams: California's Immigration Crisis." *San Francisco Chronicle*, February 21.

Gilligan, Carol. 1982. *In a Different Voice: Psychological Theory and Women's Development*. Cambridge, MA: Harvard University Press.

Gilligan, Carol. 2002. *The Birth of Pleasure: A New Map of Love*. London: Chatto and Windus.

Gimlin, Debra L. 2002: *Body Work. Beauty and Self-Image in American Culture*. Berkeley: University of California Press.

Ginzburg, Carlo. 1980. *The Cheese and the Worms: The Cosmos of a Sixteenth-Century Miller*. Tr. J. Tedeschi and A. Tedeschi. New York: Penguin.

Ginzburg, Carlo. 1983. *The Night Battles: Witchcraft and Agrarian Cults in the Sixteenth and Seventeenth Centuries*. Tr. J. Tedeschi and A. Tedeschi. Baltimore: Johns Hopkins University Press.

Giroux, Henry A. 2004. *The Terror of Neoliberalism: Authoritarianism and the Eclipse of Democracy*. Boulder: Paradigm Publishers.

Gladney, D.C. 2004. *Dislocating China: Muslims, Minorities and other Subaltern Subjects*. London: Hurst.

Glenn, Norval D. 1987. "The Trend in 'No Religion' Respondents to U.S. National Surveys, Late 1950s to Early 1980s." *Public Opinion Quarterly* 51(Fall): 293–314.

Goffman, Erwing. 1963. *Stigma: Notes on the Management of Spoiled Identity*. New York: Simon & Schuster.

Goldberg, Michelle. 2007. *Kingdom Coming: The Rise of Christian Nationalism*. New York: W.W. Norton.

Göle, Nilüfer. 1996. *The Forbidden Modern: Civilization and Veiling*. Ann Arbor: University of Michigan Press.

Göle, Nilufer. 2003. "The Voluntary Adoption of Islamic Stigma Symbols." *Social Research* 70(3): 809–828.

Gondolf, E. 2002. *Batterer Intervention Systems: Issues, Outcomes and Recommendations*. Thousand Oaks: Sage Publications.

Goodstein, Laurie. 2005. "Methodists Reinstate Defrocked Minister." *New York Times*, April 30, A9.

Gorski, Philip S. 2000. "Historicizing the Secularization Debate: Church, State, and Society in Late Medieval and Early Modern Europe, ca. 1300 to 1700." *American Sociological Review* 65(February): 138–167.

Goss, R. 1993. *Jesus Acted Up*. San Francisco: Harper-San Francisco.

Goss, R. 2002. *Queering Christ: Beyond Jesus Acted Up*. Cleveland: The Pilgrim Press.

Goss, R. and M. West. 2000. *Take Back the Word*. Cleveland: The Pilgrim Press.

Gottschalk, Peter. 2000. *Beyond Hindu and Muslim*. Oxford and New York: Oxford University Press.

Gramsci, Antonio. 1972. *Selections from the Prison Notebooks of Antonio Gramsci*. Ed. and tr. Quintin Hoare and Geoffrey Nowell Smith. New York: International Publishers.

Gramsci, Antonio. 1992. *Prison Notebooks*. Ed. Joseph A. Buttigieg, tr. Joseph A. Buttigieg and Antonio Callari. New York: Columbia University Press.

Gramsci, Antonio. 1995. *Further Selections from the Prison Notebooks*. Ed. and tr. Derek Boothman. Minneapolis: University of Minnesota Press.

Grant, Linda. 1993. *Sexing the Millennium: A Political History of the Sexual Revolution*. London: HarperCollins.

Greeley, Andrew M. 1972 *The Denominational Society: A Sociological Approach to Religion in America*. Glenview: Scott, Foresman

Greeley, Andrew M. 1989. *Religious Change in America*. Cambridge, MA: Harvard University Press.

Greeley, Andrew M. 1990. *The Catholic Myth: The Behavior and Beliefs of America's Catholics*. New York: Scribner's.

Greeley, Andrew M. 1994. "A Religious Revival in Russia." *Journal for the Scientific Study of Religion* 33(3): 253–272.

Green, M. and P. Numrich. 2001. *Religious Perspectives on Sexuality*. Chicago: The Park Ridge Center.

Grewal, Inderpal and Caren Kaplan, eds. 1994. *Scattered Hegemonies: Postmodernity and Transnational Feminist Practices*. Minneapolis: University of Minnesota Press.

Griffith R. Marie. 1997. *God's Daughters: Evangelical Women and the Power of Submission*. Berkeley: University of California Press.

Gross, Martin. 1979. *The Psychological Society*. New York: Simon & Schuster.

Grosz, Elizabeth. 1994. *Volatile Bodies: Toward a Corporeal Feminism*. Bloomington: Indiana University Press.

Guardian. 2003. "Letter that Started the Row." June 19.

Guest, K.J. 2003. *God in Chinatown: Religion and Survival in New York's Evolving Immigrant Community*. New York: New York University Press.

Gutierrez, G. 2001. *A Theology of Liberation*. London: SCM Press.

Gutierrez, Lorraine, Anne Alvarez, Howard Nemon and Edith Lewis. 1996. "Multicultural Community Organizing: A Strategy for Change." *Social Work* 5: 501–508.

Häbibolla, A. 1993. *Uyghur etnografisi*. Urumchi: Xinjiang Hälk Näshriati.

Hacking, Ian. 2002. *Historical Ontology*. Cambridge, MA: Harvard University Press.

Hadaway, C. Kirk and Penny Long Marler. 1991a. "All in the Family: Religious Mobility in America." Paper presented at annual meeting of Society for the Scientific Study of Religion, Pittsburgh.

Hadaway, C. Kirk, Penny Long Marler and Mark Chaves. 1993. "What the Polls Don't Show: A Closer Look at US Church Attendance." *American Sociological Review* 58: 741–752.

Hadden, J. 1987. "Toward Desacralizing Secularization Theory." *Social Forces* 65(3): 587–611.

Halbwachs, Maurice. 1992. *On Collective Memory*. Chicago: University of Chicago Press.

Hall, David D. 1989. *Worlds of Wonder, Days of Judgment: Popular Religious Belief in Early New England*. New York: Knopf.

Hall, John R. 1987. *Gone From the Promised Land: Jonestown in American Cultural History*. New Brunswick: Transaction Books.

Hall, John R. 1995. "Public Narratives and the Apocalyptic Sect: From Jonestown to Mt. Carmel." In *Armageddon in Waco: Critical Perspectives on the Branch Davidian Conflict*, ed. Stuart A. Wright, 207. Chicago: University of Chicago Press.

Hall, Peter A. 1999. "Social Capital in Britain." *British Journal of Politics* 29: 417–461.

Hall, Stuart. 1996. "Introduction: Who Needs 'Identity'?" In *Questions of Cultural Identity*, ed. Stuart Hall and Paul du Gay, 1–17. London: Sage.

Hallaq, Wael, ed. 1990. *Humūm al-mar'a al-muslima wal-dā'ya Zaynab al-Ghazali*. Cairo: Dār al-i'tisām. Cambridge: Cambridge University Press.

Hallaq, Wael. 1997. *A History of Islamic Legal Theories: An Introduction to Sunnī usūl alfiqh*. Cambridge: Cambridge University Press.

Halsey, P. 1984. *Abuse in the Family: Breaking the Church's Silence*. Office of Ministries with Women in Crisis, General Board of Global Ministries, United Methodist Church.

Hamilton, Clive. 2003. *Downshifting in Britain. A Sea-Change in the Pursuit of Happiness*. Discussion Paper Number 58. Canberra: The Australia Institute.

Hammond, Phillip E. 1988. "Religion and the Persistence of Identity." *Journal for the Scientific Study of Religion* 27 (March): 1–11.

Hammond, Phillip E. 1992. *Religion and Personal Autonomy: The Third Disestablishment in America*. Columbia: University of South Carolina Press.

Handlin, O. 1951. *The Uprooted*. New York: Grosset & Dunlap.

Hann, C.M. *et al.* 2006. *The Postsocialist Religious Question: Faith and Power in Central Asia and East-Central Europe*. Berlin: Lit Verlag.

Hann, C.M. 2008. "*Laiklik* in rural Xinjiang." Paper presented at the Workshop Varieties of Secularism in Asia, Aarhus University, May.

Hannerz, Ulf. 2004. *Foreign News: Exploring the World of Foreign Correspondents*. Chicago: University of Chicago Press.

Harré, R. 1981. "Psychological Variety." In *Indigenous Psychologies*, ed. P. Heelas and A. Lock. London: Academic Press.

Harrell, S. 1995. "Civilizing Projects and Reactions to Them." In *Cultural Encounters on China's Ethnic Frontiers*, ed. S. Harrell. Seattle: University of Washington Press.

Harris, Fredrick C. 1999. *Something Within: Religion in African–American Political Activism*. New York: Oxford University Press.

Harris Interactive Service Bureau. 2003. Yoga in America, www.yogajournal. com/about_press061603.cfm.

Harrison, Peter. 1990. *"Religion" and the Religions in the English Enlightenment*. Cambridge: Cambridge University Press.

Hartz, Louis. 1955. "The Feudal Dream of the South." Pt. 4 in *The Liberal Tradition in America*. New York: Harcourt, Brace & Co.

Hass, Aaron. 1990. *In the Shadow of the Holocaust: The Second Generation*. London: Cambridge University Press.

Hayes, Dawn Marie. 2003. *Body and Sacred Place in Medieval Europe, 1100–1389*. London: Routledge.

Heald, Gordon. 2000. *Soul of Britain*. London: The Opinion Research Business.

Hedges, Chris. 2007. *American Fascists: The Christian Right and the War on America*. New York: Free Press.

Hedges, Ellie and James A. Beckford. 2000. "Holism, Healing and the New Age." In *Beyond New Age: Exploring Alternative Spirituality*, ed. Steven Sutcliffe and Marion Bowman, 169–187. Edinburgh: Edinburgh University Press.

Heelas, Paul and Benjamin Seel. 2003. "An Ageing New Age?" In *Predicting Religion. Christian, Secular and Alternative Futures*, ed. Grace Davie, Paul Heelas and Linda Woodhead, 229–247. Aldershot: Ashgate.

Heide, N. van der. 2008. "Spirited Performance: The Manas Epic and Society in Kyrgyzstan." PhD thesis, Tilburg, Universiteit van Tilburg.

Heilman, Samuel C. 1990. "The Jews: Schism or Division." In *In Gods We Trust: New Patterns of Religious Pluralism in America*, ed. Thomas Robbins and Dick Anthony, 185–198. New Brunswick: Transaction.

Hekma, G. 2002. "Imams and Homosexuality: A Post-gay Debate in the Netherlands." *Sexualities* 5(2): 237–248.

Hénaff, Marcel. 1999. *Sade: The Invention of the Libertine Body*. Minneapolis: University of Minnesota Press.

Herberg, Will. 1950. *Protestant, Catholic, and Jew: An Essay in American Religious Sociology*. Chicago: University of Chicago Press.

Herberg, Will. 1955. *Protestant—Catholic—Jew: An essay in American religious sociology*. Garden City, NY: Doubleday.

Herberg, Will. 1960. *Protestant, Catholic, Jew: An Essay in American Religious Sociology*, 2d ed. Garden City, N.Y.: Anchor.

Herman, Judith. 1992. *Trauma and Recovery*. New York: Basic Books.

Hermansen, Marcia. 2003. "How to Put the Genie Back in the Bottle? 'Identity' Islam and Muslim Youth Cultures in America." In *Progressive Muslims: On Justice, Gender, and Pluralism*, ed. Omid Safi, 303–319. Oxford: Oneworld Publications.

Herndon, William Henry. 1941. In Sherwood Eddy, *The Kingdom of God and the American Dream*, 162. New York: Harper & Row.

Hervieu-Léger, Danièle. 1998. "The Transmission and Formation of Socioreligious Identities in Modernity." *International Sociology* 13(2): 213–228.

Hervieu-Léger, Danièle. 2000. *Religion as a Chain of Memory*. Cambridge: Polity Press.

Hervieu-Léger, Danièle. 2001a. "The Twofold Limit of the Notion of Secularization." In *Peter Berger and the Study of Religion*, ed. L. Woodhead, P. Heelas and D. Martin. New York: Routledge.

Hervieu-Léger, Danièle. 2001b. "Individualism, the Validation of Faith, and the Social Nature of Religion in Modernity." In *The Blackwell Companion to Religion*, ed. Richard K. Fenn, 303–319. Malden: Blackwell Publishing.

Heyat, F. 2004. "Re-Islamization in Kyrgyzstan: Gender, New Poverty and the Moral Dimension." *Central Asian Survey* 23(3–4): 275–287.

Hilgers, I. 2006. "The Regulation and Control of Religious Pluralism in Uzbekistan." In *The Postsocialist Religious Question: Faith and Power in Central Asia and East-Central Europe*, ed. C.M. Hann *et al.* Berlin: Lit Verlag.

Hill, Paul. n.d. "I Shot an Abortionist," on the Army of God website, www.armyof-god.com/PHill_ShortShot.html.

Hill, Paul. *Paul Hill Speaks*. Pamphlet published by Reformation Press, Bowie, Maryland, June 1997.

Hill, Samuel S. 1985. "Religion and Region in America." *Annals of the American Academy of Political and Social Science* 480(July): 132–141.

Hilton, Lisa. 2002. *Athénaïs: The Life of Louis XIV's Mistress, the Real Queen of France*. Boston: Little, Brown.

Hindawi, Khayriyya. 1997. "Naṣīḥat Zaynab al-Ghazali lil-mar'a al-muslima: al-Zauja la taqūl 'la' li-zaujiha abadan illa fi ma yaghḍab allāh." *Sayyidati*, January 24, 70–75.

Hirschkind, Charles. 2001. "The Ethics of Listening: Cassette-sermon Audition in Contemporary Egypt." *American Ethnologist* 28(3): 623–649.

Hirschman, C. 2004. "The Role of Religion in the Origins and Adaptation of Immigrant Groups in the United States." *International Migration Review* 38(3): 1206–1233.

Hirsh, F. 2005. *Empire of Nations: Ethnographic Knowledge and the Making of the Soviet Union*. Ithaca: Cornell University Press.

Hoare, T. 2004. "Facts about Friends," www.quaker.org/friends/html (accessed September 29, 2004).

Hochschild, Arlie R. 1983. *The Managed Heart: Commercialization of Human Feeling*. Berkeley and London: University of California Press.

Hochschild, Arlie R. 1989. *The Second Shift: Working Parents and the Revolution at Home*. New York: Viking.

Hochschild, Arlie R. 1997. *The Time Bind. When Work Becomes Home and Home Becomes Work*. New York: Metropolitan Books.

Hochschild, Arlie R. 2003. *The Commercialization of Intimate Life. Notes from Home and Work.* Berkeley, Los Angeles and London: University of California Press.

Hoffman, David. 1998. *The Oklahoma City Bombing and the Politics of Terror.* Venice, CA: Feral House.

Hoffman, Valerie. 1985. "An Islamic Activist: Zaynab al-Ghazali." In *Women and the Family in the Middle East: New Voices of Change*, ed. E. Fernea, 233–254. Austin: University of Texas Press.

Hoffmann, D.L. 2003. *Stalinist Values: The Cultural Norms of Soviet Modernity, 1917–1941.* Ithaca: Cornell University Press.

Hofstadter, D. 1979. *Gädel, Escher, Bach: An Eternal Golden Braid.* New York: Basic Books.

Hofstede, Geert. 2001. *Culture's Consequences.* London: Sage.

Hoge, Dean R. 1979. "A Test of Theories of Denominational Growth and Decline." In *Understanding Church Growth and Decline: 1950–1978*, ed. D.R. Hoge and D.A. Roozen, 179–223. New York: The Pilgrim Press.

Hoge, Dean R. and David A. Roozen, eds. 1979. *Understanding Church Growth and Decline 1950–1978.* New York: The Pilgrim Press.

Hoge, Dean R. with Kenneth McGuire and Bernard F. Stratman. 1981. *Converts, Dropouts, Returnees: A Study of Religious Change Among Catholics.* Washington, DC: U.S. Catholic Conference; New York: Pilgrim Press.

Hollywood, Amy. 2002. "Performativity, Citationality, Ritualization." *History of Religions* 42(2): 93–115.

Hollywood, Amy. 2004. "Gender, Agency, and the Divine in Religious Historiography." *The Journal of Religion* 84(4).

Holmes, Jeremy. 1999. "Ghosts in the Consulting Room: An Attachment Perspective on Intergenerational Transmission." *Attachment and Human Development* 1: 115–131.

Hopkins, Dwight. 2001. "The Religion of Globalization." In *Religions/Globalizations: Theories and Cases*, ed. N. Hopkins Dwight, Lois Ann Lorentzen, Eduardo Mendieta and David Batstone. Durham, NC and London: Duke University Press.

Hopkirk, P. 1992. *The Great Game: The Struggle for Empire in Central Asia.* New York: Kondansha International.

Hoppe, T. 1998. *Die ethnischen Gruppen Xinjiangs; Kulturunterschiede und interethnische Beziehungen*, Mitteilung 290. Hamburg: Institut für Asienkunde.

Horton, A. and J. Williamson, eds. 1988. *Abuse and Religion: When Praying isn't Enough.* New York: D.C. Heath and Company.

House of Representatives. 1996. *Investigation into the Activities of Federal Law Enforcement Agencies toward the Branch Davidians: Thirteenth Report by the Committee on Government Reform and Oversight Prepared in Conjunction with the Committee on the Judiciary together with Additional and Dissenting Views*, Report 104–749. Washington, DC: U.S. Government Printing Office, 65.

Houtman, Dick and Peter Mascini. 2002. "Why do Churches become Empty, While New Age Grows? Secularization and Religious Change in the Netherlands." *Journal for the Scientific Study of Religion* 41(3): 455–473.

Hower, T. 2003. "The GLBT Religious Experience." *San Diego Gay and Lesbian Times*, September 11.

Hoyt, Joshua. 2002. "Reflections on Immigrant Organizing and the 'Universals'." *Social Policy* 2: 37–42.

Hunter, James Davison. 1987. *Evangelicalism: the Coming Generation.* Chicago: University of Chicago Press.

Hunter, James Davison. 1990. *Culture Shift in Advanced Industrial Society.* Princeton: Princeton University Press.

Hunter, James Davison. 1991. *Culture Wars: The Struggle to Define America.* New York: Basic Books.

Hurh, W.M. and K.C. Kim. 1990. "Religious Participation of Korean Immigrants in the United States." *Journal for the Scientific Study of Religion* 29(1): 19–34.

Husband, W.B. 2000. *"Godless Communists": Atheism and Society in Soviet Russia.* DeKalb: Northern Illinois University Press.

Husian, F. and M. O'Brien. 2001. "South Asian Muslims in Britain: Faith, Family and Community." In *Maintaining Our Difference*, ed. C. Harvey, pp. 15–28. Aldershot: Ashgate.

Huysmans, J.K. 1958. *Down There (Là bas): A Study in Satanism.* Tr. Keene Wallis. New Hyde Park: University Books.

Iannaccone, Laurence R. 1990. "Religious Practice: A Human Capital Approach." *Journal for the Scientific Study of Religion* 29(September): 297–314.

Iannaccone, Laurence R. 1991. "The Consequences of Religious Market Structure." *Rationality and Society* 3(April): 156–177.

Iannaccone, Laurence. 1994. "Why Strict Churches Are Strong." *American Journal of Sociology* 99(5): 1180–1211.

Information Office of the State Council of the People's Republic of China. 1997. "White Paper on Freedom of Religious Belief in China," www.china. org.cn/e-white/Freedom/f-1.htm (last accessed Ocotber 10, 2005).

Inglehart, Ronald. 1990. *Culture Shift in Advanced Industrial Society*. Princeton: Princeton University Press.

Inglehart, Ronald. 1997. *Modernization and Postmodernization: Cultural, Economic and Political Change in 43 Societies*. Princeton: Princeton University Press.

Inglehart, Ronald, Miguel Basanez and Alejandro Moreno. 1998. *Human Values and Beliefs: A Cross-Cultural Sourcebook*. Ann Arbor: University of Michigan Press.

International Court of Justice. 1995–1998. *Legality of the Threat or use of Nuclear Weapons, Advisory Opinion of 8 July 1996, 49/75 K. General List No. 95*.

International Crisis Group. 2003. *Cracks in the Marble: Turkmenistan's Failing Dictatorship*, ICG Asia Report 44. Osh/Brussels: International Crisis Group.

Isasi-Díaz, Ada María and Yolanda Tarango. 1988. *Hispanic Women: Prophetic Voice in the Church*. San Francisco: Harper & Row.

Ismail, Salwa. 2004. "Being Muslim: Islam, Islamism and Identity Politics." *Government and Opposition* 39(4): 614–631.

Ismail, Salwa. 2006. *Rethinking Islamist Politics: Culture, the State and Islamism*. London: I.B. Tauris.

Jacobsen, Christine M. 2006. "Staying on the Straight Path: Religious Identities and Practices among Young Muslims in Norway." Unpublished dissertation for the degree of Doctor Rerum Politicarum (dr.polit.), University of Bergen, Norway.

Jamal, A. 2001. "The Story of Lot and the *Qur'an's* Perception of the Morality of Same-sex Sexuality." *Journal of Homosexuality* 41(1): 1–88.

James, William. 1994 [1902]. *The Varieties of Religious Experience: A Study in Human Nature*. New York: Modern Library.

Järvinen, Margaretha. 1993. *Of Vice and Women: Shades of Prostitution*. Oslo: Scandinavian University Press.

Jasso, G. *et al*. 2000. "Family, Schooling, Religiosity, and Mobility among New Legal Immigrants to the United States: Evidence from the New Immigrant Survey Pilot Study." In *Immigration Today: Pastoral and Research Challenges*, ed. L.F. Tomasi and M.G. Powers. Staten Island: Center for Migration Studies.

Jasso, G. *et al*. 2003. "Exploring the Religious Preferences of Recent Immigrants to the United States: Evidence from the New Immigrant Survey Pilot." In *Religion and Immigration: Christian, Jewish, and Muslim Experiences in the United States*, ed. Y.Y. Haddad, J.I. Smith and J.L. Esposito. Walnut Creek: AltaMira Press.

Jasso, G. *et al*. Forthcoming. "The U.S. New Immigrant Survey: Overview and Preliminary Results Based on the New-immigrant Cohorts of 1996 and 2003." In *Longitudinal Surveys and Cross-Cultural Survey Design*, ed. B. Morgan and B. Nicholson. UK Immigration Research and Statistics Service.

Jeffreys, Sheila. 1990. *Anticlimax: A Feminist Perspective on the Sexual Revolution*. Washington Square: New York University Press.

Jenkins, Richard. 1996. *Social Identity*. London: Routledge.

Jessa, P. 2006. "Religious Renewal in Kazakhstan: Redefining 'Unofficial Islam'." In *The Postsocialist Religious Question: Faith and Power in Central Asia and East-Central Europe*, ed. C.M. Hann *et al*. Berlin: Lit Verlag.

Jeung, Russell. 2004. *Faithful Generations: Race and the New Asian American Churches*. New Brunswick: Rutgers University Press.

Joas, Hans. 2004. *Braucht der Mensch Religion? Über Erfahrungen der Selbsttranszendez*. Freiburg: Herder.

Jobling, J. 2002. *Feminist Biblical Interpretation in Theological Context*. London: Ashgate.

Johnson, Clair. 1996. "Freemen Deal Includes 5: Negotiator Spells Out Points in Agreement." *Billings Gazette Online*, June 19.

Johnson, J. 2003. "Faith Family Photo Albums: Reclaiming Theological Traditions in the Transgressive Blend of Text and Practice." *Theology and Sexuality* 9(2): 155–166.

Jones, Constance A. 2003. "Students in Ramtha's School of Enlightenment: A Profile from a Demographic Survey, Narrative, and Interview." In *New Religions in a Postmodern World*, ed. Mikael Rothstein and Reender Kranenborg, 257–285. Aarhus: Aarhus University Press.

Jordan, Judith V., Alexandra G. Kaplan, Jean Baker Miller, Irene P. Stiver and Janet L. Surrey. 1991. *Women's Growth in Connection*. New York: Guilford.

Jordan, M. 2000. *The Silence of Sodom*. Chicago: University of Chicago Press.

Juergensmeyer, Mark. 1993. *The New Cold War? Religious Nationalism Confronts the Secular State*. Berkeley and Los Angeles: University of California Press.

Juergensmeyer, Mark. 2000. *Terror in the Mind of God. The Global Rise of Religious Violence*. Berkeley and Los Angeles: University of California Press.

Kaelber, Lutz. 1998. *Schools of Asceticism: Ideology and Organization in Medieval Religious Communities*. University Park: Pennsylvania State University Press.

Kant, I. 1991. *Kant: Political Writings*. Ed. H. Reiss. Cambridge: Cambridge University Press.

Kaplan, Jeffrey. 1997. *Radical Religion in America: Millenarian Movements from the Far Right to the Children of Noah*. Syracuse: Syracuse University Press.

Karakasoglu, Yasemine. 2003. "Custom Tailored Islam: Second Generation Female Students of Turko-Muslim Origin in Germany and their Concept of Religiousness in Light of Modernity and Education." In *Identity and Integration: Migrants in Western Europe*, ed. Rosemarie Sackmann, Thomas Faist and Bernd Peters, 107–226. London: Ashgate.

Kaschuba, Wolfgang. 2007. "Ethnische Parallelgesellschaften? Zur Kulturellen Konstruktion des Fremden in der Europäischen Migration." *Zeitschrift für Volkskunde* 103(1): 65–85.

Kaufman, Debra Renée. 1991. *Rachel's Daughters: Newly Orthodox Jewish Women*. New Brunswick: Rutgers University Press.

Kehati, Pinchas. 1996. *The Mishnah: A New Translation with a Commentary by Rabbi Pinchas Kehati*. Tr. Rafael Fisch. Jerusalem: Eliner Library, Department for Torah Education and Culture in the Diaspora.

Kehl-Bodrogi, K. 2006. "Islam Contested: Nation, Religion, and Tradition in Post-Soviet Turkmenistan." In *The Postsocialist Religious Question: Faith and Power in Central Asia and East-Central Europe*, ed. C.M. Hann *et al.* Berlin: Lit Verlag.

Kellerman, Natan. 2001a. "The Long-term Psychological Effects and Treatment of Holocaust Trauma." *Journal of Loss and Trauma* 6: 197–218.

Kellerman, Natan. 2001b. "Transmission of Holocaust Trauma—An Integrative View." *Psychiatry* 64: 256–267.

Kelley, Dean. 1972. *Why the Conservative Churches are Growing*. New York: Harper & Row.

Kelley, Dean M. [1972] 1995. *Why Conservative Churches Are Growing*. Macon: Mercer University Press/Rose.

Kellstedt, Lyman A., John C. Green, James L. Guth and Corwin E. Smidt. 1996. "Grasping the Essentials: The Social Embodiment of Religion and Political Behavior." In *Religion and the Culture Wars*, ed. John C. Green, James L. Guth, Corwin E. Smidt and Lyman A. Kellstedt, 174–192. Lanham: Rowman & Littlefield.

Kent, S.A. and J.V. Spickard. 1994. "The 'Other' Civil Religion and the Tradition of Radical Quaker Politics." *Journal of Church and State* 36(2): 373–388.

Khalid, A. 1998. *The Politics of Muslim Cultural Reform: Jadidism in Central Asia*. Delhi: Oxford University Press.

Khalid, A. 2006. *Islam After Communism: Religion and Politics in Central Asia*. Berkeley: University of California Press.

Khalid, A. 2007. "The Soviet Union as an Imperial Formation: A View from Central Asia." In *Imperial Formations*, ed. A. Stoler, C. McGranahan and P. Perdue. Santa Fe: School for Advanced Research Press.

Khosrokhavar, Farhad. 1997. *L'islam des Jeunes*. Paris: Flammarion.

Kidd, Colin. 1999. *British Identities Before Nationalism: Ethnicity and Nationhood in the Atlantic World, 1600–1800*. Cambridge: Cambridge University Press.

Kimball, Charles. 2002. *When Religion Becomes Evil*. New York: HarperSan-Francisco.

King, C. 2000. "A Love as Fierce as Death: Reclaiming the Song of Songs for Queer Lovers." In *Take Back the Word*, ed. R. Goss and M. West, 126–142. Cleveland: The Pilgrim Press.

King, Francis. 1971. *Sexuality, Magic, and Perversion*. Secaucus: Citadel.

King, Richard. 1999. *Orientalism and Religion: Postcolonial Theory India and "the Mystic East."* New York and London: Routledge.

Kittredge, C. and Z. Sherwood. 1995. *Equal Rites*. Louisville: Westminster John Knox Press.

Knott, Kim and Sadja Khokher. 1993. "Religious and Ethnic Identity among Young Muslim Women in Bradford." *New Community* 19: 593–610.

Knowles, M.D. 1963. *The Monastic Order in England: 940–1216*. 2nd edn. Cambridge: Cambridge University Press.

Koch, T. 2001. "A Homoerotic Approach to Scripture." *Theology & Sexuality* 14(March): 10–22.

Kohn, Hans. 1961. *The Idea of Nationalism*. New York: Macmillan Co.

Kokosalakis, Nikos. 1987. "The Political Significance of Popular Religion in Greece." *Archives des Sciences Sociales des Religions* 64: 37–52.

Kokosalakis, Nikos. 1995. "Icons and Non-verbal Religion in the Orthodox Tradition." *Social Compass* 42(4): 433–450.

Kosmin, Barry A., Ariela Keysar and Nava Lerer. 1991. "Secular Education and the Religious Profile of Contemporary Black Americans." Paper presented at annual meeting of the Society for the Scientific Study of Religion, Pittsburgh.

Kroeber, A.L. and C. Kluckhohn. 1952. *Culture: A Critical Review of Concepts and Definitions*. Papers of the Peabody Museum, vol. 47, no. 1. Cambridge, MA: Peabody Museum.

Kroeger, C. and N. Nason-Clark. 2001. *No Place for Abuse: Biblical and Practical Resources to Counteract Domestic Violence*. Downers Grove: InterVarsity Press. Second edition, 2010.

Kuhn, Thomas S. 1970. *The Structure of Scientific Revolutions*. 2nd enlarged edn. Chicago: University of Chicago Press.

Kurien, P.A. 1998. "Becoming American by Becoming Hindu: Indian Americans Take Their Place at the Multicultural Table." In *Gatherings in the Diaspora: Religious Communities and the New Immigration*, ed. R.S. Warner and J.G. Wittner. Philadelphia: Temple University Press.

Kurien, P.A. 2001. "Religion, Ethnicity, and Politics: Hindu and Muslim Indian Immigrants in the United States." *Ethnic and Racial Studies* 24(2): 263–293.

Kwilecki, Susan. 1987. "Contemporary Pentecostal Clergywomen: Female Christian Leadership, Old Style." *Journal of Feminist Studies of Religion* 3(Fall): 57–75.

LaBarre, Weston. 1970. *The Ghost Dance: The Origins of Religion*. New York: Dell.

LaHaye, Tim F. and Jerry Jenkins. 2000. *Left Behind: A Novel of the Earth's Last Days*. Carol Stream: Tyndale Publishing House.

Lambert, Yves. 1999. "Religion in Modernity as a New Axial Age: Secularization or New Religious Forms?" *Sociology of Religion* 60(3): 303–333.

Lame Deer, John and Richard Erdoes. 1972. *Lame Deer, Seeker of Visions*. Englewood Cliffs: Simon & Schuster.

Langer, Lawrence. 1991. *Holocaust Testimonies: The Ruins of Memory*. New Haven: Yale University Press.

Langford, Wendy. 1999. *Revolutions of the Heart: Gender, Power and the Dimensions of Love*. London: Routledge.

"Largest UCC Church in New England Votes to become Independent." 2004. *Boston Globe*, June 7. www.boston.com/news/local/connecticut/articles/2004/ 06/07/largest_ucc_church_in_new_england_votes_to_become_independent (accessed October 17, 2006).

Larson, Carin, David Madland and Clyde Wilcox. 2006. "Religious Lobbying in Virginia: How Institutions can Quiet Prophetic Voices." In *Representing God at the Statehouse: Religion and Politics in the American states*, ed. Edward Cleary and Allen Hertzke, 55–72. Lanham: Rowman & Littlefield.

Larson, Carin. 2004. "From Every Tribe and Nation? Blacks and the Christian Right." Paper presented at the Annual Meeting of the American Political Science Association, Chicago, IL. September 2–5.

LaVey, Anton Szandor. 1969. *The Satanic Bible*. New York: Avon.

LaVey, Anton Szandor. 1972. *The Satanic Rituals*. New York: Avon.

LaVey, Anton Szandor. 1989. *The Satanic Witch*. Los Angeles: Feral House.

Le Roy Ladurie, Emmanuel. 1978. *Montaillou: The Promised Land of Error*. New York: Vintage.

Lechner, F.J. 1991. "The Case against Secularization: A Rebuttal." *Social Forces* 69(4): 1103–1119.

Lefebvre, Henri. 1991. *The Production of Space*. Tr. Donald Nicholson-Smith. Oxford: Basil Blackwell.

Legality of the Threat or use of Nuclear Weapons, International Court of Justice. 1996. "Advisory Opinion, 49/75 K," www.icj-cij.org/icjwww/icases/iuna n/iunanframe.htm (accessed December 7, 2004).

Legué, Gabriel. 1903. *La Messe Noire*. Paris: E. Fasquelle.

Lemercier-Quelquejay, C. 1984. "From Tribe to Umma." *Central Asian Survey* 3(3): 15–38.

Leming, Laura M. 2007. "Sociological Explorations: What Is Religious Agency?" *The Sociological Quarterly* 48: 73–92.

Leonardo, Micaela di. 1987. "The Female World of Cards and Holidays: Women, Families and the World of Kinship." *Signs* 12(3): 440–453.

León-Portilla, Miguel. 1990. *Endangered Cultures*. Dallas: Southern Methodist University Press.

Lerner, Robert. 1972. *The Heresy of the Free Spirit in the Later Middle Ages*. Berkeley: University of California Press.

Leung, Beatrice. 1995. "Religious Freedom and the Constitution in the People's Republic of China: Interpretation and Implementation." *DISKUS* 3(1): 1–18.

Lévi-Strauss, Claude. 1970. *The Savage Mind*. Chicago: University of Chicago Press.

Levitt, P. 2007. *God Needs No Passport: Immigrants and the Changing American Religious Landscape*. New York: The New Press.

Lewis, D. 2008. *The Temptations of Tyranny in Central Asia*. London: Hurst.

Lienhardt, G. 1961. *Divinity and Experience*. Oxford: Clarendon.

Lincoln, Bruce. 1986. *Myth, Cosmos, and Society: Indo-European Themes of Creation and Destruction*. Harvard: Harvard University Press.

Lincoln, Bruce. 1989. *Discourse and the Construction of Society: Comparative Studies of Myth, Ritual, and Classification*. New York: Oxford University Press.

Lincoln, Bruce. 1996. "Theses on Method." *Method and Theory in the Study of Religion* 8(3): 225–227.

Lincoln, Bruce. 1998. "Conflict." In *Critical Terms for Religious Studies*, ed. Mark C. Taylor, 55–69. Chicago: University of Chicago Press.

Lincoln, Bruce. 2003. *Holy Terrors. Thinking About Religion After September 11*. Chicago: University of Chicago Press.

Lincoln, C. Eric and Lawrence H. Mamiya. 1990. *The Black Church in the African American Experience*. Durham, NC: Duke University Press.

Lindquist, G. 2005. *Conjuring Hope: Healing and Magic in Contemporary Russia*. Oxford: Berghahn Books.

Lipset, Seymour Martin. 1964. "Religion and American Values." In *The First New Nation*, ch. 4. New York: Basic Books.

Lipset, Seymour M. and Stein Rokkan, eds. 1967. *Party Systems and Voter Alignments: Cross-National Perspectives*. New York and London: Free Press.

Littel, Franklin Hamlin. 1962. *From State Church to Pluralism*. Chicago: Aldine.

Lloyd Warner, W. 1962. *American Life*. Chicago: University of Chicago Press.

Longhurst, John E. 1962. *The Age of Torquemada*. Lawrence: Coronado.

Lopez Jr, Donald. 1998. "Belief." In *Critical Terms for Religious Studies*, ed. Mark C. Taylor, 21–35. Chicago: University of Chicago Press.

Loseke, D.R. 1992. *The Battered Woman and Shelters: The Social Construction of Wife Abuse*. New York: State University of New York Press.

Louie, Miriam Ching. 1992. "Immigrant Asian Women in Bay Area Garment Sweatshops: 'After Sewing, Laundry, Cleaning and Cooking, I Have No Breath Left to Sing.' " *Amerasia Journal* 1: 1–26.

Löwendahl, Lena. 2002. *Med Kroppen som Instrument*. Lunds Universitet: Lund Studies in History of Religions.

Lowman, Catherine. 1988. *Annie Besant and Progressive Messianism*. Lewiston: Edwin Mellen Press.

Loy, David. 2002. *A Buddhist History of the West: Studies in Lack*. Albany: State University of New York Press.

Lozada, F. 2000. "Identity." In *Handbook of Postmodern Biblical Interpretation*, ed. A.K.M. Adam, 113–119. St. Louis: Chalice Press.

Lucas, Phillip. 1994. "How Future Wacos Might Be Avoided: Two Proposals," In *From the Ashes*, ed. James R. Lewis, 209–212. Lanham: Rowman & Littlefield

Luckman, T. 1967. *The Invisible Religion*. New York: Macmillan.

Luijpen, W.A. 1973. *Theology as Anthropology*. Pittsburgh: Duquesne University Press.

Lukenbill, B. 1998. "Observations of the Corporate Culture of a Gay and Lesbian Congregation." *Journal for the Scientific Study of Religion* 37(3): 440–552.

Luker, Kristin. 1985. *Abortion and the Politics of Motherhood*. Berkeley and Los Angeles: University of California Press.

Lukes, Steven. 1973. *Individualism*. Oxford: Basil Blackwell.

Luo, Zhufeng. 1991. *Religion under Socialism in China*. Armonk: M.E. Sharpe.

Luria, A.R. and F.I. Yudovich. 1971. *Speech and the Development of Mental Processes in the Child*. Harmondsworth: Penguin.

Luria, Keith P. 1989. "The Counter-Reformation and Popular Spirituality." In *Christian Spirituality: Post-Reformation and Modern*, ed. L. Dupré and D.E. Saliers, 93–120. New York: Crossroad.

Luria, Keith P. 1991. *Territories of Grace: Cultural Change in the Seventeenth-Century Diocese of Grenoble*. Berkeley: University of California Press.

Lynch, Gordon. 2002. *After Religion: 'Generation X' and the Search for Meaning*. London: Darton, Longman and Todd.

Lyons, Arthur. 1970. *The Second Coming: Satanism in America*. New York: Dodd, Mead.

Lyons, Arthur. 1988. *Satan Wants You: The Cult of Devil Worship in America*. New York: Mysterious Press.

Macdonald, Andrew [William Pierce]. 1996. *The Turner Diaries*. New York: Barricade Books. Originally published by National Alliance Vanguard Books, Arlington, in 1978.

MacInnis, D.E. 1989. *Religion in China Today: Policy and Practice*. Maryknoll: Orbis Books.

MacIntyre, Alisdair. 1966. *A Short History of Ethics: A History of Moral Philosophy from the Homeric to the Twentieth Century*. New York: Macmillan.

MacIntyre, A. 1971. *Against the Self-images of the Age*. London: Duckworth.

Mackerras, C. 1994. *China's Minorities: Integration and Modernization in the Twentieth Century*. Hong Kong: Oxford University Press.

Madsen, Richard. 1998. *China's Catholics: Tragedy and Hope in an Emerging Civil Society*. Berkeley: University of California Press.

Maduro, Otto. 1982. *Religion and Social Conflicts*. Maryknoll: Orbis Books.

Mahaffy, K. 1996. "Cognitive Dissonance and its Resolution: A Study of Lesbian Christians." *Journal for the Scientific Study of Religion* 35(4): 392–402.

Mahmood, Saba. 1996. "Interview with Talal Asad: Modern Power and the Reconfiguration of Religious Traditions." *SEHR* 5(1): Contested Polities (updated February 27, 1996). www.stanford.edu/group/SHR/5–1/text/asad.html (accessed March 5, 2008).

Mahmood, Saba. 1998. "Women's Piety and Embodied Discipline: The Islamic Resurgence in Contemporary Egypt." Unpublished Ph.D. Dissertation, Department of Anthropology, Stanford University.

Mahmood, Saba. 2005. *Politics of Piety: The Islamic Revival and the Feminist Subject*. Princeton: Princeton University Press.

Malik, F. 2003. *Queer Sexuality and Identity in the Qur'ān and Hadith*, www.well.com/user/aquarius/Qurannotes.htm (accessed April 2004).

Mandaville, Peter. 2005. "Sufis and Salafis: The Political Discourse of Transnational Islam." In *Remaking Muslim Politics: Pluralism, Contestation, Democratization*, ed. Robert W. Hefner, 302–326. Oxford: Princeton University Press.

Mandel, Ruth. 1989. "Turkish Headscarves and the 'Foreigner Problem': Constructing Difference through Emblems of Identity." *New German Critique* 46: 27–46.

Mandel, Ruth. 1996. "A Place of their Own: Contesting Spaces and Defining Places in Berlin's Migrant Community." In *Making Muslim Space in North America and Europe*, ed. Barbara Metcalf, 147–166. Los Angeles and London: University of California Press.

Mani, Lata. 1998. *Contentious Traditions: The Debate on Sati in Colonial India*. Berkeley and Los Angeles: University of California Press.

"Manifesto for the Christian Church," *Crosswinds*. Quoted in Berlet, Chip and John Salvi. 1996. *Abortion Clinic Violence, and Catholic Right Conspiracism*. Somerville: Political Research Associates, p. 8.

Manji, T. 2003. *The Trouble with Islam*. New York: Random House.

Marat, E. 2008. "Imagined Past, Uncertain Future: The Creation of National Ideologies in Kyrgyzstan and Tajikistan." *Problems of Post-Communism* 55(1): 12–24.

Marcos, Sylvia. 1995. "The Sacred Earth." *Concilium*, ed. Leonardo Boff and Virgilio Elizondo, 5(261): 27–37.

Martin, D. 1981. *Battered Wives*. San Francisco: New Glide.

Martin, David. 1998. *Does Christianity Cause War*. Oxford: Oxford University Press.

Martin, Emily. 1987. *The Woman in the Body: A Cultural Analysis of Reproduction*. Boston: Beacon Press.

Martin, John. 1987. "Popular Culture and the Shaping of Popular Heresy in Renaissance Venice." In *Inquisition and Society in Early Modern Europe*, ed. S. Haliczer, 115–128. Totowa: Barnes and Noble Books.

Martin, John. 1993. *Venice's Hidden Enemies: Italian Heretics in a Renaissance City*. Berkeley: University of California Press.

Martin, John. 1994. "Theories of Practice: Inquisition and the Discovery of Religion." Unpublished paper presented at Trinity University Humanities Symposium, Trinity University, San Antonio, Texas, November 17.

Martin, John. 1995. *Material Christianity: Religion and Popular Culture in America*. New Haven: Yale University Press.

Martin, T. D. 2001. *The Affirmative Action Empire: Nations and Nationalism in the Soviet Union, 1923–1939*. Ithaca: Cornell University Press.

Martin, V. 2001. *Law and Custom in the Steppe: The Kazakhs of the Middle Horde and Russian Colonialism in the Nineteenth Century*. Richmond: Curzon Press.

Martin, William. 2005. *With God on Our Side: The Rise of the Religious Right in America*. New York: Broadway.

Marx, Karl. 1974. *On Religion*. Ed. Saul K. Padover. New York: McGraw-Hill.

Massey, D.S. 1990. "The Social and Economic Origins of Migration." *The Annals of the American Academy of Political and Social Science* 510(1): 60–72.

Massey, D.S., J. Durand and N.J. Malone. 2002. *Beyond Smoke and Mirrors: Mexican Immigration in an Era of Economic Integration*. New York: Russell Sage

Massumi, Brian. 2002. *Parables for the Virtual: Movement, Affect, Sensation*. Durham, NC: Duke University Press.

Masuzawa, Tomoko. 2005. *The Invention of World Religions Or, How European Universalism Was Preserved in the Language of Pluralism*. Chicago and London: University of Chicago Press.

Matley, I.M. 1994. "The Population and the Land." In *Central Asia: 130 Years of Russian Dominance, a Historical Overview*, ed. E. Allworth. 3rd edn. Durham, NC and London: Duke University Press.

Matovina, Timothy and Gary Riebe-Estrella. 2002. "Días de los Muertos." In *Horizons of the Sacred: Mexican Catholic Traditions in U.S. Catholicism*, ed. Timothy Matovina and Gary Riebe-Estrella. Ithaca: Cornell University Press.

Matters, Michael D. 1992. "Some Cultural Correlates of Congregational Participation in the Sanctuary Movement." Paper prepared for the annual meeting of the Midwest Sociological Society, Kansas City.

Maxwell, Carol. 2002. *Pro-life Activists in America: Meaning, Motivation and Direct Action*. Cambridge: Cambridge University Press.

Mayer, J. 2002. *Nuclear Peace: The Story of the Trident Three*. London: Mackays of Chatham.

McAdam, Doug. 1982. *Political Process and the Development of Black Insurgency, 1930–1970*. Chicago: University of Chicago Press.

McBrien, J. 2006a. "Listening to the Wedding Speaker: Discussing Religion and Culture in Southern Kyrgyzstan." *Central Asian Survey* 25(3): 341–357.

McBrien, J. 2006b. "Extreme Conversations: Secularism, Religious Pluralism, and the Rhetoric of Islamic Extremism in Southern Kyrgyzstan." In *The Postsocialist Religious Question: Faith and Power in Central Asia and East-Central Europe*, ed. C.M. Hann et al. Berlin: Lit Verlag.

McBrien, J. and M. Pelkmans. 2008. "Turning Marx on His Head: 'Extremists', Missionaries, and Archaic Secularists in Post-Soviet Kyrgyzstan." *Critique of Anthropology* 28(1): 87–103.

McCormick Maaga, Mary. 1996. "Triple Erasure: Women and Power in Peoples Temple." Ph.D. diss. Drew University.

McCutcheon, Russell. 1997. *Manufacturing Religion: The Discourse on* Sui Generis *Religion and the Politics of Nostalgia*. Oxford: Oxford University Press.

McFadyen, A. 2000. *Bound to Sin*. Cambridge: Cambridge University Press.

McGuire, Meredith B. 1983. "Discovering Religious Power." *Sociological Analysis* 44(1): 1–10.

McGuire, Meredith B. 1996. "Religion and Healing the Mind/Body/Self." *Social Compass* 43(1): 101–116.

McGuire, Meredith B. 2008. *Lived Religion: Faith and Practice in Everyday Life*. New York: Oxford University Press.

McGuire, Meredith B., with Debra Kautor. 1988. *Ritual Healing in Suburban America*. New Brunswick: Rutgers University Press.

McIntosh, A. 2001. "God versus Trident: Constitutional Theology in Legal Defense of Ellen Moxley of the 'Greenock Three' Peace Women. God v. Trident Nuclear Submarines," www.alastairmcintosh.com/articles/2000_trident.htm (accessed June 1, 2005).

McLoughlin, William G. 1978. *Revivals, Awakenings, and Reform: An Essay on Religion and Social Change in America, 1607–1977*. Chicago: University of Chicago Press.

McNeill, J.T. 1933. "Folk-Paganism in the Penitentials." *Journal of Religion* 13.

McNeill, J.T. and H.M. Gamer, eds. 1938. *Medieval Handbooks of Penance*. New York: Columbia University Press.

Mead, Sidney E. 1963. *The Lively Experiment: The Shaping of Christianity in America*. New York: Harper & Row.

Melech, Aubrey. 1986. *Missa Niger: La Messe Noire*. Northampton: Sut Anubis.

Mellor, Philip A. and Chris Shilling. 1994. "Reflexive Modernity and the Religious Body." *Religion* 24: 23–42.

Menjívar, Cecilia. 1999. Religious institutions and transnationalism: A case study of Catholic and evangelical Salvadoran immigrants. *International Journal of Politics, Culture, and Society* 12: 589–612.

Mercer, Calvin and Thomas W. Durham. 1999. "Religious Mysticism and Gender Orientation." *Journal for the Scientific Study of Religion* 38(1): 175–182.

Mernissi, F. 1991. *The Veil and the Male Elite*. Reading, MA: Addison-Wesley.

Midelfort, H.C. Erik. 1982. "Witchcraft, Magic and the Occult." In *Reformation Europe: A Guide to Research*, ed. S. Ozment, 183–209. St. Louis: Center for Reformation Research.

Miller, David. 2005. Interview by Carin Robinson, March 22.

Miller, Donald E. 1997. *Reinventing American Protestanism: Christianity in the New Millennium*. Berkeley and Los Angeles: University of California Press.

Miller, Jean Baker. 1991. "The Development of Women's Sense of Self." In *Women's Growth in Connection*, ed. J.V. Jordan, A.G. Kaplan, J. Baker Miller, I.P. Stiver and J.L. Surrey, 11–26. New York: Guildford.

Mills, C. 2005. "Turkmenbashy: The Propagation of Personal Rule in Contemporary Turkmenistan." Ph.D. thesis, St Andrews, University of St Andrews.

Millward, J.A. 1998. *Beyond the Pass: Economy, Ethnicity, and Empire in Qing Central Asia, 1759–1864*. Stanford: Stanford University Press.

Millward, J.A. 2007. *Eurasian Crossroads: A History of Xinjiang*. New York: Columbia University Press.

Min, P.G. 1992. "The Structure and Social Functions of Korean Immigrant Churches in the United States." *International Migration Review* 26(4): 1370–1394.

Min, P.G. and J.H. Kim. 2003. *Religious in Asian America: Building Faith Communities*. Walnut Creek: AltaMira Press.

Mitani Takashi. 1978. "Nankinseifu to meishindaha undō, 1928–1929" (The Nanjing Government and the Smashing Superstition Movement, 1928–1929). *Rekishigaku kenkyū* (Journal of History) 455: 1–14.

Mitchell, Arnold. 1983. *The Nine American Lifestyles*. New York: Macmillan.

Moghadam, Valentine. 1994. *Identity, Politics and Women: Cultural Reassertions and Feminisms in an International Perspective*. Boulder: Westview Press.

Moghissi, Haideh. 1999. *Feminism and Islamic Fundamentalism: The Limits of Postmodern Analysis*. New York: Zed Books.

Monter, William. 1983. *Ritual, Myth, and Magic in Early Modern Europe*. Brighton: Harvester.

Mooney, M.A. 2009. *Faith Makes Us Live: Surviving and Thriving in the Haitian Diaspora*. Los Angeles: University of California Press.

Moore, Carol. 1995. *The Davidian Massacre: Disturbing Questions about Waco Which Must Be Answered*. Franklin and Springfield: Legacy Communications and Gun Owners Foundation.

Moore, S. 2001. *God's Beauty Parlour and Other Queer Spaces in and Around the Bible*. Stanford: Stanford University Press.

Morganthau, Tom, Michael Isikoff and Bob Cohn. 1995. "The Echoes of Ruby Ridge." *Newsweek*, August 28, 25–28.

Morris, Colin. 1989. *The Papal Monarchy: The Western Church from 1050 to 1250*. Oxford: Clarendon Press.

Mossman, M.J. 1987. "Feminism and Legal Method: The Difference it Makes." *Wisconsin Women's Law Journal* 3: 142–168.

Muir, Edward. 1997. *Ritual in Early Modern Europe*. Cambridge: Cambridge University Press.

Mulgan, Geoffrey. 1994. *Politics in an Antipolitical Age*. Cambridge: Polity.

Mullett, Michael. 1987. *Popular Culture and Popular Protest in Late Medieval and Early Modern Europe*. London: Croom Helm.

Murphy, Kim. 1999a. "Hate's Affluent New Godfathers." *Los Angeles Times*, January 10, A14.

Murphy, Kim. 1999b. "Last Stand of an Aging Aryan." *Los Angeles Times*, January 10, A1.

Murzakhalilov, K. 2004. "Proselytism in Kyrgyzstan." *Central Asia and the Caucasus: Journal of Social and Political Studies* 25(1): 83–7.

Muslimische Jugend Deutschland (MJD). Homepage. www. ijd-net.de (accessed January 2, 2008).

Musson, A.E. and E. Robinson. 1969. *Science and Technology in the Industrial Revolution*. Manchester: Manchester University Press.

Nahas, O. 1998. *Islamic Studies on Homosexuality*. YOESUF Foundation, www.yoesuf.nl/engels/islamic_studies.html (accessed September 2004).

Nahas, O. 2001. *Islam en Homoseksualiteit*. Amsterdam: Bulaaq.

Nahas, O. 2004. "Yoesuf: An Islamic Idea with Dutch Quality." *Journal of Gay and Lesbian Social Services* 16(1): 53–64.

Nason-Clark, N. 1995. "Conservative Protestants and Violence against Women: Exploring the Rhetoric and the Response." In *Sex, Lies and Sanctity: Religion and Deviance in Modern America*, ed. M.J. Neitz and M. Goldman, 109–130. Greenwich, CT: JAI Press.

Nason-Clark, N. 1996. "Religion and Violence against Women: Exploring the Rhetoric and the Response of Evangelical Churches in Canada." *Social Compass* 43(4): 515–536.

Nason-Clark, N. 1997. *The Battered Wife: How Christians Confront Family Violence.* Louisville: Westminster John Knox Press.

Nason-Clark, N. 1998. "The Evangelical Family is Sacred, but is it Safe?" In *Healing the Hurting: Giving Hope and Help to Abused Women,* ed. C.C. Kroeger and J. Beck, 109–125. Grand Rapids: Baker Publishing House.

Nason-Clark, N. 1999. "Shattered Silence or Holy Hush: Emerging Definitions of Violence against Women." *Journal of Family Ministry* 13(1): 39–56.

Nason-Clark, N. 2000a. "Making the Sacred Safe: Woman Abuse and Communities of Faith." *Sociology of Religion* 61(4): 349–368.

Nason-Clark, N. 2000b. "Has the Silence been Shattered or does a Holy Hush still Prevail? Defining Violence against Women within Christian Churches." In *Bad Pastors: Clergy Malfeasance in America,* ed. A. Shupe, 69–89. Albany: New York University Press.

Nason-Clark, N. 2004. "When Terror Strikes at Home: The Interface between Religion and Domestic Violence." *Journal for the Scientific Study of Religion* 42(3): 303–310.

Nason-Clark, N. 2006. "When Terror Strikes at Home: The Role of Religious Professionals." *Faith-Based Forum on Family Violence for Justice Professionals and Clergy.* West Palm Beach.

Nason-Clark, N. and B. Fisher-Townsend. 2005. "Gender." In *Handbook on Sociology of Religion and Social Institutions,* ed. H.R. Ebaugh, 207–223. New York: Plenum Press.

Nason-Clark, N. and B. Fisher-Townsend. 2008. *Acting Abusively: Faith, Hope and Charity in the Lives of Violent Men.* Manuscript in progress.

Nason-Clark, N. and C.C. Kroeger. 2004. *Refuge from Abuse: Hope and Healing for Abused Christian Women.* Downers Grove: InterVarsity Press.

Nason-Clark, N., L. Mitchell and L.G. Beaman. 2004. *Bridge Building between Churches and Community Resources: An Overview of the Work of the Religion and Violence Research Team.* Unpublished manuscript.

Nason-Clark, N., S. McMullin, V. Fahlberg and D. Schaefer. 2009. *Referal Networks between Sacred and Secular Sources of Assistance for Abuse in Religious Families.* Manuscript submitted for review.

Nason-Clark, N., N. Murphy, B. Fisher-Townsend and L. Ruff. 2003. "An Overview of the Characteristics of the Clients at a Faith-based Batterers' Intervention Program." *Journal of Religion and Abuse* 5(4): 51–72.

Naz Project. 1999. *How to Reach, Hard to Teach.* London: Naz Project.

Naz Project. 2000. *Emerging Sexualities.* London: Naz Project.

Needham, R. 1972. *Belief, Language, and Experience.* Oxford: Basil Blackwell.

Neitz, Mary Jo. 1987. *Charisma and Community: A Study of Religious Commitment within the Charismatic Renewal.* New Brunswick: Transaction.

Nevins, Allan ed. 1964. *Lincoln and the Gettysburg Address.* Urbana: University of Illinois Press.

Newman, Andy. 2005. "Connecticut Episcopalians Defy Bishop over Gay Issues." *New York Times,* April 14, B1.

Niebuhr, Reinhold. 1963. *The Religion of Abraham Lincoln.* New York.

Nietzsche, Friedrich. [1883–1885] 1981. *Thus Spoke Zarathustra.* Harmondsworth: Penguin.

Noden, Kirk. 2002. "Building Power in Forty Languages: A Story about Organizing Immigrants in Chicago's Albany Park." *Social Policy* 2: 47–52.

Nökel, Sigrid. 2002. *Die Töchter der Gastarbeiter und der Islam. Zur Soziologie alltagsweltlicher Anerkennungspolitiken. Eine Fallstudie.* Bielefeld Transcript Verlag.

Norris, P. and R. Inglehart. 2004. *Sacred and Secular: Religion and Politics Worldwide.* Cambridge: Cambridge University Press.

North, Gary. 1973. *An Introduction to Christian Economics.* Tyler: Institute for Christian Economics.

North, Gary. 1984. *Backward, Christian Soldiers? An Action Manual for Christian Reconstruction.* Tyler: Institute for Christian Economics.

North, Gary. 1988. *Unconditional Surrender: God's Program for Victory.* Tyler: Institute for Christian Economics.

North, Gary. 1990. *Millennialism and Social Theory.* Tyler: Institute for Christian Economics.

North, Gary. 1994. *Lone Gunners for Jesus: Letters to Paul J. Hill.* Tyler: Institute for Christian Economics.

Nussbaum, Martha and Jonathan Glover, eds. 1996. *Women, Culture, and Development: A Study of Human Capabilities.* Oxford: Oxford University Press.

Nye, Robert A., ed. 1999. *Sexuality: A Reader.* Oxford: Oxford University Press.

Obelkevich, James, ed. 1979. *Religion and the People, 800–1700*. Chapel Hill: University of North Carolina Press.

Ochs, Mary and Mayron Payes. 2003. "Immigrant Organizing: Patterns, Challenges and Opportunities." *Social Policy* 4: 19–24.

Ohira Kōji. 2000. "Chūgoku Bukkyō no kindaika wo saguru: Taikyo no shoki Bukkyō kaika undō" (A Study of the Modernization of Chinese Buddhism: The Early Period of Taixu's Chinese Buddhism Reform Movement). *Ritsumeikan tōyō shigaku* (Ritsumeikan Journal of Oriental Studies) 23.

Ohira Kōji. 2002. "Nankin kokuminseifu seirituki no byōsankogaku undō to Bukkyōkai" (The Convert Temples to Schools Movement and Buddhist Society during the Formative Period of the Nanjing Government: On Utilizing the Property of Temples and Monks). *Ritsumeikan gengo bunka kenkyū* (Ritsumeikan Journal of Language and Cultural Studies) 13(4): 21–38.

Okin, Susan Moller. 1997. "Is Multiculturalism Bad for Women?" *Boston Review*, http://bostonreview.net/BR22.5/okin.html (accessed October 6, 2008).

Olds, Linda E. 1981. *Fully Human: How Everyone Can Integrate the Benefits of Masculine and Feminine Sex Roles*. Englewood Cliffs: Prentice-Hall.

Orsi, Robert Anthony. 1997. "Everyday Miracles: The Study of Lived Religion." In *Lived Religion in America: Towards a History of Practice*, ed. David H. Hall, 3–21. Princeton: Princeton University Press.

Orsi, Robert Anthony. 2003. "Is the Study of Lived Religion Irrelevant to the World We Live in? Special Presidential Plenary Address." *Journal for the Scientific Study of Religion* 42(2): 169–174.

Orsi, Robert Anthony. 2005. *Between Heaven and Earth: The Religious Worlds People Make and the Scholars Who Study Them*. Princeton: Princeton University Press.

Overmyer, Daniel, ed. 2003. *Religion in China Today*. Cambridge: Cambridge University Press.

Pagnucco, R. 1996. "A Comparison of the Political Behavior of Faith-Based and Secular Peace Groups." In *Disruptive Religion: The Force of Faith in Social-movement Activism*, ed. C. Smith, 205–222. New York: Routledge.

Pandey, Gyanendra. 1992. "In Defense of the Fragment: Writing About Hindu-Muslim Riots in Indian Today." *Representations* 37, Special issue: *Imperial Fantasies and Postcolonial Histories* (Winter): 27–55.

Pape, Robert. 2005. *Dying to Win: The Strategic Logic of Suicide Terrorism*. New York: Random House.

Parker G., Cristián. 1994. "La Sociología de la Religión y la Modernidad: Por una Revisión Crítica de las Categorías Durkheimianas desde América Latina." *Revista Mexicana de Sociología* 4: 229–254.

Parrinder, G. 1996. *Sexual Morality in the World's Religions*. Oxford: Oneworld.

Payne, Neill H. 1996. "Shades of Waco: CAUSE Negotiates Peaceful End to Siege of Justus Township Standoff." *The Balance: A Newsletter of Civil Rights and Current Events* 7(2): 1–3.

Peirce, C.S. 1986. *Writings of C. S. Peirce*. Vol. 3. Bloomington: Indiana University Press.

Pelkmans, M. 2006a. "Asymmetries on the 'Religious Market' in Kyrgyzstan." In *The Postsocialist Religious Question: Faith and Power in Central Asia and East-Central Europe*, ed. C.M. Hann *et al.* Berlin: Lit Verlag.

Pelkmans, M. 2006b. *Defending the Border: Identity, Religion, and Modernity in the Republic of Georgia*. Ithaca: Cornell University Press.

Pelkmans, M. 2007. " 'Culture' as a Tool and an Obstacle: Missionary Encounters in Post-Soviet Kyrgyzstan." *Journal of the Royal Anthropological Institute* 13(4): 881–899.

Pelkmans, M. 2009. "Temporary Conversions: Encounters with Pentecostalism in Muslim Kyrgyzstan." In *Conversion after Socialism: Disruptions, Modernisms, and Technologies of Faith in the Former Soviet Union*, ed. M. Pelkmans. Oxford: Berghahn Books.

Percy, Martyn. 1996. *Words, Wonders and Power*. London: SPCK.

Perdue, P.C. 2005. *The Qing Conquest of Central Eurasia*. Cambridge, MA: Harvard University Press.

Perrin, Robin D. and Armand L. Mauss. 1991. "Saints and Seekers: Sources of Recruitment to the Vineyard Christian Fellowship." *Review of Religious Research* 33(December): 97–111.

Perry, Everett and Dean Hoge. 1981. "Faith Priorities of Pastor and Laity as a Factor in the Growth or Decline of Presbyterian Congregations." *Review of Religious Research* 22(3): 221–232.

Peterson, Anna Lisa, Manuel A. Vásquez and Philip J. Williams, eds. 2001. *Christianity, Social Change, and Globalization in the Americas*. New Brunswick: Rutgers University Press.

Peterson, Derek and Darren Walhof. 2002. *The Invention of Religion: Rethinking Belief in Politics and*

History. New Brunswick, NJ and London: Rutgers University Press.

Peyrouse, S. 2004. "Christianity and Nationality in Soviet and Post-Soviet Central Asia: Mutual Intrusions and Instrumentalizations." *Nationalities Papers* 32(3): 651–674.

Phelps Stokes, Anson. 1950. *Church and State in the United States*, vol. 1. New York: Harper & Co.

Phillips, Kevin. 2007. *American Theocracy: The Peril and Politics of Radical Religion, Oil, and Borrowed Money in the 21st Century*. New York: Penguin.

Philpott, Daniel. 2001. *Revolutions in Sovereignty: How Ideas Shaped Modern International Relations*. Princeton: Princeton University Press.

Piore, Michael J. and Charles F. Sabel. 1984. *The Second Industrial Divide: Possibilities for Prosperity*. New York: Basic Books.

Pittman, Don A. 2001. *Toward a Modern Chinese Buddhism: Taixu's Reforms*. Honolulu: University of Hawai'i Press.

Plummer, Don. 2005. "Sharpton Knocks Bush; Gays are Used to Duck Real Issues, He Says Here." *Atlanta Journal-Constitution*, January 10, 3B.

Poloma, Margaret M. 1989. *The Assemblies of God at the Crossroads: Charisma and Institutional Dilemmas*. Knoxville: University of Tennessee Press.

Poloma, Margaret M. and Lynette F. Hoelter. 1998. "The 'Toronto Blessing': A Holistic Model of Healing." *Journal for the Scientific Study of Religion* 66: 257–271.

Ponticelli, C.M. 1996. "The Spiritual Warfare of Exodus: A Postpositivist Research Adventure." *Qualitative Inquiry* 2(2): 198–219.

Portes, A., C. Escobar and A.W. Radford. 2007. "Immigrant Transnational Organizations and Development: A Comparative Study." *International Migration Review* 41(1): 242–281.

Potter, H. 2007. "Battered Black Women's Use of Religious Services and Spirituality for Assistance in Leaving Abusive Relationships." *Violence Against Women* 13(3): 262–284.

Potter, P.B. 2003. "Belief in Control: Regulation of Religion in China." In *Religion in China Today*, ed. d. Overmyer. Cambridge: Cambridge University Press.

Pratt, Richard. 1982. *Every Thought Captive*. Phillipsburg: Presbyterian and Reformed Publishing Company.

Prell, Riv-Ellen. 1989. *Prayer and Community: The Havurah in American Judaism*. Detroit: Wayne State University Press.

Prince, Robert. 1985. *The Legacy of the Holocaust: Psychological Themes in the Second Generation*. Ann Arbor: UMI Research Press.

Pringle, Rosemary. 1989. *Secretaries Talk: Sexuality, Power and Work*. Sydney: Allen and Unwin.

Pritchard, Linda. 1984. "The Burned-over District Reconsidered: A Portent of Evolving Religious Pluralism in the United States." *Social Science History* 8(Summer): 243–265.

Privratsky, B.G. 2001. *Muslim Turkistan: Kazak Religion and Collective Memory*. Richmond: Curzon.

Ptacek, J. 1988a. "How Men Who Batter Rationalize Their Behavior." In *Abuse and Religion: When Praying isn't Enough*, ed. A. Horton and J. Williamson, 247–258. New York: DC Heath and Company.

Ptacek, J. 1988b. "Why Do Men Batter Their Wives?" In *Feminist Perspectives on Wife Abuse*, ed. K. Yllo and M. Bograd, 133–158. Newbury Park: Sage Publications Inc.

Ptak, R. 2007. *Die maritime Seidenstrasse. Küstenräume, Seefahrt und Handel in vorkolonialer Zeit*. München: Beck.

Putnam, Robert. 2000. *Bowling Alone: The Collapse and Revival of American Community*. New York: Simon & Schuster.

Quaker Peace Service. 1987. *Speaking our Peace: Exploring Nonviolence and Conflict Resolution*. London: Friends House, Quaker Peace and Service.

Quarles, Chester L. 2004. *Christian Identity: The Aryan American Bloodline Religion*. Jefferson: McFarland & Co.

Quijano, Anibal. 2000. "Coloniality of Power, Eurocentrism and Latin America." *Nepantla* 1(3): 533–580.

Radcliffe-Brown, A.R. 1952 [1939]. "Taboo." In *Structure and Function in Primitive Society*. London: Cohen and West.

Rambo, Lewis R. 1999. "Theories of Conversion: Understanding and Interpreting Religious Change." *Social Compass* 46(3): 259–271.

Rantanen, Terhi. 2005. "The Message is the Medium: An Interview with Manuel Castells." *Global Media and Communication* 1: 135–147.

Ray, Paul H. and Sherry Ruth Anderson. 2000. *The Cultural Creatives*. New York: Three Rivers Press.

Reader, Ian. "Imagined Persecution: Aum Shinrikyo, Millennialism, and the Legitimation of Violence." In *Millennialism, Persecution, and Violence: Historical Cases*, ed. Catherine Wessinger, 138–152. Syracuse: Syracuse University Press.

Reader, Ian. 1996. *A Poisonous Cocktail? Aum Shinrikyo's Path to Violence*. Copenhagen: Nordic Institute of Asian Studies Books.

Reavis, Dick J. 1995. *The Ashes of Waco: An Investigation*. New York: Simon & Schuster.

Redstone, I. and D.S. Massey. 2004. "Coming to Stay: An Analysis of the U.S. Census Question on Year of Arrival." *Demography* 41(4): 721–738.

Repstad, P. 2003. "The Powerlessness of Religious Power in a Pluralist Society." *Social Compass* 50(2): 161–173.

Richardson, James T. 1995. "Manufacturing Consent about Koresh: A Structural Analysis of the Role of Media in the Waco Tragedy." In *Armageddon in Waco: Critical Perspectives on the Branch Davidian Conflict*, ed. Stuart A. Wright. Chicago: University of Chicago Press, 153–176.

Richardson, James T. 2004. "A Critique of 'Brainwashing' Claims about New Religious Movements." In *Cults in Context: Readings in the Study of New Religious Movements*, ed. Lorne L. Dawson, 217–228. New Brunswick: Transaction Publishers.

Richter, Philip and Leslie J. Francis. 1998: *Gone but not Forgotten: Church Leaving and Returning*. London: Darton, Longman and Todd.

Ridgeon, L. 2003. *Major World Religions*. London: RoutledgeCurzon.

Rieff, Philip. 1987. *The Triumph of the Therapeutic*. London: Chatto and Windus.

Ro'i, Y. 2000. *Islam in the Soviet Union: From the Second World War to Gorbachev*. London: Hurst.

Roald, A. 1997. "Feminist Reinterpretation of Islamic Sources: Muslim Feminist Theology in the Light of Christian Tradition of Feminist Thought." In *Women and Islamisation*, ed. K. Ask and M. Tjomsland, 14–36. Bergen: Chr. Michelsen Institute.

Roald, A. 2001. *Women in Islam*. London: Routledge.

Robbins, J. 2004. "The Globalization of Pentecostal and Charismatic Christianity." *Annual Review of Anthropology* 33: 117–143.

Robbins, Thomas and Dick Anthony. 1995. "Sects and Violence: Factors Enhancing the Volatility of Marginal Religious Movements." In *Armageddon in Waco: Critical Perspectives on the Branch Davidian Conflict*, ed. Stuart A. Wright, 236–259 (Chicago: University of Chicago Press, 1995).

Robinson, Carin. 2006. "From Every Tribe and Nation? Blacks and the Christian Right." *Social Science Quarterly* 87: 591–601.

Rodriguez, E.M. and S.C. Ouellette. 2000. "Gay and Lesbian Christians: Homosexual and Religious Identity Integration in the Members of a Gay-Positive Church." *Journal for the Scientific Study of Religion* 39(3): 333–347.

Roof, Wade Clark. 1993. *A Generation of Seekers: The Spiritual Journeys of the Baby Boom Generation*. San Francisco: Harper.

Roof, Wade Clark. 1996. "God is in the Details: Reflections on Religion's Public Presence in the United States in the Mid-1990s." *Sociology of Religion* 57: 149–162.

Roof, Wade Clark. 1999. *Spiritual Marketplace: Baby Boomers and the Remaking of American Religion*. Princeton: Princeton University Press.

Roof, Wade Clark and William McKinney. 1987. *American Mainline Religion: Its Changing Shape and Future*. New Brunswick: Rutgers University Press.

Roozen, David A., William McKinney and Wayne Thompson. 1990. "The 'Big Chill' Generation Warms to Worship." *Review of Religious Research* 31(March): 314–322.

Rose, Nikalas. 1999. *Inventing Our Selves: Psychology, Power and Personhood*. Cambridge: Cambridge University Press.

Rose, Stuart. 1998. "An Examination of the New Age Movement: Who is Involved and What Constitutes its Spirituality." *Journal of Contemporary Religion* 13(1): 5–22.

Rose, Susan D. 1987. "Women Warriors: The Negotiation of Gender in a Charismatic Community." *Sociological Analysis* 48(Fall): 245–258.

Rothkrug, Lionel. 1979. "Popular Religion and Holy Shrines: Their Influence on the Origins of the German Reformation and Their Role in German Cultural Development." In *Religion and the People, 800–1700*, ed. J. Obelkevich, 20–87. Chapel Hill: University of North Carolina Press.

Rotunda, R.J., G. Williamson and M. Penfold. 2004. "Clergy Response to Domestic Violence: A Preliminary Survey of Clergy Members, Victims and Batterers." *Pastoral Psychology* 52(4): 353–365.

Rowe, Henry K. 1924. *The History of Religion in the United States*. New York: Macmillan.

Roy, Oliver. 2004. *Globalized Islam: The Search for a New Umma*. New York: Colombia University Press.

Rudelson, J.J. 1997. *Oasis Identities: Uyghur Nationalism along China's Silk Road*. New York: Columbia University Press.

Rushdoony, R.J. 1978. *By What Standard?* Tyler: Thoburn Press.

Rushdoony, Rousas John. 1973. *Institutes of Biblical Law*. Nutley: Craig Press.

Russell, Jeffrey Burton. 1972. *Witchcraft in the Middle Ages*. Ithaca: Cornell University Press.

Ryan, Mary. 1981. *Cradle of the Middle Class: The Family in Oneida County, New York, 1790–1865*. Cambridge: Cambridge University Press.

Sade, Marquis de. 1797. *Juliette*. Reprint, New York: Grove Press, 1968.

Sade, Marquis de. 2000. *Philosophy in the Boudoir*. Tr. Meredith X. New York: Creation Books.

Safra Project. 2002. *Identifying the Difficulties Experienced by Muslim Lesbian, Bisexual and Transgender Women in Accessing Social and Legal Services*. London: Safra Project.

Saghal, Sita and Nira Yuval-Davis. 1992. *Refusing Holy Orders: Women and Fundamentalism in Britain*. London: Virago.

Sakamoto Hiroko. 1998. "Yō Bunkai" (Yang Wenhui). In *Kindai Chūgoku no shisakushatachi* (Modern Chinese Thinkers), ed. Satō Shinichi. Tokyo: Taishukan shoten.

Saletan, William. 2003. *Bearing Right: How Conservatives Won the Abortion War*. Berkeley: University of California Press.

Salih, Ruba. 2003. *Gender in Transnationalism: Home, Longing and Belonging among Moroccan Migrant Women*. London: Routledge.

Samad, Y. 1998. "Media and Muslim Identity: Intersections of Generation and Gender." *Innovation* 11(4): 425–438.

Sanktanber, Ayse. 2002. " 'We Pray like You Have Fun': New Islamic Youth in Turkey between Intellectualism and Popular Culture." In *Fragments of Culture*, ed. Deniz Kandiyoti and Ayse Saktanber, 254–277. London: I.B. Tauris & Co.

Saroyan, M. 1997. *Minorities, Mullahs and Modernity: Reshaping Community in the Former Soviet Union*. Ed. Edward W. Walker. University of California Press/University of California International and Area Studies Digital Collection, Edited Volume #95, available at: http://repositories.cdlib.org/uciaspubs/research/95 (accessed July 22, 2009).

Scheff, Thomas. 1979. *Catharsis in Healing, Ritual and Drama*. Berkeley: University of California Press.

Schiffer, Sabine. 2005. "Der Islam in Deutschen Medien." *Muslime in Europa*, Aus Politik und Zeitgeschichte 20: 23–30.

Schmitt, Jean Claude. 1983. *The Holy Greyhound: Guinefort, Healer of Children since the Thirteenth Century*. Cambridge: Cambridge University Press.

Schmitz, Dan. 2001. "Landlord Lawsuit Puts Gospel into Real-Life Context." *Covenant News*, April 26. Accessed at www.covchurch.org/cov/news/item1505.html.

Scott, David. 2000. "Toleration and Historical Traditions of Difference." *Subaltern Studies* XI: 288–289.

Scott, K.L. and Wolfe, D.A. 2000. "Change among Batterers: Examining Men's Success Stories." *Journal of Interpersonal Violence* 15(8): 827–842.

Scribner, Robert W. 1984a. "Cosmic Order and Daily Life: Sacred and Secular in Pre-industrial German Society." In *Religion and Society in Early Modern Europe, 1500–1800*, ed. K. von Greyerz, 17–32. London: Allen and Unwin.

Scribner, Robert W. 1984b. "Ritual and Popular Religion in Catholic Germany at the Time of the Reformation." *Journal of Ecclesiastical History* 35(1): 47–77.

Scribner, Robert W. 1990. "The Reformation Movements in Germany." In *The New Cambridge Modern History*, vol. 2, 2nd edn, ed. G.R. Elton, 69–93. Cambridge: Cambridge University Press.

Scribner, Robert W. 1993. "The Reformation, Popular Magic, and the 'Disenchantment of the World'." *Journal of Interdisciplinary History* 23(3): 475–494.

Scribner, Robert W. 1994. "Elements of Popular Belief." In *Handbook of European History, 1400–1600: Late Middle Ages, Renaissance, and Reformation*, ed. T.A. Brady Jr., H.A. Oberman and J.D. Tracy, 231–255. Leiden: Brill.

Seidman, Steven. 1991. *Romantic Longings: Love in America, 1803–1989*. London: Routledge.

Seminare Docherty, Jayne. 1998. "When the Parties Bring Their Gods to the Table: Learning Lessons from Waco." Ph.D. diss., George Mason UniversityCary R. W. Voss, Communications, University of Kansas.

Sennett, Richard. 1977. *The Fall of Public Man*. Cambridge: Cambridge University Press.

Shahrani, N. 1984. " 'From Tribe to Umma': Comments on the Dynamics of Identity in Muslim Soviet Central Asia." *Central Asian Survey* 3(3): 27–38.

Sharma, Ursula. 1995. *Complementary Medicine Today: Practitioners and Patients*. London: Routledge.

Sharma, Ursula and Paula Black. 1999. *The Sociology of Pampering: Beauty Therapy as a Form of Work*.

Working Paper. University of Derby: Centre for Social Research.

Sharot, Stephen. 2001. *A Comparative Sociology of World Religions: Virtuosos, Priests; and Popular Religion.* New York: New York University Press.

Shaw, Rosalind and Charles Stewart. 1994. "Introduction: Problematizing Syncretism." In *Syncretism/Anti-Syncretism: The Politics of Religious Synthesis,* ed. Rosalind Shaw and Stewart Charles, 1–26. London: Routledge.

Sheth, N.R. 1994. "Children of the Same God: A Spiritual Approach to Social Transformation." Working Paper No. 59, Gujarati Institute of Development Research, Ahmedabad.

Shibley, Mark A. 1996. *Resurgent Evangelicalism in the United States: Mapping Cultural Change Since 1970.* Columbia: University of South Carolina Press.

Shuck, Glenn. 2004. *Marks of the Beast: The* Left Behind *Novels and the Struggle for Evangelical Identity.* New York: New York University Press.

Shupe, A., W.A. Stacey and L.R. Hazlewood. 1987. *Violent Men, Violent Couples: The Dynamics of Domestic Violence.* Lexington: D.C. Heath and Company.

Sklair, Leslie. 2001. *The Transnational Capitalist Class.* Oxford: Blackwell.

Skovgaard-Petersen, Jakob. 1997. *Defining Islam for the Egyptian State Muftis and Fatwas of the Dār al-Iftā.* Leiden: Brill.

Slatter, Allison. 2004. Interview by Carin Robinson, November 9.

Slezkine, Y. 1994. "The USSR as a Communal Apartment, or How a Socialist State Promoted Ethnic Particularism." *Slavic Review* 53(2): 414–452.

Slocum, J.W. 1998. "Who, and When, Were the Inorodtsy? The Evolution of the Category of 'Aliens' in Imperial Russia." *The Russian Review* 57(2): 173–190.

Smart, C. 1989. *Feminism and the Power of Law.* London: Routledge.

Smith, C. 1996. *Disruptive Religion: The Force of Faith in Social Movement Activism.* New York: Routledge.

Smith, Christian. 1998. *Evangelicalism: Embattled and Thriving.* Chicago: University of Chicago Press.

Smith, Dorothy E. 1974. "Women's Perspective as a Radical Critique of Sociology." *Sociological Inquiry* 44(1): 7–13.

Smith, J. 2002. "Introduction." In *Muslims in the West,* ed. Y. Haddad, 3–35. Oxford: Oxford University Press.

Smith, Jonathan Z. 1978. *Map is not Territory: Studies in the History of Religions.* Leiden: Brill.

Smith, Jonathan Z. 1982. *Imagining Religion: From Babylon to Jonestown.* Chicago: University of Chicago Press.

Smith, L. 2006. "Lives Lived in Spirit: Quaker Service for Peace and Social Justice in the Canadian Context." Montreal: Concordia University, M.A. Thesis.

Smith, T.L. 1978. "Religion and Ethnicity in America." *American Historical Review* 83(5): 1155–1185.

Smith, W.R. 1912. *Lectures of William Robertson Smith.* Ed. J.S. Black and G. Chrystal. London: A. and C. Black.

Smith, Wilfred Cantwell. 1962. *The Meaning and End of Religion.* Minneapolis: Fortress Press.

Sobrino, Jon. 1978. *Christology at the Crossroads.* New York: Orbis Books.

Sointv, Eeva. 2004. *The Wellbeing Society.* Lancaster: Lancaster University Library.

Solnin, Amy C. 1995. *William L. Pierce, Novelist of Hate: Research Report of the Anti-Defamation League.* New York: Anti-Defamation League.

Sorscher, Nechma and Lisa J. Cohen. 1997. "Trauma in Children of Holocaust Survivors: Transgenerational Effects." *American Journal of Orthopsychiatry* 67: 493–500.

Southern, R.W. 1970. *Western Society and the Church in the Middle Ages.* Harmondsworth: Penguin.

Southwold, M. 1979. "Religious Belief." *Man,* n.s. 14.

Soysal, Levent. "Labor to Culture: Writing Turkish Migration to Europe." *The South Atlantic Quarterly* 102(2/3): 491–508.

Sperber, D. 1975. *Rethinking Symbolism.* Cambridge: Cambridge University Press.

Spickard, James V. 2006. "What is Happening to Religion? Six Visions of Religion's Future." *Nordic Journal of Religion and Society* 19(1): 13–29.

Spickard, James V., J. Shawn Landres and Meredith B. McGuire, eds. 2002. *Personal Knowledge and Beyond: Reshaping the Ethnography of Religion.* New York: New York University Press.

Spiegel Online. Deutsch-Türken gegen Kopftuch. "Symbol der Unterdrückung." (German-Turks against the Headscarf. "Symbol of suppression"). www.spiegel.de/politik/deutschland/0,1518,442656,00.html (accessed October 20, 2006).

Spielhaus, Riem. 2006. "Religion und Identität: Vom Deutschen Versuch, Ausländer zu Muslimen zu Machen." *Migration und Sicherheit* (März): 28–36.

Spielhaus, Riem and Alex F#akarber, eds. 2006. *Islamisches Gemeindeleben in Berlin*. Berlin: der Beaftragte des Senats für Integration und Migration.

Spivak, Gayatri. 1988. "Can the Subaltern Speak?" In *Marxism and the Interpretation of Culture*, ed. C. Nelson and L. Grossberg, 271–313. Urbana: University of Illinois Press.

Spivak, Gayatri Chakravorty. [1992] 1996. "More on Power/Knowledge." In *The Spivak Reader*, ed. Donna Landry and Gerald Maclean, 141–174. London: Routledge.

Spong, J. 1991. *Reclaiming the Bible from Fundamentalism*. San Francisco: Harper-San Francisco.

Srivastava, Raj Krishan. 1998. *Vital Connections: Self, Society, God: Perspectives on Swadhyaya*. New York: Weatherhill.

Stacey, Jackie. 2000. "The Global Within: Consuming Nature, Embodying Health." In *Global Nature, Global Culture*, ed. Sarah Franklin, Celia Lury and Jackie Stacey, 97–145. London: Sage.

Standaert, Michael. 2006. *Skipping Towards Armageddon: The Politics and Propaganda of the* Left Behind *Novels*. Brooklyn: Soft Skull Press.

Stanley, Liz and Sue Wise. 1983. *Breaking Out: Feminist Consciousness and Feminist Research*. London: Routledge.

Starhawk. 1979. *The Spiral Dance: A Rebirth of the Ancient Religion of the Great Goddess*. San Francisco: Harper & Row.

Stark, Rodney. 1985. "Europe's Receptivity to Religious Movements." In *Religious Movements*, ed. Rodney Stark, 301–339. New York: Paragon House.

Stark, Rodney. 1999. "Secularization, R.I.P." *Sociology of Religion* 60(3): 249–273.

Stark, Rodney. 2000. "Secularization, R.I.P." In *The Secularization Debate*, ed. W.H. Swatos Jr. and D.V.A. Olson. New York: Rowman & Littlefield.

Stark, Rodney and Roger Finke. 2000. *Acts of Faith: Explaining the Human Side of Religion*. Berkeley: University of California Press.

Steensland, Brian, Jerry Z. Park, Mark D. Regnerus, Lynn D. Robinson, W. Bradford Wilcox and Robert D. Woodberry. 2000. "The Measure of American Religion: Toward Improving the State of the Art." *Social Forces* 79(1): 291–318.

Stein, Stephen J. 2002. "The Web of Religion and Violence." *Religious Studies Review* 28: 103–108.

Stephan, M. 2006. "'You Come to Us Like a Black Cloud': Universal versus Local Islam in Tajikstan." In *The Postsocialist Religious Question: Faith and Power in Central Asia and East-Central Europe*, ed. C.M. Hann *et al*. Berlin: Lit Verlag.

Stevens-Arroyo, Anthony M. 1998. "The Evolution of Marian Devotionalism within Christianity and the Ibero-Mediterranean Polity." *Journal for the Scientific Study of Religion* 37(1): 50–73.

Stirling, M.L., C.A. Cameron, N. Nason-Clark and B. Miedema, eds. 2004. *Understanding Abuse: Partnering for Change*. Toronto: University of Toronto Press.

Stone, K. 2001a. *Queer Commentary and the Hebrew Bible*. Sheffield: Sheffield Academic Press.

Stone, K. 2001b. "Homosexuality and the Bible or Queer Reading? A Response to Martti Nissinen." *Theology & Sexuality* 14 (March): 107–118.

Stout, Harry S. 1991. *The Divine Dramatist: George Whitefield and the Rise of Modern Evangelicalism*. Grand Rapids: Eerdmans.

Strathern, Marilyn. 1988. *The Gender of the Gift: Problems with Women and Problems with Society in Melanesia*. Berkeley and Los Angeles: University of California Press.

Stuart, E. 1992. *Dare to Speak Love's Name*. London: Hamish Hamilton.

Stuart, E. 1995. *Just Good Friends*. London: Mowbray.

Stuart, E. 1997a. "Learning to Trust Our Own Experience." In *Religion is a Queer Thing*, ed. E. Stuart, A. Braunston, J. McMahon and T. Morrison, 20–28. London: Cassell.

Stuart, E. 1997b. "Prophets, Patriarchs and Pains in the Neck: The Bible." In *Religion is a Queer Thing*, ed. E. Stuart, A. Braunston, J. McMahon and T. Morrison, 37–46. London: Cassell.

Stuart, E. 2003. *Lesbian and Gay Theologies*. Aldershot: Ashgate.

Sueki Fumihiko and Cao Zhangqi. 1996. *Gendai Chūgoku no Bukkyō* (Buddhism in Contemporary China). Tokyo: Hirakawa shuppansha.

Suh, S.A. 2009. "Buddhism, Rhetoric, and the Korean American Community: The Adjustment of Korean Buddhist Immigrants to the United States." In *Immigration and Religion in America: Comparative and Historical Perspectives*, ed. R. Alba, A.J. Raboteau and J. Dewind. New York: New York University Press

Sullins, Donald Paul. 1992. "Switching Close to Home: Volatility or Coherence in Protestant

Affiliation Patterns." Paper presented at annual meeting of the Society for the Scientific Study of Religion, Arlington.

The Sunday Times. 2003. "Gay Love's Fine. It's All in the Bible." June 29.

Sykes, N. 1975. "The Religion of Protestants." In *The Cambridge History of the Bible*. Vol. 3, ed. S.L. Greenslade. Cambridge: Cambridge University Press.

Tabor, James. 1994. "The Waco Tragedy: An Autobiographical Account of One Attempt to Prevent Disaster." In *From the Ashes*, ed. James R. Lewis, 13–21. Lanham: Rowman & Littlefield

Tabor, James. "The Events at Waco: An Interpretive Log," http://home.maine.rr.com/waco/ww.html.

Tabor, James D. and Eugene V. Gallagher. 1995. *Why Waco? Cults and the Battle for Religious Freedom in America*. Berkeley: University of California Press.

Tambiah, S.J. 1990. *Magic, Science, Religion, and the Scope of Rationality*. Cambridge: Cambridge University Press.

Tamney, Joseph B. 2002: *The Resilience of Conservative Religion: The Case of Popular, Conservative Protestant Congregations*. Cambridge: Cambridge University Press.

Tantawi, Muhammed Sayyid. 1994. "Bal al-ḥijāb farīda islāmiyya." *Rūz al-Yūsuf*, June 27, 68.

Task Force on Policy Regarding Emigrants. 2002. "Ireland and the Irish Abroad: Report to the Minister for Foreign Affairs, Brian Cowen, T.D." Available at http://www.foreign affairs.gov.ie/policy/emigrant_taskforce.asp.

Taylor, Charles. 1991. *The Ethics of Authenticity*. Cambridge, MA: Harvard University Press.

Taylor, Lawrence J. 1995. *Occasions of Faith: An Anthropology of Irish Catholics*. Philadelphia: University of Pennsylvania Press.

Tedeschi, John, ed. 1991. *The Prosecution of Heresy: Collected Studies on the Inquisition in Early Modern Italy*. Binghamton: Center for Medieval and Renaissance Studies.

ter Haar, G. 2005. "Religion: Source of Conflict or Resource for Peace?" In *Bridge or Barrier: Religion, Violence and Visions for Peace*, ed. G. ter Haar and J.J. Busuttil, 3–34. Leiden: Brill.

Thomas, George M. 1989. *Revivalism and Cultural Change: Christianity, Nation Building, and the Market in the Nineteenth-Century United States*. Chicago: University of Chicago Press.

Thomas, K.J., J.P. Nicholl and P. Coleman. 2001. "Use and Expenditure on Complementary Medicine in England: A Population Based Survey." *Complementary Therapies in Medicine* 9: 2–11.

Thomas, Keith. 1971. *Religion and the Decline of Magic*. New York: Scribner's.

Thompson, Wayne L., Jackson W. Carroll and Dean R. Hoge. 1993. "Growth or Decline in Presbyterian Congregations." In *Church and Denominational Growth*, ed. David A. Roozen and C. Kirk Had-away, 188–207. Nashville: Abingdon Press.

Thornton, Sarah L. 1995. *Club Culture: Music, Media and Subcultural Capital*. Cambridge: Polity Press.

Tietze, Nikola. 2006. "Religiosity among Young Male Muslims in France and German Public Spheres." In *Islam in Public: Turkey, Iran and Europe*, ed. Ludwig Ammann Nilüfer Göle, 335–369. Istanbul: Bilgi University Press.

Timmins, L., ed. 1995. *Listening to the Thunder: Advocates Talk about the Battered Women's Movement*. Vancouver: Women's Research Center.

Tipton, Steven M. 1982. *Getting Saved from the Sixties*. Berkeley: University of California Press.

Tiryakian, Edward A. 1991. "L'exceptionnelle vitalité religieuse aux Etats-Unis: Une relecture de *Protestant—Catholic—Jew*" (The Exceptional Religious Vitality of the United States: A Re-reading of *Protestant—Catholic—Jew*). *Social Compass* 38(September): 215–238.

Toops, S.W. 2004. "The Demography of Xinjiang." In *Xinjiang: China's Muslim Borderland*, ed. S.F. Starr. New York: M.I. Sharpe.

Trident Ploughshares. 1999. *Loch Goil and Greenock Trial: Summary of Sheriff Gimblett's Ruling*, www.tridentploughshares.org/article729 (accessed June 22, 2004).

Trident Ploughshares. 2001a. *Speed the Plough*.

Trident Ploughshares. 2001b. "Overview of Trident Ploughshares. Trident Ploughshares. Tri-denting It Handbook 3rd Edition," www. tridentploughshares.org/hb3/part1.php (accessed December 7, 2004).

Trident v. Angela Zelter, Ellen Moxley, Ulla Roder. 2001. "Lord Prosser, Lord Penrose, Lord Kirkwood, Appeal Court, 1–35, H.C.J. Scot."

Trilling, Lionel. 1974. *Sincerity and Authenticity*. London: Oxford University Press.

Tschannen, Olivier. 1991. "The Secularization Paradigm: A Systematization." *Journal for the Scientific Study of Religion* 30 (December): 395–415.

Turkmenbashy, S. 2005. *Rukhnama: Reflection on the Spiritual Values of the Turkmen*. Ashgabat: State Publishing Service Turkmenistan.

Turner, Victor. 1969. *The Ritual Process*. Chicago: Aldine.

Turning the Tide: A Quaker Programme on Active Nonviolence. *Nonviolence and Active Nonviolence*, www.turning-the-tide.org/files/ Taster%20 Nonviolence.pdf (accessed December 7, 2004).

Tylor, E.B. 1871. *Primitive Culture*. London: J. Murray.

U.S., *Congressional Record*, House, March 15, 1965, pp. 4924, 4926.

Ummah Films. http://youtube.com/ummahfilms (accessed November 20, 2008).

Underwood, Grant. "Millennialism, Persecution, and Violence: The Mormons." In *Millennialism, Persecution, and Violence: Historical Cases*, ed. Catherine Wessinger, 43–61. Syracuse: Syracuse University Press.

USA Today. 2003. "A Battle for a Church's Soul." October 7.

Valentine, Daniel. 2002. "The Arrogation of Being by the Blind-Spot of Religion." In *Discrimination and Toleration*, ed. K. Hastrup and G. Ulrich, 31–53. London: Kluwer International.

Valentine, David. 2007. *Imagining Transgender: An Ethnography of a Category*. Durham, NC: Duke University Press.

van der Leeuw, Gerardus. 1938. *Religion in Essence and Manifestation: A Study in Phenomenology*. New York: Macmillan.

van der Veer, Peter. 1994. *Religious Nationalism. Hindus and Muslims in India*. Berkeley, Los Angeles and London: University of California Press.

Van Tubergen, F. 2006. "Religious Affiliation and Attendance among Immigrants in Eight Western Countries: Individual and Contextual Effects." *Journal for the Scientific Study of Religion* 45(1): 1–22.

Vauchez, André. 1993. *The Laity in the Middle Ages: Religious Beliefs and Devotional Practices*. Tr. M.J. Schneider. Ed. D.E. Bornstein. Notre Dame, IN: University of Notre Dame Press.

Veroff, Joseph, Elizabeth Douvan and Richard Kulka. 1981. *The Inner American: A Self-Portrait from 1957 to 1976*. New York: Basic Books.

Vertovec, Steven. 2000. "Religion and Diaspora." Paper presented at the conference on New Landscapes of Religion in the West, University of Oxford, September 27–29. www.transcomm.ox.ac. uk/working%20papers/Vertovec01.PDF (accessed May 12, 2004).

Victoria, Brian. 1997. *Zen At War*. New York: Weatherhill.

Victoria, Brian. 2003. *Zen War Stories*. London and New York: RoutledgeCurzon.

von Below, Susanne and Ercan Karakoyun. 2007. "Sozialstruktur und Lebenslagen Junger Muslime in Deutschland." In *Junge Muslime in Deutschland. Lebenslagen, Aufwachsprozesse und Jugendkulturen*, ed. Hans-Jürgen von Wensierski and Claudia Lübcke, 33–55. Farmington Hills: Barbara Budrisch.

Vygotsky, L.S. 1962 [1934]. *Thought and Language*. Cambridge, MA: MIT Press.

Vygotsky, L.S. 1978. *Mind in Society*. Cambridge, MA: Harvard University Press.

Waite, A.E. 1961. *The Book of Ceremonial Magic*. New York: University Books.

Waite, E. 2010. *Muslims on the Edge of China. Religious Knowledge and Authority amongst the Uyghurs of Xinjiang*. London: Routledge.

Waldron, Andrew. 1998. "Religious Revivals in Communist China." *Orbis* 42(2): 325–334.

Walter, Jess. 1995a. "'Every Knee Shall Bow': Exclusive Book Excerpt." *Newsweek*, August 28, 29–33.

Walter, Jess, 1995b. *Every Knee Shall Bow: The Truth and Tragedy of Ruby Ridge and the Randy Weaver Family*. New York: Harper Paperbacks.

Wank, David L. 2000. "Bukkyōfukkō no seijigaku: kyōgō suru kikō to seitōsei" (The Politics of the Revival Movement of Buddhism: Competing Institutions and Legitimacy). In *Kokka-shakai tono kyōsei kankei: gendai Chūgoku no shakai koōzō no henyō* (The Symbiotic Relationship of State and Society: The Transformation of Social Structure in Contemporary China), ed. Hishida Masaharu *et al.*, 275–304. Tokyo: Tōkyō daigaku shuppankai.

Wanner, C. 2007. *Communities of the Converted: Ukrainians and Global Evangelism*. Ithaca: Cornell University Press.

Warner, R. Stephen. 1993. "Work in Progress toward a New Paradigm for the Sociological Study of Religion in the United States." *American Journal of Sociology* 98(5): 1044–1094.

Warner, R. Stephen. 2005. *A Church of Our Own: Disestablishment and Diversity in American Religion*. New Brunswick: Rutgers University Press.

Warner, R. Stephen. 1988. *New Wine in Old Wineskins: Evangelicals and Liberals in a Small-Town Church.* Berkeley and Los Angeles: University of California Press.

Warner, R. Stephen 1998. "Immigration and Religious Communities in the United States." In *Gatherings in Diaspora: Religious Communities and the New Immigration*, ed. Stephen R. Warner and Judith G. Wittner, 3–34. Philadelphia: Temple University Press.

Warner, R.S. and J.G. Wittner. 1998. *Gatherings in the Diaspora: Religious Communities and the New Immigration.* Philadelphia: Temple University Press

Warren, Mark R. 2001. *Dry Bones Rattling: Community Building to Revitalize American Democracy.* New York: Oxford University Press.

Wasilewska, E. 1997. "The Past and the Present: The Power of Heroic Epics and Oral Tradition—Manas 1000." *Central Asian Survey* 16(1): 81–95.

Watkins, O.D. 1920. *A History of Penance.* 2 vols. London: Longmans.

Watson, J.L., ed. 1997. *Golden Arches East: McDonalds in East Asia.* Stanford: Stanford University Press.

Waugh, M. 2001. "Quakers, Peace, and the League of Nations: The Role of Bertram Pickard." *Quaker Studies* 6(1): 59–80.

Weaver, A.J. 1993. "Psychological Trauma: What Clergy Need to Know." *Pastoral Psychology* 41: 385–408.

Weber, Max. [1920] 1958. *The Protestant Ethic and the Spirit of Capitalism.* Tr. T. Parsons. New York: Scribner's.

Weber, Max. [1922]. *The Sociology of Religion.* Tr. E. Fischoff. Boston: Beacon Press.

Weber, Max. 1978. *Economy and Society: An Outline of Interpretive Sociology.* Ed. Guenther Roth and Claus Wittich, tr. Ephraim Fischoff *et al.* Berkeley: University of California Press.

Weeks, Jeffrey. 1981. *Sex, Politics, and Society: The Regulation of Sexuality since 1800.* London: Longman.

Welch, Holmes. 1967. *The Practice of Chinese Buddhism, 1900–1950.* Cambridge, MA: Harvard University Press.

Welch, Holmes. 1968. *The Buddhist Revival in China.* Cambridge, MA: Harvard University Press.

Welch, Holmes. 1972. *Buddhism under Mao.* Cambridge, MA: Harvard University Press.

Wenweipo (online edition). 2007. "300 Million Citizens' Belief in Religion, Popular Beliefs Are Flourishing." March 3. http://paper.wenweipo. com/2007/03//03NS0703030001.htm (last accessed November 15, 2007).

Wessinger, Catherine. 1997a. "Millennialism With and Without the Mayhem: Catastrophic and Progressive Expectations." In *Millennium, Messiahs, and Mayhem: Contemporary Apocalyptic Movements*, ed. Thomas Robbins and Susan J. Palmer, 47–59. New York: Routledge.

Wessinger, Catherine. 1997b. "Review Essay: Understanding the Branch Davidian Tragedy." *Nova Religio: The Journal of Alternative and Emergent Religions* 1(October): 122–138.

Wessinger, Catherine. 2000. "The Interacting Dynamics of Millennial Beliefs, Persecution, and Violence. In *Millennialism, Persecution, and Violence: Historical Cases*, ed. Catherine Wessinger, 3–39. Syracuse: Syracuse University Press.

Wheatley, Dennis. 1953. *To the Devil, a Daughter.* London Hutchinson.

Wheatley, Dennis. 1954. *The Devil Rides Out.* London: Hutchinson.

Whipple, V. 1987. "Counseling Battered Women from Fundamentalist Churches." *Journal for Marital and Family Therapy* 13(3): 251–258.

Widdicombe, Sue and Robin Wooffitt. 1995. *The Language of Youth Subcultures.* Hertfordshire: Harvester Wheatsheaf.

Wilcox, Clyde and Carin Larson. 2006. *Onward Christian Soldiers: The Religious Right in American Politics.* Boulder: Westview Press.

Wilcox, Clyde and Barbara Norrander. 2002. "Of Moods and Morals: The Dynamics of Opinion on Abortion and Gay Rights." In *Understanding Public Opinion*, 2nd edn, ed. Barbara Norrander and Clyde Wilcox, 121–148. Washington, DC: CQ Press.

Wilcox, Melissa M. 2002. "When Sheila's a Lesbian: Religious Individualism among Lesbian, Gay, Bisexual, and Transgendered Christians." *Sociology of Religion* 63(4): 497–513.

Wilcox, Melissa M. 2003. *Coming Out in Christianity.* Bloomington: Indiana University Press.

Wilcox, Melissa M. 2006. "Discourse Bless America: Rebuilding the National Mythos after September 11." In *Religion, Politics, and the American Experience: New Perspectives, New Directions*, ed. David S. Gutterman and Andrew R. Murphy, 25–48. Lanham: Lexington Books.

Wilcox, Melissa M. 2009. *Queer Women and Religious Individualism.* Bloomington: University of Indiana Press.

Willey, B. 1934. *The Seventeenth-Century Background.* London: Chatto and Windus.

Williams, Gerhild Scholz. 1995. *Defining Dominion: The Discourses of Magic and Witchcraft in Early Modern France and Germany*. Ann Arbor: University of Michigan Press.

Williams, Rhys. 1995. "Constructing the Public Good: Social Movements and Cultural Resources." *Social Problems* 42(1): 124–144.

Williams, Rhys. 1996. "Religion as Political Resource: Culture or Ideology?" *Journal for the Scientific Study of Religion* 35(4): 368–378.

Williams, Raymond Brady. 1998. "Americans and Religions in the Twenty-first Century: Asian Indian and Pakistani Religions in the United States." *The Annals of the American Academy of Political and Social Science* 558: 178–195.

Williams, Raymond Brady. 1988. *Religions of Immigrants from India and Pakistan: New Threads in the American Tapestry*. Cambridge: Cambridge University Press.

Williams, Raymond Brady. 2001. *An Introduction to Swaminarayan Hinduism*. Cambridge: Cambridge University Press.

Williams, Rhys and Kubal, T. 1999. "Movement Frames and the Cultural Environment: Resonance, Failure, and the Boundaries of the Legitimate." *Research in Social Movements, Conflicts and Change* 21: 225–248.

Williams, Sherri. 2004. "Comparing Gay, Civil Rights a Divisive Issue for Blacks." *Columbus Dispatch*, July 2, A8.

Wilson, Charles Reagan. 1980. *Baptized in Blood: The Religion of the Lost Cause, 1865–1920*. Athens, GA: University of Georgia Press.

Wilson, Stephen. 2000. *The Magical Universe: Everyday Ritual and Magic in Pre-modern Europe*. London: Hambledon and London.

Wiltfang, Gregory and Doug McAdam. 1991. "The Costs and Risks of Social Activism: A Study of Sanctuary Movement Activism." *Social Forces* 69(June): 987–1010.

Winwar, Frances. 1948. *The Saint and the Devil: Joan of Arc and Gilles de Rais*. New York: Harper & Brothers.

Wolf, E. 1982. *Europe and the People Without History*. Berkeley: University of California Press.

Wolfe, Burton H. 1974. *The Devil's Avenger*. New York: Pyramid Books.

Wolff, Eric R. 1990. "Facing Power—Old Insights, New Questions." *American Anthropologist* 92: 586–596.

Wong, David. 2004. Interview by Carin Robinson, November 12.

Wong, Janelle. 2006. *Democracy's Promise: American Civic Institutions and Political Mobilization among Asian American and Latino Immigrants*. Ann Arbor: University of Michigan Press.

Wood, Richard. 1997. "Social Capital and Political Culture: God Meets Politics in the Inner City." *American Behavioral Scientist* 5: 595–606.

Wood, Richard. 2002. *Faith in Action: Religion, Race and Democratic Organizing in America*. Chicago: University of Chicago Press.

Woodhead, L., P. Heelas and D. Martin. 2001. *Peter Berger and the Study of Religion*. New York: Routledge.

Wootton, J.C. and Sparber, A. 2001. "Surveys of Complementary and Alternative Medicine. Part 1. General Trends and Demographic Groups." *Journal of Alternative and Complementary Medicine* 7(2): 195–208.

Worth, Robert F. 2002. "Truth, Right and the American Way; A Nation Defines Itself By Its Evil Enemies." *New York Times*, February 22.

Wright, Lawrence. 1991. "It's Not Easy Being Evil in a World That's Gone to Hell." *Rolling Stone*, September 5, 63–68, 105–106.

Wu, Jiao. 2007. "Religious Believers Thrice the Estimate." *China Daily*, February 7 (online edition), www.chinadaily.com.cn/china/2007–02/07/content_802994.htm (last accessed November 15, 2007).

Wuthnow, Robert. 1988. *The Restructuring of American Religion: Society and Faith since World War II*. Princeton: Princeton University Press.

Wuthnow, Robert. 1998. *After Heaven: Spirituality in America since the 1950s*. Berkeley: University of California Press.

Wuthnow, Robert and K. Christiano. 1979. "The Effect of Residential Migration on Church Attendance in the United States." In *The Religious Dimension: New Directions in Quantitative Research*, ed. R. Wuthnow. New York: Academic Press.

Yamane, D. 1997. "Secularization on Trial: In Defense of a Neosecularization Paradigm." *Journal for the Scientific Study of Religion* 36(1): 109–122.

Yang, F. 2000. "The Hsi-Nan Chinese Buddhist Temple: Seeking to Americanize." In *Religion and the New Immigrants: Continuities and Adaptations in Immigrant Congregations*, ed. H.R. Ebaugh and J.S. Chafetz. Walnut Creek: AltaMira Press

Yang, F. and H.R. Ebaugh. 2001. "Transformations in New Immigrant Religions and their Global Implications." *American Sociological Review* 66(2): 269–288.

Yankelovich, Daniel. 1981. *New Rules*. New York: Random House.

Yip, A.K.T. 1997. *Gay Male Christian Couples: Life Stories*. Westport: Praeger.

Yip, A.K.T. 2000. "Leaving the Church to Keep my Faith: The Lived Experiences of Non-heterosexual Christians." In *Joining and Leaving Religion*, ed. L.J. Francis and Y.J. Katz, 129–145. Leominster: Gracewing.

Yip, A.K.T. 2002. "The Persistence of Faith among Nonheterosexual Christians: Evidence for the Neosecularization Thesis of Religious Transformation." *Journal for the Scientific Study of Religion* 41(2): 199–212.

Yip, A.K.T. 2003a. "The Self as the Basis of Religious Faith: Spirituality of Gay, Lesbian, and Bisexual Christians." In *Predicting Religion*, ed. G. Davie, L. Woodhead and P. Heelas, 135–146. Aldershot: Ashgate.

Yip, A.K.T. 2003b. "Spirituality and Sexuality: An Exploration of the Religious Beliefs of Non-heterosexual Christians in Great Britain." *Theology & Sexuality* 9(2): 137–154.

Yip, A.K.T. 2003c. "Sexuality and the Church." *Sexualities* 6(1): 60–64.

Yip, A.K.T. 2004. "Embracing Allah and Sexuality? South Asian Non-heterosexual Muslims in Britain." In *South Asians in the Diaspora*, ed. P. Kumar and K. Jacobsen, 294–310. Leiden: EJ Brill.

Yip, A.K.T. and M. Keenan. 2004. "By Name United, by Sex Divided: A Brief Analysis of the Current Crisis Facing the Anglican Community." *Sociological Research Online*, www.socresonline. org.uk/9/1/yip. html (accessed September 2004).

Yoo, David. 1999. *New Spiritual Homes: Religion and Asian Americans*. Honolulu: University of Hawaii Press.

Young, Iris Marion. 1990. *Throwing it Like a Girl and Other Essays in Feminist Philosophy and Social Theory*. Bloomington and Indianapolis: Indiana University Press.

Zarcone, T. 1999. "Quand le saint légitime le politique: Le mausolée de Afaq Khwaja à Kashgar." *Central Asian Survey* 18(2): 225–241.

Zarcone, T. 2001. " 'Le Culte des saints au Xinjiang de 1949 à nos jours' in Saints and heroes on the Silk Road. Saints et héros sur la Route de la Soie." *Journal of the History of Sufism* III: 133–172.

Zelter, A. 2001. *Trident on Trial: The Case for People's Disarmament*. Edinburgh: Luath Press Limited.

Zeskind, Leonard. 1986. *The "Christian Identity" Movement: Analyzing Its Theological Rationalization for Racist and Anti-Semitic Violence*. New York: Division of Church and Society of the National Council of Churches of Christ in the U.S.A..

Zizek, Slavoj. 1990. "Eastern Europe's Republics of Gilead." *New Left Review* 183: 50–62.

Credits

Glossary Index